# THE TIME OF OUR TIME

ALSO BY NORMAN MAILER

*The Naked and the Dead*
*Barbary Shore*
*The Deer Park*
*Advertisements for Myself*
*Deaths for the Ladies (and Other Disasters)*
*The Presidential Papers*
*An American Dream*
*Cannibals and Christians*
*Why Are We in Vietnam?*
*The Deer Park—a Play*
*The Armies of the Night*
*Miami and the Siege of Chicago*
*Of a Fire on the Moon*
*The Prisoner of Sex*
*Maidstone*
*Existential Errands*
*St. George and the Godfather*
*Marilyn*
*The Faith of Graffiti*
*The Fight*
*Genius and Lust*
*The Executioner's Song*
*Of Women and Their Elegance*
*Pieces and Pontifications*
*Ancient Evenings*
*Tough Guys Don't Dance*
*Harlot's Ghost*
*Oswald's Tale: An American Mystery*
*Portrait of Picasso as a Young Man*
*The Gospel According to the Son*

# THE TIME OF OUR TIME

# THE TIME
# OF OUR
# TIME

## NORMAN
## MAILER

LITTLE, BROWN AND COMPANY

A *Little, Brown* Book

First published in the United States of America by
Random House, Inc., 1998
First published in Great Britain by
Little, Brown and Company 1998

Acknowledgements of permission to reprint previously
published material appear on pages 1283–86

A CIP catalogue record for this book
is available from the British Library.

ISBN 0 316 64571 0

Printed and bound in Great Britain by Clays Ltd, St Ives plc

Little, Brown and Company (UK)
Brettenham House
Lancaster Place
London WC2E 7EN

TO

ROBERT F. LUCID

AND

J. MICHAEL LENNON

# Foreword

Some time ago it occurred to me that May 6, 1998, was going to be the fiftieth anniversary of the publication of *The Naked and the Dead* and I would then be seventy-five. Fifty and seventy-five are not unhappy numbers when it comes to stirring a publisher's interest. Soon, there was agreement that I should do a literary retrospective. That was nice—nice indeed—but how was I to put the collection together? Commemoration can be enjoyed by the old fellow who bathes in the honors, but it does skirt one big bog. Wonderful, everyone will exclaim—let's move on.

Form, however, is a handmaiden to take us through many a literary impasse. Should one put together an anthology of excerpts from one's novels, a file of essays on politics and philosophy, some poetry and set-pieces full of place, plus journalism, action, drama, speculation, fulmination, theology? Equal to a row of potted plants might be the final effect.

Or could it be assembled in the order published—a useful presentation for a biographer. If one wished, however, to keep some emphasis on what was written rather than on how one had lived while managing, incidentally, to be a writer, then it would be wise to keep to the background. Re-reading the bulk of my work in the course of a spring and summer, one theme came to predominate—it was apparent that most of my writing was about America. How much I loved my country—that was evident—and how much I didn't love it at all! Our noble ideal of democracy was forever being traduced, sullied, exploited, and downgraded through a non-stop reflexive patriotism. And every decade our great land lay open more and more to all the ravages of greed. So, yes, the question was alive—would greed and the hegemony of the mediocre—the media!—triumph over democracy? Or could we also celebrate some happy reading—well, yes, we could!

As a working writer I had lived, after all, through fifty years of American time, and my sense of the character of our nation had shifted in each decade. If I had often written in the very season of each happening, so had I also come back to events now ten and twenty, thirty and forty years old. That suggested a solution. I would not have to attach each episode to the year in which it was written, no, it would be better to connect it to the year I had been writing about. If in 1990 I wrote about 1951, why, then, place the piece back in 1951. The perceptions of a man no longer young could now be posed against insights the writer had once set down decades earlier.*

Over the course of our lives, most of us compose in the privacy of our minds a social and cultural history of the years through which we have passed. We often think of it as a collective remembrance that others will share with us. We even speak of it as *our* time. In fact, it is only one's personal time, one's own intimate social, cultural, and historic time, one's image of what transpired in the world. Can it be, possibly, the message we hope to bring back to eternity? Perhaps there is an angel ready to inscribe it. In any event, we are forever working to obtain some understanding of our lives and our time. So we are forever revising our personal history of the past until it includes everyone toward whom we have reacted over our years, our friends, relatives, enemies, our movie stars, athletes, heroes, and public figures, not to mention all the large, historic, and minuscule occurrences through which we have passed, plus all the books we retain—the ones that helped to change our lives.

If that was so, then I could look upon myself as blessed. Because I had had the good fortune to be able to write about my time as if it were *our* time.

Once, in describing how I came to have the confidence to write a long novel about the CIA, I remarked: "It is a fictional CIA and its only real existence is in my mind, but I would point out that the same is true for men and women who have spent forty years working within the Agency. They have only their part of the CIA to know, even as each of us has his own America, and no two Americas will prove identical. If I have an argument to make then, on grounds of verisimili-

---

*If I have the reputation of being a rebel against authority, it might be added that I am also ready to rebel against my own strictures. The premise of this book having just been declared—to wit, each piece appears in accordance with the year it refers to rather than the year in which it was written—it is, like many a good scheme, flawed at the climax. Indeed, I all but abandon the premise in the last two hundred pages. Excerpts appear that refer to Egypt in the eighteenth and twentieth dynasties (1200–1000 B.C.) and to the eighty years from Christ's birth to the writing of the Gospels. There are only three words to cover this occasion: Nobody is perfect.

tude I will claim that my imaginative CIA is as real or more real than nearly all the lived-in ones."

Let me make something of the same claim here. My America is as real as *almost* all of the other Americas that readers and writers around the world have fashioned for themselves. Nor can I pretend that I have not had this feeling for many years.

Speaking at the MacDowell Colony in the early Seventies, I found myself saying: "There is no reason to believe the novelist is not better equipped to deal with the possibilities of a mysterious and difficult situation than anyone else, since he or she is always trying to discover what the nature of reality might be. It's as if the novelist is out there, sprung early, with something most people never contemplate—which is 'How and what is the nature of this little reality before me?' The novelist is the first to ask, 'Do I love my wife? Does she love me? What is the nature of love? Do we love our child? How do we love? Would we die for our child? Or do we let the child die for us?' The novelist has to deal with these unholy questions because living with them is the only way to improve his or her brain. Without improving that brain, without refining the edge of one's perception, it is almost impossible to continue to work as a writer. Because if there is one fell rule in art, it is that repetition kills the soul. So the novelist is out there early with a particular necessity that may become the necessity of us all. It is to deal with life as something God did not offer us as eternal and immutable. Rather, it is our human destiny to enlarge what we were given. Perhaps we are meant to clarify a world which is always different in one manner or another from the way we have seen it on the day before."

By that measure, nearly everything I have written derives from my sense of the value of fiction. There is little in this book, even when it comes under the formal category of non-fiction or argument, that has not derived, then, from my understanding of how one writes fiction. It has always seemed to me that our best chance of improving those private charts of our own most complicated lives, our unadmitted maps of reality, our very comprehension, if you will, of the way existence works, seems to profit most if we can have some little idea, at least, of the warp of the observer who passes on the experience. Fiction, as I use the word, is a reality that does not cohere to received axes of fact but is breathed in through the swarm of our male and female movements about one another, a novelistic assumption, for we perceive the truth of a novel by way of the personality of the writer. We tend to know, in our unconscious at least, whether the author is to be trusted, and where we suspect he is more ignorant than ourselves.

That is the flavor of fiction. We observe the observer. Maybe that is why there is less dead air in fiction, and usually more light. It is because we have the advantage of seeing around a corner, and that is aesthetically analogous to a photograph of a mountain when early evening offers its back-lighting to the contours. Be certain the journalistic flashbulb is better for recording the carnage of an auto crash. But little else.

Such is my belief. So I can have the hope that this book may stimulate your sense of our time, and will even offer its marrow to all the years in which so many of us have met as friends and antagonists, as fools and philosophers, witnesses and protagonists, alive in our actions and upon occasion rich in our power to meditate upon the perversities and wonders of our world, our arena. In effect, this is a book that nearly all of us have created in our own minds; each book vastly different yet still related by the web of history, the style of our lives, and the river of becoming that we refer to by the most intimate and indefinable of words, the most mysterious word of them all—*time*. Time!

# Contents

# THE TIME OF OUR TIME

# PRELUDE—I

## Boxing with Hemingway

Talking to Callaghan one day, Fitzgerald referred to Hemingway's ability as a boxer, and remarked that while Hemingway was probably not good enough to be heavyweight champion of the world, he was undoubtedly as good as Young Stribling, the light-heavyweight champion. "Look, Scott," said Callaghan, "Ernest is an amateur. I'm an amateur. All this talk is ridiculous." Unconvinced, Fitzgerald asked to come along to the gym at the American Club and watch Hemingway and Callaghan box. But Callaghan has let the reader in earlier on one small point. Hemingway, four inches taller and forty pounds heavier than Callaghan, "may have thought about boxing, dreamed about it, consorted with old fighters and hung around gyms," but Callaghan "had done more actual boxing with men who could box a little and weren't just taking exercise or fooling around."

So on an historic afternoon in June in Paris in 1929, Hemingway and Callaghan boxed a few rounds, with Fitzgerald serving as timekeeper. The second round went on for a long time. Both men began to get tired, Hemingway got careless. Callaghan caught him a good punch and dropped Hemingway on his back. At the next instant Fitzgerald cried out, "Oh, my God! I let the round go four minutes."

"All right, Scott," Ernest said. "If you want to see me getting the shit knocked out of me, just say so. Only don't say you made a mistake."

According to Callaghan's estimate, Scott never recovered from that moment. One believes it. For months later, a cruel and wildly inaccurate story about this episode appeared in the *Herald Tribune* book

4 THE TIME OF OUR TIME

section. It was followed by a cable sent collect to Callaghan by Fitzgerald at Hemingway's insistence. "HAVE SEEN STORY IN HERALD TRIBUNE. ERNEST AND I AWAIT YOUR CORRECTION. SCOTT FITZGERALD."

Since Callaghan had already written such a letter to the paper, none of the three men could ever forgive each other.

The story offers a fine clue to the logic of Hemingway's mind, and tempts the prediction that there will be no definitive biography of Hemingway until the nature of his personal torture is better comprehended. It is possible Hemingway lived every day of his life in the style of the suicide. What a great dread is that. It is the dread that sits in the silences of his short declarative sentences. At any instant, by any failure in magic, by a mean defeat, or by a moment of cowardice, Hemingway could be thrust back again into the agonizing demands of his courage. For the life of his talent must have depended on living in a psychic terrain where one must either be brave beyond one's limit, or sicken closer into a bad illness, or, indeed, by the ultimate logic of the suicide, must advance the hour in which one would make another reconnaissance into one's death.

That may be why Hemingway turned in such fury on Fitzgerald. To be knocked down by a smaller man could only imprison him further into the dread he was forever trying to avoid. Each time his physical vanity suffered a defeat, he would be forced to embark on a new existential gamble with his life. So he would naturally think of Fitzgerald's little error as an act of treachery, for the result of that extra minute in the second round could only be a new bout of anxiety that would drive his instinct into ever more dangerous situations. Most men find their profoundest passion in looking for a way to escape their private and secret torture. It is not likely that Hemingway was a brave man who sought danger for the sake of the sensations it provided him. What is more likely the truth of his long odyssey is that he struggled with his cowardice and against a secret lust to suicide all of his life, that his inner landscape was a nightmare, and he spent his nights wrestling with the gods. It may even be that the final judgment on his work may come to the notion that what he failed to do was tragic, but what he accomplished was heroic, for it is possible he carried a weight of anxiety within him from day to day that would have suffocated any man smaller than himself. There are two kinds of brave men: those who are brave by the grace of nature, and those who are brave by an act of will. It is the merit of Callaghan's long anecdote that the second condition is suggested to be Hemingway's own.

From *Cannibals and Christians* (1966)

**PRELUDE—II**

## Our Man at Harvard

Let me tell you about the Somerset Maugham party that we gave at *The Advocate* in the spring of 1942. The magazine was housed then in a dark gray flat-roofed three-story building across the street from the stern of *The Lampoon* (and indeed we were much aware of being in their wake—*Lampoon* editors usually went to *Time;* ours to oblivion). In those days *The Advocate* building was as ugly from the exterior as it is now. A few small and dingy stores occupied the ground floor; some mysterious never-seen tenants were on the second; and *The Advocate* offices took up the third. They were beautiful to me. One climbed a dull, carpeted staircase as dusty as a back road in Guerrero, used one's *Advocate* key to go through the door at the top, and opened the suite, an entire floor-through of five rooms, five mystical chambers full of broken-down furniture and the incomparable odor that rises from old beer stains in the carpet and syrup-crusted empty Coke bottles in the corners. It is a better odor than you would think, sweet and alcoholic and faintly debauched—it spoke of little magazines and future lands of literature, and the offices were almost always empty in late afternoon, when the sunlight turned the dust into a cosmos of angels dancing on a pin. Maybe I loved the *Advocate* offices more than anyone who was taken in my competition—I spent the spring of sophomore year at Harvard drinking Cokes by a table at the window that faced on *The Lampoon,* and I read old issues of the magazine. Once I was an authority on the early published work in *The Advocate* of T. S. Eliot, Van Wyck Brooks, Conrad Aiken, E. E. Cummings, and Malcolm Cowley—it must have been the nearest I ever came to extracting genealogical marrow from old print. Occasionally, our President, or our Pegasus, would come through the office, give a start at seeing me at the same chair and table where he had glimpsed me on the last visit and go off to do his work.

The following academic year, '41–'42, Bruce Barton, Jr., was elected President and John Crockett became Pegasus. We had troubles instantly. Pete Barton was the nicest guy a lot of us met at Harvard, and with his blond hair, good if somewhat pinched features, and fundamental decency, he could have passed for Billy Budd if he had not gone to Deerfield Academy, which left him a little more patrician than yeoman in manner. But he was gentle, he was quietly literary, and his father had millions. Since *The Advocate* was in its usual cauldron of debt, no other man would have been so appropriate to serve as President. Barton might even have had a benign, well-financed, and agreeable administration if not for the new Pegasus, John Crockett, a man as talented as Claggart and equally riven in his soul by detestation of our Billy Budd.

Being innocent of Crockett's propensities for literary evil, we were a happy group coming into the office. The magazine would be ours. We would print what we wished. Our first issue, therefore, consisted of each of us putting in his own story. Crockett then took our gems to a printer in Vermont. This was, I think, in November. By February we still did not have a magazine. Crockett kept assuring us the printer would soon deliver. None of us ever called him. Crockett had promised us that the inexpensive rate he had managed to extract from the Linotype mills of the Vermont woods would be ruined forever if we broke any of our voices on the printer's ear. Therefore, we waited. Nervously, impatiently, suspiciously, we waited for the issue with our stories.

Instead, Crockett came back with the seventy-fifth anniversary edition of *The Advocate,* a little work of love Crockett had gotten together by himself over the last year—collecting poems, pieces, and comment from the fine ranks of Wallace Stevens, Horace Gregory, Djuna Barnes, Marianne Moore, Robert Hillyer, Frederic Prokosch, Mark Schorer, John Malcolm Brinnin, Richard Eberhart, Bowden Broadwater, William Carlos Williams, plus a poem by John Crockett, "The Sulky Races at Cherry Park." None of us on *The Advocate* had had the first clue as to what Crockett was cooking. As for the issue with our stories—Crockett promised to get to that next. The expression on his young but sour face told us what he thought of our stories. Crockett, incidentally, while not as well-featured as John Dean had a great resemblance to him—I remember his tortoiseshell glasses, high forehead, and thin pale hair.

Pete Barton had been agitated for weeks at the long wait on our first issue. Painfully aware of his father's weight in the world, he was invariably overscrupulous never to push his own. He had suspended himself into a state of forbearance worthy of a Zen warrior considering the immense agitation the late appearance of the magazine had caused. When the anniversary issue appeared (to rich critical reception in the Boston papers, worse luck!) Barton finally demonstrated his father's blood. He called an emergency meeting, where he calumniated himself for his derelictions of attention, took the full blame for the financial disaster of the issue (it had cost something like three times as much as more modest issues; our debt on the consequence had doubled overnight) and—Billy Budd to the last, absent even to intimations of a further notion to evil—stated that he would not ask for Crockett's resignation if he could expect his cooperation on future projects.

Crockett replied with a nod of his head and a profound turning of our collective head. Having heard, he said, that Somerset Maugham would be in the Boston area during April, he had sent an invitation to Maugham to come to a party that *The Advocate* would be happy to throw in his honor, and Maugham had accepted. Maugham had accepted.

This piece of news ran around the ring of Cambridge like a particle in a cyclotron. Nothing in four years at Harvard, not Dunkirk, Pearl Harbor, or the blitz, not even beating Yale and Princeton in the same season for the first time in years, could have lit Harvard up more. Not to be invited to that party was equal to signifying that one had mismanaged one's life.

The literary grandees of the faculty sent their early acceptance. The officers of *The Lampoon* sucked around. Housemasters' wives asked how things were *going* at *The Advocate*. On the night of the party, four hundred souls in four hundred bodies as large as Patrick Moynihan's and as delicate as Joan Didion's came to the small rooms on the third floor and packed themselves in so completely that you ended by bringing your drink to your lips around the wrist of the strange forearm in front of your face. The noise of cocktail gabble anticipated the oncoming shapings of time—one would not hear the sound again until the first jet planes fired up their engines at an airport. Drinks were passed overhead. If you did not reach at the right time, another hand plucked the drink. It did not matter. More was on its way. Glasses bounced like corks over white choppy Harvard hands. From time to time, word would pass like wind through grass that Maugham had just entered the building, Maugham was having trouble getting up the stairs, Maugham was through the door. Maugham was in the other room. We formed phalanxes to move into the other room; we did not budge. A phalanx cannot budge a volume that is impacted. The lovely smile of resignation was on the lips of faculty wives: It is the establishment smile that says, "Life is like that—the nearest pleasures are not to be tasted." After a half hour of such smiling into the face of a stranger as one brought one's arm around her neck to get at one's drink, the wind came through the grass again. Maugham, we heard, was at the door. Maugham was slowly going down the stair. Somerset Maugham was gone.

Hands passed drinks above the impacted mass. Eyes flashed in that hard gemlike smile of pride retained when opportunity is lost. In another half hour, there was a lessening of pressure on one's chest, and bodies began to separate. After a while, one could walk from room to room. What was the point? Maugham was gone.

It was only on the next day, after the claims of liars had been checked against the quiet evidence of reliable witnesses who had found themselves analogously empretzeled in every room and on the stairs, that the news came back. By every sound measure of verification, Somerset Maugham had never been in *The Advocate* building that night. Crockett, now confronted, confessed. Out of his unflappable funds of phlegm, he allowed that he had known for weeks Somerset Maugham was not coming—the great author had been kind enough to send a telegram in answer to the invitation. "Certainly not," it said.

It was too late to ask Crockett to resign. Due to the war and an accelerated graduation, our term as *Advocate* officers was up; the new President and Pegasus were in. Because of the party, we left with a debt that had just doubled again. *The Advocate* has never been solvent since.

A postscript: Pete Barton became a Navy officer and commanded a ship, came home, worked as quietly for *Time* as if he had been a *Lampoon* man, and died before he was forty. The only time I saw John Crockett again was about ten years ago in New York on a reunion at the Harvard Club. He was now in the State Department and had been stationed for years in Yugoslavia. He told delicious stories about idiotic conversations with Madame Tito at banquets in Zagreb. He looked to be as wicked as ever. Our cause was being well served in Yugoslavia.

From *Pieces and Pontifications* (1982)

# THE SECOND
# WORLD WAR—I

## The Attack Across the River

A soldier came walking toward them. "Are you guys Recon?" he asked.

"Yeah," Croft said.

"Okay, you want to follow me?"

They picked up their packs and began walking through the darkness. It was difficult to see the man ahead. After they had gone a few hundred feet, the soldier who was leading them halted and said, "Wait here."

Red swore. "Next time, let's do it by the numbers," he said. Cannon company fired again, and the noise sounded very loud. Wilson dropped his pack and muttered, "Some poor sonsofbitches are gonna catch hell in 'bout half a minute." He sighed and sat down on the wet ground. "You'd think they had somepin better to do than have a whole squad of men walkin' around all night. Ah can't make up m' mind if Ah'm hot or cold." There was a wet heavy mist over the ground, and alternately they shivered in their wet clothing and sweltered in the airless night. Some Japanese artillery was landing about a mile away, and they listened to it quietly.

A platoon of men filed by, their rifles clanking against their helmets and pack buckles. A flare went up a short distance away, and in its light the men looked like black cutouts moving past a spotlight. Their rifles were slung at odd angles, and their packs gave them a humped misshapen appearance. The sound of their walking was confused and intricate; like the truck convoy, it resembled the whisper of surf. Then the flare died, and the column of men passed. When they were some distance away, the only sound that still remained was the soft metallic jingle of their rifles. A skirmish had started at some distance and Jap rifles were firing. Red turned to Wyman and said, "Listen to them. Tick-boom, tick-boom. You can't miss it." A few American rifles answered, their fire sounding more powerful, like a leather belt slapped on a table. Wyman shifted uneasily. "How far away do you figure the Japs are?" he asked Croft.

"Damned if I know. You'll see 'em soon enough, boy."

"Hell he will," Red said. "We're going to be sitting around all night."

Croft spat. "You wouldn't mind that, would you, Valsen?"

"Not me. I'm no hero," Red said.

Some soldiers walked past in the darkness, and a few trucks pulled into the bivouac. Wyman lay down on the ground. He was a little chagrined that he would spend his first night in combat trying to fall asleep. The water soaked through his shirt, which was already wet, and he sat up again, shivering. The air was very sultry. He wished he could light a cigarette.

They waited another half hour before receiving the order to move. Croft stood up and followed their guide while the rest trailed behind. The guide led them into a patch of brush where a platoon of men was grouped around six antitank guns. They were 37s, small guns about six feet long with very slender barrels. One man could pull one gun without too much difficulty over level hard ground.

"We're going along with antitank up to First Battalion," Croft said. "We got to pull two of them guns."

Croft told them to gather around him. "I don't know how muddy the damn trail is going to be," he began, "but it ain't too hard to guess. We're going to be in the middle of the column, so I'm going to cut us into three groups of three men each, and they'll be one group restin' all the time. I'll take Wilson and Gallagher, and Martinez can take Valsen and Ridges, and Toglio, you got what's left—Goldstein and Wyman. We're scrapin' the barrel," he added dryly.

He went up to talk to an officer for a few seconds. When he came back, he said, "We'll let Toglio's group have the first rest." He got behind one of the guns and gave it a tug. "The sonofabitch is going to be heavy." Wilson and Gallagher started pulling it with him, and the other platoon, which had already divided into a few men on each gun, began to move out. They tugged the guns across the bivouac area, and passed through a gap in the barbed wire where there was a machine gun emplacement. "Have a good time, men," the man at the machine gun said.

"Blow it out," Gallagher answered. The gun was beginning to drag on his arms already.

There were about fifty men in the column, and they moved very slowly down a narrow trail through the jungle. After they had moved a hundred feet, they were no longer able to see the men in front of them. The branches of the trees on either side of the trail joined overhead, and they felt as though they were groping through an endless tunnel. Their feet sank into the deep mud and, after a few yards, their boots were covered with great slabs of muck. The men on the guns would lunge forward for a few feet and then halt, lunge forward, and halt. Every ten yards a gun would bog down and the three men assigned to it would have to tug until their strength seeped from their fingers. They would wrestle the gun out of its rut and plunge it forward for fifteen feet before their momentum was lost. Then they would pull it and lift it for another few yards until it sank into a hole once more. The entire column labored and stumbled at a miserable pace along the trail. In the darkness they kept ganging up on each other, the men on one gun sometimes riding it up onto the muzzle of the one ahead, or falling behind so far that the file at last broke into separate wriggling columns like a worm cut into many parts and still living. The men at the rear had the worst of it. The guns and men that preceded them had churned the trail until it was almost a marsh, and there were places where two teams would have to combine on one gun and carry it above the ground until they had passed the worst of the slime.

The trail was only a few feet wide. Huge roots continually tripped the men, and their faces and hands became scratched and bleeding from the branches and thorns. In the complete darkness they had no idea of how the trail might bend, and sometimes on a down slope, when they could let the gun roll a little distance, they would land at the bottom with the field piece completely off the trail. Then they would have to fumble in the brush, covering their eyes with their arms to protect them from the vines, and a painful struggle to bring the gun back on the path would begin.

Some Japanese might easily have been waiting in ambush, but it was impossible to keep silent. The guns squeaked and lumbered, made sucking sounds as their tires sank into the mud, and the men swore helplessly, panted with deep sobbing sounds like wrestlers at the end of a long bout. Voices and commands echoed hollowly, were lost in a chorus of profanity and hoarse sobbing, the straining sweating noises of men in great labor. By the time an hour had passed, nothing existed for them but the slender cannon they had to get down the track. The sweat drenched their clothing and filled their eyes, blinding them. They grappled and blundered and swore, advanced the little guns a few feet at a time with no consciousness any longer of what they were doing.

When one team was relieved by another, they would stagger alongside the guns trying to regain their wind, falling behind sometimes to rest for a little while. Every ten minutes the column would stop to allow the stragglers to catch up. During the halts the men would sprawl in the middle of the trail not caring how the mud covered them. They felt as though they had been running for hours; they could not regain their breath, and their stomachs retched emptily. The air was unbearably hot under the canopy of the jungle, and the darkness gave no relief from the heat of the day; if anything, walking the trail was like fumbling through an endless closet stuffed with velvet garments.

During one of the halts, the officer leading the file worked his way back to find Croft. "Where's Sergeant Croft?" he shouted, his words repeated by the men along the trail until it reached Croft.

"Here, sir." They stumbled toward each other through the mud.

"How're your men?" the officer asked.

"Okay."

Croft, with his lean ropy body, had borne the labor comparatively well, but his voice was unsteady and he had to talk with short quick spates of words. "How far?" he asked.

"Have to go one mile . . . one mile yet. More than halfway there, I think. Never should have tried it."

"They need the guns bad?"

The officer halted for a moment and tried to speak normally. "I think so . . . there's no tank weapons there . . . up on the line. We stopped a tank attack two hours ago . . . at Third Battalion. Orders came to move some thirty-sevens over to First Battalion. Guess they expect attack there."

"Better get them through," Croft said. He was contemptuous because the officer had to talk to him. The man ought to be able to do his own job.

"Have to, I guess." The officer stood up and leaned for a moment against a tree. "If you get a gun stuck, let me know. Have to cross a stream . . . up ahead. Bad place, I think."

He began to feel his way forward, and Croft turned around and worked his way back to the gun he was pulling. The column was over two hundred yards long by now. They started to move, and the labor continued. Once or twice a flare filtered a wan and delicate bluish light over them, the light almost lost in the dense foliage through which it had to pass. In the brief moment it lasted, they were caught at their guns in classic straining motions that had the form and beauty of a frieze. Their uniforms were twice blackened, by the water and the dark slime of the trail. And for the instant the light shone on them their faces stood out, white and contorted. Even the guns had a slender articulated beauty like an insect reared back on its wire haunches. Then darkness swirled about them again, and they ground the guns forward blindly, a line of ants dragging their burden back to their hole.

They had reached that state of fatigue in which everything was hated. A man would slip in the mud and remain there, breathing hoarsely, having no will to get to his feet. That part of the column would halt, and wait numbly for the soldier to join them. If they had breath, they would swear.

"Fug the sonofabitchin' mud."

"Get up," somebody would cry.

"Fug you. Fug the goddamn gun."

"Let me lay here. I'm okay, they ain't a thing wrong with me, I'm okay, let me lay."

"Fug you, *get up!*"

And they would labor forward a few more yards and halt. In the darkness, distance had no meaning, nor did time. The heat had left their bodies; they shivered and trembled in the damp night, and everything about them was sodden and pappy; they stank but no longer with animal smells; their clothing was plastered with the foul muck of the jungle mud, and a chill dank rotting smell somewhere between leaf mold and feces filled their nostrils. They knew only that they had to keep moving, and if they thought of time it was in so many convulsions of nausea.

Wyman was wondering why he did not collapse. His breath came in long parched shudders, his pack straps galled, his feet were ablaze, and he could not have spoken, for his throat and chest and mouth seemed covered with a woolly felt. He was no longer conscious of the powerful and fetid stench that rose from his clothes. Somewhere deep inside himself was a wonder at the exhaustion his body could endure. He was normally a sluggish youth who worked no more than he was obliged to, and the sensations of labor, the muscle strains, the panting, the taste of fatigue were things he had always tried to avoid. He had had vague dreams about being a hero, assuming this would bring him some immense reward that would ease his life and remove the problems of supporting his mother and himself. He had a girl and he wanted to dazzle her with his ribbons. But he had always imagined combat as exciting, with no misery and no physical exertion. He dreamed of himself charging across a field in the face of many machine guns; but in the dream there was no stitch in his side from running too far while bearing too much weight.

He had never thought he would be chained to an inanimate monster of metal with which he would have to grapple until his arms trembled helplessly and his body was ready to fall. Certainly he had never imagined he would stumble down a path in the middle of the night with his shoes sucking and dragging in slime. He pushed at the gun, he lifted it with Goldstein and Toglio when it became mired in a hole, but the motions were automatic by now; he hardly even felt the added pain when they had to pull it out by the wheel hubs. His fingers were no longer able to close, and often he would tug helplessly until his hands slipped away with the gun still mired.

The column was proceeding even more slowly than it had at the start, and sometimes fifteen minutes would elapse before a gun could be moved a hundred yards.

At last a message began to carry back along the trail, "Keep going, we're almost there," and for a few minutes it served as a stimulant so that the men labored with some hope again. But when each turning in the trail discovered only another ribbon of mud and darkness, the men began to feel a hopeless dejection. Sometimes for as much as a minute they would not move at all. It became harder and harder to pitch themselves against the guns again. Every time they stopped they felt like quitting.

There was a draw they had to cross a few hundred feet before they reached 1st Battalion, and its banks sloped very steeply down to a little stony brook, then ascended again abruptly to about fifteen feet above the bottom. This was the stream the officer had mentioned. When the men reached it, the column stopped completely, and the stragglers caught up. Each team of soldiers waited for the men and gun in front of them to cross the stream. In the night it was an extremely difficult business at best and took a long time. The men would go sliding down the bank trying to restrain their field piece from turning over at the bottom, and then they would have to lift it over the slippery rocks of the brook before attempting to wrestle it up the other side. The banks were slimy, and there was no foothold; time and again a team would force its gun up almost to the top of the draw only to slip back again futilely.

By the time Wyman and Toglio and Goldstein had to move their gun, a half hour had passed and they were a little rested. Their wind had returned and they kept shouting instructions to each other as they nosed the gun over the edge of the bank. It began to pull away from them, and they had to resist desperately to keep it from crashing to the bottom. The exertion drained most of the strength they had recovered, and after they had carried the piece across the stream, they were as exhausted as they had been at any time during the march.

They stopped for a few moments to gather whatever force was left in them and began the struggle up the bank. Toglio was wheezing like a bull, and his commands had a hoarse urgent sound as if he were wrenching them from deep inside his body. "Okay, PUSH . . . PUSH," he growled, and the three of them strove numbly to roll the gun. It resisted them, moved sluggishly and treacherously, and the strength began to flow out of their trembling legs. "HOLD IT!" Toglio shouted. "DON'T LET IT SLIP!" They braced themselves behind the gun, trying to wedge their feet into the wet clay of the bank. "PUSH AGAIN!" he shouted, and they forced it upward a few more feet. Wyman felt a band was stretching dangerously inside his body and would snap at any moment. They rested again, and then shoved the gun another few yards. Slowly, minute by minute, they came closer to the top. They were perhaps four feet from the crest when Wyman lost the last reserves of his strength. He tried to draw some few shreds of effort from his quivering limbs, but he seemed to collapse all at once, and just lay stupidly behind the gun supporting it with no more than the weight of his sagging body. The gun began to slip, and he pulled away. Toglio and Goldstein were left at each of the hubs. When Wyman let go, they felt as though someone were pushing down against the gun. Goldstein held on until the sliding wheels pulled his fingers loose, one by one, and then he just had time to shout hoarsely, "WATCH IT!" to Toglio, before the gun went crashing down to the bottom. The three men fell after it, rolling in its wake. The gun struck some rocks at the bottom, and one of the wheels was knocked completely awry. They felt for it in the darkness like pups licking the wounds of their mother. Wyman began to blubber with exhaustion.

The accident caused a great deal of confusion. Croft's team was on the gun waiting behind them, and he began to shout, "What's holdin' you up? What's happening down there?"

"We had . . . trouble," Toglio shouted back. "Wait!" He and Gold-stein succeeded in turning the gun on its side. "The wheel's shot," Toglio shouted. "We can't move the gun."

Croft swore. "Get her out of the way."

They tried, and couldn't budge it.

"We need help," Goldstein shouted.

Croft swore again, and then he and Wilson slid down the bank. After a while they were able to tumble the gun over enough times to move it down the creek bed. Without saying anything, Croft went back to his gun, and Toglio and the others climbed up the far bank and went staggering down the trail till they reached 1st Battalion's bivouac. The men who had arrived before them were lying on the ground motionless. Toglio stretched out in the mud, and Wyman and Goldstein lay down beside him. None of them spoke for ten minutes. Occasionally, a shell might burst somewhere in the jungle about them and their legs might twitch, but this was the only sign they gave of being conscious. Men were moving about constantly, and the sounds of the fighting were closer, more vicious. Voices kept coming to them out of the darkness. Someone would shout, "Where's the pack train for B Company?" and the answer would be muffled to the men lying on the ground. They hardly cared. Occasionally they would be aware of the sounds of the night; for a few instants they might concentrate on the constant thrumming that emanated from the jungle, but they always relapsed into a stupor, thinking of nothing once more.

Croft and Wilson and Gallagher brought their gun in a short while later, and Croft shouted for Toglio.

"What do you want? I'm here," Toglio said. He hated to move.

Croft came toward him in the darkness and sat down beside him. His breath was coming in long slow gasps like a runner's after a race. "I'm going to see the Lieutenant . . . tell him about the gun. How the hell did it happen?"

Toglio propped himself on an elbow. He loathed the explanations that were to come, and he was confused. "I don't know," he said. "I heard Goldstein yell 'Watch out' and then it just seemed to rip out of our hands." Toglio hated to give excuses to Croft.

"Goldstein yelled, huh?" Croft asked. "Where is he?"

"Here I am, Sergeant." Goldstein's voice came out of the dark-ness beside them.

"Why'd you yell 'Watch out'?"

"I don't know. I felt suddenly as if I couldn't hold it anymore. Something pulled it away from me."

"Who was the other man?"

Wyman roused himself. "I guess I was." His voice sounded weak. "Did you let go?" Croft asked.

Wyman felt a trace of fear as he thought of admitting that to Croft. "No," he said. "No, I don't think so. I heard Goldstein yell, and then the gun started to come down on me. It was rolling back so I got out of the way." Already he was uncertain exactly how it had occurred, and a part of his mind was trying to convince him that he spoke the truth. With it, however, he felt a surprising flush of shame. "I guess it was my fault," he blurted out honestly, but his voice was so tired that it lacked sincerity, and Croft thought he was trying to protect Goldstein.

"Yeah," Croft said. A spasm of rage worked through him, and he turned on Goldstein and said, "Listen, Izzy."

"My name isn't Izzy," Goldstein said angrily.

"I don't give a damn what it is. The next time you pull a goddamn trick like that, I'm going to put you in for a court-martial."

"But I don't think I let go," Goldstein protested weakly. By now, he too was no longer sure. The sequence of his sensations when the gun had begun to pull out of his hands was too confused for him to feel righteous. He had thought that Wyman stopped pushing first, but when Wyman declared he was to blame, Goldstein had a moment of panic. Like Croft, he believed Wyman was protecting him. "I don't know," he said. "I don't think I did."

"You don't think," Croft cut him off. "Listen, for as long as you've been in the platoon, Goldstein, you've done nothing but have ideas about how we could do something better. But when it comes down to a little goddamn work, you're always dicking off. I've had enough of that bullshit from you."

Once again Goldstein was feeling a helpless anger. A reaction he could not control, his agitation was even greater than his resentment and choked him so that he could not speak. A few tears of frustration welled in his eyes, and he turned away and lay down again. His anger was now directed toward himself and he felt a hopeless shame. Oh, I don't know, I don't know, he said.

Toglio had a mingled relief and pity. He was glad the onus of losing the gun was not his, and yet he was unhappy anyone should be blamed. The bond of common effort that the three men had known while struggling with the weapon was still with him, and he said to himself, Poor Goldstein, he's a good guy; he just had hard luck.

Wyman was too exhausted to think clearly. After he declared it was his fault, he was relieved to discover he was not to be blamed after all. He was actually too depleted to think consecutively about anything, or indeed remember anything. By now, he was convinced it was Goldstein who had deserted the gun, and his main reaction was one of comfort. The image still most vivid to him was the agony he had felt in his chest and groin as they had started up the embankment, and he thought, I would have let go two seconds later if he didn't. For this reason, Wyman felt a dulled sense of affection for Goldstein.

Croft stood up. "Well, that's one gun they ain't going to rescue for a little while," he said. "I bet it stays there for the whole campaign." He was enraged enough to strike Goldstein. Without saying anything more, Croft left them and went in search of the officer who had led the column.

The men in the platoon settled down and began to sleep. Occasionally a shell would burst in the jungle nearby, but they hardly cared. The battle had been threatening all evening like a thunderstorm that never breaks, and by now it would have taken a barrage to move them. Besides, they were too weary to dig holes.

It took Red longer to fall asleep than any of the others. For many years his kidneys had bothered him whenever he had too much exposure to dampness. They were throbbing now, and he turned several times on the wet ground, trying to decide if it would be less painful to sleep with his back against the moist earth or exposed to the night air. He lay awake for a long time thinking, his mood turning through a small gamut from weariness to sadness. He was thinking of a time when he had been caught in a small town in Nebraska with no jobs to be had, and had had to wait until he could catch a boxcar out of town. It had seemed very important to him then not to beg for something to eat, and he wondered if he still had that pride. "Oh, I've been tough in my time," he muttered to himself. "Lot of good it does me." The air was cold on his back, and he turned over. It seemed to him that all his life he had been sleeping in bare wet places, seeking for warmth. He thought of an old hobo saying, "Half a buck in your pocket and winter coming," and felt some of the gloom he had known on cold October twilights. His stomach was empty, and he got up after a while and rummaged through his pack. He found a K ration and chewed the fruit bar, washing it down with water from his canteen. His blanket was still wet from the evening storm, but he wrapped it about him and found a little warmth. Then he tried to go to sleep again, but his kidneys were aching too much. At last he sat up, fumbled in the first-aid kit on his cartridge belt, and withdrew the little paper bag of wound tablets. He swallowed half of them and drank about half the water remaining in his canteen. For a moment he thought of using them all, but then he remembered that he might be wounded and need them. It brought back his dejection, and he stared solemnly into the darkness, being able to discern after a time the bodies of the sleeping men around him. Toglio was snoring, and he heard Martinez mutter softly in Spanish and then cry out, "I no kill Jap, God, I no kill him." Red sighed and lay down again. What men sleep easy? he thought.

A trace of an old anger passed through him. I don't give a damn about anything, he said to himself, and listened uneasily to a shell sighing overhead. This time it sounded like the branches of a tree murmuring in a winter wind. He remembered once striding along a highway as evening came. It had been in the eastern coal-mining towns of Pennsylvania and he had watched the miners driving home in their battered Fords, their faces still dark with the day's accumulation of soot and coal dust. It had not looked anything like the mining country in Montana he had left years before, and yet it had been the same. He had walked along brooding about home, and someone had given him a ride and treated him to a drink in a noisy bar. That night had a beauty about it now, and he remembered for a moment the sensation of leaving a strange town on a dark freight. Things like that were only glints of light in the long gray day of those years. He sighed again as if to grasp something of the knowledge he had felt for an instant. Nobody gets what he wants, he said to himself, and this deepened his mood of pleasurable sorrow. He was growing drowsy, and he burrowed his head under his forearm. A mosquito began to whine near his ear and he lay still, hoping it would go away. The ground seemed crawling with insects. The little buggers are one thing I'm used to, he thought. For some reason this made him smile.

It was beginning to rain, and Red covered his head with the blanket. His body was slowly sinking into a weary slumber in which different parts of him fell asleep at separate intervals, so that long after he had stopped thinking, a portion of his mind could feel the quivering of an exhausted limb or a cramp in one of his limbs. The shelling was becoming steady, and a half mile away from him a machine gun kept firing. Almost asleep, he watched Croft return and spread out a blanket. The rain continued. After a time, he no longer heard the artillery. But even when he was completely asleep, one last area of his mind noticed what was happening. Although he didn't remember it when he awoke, he heard a platoon of men march by, and was conscious of some other men beginning to push the antitank guns to the other side of the bivouac. There's a Jap road leads into the bivouac, he said in his sleep. They're going to protect it now. Probably he was feverish.

He dreamed until he heard a voice shout, "Recon? Where's Recon?" The dream ebbed away, and he lay there drowsily, listening to Croft spring to his feet and holler, "Here, over here!" Red knew he would have to be moving in a few minutes, and he burrowed deeper into his blankets. His body ached and he knew that when he stood up he would be stiff. "All right, men, on your feet." Croft was shouting. "Come on, get up, we got to move."

Red pulled the cover off his face. It was still raining and his hand came away wet from the top surface of the blanket. When he replaced the blanket in his pack, his pack also would become wet. "Aaaahhh-hhrr." He cleared his throat with disgust and spat once or twice. The taste in his mouth was foul. Gallagher sat up beside him and groaned. "Goddamn Army, why don't they let a guy sleep? Ain't we done enough tonight?"

"We're heroes," Red said. He stood up and began to fold his blanket. It was sopping wet on one side and muddy on the other. He had slept with his rifle beside him, covered under the blanket, but it too was wet. Red wondered how long it had been since he was dry. "Fuggin jungle," he said.

"Come on, you men, snap it up," Croft said. A flare lit the wet ugly shrubs about them and flickered dully against their wet black clothing. Red saw that Gallagher's face was covered with mud, and when he felt his own face, his hands came away soiled. "Show me the way to go home," he hummed. "I'm tired and I want to go to bed."

"Yeah," Gallagher said. They made their packs together and stood up. The flare had gone out and they were blinded for a moment in the returning darkness. "Where we going?" Toglio asked.

"Up to A Company. They expect an attack there," Croft said.

"We sure are a hard-luck platoon," Wilson sighed. "At least we're done with them antitank guns. Ah swear Ah'd fight a tank with mah bare hands 'fore Ah'd rassle with one of them sonsofbitches again."

The squad formed a single file and began to move out. First Battalion's bivouac was very small and in thirty seconds they had reached the gap in the barbed wire. Martinez led them cautiously down the trail leading to A Company. His drowsiness vanished quickly, and he became alert. Actually, he could not see anything, but some sense seemed to guide him along the bends in the path so that he rarely stumbled or blundered off the trail. He was proceeding about thirty yards ahead of the other men and he was completely isolated. If some Japanese had been waiting in ambush along the path, he would have been the first to be trapped. Yet he had very little fear; Martinez's terror developed in a void; the moment he had to lead men, his courage returned. At this instant, his mind was poised over a number of sounds and thoughts. His ears were searching the jungle ahead of him for some noise which might indicate that men were waiting in the brush beside the trail; they were also listening with disgust to the stumbling and muttering of the men following behind him. His mind recorded the intermittent sounds of battle and tried to classify them; he looked at the sky whenever they passed through a partial clearing in order to find the Southern Cross and determine in which direction the trail was bending. Wherever he could, he made a mental note of some landmark they were passing and added it to the ones he had observed previously. After a time he kept repeating a jingle to himself, which went, Tree over trail, muddy creek, rock on trail, bushes across. Actually there was no reason for him to do it; the trail led only from 1st Battalion to A Company. But this was a habit he had formed on his first patrols. He did it instinctively by now.

And another part of his mind had a quiet pride that he was the man upon whom the safety of the others depended. This was a sustaining force that carried him through dangers his will and body would have resisted. During the march with the antitank guns, there had been many times when he wanted to quit; unlike Croft, he had felt it no contest at all. He would have been perfectly willing to declare the task beyond his strength and give up, but there was a part of his mind that drove him to do things he feared and detested. His pride with being a sergeant was the core about which nearly all his actions and thoughts were bound. Nobody see in the darkness like Martinez, he said to himself. He touched a branch before his extended arm and bent his knees easily and walked under it. His feet were sore and his back and shoulders ached, but they were ills with which he no longer concerned himself; he was leading his squad, and that was sufficient in itself.

The rest of the squad, strung out behind, was experiencing a variety of emotions. Wilson and Toglio were sleepy, Red was alert and brooding—he had a sense of foreboding. Goldstein was miserable and bitter, and the tension of creeping down a trail in the black early hours of the morning made him gloomy and then sad. He thought of himself dying without friends nearby to mourn him. Wyman had lost his power to recuperate; he was so tired that he plodded along in a stupor, not caring where he went or what happened to him. Ridges was weary and patient; he did not think of what the next hours would bring him, nor did he lose himself in contemplation of his aching limbs; he just walked and his mind drifted slowly like a torpid stream.

And Croft; Croft was tense and eager and impatient. All night he had been balked by the assignment of the squad to a labor detail. The sounds of battle he had been hearing all night were goading to him. His mind was buoyed by a recurrence of the mood he had felt after Hennessey's death. He felt strong and tireless and capable of anything; his muscles were as strained and jaded as any of the men's, but his mind had excluded his body. He hungered for the fast taut pulse he would feel in his throat after he killed a man.

On the map there was only a half mile between 1st Battalion and A Company, but the trail doubled and curved so often that it was actually a mile. The men in recon were clumsy now and uncertain of their footing. Their packs sagged; their rifles kept sliding off their shoulders. The trail was crude. Originally a game wallow, it had been partially enlarged, and in places it was still narrow. A man could not walk without being scratched by the branches on either side. The jungle was impenetrable at that point, and it would have taken an hour to cut one's way a hundred feet off the path. In the night it was impossible to see anything and the smell of the wet foliage was choking. The men had to walk in single file, drawn up close. Even at three feet they could not see one another, and they plodded down the trail with each man grasping the shirt of the man before him. Martinez could hear them and judge his distance accordingly, but the others stumbled and collided with one another like children playing a game in the dark. They were bent over almost double, and the posture was cruel. Their bodies were outraged; they had been eating and sleeping with no rhythm at all for the last few hours. They kept loosing gas whose smell was nauseating in the foul dense air. The men at the rear had the worst of it; they gagged and swore, tried not to breathe for a few seconds, and shuddered from fatigue and revulsion. Gallagher was at the end of the file, and every few minutes he would cough and curse. "Cut out the goddamn farting," he would shout, and the men in front would rouse themselves for a moment and laugh.

"Eatin' dust, hey, boy," Wilson muttered, and a few of them began to giggle.

Some of them began to fall asleep as they walked. Their eyes had been closed almost the entire march, and they drowsed for the instant their foot was in the air and awakened as it touched the ground. Wyman had been plodding along for many minutes with no sensation at all; his body had grown numb. He and Ridges drowsed continually, and every now and then for ten or fifteen yards they would be completely asleep. At last they would weave off the trail and go pitching into the bushes stupidly before regaining their balance. In the darkness such noises were terrifying. It made the men uncomfortably aware of how close they were to the fighting. A half mile away some rifles were firing.

"Goddammit," one of them would whisper, "can't you guys keep quiet?"

The march must have taken them over half an hour, but after the first few minutes they no longer thought about time. Crouching and sliding through the mud with their hands on the man in front became the only thing they really knew; the trail was a treadmill and they no longer concerned themselves with where they were going. To most of them the end of the march came as a surprise. Martinez doubled back and told them to be quiet. "They hear you coming for ten minutes," he whispered. A hush settled over the men, and they trod the last hundred yards with ridiculous precautions, tensing every muscle whenever they took a step.

There was no barbed wire, nor any clearing at A Company. The trail divided in a quadruple fork that led to different emplacements. A soldier met them where the path broke up and led the squad along one of the footpaths to a few pup tents pitched in the middle of some foliage. "I got Second Platoon," he told Croft. "I'm just about a hundred yards down the river. Your squad can sleep in these holes tonight, and set up a guard right along here. They's two machine guns set up for you."

"What's doing?" Croft whispered.

"I dunno. I heard they expect an attack all up and down the line about dawn. We had to send a platoon over to C Company early tonight, and we been holding down the whole outpost here with less than a platoon." He made a rustling sound in the darkness as he wiped his hand against his mouth. "C'mere, I'll show you the setup," he said, grasping Croft's elbow. Croft slipped his arm free; he hated to have anyone touch him.

They went a few feet along the path, until the sergeant from A Company halted before a foxhole. There was a machine gun mounted in front, its muzzle just projecting through a fringe of bushes. Croft peered through the foliage and in the faint moonlight was able to see a stream of water and a strip of beach bordering it on either side. "How deep is the river?" he asked.

"Aw, it's four, five feet maybe. That water ain't going to stop them."

"Any outposts forward of here?" Croft asked.

"Nothing. And the Japs know right where we are. Had some patrols up." The soldier wiped his mouth again and stood up. "I'll show you the other machine gun." They walked along a stubbly path cut through the jungle about ten feet from the river's edge. Some crickets were chirping loudly, and the soldier trembled a little. "Here's the other one," he said. "This is the flank." He peered through the bushes and stepped out onto the strip of beach. "Look," he said. Croft followed him. About fifty yards to their right, the bluffs of Watamai Range began. Croft looked up. The cliffs rose almost vertically for perhaps a thousand feet. Even in the darkness, he felt them hovering above him. He strained his eyes and thought he saw a swatch of sky where they ended but could not be certain. He had a curious thrill. "I didn't know we were that close," he said.

"Oh, yeah. It's good and it's bad. You don't have to worry about them coming around that end, but still we're the flank. If they ever hit here hard, there ain't much to hold them." The soldier drew into the bushes again and exhaled his breath slowly. "I'll tell you these two nights we been out here give me the creeps. Look at that river. When there's a lot of moonlight it just seems to shine, and you get jittery after a while looking at it."

Croft remained outside the jungle edge, looking at the stream that curved away at the right and flowed parallel to the mountains. It took a turn toward the Japanese lines just a few yards before the first walls of the bluff began, and he would be able to see everything on that side. To the left the stream ran straight for a few hundred yards like a highway at night, sunk between high grassy banks. "Where are you?" he asked.

The soldier pointed to a tree that projected a little from the jungle. "We're just on this side of it. If you got to get to us, go back to the fork and then take the trail at the far right going away from here. Yell 'Buckeye' when you come up."

"Okay," Croft said. They talked for a few more minutes, and then the other soldier hooked his cartridge belt. "Jesus, I'll tell ya, it'll drive ya crazy spending a night here. Just wilderness, that's all, and you stuck out at the end of it with nothing but a lousy machine gun." He slung his rifle and struck off down the trail. Croft looked at him for a moment and then went back to Recon. The men were waiting by the three pup tents, and he showed them where the two machine guns were placed. Briefly he told them what he had learned and picked a guard. "It's three A.M. now," he told them. "There's gonna be four of us on one post and five on the other. We'll do it in two-hour shifts.

Then the post that's only got four men will get the extra one for the next time around." He divided them up, taking the first shift at the flank gun himself. Wilson volunteered to take the other gun. "After Ah'm done, Ah'm gonna want to sleep right on through," Wilson said. "Ah'm tired of gittin' up right when Ah'm havin' a good dream."

The men smiled wanly.

"An' listen," Croft added, "if any trouble starts, the men that are sleeping are to git up goddamn fast and move to help us. It's only a couple of yards from our tents to Wilson's machine gun, and it ain't much further to mine. It shouldn't be takin' you all more than about three hours to reach us." Again, a couple of men smiled. "Okay, that's about it," Croft said. He left them and walked over to his machine gun.

He sat down on the edge of the hole and peered through the bushes at the river. The jungle completely surrounded him, and, now that he was no longer active, he felt very weary and a little depressed. To counteract this mood, he began to feel the various objects in the hole. There were three boxes of belt ammunition and a row of seven grenades lined up neatly at the base of the machine gun. At his feet were a box of flares and a flare gun. He picked it up and broke open the breech quietly, loaded it, and cocked it. Then he set it down beside him.

A few shells murmured overhead and began to fall. He was a little surprised at how near they landed to the other side of the river. Not more than a few hundred yards away, the noise of their explosion was extremely loud; a few pieces of shrapnel lashed the leaves on the trees above him. He broke off a stalk from a plant and put it in his mouth, chewing slowly and reflectively. He guessed that the weapons platoon of A Company had fired, and he tried to determine which trail at the fork would lead to them in case he had to pull back his men. Now he was patient and at ease; the danger of their position neutralized the anticipation for some combat he had felt earlier, and he was left cool and calm and very tired.

The mortar shells were falling perhaps fifty yards in front of the platoon at his left, and Croft spat quietly. It was too close to be merely harassing fire; someone had heard something in the jungle on the other side of the river or they would never have called for mortars so close to their own position. His hand explored the hole again and discovered a field telephone. Croft picked up the receiver, listened quietly. It was an open line, and probably confined to the platoons of A Company. Two men were talking in voices so low that he strained to hear them.

"Walk it up another fifty and then bring it back."

"You sure there're Japs?"

"I swear I heard them talking."

Croft stared tensely across the river. The moon had come out, and the strands of beach on either side of the stream were shining with a silver glow. The jungle wall on the other side looked impenetrable.

The mortars fired again behind him with a cruel flat sound. He watched the shells land in the jungle, and then creep nearer to the river in successive volleys. A mortar answered from the Japanese side of the river, and about a quarter of a mile to the left Croft could hear several machine guns spattering at each other, the uproar deep and irregular. Croft picked up the phone and whistled into it. "Wilson," he whispered. *"Wilson!"* There was no answer and he debated whether to walk over to Wilson's hole. Silently Croft cursed him for not noticing the phone, and then berated himself for not having discovered it before he briefed the others. He looked out across the river. Fine sergeant I am, he told himself.

His ears were keyed to all the sounds of the night, and from long experience he sifted out the ones that were meaningless. If an animal rustled in its hole, he paid no attention; if some crickets chirped, his ear disregarded them. Now he picked a muffled slithering sound that he knew could be made only by men moving through a thin patch of jungle. He peered across the river, trying to determine where the foliage was least dense. At a point between his gun and Wilson's there was a grove of a few coconut trees sparse enough to allow men to assemble; as he stared into that patch of wood, he was certain he heard a man move. Croft's mouth tightened. His hand felt for the bolt of the machine gun, and he slowly brought it to bear on the coconut grove. The rustling grew louder; it seemed as if men were creeping through the brush on the other side of the river to a point opposite his gun. Croft swallowed once. Tiny charges seemed to pulse through his limbs and his head was as empty and shockingly aware as if it had been plunged into a pail of freezing water. He wet his lips and shifted his position slightly, feeling as though he could hear the flexing of his muscles.

The Jap mortar fired again and he started. The shells were falling by the next platoon, the sound painful and jarring to him. He stared out on the moonlit river until his eyes deceived him; he began to think he could see the heads of men in the dark swirls of the current. Croft gazed down at his knees for an instant and then across the river again. He looked a little to the left or right of where he thought the Japanese might be; from long experience he had learned a man could not look directly at an object and see it in the darkness. Something seemed to move in the grove, and a new trickle of sweat formed and rolled down his back. He twisted uncomfortably. Croft was unbearably tense, but the sensation was not wholly unpleasant.

He wondered if Wilson had noticed the sounds, and then in answer to his question, there was the loud unmistakable clicking of a machine gun bolt. To Croft's keyed senses, the sound echoed up and down the river, and he was furious that Wilson should have revealed his position. The rustling in the brush became louder and Croft was convinced he could hear voices whispering on the other side of the river. He fumbled for a grenade and placed it at his feet.

Then he heard a sound that pierced his flesh. Someone called from across the river, "Yank, Yank!" Croft sat numb. The voice was thin and high-pitched, hideous in a whisper. "That's a Jap," Croft told himself. He was incapable of moving for that instant.

"Yank!" It was calling to him. "Yank. We you coming-to-get, Yank."

The night lay like a heavy stifling mat over the river. Croft tried to breathe.

*"We you coming-to-get, Yank."*

Croft felt as if a hand had suddenly clapped against his back, traveled up his spine over his skull to clutch at the hair on his forehead. "Coming to get you, Yank," he heard himself whisper. He had the agonizing frustration of a man in a nightmare who wants to scream and cannot utter a sound. "We you *coming-to-get,* Yank."

He shivered terribly for a moment, and his hands seemed congealed on the machine gun. He could not bear the intense pressure in his head.

"We you coming-to-get, Yank," the voice screamed.

"COME AND GET ME YOU SONSOFBITCHES," Croft roared. He shouted with every fiber of his body as though he plunged at an oaken door.

There was no sound at all for perhaps ten seconds, nothing but the moonlight on the river and the taut rapt buzzing of the crickets. Then the voice spoke again. "Oh, we come, Yank, we come."

Croft pulled back the bolt on his machine gun, and rammed it home. His heart was still beating with frenzy. "Recon . . . RECON, UP ON THE LINE," he shouted with all his strength.

A machine gun lashed at him from across the river, and he ducked in his hole. In the darkness, it spat a vindictive white light like an acetylene torch, and its sound was terrifying. Croft was holding himself together by the force of his will. He pressed the trigger of his gun and it leaped and bucked under his hand. The tracers spewed wildly into the jungle on the other side of the river.

But the noise, the vibration of his gun, calmed him. He directed it to where he had seen the Japanese gunfire and loosed a volley. The handle pounded against his fist, and he had to steady it with both hands. The hot metallic smell of the barrel eddied back to him, made what he was doing real again. He ducked in his hole waiting for the reply and winced involuntarily as the bullets whipped past.

BEE-YOWWWW! . . . BEE-YOOWWWW! Some dirt snapped at his face from the ricochets. Croft was not conscious of feeling it. He had the surface numbness a man has in a fight. He flinched at sounds, his mouth tightened and loosened, his eyes stared, but he was oblivious to his body.

Croft fired the gun again, held it for a long vicious burst, and then ducked in his hole. An awful scream singed the night, and for an instant Croft grinned weakly. Got him, he thought. He saw the metal burning through flesh, shattering the bones in its path. "AII-YOHHHH." The scream froze him again, and for an odd disconnected instant he experienced again the whole complex of sounds and smells and sights when a calf was branded. "RECON, UP . . . UP!" he shouted furiously and fired steadily for ten seconds to cover their advance. As he paused he could hear some men crawling behind him, and he whispered, "Recon?"

"Yeah." Gallagher dropped into the hole with him. "Mother of Mary," he muttered. Croft could feel him shaking beside him.

"Stop it!" he gripped his arm tensely. "The other men up?"

"Yeah."

Croft looked across the river again. Everything was silent, and the disconnected abrupt spurts of fire were forgotten like vanished sparks from a grindstone. Now that he was no longer alone, Croft was able to plan. The fact that men were up with him, were scattered in the brush along the bank between their two machine guns, recovered his sense of command. "They're going to attack soon," he whispered hoarsely in Gallagher's ear.

Gallagher trembled again. "Ohh. No way to wake up," he tried to say, but his voice kept lapsing.

"Look," Croft whispered. "Creep along the line and tell them to hold fire until the Japs start to cross the river."

"I can't, I can't," Gallagher whispered.

Croft felt like striking him. "Go!" he whispered.

"I can't."

The Jap machine gun lashed at them from across the river. The bullets went singing into the jungle behind them, ripping at leaves. The tracers looked like red splints of lightning as they flattened into the jungle. A thousand rifles seemed to be firing at them from across the river, and the two men pressed themselves against the bottom of the hole. The sounds cracked against their eardrums. Croft's head ached. Firing the machine gun had partially deafened him. BEE-YOWWWW! A ricochet slapped some more dirt on top of them. Croft felt it pattering on his back this time. He was trying to sense the moment when he would have to raise his head and fire the gun. The firing seemed to slacken, and he lifted his eyes cautiously. BEE-YOWWW, BEE-YOWWWW! He dropped in the hole again. The Japanese machine gun raked through the brush at them.

There was a shrill screaming sound, and the men covered their heads with their arms. BAA-ROWWMM, BAA-ROWWMM, ROWWMM, ROWWMM. The mortars exploded all about them and something picked Gallagher up, shook him, and then released him. "Oh, God," he cried. A clod of dirt stung his neck. BAA-ROWWMM, BAA-ROWWMM.

"Jesus, I'm hit," someone screamed, "I'm hit. Something hit me." BAA-ROWWMM.

Gallagher rebelled against the force of the explosions. "Stop, I give up," he screamed. "STOP! . . . I give up! I give up!" At that instant he no longer knew what made him cry out.

BAA-ROWWMM, BAA-ROWWMM.

"I'm hit, I'm hit," someone was screaming. The Japanese rifles were firing again. Croft lay on the floor of the hole with his hands against the ground and every muscle poised in its place.

BAA-ROWWMM. TEEEEEEEEN! The shrapnel was singing as it scattered through the foliage.

Croft picked up his flare gun. The firing had not abated, but through it he heard someone shouting in Japanese. He pointed the gun in the air.

"Here they come," Croft said.

He fired the flare and shouted, "STOP 'EM!"

A shrill cry came out of the jungle across the river. It was the scream a man might utter if his foot was being crushed. "AAAIIIIII, AAAIIIIIIII."

The flare burst at the moment the Japanese started their charge. Croft had a split perception of the Japanese machine gun firing from a flank, and then he began to fire automatically, not looking where he fired, but holding his gun low, swinging it from side to side. He could not hear the other guns fire, but he saw their muzzle blasts like exhausts.

He had a startling frozen picture of the Japanese running toward him across the narrow river. "AAAAIIIIIIIIIIH," he heard again. In the light of the flare the Japanese had the stark frozen quality of men revealed by a shaft of lightning. Croft no longer saw anything clearly. He could not have said at that moment where his hands ended and the machine gun began. He was lost in a vast moil of noise out of which individual screams and shouts etched in his mind for an instant. He could never have counted the Japanese who charged across the river; he knew only that his finger was rigid on the trigger bar. He could not have loosened it. In those few moments he felt no sense of danger. He just kept firing.

The line of men who charged across the river began to fall. In the water they were slowed considerably and the concentrated fire from Recon's side raged at them like a wind across an open field. They began to stumble over the bodies ahead of them. Croft saw one soldier reach into the air behind another's body as though trying to clutch something in the sky and Croft fired at him for what seemed many seconds before the arm collapsed.

He looked to his right and saw three men trying to cross the river where it turned and ran parallel to the bluff. He swung the gun about and lashed them with it. One man fell, and the other two paused uncertainly and began to run back toward their own bank of the river. Croft had no time to follow them; some soldiers had reached the beach on his side and were charging the gun. He fired point blank at them, and they collapsed about five yards from his hole.

Croft fired and fired, switching targets with the quick reflexes of an athlete shifting for a ball. As soon as he saw men falling he would attack another group. The line of Japanese broke into little bunches of men who wavered, began to retreat.

The light of the flare went out and Croft was blinded for a moment. There was no sound again in the darkness and he fumbled for another flare, feeling an almost desperate urgency. "Where is it?" he whispered to Gallagher.

"What?"

"Shit." Croft's hand found the flare box, and he loaded the gun again. He was beginning to see in the darkness, and he hesitated. But something moved on the river and he fired the flare. As it burst, a few

Japanese soldiers were caught motionless in the water. Croft pivoted his gun on them and fired. One of the soldiers remained standing for an incredible time. There was no expression on his face. He looked vacant and surprised even as the bullets struck him in the chest.

Nothing was moving now on the river. In the light of the flare, the bodies looked as limp and unhuman as bags of grain. One soldier began to float downstream, his face in the water. On the beach near the gun, another Japanese soldier was lying on his back. A wide stain of blood was spreading out from his body, and his stomach, ripped open, gaped like the swollen entrails of a fowl. On an impulse Croft fired a burst into him, and felt a twitch of pleasure as he saw the body quiver.

A wounded man was groaning in Japanese. Every few seconds he would scream, the sound terrifying in the cruel blue light of the flare. Croft picked up a grenade. "That sonofabitch is makin' too much noise," he said. He pulled the pin and lobbed the grenade over to the opposite bank. It dropped like a beanbag on one of the bodies, and Croft pulled Gallagher down with him. The explosion was powerful and yet empty like a blast that collapses windowpanes. After a moment, the echoes ceased.

Croft tensed himself and listened to the sounds from across the river. There was the quiet furtive noise of men retreating into the jungle. "GIVE 'EM A VOLLEY!" he shouted.

All the men in Recon began to fire again, and Croft raked the jungle for a minute in short bursts. He could hear Wilson's machine gun pounding steadily. "I guess we gave 'em something," Croft told Gallagher. The flare was going out, and Croft stood up. "Who was hit?" he shouted.

"Toglio."

"Bad?" Croft asked.

"I'm okay," Toglio whispered. "I got a bullet in my elbow."

"Can you wait till morning?"

There was silence for a moment, then Toglio answered weakly, "Yeah, I'll be okay."

Croft got out of his hole. "I'm coming down," he announced. "Hold your fire." He walked along the path until he reached Toglio. Red and Goldstein were kneeling beside him, and Croft spoke to them in a low voice. "Pass this on," he said. "We're all gonna stay in our holes until mornin'. I don't think they'll be back tonight, but you cain't tell. And no one is gonna fall asleep. They's only about an hour till dawn, so you ain't got nothin' to piss about."

"I wouldn't go to sleep anyway," Goldstein breathed. "What a way to wake up." It was the same thing Gallagher had said.

"Yeah, well, I just wasn't ridin' on my ass either, waitin' for them to come," Croft said. He shivered for a moment in the early morning air and realized with a pang of shame that for the first time in his life he had been really afraid. "The sonsofbitchin' Japs," he said. His legs were tired and he turned to go back to his gun. I hate the bastards, he said to himself, a terrible rage working through his weary body.

"One of these days I'm gonna really get me a Jap," he whispered aloud. The river was slowly carrying the bodies downstream.

"At least," Gallagher said, "if we got to stay here a couple of days, the fuggers won't be stinkin' up the joint."

From The Naked and the Dead (1948)

# THE SECOND
# WORLD WAR—II

## The Four Dead Germans

I met Jack Kennedy in November 1946. We were both war heroes, and both of us had just been elected to Congress. We went out one night on a double date and it turned out to be a fair evening for me. I seduced a girl who would have been bored by a diamond as big as the Ritz.

She was Deborah Caughlin Mangaravidi Kelly, of the Caughlins first, English-Irish bankers, financiers, and priests; the Mangaravidis, a Sicilian issue from the Bourbons and the Hapsburgs. Kelly's family was just Kelly, but he had made a million two hundred times. So there was a vision of treasure, far-off blood, and fear. The night I met her we had a wild ninety minutes in the back seat of my car parked behind a trailer truck on a deserted factory street in Alexandria, Virginia. Since Kelly owned part of the third largest trucking firm in the Midwest and West, I may have had a speck of genius to try for his daughter where I did. Forgive me. I thought the road to President might begin at the entrance to her Irish heart. She heard the snake rustle however in *my* heart; on the telephone next morning she told me I was evil, awful and evil, and took herself back to the convent in London where she had lived at times before. I did not know as yet that ogres stand on guard before the portal of an heiress. Now in retrospect I can say with cheer: That was the closest *I* came to being President. (By the time I found Deborah again—all of seven years later in Paris—she was no longer her father's delight, and we were married in a week. Like any tale that could take ten books, it is best to quit it by a parenthesis—less than ten volumes might be untrue.)

Of course Jack Kennedy has gone on a bit since those days, and I have traveled up and I have voyaged down and I've gone up and down, but I remember a full moon the night we had our double date, and to be phenomenologically precise, there was also a full moon on the night I led my patrol to the top of a particular hill in Italy, and a full moon the night I met another girl, and a full moon. . . . There are times when I like to think I still have my card in the intellectuals' guild, but I seem to be joining company with that horde of the mediocre and the mad who listen to popular songs and act upon co-incidence. The real difference between the President and myself may be that I ended with too large an appreciation of the moon, for I looked down the abyss on the first night I killed: four men, four very separate Germans, dead under a full moon—whereas Jack, for all I know, never saw the abyss.

Of course, I did not have any illusion that my heroism was the equal of his. I got good for one night. I was a stiff, overburdened, nervous young Second Lieutenant, fresh from Harvard, graduated a year behind Prince Jack (we never met—not there). I had gone into the Army with a sweaty near-adolescent style, Harvard on the half-shell ("Raw-Jock" Rojack was the sporting name bestowed on me in House Football) and I had been a humdrum athlete and, as a student, excessively bright: Phi Beta Kappa, *summa cum laude*, Government.

Small wonder I was thus busy working to keep some government among the hard-nosed Southerners and young Mafiosos from the Bronx who made up the double nucleus of my platoon, working so busily that death this night first appeared to me as a possibility considerably more agreeable than my status in some further disorder. I really didn't care much longer whether I stayed alive. When I steered us up the hill therefore to get pinned down in a long, bad line, one hundred feet from the summit, a modest twin dome, a double hill with a German machine gun on one knoll and a German machine gun on the other, I was so ready to die in atonement I was not even scared.

Trapped beneath a rusty sputter—the guns had not quite found me nor any of the others—the full moon giving a fine stain to the salient of our mood (which was fear and funk and a sniff of the grave), I could nonetheless feel danger withdraw from me like an angel, withdraw like a retreating wave over a quiet sea, sinking quietly into the sand, and I stood and then I ran. I ran up the hill into the aisle of safety I felt opening for me, which is part of what captured that large decoration later, because the route I took was under the separate fire of each of those guns and the two together could stitch you to a pulp. Their fire was jagged, however. It was startled. And as I ran, I threw my carbine away, out ten yards to the front of me, crossed my arms to pull a grenade from each shirt pocket, pulled the rings with my teeth, which I had hardly been able to do in practice (much too hard on the teeth), released the spoon handles, the fuse now lit and spitting, and shot my arms out like the wings of the letter Y. The grenades sailed away in separate flights and I had time to stop, turn around, and dive back for my carbine, which I had overrun.

Years later I read *Zen in the Art of Archery* and understood the book. Because I did not throw the grenades on that night on the hill under the moon, *it* threw them, and *it* did a near-perfect job. The grenades went off somewhere between five and ten yards over each machine gun, *blast, blast,* like a boxer's tattoo, one-two, and I was exploded in the butt from a piece of my own shrapnel, whacked with a delicious pain clean as a mistress' sharp teeth going "Yummy" in your rump, and then the barrel of my carbine swung around like a long fine antenna and pointed itself at the machine-gun hole on my right, where a great bloody sweet German face, a healthy spoiled overspoiled young beauty of a face, mother-love all over its making, possessor of that overcurved mouth which only great fat sweet young faggots can have when their rectum is tuned and entertained from adolescence on, came crying, sliding, smiling up over the edge of the hole, "Hello death!" blood and mud like the herald of sodomy upon his chest, and I pulled the trigger as if I were squeezing the softest breast of the softest pigeon that ever flew, still a woman's breast takes me now and then to the pigeon on that trigger, and the shot cracked like a birch twig across my palm, *whop!* and the round went in at the base of his nose and spread and I saw his face sucked in backward upon the gouge of the bullet, he looked suddenly like an old man, toothless, sly, reminiscent of lechery. Then he whimpered *"Mutter,"* one yelp from the first memory of the womb, and down he went into his own blood just in time, timed like the interval in a shooting gallery, for the next was up, his hole-mate, a hard avenging specter with a pistol in his hand and one arm off, blown off, rectitude like a stringer of saliva across the straight edge of his lip, the straightest lip I ever saw, German-Protestant rectitude. *Whap!* went my carbine and the hole was in his heart and he folded back the long arm with the pistol, back across his chest to cover his new hole and went down straight and with a clown's deep gloom as if he were sliding down a long thin pipe, and then I turned, feeling something tear in my wound, nice in its pain, a good blood at liberty, and I took on the other two coming out of the other hole, one short stocky ape-like wretch with his back all askew, as if he'd had a false stuffed hump that shrapnel had disgorged beyond his shoulder blade. I fired at him and he went down and I never knew where it hit nor quite saw his face. Then the last stood up straight with a bayonet in his hand and invited me to advance. He was bleeding below his belt. Neat and clean was his shirt, level the line of his helmet, and nothing but blood and carnage below the belt. I started to rise. I wanted to charge as if that were our contract, and held, for I could not face his eyes: They now contained all of it—the two grenades, the blood on my thigh, the fat faggot, the ghost with the pistol, the hunch-back, the blood, those bloody screams that never sounded, it was all in his eyes. He had eyes I was to see once later on an autopsy table in a small town in Missouri, eyes belonging to a redneck farmer from a deep road in the Ozarks, eyes of blue, so perfectly blue and mad they go all the way in deep into celestial vaults of sky, eyes that go back all the way to God is the way I think I heard it said once in the South, and I faltered before that stare, clear as ice in the moonlight, and hung on one knee, not knowing if I could push my wound, and suddenly it was all gone, the clean presence of *it,* the grace, *it* had deserted me in the instant I hesitated, and now I had no stomach to go, I could charge his bayonet no more. So I fired. And missed. And fired again. And missed. Then he threw his bayonet at me. It did not reach. He was too weak. It struck a stone instead and made a quivering whanging sound like the yowl of a tomcat on the jump. Then it stopped between us. The light was going out in his eye. It started to collect, to coagulate into the thick jelly that forms on the pupil of a just-dead dog, and he died then, and fell over. Like a noble tree with rotten roots. And the platoon was up around me, shooting a storm into those two holes, and they were cheering, buzzing, kissing my mouth (one of the Italians for certain), pounding my back. "Get off him, he's wounded," shouted somebody, the Sergeant, and I felt like a halfback who has caught a fifty-yard pass and run another forty-eight for the longest touchdown in the history of the school, except that the final excellence of it was smuggled away since the ball squiggled out of my arms as I ran it out past the end zone. I had scored, but no football in my belly at the end, just six points. And those blue eyes kept staring into the new flesh of my memory until I went over with a thud, a wave from the wound car-rying me back, forcing my head to the ground with some desire of its own. "Medics," I heard a man yell.

I was carried out later on a stretcher—an X-ray showed a minor crack and small split in the girdle of the pelvis. I was evacuated to a base hospital, then sent to New York, where I was given a Distinguished Service Cross, not anything less, and was used for the last year to bring good public relations for the Army. Which I did, showing the trace of a distinguished limp. A hero in mid-'44, a hero for all of '45, surviving even V-J Day, I had my pick of opportunities and used them. I went around for a time speaking with Mrs. Roosevelt at one honorable drive after another, and she liked me. She encouraged me to think of politics. Those became the years when the gears worked together, the contacts and the insights, the style and the manufacture of oneself. It all turned together very well. I was a curiosity after all, a most special product. I was the one intellectual in America's history with a DSC and I spoke in public with a modest warrior's charm.

About the time the Party machine in New York County was sorting through its culls and giving me odd off-hand invitations to lunch with the Cardinal and the Bishop ("One question, son," asked the first Eminence, "do you believe in God?" "Yes, your Eminence") Mrs. Roosevelt was introducing me to Protestant gentry and Jewish gentry and, yes, it all began to fit and fit so well I came out, by the end, a candidate for Congress, and was then elected. Congressman Stephen Richards Rojack, Democrat from New York.

Now, I could go into more detail about the precise sequence of steps that left me a young Congressman in 1946 at the age of twenty-six—the moves were not automatic after all, but would merely describe the adventures of the part that I as a young actor was playing. There are any number of movie stars who capture the love of women they have never seen; the poor husbands of those women are in competition with a man they cannot meet. But I think of those particular few movie stars who are not only profiles for a great lover, but homosexual and private in their life. They must live with insanity on every breath. And something that could correspond to this was true for me. Where many another young athlete or hero might have had a vast and continuing recreation with sex, I was lost in a private kaleidoscope of death. I could not forget the fourth soldier. His eyes had come to see what was waiting on the other side, and they told me then that death was a creation more dangerous than life. I could have had a career in politics if only I had been able to think that death was zero, death was everyone's emptiness. But I knew it was not. I remained an actor. My personality was built upon a void. Thus I quit my place in politics almost as quickly as I gained it, for by '48 I chose to bolt the Democratic Party and run for office on the Progressive ticket. Henry Wallace, Glen Taylor, and me. I had reasons for the choice, some honorable, some spurious, but one motive now seems clear—I wanted to depart from politics before I was separated from myself forever by the distance between my public appearance, which had become vital on television, indeed nearly robust, and my secret frightened romance with the phases of the moon. About the month you decide not to make a speech because it is the week of the full lunar face you also know if still you are sane that politics is not for you and you are not for politics.

From *An American Dream* (1965)

# THE SECOND
# WORLD WAR—III

## The Death of Mary Gallagher

The campaign was over, and Recon was working on a road. One day, after the midday meal, Gallagher was sitting in his tent when Croft called him. "What is it?" Gallagher asked.

"The chaplain wants to see you," Croft said.

"What about?"

"I don't know," Croft shrugged. "We'll be gone when you get back, so you'll have perimeter guard for the afternoon."

Gallagher walked through the bivouac and stopped at the chaplain's tent. His heart was beating quickly, and he was trying to suppress the hope he was feeling. Before they had landed on Anopopei, he had asked the chaplain if he needed another assistant, and the chaplain had promised to consider him. To Gallagher it meant getting out of combat, and he had allowed himself to dream about the possibility several times.

"Good afternoon, Father Leary," he said. "I heard you wanted to see me." His voice was polite and uncomfortable, and he was perspiring from the effort of having to watch his profanity.

"Sit down, Gallagher." Father Leary was a tall slim middle-aged man with light hair, and a caressing voice.

"What is it, Father?"

"Go ahead and smoke, son." Father Leary lit a cigarette for him. "You get much mail from home, Gallagher?"

"My wife writes to me every day, almost, Father. She's gonna be having a baby any day now."

"Yes." Father Leary was silent; he fingered his lip, and then sat down abruptly. He put his hand on Gallagher's knee. "Son, I have some pretty bad news for you."

Gallagher felt a chill. "What is it, Father?"

"You know, son, there're a lot of things that are difficult to understand. You just have to believe that it's right, and that there's a good reason for it, that God understands and sees and does what is best, even if we don't understand right away."

Gallagher was ill at ease and then abruptly frantic. All kinds of wild thoughts passed through his mind. He blurted out, "My wife didn't leave me, did she?" He felt shame as soon as he had spoken.

"No, son, but there has been a death."

"My mother?"

Father Leary shook his head. "Not your parents."

Gallagher thought his child had died in birth. He felt a quick passage of relief. That ain't so bad, went through his mind. For an instant he wondered again dumbly if Father Leary had called him in to give him the job as chaplain's assistant.

"No, son, I'm afraid it was your wife."

The words passed through Gallagher numbly. He sat there without any response, without thinking of anything at all. An insect buzzed in through the folded flaps of the tent, and he watched it. "Wha-a-a-at?" he asked.

"Your wife died in childbirth, Gallagher." Father Leary looked away. "They were able to save your child, though."

"Mary wasn't very big," Gallagher said. The word "dead" formed for him, and because it now had only one meaning to him, he saw Mary quivering and twitching like the Japanese soldier who had been killed in the draw. He began to shiver uncontrollably. "Dead," he said. The word had no sense. He sat there very numb. His thoughts had retreated into some deep secure closet of his mind and the words of the chaplain fell abstractly on the anesthetized surface of his brain. For a few seconds he felt as if he were hearing a story about someone else in which he was not very interested. Oddly, the only thing he told himself was that he had to look alert to impress the chaplain. "Ohhhhhh," he said at last.

"The information they gave me was very slight, but I'll give you the details when I hear them, son. It's terribly hard to be so far away from home, and be unable to see your beloved ones for a last time."

"Yeah, it's hard, Father," Gallagher said automatically. Like the rising of the dawn, Gallagher was slowly becoming able to distinguish the objects about him, and understand the news he had heard. His mind was telling him something bad had happened, and he thought, I hope Mary don't worry over the news. He realized suddenly that Mary would not be worrying, and before the contradiction, he retreated. He gazed dully at the wood of the chair upon which the chaplain was sitting. He felt as if he were in a church, and mechanically he looked at his hands and tried to assume a serious expression.

"Life goes on. It's not without meaning that your child was saved. If you wish, I'll inquire for you as to who will take care of her. Perhaps we can arrange a furlough for you."

Gallagher's spirits rose. He would be seeing his wife. But Mary was dead; this time his mind did not retreat quite so far. He sat there thinking of how pleasant the sunlight had been that morning as he climbed on the truck, and dumbly he understood that he wanted to go back to that moment.

"Son, you've got to have courage."

"Yes, Father." Gallagher stood up. He could not feel the soles of his feet, and when he rubbed his mouth it felt swollen and alien under his fingers.

"Go to your tent, son, and lie down," Father Leary said.

"Okay, Father." Gallagher walked through the bivouac area. It was almost deserted now that the men were out on detail, and this gave him a secure feeling of isolation. He came to his tent, dropped in the hole, and stretched out on his blanket. He was feeling nothing except an extreme weariness. His head ached and he wondered idly if he should take an atabrine tablet from his jungle aid kit. Maybe I got malaria, he said to himself. The heat of the sun was oppressive, and he became drowsy, and slept at last. In his slumber his body would twitch from time to time.

In the days that followed the news of Mary's death Gallagher worked furiously on the road, shoveling without pause in the drainage ditches, and chopping down tree after tree whenever they had to lay a corduroy. He would rarely halt in the breaks they were given every hour, and at night he would eat his supper alone and curl into his blankets, sleeping exhaustedly with his knees near his chin. Wilson would hear him shuddering in the middle of the night, and would throw his blanket over him, clucking to himself at the misery Gallagher was undergoing. Gallagher showed no sign of his grief except that he became even leaner and his eyes and eyelids were swollen as if he had been on a long drinking bout or had played poker for forty-eight hours at a stretch.

The men tried to feel sorry for him, but the event had given a variation to the monotonous sweep of their days on the road. For a short time they sustained a quiet compassion when he was near and spoke in soft voices, uncomfortable in his presence. They ended by feeling merely uncomfortable and were resentful when he sat by them, for it inhibited their speech and made them acutely uneasy. Red felt a little shame and brooded over it one night on guard, deciding there was nothing he could do about it. It's tough, but I can't change it. He looked off into the night and shrugged. To hell with it, it's Gallagher's bloody nose, not mine.

The mail began to come in almost daily, and a frightening thing happened. Gallagher continued to receive letters from his wife. The first one came a few days after Father Leary had told him about her death; it had been mailed almost a month before. Wilson collected the letters for the platoon that night from the orderly room, and he debated whether to give it to Gallagher. "It's gonna make him feel mighty funny," he said to Croft.

Croft shrugged. "You can't tell. He may want it." Croft was curious to see what happened.

Wilson's voice was casual when he gave it to Gallagher. "Some mail for ya, boy." He felt embarrassed and looked away.

Gallagher's face whitened as he gazed at the letter. "That ain't for me," he muttered. "Some mistake."

"It's your letter, boy." Wilson put an arm on his shoulder, and Gallagher shook it off. "You want me to throw it away?" Wilson asked.

Gallagher looked at the date on the envelope. He shivered a little. "No, give it to me," he blurted. He walked away a few yards and ripped it open. The words were indistinguishable to him, and he could not read it. He began to tremble. Holy Mary, Joseph, and Jesus, he said to himself. His eyes were able to focus on a few lines, and their meaning seeped into his mind. "I been worrying about you, Roy, you're allways so angrie about everthing, and I pray for your safety every night. I love you so much when I think of the baby, only sometimes I can't beleive that its going to come so soon. Only three weeks now, the doctor said." Gallagher folded the letter, and walked around blindly. The purple lump on his jawbone twitched dully. "Oh, Christ Savior," he said aloud. He began to tremble again.

Gallagher could not accept Mary's death. At night, on guard, he would catch himself thinking of his return, and he would imagine

ing against the shore with their motors running, and two columns of men were filing between the supply dump and the boats. A haze was spreading over the sea almost obscuring the few freighters riding at anchor offshore. He walked around the bend, and saw a few squad tents just off the beach. The flaps were rolled and he could see several men lying on cots and talking to each other. Dully, he read the sign, "5279 Quartermaster Trucking Company." He sighed and continued to walk. Goddamn quartermaster's got all the breaks, he told himself, but without any real bitterness.

He passed by the strip of beach where Hennessey had been killed. It roused a mood of pity, and he halted to sift a handful of sand through his fingers. "Young kid, didn't even know what the fuggin score was," he thought. He remembered abruptly that when they had picked Hennessey up to move him farther away from the water, his helmet had fallen off. It had landed with a dull grating sound, and it spun once with a gritty noise in the sand. Guy's dead, and that's all he gets. He began to tremble as he remembered the letter in his shirt pocket. He had taken one look at the date, and he had known it would be the last one he would ever get. Maybe she wrote another one, he thought, and kicked some sand. He sat down, looked about him with the suspicious attitude of an animal about to eat in its lair, and then ripped open the flap. The sound tore at his nerves. He was beginning to feel the finality of each of his motions now. Abruptly, he realized the irony of pitying Hennessey. "I got my own fuggin troubles," he muttered. The sheets of paper felt pitifully flimsy in his hands.

He reread the last paragraph when he had finished. "Roy, honey, this'll be the last letter I'll write for a coupel of days, the pain started just a little while ago, and Jamie went down to get Dr Newcome. I'm awful scared cawse he said I'm going to have a hard time, but dont worrie cawse everything will be alright, I know it. I wish you could be with me, you got to take awful good care of youeself cawse I would be afraide to be alone. I love you so much, honey."

He folded the letter and put it back in his pocket. He felt a dull ache; his forehead was burning. For several minutes he did not think of anything at all, and then he spat bitterly. Aaah, the fuggin women, that's all they know, love, I love you, honey, just want to hold a man down. He trembled again; he was remembering the frustrations and annoyances of his marriage for the first time in many months. All a woman wants is to get a man and then she goes to pot, to hell with it all. He was thinking of how wan Mary looked in the morning, and how the left side of her jaw would swell in sleep. Incidents, unpleasant fragments of their life churned turgidly in his brain like a pot of thick stew coming to a boil.

She used to wear a tight hair net in the house, and always of course her habit of sitting around in a slip that had a frayed edge. Worst of all was something he had never quite admitted to himself; the walls of the bathroom were thin and he could hear the sounds she made. She had faded in the three years they had been married. She didn't take the right care of herself, he thought bitterly. At this moment he hated the memory of her, hated the suffering she had caused him in the past few weeks. Always that love-dove stuff, and they don't give a fug how they look. He spat again. Don't even have any . . . any manners. He meant "modesty." Gallagher thought of Mary's mother, who was fat and very dowdy, and he felt an inarticulate rage at a variety of things—at the very fact that she was so immense, at the lack of money that had made him live in a tiny drab apartment, at all the breaks he had never got, because his wife in dying had caused him so much pain. Never get a goddamn thing. He thought of Hennessey and his mouth tightened. Get your head blown off . . . for what, for what? He lit a cigarette, and tossed the match away, looking at where it fell in the sand. Goddamn Yids, fight a war for them. He thought of Goldstein. Bunch of fug-ups, lose a goddamn gun, won't even take a drink when it's free. He lurched to his feet, and began to walk again. A dull pain and hatred beat through his head.

On the beach giant kelp had washed ashore, and he walked down to the water's edge and looked at it. It was dark brown and very long, perhaps fifty feet, and its dark rubbery skin glistened like snakes, and gave him a jolt of horror. He was remembering the bodies in the cave. "What drunken bastards we were," he said. He was remorseful, or more correctly he generated remorse in himself because he felt he had done something bad. The kelp frightened him—he walked away.

After a few hundred yards, he sat down on the top of a dune that looked out to sea. A storm was coming up, and he felt suddenly cold. A great cloud perhaps thirty miles long, shaped like a flat fish and very dark, had covered most of the sky. A wind had sprung up and was lashing the sand in horizontal sheets along the beach. Gallagher sat there and waited for the rain that did not come. He was feeling pleasurably moody; he was enjoying the barrenness and brooding of the scene, the remote froth of the waves against the shore. Without quite realizing it, he began to draw a woman in the sand. She had great breasts and a narrow waist and very wide full hips. He looked at it soberly, and remembered that Mary was very ashamed of her tiny breasts. She had once said, "I wish they were big."

"Why?"

"I know you like them better that way."

He had lied. "Naw, they're just right the way they are."

An eddy of tenderness wound through him. She had been very small, and he thought of how she had seemed like a little girl to him at times, and how he had been amused at her seriousness. He laughed softly, and then abruptly, with no defenses raised, he realized that she was utterly dead and he would never see her any more. The knowledge flowed through him without resistance, like a torrent of water when a floodgate is lowered. He heard himself sob, and then was no longer conscious of the choking sounds of his anguish. He felt only a vast grief that mellowed him, dissolved the cysts of his bitterness and resentment and fear, and left him spent and weeping on the sand. The softer gentler memories of Mary were coming back to him. He recalled the sweltering liquid rhythms of their bodies against each other in heat and love; he felt dumbly the meaning of her smile when she handed him his lunch box as he went to work in the morning; he recalled the sad clinging tenderness they had felt for each other on the last night of his last furlough before he went overseas. They had gone on a moonlight excursion in Boston Harbor and he remembered with a pang how they had sat silently in the stern of the ship, holding each other's hands, and watching with a tender absorbed silence the turbulence of the wake. She was a good girl, he said to himself. He was thinking without quite phrasing it that no other person had ever understood him so fully, and he felt a secret relief as he realized that she had understood him and still loved him. This opened again the wound of all his loss, and he lay weeping bitterly for many minutes, unconscious of where he was, feeling nothing but the complete sorrow in his body. He would think of the last letter every now and then, and this would send him off into a new spasm of grief. He must have cried for almost an hour.

At last he was spent, and he felt clean and gentle. For the first time he remembered that he had a child, and he wondered what it looked like and what its sex might be. It gave him a delicate joy for an instant, and he thought, If it's a boy, I'm gonna train him early. He'll be a pro baseball player; that's where the money is. His thoughts eddied away, and his mind became rested and empty. He looked moodily at the dense jungle behind him, and wondered how far he would have to walk back. The wind was still sweeping along the beach, and his emotions became vague and shifted about like vapors. He was sad again and thought of cold and lonely things like wind on a winter beach.

From *The Naked and the Dead* (1948)

**1946–1949**　　**AFTERMATH**

Once it became obvious that *The Naked and the Dead* was going to be a best seller, and I would therefore receive that small fame which comes upon any young American who makes a great deal of money in a hurry, I remember that a depression set in on me. I was twenty-five, living in Paris with my first wife, Beatrice, and I had gone through a long leaky French winter in which I discovered once again that I knew very little and had everything still to learn. So I think I probably had been hoping *The Naked and the Dead* would have a modest success, that everyone who read it would think it was extraordinary, but nonetheless the book would not change my life too much. I wished at that time to protect a modest condition. Many of my habits, even the character of my talent, depended on my humility—that word which has become part of the void in our time. I had had humility breathed into me by the war. After four serious years of taking myself seriously at Harvard, the Army gave me but one lesson over and over again: When it came to taking care of myself, I had little to offer next to the practical sense of an illiterate sharecropper. Sometimes I think courage is the most exhaustible of the virtues, and I used up a share of mine in getting through the war with my lip buttoned, since it took all of me to be at best a fair rifleman. No surprise then if I was a modest young man when it was all over. I knew I was not much better and I was conceivably a little less than most of the men I had come to know. At least a large part of me felt that way, and it was the part in command while I was writing *The Naked and the Dead*.

But once free of the Army, I came back to some good luck. My first wife and I had saved some money during the war, and I did not have to work for a year. She believed in me and my family believed in me, and I was able to do my book. *The Naked and the Dead* flowed—I used to write twenty-five pages of first draft a week, and with a few weeks lost here and there, I still was able to write the novel and rewrite it in fifteen months, and I doubt if ever again I will have a book that is so easy to write. When once in a while I look at a page or two these days, I like its confidence—it seems to be at dead center— "Yes," it is always saying, "this is about the way it is."

Naturally, I was blasted a considerable distance away from dead center by the size of its success, and I spent the next few years trying to gobble up the experiences of a victorious man when I was still no man at all, and had no real gift for enjoying life. Such a gift usually comes from a series of small victories artfully achieved—my experience had consisted of many small defeats, a few victories, and one explosion. So success furnished me great energy, but I wasted most of it in the gears of old habit, and had experience that was overheated, brilliant, anxious, gauche, grim—even, I suspect—killing. My farewell to an average man's experience was too abrupt; never again would I know, in the dreary way one usually knows such things, what it was like to work at a dull job, or take orders from a man one hated. If I had had a career of that in the Army, it now was done—there was nothing left in the first twenty-four years of my life to write about; one way or another, my life seemed to have been mined and melted into the long reaches of the book. And so I was prominent and empty, and I had to begin life again. From now on, people who knew me would never be able to react to me as a person whom they liked or disliked in small ways, *for myself alone* (the inevitable phrase of all tear-filled confessions); no, I was a node in a new electronic landscape of celebrity, personality, and status. Other people, meeting me, could now unconsciously measure their own status by sensing how I reacted to them. I had been moved from the audience to the stage—I was, on the instant, a man—I could arouse more emotion in others than they could arouse in me; if I had once been a cool observer because some part of me knew that I had more emotion than most and so must protect myself with a cold eye, now I had to guard against arousing the emotions of others, particularly since I had a strong desire to do just that—exhaust the emotions of others.

From *Advertisements for Myself* (1959)

# PORTRAIT—I

## Dorothy Parker

Anyone who had read Dorothy Parker, and was expecting a lady of immaculate and elegant savagery of tongue, would feel on the consequence when meeting her a discernible shock. She was tiny, and she tended to be plump. She had bags under her eyes (from the fatigues of three good decades of drinking) and these bags touched the heart in a way few middle-aged women and only a very few middle-aged men with wondrously lugubrious bags can so touch us. (Perhaps it is by way of the sorrows they have bottomed out on while drinking.) Dorothy Parker looked like a bird at the mercy of every beast with teeth, a flurry of feathers up in a tree with wonderful bags under her eyes. And in the middle of her sad little face, sad as the ghost of tenderness itself, was her nose, the tip of which was always overpowdered. She would dust it once with a swipe to one nostril, and again with a swipe to the other, the overlay thereby suggesting the white painted button of a clown who is more lugubrious than his bulbous red-tipped colleagues.

She also wore a series of black shawls and garments to give her the appearance of a British witch. The garments looked to have come from an attic. Since Norman met her first in Los Angeles in 1949, he could not imagine at the time where she found her clothes. Los Angeles was a city whose homes were conspicuously without attics.

She also had a manner that was gentle, full of praise, and treacherous as a scorpion. The day he was introduced, an agent who would later be powerful enough to deal with the memoirs of Presidents and kings was in Dorothy Parker's room at the Chateau Marmont, and she gave the agent nothing but compliments, sweet compliments in a tender threadbare little voice that spoke of his energy (boundless!), his goodwill (Christly), and his genius (large enough to sell one of her poor scripts; he, he alone, could do it!) and the agent having left in all the happiness of being given these compliments by a great American writer—he was still a young agent, pushy, and prematurely bald—she said, so soon as the door was closed, "Agggrhh"—a clearing of the throat in pure facsimile to that first blast of the interior when vomiting—and added, "What an awful man. What a dreadful dreadful man!"

After that meeting, Mailer always did his best to be the last to leave Dottie Parker's sitting room at the Chateau Marmont. Once, confessing to Lillian Hellman his concern at how Dorothy Parker might describe him in his absence, Miss Hellman laughed with the happiness she always felt in being generous, instructive, and superior to the innocence of her friends, and said, "Norman, everyone knows that Dottie will talk about you after you leave the room. It will amount to no more than the compliments she's just given you. Everybody who cares about Dottie knows that's the price to pay." And she laughed gaily.

Still, Norman wanted Dottie Parker's real affection. He wanted the lovely things she said to him on one side of the door to be repeated on the other. Since they got along very well, and he was always proud to invite her to his rented house, and pleased to be invited back to her poor suite at the Marmont (she had no money in those years—all the splendid short stories and no money!) he even entertained the illusion that she might offer a dispensation.

He would never find out, however, because of her dog. She had a Boxer, not a year old, named Bruce, who had been badly mistreated by his first owners, and now whimpered at harsh looks. Dottie did her best to give the dog more courage—she raised him like the child she had never had, ready to take Bruce up each rung of the mile-high ladder that climbs from abysmal cowardice to transcendental courage; she would tell her friends of each new advance Bruce and she had made. One would learn that Bruce had gotten up his nerve sufficiently one day to take a walk around the block with her.

These methods seemed intolerably slow to Norman. He kept telling her that she ought to bring Bruce over to meet his dog. Since Dorothy Parker had by now made friends with Karl, she was tempted. Timid people were invariably proud of such a friendship for Karl was a black German Shepherd, huge and ferocious to strangers. Since his first allegiance was to the house, his master became whoever lived in the house (and incidentally fed him). Norman, renting the place, was therefore the master and thus became the only man in Laurel Canyon who could drive up to the house, get out of his car, and not be attacked. No one else dared. Our best-selling young author used to run out to the driveway when guests came; otherwise visitors were obliged to cower inside their vehicle while the dog would lunge at the windows. Once Norman got out, however, and barked, "Karl!" the Shepherd immediately subsided. He could now recognize that these intruders would be acceptable to the house. After they were admitted to the living room, Karl would even go over, sit down on the floor, and make a point of shaking hands with them. Delighted that the dog had become well-disposed, the new arrival would make much of this. Karl would extend his paw for a second greeting. His tongue would loll and he would pant a little. After the third handshake, Karl would get a hard-on. "*Karl!*" his master would say, and the hard-on would go away. Under such circumstances, it became easy to think of him as an overrated danger.

So when Dorothy Parker finally decided that she might bring Bruce to the house, Mailer thought it was a terrific idea. He would take care of bringing them together peacefully, he promised. Good to his word, he put Karl away in the bedroom before Dorothy Parker arrived with Bruce. The Boxer, however, did not want to quit the car. He could hear the other beast.

"It'll be all right," said Mailer cheerfully, "once Bruce is inside. Karl is really lonesome."

Coaxed within the house, however, Bruce urinated on the carpet. It was not difficult to forgive him. In the bedroom, Karl was making that sound a cat will make when a dog is near, and she is ready to fight for her life. It is a more awesome sound when it comes from a large hound.

"Don't you think this is a mistake?" said Dottie Parker. "I can put Bruce in the car and go home now."

That would be a loss for Bruce, he answered. "Why don't I put Karl on a leash, and bring them together slowly? It'll be so good for Bruce if he and Karl can make friends."

This liberal and romantic expectation prevailed. Karl was brought out of the bedroom. The dog came quietly on his tether, and looked at Bruce without a sound. He sniffed the other's nose. A pause. Bruce peed. Karl's head went off in a roar as loud as a howitzer. His mouth opened into shark's teeth and flayed the air with strings of saliva; at this point his master was sufficiently outraged to yank him back by the neck, and manhandle him to the bedroom. In the space this took, Dottie Parker was out the door, and in her car. Before she could drive away, Norman came running out to find Bruce collapsed in the rear seat. The dog's limbs were vibrating. It was that quiver which will not cease until the nerve dies.

"I said it wouldn't work," said Dottie Parker face to face. She imparted this in a tone of whole reproach as if to tell him that the worst damage a friend can wreak is to convince you to be brave when you know you are right to be cautious, and then proceed to prove that indeed you were right. It throws you back even further upon yourself when that is no place to be.

As she drove off, he knew that he had wanted to bring Karl from the bedroom because he wished to show how well he could control the dog. Besides he had been curious on the outcome. He noticed that he did not feel very sorry. Only chagrined. But then the wicked are famous for offering small remorse.

From *Pieces and Pontifications* (1982)

# THE SECOND NOVEL—II

## A Preface to *Barbary Shore* (written eight years later)

If once I had been a young man whom many did not notice, and so was able to take a delayed revenge—in my writing I could analyze the ones who neglected to look at me—now I came to know that I could bestow the cold tension of self-hatred, or the warmth of liking oneself again, to whichever friends, acquaintances, and strangers were weak, ambitious, vulnerable, and in love with themselves—which must be of course half the horde of my talented generation.

This was experience unlike the experience I had learned from books, and from the war—this was experience without a name—at the time I used to complain that everything was unreal. It took me years to realize that it was my experience, the only one I would have to remember, that my apparently unconnected rat-scufflings and ego-gobblings could be fitted finally into a drastic vision, an introduction of the brave to the horrible, a dream, a nightmare. Willy-nilly I had had existentialism forced upon me. I was free, or at least whatever was still ready to change in my character had escaped from the social obligations that suffocate others. I could seek to become what I chose to be, and if I failed—there was the ice pick of fear! I would have nothing to excuse failure. I would fail because I had not been brave enough to succeed. So I was much too free. Success had been a lobotomy to my past, there seemed no power from the past that could help me in the present, and I had no choice but to force myself to step into the war of the enormous present, to accept the private heat and fatigue of setting out by myself to cut a track through a new wild.

Now of course this way of describing my past has a protective elegance. I could as well have described the years that followed the appearance of *The Naked and the Dead* by saying that I traveled scared, excited, and nervous, ridden by the question which everyone else was ready to ask and which I was forever asking of myself—had this first published novel been all of my talent? Or would my next book be better?

In a sense, I may have tried to evade the question by writing *Barbary Shore*, but there was no real choice. If my past had become empty as a theme, was I to write about Brooklyn streets, or my mother and father, or another war novel *(The Naked and the Dead Go to Japan)*, was I to do the book of the returning veteran when I had lived like a mole writing and rewriting seven hundred pages in those fifteen months? No, those were not real choices. I was drawn instead to write about an imaginary future that was formed by the powerful intellectual influence of my friend Jean Malaquais, and by the books I had read, and the aesthetics I considered desirable, but *Barbary Shore* was really a book to emerge from the bombarded cellars of my unconscious, an agonized eye of a novel that tried to find some amalgam of my new experience and the larger horror of a world which might be preparing to destroy itself. I was obviously trying for something at the very end of my reach, and then beyond it, and toward the end my second novel collapsed into a chapter of political speech and never quite recovered. Yet, it could be that if my work is alive one hundred years from now, *Barbary Shore* may still be read occasionally for its odd shadow and theme-maddened light, its sense of authority and nihilism stalking one another through the middle of the century. I must admit that would not bother me at all, for on publication day, its reviews proved to be as bad as the reviews for *The Naked and the Dead* had been good. *Time* magazine even described *Barbary Shore* as "paceless, tasteless, graceless . . . marooned on a point of no intellectual return."

From *Advertisements for Myself* (1959)

# Excerpts from *Barbary Shore*

### GUINEVERE

A jewel. But set in brass. This morning she had sported a house dress and covered it with a bathrobe. Her red hair, with which undoubtedly she was always experimenting, had been merely blowzy and flew out in all directions from her head. Yet there had been opera pumps on her feet, her nails had been painted, her lipstick was fresh. She was a house whose lawn was landscaped and whose kitchen was on fire. I would not have been startled if she had turned around and like the half-dressed queen in the girlie show: surprise! her buttocks are exposed.

## GUINEVERE'S GREAT AMERICAN SOAP OPERA

"I've been trying to make up my mind which stars ought to play it, but so far I'm not sure, although I suppose they decide it all in Hollywood anyway. Just to think about it gets me excited.

"Here," she offered. "It takes place in this city in New York State, and the main characters are a doctor, a real good-looking guy with a mustache, big you know, and his nurse, she looks like some of those blond stars, and then he's got a girl friend, a dark-haired girl, any feature player could do that part." Guinevere lit a cigarette. "Now, this guy, the doctor, he's a pretty good guy, good heart and so forth, and he's a wow with the women. He's got the biggest whang on him in the whole town, and maybe he don't know it. He's got dozens of girl friends, and there isn't one of them who won't surrender herself to him, you know. But he's got a favorite, the blond star one, his nurse, and she's a good kid too, worked hard all her life, and she goes for him. You know she's really in love, but she don't show it, puts up a tough front." Guinevere sighed with content. "Now the other one is a society girl, hoity-toity, and she comes to see him about something or other, woman trouble maybe, and he seduces her in his medical chambers, and they really tie a can on. You know for weeks he just goes around with her, to night clubs and to the beach, the country club, and he can't get her out of his system, it's chemical. Only all the time, at the same time, he still keeps the nurse on the string, and they get together once in a while, and it's love with them, it's just passion with the other."

"That is," I interposed, "it's the blond star one he's really in love with?"

"Yeah." Without missing a breath, she continued. "Well, all this time, there's been a hullabaloo with the brunette society one's parents, you know they don't like the doctor because he's also from lowly origin like the nurse. But there's nothing they can do, it's real flaming youth." She halted, and murmured in aside, "Some of this I'm drawing from my own experiences." Guinevere tapped the ash from her cigarette. "Well, this goes on for a while and there's a climax. One night just for the hell of it he has one on the house with the society gal, and she gets pregnant. Only in the meantime before she finds out, he's decided that he's really more interested in the nurse, and they're thinking of getting married. When the society girl comes in, you know, knocked up, he talks to her for a while and convinces her he's not in love, and that she ought to have an operation. And so here's the first big scene. The doctor makes an operation on this dame he's had a hot affair with, and the nurse, the woman he's in love with, assists him right at it. I mean you see how this would make a movie even though they'd have trouble with such a scene. I imagine they could work it out, though. She could have a brain tumor, or something of that nature. It would be a good scene the operation, you know with him giving directions to the nurse, scalpel nurse, forceps nurse, sponge, acting cold because he's a good doctor, and he's got lots of responsibility." Guinevere stared at me blankly. "The operation turns out a failure. She isn't going to have the baby any more, but at the same time he does something, he makes a mistake, and the society girl can't make love any more. She looks perfectly okay, but she's crippled there, a beautiful girl and yet she can't do it any more. Well, when she finds out, she's mad, and she's going to expose him, but the nurse who's a wonderful character convinces him he ought to marry the society girl, and he does even though there can't be anything between them, and for a while they all keep living in the same town, and he keeps up his affair with the blond nurse. They're still in love, and it's gotten very chemical like it used to be with the society girl, he goes down on her and everything, and she loves him. But the wife who's now turned out a bitch is going to expose him all over again, and so the nurse takes off and goes to New York, and the doctor gets richer and richer, fooling around with a lot of dames on the side, but his heart is still with the blond nurse. Only they don't see each other for years." She stopped. "Guess what the ending's going to be?"

I was not to hear it so quickly. Guinevere went on developing wondrous detail upon detail; my attention flagged, and I listened indifferently. For Monina stood in the hall entrance performing a dance. The child was still nude, but somewhere she had picked up a coaster for a highball glass, and now in a posture of unbelievable provocation, she held it like a fig leaf, writhing her limbs sinuously through a parody of amorous advance and retreat. She would approach a few steps, her blond head cocked to one side in sensuous repose as if she were stirred by an exotic music, and then abruptly, with a tiny pout upon her lips, she would draw back, an attitude of feigned horror in the pose of her limbs. As her mother spoke she danced silently, an interpreter. The story drew to a close, and with it the dance. Monina reclined against the doorway, her arm caressing her thigh. She never looked in my direction, yet everything was done for me. Her blond eyelashes fluttered upon her cheek, her eyes opened to gaze boldly at the wall. And all the while, Guinevere, unheeding, continued to talk.

"They meet again in New York, just about a year ago, the nurse and the doctor, and the doctor's wife is dead, and whammo do they get together. I mean drinking and making love, nothing can stop them. And the nurse doesn't tell him about that baby she had from him after she left 'cause she knows he won't believe her; he'll think it belongs to some other guy. And the doctor wants to get married, and she holds him off 'cause she doesn't know what to do with the kid. And then what do you think, she can't tell him so she murders the kid, her own child, and she's caught, and the doctor too. I forgot to say he made out the death certificate 'cause she brought him in on it at the end, and then in prison, which'll be the last chapter, they're brought together for a final hour by the warden who's a pretty good guy, and there in the cell behind the bars they have a last one that really makes it worth while being killed."

And Monina, resolving the chord, ran toward me on tiptoe, nude nymph, halted within the reach of my arm, and in a child's counterfeit of a leer raised the fig leaf above her head, exposed and triumphant.

For the first time she stared at me as though I were real.

In the next instant a look of confusion mounted upon her face, deepened into terror. Abruptly, her mouth crumpled, her eyebrows knotted, and she began to wail in panic. Within a minute she was hysterical.

### McLEOD'S SOLILOQUY

"Think of it, you've got to make the imaginative reconstruction, don't forget you're dedicated to the land across the sea, you've come to understand finally the gory unremitting task of history and the imperfect men with whom you change it, and it's a whole choice, you tell yourself, with all the good and bad of one against all the bad and good of the other, until I can tell you it's with a gloomy but nonetheless delicious satisfaction that you hear about some particularly unpleasant piece of work by the side you're on because it's a test of yourself, and you don't shrink back. It's hard is it, well then make it harder, burn out the pap and the syrup and make yourself harder because it takes that; it takes all of that." He halted in the middle of the floor, looking at me expectantly with a puckering of his mouth. If there had been a glass of water in his hand, he would have swallowed it at a gulp. "And that's only the preliminary, because soon you know that it's all renounced for yourself, all the pleasures of the plump belly, and you're burned out, burned out for the generations to come, and so you can only drive yourself. Cannot you understand, you crippled prig," he shouted at my impassive face, "why we remained so long in a situation now reactionary and stoked fuel to the counterrevolution? You have no life, and so you do not know what it means to deny what has been the meaning of your life, for if you've been wrong, mark you now, if you've been wrong, then what of the decamillion of graves, and so you're committed, you're committed wholly, do you understand? And each action you perform can only confirm you further in your political position or what I would now call the lack of one, and there's only the nightmare of yourself if you're wrong, for you see it gets turned inside out and after a while the only path to absolution is to do more of the same so that you end up religious and climb to salvation on the steps of your crimes. And in all this, in all the activity and activity, do you dare lie awake and resurrect all the old tools of surplus value and accumulation and the exploitation of one class by another, or do you sink your teeth into the meat you're permitted, no private ownership and therefore . . . therefore therefore . . . I exist, therefore I am, and so there must be socialism, except that the weirdest statements go through your head, and once I jotted it down on a piece of paper, a perfectly ridiculous remark, 'The historical function of La Sovietica is to destroy the intellectual content of Marxism.' "

### LANNIE TO LOVETT'S EAR

"Have you forgotten? Do you remember how the poorest of the poor used to be driven to the room where they were given death by gas? How was it done, and with what nobility do we all die? Let me tell you. The guards were chosen from a list, so they would come from the kitchen or standing before the gate with their gun at present arms, and they would all assemble in a room and an officer would give them orders, and each of them would rate an extra cup, and they would drink it and go to collect the prisoners, who had been selected already by other men. And the prisoners would march along, and if one of them weighed a hundred pounds, he was a giant to the rest, and they would shuffle and smile and try to catch the guard's eye. And the guards were drunk, and you would be amazed how happy a man may feel at such a moment. For the comedy is about to begin. They come to the antechamber, a room with gray walls and without windows, and it's men to the right and women to the left and strip your clothes, but only a moment. The clothes off, the guards are driving them into the other room, and smack their hands on skinny flesh and bony flesh, it's bag a tittie and snatch a twot, and they can smell them stinking all those naked people, while in the heart of their own pants it's sweet with brandy so slap an ass and laugh like mad while the naked go stumbling, screaming into the last room of them all. And there one might suppose they prepare to die. For, mark you, this has been a long road, and each step of the way they have been deceived.

"Yet my story is not done," she said, holding up a hand, her eyes clear, her speech distinct as though she were reciting before a mirror. "The guards have one more resource. As they are about to close the door to the last room, an announcement is made. The State in its infinite mercy will allow one of them to be saved, the strongest. The one who can beat the others will be given a reprieve. This declaration, although it is worthy of the State, is due actually to the genius of a single guard, who has conceived it at the very moment. And so through a window the guards may watch while one naked pygmy tears the hair of another, and blood runs where one thought no blood was left, and half of them are dead and scream like pigs with the head down and waiting for the knife, and as they scratch and sob and bite each other's rind, the guards turn on the gas and roar like mad for the fools thought one would be saved and so ate each other.

"This is the world, Mickey. If there had been one who said, 'Let us die with dignity,' but they went choking into the gas with the blood of a friend in their mouth."

"It was too late then," I murmured.

"Listen, my friend," she said softly, "the grass waves, and we are lost again in childhood souvenir. It is too late now. Do you understand? There are no solutions . . . All that is left is to love the fire."

From *Barbary Shore* (1951)

# THE COLD WAR—I

## Lunch at 21

Let me offer the primary fact. I am a Hubbard. Bradford and Fidelity Hubbard arrived in Plymouth seven years after the *Mayflower* and branches of the clan are to be found today in Connecticut, Maine, New Hampshire, Rhode Island, and Vermont. To my knowledge, however, I am the first Hubbard to make public admission that the sound of the family name is not quite as impressive as our share of lawyers and bankers, doctors and legislators, one Civil War general, several professors, and my grandfather, Smallidge Kimble Hubbard, Headmaster of St. Matthew's. He remains a legend to this day. At the age of ninety, he still managed on warm summer mornings to get into his single shell and row one hundred strokes out into Blue Hill Bay. Of course, one stroke missed and over he would have gone into cold Maine waters, a near-fatal proposition, but he died in bed. My father, Boardman Kimble Hubbard, known to his friends as Cal (for Carl "Cal" Hubbell the New York Giants pitcher, whom he revered), was equally exceptional, but so divided a man that my wife, Kittredge, used him as a source of private reference for her work *The Dual Soul*. He was a swashbuckler and yet a deacon; a bold, powerful man who showered in cold water with the same morning certainty that others used to feel while eating eggs and bacon. He went to church each Sunday; he was a prodigious philanderer. During the time shortly after World War II, when J. Edgar Hoover was doing his best to convince Harry Truman that the proposed CIA was not necessary and the FBI could take over all such jobs, my father went on a save-our-outfit mission. He seduced a few key secretaries in the State Department, thereby picking up a flood of in-office secrets which he then passed to Allen Dulles, who promptly sent such product on to the White House with a cover story to protect the secretaries. It certainly helped to convince the White House that we might need a separate Intelligence body. Allen Dulles was fond of Cal Hubbard after that, and said to me once, "Your father won't admit it, but that month with the secretaries was the best time of his life."

I loved my father outrageously and thereby had a frightened childhood, worried, strained, and cold within. I wished to be the salt of his salt but my stuff was damp. Much of the time I came near to hating him because he was disappointed in me and I did not hear from him often.

My mother was a different matter. I am the product of a marriage between two people so quintessentially incompatible that they might as well have come from separate planets. Indeed, my parents were soon separated and I spent my boyhood trying to keep two disjointed personalities together.

My mother was small-boned, attractive, and blond, and she lived, but for summer at Southampton, in that social nucleus of New York which is bounded by Fifth Avenue on the west, Park Avenue to the east, the Eighties to the north, and the Sixties to the south. She was a Jewish Princess but the emphasis can be put on the second word. She could not have told you the difference between the Torah and the Talmud. She brought me up to be ignorant of every Jewish subject but one: the names of prominent New York banking houses with Semitic roots. I think my mother thought of Salomon Brothers and Lehman Brothers as ports of call in some future storm.

It was sufficient that my mother's great-great-grandfather was a remarkable man named Chaim Silberzweig (who had his name streamlined by immigration officials to Hyman Silverstein). He came over as an immigrant in 1840 and rose from a street peddler to the clear-cut status of a department-store owner. His sons became merchant princes and his grandsons were among the first Jews tolerated in Newport. (The name by now was Silverfield.) If each generation of my mother's family was more spendthrift than the one before, it was never at a catastrophic rate: My mother was worth about as much in real money as the first Silverstein had left for his immediate heirs— and she possessed about a quarter of his Jewish blood. The Silverfield men married golden gentile women.

That is my mother's family. Although I saw more of her when young than of my father, it was my paternal grandfather with his single shell that I deemed to be true kin. My mother's side I tried to ignore. A man on death row once said: "We owe nothing to our parents—we just pass through them." I felt that way about my mother. From an early age I did not take her seriously. She could be charming and full of interesting follies; she was certainly a lot better than average at giving merry dinner parties. She was also, unfortunately, the owner of a terrible reputation. The Social Register dropped her a few years after Jessica Silverfield Hubbard became an ex-Hubbard, but it took another ten years before her best friends stopped seeing her. The reason, I suspect, was not her succession of affairs so much as her propensity to lie. She was a psychopathic liar, and finally her memory became her only lasting friend. It always told her what she wished to remember about the present and the past. In consequence, you never could know what anyone was up to if you listened to her. I make this point because my mother equipped me, I believe, for counterespionage, a field where we do, after all, attempt to implant errors in our opponent's knowledge.

At any rate, I can hardly pretend that I ended as any good fraction of a Jew. My only kinship with "that herring baron," as my mother referred to great-great-grandfather Chaim Silberzweig, is that anti-Semitic slurs made me tense. I might as well have grown up in a ghetto for the size of the fury aroused in me. For I would then feel Jewish. Of course, my idea of feeling Jewish was to be reminded of the strain on people's faces in the rush hour on the New York subway as they stood prey to harsh and screeching sounds.

I had, however, a privileged boyhood. I went to the Buckley School and was a Knickerbocker Gray until asked to withdraw, a reflection of my serious incompetence at close-order drill. While marching, I would generate headaches of such intensity that I would fail to hear commands.

Of course, the bad reputation of my mother may have been another factor, and I take confirmation for this suspicion by the manner in which my father had me reinstated. As a cold-shower warrior he was not inclined to ask for favors for his progeny. This time, however, he called on people one saves for emergencies. The Hubbards had well-placed friends in New York, and my father took me to meet a few alumni of the Grays. "It's unfair. They're blaming the boy for *her*," was part of what I overheard, and it must have done the work. I was reinstated, and managed to soldier my way thereafter with fewer headaches, although I never knew one relaxed breath as a cadet.

I suppose people who were happy when young may recall their childhood well. I remember little. Summary disposes of the years and I collect memories by subjects. I can always answer such absurd essay questions as "What was the most important day you spent with a parent?" I would reply: "When my father took me to Twenty-One for lunch on my fifteenth birthday."

Twenty-One was the perfect place to take me. While my father did not know "one superior hell of a lot"—his phrase—about boys, he knew enough to be standing at the bar waiting for me.

I cannot swear in all confidence that the downstairs dining room has not been altered since 1948, but I might bet on the possibility. I think the same model toys are still suspended from the low dark ceiling, same steamships, 1915 Spad biplanes, railroad locomotives, and trolley cars. The little coupe with its rumble seat and spare tire in the white slipcover is still above the bar. Above the bottle cabinet hang the same hunting horns, cutlasses, elephant tusks, and one pair of boxing gloves small enough to fit an infant. My father told me that Jack Dempsey gave those gloves to the owner of 21, Jack Kriendler, and while I would hope the story is true, my father did not mind polishing legends of his own devising. I think he had concluded that good feeling was always in danger of being wiped out; ergo, he gilded the stories he told. He had, by the way, a degree of resemblance to Ernest Hemingway—he was at least equally vivid in presence—and he cultivated the same large dark mustache. He also had Hemingway's build. Sporting relatively spindly legs for a man of strength, he often said, "I might have made first team All-American fullback if not for my pins." He also had a great barrel of a chest, which bore a distinct likeness to the antique bronze cash register on the bar at 21. My father's heart beat with pride.

Of course, the pride was for himself. If I state that my father was vain and self-centered, I do not wish to demean him. While he carried the complacent look of a successful college athlete, his fundamental relation to others was a reflection of his concealed but endless negotiations with himself: The two halves of his soul were far apart. The deacon and the swashbuckler had miles to walk each night before they slept; I think his strength was that he had managed to find some inner cooperation between these disparate halves. When the headmaster's son, impacted with Cromwellian rectitude, was able to hook up with a venture that the conquistador could also applaud, well, the energy poured forth. My father, while not uncommonly reflective, did say once: "When your best and worst motive agree on the same action, watch the juices flow."

On this day in December 1948, my father was dressed in what I would come to call his "battle tweeds." That once had been a suit of light brown Scotch tweed (light in hue, but as heavy and hard to the touch as a horse-blanket). He bought his suits from Jones, Chalk and Dawson on Savile Row, and they knew how to outfit a horseman. I had seen this same suit on him for ten years. By now, patched with leather at elbows and cuffs, and become more malleable, it could still stand on its legs when taken off. It fit him, however, with a comfortable surround of dignity to suggest that these two materials—his manly flesh and that iron cloth—had lived together long enough to share a few virtues. In fact, he no longer owned a business suit and so had nothing more formal to wear until you got to his black velvet dinner jacket. Needless to say, on such nightly occasions, he was a lady's vision. "Oh, Cal," they would say of him, "Cal's *divine*. If only he didn't drink so much."

I think my father would have broken relations with any friend who dared to suggest Alcoholics Anonymous was waiting for him, and he could have been right. His contention was that he drank no more than Winston Churchill and held it as well. He never got drunk. That is to say, his speech never slurred and he never staggered, but he did move through moods powerful enough to alter the electromagnetic fields through which he passed. It is a way of remarking that he had charisma. He had no more than to say "Bartender" in a quiet tone, and the man, if his back were turned, and had never heard my father's voice before, would nonetheless spring around as if starting a new page in his bar accounts. My father's emotional temperature seemed to rise and fall as he drank. His eyes, by the shift of the hour, could blaze with heat, or install you in a morgue; his voice would vibrate into your feet. Doubtless I exaggerate, but he was my father, and I saw him so seldom.

On this day, as I came in, he and his battle tweeds were sheeted in anger. For practical purposes, I was not unlike one of those little wives who are married to huge sea captains: I could feel his thoughts. He had been busy on some serious job before lunch, and had nearly cracked its difficulty; now he was putting down his first martini with all the discontent of interrupted concentration. I could imagine how he said to some assistant, "Damn, I've got to see my son for lunch."

To make matters worse, I was late. Five minutes late. When it came to promptitude, he was always on the mark, a headmaster's son. Now, waiting for me, he had had time to finish the first drink and review in his mind an unpromising list of topics about which we might converse. The sad truth is that he invariably gave off gloom on those rare occasions when we were alone with each other. He did not know what to talk to me about, and I, on my side, filled with my mother's adjurations, injunctions, and bitch-fury that I was going to see a man who was able to live in whole comfort apart from her, was jammed up. "Get him to talk about your education," she'd say before I was out the door. "He's got to pay for it, or I'll take him to law. Tell him that." Yes, I would be in great haste to tell him. "Watch out for his charm. It's as real as a snake," and, as I was going out the door, "Tell him I said hello—no, don't you tell him that."

I gave a nod with one quick bob of my head and got onto the barstool next to him. Naturally, I scrunched my larger testicle by too abruptly lowering my butt to the seat. Then I sat there through the small wave of discomfort this brought on and tried to study the signs above the bar.

YO, HO, HO, AND A BOTTLE OF RUM, said one old wooden placard.

21 WEST ZWEI UND FÜNFZIGSTE STRASSE, said a painted street sign.

"Oh," I said, "is that German, Dad?"

"Fifty-second Street," he told me.

We were silent.

"How do you like St. Matthew's?" he said.

"Okay."

"Better than Buckley?"

"It's tougher."

"You're not going to flunk out?"

"No, I get B's."

"Well, try to get A's. Hubbards are expected to get A's at St. Matt's."

We were silent.

I began to look at another sign hanging over the bar. It obviously enjoyed its misspelling. CLOSE SATURDAYS AND SUNDAYS, it said.

"I've had one superior hell of a lot of work lately," he said.

"I guess," I said.

We were silent.

His gloom was like the throttled sentiments of a German shepherd on a leash. I think I was something of a skinny version of him, but I believe he always saw every bit of resemblance I had to my mother during the first five minutes of every one of our meetings, and I even came to understand over the years that she might have done him a real damage. There was probably never a human he wished to kill more with his bare hands than this ex-wife; of course, he had had to forgo such pleasure. Blocked imperatives brought my father that much nearer to stroke.

Now he said, "How's your leg?"

"Oh, it's recovered. It's been all right for years."

"I bet it's still stiff."

"No, it's all right."

He shook his head. "I think you had your trouble with the Grays because of that leg."

"Dad, I was just no good at close-order drill." Silence. "But I got better." The silence made me feel as if I were trying to push a boat off the shore and it was too heavy for me.

"Dad," I said, "I don't know if I can get A's at St. Matthew's. They think I'm dyslexic."

He nodded slowly as if not unprepared for such news. "How bad is it?" he asked.

"I can read all right, but I never know when I'm going to reverse numbers."

"I had that trouble." He nodded. "Back on Wall Street before the war, I used to live in fear that one bright morning my touch of dyslexia would make the all-time mistake in the firm. Somehow, it never did." He winked. "You need a good secretary to take care of those things." He clapped me on the back. "One more lemonade?"

"No."

"I'll have another martini," he said to the bartender. Then he turned back to me. I still remember the bartender's choice of a keen or sour look. (Keen when serving gentlemen; sour for the tourists.) "Look," my father said, "dyslexia is an asset as well as a loss. A lot of good people tend to have dyslexia."

"They do?" Over the past term a few boys at school had taken to calling me Retardo.

"No question." He put his eyes on me. "About ten years ago in Kenya we were going for leopards. Sure enough, we found one, and it charged. I've hit elephants coming at me, and lions and water buffalo. You hold your ground, look for a vulnerable area in the crosshairs, then squeeze off your shot. If you can steer between the collywobbles, it's as easy as telling it to you now. Don't panic and you have yourself a lion. Or an elephant. It's not even a feat. Just a measure of inner discipline. But a leopard is different. I couldn't believe what I saw. All the while it was charging it kept leaping left to right and back again, but so fast I thought I was watching a movie with pieces missing. You just couldn't get your crosshairs on any part of that leopard. So I took him from the hip. At twenty yards. First shot. Even our guide was impressed. He was one of those Scotsmen who sneer at all and anything American, but he called me a born hunter. Later I figured it out for myself: I was a good shot because of my dyslexia. You see, if you show me 1-2-3-4, I tend to read it as 1-4-2-3 or 1-3-4-2. I suppose I see like an animal. I don't read like some slave—yessir, boss, I'm following you, yessir, 1-2-3-4—no, I look at what's near me and what's in the distance and only then do I shift to the middle ground. In and out, back and forth. That's a hunter's way of looking. If you have a touch of dyslexia, that could mean you're a born hunter."

He gave my midriff a short chop with his elbow. It proffered enough weight to suggest what a real blow would do.

"How's your leg?" he asked again.

"Good," I said.

"Have you tried one-legged knee raises?"

The last time we had been to lunch, eighteen months ago, he had prescribed such an exercise.

"I've tried it."

"How many can you do?"

"One or two." I was lying.

"If you're really working at it, you would show more progress."

"Yessir."

I could feel his wrath commencing. It began slowly, like the first stirring of water in a kettle. This time, however, I could also sense the effort to pull back his annoyance, and that puzzled me. I could not recollect when he had treated me to such courtesy before.

"I was thinking this morning," he said, "of your ski accident. You were good that day."

"I'm glad I was," I said.

We were silent again, but this time it was a pause we could inhabit. He liked to recall my accident. I believe it was the only occasion on which he ever formed a good opinion of me.

When I was seven, I had been picked up at school one Friday in January by my mother's chauffeur and driven to Grand Central Station. On this day, my father and I were going to board the weekend special to Pittsfield, Mass., where we would ski at a place called Bousquet's. How the great echoes of Grand Central matched the reverberation of my heart! I had never been skiing and therefore believed I would be destroyed next day flying off a ski jump.

Naturally, I was taken over no such towering jump. I was put instead on a pair of rented wooden slats and, after a set of near-fiascoes on the long rope-tow up, attempted to follow my father down. My father had a serviceable stem turn, which was all you needed to claim a few yodeling privileges in the Northeast back in 1940. (People who could do a parallel christie were as rare then as tightrope artists.) I, of course, as a beginner, had no stem turn, only the impromptu move of falling to either side when my snow plow got going too fast. Some spills were easy, some were knockouts. I began to seek the fall before I needed to. Soon, my father was shouting at me. In those days, whether riding, swimming, sailing, or on this day, skiing, he lost his temper just so quickly as first returns made it evident that I was without natural ability. Natural ability was closer to God. It meant you were wellborn. Bantu blacks in Africa, I came to learn in CIA, believed that a chieftain should enrich himself and have beautiful wives. That was the best way to know God was well disposed toward you. My father shared this view. Natural ability was bestowed on the deserving. Lack of natural ability spoke of something smelly at the roots. The clumsy, the stupid, and the slack were fodder for the devil. It is not always a fashionable view today, but I have pondered it all my life. I can wake up in the middle of the night thinking, What if my father was right?

Soon he grew tired of waiting for me to get up.

"Just do your best to follow," he said, and was off, stopping long enough to call back, "Turn when I turn."

I lost him at once. We were going along a lateral trail that went up and down through the woods. Going uphill, I did not know how to herringbone. I kept getting farther behind. When I came to the top of one rise and saw that the next descent was a full-fledged plunge followed by an abrupt rise, and my father was nowhere in sight, I decided to go straight down in the hope such a schuss would carry me a good way up. Then he would not have to wait too long while I climbed. Down I went, my skis in a wobbly parallel, and almost at once was moving twice as fast as I had ever traveled before. When I lost my nerve and tried to switch to a snowplow, my skis crossed, dug into the soft snow, and I wrenched over in a somersault. There was no release to the bindings in those days. One's feet stayed in the skis. I broke my right tibia.

I did not know that at first. I only knew more pain than ever felt before. Somewhere in the distance my father was bellowing, "Where are you?" It was late in the afternoon and his voice echoed through the hills. No other skiers were coming by. It started to snow and I felt as if I were in the last reel of a movie about Alaska; soon the snow would cover all trace of me. My father's roars were, in this silence, comforting.

He came climbing back, angry as only a man with a powerful, sun-wrinkled neck can be angry. "Will you rise to your feet, you quitter," he cried out. "Stand up and ski."

I was more afraid of him than the five oceans of pain. I tried to get up. Something, however, was wrong. At a certain point, my will was taken away from me completely. My leg felt amputated.

"I can't, sir," I said, and fell back.

Then he recognized there might be more than character at issue here. He took off his ski jacket, wrapped me in it, and went down the mountain to the Red Cross hut.

Later, in the winter twilight, after the ski patrol had put on a temporary splint and worked me down to the base in a sled, I was put in the back of a small truck, given a modest dose of morphine, and carried over some frozen roads to the hospital in Pittsfield. It was one hell of a ride. The spirit of the morphine was kind, but the pain still rasped like a rough-toothed saw into my broken bone each time we hit an evil bump (which was every fifty yards). The drug enabled me, however, to play a kind of game. Since the shock from every bump shivered through my teeth, the game became the art of not making a sound. I lay there on the floor of the truck with a wadded ski jacket under my head and another beneath my leg, and must have looked like an epileptic: My father kept wiping froth from my mouth.

I made, however, no sound. After a time, the magnitude of my personal venture began to speak to him for he took my hand and concentrated upon it. I could feel him trying to draw the pain from my body into his, and this concern ennobled me. I felt they could tear my leg off and I might still make no outcry.

He spoke: "Your father, Cal Hubbard, is a fathead." That may be the only occasion in his life when he used the word in reference to himself. In our family, *fathead* was about the worst expression you could use for another person.

"No, sir," I said. I was afraid to speak for fear that the groans would begin, yet I also knew the next speech was one of the most important I would ever make. For a few moments I twisted through falls of nausea—I must have been near to fainting—but the road became level for a little while, and I succeeded in finding my voice. "No, sir," I said, "my father, Cal Hubbard, is not a fathead."

It was the only time I ever saw tears in his eyes.

"Well, you silly goat," he said, "you're not the worst kid, are you?"

If we had crashed at that moment I could have died in a happy state. But I came back to New York in a cast two days later—my mother sent chauffeur and limousine up for me—and a second hell began. The part of me that was ready to go through a meat grinder for my father could hardly have been the poor seven-year-old boy who sat home in New York in his Fifth Avenue apartment with a compound fracture surrounded by a plaster cast that itched like the gates of sin. The second fellow seethed with complaints.

I could not move. I had to be carried. I went into panic at the thought of using crutches. I was certain I would fall and break the leg again. The cast began to stink. In the second week the doctor had to cut the plaster off, clean my infection, and encase me again. I mention all this because it also cut off my father's love affair with me nearly as soon as it had begun. When he came over to visit—after an understanding with my mother that she would not be there—he would be obliged to read the notes she left—"You broke his leg, now teach him to move."

Allowing for his small patience, he finally succeeded in getting me up on crutches, and the leg eventually mended, just a bit crooked, but it took too long. We were back in the land of paternal disillusion. Besides, he had more to think about than me. He was happily remarried to a tall, Junoesque woman absolutely his own size, and she had given him twin boys. They were three years old when I was seven, and you could bounce them on the floor. Their nicknames—I make no joke— were Rough and Tough. Rough Hubbard and Tough Hubbard. Actually, they were Roque Baird Hubbard and Toby Bolland Hubbard, my father's second wife being Mary Bolland Baird, but rough and tough they promised to be, and my father adored them.

Occasionally I would visit the new wife. (They had been married four years but I still thought of her as *the new wife.*) It was just a trip of a few blocks up the winter splendor of Fifth Avenue, that is to say, an education in the elegance of gray. The apartment houses were lilac-gray, and Central Park showed field-gray meadows in winter and mole-gray trees.

Since finding myself on crutches, I no longer ventured from my apartment house. In one of the later weeks of convalescence, however, I had a good day, and my limb did not ache in its cast. By afternoon, I was restless and ready for adventure. I not only went down to the lobby and talked to the doorman but, on impulse, set out to circumnavigate the block. It was then the idea came to me to visit my stepmother. She was not only large but hearty, and succeeded at times in making me think she liked me; she would certainly tell my father that I had visited, and he would be pleased I was mastering the crutches. So I decided to attempt those five blocks uptown from 73rd to 78th Street and immediately went through a small palsy the first time I put my crutches out from the curb down six inches to the gutter. This small step accomplished, however, I began to swing along, and by the time I reached their apartment house, I was most talkative with the elevator man and pleased with how much pluck I was showing for a seven-year-old.

At their door a new maid answered. She was Scandinavian and hardly spoke English, but I gathered that the nurse was out with the twins and "the Madame" was in her room. After some confusion the new girl let me in and I sat on a couch, bored by the wan afternoon sun as it reflected on the pale silk colors of the living room.

It never occurred to me that my father was home. Later, much later, I would gather that this was about the time he had given up his broker's slot in Merrill Lynch to volunteer for the Royal Canadian Air Force. To celebrate, he was taking the afternoon off. I, however, thought Mary Bolland Baird Hubbard was alone and reading, and might be as bored as I was. So I hopped across the living room and down the hall to their bedroom, making little sound on the pile carpet, and then, without taking the time to listen—all I knew was that I did not wish to return home without having spoken to someone, but would certainly lose my nerve if I waited at the door—I turned the knob, and, to keep my balance, took two big hops forward on my crutches. The sight that received me was my father's naked back, then hers. They were both pretty big. They were rolling around on the floor, their bodies plastered end to end, their mouths on each other's—if I say *things,* it's for want of remembering the word I had then. Somehow I had an idea what they were doing. Importuning sounds came out of them, full of gusto, that unforgettable cry which lands somewhere between whooping and whimpering.

I was paralyzed for the time it took to take it all in; then I tried to escape. They were so deep in their burrow they did not even see me, not for the first instant, the second, nor even the third as I backed my way to the door. Right then, they looked up. I was nailed to the door frame. They stared at me, and I stared at them, and I realized they did not know for how long I had been studying them. For heavens, how long? "Get out of here, you dodo," my father roared, and the worst of it was that I fled so quickly on the crutches that they thumped like ghost-bumpers on the carpet while I vaulted down the hall. I think it was this sound, the thump-thump of a cripple, that must have stayed in her ears. Mary was a nice woman, but she was much too proper to be photographed by anyone's memory in such a position, let alone a slightly creepy stepson. None of us ever spoke of it again; none of us forgot it. I remember that in the time it took to reach my mother's apartment, I generated a two-ton headache, and it was the first of a chronic run of migraines. This pressure had been paying irregular visits from that day. Right now, here at lunch, I could feel it on the edge of my temples, ready to strike.

"How are your headaches?" asked my father at the bar at 21.

"No worse," I said.

"But they don't get better?"

"They don't, I guess."

"I'd like to reach in and pull out what's bothering you," he said. It was not a sentimental remark so much as a surgeon's impulse.

I shifted the subject to Rough and Tough. They were now Knickerbocker Grays, and doing well, he told me. I was tall for my age, almost as tall as my father, but they gave every promise of outstripping me. As he spoke, I knew there was some other matter on his mind.

It was his inclination to pass me tidbits about his work. This presented curious debits to his duty. In his occupation, you were supposed to encapsulate your working life apart from your family. On the other hand, he had formed his reflexes for security, such as they were, working for the OSS in Europe during World War II. Nobody he knew then had been all that cautious. Today's secret was next week's headline, and it was not uncommon to give a hint of what one was up to when trying to charm a lady. Next day, after all, an airplane was going to parachute you into a strange place. If the lady were made aware of this, well, she might feel less absolutely loyal to her husband (also away at war).

Besides, he wanted to fill me in. If he was not an attentive parent, he was at least a romantic father. Moreover, he was a team man. He was in the Company and his sons ought to be prepared as well: While Rough and Tough were a foregone conclusion, he could hardly swear on me.

"I'm all riled up today," said my father. "One of our agents in Syria got shot on a stupid business."

"Was he a friend of yours?" I asked.

"Neither here nor there," he replied.

"I'm sorry."

"No, I'm just so goddamn mad. This fellow was asked to obtain us a piece of paper that wasn't really needed."

"Oh."

"I'll tell you, darn it all. You keep this to yourself."

"Yes, Dad."

"One of those playboys at State decided to be ambitious. He's doing his Ph.D. thesis on Syria over at Georgetown. So he wanted to present a couple of hard-to-get details that nobody else has. He put through a request to us. Officially. From State. Could we furnish the poop? Well, we're green. You could grow vegetables with what they scrape off our ignorance. We try to oblige. So we put a first-rate Syrian agent on it, and there you are—lost a crack operator because he was asked to reach for the jam at the wrong time."

"What'll happen to the fellow in the State Department?"

"Nothing much. Maybe we'll slow down a promotion for that idiot by talking to a guy or two at State, but it's horrifying, isn't it? Our man loses his life because somebody needs a footnote for his Ph.D. thesis."

"I thought you looked upset."

"No," he said quickly, "it's not that." Then he hoisted his martini, stepped off the stool, raised his hand as if calling a cab, and the captain was there to bring us to our table, which was, I already knew, in his favored location against the rear wall. There my father placed me with my back to the room. At the table to my left were two men with white hair and red faces who looked like they might have gout, and on the right was a blond woman with a small black hat supporting a long black feather. She was wearing pearls on a black dress and had long white gloves. Sitting across from her was a man in a pencil-thick pinstripe. I mention these details to show a facet of my father: He was able, in the course of sitting down, to nod to the two gentlemen with gout as if, socially speaking, there was no reason why not to speak to one another, and freeze the man in the pencil-stripe suit for the width of his stripes while indicating to the blond lady in black that she was blue ribbon for blond ladies in black. My father had a gleam in his eye at such times that made me think of the Casbah. I always supposed a Levantine would come up to you in the Casbah and give a flash of what he had in his hand. There!—a diamond peeked out. That made me recollect Cal Hubbard rolling with Mary Baird on the carpeted floor, which in turn caused me to look down quickly at my plate.

"Herrick, I haven't seen a superior hell of a lot of you lately, have

I?" he asked, unfolding his napkin, and sizing up the room. I wasn't too happy being placed with my back to everyone, but then he gave a wink as if to suggest that he had his reasons. It was incumbent on his occupation, as he once explained, that he be able to *eye* a joint. I think he may have picked up the phrase from Dashiell Hammett, with whom he used to drink before word went around that Hammett was a Communist. Then, since he considered Hammett smarter than himself, he gave up the acquaintance. A loss. According to my father, he and Dashiell Hammett could each put down three double Scotches in an hour.

"Well, there's a reason I haven't seen a lot of you, Rick." He was the only one to call me Rick, rather than Harry, for Herrick. "I have been traveling an unconscionable amount." This was said for the blond woman as much as for me. "They don't know yet whether I'll be one of the linchpins in Europe or the Far East."

Now the man in the pencil-stripe suit began his counteroffensive. He must have put a curve on what he said, for the woman gave a low intimate laugh. In response, my father leaned toward me across the table and whispered, "They've given OPC the *covert* operations."

"What's covert?" I whispered back.

"The real stuff. None of that counterespionage where you drink out of my teacup and I drink out of yours. This is war. Without declaring it." He raised his voice sufficiently for the woman to hear the last two phrases, then dropped back to a murmur as if the best way to divide her attention was to insinuate himself in and out of her hearing.

"Our charter calls for economic warfare," he said in a highly shaped whisper, "plus underground resistance groups." Loudly: "You saw what we did in the Italian elections."

"Yessir."

He enjoyed the *yessir.* I had broadcast it for the blond lady.

"If not for our little operation, the Communists would have taken over Italy," he now stated. "They give the credit to the Marshall Plan but that's wrong. We won in Italy in spite of the money that was thrown around."

"We did?"

"Count on it. You have to take into account the Italian ego. They're an odd people. Half sharp, half meatball."

By the way in which the man in the pencil-stripe reacted, I suspected he was Italian. If my father sensed that, he gave no sign. "You see, the Romans themselves are civilized. Minds quick as stilettos. But the Italian peasant remains as backward as a Filipino. In consequence, you mustn't try to motivate their self-interest too crudely. Self-esteem means more to them than filling their bellies. They're always poor, so they can live with hunger, but they don't want to lose their honor. Those Italians really wanted to stand up to us. They would have derived more pleasure spitting in our face than sucking up to us with their phony gratitude. Nothing personal. The Italians are like that. If Communism ever takes over in Italy, those Red wops will drive the Soviets just as crazy as they're driving us."

I was feeling the wrath of the Italian man next to me. "Dad, if that's what you think," I blurted out, scurrying to save the peace, "why not let the Italians choose their path? They're an ancient and civilized people."

My father had to ponder this. Allen Dulles may have said that the happiest week of Cal Hubbard's life was spent seducing secretaries, but I expect no period could have been equal to the year he spent with the partisans. If Italy had gone Communist in 1948, my father would probably have gone right over to form an anti-Communist underground. In recesses of his brain so secret he could not even reach them in his dreams, I believe he would have enjoyed a Communist takeover of America. What an American underground he could have helped to set up then! The thought of dynamite Americans waging an underground war up and down our countryside against an oppressive enemy would have been a tonic to keep him young forever.

So my father may have been on the edge of saying "You bet," but he didn't. Instead, he answered dutifully, "Of course, we can't afford to let the Russians in. Who knows? Those guineas might get along with the Russians."

We had an interruption here. The man next to us suddenly called out for his check, and my father immediately stopped our conversation in order to look appreciatively at the blond lady.

"Weren't we introduced at Forest Hills this fall?" he said to her.

"Nah, I don't think so," she answered in a muffled voice.

"Please tell me your name," said my father, "and I'm certain I'll recollect where it was."

"Think of nowhere," said the man in the striped suit.

"Are you trying to give directions?" asked my father.

"I heard of people," said the man, "who lose their nose by poking it around the corner."

"Al!" said the blond lady.

Having stood up abruptly, Al was now putting money on the table to cover his tab. He dropped each new bill like a dealer snapping cards, signally upset that one of the players had called for another deck. "I've heard of people," repeated Al, and now he looked sideways at my father, "who stepped off the curb and broke a leg."

Into my father's eyes came that diamond of the Casbah. He, too, stood up. They each took a long look at the other. "Buster," said my father in a happy, husky voice, "don't get tough!"

It was his happiness that did the job. Al thought of replying, then thought better. His jaw did not work. He folded his napkin as if folding his tent, looked for the opportunity to throw a sneak punch, did not find what he was looking for, and gave his arm to the blond lady. They left. My father grinned. If he couldn't have her, he had at least broken a couple of eggs.

Now my father began to talk a good deal. Any victory over a stranger was kin to triumph over rival hordes. Al was out there with the Russians. "There are six million soldiers in the Red Army," said my father, "and only a million of us. That's counting NATO. The Russians could take all of Europe in two months. It's been true for the last three years."

"Then why haven't they?" I asked. "Dad, I read that twenty million Russians were killed in the war. Why would they want to start one now?"

He finished his drink. "Damned if I know." As the waiter sprang for the refill, my father leaned forward: "I'll tell you why. Communism is an itch. What does that mean, to have an itch? Your body is out of whack. Little things take on large proportions. That's Communism. A century ago, everybody had their place. If you were a poor man, God judged you as such, a poor man. He had compassion. A rich man had to pass more severe standards. As a result, there was peace between the classes. But materialism came down on us. Materialism propagated the idea that the world is nothing but a machine. If that's true, then it's every man's right to improve his piece of the machine. That's the logic of atheism. So, now everybody's ears are being pounded to bits, and nothing tastes right any more. Everybody is too tense, and God is an abstraction. You can't enjoy your own land so you begin to covet the next guy's country."

He took a long, thoughtful swallow from his drink. My father could always bring a cliché to life. Many have been described as taking long thoughtful swallows of their drinks, but my father drank like an Irishman. He took it for granted that real and true spirits were entering with the fire of the liquor. He inhaled the animation around him and could breathe back his own excitement. Emotion must never be wasted. "Rick, keep clear on one matter. There's a huge war brewing. These Communists are insatiable. We treated them as friends during the war and they'll never get over that. When you're older, you may have the bad luck to get into an affair with an ugly woman who happens to enjoy what you offer but has never been on daily terms with a man. She's too ugly. Fellow, you're going to have trouble on your hands. Before long, she's insatiable. You've given the taste of the forbidden to her. That's the Russians. They got ahold of Eastern Europe; now they want it all."

He did not halt long at this place. "No," he said, "it's not a good analogy. It's really worse than that. We're in an ultimate struggle with the Russians, and that means we have to use everything. Not only the kitchen sink, but the vermin that come with the sink."

My father was interrupted at this moment by the two white-haired gentlemen seated on his right. They were getting up to leave and one said, "I couldn't help hearing what you were explaining to your son, and I wish to say, couldn't agree more. Those Russians want to crack our shell and get all the good meat. Don't let them."

"No, sir," said my father, "not one knuckle will they get," and he stood up on that remark. The rich compact that comes from a common marrow guarded us all. Honor, adventure, and sufficient income were in the air of 21. Even I could prosper there.

When we sat down again, my father said, "Keep this most strictly to yourself. I'm going to trust you with a weighty secret. Hitler used to say, 'Bolshevism is poison.' That idea is not to be rejected out of hand just because Adolf said it. Hitler was so awful that he ruined the attack on Bolshevism for all of us. But the fundamental idea is right. Bolshevism *is* poison. We've even come to the point"—and here he dropped his voice to the lowest whisper of the lunch—"where we've got to employ a few of those old Nazis to fight the Reds."

"Oh, no," I said.

"Oh, yes," he said. "There's hardly a choice. The OSO is not all that competent. We were supposed to put agents in place all over the Iron Curtain countries and couldn't even seed it with birdfeed. Every time we built a network, we discovered the Russians were running it. The great Russian bear can move his armies anywhere behind the Iron Curtain, and we don't have an effective alert system. If, two years ago, the Soviets had wanted to march across Europe, they could have. We would have gotten out of bed in the morning to hear their tanks in the streets. No reliable intelligence. That's fearful. How would you like to live blindfolded?"

"No good, I guess."

"It came down to this: We had to use a Nazi general. I call him General Microfilm. I can't reveal his name. He was top intelligence man for the Germans on the Russian front. He would weed out the most promising of the Russians captured by the Germans and manage to infiltrate them back behind Russian lines. For a while, they honeycombed the Red Army, even worked a few of their boys into the Kremlin. Just before the war ended, this general, prior to destroying his files, buried fifty steel boxes somewhere in Bavaria. They were the microfilm copies of his files. A voluminous product. We needed it. Now he's dealing with us. He has built up new networks all through East Germany, and there isn't much those East German Communists don't tell his West German agents about what the Reds are planning to do next in Eastern Europe. This general may be an ex-Nazi, but, like it or not, he's invaluable. That's what my business is about. You work with the next-to-worst in order to defeat the worst. Could you do that?"

"Maybe."

"You might be too liberal, Herrick. Liberals refuse to look at the whole animal. Just give us the tasty parts, they say. I think God has need of a few soldiers."

"Well, I believe I could be a good one."

"I hope so. When you broke your leg, you were a great soldier."

"Do you think so?" This moment alone made the lunch superlative for me. So I wanted him to say it again.

"Not in question. A great soldier." He paused. He played with his drink. His free hand made a rocking motion on the table from thumb to little finger. "Rick," he announced, "you're going to have to pull up your gut again."

It was like coming in for a landing. My focus moved closer to my father's with every instant.

"Is it medical?" I asked. Then answered myself. "It's the tests I took."

"Let me give you the positive stuff first." He nodded. "It's operable. There's an 80-percent likelihood it's benign. So when they take it out, they've got it all."

"A benign tumor?"

"As I say, they are 80-percent certain. That's conservative. I believe it's 95-percent certain."

"Why do you think that?"

"You may have bad headaches but the powers that be aren't ready to lift you from the board. It makes no sense."

"Maybe the whole thing makes no sense," I said.

"Don't you ever believe that. I'd rather you took a dump right here in public, right in the middle of my favorite restaurant, than that you descend into that kind of sophomoric nihilism. No, look at it this way. Assume the Devil made a mistake and put all his eggs in one basket concerning you"—again my father was whispering as if any loud statement of Satan's name could summon him to your side—"and we're going to remove him all at once. Excise him. Rick, your headaches will be gone."

"That's good," I said. I was ready to cry. Not because of the operation. I had not realized an operation was this near, but it had been part, certainly, of my inner horizon. I had been taking tests for three months. No, I was ready to cry because now I knew why my father had taken me to lunch and favored me with professional secrets.

"I convinced your mother," he said. "She's a very difficult woman under any and all circumstances, but I got her to recognize that one of the best neurosurgeons in the country is available for this. I can tell you in confidence he also works for *us*. We've talked him into putting his toe in the water for some studies we're doing on brainwashing techniques. We need to keep up with the Russians."

"I guess he'll learn a little more about brainwashing with me."

My father gave a half-smudged smile for the joke. "He'll give you every chance to become the man you want to be."

"Yes," I said. I had an awful feeling I could not explain. There was no doubt in my mind that the tumor was the worst part of me. Everything rotten must be concentrated there. I had always supposed, however, that sooner or later it would go away by itself.

"What if we don't have surgery? I can keep living with my headaches," I said.

"There's a chance it is malignant."

"You mean when they open my head, they could discover cancer?"

"There's one chance in five."

"You said 95 percent. Isn't that one chance in twenty?"

"All right. One in twenty."

"Dad, that's twenty to one in our favor. Nineteen to one, actually."

"I'm looking at other kinds of odds. If you're debilitated with headaches during all the formative years to come, you'll end up half a man." I could hear the rest. "Shape up" were the words he was inclined to speak.

"What do the doctors think?" I asked at last.

I had given up the game by asking this question. "They say you must have the operation."

Years later, a surgeon would tell me that the operation would have been elective, not mandatory. My father had lied. His logic was simple. He would not manipulate me or any other family member who was arguing a point out of his own feelings; if third parties, however, were consulted, then the debate had become a recourse to authority. Since I asked what the doctors said, my father was ready to substitute himself as final authority.

Now he got out his wallet to pay the check. Unlike Al, my father did not snap his money down. He laid it like a poultice on the plate.

"When this is over," he told me, "I'm going to introduce you to a dear friend of mine whom I've asked to be your godfather. It's not customary to have a brand-new godfather at the age of fifteen, but the one we gave you at birth was a friend of your mother's and he's dropped out of sight. The guy I'm bringing in is wholly superior. You'll like him. He's named Hugh Montague, and he's one of us. Hugh Tremont Montague. He did wonderful stuff for OSS while on liaison with the Brits. During the war he worked with J. C. Masterman—I can tell you that name. An Oxford don. One of their spymasters. Hugh will fill you in on all of that. The English are such aces in this kind of work. In 1940, they captured a few of the first German agents sent over to England and succeeded in turning them. As a result, most of the German spies who followed were picked up on arrival. For the rest of the war, the Abwehr was fed the niftiest disinformation by their own agents in England. And, oh, how the Brits got to love their German agents. Just as loyal to them as to their favorite foxhounds, yes, they were." Here my father began laughing heartily. "You have to," he added, "get Hugh to tell you about the code names the English gave their little Germans. Perfect names for peachy dogs. CELERY," said my father, "SNOW, GARBO, CARROT, COBWEB, MULLET, LIPSTICK, NEPTUNE, PEPPERMINT, SCRUFFY, ROVER, PUPPET, BASKET, BISCUIT, BRUTUS. Is that, or is that not, the English?"

For years, I would fall asleep surrounded by men and women holding brass nameplates in capitals: BRUTUS, COBWEB, TREASURE, RAINBOW. As I grew ready in the last of this lunch at 21 to lose a part, forever, of the soft meats of my brain, so were old spies with the code names of hunting dogs filing one by one into the cavity waiting for them.

From *Harlot's Ghost* (1991)

**THE COLD WAR—II**

## The Man Who Studied Yoga

### 1.

I would introduce myself if it were not useless. The name I had last night will not be the same as the name I have tonight. For the moment, then, let me say that I am thinking of Sam Slovoda. Obligatorily, I study him, Sam Slovoda who is neither ordinary nor extraordinary, who is not young nor yet old, not tall nor short. He is sleeping, and it is fit to describe him now, for like most humans he prefers sleeping to not sleeping. He is a mild pleasant-looking man who has just turned forty. If the crown of his head reveals a little bald spot, he has nourished in compensation the vanity of a mustache. He has generally when he is awake an agreeable manner, at least with strangers; he appears friendly, tolerant, and genial. The fact is that like most of us, he is full of envy, full of spite, a gossip, a man who is pleased to find others are as unhappy as he, and yet—this is the worst to be said—he is a decent man. He is better than most. He would prefer to see a more equitable world, he scorns prejudice and privilege, he tries to hurt no one, he wishes to be liked. I will go even further. He has one serious virtue—he is not fond of himself; he wishes he were better. He would like to free himself of envy, of the annoying necessity to talk about his friends. In fact, he would like to love people more. Specifically, he would like to love his wife more, and to love his two daughters without the tormenting if nonetheless irremediable vexation that they closet his life in the dusty web of domestic responsibilities and drudging for money.

How often he tells himself with contempt that he has the cruelty of a kind weak man.

May I state that I do not dislike Sam Slovoda; it is just that I am disappointed in him. He has tried too many things and never with a whole heart. He has wanted to be a serious novelist and now merely indulges the ambition; he wished to be of consequence in the world, and has ended, temporarily perhaps, as an overworked writer of continuity for comic magazines. When he was young he tried to be a bohemian and instead acquired a wife and family. Of his appetite for a variety of new experience I may say that it is matched only by his fear of new people and novel situations.

I will give an instance. Yesterday, Sam was walking along the street and a bum approached him for money. Sam did not see the man until too late; lost in some inconsequential thought, he looked up only in time to see a huge wretch of a fellow with a red twisted face and an outstretched hand. Sam is like so many. Each time a derelict asks for a dime, he feels a coward if he pays the money, and is ashamed of himself if he doesn't. This once, Sam happened to think, I will not be bullied, and hurried past. But the bum was not to be lost so easily. "Have a heart, Jack," he called after in a whisky voice, "I need a drink bad." Sam stopped. Sam began to laugh. "Just so it isn't for coffee, here's a quarter," he said, and he laughed, and the bum laughed. "You're a man's man," the bum said. Sam went away pleased with himself, thinking about such things as the community that existed between all people. It was cheap of Sam. He should know better. He should know he was merely relieved the situation had turned out so well. Although he thinks he is sorry for bums, Sam really hates them. Who knows what violence they can offer?

At this time, there is a powerful interest in Sam's life, but many would ridicule it. He is in the process of being psychoanalyzed. Myself, I do not jeer. It has created the most unusual situation between Sam and me. I could go into details but they are perhaps premature. It would be better to watch Sam awaken.

His wife, Eleanor, has been up for an hour, and she has shut the window and neglected to turn off the radiator. The room is stifling. Sam groans in a stupor that is neither sleep nor refreshment, opens one eye, yawns, groans again, and lies twisted, strangled, and trussed in pajamas that are too large for him. How painful it is for him to rise. Last night there was a party, and this morning, Sunday morning, he is awakening with a hangover. Invariably, he is depressed in the morning, and it is no different today. He finds himself in the flat and familiar dispirit of nearly all days.

It is snowing outside. Sam finally lurches to the window, and opens it for air. With the oxygen of a winter morning clearing his brain, he looks down six stories into the giant quadrangle of the Queens housing development in which he lives, staring morosely at the inch of slush which covers the monotonous artificial park that separates his apartment building from an identical structure not two hundred feet away. The walks are black where the snow has melted, and in the children's playground, all but deserted, one swing oscillates back and forth, pushed by an irritable little boy who plays by himself among the empty benches, swaddled in galoshes, muffler, and overcoat. The snow falls sluggishly, a wet snow that probably will turn to rain. The little boy in the playground gives one last disgusted shove to the swing and trudges away gloomily, his overshoes leaving a small animal track behind him. Back of Sam, in the four-room apartment he knows like a blind man, there is only the sound of Eleanor making breakfast.

Well, thinks Sam, depression in the morning is a stage of his analysis, Dr. Sergius has said.

This is the way Sam often phrases his thoughts. It is not altogether his fault. Most of the people he knows think that way and talk that way, and Sam is not the strongest of men. His language is doomed to the fashion of the moment. I have heard him remark mildly, almost apologetically, about his daughters: "My relation with them still suffers because I haven't worked through all my feminine identifications." The saddest thing is that the sentence has meaning to Sam even if it will not have meaning to you. A great many ruminations, discoveries, and memories contribute their connotation to Sam. It has the significance of a cherished line of poetry to him.

Although Eleanor is not being analyzed, she talks in a similar way. I have heard her remark in company, "Oh, you know Sam, he not only thinks I'm his mother, he blames me for being born." Like most women, Eleanor can be depended upon to employ the idiom of her husband.

What amuses me is that Sam is critical of the way others speak. At the party last night he was talking to a Hollywood writer, a young man with a great deal of energy and enthusiasm. The young man spoke something like this: "You see, boychick, I can spike any script with yaks, but the thing I can't do is heartbreak. My wife says she's gonna give me heartbreak. The trouble is I've had a real solid-type life. I mean I've had my ups and downs like all of humanity, but there's never been a shriek in my life. I don't know how to write shrieks."

On the trip home, Sam had said to Eleanor, "It was disgraceful. A writer should have some respect for language."

Eleanor answered with a burlesque of Sam's indignation. "Listen, I'm a real artist-type. Culture is for comic-strip writers."

Generally, I find Eleanor attractive. In the ten years they have been married she has grown plump, and her dark hair, which once was long, is now cropped in a mannish cut of the prevailing mode. But this is quibbling. She still possesses her best quality, a healthy exuberance that glows in her dark eyes and beams in her smile. She has beautiful teeth. She seems aware of her body and pleased with it. Sam tells himself he would do well to realize how much he needs her. Since he has been in analysis he has come to discover that he remains with Eleanor for more essential reasons than mere responsibility. Even if there were no children, he would probably cleave to her.

Unhappily, it is more complicated than that. She is always—to use their phrase—competing with him. At those times when I do not like Eleanor, I am irritated by her lack of honesty. She is too sharp-tongued, and she does not often give Sam what he needs most, a steady flow of uncritical encouragement to counteract the harshness with which he views himself. Like so many who are articulate on the subject, Eleanor will tell you that she resents being a woman. As Sam is disappointed in life, so is Eleanor. She feels Sam has cheated her from a proper development of her potentialities and talent, even as Sam feels cheated. I call her dishonest because she is not so ready as Sam to put the blame on herself.

Sam, of course, can say all this himself. It is just that he experiences it in a somewhat different way. Like most men who have been married for ten years, he finds that Eleanor is not quite real to him. Last night at the party, there were perhaps half a dozen people whom he met for the first time, and he talked animatedly with them, sensing their reactions, feeling their responses, aware of the life in them, as they were aware of the life in him. Eleanor, however, exists in his nerves. She is a rather vague embodiment. He thinks of her as "she" most of the time, someone to conceal things from. Invariably, he feels uneasy with her. It is too bad. No matter how inevitable, I am always sorry when love melts into that pomade of affection, resentment, boredom, and occasional compassion that is the best we may expect of a man and woman who have lived together a long time. So often, it is worse, so often no more than hatred.

They are eating breakfast now, and Eleanor is chatting about the party. She is pretending to be jealous about a young girl in a strapless evening gown, and indeed, she does not have to pretend altogether. Sam, with liquor inside him, had been leaning over the girl; obviously he had coveted her. Yet, this morning, when Eleanor begins to talk about her, Sam tries to be puzzled.

"Which girl was it now?" he asks a second time.

"Oh, you know, the hysteric," Eleanor says, "the one who was parading her bazooms in your face." Eleanor has ways of impressing certain notions upon Sam. "She's Charlie's new girl."

"I didn't know that," Sam mutters. "He didn't seem to be near her all evening."

Eleanor spreads marmalade over her toast and takes a bite with evident enjoyment. "Apparently, they're all involved. Charles was funny about it. He said he's come to the conclusion that the great affairs of history are between hysterical women and detached men."

"Charles hates women," Sam says smugly. "If you notice, almost everything he says about them is a discharge of aggression." Sam has the best of reasons for not liking Charles. It takes more than ordinary character for a middle-aged husband to approve of a friend who moves easily from woman to woman.

"At least Charles discharges his aggression," Eleanor remarks.

"He's almost a classic example of the Don Juan complex. You notice how masochistic his women are?"

"I know a man or two who's just as masochistic."

Sam sips his coffee. "What made you say the girl was an hysteric?"

Eleanor shrugs. "She's an actress. And I could see she was a tease."

"You can't jump to conclusions," Sam lectures. "I had the impression she was a compulsive. Don't forget you've got to distinguish between the outer defenses and the more deeply rooted conflicts."

I must confess that this conversation bores me. As a sample it is representative of the way Sam and Eleanor talk to each other. In Sam's defense I can say nothing; he has always been too partial to jargon.

I am often struck by how eager we are to reveal all sorts of supposedly ugly secrets about ourselves. We can explain the hatred we feel for our parents, we are rather pleased with the perversions to which we are prone. We seem determinedly proud to be superior to ourselves. No motive is too terrible for our inspection. Let someone hint, however, that we have bad table manners and we fly into a rage. Sam will agree to anything you may say about him, provided it is sufficiently serious—he will be the first to agree he has fantasies of murdering his wife. But tell him that he is afraid of waiters, or imply to Eleanor that she is a nag, and they will be quite annoyed.

Sam has noticed this himself. There are times when he can hear the jargon in his voice, and it offends him. Yet, he seems powerless to change his habits.

An example: He is sitting in an armchair now, brooding upon his breakfast, while Eleanor does the dishes. The two daughters are not home; they have gone to visit their grandmother for the weekend. Sam had encouraged the visit. He had looked forward to the liberty Eleanor and himself would enjoy. For the past few weeks the children had seemed to make the most impossible demands upon his attention. Yet now they are gone and he misses them; he even misses their noise. Sam, however, cannot accept the notion that many people are dissatisfied with the present, and either dream of the past or anticipate the future. Sam must call this "ambivalence over possessions." Once he even felt obliged to ask his analyst, Dr. Sergius, if ambivalence over possessions did not characterize him almost perfectly, and Sergius, whom I always picture with the flat precision of a coin's head—bald skull and horn-rimmed glasses—answered in his German accent, "But, my dear Mr. Slovoda, as I have told you, it would make me happiest if you did not include in your reading, these psychoanalytical text-works."

At such rebukes, Sam can only wince. It is so right, he tells himself. He is exactly the sort of ambitious fool who uses big words when small ones would do.

### 2.

While Sam sits in the armchair, gray winter light is entering the windows, snow falls outside. He sits alone in a modern seat, staring at the gray, green, and beige décor of their living room. Eleanor was a painter before they were married, and she has arranged this room. It is very pleasant, but like many husbands, Sam resents it, resents the reproductions of modern painters upon the wall, the slender coffee table, a free-form poised like a spider on wire legs, its feet set onto a straw rug. In the corner, most odious of all, is the playmate of his children, a hippopotamus of a television-radio-and-phonograph cabinet with the blind monstrous snout of the video tube.

Eleanor has set the Sunday paper near his hand. Soon, Sam intends to go to work. For a year, he has been giving a day once or twice a month to a bit of thought and a little writing on a novel he hopes to begin sometime. Last night, he told himself he would work today. But he has little enthusiasm now. He is tired, he is too depressed. Writing for the comic strips seems to exhaust his imagination.

Sam reads the paper as if he were peeling an enormous banana. Flap after flap of newsprint is stripped away and cast upon the straw rug until only the Magazine Section is left. Sam glances through it with restless irritability. A biography of a political figure runs its flatulent prose into the giant crossword puzzle at the back. An account of a picturesque corner of the city becomes lost in statistics and exhortations on juvenile delinquency, finally to emerge with photographs about the new style of living that desert architecture provides. Sam looks at a wall of windows in rotogravure with a yucca tree framing the pool.

There is an article about a workingman. His wife and his family are described, his apartment, his salary, and his budget. Sam reads a description of what the worker has every evening for dinner, and how he spends each night of the week. The essay makes its point; the typical American workingman must watch his pennies, but he is nonetheless secure and serene. He would not exchange his life for another.

Sam is indignant. A year ago he had written a similar article in an attempt to earn some extra money. Subtly, or so he thought, he had suggested that the average workingman was raddled with insecurity. Naturally, the article had been rejected.

Sam throws the Magazine Section away. Moments of such anger torment him frequently. Despite himself, Sam is enraged at editorial dishonesty, at the smooth strifeless world that such articles present. How angry he is—how angry and how helpless. It is the actions of men and not their sentiments that make history, he thinks to himself, and smiles wryly. In his living room he would go out to tilt the windmills of a vast, powerful, and hypocritical society; in his week of work he labors in an editorial cubicle to create spaceships, violent death, women with golden tresses and wanton breasts, men who act with their fists and speak with patriotic slogans.

I know what Sam feels. As he sits in the armchair, the Sunday papers are strewn around him, carrying their war news, their murders, their parleys, their entertainments, mummery of a real world that no one can grasp. It is terribly frustrating. One does not know where to begin.

Today, Sam considers himself half a fool for having been a radical. There is no longer much consolation in the thought that the majority of men who succeed in a corrupt and acquisitive society are themselves obligatorily corrupt, and one's failure is therefore the price of one's idealism. Sam cannot recapture the pleasurable bitterness which resides in the notion that one has suffered for one's principles. Sergius is too hard on him for that.

They have done a lot of work on the subject. Sergius feels that Sam's concern with world affairs has always been spurious. For example, they have uncovered in analysis that Sam wrote his article about the worker in such a way as to make certain it would be refused. Sam, after all, hates editors. To have such a piece accepted would mean he is no better than they, that he is a mediocrity. So long as he fails he is not obliged to measure himself. Sam, therefore, is being unrealistic. He rejects the world with his intellect, and this enables him not to face the more direct realities of his present life.

Sam will argue with Sergius but it is very difficult. He will say, "Perhaps you sneer at radicals because it is more comfortable to ignore such ideas. Once you became interested it might introduce certain unpleasant changes in your life."

"Why," says Sergius, "do you feel it so necessary to assume that I am a bourgeois interested only in my comfort?"

"How can I discuss these things," says Sam, "if you insist that my opinions are the expression of neurotic needs, and your opinions are merely dispassionate medical advice?"

"You are so anxious to defeat me in an argument," Sergius will reply. "Would you admit it is painful to relinquish the sense of importance that intellectual discussion provides you?"

I believe Sergius has his effect. Sam often has thoughts these days that would have been repellent to him years ago. For instance, at the moment, Sam is thinking it might be better to live the life of a worker, a simple life, to be completely absorbed with such necessities as food and money. Then one could believe that to be happy it was necessary only to have more money, more goods, less worries. It would be nice, Sam thinks wistfully, to believe that the source of one's unhappiness comes not from oneself, but from the fault of the boss, or the world, or bad luck.

Sam has these casual daydreams frequently. He likes to think about other lives he might have led, and he envies the most astonishing variety of occupations. It is easy enough to see why he should wish for the life of an executive with the power and sense of command it may offer, but virtually from the same impulse Sam will wish himself a bohemian living in an unheated loft, his life a catch-as-catch-can from day to day. Once, after reading an article, Sam even wished himself a priest. For about ten minutes it seemed beautiful to him to surrender his life to God. Such fancies are common, I know. It is just that I, far better than Sam, know how serious he really is, how fanciful, how elaborate, his imagination can be.

The phone is ringing. Sam can hear Eleanor shouting at him to answer. He picks up the receiver with a start. It is Marvin Rossman, who is an old friend, and Marvin has an unusual request. They talk for several minutes, and Sam squirms a little in his seat. As he is about to hang up, he laughs. "Why, no, Marvin, it gives me a sense of adventure," he says.

Eleanor has come into the room toward the end of this conversation. "What is it all about?" she asks.

Sam is obviously a bit agitated. Whenever he attempts to be most casual, Eleanor can well suspect him. "It seems," he says slowly, "that Marvin has acquired a pornographic movie."

"From whom?" Eleanor asks.

"He said something about an old boy friend of Louise's."

Eleanor laughs. "I can't imagine Louise having an old boy friend with a dirty movie."

"Well, people are full of surprises," Sam says mildly.

"Look, here," says Eleanor suddenly. "Why did he call us?"

"It was about our projector."

"They want to use it?" Eleanor asks.

"That's right." Sam hesitates. "I invited them over."

"Did it ever occur to you I might want to spend my Sunday some other way?" Eleanor asks crossly.

"We're not doing anything," Sam mumbles. Like most men, he feels obliged to act quite nonchalantly about pornography. "I'll tell you, I am sort of curious about the film. I've never seen one, you know."

"Try anything once, is that it?"

"Something of the sort." Sam is trying to conceal his excitement. The truth is that in common with most of us, he is fascinated by pornography. It is a minor preoccupation, but more from lack of opportunity than anything else. Once or twice, Sam has bought the sets of nude photographs that are sold in marginal bookstores, and with guilty excitement has hidden them in the apartment.

"Oh, this is silly," Eleanor says. "You were going to work today."

"I'm just not in the mood."

"I'll have to feed them," Eleanor complains. "Do we have enough liquor?"

"We can get beer." Sam pauses. "Alan Sperber and his wife are coming too."

"Sam, you're a child."

"Look, Eleanor," says Sam, controlling his voice, "if it's too much trouble, I can take the projector over there."

"I ought to make you do that."

"Am I such an idiot that I must consult you before I invite friends to the house?"

Eleanor has the intuition that Sam, if he allowed himself, could well drown in pornography. She is quite annoyed at him, but she would never dream of allowing Sam to take the projector over to Marvin Rossman's, where he could view the movie without her—that seems indefinably dangerous. Besides, she would like to see it, too. The mother in Eleanor is certain it cannot hurt her.

"All right, Sam," she says, "but you are a child."

More exactly, an adolescent, Sam decides. Ever since Marvin phoned, Sam has felt the nervous glee of an adolescent locking himself in the bathroom. Anal fixation, Sam thinks automatically.

While Eleanor goes down to buy beer and cold cuts in a delicatessen, Sam gets out the projector and begins to clean it. He is far from methodical in this. He knows the machine is all right, he has shown movies of Eleanor and his daughters only a few weeks ago, but from the moment Eleanor left the apartment, Sam has been consumed by an anxiety that the projection bulb is burned out. Once he has examined it, he begins to fret about the motor. He wonders if it needs oiling; he blunders through a drawer of household tools looking for an oilcan. It is ridiculous. Sam knows that what he is trying to keep out of his mind are the reactions Sergius will have. Sergius will want to "work through" all of Sam's reasons for seeing the movie. Well, Sam tells himself, he knows in advance what will be discovered: detachment, not wanting to accept Eleanor as a sexual partner, evasion of responsibility, etc. etc. The devil with Sergius. Sam has never seen a dirty movie, and he certainly wants to.

He feels obliged to laugh at himself. He could not be more nervous, he knows, if he were about to make love to a woman he had never touched before. It is really disgraceful.

When Eleanor comes back, Sam hovers about her. He is uncomfortable with her silence. "I suppose they'll be here soon," Sam says.

"Probably."

Sam does not know if he is angry at Eleanor or apprehensive that she is angry at him. Much to his surprise he catches her by the waist and hears himself saying, "You know, maybe tonight when they're gone . . . I mean, we do have the apartment to ourselves." Eleanor moves neither toward him nor away from him. "Darling, it's not because of the movie," Sam goes on, "I swear. Don't you think maybe we could . . ."

"Maybe," says Eleanor.

**3.**

The company has arrived, and it may be well to say a word or two about them. Marvin Rossman, who has brought the film, is a dentist, although it might be more accurate to describe him as a frustrated doctor. Rossman is full of statistics and items of odd information about the malpractice of physicians, and he will tell these things in his habitually gloomy voice, a voice so slow, so sad, that it almost conceals the humor of his remarks. Or, perhaps, that is what creates his humor. In his spare time, he is a sculptor, and if Eleanor may be trusted, he is not without talent. I often picture him working in the studio loft he has rented, his tall bony frame the image of dejection. He will pat a piece of clay to the armature, he will rub it sadly with his thumb, he will shrug—he does not believe that anything of merit could come from him. When he talked to Sam over the phone, he was pessimistic about the film they were to see. "It can't be any good," he said in his melancholy voice. "I know it'll be a disappointment." Like Sam, he has a mustache, but Rossman's will droop at the corners.

Alan Sperber, who has come with Rossman, is the subject of some curiosity for the Slovodas. He is not precisely womanish; in fact, he is a large plump man, but his voice is too soft, his manners too precise. He is genial, yet he is finicky; waspish, yet bland. He is fond of telling long rather affected stories, he is always prepared with a new one, but to general conversation he contributes little. As a lawyer, he seems miscast. One cannot imagine him inspiring a client to confidence. He is the sort of heavy florid man who seems boyish at forty, and the bow ties and gray flannel suits he wears do not make him appear more mature.

Roslyn Sperber, his wife, used to be a schoolteacher, and she is a quiet nervous woman who talks a great deal when she is drunk. She is normally quite pleasant, and has only one habit that is annoying to any degree. It is a little flaw, but social life is not unlike marriage in that habit determines far more than vice or virtue. This mannerism, which has become so offensive to the friends of the Sperbers, is Roslyn's social pretension. Perhaps I should say intellectual pretension. She entertains people as if she were conducting a salon, and in her birdlike voice is forever forcing her guests to accept still another intellectual canapé. "You must hear Sam's view of the world market," she will say, or, "Has Louise told you her statistics on divorce?" It is quite pathetic, for she is so eager to please. I have seen her eyes fill with tears at a sharp word from Alan.

Marvin Rossman's wife, Louise, is a touch grim and definite in her opinions. She is a social welfare worker, and will declare herself with force whenever conversation impinges on those matters where she is expert. She is quite opposed to psychoanalysis, and will say without quarter, "It's all very well for people in the upper-middle area"—she is referring to the upper middle class—"but, it takes more than a couch to solve the problems of . . ." and she will list narcotics, juvenile delinquency, psychosis, relief distribution, slum housing, and other descriptions of our period. She recites these categories with an odd anticipation. One would guess she was ordering a meal.

Sam is fond of Marvin but he cannot abide Louise. "You'd think she discovered poverty," he will complain to Eleanor.

The Slovodas do feel superior to the Rossmans and the Sperbers. If pressed, they could not offer the most convincing explanation why. I suppose what it comes down to is that Sam and Eleanor do not think of themselves as really belonging to a class, and they feel that the Sperbers and Rossmans are petit-bourgeois. I find it hard to explain their attitude. Their company feels as much discomfort and will apologize as often as the Slovodas for the money they have, and the money they hope to earn. They are all of them equally concerned with progressive education and the methods of raising children to be well adjusted—indeed, they are discussing that now—they consider themselves relatively free of sexual taboo, or put more properly, Sam and Eleanor are no less possessive than the others. The Slovodas' culture is not more profound. I should be hard put to say that Sam is more widely read, more seriously informed, than Marvin or Alan or, for that matter, Louise. Probably, it comes to this: Sam, in his heart, thinks himself a rebel, and there are few rebels who do not claim an original mind. Eleanor has been a bohemian and considers herself more sophisticated than her friends who merely went to college and got married. Louise Rossman could express it most soundly. "Artists, writers, and people of the creative layer have in their occupational ideology the belief that they are classless."

One thing I might remark about the company. They are all being the most unconscionable hypocrites. They have rushed across half the city of New York to see a pornographic film, and they are not at all interested in each other at the moment. The women are giggling like tickled children at remarks that cannot possibly be so funny. Yet, they are all determined to talk for a respectable period of time. No less, it must be serious talk. Roslyn has said once, "I feel so funny at the thought of seeing such a movie," and the others have passed her statement by.

At the moment, Sam is talking about value. I might note that Sam loves conversation and thrives when he can expound an idea.

"What are our values today?" he asks. "It's really fantastic when you stop to think of it. Take any bright talented kid who's getting out of college now."

"My kid brother, for example," Marvin interposes morosely. He passes his bony hand over his sad mustache, and somehow the remark has become amusing, much as if Marvin had said, "Oh, yes, you have reminded me of the trials, the worries, and the cares which my fabulous younger brother heaps upon me."

"All right, take him," Sam says. "What does he want to be?"

"He doesn't want to be anything," says Marvin.

"That's my point," Sam says excitedly. "Rather than work at certain occupations, the best of these kids would rather do nothing at all."

"Alan has a cousin," Roslyn says, "who swears he'll wash dishes before he becomes a businessman."

"I wish that were true," Eleanor interrupts. "It seems to me everybody is conforming more and more these days."

They argue about this. Sam and Eleanor claim the country is suffering from hysteria; Alan Sperber disagrees and says it's merely a reflection of the headlines; Louise says no adequate criteria exist to measure hysteria; Marvin says he doesn't know anything at all.

"More solid liberal gains are being made in this period," says Alan, "than you would believe. Consider the Negro—"

"Is the Negro any less maladjusted?" Eleanor shouts with passion.

Sam maneuvers the conversation back to his thesis. "The values of the young today, and by the young, I mean the cream of the kids, the ones with ideas, are a reaction of indifference to the culture crisis. It really is despair. All they know is what they don't want to do."

"That is easier," Alan says genially.

"It's not altogether unhealthy," Sam says. "It's a corrective for smugness and the false value of the past, but it has created new false value." He thinks it worth emphasizing. "False value seems always to beget further false value."

"Define your terms," says Louise, the scientist.

"No, look," Sam says, "there's no revolt, there's no acceptance. Kids today don't want to get married, and—"

Eleanor interrupts. "Why should a girl rush to get married? She loses all chance for developing herself."

Sam shrugs. They are all talking at once. "Kids don't want to get married," he repeats, "and they don't want not to get married. They merely drift."

"It's a problem we'll all have to face with our own kids in ten years," Alan says, "although I think you make too much of it, Sam."

"My daughter," Marvin states. "She's embarrassed I'm a dentist. Even more embarrassed than I am." They laugh.

Sam tells a story about his youngest, Carol Ann. It seems he had a fight with her, and she went to her room. Sam followed; he called through the door.

"No answer," Sam says. "I called her again, 'Carol Ann.' I was a little worried, you understand, because she seemed so upset, so I said to her, 'Carol-Ann, you know I love you.' What do you think she answered?"

"What?" asks Roslyn.

"She said, 'Daddy, why are you so anxious?' "

They all laugh again. There are murmurs about what a clever thing it was to say. In the silence that follows, Roslyn leans forward and says quickly in her high voice, "You must get Alan to tell you his wonderful story about the man who studied yogi."

"Yoga," Alan corrects. "It's too long to tell."

The company prevails on him.

"Well," says Alan, in his genial courtroom voice, "it concerns a friend of mine named Cassius O'Shaugnessy."

"You don't mean Jerry O'Shaugnessy, do you?" asks Sam.

Alan does not know Jerry O'Shaugnessy. "No, no, this is Cassius O'Shaugnessy," he says. "He's really quite an extraordinary fellow." Alan sits plumply in his chair, fingering his bow tie. They are all used to his stories, which are told in a formal style and exhibit the attempt to recapture a certain note of urbanity, wit, and *élan* that Alan has probably copied from someone else. Sam and Eleanor respect his ability to tell these stories, but they resent the fact that he talks *at* them.

"You'd think we were a jury of his inferiors," Eleanor has said. "I hate being talked down to." What she resents is Alan's quiet implication that his antecedents, his social position, in total his life outside the room is superior to the life within. Eleanor now takes the promise from Alan's story by remarking, "Yes, and let's see the movie when Alan has finished."

"Sssh," Roslyn says.

"Cassius was at college a good while before me," says Alan, "but I knew him while I was an undergraduate. He would drop in and visit from time to time. An absolutely extraordinary fellow. The most amazing career. You see, he's done about everything."

"I love the way Alan tells it," Roslyn pipes nervously.

"Cassius was in France with Dos Passos and Cummings—he was even arrested with e.e. After the war, he was one of the founders of the Dadaist school, and for a while I understand he was Fitzgerald's guide to the gold of the Côte D'Azur. He knew everybody, he did everything. Do you realize that before the twenties had ended, Cassius had managed his father's business and then entered a monastery? It is said he influenced T. S. Eliot."

"Today, we'd call Cassius a psychopath," Marvin observes.

"Cassius called himself a great dilettante," Alan answers, "although perhaps the nineteenth-century Russian conception of the great sinner would be more appropriate. What do you say if I tell you this was only the beginning of his career?"

"What's the point?" Louise asks.

"Not yet," says Alan, holding up a hand. His manner seems to say that if his audience cannot appreciate the story, he does not feel obliged to continue. "Cassius studied Marx in the monastery. He broke his vows, quit the Church, and became a Communist. All through the thirties he was a figure in the Party, going to Moscow, involved in all the Party struggles. He left only during the Moscow trials."

Alan's manner while he relates such stories is somewhat effeminate. He talks with little caresses of his hand, he mentions names and places with a lingering ease as if to suggest that his audience and he are aware, above all, of nuance. The story as Alan tells it is drawn overlong. Suffice it that the man about whom he is talking, Cassius O'Shaugnessy, becomes a Trotskyist, becomes an anarchist, is a pacifist during the Second World War, and suffers it from a prison cell.

"I may say," Alan goes on, "that I worked for his defense, and was successful in getting him acquitted. Imagine my dolor when I learned that he had turned his back on his anarchist friends and was living with gangsters."

"This is weird," Eleanor says.

"Weird, it is," Alan agrees. "Cassius got into some scrape, and disappeared. What could you do with him? I learned only recently that he had gone to India and was studying yoga. In fact, I learned it from Cassius himself. I asked him of his experiences at Brahna-puth-thar, and he told me the following story."

Now Alan's voice alters. He assumes the part of Cassius and speaks in a tone weary of experience, wise and sad in its knowledge.

" 'I was sitting on my haunches contemplating my navel,' Cassius said to me, 'when of a sudden I discovered my navel under a different aspect. It seemed to me that if I were to give a counterclockwise twist, my navel would unscrew.' "

Alan looks up, he surveys his audience. They are now rapt and uneasy, not certain as yet whether a joke is to come. Alan's thumb and forefinger pluck at the middle of his ample belly, and his feet are crossed upon the carpet in symbolic suggestion of Cassius upon his haunches.

" 'Taking a deep breath, I turned, and the abysses of Vishtarni loomed beneath. My navel had begun to unscrew. I knew I was about to accept the reward of three years of contemplation. So,' said Cassius, 'I turned again, and my navel unscrewed a little more. I turned and I turned,' " Alan's fingers now revolving upon his belly, " 'and after a period I knew that with one more turn my navel would unscrew itself forever. At the edge of revelation, I took one sweet breath, and turned my navel free.' "

Alan looks up at his audience.

" 'Damn,' said Cassius, 'if my ass didn't fall off.' "

### 4.

The story has left the audience in an exasperated mood. It has been a most untypical story for Alan to tell, a little out of place, not offensive exactly, but irritating and inconsequential. Sam is the only one to laugh with more than bewildered courtesy, and his mirth seems excessive to everyone but Alan, and of course, Roslyn, who feels as if she has been the producer. I suppose what it reduces to is a lack of taste. Perhaps that is why Alan is not the lawyer one would expect. He does not have that appreciation—as necessary in his trade as for an actor— of what is desired at any moment, of that which will encourage as opposed to that which does not encourage a stimulating but smooth progression of logic and sentiment. Only a fool would tell so long a story when everyone is awaiting the movie.

Now, they are preparing. The men shift armchairs to correspond with the couch, the projector is set up, the screen is unfolded. Sam attempts to talk while he is threading the film, but no one listens. They seem to realize suddenly that a frightful demand has been placed upon them. One does not study pornography in a living room with a beer glass in one's hand and friends at the elbow. It is the most unsatisfactory of compromises; one can draw neither the benefits of solitary contemplation nor of social exchange. There is, at bottom, the same exasperated fright that one experiences in turning the shower tap and receiving cold water when the flesh has been prepared for heat. Perhaps that is why they are laughing so much now that the movie is begun.

A title, *The Evil Act*, twitches on the screen, shot with scars, holes, and the dust lines of age. A man and woman are sitting on a couch; they are having coffee. They chat. What they say is conveyed by printed words upon an ornately flowered card, interjected between glimpses of their casual gestures, a cup to the mouth, a smile, a cigarette being lit. The man's name, it seems, is Frankie Idell. He is talking to his wife, Magnolia. Frankie is dark, he is sinister, he confides in Magnolia, his dark counterpart, with a grimace of his brows, black from make-up pencil.

This is what the titles read:

FRANKIE: She will be here soon.
MAGNOLIA: This time the little vixen will not escape.
FRANKIE: No, my dear, this time we are prepared.
   (*He looks at his watch.*)
FRANKIE: Listen, she knocks!

There is a shot of a tall blond woman knocking on the door. She is probably over thirty, but by her short dress and ribboned hat it is suggested that she is a girl of fifteen.

FRANKIE: Come in, Eleanor.

As may be expected, the audience laughs hysterically at this. It is so wonderful a coincidence. "How I remember Frankie," says Eleanor Slovoda, and Roslyn Sperber is the only one not amused. In the midst of the others' laughter, she says in a worried tone, obviously adrift upon her own concerns, "Do you think we'll have to stop the film in the middle to let the bulb cool off?" The others hoot, they giggle, they are weak from the combination of their own remarks and the action of the plot.

Frankie and Magnolia have sat down on either side of the heroine, Eleanor. A moment passes. Suddenly, stiffly, they attack. Magnolia from her side kisses Eleanor, and Frankie commits an indecent caress.

ELEANOR: How dare you? Stop!
MAGNOLIA: Scream, my little one. It will do you no good. The walls are soundproofed.

FRANKIE: We've fixed a way to make you come across.
ELEANOR: This is hideous. I am hitherto undefiled. Do not touch me!

The captions fade away. A new title takes their place. It says, *But There Is No Escape From The Determined Pair.* On the fade-in, we discover Eleanor in the most distressing situation. Her hands are tied to loops running from the ceiling, and she can only writhe in helpless perturbation before the deliberate and progressive advances of Frankie and Magnolia. Slowly they humiliate her; with relish they probe her.

The audience laughs no longer. A hush has come upon them. Eyes unblinking, they devour the images upon Sam Slovoda's screen.

Eleanor is without clothing. As the last piece is pulled away, Frankie and Magnolia circle about her in a grotesque of pantomime, a leering of lips, limbs in a distortion of desire. Eleanor faints. Adroitly, Magnolia cuts her bonds. We see Frankie carrying her inert body.

Now, Eleanor is trussed to a bed, and the husband and wife are tormenting her with feathers. Bodies curl upon the bed in postures so complicated, in combinations so advanced, that the audience leans forward, Sperbers, Rossmans, and Slovodas, as if tempted to embrace the moving images. The hands trace abstract circles upon the screen, passes and recoveries upon a white background so illumined that hollows and swells, limb to belly and mouth to undescribables, tip of a nipple, orb of a navel, swim in giant magnification, flow and slide in a lurching yawing fall, blotting out the camera eye.

A little murmur, all unconscious, passes from their lips. The audience sways, each now finally lost in himself, communing hungrily with shadows, violated or violating, fantasy triumphant.

At picture's end, Eleanor the virgin whore is released from the bed. She kisses Frankie; she kisses Magnolia. "You dears," she says, "let's do it again." The projector lamp burns empty light, the machine keeps turning, the tag of film goes *slap-tap, slap-tap, slap-tap, slap-tap, slap-tap, slap-tap.*

"Sam, turn it off," says Eleanor.

But when the room lights are on, they cannot look at one another. "Can we see it again?" someone mutters. So, again, Eleanor knocks on the door, is tied, defiled, ravished, and made rapturous. They watch it soberly now, the room hot with the heat of their bodies, the darkness a balm for orgiastic vision. To the Deer Park, Sam is thinking, to the Deer Park of Louis XV were brought the most beautiful maidens of France, and there they stayed, dressed in fabulous silks, perfumed and wigged, the mole drawn upon their cheek, ladies of pleasure awaiting the pleasure of the king. So Louis had stripped an empire, bankrupt a treasury, prepared a deluge, while in his garden on summer evenings the maidens performed their pageants, eighteenth-century tableau of the evil act, beauteous instruments of one man's desire, lewd translation of a king's power. That century men sought wealth so they might use its fruits; this epoch men lusted for power in order to amass more power, a compounding of power into pyramids of abstraction whose yield are cannon and wire enclosure, pillars of statistics to the men who are the kings of this century and do no more in power's leisure time than go to church, claim to love their wives, and eat vegetables.

Is it possible, Sam wonders, that each of them here, two Rossmans, two Sperbers, two Slovodas, will cast off their clothes when the movie is done and perform the orgy that tickles at the heart of their desire? They will not, he knows. They will make jokes when the projector is put away. They will gorge the plate of delicatessen Eleanor provides, and swallow more beer, he among them. He will be the first to make jokes.

Sam is right. The movie has made him extraordinarily alive to the limits of them all. While they sit with red faces, eyes bugged, glutting sandwiches of ham, salami, and tongue, he begins the teasing.

"Roslyn," he calls out, "is the bulb cooled off yet?"

She cannot answer him. She chokes on beer, her face glazes, she is helpless with self-protecting laughter.

"Why are you so anxious, Daddy?" Eleanor says quickly.

They begin to discuss the film. As intelligent people they must dominate it. Someone wonders about the actors in the piece, and discussion begins afresh. "I fail to see," says Louise, "why they should be hard to classify. Pornography is a job to the criminal and prostitute element."

"No, you won't find an ordinary prostitute doing this," Sam insists. "It requires a particular kind of personality."

"They have to be exhibitionists," says Eleanor.

"It's all economic," Louise maintains.

"I wonder what those girls felt?" Roslyn asks. "I feel sorry for them."

"I'd like to be the cameraman," says Alan.

"I'd like to be Frankie," says Marvin sadly.

There is a limit to how long such a conversation may continue. The jokes lapse into silence. They are all busy eating. When they begin to talk again, it is of other things. Each dollop of food sops the agitation that the movie has spilled. They gossip about the party the night before, they discuss which single men were interested in which women, who got drunk, who got sick, who said the wrong thing, who went home with someone else's date. When this is exhausted, one of them mentions a play the others have not seen. Soon they are talking about books, a concert, a one-man show by an artist who is a friend. Dependably, conversation will voyage its orbit. While the men talk of politics, the women are discussing fashions, progressive schools, and recipes they have attempted. Sam is uncomfortable with the division; he knows Eleanor will resent it, he knows she will complain later of the insularity of men and the basic contempt they feel for women's intelligence.

"But you collaborated," Sam will argue. "No one forced you to be with the women."

"Was I to leave them alone?" Eleanor will answer.

"Well, why do the women always have to go off by themselves?"

"Because the men aren't interested in what we have to say."

Sam sighs. He has been talking with interest, but really he is bored. These are nice pleasant people, he thinks, but they are ordinary people, exactly the sort he has spent so many years with, making little jokes, little gossip, living little everyday events, a close circle where everyone mothers the other by his presence. The womb of middle-class life, Sam decides heavily. He is in a bad mood indeed. Everything is laden with dissatisfaction.

Alan has joined the women. He delights in preparing odd dishes when friends visit the Sperbers, and he is describing to Eleanor how he makes blueberry pancakes. Marvin draws closer to Sam.

"I wanted to tell you," he says, "Alan's story reminded me. I saw Jerry O'Shaugnessy the other day."

"Where was he?"

Marvin is hesitant. "It was a shock, Sam. He's on the Bowery. I guess he's become a wino."

"He always drank a lot," says Sam.

"Yeah." Marvin cracks his bony knuckles. "What a stinking time this is, Sam."

"It's probably like the years after 1905 in Russia," Sam says.

"No revolutionary party will come out of this."

"No," Sam says, "nothing will come."

He is thinking of Jerry O'Shaugnessy. What did he look like? what did he say? Sam asks Marvin, and clucks his tongue at the dispiriting answer. It is a shock to him. He draws closer to Marvin; he feels a bond. They have, after all, been through some years together. In the thirties they were in the Communist Party, they quit together. Now they are both weary of politics today, still radicals out of habit, but without enthusiasm and without a cause. "Jerry was a hero to me," Sam says.

"To all of us," says Marvin.

The fabulous Jerry O'Shaugnessy, thinks Sam. In the old days, in the Party, they had made a legend of him. All of them with their middle-class origins and their desire to know a worker-hero.

I may say that I was never as fond of Jerry O'Shaugnessy as was Sam. I thought him a showman and too pleased with himself. Sam, however, with his timidity, his desire to travel, to have adventure and know many women, was obliged to adore O'Shaugnessy. At least he was enraptured with his career.

Poor Jerry who ends as a bum. He has been everything else. He has been a trapper in Alaska, a chauffeur for gangsters, an officer in the Foreign Legion, a labor organizer. His nose was broken; there were scars on his chin. When he would talk about his years at sea or his experiences in Spain, the stenographers and garment workers, the radio writers and unemployed actors would listen to his speeches as if he were the prophet of new romance, and their blood would be charged with the magic of revolutionary vision. A man with tremendous charm. In those days it had been easy to confuse his love for himself with his love for all underprivileged workingmen.

"I thought he was still in the Party," Sam says.

"No," says Marvin, "I remember they kicked him out a couple of years ago. He was supposed to have piddled some funds, that's what they say."

"I wish he'd taken the treasury," Sam remarks bitterly. "The Party used him for years."

Marvin shrugs. "They used each other." His mustache droops. "Let me tell you about Sonderson. You know he's still in the Party. The most progressive dentist in New York." They laugh.

While Marvin tells the story, Sam is thinking of other things. Since he has quit Party work, he has studied a great deal. He can tell you about prison camps and the secret police, political murders, the Moscow trials, the exploitation of Soviet labor, the privileges of the bureaucracy; it is all painful to him. He is straddled between the loss of a country he has never seen and his repudiation of the country in which he lives. "Doesn't the Party seem a horror now?" he bursts out.

Marvin nods. They are trying to comprehend the distance between Party members they have known, people by turn pathetic, likable, or annoying—people not unlike themselves—and in contrast the immensity of historic logic, which deploys along statistics of the dead.

"It's all schizoid," Sam says. "Modern life is schizoid."

Marvin agrees. They have agreed on this many times, bored with the petulance of their small voices, yet needing the comfort of such complaints. Marvin asks Sam if he has given up his novel, and Sam says, "Temporarily." He cannot find a form, he explains. He does not want to write a realistic novel, because reality is no longer realistic. "I don't know what it is," says Sam. "To tell you the truth, I think I'm kidding myself. I'll never finish this book. I just like to entertain the idea I'll do something good some day." They sit there in friendly depression. Conversation has cooled. Alan and the women are no longer talking.

"Marvin," asks Louise, "what time is it?"

They are ready to go. Sam must say directly what he had hoped to approach by suggestion. "I was wondering," he whispers to Rossman, "would you mind if I held on to the film for a day or two?"

Marvin looks at him. "Oh, why of course, Sam," he says in his morose voice. "I know how it is." He pats Sam on the shoulder as if, symbolically, to convey the exchange of ownership. They are fellow conspirators.

"If you ever want to borrow the projector," Sam suggests.

"Nah," says Marvin, "I don't know that it would make much difference."

### 5.

It has been, when all is said, a most annoying day. As Sam and Eleanor tidy the apartment, emptying ash trays and washing the few dishes, they are fond neither of themselves nor each other. "What a waste today has been," Eleanor remarks, and Sam can only agree. He has done no writing, he has not been outdoors, and still it is late in the evening, and he has talked too much, eaten too much, is nervous from the movie they have seen. He knows that he will watch it again with Eleanor before they go to sleep; she has given her assent to that. But as is so often the case with Sam these days, he cannot await their embrace with any sure anticipation. Eleanor may be in the mood or Eleanor may not; there is no way he can control the issue. It is depressing. Sam knows that he circles about Eleanor at such times with the guilty maneuvers of a sad hound. Resent her as he must, be furious with himself as he will, there is not very much he can do about it. Often, after they have made love, they will lie beside each other in silence, each offended, each certain the other is to blame. At such times, memory tickles them with a cruel feather. Not always has it been like this. When they were first married, and indeed for the six months they lived together before marriage, everything was quite different. Their affair was very exciting to them; each told the other with some hyperbole but no real mistruth that no one in the past had ever been comparable as lover.

I suppose I am a romantic. I always feel that this is the best time in people's lives. There is, after all, so little we accomplish, and that short period when we are beloved and triumph as lovers is sweet with power. Rarely are we concerned then with our lack of importance; we are too important. In Sam's case, disillusion means even more. Like so many young men, he entertained the secret conceit that he was an extraordinary lover. One cannot really believe this without supporting at the same time the equally secret conviction that one is fundamentally inept. It is—no matter what Sergius would say—a more dramatic and therefore more attractive view of oneself than the sober notion, which Sam now accepts with grudging wisdom, that the man as lover is dependent upon the bounty of the woman. As I say, he accepts the notion, it is one of the lineaments of maturity, but there is a part of him which, no matter how harried by analysis, cannot relinquish the antagonism he feels that Eleanor has respected his private talent so poorly, and has not allowed him to confer its benefits upon more women. I mock Sam, but he would mock himself on this. It hardly matters. Mockery cannot accomplish everything, and Sam seethes with that most private and tender pain: Even worse than being unattractive to the world is to be unattractive to one's mate, or, what is the same and describes Sam's case more accurately, never to know in advance when he shall be undesirable to Eleanor.

I make perhaps too much of the subject, but that is only because it is so important to Sam. Relations between Eleanor and him are not really that bad—I know other couples who have much less or nothing at all. But comparisons are poor comfort to Sam; his standards are so high. So are Eleanor's. I am convinced the most unfortunate people are those who would make an art of love. It sours other effort. Of all artists, they are certainly the most wretched.

Shall I furnish a model? Sam and Eleanor are on the couch and the projector, adjusted to its slowest speed, is retracing the elaborate pantomime of the three principals. If one could allow these shadows a life . . . but indeed such life has been given them. Sam and Eleanor are no more than an itch, a smart, a threshold of satisfaction; the important share of themselves has steeped itself in Frankie-, Magnolia-, and Eleanor-of-the-film. Indeed the variations are beyond telling. It is the most outrageous orgy performed by five ghosts.

Self-critical Sam! He makes love in front of a movie, and one cannot say that it is unsatisfactory any more than one can say it is pleasant. It is dirty, downright porno dirty, a lewd slop-brush slapped through the middle of domestic exasperations and breakfast eggs. It is so dirty that only half of Sam—he is quite divisible into fractions—can be exercised at all. The part that is his brain worries along like a cuckolded burgher. He is taking the pulse of his anxiety. Will he last long enough to satisfy Eleanor? Will the children come back tonight? He cannot help it. In the midst of the circus, he is suddenly convinced the children will walk through the door. "Why are you so anxious, Daddy?"

So it goes. Sam the lover is conscious of exertion. One moment he is Frankie Idell, destroyer of virgins—take that! you whore!—the next, body moving, hands caressing, he is no more than some lines from a psychoanalytical text. He is thinking about the sensitivity of his scrotum. He has read that this is a portent of femininity in a male. How strong is his latent homosexuality worries Sam, thrusting stiffly, warm sweat running cold. Does he identify with Eleanor-of-the-film?

Technically, the climax is satisfactory. They lie together in the dark, the film ended, the projector humming its lonely revolutions in the quiet room. Sam gets up to turn it off. He comes back and kisses Eleanor upon the mouth. Apparently, she has enjoyed herself more than he; she is tender and fondles the tip of his nose.

"You know, Sam," she says from her space beside him, "I think I saw this picture before."

"When?"

"Oh, you know when. That time."

Sam thinks dully that women are always most loving when they can reminisce about infidelity.

"That time!" he repeats.

"I think so."

Racing forward from memory like the approaching star that begins as a point on the mind and swells to explode the eyeball with its odious image, Sam remembers, and is weak in the dark. It is ten years, eleven perhaps, before they were married, yet after they were lovers. Eleanor has told him, but she has always been vague about details. There had been two men it seemed, and another girl, and all had been drunk. They had seen movie after movie. With reluctant fascination, Sam can conceive the rest. How it had pained him, how excited him. It is years now since he has remembered, but he remembers. In the darkness he wonders at the unreasonableness of jealous pain. That night was impossible to imagine any longer—therefore it is more real; Eleanor his plump wife who presses a pigeon's shape against her housecoat, forgotten heroine of black orgies. It had been meaningless, Eleanor claimed; it was Sam she loved, and the other had been no more than a fancy of which she wished to rid herself. Would it be the same today, thinks Sam, or had Eleanor been loved by Frankie, by Frankie of the other movies, by Frankie of the two men she never saw again on that night so long ago?

The pleasure I get from this pain, Sam thinks furiously.

It is not altogether perverse. If Eleanor causes him pain, it means after all that she is alive for him. I have often observed that the reality of a person depends upon his ability to hurt us; Eleanor as the vague accusing embodiment of the wife is different, altogether different, from Eleanor who lies warmly in Sam's bed, an attractive Eleanor who may wound his flesh. Thus, brother to the pleasure of pain is the sweeter pleasure that follows pain. Sam, tired, lies in Eleanor's arms, and they talk with the cozy trade words of old professionals, agreeing that they will not make love again before a movie, that it was exciting but also not without detachment, that all in all it has been good but not quite right, that she had loved this action he had done, and was uncertain about another. It is their old familiar critique, a sign that they are intimate and well disposed. They do not talk about the act when it has failed to fire; then they go silently to sleep. But now, Eleanor's enjoyment having mollified Sam's sense of no enjoyment, they talk with the apologetics and encomiums of familiar mates. Eleanor falls asleep, and Sam falls almost asleep, curling next to her warm body, his hand over her round belly with the satisfaction of a sculptor. He is drowsy, and he thinks drowsily that these few moments of creature-pleasure, this brief compassion he can feel for the body that trusts itself to sleep beside him, his comfort in its warmth, is perhaps all the meaning he may ask for his life. That out of disappointment, frustration, and the passage of dreary years come these few moments when he is close to her, and their years together possess a connotation more rewarding than the sum of all which has gone into them.

But then he thinks of the novel he wants to write, and he is wide-awake again. Like the sleeping pill that fails to work and leaves one warped in an exaggeration of the ills which sought the drug, Sam passes through the promise of sex-emptied sleep, and is left with nervous loins, swollen jealousy of an act ten years dead, and sweating irritable resentment of the woman's body that hinders his limbs. He has wasted the day, he tells himself. He has wasted the day as he has wasted so many days of his life, and tomorrow in the office he will be no more than his ten fingers typing plot and words for Bramba the Venusian and Lee-Lee Deeds, Hollywood Star, while that huge work with which he has cheated himself, holding it before him as a covenant of his worth, that enormous novel which would lift him at a bound from the impasse in which he stifles, whose dozens of characters would develop a vision of life in bountiful complexity, lies foundered, rotting on a beach of purposeless effort. Notes here, pages there, it sprawls through a formless wreck of incidental ideas and half-episodes, utterly without shape. He has not even a hero for it.

One could not have a hero today, Sam thinks, a man of action and contemplation, capable of sin, large enough for good, a man immense. There is only a modern hero damned by no more than the ugliness of wishes whose satisfaction he will never know. One needs a man who could walk the stage, someone who—no matter who, not himself. Someone, Sam thinks, who reasonably could not exist.

The novelist, thinks Sam, perspiring beneath blankets, must live in paranoia and seek to be one with the world; he must be terrified of experience and hungry for it; he must think himself nothing and believe he is superior to all. The feminine in his nature cries for proof he is a man; he dreams of power and is without capacity to gain it; he loves himself above all and therefore despises all that he is.

He is that, thinks Sam. He is part of the perfect prescription, and yet he is not a novelist. He lacks energy and belief. It is left for him to write an article some day about the temperament of the ideal novelist.

In the darkness, memories rise, yeast-swells of apprehension. Out of bohemian days so long ago comes the friend of Eleanor, a girl who had been sick and was committed to an institution. They visited her, Sam and Eleanor. They took the suburban train and sat on the lawn of the asylum grounds while patients circled about intoning a private litany, or shuddering in boob-blundering fright from an insect that crossed their skin. The friend had been silent. She had smiled, she had answered their questions with the fewest words, and had returned again to her study of sunlight and blue sky. As they were about to leave, the girl had taken Sam aside. "They violate me," she said in a whisper. "Every night when the doors are locked, they come to my room and they make the movie. I am the heroine and am subjected to all variety of sexual viciousness. Tell them to leave me alone so I may enter the convent." And while she talked, in a horror of her body, one arm scrubbed the other. Poor tortured friend. They had seen her again, and she babbled, her face had coarsened into an idiot leer.

Sam sweats. There is so little he knows, and so much to know. Youth of the depression with its economic terms; what can he know of madness or religion? They are both so alien to him. He is the mongrel, Sam thinks, brought up without religion from a mother half Protestant and half Catholic, and a father half Catholic and half Jew. He is the quarter-Jew, and yet he is a Jew, or so he feels himself, knowing nothing of Gospel, tabernacle, or Mass, the Jew through accident, through state of mind. What . . . whatever did he know of penance? self-sacrifice? mortification of the flesh? the love of his fellow man? Am I concerned with my relation to God? ponders Sam, and smiles sourly in the darkness. No, that has never concerned him, he thinks, not for better nor for worse. "They are making the movie," says the girl into the ear of memory, "and so I cannot enter the convent."

How hideous was the mental hospital. A concentration camp, decides Sam. Perhaps it would be the world some day, or was that only his projection of feelings of hopelessness? "Do not try to solve the problems of the world," he hears from Sergius, and pounds a lumpy pillow.

However could he organize his novel? What form to give it? It is so complex. Too loose, thinks Sam, too scattered. Will he ever fall asleep? Wearily, limbs tense, his stomach too keen, he plays again the game of putting himself to sleep. "I do not feel my toes," Sam says to himself, "my toes are dead, my calves are asleep, my calves are sleeping . . ."

In the middle from wakefulness to slumber, in the torpor that floats beneath blankets, I give an idea to Sam. "Destroy time, and chaos may be ordered," I say to him.

"Destroy time, and chaos may be ordered," he repeats after me and, in desperation to seek his coma, mutters back, "I do not feel my nose, my nose is numb, my eyes are heavy, my eyes are heavy."

So Sam enters the universe of sleep, a man who seeks to live in such a way as to avoid pain, and succeeds merely in avoiding pleasure. What a dreary compromise is our life!

From *Advertisements for Myself* (1959)

**THE COLD WAR—III**

## The Face of the Rock

In adolescence, I had only to say "God," and I would think of my groin. God was lust to me. God was like the image of the Devil offered to us at St. Matthew's. Chapel was daily and devoted to Christ, but once a week on average we might hear of the temptings of a somewhat legendary master-ghost named Satan. Chapel kept God and Satan well separated, but I, unlike other Matties, kept mixing them up. I had my reasons: I was introduced to carnal relations during my first year in the school by an assistant chaplain of St. Matthew's who *glommed*—I choose the word to convey the sensation of that rubbery, indefatigable seal—my fourteen-year-old penis in his tight, unhappy lips.

We were in Washington, D.C., on a school trip. Maybe that is one more reason I dislike our subtle, oppressive capital, that broad, well-paved swamp. Boredom and bad memory are at the root of many an oppression, I would suppose, and that night I was sharing a double bed with the assistant chaplain in an inexpensive hotel not far from H Street, NW, and was unable to sleep and feeling full of apprehension just about the time that the chaplain came out of a millrace of stentorian snoring, murmured his wife's name several times, "Bettina, Bettina," and proceeded to embrace my hips and strip my bewildered young privates of their primeval dew. I remember lying there with a complete sense of the sixteen other members of my class who were also on the trip and in the hotel. I visualized them, two by two, and four by four, in all the other six bedrooms where they had been placed. On this annual trip to Washington the assistant chaplain was our guide, and since I had not succeeded in my first year at the school in being associated in anyone's mind with anyone else, and was marked as a loner, the assistant chaplain, a sympathetic fellow, had assigned me to his room.

In the other cubicles, who knew what might be going on? At St. Matthew's, they used to call it "kidding around." Since my memory was seared with images of the two-backed beast of my father and stepmother (it was a two-backed beast long before I ever encountered the phrase in *Othello*), I stayed far apart from such gang play. All of us knew, however, that there were goings-on all up and down the dorm. Boys would stand side by side and stroke themselves into erections to see who was longer. It was the age of innocence. Being wider was not even a concept to us, for it would have suggested penetration. The nearest any of the boys came to that was by mounting a sweet, fat little creature named Arnold; we called him St. Matthew's Arnold. Even at the age of fourteen, literary wit was not discouraged among us, and St. Matthew's Arnold used to drop his pants and lie on a bed, buttocks exposed. Six or eight of us would watch while two or three of the more athletic of our skulk would take turns slapping their brand-new instruments onto the crack between St. Matthew's Arnold's cheeks. "Ugh, you're disgusting," they'd say, and he'd whine back, "Aaah, shut up. *You're* doing it too."

It was never homosexual. It was "kidding around." Once done, it was not uncommon for the budding jock to leap off the body, wipe himself, and say, "Why can't you be a girl? You look just like a girl." Which was true—Arnold's cheeks were cousins to the moon—and Arnold, having his own male dignity to defend, would reply, "Aaaah, shut up." He was smaller than the boys who did it to him, so they barely cuffed him for being rude.

I would, as I say, merely watch. I was not up for studies in comparative phallitude. I was electrified by them, but even at fourteen I had already acquired some of our Hubbard insulation. I didn't show a spark.

My own relation to these sports and circuses was revealed to me, however, by the sweet-edged shudder that the chaplain's mean little lips pulled from me. When it was over, and I had been given an adolescent's peek into the firmament, he swallowed all the nourishment offered the parching of his mouth and began to sob in shame. Deep sobs. He was not a weak man physically, and his strength, like my father's, was in his upper body. So his sobs were strong.

I felt injected with ten tons of novocaine. Except, that is not true either. Two rivers were flowing in me, although to opposite directions. I felt relief I had never known before in my limbs, yet my heart, liver, head, and lungs were in a boil. This was even worse than seeing Mary Bolland Baird and my father in their roll-around. I knew myself to be the compliant apprentice of a monster.

After his sobbing, the man began to weep. I knew he was worried about his wife and children. "Don't worry," I said, "I'll never tell." He hugged me. Gently, I disengaged myself. I did it gently out of no noble funds of generosity, rather in the fear he would turn angry and grow rough. I think my secret instinct knew he wished me to have, in turn, a thirst I would slake on him. If I had none (and I did not), well, went his unspoken imperative: Generate some! You damn well better generate some.

How the poor man must have been hung between his lust for one good, reciprocal suck on his charged-up end and the horror of knowing that he was inching out along the precipice of his career. When I remained still and did not move at all, his sobbing finally ceased and he lay still as well. I did my best to picture him officiating at a High Mass in school chapel, white silk surplice over white linen cassock, his ritual gestures a talisman I could employ against him. It may have been a real magic. After an interval of silence, equal in weight to the darkness of our hotel room, he gave a sigh, slipped out of bed, and spent the rest of the night on the floor.

That was the extent of my homosexual experience, but what a bend it put into the shape of my psyche. I stayed away from sex as though it were a disease. I had bog-and-marsh dreams where I was Arnold and the chaplain released streams of the foulest suppurations over me. In turn, I would awaken to feel infected. My sheets were wet, sprayed with nothing less than the pus, I was certain, of my unholy infections. The headaches grew worse. When the boys got ready to kid around, I took off for the library. I believe I finally accepted my father's desire to have an operation on my head because I could not overcome the part of me that was certain there was awful matter in the brain to be cut out.

Conceivably, something may have altered. When I went back to St. Matthew's in the fall of 1949, after my summer of convalescence, the school seemed at last a reasonable place. Our soccer teams (it was the first prep school I knew to take soccer seriously), our football scrimmages at every class level, our Greek, Latin, daily chapel, and prayers before meals, our ice-cold showers from October to May (lukewarm in June and September), our button-down shirts and school ties for all occasions but sports (starched white collar and shirt on Sundays) had now become an agreeable order of the day. My dyslexia seemed to wane after the operation. (As a result, my case was written about in neurosurgical papers.) I felt more like others, and stronger for average tasks. I had a B-plus average.

Left to myself, I think I might have ended like most of my classmates. From Yale, where many a good Mattie went in those days, I would have continued on to Wall Street or the Bar. I probably would have made an acceptable, even a good, estate lawyer, my experience with the chaplain keeping me alert to the pits of horrible possibility in the most proper affairs, and like many another not quite notable prep school product, I might even have improved with the years. The odds are favorable if you can hold your liquor.

Hugh Tremont Montague intervened. My father, who always kept his promises, if late by many a season, finally arranged for the meeting a year and a half after our lunch at 21. My operation had come and gone, as well as my convalescence. I was now a senior, and a responsible figure to my younger cousins and brothers in the summer frolics at Doane, curious frolics—the eight-hundred-yard swimming race around the island, four hundred with the current, four hundred back in the channel against it, and the all-day hike that commenced at The Precipices south of Bar Harbor at eight in the morning, went over Cadillac Mountain to Jordan Pond at noon, then up to Sargent Mountain and down all the way to Somesville; next, Acadia Mountain descending to Man of War Creek. We ended at the dock in Manset by eight in the evening. There a lobster boat came to meet us for the trip by water around the Western Way, up to Blue Hill Bay and Doane. A platoon of Marines would have complained of a twenty-mile march over hills like that, but we were rewarded by explorations in the lobster boat over the next few days to islands scattered around the bay, islands so small their names were in dispute, and their topography eccentric—great grass meadows on one, guano-encrusted sea ledges on another, forests with unearthly trees warped by long-lost winds. We would feast on lobsters boiled over driftwood fires and clams baked in the coals—even the charred hot dogs tasted as good as wild game caught with bow and arrow. To this day, Kittredge and I are visited in summer by cousins who have shared these Hubbard gymkhanas. No great tennis players ever came out of such a regimen, but our family life was our social life.

When Hugh Tremont Montague came up one weekend with my father in a light chartered plane from Boston, it was, therefore, an event of the first measure. We had a much spoken-of visitor. I might have heard of my anointed godfather for the first time during lunch at 21, but his name seemed present everywhere thereafter at school. A new file in my personal history had been opened. He was, as I now discovered, one of the myths of St. Matthew's. All through my first year at school, teachers must have spoken of him, but the name never entered my ear. Once my father inscribed his importance on my attention, however, accounts of him popped up everywhere. One spoke of him now as if he had been headmaster. By actual record, he was coach of the soccer team and founder of the Mountaineering Club. A graduate of St. Matthew's, '32, and of Harvard, '36, he taught at the school until he joined the OSS. Instructor in English and in Divine Studies, he installed his own dicta in our dogma and lore. At St. Matthew's I had heard of the Egyptian goddess Maat before I ever heard of Hugh Montague. Maat had the body of a woman and a large feather for her neck and head. As the Egyptian Goddess of Truth, she embodied a curious holy principle: In the depths of one's soul, the difference between a truth and a falsehood weighed no more than a feather. St. Matthew's tended to equate this weight to the presence of Christ, and Montague was the determined author of that addition. St. Matthew's had always taken Divine Studies seriously, but after Montague's influence on us, we felt we had a greater contribution to make than any other school of our ilk in New Hampshire or Massachusetts, or, if one is to lower the bars, Connecticut. We were closer to God than the others and Mr. Montague had given the clue: Christ was Love, but Love lived only in the Truth. Why?—because one's ability to recognize the presence of Grace (which I always saw as a leavening in the region of the chest) could be injured by a lie.

Harlot left other precepts at St. Matthew's. God the Father—awesome, monumental Jehovah—was the principle of Justice. Mr. Montague added that Jehovah was also the embodiment of Courage. Just as Love was Truth and there could be no compassion without honesty, so was Justice equal to Courage. There was no justice for the coward. There was only the purgatory of his daily life. Did a student feel despair? Look to the root. A cowardly act had been committed, or a lie told. Somewhere in the school pamphlets sent out to increase St. Matthew's endowment, there are a few lines quoted from an address Hugh Montague gave on a special occasion to a senior class in chapel. "The first purpose of this school," he said, "is not to develop your potentialities—although some of you do indeed bear the unruly gift of quick mentality—but to send out into American society young men keen to maintain their honesty and sense of purpose. It is this school's intention that you grow into good, brave young men."

I will say it for Mr. Montague and St. Matthew's. Our theology was more complex than that. There was the special temptation of evil for the good and brave. The Devil, Montague warned, employed his finest wits to trap the noblest soldiers and scholars. Vanity, complacency, and indolence were a curse, since bravery was an ascending slope and one could not rest on it. One must succeed in rising to every challenge except the ones that would destroy us needlessly. Prudence was the one amelioration God allowed to the imperative of Courage; Love, on fortunate occasions, could offer support to Truth.

Competition on the playing field became, therefore, an avatar of Courage and Prudence, Love and Truth. On the playing field, one could find the unique proportions of one's heart. Later, properly prepared, out in the world, one might be able to deal with the Devil. Although it was never stated so at St. Matthew's, we all knew that women—as opposed to mothers, sisters, cousins, and ladies—had to be one more word for the world.

Since Mr. Montague had been gone for six years before I entered, I had no notion of the dialectical niceties of his mind. Only the precepts came down to us in strong doses imparted by instructors who lived with the conclusions. So hypocrisy also abounded at St. Matthew's. We were all smaller than our precepts. Indeed, the assistant chaplain who minted my adolescent glans was a disciple of Hugh Tremont Montague, even a rock climber, although I heard he was not a good one.

Rock climbing, after all, was the objective correlative of Virtue, which is to say, the meeting of Truth and Courage. I was soon to find out. That night in the summer of 1949 when Hugh Montague came to the Keep for the first time, he was thirty-five and I was seventeen, and much as I expected, he looked half a British officer with his erect posture and mustache and half an Anglican clergyman by way of his wire-rimmed eyeglasses and high forehead. Let me say that he could have been taken for a man of forty-five, but continued to look no older for the next twenty years, right up to his dreadful fall.

On shaking hands, I knew immediately why Christ was Truth not Love for Mr. Montague. He had a grip to remind you of the hard rubber pads that are put on vise-jaws to keep them from injuring any object in their grasp. Heaven help me, went my thought, this man is a real prick.

Accurate was my instinct! Decades later, over the seasons of my marriage to Kittredge, I learned the innermost secrets of Harlot's young manhood even as he had confessed them one by one to her; what other gift could measure his profound love for Kittredge? He had indeed been a prick, and of the worst sort. His personal devil had been a great desire to ream young pits. There was hardly a good-looking boy in his instruction whom he had not wanted to bugger. According to Kittredge, he never had: at least, not if he was telling the truth—which was always the question—but he avowed that until he met her, this impulse was the ongoing daily torment of his years at Harvard, then later at St. Matthew's, where he ground his teeth in sleep. Indeed, he had not entered the ministry for fear that he would, one good day, dive deep into his impulses and betray his church. The sexual energies, in consequence, were in-held. As he took my hand on introduction and stared into my eyes, he was a force and I was a receptacle: He was clean as steel and I was a punk.

I remember how my father, forty pounds heavier than Hugh Tremont Montague, circled nonetheless around our introduction like an anxious relative, a facet of Cal Hubbard's personality I had never seen before. I not only realized how much this meeting had to mean to my father, but even why it had taken so long to arrange—Cal Hubbard's expectations would suffer a dull return if it did not work.

I describe our meeting as if there were no one else in the house. In fact, something like seventeen of us, Mary Bolland Baird, Rough, Tough, cousins, fathers and mothers of cousins, aunts, uncles, numerous Hubbards were there. It was our last summer in that period at the Keep. My father was in the process of selling the place to Rodman Knowles Gardiner, Kittredge's father, and we were all taking a long farewell to our summer house. There might have been five people present when we were introduced, or ten, or we could have been alone. All I remember is that my father circled Mr. Montague and me, and my father was soon gone. I have some recollection that we then went down to the den to have a talk. That comes to me with clarity.

"You're out of the dyslexia, your father says."

"I think so."

"Good. What are your subjects at St. Matthew's?"

I named them.

"Your favorite?"

"English," I said.

"What's the best novel you've read this year?"

"*Portrait of a Lady*. We had it assigned, but I liked it a lot."

He nodded sourly. "Henry James is a quince pie as large as the Mojave Desert. It's a pity. Put Hemingway's heart in him and James would have been a writer to equal Stendhal or Tolstoy."

"Yessir," I said. I was such a liar. I had gotten an A for my paper on *Portrait of a Lady,* but I had merely parroted a few critical appreciations. *The Young Lions* was what I had enjoyed most last year. Noah Ackerman, the Jew, had appealed to me.

"Let's go out tomorrow," he said. "Your father wants me to take you on a climb. I hear there's dependable rock suitable for beginners over at a place called Otter Cliffs. We'll pick a route that's feasible."

"Yessir." I was hoping that what he called Otter Cliffs was some other Otter Cliffs than the one I knew. That was black rock and dropped a straight eighty feet down to the sea. Sometimes on the rise of the tide, there was a heavy roll of surf in Frenchman's Bay, and I had heard the growl of black waters on black rock at Otter Cliffs. Indeed, the fall was so steep I could never look over the edge.

"Guess I haven't done any rock climbing," I said, and regretted the remark on the instant.

"You'll know a little more tomorrow than you know right now."

"Yessir."

"Your father asked me to be your godfather."

I nodded. My quick fear at the thought of tomorrow had already commandeered the lower register of my voice. If I said "yessir" one more time it would come out like ship's pipes.

"I have to tell you," he said, "I was inclined to refuse." He fixed me front and center with his stare. "One must have a close personal interest to be a godfather."

"That's true, I suppose." I croaked it forth.

"I don't like close personal interest."

I nodded.

"On the other hand, I have regard for your father. No one will ever know how good his war record was until the secrets can be told."

"Yessir." But I beamed. Absolutely unexpected to myself, I experienced such happiness at this confirmation of my father's qualities that I knew the value, on the spot, of family pride and could have been filled from head to toe with well-nourished blood.

"Some day," he said drily, "you must try to equal him."

"Never," I said. "But I intend to try."

"Harry," he said, giving me back my name for the first time, "you're fortunate to be carrying that kind of burden. I don't tell people often, but since you and I are obviously embarked on a special venture, at least personally speaking, I choose to inform you that a father one admires extravagantly may be less of an impost than growing up without one. Mine was killed in Colorado in a shooting accident."

"I'm sorry to hear that."

"I was eleven when it occurred. I must say I didn't have to grow up altogether without him. He was always a presence in my life."

It took a few more years before I was to learn that David Montague, Harlot's father, had been shot by Harlot's mother, Imogene, as David entered the master bedroom one night. It was never clear whether he had lost his keys and was climbing through the window or walking through the door. There was too much blood on the floor. Either he had traveled on his belly, mortally wounded, from the window to the door, as was her claim, or had been dragged by Hugh's mother from the door to the window, then back to the door, to support the story that his unexpected entrance by the window caused her to believe he was an intruder. I understand Ty Cobb's father was shot under similar circumstances and there are some who believe it accounts for the tigerish rapacity of Ty Cobb on the base paths. If that is the formula for generating ungodly determination, I see no reason why it could not apply to Harlot.

Next day, true to his promise, he drove me out to Otter Cliffs. In anticipation, I spent a sleepless night. First I hoped it would rain, then that it would not. I was certain Mr. Montague would say the essence of rock climbing was to accept the given. If the rock was slippery, we would still have a go. So I began to pray it would not rain.

It was misty at 6:30 in the morning, but I knew the weather on Mount Desert well enough to see that the sky would be clear by eight. To avoid a family breakfast, we had fried eggs and coffee at a hashhouse (no granola for outdoorsmen then!) and I ate my food in all somber duty, the yolk and biscuits going down like sulphur and brimstone, after which we took the Park Drive along the eastern shore of Mount Desert. As we drove I named for him places long familiar to me, the Beehive, Sand Beach, Thunder Hole, Gorham Mountain, a guide leading the way to his own terminal hour. Or so I was convinced. Rock climbing was familiar to me, if only in sleep. I always knew when a dream had become a nightmare, for there was I clinging to a wall.

We parked. We walked along a wooded trail for a hundred yards, and suddenly had, all to ourselves, the precipice of a cliff. Our view was open to the boom and hiss of the Atlantic pounding on rocks below. I took a quick glimpse down. It proved no easier than standing on the edge of a roof seven stories high that had no railing. My impulse was to ask Mr. Montague if this was, for certain, the right place.

He was scouting, his boots six inches from the lip. He strode along, frowning and clucking, weighing one ascent against another, while I sat beside his pile of climbing gear, nerveless, and for all I knew, limbless. The stone on which I perched was pale pink and friendly, but the straight rock-fall below was dark gray, and black at the bottom. Years later, in Saigon, I was to have an outrageous attack of anxiety one night while staring at a Vietnamese prostitute's out-spread legs. Her open vagina looked as sinister to me as an exotic or-chid. Only then did I realize that the contrast of her pink petals and near-black overleaves had brought me back to the fearful minutes I waited for Harlot to take the measure of where to commence my instruction.

Finally he settled on the right place. "This will do," he told me, and unstrapped his gear, took out two coiled nylon ropes from the tote bag, and tugged on a few trees near the edge. "We'll rappel down," he said. "It's easy. Beginners like it. I, however, confess to you—it terrifies me."

Somehow, that was reassuring. "Why?" I managed to ask.

"You're dependent on things external to yourself," he answered, as if that were the only reply. "There's no sure means of knowing when a little tree like this gives way."

He was taking precautions. I will not try to describe all that he did, but I could see that he anchored one end of the rappel rope not only to the tree, but to an adjacent rock through the agency of a long sling of webbing. These various ties converged through an oval chromium ring smaller than my palm, which I knew was called a cara-biner.

"Are you going to use pitons?" I asked, trying to give a warrant of knowledgeability.

"Oh, no need," he said. "Not for this."

Old as he was, we were acting as if both of us were seventeen. Which made it worse—he was vastly superior.

"All right, you wait here," he said when done, "and I'll go down, look it over, and come back. Then you'll do it."

I found it hard to believe that he was going to make a voyage up and down that cliff as casually as taking reconnaissance of a few floors on an elevator, but indeed, he gave one mighty yank on the anchor of his rappelling rope, and, satisfied with such security, stood on the edge of the cliff, back to the sea, the rope wound once around his waist, and stated, "You'll find this the hardest part of the rappel. Just slack off some rope and consign your butt to the void. Then, sit back on the rope." Which he did by placing the sole of his shoes on the lip and leaning backward, until his extended legs were in a horizontal line with the ground. "Now," he said, "just walk down, step by step.

Keep your legs stiff, your feet against the rock, and give yourself slack when you need it."

He made a few moves slowly, simulating the step-by-step technique a beginner should employ, the performance going on for five or six steps of descent. After which, bored with the sluggishness of this method, he gave a little whoop, shoved off with his feet from the rock, and slackened ten feet of rope in a rush. When he bounced, toes first, back into the wall, he was a good piece further down already, and with three or four more such springs out from the wall, there he was below, standing on a ledge of flat, black, wet stone.

He slipped the rope from around his waist, called to me to pull it up. Then he climbed right after. It seemed to take him no longer than he would have spent on five or six flights of stairs.

"Nice rock," he said. "You'll have a good time."

I did not say a word. I thought of every excuse I could make. I had had no sleep. My operation left me dizzy at unexpected times. I would like to approach this more slowly: Could we warm up on a trail that did not require ropes? Below, tolling loudly on the rocks, the surf reverberated among my fears.

I said nothing. My own destruction was by now superior to whimpering out of this situation. Since I could find no excuse to survive, I stood as passively as a martyr before faggots and flames, but I was only a numb body suffering the rope to be fastened about me. Later there would be much sophistication of apparatus, but on this occasion, he merely knotted one end of a mountain cord around my waist and dropped the rest of the coil on the ground beside him. He took another rope, doubled it, and slipped it through the carabiner attached to the tree, after which he passed it through two carabiners linked onto my harness at the waist, these carabiners to serve as brake, he explained, during the rappel. Then he ran this double rope under my thigh, passed it diagonally across my chest, and around my back to the other arm. So holding each end of its snakelike embrace of me, one hand guiding the slack, the other out for balance, I prepared to go off the lip.

To put one's heels on a ledge and lean backward into space, holding only to a rope, is equal to the wail one hears in childhood on falling out of bed. One discovers the voice is one's own. My first few steps, feet pressed flat against the vertical rock, were as clumsy as if my legs were concrete posts.

It was only after I descended five or six steps that I began to comprehend that the act of rappelling could actually be accomplished; indeed, it was a good deal easier than learning to use crutches.

How intimate was the surface of the rock, however! Each pock before me was an eye-socket; each large crack, a door ajar. Faces of intricate benignity and malevolence looked back at me from the lines and knobs of the rock. I felt as if I were lowering myself around the flank of Leviathan. Yet such was my relief at being able to perform these acts that before I reached the bottom, I actually gave a few thrusts out with my legs and tried running off slack through the double carabiners at my waist, these tentative efforts not dissimilar, I am certain, to the first stir of the lower throat that a six-week-old dog will make in preparation for barking.

I reached the ledge. The surf was steaming just below, and the wet, black stone under my sneakers felt as oily as a garage floor. I released the double rappel rope from the double carabiner and only then realized I had been attached all the while by my harness itself to the coil of cord Mr. Montague had held. If all had gone wrong, and I had lost balance on the rappel, Mr. Montague would have been there to support me by the second connection. Now my initial fear felt absurd to me. I was commencing to learn that fear was a ladder whose rungs are surmounted one by one, and at the summit—as Mr. Montague would probably say—lay Judgment itself.

He now plummeted down in three long swoops to stand beside me on the wet ledge. "This climb will test you," he said. "However, it's not unreasonable. Just a matter of learning a new vocabulary."

"What do you mean?" I murmured. I now had had my first good look at the ascent, and fear returned.

He gave the smallest smile—the first he had been ready to offer since his arrival. "You'll find I picked a climb with a few buckets."

Unattached to any rope, he started up. "Try to recall my route when you're here," he called down from fifteen feet above, "but don't fret if you lose it. Part of the fun is to come on your own finds." Whereupon he mounted the face in one continuous series of easy moves and was at the top before I became aware again that the rope attached to my waist was still very much in place, and its other end was tied to some tree above the lip and out of sight. Mr. Montague appeared on the edge, some eighty agonizing feet above, sitting on the brink in all comfort, his feet dangling over, my rope—the rope, that is, with which he would belay me—wound casually, and only once, around his waist.

"Won't I pull you with me if I fall?" I asked. My voice emerged in a reasonably clear little croak, but the effort was analogous to putting the shot.

"I'm anchored to the tree." He beamed down on me. "Get started. I'll send you clues by carrier pigeon." I was beginning to understand what animated him. The air of funk in others can taste, I suppose, like caviar.

How to speak of the beauty that rises from one's fear of the rock? I was shriven. I understood the logic of God: The seed of compassion is to be found in the harsh husk of the demand.

As I started up the wall, I could not believe how vertical was the ascent. I thought there might be some slant in my favor, but no. Vertical. True, the rock was cracked and scarred and nubbled and pitted, a raw acne of surface that you could certainly get a grip on. Feeling a friendly knob of a hold at the top of my reach, and seeing a small slot for my foot, I stepped in, reached up, and pulled myself one foot off the bottom ledge. I knew something of the emotions of the first great day at Kitty Hawk then. Yes, this was as good as the virgin jump from the balcony deck into Blue Hill Bay. To fortify me, Mr. Montague pulled slightly on my harness. "If you need a little help," he yelled down, "call: 'Tension,'" on which, by demonstration, he pulled harder so that I felt somewhat less than my own full weight and more inclined to climb. I found another grip and foothold just above, took the move, took another, and another, glanced down. I was eight feet above the ledge. Splendid! I found another knob and just above my knee was one of the buckets of which he spoke, a hole about as large as a pool-table pocket in which I could rest my foot. There I halted, catching my breath. The rock felt alive. It had odors, grooves filled with dirt, overhanging elbows, armpits; it had pubic corners. I do not wish to exaggerate, but I was not prepared for the intimacy of the activity. It was as if I were climbing up the body of a giant put together of the bones and flesh and pieces and parts of a thousand humans.

Now, soon enough, I entered a more difficult portion of the ascent. About halfway up, I came to a place where I did not know how to continue. There were no good grips to reach with my hands, and not a quarter inch of rock-wrinkle to support the next push with my foot. In deadlock, straddled, I encountered the agonizing indecision of the rock climber. All the while that one's limbs are burning from expenditures of anxiety, one does not know whether to try to continue up or look to descend a few feet in order to veer onto another route. Frozen on the rock; my voice scorched in my throat. The open depths below were falling away into the unrecoverable past. I stared like a pawnbroker at the dubious possibilities presented by each ripple in the rock. I think half of all I ever learned about rock climbing came

from these first five minutes on Otter Cliffs; I was given a quick introduction to the great social world of vertical stone. There the smallest
bit of irregularity can prove an immensely useful friend, a treacherous
if conceivably employable associate, a closed door, or an outright
enemy. I had by now managed to maneuver myself into a coffin's corner just beneath an overhang.

There I rested, sobbing for breath, altogether bewildered what to
do next. The more I squeezed myself into this perch, which accommodated only a part of my body, the more I had to consume the
strength of my arms in unhappy holds. I heard Montague call out,
"Don't build your nest there. It's no place to breed."

"I don't know what to do," I said.

"Back down a few feet. Work to your right."

Here I discovered the curious nature of one's own virtue. It is so
inaccessible to us on normal occasions that we are doomed to become
more intimate with our vices. Even as I took my first step in retreat,
eyeing already the potentialities he had suggested on the right, I saw
what might be a quicker way around the overhang if I tried a route to
the left. It was riskier. To the right, I had his word at least, whereas to
the left I could see one good move and then another, but there appeared to be a straddle ten feet above—a smooth rock face with two
vertical cracks five feet apart—perhaps a grip or two, I could not tell.
What appears to be a hold from below can prove only the shadow of a
bulge; what promises an edge for one's foot comes out to no more
than a striation in the stone.

I took the option to the left. It was mine. It had not been given to
me and so could become my virtue. Such was the state of my logic.
Panting for breath as unashamedly as a woman in labor (which image
I account for by my adolescent, film-sophisticated understanding of
how a woman acts in labor), I could feel my religious education advancing by leaps. Virtue was grace. The impossible could be traversed
by the intuitions of one's heart. Scaling off to the left, I had to make
moves I would not have attempted before. Desperate to prove my
choice, I had to include one fancy scrabble from one welt of rock up
to another, neither step of which could have held me for more than a
second, but I did it all in one continuous move as if I were Montague,
and in reward found myself able to stand and rest on the small ledge
above the overhang.

Montague called down, "Three cheers, boy. You're past the crux."

It came on me. I had gotten through the worst. I continued on to
the top in a state of elation that was potentially as dangerous as an all-

out funk. "Perfect," he said when I joined him. "Now we'll try you on tougher stuff," and began packing the gear for the drive to the next step.

One's fears on the rock soon gain proportion. If one does not take the lead like Montague, but is belayed from above by a good climber, it soon becomes clear: You can afford on occasion to fall. Unaware my first time up of such relative security, I made every move as if a mistake might be my death. It took a second ascent that afternoon on a vertical column in The Precipices to make me aware that I was living in comparative safety. For when one move I made did not work and I slipped from a fractional foothold, I plunged but a couple of feet, suffering no more than a scrape to my knee. The rope was belaying me from above.

I made progress after that. Mr. Montague had accepted my father's invitation to take his two-week summer vacation at Doane. So for two weeks I went out every day with him. (And often in the rain.) Once, he took along two of my cousins, but I took no pleasure in their fears. I felt—rare emotion—like a veteran.

Mr. Montague and I preferred to be alone. Each day he took me over a different kind of hazard. I was introduced to finger jams and pressure holds. I learned how to *smear* smooth rock with the heel of my hand. Lie-back holds and crack-backs were shown to me, foot jams and chimneys. He took me up squeeze chimneys and over slabs, gave me problems in mantling and hand traverses. Forgive me, but I mention these techniques to keep track of the different rock faces on which we spent our days. There were nights when the proper placement of pitons and bongs clanged in my head as I went to sleep, and I heard the hiss of the rope as Mr. Montague, on the lead, tugged it through the carabiner above me.

I had fallen in love with the illimitable skill of the rock climber. Clumsy, using my arms more than my legs, and my will as a substitute for wisdom, I scratched my way up many a face, growing filthy with the effluvia of the stone. For those two weeks of summer, I did not have a finger, an elbow, or a knee that was not raw, and my thighs and shins acquired a hundred bruises, but I was happy. I expect I was more happy than not for the first time in my life, and thereby, at the age of seventeen, grasped a truth some choose never to go near: Happiness is experienced most directly in the intervals between terror. As each climb he led me to was, in general, more difficult than the one before, so did I rarely have a day in which I was not washed in sweat. I spent time with fear as intimately as a body down with flu knows fever. I learned the implacable law of fear. It has to be conquered or it collects, then invades one's dreams. There were days when I could not complete a climb and had to go down. In rock climbing, it is harder, however, to descend than to climb—one's feet have to search for the holds, and they see less well than the fingers. So I slipped often, and dangled on the rope, and sweated, and knew myself doubly abject, and could not sleep that night for confronting my terror: I would have to return next day and do it properly. A compelling transaction. One is raising at such times all the ships that sank in childhood from loss of courage, yes, hoisting them up from the sea bottom of oneself. I felt as if all the childhood fears that weighed me down had begun their ascent to the surface—I was being delivered from the graveyard of expired hope. But what a chancy operation! Each time I failed to complete a climb, the fear I was hoping to cure was not consumed but turned corrupt.

Yet each time I succeeded, I received my dependable reward. For an hour, or for a night, I was happy. On the best day I had in those two weeks, which was next to the last day, Montague brought me back to Otter Cliffs and told me to take the lead. Notwithstanding all I had learned, going up first on the same ascent where I had begun proved several times more difficult. Taking the lead, I had to hammer in my pitons as I went, my arm in such a catalepsy of controlled panic that it would cramp after every few raps of the hammer. Now the prospect of a fall was serious again. On the lead, I tried to put a piton in every five feet, knowing each prospective fall could double the length since one might plummet from five feet above the last piton to five feet below. And that ten feet would double again should the lower piton pull out. Facing such a prospect, easy climbs became difficult.

Once I did fall. It was for ten feet, no more. My piton held, but I bounced on the end of the rope, then took a mean swing into the rock. Scraped, bruised, and feeling as shattered as a cat who has been plunged into a pail of ice water, I held my breath against the long temptation to whimper, took a full minute to call back the wide-flying streamers of my will, and, hard to believe that I was exacting this on myself, took on the climb again and searched for a way through the crux. It happened to be the same overhang as on the first day, but now I was dragging a rope behind me rather than being encouraged from above. Two weeks of newly acquired knowledge made the difference. I worked my way to the lip without another fall.

Those two weeks did more for me than any operation on my skull. I had new standing in the family. My cousins gave way to my opinions in passing squabbles, and my father took me out for a night of drinking in the modest bars of Bar Harbor. Toward the end of the evening, I was feeling as relaxed as a piece of spaghetti cooked in wine, and my male parent, giving, as usual, no more sign of drink than his massive emanations of good or bad will, said—he was obviously in a splendid spirit—"Hugh Montague has a good opinion of you. That's the accolade, Harry. He doesn't have three words to say for any ten people."

"Well, I'm glad," I said. I felt so corny I was ready to cry. Instead, I laid in a good swallow of bourbon. The flush it inspired told me for the first time how rich my father's insides must feel.

"Hugh's going to take you for a lobster dinner tomorrow," he told me. "Hugh says you're worth a good-bye party all to yourself."

In the event, Hugh Montague had a great deal to say to me. By the first drink, I had begun to babble—the intoxication of having encountered this vocation which was a sport, a skill, and an open-air monastery for the soul, augmented by my successful lead that very afternoon, not to mention my felicitous connection with bourbon the night before, as well as the great (if hitherto unadmitted) release of knowing that Mr. Montague, fearsome godfather, would be gone tomorrow, had me nattering. I was ready to take vows never to betray the new discipline, but Mr. Montague cut me off.

"Harry, I'm going to tell you something that will hurt. I advance it, however, for your benefit. I have kept a high opinion of you over these two weeks. You are going to make a good man, and I respect that doubly in your case because you were dealt paltry cards in childhood. I gather your mother is tiny."

"Yes."

"And not wholly dependable, according to your father."

"Not wholly."

"Men work to develop their evil skills. Women—it is my belief— merely summon them." When he saw my adolescent eyes were not within a hundred miles of the peak of this observation, he shrugged, and said, "When we know each other better, we might trade a few anecdotes about our respective mothers"—he came to a full stop as if startled by himself—"although, don't count on it."

"Yessir."

"From now on, when we're alone, you and I, I want you to call me by the name my associates employ. That name is Harlot. Not to be confused with Harlow, Jean Harlow, but *Harlot*."

"Yessir."

"One of the most persistent little questions over at Foggy Bottom is why Montague chose such a point of reference. Sooner or later, they all make the pilgrimage over to my good side and have the touching simplicity to ask directly. As if I were in haste to tell! Should we become exceptional friends, I'll spill the beans. In twenty years."

"Yes, Harlot." I stopped. "It doesn't sound right."

"Never fear. You'll get used to it." He picked up the knuckles of a claw, twisted them apart without getting his fingertips caught on the spurs, and proceeded with his lobster fork to pluck forth the meat.

"Harry, I'll present you with the worst first." He fixed me with his eyes. There would be no sliding off. "I want you to give up rock climbing."

He could as well have struck me in the face.

"Oh," I said. "Golly."

"It's not that you are bad. You are better than your physical skills. You have innate moxie. Of ten beginners one might instruct, I say you would probably come in second or third in the lot."

"Then why do I have to stop?" I paused. I dropped my voice. "Would I kill myself?"

"Probably not. Hurt yourself, certainly. But that's not my reason. It's more particular than that. Only the best of beginners should ever dream of going on. It's more than just a sport, you see, for brave ones like yourself." This was the first time anyone had ever called me brave.

"No," I said, "why? Why do you want me to quit?"

"It's an activity that insists on excellence. Harry, if you went on, it would take over your life. You could not rest. Whenever you failed on a climb, the memory would overpower every thought until you succeeded. Even among good people, that can be a terribly debilitating process. An addiction. One ends as a coward, a victim, or a mediocre monomaniac. It is like being an ex-alcoholic. One is able to contemplate nothing else."

I was sufficiently agitated to say to him, "I don't understand what you're saying." My voice must have been rude-edged, for I could feel his annoyance. His disciplines as a pedagogue may have saved me from a few thrusts of his temper.

"All right then," he said, "we will go further. A man who acquires high competence in rock climbing is able to become the instrument of his own will. That's what we try to arrive at. That's what we're encouraged to desire from the year one. A child is taught not to soil his pants. His bowels become the instrument of his will. And as we grow older, we often feel emotions that are as low and obstreperous as the embarrassing necessity, if caught in public, to take a *drop*." He used the word as though that were the only acceptable synonym ever to employ. "Nonetheless, we say to our good sphincter, so much the creature of our will, 'Tighten up, you fool.'

"Obviously rock climbing firms the upper regions of the will. But it's quite a process. And just as dangerous as black magic. For every fear we are ready to confront is equally open, you see, to the Devil. Should we fail, the Devil is there to soothe our cowardice. 'Stick with me,' he says, 'and your cowardice is forgiven.' Whereas, rock climbing, when well done, pinches off the Devil. Of course, if you fail, his nibs returns twofold. If you are not good enough then, you spend half your days getting the Devil out. That is marking time. And so long as we stay in place, Satan is more than satisfied. He loves circular, obsessive activity. Entropy is his meat. When the world becomes a pendulum, he will inhabit the throne."

"Maybe," I said, "I would know what I could climb and what I couldn't, and just stick with that."

"Never. You are half your father. That half is not going to rest. I could see from the first day that by one measure you were equal to the best rock climbers. You understood it. You knew you were in one damned awesome church, indeed the only one where religion comes close enough to Our Lord to give a little real sustenance."

"Yessir."

"There's a story I was told about some far-fetched, terribly intense sect of Jewish people called Hasidim. They used to inhabit village ghettos in Russia and the Ukraine. It seems that one of their folk, a rabbi, was so devotional that he prayed to God forty times a day. Finally, after forty years, the rabbi grew impatient and said, 'God, I have loved You for so long that I want You to reveal Yourself to me. Why won't You reveal Yourself to me?' Whereupon God did just that. He revealed Himself. How do you think the rabbi reacted?"

"I don't know."

Harlot began to laugh. I had never heard him give a full laugh before. It gave a clue to why he had chosen his name. Inside him were more people than one would have thought. His laugh was all over the place. "Well, Harry, the good fellow dived right under the bed and began to howl like a dog. 'Oh, God,' the rabbi said, 'please do *not* reveal Yourself to me.' That, Harry, is a useful story. Before all else, God is awesome. It's the first thing to know. If Christ had not been sent to us, no one would ever have gotten out of the cave. Jehovah was too much for all of us. There would have been no modern civilization."

"What about Egypt, or Greece and Rome? Didn't they take us out of the cave?"

"Harry, those cultures marked time. They were perfect examples of the obsessional. Devil's abodes, all three, Egypt, Greece, and Rome. Don't be impressed by how beautiful they were. The Devil, you must never forget, is the most beautiful creature God ever made. Spiritually, however, those cultures did not choose to emerge from Plato's cave. It took Christ to come along and say, 'Forgive the sons for the sins of the fathers.' That's the day, Harry, that scientific inquiry was born. Even if we had to wait a millennium and more for Kepler and Galileo. So, follow the logic: Once the father begins to believe that his sons will not suffer for his acts of sacrilege, he grows bold enough to experiment. He looks upon the universe as a curious place, rather than as an almighty machine guaranteed to return doom for his curiosity. That was the beginning of the technological sleigh ride which may destroy us yet. The Jews, of course, having rejected Christ, had to keep dealing with Jehovah for the next two millennia. So they never forgot. God is awesome. 'Oh God, do not reveal Yourself to me. Not all at once!'"

He paused. He ordered another drink for each of us, Hennessey for himself, and Old Harper's, I recollect, for me. "Let us have an Old Harper's for Young Harry," he actually said to the waitress, and went right back to his disquisition on the awesome: "I suspect that God is with us in some fashion on every rock climb. Not to save us—how I detest that tit-nibbling psychology—God saves!—God at the elbow of all misbegotten mediocrities. As if all that God had to do was preserve the middling and the indifferent. No, God is not a St. Bernard dog to rescue us at every pass. God is near us when we are rock climbing because that is the only way we get a good glimpse of Him and He gets one of us. You experience God when you're extended a long way out beyond yourself and are still trying to lift up from your fears. Get caught under a rock and of course you want to howl like a dog. Surmount that terror and you rise to a higher fear. That may be our simple purpose on earth. To rise to higher and higher levels of fear. If we succeed, we can, perhaps, share some of God's fear."

"His fear?"

"Absolutely. His fear of the great power He has given the Devil. There is no free will for man unless the Devil's powers were made equal on this embattled planet to the Lord's. That is why," he said, "I don't want you to continue rock climbing. The brute fact is that you don't have the exquisite skills that are necessary. So you will keep finding a little courage and losing it. You could end up like one of those monumentally boring golfers who work for years to improve their swing and never stop talking about it. Orotund blobs of narcissism."

"Okay," I said. Now I was angry. Awfully hurt but clearly angry.

"All this is not in disrespect for your feelings, but in true respect. I believe there is a place for you. It will make demands upon your courage, your intelligence, your will, and your wit. You will be tempted by the Devil at every turn. But you can, in my modest opinion, serve God. In a far better way, I propose, than as a rock climber."

Formidable were his gifts of transition. I had been shifted from the pits of an unexpected wound to a pitch of interest. "Are you saying what I suppose you are saying?"

"Of course. Your father asked me to spend my vacation looking you over as a prospect. Nothing less. I had other plans for these two weeks. But he said, 'More than anything, I want the boy to come aboard with us. Only, however, if you think he's right. It's too important a matter to be judged by my desires and affection.'"

"Did my father speak that way to you?"

"Most definitely."

"You told him I could come aboard?"

"Yesterday. By now, I know you better than your father does. You have nice gifts. I'll say no more. Your father is an enthusiast, and overextended, therefore, on occasion, in judgment, but I pride myself on a cold eye. You have qualities that your father, for all his splendid stuff, is lacking."

I was tempted to say, "There is nothing special about me"—is that not the most painful cry one can utter in adolescence?—but now I was gifted with judgment. I kept my mouth shut.

"You're planning to go to Yale?"

"Yessir."

"I'd say, short of a collapse on entrance exams, it can be taken for granted you will get in. Yale is perfect. I call it Uncle Eli's Cabin."

I laughed.

"Oh, yes," said my new associate, Harlot, "part of the underground railway. One of the stations on the route. At least for a few." He made a face. "As an old Harvard man, I don't like to say this, but Yale is a touch niftier to our purposes. Harvard gets quiffy about recruitment. It's a stinking irony, since half of our real people did happen to go there. Well, as I always say, trust a good fellow so long as he doesn't matriculate at Princeton."

Harlot held up his glass. We would drink to that. One knew all the merriment of drinking to the health of Annapurna as opposed to Nanda Devi. Then we shook hands and drove back to the Keep. In the morning, Harlot left. He would drop me a letter on a point of advice from time to time, but I was not to be in the same room with him again for several years.

From *Harlot's Ghost* (1991)

# HOLLYWOOD—I

## Herman Teppis at the
## Laguna Room

We came to Munshin's bungalow, and Eitel tapped the knocker on the pink-colored door. After a wait I could hear somebody running toward us, and then it flew open, and I had no more than the sight of the back of a fat man in a dressing gown who went bounding away to the phone, the gown flapping against his calves while he called over his shoulder, "Come in. Be with you in a minute, fellows." He was talking in a high-pitched easy voice to somebody in New York, holding the receiver in his left hand while with his right he was neatly mixing drinks for us, not only carrying on his business conversation but opening a big smile across his face at the introduction to me. A little under medium height, with short turned-up features, he looked like a clown, for he had a large round head on a round body and almost no neck at all.

The drinks made, he passed them over with a wink, and his right hand free again, he began to tickle his thin hair, discovering a bald spot on his head and then patting it into hiding again, only to leave his head for his belly, which he prodded gingerly as if to find out whether it concealed an ache. He certainly had a lot of energy; I had the idea it would be rare to see him doing one thing at a time.

Eitel sat down with a bored look and smiled at the producer's calisthenics. When the call was done, Munshin bounced to his feet and advanced on Eitel with an outstretched palm, a grin on his face. "*Charley!*" he said, as if Eitel had just come into the room and he was surprised to see him. "You look great. How have you been?" Munshin asked, his free hand covering their handclasp. "I've been hearing great things about you."

"Stop it, Collie," Eitel laughed, "there's nothing you can steal from me."

"Steal? Lover, I just want to steal your company." He clamped a bear-hug on Eitel's neck. "You look great," he repeated. "I've been hearing wonderful things about your script. I want to read it when it's done."

"What for?" Eitel asked.

"I want to buy it." He said this as if nothing were in the way of buying anything from Eitel.

"The only way I'll let you buy it is blind."

"I'll buy it blind. If it's from you, Charley, I'll buy it blind."

"You wouldn't buy Shakespeare blind."

"You think I'm kidding," Munshin said in a sad voice.

"Stop it, Collie," Eitel said again.

As he talked, Munshin kept on touching Eitel, pinching his elbow, patting his shoulder, jabbing his ribs. "Charley, don't show your script to anybody. Just work on it. Don't worry about your situation."

"Get your greedy little hands off me. You know I'm going to make the picture by myself."

"That's your style, Charley," Munshin said with a profound nod. "That's the way you always should work."

He told us a joke, passed a bit of gossip, and kept his hands on Eitel's body in a set of movements that called up the picture of a fat house detective searching a drunk. Then Eitel walked away from him, and we all sat down and looked at each other. After a short silence, Munshin announced, "I've thought of a great movie to make."

"What is it?" I asked, for Eitel only made a face. The producer gave the name of a famous French novel. "That author knows everything about sex," Munshin said. "I'll never be able to think I'm in love again."

"Why don't you do the life of the Marquis de Sade?" Eitel drawled.

"You think I wouldn't if I could find a gimmick?"

"Collie," Eitel said, "sit down and tell me the story you really have."

"I don't have a thing. I'm open to suggestion. I'm tired of making the same old stuff. Every man has an artistic desire in this business."

"He's absolutely unscrupulous," Eitel said with pride. Collie grinned. He cocked his head to the side with the cunning look of a dog who is being scolded.

"You're a born exaggerator," Munshin said.

"You can't stop Collie."

"I love you."

Munshin poured another drink for us. His upper lip was covered with perspiration. "Well, how *are* things?" he said.

"Just fine, Collie. How are things with you?" Eitel asked in a flat voice. I knew him well enough to know he was very much on guard.

"Charley, my personal life is in bad shape."

"Your wife?"

Munshin stared into space, his hard small eyes the only sign of bone beneath his fat. "Well, things are always the same between her and me."

"What is it then, Collie?"

"I've decided to give the brush to my girl friend."

Eitel began to laugh. "It's about time."

"Now, don't laugh, Charley. This is important to me."

I was surprised at the way Munshin talked so frankly. He hadn't known me fifteen minutes, and yet he was as ready to talk as if he were alone with Eitel. I was still to learn that Munshin, like many people from the capital, could talk openly about his personal life while remaining a dream of espionage in his business operations.

"You're not really giving her up?" Eitel said lightly. "What's the matter, has Teppis laid down the law?"

"Charley!" Munshin said. "This is a personal tragedy for me."

"I suppose you're in love with the girl."

"No, now I wouldn't say that. It's hard to explain."

"Oh, I'm sure of that, Collie."

"I'm very worried about her future," Munshin said, his fingers prodding his belly again.

"From what I've heard about her, she'll get along."

"What did you hear?" Munshin asked.

"Just that while she's known you, she's had her extracurricular activities."

Munshin's round face became tolerant and sad. "We live in a cummunity of scandal," he said.

"Spare me, Collie," Eitel murmured.

Munshin was on his feet. "You don't understand this girl," he said in a booming voice. I was left behind by the sudden transition. "She's a child. She's a beautiful, warm, simple child."

"And you're a beautiful, warm, simple father."

"I've defended you, Charley," Munshin said. "I've defended you against stories that even you wouldn't want to hear about yourself. But I'm beginning to think you're nothing but rottenness and corruption."

"Honest corruption. I don't play the saint."

"I'm not claiming I'm a saint," Munshin bellowed again. "But I have feelings." He turned in my direction. "What do you see when you look at a fellow like myself?" he asked. "You see a fat man who likes to play the clown. Does that mean I have no human sentiments?"

He was far from a clown at the moment. His mild high-pitched voice had swollen in volume and dropped deeper in tone. Standing over us, he gave me the feeling that he was a man of some physical power. "All right, Charley," he said, "I know what you think of me, but I'll tell you something. I may be a businessman, and you may be an artist, and I've great respect for your talent, great respect, but you're a cold man, and I have emotions, and that's why you can't understand me."

Through this tirade, Eitel had been drawing on his cigarette. Nonchalantly, he put it out. "Why did you invite me over, Collie?"

"For friendship. Can't you understand that? I wanted to hear your troubles, and I wanted to tell you mine."

Eitel leaned forward, his broad body hunched on itself. "I have no troubles," he said with a smile. "Let me hear yours."

Munshin relaxed. "There are pluses as well as minuses to this affair. It's easy to sneer at the girl," he said. "I've sneered at her myself. When I first set her up, I thought, 'Just another night-club dancer. A hot Italian babe with that hot Latin blood.' Well, it's a story, Charley. She may not be so brilliant, and she's obviously from a poor background." He looked at me. "I've always been full of prejudices about women," Munshin said humbly. "You know, I've wanted girls with some class and distinction to them, and I'll admit it, it's what I still hold against Elena. She doesn't match up to the people I know. But that doesn't keep her from being very human."

"Still, you're giving her the brush," Eitel said. "You're giving the brush to a very human girl."

"There's no future for us. I admit it, you see, I admit my faults. I'm a social coward like everybody else in the industry."

"So like all cowards you got tired of turning down her marriage proposals."

"Elena's not a schemer," Munshin said firmly. "You want to know something? Just a couple of days ago I tried to give her a thousand dollars. She wouldn't take it. Not once did she ever ask me to marry her. She's not the kind who threatens. It's just that I can't stand the thought she has no future with me."

"Herman Teppis can't stand the thought either."

Munshin allowed this to pass. "Let me tell you about her. She's a girl who's composed of hurts and emotion and dirt and shining love," he said in the round categorical style of a criminal lawyer who wishes to attract all the elements in a jury. "I had my analyst send her to a friend of his, but it didn't come off. She didn't have enough ego to work on. That's how serious the problem is." Munshin held out a heavy palm as if to draw our attention. "Take the way I met her. She was doing a fill-in number at a benefit I ran. I saw her in the wings, dressed up, ready to go on. A real Carmen-type. Only, a Carmen shuddering with fright," said Munshin looking at us. "She was practically clawing the hand off her partner. 'There's a human being in torment,' I said to myself, 'a girl who's as wild and sensitive as an animal.' Yet when she got up on the stage, she was all right. A good flamenco dancer. In and out, but talent. Afterward, we started talking, and she told me she couldn't even eat a piece of bread on a day she was working. I told her I thought I could help her with some of her problems and she was grateful as a puppy. That's how we started." Munshin's voice became heavy with emotion. "You, Eitel, you'd call that scheming, I suppose. I call it sensitivity and heartbreak and all kinds of hurts. She's a girl who's all hurts."

As Munshin kept on talking, I had the idea he was describing her the way he might line up a heroine in a story conference, the story conference more interesting than the film that would come from it.

"You take the business of being Italian," Munshin lectured us. "I can't tell you the things I've learned, the human subtleties, and I'm a good liberal. For instance, if she was served by a Negro waiter, she always had the idea that he was being a little intimate with her. I talked to her about such problems. I explained how wrong it is to have prejudice against a Negro, and she understood."

"Like that," Eitel said, snapping his fingers.

"You stop it, Charley," Munshin said, bobbing in his seat. "You understand what I mean. She was ashamed of her prejudice. Elena is a person who hates everything that is small in herself. She's consumed by the passion to become a bigger person than she is, *consumed*, do you understand?" and he shook his fist.

"Collie, I really think you're upset."

"Take her promiscuity," Munshin went on, as if he had not heard. "She's the sort of girl who would love a husband and kids, a decent healthy mature relationship. You think it didn't bother me, her seeing other men? But I knew it was my fault. I was to blame and I'll admit it freely. What could I offer her?"

"What could the others offer her?" Eitel interrupted.

"Fine. Fine. Just fine coming from you. I'll tell you, Charley, I don't believe in double standards. A woman's got just as much right as a man to her freedom."

"Why don't we start a club?" Eitel jeered.

"I've gone to bat for you, Eitel. I pleaded with H.T. not to suspend you after *Clouds Ahoy*. Are you so ungrateful that I have to remind you how many times I helped you make pictures you wanted to make?"

"And then you cut them to ribbons."

"We've had our disagreements, Charley, but I've always considered you a friend. I don't care what transpires between us today, it won't affect my attitude toward you."

Eitel smiled.

"I'm curious." Munshin put his hands on his knees. "What do you think of Elena the way I've described her?"

"I think she's better than you deserve."

"I'm glad you say that, Charley. It means I've been able to convey her quality." Munshin paused, and loosened the cord of his dressing gown. "You see, about an hour ago I told Elena we couldn't go on."

"An hour ago!"

Munshin nodded.

"You mean she's here?" Eitel asked. "Here in town?"

"Yes."

"You brought her out here to give her the brush?"

Munshin started to pace the floor. "I didn't plan it. A lot of times I bring her along on my trips."

"And let her stay in a separate hotel?"

"Well, I've explained the situation."

"When is your wife due?"

"She'll be here tomorrow." Munshin blew his nose. "I had no idea it would happen like this. For months I knew I couldn't go on with Elena, but I didn't expect it for today."

Eitel shook his head. "What do you want me to do? Hold her hand?"

"No, I mean . . ." Munshin looked miserable. "Charley, she doesn't know a soul in this place."

"Then let her go back to the city."

"I can't stand the thought of her being alone. There's no telling what she'll do. Charley, I'm going out of my mind." Munshin stared at his handkerchief, which he kept wadded in his hand. "Elena was the one who said we should break up. I know what it means to her. She'll put the blame on herself. She'll feel she wasn't good enough for me."

"It's the truth, isn't it?" Eitel said. "That's how you feel."

"All right, I'm the rotten one. I'm no good." Munshin came to a stop in front of Eitel. "Charley, I remember you saying, it's your exact words. You said that when you were a kid you always wondered how to get a woman, and now you wonder how to get rid of one."

"I was bragging."

"Can't you sympathize?"

"With you?"

"Could you pay her a visit?"

"I don't know her," Eitel said.

"You could be introduced as a friend of mine."

Eitel sat up. "Tell me, Collie," he said, "is that why you loaned me the money two weeks ago?"

"What money?" said Munshin.

"You don't have to worry about Sergius," Eitel said, and he began to laugh. "I'm ashamed of you. Two thousand dollars is a lot of money for Carlyle Munshin to pay to have a broken-down director take a girl off his hands."

"Charley, you're a corrupt man," Munshin said loudly. "I loaned you that money because I consider you my friend, and I oughtn't to have to tell you that you could be more discreet. If word ever got around, I'd be in trouble up to here." The producer held a finger to his throat. "It's Elena I'm thinking about now. Let this boy be the witness. If anything happens to her, part of it will be your fault."

"There's no limit to you, Collie," Eitel started to say, but Munshin interrupted. "Charley, that girl should not be left alone. Do I say I'm in the right? What do you want, my blood? Offer a solution at least."

"Turn her over to Marion Faye."

"You're a stone," Munshin said. "A human being is in pain, and you say things like that."

"I'll see her," I blurted suddenly.

"You're a beautiful kid," Munshin said levelly, "but this is not the job for you."

"Keep out of this," Eitel snapped at me.

"Even the kid here will go," Munshin said. "Charley, tell me, is all the heart cut out of you? Isn't there even a little bit left? Or are you getting too old to handle a real woman?"

Eitel lay back in his chair and stared at the ceiling, his legs spread before him. "Okay, Collie," he said slowly, "okay. One loan deserves another. I'll get drunk with your girl."

"You're a jewel, Charley," Munshin said huskily.

"What if you-know-what happens?" Eitel drawled.

"Are you a sadist?" Munshin said. "I don't even think of things like that."

"Then what do you think of?"

"You'll like Elena and she'll like you. It'll make her feel good to know that a fellow with your reputation and your presence admires her."

"Oh, God," Eitel said.

The phone was ringing.

Munshin tried to say something more, as if he were afraid Eitel might change his mind, but the noise of the telephone was too distracting. Obeying the irregular rhythm of the switchboard operator, it would stop, it would be silent, and then it would ring again.

"Answer it," Eitel said irritably.

Munshin pinched the receiver against his jowl. He was preparing to make another drink, but the sounds he heard through the earpiece stopped everything. We listened to a woman who was crying and laughing, and her fright quivered through the room. There was so much terror in the voice and so much pain that I stared at the floor in shock. One cry sounded, so loud in its loneliness I couldn't bear it.

"Where are you, Elena?" Munshin said sharply into the mouthpiece.

Some climax passed. I could hear the sound of quiet sobbing. "I'll be right over," Munshin said. "Now, you stay there. You stay there, do you understand, Elena?" He had no sooner hung up the phone than he was drawing on a pair of trousers, fastening the buttons to a shirt.

Eitel was pale. "Collie," he said with an effort, "do you want me to come along?"

"She's in her hotel room," Munshin said from the door. "I'll call you later."

Eitel nodded and sat back. We were silent once Munshin was gone. After a few minutes, Eitel got up and mixed a drink. "What a horrible thing," he muttered.

"How does a man," I asked, "stay with a woman who is so . . . It's messy."

Eitel looked up. "A little compassion, Sergius," he said. "Do you think we choose our mates?" And, moodily, he sipped on his drink. "I wonder if I'll ever know the answer to that one?" he said almost to himself.

Time passed, and we kept on drinking Carlyle Munshin's liquor. Slowly, the afternoon went by. It seemed pointless to remain there, just as pointless to move on. Outside, there would only be the desert sun. "I'm depressed," Eitel said with a broad grin after half a dozen drinks. I had the feeling his face was numb; slowly, with pleasure, he was patting the bald spot on his head. "Wonder how Collie is making out?" Eitel said after another pause.

As if to answer, there was a knock on the door. I went to open it, and an elderly man shouldered me aside and walked into the living room. "Where's Carlyle?" he asked of nobody in particular, and left me to follow behind him.

Eitel stood up. "Well, Mr. Teppis," he said.

Teppis gave him a sour look. He was a tall heavy man with silver hair and a red complexion, but even with his white summer suit and hand-painted tie he was far from attractive. Underneath the sun tan, his features were poor. His eyes were small and pouched, his nose was flat, and his chin ran into the bulge of his neck. He had a close resemblance to a bullfrog. When he spoke, it was in a thin hoarse voice. "All right," he said, "what are you doing here?"

"Do you know," Eitel said, "that's a good question to ask."

"Collie's up to something," Teppis announced. "I don't know why he saw you. I wouldn't even want to breathe the air a subversive breathes. Do you know what you cost me on *Clouds Ahoy*?"

"You forget the money I made for you . . . Herman."

"Hah," said Teppis, "now he calls me by my first name. They leave me and they go up in the world. Eitel, I warned Lulu against you. Marry a fine young American actress, a girl who's too good for you, and you just drag her name through the muck and the dirt and the filth. If anybody saw me talking to you, I'd be ashamed."

"You should be," Eitel said. "Lulu was a fine American girl, and you let me turn her into a common whore." His voice was cool, but I could sense it was not easy for him to talk to Teppis.

"You have a dirty mouth," Herman Teppis said, "and nothing else."

"Don't speak to me this way. I no longer work for you."

Teppis rocked forward and back on the balls of his feet as if to build up momentum. "I'm ashamed to have made money from your movies. Five years ago I called you into my office and I warned you. 'Eitel,' I said, 'anybody that tries to throw a foul against this country ends up in the pigpen.' That's what I said, but did you listen?" He waved a finger. "You know what they're talking about at the studio? They say you're going to make a comeback. Some comeback. You couldn't do a day's work without the help of the studio. I let people know that."

"Come on, Sergius, let's go," Eitel said.

"Wait, you!" Teppis said to me. "What's your name?"

I told him. I gave it with an Irish twist.

"Sergius O'Shaugnessy? What kind of name is that for a clean-cut youngster like you? You should change it. John Yard. That's the kind of name you should have." He looked me over as if he were buying a bolt of cloth. "Who are you?" said Teppis. "What do you do? I hope you're not a bum."

If he wanted to irritate me, he was successful. "I used to be in the Air Force," I said to him.

There was a gleam in his eye. "A flier?"

Standing in the doorway, Eitel decided to have his own fun. "Do you mean you never heard of this boy, H.T.?"

Teppis was cautious. "I can't keep up with everything," he said.

"Sergius is a hero," Eitel said creatively. "He shot down four planes in a day."

I had no chance to get into this. Teppis smiled as if he had been told something very valuable. "Your mother and father must be extremely proud of you," he said.

"I wouldn't know. I was brought up in an orphanage." My voice was probably unsteady, because I could see by Eitel's change of expression that he knew I was telling the truth. I was sick at giving myself away so easily. But it is always like that. You hold a secret for years, and then spill it like a cup of coffee. Or maybe Teppis made me spill it.

"An orphan," he said. "I'm staggered. Do you know you're a remarkable young man?" He smiled genially and looked at Eitel. "Charley, you come back here," he said in his hoarse voice. "What are you flying off the handle for? You've heard me talk like this before."

"You're a rude man, Herman," Eitel said from the doorway.

"Rude?" Teppis put a fatherly hand on my shoulder. "Why, I wouldn't even be rude to my doorman." He laughed and then began to cough. "Eitel," he said, "what's happened to Carlyle? Where'd he go?"

"He didn't tell me."

"I don't understand anybody any more. You're a young man, Johnny," he said, pointing to me as if I were inanimate, "you tell me, what is everything all about?" But long before I could answer that question, he started talking again. "In my day a man got married, and he could be fortunate in his selection, or he could have bad luck, but he was married. I was a husband for thirty-two years, may my wife rest in peace. I have her picture on my desk. Can *you* say that, Eitel? What do you have on your desk? Pinup pictures. I don't know people who feel respect for society any more. I tell Carlyle. What happens? He wallows. That's the kind of man my daughter wanted to marry. A fool who sneaks around with a chippie dancer."

"We all have our peculiarities, Herman," Eitel said.

This made Teppis angry. "Eitel," he shouted, "I don't like you, and you don't like me, but I make an effort to get along with everybody," and then to quiet himself down, he made a point of looking me over very carefully. "What do you do?" he asked again as if he had not heard my answer. "Are you an actor?"

"No."

"I knew it. None of the good-looking clean-cut ones are actors any more. Just the ugly ones. Faces like bugs." He cleared his throat with a barking sound. "Look, Johnny," he went on, "I like you, I'll do you a good turn. There's a little party tomorrow night. I'm giving it for our people out here. You're invited."

The moment he gave this invitation, I knew I wanted to go to his party. Everybody in Desert D'Or had been talking about it for the last few days, and this was the first big party at the resort that I had been invited to. But I was angry at myself because I was ready to say yes, and in that second I almost forgot Eitel. So I told myself that I was going to play it through, and if Teppis wanted to invite me, and I didn't know why, I was going to get him to invite Eitel.

"I don't know if I want to go alone," I said to him, and I was satisfied that my voice was even.

"Bring a girl," Teppis offered. "You got a sweetheart?"

"It's not easy to find the right girl," I said. "I lost too much time flying airplanes."

My instinct about Herman Teppis seemed to be working. He nodded his head wisely. "I see the connection," he said.

"I was thinking Charley Eitel could help me find a girl," I added.

For a second I thought I had lost it and Teppis was going to fly into a rage. He glared at both of us. "Who invited Eitel?" he said furiously.

"You didn't invite him?" I said. "I thought maybe you did."

With what an effort, Teppis smiled benevolently. "Johnny, you're a very loyal friend. You got spunk." In practically the same breath he said to Eitel, "Tell me, cross your heart, Charley, are you a Red?"

Eitel didn't rush to answer. "You know everything, Herman," he murmured at last. "Why ask questions?"

"I know!" Teppis shouted. "I know all about you. I'll never understand why you made such a spectacle of yourself." He threw up his arms. "All right, all right, I know you're clean deep-down. Come to my party." Teppis shook his head. "Only, do me a favor, Charley. Don't say I invited you. Say it was Mac Barrantine."

"This is one hell of an invitation," Eitel answered.

"You think so, well, don't look a gift horse, you know what I mean? One of these days go clear yourself with the American government, and then maybe I'll work with you. I got no objection to making money with people I don't like. It's my motto." He took my hand and shook it firmly. "Agree with me, Johnny? That's the ticket. I'll see both you boys tomorrow night."

On the drive back to Eitel's house I was in a good mood. Teppis had been just right for me. I was even overexcited. I kept talking to Eitel about how it felt the time I took my first solo. Then I began to realize that the more I talked the more depressed I made him feel, and so looking for any kind of question to change the subject I said, "What do you say about our invitation? Maybe there's going to be just a little look on people's faces when you turn up." I started to laugh again.

Eitel shook his head. "They'll probably say I've been having private talks with the Committee, or else why would Teppis have me there?" Then he grinned at the frustration of it. "Man," he said, mimicking me, "don't you just have to be good to win?" But there was more than enough to think about in this thought, and neither of us said another word until we turned into his garage. Then Eitel stopped the car with a jerk. "Sergius, I'm not going to that party," he said.

"Well, if you won't change your mind . . ." I wanted to go to the party—I was ready for it, I thought—but it was going to be harder without Eitel. I wouldn't know anybody there.

"You did well, today," he said. "You go. You'll enjoy it. But I can't go. I've been a bus boy to Teppis for too many years." We went inside, and Eitel dropped into an armchair and pressed his hands to his forehead. The script was on the end table next to him. He picked it up, rustled the pages, and dropped it to the floor. "Don't tell anybody, Sergius," he said, "but this script stinks."

"Are you sure?"

"I don't know. I can't get out of myself long enough to look at it." He sighed. "If I ever bring it off, remind me, will you, of this conversation? You see, I've been trying to remember if I was as depressed in the old days when the work would come out well."

"I'll remind you," I said.

A short while later, Munshin phoned Eitel. Elena was all right, he told him. She was sleeping. Tonight, he would take care of her. But for tomorrow he begged Eitel to show her a good time.

Eitel said he would. When the call was finished, his eyes were dancing. "Do you know," he said, "I can hardly accuse myself of running after Teppis if I take Collie's girl along."

"But what about the girl?"

"It could be the best way to get over Mr. Munshin. She'll see that a stranger will do more for her in a night than he did in three years."

"What are you up to?" I asked.

"Yes, I'm going to take her to the party," Eitel said.

The Laguna Room at the Yacht Club, which Herman Teppis had rented for his party, was not a room at all. Painted in the lemon-yellow of the Yacht Club, it was open to the sky, an amoebic pool strayed between the tables, rounded a portion of the dance floor, and ended behind the bar, a play of colored lights changing the water into a lake of tomato aspic, lime Jell-O, pale consommé, and midnight ink. On an island not twenty feet long, in the middle of the pool, the bandstand was set up, and the musicians played their dance numbers free of any passing drunk who might want to take a turn on the drums.

Since the party was given by Herman Teppis, the management of the Yacht Club had added some special old-fashioned effects. A big searchlight threw its column into the air, placed at such an angle as not to burn into the eyes of the guests, and a collection of spotlights and flood lamps was arranged to make it look like a party on a movie set, even to the expense of a tremendous papier-mâché camera on a wooden boom, directed by a bellhop wearing the outfit of a silent-film cameraman with the peak of his cap turned backward and a pair of knickers that reached his knees. All through the evening the camera was rotated on its boom, lowered almost into the water or raised so high it threw a long shadow across the colors of the Laguna Room.

I had trouble getting in. Eitel had left earlier in the evening to meet Elena and had still not returned by eleven, so I decided to go alone, and I put on my Air Corps uniform with its ribbons. At the entrance to the Laguna Room, which was garnished with a gangplank, a man dressed like a purser stood checking the invitations. There was no record of my name on the guest list.

I said, "Maybe I'm down there as John Yard."

There was no John Yard on the purser's scratchboard.

"How about Charles Eitel?" I asked.

"Mr. Eitel is listed, but you would have to come in with him."

Yet it was the purser who discovered my name. In a last-minute addition, Teppis had recorded me as "Shamus Something-or-other," and so as Shamus Something-or-other, I got into his party.

Near the purser's stand, seated on two couches that faced each other, were half a dozen women. They were all dressed expensively, and their make-up, to make up for such faults as thin mouths, small eyes, and mouse-colored hair, had curved their lips, slimmed their cheeks, and given golden or chestnut tints to their coiffures. Like warriors behind their painted shields, they sat stiffly, three and three, staring at one another, talking with apathy. I bobbed my head at them, not knowing whether to introduce myself or to move on, and one of them looked up, and in a voice that was harsh, asked, "You under contract at Magnum?"

"No," I said.

"Oh, I thought you were somebody else," she said, and looked away again.

They were talking about their children and I guessed, as Eitel later confirmed, that they were the wives of important men and men who wanted to be important, the husbands off in chase of one another through the Laguna Room while the women were left behind.

"What do you mean, California is no good?" one of them said fiercely. "It's wonderful for children."

When a man went by, they tried to pay no notice. I realized that in walking past with a clumsy smile, showing how I didn't know if I was supposed to talk to them or not, I had done the dirty service of reflecting their situation. A few other men came in after me, and I saw that they either walked by without a look, or stopped for a brief but wild gallantry that went something like this:

"Carolyn!" the man would say, as if he could not believe he saw the woman here and was simply overcome.

"Mickey!" one of the six women would say.

"My favorite girl," the man would say, holding her hand.

"The only real man I know," the deserted wife would say. Mickey would smile. He would shake his head; he would hold her hand. "If I didn't know you were kidding, I could give you a tumble," he would say.

"Don't be too sure I'm kidding," the wife would say.

Mickey would straighten up; he would release her hand. There would be a silence until Mickey murmured, "What a woman." Then, in the businesslike tone that ends a conversation, he would say, "How are the kids, Carolyn?"

"They're fine."

"That's great. That's great." He would start to move away, and give a smile to all the women. "We have to have a long talk, you and me," Mickey would say.

"You know where to find me."

"Great kidder, Carolyn," Mickey would announce to nobody in particular, and disappear into the party.

All through the Laguna Room, wherever there was a couch, three wives were sitting in much that way. Since a lot of the men had come without women, the result was that men got together with men, standing near the pool, off the dance floor, at the café tables, or in a crowd near the bar. I picked up a drink and wandered through the party looking for a girl to talk to. But all the attractive girls were surrounded, though by fewer men than squeezed up to listen to a film director or a studio executive, and besides I did not know how to get into the conversations. They were all so private. I had been thinking that my looks and my uniform might not do me any harm, but most of the girls seemed to like the conversation of fat middle-aged men and bony middle-aged men, the prize going to a German movie director with a big paunch who had his arms around the waists of two starlets. Actually I wasn't really that eager. Being stone sober, the fact was that it was easier to drift from one circle of men to another.

In a cove of the bar formed by two tables and the tip of one of the pool's tentacles, I found Jennings James telling a joke to several feature actors of no particular celebrity. Jay-Jay rambled on, his eyes blurred behind his silver-rimmed glasses. When he was done, other jokes were told, each more stray than the one that went before. I quit them after a while, and Jay-Jay caught up to me.

"What a stinking party this is," he said. "I'm supposed to work tonight, show the photographers a good time." He coughed with stomach misery. "I left all those photographers over at the canopy table. You know it's the truth about photographers, they'd rather eat than drink." Jay-Jay had an arm on my shoulder, and I realized he was using me as an escort to reach the men's room. "You know the line of poetry, 'Methought I saw the grave where Laura lay'?" he started to say. But whatever it was he wanted to add was lost, and he stood looking at me sheepishly. "Well, that's a beautiful line of poetry," he finished, and like a kid who has clung to the back of a streetcar while it climbs the hill, and drops off once the top is reached, Jay-Jay let go my arm and, listing from the change in balance, went careening to the urinal.

I was left to stand around the edge of one group or another. A director finished a story of which I heard no more than the last few

lines. "I sat down and I told her that to be a good actress, she must always work for the truth in what she's playing," the man said in a voice
not empty of self-love, "and she said, 'What's the truth?' and I said it
could be defined as the real relation between human beings. You saw
the performance I got out of her." He stopped, the story was over, and
the men and women around him nodded wisely. "That's wonderful
advice you gave her, Mr. Sneale," a girl said, and the others murmured in agreement.

"Howard, tell the story about you and Mr. Teppis," one of them
begged.

The director chuckled. "Well, this story is on Herman, but I know
he wouldn't mind. There are enough stories on me in my dealings
with him. H.T.'s got an instinct that is almost infallible. There's a reason why he's such a great movie-maker, such a creative movie-maker."

"That's very true, Howard," the same girl said.

I moved on without listening any more and almost bumped into
the subject of the story. In a corner, off on a discussion, were Herman
Teppis and two other men who were not too different from Teppis.
They had been pointed out to me already as Eric Haislip, head of
Magnum, and Mac Barrantine from Liberty Pictures, but I think I
would have guessed in any case, for the three men were left alone. If
I had drunk my liquor more slowly, I might have felt the social paradox that allowed only these men to be able to talk without the attention of a crowd, but instead I placed myself at the elbow of the
producer named Mac Barrantine. They continued their conversation
without paying any attention to me.

"What do you think you'll gross on *The Tigress*?" Eric Haislip was
saying.

"Three-and-a-half to four," Herman Teppis said.

"Three-and-a-half to four?" Eric Haislip repeated. "H.T., you're
not talking to the New York office. You'll be lucky to get your money
out."

Teppis snorted. "I could buy your studio with what we'll make."

Mac Barrantine spoke slowly out of the side of a cigar. "I claim
that you just can't tell any more. There was a time when I could say,
'Bring it in at one-and-a-half, and we'll gross a million over.' Today,
picture-making is crazy. A filthy bomb I'm ashamed of makes money,
a classical musical comedy vehicle like *Sing, Girls, Sing* lays an egg. You
figure it out."

"You're wrong," Herman Teppis said, prodding him with a finger. "You know the trouble? People are confused today. So what do

they want? They want a picture that confuses them. Wait till they get really confused. Then they'll want a picture that sets them straight."

"Now you're required to show them real things on the screen," Eric Haislip sighed.

"Real things?" Teppis exploded. "We bring real things to them. Realism. But because a fellow in an Italian movie vomits all over the place and they like it in some art theater doesn't even have air-cooling, we should bring them vomit?"

"There's no discipline," Mac Barrantine said. "Even a director, a man with a high-powered tool in his hands. What does he do? He runs amok like a gangster."

"Charley Eitel cut your throat," Eric Haislip said.

"They all cut my throat," Teppis said passionately. "You know something? My throat don't cut." He glared at them as if remembering times when each of them had tried to treat him to a razor. "Bygones. Let it be bygones," Teppis said. "I get along with everybody."

"There's no discipline," Barrantine repeated. "I got a star, I won't mention her name. She came to me, she knew that in two months we were starting production on a really big vehicle for her, and you know what she had the gall to say? 'Mr. Barrantine, my husband and I, we're going to have a baby. I'm six weeks along.' 'You're going to have a baby?' I said. 'Where in hell's your loyalty? I know you, you're selfish. You can't tell me you want the heartache of bringing up an infant.' 'Mr. Barrantine, what should I do?' she bawled to me. I gave her a look and then I told her. 'I can't take the responsibility for advising you what to do,' I said, 'but you damn well better do something.' "

"She's going to be in the picture, I hear," Eric Haislip said.

"Of course she's going to be in the picture. She's an ambitious girl. But discipline and consideration. Do any of them have that?"

Eric Haislip was looking at me. "Who are you? What do you want here, kid?" he asked suddenly, although he had been aware of me for several minutes.

"I've been invited," I said.

"Did I invite you to sit on my lap?" Mac Barrantine said.

"You'd be the first," I muttered.

To my surprise, Teppis said, "Leave the boy alone. I know this boy. He's a nice young fellow."

Barrantine and Haislip glowered at me, and I scowled back. We all stood nose to nose like four trucks meeting at a dirt crossroad. "The youth, the young people," Teppis announced. "You think you know something? Listen to a young fellow's ideas. He can tell you something. This boy has a contribution."

Barrantine and Haislip did not seem particularly enthusiastic to hear my contribution. Conversation ground along for several minutes, and then they left on the excuse of filling their drinks. "I'll call the maître dee," Teppis offered. They shook their heads. They needed a walk, they announced. When they were gone, Teppis looked in a fine mood. I had the suspicion he had come to my defense in order to insult them. "First-rate fellows," he said to me. "I've known them for years."

"Mr. Teppis," I said irritably, "why did you invite me to your party?"

He laughed and clamped a hand on my shoulder. "You're a clever boy," he said, "you're quick-tongued. I like that." His hoarse thin voice drew a conspiratorial link between us whether I wanted it or not. "You take the desert," he confided to me. "It's a wonderful place to make a human being feel alive. I hear music in it all the time. A musical. It's full of cowboys and these fellows that live alone, what do you call them, hermits. Cowboys and hermits and pioneers, that's the sort of place it is. Fellows looking for gold. As a young fellow, what do you think, wouldn't you like to see such a movie? I like history," he went on before I could answer. "It would take a talented director to make such a story, a fellow who knows the desert." He poked me in the ribs as though to leave me breathless and therefore honest. "You take Eitel. Is he still hitting the booze?" Teppis said suddenly, his small flat eyes studying my reaction.

"Not much," I said quickly, but my look must have wandered, because Teppis squeezed my shoulder again.

"We got to have a long talk, you and me," Teppis said. "I like Charley Eitel. I wish he didn't have such a stain on his character. Politics. Idiotic. What do you think?"

"I think he's going to make the best movie of his life," I said with the hope I could worry Teppis.

"For the art theaters," Teppis stated, and he pointed a finger to his brain. "It won't be from the heart. You're too fresh for your own good," he continued with one of his fast shifts. "Who's interested in your ideas? I'll tell you what the story is. Eitel is through."

"I disagree," I said, cheered to realize I was the only one at this party who did not have to be polite to Herman Teppis.

"You disagree? What do you know? You're a baby." But I thought I understood what went on in him, the fear that he might be wrong chewing at the other fear that he might make a fool of himself by considering Eitel again. "Now listen, you," he started to say, but we were interrupted.

"Good evening, Daddy," a woman said.

"Lottie," Teppis said moistly, and embraced her. "Why didn't you call me?" he asked. "Ten o'clock this morning and no call from you."

"I had to miss it today," said Lottie Munshin. "I was packing for the trip."

Teppis began to ask her about his grandchildren, turning his back almost entirely on me. While they spoke I watched Carlyle Munshin's wife with interest. She was one of those women who are middle-aged too soon, her skin burned into the colors of false health. Thin, nervous, her face was screwed tight, and in those moments when she relaxed, the lines around her forehead and mouth were exaggerated, for the sun had not touched them. Pale haggard eyes looked out from sun-reddened lids. She was wearing an expensive dress but had only succeeded in making it look dowdy. The bones of her chest stood out, and a sort of ruffle fluttered on her freckled skin with a parched rustling movement like a spinster's parlor curtains. "I was delayed getting here," she said to her father in so pinched a voice I had the impression her throat was tight. "You see, Doxy was littering today. You know Doxy?"

"It's one of the mutts?" Teppis asked uncomfortably.

"She took the state-wide blue ribbon for her class," Lottie Munshin said. "Don't you remember?"

"Well, that's good." Teppis coughed. "Now, why don't you leave those dogs out of your mind for a couple of weeks, and you take a good vacation. You relax. You have a good time with Collie."

"I can't leave them for two weeks," she said with something like panic. "Salty litters in the next ten days, and we have to start training Blitzen and Nod for the trials."

"Well, that's fine," Teppis said vaguely. "Now, there's a fellow I got to see, so I'll leave you in the company of this young man. You'll enjoy talking to him. And, Lottie, you remember," he said, "there's more important things than those dogs."

I watched him walk away, nodding his head to the people who swarmed to greet him, carrying them one at a time like parasite fish. One couple even moved off the dance floor and came hurrying toward him.

"Do you like dogs?" Lottie Munshin asked me. She gave a short rough laugh for punctuation, and looked at me with her head cocked to one side.

I made the mistake of saying, "You breed them, don't you?"

She replied; she replied at length—she insisted on going into details that led into other details. She was a fanatic, and I stood listening to her, trying to find the little girl who had grown into this woman. "Collie and I have the best ranch within the county limits of the capital," she said in that pinched voice, "although of course keeping it up devolves upon me. It's quite a concern, I can tell you. I'm up at six every morning."

"You keep an early schedule," I offered.

"Early to bed. I like to be up with the sun. With such hours everybody could keep themselves in fine condition. You're young now, but you should take care of yourself. People should follow the same hours animals do, and they would have the natural health of an animal."

Over her shoulder I could see the dance floor and the swimming pool, and I was pulled between my desire to quit her for people who were more interesting and my reluctance to leave her alone. While she spoke, her bony fingers plucked at her chin. "I've got a green thumb," she said. "It's an unusual combination. I breed dogs and things grow under my thumb. Sometimes I think my father must have been meant to be a farmer, because where else could it have developed in me?"

"Oh, look. There's your husband," I said with relief.

She called to him. He was some distance away, but at the sound of her voice he looked up with an exaggeration of surprise that betrayed he was not surprised at all, and came moving toward us. As he recognized me his expression changed for a moment, but all the same he shook my hand warmly. "Well, we meet again," he said broadly.

"Carlyle, I meant to ask you," Lottie Munshin went on in a worried voice, "are you going to try that favorite-food diet?"

"I'll give it a look," he said in a bored tone, and caught me by the arm. "Lottie, I have something to talk over with Sergius. You'll excuse us." And with no more than that he steered me under a yucca tree, and we stood in the harsh shadow made by a flood lamp above the fronds.

"What are you doing here?" he asked.

Once again I explained that I had been invited by Herman Teppis.

"Eitel, too?"

When I nodded, Munshin burst out, "I wouldn't put it past Eitel to bring Elena here." As he shook his head with indignation, I began to laugh.

"It's a rotten party," I said. "It needs some kicks."

Munshin surprised me. A calculating expression came over his face and suddenly he looked like a very tough clown to me, a clown who in a quiet private way knew more than a few corners of the world. "It would be worth a lot of money to know what's in H.T.'s head," he muttered to himself, and walked away leaving me beside the yucca tree.

The party was becoming more active. People were going off by couples, or coming together at one center of interest or another. In a corner a game of charades was going on, the dance floor was nearly filled, a well-known comedian was performing for nothing, and an argument about a successful play almost killed the music of the rumba band. A drunk had managed to climb the boom that supported the papier-mâché camera, and he was quarreling with the cameraman, who was trying to get him to go down. Nearby, his wife was laughing loudly. "Ronnie's a flagpole sitter," she kept announcing. The swimming instructor of the hotel was giving a diving exhibition in a roped-off portion of the pool, but only a few were watching her. I had a couple of drinks at the bar, and tried to work into one circle or another without success. Bored, I listened to a folk singer dressed like a leatherstocking, who sang old ballads in a quavery twang that could be heard above the dance orchestra. "Isn't he talented?" a woman said nearby.

I felt a tap on my shoulder. A blond man whom I recognized as the tennis professional of the Yacht Club smiled at me. "Come on over," he said, "somebody would like to meet you." It turned out to be the movie star Teddy Pope. He was a tall man with an open expression and dark-brown hair, which fell in a cowlick over his forehead. When I came up with the tennis player, he grinned at me.

"Isn't this party a dog?" Teddy Pope said.

We all smiled at one another. I could think of nothing to say. Beside Pope sat Marion Faye, looking small and bored. He only nodded at me.

"Do you know roulette?" the tennis player asked. "Teddy's an *aficionado*."

"I've been trying to get a system," Teddy said. "I had a theory about the numbers. But mathematically it was too much for my low intelligence. I hired a statistician to try to figure it out." He grinned at me again. "You a weight-lifter?" Teddy asked me.

"No. Should I be?"

This turned out to be very amusing. Pope and the tennis player and Marion Faye shared a long run of laughter. "I can bend an iron bar," Teddy said to me. "That is, if it's a slim enough iron bar. I just stay in weight-lifting to keep from getting fat. I'm getting so fat now." He pinched his belly to give a demonstration and was able to show an excess of flesh no thicker than a pencil. "It's disgusting."

"You look in good shape," I said uncomfortably.

"Oh, I'm pudgy," Pope said.

"Weight-lifting ruined your forehand," the tennis player said.

Teddy Pope made no answer. "I can see you're a flier," he said. "Is it true that most of you live for drinking and sex?" He leaned back and smiled at the sky. "Oh, there's a beauty," he said as a girl passed. "Would you like to meet her? Marion says you're a little shy."

"I'll make out."

"Why don't you help him, Teddy?" Marion jeered.

"I would just be a drag," Pope said.

"Sit down, Sergei," said the tennis player.

"No. Well, you see," I said, "I promised to bring a drink to somebody."

"Come back if you get bored," Teddy said.

I was approached beneath another yucca tree by a little bald-headed man in a sky-blue tropical suit who had a tall red-headed girl by the hand. "Ah, there you are, I missed you before," he said briskly. "I'd like to introduce myself. I'm Bunny Zarrow, you may have heard of me. Actor's representative." I must have looked at him with surprise, for he added, "I see you were talking to Mr. Teppis. May I ask what you were talking about?"

"He wanted my advice on a movie."

"That's interesting. That's unusual. And what is your name?"

"John Yard," I said.

"You're under contract, I take it?"

"Of course."

"Well, a contract can sometimes be bettered. I wish I could place your name. I will say this is neither the time nor the opportunity, but you and I must have lunch to discuss it. I'll call you at the studio." He pointed to the girl beside him. "I'd like you to meet Candy Ballou." The girl yawned and then tried to smile. She was very drunk.

Bunny drew me aside. "Let me give you her phone number. She's a charming, outgoing girl." He blinked his eyes. "I'm glad to do you a favor. If I weren't so overworked, I would keep her number, but it's a shame to keep such a girl to myself." He returned me to Candy Ballou and placed our hands together. "Now, kiddies, I'm sure you two have a great deal in common," he said, and left us looking at one another.

"Would you like to dance?" I asked the redheaded girl.

"Don't panic, love-bucket." She said this as if it were a password, and then opened her eyes to focus on me. "What studio you at?" she blurted.

"That's just a joke, Candy," I said.

"A joke on Zarrow, huh?"

"That's right."

"What do you do?"

"Nothing," I said.

"No dough. I might have known." She swayed her body to the rhythms of the rumba music and yawned fiercely. "Oh, honey," she said in a little broken voice, "if you had class, you'd help me to the ladies' room."

On my return from that errand with no more for company than a new highball, I saw Eitel come in at last. He was with a girl. Elena, I knew.

She was a near-beauty. Elena's hair was a rich red-brown and her skin was warm. She walked with a sense of her body, and I had always been drawn to that in a girl since my first year in the Air Force, when like every other fly at an enlisted man's dance, I would cock my hat and try to steal prizes like Elena with my speed. Although she wore a lot of lipstick, and her high heels would have satisfied a show-girl, there was something delicate about her and very proud. She carried herself as if she were tall, and her strapless evening gown showed round handsome shoulders. Her face was not exactly soft, but it was heartshaped, and above a tender mouth and chin, the nares of her long narrow nose suggested ample aptitude to me. Munshin's description seemed passing poor.

Except that she was obviously not at ease. As I watched Eitel lead her into the mouth of the party she reminded me of an animal, ready for flight. Their appearance at the party had set off a ripple of confusion, and very few of the people who saw him knew what to do. There were several who smiled and even said hello, there were some who nodded, and even more who turned away, but I had the feeling they were all frightened. Until they knew the reason why Eitel had been invited, they could only feel the panic that whatever they did could be a mistake. It was grim the way he and Elena were left to cross the floor of the party without catching anybody to accompany them, and I saw

Eitel stop finally at an empty table near the pool, set out a chair for Elena, and then sit down himself. From a distance, I had to like the way he succeeded in looking bored.

I went up to their table. "Can I join you?" I said clumsily.

Eitel gave me a quick grateful smile. "Elena, you must meet Sergius, he's the best person here."

"Oh, shut up," I told him, and turned to her. "I'm awfully sorry, I didn't catch your last name," I said.

"It's Esposito," Elena muttered, "an Italian name." Her voice was just a little hoarse, and surprisingly deep, which made it considerably less useful to her than her face, but it was a voice that had muffled strength in it. I had heard accents like that since I was a kid.

"Doesn't she look like a Modigliani?" Eitel said enthusiastically, and then added, "Elena, I know you've been told that more than once."

"Yes," Elena said, "that is, someone once told me. As a matter of fact it was your friend."

Eitel passed over the reference to Munshin. "But where did you get those green eyes?" he teased her. From the angle where I sat, I could see his fingers tapping restlessly on his knee.

"Oh, that's from my mother," Elena said. "She's half Polish. I guess I'm one-quarter Polish and three-quarters Italian. Oil and water." We all worked a little to laugh, and Elena shifted uncomfortably. "What a funny subject," she said.

Eitel made a play of studying the Laguna Room and said, "What do you think this party needs?"

"What?" I asked.

"A roller coaster."

Elena burst into laughter. She had a nice laugh that showed her white teeth, but she laughed too loudly. "Oh, that's so funny," she said.

"I love roller coasters," Eitel went on. "It's that first drop. Like the black hole of death. There's nothing to compare with it." And for the next two minutes he talked about roller coasters, until I could see by the look in Elena's eyes how alive he made the subject seem. He was in good form, and to draw him out, Elena was a good listener. I found myself thinking that she was not stupid, and yet she would only answer with a laugh or some little remark. It was the style of her attention. Her face gave back the shadow of everything he said, until Eitel was carried away. "It proves an old idea of mine," he said. "One gets on a roller coaster in order to feel certain emotions, and I wonder if it's not the same with an affair. When I was younger, I used to think it was ugly, even unclean I suppose, that a man who thought he was in love would find himself using the same words with one girl after another. Yet there's nothing wrong about it really. The only true faithfulness people have is toward emotions they're trying to recapture."

"I don't know," Elena said. "I think a man like that wouldn't be feeling anything for the woman."

"On the contrary. At that moment, he adores her."

This confused her. "I mean," she interrupted, "you know, it's . . . oh, I'm not sure." But she could not let it pass. "A man like that isn't relating to the woman. He's detached."

Eitel looked pleased. "You're right," he reversed himself. "I suppose it's the proof of how detached I am."

"Oh, you can't be," she said.

"I certainly am," he smiled, as though to flag an advance warning.

It must have been hard to believe. His eyes were bright, his body leaned toward her, and his dark hair looked charged with energy. "Don't judge by appearances," Eitel began. "Why, I can tell you . . ."

He broke off. Munshin was coming toward us. Elena's face lost all expression, and Eitel began to smile in an unnatural way.

"I don't know what it is you got," Collie boomed, "but H.T. told me to come over and say hello. He wants to talk to you later."

When none of us answered, Munshin contented himself with staring at Elena.

"Collie, how are you?" Eitel said finally.

"I've been better." He nodded his head. "I've been a lot better," he said, continuing to look at Elena.

"Aren't you having a good time?" she asked.

"No, I'm having a rotten time," Munshin answered.

"I was looking for your wife," Elena said, "but I don't know who she is."

"She's around," Munshin said.

"And your father-in-law? He's here, I heard you say."

"What difference does it make?" Munshin asked with a moist look, as if he were really saying, "Someday you won't hate me anymore."

"Oh, yes, no difference at all. I wouldn't want to embarrass you," Elena said, her voice all but out of control. It gave a hint of how badly she would act in a quarrel.

"I met Teddy Pope tonight," I interrupted as best I could. "What is he like?"

"I can tell you," Eitel said nimbly, "he's been in several of my pictures. And do you know, I think he's really sort of decent as an actor. Some day he may be very good."

At that moment, a beautiful blond girl in a pale-blue evening gown came up behind Munshin and covered his eyes with her hands. "Guess who?" she said in a throaty voice. I had a glimpse of a little turned-up nose, a dimpled chin, and a pouting mouth I had seen before. At the sight of Eitel she made a face.

"Lulu," Munshin said, half rising from his chair, and not knowing if her interruption had helped the situation or made it worse, he hugged Lulu with fatherly arms, smiling at Elena and Eitel, while with his free hand visible only to me, he patted the small of her back as though to tell her she might do worse than to hug him again.

"Miss Meyers, Miss Esposito," Eitel said smoothly, and Lulu gave a passing nod to Elena. "Collie, we have to talk," Lulu said. "I have something I definitely want to tell you about." Then she gave a sweet smile to Eitel. "Charley, you're getting fat," she said.

"Sit down," Eitel offered.

She took a chair next to him, and told Munshin to sit on the other side. "Isn't anybody going to introduce the Air Force?" she asked directly of me, and when that was done, she made a game of studying my face. I forced myself to stare her down but it took something out of me. "What a pretty boy you are," said Lulu Meyers. She could not have been much more than twenty herself.

"She's great," Munshin said. "What a tongue."

"Would you like a drink?" I asked Elena. She hadn't said a word since Lulu had come, and by comparison she did not seem as attractive as I thought her before. Maybe aware of this herself, she picked nervously and savagely at the cuticle on her nail. "Oh, yes, I'd like a drink," Elena agreed, and as I started away, Lulu handed me her glass. "Get me a small Martin, will you?" she asked, turning violet-blue eyes on me. I realized she was as nervous as Elena, but in a different way; Lulu made herself sit easily in the chair—I had learned the same trick in flying school.

When I came back, she was talking to Eitel. "We miss you, old ham," she was saying. "I don't know anybody I'd rather get drunk with than Eitel."

"I'm on the wagon," Eitel said with a grin.

"You're on the wagon as far as I'm concerned," Lulu said with a glance at Elena.

"I hear you're going to marry Teddy Pope," Eitel answered.

Lulu turned on Munshin. "You tell H.T. to lay off the drums," she said, and flipped her cigarette to the floor, grinding it out with a quick impatient motion. I had a peep at her legs and of little feet covered by silver slippers. Those legs were as familiar as the contour of her mouth, each drawn on one's memory by a hundred photographs, or was it a thousand? "Collie, this propaganda has got to stop, I tell you."

Munshin gave his sheepish smile. "Now, you relax, doll. Who's forcing you into anything?"

"I approve of Lulu marrying Teddy," Eitel drawled.

"Charley, you're a troublemaker," Munshin said quickly.

Elena and I looked at each other. She was trying very hard to be a part of this, her eyes following everyone who spoke, her smile forced as if she didn't want to seem ignorant. Probably I was acting the same way. We sat at opposite flanks of the conversation, no more than social book-ends.

"I'm serious," Lulu said. "You can tell Mr. T. I'll marry this pretty boy first," and she inclined a finger toward me.

"You haven't proposed yet," I said.

Elena laughed with enough pleasure to have said it herself. Again her laugh was too loud, and the others stared at her.

"Don't panic, love-bucket," Lulu said with an authority the red-headed girl, Candy Ballou, had not been able to muster. She held her empty glass up for us all to see, and poured its last drop on the floor. "I'm sad, Collie," she announced, and laid her head on Munshin's shoulder.

"I saw your last picture," Eitel said to her.

"Wasn't I just awful in it?" Lulu made a face again. "They're ruining me. What did you think, Eitel?"

He smiled noncommittally. "I'll talk to you about it."

"I know what you'll say. I was performing too much, wasn't I?" She raised her head and pinched Collie on the cheek. "I hate acting." And with hardly a pause she leaned forward to ask a question. "What do you do, Miss Esposo?"

"Esposito," Eitel said.

Elena was uncomfortable. "I've been . . . not exactly, a dancer, I guess."

"Modeling now?" Lulu said.

"No . . . I mean, of course not. . . ." Elena was not altogether helpless before her. "Different things," she finished at last. "Who wants to be a skinny model?"

"Oh, I'll bet," Lulu said, and spoke to me again. "You the latest tail on Eitel's old tattered kite?"

I could feel myself turning red. Her attacks came so fast that it was a little like waiting for the sound to stop in musical chairs. "They say you're through, Charley," Lulu went on.

"They certainly do talk about me," Eitel said.

"Not as much as you think. Time passes."

"I'll always be remembered as your second ex-husband," Eitel drawled.

"It's a fact," she said. "When I think of Charley Eitel, I think of number two."

Eitel smiled cheerfully. "If you want to put on the brass knuckles, Lulu, just give the word."

There was a moment, and then Lulu smiled back. "I'm sorry, Charley, I apologize." She turned to all of us, and in that husky voice which went along so nicely with her blond hair and blue eyes, she said, "I saw an awful picture of me today in the papers."

"Lulu," Munshin said quickly, "we can rectify that. The photographers will be working soon."

"I won't be mugged with Teddy Pope," Lulu declared.

"Who's forcing you?" Munshin said.

"No tricks, Collie."

"No tricks," Munshin promised, wiping his face.

"Why are you perspiring so?" Lulu asked, and then broke off to stand up. "Jay-Jay!" she cried aloud, and opened her arms. Jennings James, who had just walked toward us, wrapped her to his skinny body in a parody of Munshin's bear-hug. "My favorite girl," he said in his high Southern voice.

"That was a bitchy release you had on me day before yesterday," Lulu said.

"Honey, you're paranoidal," Jennings James told her. "I wrote it as a work of love to you." He nodded to all of us. "How are you, Mr. Munshin?" he said. The trip to the men's room seemed to have revived him.

"Take a chair, Jay-Jay," Munshin said. "This is Miss Esposito."

Jennings James bowed formally to her. "I love the dignity of Italian women, Miss Esposito." His freckled hand smoothed his red hair. "Are you going to stay with us long in Desert D'Or?"

"I'm going back tomorrow," Elena said.

"Oh, you're not," Eitel said.

"Well, I'm not sure," Elena corrected herself.

A waiter brought ice cream. It was melted on the plates, and only Elena took a dish. "This is soft ice cream, isn't it?" she said. "That's the expensive kind, I've heard." When everybody looked puzzled by the remark, Elena became a little desperate in the attempt to prove it. "I don't remember where I heard, but I did see it advertised, soft ice cream, I mean, or maybe I was eating it, I don't know."

Eitel came to her aid. "It's true. Duvon's in the city features a sort of melted ice cream. I've had it myself. But I don't think this is Duvon's, Elena."

"Oh, no, I know it isn't," she said quickly.

Jay-Jay turned back to Lulu. "Honey, we're ready for the pictures. Those photographers have finished grossifying themselves, and it all waits on you."

"Well, let it wait," said Lulu. "I want another drink."

"Mr. T. asked me specially to get you."

"Come on, let's go," said Munshin, "everybody." I think he included Elena, Eitel, and myself to prevent Lulu from deciding she wanted to stay with us. Once on his feet, Munshin took her arm and started along the edge of the pool past the dance floor toward a group of photographers I could see gathered near the papier-mâché movie camera.

Jay-Jay brought up the rear with me. "That Esposito dame," he said. "She's Munshin's little gal, I hear."

"I don't know," I said.

"Oh, man, she's a dish. I never got my hooks into her, but I know some who have. When old Charley Eitel gets done with Esposito, you ought to spend a couple of delicious hours with her." He then started to give me details of how good she was supposed to be. "And she looks like a sweet kid, too," he added gallantly. "It's hard for a girl living in the capital. I don't hold it against any of them. Why, Teppis himself, that son of a bitch . . ." But Jay-Jay had no time to finish the sentence, for we had come up to the photographers.

I could see Teddy Pope moving in from another direction. The tennis player still was with him, and they were laughing at some private joke. "Lulu, honey," Pope said, and held out his hand to shake hers. They touched fingertips and stood side by side.

"Now, fellows," said Jay-Jay, springing forward and talking to the three photographers who stood phlegmatically in front of the camera boom, "we want some human-interest stills. Nothing elaborate. Just how cinema folks live and entertain each other. You got the idea." People were coming over from various corners of the Laguna Room.

"Honeybun, you look lovely," Dorothea O'Faye called out, and Lulu smiled. "Thank you, sweetie," she called back. "Hey, Teddy," a man said, "have your autograph?" and Teddy laughed. Now that he was standing before an audience, his manner had changed. He seemed more boyish and more direct. "Why, here comes Mr. T. now," he said aloud, and showing a crack disdain to those who could see it, he began to clap his hands, and at least a dozen of the people near him, trapped into obedience, applauded as well. Teppis held his arm aloft. "We're taking some pictures tonight of Teddy and Lulu, not only for interest on their picture, or should I say *our* picture, *An Inch from Heaven,* but as a symbol, as I would call it, of tonight and the kind of good time we've had." Teppis cleared his throat and smiled sweetly. His presence had succeeded in drawing even more people, and for a while the scene was busy with the flash-bulbs of the cameras, the shifting of positions, and the directions given by the photographers. I saw Teppis in place between Teddy and Lulu, Lulu between the two men, Teddy and Lulu together, Teddy and Lulu apart, Teppis holding Lulu's hand in a fatherly way, Teppis photographed with his hand on Teddy's elbow. I was struck by how well they did it, Teddy smiling, happy, healthy, and Lulu sweet. Lulu demure, Lulu ready, all with an ease that balanced the pride of Herman Teppis. It was just about perfect. Teddy Pope turned his face to every instruction of the photographers, his voice had sincerity, his smile seemed to enjoy his surroundings. He waved his hands in the air like a prizefighter, and gave a play of having wrenched his shoulder from the exercise; he put his arm around Lulu's waist, he bussed her cheek. And Lulu with a cuddling curving motion slipped against his side. She seemed to bounce when she walked, her shoulders swayed in a little rhythm with her hips, her neck curved, her hair tumbled in gold ringlets over her head, and her husky voice laughed at everyone's jokes. I thought she was about as beautiful as any girl I had ever seen.

When the photographers were done, Teppis made another speech. "You never know. We're a big family at Supreme. I'll tell you something. I don't think these two kids were acting." And with a hand against each of their backs, he pushed them together until they had to hug each other in order not to trip. "What's this I hear, Lulu?" he said aloud to the laughter of the guests. "A little ladybug has told me you and Teddy are dear friends."

"Oh, Mr. Teppis," Lulu said in her sweetest voice, "you should have been a marriage broker."

"It's a compliment. I take it as a compliment," Teppis said. "A producer is always making marriages. Art and finance. Talent and an audience. Are you all having a good time tonight?" he asked of the guests watching, and I listened to more than one answer that a good time was being had. "Treat the camera boys," Teppis said to Jay-Jay, and walked off with Lulu on his arm. The crowd faded; the photographers were left to pack their equipment. Beside the pool, I saw Teppis stop to talk to Eitel, and while he spoke he looked at Elena.

I could see that Teppis recognized her name the moment Eitel introduced her, for Teppis' reaction followed quickly. His back stiffened, his ruddy face seemed to swell, and he said something, something to the point, since Eitel and Elena turned away immediately.

Alone with Lulu, Teppis was mopping his forehead with a silk handkerchief. "Go dance with Teddy," I heard him say hoarsely as I approached. "Do it as a favor for me."

Because of the crowd I could no longer see what had happened to Eitel.

Lulu caught my eye. "Mr. T., I want to dance with Sergius first," she said with a pout, and slipping away from Teppis she put her hand in my palm and drew me to the dance floor. I held her tightly. The liquor I had been drinking all evening was finally beginning to do its work.

"How long will it take," I said in her ear, "before you start to look for Teddy?"

To my surprise she took this meekly. "You don't know what I'm up against," Lulu said.

"Why? Do you know?"

"Oh, don't be like that, Sergius. I like you." At the moment she seemed no more than eighteen. "It's harder than you think," she whispered, and by the softness with which she held herself, I found it hard to believe in the first impression she made on me. She seemed young; spoiled maybe, but very sweet.

We danced in silence. "What did Teppis say to Eitel?" I asked finally.

Lulu shook her head and then giggled. "He told Charley to get the hell out."

"Well, then I guess I have to go too," I told her.

"You weren't included."

"Eitel is my friend," I said.

She pinched my ear. "Wonderful. Charley will love that. I have to tell him when I see him."

"Leave with me," I said.

"Not yet."

I stopped dancing. "If you want," I said, "I'll ask Mr. T. for permission."

"You think I'm afraid of him."

"You're not afraid of him. You'll just end up dancing with Teddy."

Lulu began to laugh. "You're different from what I thought at first."

"That's just liquor."

"Oh, I hope not."

Reluctantly, in a sort of muse, she allowed me to take her from the dance floor. "This is an awful mistake," she whispered.

Yet Lulu was not exactly timorous when we passed Teppis. Like a promoter who counts the seats in the house, he stood near the entrance, his eyes adding up the scene. "Girlie," he said, gripping her by the arm, "where are you going?"

"Oh, Mr. T.," Lulu said like a bad child, "Sergius and I have so much to talk about."

"We want to get some air," I said, and I took the opportunity to give him a finger in the ribs.

"Air?" He was indignant as we left. "Air?" I could see him looking for the ceiling of the Laguna Room. Behind us, still in operation, the papier-mâché camera rotated on its wooden boom, the searchlights lifting columns to the sky. A pall lay over the party. The zenith had passed, and couples were closed into tête-à-têtes on the couches, for the drunken hour had come where everything is possible and everybody wants everybody; if desires were deeds, the history of the night would end in history.

"You say to Charley Eitel," Teppis shouted after me, "that he's through. I tell you he's through. He's lost his chance."

Giggling at the sound of his rage, Lulu and I ran along the walks and over the little trellised bridges of the Yacht Club until we came to the parking circle. Once, underneath a Japanese lantern, I stopped to kiss her, but she was laughing too hard and our mouths didn't meet. "I'll have to teach you," she said.

"Teach me nothing. I hate teachers," I said and, holding her hand, pulled her behind me, her heels clicking, her skirt rustling in the promising tap-and-whisper of a girl trying to run in an evening gown.

We had an argument over whose car to take. Lulu insisted on using her convertible. "I'm cooped up, Sergius," she said. "I want to drive." "Then drive my car," I compromised, but she would have no other way than her own. "I won't leave," she said, driven to a pitch of stubbornness, "I'll go back to the party."

"You're frightened," I taunted her.

"I'm not."

She drove badly. She was reckless, which I expected, but what was worse, she could not hold her foot steady on the pedal. The automobile was always slowing or accelerating, and drunk as I was she made me aware of danger. But that wasn't the danger I was worrying about.

"I'm a nut," she'd say.

"Let's park, nut," I would answer. "Let's cut the knot."

"Did you ever go to the crazy doctor?" Lulu asked.

"You don't need him."

"Oh, I need something," she said, and with a wrench, gravel stinging our fenders, she brought the car off the shoulder and on the road again.

"Let's park," I said.

She parked when she would have it. I had given up hope. I was prepared to sit politely while she skidded us off the highway and we rolled and smacked at seventy miles an hour through the cactus and desert clay. But Lulu decided we might just as well live a little while longer. Picking a side road at random, she screamed around the turn, slowed down once it was past, drifted along, and finally pulled off in some deserted flat, the night horizon lying all around us in a giant circle.

"Lock the windows," she said, engrossed in pressing the button that raised the canvas top.

"It'll be too hot," I argued.

"No, the windows have to be closed," she insisted.

All preparations spent, she turned in her seat and took my kiss. She must have felt she had let loose a bull, and in fact she had; for the first time in almost a year I knew that I would be all right.

Yet it was not so easy as that. She would give herself to my mouth and my arms, she would be about to be caught, and then she would start away, looking fearfully through the car window. "There's a man coming," she would whisper, her nails digging my wrist, and I would be forced to lift my head and scan the horizon, forced to stop and say, "There's no one around, can't you see?"

"I'm scared," she would say, and give her mouth to me again. How long it went on I do not know, but it was a classic. She coaxed me forward, she pushed me back, she allowed me a strip of her clothing only to huddle away like a bothered virgin. We could have been kids on a couch. My lips were bruised, my body suffered, my fingers were thick, and if I succeeded finally in capturing what clothing she wore beneath her evening dress, pushing it behind me in the seat like a mad jay stuffing its nest, I still could not inspire Lulu to give up her gown. Though she allowed the most advanced forays and even let me for one, two, and three beats of the heart, she sat up with a little motion that pushed me away, and looked through the windows. "There's someone coming. There's somebody on the road," she said, and pinched me when I tried to come near her.

"This is it," I told her, but for all I told her, high-water mark had been reached. For another hour, no matter what I did, how I forced, how I waited, and how I tried, I could not get so close again. The dawn must have been not too far away when, exhausted, discouraged, and almost indifferent, I shut my eyes and murmured, "You win." With a weary hand I passed over my cache of her door-prizes and lay back against the seat.

Tenderly, she kissed my lashes, her fingernails teased my cheek. "You're sweet," she whispered, "you're really not so rough." To revive me, she pulled my hair. "Kiss me, Sergius," she said as if I had not yet done anything at all, and in the next minute while I lay back on the seat, not believing and almost dumb to her giving, I was led to discover the mysterious brain of a movie star. She gave herself gently to me, she was delicate, she was loving, loving even to the modesty with which she whispered that this was all very unplanned, and I must be considerate. So I was obliged to take the trip alone, and was repaid by having her cuddle in my arms.

"You're wonderful," she said.

"I'm just an amateur."

"No, you're wonderful. Oooh, I like you. You!"

On the way back I drove the car while she curled beside me, her head on my shoulder. The radio was on and we hummed to the music. "I was crazy tonight," she said.

I adored her. The way she had treated everybody when I met her made this even better. For on that long drive she took me before we parked, I had told myself that absolutely I had to succeed with her, and the memory of this feeling now that I had succeeded was fine. Maybe it was no more than that enough time had gone by, but I felt all right, I felt ready—for what, I hardly knew. But I had made it, and with what a girl.

Lulu was tense when we kissed good night outside her door. "Let me stay," I said.

"No, not tonight." She looked behind her to see if the walks were deserted.

"Then come to my house."

She kissed me on the nose. "I'm just beaten, Sergius." Her voice was the voice of a child.

"All right, I'll see you tomorrow."

"Call me." She kissed me again, she blew a kiss as she disappeared through the door, and I was left alone in the labyrinth of the Yacht Club, the first sun of desert morning not far away, the foliage a pale-blue like the pale-blue of her gown.

It may sound weird, but I was so excited with enthusiasm that I had to share it, and I could think of nobody but Eitel. It did not even occur to me that he might still be with Elena, or that as the ex-husband of little Lulu, he would not necessarily find my story a dream. I don't know whether I even remembered that Lulu had been married to him. In a way, she had no existence for me before tonight, and if she seemed bigger than life, she was also without life. How I loved myself then. With the dawn spreading out from me until it seemed to touch the Yacht Club with its light, I began to think of those mornings when I was out on a flight that started in the darkness of the hangars, the syrup of coffee on my tongue, the blast of my plane flaring two long fires into the night. We would take off an hour before dawn, and when morning came to meet us five miles high in the air with the night clouds warmed by a gold and silver light, I used to believe I could control the changes of the sky by a sway of my body as it was swelled by the power of the plane, and I had played with magic. For it was magic to fly an airplane. We knew that no matter what happened on ground, no matter how little or confusing we ourselves could be, there would always come those hours when we were alone in formation and on top of life, and so the magic was in the flight and the flight made us cool, and there was nothing that could happen once we were down which could not be fixed when the night went into the west and we ganged after it on our wings.

I had been careful to forget all of this; I had liked it too much, and it had not been easy to think that I probably would never have any magic again. But on this dawn with the taste of Lulu still teasing me, I knew that I could have something else, and I could be sad for those airplanes I deserted because there was something to take their place.

Thinking this, or thinking of such things, I started up the path to where I had parked my car. Halfway, I sat on a bench underneath a bower of shrubbery, breathing the new air. Everything had come to rest around me. Then, in a cottage nearby I heard sudden brawling sounds, a mixed dialogue or two, and a door in the wall opened and Teddy Pope lurched out, wearing a sweater and dungarees, but his feet were bare. "You bitch," he shouted at the door.

"Stay out," came the voice of the tennis player. "I don't want to tell you again." Teddy cursed. He cursed at such length and in so loud a voice that I was sure everybody sleeping nearby must be reaching for their pills. The door in the bungalow opened again, and Marion Faye came outside. "Go beat your meat, Teddy," he said in his quiet voice, and then he stepped back inside and shut the door. Teddy turned around once and looked past me with blank eyes that took me in, or maybe didn't see anything at all.

I watched him stagger along the wall, and in spite of myself I followed at a distance. In one of the minor patios of the Yacht Club where a fountain, a few yucca trees, and a hedge of bougainvillea set up an artificial nook, Teddy Pope stopped and made a phone call from an outdoor booth set under a trellis of rambler roses. "I can't go to sleep like this," he said into the receiver. "I've got to talk to Marion." The voice at the other end made some answer.

"Don't hang up," Teddy Pope said loudly.

Like a night watchman making his rounds, Herman Teppis came into sight along one of the walks. He approached Teddy Pope, came up beside him, and slammed the receiver on its cradle.

"You're a disgraceful human being," Herman Teppis said, and kept on down the walk without saying another word.

Teddy Pope wobbled away and came to rest against a joshua tree. He leaned on it as if it were his mother. Then he began to cry. I had never seen a man so drunk. Sobbing, hiccupping, he tried to chew on the bark of the tree. I backed away, I wanted nothing so much as to disappear. When I was out of sight, I heard Pope scream. "You bastard, Teppis," he cried out into the empty dawn, "you know what you can do, you fat bastard, Teppis," and I could picture his cheek on the joshua tree. I drove slowly home, making no attempt to find Eitel after all.

I had never known a girl like Lulu, nor had I ever been in such a romance. Of course I had had my share of other girls—one doesn't go through the Air Force without learning something about women—but I had always been a poor detective and ladies were way ahead of me.

Yet I think Lulu would have had her surprises for any man. I couldn't tell from one hour to the next if we were in love or about to break up, whether we would make love or fight, do both or do nothing at all. The first time I saw her again, she was with friends and never let me be alone with her; the next day she came to visit my house and not only made it easy, but told me she was in love. Naturally, I told her the same. It would have been hard not to, and for sure I was in love if love is the time to do nothing else. Before she left, we had a quarrel; we would never see each other again. A half hour later she telephoned me from the Yacht Club and burst into tears. We loved each other after all.

It was out of control, beyond a doubt. I was able to discover emotions I never knew I owned, and I must have enjoyed it as much as Lulu. So I thought by virtue of the things we did I would put my mark on her forever. What she may have intended as a little dance was a track and field event to me, and I would snap the tape with burning lungs, knotted muscles, and mind set on the need to break a record. It was the only way I could catch her and for three minutes keep her. Like a squad of worn-out infantrymen who are fixed for the night in a museum, my pleasure was to slash tapestries, poke my fingers through nude paintings, and drop marble busts on the floor. Then I could feel her as something I had conquered, could listen to her wounded breathing, and believe that no matter how she acted other times, these moments were Lulu, as if her flesh murmured words more real than her lips. To the pride of having so beautiful a girl was added the bigger pride of knowing that I took her with the cheers of millions behind me. Poor millions with their low roar! They would never have what I had now. They could shiver outside, make a shrine in their office desk or on the shelf of their olive-drab lockers, they could look at the pin-up picture of Lulu Meyers. I knew I was good when I carried a million men on my shoulder.

But if I caught her in bed, I caught her nowhere else. There were days when Lulu told me to leave her alone, there were other days when she would not let me quit her for a minute, but the common denominator was that I had to follow every impulse. I could go over at noon to her suite in the Yacht Club after a summons by phone; she would be decided that we go horseback riding in the desert. I would arrive to find her still in bed. Breakfast had not yet come; would I have coffee with her? The moment room service left a tray, Lulu told me she wanted a Stinger.

"I don't know how to make Stingers," I would answer.

"Oh, sweetie, everybody knows how to make a Stinger. There's brandy, crème de menthe. What did you do in the Air Force, milk a cow?"

"Lulu, are we going horseback riding?"

"Yes, we're going horseback riding." She would hold up a mirror, study her face with the stare of a beauty-parlor operator, and stick out her tongue at the reflection. "Do I look good without make-up?" she would ask in a professional tone that allowed no nonsense.

"You look very good."

"My mouth's a little too thin."

"It wasn't last night," I would say.

"Oh, you. A corpse could satisfy you." But she would hug me matter-of-factly. "I love you, darling," she would say.

"Let's go horseback riding."

"Do you know, Sergius, you're neurotic."

"I'm neurotic. I can't stand to waste a day."

"Well, I don't feel like getting on a horse," Lulu would decide.

"I knew you wouldn't. I didn't want to either."

"Then why did you wear jodphurs?"

"Because if I didn't wear them, you would want to go."

"Oh, I'm not like that." Sitting in bed, she would hug herself, her beautiful face arched above her cool throat. "Honest, I'm not."

The phone would ring. It would be a call from New York. "No, I'm not marrying Teddy Pope," she would say to a columnist. "Of course, he's a son of a bitch. Yes, say we're good friends and that's all. Good-bye, sweetie." She would hang up, she would groan. "That stupid press agent I've got. If you can't handle a gossip columnist what kind of press agent are you?"

"Why don't you let him try?"

"He's beyond hunger."

So it would go. About the time I was past exasperated she would begin to dress. The coffee was cold she would tell me and call room service for more. I would lose my temper. I was definitely leaving, I would tell her. She would run after me and catch me at the door. She knew I was willing to be caught. "I'm a bitch, I tell you," she would say. "I was trying to get you mad."

"You never came near."

"You'll end up hating me. You will. Nobody likes me who really knows me. Even I don't like myself."

"You love yourself."

She would grin delightfully. "It's not the same thing. Sergius, let's go horseback riding."

Finally we would go. She was always dawdling or at a gallop. One time we were riding around an abandoned wooden fence and she told me to jump it. I told her I wouldn't because I was a bad jumper. It was an honest estimate. I had been riding for a month.

"The lousiest stunt man will fall on his ass for fifty bucks," she said, "but you won't try anything."

Actually, I wanted to jump. I had the anticipation of falling and Lulu nursing me. That was a part of our affair that had never been tried. When I took the jump, and I thought it was a good one, I turned around for her applause and saw her trotting away in the opposite direction. For all I knew she hadn't even looked. After I caught up to her she turned on me. "You're a baby. Only a second-rater would take a stupid dare like that."

We rode back without a word. When we reached the Yacht Club, she went into her cabaña, came out in a bathing suit, and talked to everybody but me. The only time our eyes met, she held out her glass as she had done the night of the party, and said, "Sugar, get me a small Martin."

Her caution when our affair began was often a chore. She used to come to my house on foot, or she would admit me to her room only after dark. "They'll crucify me when they find out," she would complain, "look at Eitel," that way comparing me to Elena. About his affair she was furious. "Eitel never had any taste," she would say. "Any tramp who tells him he's terrific can always sell him a ticket to her favorite charity." And once when we met them on the street, she was hardly easy on Elena. "I bet she has dirty underwear," Lulu said. "You watch. She's going to be fat as a bull." When I argued that I liked Elena, Lulu became sullen. "Oh, sure, she's the underdog," Lulu snapped. Yet, a few hours later, she said to me, "You know, Sugar, maybe it would have been better if I had to struggle. Maybe my character would be better." Her finger to her chin, she asked, "Am I really a bore?"

"Only when you're vertical . . ."

"You'll pay for that." And she chased me around with a pillow. When she had finished pounding me, she made me lie down beside her. "I'm awful, but Strong-Arm O'Shaugnessy, I want to be good. It was terrible with Eitel. He would laugh at me and some of his friends were intellectually very overbearing." She giggled. "When I was with Eitel, I used to study to be an intellectual."

If she had decided to keep our affair a secret, she changed her mind one day by sitting on my lap at the Yacht Club pool. "You ought to try Sugar some time," she said to several of her women friends, "he's not bad at all." Which depressed me. Because I knew if I was really good, she wouldn't give her friends a clue. For a few days she couldn't walk in public without my arm around her. Pictures were taken of us by night-club photographers. I got up one morning to find Lulu by my bed, a gossip column in her hand. "Look at it. How awful!" she said to me. I read the following:

> Atom Bomb Lulu Meyers and the potential next Mr. Meyers, ex-Marine Corps Captain Silgius McShonessy, scion of an Eastern-or-is-it-Midwestern fortune, are setting off those Geiger counters in Desert D'Or.

I didn't know if I was more pleased or more horrified. "Don't they ever get a name right?" I blustered. Lulu began to tickle me. "You know that's not bad. They could have been a lot nastier," she said. "Atom Bomb Lulu Meyers. Do you think people really think of me that way?"

"Of course they don't. You know your press agent wrote it."

"I don't care. It's still interesting." Like so many name-people in Desert D'Or, it didn't matter to Lulu that the news came from her. Seeing the printed lines made an alchemy—I know our affair was more real to her. "Geiger counters," Lulu said thoughtfully, "that's a smart line, publicity-wise. Oh, he's a good press agent. I'm going to call him in a day or two."

Now that our romance was publicly big, or better, torrid, Lulu started to confuse people again. "They make Sugar sound so good in the newspapers," she said one night to some people in a bar, "that I'll really try him. I really will, Sugar." And she gave me a sisterly kiss. Older sister.

We soon found something new to fight about. I discovered that to make love to Lulu was to make myself a scratch-pad to the telephone. It was always ringing, and no moment was long enough to keep her from answering. Her delight was to pass the first few rings. "Don't be so nervous, Sugar," she would say, "let the switchboard suffer," but before the phone had screamed five times, she would pick it up. Almost always, it was business. She would be talking to Herman Teppis, or Munshin who was back in the capital, or a writer, or her director for the next picture, or an old boy friend, or once her hairdresser—Lulu was interested in a hair-do she had seen. The conversation could not go on for two minutes before she was teasing me again; to make love and talk business was a double-feature to her.

"Of course I'm being a good girl, Mr. Teppis," she would say, giving me a wink. "How can you think these things of me?" As the end in virtuosity, she succeeded one time in weeping through a phone call with Teppis while rendering a passage with me.

I would try to get her to visit my place but she had grown an aversion. "It depresses me, Sugar, it's in such bland taste." For a while everything would be bland. Her own place was now spoiled by that word, and one day she told the management to have her room suite redecorated. Between morning and evening its beige walls were painted to a special blue, which Lulu claimed was her best color. Now she lay with her gold head on pale-blue linen, ordering pink roses and red roses from the telephone; the florist at the Yacht Club promised to arrange them himself. She would buy a dress and give it to her maid before she had even worn it; she would complain she had not a thing to wear. Her new convertible she traded in one afternoon for the same model in another color, and yet the exchange cost her close to a thousand dollars. When I reminded her that she had to drive the new car slowly until it accumulated the early mileage, she hired a chauffeur to trundle it through the desert and spare her the bother. Her first phone bill from the Yacht Club was five hundred dollars.

Yet when it came to making money she was also a talent. While I knew her, negotiations were on for a three-picture contract. She would phone her lawyers, they would call her agent, the agent would speak to Teppis, Teppis would speak to her. She asked a big price and got more than three quarters of it. "I can't stand my father," she explained to me, "but he's a gambler at business. He's wonderful that way." It came out that when she was thirteen and going to a school for professional children in the capital, Magnum Pictures wanted to sign her to a seven-year contract. "I'd be making a stinking seven hundred and fifty a week now like all those poor exploited schnooks, but Daddy wouldn't let me. 'Free-lance,' he said, he talks that way, 'this country was built on free-lance.' He's just a chiropodist with holdings in real estate, but he knew what to do for me." Her toes nibbled at the telephone cord. "I've noticed that about men. There's a kind of man who never can make money for himself. Only for others. That's my father."

Of her father and mother, Lulu's opinion changed by the clock. One round it would be her father who was marvelous. "What a bitch my mother is. She just squeezed all the manhood out of him. Poor Daddy." Her mother had ruined her life, Lulu explained. "I never wanted to be an actress. She made me one. It's her ambition. She's just an . . . octopus." Several phone calls later, Lulu would be chatting with her mother. "He's what? . . . He's acting up again. . . . Well, you tell him to leave you alone. I wouldn't put up with it if I were you. I would have divorced him long ago. I certainly would. . . ."

"I don't know what I'd do without her," Lulu would say on hanging up the phone, "men are terrible," and she would have nothing to do with me for the next half hour.

It took me longer than it need have taken to realize that the heart of her pleasure was to show herself. She hated holding something in. If Lulu felt like burping, she would burp; if it came up that she wanted to put cold cream on her face, she would do it while entertaining half a dozen people. So it went with her acting. She could say to a stranger that she was going to be the greatest actress in the world. Once, talking to a stage director, she was close to tears because the studio never gave her a part in a serious picture. "They ruin me," she complained. "People don't want glamour, they want acting. I'd take the smallest role if it was something I could get my teeth into." Still, she quarreled for three days running, and how many hours on the telephone I could never guess, because Munshin, who was producing her next picture, would not enlarge her part. Publicity, she announced, was idiotic, but with her instinct for what was good to an adolescent, she did better than co-operate with photographers. The best ideas always came from Lulu. One sortie when she was photographed sipping a soda she shaped the second straw into a heart, and the picture as it was printed in the newspapers showed Lulu peeping through the heart, coy and cool. On the few times I would be allowed to spend the night with her, I would wake up to see Lulu writing an idea for publicity in the notebook she kept on her bed table, and I had a picture of her marriage to Eitel, each of them with his own notebook and own bed table. With pleasure, she would expound the subtleties of being well photographed. I learned that the core of her dislike for Teddy Pope was that each of them photographed best from the left side of the face, and when they played a scene together Teddy was as quick as Lulu not to expose his bad side to the camera. "I hate to play with queers," she complained. "They're too smart. I thought I had mumps when I saw myself. Boy, I threw a scene." Lulu acted it for my private ear. "You've ruined me, Mr. Teppis," she shrieked. "There's no chivalry left."

For odd hours, during those interludes she called at her caprice, things had come around a bit. To my idea of an interlude that must have left her exhausted, she coached me by degrees to something different. Which was all right with me. Lulu's taste was for games, and if

she lay like a cinder under the speed of my sprints, her spirits improved with a play. I was sure no two people ever had done such
things nor even thought of them. We were great lovers, I felt in my
pride; I had pity for the hordes who could know none of this. Yes,
Lulu was sweet. She would never allow comparison. This was the best.
I was superb. She was superb. We were beyond all. Unlike Eitel, who
now could not bear to hear a word of Elena's old lovers, I was charitable to all of Lulu's. Why should I not be? She had sworn they were
poor sticks to her Sugar. I was even so charitable that I argued in
Eitel's defense. Lulu had marked him low as a lover, and in a twist of
friendship my heart beat with spite. I stopped that quickly enough. I
had an occasional idea by now of when Lulu was lying, and I wanted
to set Eitel at my feet, second to the champion. It pleased me in my big
affair that I had such a feel for the ring.

We played our games. I was the photographer and she was the
model; she was the movie star and I was the bellhop; she did the
queen, I was slave. We even met even to even. The game she loved
was to play the bobby-soxer who sat with a date in the living room and
was finally convinced, always for the first time naturally enough. She
was never so happy as when we acted at theater and did the mime on
clouds of myth. I was just young enough to want nothing but to be
alone with her. It was not even possible to be tired. Each time she gave
the signal, and I could never know, not five minutes in advance, when
it would happen, my appetite was sharp, dressed by the sting of what
I suffered in public.

To eat a meal with her in a restaurant became the new torture. It
didn't matter with what friends she found herself nor with what enemies—her attention would go, her eye would flee. It always seemed to
her that the conversation at another table was more interesting than
what she heard at her own. She had the worry that she was missing a
word of gossip, a tip, a role in a picture, a financial transaction, a . . . it
did not matter; something was happening somewhere else, something
of importance, something she could not afford to miss. Therefore,
eating with her was like sleeping with her; if one was cut by the telephone, the other was rubbed by her itch to visit from table to table,
sometimes dragging me, sometimes parking me, until I had to wonder what mathematical possibility there was for Lulu to eat a meal in
sequence, since she was always having a bit of soup here and a piece of
pastry there, joining me for breast of squab, and taking off to greet
new arrivals whose crabmeat cocktail she nibbled on. There was no
end, no beginning, no surety that one would even see her during a

meal. I remember a dinner when we went out with Dorothea O'Faye and Martin Pelley. They had just been married and Lulu treasured them. Dorothea was an old friend, a dear friend, Lulu promised me, and before ten minutes she was gone. When Lulu finally came back, she perched on my lap and said in a whisper the others could hear, "Sugar, I tried, and I couldn't make doo-doo. Isn't that awful? What should I eat?"

Five minutes later she outmaneuvered Pelley to pick up the check.

From *The Deer Park* (1955)

# GETTING TO KNOW YOU—I

## Miking It

Back in 1953, stoned on pot, wafted up and down on Seconal, jammed with ambition, terror, and the common lust to learn the secrets of the world some easy way, the immersion into TV was profound. By it, one could study the world, and the tricks of the world. Watching Steve Allen taught much, for example, about American fellatio. A twinkle would light up in Allen's eye as he took the mike and cord down the aisle and in and out of impromptu interviews with his audience, snaking the rounded knob right up to the mouth of some starched skinny Middle West matron, lean as whipcord, tense as rectitude, a life of iron disciplines in the vertical wrinkles of the upper lip. The lady would bare her teeth in a snarl and show a shark's mouth as she brought her jaws around to face and maybe bite off that black dob of a knob so near to touching her tongue.

A high school girl would be next, there with the graduating class on a trip to New York, her folks watching back home. She would swoon before the mike. She could not get her mouth open. She would keep dodging in her seat, and Steve would stay in pursuit, mike extended. Two nights ago she had dodged for two hours in the back seat of a car. My God, this was in public.

A young housewife, liberal, sophisticated, happy to present her congenial point of view, compliments Mr. Allen on the quality of his show. "We watch you regularly, Steve, and like to think we're not too far behind the times up in Norfolk, Connecticut. That's right, Nor-

folk, not Norwalk." Her mouth, which has regular lips, is held a regular distance from the microphone. She shows no difficulty with it, no
more than she would have with a phallus; two fingers and a thumb
keep the thing canted right. There can be nothing wrong, after all, in
relations between consenting adults. So speaks her calm.

Then there is a big heavy-set man who owns a grain-and-feed
store in Ohio. He prides himself on imperturbable phlegm, and some
thrift with words. He is not quite aware of the mike. If a man came
into his store and proceeded to expose himself, this proprietor would
not see it right away. He might, after all, be explaining the merits and
demerits of one feed-mix compared to another. Since he chews no
gum when he walks, neither does he offer attention to tangentia as he
talks. Now, singled out from the audience to be interviewed, he is stiff-
necked, and responds only from that side of his mouth adjacent to the
cheek on which Steve is asking the questions. He allows, "New York is
a good place to visit, but, yessir, I'll be glad to start up for home," then,
bla-looh! he sees it, black blimp-like little object! He blinks, he swallows, he looks at Steve: "I guess I've had my say, Mr. Allen," he says,
and shuts up shop. Later he will tell a pinochle partner about the
crazy people in New York. "Yes," the friend will acknowledge.

"You bet, Steve," says the next fellow, "I'm awfully glad you selected me. I've always wanted to talk to you." He is fully aware of the
mike and what it portends. "Yes, yes, I'm a male secretary, love the
work." "It doesn't bother you," asks Steve, "if people say, 'What is that,
a male secretary, isn't it supposed to be women's work?' " "Oh, Steve,
that doesn't bother me a bit. Here," he says, reaching for the mike.
"Do you mind? I'm much more comfortable when I hold it."

"Help yourself," says Steve.

"Oh, I intend to," says the guest. "Life is a feast, and I think we
should all get what we can, don't you?"

From *Pieces and Pontifications* (1982)

# GETTING TO
# KNOW YOU—II

## Homage to El Loco

The mind returns to the comedy and the religious dedication of the bullfight. Late afternoons of color—hues of lavender, silver, pink, orange silk, and gold in the *traje de luces*—now begin to play in one's mind against the small sharp impact on the eyes of horseballs falling like eggs between the frightened legs of the horse, and the flanks of the bull glistening with the sheen of a dark wet wood. And the blood. The bullfight always gets back to the blood. It pours in gouts down the forequarters of the bull—it wells from the hump of his *morrillo,* and moves in waves of bright red along the muscles of his chest and the heaving of his sides. If he has been killed poorly and the sword goes through his lung, then the animal dies in vomitings of blood. If the matador is working close to the animal, the suit of lights becomes stained—the dark bloodstain is honorable. It is also steeped in horror. The life of the bright red blood of an animal river pouring forth becomes some other life as it darkens down to the melancholy hues of an old dried blood that speaks in some lost primitive tongue about the mysteries of death, color, and corruption. The dried blood reminds you of the sordid glory of the bullfight, its hint of the Renaissance when noble figures stated their presence as they paraded through the marketplace and passed by cripples with stumps for legs, a stump for a tongue, and the lewdest grin of the day. Yes, the spectrum of the bullfight goes from courage to gangrene.

In Mexico, the hour before the fight is always the best hour of the week. It would be memorable not to sound like Hemingway, but in fact you would get happy the night before just thinking of that hour next day. Outside the Plaza Mexico, cheap cafés open only on Sunday and huge as beer gardens, filled with the public (us tourists, hoodlums, pimps, pickpurses, and molls, Mexican variety—which is to say the whores had headdresses and hindquarters not to be seen elsewhere on earth, for their hair rose vertically twelve inches from the head, and their posteriors projected horizontally twelve inches back into that space the rest of the whore had just marched through). The mariachis were out with their romantic haunting caterwauling of guitar, violin, songs of carnival, and trumpet, their song told of hearts that were true and hearts which were broken, and the wail of the broken heart went right into the trumpet until there were times when drunk the right way on tequila or Mexican rum—it was perhaps the best sound heard this side of Miles Davis. You hear a hint of all that in the Tijuana Brass.

You see, my friends, the wild hour was approaching. The horrors of the week in Mexico were coming to term. Indeed, no week in Mexico is without its horrors for every last Mexican alive—it is a city and a country where the bones of the dead seem to give the smell of their char to every desert wind and auto exhaust and frying tortilla. The mournfulness of unrequited injustice hangs a shroud across the centuries. Every Mexican is gloomy until the instant he becomes happy, and then he is a maniac. He howls, he whistles, smoke of murder passes off his pores, he bullies, he beseeches friendship, he is a clown, a brigand, a tragic figure suddenly merry. The intellectuals and the technicians of Mexico abominate their national character because it is always in the way. It puts the cracks in the plaster of new buildings, it forgets to cement the tiles, it leaves rags in the new pipes of new office buildings and forgets to put the gas cap back on the tank. So the intellectuals and the technicians hate the bullfight as well. You cannot meet a socialist in Mexico who approves of the running of the bulls. They are trying to turn Mexico into a modern country, and thus the same war goes on there that goes on in three-quarters of the world— battlefront is the new highways to the suburbs, and the corporation's office buildings, the walls of hospital white, and the myopic sheets of glass. In Mexico, like everywhere else, it is getting harder and harder to breathe in a mood through the pores of the city, because more and more of the city is being covered with corporation architecture, with surgical dressing. To the vampires and banshees and dried blood on the curses of the cactus in the desert is added the horror of the new technology in an old murder-ridden land. And four o'clock on Sunday is the beginning of release for some of the horrors of the week. If many come close to feeling the truth only by telling a lie, so Mexicans come close to love by watching the flow of blood on an animal's flanks and the certain death of the bull before the bravery and/or humiliation of the bullfighter.

I could never have understood it if someone tried to explain ahead of time, and in fact, I came to love the bullfight long before I comprehended the first thing about why I did. That was very much to the good. There are not too many experiences a radical American intellectual could encounter in those days (when the youngest generation was called the silent generation) that invaded his sure sense of his own intellectual categories. I did not like the first bullfights I saw—the formality of the ritual bored me, the fights appeared poor (indeed they were), and the human content of the spectacle came out atrocious. Narcissistic matadors, vain when they made a move, pouting like a girl stood up on Saturday night when the crowd turned on them, clumsy at killing, and the crowd, brutal to a man. In the Plaza Mexico, the Indians in the cheap seats buy a paper cup of beer and when they are done drinking, the walk to the W.C. is *miles* away, and besides they are usually feeling sullen, so they urinate in their paper cup and hurl it down in a cascade of harvest gold, Indian piss. If you are an American escorting an American girl who has blond hair, and you have tickets in *Sol,* you buy your girl a cheap sombrero at the gate, for otherwise she will be a prime target of attention. Indeed, you do well not to sit near an American escorting a blonde whose head is uncovered, for the aim of a drunken Indian is no better than you when your aim is drunk. So no surprise if one's early detestation of the bullfight was fortified in kidney brew, Azteca.

Members of a minority group are always ready to take punishment, however, and I was damned if I was going to be excluded from still another cult. So I persisted in going to bullfights, and they were a series of lousy bullfights, and then the third or fourth time I got religion. It was a windy afternoon, with threats of rain, and now and then again ten minutes of rain, poisonous black clouds overhead, the chill gloom of a black sky on Sundays in Mexico, and the particular torero (whose name I could not recall for anything) was a clod. He had a nasty build. Little spindly legs, too big a chest, a butt that was broad and stolid, real peasant ass, and a vulgar worried face with a gold tooth. He was engaged with an ugly bull who kept chopping at the muleta with his horns, and occasionally the bull would catch the muleta and fling it in the air and trample it and wonder why the object was either dead or not dead, the bull smelling a hint of his own blood (or the blood of some cousin) on the blood of the muleta, and the crowd would hoot, and the torero would go over to his sword handler at the barrera, and shake his head and come out with a new muleta, and the bull would chop, and the wind would zig the muleta out of control, and then the matador would drop it and scamper back to the barrera, and the crowd would jeer and the piss would fly in yellow arcs of rainbow through the rain all the way down from the cheap seats, and the whores would make farting sounds with their spoiled knowledgeable mouths, while the aficionados would roll their eyes, and the sound of Mexican laughter, that operative definition of the echo of total disgust, would shake along like jelly-gasoline through the crowd.

I got a look at the bullfighter who was the center of all this. He was not a man I could feel something for. He had a cheap pimp's face and a dull, thoroughgoing vanity. His face, however, was now in despair. There was something going on for him more humiliating than humiliation—as if his life were going to take a turn into something more dreadful than anything it had encountered until now. He was in trouble. The dead dull fight he was giving was going to be death for certain hopes in his psyche. Somehow it was going to be more final than the average dead dull fight to which he was obviously all too accustomed. I was watching the despair of a profoundly mediocre man.

Well, he finally gave up any attempt to pass the bull, and he worked the animal forward with jerks of his muleta to left and right, a competent rather than a beautiful technique at best, and even to my untutored eye he was a mechanic at this, and more whistles, and then, desperation all over that vain incompetent pimp's face, he profiled with his sword, and got it halfway in, and the animal took a few steps to one side and the other and fell over quickly.

The art of killing is the last skill you learn to judge in bullfighting, and the kill on this rainy afternoon left me less impressed than the crowd. Their jeers were replaced by applause (later I learned the crowd would always applaud a kill in the lung—all audiences are Broadway audiences) and the approbation continued sufficiently for the torero to take a tour of the ring. He got no ears, he certainly didn't deserve them, but he had his tour and he was happy, and in his happiness there was something suddenly likable about him, and I sensed that I was passing through some interesting emotions since I had felt contempt for a stranger and then a secret and most unsocialistic desire to see this type I did not like humiliated a little further, and then in turn I was quietly but most certainly overcome by his last-minute success sufficiently to find myself liking a kind of man I had never considered near to human before. So this bad bullfight in the rain had given a drop of humanity to a very dry area of my heart, and now I knew a little more and had something to think about which was no longer altogether in category.

We have presented the beginning of a history then—no, say it better—the origin of an addiction. For a drug's first appeal is always existential—our sense of life is thereupon so full of need as the desire for a breath of air. The sense of life comes alive in the happy days when the addict first encounters his drug. But all histories of addiction are the same—particularly in the beginning. They fall into the larger category of the history of a passion. So I will spare each and every one of us the titles of the books I read on the running of the bulls, save to mention the climactic purchase of a three-volume set in leather for fifty 1954 dollars (now doubtless in value one hundred) of *Los Toros* by Cossío. Since it was entirely in Spanish, a language I read with about as much ease and pleasure as Very Old English, *Los Toros* remains in my library as a cornerstone of my largest mental department—*The Bureau of Abandoned Projects:* I was going to write *the* novel about bullfight, dig!

Nor will I reminisce about the great bullfighters I saw, of the majesties of Arruza and the *machismo* of Procuna, the liquidities of Silverio and the solemnity of César Girón, no, we will not micturate the last of such memory to tell a later generation about El Ranchero and Ortiz of the Orticina, and Angel Peralta the Rejoneador, nor of Manolete, for he was dead long before I could with confidence distinguish a bull from a heifer or a steer, and no more can I talk of Luis Miguel and Antonio, for neither of them have I seen in a fight, so that all I know of Ordóñez is his reputation, and of Dominguín his style, for I caught his work in a movie once and it was not work the way he made it look. No, enough of these qualifications for *afición.* The fact is that I do not dwell on Arruza and Procuna and Silverio and Girón and Peralta and Ranchero because I did not see them that often and in fact most of them I saw but once. I was always in Mexico in the summer, you see, and the summer is the *temporada de novillos,* which is to say it is the time when the *novilladas* are held, which is to say it is the time of the novices.

Now the fellow who is pushing up this preface for you is a great lover of the bullfight—make on it no mistake. For a great bullfight he would give up just about any other athletic or religious spectacle—the

World Series in a minute, a pro football championship, a mass at the Vatican, perhaps even a great heavyweight championship—which is really saying it. No love like the love for four in the afternoon at the Plaza Mexico. Yet all the great matadors he saw were seen only at special festivals when they fought very small bulls for charity. The novillada is, after all, the time of the novilleros, and a novillero is a bullfighter approximately equal in rank to a Golden Gloves fighter. A very good novillero is like a very good Golden Gloves finalist. The Sugar Ray Robinsons and the Rocky Marcianos of the bullfighting world were glimpsed by me only when they came out of retirement long enough to give the equivalent of a snappy two-round exhibition. My love of bullfighting, and my experience of it as a spectator, was founded then by watching novilleros week after week over two separate summers in Mexico City. So I know as much about bullfighting as a man would know about boxing if he read a lot and heard a lot about great fighters and saw a few movies of them and one or two exhibitions, and also had the intense, if partial, fortune to follow two Golden Gloves tournaments all the way and to follow them with some lively if not always dependable instinct for discerning what was good and what was not so good in the talent before him.

After a while I got good at seeing the flaws and virtues in novilleros, and in fact I began to see so much of their character in their style, and began to learn so much about style by comprehending their character (for nearly everything good or bad about a novice bullfighter is revealed at a great rate), that I began to take the same furious interest and partisanship in the triumph of one style over another that is usually reserved for literary matters (is Philip Roth better than John Updike?—you know) or what indeed average Americans and some not so average might take over political figures. To watch a bullfighter have an undeserved triumph on Sunday afternoon when you detest his style is not the worst preparation for listening to Everett Dirksen nominate Barry Goldwater or hearing Lyndon Johnson give a lecture on TV about Amurrican commitments to the free universe. Everything bad and God-awful about the style of life got into the style of bullfighters, as well as everything light, delightful, honorable, and good.

At any rate, about the time I knew a lot about bullfighting, or as much as you could know watching nothing but novilleros week after week, I fell in love with a bullfighter. I never even met this bullfighter, I rush to tell you. I would not have wanted to meet him. Meeting him could only have spoiled the perfection of my love, so pure was my affection. And his name—not one in a thousand of you out there can have heard of him—his name was El Loco. El Loco, the Crazy One. It is not a term of endearment in Mexico, where half the populace is crazy. To amplify the power of nomenclature, El Loco came from the provinces, he was God's own hick, and his real name was Amado Ramírez, which is like being a boy from Hicksville, Georgia, with a name like Beloved Remington. Yet there was a time when I thought Beloved Remington, which is to say Amado Ramírez, would become the greatest bullfighter in the whole world, and there were critics in Mexico City hoary with *afición* who held the same opinion (if not always in print). He came up one summer a dozen years ago like a rocket, but a rocket with one tube hot and one tube wet, and he spun in circles all over the bullfighting world of Mexico City all through the summer and fall.

But we must tell more of what it is like to watch novilleros. You see, novice bullfighters fight bulls who are called *novillos,* and these bulls are a year younger and two to four hundred pounds lighter than the big fighting bulls up around a thousand pounds that matadors must face. So novillo bulls are less dangerous. They can still kill a man, but not often does that happen—they are more likely to pound and stomp and wound and bruise a novillero than to catch him and play him in the air and stab him up high on the horns the way a terrible full-grown fighting bull can do. In consequence, the analogy to the Golden Gloves is imperfect, for a talented novillero can at his best look as exciting as, or more exciting than, a talented matador—the novice's beast is smaller and less dangerous, so his lack of experience is compensated for by his relative comfort—he is in less danger of getting killed. (Indeed, to watch a consummate matador like Carlos Arruza work with a new young bull is like watching Norman Mailer box with his three-year-old son—absolute mastery is in the air.)

Novilleros possess another virtue. Nobody can contest their *afición.* For every novillero who has a manager, and a rich man to house and feed him, and influential critics to bring him along on the sweet of a bribe or two, there are a hundred devoted all but unknown novilleros who hitch from *poblado* to *poblado* on back dirt roads for the hint of a chance to fight at some fiesta so small the results are not even phoned to Mexico City. Some of these kids spend years in the provinces living on nothing, half-starved in the desire to spend a life fighting bulls, and they will fight anything—bulls who are overweight, calves who are under the legal limit, beasts who have fought before and so are sophisticated and dangerous. These provincial novilleros get hurt badly by wounds that show no blood, deep bruises in the liver and kidney from the flat of a horn, deep internal bleedings in the gut, something lively taken off the groin—a number of them die years later from malnutrition and chronic malfunctions of some number of those organs. Their deaths get into no statistics on the fatalities of the bullfight.

A few of these provincial novilleros get enough fights and enough experience and develop enough talent, however, to pick up a reputation of sorts. If they are very lucky and likable, or have connections, or hump themselves—as some will—to rich homosexuals in the capital, then they get their shot. Listen to this. At the beginning of the novillada, six new bullfighters are brought in every Sunday to fight one bull each in the Plaza Mexico. For six or eight weeks this goes on. Perhaps fifty fighters never seen before in Mexico City have their chance. Maybe ten will be seen again. The tension is enormous for each novillero. If he fails to have a triumph or attract outstanding attention, then his years in the provinces went for nothing. Back again he will go to the provinces as a punishment for failing to be superb. Perhaps he will never fight again in the Plaza Mexico. His entire life depends on this one fight. And even this fight depends on luck. For any novillero can catch a poor bull, a dull mediocre cowardly bull. When the animal does not charge, the bullfighter, unless possessed of genius, cannot look good.

Once a novillero came into the Plaza on such an occasion, was hit by the bull while making his first pass, a veronica, and the boy and cape sailed into the air and came down together in such a way that when the boy rolled over, the cape wrapped around him like a tortilla, and one wit in *Sol,* full of the harsh wine of Mexico's harsh grapes, yelled out, "*Suerte de Enchiladas.*" The young bullfighter was named The Pass of the Enchiladas. His career could never be the same. He went on to fight that bull, did a decent honorable job—the crowd never stopped laughing. Suerte de Enchiladas. He was branded. He walked off in disgrace. The one thing you cannot be in any land where Spanish is spoken is a clown. I laughed with the rest. The bullfight is nine-tenths cruelty. The bullfight brews one's cruelty out of one's pores—it makes an elixir of cruelty. But it does something else. It reflects the proportions of life in Latin lands. For in Mexico it does not seem unreasonable that a man should spend years learning a dangerous trade, be rapped once by a bull, and end up ruined, a Suerte de Enchiladas. It is unfair, but then life is monstrously unfair, one knows that—one of the few gleams in the muck of all this dubious Mexican majesty called existence is that one can on occasion laugh bitterly with the gods. In the Spanish-Indian blood, the substance of one's dignity is found in sharing the cruel vision of the gods. In fact, dignity can be found nowhere else. For courage is seen as the servant of the gods' cruel vision.

On to Beloved Remington. He arrived in Mexico City at the end of the beginning of the novillada in the summer of 1954. He was there, I think, on the next to last of the early Sundays when six bulls were there for six novilleros. (In the full season of the novillada, when the best new young men have been chosen, there are six bulls for only three toreros—each kid then has two bulls, two chances.) I was not yet in Mexico for Amado Ramírez's first Sunday, but I heard nothing else from my bullfighting friends from the day I got in. He had appeared as the last of six novilleros. It had been a terrible day. All of the novilleros had been bad. He apparently had been the last and the worst, and had looked so clumsy that the crowd in derision had begun to applaud him. There is no sign of displeasure greater among the Mexican bullfighting public than to turn their ovations upside down. But Ramírez had taken bows. Serious solemn bows. He had bowed so much he had hardly fought the bull. The Plaza Mexico had rung with merriment. It took him forever to kill the beast—he received a tumultuous ovation. He took a turn of the ring. A wit shouted *"Ole, El Loco."* He was named. When they cheer incompetence they are ready to set fire to the stadium.

El Loco was the sensation of the week. A clown had fought a bull in the Plaza Mexico and gotten out alive. The promoters put him on the following week as a seventh bullfighter, an extra added attraction. He was not considered worth the dignity of appearing on the regular card. For the first time that season, the Plaza was sold out. It was also the first fight I was to see of my second season.

Six young novilleros fought six mediocre bulls that day, and gave six mediocre fights. The crowd grew more and more sullen. When there is no good bullfight, there is no catharsis. One's money has been spent, the drinks are wearing down, and there has been no illumination, no moment to burn away all that spiritual sewer gas from the horrors of the week. Dull violence breeds, and, with it, contempt for all bullfighters. An ugly Mexican bullfighting crowd has the temper of a street corner in Harlem after the police wagon has rounded up the nearest five studs and hauled them away.

Out came the clown, El Loco. The special seventh bullfighter. He was an apparition. He had a skinny body and a funny ugly face with little eyes set close together, a big nose, and a little mouth. He had very black Indian hair, and a tuft in the rear of his head stood up like the spike of an antenna. He had very skinny legs and they were bent at the knee so that he gave the impression of trudging along with a lunchbox in his hand. He had comic buttocks. They went straight back like a duck's tail feathers. His suit fit poorly. He was some sort of grafting between Ray Bolger and Charlie Chaplin. And he had the sense of self-importance to come out before the bull—he was indeed given a turn of the ring before he even saw the bull. An honor granted him for his appearance the week before. He was altogether solemn. It did not seem comic to him. He had the kind of somber extravagant ceremoniousness of a village mayor in a mountain town come out to greet the highest officials of the government. His knees stuck out in front. The Plaza rocked and rocked. Much applause followed by circulating zephyrs of laughter. And under it all, like a croaking of frogs, the beginnings of the biggest thickest Bronx raspberry anybody living ever heard.

Amado Ramírez went out to receive the bull. His first pass was a yard away from the animal, his second was six feet. He looked like a fifty-five-year-old peon ready to retire. The third pass caught his cape, and as it flew away on the horns, El Loco loped over to the barrera with a gait like a kangaroo. A thunderstorm of boos was on its way. He held out his arm horizontally, an injunction to the crowd, fingers spread, palm down, a mild deprecatory peasant gesture, as if to say, "Wait, you haven't seen nothing yet." The lip-farters began to smack. Amado went back out. He botched one pass, looked poor on a basic veronica. Boos, laughter, even the cops in the aisle were laughing. *Que payaso!*

His next pass had a name, but few even of the *afición* knew it, for it was an old-fashioned pass of great intricacy that spoke of the era of Belmonte and El Gallo and Joselito. It was a pass of considerable danger, plus much formal content (for a flash it looked like he was inclining to kiss a lady's hand, his cape draped over his back, while the bull went roaring by his unprotected ass). If I remember, it was called a *gallicina,* and no one had seen it in five years. It consisted of whirling in a reverse *serpentina* counterclockwise into the bull, so that the cape was wrapped around your body just like the Suerte de Enchiladas, except you were vertical; but the timing was such that the bull went by at the moment your back was to him and you could not see his horns. Then the whirling continued, and the cape flared out again. Amado was clumsy in his approach and stepped on his cape when he was done, but there was one moment of lightning in the middle when you saw clear sky after days of fog and smelled the ozone. There was an instant of heaven—finest thing I had yet seen in the bullfight—and in a sob of torture and release, "Olé" came in a panic of disbelief from one parched Mexican throat near to me. El Loco did the same pass one more time and then again. On the second pass, a thousand cried "Olé," and on the third, the Plaza exploded and fifty thousand men and women gave up the word at the same time. Something merry and corny as a gypsy violin flowed out of his cape.

After that, nothing but comedy again. He tried a dozen fancy passes—none worked well. They were all wild, solemn, courtly, and he was there with his knobby knees. The crowd laughed with tears in their eyes. With the muleta he looked absurd, a man about to miss a train and so running with his suitcase. It took him forever to kill and he stood out like an old lady talking to a barking dog, but he could do no wrong now for this crowd—they laughed, they applauded, they gave him a tour of the ring. For something had happened in those three passes that no one could comprehend. It was as if someone like me had gotten in the ring with Cassius Clay and for twenty seconds had clearly outboxed him. The only explanation was divine intervention. So El Loco was back to fight two bulls next week.

If I remember, he did little with either bull, and killed the second one just before the third *aviso*. In a good season, his career would have been over. But it was a dreadful season. A couple of weeks of uneventful bullfights and El Loco was invited back. He looked awful in his first fight, green of face, timid, unbelievably awkward with the cape, morose, and abominably prudent with the muleta. He killed badly. So badly in fact that he was still killing the bull when the third *aviso* sounded. The bull was let out alive. A dull sullen silence riddled with Mexican whistles. The crowd had had a bellyful of laughs with him. They were now getting very bored with the joke.

But the second bull he liked. Those crazy formal courtly passes, the *gallicinas*, whirled out again, and the horns went by his back six inches away. Olé. He went to put the banderillas in himself and botched the job, had to run very fast on the last pair to escape the bull and looked like a chicken as he ran. The catcalls tuned up again. The crowd was like a bored lion uncertain whether to eat entrails or lick a face. Then he came out with the muleta and did a fine series of *derechazos*, the best seen in several weeks, and to everyone's amazement, he killed on the first *estocada*. They gave him an ear. He was the *triunfador* of the day.

This was the afternoon which confirmed the beginning of a career. After that, most of the fights are mixed in memory because he had so many, and they were never without incident, and they took place years ago. All through the summer of 1954, he fought just about every week, and every week something happened which shattered the comprehension of the most veteran bullfighting critic. They decided after this first triumph that he was a mediocre novillero with nothing particular to recommend him except a mysterious flair for the *gallicina* and a competence with the *derechazo*. Otherwise, he was uninspired with the cape and weak with the muleta. So the following week he gave an exhibition with the muleta. He did four *pases de pecho* so close and luminous (a pass is luminous when your body seems to lift with breath as it goes by) that the horns flirted with his heart. He did *derechazos* better than the week before, and finished with *manoletinas*. Again he killed well. They gave him two ears. Then his second bull went out alive. A *fracaso*.

Now the critics said he was promising with the muleta but weak with the cape. He could not do a veronica of any value. So in one of the following weeks he gave five of the slowest, most luminous, most soaring veronicas anyone had ever seen.

Yet for three weeks in a row, if he cut ears on one bull, he let the other go out alive. A bullfighter is not supposed to let his animal outlive three *avisos*. Indeed if the animal is not killed before the first *aviso*, the torero is in disgrace already. Two *avisos* is like the sound of the knell of the bell in the poorhouse, and a bullfighter who hears the third *aviso* and has to let his bull go out alive is properly ready for hara-kiri. No sight, you see, is worse. It takes something like three to five minutes from the first *aviso* to the last, and in that time the kill becomes a pigsticking. Because the torero has tried two, three, four, five times, even more, to go in over the horns, and he has hit bone, and he has left the sword half in but in some abominable place like the middle of the back or the flank, or he has had a perfect thrust and the bull does not die and minutes go by waiting for it to die and the peons run up with their capes and try to flick the sword out by swirling cloth around the pommel guard and giving a crude Latin yank—nothing is cruder than a peon in a sweat for his boss. Sometimes they kick the bull in the nuts in the hope it will go down, and the crowd hoots. Sometimes the bull sinks to its knees and the puntillero comes in to sever its neck with a thrust of his dagger, but the stab is off-center, the spinal cord is not severed. Instead it is stimulated by the shock and the dying bull gets up and wanders all over the ring looking for its *queren-*

*cia* while blood drains and drips from its wounds and the bullfighter, looking ready to cry, trots along like a farmer accompanying his mule down the road. And the next *aviso* blows. Such scenes are a nightmare for the torero. He will awaken from dreams where he is stabbing and stabbing over the horns with the *descabellar* and the bull does not drop but keeps jerking his head. A bull going out alive because the torero was not able to kill him in the allotted time is a sight about as bloody and attractive as a victim getting out of a smashed car and stumbling down the road, and the matador is about as popular as the man who caused the accident. The average torero can afford less than one occasion a year when three *avisos* are heard. El Loco was allowing an average of one bull a week to go out unkilled. One may get an idea of how good he was when he was good, if one appreciates a prizefighter who is so good that he is forgiven even if every other fight he decides to climb out of the ring and quit.

For a period, criticism of El Loco solidified. He had brilliant details, he was able on occasion to kill with inspiration, he had huge talent, but he lacked the indispensable ingredient of the bullfighter—he did not know how to get a good performance out of a bad bull. He lacked tenacity. So Ramírez created the most bizarre *faena* in anyone's memory, a fight that came near to shattering the rules of bullfighting. For on a given Sunday, he caught a very bad bull, and worked with him in all the dull, technical, unaesthetic ways a bullfighter has to work with an unpromising beast, and chopped him to left and to right, and kept going into the bull's *querencia* and coaxing him out— and this went on for minutes, while the public demonstrated its displeasure. And El Loco paid no attention and kept working with the bull, and then finally got the bull to charge and he made a few fine passes. But then the first *aviso* sounded and everyone groaned. Because finally the bull was going good, and yet Amado would have to kill him now. But Amado had his bull in shape and he was not going to give him up yet, and so with everyone on the scent of the loss of each second, he made derechazos and the pass with the muleta that looks like the *gaonera* with the cape, and he did a deliberate *adorno* or two and the second *aviso* sounded and he made an effort to kill and failed, but stayed very cool and built up the crowd again by taking the bull through a series of *naturales,* and with twenty seconds left before the third *aviso* and the Plaza in pandemonium he went in to kill and had a perfect *estocada* and the bull moved around softly and with dignity and died about ten seconds after the third *aviso*, but no one could hear the trumpet, for the crowd was in a delirium of thunder, and every white handkerchief in the place was out. And Amado was smiling, which is why you could love him, because his pinched ugly little peasant face was full of a kid's decent happiness when he smiled. And a minute later there was close to a riot against the judges, for they were not going to give him tail or two ears or even an ear—how could they if the bull had died after the third *aviso?*—and yet the tension of fighting the bull on the very edge of his time had given a quality to this fight that had more than a hint of the historic, for new emotions had been felt. The bullfighting public has a taste for new emotions equaled only by the lust of a lady greedy for new pleasures.

This record is in danger of becoming as predictable as any account of the triumphs of Caesar. Let us keep it alive with the fiascos. Amado was simply unlike any bullfighter who had ever come along. When he had a great fight, or even a great pass, it was unlike the passes of other fine novilleros—the passes of El Loco were better than anything you had ever seen. It was as if you were looking at the sky and suddenly a bird materialized in the air. And a moment later disappeared again. His work was frightening. It was simple, lyrical, light, illumined, but it came from nowhere and then was gone. When El Loco was bad, he was not mediocre or dull, he was simply the worst, most inept, and most comical bullfighter anyone had ever seen. He seemed to have no technique to fall back on. He would hold his cape like a shroud, his legs would bend at the knees, his sad ass seemed to have an eye for the exit, his expression was as morose as Fernandel's, and his feet kept tripping. He looked like a praying mantis on its hind legs. And when he was afraid he had a nerveless incapacity to kill which was so hopeless that the moment he stepped out to face his animal you knew he could not go near this particular bull. Yet when he was good, the comic body suddenly straightened, indeed took on the camber of the best back any Spanish aristocrat chose to display—the buttocks retired into themselves like a masterpiece of poise, and the cape and the muleta moved slowly as full sails, or whirled like the wing of that mysterious bird. It was as if El Loco came to be every comic Mexican who ever breathed the finest Spanish grace into his pores. For five odd minutes he was as completely transformed as Charlie Chaplin's tramp doing a consummate impersonation of the one and only Valentino, long-lost Rudolph.

Let me tell then of Amado's best fight. It came past the middle of that fine summer when he had an adventure every week in the Plaza and we had adventures watching him, for he had fights so mysterious that the gods of the bulls and the ghosts of dead matadors must have

come with the mothers and the witches of the centuries, homage to
Lorca! to see the miracles he performed. Listen! One day he had a
sweet little bull with nice horns, regular, pleasantly curved, and the
bull ran with gaiety, even abandon. Now we have to stop off here for
an imperative explanation. I beg your attention, but it is essential to
discuss the attitudes of *afición* to the *natural*. To them the *natural* is the
equivalent of the full parallel turn in skiing or a scrambling T-
formation quarterback or a hook off a jab—it cannot be done well by
all athletes no matter how good they are in other ways, and the *natural*
is, as well, a dangerous pass, perhaps the most dangerous there is.
The cloth of the muleta has no sword to extend its width. Now the
cloth is held in the left hand, the sword in the right, and so the target
of the muleta that is presented for the bull's attraction is half as large
as it was before and the bullfighter's body is thus so much bigger and
so much more worthy of curiosity to the beast—besides the bull is
wiser now, he may be ready to suspect it is the man who torments him
and not the swirling sinister chaos of the cloth in which he would bury
his head. Moreover—and here is the mystique of the *natural*—the
bullfighter has a psychic communion with the bull. With the muleta
he fights him usually with his right hand from a position of authority.
Switching the cloth to the left hand exposes his psyche as well as his
body. He feels less authority—in compensation his instinct plays closer
to the bull. But he is so vulnerable! So a *natural* inspires a bullfighting
public to hold their breath, for danger and beauty come close to meeting here.

It was *naturales* Amado chose to perform with this bull. He had
not done many this season. The last refuge of his detractors was that
he could not do *naturales*. So here on this day he gave his demonstration.

He began his *faena* by making no exploratory pass, no *pase de
muerte*, no *derechazos*—he never chopped, no, he went up to this sweet
bull and started his *faena* with a series of five *naturales* that were all
linked and all beautiful and had the Plaza in pandemonium because
where could he go from there? And Amado came up sweetly to the
bull, and did five more *naturales* as good as the first five, and then did
five more without moving from his spot—they were superb. Then, he
furled his muleta until it was the size of this page and he passed the
bull five more times in the same way, the horns going around his left
wrist. The man and the bull looked in love with each other.

After these twenty *naturales*, Amado did five more with almost no
muleta at all, five series of five *naturales* had he performed, twenty-five

*naturales*—it is not much easier than making love twenty-five times in a row—and then he knelt and kissed the bull on the forehead he was so happy, and got up delicately, and went to the barrera for his sword, came back, profiled to get ready for the kill. Everyone was sitting on a collective fuse. If he managed to kill on the first *estocada* this could well be the best *faena* anyone had ever seen a novillero perform—who knew, it was all near to unbelievable—and then just as he profiled, the bull charged prematurely, and Amado, determined to get the kill, did not skip away but held ground, received the charge, stood there with the sword, turned the bull's head with the muleta, and the bull impaled himself on the point of the torero's blade, which went right into the proper space between the shoulders, and the bull ran right up on it into his death, took several steps to the side, gave a toss of his head at heaven, and fell. Amado had killed *recibiendo*. He had killed standing still, receiving the bull while the bull charged. No one had seen that in years. So they gave him everything that day, ears, tail, *vueltas* without limit—they were ready to give him the bull.

He concluded the summer in a burst of honors. He had more great fights. Afterward they gave him a day where he fought six bulls all by himself, and he went on to take his *alternativa* and become a full-fledged matador. But he was a Mexican down to the bones. The honors all turned damp for him. I was not there the day he fought six bulls—I had had to go back to America and never saw him fight again. I heard about him only in letters and in bullfighting newspapers. But the day he took on the six bulls I was told he did not have a single good fight, and the day he took his *alternativa* to become a matador, both his bulls went out alive, a disgrace too great even for Amado. He fought a seventh bull. Gypsy magic might save him again. But the bull was big and dull and El Loco had no luck and no magic and just succeeded in killing him in a bad difficult dull fight. It was obvious he was afraid of the big bulls. So he relinquished his *alternativa* and went back to the provinces to try to regain his reputation and his nerve. And no one ever heard much of him again. Or at least I never did, but then I have not been back to Mexico. Now I suspect I'm one of the very few who remember the happiness of seeing him fight. He was so bad when he was bad that he gave the impression you could fight a bull yourself and do no worse. So when he was good, you felt as if you were good too, and that was something no other torero ever gave me, for when they were good they looked impenetrable, they were like gods, but when Beloved Remington was good, the whole human race was good—he spoke of the great distance a man can go from the worst in himself to the best, and that finally is what the bullfight might be all about, for in dark bloody tropical lands possessed of poverty and desert and swamp, filth and treachery, slovenliness, and the fat lizards of all the worst lust, the excretory lust to shove one's own poison into others, the one thing that can keep the sweet nerve of life alive is the knowledge that a man cannot be judged by what he is every day, but only in his greatest moment, for that is the moment when he shows what he was intended to be. It is a romantic self-pitying impractical approach to the twentieth century's demand for predictable ethics, high production, dependability of function, and categorization of impulse, but it is the Latin approach. Their allegiance is to the genius of the blood. So they judge a man by what he is at his best.

By that logic, I will always have love for El Loco because he taught me how to love the bullfight, and how to penetrate some of its secrets. And finally he taught me something about the mystery of form. He gave me the clue that form is the record of a war. Because he never had the ability most bullfighters, like most artists, possess to be false with their art, tasty yet phony, he taught something about life with every move he made, including the paradox that courage can be found in men whose conflict is caught between their ambition and their cowardice. He even taught me how to look for form in other places. Do you see the curve of a beautiful breast? It is not necessarily a gift of God—it may be the record life left on a lady of the balance of forces between her desire, her modesty, her ambition, her timidity, her maternity, and her sense of an impulse that cannot be denied. If we were wise enough, bold enough, and scholars from head to motorcyclist's boot, we could extract the real history of Europe from the form elucidated between man and beast that we glimpse again in recall of the bullfight. Indeed where is a writer or a lover without a knowledge of what goes on behind that cloth where shapes are born? *Olé*, Amado!

From *Existential Errands* (1972)

# THE COLD WAR—IV

## Imbibing Thursdays

The summer in D.C. was hot. The Thursdays were what I waited for.

They were certainly talked about. Over lunch in the cafeteria one hot day, two senior officers, friends of Cal, offered me disparate evaluations: "Much ado about nothing," said one. "He's so brilliant it's unholy," said the other. "Why, you don't know how fortunate you are to be selected."

The class, now in its third year, had been commenced as a seminar on Thursday afternoons for some of Harlot's staff plus young officers who had been recommended for a few of his projects. Those were Low Thursdays, but once a month, on what soon came to be called the High Thursdays, important guests showed up by invitation, as did visiting professionals whose Company labors had brought them back to D.C. from various lairs abroad.

On all occasions, we would meet around the conference table in Hugh Montague's outer office, a large room on the second floor of the yellow brick villa that Allen Dulles used for his headquarters. Situated on E Street, well away from the Reflecting Pool and Cockroach Alley, it was an elegant building larger than most of the foreign embassies in Washington. Harlot was one of the few high-ranking officers to work in such proximity to Dulles, and so an added zest was brought to the occasion by the importance of our surroundings. Indeed, Allen Dulles would keep popping in and out, a beeper in his breast pocket prodding him back to his own office, and once, I remember, he made a point of letting us know that he had just gotten off the phone with President Eisenhower.

The lectures on High Thursday were, of course, the most exceptional. Harlot's voice became even more commodious then, and he could not have been more unabashed in his use of rich syntax. How much one learned directly, however, is not easy to measure. He gave no assignments. He might recommend a book from time to time, but never pursued our diligence, no, it was more a matter of sowing the seeds. A few might sprout. Since the Director himself was not only our peripatetic guest but had obviously given his imprimatur, and would often nod at the sheer wonderful glory of the subject—"Ah," one could almost hear Mr. Dulles say, "this wonderfully shrewd and metaphysical and monumental world of Intelligence itself!"—it took no vast acumen on my part to recognize that come a High Thursday, Harlot would teach our group from the top down. His preference was to stimulate his equals: On such occasions, the rest of us could scramble how we might. Low days were of more use to us. Then, the course served, as Harlot once remarked, "to rev up the Mormons." There were five of them, Ph.D.s from state universities in the Midwest, and they were always taking notes, always in crew cut, white shirt with short sleeves, pens in the breast pocket, dark thin ties, eyeglasses. They looked like engineers, and I recognized after a time that they were the galley slaves over in Montague's counterespionage shop at TSS, marooned in prodigiously demanding tasks of cryptography, file-searching, estimate-vetting, etc. You could see it in their faces: They were signed up for a career of the highest level of clerking. I was, I admit, snobby, but then, as the son of a Bold Easterner, and thus, by titular descent, a Junior Bold Easterner, Ivy League out of Andover, Exeter, Groton, Middlesex, or Saints Paul, Mark, or Matthew, how could I not begin to feel well installed while listening to Hugh Montague? At full throttle on a High Thursday, he could employ rhetoric that was equal to high adventure. Since memory, for all its vicissitudes, can also be immaculate, I am tempted to swear that, word for word, this has to be close to the way he offered it.

"An understanding of counterespionage presents difficulties to which we must return again and again," he would remark, "but it helps for us to recognize that our discipline is exercised in the alley between two theaters—those separate playhouses of paranoia and cynicism. Gentlemen, select one rule of conduct from the beginning: Too much attendance at either theater is imprudent. One must keep shifting one's seat. For what, after all, are our working materials? Facts. We live in the mystery of facts. Obligatorily, we become expert observers on the permeability, malleability, and solubility of so-called hard facts. We discover that we have been assigned to live in fields of distortion. We are required to imbibe concealed facts, revealed facts, suspicious facts, serendipitous facts."

Rosen had the temerity on this particular High Thursday to interrupt Harlot long enough to ask, "Sir, I know the meaning of the word, but not its application here. What are serendipitous facts?"

"Rosen," said Harlot, "let us search for the answer." Harlot paused. I was all too aware of the way he played with the name. There had been just a hint of mournful woe in the long *o* of Rosen. "Rosen," he said, "assume that you are on a tour of duty in Singapore and a scrumptious blonde, a veritable *bagatelle,* happens to knock on your hotel room door at 2:00 A.M., and she is—let us say it is 90-percent ver-ifiable—*not* employed by the KGB, but chooses to knock because she likes you. That, Arnold, is a serendipitous fact."

Guffaws popped forth. Rosen managed to smile. Indeed, I felt his gleam of happiness at arousing the wit of the master. "I thrive on de-rision," said his manner.

Harlot resumed. "Gentlemen," he declared, "in the more ad-vanced regions of our work, sound judgment is paramount. Is the ap-parently unsuccessful operation that we are trying to analyze no more than an error by our opponents, a bureaucratic fumble, a gaffe, or, to the contrary, do we have before us an aria with carefully chosen disso-nances?" He paused. He glared at us. Just as a great actor can give the same soliloquy to beggars or kings—it does not matter—he was here to expatiate on a theme. "Yes," he said, "some of you, on such occa-sions, will be in an unholy rush toward the Theater of Paranoia; others will leave their name at the Cinema of Cynicism. My esteemed Director"—he nodded in the general direction of Mr. Dulles—"has sometimes assured me that I hold forth at times too long over at Para-noia House."

Dulles beamed. "Oh, Montague, you can tell as many stories on me as I can on you. Let's assume there's nothing wrong with suspi-cion. It tends to keep the mind alive."

Harlot nodded. Harlot said: "The man with talent for counteres-pionage, the true *artist,*"—now using the word with as much nesting of his voice as an old Russian lady saying *Pushkin*—"draws on his para-noia to perceive the beauties of his opponent's scenario. He looks for ways to attach facts properly to other facts so that they are no longer separated objects. He tries to find the picture that no one else has glimpsed. All the same, he never fails to heed the warnings of cynicism.

"For cynicism has its own virtues. It is analogous to the oil that wells up from every crushed seed, every damn plan that went wrong." Sitting near Allen Dulles on this day, I heard him grunt in pleasure. It was a small but enjoyable sound. "Hear, hear," he said softly, and I heard him. "Do not," continued Harlot, "attempt to comprehend the KGB, therefore, until you recognize that they have some of the most flexible and some of the most rigid minds in intelligence work, and their people clash with each other, even as some of ours have been known to do. We must always feel the play of forces in our opponent's scheme. It teaches us to beware of divinations that are too comprehensive, too satisfying. Cynicism teaches you to distrust the pleasure you may feel when previously scattered facts come into a nice pattern. If that happens just a little too quickly, you may have come upon your first hint that you are dealing with a precalculated narrative. In a word, disinformation."

Advanced were the High Thursdays, awfully advanced for the Lows. I would ponder some of his conclusions for many a year. If Montague's method of discourse on such days threw the more inexperienced of us over such high hurdles as the Theater of Paranoia and the Cinema of Cynicism, he could on any Low Thursday return us to the threading of a rusty nut to a dirt-grimed bolt. Indeed, the first day of the first Low had us working for two hours to construct a scenario on the basis of a torn receipt, a bent key, a stub of pencil, a book of matches, and a dried flower pressed into a cheap unmarked envelope. These items, he told us, happened to be the pocket litter left by an agent under suspicion who had decamped in unholy haste from a furnished room. For two hours we fingered these objects, brooded upon them, and offered our theories. I forget mine. It was no better than the others. Only Rosen was to distinguish himself that day. Once all the others had finished their expositions, Arnie continued to look unhappy. "In my opinion," he said, "too many pieces are missing."

"This is the sum of your contribution?" asked Harlot.

"Yessir. Given the paucity of facts, no viable scenario is available."

"Rosen," Harlot told us, "is on the nose. These objects were selected arbitrarily. A correct solution does not exist."

Explanation: The exercise was to alert us to the risk of autointoxication when formulating scenarios. Deductive passions could be loosed all too easily by a dried flower, a cheap envelope, a stub of pencil, the bent key, the torn receipt for $11.08. Our first lesson had been designed to make us aware (in retrospect) of any subtle discomfort we had ignored in the course of working up our explanation. "Respect that subtle hollow," Harlot told us. "When a scenario feels absolutely right, it is usually right, but if your story feels almost right, yet just a little empty, well, then, it's all wrong." The next Low, he told us, would be devoted to espionage itself. Espionage, plain and simple, as opposed to counterespionage.

Back at the Farm, there had been a course called *Agent Recruitment;* it gave no clear picture of the reality. Montague moved us quickly from conventional formulations to the marrow. "Espionage," he told us, "is the selection and development of agents. That can be comprehended by two words: disinterested seduction."

Taking his pause, he added: "If you see me as an advocate of unbridled carnality, you are in the wrong room. We are speaking of *disinterested* seduction. That is not, if you reflect on it, physical. It is psychological. Manipulation lies at the heart of such seduction.

"In our Judeo-Christian culture, therefore, difficulties arise. Manipulation is Machiavellian, we say, and are content to let the name judge the matter. Yet if a good man working for his beliefs is not ready to imperil his conscience, then the battlefield will belong to those who manipulate history for base ends. This is not an inquiry into morality, so I pursue the matter no further than to say that a visceral detestation of manipulation is guaranteed to produce an incapacity to find agents and run them. Even for those of us who accept the necessity, it may prove difficult. There are case officers who have spent their working lives in foreign capitals but cannot point to a single on-site agent they managed to recruit. Such failure tends to produce the kind of unhappiness you see on the face of a dedicated hunter who dependably fails to bag his deer. Of course, the odds in certain countries are very much against us."

I do not think any of us were too bothered by the idea of manipulation at this point. To the contrary—we wondered: Would we be able to do the job? We sat there in a mixture of anticipation and worry.

"At this point," said Harlot, "you may be thinking: So incredible a purpose, so difficult an achievement! How do I begin? Rest somewhat assured. The Agency knows better than to depend on your first instinctive efforts. Recruitment is usually the product of the time and care that is spent in studying each prospective client or target. If, for example, the condition of steel production in a certain country interests us, then a cleaning woman who has access to the wastebaskets of a high official in machine-tool production can, for the moment, serve us better than a high functionary in Agriculture. There is logic to this work, and to a degree, one can instruct you in it."

Everyone nodded profoundly, as if we had come to the same conclusion.

"Today, we will place ourselves in a specific milieu," Harlot said. "Let us suppose we are stationed in Prague, yet can only speak a minimal Czech. How is one to cook the omelette when the pan has no handle? Well, gentlemen, we have a support system. In the labyrinth, we are never alone. It is not expected that you, personally, will try to handle Czech agents who speak nothing but their own tongue. Obviously, there has to be an intermediary whom we can employ, a working native. This fellow is called a principal. The principal agent is the Czech who will solicit his countrymen for you. You will merely guide his work."

"Sir, are you saying that we don't really get out in the field?" asked one of the Junior Bold Easterners.

"In the satellite countries, you won't get out," answered Harlot.

"Then why are we studying recruitment?" he asked.

"To be able to think like a principal. Today, in fact, working in company, we will try to perceive ourselves as one such principal. All of you will now convert into one imaginary Czechoslovakian, an official in the Prague government who has already been recruited by the Agency. Now he—by which, of course, we now mean I, our surrogate principal—is trying to bring in a few more Czechs from nearby government offices. Manipulation commences. The first clue to effective manipulation happens to be the cardinal law of salesmanship. Would any of you be familiar with that precept?"

Rosen's hand shot up. "The customer," he said, "doesn't buy the product until he accepts the salesman."

"How do you know that?"

Rosen shrugged. "My father used to own a store."

"Perfect," said Harlot. "I, as the principal, am there to inspire the putative agent—my client—with one idea. It is that I am good for his needs. If my client is a lonely person with a pent-up desire to talk, what should be my calculated response, therefore?"

"Be there to listen," said several of us at once.

"But what if I am dealing with a lonely man who dwells in isolation out of personal choice?"

"Well, just sit beside him," said one of the Mormons, "enjoy the quiet."

"Clear enough," said Harlot. "In doubt, always treat lonely people as if they are rich and old and very much your relative. Look to provide them with the little creature comfort that will fatten your share of the will. On the other hand, should the client prove to be a social climber who gnashes his teeth at the mention of every good party he was not invited to, then sympathy won't get you much. Action is needed. You have to bring this person to a gala gathering." Harlot snapped his fingers. "Next problem. The client has just confessed to you a secret or two about his sexual needs. What would you do about that?"

Savage, a former football player from Princeton, said, "Satisfy them."

"Never! Not in the beginning."

We were at a loss. Discussion circulated aimlessly until Harlot cut it off. "Confess to similar sexual needs," he said. "Of course, this assumes our client is not a homosexual." We laughed uneasily. "All right," said Harlot, "I will provide an easier example: Suppose the client is ready to be unfaithful to his wife. Not an uncommon possibility in Czechoslovakia. Well, you, good principal, do not try to provide him with a mistress. Do not complicate the relationship by adding so dramatic and unstable an element as a mistress. Instead . . . well, what does one do? Rosen?"

"I'm temporarily at a loss."

"Savage?"

"Ditto."

"Hubbard?"

It seemed to me that the answer had already been provided. "Perhaps you should confess to the same longing yourself?"

"Yes. Hubbard listens to what I say. Confess to similar sexual needs."

"But we still don't know," said Rosen, "what to do if the client's desires are frankly and actively homosexual."

We went around the room again. It was my day in class. This time I had a small inspiration. "I think you should show sympathy, not identity," I said.

"Keep on," said Harlot.

"I suppose you could say that while not a homosexual yourself, you do have a younger brother who is, so you understand the need."

"Well," said Harlot, "we now have an approach. Let us apply it to other vices. Suppose the client happens to gamble?"

The most effective response, we agreed, would be to tell him that one's father also gambled.

We moved on. What if the client wanted to get his oldest son accepted at a prestigious university? The principal might then have to call on influential friends. Some preparations took years.

"One has, however," said Harlot, "to keep a firm grasp on the intrinsic problem. An exceptional friendship is being forged. One is acting as generously as a guardian angel. That can arouse suspicion in the client. He has to be aware, after all, that his job deals with government secrets. Your official might be as suspicious as a rich girl with a plain face who is being rushed by an enthusiastic suitor. Depend on it. Espionage has its parallels to matchmaking. Ministers sitting on large secrets are the most difficult to woo. One more reason to focus on the easier target—the petty official. Even in such modest purlieus, however, you, as the guardian angel, have to be ready to dissolve the client's distrust as it forms. It is reasonable to assume that the client, in some part of himself, knows what you are up to, but is amenable to your game. Now is the time to talk him into taking the first step—that same first step which will lead him into becoming an espionage agent. The success of this transition—term it the *pass*—depends on one procedure so well established that it is a rule of thumb. Do any of you have a contribution?"

We were silent.

"I guess one has got to move slow," said a Mormon.

"No," said another Mormon, who had done missionary work in the Philippines. "Fast or slow, make it seem natural."

"You're on track," said Harlot. "The rule is to reduce the drama."

"Is this always true?" asked Rosen.

"None of what I tell you is true," replied Harlot. "At this point, you are being provided with scenarios to substitute for your lack of experience. Out in the field, count on it, your agents are going to act in unforeseen patterns."

"I know that," said Rosen. "It's just I have this idea that the pass, as you call it, can make matters more dramatic."

"Only in counterespionage," said Harlot. "In time, we will take a look at that arcane subject. For now, however, keep the transition modest, uneventful, dull. Reduce the drama. Request something minor. Your purpose, at this point, is not to net information, but to relax your client's conscience. A salesman, as Mr. Rosen's father can no doubt tell us, wants to keep a potential buyer from wondering whether he really needs the product. What procedure is analogous to our circumstances, Hubbard?"

"Do not let the client recognize how much he's getting into."

"Good. You, the principal, are there to allay anxiety. Warm the soup slowly. 'Look, friend,' you might complain to your budding little agent, 'when I want to speak to someone in your office, the number is not available. I cannot pick up the phone and call them—I have to send a letter. No wonder our socialist economy creeps along. If you could let me borrow your department's telephone registry for one night, it would make my work so much easier.' Well, how can the client refuse after all you've done for him? It is, after all, a modest request. The intraoffice phone book is thin. One can slip it into the torn lining of one's overcoat. So the client brings it out to you, and you get it copied immediately, and return it early the next morning before work. Now what do you do?"

We were silent.

"You let a week go by. If any anxiety was aroused in the client's tender breast, it should have settled. Now, ask for a bit more. Can your friend let you have a look at X report? You happen to know that this X report is sitting on one of the desks in his bureau. Nothing weighty, just something your boss would be pleased to see. It could advance your boss's interests to have such information available to him.

"An unhappy sigh from the client," said Harlot, "but he agrees. The report is carried out in his briefcase that night, and is returned to him in the morning.

"The major shift, however, is yet to come. In order for the client to develop into a reliable agent willing to work in place for years, what now is necessary?"

Rosen had his hand up. So did the Mormons. Soon, everyone around the table but myself had raised his hand. I was the only one not to realize that the next step would lead our new agent into taking money for his services.

"It is easier," said Harlot, "than you would suppose. Just as many a woman prefers to receive kisses *and* gifts, rather than kisses solo, so your just-hatched agent won't mind being paid for his sins. A little corruption warms the chill. Remember, however, that hypocrisy is indispensable here. Keep to the model of the young lady. Offer presents before you get around to money. Avoid any hint of the crass. Pay off, for instance, some old nagging debt of the client. Just one more favor.

"Sooner than you would believe, our novice agent is ready for a more orderly arrangement. If he senses that he is entering into a deeper stage of the illicit, money can relieve some of his anxiety. For criminals, this is always true, and an agent is, at the least, a white-collar criminal. In our case, he has just emerged from an orderly but hitherto unsatisfactory middle-class life. Money becomes awfully attractive when one is perched on the edge. Strike your bargain then. You, as the principal, can bring in an offer from your boss. In return for regular removal of selected official documents, a weekly stipend can be arranged."

Harlot nodded. "An interesting period commences. Our novice's secret work now provides him with excitement. If he is middle-aged, you could say he is having a fling. If young, he might actually be stimulated by discovery of this potentiality for deceit in himself."

Here, Harlot looked around our conference table. Did I have the impression that his eyes rested just a little longer on mine? His gaze moved on. "I cannot repeat often enough," he said, "the importance of this regular cash stipend. It must, however, not be so large as to show up in a bank account, or a new home. Yet it has to be enough to quiet anxiety. Again, we rely on a rule of thumb. A good measure is to peg the supplements at not less than one-third and not more than one-half of the agent's weekly salary. Regularity of payment serves the same purpose here as dependable meetings with a lady-love. Hysteria, always ready to flare up, is abated to some degree by predictable performance on your side. Questions?"

One of the Mormons put up his hand. "Can you afford to let the agent become witting of who he is working for?"

"Never. If you are able to manage it, don't let him know it is the Company. Especially in an Eastern satellite. His anxiety would be excessive. If, for example, he is a Czech Communist, let him acquire the notion that he is working for the Russians. Or if, like a few Slovaks I know, he is an Anglophile, you might slip across the idea that MI6 is funding all this. If he likes to see himself as a spiritual descendant of Frederick the Great, nominate the BND. Question?"

"What if the new agent doesn't want to take money?" I asked. "What if he hates Communism so much he wants to fight against it? Aren't we abusing his idealism?"

"In the rare case, yes," said Harlot. "But an idealistic agent can burn out quickly, and turn on you. So, the financial connection is, if anything, even more desirable with idealists."

"Isn't the real purpose of the money," Rosen now asked, "to keep the agent intimidated? He has to sign a receipt, doesn't he?"

"Absolutely."

"Well, then we've handcuffed him to the job. There's evidence against him."

"The KGB uses such tactics. We prefer not to," said Harlot. "Of course, there will be times when a signed receipt does *underline* the situation. I would argue, however, that the true purpose of the stipend is to give a sense of participation, even if the agent does not know exactly who we are. When you are living at the end of a network, nothing is more crucial than to feel you are not wholly alone. I repeat: Money confirms—here is our paradox—money confirms the virtue of the vice.

"Let us count our gains," Harlot said. "As principal, you have done your favors, avoided traps, made the pass, put the client on regular stipend, and concealed the source. A perfect performance to this point. Only one major step remains. What might that be?"

"Well, you have to train him," said one of the Junior Bold Easterners, "you know, weapons, illegal entry, one-time pads, all the stuff that's got to be learned."

"No," said Harlot, "training is kept to a minimum. He is not an intelligence officer, but an agent. Use him as you have found him. He will be asked to take out official papers from his office. He will be taught to photograph documents that cannot be removed. He must never be pushed, however, unless we are desperate to obtain relatively inaccessible material. That is dangerous use of an asset. A good agent ends up not unlike a good hardworking animal on a farm. We teach it not to gallop, but to pull its load. We regulate its diet. The end we seek is an industrious performer who will help us to harvest dependable product on a regular basis year after year. That is a valuable commodity never to be risked for too little, and never to be asked for too much. Underline this in your thoughts: The *stability* of espionage work is the element that generates good results. As far as possible, crises are to be avoided. Therefore, gentlemen, ask yourselves: What is the last step to be taken in the relationship between the principal and the agent?"

I do not know how the next answer came to me. Either I had developed some small ability to read Harlot's thoughts, or was growing familiar with his intellectual style, but I spoke out quickly, wanting credit for the answer. "Withdrawal," I said. "The principal withdraws from a close relation with the agent."

"How," he asked, "do you know that?"

"I can't say," I said. "It just feels right."

"Hubbard, who would have thought it? You are exhibiting the instincts of an intelligence officer." The class laughed, and I flushed, but I knew why he had done this. I had been sufficiently indiscreet once to confess to Rosen that Hugh Montague was my godfather; now the class knew it, and Harlot must have picked that up. "Well," he said, "instincts are indispensable in our occupation, but I will spell it out for those of you who are not as endowed as Hubbard. Some of us have spent a few years here brooding professionally, you might say, on how to keep an agent in quiet working balance. We have come to conclude that sooner or later, the principal must separate himself from his agent. Look upon it as analogous to the shift from early parental warmth to the increasing discipline that a child has to accept as it grows older."

"Does this have anything to do with the agent's sense of his new identity?" asked Rosen.

"Excellent. Identity is no more than how we perceive ourselves. To become an agent, therefore, is equal to assuming a new identity. But, note: With each change of identity, we are born again, which is to say that we have to take another voyage through childhood. So now the principal will reward the agent only for disciplined behavior. Of course, the agent, if he has been developed properly, should be in less need of an emotional bond than of good advice. He no longer requires a one-sided friendship nearly so much as he can use someone with the skill and authority to steer him through hazards. Given the danger, he wishes to believe that so long as he does exactly as he is told, his new life is safe and moderately prosperous. Of course, he must learn to take precise instructions. Certain precautions may seem onerous, but spontaneity is forbidden. In effect, the agent has a contract, and the free insurance that goes with it. After all, in the event of serious trouble, the principal is ready to pluck the agent and his family out of the country.

"All right, then. Their new roles established, the principal can complete his withdrawal from the agent. They still meet, but less often. After a few years, agent and principal may not even see each other. The agent, furnished with a dead drop, leaves his papers and picks up his instructions. On those rare occasions when it is crucial for the agent to talk to the principal, a meeting is arranged in a safe house, but since this is time-consuming in a hostile land, they usually stay apart. The principal is out breaking ground with new clients.

"This, gentlemen," said Harlot, "is espionage—a middle-class activity that depends on stability, money, large doses of hypocrisy on both sides, insurance plans, grievances, underlying loyalty, constant inclinations toward treachery, and an immersion in white-collar work. See you next week. Before too long, we will come to more damnable stuff—counterespionage. That is where we say farewell to white-collar mentality." He waved at us and walked from the room.

From *Harlot's Ghost* (1991)

# MORE
# THAN A BIT
# OF VIOLENCE
# IN ME

## Literary Pain and Shame

By the time *The Deer Park* was published I had come to recognize that
I was concerned with living in Hemingway's discipline, by which I do
not mean I was interested in trying for some imitation of the style, but
rather that I shared with Papa the notion, arrived at slowly in my case,
that even if one dulled one's talent in the punishment of becoming a
man, it was more important to be a man than a very good writer, that
probably I could not become a very good writer unless I learned first
how to keep my nerve, and what is more difficult, learned how to find
more of it.

Filled with this hard new knowledge that the secret to everything
was never to cheat life, I set out immediately to try to cheat life. *The
Deer Park* was done; it would be out in six weeks. I could not keep myself from thinking that twenty good words from Ernest Hemingway
would make the difference between half-success and a breakthrough.
He would like the book, he would have to—it would be impossible for
him not to see how much there was in it. So I cracked the shell of my
pride, got his address from a reliable source, and sent him an inscribed copy. But because I was furious with myself, I turned on my
intent, and put the following words on Father Ernest's copy:

> TO ERNEST HEMINGWAY
>
> —because finally after all these
> years I am deeply curious to know

what you think of this.
—but if you do not answer, or if you
answer with the kind of crap you
use to answer unprofessional writers,
sycophants, brown-nosers, etc., then
fuck you, and I will never attempt
to communicate with you again.

About ten days later, the book came back in the mail, same wrapper and maybe the same string enclosing the package. Stamped all over it was the Spanish equivalent of *Address Unknown*. So I had the following possibilities to choose from:

1. The address was not correct, and the mail clerk in the Havana post office had never heard of Ernest Hemingway.

2. By Standard-Operating-Procedure, all unsolicited books received by Mr. and Mrs. Hemingway were returned unreceived to insure the minimum of bile for the sender.

3. Good wife Mary saw the inscription first, thought it best to leave the husband to his work, and made a lady's executive decision.

4. Hemingway looked at *The Deer Park,* decided he wasn't ready to say yes or no, called up his good friend Colonel C. —— in the Cuban postal service, had the island searched for shipping paper similar to mine (the original wrapper having been torn by a Latin houseboy on reception), had the best Havana forger copy the handwriting, gave a *mordida* to the proper authorities for this breach of postal etiquette, and broke a bottle of champagne over the book just before it was stamped by some of the best bureaucratic hands in Havana and sent on its way back to Putnam, where Walter Minton, then my publisher, put it in his desk, figuring the copy might be worth half a grand to the grandchildren.

Or, 5. The inscription was read, and that carried the day. "If you want to come on that hard, Buster, don't write words like 'deeply curious,'" Papa said, had the original wrapper put back on, stamped it with his private Address Unknown stamp (purchased at Abercrombie and Fitch), and started to drink fifteen minutes early that day.

This is all fine in its way, but once on television in the eighth round, as I remember, I saw Carmen Basilio take one of Paddy De Marco's best punches, go out on his feet, start to sit down on the canvas, and then with his butt three inches from the ground, Basilio did a one-legged knee stand, pushed up, avoided the knockdown (he had never been knocked down in a fight before or since), and went on to knock out De Marco in a few rounds. The story in the newspapers the next day, which I would like to think is true, was that Basilio, when asked why he didn't take an eight-count and get some rest, answered, "I didn't want to start any bad habits."

I could have followed that advice. Moderation is the last virtue I'll capture, and a day or two after the book went off to Hemingway, the broken shell of my pride collapsed into powder, and I sent off inscribed copies to Graham Greene, Cyril Connolly, Philip Rahv, and a dozen others whom I no longer remember. The only one who answered was Moravia, but then we knew each other, and I had told him I didn't want his comment for advertising copy.

This confession off my liver forever, it occurs to me now that I must have carried the memory as a silent shame which helped to push me further and deeper into the next half year of bold assertions, half-done work, unbalanced heroics, and an odd notoriety of my own choice. I was on the edge of many things and I had more than a bit of violence in me.

# Quickly: A Column for Slow Readers

Many years ago I remember reading a piece in the newspapers by Ernest Hemingway and thinking: "What windy writing." That is the penalty for having a reputation as a writer. Any signed paragraph that appears in print is examined by the usual sadistic literary standards, rather than with the easy tolerance of a newspaper reader pleased to get an added fillip for his nickel.

But this is a fact of life which any professional writer soon learns to put up with, and I know that I will have to put up with it since I doubt very much if this column is going to be particularly well-written. That would take too much time, and it would be time spent in what is certainly a lost cause. Greenwich Village is one of the bitter provinces—it abounds in snobs and critics. That many of you are frustrated in your ambitions, and undernourished in your pleasures, only makes you more venomous. Quite rightly. If I found myself in your position, I would not be charitable either. Nevertheless, given your general animus to those more talented than yourselves, the only way I see myself becoming one of the cherished traditions of the Village is to be actively disliked each week.

At this point it can fairly be asked: "Is this your only reason for writing a column?" And the next best answer I suppose is: "Egotism. My search to discover in public how much of me is sheer egotism." I find a desire to inflict my casual opinions on a half-captive audience. If I did not, there would always be the danger of putting these casual opinions into a new novel, and we all know what a terrible thing that is to do.

I also feel tempted to say that novelists are the only group of people who should write a column. Their interests are large, if shallow, their habits are sufficiently unreliable for them to find something new to say quite often, and in most other respects they are more columnistic than the columnists. Most of us novelists who are any good are invariably half-educated; inaccurate, albeit brilliant upon occasion; insufferably vain of course; and—the indispensable requirement for a good newspaperman—as eager to tell a lie as the truth. (Saying the truth makes us burn with the desire to convince our audience, whereas telling a lie affords ample leisure to study the result.)

We good novelists also have the most unnewspaperly virtue of never praising fatherland and flag unless we are sick, tired, generally defeated, and want to turn a quick dishonest buck. Nobody but novelists would be asked to write columns if it were not for the sad fact that newspaper editors are professionally and obligatorily patriotic, and so never care to meet us. Indeed, even *The Village Voice*, which is remarkably conservative for so young a paper, and deeply patriotic about all community affairs, etc., etc., would not want me either if they were not so financially eager for free writing, and a successful name to go along with it, that they are ready to put up with almost anything. And I, as a minority stockholder in the *Voice* corporation, must agree that this paper does need something added to its general languor and whimsy.

At any rate, dear reader, we begin a collaboration that may go on for three weeks, three months, or, the Lord forbid, for three-and-thirty years. I have only one prayer—that I weary of you before you tire of me. And therefore, so soon as I learn to write columnese in a quarter of an hour instead of the unprofitable fifty-two minutes this has taken, we will all know better if our trifling business is going to continue. If it does, there is one chance in a hundred—make it a hundred-thousand—that I will become an habitual assassin-and-lover columnist who will have something superficial or vicious or inaccurate to say about many of the things under the sun, and who knows but what some of the night.

# The White Negro: Superficial Reflections on the Hipster

### 1.

Probably, we will never be able to determine the psychic havoc of the concentration camps and the atom bomb upon the unconscious mind of almost everyone alive in these years. For the first time in civilized history, perhaps for the first time in all of history, we have been forced to live with the suppressed knowledge that the smallest facets of our personality or the most minor projection of our ideas, or indeed the absence of ideas and the absence of personality, could mean equally well that we might still be doomed to die as a cipher in some vast statistical operation in which our teeth would be counted, and our hair would be saved, but our death itself would be unknown, unhonored, and unremarked, a death that could not follow with dignity as a possible consequence to serious actions we had chosen, but rather a death by *deus ex machina* in a gas chamber or a radioactive city; and so in the midst of a civilization founded upon the Faustian urge to dominate nature, our psyche was subjected to the intolerable anxiety that death being causeless, life was causeless as well, and time deprived of cause and effect had come to a stop.

The Second World War presented a mirror to the human condition that blinded anyone who looked into it. For if tens of millions were killed in concentration camps out of the inexorable agonies and contractions of super-states founded upon the always insoluble contradictions of injustice, one was then obliged also to see that no matter how crippled and perverted an image of man was the society he had created, it was nonetheless his creation, his collective creation (at least his collective creation from the past), and if society was so murderous, then who could ignore the most hideous of questions about his own nature?

Worse. One could hardly maintain the courage to be individual, to speak with one's own voice, for the years in which one could com-

placently accept oneself as part of an elite by being a radical were forever gone. A man knew that when he dissented, he gave a note upon
his life that could be called in any year of overt crisis. No wonder then
that these have been the years of conformity and depression. A stench
of fear has come out of every pore of American life, and we suffer
from a collective failure of nerve. The only courage, with rare exceptions, that we have been witness to has been the isolated courage of
isolated people.

## 2.

It is on this bleak scene that a phenomenon has appeared: the American existentialist—the hipster, the man who knows that if our collective condition is to live with instant death by atomic war, relatively
quick death by the State as *l'univers concentrationnaire,* or with a slow
death by conformity with every creative and rebellious instinct stifled
(at what damage to the mind and the heart and the liver and the
nerves no research foundation for cancer will discover in a hurry), if
the fate of twentieth-century man is to live with death from adolescence to premature senescence, why then the only life-giving answer
is to accept the terms of death, to live with death as immediate danger,
to divorce oneself from society, to exist without roots, to set out on that
uncharted journey into the rebellious imperatives of the self. In short,
whether the life is criminal or not, the decision is to encourage the
psychopath in oneself, to explore that domain of experience where
security is boredom and therefore sickness, and one exists in the
present, in that enormous present which is without past or future,
memory or planned intention, the life where a man must go until he
is beat, where he must gamble with his energies through all those
small or large crises of courage and unforeseen situations that beset
his day, where he must be with it or doomed not to swing. The unstated essence of Hip, its psychopathic brilliance, quivers with the
knowledge that new kinds of victories increase one's power for new
kinds of perception; and defeats, the wrong kind of defeats, attack the
body and imprison one's energy until one is jailed in the prison air of
other people's habits, other people's defeats, boredom, quiet desperation, and muted icy self-destroying rage. One is Hip or one is Square
(the alternative that each new generation coming into American life is
beginning to feel), one is a rebel or one conforms, one is a frontiers-
man in the Wild West of American night life or else a Square cell,
trapped in the totalitarian tissues of American society, doomed willy-
nilly to conform if one is to succeed.

A totalitarian society makes enormous demands on the courage of men, and a partially totalitarian society makes even greater demands, for the general anxiety is greater. Indeed if one is to be a man, almost any kind of unconventional action often takes disproportionate courage. So it is no accident that the source of Hip is the Negro, for he has been living on the margin between totalitarianism and democracy for two centuries. But the presence of Hip as a working philosophy in the sub-worlds of American life is probably due to jazz, and its knifelike entrance into culture, its subtle but so penetrating influence on an avant-garde generation—that postwar generation of adventurers who (some consciously, some by osmosis) had absorbed the lessons of disillusionment and disgust of the twenties, the depression, and the war. Sharing a collective disbelief in the words of men who had too much money and controlled too many things, they knew almost as powerful a disbelief in the socially monolithic ideas of the single mate, the solid family, and the respectable love life. If the intellectual antecedents of this generation can be traced to such separate influences as D. H. Lawrence, Henry Miller, and Wilhelm Reich, the viable philosophy of Hemingway fit most of their facts. In a bad world, as he was to say over and over again (while taking time out from his parvenu snobbery and dedicated gourmandize), in a bad world there is no love nor mercy nor charity nor justice unless a man can keep his courage, and this indeed fitted some of the facts. What fitted the need of the adventurer even more precisely was Hemingway's categorical imperative that what made him feel good became therefore The Good.

So no wonder that in certain cities of America, in New York, of course, and New Orleans, in Chicago and San Francisco and Los Angeles, in such American cities as Paris and Mexico, D.F., this particular part of a generation was attracted to what the Negro had to offer. In such places as Greenwich Village, a ménage-à-trois was completed— the bohemian and the juvenile delinquent came face-to-face with the Negro, and the hipster was a fact in American life. If marijuana was the wedding ring, the child was the language of Hip, for its argot gave expression to abstract states of feeling that all could share, at least all who were Hip. And in this wedding of the white and the black it was the Negro who brought the cultural dowry. Any Negro who wishes to live must live with danger from his first day, and no experience can ever be casual to him, no Negro can saunter down a street with any real certainty that violence will not visit him on his walk. The cameos of security for the average white—mother and the home, job and the family—are not even a mockery to millions of Negroes; they are impossible. The Negro has the simplest of alternatives: live a life of constant humility or ever-threatening danger. In such a pass where paranoia is as vital to survival as blood, the Negro had stayed alive and begun to grow by following the need of his body where he could. Knowing in the cells of his existence that life was war, nothing but war, the Negro (all exceptions admitted) could rarely afford the sophisticated inhibitions of civilization, and so he kept for his survival the art of the primitive. He lived in the enormous present, he subsisted for his Saturday night kicks, relinquishing the pleasures of the mind for the more obligatory pleasures of the body, and in his music he gave voice to the character and quality of his existence, to his rage and the infinite variations of joy, lust, languor, growl, cramp, pinch, scream, and despair of his orgasm. For jazz is orgasm, it is the music of orgasm, good orgasm and bad, and so it spoke across a nation. It had the communication of art even where it was watered, perverted, corrupted, and almost killed. It spoke in no matter what laundered popular way of instantaneous existential states to which some whites could respond. It was indeed a communication by art, because it said, "I feel this, and now you do too."

So there was a new breed of adventurers, urban adventurers who drifted out at night looking for action with a black man's code to fit their facts. The hipster had absorbed the existentialist synapses of the Negro, and for practical purposes could be considered a white Negro.

To be an existentialist, one must be able to feel oneself—one must know one's desires, one's rages, one's anguish; one must be aware of the character of one's frustration and know what would satisfy it. The overcivilized man can be an existentialist only if it is chic, and deserts it quickly for the next chic. To be a real existentialist (Sartre admittedly to the contrary) one must be religious; one must have one's sense of the "purpose"—whatever the purpose may be. But a life which is directed by one's faith in the necessity of action is a life committed to the notion that the substratum of existence is the search, the end meaningful but mysterious; it is impossible to live such a life unless one's emotions provide their profound conviction. Only the French, alienated beyond alienation from their unconscious, could welcome an existential philosophy without ever feeling it at all. Indeed, only a Frenchman by declaring that the unconscious did not exist could then proceed to explore the delicate involutions of consciousness, the microscopically sensuous and all but ineffable *frissons* of mental becoming, in order finally to create the theology of atheism and so submit that in a world of absurdities the existential absurdity is most coherent.

In the dialogue between the atheist and the mystic, the atheist is on the side of life, rational life, undialectical life. Since he conceives of death as emptiness, he can, no matter how weary or despairing, wish for nothing but more life. His pride is that he does not transpose his weakness and spiritual fatigue into a romantic longing for death, for such appreciation of death is then all too capable of being elaborated by his imagination into a universe of meaningful structure and moral orchestration.

Yet this masculine argument can mean very little for the mystic. The mystic can accept the atheist's description of his weakness, he can agree that his mysticism was a response to despair. And yet . . . and yet his argument is that he, the mystic, is the one finally who has chosen to live with death, and so death is his experience and not the atheist's, and the atheist by eschewing the limitless dimensions of profound despair has rendered himself incapable to judge the experience. The real argument that the mystic must always advance is the very intensity of his private vision—his argument depends from the vision precisely because what was felt in the vision is so extraordinary that no rational argument, no hypotheses of "oceanic feelings," and certainly no skeptical reductions can explain away what has become for him the reality more real than the reality of closely reasoned logic. His inner experience of the possibilities within death is his logic. So, too, for the existentialist. And the psychopath. And the saint and the bullfighter and the lover. The common denominator for all of them is their burning consciousness of the present, exactly that incandescent consciousness which the possibilities within death has opened for them. There is a depth of desperation to the condition which enables one to remain in life only by engaging death, but the reward is their knowledge that what is happening at each instant of the electric present is good or bad for them, good or bad for their cause, their love, their action, their need.

It is this knowledge that provides the curious community of feeling in the world of the hipster, a muted cool religious revival to be sure; but the element which is exciting, disturbing, nightmarish perhaps, is that incompatibles have come to bed—the inner life and the violent life, the orgy and the dream of love, the desire to murder and the desire to create, a dialectical conception of existence with a lust for power, a dark, romantic, and yet undeniably dynamic view of existence, for it sees every man and woman as moving individually through each moment of life forward into growth or backward into death.

### 3.

It may be fruitful to consider the hipster a philosophical psychopath, a man interested not only in the dangerous imperatives of his psychopathy but in codifying, at least for himself, the suppositions on which his inner universe is constructed. By this premise the hipster is a psychopath, and yet not a psychopath but the negation of the psychopath, for he possesses the narcissistic detachment of the philosopher, that absorption in the recessive nuances of one's own motive that is so alien to the unreasoning drive of the psychopath. In this country, where new millions of psychopaths are developed each year, stamped with the mint of our contradictory popular culture (where sex is sin and yet sex is paradise), it is as if there has been room already for the development of the antithetical psychopath who extrapolates from his own condition, from the inner certainty that his rebellion is just, a radical vision of the universe, which thus separates him from the general ignorance, reactionary prejudice, and self-doubt of the more conventional psychopath. Having converted his unconscious experience into much conscious knowledge, the hipster has shifted the focus of his desire from immediate gratification toward that wider passion for future power which is the mark of civilized man. Yet with an irreducible difference. For Hip is the sophistication of the wise primitive in a giant jungle, and so its appeal is still beyond the civilized man. If there are ten million Americans who are more or less psychopathic (and the figure is most modest), there are probably not more than one hundred thousand men and women who consciously see themselves as hipsters. Yet their importance is that they are an elite with the potential ruthlessness of an elite, and a language most adolescents can understand instinctively, for the hipster's intense view of existence matches their experience and their desire to rebel.

Before one can say more about the hipster, there is obviously much to be said about the psychic state of the psychopath—or, clinically, the psychopathic personality. Now, for reasons that may be more curious than the similarity of the words, even many people with a psychoanalytical orientation often confuse the psychopath with the psychotic. Yet the terms are polar. The psychotic is legally insane; the psychopath is not. The psychotic is almost always incapable of discharging in physical acts the rage of his frustration, while the psychopath at his extreme is virtually as incapable of restraining his violence. The psychotic lives in so misty a world that what is happening at each moment of his life is not very real to him, whereas the psychopath seldom knows any reality greater than the face, the voice, the being of the particular people among whom he may find himself at any moment. Sheldon and Eleanor Glueck describe him as follows:

> The psychopath . . . can be distinguished from the person sliding into or clambering out of a "true psychotic" state by the long tough persistence of his anti-social attitude and behaviour and the absence of hallucinations, delusions, manic flight of ideas, confusion, disorientation, and other dramatic signs of psychosis.

The late Robert Lindner, one of the few experts on the subject, in his book *Rebel Without a Cause—The Hypnoanalysis of a Criminal Psychopath* presented part of his definition in this way:

> . . . the psychopath is a rebel without a cause, an agitator without a slogan, a revolutionary without a program: in other words, his rebelliousness is aimed to achieve goals satisfactory to himself alone; he is incapable of exertions for the sake of others. All his efforts, hidden under no matter what disguise, represent investments designed to satisfy his immediate wishes and desires. . . . The psychopath, like the child, cannot delay the pleasures of gratification; and this trait is one of his underlying, universal characteristics. He cannot wait upon erotic gratification which convention demands should be preceded by the chase before the kill: he must rape. He cannot wait upon the development of prestige in society: his egoistic ambitions lead him to leap into headlines by daring performances. Like a red thread the predominance of this mechanism for immediate satisfaction runs through the history of every psychopath. It explains not only his behaviour but also the violent nature of his acts.

Yet even Lindner, who was the most imaginative and most sympathetic of the psychoanalysts who have studied the psychopathic personality, was not ready to project himself into the essential sympathy—which is that the psychopath may indeed be the perverted and dangerous front-runner of a new kind of personality, which could become the central expression of human nature before the twentieth century is over. For the psychopath is better adapted to dominate those mutually contradictory inhibitions upon violence and love that civilization has exacted of us, and if it be remembered that not every psychopath is an extreme case, and that the condition of psychopathy is present in a host of people, including many politicians, professional soldiers, newspaper columnists, entertainers, artists, jazz musicians, call-girls, promiscuous homosexuals, and half the executives of Hollywood, television, and advertising, it can be seen that there are aspects of psychopathy that already exert considerable cultural influence.

What characterizes almost every psychopath and part-psychopath is that they are trying to create a new nervous system for themselves. Generally we are obliged to act with a nervous system which has been formed from infancy; it carries in the style of its circuits the very contradictions of our parents and our early milieu. Therefore, we are obliged, most of us, to meet the tempo of the present and the future with reflexes and rhythms that come from the past. It is not only the "dead weight of the institutions of the past" but indeed the inefficient and often antiquated nervous circuits of the past that strangle our potentiality for responding to new possibilities which might be exciting for our individual growth.

Through most of modern history, "sublimation" was possible: At the expense of expressing only a small portion of oneself, one could express that small portion intensely. But sublimation depends on a reasonable tempo to history. If the collective life of a generation has moved too quickly, the "past" by which particular men and women of that generation may function is not, let us say, thirty years old, but relatively a hundred or two hundred years old. And so the nervous system is overstressed beyond the possibility of such compromises as sublimation, especially since the stable middle-class values so prerequisite to sublimation have been virtually destroyed in our time, at least as nourishing values free of confusion or doubt. In such a crisis of accelerated historical tempo and deteriorated values, neurosis tends to be replaced by psychopathy, and the success of psychoanalysis (which even ten years ago gave promise of becoming a direct major force) diminishes because of its inbuilt and characteristic incapacity to handle patients more complex, more experienced, or more adventurous than the analyst himself. In practice, psychoanalysis has by now become all too often no more than a psychic blood-letting. The patient is not so much changed as aged, and the infantile fantasies that he is encouraged to express are condemned to exhaust themselves against the analyst's nonresponsive reactions. The result for all too many patients is a diminution, a "tranquilizing" of their most interesting qualities and vices. The patient is indeed not so much altered as worn out—less bad, less good, less bright, less willful, less destructive, less creative. He is thus able to conform to that contradictory and unbearable society which first created his neurosis. He can conform to what he loathes because he no longer has the passion to feel loathing so intensely.

The psychopath is notoriously difficult to analyze, because the fundamental decision of his nature is to try to live the infantile fantasy, and in this decision (given the dreary alternative of psychoanalysis) there may be a certain instinctive wisdom. For there is a dialectic to changing one's nature, the dialectic that underlies all psychoanalytic method: it is the knowledge that if one is to change one's habits, one must go back to the source of their creation, and so the psychopath exploring backward along the road of the homosexual, the orgiast, the drug-addict, the rapist, the robber, and the murderer seeks to find those violent parallels to the violent and often hopeless contradictions he knew as an infant and as a child. For if he has the courage to meet the parallel situation at the moment when he is ready, then he has a chance to act as he has never acted before, and in satisfying the frustration—if he can succeed—he may then pass by symbolic substitute through the locks of incest. In thus giving expression to the buried infant in himself, he can lessen the tension of those infantile desires and so free himself to remake a bit of his nervous system. Like the neurotic, he is looking for the opportunity to grow up a second time, but the psychopath knows instinctively that to express a forbidden impulse actively is far more beneficial to him than merely to confess the desire in the safety of a doctor's room. The psychopath is ordinately ambitious, too ambitious ever to trade his warped brilliant conception of his possible victories in life for the grim if peaceful attrition of the analyst's couch. So his associational journey into the past is lived out in the theatre of the present, and he exists for those charged situations where his senses are so alive that he can be aware actively (as the analysand is aware passively) of what his habits are, and how he can change them. The strength of the psychopath is that he knows (where most of us can only guess) what is good for him and what is bad for him at exactly those instants when an old crippling habit has become so attacked by experience that the potentiality exists to change it, to replace a negative and empty fear with an outward action, even if— and here I obey the logic of the extreme psychopath—even if the fear is of himself, and the action is to murder. The psychopath murders— if he has the courage—out of the necessity to purge his violence, for if he cannot empty his hatred then he cannot love; his being is frozen

with implacable self-hatred for his cowardice. (It can of course be suggested that it takes little courage for two strong eighteen-year-old
hoodlums, let us say, to beat in the brains of a candy-store keeper, and
indeed the act—even by the logic of the psychopath—is not likely to
prove very therapeutic, for the victim is not an immediate equal. Still,
courage of a sort is necessary, for one murders not only a weak fifty-
year-old man but an institution as well. One violates private property;
one enters into a new relation with the police and introduces a dangerous element into one's life. The hoodlum is therefore daring the
unknown, and so no matter how brutal the act, it is not altogether
cowardly.)

At bottom, the drama of the psychopath is that he seeks love. Not
love as the search for a mate, but love as the search for an orgasm
more apocalyptic than the one that preceded it. Orgasm is his therapy—he knows at the seed of his being that good orgasm opens his
possibilities and bad orgasm imprisons him. But in this search, the
psychopath becomes an embodiment of the extreme contradictions of
the society that formed his character, and the apocalyptic orgasm
often remains as remote as the Holy Grail, for there are clusters and
nests and ambushes of violence in his own necessities and in the imperatives and retaliations of the men and women among whom he
lives his life, so that even as he drains his hatred in one act or another,
so the conditions of his life create it anew in him until the drama of his
movements bears a sardonic resemblance to the frog who climbed a
few feet in the well only to drop back again.

Yet there is this to be said for the search after the good orgasm:
When one lives in a civilized world, and still can enjoy none of the cultural nectar of such a world because the paradoxes on which civilization is built demand that there remain a cultureless and alienated
bottom of exploitable human material, then the logic of becoming a
sexual outlaw (if one's psychological roots are bedded in the bottom)
is that one has at least a running competitive chance to be physically
healthy so long as one stays alive. It is therefore no accident that psychopathy is most prevalent with the Negro. Hated from outside and
therefore hating himself, the Negro was forced into the position of exploring all those moral wildernesses of civilized life that the Square
automatically condemns as delinquent or evil or immature or morbid
or self-destructive or corrupt. (Actually the terms have equal weight.
Depending on the telescope of the cultural clique from which the
Square surveys the universe, "evil" or "immature" are equally strong
terms of condemnation.) But the Negro, not being privileged to grat-

ify his self-esteem with the heady satisfactions of categorical condemnation, chose to move instead in that other direction where all situations are equally valid, and in the worst of perversion, promiscuity, pimpery, drug addiction, rape, razor-slash, bottle-break, what-have-you, the Negro discovered and elaborated a morality of the bottom, an ethical differentiation between the good and the bad in every human activity from the go-getter pimp (as opposed to the lazy one) to the relatively dependable pusher or prostitute. Add to this the cunning of their language, the abstract ambiguous alternatives in which from the danger of their oppression they learned to speak ("Well, now, man, like I'm looking for a cat to turn me on . . ."), add even more the profound sensitivity of the Negro jazzman who was the cultural mentor of a people, and it is not too difficult to believe that the language of Hip that evolved was an artful language, tested and shaped by an intense experience and therefore different in kind from white slang, as different as the special obscenity of the soldier, which in its emphasis upon "ass" as the soul and "shit" as circumstance, was able to express the existential states of the enlisted man. What makes Hip a special language is that it cannot really be taught—if one shares none of the experiences of elation and exhaustion that it is equipped to describe, then it seems merely arch or vulgar or irritating. It is a pictorial language, but pictorial like nonobjective art, imbued with the dialectic of small but intense change, a language for the microcosm, in this case, man, for it takes the immediate experiences of any passing man and magnifies the dynamic of his movements, not specifically but abstractly so that he is seen more as a vector in a network of forces than as a static character in a crystallized field. (Which latter is the practical view of the snob.) For example, there is real difficulty in trying to find a Hip substitute for "stubborn." The best possibility I can come up with is: "That cat will never come off his groove, dad." But "groove" implies movement, narrow movement but motion nonetheless. There is really no way to describe someone who does not move at all. Even a creep does move—if at a pace exasperatingly more slow than the pace of the cool cats.

### 4.

Like children, hipsters are fighting for the sweet, and their language is a set of subtle indications of their success or failure in the competition for pleasure. Unstated but obvious is the social sense that there is not nearly enough sweet for everyone. And so the sweet goes only to the victor, the best, the most, the man who knows the most about how to find his energy and how not to lose it. The emphasis is on energy because the psychopath and the hipster are nothing without it, since they do not have the protection of a position or a class to rely on when they have overextended themselves. So the language of Hip is a language of energy, how it is found, how it is lost.

But let us see. I have jotted down perhaps a dozen words, the Hip perhaps most in use and most likely to last with the minimum of variation. The words are: man, go, put down, make, beat, cool, swing, with it, crazy, dig, flip, creep, hip, square. They serve a variety of purposes and the nuance of the voice uses the nuance of the situation to convey the subtle contextual difference. If the hipster moves through his life on a constant search with glimpses of Mecca in many a turn of his experience (Mecca being the apocalyptic orgasm) and if everyone in the civilized world is at least in some small degree a sexual cripple, the hipster lives with the knowledge of how he is sexually crippled and where he is sexually alive, and the faces of experience that life presents to him each day are engaged, dismissed, or avoided as his need directs and his lifemanship makes possible. For life is a contest between people in which the victor generally recuperates quickly and the loser takes long to mend, a perpetual competition of colliding explorers in which one must grow or else pay more for remaining the same (pay in sickness, or depression, or anguish for the lost opportunity), but pay or grow.

Therefore one finds words like go, and make it, and with it, and swing: "Go" with its sense that after hours or days or months or years of monotony, boredom, and depression one has finally had one's chance; one has amassed enough energy to meet an exciting opportunity with all one's present talents for the flip (up or down) and so one is ready to go, ready to gamble. Movement is always to be preferred to inaction. In motion a man has a chance. His body is warm, his instincts are quick, and when the crisis comes, whether of love or violence, he can make it, he can win, he can release a little more energy for himself, since he hates himself a little less. He can make a little better nervous system, make it a little more possible to go again, to go faster next time and so make more and thus find more people with whom he can swing. For to swing is to communicate, is to convey the rhythms of one's own being to a lover, a friend, or an audience, and—equally necessary—be able to feel the rhythms of their response. To swing with the rhythms of another is to enrich oneself—the conception of the learning process as dug by Hip is that one cannot really learn until one contains within oneself the implicit rhythm of the subject or the person. As an example, I remember once hearing a Negro friend have an intellectual discussion at a party for half an hour with a white girl who was a few years out of college. The Negro literally could not read or write, but he had an extraordinary ear and a fine sense of mimicry. So as the girl spoke, he would detect the particular formal uncertainties in her argument, and in a pleasant (if slightly Southern) English accent, he would respond to one or another facet of her doubts. When she would finish what she felt was a particularly well-articulated idea, he would smile privately and say, "Other-direction . . . do you really believe in that?"

"Well . . . no," the girl would stammer. "Now that you get down to it, there is something disgusting about it to me," and she would be off again for five more minutes.

Of course the Negro was not learning anything about the merits and demerits of the argument, but he was learning a great deal about a type of girl he had never met before, and that was what he wanted. Being unable to read or write, he could hardly be interested in ideas nearly as much as in lifemanship, and so he eschewed any attempt to obey the precision or lack of precision in the girl's language, and instead sensed her character (and the values of her social type) by swinging with the nuances of her voice.

So to swing is to be able to learn, and by learning take a step toward making it, toward creating. What is to be created is not nearly so important as the hipster's belief that when he really makes it, he will be able to turn his hand to anything, even to self-discipline. What he must do before that is find his courage at the moment of violence, or equally make it in the act of love, find a little more between his woman and himself, or indeed between his mate and himself (since many hipsters are bisexual), but paramount, imperative, is the necessity to make it, because in making it one is making the new habit, unearthing the new talent that the old frustration denied.

Whereas if you goof (the ugliest word in Hip), if you lapse back into being a frightened stupid child, or if you flip, if you lose your control, reveal the buried weaker part of your nature, then it is more difficult to swing the next time; your ear is less alive, your bad and energy-wasting habits are further confirmed, you are farther away from being with it. But to be with it is to have grace, is to be closer to the secrets of that inner unconscious life that will nourish you if you can hear it, for you are then nearer to that God which every hipster believes is located in the senses of his body, that trapped, mutilated, and nonetheless megalomaniacal God who is It, who is energy, life, sex, force, the Yoga's *prana*, the Reichian's orgone, Lawrence's "blood," Hemingway's "good," the Shavian life-force; "It"; God; not the God of the churches but the unachievable whisper of mystery within the sex, the paradise of limitless energy and perception just beyond the next wave of the next orgasm.

To which a cool cat might reply, "Crazy, man!"

Because, after all, what I have offered above is an hypothesis, no more, and there is not the hipster alive who is not absorbed in his own tumultuous hypotheses. Mine is interesting, mine is way out (on the avenue of the mystery along the road to "It"), but still I am just one cat in a world of cool cats, and everything interesting is crazy, or at least so the Squares who do not know how to swing would say.

(And yet crazy is also the self-protective irony of the hipster. Living with questions and not with answers, he is so different in his isolation and in the far reach of his imagination from almost everyone with whom he deals in the outer world of the Square, and meets generally so much enmity, competition, and hatred in the world of Hip, that his isolation is always in danger of turning upon itself, and leaving him indeed just that—crazy.)

If, however, you agree with my hypothesis, if you as a cat are way out too, and we are in the same groove (the universe now being glimpsed as a series of ever-extending radii from the center), why then you say simply, "I dig," because neither knowledge nor imagination comes easily. It is buried in the pain of one's forgotten experience, and so one must work to find it, one must occasionally exhaust oneself by digging into the self in order to perceive the outside. And indeed it is essential to dig the most, for if you do not dig you lose your superiority over the Square, and so you are less likely to be cool (to be in control of a situation because you have swung where the Square has not, or because you have allowed to come to consciousness a pain, a guilt, a shame, or a desire that the other has not had the courage to face). To be cool is to be equipped, and if you are equipped it is more difficult for the next cat who comes along to put you down. And of course one can hardly afford to be put down too often, or one is beat, one has lost one's confidence, one has lost one's will, one is impotent in the world of action and so closer to the demeaning flip of becoming a queer, or indeed closer to dying, and therefore it is even more difficult to recover enough energy to try to make it again, because once a cat is beat he has nothing to give, and no one is interested any longer in making it with him. This is the terror of the hipster—to be beat—because once the sweet of sex has deserted him, he still cannot give up the search. It is not granted to the hipster to grow old gracefully—he has been captured too early by the oldest dream of power, the gold fountain of Ponce de León, the fountain of youth where the gold is in the orgasm.

To be beat is therefore a flip; it is a situation beyond one's experience, impossible to anticipate—which indeed in the circular vocabulary of Hip is still another meaning for flip, but then I have given just a few of the connotations of these words. Like most primitive vocabularies, each word is a prime symbol and serves a dozen or a hundred functions of communication in the instinctive dialectic through which the hipster perceives his experience, that dialectic of the instantaneous differentials of existence in which one is forever moving forward into more or retreating into less.

### 5.

It is impossible to conceive a new philosophy until one creates a new language, but a new popular language (while it must implicitly contain a new philosophy) does not necessarily present its philosophy overtly. It can be asked then what really is unique in the life-view of Hip that raises its argot above the passing verbal whimsies of the bohemian or the lumpenproletariat.

The answer would be in the psychopathic element of Hip, which has almost no interest in viewing human nature or, better, in judging human nature, from a set of standards conceived a priori to the experience, standards inherited from the past. Since Hip sees every answer as posing immediately a new alternative, a new question, its emphasis is on complexity rather than simplicity (such complexity that its language without the illumination of the voice and the articulation of the face and body remains hopelessly incommunicative). Given its emphasis on complexity, Hip abdicates from any conventional moral responsibility because it would argue that the result of our actions are unforeseeable, and so we cannot know if we do good or bad, we cannot even know (in the Joycean sense of the good and the bad) whether we have given energy to another, and indeed if we could, there would still be no idea of what ultimately the other would do with it.

Therefore, men are not seen as good or bad (that they are good-and-bad is taken for granted) but rather each man is glimpsed as a collection of possibilities, some more possible than others (the view of character implicit in Hip) and some humans are considered more capable than others of reaching more possibilities within themselves in less time, provided, and this is the dynamic, provided the particular character can swing at the right time. And here arises the sense of context that differentiates Hip from a Square view of character. Hip sees the context as generally dominating the man, dominating him because his character is less significant than the context in which he must function. Since it is arbitrarily five times more demanding of one's energy to accomplish even an inconsequential action in an unfavorable context than a favorable one, man is then not only his character but his context, since the success or failure of an action in a given context reacts upon the character and therefore affects what the character will be in the next context. What dominates both character and context is the energy available at the moment of intense context.

Character being thus seen as perpetually ambivalent and dynamic enters then into an absolute relativity, where there are no truths other than the isolated truths of what each observer feels at each instant of his existence. To take a perhaps unjustified metaphysical extrapolation, it is as if the universe, which has usually existed conceptually as a Fact that was the aim of all science and philosophy to reveal, becomes instead a changing reality whose laws are remade at each instant by everything living, but most particularly man, man raised to a neo-medieval summit, where the truth is not what one has felt yesterday or what one expects to feel tomorrow but rather truth is no more nor less than what one feels at each instant in the perpetual climax of the present.

What is consequent therefore is the divorce of man from his values, the liberation of the self from the Super-Ego of society. The only Hip morality (but of course it is an ever-present morality) is to do what one feels whenever and wherever it is possible, and—this is how the war of the Hip and the Square begins—to be engaged in one primal battle: to open the limits of the possible for oneself, for oneself alone, because that is one's need. Yet in widening the arena of the possible, one widens it reciprocally for others as well, so that the nihilistic fulfillment of each man's desire contains its antithesis of human cooperation.

If the ethic reduces to Know Thyself and Be Thyself, what makes it radically different from Socratic moderation, with its stern conservative respect for the experience of the past, is that the Hip ethic is immoderation, childlike in its adoration of the present (and indeed to respect the past means that one must also respect such ugly consequences of the past as the collective murders of the State). It is this adoration of the present which contains the affirmation of Hip, because its ultimate logic surpasses even the unforgettable solution of the Marquis de Sade to sex, private property, and the family, that all men and women have absolute but temporary rights over the bodies of all other men and women—the nihilism of Hip proposes as its final tendency that every social restraint and category be removed, and the affirmation implicit in the proposal is that man would then prove to be more creative than murderous and so would not destroy himself. Which is exactly what separates Hip from the authoritarian philosophies that now appeal to the conservative and liberal temper—what haunts the middle of the twentieth century is that faith in man has been lost, and the appeal of authority has been that it would restrain us from ourselves. Hip, which would return us to ourselves, at no matter what price in individual violence, is the affirmation of the barbarian, for it requires a primitive passion about human nature to believe that individual acts of violence are always to be preferred to the collective violence of the State; it takes literal faith in the creative possibilities of the human being to envisage acts of violence as the catharsis that prepares growth.

Whether the hipster's desire for absolute sexual freedom contains any genuinely radical conception of a different world is of course another matter, and it is possible, since the hipster lives with his hatred, that many of them are the material for an elite of storm troopers ready to follow the first truly magnetic leader whose view of mass murder is phrased in a language that reaches their emotions. But given the desperation of his condition as a psychic outlaw, the hipster is equally a candidate for the most reactionary and most radical of movements, and so it is just as possible that many hipsters will come—if the crisis deepens—to a radical comprehension of the horror of society, for even as the radical has had his incommunicable dissent confirmed in his experience by precisely the frustration, the denied opportunities, and the bitter years that his ideas have cost him, so the sexual adventurer deflected from his goal by the implacable animosity of a society constructed to deny the sexual radical as well, may yet come to an equally bitter comprehension of the slow relentless inhumanity of the conservative power that controls him from without and from within. And in being so controlled, denied, and starved into the attrition of conformity, indeed the hipster may come to see that his condition is no more than an exaggeration of the human condition, and if he would be free, then everyone must be free. Yes, this is possible too, for the heart of Hip is its emphasis upon courage at the moment of crisis, and it is pleasant to think that courage contains within itself (as the explanation of its existence) some glimpse of the necessity of life to become more than it has been.

It is obviously not very possible to speculate with sharp focus on the future of the hipster. Certain possibilities must be evident, however, and the most central is that the organic growth of Hip depends on whether the Negro emerges as a dominating force in American life. Since the Negro knows more about the ugliness and danger of life than the white, it is probable that if the Negro can win his equality, he will possess a potential superiority, a superiority so feared that the fear itself has become the underground drama of domestic politics. Like all conservative political fear it is the fear of unforeseeable consequences, for the Negro's equality would tear a profound shift into the psychology, the sexuality, and the moral imagination of every white alive.

With this possible emergence of the Negro, Hip may erupt as a psychically armed rebellion whose sexual impetus may rebound against the antisexual foundation of every organized power in America, and bring into the air such animosities, antipathies, and new conflicts of interest that the mean empty hypocrisies of mass conformity will no longer work. A time of violence, new hysteria, confusion, and rebellion will then be likely to replace the time of conformity. At that time, if the liberal should prove realistic in his belief that there is peaceful room for every tendency in American life, then Hip would end by being absorbed as a colorful figure in the tapestry. But if this is not the reality, and the economic, the social, the psychological, and finally the moral crises accompanying the rise of the Negro should prove insupportable, then a time is coming when every political guidepost will be gone, and millions of liberals will be faced with political dilemmas they have so far succeeded in evading, and with a view of human nature they do not wish to accept. To take the desegregation of the schools in the South as an example, it is quite likely that the reactionary sees the reality more closely than the liberal when he argues that the deeper issue is not desegregation but miscegenation. (As a radical I am of course facing in the opposite direction from the White Citizen's Councils—obviously I believe it is the absolute human right of the Negro to mate with the white, and matings there will undoubtedly be, for there will be Negro high school boys brave enough to chance their lives.) But for the average liberal, whose mind has been dulled by the committee-ish cant of the professional liberal, miscegenation is not an issue because he has been told that the Negro does not desire it. So, when it comes, miscegenation will be a terror, comparable perhaps to the derangement of the American Communists when the icons to Stalin came tumbling down. The average American Communist held to the myth of Stalin for reasons that had little to do with the political evidence and everything to do with their psychic necessities. In this sense it is equally a psychic necessity for the liberal to believe that the Negro and even the reactionary Southern white are eventually and fundamentally people like himself, capable of becoming good liberals too if only they can be reached by good liberal reason. What the liberal cannot bear to admit is the hatred beneath the skin of a society so unjust that the amount of collective violence buried in the people is perhaps incapable of being contained, and therefore if one wants a better world one does well to hold one's breath, for a worse world is bound to come first, and the dilemma may well be this: Given such hatred, it must either vent itself nihilistically or become turned into the cold murderous liquidations of the totalitarian state.

6.

No matter what its horrors the twentieth century is a vastly exciting century, for its tendency is to reduce all of life to its ultimate alternatives. One can well wonder if the last war of them all will be between the blacks and the whites, or between the women and the men, or between the beautiful and ugly, the pillagers and managers, or the rebels and the regulators. Which of course is carrying speculation beyond the point where speculation is still serious, and yet despair at the monotony and bleakness of the future have become so engrained in the radical temper that the radical is in danger of abdicating from all imagination. What a man feels is the impulse for his creative effort, and if an alien but nonetheless passionate instinct about the meaning of life has come so unexpectedly from a virtually illiterate people, come out of the most intense conditions of exploitation, cruelty, violence, frustration, and lust, and yet has succeeded as an instinct in keeping this tortured people alive, then it is perhaps possible that the Negro holds more of the tail of the expanding elephant of truth than the radical, and if this is so, the radical humanist could do worse than to brood upon the phenomenon. For if a revolutionary time should come again, there would be a crucial difference if someone had already delineated a neo-Marxian calculus aimed at comprehending every circuit and process of society from ukase to kiss as the communications of human energy—a calculus capable of translating the economic relations of man into his psychological relations and then back again, his productive relations thereby embracing his sexual relations as well, until the crises of capitalism in the twentieth century would yet be understood as the unconscious adaptations of a society to solve its economic imbalance at the expense of a new mass psychological imbalance. It is almost beyond the imagination to conceive of a work in which the drama of human energy is engaged, and a theory of its social currents and dissipations, its imprisonments, expressions, and tragic wastes, are fitted into some gigantic synthesis of human action where the body of Marxist thought, and particularly the epic grandeur of *Das Kapital* (that first of the major *psychologies* to approach the mystery of social cruelty so simply and practically as to say that we are a collective body of humans whose life-energy is wasted, displaced, and procedurally stolen as it passes from one of us to another)— where particularly the epic grandeur of *Das Kapital* would find its place in an even more God-like view of human justice and injustice, in some more excruciating vision of those intimate and institutional processes that lead to our creations and disasters, our growth, our attrition, and our rebellion.

All selections from *Advertisements for Myself* (1959)

# URUGUAY—I

## The Car Windows Were Clouded

2:00 A.M.

Kittredge,

Brand new subject. Please save judgments until you've read all. What I have to tell will not, I pray, affect our friendship. You see, I am now embarked on what may yet prove an ongoing affair. While in Washington you were always trying to find some attractive young lady for me, the woman I'm now meeting *on the sly*—this slippery cliché certainly has the feel of it!—is, I fear, not suitable. In fact, she is married, has two children, and is the spouse, worse luck, of one of my colleagues.

All right, I know you'll ask how it began, and who she is, and I'll reply that she is Sally Porringer, the wife of Oatsie.

Let me give the facts. It began one evening about a week before Christmas after a party at Minot Mayhew's house. Mayhew, having received word that E. Howard Hunt is finally coming to replace him as Chief of Station toward the end of January, threw a farewell party for himself. He invited the Station folk and wives, plus a number of his State Department cronies, plus an even larger number of relatively—I thought—undistinguished Uruguayan businessmen and their wives, and I must say it proved nothing remarkable, what with all the other Christmas parties going on.

For that matter, Christmas down here is curiously discordant. That sense of a rose-chill to winter twilight, sweet as fine sorbet, is missed in the heat of summer. One is angry and compassionate in bursts. I mention this because Mayhew's party in his well-appointed house, filled with career mementos and hacienda-type furniture (armchairs with steer's horns), and paid for, no doubt, with his stock-market profits, did improve once he sat down to the piano. "Every man I know," my father told me once, "has an unexpected skill." Mayhew's is to sing and play. He led us through all the expected. We did "Deck the Halls," and "Hark! The Herald Angels Sing," "Noel, Noel," "Jingle Bells," "Silent Night," of course, and then somewhere in "O Come, All Ye Faithful," there was Sally Porringer next to me, her arm around my waist, and swaying in rhythm as we and thirty other people sang along with Mayhew.

I'm no great vocalist, you know. There are all too many inhibiting influences ravaging my impulse to utter golden notes, but I do my best to get along. Sally, however, elucidated something better from limited talents. I don't know if it was due to the fact that I had never before swayed rhythmically while singing, but I heard my voice coming forth, thank you, and this freedom to sing and feel the beauty— not of the words, so much, but all the nuances and timbre of an ice-cold rose-sweet time of year—was going through me again. I felt as if it was really Christmas, even in Uruguay. I had the epiphany I always wait for as December descends into its climactic week, that feeling so hard to live without through most of the year—the conviction (I whisper it) that He may really be near.

Well, I was transported just enough to be fond suddenly of all my cohorts and their wives, and I thought of all the sweet solemn calls of country, duty, rich endeavor, and one's dearest friends. Most of all, I thought of you, because I can often feel that Christmas is near to me again by recollecting your beauty—there, I've said it—and then, even as I'm singing out, "O come, let us adore Him," I look down and see Sally Porringer's face and she smiles back with a warmth and energy that is part of my own sudden good voice, and I liked her for the first time.

After the carols, we sat on the sofa for a while, and I asked her a question about herself. She gave me a considerable amount of her life story in return. Her father was a rodeo rider, but drank too much and left her mother, who remarried a nice grain-and-feed man. Sally and Sherman knew each other in high school (Stillwater, Oklahoma), went on to Oklahoma State in the same class, but never saw much of each other the first three years. He was a grind, getting all kinds of academic honors, and she was on the cheerleaders' team. (I was right

about that!) I took a second look at her then. She's pretty enough, if
in no striking way, small turned-up nose, freckles, pale green eyes,
sandy hair, a slightly harried housewife in her present cast, but I could
see how it must have been ten or twelve years ago. She was probably
healthy and vivacious then, and was having, as she now indicated,
some kind of all-out affair with one of the football players. I expect he
ditched her, since in senior year Sherman and she found each other
and were married after graduation.

I knew I was now expected to reply in kind, but I didn't feel like
raiding my own meager cupboard. So I sat there, and smiled, knowing I had to come up with something. Will you believe it? I went on
and on about discovering Skeat at Yale, and I expect she did her best
to keep from falling asleep in disappointment. A minute later, just as
we were about to move away from one another, Sherman came up. He
was Duty Officer tonight at the Embassy. That meant he had to take
his car to work and was leaving now. She wanted to stay on. I, being
equipped for the evening with a Chevrolet two-door from the Embassy motor pool, offered to drop her off on my way back. I hardly
wanted to, I would just as soon have departed right behind Porringer—I did not like the idea of those paranoid eyes staring at me
through the malign screen of his thick spectacles, but she looked so
sad at having to leave that I stayed.

A little later, I danced with her. Minot Mayhew was now playing
all kinds of what I call Charleston rags, although I know the term is
not accurate for dances like the Shag and the Lindy and the Lambeth
Walk. I didn't know how to do them, but she did, and we had fun.
When he played a couple of slow foxtrots from the thirties—"Deep
Purple" and "Stardust" are the ones I remember—she danced just a
little too intimately, I thought. It was the sort of semiflirtatious stuff
that's acceptable, I suppose, if the husband is still in the room. Which
he wasn't. Then, Barry Kearns, our Commo Officer, cut in—to my relief. When I sat down, however, I was irked because she seemed to be
enjoying herself just as much with Barry.

Sally was right there with me, however, on the turn of the party
tide, and we left. On the drive back to Montevideo from Carrasco, I
searched for subjects to discuss, but we were silent. I was feeling the
same kind of tension I used to have years ago at the Keep playing kissing games with the neighbors' girls; there was that awful silence as you
marched out of the room with a girl. I remember that I always felt
then as if I were passing through the woods during a thaw and every
sound of melting water had the composure of a far-seeing purpose.

So soon as I parked in front of her house, she said, "Drive around the block."

I did. The Porringers were living in a small stucco house on one of the medium-income, medium-horizon, only-slightly-crumbling streets in an anonymous area back of the Legislative Palace. Even in summer, the streets are relatively deserted, and the block behind her house was distinguished by several empty lots. We parked, and she waited, and I did nothing. Then she reached around to lock the doors and close the windows. I still did nothing. I think my heart was beating loud enough for her to hear it. I did not really want to make love to her, and I did not want to cuckold Sherman Porringer, although there was, I admit, some dirty little rise somewhere down there. Then she said,

"May I ask you a personal question?"

"Yes," I said.

"Are you a queer?"

"No," I said.

"Then why won't you kiss me?"

"I don't know."

"Prove to me you're not a queer."

"Why do you think I am?"

"You talk so upper-class. Sherman says you're a prep-school kid."

I plunged. She went off like a firecracker. I confess to you, Kittredge, I didn't know that women could be so passionate.


This last sentence betrayed what I had known from the beginning—I was not going to go to conclusion. The details were not to be put into a letter. So I sat back in my chair, looked out my hotel room window at the grim building across the street from me, and recalled how her lips had kissed mine as if our mouths were in combat. Her hands, free of any conceivable embarrassment, hooked onto the buttons of my fly. Her breasts, which she soon freed of her brassiere, were in my mouth whenever she had need to lift her head to breathe, and then, to my horror, as if a long string of underground ammunition dumps in the sexual field of my fantasies were all to be detonated at once, she twisted, quick as a cat, bent down, and wrapped her mouth around the prow of my phallus (which seemed to me at that moment not only larger than I could ever remember, but worthy of the word phallus) and proceeded to take into her mouth the six, eight, nine, eleven jackhammer thrusts of the battering ram she had made of me. Then, in the midst of the extreme ejaculations of such ammo dumps blowing up, she added insult to injury and stuck her finger without a by-your-leave up my anus. I had obviously had one good Oklahoma cow-poke of a fuck, and we hadn't even had sexual intercourse yet.

That was remedied in surprisingly little time. I was amazingly hell-bent on enjoying all I could, as much as I could, as fast as I could, and yet, how I was repelled! It seemed manifestly unfair to raid the treasury of sex. In the middle of all my elation, exuberance, sexual wrath, and jubilee, in the midst of all my sense of something awfully strong in each of us smacked totally up against one another, there was the long, faint, elevated horror that Kittredge—for whom I had saved myself—was now forever removed from my first taste of all-out frenzy and lust. I had always assumed this kind of heat could only arrive at the end of the deepest sort of love affair, and with momentum as gravely joyous as the mount toward elation in a majestic orchestra embarked on a mighty symphony. Sex with Sally was a football mêlée with bites and bruises and chocolate squashed in your crotch.

By my third ejaculation, I was weary of her. The car windows were clouded, our clothes were a wadded-up joke, and I hardly knew if I was a stud or a rape victim. Drawing away from her, I managed to induce us to get our clothes together, Sally half-unwillingly. Her kisses—how cruel is the after-shade of desire!—had begun to seem leechlike. I wanted to get home.

I could not leave her at her door, however, like a package delivered by someone else. "I'll call you soon," I said, and felt all the powers of extortion being worked on me.

"Oh, you better," she said. "That was groovy."

Groovy! I had been offered the key to my country. I was now a charter member of that great, unknown middle land of America that I was prepared to defend. And felt a great relief as I drove off because so far as I knew, no pedestrian had passed our automobile on that lonely street. The risk of what we had undertaken was just becoming real to me.

Well, I had seen her since, of course. Once at her home while the children were out with a babysitter—a dreadful clammy occasion when we fornicated in fear that Sherman in full deployment of his paranoid powers would pop home, and we had certainly done better in my room at the Cervantes despite carnal heats on a mattress that smelled of disinfectant. Finally, I dared all the gods of precaution and took her to the safe house above Pocitos Beach, where we coupled in a chair by the twelfth-story window looking down on the passing traffic and the clay-colored waves.

No, I decided, it would have been hopeless to write about any of this to Kittredge, and I put aside the pages I had written about Sally.

Because I could not ignore the part of myself, however, that pleaded for some kind of confession, I conceived of a tale to close the gap.

2:00 A.M.

Kittredge,

Brand new subject. What I have to tell will not, I hope, affect us grievously, since our relation is dearer to me than any loyalty or pleasure I could find on the banks of the Rio Plata. You must believe that. I hope you will not be shocked if I confess that after many weeks of the most intense suffering from sexual abstention, I have at last felt bound to go to one of the better brothels here, and after a week or two of the inevitable winnowing out of choices, concerning which I will regale you someday, I have now settled on one Uruguayan girl in the Casa de Tres Árboles, and have what yet may prove to be an arrangement with her.

It makes sense to me. While you will always be the nearest embodiment I can know of the ineluctable quest, so do I also understand that you and Hugh will be together forever, as indeed you should be. There is no one I know closer to greatness than Hugh. Forgive such sententiousness, but I just want to say that I love you and Hugh together as much as I adore you separately, which, mathematically, is like trying to equate finite numbers with infinite sums—I come to full stop: All I wish to say is we must be truthful with one another as best we can, and I just had to have a woman. I know there's no conventional reason to ask your forgiveness, but I do. And I feel innocent, I confess.

I went on with the letter, spinning careful false tales of the mood of the brothel and finally signed off, not knowing whether I felt vicious or wise in using my original if now unsent letter about Sally as a guide to the false tale, but I knew myself well enough to feel a certain contentment at my guile even as I was falling asleep.

Over the next few months, I hardly knew what to do about Sally. We were more intimate than our affection for each other. And my derelictions of duty were increasing. If Porringer was working triple-time under Hunt, I took time out from my own double-time to arrange a meeting with an agent that I knew would not take place. I had not notified him. Instead, I saw Sally. A week later, I did as much again. Professionally speaking, it was easy to conceal. Agents often missed meetings. Like horses, they bolted at the sight of a leaf blowing by. I had to file bogus reports, but they were routine, and bought two hours each time with Sally in my bedroom at the Cervantes. I, waiting for her, would have my clothes off, and my bathrobe on; she, knocking on the door with a tap followed by two taps, would be out of her shoes and off with her skirt even as we embraced in the first of her powerful kisses. "Glue sandwiches" I would have labeled them if not in the mood, but I was usually in the mood, and, naked in a streak, we grappled toward the bed, stealing handfuls of each other's flesh en route before diving down into the song of the bedsprings, her mouth engorging my cock. There are a hundred words, I suppose, for a penis, but cock is the one that goes with fellatio, and her open marriage with lust, abandonment, and sheer all-out hunger for Hubbard's Yankee prong gave that fellow a mind of his own, a hound off his leash, a brute pillaging the temple of her mouth, except who could call it a temple?—she had confessed to me in one of our postcopulatory conversations that from high school on, she had had a natural appetite, or was it thirst, for this outpost of the forbidden, and, God, it was out of control by the time she came to me.

I, in my turn, was developing tastes and inclinations I did not know I had. Before long, she was presenting her navel and pubic hair toward me, and I, facing the contradictory choices of domination or equality, found my own head reaching to explore her sandy, almost weedlike bush. I am cruel enough to mention how wild and scraggly it looked because that came to mean little. It was the avid mouth behind the hair that leaped out to a part of me that did not know it existed until I was licking and tonguing away with my own abandon which I had never known could belong to my critical lips until they opened into the sheer need I knew to jump across the gap from one bare-ass universe to the next. The only way I ever felt close to Sally Porringer was when her mouth was on my cock and my face was plastered into the canyon between her legs. Who could know what things we had to tell each other at such times? It was not love we exchanged, I expect, but all the old bruises and pinched-off desires—how much there was of that! Lust, I was deciding, had to be all the vast excitement of releasing the tons of mediocrity in oneself. (Then, afterward, when alone in my bed, I would wonder if new mediocrity had been ingested just as much as the old had been purged.) I was discovering that I had the gusto of a high school athlete and the chill estimates of a man so noble in perception of each unhappy nuance as T. S. Eliot.

Say this for the act. When we rose dripping from the sweet and sour mire of feeding on each other, my copulation came pounding happily out of me. To fuck fast was to throw one's heart into the breach and pound enough blood to the head to banish Thomas Stearns of the Eliot family. One gunned the motors of one's soul and the sugar of one's scrotum—what a joy to discover that Hubbards also secreted scrotum sugar—up, up, over the hill, and into the unchartable empyrean beyond. That vision seemed to disappear almost as soon as it afforded its glimpse. I would be happy for a while to know I was a man and that she wanted me and I gave her pleasure. Soon enough she would be stirring once more. She was not insatiable, but near enough. By the third time, I would be thinking that the worst of all this passion was the knowledge that when we were done, we would not know how to talk. We were about as essentially happy with each other in this situation as two strangers who attempt to make conversation on a train.

From *Harlot's Ghost* (1991)

# URUGUAY—II

## A Course in Counterespionage

Jan. 11, 1958

Dearest Kittredge,

Let me introduce you to my new KGB cronies, Boris Gennadye-vitch Masarov and his gypsy wife, Zenia. (She told me once that she was one-nineteenth gypsy.)

"One-nineteenth?" I asked her.

"You are brutal as Russian with fascination for facts, figures, num-bers," she responded.

"One-nineteenth?" I inquired again.

"Are good-looking young man. Why ask silly question?"

Having set down this exchange, I see that I have failed to present her quality. She is not shallow. She carries herself as if nothing has tran-spired in Russia of any moment since Dostoyevsky was saved from the firing squad by the czar's reprieve. I suppose I am saying that she elic-its a chord in one's historical appreciation. I now know how an aristo-cratic woman of the provinces might appear to us in the middle of the nineteenth century. The best of Russian literature comes alive for me when I am around Zenia. So many of Turgenev's dissatisfied women come to mind, and Chekhov's incomparable glimpses of the Russian provinces. Zenia is all of them for me, and more. Yet, she is also a woman who has lived under the horrors of Stalin. Kittredge, you can feel the depredations of Soviet history through the sense one receives of her much-battered soul. While she looks over forty, the Russians show their age in ways we do not. Do you know, I believe they take a certain grim satisfaction in wearing their souls on the wrinkled surface of their face. We Americans would, of course, go squeak before we'd ever let anyone have the satisfaction of thinking he was looking into our spiritual depths, but that may be exactly what the Russians have to offer. "I have passed through cataclysmic days, and permitted state horrors to be visited on friends, but I have never lied to my soul." That is what her face says to me. (She has the most extraordinary deep dark eyes—operative definition of "Otchi Chorniya.") Yet she has to have been around frightful events. She is KGB, after all. Or at least her husband is. Then she tells me that she is thirty-three. Yes, history has cut its lines into Russian faces.

Well, here I am, rushing new people on to you without the courtesy of a little development, but then this friendship with the Masarovs is the most interesting relation I have at present with anyone in Uruguay, even if it has been put together like an arranged marriage with brokers on both sides.

It began because here in Montevideo we are sometimes a working part of the State Department. "Our cover folds us into the crust" has become one of Hunt's sayings. Of course, he doesn't exactly hate the idea of pretending to be First Secretary to the American Ambassador. As you may recall, that worthy, Jefferson Patterson, Eisenhower's appointee, is a genteel man with a hopeless stammer in English and it gets worse when he attempts Spanish. So, Patterson continues to avoid functions. His deputy, the Counselor, is all right, but his wife, a lush, has been known to take off her shoes at Embassy dances and embark on impromptu high kicks—"*Grands jetés*," she announces. Needless to say, they took her off the circuit. Which leaves the field open to the Hunts, and, on occasion, the Porringers, and myself.

Combine this with the State Department's estimate that Khrushchev's constant appeals lately for armament reductions, while clearly not to be trusted, must be met, nonetheless, with compensatory American moves. We-cannot-lose-another-contest-for-world-opinion is the present State Department stance. Word has even come to us from Western Hemisphere Division: Carefully monitored fraternizing with the Soviets is a viable option. Theoretically, we're always prepared to get friendly with any Soviet who throws us a side glance, but as a practical matter, whenever small conversations commence around the canapé tables, we comport ourselves as if we are offering Christmas politesse to lepers. You don't put a career on the line by fraternizing for too little.

Well, the directive has come in. And we have certainly heated up our telephoto outpost now that the Russian garden parties are going again. The Sourballs thought enough of this opportunity to send down two of their operators. Nearly all of Soviet Russia Div's people are anti-Soviet Russians, or Poles, or Finns, intensely fluent in Russian. They do make an odd breed. Paranoid and insular to an extraordinary degree, they give off about as much warmth as a barnacle. Yet they sport what could be Irish names if not for the odd spelling. Monikers like Heulihaen (pronounced Hoolihan) and Flarrety (pronounced Flaherty). Heulihaen and Flarrety have been installed on separate eight-hour stints at GOGOL for the last month, and have been photographing the very hell out of the lawn parties in the Soviet Embassy garden.

Hunt calls them our Finnish Micks. Left to themselves, the Finnish Micks would pass over to us about as much information as you could get from a Mickey Finn, but Hunt knows how to play the web back at Cockroach Alley. Result: The Finnish Micks grudgingly provide us with bits of poop and scam.

The largest discovery (accomplished by way of filming the Russians and their guests in the garden, then studying these home movies around the clock) is that a bit of infidelity is going on behind Soviet Embassy walls. There seems a likely connection between the new Soviet KGB chief, the *Resident,* named Varkhov, Georgi Varkhov, who looks exactly as he should, built like a tank, shaved head like a bullet, and—are you wholly prepared?—our own soulful Zenia.

Now, I was apprised of this item after I became friendly, all proportions kept, with the Masarovs. I still think Zenia is soulful, although her taste for Varkhov, if true, puts me off. The Finnish Micks, however, seem pretty certain of their ground. The working logic for such conclusions, as I piece it out, comes to this: In social life, we are always surrounded by hints of infidelity at every party. We see smiles, whispers, glances—all that movie-business sign language. Yet our perceptions are transitory. Hints of behavior are everywhere, but we usually cannot confirm what we have seen. On film, however, if we expend the patience to reexamine each move of our actors, the indeterminate can crystallize into the concrete. By such methods are we provided with a 75-percent certainty that Zenia Masarov and Georgi Varkhov are having a liaison, and Boris Gennadyevitch Masarov is aware of the situation.

Some time ago, Varkhov, the Resident at the Russian Embassy, invited us to a large party. After cable exchanges with the Groogs and the Sourballs, we accepted. Hunt led the State Department delegation, and Porringer and I took up our cover as First Assistant and Second Assistant to the First Secretary to the Ambassador—shades of Gilbert and Sullivan! Hunt, looking over our team, decided that I needed a date.

"How about Nancy Waterston," he decided.

I'm sure it's been so long since I mentioned our Administrative Officer that I must refresh your memory. I believe I described Nancy once as sweet, bright, and hardworking but undeniably plain and very much a spinster. She used to be devoted to Mayhew, and Hunt now gets ditto loyalty. In the beginning, I took her out a couple of times when Mrs. Sonderstrom or Mrs. Porringer or Mrs. Gatsby or Mrs. Kearns couldn't find an unattached single girl for me. Nancy has to be ten years older than myself, and I would guess that she has never been to bed with a man.

Well, if it had been the Swiss Embassy, or even the Embajada de Gran Bretaña, I would have accepted the chore, but I felt curiously diminished to enter the Soviet lair with Nancy on my arm.

Hunt would have none of these niceties. "Do you know the meaning of 'The Colonel requests'?" he asked.

"Howard, Nancy won't enjoy herself."

"She will."

He laughed a lot at that in the sky-high skinny whinny you so detest.

"What is your motive?" I asked about as coldly as I dared.

"It's a ploy, Harry. The King Brothers won't know what to make of you and Nancy."

"They'll see right through it."

"Well, kid, they might not. Because I want you to introduce Nancy as your fiancée."

"Have you asked her?"

"She's amenable. It'll be fun for her."

"Howard," I said, "tell me the real motive. It will go down easier."

"The Sovs are always running a dupe-show on us. I've seen one of their joy-boys with three different Russian tomatoes at three different foreign embassy functions. Each time, the same fellow has the gall to introduce the *lady*"—he held both hands far apart and dipped quotation marks with bent fingers—"as his wife. The time has come to show them a little of our dipsy doodle."

Well, Kittredge, it ended up being quite an evening. We arrived at the Russian Embassy on a Saturday in late afternoon and the light was kind to the soft yellow tones of their stone manse. Like much of Montevideo architecture, it is a hodgepodge of Italian Renaissance, French Baroque, Transylvanian Gothic, Oak Park, Illinois, circa 1912, and plain old Russian samovar, a big sprawling villa with massive doors and turrets and ingrown balconies that look like ingrown toenails, dwarf windows and magnum windows, forbidding outer gates, black-spiked fence with painted gold tips on the spearheads. "Bluebeard's castle," I whispered to Nancy as we entered the outer gate and were steered by a wholly uncompromising young Russian marine to the garden. I had an unruly impulse to look up at our villa window where our Bolex H-16 is posted, and give a clenched fist of a Communist salute to the Finnish Micks.

Well, I've never described an embassy party on the theory that you're familiar enough with them in Washington, so why be offered details of our lesser spread? Still, the Russians do it up. They had invited about every foreign gang in town—Norway, Greece, Japan, Portugal, Costa Rica, name it, even the Orden Soberana de Malta, the Reino de Bélgica, and the República Socialista de Checoslovaquia. By the time the international tide was in, there may have been one hundred and fifty people on that lawn drawn from as many as forty embassies and consulates. A Soviet offering of hospitality to the world: one ton of black caviar, endless supplies of vodka, plus the usual array of appetizers, most of which struck the eye like a bead of acid-green pigment on a mound of cadmium orange. They also serve red wine and white wine from the Caucasus—some of the worst stuff ever corked—and all the foreign embassy types did their best to practice English on me. There is something so prodigiously fraudulent about the congealed friendliness of these embassy types. Such anxiety in the air. Everyone stirs with the restlessness of birds.

All this was exacerbated by the presence of Americans in the Russian garden. How I wish you could have been here. Your beauty would have polarized the greensward. As it was, I anticipated in advance just how it was going to show in the films. From above, each American and each Russian was the center of a cluster of foreign embassy types. Caught by a telephoto lens, pieces of information seem equal to particles of food. Tongues dart out to snatch each morsel.

Afternoon opened onto twilight, and another mood settled in. Everyone got a little wild (by which I mean no more than a shade over into the indiscreet). Hunt tells me that movie people call this time of day the magic hour since the natural light is soft and wonderful, but the scene has to be captured on film in thirty minutes. (If I ever have to face a firing squad, I hope it's in a garden at twilight—what a thought!) I kept picturing the frustrations of Heulihaen and Flarrety as they bore down on us with their lens and (it better be) ultra-high-speed film. Of course, the more we all acted up at the party, the less light there was to satisfy our Finns.

Pretty soon, those minor and major embassies who happen on this day to have no particular business to initiate begin to leave, and the lawn opens for dramatic action. Now you can pick up what is happening across the garden. Hunt is talking to Varkhov, who in turn is paying court to Dorothy. Before long, Zenia takes a stroll from the Foreign Office to the KGB, which is to say leaves two of Great Britain's officials to join her Resident, and she and Varkhov now laugh loudly at Hunt's jokes, and I, giddy from caviar, after a year of eating meat twice a day, and not impervious to the vodka, move in on Boris Masarov, keeping Nancy at my side. "I want you to meet my fiancée," I say in the best good humor, as if the idea were mine all along.

Kittredge, I must tell you. Given my schooling, I am only now learning what wonderful and mysterious beings women are. I confess it. Nancy Waterston, whose face on a good day would give competition to a parson's daughter, narrow, pinched, and all her features pulled by duty, her small bust unable to protrude beyond the forward hunch of her shoulders, now looked as attractive as if sparklers had been set off on her wedding cake. When a plain woman looks dazzling for an instant, one's breath stands still; the universe is full of surprise. (Which is equal to saying, I suppose, that the universe is meaningful.)

Masarov reacted formally. "I congratulate you," he said. "I lift glass to toast vital spirit of future marriage."

"Mr. Masarov, that is a distinguished toast," said Nancy in her good Midwestern accent so cram-packed with honest step-by-step sentiment. But then she gave a little laugh as such honesty came face to face with her present role. "Maybe you will attend our wedding," she said.

"It will be when?" he asked, and I could not help but notice that he was looking down the length of the lawn to where Zenia and Varkhov were still talking to Hunt and Dorothy. The anguish on Masarov's face (which I cannot say I would have perceived had not the Zenia-Varkhov liaison been advertised to me as a 75-percent likelihood) now seemed analogous to the wound of a tired animal who pauses, blood dripping, before gathering itself to climb one more hill. He downed his drink in a shot and stopped a Uruguayan waiter who was carrying an ice-cold bottle of vodka on a tray.

"We don't know the date yet," said Nancy, "because I believe in long engagements." Was she drunk, I wondered, or merely intoxicated by newfound talents? "That's an old family institution," she told him. "My father and mother went together seven years before their wedding bells spoke up long enough to say, 'Enough of this. Please ring us. We're rusty.' "

"Yes," he said, "may I ask? What does your father do?"

"He's a circus acrobat," said Nancy, and giggled again. Her eyes were dancing behind her eyeglasses. I realized, as if I were cleansing the inside of myself with the nicest pomade of compassion and sweet sorrow, that this must be the liveliest evening she had had in Uruguay. "No," she said, "our country was founded on the idea that you cannot tell a lie. My father is retired, but he used to be a corporate executive in insurance in Akron, Ohio."

Masarov looked relieved, as if a piece of intelligence had just checked out. "My country was not founded," he said in reply. "More likely, was shot out of a cannon."

Be certain, I underlined that last remark for referral to Hunt.

Masarov held up his glass. "Toast to future nuptials."

"I like being toasted," said Nancy.

"First, however, learn to drink our vodka. Americans are always telling me is hard to keep up with Russian banquets. Because they do not know secret."

"Oh, give me the secret," she said.

At just this juncture, Varkhov, who was making a tour of his remaining guests, joined us, and jumped in so quickly on Masarov's speech that I realized both men were equally well used to informing all and sundry how to imbibe Russian spirits. Varkhov's syntax in English, however, was what an instructor at the Farm once called *Russky Tarzan*. Articles, pronouns, and the verb *to be* withered away. Primeval grunts were substituted.

"Not sipping," he said. "Never sipping. Gulp vodka. Only"—Varkhov held up one Russian commissar of a flat, heavy palm—"offer toast. First! Deepest toast. Appraisal of relationship. From heart. Offered from heart, drink vodka in gulp." Which he did, and whistled for the waiter to come back. "Fill glasses. Not worry. Small glasses."

We filled glasses. "After vodka," he said, "eat caviar. Better, eat *zakushki*. Appetizer."

"Yes," said Nancy, as if she were well used to obeying orders.

"Then, darling lady never drunk."

"Ho, ho, ho," said I.

"Cynic," said Varkhov.

He held up his glass again. "Toast," he said. "To evening, to future of peace, to lovely lady, to American with mission," and he winked at me. We were all drunk, yessiree baby.

Outside on the Bulevar España you could hear the traffic going to and fro between the city to our right and Pocitos Beach, with its high-rise apartment houses, down to the left. From side streets, the tangential whoops of adolescents ricocheted through the evening air. Quite as abruptly as he had joined us, Varkhov bowed and left for another group.

"Do you play chess?" Masarov asked me.

"Yes," I said, "not all that well."

"But not so badly?"

"I can play," I said.

"Good. You must be very good. I will invite you to my home. It is nearby. And you, Miss Waterston."

"Name the date, I'll bring the cake," she said.

"An old American expression?" he asked. Was I reading too much into him, or was it said with something like longing? He not only spoke reasonably good English but seemed to take pleasure in it.

"No," she answered, "it's as hometown and hicky as you can get."

"Hometown and hicky," he repeated. "Hicky is . . . pustule, pimple?"

"Just about," said Nancy.

Kittredge, this was the hot core of the evening. The string was thrown across the abyss and now the cord and rope will follow. Indeed, it has. I will tell you in my next letter about the evening with the Masarovs.

> My love to you, to Hugh, and to Christopher,
> Harry the Betrothed


In my letter, I had jumped conveniently over the rest of the evening. Nancy was drunk and said she had eaten too many appetizers, so I took her home. Home proved to be three rooms on the second floor of a modest villa on the Calle Doctor Geraldo Ramón not three blocks from the Embassy. "I think freedom consists of being able to walk to work in the morning," she told me in most certain, if inebriated, terms. She certainly had a second voice installed behind the first. I made the mistake of kissing her.

She kissed back as if we were indeed betrothed and getting married tomorrow. I was discovering that the mouth of a virgin spinster was not like others. Her lips pressed against mine, a family seal upon wax. Her teeth offered the faint odor of dentifrice, mouthwash, and tooth inlay, but her breath was a furnace, and back of that was some baleful neutral zone inspired by her stomach. I had an awful set of impulses I could never have been able to confess to Kittredge in a letter. I knew that Nancy Waterston could be mine forever if I chose, and the centrality of such power stirred something awfully cold in me. It was then I assured her that it had been a remarkable evening and perhaps we would visit the Masarovs together, and made my exit much impressed with the ability of one kiss to conduct me right up to the edge of a possible marriage.

January 27, 1958

Dearest Kittredge,

I was hoping for a letter, but perhaps you are waiting to hear more about the Masarovs. In any event, I feel like writing. You see, I'm obliged to report these days on each step taken with Boris and Zenia. Then the Groogs and Sourballs masticate my cables down to the molecules.

As one example of the present work mode, the Groogs and Sours decide in concert with Hunt (for he refuses to be bypassed on any decision, minor or major) that Nancy should not accompany me to the Masarov home. Their reasoning is that a continuing presentation of Miss Waterston and myself as prospective bride and groom might put our histrionic abilities to too great a test—Nancy's, anyway, Hunt allows. I suspect that Hunt messed up in the first place by putting an Administrative Officer like Nancy into such a slot.

At any rate, Miss Waterston was sufficiently disappointed to show chagrin. "Oh, fudge," she said, "oh, fudge and yee-God crackers," so help me, Kittredge, is what she said. Then, with a sigh and a formal, professional smile—Lord, she is professional—she went back to auditing accounts. Poor Nancy—she is so weathered by disappointment.

Meanwhile, I get ready to visit the Masarovs. I call, and, via Hunt's specific instructions, make the date for Nancy and myself. The idea is to keep Zenia at home with Boris. If she knows Nancy is not accompanying me, she may absent herself, and Howard is trying to forestall that. It's deemed more rewarding to get a take on husband and wife together. If the Masarovs are near to a breakup, there may be indications which of the two could be more likely to defect. On the off chance that they present themselves as a strong, well-knit couple, maybe they'll fly the coop together. Such is our advance reasoning.

The day arrives. I trot over for tea and make my apologies about Nancy's indisposition. They seem disappointed. I cannot help thinking that Hunt was right. If Zenia had been told in advance, she might not have been there.

Given the limited supply of desirable real estate in Montevideo, my friendly Russian couple is living in a high-rise apartment house just two blocks further down the Rambla from the similar high-rise in which is located our safe house. The Masarovs are on the tenth floor, and also have a view through their picture window of Pocitos Beach and the sea. There, all resemblances end. They have truly furnished their place. I do not know if it is to my taste, but their belongings do fill the living room. There are heavy velvet drapes looped around the picture window, several fat armchairs and a plump sofa with lace antimacassars, a small oriental carpet on top of a large one, two samovars—one in brass, the other in silver—a number of standing lamps with beaded shades, a large piece of mahogany furniture with open glass cases for the display of their plates and dishes, small casts of heavy nineteenth-century sculpture on every table, a bronze maiden, for example, with a filmy bronze gown clinging to her half-exposed breasts, then Apollo, standing on the ball of one foot, and gold-framed prints of paintings wherever there is space: Cézanne, Gauguin, Van Gogh, plus a couple of Russian painters I do not recognize who portray czars flanked by Russian Orthodox high priests, and nobles dressed half like pirates—must be boyars. In the corner of one painting, a defeated boyar is bleeding to death from a wound in his neck. The agony on his mouth is expressive. Quite a picture to look at every day.

There are also oriental carpets put up as wall hangings, and I count four chess sets, two of which look to be of value. One of the boards is made of inlaid wood.

I can't help contrasting this old-fashioned, middle-class opulence with Sherman Porringer's child-scuffed, dog-chewed, blond-wood furniture and bookshelves on bricks. The Masarovs, possessing not all that much space (now that they've filled it), have converted the hallway that ties their three and a half rooms together into a long, very narrow library. It is a squeeze for two people to walk side by side, yet both walls are lined with dark-stained oak bookcases. Later I get to look at Boris' collection of tomes, and will tell you that he reads French, German, English, Spanish, Italian, and several Soviet languages whose names I would not know how to spell. That is a lot for him to have learned, but then he says he is thirty-seven. While this conflicts with the Sourball dossier, which pegs him at thirty-two, I must say it adds up. He speaks of the Second World War, where he rose to the rank of captain, and countless framed photographs on a collection of end tables are certainly there to verify his military career. I do take mental note of the shoulder-board epaulets in these photographs so the Sours can check it out. Of course, I am not able to swear these are World War II snapshots, but they do have the feel of those times, and on one photograph you can witness for background an incredibly littered city of rubble and jagged artifacts. "Berlin," he told me, "in the last days. That is why we are smiling."

"Yes, you must have been happy the war was coming to an end."

He shrugged. Suddenly, he was gloomy. "Half happy," he replied gnomically, but then, as if it were not congenial to speak in such fashion to a guest, he added, "There is always question. Does one deserve life? Better men have perished."

"Still, you laugh in photograph," remarked Zenia.

"I am happy," he said, contradicting himself.

"We were meeting two days before," said Zenia. "Brishka and myself. First time."

"You, too, happened to be in Berlin?" I asked.

"Entertain troops."

"Zenia is a poet," said Masarov.

"Was," said Zenia.

"She has not written a poem in two years."

"Oh," I said.

"Close to goofy," said Zenia. *"Moi."*

"Well," I said. (Kittredge, I swear, we have to be as bad as the English when it comes to receiving sudden confession.) "Well, it must be difficult to sit in these well-furnished rooms when one's pen is dry." (To myself, I sounded like the Earl of Phumpherdom.)

The Russians have one virtue, however. They are so abrupt that no deadening remark can keep a half-life of more than three seconds. "Well-furnished?" asked Zenia. "Aggregate. Is but aggregate."

I heard "aggravate" at first, so was, of course, confused, until her next speech brought clarification. "His family, my family. Aggregate of Moscow apartment—his father; Leningrad apartment—my mother. Remnants of families now complete."

"None of it yours?"

"All mine. All belongs to Boris. *Aussi.* Also."

"Yes," I said, "and your government shipped it over here for you?"

"Of course," she said, "why not?"

"But your apartment in Moscow must be empty."

She shrugged. "People in it."

We sat down at this point before the second-best chess set and Boris handed me the white pawn. "You are my guest," he said.

Kittredge, you know I am not at all in Hugh's class as a player, but I'm not bad—once I won a low-level tournament of *patzers,* as modest players are referred to, and in a simultaneous exhibition with a ranked master who was taking on twenty Yale students at twenty boards, I happened to be one of three who came away with a draw. The other seventeen all lost. All the same, I am, when it comes to real levels of chess, essentially talentless.

I could sense, however, as soon as we commenced, that the game meant much to him. As if a first whiff of the great international contest for the soul of man had finally entered our mood, I was aware of his tension, and then, reciprocally, of mine. "When in doubt, open with a king's pawn," I said cheerfully to him, and did just that. He nodded curtly, but then was rude enough for the first time—since his manners, as I hope I've indicated, are the best of that whole Russian gang on Bulevar España—to sit in his chair and study me openly for a minute. He did not look at the board, rather at my face, my posture, my uncertain smile, my—in short—my emanations. He made me feel as if I were back in the gym at St. Matthew's, and was going to wrestle with the determined-looking fellow at the other end of the mat in just twenty seconds.

"I think," he said at last, "Sicilian Defense is appropriate reply," and he advanced a queen's bishop's pawn to the fourth rank. Kittredge, I remember clearly that you spoke once of giving chess up at the age of twelve because you could think of nothing else. I would not wish to stir any half-buried cerebration, but I have to tell you this much: The black reply that always puts my king's-pawn opening into trouble is the Sicilian Defense. It seems to take a different turn every time, and I never get to play my game. I'm white, but I'm reacting all the while to what black is up to. It was uncanny of Boris to look me over so carefully, then pick the Sicilian.

Well, that's all you need to know. By the sixth move I was uncomfortable, by the eighth I was beginning to glimpse future defeat, and by the tenth move he had gotten up from his chair in impatience at how long it was taking me—we employed no clock—and came back with a book, and was impolite enough, or superior enough, or maybe it is elegant enough, to sit there reading while I cogitated over my next move. Then, as soon as I had come to a decision, he would look up, pull his upper teeth over his lower lip with the gentlest sound of tasteful appreciation, reach forward, make his move, which always took immediate account of whatever small positional scheme I was hoping to advance, and then without a by-your-leave, go back to his book, which happened to be—do you believe this?—the Modern Library Giant of *Moby-Dick*. He was, incidentally, well into it.

Masarov took a knight on the fourteenth move, and I gave up on the fifteenth. He had all the position by then and his rooks were ready to go. I never succeeded in castling. He kept me too busy.

Now Zenia brings out the tea. There is, in the wake left by the game, nothing to talk about. I comment that she does not use the samovars but a teapot. "English tea," she replies. I ask for her patronymic. "My father's name—Arkady. I am Zenia Arkadyova."

"The sounds are beautiful," I say. "Zenia Arkadyova."

We make a little game of getting the accent right. "Many sounds in Russian," she tells me, "woods, earth, small animals in forest, rivers. English different. Derives from roads, hills, beaches. Surf of sea."

The largest generalizations are always begging to be adopted by me, but this is too basic.

"I'm sure you are right," I say.

She stares at me. It is disconcerting. She seems to be searching for some person in hiding just behind myself. "May I look at your library?" I ask Boris.

He pulls himself out of the deep depression in which he has sat since the end of the game. He passes with a wave of his hand over the three-quarters of his books that are in Cyrillic, and brings me to his American section. In English, is all of Hemingway and most of Faulkner. Also Mary McCarthy, Tennessee Williams, Arthur Miller, William Inge, Sidney Howard, Elmer Rice, all of O'Neill, Clifford Odets, and T. S. Eliot—*The Cocktail Party*.

"Do you have ambitions to be a playwright?" I asked.

He grunted. "A playwright?" he replied. "I would not know how to talk to actors."

"Nonsense," said Zenia.

He shrugged. "Hemingway I like," he said. " 'Tis the essence of pre–World War Two America, would you agree?" (" 'Tis!") We had taken another step along the bookcase and were passing the works of Henry James. "Much studied by Lenin and Dzerzhinsky," said Masarov, tapping the binding of *The Golden Bowl*.

"Is that really true?" I asked. I was overcome by such news.

"No," said Zenia. "Brishka makes jokes."

"Not at all. *Golden Bowl*. Perfect symbol for capitalism. Of course Dzerzhinsky would read such work."

"Boris, ridiculous. Is insult to our guest."

He shrugged. "I apologize," he said, and looked me in the eye. "Who do you like? Tolstoy or Dostoyevsky?"

"Dostoyevsky," I said.

"Good. Dostoyevsky writes semi-atrocious Russian, but is, in fact, my preference. So we have possibility for friendship."

"First, I must improve my chess."

"Cannot be done," he said. His candor caught me by surprise, and I began to laugh. He soon joined me. He's got this heavy body and prematurely graying hair, much-lined face, one tough guy, but there's an odd youth lurking in the corners of his expression, as if he hasn't figured everything out yet.

"*Zakuski*," said Zenia. "Have *zakuski* with more tea. Or vodka."

I declined. She protested. Despite an atrocious accent, her voice is deep and suggestive. At public functions, she seems like a mysterious and sensuous woman, exotic, occult, as removed from both of us as an oracle; this afternoon, she is middle-aged, fussy, maternal, the mistress of a small and very bourgeois establishment. I am finding it hard to piece together any sense of these two people as KGB, whether together or apart. Yet he has gone out of his way to mention Dzerzhinsky—that is obliged to be some sort of signal.

We sit down and chat about cultural matters American. He is interested in Jack Kerouac and William Burroughs, in Thelonius Monk, in Sonny Rollins, whom I have never heard of. He has a record of Sonny Rollins and plays it for me and beams when I say that I have never heard a better tenor saxophone.

Abruptly, he opens a new direction. "Zenia was telling untruth," he says.

"Zenia Arkadyova was lying?" I ask.

He smiles at my use of the patronymic. "She has, actually, written one poem in last two years."

"No, is awful. Do not show," says Zenia.

"In English," says Masarov. "This year, in Russian tongue, Zenia cannot express herself. Not this year. Is total block. So, in your language, she has essayed . . . attempted . . ."

"*Zakuski*. Little poem. Appetizer," says Zenia. She is wholly flushed now, and her ample bosom is, I could swear, surging. "Nugatory," she says. "Trivial." (Sounds like tree-vee-*owl*.)

"Let him read it," says Brishka.

They argue in Russian. She yields. She goes to the bedroom and comes back with a sheet of cheap notebook paper. On it, in a somewhat unwieldy hand, she has put this head: "Vertigo Is Joy."

You can believe that after encountering such a title, I picked up her offering with no happiness, but . . . let me write it out for you. Lord knows, I've not only got a copy, but can recite it by heart after the workout it got from the Sourballs.

VERTIGO IS JOY

*Our bird passed away in my hand,*
  *its feathers a shroud.*
*I knew the moment,*
*Its last heartbeat*
*spoke to my palm.*
*Comrade, said bird,*
*do not wait in line*
*to mourn for me.*
*I fall into depths*
*that are great heights.*

"Better if in Russian," said Zenia, "but cannot find *les mots justes.* Not for Russian. Words speak from English. Boris gives correct grammar? Correct punctuation? Is correct?"

"Yes," I said.

"Is good? Good poem?"

"I think so."

"Zenia is recognized in Russia," said Boris, "although perhaps not recognized enough."

"Is good for printing in America?" asked Zenia.

"Probably," I said. "Let me take it. I have two friends who edit literary magazines."

"Yes," she said, "yours," and folded it into my hand, and looked at me with embarrassing intimacy considering that we were standing there in front of her husband. "Print with pseudonym for me," she said.

"No," said Boris. "Present as work of a Soviet poet."

"Madness," she muttered.

"I think you might change the title," I said. "It's a little too direct for English."

She would not change her title. She loved the sound. "Am adamant for *vertigo*," she said. In her pronunciation, it rhymes with tuxedo. Ver-*te*-go.

I left after some discussion of when we would visit again. Masarov proposed a picnic with Nancy and me. I agreed. But by the time that day arrived, Nancy was not on board, and Zenia had decamped for the day. Boris and I went on the picnic together.

I am beginning to rush, however, and would rather wait for a day or two and finish this off with another letter.

Yours,
Harry

February 16, 1958

Dear Kittredge,

It was my intent to get back to you a couple of weeks ago. The Sourballs, however, have been taking me through session after session, and I come back to my hotel room each night hoping to empty my head long enough to find sleep. In addition, I am concerned by your lack of response. Sometimes I even wonder whether my letters pile up unread. Ah, well, if you are interrogated often enough by the Sourballs, there is no drear scenario that will not raise its paranoid head.

You may recollect how modest was my meeting with the Masarovs. Well, the Soviet Russia Division did not think so. After I sent off a lengthy cable to Washington concerning my little get-together with the new Soviet friends, I received by return cable a questionnaire about as long as my last letter to you. Answering it kept me busy for a day and a half. Then, a man flew down to us, care of Soviet Russia Division, to interrogate me personally. By accent and appearance, he has to be another Finnish Mick. He calls himself Omaley. (Pronounced like "homily" without the *h*.) He is not too tall, and very thin, and has horns, yes, horns of hair on an otherwise near-bald head. He also has a profusion of what I am tempted to call reverse whiskers. His chest thatch is apparently so thick that it grows out of his shirt and half up his neck. It gives him a ruff above his collar. He looks like a malnourished wild boar. You can imagine how well Howard Hunt takes to Hjalmar Omaley.

Well, Hjalmar Omaley doesn't care one goddamn what anyone thinks of him. He lives to do his work. Around the second day of living in his implacably chill company, I recognize that he reminds me of the exterminator who used to come to my mother's Park Avenue apartment on those cheerful mornings when cook discovered cockroaches in the oven and was ready to quit because maid was not washing the grill. I don't want to throw your stomach into the next meal, but Omaley looks like a liquidator ready to leave nothing of our enemy but the last of its bodily seepage. Communists are vermin, Soviet Communists are rabid vermin, KGB Communists are rabid *occult* vermin, and I had been in contact with the latter.

Now, I exaggerate. Except, I don't. I was queried on what I could remember of the Masarovs' war photographs until I began to feel profoundly guilty that I could not remember more, indeed, I began to wonder at my lack of motivation in memorizing relatively so little. Hjalmar, who must have simmered in sperm-soups of suspicion before being received by the clear-eyed ovum in his mother's womb, led me through endless rephrasings of each question. I had made the large mistake in my first cable of describing Boris and Zenia as "reasonably agreeable." I had intended to give an objective appraisal, but it stirred frightful concerns in the counterintelligence gang at Soviet Russia Division. I can tell you that I was interrogated on every aspect of the meeting. Could I remember the exact sequence of moves in the chess game? I did my best to replay the game to their satisfaction but could not connect the opening to our final position. This infuriated Hjalmar Omaley. Apparently, Masarov is so good at chess (at least by their original dossier on him—which, I would remind you, places him at age thirty-two, not thirty-seven) that they wanted to see whether he was carrying me in the game; that might indicate whether his motive was to charm me. No, I told them over and over, he was not carrying me—it was embarrassing to have to resign by the fifteenth move.

Next, we catalogued the furniture. The Sourballs are looking into their sources to see if more can be learned about Masarov's father's Moscow apartment and Zenia's mother's Leningrad apartment. After which, they proceeded to interrogate me about the American novels and plays in his bookcase. How new were the volumes? How well thumbed? The question is how close he is to what he presents himself as being—a Russian official with specialties on American cultural affairs.

Then we went to the poem. I had been wired with a sneaky that possessed only an hour's capacity, so the tape was finished before we came to the poem. I was asked, therefore, to reconstruct all dialogue not recorded. In what ways did the couple react to my suggestion that the poem was printable in America? Am I certain that Zenia muttered the word *madness*?

I won't bore you with how long they spent on "I fall into depths that are great heights." (It is, of course, being interpreted as the Masarov offer to defect.)

On the second day, I said to Omaley, "Do you always pursue details this intensively after Agency meetings with Russians?"

He smiled as if only an idiot like myself could ask such a question. I felt as if I were in the dentist's chair.

On the third day, Howard Hunt took me to El Águila, his favorite restaurant, for lunch. The Sourballs were in an uproar, he confided, over the discrepancy in Boris' dossier. Since my report that he was thirty-seven gummed up their Soviet Personnel Record file, they were damned upset. The question now is whether our present Boris is the original, or a new body. "Next question," said Hunt. "Does Boris want to defect, or does he wish to entrap you?"

"For practical purposes, he has," I said. "I can't get any of my other work done."

"This will pass," he answered. "Just keep to the positive side of the equation. Get Boris to defect and you will hold all the bouquets." He nodded. "But, buddy, you've got to be more observant next time."

"It doesn't add up," I said. "If Boris wants to come over to us, why would he entertain me and put himself at risk?"

"Given Zenia's affair with Varkhov, Boris' judgment might be off." Hunt now tasted the first glass of wine from the bottle just opened for him, and made a face. "*Joven,*" he said to the waiter, "*esta botella es sin vergüenza. Por favor, trae un otro con un corcho correcto.*"

"Bottom line," he said to me. "The situation does not add up. Why fraternize with you? What can you give them, Harry Hubbard? Maybe they believe you can offer them something."

"Way beyond me," I said.

"Back to basics," said Howard. "What do we know for certain? It is that Boris, whether Masarov One or Masarov Two, is KGB. As the Montevideo *residentura,* he is definitely Number Two man under Varkhov."

"Definitely?"

"Heulihaen and Flarrety have studied their films comprehensively enough to establish an authoritative pecking order. They can document precisely whose ass is exposed to whose beak. Varkhov has precedence over the Soviet Ambassador and his minions. And Masarov is Number Two. Meanwhile, Number One is banging the boobies off the wife of his own Number Two, while Number Two seeks to fraternize with you."

"I'm dreading the picnic," I said. "It's not the picnic. It's the three days with Omaley that are going to follow."

"Get a couple of real pieces of Masarov meat, and I will grind Hjalmar's testes into powder. But do your best to avoid inconclusive results."

Thus armed, Kittredge, thus armed. Yesterday, Zenia phoned to ask if Nancy was coming. When I said that she was still indisposed, Zenia gave a grunt that sounded much like Boris. Zenia will not be with us either.

Then, today, Sunday morning—it is now late Sunday evening as I write to you—Boris and I drove out to the country. He took along his fishing gear, and little else since Zenia had neglected to pack a hamper. I felt wrung out and distracted; so, I suspected, was Boris. We hardly talked. After half an hour on the road, he reached over to his glove compartment and handed me a flask of Scotch, which was, under the circumstances, agreeable. On the *laissez-passer* of the booze, we uttered a word or two.

"Do you like the countryside?" he asked.

"Not much."

Kittredge, this was only my second trip out of Montevideo. In almost a year and a half! I can't believe the fact even as I write this; I am such an underground animal! At Yale, I never left New Haven. Here, all my world is contained within the Embassy, the safe house, Hunt's villa in Carrasco, and my cheap hotel room. I think it is because everything I do means so much to me that I simply don't notice from month to month how circumscribed are my movements. I saw more of the city in my first three days than in all the time since.

Of course, outside Montevideo, there is not much to look at. Along the sea are third-rate resorts trying to rise to the second level. Stucco debris stirs dust in half-finished villas by the side of the road. Inland are no more than gently rolling grassy plains, occasionally fenced in with cattle, but, over the whole, monotonous.

Masarov speaks out of a silence. *"Cuando el Creador llegó al Uruguay, ha perdido la mitad de Su interés en la Creación."* We laugh. His Spanish is not as good as his English, but I laugh heartily—partly at the Russian accent in Spanish. It's true. God did lose half His interest in creating the world after He came to Uruguay.

"Yet I like this country," he says. "Conducive to inner calm."

I am not feeling much of that. The highway has dwindled into a narrow two-lane road, much broken and humped and oil-stained by the weight and effluvia of truck commerce, and when we pull over to have lunch at a café *cum* gas station, it is for the omnipresent hamburg-

ers, the local *cerveza,* and the smell of rendered beef fat and onions—
what Porringer has called "the whorehouse-full-of-traffic smell."

Yet, Masarov is known in this café. We are apparently near his
fishing hole, and he must have stopped here often. I am wondering if
these poor roads, flat country, and functional little roadhouse do not
remind him of his native country, and, as if we are curiously tuned to
one another, he now says on the first sip of beer, "Uruguay is like small
corner of Russia. Nondescript. To my liking."

"Why?"

"When nature grows awesome, man turns small." He lifts his
mug. "Homage to the Swiss!"

"Whereas here, you feel larger than nature?"

"On good days." He looks at me carefully. "You know Uruguayans?"

"Not many."

"Me neither." He sighs and lifts his beer. "To Uruguayans."

"Why not?"

We click glasses. We eat in silence. It occurs to me that Boris may
be under as much tension as myself. I remember Hunt's injunction:
Avoid inconclusive results.

"Boris," I say. "What are we up to?"

"That will develop."

I feel as if I am back in the chess game. Does he long for a book
to read while waiting for each of my cautious moves?

"Let me put it," he says. "I know who you are, and you know who
I am."

Now I have to turn on the sneaky. The switch is in my pants
pocket, but the shift of position entailed to get my left hand over (for
it is the left hand that has been holding the hamburger) cannot possibly appear as clumsy to him as it feels to me.

"Yes," I say, now that I have pressed the recording button, "you
claim to know who I am, and that I know who you are."

He will not keep from smiling at this obvious move. "Of such nature," he replies.

"What does that promise?" I ask.

"Extended discourse. Is a possibility?"

"Only if we trust each other."

"Half-trust," he says, "sufficient for such discussion."

"Why choose me?"

He shrugs. "You are here."

"Yes."

"Seem cautious," he says.

"Apparently I am."

He drinks a good portion of his beer at a gulp. "I have more to lose," he says, "than you."

"Well, that," I say, "depends on what you want."

"Nothing," he says.

"Do you want to come over to us?" I ask.

"Are you mad, or clumsy?" he replies in a gentle voice.

Kittredge, I am thinking of how bad this is going to look on the typed transcript. It will not convey the lack of personal offense in his voice. It will, to the contrary, project me as maladroit.

"No, Boris," I say, "I am neither mad nor clumsy. You approach me. Your overtures are friendly. You suggest that we have much to talk about. What can I suppose that to be but an indication of your desire to come nearer to us?"

"Or demonstration," he says, "of absolute ignorance of your people about mine."

"Are you prepared to tell me why we are here?"

"Could disappoint you."

"May I be the judge?"

He said nothing, and we sat side by side at our table looking out to the open end of the café, which had no front window but only an awning that flapped with a sound as sharp as a pistol shot each time a truck went by.

"Let's approach this again," I said. "What do you really want?"

"Political intelligence." He smiled, however, as if to deny the remark.

"I may be more ready to receive than to give."

"Could not be otherwise," he said. He gave a weary sigh. "KGB," he said, "stands for Komitet Gosudarstvennoi Bezopasnosti. Committee for State Security."

"I know all that," I said. "Even a Foreign Service Officer in the State Department knows that much."

He looked amused that I would still insist on maintaining cover. "Many Directorates in KGB," he said.

"I know that as well."

"Will speak of First Directorate, and Second. First is for Soviet officers abroad; Second for home security. Respectively, CIA, FBI."

"Yes," I said.

"Our FBI, Second Directorate, has fine reputation in America. Is seen as effective. But, by many of us, is considered stupid. Wish to hear joke?"

"Yes," I said. "I would."

"Of course," he said. "Why not?"

Now, we both laughed. It was droll. We both knew that my sneaky was on, and everything said would generate analysis. We quaffed our beer. Down the hatch. He clapped his hands and *el patrón* came forward with two more mugs, and a bottle of vodka. It occurred to me that this café could conceivably be a Russian outpost with microphones in the woodwork and a camera in the ceiling cranking away.

Or—Masarov merely came here often enough for the owner to stock a few bottles of vodka.

Yes, Kittredge, droll. Masarov, with a glass in his hand was not unlike other sturdy souls who live for a booze-up—he mellowed quickly.

"Two men," he said, "from Second Directorate are in car following boy and girl in other car through multitudes of Moscow streets, then zip out to highway. The boy and girl have been with foreigners they should not visit, but are children of very high officials, so not frightened. Say to each other, 'We get rid of these yeggs, yes?'" He stopped. "Yeggs?"

"Perfect use of the word."

"Dumb cops. Yeggs. Yes?"

"Perfect."

"So boy and girl pull their car over to side of road. Behind them, other car also stops hundred meters back. Our brave boy gets out. Lifts car hood to indicate motor trouble. What do yeggs do?"

"Tell me," I said.

"Get out of car," Boris said solemnly, "and lift *their* hood. Copycats, yes?"

"Yes," I said, "stupid."

"Our Second Directorate," he said, "has undue complement of stupid people."

"Why do you tell me this?"

"Because your CIA should distinguish between First and Second Directorate. Your CIA sees all KGB as brutes."

"Oh, that's not true," I said. "We spend weeks analyzing what Dzerzhinsky learned from *The Golden Bowl*."

Now he starts to roar. He laughs with a great bellow and smacks me on the back. Boris is one hell of a strong man.

"I like you," he says.

"Vertigo is joy," I reply.

We both laugh again. We are practically hugging one another. When the mirth ceases, he is suddenly and powerfully serious.

"Yes," he says, "in First Directorate, we go abroad. By our work, are obliged to study other nations. Become aware, sometimes painfully, of deficiencies in Soviet system. Within limitations of bureaucratic tact, we give accurate picture to home base. We try to help rectify our great Soviet dream. Yes. Even when answers are ugly and show it is our fault. The leaders of the First Directorate know more of everything wrong in the Soviet Union than anyone in your country."

"That's not the impression we get."

"Of course not. For you, KGB is equal to killers."

"It's a little more sophisticated than that."

"No! Low level! You speak of us as killers. We are professionals. Name one CIA officer who loses one little finger because of us."

"It's the hired help who get it," I said. I was thinking suddenly of Berlin.

"Yes," said Boris, "hired help get hell. True for you, true for us."

I was silent. "When do we go fishing?" I said at last.

"Fuck fishing," he said. "Let's drink."

We did. After a while I began to feel as if he had been waiting all his life to have a dialogue with one American. I was getting to know him so well that it was almost carnal, by which I mean that like most Russians he spoke with his face in mine (I suppose it is due to their small, crowded apartments) and so I came to know his exterior intimately—the places where his razor had missed some stubble, the spike-hairs in his nose, the breath of hamburgers, Turkish tobacco, onions, vodka, beer, and just enough caries to be, I swear, half-agreeable, as if a touch of rot in the mouth keeps a man honest. Hugh once imparted to me that unforgettable line of Engels—quantity changes quality—well, a touch of bad breath is altogether different from the odor of a badly corrupted mouth. I offer this aside because I lived for so long at a café table with Brishka, as he soon insisted I call him—Brishka and Harry, for sure—that the lunch drank itself down into the late afternoon, and the sun glared out of the west into the corner of our eyes as it dipped below the awning open to the road, and once in a while, a car went by or a drunk wandered in or out.

Masarov must have gone on for an hour about Nikita Khrushchev. Nobody in America could understand the Soviet Union, said Brishka, unless they came to comprehend the Premier. He was a great man. "Great in relation to present situation of Soviet Union." And he recited a litany to me. *Countless killed,* was the phrase. Countless Russians had been killed in the First World War, countless were also killed in the Russian Civil War, initiated, he would remind me, by Americans, British, and French, countless killed by Stalin in collectivization of the farms, and countless-countless Soviet soldiers and citizens killed by Hitler, countless-countless killed again by Stalin after the war. The Soviet Union had been battered more than "a wife," he said, "who is beaten every day by an ugly husband. For forty years! If it were American wife, she would hate such husband. But Russian wife knows better. Underneath everything in such marriage is man's desire for improvement."

"I'm lost," I said. "Who is the Russian wife, and who is the husband?"

"Oh," he said, "obvious. Russian wife is Russia. Husband is the Party. Some days, one must recognize that Russian wife is at fault. She may deserve her beating. Looks at ground. Won't move forward. Husband may be drunk, but looks at sky." He stopped here and slapped himself across the cheek with a blow hard enough to rattle the crockery in the kitchen (if it were listening). "Drunk," he said, and ordered black coffee.

Now his syntax improved. "What I said before is *kvatch*."

"*Kvatch?*"

"Of no value. Too general. The relation of Communist Party to people not easy to explain. Soviet children grow up with belief that one becomes a better person by sheer force of will. *They* will to be good and unselfish. We try to destroy interest in enriching ourselves personally. Very hard to do. In my childhood, I would feel ashamed of greedy desires. Weight upon the leader of such a people has to be immense. All trying to be better than they are. Stalin—I am ashamed to confess this—lost inner balance. Then Khrushchev, one of the brave, replaced Stalin. I love Khrushchev."

"Why?" I asked.

He shrugged. "Because he was bad man. And gets better."

"Bad? He was the Butcher of the Ukraine."

"Oh, *they* teach you. *They* give you good course for the winter, Harry. But, *they* forget spring."

"Who is they?"

"Your teachers. Miss huge point. Take question from Russian point of view. We see cruel people magnetized by power."

"Isn't this a little beyond Marx?"

"Ultra-Marxist," said Brishka. "Comes from Russian people. Not Marx. We expect cruel leaders. Our question is how can leaders transcend origins? Become better men. Stalin was great, but Stalin would not transcend. Turned worse. Evil deeds drive him crazy. Khrushchev *is the* opposite." He slapped himself again as if English were about to misprint itself on his tongue, and he had to jar his brain into line with his mouth. His English might be relatively polished, but underneath, Russky Tarzan lurked. As Boris got drunk, I could feel a cruder mode of expression come nearer and nearer to asserting itself. Of course, he would never say "Khrushchev opposite," but you could feel the words he was ready to leave out. "Khrushchev *is the* opposite."

"Yes," he said, "contemplate Khrushchev. *He is* not wholly popular. Many Russian detractors. Some say *he is* too emotional. Yes," he said, "almost all agree Khrushchev is *nyet kulturny.* You comprehend *nyet kulturny?*"

"I speak no Russian."

"Stick to your story." He laughed at this. Like Zenia, he has two persons in him, and they are not accommodated to each other. He had been drunk, and heavy in his sentiments; now, the irony of the chess master leaped out again. "Stick to your story," he said once more, as if he had a clear dossier on me. (Probably he did, and doubtless it was as inaccurate as ours on him.)

"Does *nyet kulturny* mean not cultured?"

"Of course. Crystal clear. Not cultured. Gross. That is worst thing you can say of a Russian"—yes, his better English was still with him. "Hordes of my people lived for centuries in huts. Nobody need to wipe his shoes. Floors were dirt. Animals slept with family. *Nyet kulturny.* Crude. Void of high culture. So, Khrushchev embarrasses many. Will ruin him yet."

"But he's a great man, you say?"

"Believe me. Gross, brutal, minion of Stalin. Yet, grows in stature. Immeasurable bravery to repudiate Stalin. You should try explaining to your people. In Moscow now, many high party leaders say to Khrushchev, 'U.S. has four times more nuclear capacity. We are obliged to catch up.' Khrushchev says, 'If U.S. attacks, we answer. Both nations *are* destroyed. So, will be no war. Our Soviet need is to develop *our* economy.' Khrushchev resists huge military pressure. Khrushchev a good man."

"On our side, we find that a little harder to believe. We think you are responsible for your past, and you don't shake it so quickly."

He nodded. "That is because you represent corporate capitalism. Linear. Unilinear people in corporation." He took a large swallow of his black coffee, which was thick as filtered mud, and nodded. "Yes," he said, "Americans never understand how Communist Party works. See us as living under total relation to ideology. Grave error. Only corporate capitalism lives in total relation to ideology. We, who you call slave people, more individual."

"I believe you really think that."

"Of course. No two Russians alike. All Americans, to me, are same breed."

"In no way could this be a misapprehension on your part?"

He touched my elbow in amelioration. "Speak of corporate capitalist Americans. Managers. Executive class. They believe American ideology. We believe, but only by half."

"By half?"

"By half, Harry, you bet." Again, his heavy hand clapped me on the back.

"And the other half?"

"Our secret half. We brood."

"Over what?"

"Our soul. I taste *my* soul. American people speak of free-floating anxiety, yes? Lack of identity, yes? But Russian says: I am losing my soul. Americans used to be like Russians. In nineteenth century. When were individual entrepreneurs. Then, still *the* baroque spirit. In your hearts. In American architecture. Individual people, eccentric. Now, Americans are corporate capitalists. Brainwashed."

There was a glint in his eye at the expression on my face. "Khrushchev does not want to lose his soul," Masarov said, "so, works hard to improve *the* world."

"You tell me all this with a straight face?" I confess I was getting angry at his consummate gall.

"Straight face."

"Tell me about your prison camps."

His good mood vanished. "The Russian Bear," he said, "lives with dinosaur's tail. Tail crawls with infestations. From *the* past. Eventually, eat *the* tail. *We* will absorb horrendous history. But, as of now, immense convulsions. Tragedies. Horrors. Still."

I could hardly believe he had said this much. He was scowling at his coffee as if it had been a mistake to leave his old comrade-in-arms, vodka, for this new acquaintance. Then he gave a great sigh as if to clean his breath of old memories. "Do you know about *beriozhka*?" he asked. "Birch trees."

"Yes. You are all said to love them."

"Yes." He nodded. "Zenia wrote beautiful poem in Russian about *beriozhka*. Translated into English by me. With liberties, however. Zenia would not recognize it. She would leave me." He looked as if he were about to cry, but instead took out a piece of paper and read aloud to me.

### TO THE BIRCHES

*pale sentinels*
*silent arrows*
*light and moonlight*
*our silver sun*

"Uruguay is not like Russia," he said. "Are no birches here."

Then he tore off the unmarked bottom half of the sheet on which the poem was written, scribbled a note upon it for me, and passed it over. The wording, Kittredge (and you will soon see why), is offered to you from memory.

Caution. Just as one of ours may be, in secret, yours, so one of yours may be ours. Do not trust the people in your Soviet Russia Division. Such remarks can hang me. Silence. Caution. Speak only to your most trusted own.

I had time to read it carefully before he whipped back the note and held it in his hands. I do not know if I was inhabiting his mind at that point, but I did envision him setting this half sheet of paper on fire in the ashtray, which, I swear to you, he proceeded to do just then, as if I had either willed him to do it, or had read his mind before he expressed it.

Kittredge, that was indeed the curious tone on which we left the café and took the drive back to Montevideo in the late summer dusk of February. It is late now, and I am weary, but we are, at last, caught up.

Devotedly,
Harry

It was understood that I would call Howard so soon as I came back from the picnic, but I found myself in a peculiar and rebellious state. I did not wish to be debriefed into the late hours of Sunday night. Instead, I chose to write to Kittredge. It was as if my best hope of understanding what had taken place between Masarov and myself would be obtained by setting it down for her. I knew that once my formal report was perused by Hjalmar Omaley, converted to cable traffic, and subjected to the Soviet Russia Division's questionnaires, the experience would be altered, and I felt some need, no matter how unprofessional, to keep it intact.

I was in a dilemma, however. *"Do not trust the people in your Soviet Russia Division,"* was a dangerous remark to bring back. Since I now had no evidence of Boris' note other than my personal description of it, I was bound to be seen as the untrustworthy bearer of a wholly disturbing communication. Maybe the KGB had designed the afternoon to get me to return with a message that would disrupt our Soviet Russia Division. In that case, it might be prudent not to mention the note.

Of course, there was the real possibility that a movie camera had been installed behind a peephole in the café to record the moment when Boris passed his written message over to me and I read it and he then incinerated it in the ashtray, both of us watching solemnly. In such a case, if I did not report the incident to Hunt and Omaley, and there was indeed a KGB mole at Soviet Russia Division in position to see my report on the picnic, then I would be prey to blackmail if I made no mention of Masarov's message.

I decided to state in my report, therefore, that the note had been passed to me; I would, however, leave out the reference to the Soviet Russia Division. If the intent of the KGB was to increase our suspicion of our own people, then I would be thwarting their purpose. The remaining contents of the note would prove vague. I decided to accept the risk.

Why? As if someone had poked a rude finger into my stomach, the question hit with force. Why, indeed? Why not tell the truth? If it disrupted the Soviet Russia Division, well, they had suffered, no doubt, in such fashion before. Yet I knew I would not change my mind. Not only was living in close quarters with Al Omaley much like cohabiting with a contagious disease, but I did not feel ready to face his meticulous paranoia. I, the messenger, had to be tainted by the message.

All the same, my private motive remained inaccessible to me. Some stubborn depth of instinct was speaking.

It was now ten o'clock on Sunday night, and one could put off calling Howard Hunt no longer. I went down to the street and found a pay phone. On the Avenue of the 18th of July, the night was as quiet as a midnight Tuesday in Green Bay, Wisconsin.

"Where in hell have you been?" was his opening remark.

"Getting drunk with our friend."

"Until now?"

"A confession, Howard. I got back to the hotel at seven, started to call just to say that I was back and would ring again from downstairs in ten minutes, but, so help me, I fell asleep with the phone in my hand."

"Oh, no."

"Did you ever match vodka for vodka with the Russians?"

"Yes. And successfully. Don't you know enough to drink olive oil before you start?"

"Well, maybe I do now."

"All right. One question. Was it conclusive?"

"Not wholly affirmative on that."

"Shit."

"A fair amount of stuff, all the same."

"Enough to begin an all-night session right now?"

"I doubt it."

"Then, I will let it keep till tomorrow. But you get over to the Embassy now. Nancy is waiting to type up the tape."

"Well, yes."

"Hang around to help her with garbled transmission."

"Of course."

"I know this is open wire, boy, but give a clue. What was our friend up to?"

"Wiser minds than mine will determine that."

"Any chance of your buddy riding down the river?"

"Twenty-percent possibility."

"Only twenty percent," repeated Hunt. I could picture his study at Carrasco; I could all but hear his long fingers tapping on the desk. "That's a bit of a disappointment," he said.

"All the same," I told him, "there are a few new flowers in the nosegay."

"We'll be busy tomorrow," said Hunt. "Get some sleep."

"I intend to—after the next three hours with Nancy."

"That's all right, Harry. You were snoring it off while I was pacing my study worrying over what to say at your grave."

My relations with Nancy during the hours it took to transcribe the tape proved as formal as the muted aftereffect of our single kiss, a sad void for her, I was certain, but by two in the morning, the transcript was done, and so was my accompanying report. I went back to the hotel, while Nancy, loyal to the code of all the unsung soldiers, was still sending our text on the encoding machine. Our five-letter groups would be deciphered by communications people in Washington before the dawn.

Hjalmar Omaley, whether alerted by Hunt or paranoically instinctive, came by some twenty minutes in advance of my departure, a precise timing that enabled him to read my report and go through the transcript just as Nancy was finishing the last page. He had the oddest style of perusal. He all but crooned into the contents. "Holy hooligans, Hjalmar, holy hooligans," he kept saying as he read, but whether this was praise for the operation or astonished disapproval, I had no idea. Just as I was leaving, Nancy, quick as a bird darting into the eaves (for I was not supposed to see it), flashed one tender smile at Hjalmar. It seemed to me then that I would be wiser to worry over the empty space in my own heart rather than the void in others'.

By the middle of Monday morning, Howard was in a state of great excitement. The Sourballs had succeeded in closing the discrepancy on Masarov's age. Their Soviet Personnel Record dossier was now in order. While Hunt would not, or could not, provide me with more detail than to say, "Masarov is not thirty-two but thirty-nine, not, as he claims, thirty-seven. Get set for this: He is higher echelon than we thought. Considerably above Varkhov in rank."

"I thought the Finnish Micks had concluded Boris was Number Two KGB here."

"They did, but the Sovs must have been sending contrived signals. It's a kangaroo pouch."

While I had never heard the expression before, the metaphor obviously spoke of an operation where the number-one man is concealed.

"What of Zenia and Varkhov?" I asked.

"In for reappraisal. One thing is nailed down, though. Our Masarov here in Uruguay is one of the leading KGB experts on America."

"Why, then, is he in these parts?"

"That may be the focal enigma, may it not?" said Howard.

If my visit to the home of Boris and Zenia had taken me through heavy cross-examination, the picnic subjected me to an eighteen-hour day with Hjalmar, followed by two more eighteen-hour days responding to questionnaires from Washington. More than once I came close to confessing what I now called (in the last redoubts of the privacy of my mind) "The Abominable Omission," for the questionnaires certainly kept returning to the contents of Boris' note. What certainty could I submit that the message, as recollected by me, was complete: 60 percent? 70 percent? 80 percent? 90 percent? 95 percent? 100 percent? I made the mistake of answering 80 percent. As if they were psychically attuned to the topography of culpability, the Sourballs' follow-up question stated: *In your reconstruction, the note has three full statements plus three one-word exhortations. If recall is 80% complete, what is the possibility that a fourth sentence is missing?*

To which I replied: *Zero possibility.*

*Repeat query: 50%? 40%? 30%? 20%? 10%? 5%? 0%?*

*Zero possibility.*

*Boris note lacks concerted impact. How do you account for that?*

I was sitting at a typewriter console hooked up to our Encoder-Decoder. An encrypted question would come in from Washington, go through the decoder, activate the keys of my typewriter, and come out in deciphered five-letter groups on my typewriter page, which I could read, by now, as quickly as plain text. BORIS NOTEL ACKSC ONCER TEDIM PACT didn't cost me one-tenth of a second more. Then, so soon as I typed out a reply to the comment, my five-letter groups would begin their trip back through the same typewriter and Encoder-Decoder to the Sourballs in Cockroach Alley. I would sit and wait for my typewriter to commence clacking again. After hours of such back and forth, I began to feel as if I were playing chess with an opponent in another room. Over my shoulder, Hjalmar Omaley read the questions and my answers.

On this last comment, *Boris note lacks concerted impact,* I turned to him.

"What is that supposed to mean?"

He had an irritating smile. His teeth would gleam in concert with the gleam that came off his eyeglasses. "It means," said Hjalmar, "precisely what it says."

This annoyed me sufficiently to type for my reply exactly what I had said to him. WHATD OESTH ISMEA N

PRECI SELYW HATIT SAYS came back.

"All right, we have a problem," I said. "I can't comment if I don't know what I'm replying to."

At Yale, I had always detested the superior sort of graduate student who looked like Hjalmar Omaley. Their heads were invariably held at odd angles. They listened with a half-smile. They appeared to be sniffing the inferior odor of your turds as compared to the integrated concert of their own. They would answer inquiries with questions or with such throwaways as *precisely what it says.* When, however, they finally took account of the subject, they left you in no doubt of their credentials. "We have under consideration," said Hjalmar, "a high-echelon member of the KGB, expert in American studies, who dallies with a minor case officer in a country with small to negligible geopolitical impact. Said KGB officer then proceeds to incriminate himself to said minor case officer by dint of extreme remarks, allusions, and unorthodox comparisons of his country and party to a sordid husband and wife. He abuses Marxist tenets. All such product would guarantee, at the least, his recall, and imprisonment if we were to forward transcript obtained to the KGB and they were to believe it. Do you follow me now?"

"Yes."

"Good. Since he is, however, heading up the KGB cadres here, his own transcript, if he has one, need not be of concern to him. He has obviously been given sanction. There are elements in the KGB who do have sanction to speak freely and, on occasion, act freely. Such post-Neanderthals can be seen as the equivalent of seventeenth-century Jesuits. Are you still capable of following me?"

"Yes."

"Good. We now encounter the specific implausibility of the entire situation. To summarize what I have just said: A major KGB operative who, so far as we can see, has no intention of defecting, nonetheless engages in major conversational indiscretions with the opposition. If there is an entelechy in his process—and there must be entelechy, or else, why commence?—he succeeds in presenting a note which is destroyed almost immediately after it is delivered. That is a dubious business, since the message has no incisive content. It names no person, attacks specifically none of our departments, and in sum, is too general to be disruptive. He has given you a shovel without a handle. What explanation do you offer?"

I was about to reply, but he said, "Wait," and turned on a tape recorder placed next to the Encoder-Decoder. "Speak your piece into that."

The position of the microphone placed my back to Omaley, and I could feel his malign presence leaning in full psychic drapery upon my shoulders.

"Repeat your question," I said.

"What explanation do you offer of your meeting?"

"I think we are dealing with a man rather than a scenario."

"Expatiate."

"I'm not as certain as all of you that Masarov has a clear message to pass on. If he is the number-one man, and his wife is indeed in love with Varkhov, who now, it seems, is his assistant, I believe that could prove disorienting to his behavior."

"Masarov is ruthless, skillful, and highly capable of discharging ultimate functions. It is difficult to believe that his marital troubles, if bona fide, would prove unsettling. In 1941, at the age of twenty-two, as a young officer in the NKVD, he was present in the Katyn Forest during the Soviet massacre of the Polish officers. He is a man, therefore, who has shot others in the back of the head." Standing behind me, Hjalmar did tap me lightly on the head.

Could I place Boris into this new portrait? My stomach was reacting. "Katyn Forest helps to explain his appraisal of Khrushchev," I said.

"To employ Masarov's own terminology—*kvatch.* An attempt to beguile you, misdirect you, have you, in short, follow the wrong shell in his game."

"If you know all of it, why do you keep questioning me?"

" 'Boris note lacks concerted impact.' Try replying to that on the E-D."

I turned to my typewriter and sent the following into the Encoder-Decoder.

ICANN OTDOA NYTHI NGTOR ESOLV ETHIS IMPAS SEIWI LLALT ERMYE STIMA TEOFP ROBAB ILITY OFREC OLLEC TIONO FTHEN OTEFR OM80% TO95%

There was a long pause. Omaley sat there shaking his head slowly from side to side like a metronome oscillating alone in a vault. It was late at night and we were the only two people left in our wing of the Embassy.

FINAL, asked the E-D.

FINAL, I typed back.

This time the pause was short. DOYOU AGREE TOTAK INGAL IEDET ECTOR TEST

Omaley looked happy for the first time in three days.

INPRI NCIPL EYESP ROVID EDJUR ISDIC TIONA LHEGE MONIE SDONO TOVER RIDET HEPRI NCIPL E

"In principle, yes," read Hjalmar over my shoulder, and very much aloud, "provided jurisdictional hegemonies do not override the principle." He laughed. "What would you suppose are the probabilities that your Chief of Station will enable you to avoid the flutter box? Fifty percent? Forty percent?"

There was a high-pitched note so hateful in his voice that I came very close to hitting him. I was still smarting from the tap on the back of my head.

"Preposterous," said Howard next morning, "outrageous. You have been doing your best to stay afloat with a KGB heavyweight, and they want to flutter you because they are not happy with the results? You are absolutely right. This is jurisdictional. I'm not letting any paranoid peacocks drive a truck right through the middle of my Station."

"I'm ready to take the test if it comes to it," I said.

"Glad you said that, but I'm here to protect my people fully as much as I am ready to expose them to appropriate risk-taking." He paused. "I want all the tarps tied down on this one, however. Are you really 95-percent sure of your accuracy about this note? That's what ticked them off, you know. You can't get cheeky with their evaluation process. It's like defiling the Torah or the Koran." He looked most carefully at me. "Between us, cozy as thieves, what is your real estimate?"

"Ninety percent."

"Okay. I have to buy that. But why is Masarov's message so anemic? The name of the game is to maim someone's name."

"Howard, I put it in my report. I have a theory that no one gives credence to: Just a couple of weeks ago, the Russians asked for a summit meeting. I think Masarov wanted me to bear the same message that the Russians are sending in a thousand different ways all over the world. 'Give the summit a try, Khrushchev is okay.' Part of their personal propaganda approach."

"All right. Those lines of possibility do stand out in the transcript. But why confuse matters? Boris is an old pro. He knows the cardinal differences between a clandestine note and a political pitch—which, by the way, I don't trust for one minute, those Sovietskys don't want peace ever, just a breathing space to find a new way to screw us." He paused. "But, all right. Boris gives his sermon. We can all cry for the Soviet Union. Countless-countless killed. Yes, and how about the five thousand Polish officers Masarov helped to shoot in the back of the head, and the other ten thousand Polish officers that remain missing? Stalin knew what he was doing. He was killing the cadres of a possible future independent Poland, yeah, those Sovs want peace—I'll believe that when pimps stop taking their cut." He tapped his desk as if it were a podium.

"You ought to be in politics, Howard," I said.

"I could have been in many things. It kills me to look at the properties you could develop out in Carrasco. We pay a stiff price, Harry, for giving our allegiance to the Company. A CIA man makes a whole financial sacrifice for life. But that's another matter. Let's keep the target in our sights. Explain to me one more time your understanding of Masarov's note."

"Howard, I think Boris was drunk and full of misery, half ready to defect and knows he won't—unless he does—he's a Russian, after all, he's half crazy, he loves his wife, he's sinking in guilt, he has a lot on his conscience, he wants to save his soul, and if you add it all up, he must be very self-destructive. He loves Dostoyevsky. I think he wanted to hang himself with that meaningless note, but then he changed his mind and burned it."

"So you buy his speech at face value?"

"I think I do. Why else write a meaningless note?"

"God, you're young."

"I guess I am."

Actually, I was amazed at the felicity with which I was able to lie. How much of my mother was in me after all. For the first time I understood her pleasure in little creations. Lies were also a species of spiritual currency.

"Well, I'm going to bat for you," said Howard.

"I appreciate that."

"Kid, do you have any idea how expensive this could prove for yours truly?"

"I think a lot of people up and down the line will respect you for taking a tough stand," I said.

"Yes. How much won in respect, and how much lost to future deep-dyed, unalloyed enmity. Yes. Tell me, Harry, why are you reluctant to take the test?"

"I'll take it, Howard. I'm ready to. I'm innocent. It's just that they get you feeling so goddamn guilty once they put those electrodes on."

"Say that again. I remember my indignation when they asked me if I was homosexual. Years ago. I controlled myself long enough to say no—when in doubt, observe the proprieties—but, I tell you, fellow, if any man was ever crazy enough to try to put his pecker in my mouth, and I don't care if that man is a buck nigger, six feet six inches tall, I would bite his masterpiece off at the root. So, yes, I can hook on to your feelings. I hate lie detectors too. We'll stop those bastards right where they live. This is, after all, my Station."

I caught a whiff of his breath. He had had a few belts, and that was certainly not his habit for the morning. It was possible that he was more agitated than me.

Howard left soon after to keep a date for lunch with one of his Uruguayan friends. "I'm going to hold the line," he said.

As if to show his trust in me, he quit his office while I was still in it. That was not customary. He usually locked his door. Now, he merely left it ajar so that from her desk just outside, Nancy Waterston could certainly check on whether I was looking into any of his drawers. Just then, the secure phone in the locked closet began to ring.

"Nancy," I said, "do you hear that?"

She did after a moment.

"I think," I told her, "we had better answer it. Do you have a key?"

She did. She made a point of unlocking the closet door herself. By the time she lifted the receiver, there had been twelve rings. "Yes," she said, "He's here. Who wishes to speak to him?" A pause. "Oh, it's classified. Oh, I'm afraid I don't know the protocol on classified secure phone referrals." Meanwhile, she was stabbing her finger directly into the air between us. "For you," her finger was saying.

"I'll take it," I said.

"I don't know," she said, covering the mouthpiece, "who is asking for you."

"Never fear. It's more routine than you'd expect."

"I don't know," she repeated, "who is asking for you."

"Nancy, I could, if necessary, tell you what this is all about, but I won't. You are interfering with a priority."

"All right," she said, then added as she handed me the phone, "it's a woman."

"Hello," I said into the mouthpiece.

"Is that other person standing at your elbow?" said Kittredge in my ear.

"More or less."

"Banish her."

"It'll take some doing."

"All the same!"

"Nancy," I said, "this is a secure phone. I'd like privacy. That is the designated purpose of these phones."

"Only intended for use," said Nancy, "by the Chief of Station."

"In his absence, I have entitlement. This involves something co-developed by Howard and me."

Nancy receded, but grudgingly, like a tide not yet ready to accept its summons back from high water. She left Howard's door still ajar. I, in turn, did not feel ready to close the closet. Under these exceptional circumstances, Nancy might feel emboldened to listen at the keyhole. So, through two half-opened doors, we managed to keep an eye on each other even as I spoke in the lowest tones.

"Are we clear?" asked Kittredge.

"Yes."

"Harry, I love your letters. I know I haven't been responding lately, but I love them. Particularly the last one. It's invaluable."

"Are you all right?"

"Couldn't be better. It's all turned around now. I'm in splendid shape."

Her voice, however, was coming to me out of the long reverberations of the secure phone. All I could determine about her state of being was that she was speaking quickly.

"Yes," she said, "I want your permission on a small but precise fabrication."

"You've got it," I said. Given the proportions of the Abominable Omission, why deny anything small and precise?

"I'm not ready to inform Hugh we're corresponding, because that would upset him much too much, but I do ask for your permission to tell him that you were sufficiently concerned by what took place on your Soviet picnic to place a call to the Stable's secure phone. He was out, I'll say, and so you told me all. Then you and he can get together tonight on this same lovely red phone."

"The first thing wrong with your proposal," I said, "is that your call right now has already ticked off a nasty response. Unless I can come up with a feasible explanation, I'll never be able to get a second call out tonight on my lovely red phone, which, incidentally, dear lady, is housed in a stifling closet—"

"Don't talk so much," she said, "there's an off-putting echo."

"The second difficulty," I said, "is that I don't believe you. I think you've told Hugh already."

"I have," she said.

"About my last letter?"

"No, never the letter. About Masarov's crazy note. Your letter arrived yesterday, yes, yesterday, Wednesday, and I made up the story of your phone call, said it was at 4:00 P.M., and Hugh was sufficiently exercised—"

"Speak more slowly. Did you say exercised?"

"Exercised, not ex-or-cised. Hugh tapped into his source over at

Soviet Russia Division, and, yes, the Sourballs are agog. Darling boy, you must have tampered with the message. Hugh gave me the wording. It's not what you put in the letter to me. They must be trying to sweat the last gamma globulin—"

"Slower, please."

"Not getting their last bit of fat, are they?"

"No." Pause. "What does Hugh think of what I did?"

"Thinks your natural instinct has a touch of the divine tar."

"Divine tar?"

"Harry, that's Hugh's accolade. The stuff God filched back from the Devil. Divine tar."

"Well, Kittredge, you've left me impressed with myself."

Suddenly, however, all amusement was gone. "Oh, Harry, it just occurred to me. When you speak to Hugh, do get *our* little story straight. When you phoned me yesterday, you did impart the missing contents to me."

"Yes, I'll keep the new chronology in place," I said.

"I think you're wonderful. However, that's not what's at issue. How are you and my spouse going to speak if you can't get a secure phone?"

"I guess," I said, "that Hugh should ring me at eleven o'clock tonight," and I gave the number of a street phone near my hotel that I sometimes used to call Chevi Fuertes.

"Is it virgin?" she asked.

"Hell, no."

"You must select another pay phone you've never used before. Then phone us at home around eleven tonight on any pay phone. Hugh will pick up. Don't speak to him by name. Just give the color code for the selected phone and hang up. Of course, you had better skew the color code."

"By how many digits?"

"Choose a number."

"Four . . ."

"I just picked two. Make it three then," Kittredge said.

"Three."

"Skewed by three."

"Shouldn't it be a continuing skew?"

"Agreed."

"By the way, only six digits on phones here, not seven," I said. "And I will call at eleven o'clock. If I can't make it, then by midnight."

"Agreed," she said.

"By the way, they want to put me in the flutter box."

"Hugh will probably get you out of that."

"How?"

"Harry, be content."

She hung up before I could say good-bye.

It was a long afternoon and made more nervous by thoughts of the skew. My recall of the color code for phone numbers was still absolute—on that I could feel well trained. Zero was white; 1, yellow; 2, green; 3, blue; 4, purple; 5, red; 6, orange; 7, brown; 8, gray; 9, black. A full skew turned zero into 9, 1 to 8, 2 to 7, so forth. A skew of three changed 3 to 9, 4 to 8, 5 to 7, 6 to 6, 7 to 5, so forth. But continuing skew was a misery. The first digit in the telephone number was skewed by three, the next by three more, or six, the third by nine, the fourth by three again, the fifth by six again, the sixth by nine once more. One didn't dare do it in one's mind, but reached for pencil and pad. The virtue of the continuing skew, however, was that anyone tapping in on the first conversation who happened to be familiar with the color code would still, if he did not know the continuing skew, need time to break down the number. By then, presumably, the pay phone would have been used and never employed again.

Hunt returned from lunch and locked his door. I surmised he was on the phone to Washington. Then he called in Hjalmar Omaley, who looked expressionless when he came out. It took no great acumen to recognize that the demand by SR Division for a lie-detector test was not going to be decided by Hunt but back in Cockroach Alley. The Encoder-Decoder was certainly silent.

Porringer went home at five, ditto Gatsby. Nancy Waterston quit at six, which was as early as she had left in several weeks. Hjalmar soon followed; I had the idea he and Nancy would meet for dinner tonight.

Hunt stopped at my desk as he was leaving. "What was that secure phone call about? More illness in the family?"

"Yessir."

He lost his temper. Mean storm warnings passed across his face. "I don't want you using the red box again."

"I won't."

He slammed out of the office. I understood his fury. He was not going to circle the encampment with our wagons after all.

Alone in the office, I felt gainfully employed for the first time since Sunday afternoon. My regular meeting with Chevi Fuertes was scheduled for Friday at the safe house, and I had to go over his file.

Then my accounts with AV/ALANCHE, sadly screwed up. I had not been out with them in two weeks and they were in a state of disarray from a couple of bloody street fights. My undone account books concerned not only AV/OCADO and AV/ALANCHE, but AV/OUCH-1, AV/OUCH-2, and AV/ERAGE, all on my desk to be brought up to date for Nancy Waterston. As I sat alone in the office, I could even feel AV/ERAGE, my homosexual society journalist, sulking—I had not met him this week for a drink. Yet the thought of all these unaccomplished tasks was curiously soothing, as if I could wrap them about myself like a poultice against the raw adrenaline of the last three days.

That evening, after choosing the critical phone for my serious conversation with Harlot, I ate alone in a trucker's café in the Old City, an uneasy but pleasurable anticipation suffusing itself into my broiled meats and wine as if I were getting ready to meet Sally on a good night for me. I obtained from the waiter a fistful of change, and my pants pocket, on leaving the restaurant, lolled concupiscently against my thigh.

By ten-thirty, I had chosen the phone booth for the first call, and at ten of eleven, I called the international operator, gave her the number of the Stable in Georgetown, and deposited my coins. When I heard Harlot's voice, I said, "In front of a yellow wall is a white table with a purple lamp. A man in a brown jacket, yellow pants, and red shoes is standing. There is no chair."

"Repeat in brief," said Harlot's voice.

"Yellow, white, purple, brown, yellow, red." That would convert to 10-47-15.

"Twelve to fifteen minutes," said Harlot, and hung up.

Ten-47-15 was but the immediate conversion. Calculated for a continuing skew of three, it would come out to 15-45-45.

I had chosen to receive the second telephone call in a nearby bar of reasonable decorum. It had two phones in private booths and thereby offered less likelihood that some stranger would be kept waiting if our conversation should take a while. Indeed, I was in the booth five minutes in advance with the phone up to my ear and my other hand on the hang-up lever so that the apparatus would be able to ring.

In the fourteenth minute, it did.

"Well," said Harlot, "back to the old rigamarole. I dislike pay phones quite as much as you do."

"This one has been interesting," I said.

"Time-consuming." He paused. "Here is the hygiene. If necessary, for purposes of clarity, names are permissible. Should we, for any reason, disconnect, hold your place and I will call again. If you don't hear in five minutes, wait until midnight. I'll call then."

"Make it eleven-forty," I said. "This place shuts down at midnight. I've asked."

"Good fellow. Now, purpose of my call. Verification. There is no doubt in your mind that your drinking pal named the Soviet Russia Division?"

"Zero doubt," I said.

"Why did you not report it?"

"My drinking partner had obviously set me up to do so. I thought I'd spike his game."

"Presumptuous of you."

"I can only say that my deepest instinct told me to follow such a course," I said. "I had a hunch you would want me to follow such a course."

"This is amazing," said Harlot. "Do you know, if you had consulted me, I would have told you to do just what you did. The real object of the Russian's billet-doux was not SR Division but closer to home, in fact, right in the *Sanctum Sanctorum*."

"My God," I said.

"Yes. GHOUL. I think there is a furry little creature loose in the Soviet Russia Division. We all agree that the Agency is suffering a penetration, but Sov Russ Div wants to place the mole in GHOUL. Dear boy, you were instinctively bright. Since you and I, for better or worse, are seen by now as umbilically attached, even Allen would have had to give some credence to SR's claim that the mole is in my cellar, if you had, that is, reported your meeting accurately. I expect Masarov chose you precisely for that reason. No question, you see—they're after me. The Russkys do appreciate my value more than the Agency. And I appreciate your new drinking pal even more than the KGB does. He's a hell of a fellow. Stay away from him. Competitively speaking, he's nearly as competent as myself."

"Good Lord," I said.

"You wouldn't care to trade wits with me yet, would you?"

"No, sir. Not yet."

"Ho. Good for you. Not yet. Well, by the same logic, stay away from your new friend."

"If I will be permitted to."

"You will." Pause. "Now, about the lie detector test. You won't have to take it."

"May I query you further?"

"Lord, no. You've got all you need. This call is costing a lot, and I can hardly put it on my expense account."

"Well, good-bye, then."

"Yes. Remember that I'm pleased with you." He hung up.

February 22, 1958

Dearest Harry,

There will be no flutter test. If my husband is Byzantine on matters so minor as a dinner party, I assure you that he is Bach's harpsichordist when it comes to tweaking Company strings. So, to pull you out of the clutches of Soviet Russia Division, Hugh chose the Right Gobsloptious Baron of your Western Hemisphere Division, J. C. King. J.C. is not the sort of fellow to welcome Soviet Russia Division's poachers onto his preserve. You are saved. Isn't it a fact that my husband can take care of everyone's career but his wife's?

Actually, Hugh and I have been getting along far better than ever, and since my illness he has been sharing a good deal more of his work with me. So I may know more now about your situation than you. I wish to give you a warning. The KGB, according to Hugh, has taken great strides in these last few years since Stalin's death. The all-out reign of terror is over, and they have begun to get fearfully skillful again. You might try worrying about them in serious respectful fashion. Hugh's estimate of the Masarov picnic is as follows: The KGB has succeeded in placing a mole in the Soviet Russia Division. The best way to protect said mole is to insinuate a notion into the upper reaches of the Agency that the fellow is to be found in GHOUL. By Hugh's estimate, the KGB set up the picnic in order to hand you a note that would point directly to Soviet Russia Division. This was done on the firm premise that Allen Dulles would then conclude the furry creature was to be located anywhere but in SR Div. Since you were the recipient of the note but could not produce it, inasmuch as Boris had taken it back, a shadow would fall on GHOUL. The antipathy between GHOUL and SR Division is, after all, no secret. So we would have one more bad mark against Hugh. A provocation set up by the KGB in Uruguay would have been manipulated to great effect by the mole in SR Div back at Headquarters.

The purpose of the picnic, therefore, was not merely to injure GHOUL but to crimp Hugh's influence in the Agency. That would be a disaster. Hugh is not the man to make such a claim aloud, but I know he feels the KGB are going to be able to penetrate to the very top of the Agency if he is not there to stop them. And it won't take all that many years.

Harry, I know you hate the idea of backing off from Masarov, so I'm going to offer the sum of my modest wisdom. I believe that people like you and me go into intelligence work in the first place because to a much greater degree than we realize, we've been intellectually seduced. And often by nothing more impressive than good spy novels and movies. We want, secretly, to act as protagonists in such ventures. Then we go to work for the Company, and discover that, whatever we are, we are never protagonists. We pop into the spy novel at chapter six but rarely find out what was going on in chapter five, let alone earlier times. Just as seldom are we privy to what happens in the rest of the book. I offered this once to Hugh, and he said, "If you must feel sorry for yourself, read a book on the calculus of partial derivatives. That will give you paradigmatic solace, darling." The key to our lives, Harry, is in the drear word *patience*. We are incompetent without it.

Love,
Kittredge

From *Harlot's Ghost* (1991)

**1958**     # GETTING TO KNOW YOU—III

## Night Beat

His first appearance on a television show happened to be *Night Beat,* Mike Wallace the host. Mailer got ready like a Depression fighter going into the main bout at the Garden on Friday night. Since his anticipation of such experiences had been formed by films of the Thirties, and his wife would in fact have their first baby in two weeks— since he also saw his opponent as tough—the pressure might be immense, but, as he saw it, he had to win. On just such trinities as poverty, babies, and tough opponents had John Garfield's movies been built.

Two decades later, Norman would not bother to think about a TV show until he was on it. He had learned over the years that the inner condition for projecting a firm and agreeable presence for TV was to be bored. Ideally, it was best to feel no more desire than a prostitute can muster toward the tenth client of the night. This abyss between the luminosity of the outer appearance and the void of the inner dark was a phenomenon unique to TV participants, and might be the very health of the malignancy; it was certainly what kept television such a formidable foe. How could one battle a process that accommodated the emptiest space in oneself?

Of course, on the afternoon before his first television appearance, Mailer was hardly in possession of such wisdom. Rather, he was as tight as a man going to the electric chair. While trying to relax on his bed, adrenaline would take the best of him, and he would pace the room, and proceed to interrogate himself, asking the worst questions Mike Wallace might dare to ask, then search himself for the best of eight possible answers, a true fever! Young fighters dropped fights by squandering adrenaline before they reached the ring; they, too, were overcome with the monumental significance of whether they won or lost. Mailer, possessed of all the innocence of a protagonist who had never been on TV, did not understand he was entering no main event, but seeing the floor plans for a future mansion of Limbo. How was there a way to comprehend that he would not make history but probably stifle it a little more?

It was a natural error to make. He could not, after all, get beyond the idea that he would be on the virgin air. If one said what one had to say with wit, conviction, and passion, if one said the unsayable, if people therefore heard something for the first time, passions ought to commence, buried sentiments could take life. But first he must be able to hold his own with Mike Wallace, and given Mailer's massive incapacity to stay cool, that was not automatic.

Wallace had become a success by way of a personality considerably at contrast to other TV hosts'. His manner was not friendly but adversary. His straight black hair and craggy face gave off a presence as formidable as an Indian in a gray flannel suit. To this he added a humorless mind of which he was utterly unashamed, and used therefore as a weapon—no wit could slow his attack. His badly pitted skin suggested the unremitting stubbornness of a district attorney bitten hard enough in his youth to offer little mercy now. He was obviously not, like other interviewers, full of the very lard of companionability. Instead, Wallace gave the impression of wanting to interrogate further than the family manners of television permitted. Something of solemn, even heavy, purpose came off him, a distrust of human nature that was ready to focus on the probable insincerities of his guest. It was therefore a show to attract jokes about the masochism of people who would accept invitations from Mike Wallace, but Mailer, having studied the format for months, saw it as a rite of passage. If one wanted to make an impact on TV, *Night Beat* was the proper test.

By now, his own approach was as humorless as Wallace's. He had so fired up the household that his wife, in her ninth month, also took it as a test and put on a low-cut black velvet dress, thereby mustering her best appearance. Her hair was as black as Mike Wallace's, and being a real Indian (Peruvian), she did her best to help her husband make a decent entrance. Indeed, she looked splendid and sent out the beauty of her pregnancy like a promulgation of status. Her mate might have been happier to come into a real ring with a trainer to massage the back of his neck, and he certainly had the ravenous flare in his throat that only true desire for whiskey can bring, but he also knew the happiness of the fighter—at long last, love! even if love is the pow of a glove and the rocketing of the ring lights. He felt equal to expectation itself—maybe he had never been as aware before of all of America out there—a pregnancy in the night itself equal to his awareness of a million homes tuning into *Night Beat*. In later years, when everything was taped, he would not often feel the sensation that everyone was listening as the sounds came out of his throat.

Now, the program began, that is, they took seats that had been set out facing each other, chatted a little—it was a false and most unnatural kind of chatting, like fighters meeting at a weigh-in—and then with thirty seconds to air-time, to Wallace's small but somewhat superior annoyance, Mailer poured his water back into the carafe, took a small flask of gin out of his pocket, and decanted half of it into the empty glass.

He was sipping the gin as they went on the air. Since his mind had been overworked for hours, the liquor did not relax his tongue so much as disconcert his head and burn his stomach.

"*Life* magazine accuses your novel, *The Deer Park*," said Wallace in his opening and hortatory tones, "of dealing with immorality, alcoholism, perversion, and political terror in Hollywood. Why do you emphasize these themes?"

Mailer laid out the rights of a novelist to choose his subject, but his answer went on too long, and Wallace merely looked quizzical, self-centered, and superior in his lack of comprehension even as Norman said, "Only hypocrisy and insincerity are dirty. *Life* magazine is a dirty magazine."

So he felt uncomfortable through the early questions, going too long for one answer, too flippantly for another, only to be brusque on the third reply. He was like a tight-muscled fighter and could not seem to fake Wallace the least bit out. His voice began to grow dogged. On the other hand, Wallace did not seem comfortable either. Before one could expect it, the first commercial had come. One-third of the show was over, and it wasn't going as he had hoped.

He raised the ante. Mailer had an instinct for the wicked. If evil was to discover what was good and proceed to destroy it, then how many people could ever learn enough to be evil? Wickedness was more available. Wickedness would consist of raising the ante without knowing what the consequences might be. It was a way of asking for peril without a clue to who would be hurt. Wickedness was what he leaped into tonight. It was as if the only means for dealing with Mike Wallace's imperturbable certainty that the people who ran things knew more than the people who didn't was to keep raising the ante of his replies. Before long, he was saying, "America is a great and prosperous country, but it is not a brave or noble country. Our leaders are drowning in conformity and act like *women*."

(May it return a full sense of the Eisenhower period to recognize that our author was not near to suspecting a powerful movement would arise one day to banish men from public life for failing to refer to women as persons.)

Wallace, being equally ignorant of the future, looked awfully confident. "Who in high office," he asked in his deepest voice, "would you say is so feminine?"

Mailer came back with the first happiness he was ever to know on television. "President Eisenhower is a bit of a woman," he said into the ring of night around them, and was certain he could feel the instant when the heart of a million TV sets missed a beat.

Wallace never looked more like an Indian. His eyes grew as flat as the eyes of a movie Apache who has just taken a rifle bullet to the stomach.

"Come off it," he said. He, too, was listening to the silence in the living rooms.

"I mean just that," said Mailer.

They went on. The atmosphere was not dissimilar to the tension in a bar when a glass has been shattered and no apologies are made. They went through the half-hour to conclusion, and Mailer did a little better, and Wallace might have done a little less well, and the show came to its end. Mailer felt a great glow. He was immensely pleased with himself. In the elevator, going down to the street, his wife said, "Maybe we'll be dead tomorrow, but it was worth it." It is possible they never had a better moment together. They had been with each other for years, yet always fought in the animal rage of never comprehending one another. On this night, however, with the baby two weeks away, they were ready, for one hour, at least, to die together. For once Mailer felt like a hero. In those days saying something bad about Dwight D. Eisenhower was a not great deal less atrocious than deciding Jesus Christ has something wrong with Him.

Our new TV talent waited therefore on large and scandalized results from this Wallace show. Nothing seemed to happen. Occasionally he would run into an old friend who had happened to see it, and would chuckle over his remark. Weeks later, he learned that James Hagerty, the Press Secretary to President Eisenhower, asked for a transcript. That was all he ever heard. The phone did not ring with invitations from network executives to discuss a new show built around his controversial personality. Indeed, he was not invited on other shows for a while. It was more than another year before he was asked by David Susskind to come on *Open End* with Dorothy Parker and Truman Capote.

From *Pieces and Pontifications* (1982)

# PORTRAIT—II

## Truman Capote

When he arrived at the studio in Newark, and saw Dorothy Parker waiting, older, more fragile, close to desperately nervous and certainly not cordial, his feelings were only in a small way hurt that she was not happy to see him again, and showed an obvious preference for Truman Capote. He was, by his own measure, not the same writer she had known before. He had met her, after all, in the season after *The Naked and the Dead* when he went out to Hollywood, and much had been made of him. Now, after this early success, he had gone through a number of years in which people spoke of him as a failure. Since he had written two novels, *Barbary Shore* and *The Deer Park,* which he thought had received unfair reviews, he had a view of himself that was at odds with others, and he did not like to be snubbed by people who had been friendly to him ten years ago. All the same, it gave justification to his anger. So her unfriendliness left him in a well-balanced position. If it came to it, he would not have to be too friendly on the show.

David Susskind also gave small welcome. "We met a long time ago," Susskind said.

"I remember."

"I do, too," said Susskind in a chilly voice. It had been at a party on a very hot summer night in 1948, and they had talked on a Manhattan roof. Susskind was then a young agent, and he had wanted to sell *The Naked and the Dead* to the movies. Mailer had made fun of him.

"Don't you understand?" he had said to Susskind. "*They* can't make it into a film, and I don't want it made."

Of course, years later, he sold it after all, and *they* had made a very bad film. So he felt at a disadvantage now with Susskind and said, "Maybe I should have listened to you."

Susskind's face showed what he thought of people who were rude years ago and ready to flatter now. Their relations for this night were certainly not off to a good start.

He had only Capote. They had gotten along well on the drive out to Newark, each—they had not met before—intensely curious of the other. Since Mailer's wife accompanied him again, and again was looking her best, he had made a point of having her sit between Truman and himself. Since she was twice Truman's size and had the overpowering sexuality, on occasion—this was such an occasion—of her burgeoning Latin blood, it had been an advantage equal to playing on one's home court.

Truman did much complaining on the trip out. "I didn't want to do this show," he said in a dry little voice that seemed to issue from an unmoistened reed in his nostril. "I told Bennett Cerf it was a mistake, but Bennett thinks television is going to be very important for selling our books. I hope he's wrong," said Truman Capote, and laughed.

Once the show began, Norman thought himself splendid. Unlike the night with Mike Wallace, he felt at his best—thoughts came clearly, he was full of energy, and the others seemed bewildered. Susskind labored in the early minutes to put Dorothy Parker at ease but he was not able to succeed; she simply would not trust him. She spoke in a pained and quavering voice, hardly able to make herself heard. Truman did not add much, and Mailer, pleased with his powers, began to take over. Soon he and Susskind were doing most of the talking, that is, most of the debating, for it was obvious Susskind was irritated by what he had to say. Whenever Norman would launch on a flight of what he considered well-stated criticism of society, Susskind would make a point of looking at his watch. Whenever he could, Susskind tried to give time to the others, but it did not work. The others seemed apathetic. Once, while executing a panegyric about politicians, Norman Mailer flew so high as to say, "They're all whores."

Dottie Parker interrupted then to say with a little real force, "That's a sweeping remark."

"Well," said Mailer, "it may be sweeping, but it certainly is true."

It put Dorothy Parker back into silence—who was she, after all, to defend politicians?—and it irritated Susskind more. After close to an hour of TV time that felt wholly enjoyable to Mailer, he began to grow irritated at Susskind's efforts to slow him up. Since his host seemed determined to shut off this most interesting part of the show, Norman could see no reason not to allow the host to hang himself, and so he ceased speaking. Susskind began immediately to draw upon Truman Capote, and Capote, having digested a few of the peculiar processes of this odd medium, and measured the possible fit for himself, began at last to speak, and was, Mailer thought, not unamusing. He laughed encouragingly at Truman's remarks; he offered attention. Truman was so tiny that something gallant came to you from the fact of his existence itself. Mailer felt generous indeed. Few moods are as charitable as this sensation of being physically superior to everyone in the room.

In such a state, feeling handsome, vital, and more interesting than anyone had a right to be, he got into a discussion with Truman about the merits of Jack Kerouac. Since Mailer was not without his jealousy of the large attention paid Kerouac that year, he gave a defense of *On the Road* that was built on the basis of calling Kerouac, Jack—that is, he was two-thirds for Jack's virtues and one-third against Jack's vices.

Capote detested Kerouac. As Mailer grew benign, Capote grew precise. He rose at last to his own peroration and invoked the difficulties of the literary craft in contrast to Mr. Kerouac's undisciplined methods of work. Finally, in a tone of fearless and absolute severity, Capote said: "It is not writing. It is only typing."

"I agree," said Dorothy Parker in a hoarse voice.

"Well, I don't," said Mailer, only to give a limp defense. He was empty of vast indignation at this dreadful put-down of Kerouac. He even decided it might look good to let Truman have his winning little moment, certainly better than trying to hog the show.

*Open End* came to a finish. As they walked off the set, a few technicians were studying the kinescope of what they had just done. Therefore, Parker, Capote, Susskind, Mailer and Mrs. Mailer stopped to watch a minute of it.

Dorothy Parker did not look good on TV. She took one peek at herself, gasped, and said to Susskind, "No, I really don't want to see another instant of it." Solicitous as St. Peter, Susskind led her away.

In contrast, Norman Mailer had the pleasure of seeing himself as he wanted to look. The kinescope caught him as he was making a point, and his face looked forceful, his language was good, yes, he appeared even better on TV, he thought, than in the mirror. "Didn't I

tell you," said Truman, "that you're terrific on this? You're *telegenic!*"
It was true. But then, in every intermission, Truman had been telling
him how splendidly he was doing.

Truman groaned when the camera shifted to him. There was a
medium shot of Truman looking a hint bewildered at the beginning of
the show, and he winced as he heard his voice. "I told my publishers I
shouldn't go on," he declared with annoyance.

In the limousine on the way back to Manhattan, Truman kept
saying, "I shouldn't have done it. I didn't want to, I've never appeared
on television, not once—even though I've had many invitations—and
I certainly oughtn't to have been here tonight. What I can do is special, it's *very* literary, and I shouldn't attempt to *intrude* my personality.
I'm not good at that like you, Norman. Television is good for you."

Mailer lay back in the limousine, enjoying a winner's ride, and his
wife said encouragingly to Capote, "You were good, too, Truman. You
really got better as it went on."

"Do you think so?" asked Truman. "Do you really think so?"

Now, both Mr. and Mrs. Mailer assured Truman Capote that he
was better than he thought he had been.

"Well, at least," said Truman, "I was better than poor Dorothy
Parker. When she looked at herself afterward . . ." He shuddered in
sympathy. "Wasn't that *Disasterville?*" They laughed, but not in pleasure at her woe so much as in wonder at the clear lines of Judgment
itself.

Truman could not quite get out of his bad mood, however. Before
they said goodnight he suggested they have a drink with him at El
Morocco. Before long, they thought to have supper. Despite all the
sandwiches served on *Open End,* they were starved. Truman insisted
on treating. A prince, he seemed to hint, must play the host after a
sorry loss—it is the only way to come close to one's blood again.

It was late on Sunday night and they had the place to themselves.
Under the solicitousness of the waiters and the captain, and finally the
manager himself, who all came over to assure Capote of their unremitting attention, under the spell of this wholly superior service
Truman was obviously accustomed to receiving whenever he went
into El Morocco, his spirits not only revived but turned charming, and
he began to offer an attention to Adele Mailer that had her believing
in the unique properties of her attractiveness and her wit; yes, Truman was charming. Mailer saw why he had become the in-house author of the most important hostesses in New York, and envied him
honestly, the way one good athlete will have respect for another. Just

as a pitcher will think, "If I had as much stuff to my curve, I'd win more games because of my superior ball sense," so did Mailer think wistfully that if he could get to a few of the select parties Truman got to, why, boy, he'd have more to say about society. Of course, how could you be a radical yet intimate to the top drawer of the world—that was the iron warp of irony itself.

They had a fine time. They discovered unexpected points of agreement, and lively places to disagree; they had each had such curiosity about the other after all these years—their first novels had come out within a year of one another; both had been celebrated almost instantly. It was a grand evening, and at the end, Truman announced they would be great friends forever, and thanked them for taking him through what would otherwise have been a terribly depressing night—"God, was I awful on that show," he said as they parted, and he made a face to simulate the gargoyle of godawfulness.

There were not many nights when Norman Mailer went to bed so pleased with his wife, himself, and what they were able to do for each other as on this evening. He woke up early in the morning, enjoyed his breakfast, and could hardly wait for the phone to ring, and the praises of his friends to begin. But when he had heard from his parents (who loved the show), from an aunt and uncle (loved the show), from his sister, who liked what he had done ("generally") and was somewhat taken with Truman, "what an interesting personality he has, really," she said; and when he had gotten tired of waiting for friends to ring, and called up one instead, there was a pause at the other end, and then the friend said in sorrow, "Oh, man, did Truman take you!"

He called other friends. They seemed not to have seen the show and left a pall equal to the message of the medium itself. He went out on the street for a walk. Since he was living in Greenwich Village, it was not hard to run into a few acquaintances. One stopped, saluted, and said: "It is not writing; it is *only* typing," and gave a long phlegmy laugh as he went on down the street. Another said, "Truman; too much!" A third said, "Could you get me to meet Capote?"

More serious friends were balanced. "In terms of polemical points, I think you made the most. Of course, Capote does suggest real authority."

He called Truman a couple of days later.

"Yes," said Capote, "isn't it the *strangest* thing? Everybody has been telling me how marvelous I was. I can't believe it. 'Norman Mailer is the one who was marvelous,' I say to them, and they reply,

'Truman, you were *wunderbar.* Don't sell yourself short.' 'Honey,' I told this friend, 'I been short all my life,' " Truman guffawed with pleasure. "It certainly is a mystery," he said complacently.

Mailer couldn't bear it. He finally called *Open End* and asked to see a kinescope. It became his first introduction to our hypothesis that television is not a technological process that reproduces images of real life by way of electronics, but is rather a machine (more or less cosmically operated) to anticipate the judgments and/or anathema of Limbo; the technicians pitch in with camera angles.

He discovered that the nice close-up he had seen of himself immediately after the show was one of the few close-ups they had chosen to give him. The more he talked, and the more Susskind looked at his watch, why, the more they relegated him to medium shots and long shots. There is something pathetic about a man speaking at the bottom of a long shot: He does not sound convinced by himself. He is, after all, at the end of the tunnel.

In contrast, they gave many close-ups to Truman. Capote did not look small on the show but large! His face, in fact, was extraordinary, that young-old face, still pretty and with such promise of oncoming ugliness; that voice, so full of snide rustlings and unforgiving nasalities—it was a voice to knock New York on its ear. The voice had survived; it spoke of horrors seen and passed over; it told of judgments that would be merciless.

Watching the kinescope, Mailer realized at last what an impact Capote had made on the television viewers of New York. They had never seen anyone remotely like him. Once Truman finally opened his mouth, the camera never left his face. The camera would turn to Capote even as Norman was speaking.

His own arguments that had sounded so forceful to him a few nights ago now seemed vague and, with his beard, pious. (He shaved off the beard a week or two later.) Talking about large matters on television with all the passion and all the lack of specific detail these immense theses encouraged, speaking in a voice that came out of the depths of a medium shot, proved to be not nearly so exhilarating to a viewer as it had felt for him in the middle of articulating his thoughts. His obvious pride in his ideas now seemed fatuous. His physical superiority was gone. He was only intense, vague, and a bit out of focus. Whereas Capote took his unforgettable personality and added to it practicality, common sense, and pride. In so misty a medium, the best gift a guest could provide was pearls. The certainty of a pearl! Yes, to light upon a problem and come up with a good one-line answer was to produce a pearl of the mind. How much interest could viewers have in a point that took five minutes to make? That was something they could not do. It spoke of too good a college education. So they preferred people with a one-line answer, barroom knockouts, one-punch pearls. There is no man or woman on the street whose mind will not produce a pearl from time to time. They loved Truman because he had given them "It is not writing. It is only typing."

From now on, thought Mailer, he would not try to show how intelligent he was; he would look for pearls. That became his latest hypothesis: the light from a TV screen was flattering to a pearl.

Such were a few of Mailer's conclusions after his defeat by Capote.

The next time they met, Truman had a new assurance to put on top of the old one. In these few weeks, he confessed, there had been numerous invitations, all turned down, to appear on other shows; a difference in Truman's idea of himself had begun to appear. That personality he had presented, with all his early bravado, to a most special part of the world was, it seemed, going to be accepted by all the world. He obviously felt stronger already. And Mailer, stunned as any confident contender who has been abruptly knocked out, now felt, measure to measure, weaker. It was obvious to him (for no one understands the future reactions of a snob so well as an unsuccessful snob) that never again would Truman spend a night trying to recoup the losses of his ego out of *this* Mr. and Mrs. Mailer.

From *Pieces and Pontifications* (1982)

# A STATE OF MIND
# AS DECLARED IN 1959

## The Shits Are Killing Us

Like many another vain, empty, and bullying body of our time, I have been running for President these last ten years in the privacy of my mind, and it occurs to me that I am less close now than when I began. Defeat has left my nature divided, my sense of timing is eccentric, and I contain within *myself* the bitter exhaustions of an old man, and the cocky arguments of a bright boy. So I am everything but my proper age of thirty-six, and anger has brought me to the edge of the brutal. I find arrogance in much of my mood. It cannot be helped. The sour truth is that I am imprisoned with a perception that will settle for nothing less than making a revolution in the consciousness of our time. Whether rightly or wrongly, it is then obvious that I would go so far as to think it is my present and future work which will have the deepest influence of any work being done by an American novelist in these years. I could be wrong, and if I am, then I'm the fool who will pay the bill, but I think we can all agree it would cheat this collection of its true interest to present myself as more modest than I am.

# Hip, Hell, and the Navigator:
## *An Interview with Richard G. Stern and Robert F. Lucid*

RICHARD STERN: I've been reading "The White Negro" and a fair amount of other material on the hipster, and I must say that intellectually I resent Hip as much as I can resent anything. Now, I wonder about the extent of your allegiance to Hip. Are you using this material for fiction, or are you committed to it as a style of life, one which you want to practice yourself and recommend to others?

NORMAN MAILER: All right, good, I think the difficulty for most people who are at all interested in my work is that I started as one kind of writer and I've been evolving into another. Most serious readers like a writer to be a particular thing. It's important; it's reassuring, somehow. So, I think if I'm going in this direction, it has to be assumed at least from the outside that I'm serious.

STERN: The interesting thing about Hip is that Hip shouldn't belong to writers. If you're a genuine hipster you're committed, it seems to me, to a kind of anti-expressionism. If you're a sincere hipster you shouldn't be a writer. Then there's another thing as far as writing goes. Isn't a novel controlled by some overriding notion, by a kind of fanaticism which organizes a great deal of disparate material? In a sense, a novel is like the mind of a madman: Everything—casual looks, street signs, world news reports—is charged with meaning. That's why novelists write about ruling passions like love and ambition, passions which put their mark on all they touch, trivial or major. Now, I can't believe that Hip allows for such overriding notions and passions. For the hipster, the cool one, detail is illumined, livid, but for its own sake, unqualified by the sort of organization which novels demand. I wonder if such material can be put into fiction.

MAILER: I think it can—and not only that, but I think Hip is particularly illumined by one notion so central and so shattering that its religious resonances and reverberations are going to dominate this coming century. And I think there is one single burning pinpoint of the vision in Hip: it's that God is in danger of dying. In my very limited knowledge of theology, this never really has been

expressed before. I believe Hip conceives of Man's fate being tied
up with God's fate. God is no longer all-powerful.

STERN: Now, that's a fantastic assertion. That really makes me sit up.
What is the notion of God behind all this? Do you mean that some
kind of personal god is dying with us?

MAILER: Now, I only talk about my own vision of it, really. I think that
the particular God we can conceive of is a god whose relationship
to the universe we cannot divine—that is, how enormous He is in
the scheme of the universe we can't begin to say. But almost certainly, He is not all-powerful; He exists as a warring element in a
divided universe, and we are a part of—perhaps the most important part of—His great expression, His enormous destiny. Perhaps He is trying to impose upon the universe His conception of
being against other conceptions of being very much opposed to
His. Maybe we are in a sense the seed, the seed-carriers, the voy-
agers, the explorers, the embodiment of that embattled vision;
maybe we are engaged in a heroic activity, and not a mean one.

STERN: This is really something.

MAILER: Well, I would say it is far more noble in its conception, far
more arduous as a religious conception, than the notion of the
all-powerful God who takes care of us.

STERN: And do you take to this conception for its perilous nobility, or
do you take to it because you believe in it?

MAILER: I believe in it.

STERN: You believe in it.

MAILER: It's the only thing that makes any sense to me. It's the only
thing that explains to me the problem of evil. You see, the answer
may well be—how to put it?—that God Himself is engaged in a
destiny so extraordinary, so demanding, that He too can suffer
from a moral corruption, that He can make demands upon us
which are unfair, that He can abuse our beings in order to achieve
His means, even as we abuse the very cells of our own body.

STERN: Is it a person's duty to find out whether he's of God's party,
whether he's working with God-beneficent or God-maleficent?

MAILER: Well, look, let's go back—let's go back to something much
more modest for the moment, which I think may tie this up, to a
small extent, anyway. You asked me before why Hip is interesting
for the novel. Well, up to now, when a novelist treats someone like
a drug addict, the Square way is to treat the addict as a poor sociological cripple who is doomed and damned and goes down to
his inevitable defeat. In Hip, which has after all to a certain extent

come out of drug-taking (it's one of the elements in the growth of Hip), the attitude would be more that if taking drugs gives one extraordinary sensations, then the drug-taker is probably receiving something from God. Love, perhaps. And perhaps he is. Let's just entertain the notion and see how far we go with it. If the hipster is receiving love from God he may well be draining some of the substance of God by calling upon this love, you see, which the drug releases. And in draining the substance of God he's exhausting Him, so that the drug-taker may be indulging an extraordinarily evil act at the instant he is filled with the feeling that he is full of God and good and a beautiful mystic. This involves new moral complexities which I feel are far more interesting than anything the novel has gotten into yet. It opens the possibility that the novel, along with many other art forms, may be growing into something larger rather than something smaller, and the sickness of our times for me has been just this damn thing that everything has been getting smaller and smaller and less and less important, that the romantic spirit has dried up, that there is almost no shame today like the terror before the romantic. We're all getting so mean and small and petty and ridiculous, and we all live under the threat of extermination. In contrast, the notions of Hip enlarge us, they make our small actions not necessarily large but more meaningful. If we pick up a bottle while listening to some jazz and we feel each of our five fingertips in relation to the bottle, the bottle begins to have a kind of form for us and we begin to feel each of our fingertips is receiving a different thing from the shape and the structure of the glass, and we then begin to think that maybe the very structure of this glass could conceivably contain some kind of hell within its constitution, some inorganic frozen state of imprisoned being less being than us. I think it's a more interesting notion than just picking up a bottle and pouring out some whisky.

STERN: It's a very pretty notion.

MAILER: Hip is pretty.

STERN: But it's all action, it's all erectile, isn't it? It's all feeling and taste and touch and smell. Isn't that the trouble with it?

MAILER: The trouble is that it's enormously difficult to return to the senses. We're all civilized, and to return to the senses and keep the best parts of our civilized being, to keep our capacity for mental organization, for mental construction, for logic, is doubly difficult, and there's a great danger that the nihilism of Hip will destroy civilization. But it seems to me that the danger which is even more paramount—the danger which has brought on Hip—is that civilization is so strong itself, so divorced from the senses, that we have come to the point where we can liquidate millions of people in concentration camps by orderly process.

STERN: Every powerful and refining force involves danger and waste. Does this divorce from the senses you talk about justify cashing in two or three thousand years of continuous culture?

MAILER: Well, your argument is moot. It's too vast for this—for me. But let me try to put it this way. If the divorce from the senses I talk about is becoming a human condition, then by all means, yes, civilization must be cashed in or we will destroy ourselves in the cold insensate expressions of due process of law and atomic radiation.

STERN: All right, let's concentrate on what all this has to do with you as a practicing novelist. How are these notions going to work for you? The idea of art seems to me to be to generate emotion from the treated material, not to point out some material and some feeling and say, "Put them together, reader."

MAILER: Let me avoid answering you directly. I feel that the final purpose of art is to intensify, even, if necessary, to exacerbate the moral consciousness of people. In particular, I think the novel is at its best the most moral of the art forms, because it's the most immediate, the most overbearing, if you will. It is the most inescapable. Ideally, what I would hope to do with my work is intensify a consciousness that the core of life cannot be cheated. Every moment of one's existence one is growing into more or retreating into less. One is always living a little more or dying a little bit. That the choice is not to live a little more or to not live a little more; it is to live a little more or to die a little more. And as one dies a little more, one enters a most dangerous moral condition for oneself because one starts making other people die a little more in order to stay alive oneself. I think this is exactly the murderous network in which we all live by now.

STERN: And this is what the hipster does; he strikes out at others; he's constantly craving for more. He faces the risk of the extinction of his senses, extinction of his being, extinction of his capacity for making distinctions.

MAILER: He does certain things that are very brave in their way; he gambles for one thing with his soul—he gambles that he can be terribly, tragically wrong, and therefore be doomed, you see, doomed to Hell.

STERN: And the novelist is gambling with his talent as a novelist.

MAILER: Oh, yeah. Yeah.

STERN: The one talent he's got.

ROBERT LUCID: This is what kills me. You presume consciousness, you presume purpose, you presume direction on the part of this class—if that's the word—analogous to the novelist. And it seems to me that the whole notion of Hip is, in fact, unconscious, it is mere action. It seems to me the kind of guy we're talking about as hipster *qua* hipster is a guy who is, in fact, unconscious of risks of this kind, of the profundity . . .

MAILER: Consciously, he may think it's cutting quite a few corners as far as that goes. What I'm postulating in all this—the notion I've been working with all along that's been tacit to my remarks, implicit in my remarks, is that the unconscious, you see, has an enormous teleological sense, that it moves towards a goal, that it has a real sense of what is happening to one's being at each given moment—you see—that the messages of one's experience are continually saying, "Things are getting better," or "Things are getting worse." For me. For that one. For my future, for my past, mmm? It is with this thing that they move, that they grope forward—this navigator at the seat of their being.

Both selections from *Advertisements for Myself* (1959)

# HOLLYWOOD—II

## The Jewish Princess

There are fifty variants on one fertile idea: the Great American Brain is marrying the Great American Body. Because Marilyn is taking up the faith (Reformed Synagogue), the *New York Post*, whose base of readership is suburban liberal, trade union, middle class, and—in the absence of other sheets—progressive, goes in for tooth-sucking analyses of the wedding to come, plus an interview with Arthur Miller's mother. "She opened her whole heart to me," said Mrs. Miller, who then told how Marilyn was learning to make gefilte fish, borscht, chicken soup with matzoh balls, chopped liver, tsimis, potato pirogen.

Now the House Un-American Affairs Subcommittee provides an interruption to their plans for marriage. Looking for publicity, they summon Miller as a witness to explain why he was not granted a passport in 1954. It is four years since the peak of the McCarthy days and, next to testing a new hydrogen bomb, Miller and Marilyn are the most newsworthy item in America. Everybody in Washington understands that the Un-American Affairs Subcommittee, which has been altogether out of the news, now hopes to regain some of its lost attention by being able to cite Arthur Miller for contempt should he refuse to testify. Since publicity is a subcommittee angel, they are naturally slavish in their secret respect for Marilyn. So they also offer a secret deal: If Miss Monroe will pose for a picture with Chairman Walter of the Subcommittee, Miller's difficulties may begin to disappear. Miller refuses. He is even warned by his lawyers not to tell anyone. Who will believe such farce?

In the meantime, the hearings are given headlines. Marilyn endears herself to everyone from liberal Democrats to the *Daily Worker!* She tells the press her fiancé will win. There is a newsreel clip that shows her in the midst of an interview at this time on a lawn outside a Washington home, and she is never more beautiful. She looks in love. It could be said, if we are to invest in the logic of sentiment, that she looks deeply in love as she slowly replies out of a profound and pretty confusion to the questions that are asked of her. She seems bemused, as if thinking of pleasant hours with Miller rather than of the questions besieging her now. Of course, she is probably on sedation. We must live in two lives whenever we think of her one life.

It is still a year in which a movie star can be persecuted in the press for open left-wing associations, and so the suggestion that her fortune is committed to Miller's fortune gives her status as a heroine. She is beginning to capture the imagination of America's intellectuals; grudgingly, they are obliged to contemplate the remote possibility that she is not so much a movie star as a major figure in American life—of a new sort! Of course, they will not move too far in this direction until her death. But since European intellectuals are agog at this new portrait—America persecuting its outstanding author and most attractive movie star in a neo-McCarthian wholly sophomoric hysteria, et cetera—the State Department quietly intervenes, Chairman Walter quietly breaks his wind, and Miller and Monroe have held their first fort. He gets the passport. They can be married and go to England to make the movie with Olivier.

So Marilyn is indoctrinated by Rabbi Robert Goldberg from the environs of New Haven on some general tenets and theory of Judaism (for two hours!), embraces the faith, enters the fold, and is told there is no afterlife. (What is the pride of Reformed Judaism if it is not the absence of an afterlife?) A double-ring ceremony takes place in Katonah at the home of Kay Brown, Miller's literary agent, and follows by two days the unscheduled civil ceremony in White Plains, which had been quickly arranged on Friday evening after an horrific press conference on early Friday afternoon at Miller's farm in Connecticut. That was when Myra Sherbatoff of *Paris-Match* was killed chasing their newsworthy automobile, and four hundred people gathered around Milton Greene to hear how they would be given twenty minutes for newsreels, twenty for still photographers, thirty for reporters, a technological ceremony for the stifling midday landlocked heat of a Connecticut farm in the end of June.

"Give him a kiss, Marilyn," sing the photographers.

"One shot of the lovebirds, please."

One nightmare. Yet we have pictures of the day, and she looks happy. Death, press hysteria, Congress, and religious vows soon to come—it is all part of the *tohu-bohu* (if we are to use a good Hebrew word) of what has always been her public life.

Still, how beautiful they look in their wedding pictures. Staid Arthur Miller has been a scandal to his friends ever since he came back from Reno, for he and Marilyn sit in entwinement for hours. Like Hindu sculpture, their hands go over one another's torsos, limbs, and outright privates in next to full view of company, a questionable activity to perform in front of cynics, but it is as if the hero and heroine will each declare to the world that no matter the extent of *her* sexual scholarship and *his* meager schooling, they meet as equals in the godly art. They are lovers, and that is the only law of balance in sexual thermodynamics. They will immolate the past with the heat of the present. He buys her a gold wedding ring and inscribes it, "*A to M, June 1956. Now is Forever.*" It is a fervent response to whatever sentiments of confidence he hears pounding in his heart.

There is in retrospect a dialogue on the wedding day of Quentin and Maggie in *After the Fall.*

MAGGIE: . . . you said we have to love what happened, didn't you. Even the bad things.

QUENTIN: Sweetheart—an event itself is not important; it's what you took from it. Whatever happened to you, this is what you made of it, and I love this!

A few lines later Maggie says, "There's people who're going to laugh at you."

QUENTIN: Not any more, dear, they're going to see what I see. . . .

MAGGIE: What do you see? Tell me! ·[*Bursting out of her*] 'Cause I think . . . you were ashamed once, weren't you?

QUENTIN: I see your suffering, Maggie; and once I saw it, all shame fell away.

MAGGIE: You . . . were ashamed?

QUENTIN: [*with difficulty*]: Yes. But you're a victory, Maggie, you're like a flag to me, a kind of proof, somehow, that people can win.

It is his rallying cry. One can hardly remain a left-wing writer if one does not believe that the people who are coming up from the bottom have enough goodness to win, have enough moral wherewithal to deserve to win, yes, she is his living testament, for she—his blessed heroine—is up from the people. So she becomes the affirmation to replace all lost left-wing certainties.

Of course, Miller, like many a playwright before him, is too complex a man to remain in one consistent piece. He is also a *practical* poet and much immersed in studies of money coming in and money going out. There is more to life than affirmations of passion and sexual vaults over the past. Miller is always asking Greene about Marilyn Monroe Productions, its details, its plans, its financing, its projects, its difficulties, until Greene says to him, "Be a husband! Leave the corporation to Marilyn and me." No, there is no quick love between Miller and Milton, nor much more between Miller and the Strasbergs. Lee Strasberg will give Marilyn away at the double-ring wedding, but Arthur, still keeping his opinion to himself, does not approve of Actor's Studio, nor Strasberg's mode of teaching, which makes actors "secret people," and "makes acting secret [when] it's the most communicative art known to man." (Never has the inborn antipathy of the progressive mind for the dialectical hitch been more in evidence!) We can be witness to a small part of their first meeting. It is at Strasberg's home before the marriage, and one can anticipate Marilyn's excitement. But it all goes wrong. Marilyn begins to talk of a special record—Woody Herman playing Stravinsky—that Lee Strasberg has let her hear. Arthur wishes to share this pleasure, and Strasberg puts it on. A marvelous record, says Arthur; where can one purchase it? Can't be done, Strasberg assures him. The record is one of a kind. Arthur looks at it. It has a commercial label. May be hard to find, Arthur suggests, but not one of a kind. Most certainly is, says Strasberg, ending the discussion. It is evident to Miller that Strasberg is trapped in a boast he must have made on another occasion to Marilyn that the Woody Herman–Stravinsky record was unique. No, no quick love between Miller and Strasberg.

Still, for a honeymoon they will all go over to England to work on *The Prince and the Showgirl,* Millers, Greenes, and Strasbergs. A troika! Strasberg is no happier with Greene. A half year earlier, consulted by Milton as to the advisability of taking on Olivier to be director of the film as well as its leading man, Strasberg committed himself to no more than a mild opinion that the possibility "was a good idea." Greene immediately took this speech as his opportunity to cable Olivier a firm offer as director. A misunderstanding, they might agree, but who could be certain, including Greene himself, that the secret motive may not have been to cut off flirtation with any possibility that

Strasberg might direct his first film—or did Greene wish to ingratiate himself with Olivier for future films? Who could know? In business, ambiguity poisons several more relations than betrayal.

Marilyn travels as her own kind of queen. Shades of Zelda! The Millers fly to England with twenty-seven pieces of luggage (of which three are Arthur's—like Barry Goldwater, he is ready to hold on to his socks!). There is $1,500 in overweight luggage, of which $1,333.33 is her share, and they are deluged by hundreds of press at the airports in New York and London. Guiles reports Miller in a near state of shock as they are conducted from terminal to plane, "strange arms under their elbows . . . no air to breathe . . . voices become a muffled roar . . . a little like drowning." Miller shows just such torture in his expression for photographers. The corners of his mouth have become the creases in the smile of a stone dragon. Given the dragon's stern principles, this wrack of publicity will never end. Perhaps he will suffer most when he finds himself trying to enjoy it. There seems a will to torture himself reminiscent of Richard Nixon being jovial on command.

At London Airport they are met by Sir Laurence Olivier and wife, Vivien Leigh. A photographer is trampled in the crush. Off they go with a thirty-car caravan to a "large rented estate" at Egham in the royal grounds of Windsor Park. They have been expecting a "cottage" but find an English country mansion. All one-family homes in England, they are assured, are cottages.

Ga-ga is the prose of the English press. One London weekly prints a special Marilyn Monroe edition. That is an honor given to no human since Queen Elizabeth's coronation. "She is here," says the London *Evening News*. "She walks. She talks. She really is as luscious as strawberries and cream." *The Seven-Year Itch* has had exactly the kind of success one would expect in England, where many an Englishman can identify with Tom Ewell. Miller is naturally expected to be clever, superb, well-spoken, and romantic—a tall knight who has been ready to go to war with bloody McCarthy. England offers its oyster.

> She was invited to be the patroness of a cricket match for charity at Tichborne Park and to taste the rockbound solitude of the island of Aran; the Scottish knit goods industry was preparing for her a lifetime collection of hand-knit cashmere twin-set sweaters;

a group of teddy boys invited her to join them for a bit of fish and chips in Penge, a London suburb.

But it is comedy. For the Millers are tied in class knots. English accents, Olivier's in particular, have to certainly remind them that she is a girl from a semi-slum street and he is a boy from Brooklyn. She says the wrong things at her first press conference. The British do not care if she is witty, or refreshingly dumb, but she must choose to be one, or be the other—instead, she is pretentious.

"Do you still sleep in Chanel No. 5?"

"Considering I'm in England now, let's say I am now sleeping in Yardley's Lavender." That will waft no balm to English noses. It is like coming out four-square for Catholicism at Notre Dame—they have heard that already.

"Can you give us your tastes in music?"

"I like, well, jazz, like Louis Armstrong, you know, and Beethoven."

"Oh, *Bee*thoven?" We hear the nasal flush of Anglican tides in the Bay of Beethoven. "What *Bee*thoven numbers in *particular, Miss* Monroe?"

She gives a hopelessly American reply. "I have a terrible time with numbers." Now the recovery. "But I know it when I hear it." No worse mistake! You do not offer something to the English unless you deliver it altogether. They are not tolerant of conversations that belly-flop from one unfinished line to another.

In turn, Miller is hopelessly stiff. No more do the English need his chill. They have their own castles for chill. Miller is described to Zolotow by a London friend as "cold as a refrigerated fish." They turn down invitations to fashionable parties, and invite no one in return. Off to a very bad start.

Soon they begin to recognize new trouble. Olivier *hates* the Method. Where is Milton Greene, who had the genius to make him the director? It is possible Olivier is the foremost representative in all the world of the school of Coquelin. An actor does well to do his homework, and come to the set with characterization superbly in hand. One does not wallow in depths. One delivers the point. Eli Wallach can speak of taking Olivier to Actor's Studio to watch the Method in operation. The reactions of Sir Laurence then are to show that he is not to be party to this revolution.

It can be said with no great strain that most of the male and female population of England are good amateur actors, well schooled in Coquelin. One lives in the creation of one's manner; one delivers the manner on call. None of your crude American fumbling toward the point while gorging on the charity of all. Can we conceive of a worse situation for Marilyn? She is an extermination camp to millions of cells in each of the brains of her co-workers as she gasses their patience—yes, Tony Curtis will speak of kissing Hitler, and Olivier will tell Milton Greene he is ready to "squeak!" What makes it even worse is that her troika is pulling next to no chariot for her. Milton Greene is smooth as rum and butter with Olivier, and Miller has been lumbered by English upmanship and secretly respects Sir Laurence much too much. Strasberg delivers Big Bertha pronunciamentos from safe London, miles away from the studio. "Why does Olivier say he had difficulty with her," he remarks in later years. "I would say she had difficulty with him," but he is an outmoded gun for wars like this.

While Olivier has been warned in many a note from Joshua Logan to be patient with Marilyn, and not to raise his voice, nor expect "disciplined stage deportment," and Olivier has promised to iron himself out "nice and smooth," it is likely Olivier is contemptuous of the situation even before the film begins. He has already done *The Sleeping Prince* as a play with Vivien Leigh and so is conceivably in this for the profit rather than the glory of Marilyn Monroe's profession. Monroe, on the other hand, carrying all the secret snobbery that has led her to consider becoming Princess of Monaco, has to quicken to the thought she is playing with the monarchical actor of them all—her own secret coronation! We can measure the great and royal hollow of the orphanage by the size of her noble ambition now—yet there is Olivier brimming with hostility he cannot even begin to swallow at Logan-like injunctions to take care of darling little spoiled *lèse-majesté* wild animal actresses and Method madness and American money, upstart Millers and ogre Strasbergs, goes out, does Sir Laurence, and roils Miss Monroe's ego royally on the first week of work by saying, "All right, Marilyn, be sexy!" One might as well ask a nun to have carnal relations for Christ. Olivier has exposed that little gulf, wider than the Atlantic, between Method and Coquelin. In common-sensical Coquelin it don't take long to get sexy. If God was good enough to give it, throw it, babe! Indeed, the more unheralded English actors on the set have been looking at her with giggles. They have been waiting for the sex machine to start.

But in the Method, one does not get sexy. She calls Strasberg in London. Her voice burns wire. "Lee, how do you become sexy? What do you do to be sexy?" She cannot be soothed. Olivier has jammed into the tender roots of ontology and revealed his secret contempt for her. "The naughtiest little thing. . . ." Balzac, describing a bourgeois who purchased a false title, could do justice to her wrath. Now Olivier will get *her* treatment. He will learn, naughty little English boy, that sexiness is not a shiver in the pickle but the whole evocation of the whole woman in relation to the whole role: Marilyn proceeds to get ill. Quickly the cast is instructed by Greene not to giggle when she appears, and indeed, in reaction, are now funereal at the sight of her.

Soon they are in the familiar clutch of not knowing whether she will show up two hours late, four hours late, or not at all. Morning after morning, Miller phones that she is sick. In fact, she is back on quantities of sleeping pills. Nights go by when she cannot sleep at all. The unnumbered count of pills goes up. Then the gamble. Does she splurge for a few more and get a couple of hours sleep, thereby to stagger forth in drastic stupor for a working day, or should she pass into morning without sleep and try the job on stimulants? And red-rimmed eyes? Or does she skip the job and miss another day? Arthur is on vigil. Already there are intimations that the bucket by which she lowers herself into the well is tied to a frayed rope. It is fair to wonder if Miller is still full of love, or whether rage at her habits has now begun as well. He is a most ambitious man. In his own way, he is as ambitious as she is, and if she had only been an actor in the school of Coquelin—small detail!—and could get the work out on time, they could go far together. During those days in Washington when he fought for his passport he must have thought once or twice that no national office was necessarily too small for him. The public loved them so! Instead, after years of cramped work, he is now doing less writing than ever. He is her god, her guard, her attendant, and her flunky. Old friends, much impressed with his importance in the past, are now horrified to see Miller pasting up news clippings of Marilyn in a scrapbook, or standing around to approve her stills. Greene, who reads the situation better, senses that Miller is immersing himself in all the corners of movie business by way of preparing to replace him.

Still, how she must irritate Miller with her endless journeys to the simplest point. He is becoming all too aware of her capacity to inflict damage in secret wars. He cannot help it—he has sympathy for Olivier. Honest Jewish lover, he must write "a letter from hell" and leave it for her to see. (Perhaps he thinks it will give the proper reorientation to her heart.) When she reads these few lines (left on his desk open) she phones Strasberg again. Guiles gives the recollection:

She was so overwrought in telling the story it was not easy to determine precisely what the notebook entry had said, but Strasberg remembers there was indignation in her voice. "It was something about how disappointed he was in me. I was some kind of angel but now he guessed he was wrong. That his first wife had let him down, but I had done something worse. Olivier was beginning to think I was a troublesome bitch and that he [Arthur] no longer had a decent answer to that one."

The Strasbergs naturally would believe in later years that the episode was "the seed of her later destruction." Miller as naturally would see it as one episode among many. Marilyn, always ready to shift the burial ground of each corpse in her past, would say after she broke with Miller that he had called her a "whore." In *After the Fall,* Miller will re-create the episode and give this language to the note: "The only one I will ever love is my daughter. If I could only find an honorable way to die." What a nightmare is beginning for him. It is the cauldron in which Marilyn has spent her life, but he has no habits for it.

The movie progresses with absences, breakdowns, crises. Olivier is close to collapse himself. The irony is that when one sees *The Prince and the Showgirl,* it is better than anyone has a right to expect from the history of its making, but that is because Monroe is superb—will wonders never cease?

Dame Sybil Thorndike, who plays the Dowager Queen, is even going to say after the film is done, "I thought, surely she won't come over, she's so small scale, but when I saw her on the screen, my goodness, how it came over. She was a revelation. We theatre people tend to be so outgoing. She was the reverse. The perfect film actress, I thought. I have seen a lot of her films since then, and it's always there—that perfect quality."

She is also lovely. Milton H. Greene is indeed a genius with makeup. Never will Marilyn exhibit so marvelous a female palette, her colors living in the shades of an English garden. A hue cannot appear on her face without bearing the tone of a flower petal. Her lips are rose, her cheeks have every softened flush. Lavender shadows are lost in her hair. Once again she inhabits every frame of the film.

Of course, Olivier in his turn cannot fail to be excellent. He is too great an actor not to offer some final delineation of a Balkan Archduke. If there are a thousand virtuosities in his accent, it is because his virtuosities are always installed within other virtuosities—a consummate house of cards. It is just that he is out there playing by himself. So one can never get to believe he is attracted to Monroe. (Indeed, he is most believable when he snorts, "She has as much *comme il faut* as a rhinoceros!") Willy-nilly, he is therefore emphasizing the high level of contrivance in the plot.

A day arrives when Paula Strasberg strikes with "torrents of love and interest." She tells Olivier that his performance is artificial. It will not be long before she is banned from the set, then sent home from England. (Somehow, Olivier cannot grow accustomed to Monroe's habit of walking away from him to confer with Paula.) Mrs. Strasberg has been struck down, however, for loyalty on the right front. After this, Paula would be working with Marilyn for the rest of her life. And Milton Greene would catch the backed-up cess. From Marilyn's point of view, she was the producer of the film, but had no artistic control. Greene had given all that away to Olivier! One gets a glimpse of her rage, plus the mode in which Arthur and she have been talking about Milton, right after Greene announces to the British press *on his own* that he is ready to set up a British subsidiary of Marilyn Monroe Productions in order to make films in England. How unaware Milton must have been of Marilyn's feelings. Obviously, she had given him too small a clue.

> Miller put in a call to Greene, but his anger was such that he was shouting into the instrument and all Greene could hear was an incoherent roar. He recalls his angry reply, "If you want to talk to me, talk to me. If you're going to yell, then I'm not going to listen." When the roar continued, he slammed down the receiver.

Doubtless, he could then measure the beginning of the end of his relation to Marilyn Monroe Productions. Implicated Greene! He was also forced to serve as Olivier's emissary to inform Paula Strasberg that she was exiled. Somewhere in these embattled weeks, Monroe summons her analyst from New York and delays production another week.

For a taste of mutual relations just before the banishment, then we must trust Zolotow. If this glimpse of a scene is not true, we know it ought to be.

> One day when Monroe was being insufferably slow about everything, Olivier said something about speeding things up a bit. Mrs. Strasberg said, "You shouldn't rush Marilyn. After all, Chaplin took eight months to make a movie."
> Olivier looked from Monroe to Mrs. Strasberg to Greene. He didn't say a word. But his expression indicated that the analogy between Monroe and Chaplin was possibly the most nauseating remark he had ever heard.

Olivier is wrong. British snobbery is once again building empires and buggering them. All parties concerned finish the film in a cloud of detestations and Marilyn makes a little speech to the cast. "I hope you will all forgive me. It wasn't my fault. I've been very, very sick all through the picture. Please—please don't hold it against me."

She is introduced to the Queen. It does no good. She has lost the British press. They sniff and snipe to a fare-thee-well. She did not have the common touch, she did not know *in the way Winston Churchill did* how to take fish and chips with Cockneys.

The Millers return to America. The dream that they were destined for a great and mighty marriage may already have foundered. One would like a picture of Olivier's face as he said goodbye.

They come back to the Greenes' apartment on Sutton Place, and divide their time between New York and Miller's farm in Connecticut. The racketing assembly line of daily publicity shuts down. They begin to have some of the married life Miller once envisaged. Later he will indicate that this fall, winter, and spring, plus the summer they had together in Amagansett, was their happiest time, and if this would clash with the Strasbergs' view that the marriage was already hurt in final fashion by the discovery of Miller's notebook in Egham, it is better to recognize that their marriage requires love to enter the service of medicine. So for a period he will be the most deeply devoted physician of her life, and she will love him back—in very much the way gentile girls are supposed to love Jewish doctors. There is so much concern for healing you! In all of Miller's early plays is one progressive theme: Social evil derives from minds sickened by inhuman values. Those minds can best be cured by healing the heart. He loved her heart. It is significant that Paula Strasberg, interviewed in New York right after *The Prince and the Showgirl* (which is to say right after Egham), was sufficiently uninhibited to say, "I have never seen such tenderness and love as Arthur and Marilyn feel for each other. How he values her! I don't think any woman I've ever known has been so *valued* by a man." It seems Egham had not blown all the walls just yet.

Actually, they settle into good days and bad days. Which is the narrative line of marriage. In England he has been a failure to her. In *After the Fall*, Maggie cries, "You should've gone in there roaring! 'Stead of a polite liberal and affidavits. . . ." Greene remarked: "She wanted a fuehrer to deal with Olivier, and got a broker." No, Marilyn has not wanted Miller's insights into the complexity of the artist's working situation. So Arthur has been, yes, a failure in England, and at Egham a traitor. But the marriage can hardly be dead. She is in the deepest need of a cure. Her illness is made up of all that oncoming accumulation of ills she has postponed from the past, all that sexual congress with men she has not loved, and all those unfinished hours with men she has loved, all the lies she has told, all the lies told about her, all unavenged humiliations sleeping like unfed scorpions in the unsettled flesh. Worse!—all unfinished family insanity, plus her own abused nerves. Plus the need to come to rest in some final identity. (Even in her last *Life* interview with Meryman, she will say, "My work is the only ground I've ever had to stand on. . . . To put it bluntly, I seem to have a whole superstructure with no foundation.") If she has known the best sexual athletes of Hollywood (that capital of sex) and Miller at his worst has to be an inhibited householder from Brooklyn, nonetheless she loves him. He is the first man she has met upon whom she can found an identity, be Marilyn Monroe, the wife of Arthur Miller. That alone may provide her such happiness that she is able for this period at least to grant him that indispensable fiction for the maintenance of marriage—you are the best lover I ever had. Of course, *best lover* is its own happy category. Many a man or woman has a sexual life with oncoming lovers who appear each in turn the *best,* one lover for each face of the sexual best; somehow there are twenty best faces. It would hardly be unnatural if, feeling some tenderness with him she has not necessarily known before, she would decide tenderness was, yes, best, tenderness was best, even as the number of certified sexual arrivals—call Dr. Kinsey!—may once have been best, or some high electric discharge into the stratosphere of the shaking sexual tree, some sweet taste of liberty (the freedom to fuck!), any category can be best: lips, smell, skin, *whatever*—there is no standard to keep us from deciding that our present sex is at the maximum. Of course, we all grow old—that little problem! Still, we can always carry our sexual past into the present (even as Miller suggested in *After the Fall*), but then we are able to succeed at making the present lover equal to the sum of all which has gone before only if we are also increasing, that is becoming wiser, wittier, or possessed of more psychic strength. We have to transcend what is past—in our emotions, at least, if not in our bodies. Emotion has to work through the sorrow of the past without self-pity; so, one must find more wealth in the heart—no small requirement!

But there is small evidence that they were ever in such a state. Like everything else in Marilyn's life, she lived in the continuing condition of a half-lie, which she imposed upon everyone as an absolute truth—it was that Miller adored her out of measure. Like a *goddess*. Since Miller was also a man with such separate needs as the imperative to write well, as well as to profit from her talents as much as anyone else was prospering, yes, whenever he emerged as a *separate person*—fell phrase of romance!—this half-lie or half-truth that he adored her without limit had to collapse. Where she had claimed an absolute truth that was ill-founded, now there was an absolute denial, equally ill-founded. He did not love her at all. He wished only to use her.

A picture of just such emotional swings is revealed in her habits at Amagansett. The summer of 1957 is the period in which he works best as Young Doctor Miller, and often will get her off sleeping pills, or down to just one or two a night; sometimes she will even sleep. Restored by the least bit of rest, there are days when she will have endless energy and show exquisite sensitivity—at least to his lover's eye. She has only to study the petals of a flower to invoke the full appreciation of his adoring view—"she was able to look at a flower as if she had never seen one before," he would say in an interview—and we get a glimpse of what was most tender and attractive between them in a quotation Guiles selects for us from Miller's short story "Please Don't Kill Anything."

> The waves were breaking into the net now, but they could not yet see any fish. She put her two hands up to her cheeks and said, "Oh, now they know they're caught!" She laughed. "Each one is wondering what happened!" He was glad she was making fun of herself even if her eyes were fixed in fear on the submerged net. She glanced up at her husband and said, "Oh, dear, they're going to be caught now."
>
> He started to explain, but she quickly went on, "I know it's all right as long as they're eaten. They're going to eat them, aren't they?"
>
> "They'll sell them to the fish stores," he said softly, so the old man at the winch wouldn't hear. "They'll feed people."
>
> "Yes," she said, like a child reassured. "I'll watch it. I'm watching it," she almost announced to him. But in her something was holding its breath.

We are finally dealing with the root of human comedy, and it is tragic. She is a girl who cannot bear the death of one little fish—she is thus genuinely sensitive to the expiration of life, to the *instant* when it stirs intimations, which go to the root of her divine nerves—yet she is ready to kill herself before she can allow his will to influence her will.

During years to come when her suicide attempts will be not infrequent, he will come to recognize that her desire to kill herself would kill him almost as effectively in the eyes of society. "I'm all the evil in the world, aren't I?" Quentin says to Maggie in the middle of just such an attempt. "A suicide kills two people, Maggie, that's what it's for!"

Of course, Miller is not without his own purchase on contradiction. He is a masterpiece of love and thrift, generosity and pinch. If he comes to her as a man bursting with the desire to offer his love to someone who has need of it, she must know all the pleasure of a thief who rips off a consummate miser. What a treasure in the hoard! For the first time in her life she can live in a milieu that adores her, adores her twice, first as a star, and then because she has chosen Arthur and so prefers intelligentsia and the theatre to capitalists, professional sports, or Hollywood. Moreover, there are the near to unlimited funds of his attention—it is such a special and loving attention. She has the most talented slave in the world. And she has full need to manipulate a slave after a life in which her nerves have been pulled by the imperatives of others.

That, however, is only one side of Miller. He is also ambitious, limited, and small-minded, an intellectual who is often scorned by critics outside the theatre for his intellectual lacks. Nor has he developed to meet such criticisms. Rather, he has reinforced his old walls. He has virtually a terror of the kind of new experience that might open his ideas; so she is enough new experience to last him for a lifetime.

If these limitations have cut off his work even before he has come to live with her, the inability to do much writing in their first year together sets early patterns that will later hurt him. (Of course, the fact that he is still being harassed by congressional committees is no help to his work, either.) But from the beginning it is her money that they live on. From her work. In such a condition, it is natural to toady to her. Can anything be worse for him? He begins to develop the instincts of a servant. Since he is already full of the middle-class nose for petty increments of power, the vacuum in his own creative force has to be filled by becoming a species of business manager, valet, and in-residence hospital attendant. He manages too much. She, with her profound distrust of everyone about her, begins to suspect him. Has he married her because he can't write anymore? Is his secret ambition to become a Hollywood producer? Or does he want to use her as a meal ticket? Such mean suspicions warm up the dynamos of all throttled insanity. Over and over, through the good months at Amagansett, she will plunge into sudden depressions. They are inexplicable to him. What he cannot recognize as he comes to grips with the full incalculable complexity of a woman is that he is just as much of an enigma to her, and unlike him she sickens before mysteries. They do not offer new literary lines of work, but are connotative of the pit.

In Amagansett they also discover she is pregnant. By the sixth week she is in such pain they rush to New York for an operation. It is announced that the pregnancy is tubal. But there is ambiguity even about this. The question remains whether her pregnancies were tubal or hysterical. Greene claims she once had a fearful abortion that made it impossible for her to be pregnant. Miller, in an interview, said she could not, but then later in the same interview thought she did have a tubal pregnancy. It is a confusion that she may even have disseminated herself and it persists. What may be the best explanation, from a friend who knew Marilyn well, is that she had had many abortions, perhaps so many as twelve! And in cheap places—for a number of these abortions came in the years she was modeling or a bit player on seven-year contracts—thus her gynecological insides were unspeakably scarred, and her propensity for tubal pregnancies was increased. Since her periods were unendurable—"the pain was so great she would writhe on the floor"—a doctor began to inhibit her menstruation with a drug that anticipated the Pill, and for such duration not able to become pregnant, she would "in hysterical compensation think she was. Can you conceive what a frightful mess this had to make of her?"

"She never wore a diaphragm?"

"She hated them," said the woman friend. "What people don't understand is that Marilyn loved sex." (We are in *Rashomon* once more!) "I don't think she went a week in her life without having some man around. She took sex with men the way men used to take sex with women."

"Still, she needed sleeping pills."

"Nobody's perfect."

Now, with Miller, faithful to Miller, she will have an operation and then another to make a child possible, and will claim to have other pregnancies—what stays constant is the depth of depression each time the pregnancy, real, tubal, or hysterical, is over. It is as if Zanuck's verdict upon her as a sexual freak is being confirmed. If few women are without depression after a miscarriage—they are dealing, finally, with a mystery, which, for whatever reason, has chosen not to be born—then what an avalanche of depression for Marilyn. The unspoken logic of suicide insists that an early death is better for the soul than slow extinction through a misery of deteriorating years.

This depression lies so heavy upon her that Miller crosses his Rubicon. He has never written before with an actor or actress in mind. He derives from the high literary tradition that true theatre depends upon the play, and the script is inviolate. Great playwrights live with themes, not actors. But he will write a movie script for her. He will adapt his short story "The Misfits" into her vehicle. It is, from Marilyn's point of view, either the highest offering of his love or the first aggressive calculation of a mean and ambitious brain. Her mood rises and she is gay for a few days, but on their return from the hospital she slides back into depression and begins to increase her count of Nembutals. One day he sees her stumble into a chair and go immediately into a heavy doze. Her breathing is labored. Then for the first time he hears what will become the unmistakable sounds of a half-paralyzed diaphragm—her breath is coming with an eerie continuing sigh. The wind of death is in the winding sheet. He does not try to brew coffee or walk her around, slap her face, or pinch the back of her knees. Instead, he seeks "immediate medical help." It is in his character not to look for amateur solutions. Apparatus and technicians from a nearby clinic come *quickly*—can this be medical assistance with which any of us is familiar?—and they resuscitate her. He has saved her life. He will have to save it more than once again. In the days after this incident she will, according to Guiles, be endlessly affectionate to Miller, kiss his hands over and over.

What do we witness? Has she actually supposed (with her abominable facility for living in the unconscious of others) that he might let her die? Or has her hatred been put to rest by the look of relief in his eyes that she is still alive?

They begin to put down roots. He finds another farm in Connecticut, and they buy it. She is busy and happy with the details of alteration and studies the daily work of the carpenters, while he begins to work on *The Misfits*. It is a happy time, but will end, he knows, so soon as the alterations are finished. He is right. She is bored with the country, and begins to talk of their own apartment in New York. They move from the Greenes' apartment on Sutton Place to another at 444 East Fifty-seventh Street. Her love of Brooklyn is obviously not as intense now as it used to be. If there will be a view across the East River, it is from Manhattan that they will look at unhappy squats on the skyline of Queens. Now she picks up her classes with Strasberg again, and spends many an evening talking to other actors at the Strasberg home. Miller does not often accompany her, but he does not oppose her either. It is as if he senses that she must be forever engaged in feathering the nest of some future identity. Being among actors offers a culture she can finally acquire the way others pick up a foreign language—she is at least absorbing the milieu of the New York Method actor: his gossip, his prospects, his sophistication, his cynicism, and his sharp horizons. To live at last in a milieu must be the equivalent of oxygen to her. Yet, she is also most respectful of Miller during this time. When guests visit the New York apartment, she takes them on tiptoe past the important room of the house—it is the place where her husband writes. We must conceive of him sitting there, unable to put down a word for dint of listening to her caution the guests. Of course, during this time Milton Greene is also being sued for control of Marilyn Monroe Productions, a sordid episode. At Miller's urging, she even attempts through her lawyers to have Greene's name removed as executive producer of *The Prince and the Showgirl*. Milton has heard nothing from her in the interval. Since he has just turned down a $2,000,000 offer from television because "she isn't up to the strain of a series," he can feel he has legitimately been protecting her interests. Half of that $2,000,000 would, after all, have gone to him. While Greene threatens a lawsuit in which he will claim huge amounts, he feels small heart for the project and finally accepts $100,000, far less than Monroe's lawyers were prepared to pay. "My interest in Marilyn's career," he says with sad dignity, "was not for gain," and after three years of activity that has telescoped the focus of his life inside out, he goes back to his profession as a fashion photographer.

Whether this victory for Miller contributes a bit to the excellence of *The Misfits* is hardly knowable, but the script in any case proceeds well. He is out of his literary doldrums. Some time after a first draft of the movie is finished, he invites his old friend and neighbor, Frank Taylor, who has been a book editor *and* a Hollywood producer, to listen to the script. On an afternoon in July of 1958, Miller reads it to him, and Taylor is obviously impressed, for he suggests sending the work to John Huston in Paris—at once!—and Huston wires back within the week that it is "magnificent." He will be happy to direct it. Clark Gable is given a copy and is also anxious to do it. Taylor agrees to take a leave from publishing and be the producer. United Artists is interested in financing. Now they have not only a major production, well launched, but a sudden sense of all-surrounding excitement. And promises at last of fulfillment. They seem to have emerged onto the good-working married ground that they have an exciting job they will do together. It is a long time since so much talent and celebrity have come together on a film.

From *Marilyn* (1973)

# THE TIME
# OF HER TIME

*"The Time of Her Time" was a salacious object in its time. Secretly, I didn't be-*
*lieve it could be printed. Then my publisher, Walter Minton of G. P. Putnam's,*
*agreed it could not be included in* Advertisements for Myself. *Not as it*
*stood.*

*"You have to, Walter.* Advertisements *is no book without it."*

*"Don't I know it," he whined.*

*Walter Minton is the only man I ever met who gets stronger as he whines.*
*Before it was over, he agreed to take the chance without asking me to remove a*
*word. Then a year or two later he published* Lolita. *"You know," he confided*
*once, "I think it was publishing 'The Time of Her Time' and seeing how little*
*trouble came to us which made me realize you could do* Lolita."

*Reader, the story you are about to peruse is the godfather of* Lolita.

## 1.

I was living in a room one hundred feet long and twenty-five feet
wide, and it had nineteen windows staring at me from three of the
walls and part of the fourth. The floor planks were worn below the
level of the nails that held them down, except for the southern half of
the room, where I had laid a rough linoleum which gave a hint of
sprinkled sand, conceivably an aid to the footwork of my pupils. For
one hundred dollars I had the place whitewashed—everything: the
checkerboard of tin ceiling plates one foot square with their fleur-de-
lis stamped into the metal, the rotted sashes on the window frames (it

took twelve hours to scrape the calcimine from the glass), even parts of the floor had white drippings (although that was scuffed into dust as time went on), and yet it was worth it. When I took the loft it stank of old machinery and the paint was a liverish brown—I had tried living with that color for a week: My old furniture, which had been moved by a mover friend from the Village and me, showed the scars of being humped and dragged and flung up six flights of stairs, and the view of it sprawled over twenty-five hundred feet of living space, three beat old day beds, some dusty cushions, a broken-armed easy chair, a cigarette-scarred coffee table made from a door, a kitchen table, some peeled enamel chairs that thumped like a wooden-legged pirate when one sat in them, the bookshelves of unfinished pine butted by bricks, yes, all of this, my purview, this grand vista, the New York sunlight greeting me in the morning through the double filter of the smog yellow sky and the nineteen dirt-frosted windows, inspired me with so much content, especially those liver-brown walls, that I fled my pad like the plague, and in the first week, after a day of setting the furniture to rights, I was there for four hours of sleep a night, from five in the morning when I maneuvered in from the last closed Village bar and the last coffee-klatsch of my philosopher friends for the night to let us say nine in the morning, when I awoke with a partially destroyed brain and the certainty that the sore vicious growl of my stomach was at least the onset of an ulcer and more likely the first gone cells of a thoroughgoing cancer of the duodenum. So I lived in it that way for a week, and then following the advice of a bar-type who was the friend of a friend, I got myself up on the eighth morning, boiled my coffee on a hot-plate while I shivered in the October air (neither the stove nor the gas heaters had yet been bought), and then I went downstairs and out the front door of the warehouse onto Monroe Street, picking my way through the garbage-littered gutter that always made me think of the gangs on this street, the Negroes on the east end of the block, the Puerto Ricans next to them, and the Italians and Jews to the west—those gangs were going to figure a little in my life, I suspected that. I was anticipating those moments with no quiet bravery considering how hung was my head in the morning, for the worst clue to the gangs was the six-year-olds. They were the defilers of the garbage, knights of the ordure, and here, in this province of a capital Manhattan, at the southern tip of the island, with the overhead girders of the Manhattan and Brooklyn bridges the only noble structures for a mile of tenement jungle, yes, here the barbarians ate their young, and any type who reached the age of six without being altogether mangled by father, mother, family, or friends was a pint of iron man, so tough, so ferocious, so sharp in the teeth that the wildest alley cat would have surrendered a freshly caught rat rather than contest the meal. They were charming, these six-year-olds, as I told my up-town friends, and they used to topple the overloaded garbage cans, strew them through the street, have summer snowball fights with orange peel, coffee grounds, soup bones, slop—they threw the discus by scaling the raw tin rounds from the tops of cans, their pillow fights were with loaded socks of scum, and a debauch was for two of them to scrub a third around the inside of a twenty-gallon pail still warm with the heat of its emptied treasures. I heard that the Olympics took place in summer when they were out of school and the streets were so thick with the gum of old detritus, effluvium, and dross that the mash made by passing car tires fermented in the sun. Then the parents and the hoods and the debs and the grandmother dowagers cheered them on and promised them murder and the garbage flew all day, but I was there in fall and the scene was quiet from nine to three. So I picked my way through last night's stew of rubble on this eighth morning of my hiatus on Monroe Street, and went half down the block to a tene-ment on the boundary between those two bandit republics of the Ne-groes and the Puerto Ricans, and with a history or two of knocking on the wrong door, and with a nose full of the smells of the sick overpep-pered bowels of the poor that seeped and oozed out of every leaking pipe in every communal crapper (only as one goes north does the word take on the Protestant propriety of john), I was able finally to find my man, and I was an hour ahead of him—he was still sleeping off his last night's drunk. So I spoke to his wife, a fat masculine Negress with the face and charity of a Japanese wrestler, and when she understood that I was neither a junk-peddler nor fuzz, that I sold no numbers, carried no bills, and was most certainly not a detective (though my Irish face left her dubious of that) but instead had come to offer her husband a job of work, I was admitted to the first of three dark rooms, face to face with the gray luminescent eye of the televi-sion set going its way in a dark room on a bright morning, and through the hall curtains I could hear them talking in the bedroom.

"Get up, you son of a bitch," she said to him.

He came to work for me, hating my largesse, lugging his air com-pressor up my six flights of stairs, and after a discussion in which his price came down from two hundred to one, and mine rose from fifty dollars to meet his, he left with one of my twenty-dollar bills, the air compressor on the floor as security, and returned in an hour with so many sacks of whitewash that I had to help him up the stairs. We worked together that day—Charley Thompson his name was, a small lean Negro maybe forty years old, and conceivably sixty, with a scar or two on his face, one a gouge on the cheek, the other a hairline along the bridge of his nose, and we got along not too badly, working in sullen silence until the hangover was sweated out, and then starting to talk over coffee in the Negro hashhouse on the corner where the bucks bridled a little when I came in, and then ignored me. Once the atmosphere had become neutral again, Thompson was willing to talk.

"Man," he said to me, "what you want all that space for?"

"To make money."

"Out of which?"

I debated not very long. The people on the block would know my business sooner or later—the reward of living in a slum is that everyone knows everything that is within reach of the senses—and since I would be nailing a sign over my mailbox downstairs for the pupils to know which floor they would find me on, and the downstairs door would have to be open since I had no bell, the information would be just as open. But for that matter I was born to attract attention; given my height and my blond hair, the barbarians would notice me, they noticed everything, and so it was wiser to come on strong than to try to sidle in.

"Ever hear of an *Escuela de Torear*?" I asked him without a smile.

He laughed with delight at the sound of the words, not even bothering to answer.

"That's a bullfighter's school," I told him. "I teach bullfighting."

"You know that?"

"I used to do it in Mexico."

"Man, you can get killed."

"Some do." I let the exaggeration of a cooled nuance come into my voice. It was true, after all; some do get killed. But not so many as I was suggesting—maybe one in fifty of the successful, and one in five hundred of the amateurs like me who fought a few bulls, received a few wounds, and drifted away.

Charley Thompson was impressed. So were others—the conversation was being overheard, after all, and I had become a cardinal piece on the chaotic chessboard of Monroe Street's sociology—I felt the clear bell-like adrenalines of clean anxiety, untainted by weakness, self-interest, neurotic habit, or the pure yellows of the liver. For I had put my poker money on the table, I was the new gun in a frontier saloon, and so I was asking for it, not today, not tomorrow, but come sooner, come later, something was likely to follow from this. The weak would leave me alone, the strong would have respect, but be it winter or summer, sunlight or dark, there would come an hour so cold or so hot that someone, somebody, some sexed-up head, very strong and very weak, would be drawn to discover a new large truth about himself and the mysteries of his own courage or the lack of it. I knew. A year before, when I had first come to New York, there was a particular cat I kept running across in the bars of the Village, an expert with a knife, or indeed, to maintain the salts of accuracy, an expert with two knives. He carried them everywhere—he had been some sort of hophead instructor in the Marines on the art of fighting with the knife, and he used to demonstrate nice fluid poses, his elbows in, the knives out, the points of those blades capering free of one another—he could feint in any direction with either hand, he was an artist, he believed he was better with a knife than any man in all of New York, and night after night in bar after bar he sang the love-song of his own prowess, begging for the brave type who would take on his boast, and leave him confirmed or dead.

It is mad to take on the city of New York, there is too much talent waiting on line; this cat was calling for every hoodlum in every crack gang and clique who fancied himself with the blade, and one night, drunk and on the way home, he was greeted by another knife, a Puerto Rican cat who was defective in school and spent his afternoons and nights shadow-knifing in the cellar clubhouse of his clique, a real contender, long-armed for a Latin, thin as a Lehmbruck, and fast as a hungry wolf; he had practiced for two months to meet the knife of New York.

So they went into an alley, the champion drunk, a fog of vanity blanketing the point of all his artistic reflexes, and it turned out to be not too much of a fight: The Puerto Rican caught it on the knuckles, the lip, and above the knee, but they were only nicks, and the champion was left in bad shape, bleeding from the forearm, the belly, the chest, the neck, and the face. Once he was down, the Puerto Rican had engraved a double oval, labium majorum and minorum on the skin of the cheek, and left him there, having the subsequent consideration or fright to make a telephone call to the bar in which our loser had been drinking. The ex-champion, a bloody cat, was carried to his pad, which was not far away (a bit of belated luck), and in an hour, without undue difficulty, the brother-in-law doctor of somebody or other was good enough to take care of him. There were police reports, and as our patois goes, the details were a drag, but what makes my story sad is that our ex-champion was through. He mended by sorts and shifts, and he still bragged in the Village bars, and talked of finding the Puerto Rican when he was sober and in good shape, but the truth was that he was on the alcoholic way, and the odds were that he would stay there. He had been one of those gamblers who saw his life as a single bet, and he had lost. I often thought that he had been counting on a victory to put some charge below his belt and drain his mouth of all that desperate labial libido.

Now I was following a modest parallel, and as Thompson kept asking me some reasonable if openly ignorant questions about the nature of the bullfight, I found myself shaping every answer as carefully as if I were writing dialogue, and I was speaking particularly for the black-alerted senses of three Negroes who were sitting behind me, each of them big in his way (I had taken my glimpse as I came in), with a dull, almost Chinese, sullenness of face. They could have been anything. I had seen faces like theirs on boxers and ditch diggers, and I had seen such faces by threes and fours riding around in Cadillacs through the Harlem of the early-morning hours. I was warning myself to play it carefully, and yet I pushed myself a little further than I should, for I became ashamed of my caution and therefore was obliged to brag just the wrong bit. Thompson, of course, was encouraging me—he was a sly old bastard—and he knew even better than me the character of our audience.

"Man, you can take care of yourself," he said with glee.

"I don't know about that," I answered, obeying the formal minuet of the *macho*. "I don't like to mess with anybody," I told him. "But a man messes with me—well, I wouldn't want him to go away feeling better than he started."

"Oh, yeah, ain't that a fact. I hears just what you hear." He talked like an old-fashioned Negro—probably Southern. "What if four or five of them comes on and gangs you?"

We had come a distance from the art of the *corrida*. "That doesn't happen to me," I said. "I like to be careful about having some friends." And part for legitimate emphasis, and part to fulfill my image of the movie male lead—that blond union of the rugged and the clean-cut (which would, after all, be *their* image as well)—I added, "Good friends, you know."

There we left it. My coffee cup was empty, and in the slop of the saucer a fly was drowning. I was thinking idly and with no great compassion that wherever this fly had been born it had certainly not expected to die in a tan syrupy ring-shaped pond, struggling for the greasy hot-dogged air of a cheap Negro hashhouse. But Thompson rescued it with a deft little flip of his fingers.

"I always save," he told me seriously. "I wouldn't let nothing be killed. I'm a preacher."

"Real preacher?"

"Was one. Church and devoted congregation." He said no more. He had the dignified sadness of a man remembering the major failure of his life.

As we got up to go, I managed to turn around and get another look at the three spades in the next booth. Two of them were facing me. Their eyes were flat, the whites were yellow and flogged with red—they stared back with no love. The anxiety came over me again, almost nice—I had been so aware of them, and they had been so aware of me.

### 2.

That was in October, and for no reason I could easily discover, I found myself thinking of that day as I awoke on a spring morning more than half a year later with a strong light coming through my nineteen windows. I had fixed the place up since then, added a few more pieces of furniture, connected a kitchen sink and a metal stall shower to the clean water outlets in the john, and most noticeably I had built a wall between the bullfight studio and the half in which I lived. That was more necessary than one might guess—I had painted the new wall red. After Thompson's job of whitewash I used to feel as if I were going snow-blind; it was no easy pleasure to get up each morning in a white space so blue with cold that the chill of a mountain peak was in my blood. Now, when I opened my eyes, I could choose the blood of the wall in preference to the ice slopes of Mt. O'Shaugnessy, where the sun was always glinting on the glaciers of the windows.

But on this particular morning, when I turned over a little more, there was a girl propped on one elbow in the bed beside me, no great surprise, because this was the year of all the years in my life when I was scoring three and four times a week, literally combing the pussy out of my hair, which was no great feat if one knew the Village and the scientific temperament of the Greenwich Village mind. I do not want to give the false impression that I was one of the lustiest to come adventuring down the pike—I was cold, maybe by birth, certainly by environment: I grew up in a Catholic orphanage—and I had had my little kinks and cramps, difficulties enough just a few years ago, but I had passed through that, and I was going now on a kind of disinterested but developed competence. What it came down to was that I could go an hour with the average girl without destroying more of the vital substance than a good night's sleep could repair, and since that sort of stamina seems to get advertised, and I had my good looks, my blond hair, my height, build, and bullfighting school, I suppose I became one of the Village equivalents of an Eagle Scout badge for the girls. I was one of the credits needed for a diploma in the sexual humanities, I was par for a good course, and more than one of the girls and ladies would try me on an off-evening like comparison-shoppers to shop the value of their boy friend, lover, mate, or husband against the certified professionalism of Sergius O'Shaugnessy.

Now if I make this sound bloodless, I am exaggerating a bit—even an old habit is livened once in a while with color, and there were girls I worked to get and really wanted, and nights when the bull was far from dead in me. I even had two women I saw at least once a week, each of them, but what I am trying to emphasize is that when you screw too much and nothing is at stake, you begin to feel like a saint. It was a hell of a thing to be holding a nineteen-year-old girl's ass in my hands, hefting those young kneadables of future power, while all the while the laboratory technician in my brain was deciding that the experiment was a routine success—routine because her cheeks looked and felt just about the way I had thought they would while I was sitting beside her in the bar earlier in the evening, and so I still had come no closer to understanding my scientific compulsion to verify in the retort of the bed how accurately I had predicted the form, texture, rhythm, and surprise of any woman who caught my eye.

Only an ex-Catholic can achieve some of the rarer amalgams of guilt, and the saint in me deserves to be recorded. I always felt an obligation—some noblesse oblige of the kindly cocksman—to send my women away with no great wounds to their esteem, feeling at best a little better than when they came in, I wanted it to be friendly (what vanity of the saint!). I was the messiah of the one-night stand, and so I rarely acted like a pig in bed, I wasn't greedy, I didn't grind all my tastes into their mouths, I even abstained from springing too good a lay when I felt the girl was really in love with her man, and was using me only to give love the benefit of new perspective. Yes, I was a good sort, I probably gave more than I got back, and the only real pains for all those months in the loft, for my bullfighting classes, my surprisingly quiet time (it had been winter after all) on Monroe Street, my bulging portfolio of experiments—there must have been fifty girls who spent at least one night in the loft—my dull but doggedly advancing scientific data, even the cold wan joys of my saintliness demanded for their payment only one variety of the dead hour: When I woke in the morning, I could hardly wait to get the latest mouse out of my bed and out of my lair. I didn't know why, but I would awaken with the deadliest of depressions, the smell of the woman had gone very stale for me, and the armpits, the ammonias, and dead sea life of old semen and old snatch, the sour fry of last night's sweat, the whore scent of overexercised perfume, became an essence of the odious, all the more remarkable because I clung to women in my sleep, I was one Don John who hated to sleep alone, I used to feel as if my pores were breathing all the maternal (because sleeping) sweets of the lady, wet or dry, firm or flaccid, plump, baggy, or lean who was handled by me while we dreamed. But on awakening, hung with my head—did I make love three times that year without being drunk?—the saint was given his hour of temptation, for I would have liked nothing more than to kick the friendly ass out of bed, and dispense with the coffee, the good form, my depression and often hers, and start the new day by lowering her in a basket out of my monk-ruined retreat six floors down to the garbage pile (now blooming again in the freshets of spring), wave my hand at her safe landing, and get in again myself to the blessed isolations of the man alone.

But of course that was not possible. While it is usually a creep who generalizes about women, I think I will come on so heavy as to say that the cordial tone of the morning after is equally important to the gymkhana of the night before—at least if the profit made by a nice encounter is not to be lost. I had given my working hours of the early morning to dissolving a few of the inhibitions, chilled reflexes, and dampened rhythms of the corpus before me, but there is not a restraint in the world that does not have to be taken twice—once at night on a steam-head of booze, and once in daylight with the grace of a social tea. To open a girl up to the point where she loves you or It or some tremor in her sexual baggage and then to close her in the morning is to do the disservice that the hateful side of women loves most— you have fed their cold satisfied distrust of a man. Therefore my saint fought his private churl, and suffering all the detail of abusing the sympathetic nervous system, I made with the charm in the daylight and was more of a dear than most.

It was to be a little different this morning, however. As I said, I turned over in my bed, and looked at the girl propped on her elbow beside me. In her eyes there was a flat hatred that gave no ground— she must have been staring like this at my back for several minutes, and when I turned, it made no difference—she continued to examine my face with no embarrassment and no delight.

That was sufficient to roll me around again, my shoulder blades bare to her inspection, and I pretended that the opening of my eyes had been a false awakening. I felt deadened then with all the diseases of the dull—making love to her the night before had been a little too much of a marathon. She was a Jewish girl and she was in her third year at New York University, one of those harsh alloys of a self-made bohemian from a middle-class home (her father was a hardware wholesaler), and I was remembering how her voice had irritated me each time I had seen her, an ugly New York accent with a cultured overlay. Since she was still far from formed, there had been all sorts of Lesbian hysterias in her shrieking laugh and they warred with that excess of strength, complacency, and deprecation that I found in many Jewish women—a sort of "Ech" of disgust at the romantic and mysterious All. This one was medium in size and she had dark long hair, which she wore like a Village witch in two extended braids that came down over her flat breasts, and she had a long thin nose, dark eyes, and a kind of lean force, her arms and square shoulders had shown the flat thin muscles of a wiry boy. All the same, she was not bad, she had a kind of Village chic, a certain snotty elegance of superiority, and when I first came to New York I had dug girls like her—Jewesses were strange to me—and I had even gone with one for a few months. But this new chick had been a mistake—I had met her two weeks ago at a party, she was on leave from her boy friend, and we had had an argument about T. S. Eliot, a routine that for me had become the quintessence of corn, but she said that Eliot was the apotheosis of manner, he embodied the ecclesiasticism of classical and now futureless form, she adored him, she said, and I was tempted to tell her how little Eliot would adore the mannerless yeasts of the Brooklyn from which she came, and how he might prefer to allow her to appreciate his poetry only in step to the transmigration of her voice from all urgent Yiddish nasalities to the few high English analities of relinquished desire. No, she would not make that other world so fast—nice society was not cutting her crumpets thus quickly because she was gone on Thomas Stearns Eeeee. Her college-girl snobbery, the pith for me of eighty-five other honey-pots of the Village aesthetic whose smell I knew all too well, so inflamed the avenger of my crotch that I wanted to prong her then and there, right on the floor of the party, I was a primitive for a prime minute, a gorged gouge of a working-class phallus, eager to ram into all her nasty little tensions. I had the message again, I was one of the millions on the bottom who had the muscles to move the sex that kept the world alive, and I would grind it into her, the healthy hearty inches and the sweat of the cost of acquired culture when you started low and you wanted to go high. She was a woman, what! she sensed that moment, she didn't know if she could handle me, and she had the guts to decide to find out. So we left the party and we drank and (leave it to a Jewish girl to hedge the bet) she drained the best half of my desire in conversation because she was being psychoanalyzed, what a predictable pisser! and she was in that stage where the jargon had the totalitarian force of all vocabularies of mechanism, and she could only speak of her infantile relations to men, and the fixations and resistances of unassimilated penis-envy with all the smug gusto of a female commissar. She was enthusiastic about her analyst, he was also Jewish (they were working now on Jewish self-hatred), he was really an integrated guy, Stanford Joyce, he belonged on the same mountain as Eliot, she loved the doers and the healers of life who built on the foundationless prevalence of the void those islands of proud endeavor.

"You must get good marks in school," I said to her.

"Of course."

How I envied the jazzed-up brain of the Jews. I was hot for her again, I wanted the salts of her perspiration in my mouth. They would be acrid perhaps, but I would digest them, and those intellectual molecules would rise to my brain.

"I know a girl who went to your bullfighting school," she said to me. She gave her harsh laugh. "My friend thought you were afraid of her. She said you were full of narcissistic anxieties."

"Well, we'll find out," I said.

"Oh, you don't want me. I'm very inadequate as a lover." Her dark hard New York eyes, bright with appetite, considered my head as if I were a delicious and particularly sour pickle.

I paid the check then, and we walked over to my loft. As I had expected, she made no great fuss over the back-and-forth of being seduced—to the contrary. Once we were upstairs, she prowled the length of my loft twice, looked at the hand-made bullfighting equipment I had set up along one wall of the studio, asked me a question or two about the killing machine, studied the swords, asked another question about the cross-guard on the descabellar, and then came back to the living-room–bedroom–dining-room–kitchen of the other room, and made a face at the blood-red wall. When I kissed her she answered with a grinding insistence of her mouth upon mine, and a muscular thrust of her tongue into my throat, as direct and unfeminine as the harsh force of her voice.

"I'd like to hang my clothes up," she said.

It was not all that matter-of-fact when we got to bed. There was nothing very fleshy about the way she made love, no sense of the skin, nor smell, nor touch, just anger, anger at her being there, and another anger which was good for my own, that rage to achieve . . . just what, one cannot say. She made love as if she were running up an inclined wall so steep that to stop for an instant would slide her back to disaster. She hammered her rhythm at me, a hard driving rhythm, an all but monotonous drum, pound into pound against pound into pound until that moment when my anger found its way back again to that delayed and now recovered Time when I wanted to prong her at the party. I had been frustrated, had waited, had lost the anger, and so been taken by her. That finally got me—all through the talk about T. S. Eliot I had been calculating how I would lay waste to her little independence, and now she was alone, with me astride her, going through her paces, teeth biting the pillow, head turned away, using me as the dildo of a private gallop. So my rage came back, and my rhythm no longer depended upon her drive, but found its own life, and we made love like two club fighters in an open exchange, neither giving ground, rhythm to rhythm, even to even, hypnotic, knowing neither the pain of punishment nor the pride of pleasure, and the equality of this, as hollow as the beat of the drum, seemed to carry her into some better deep of desire, and I had broken through, she was following me, her muscular body writhed all about me with an impersonal abandon, the wanton whip-thrash of a wounded snake, she was on fire and frozen at the same time, and then her mouth was kissing me with a rubbery greedy compulsion so avid to use all there was of me, that to my distant surprise, not in character for the saint to slip into the brutal, my hand came up and clipped her mean and open-handed across the face, which brought a cry from her and broke the piston of her hard speed into something softer, wetter, more sly, more warm, I felt as if her belly were opening finally to receive me, and when her mouth kissed me again with a passing tender heat, warm-odored with flesh, and her body sweetened into some feminine embrace of my determination driving its way into her, well, I was gone, it was too late, I had driven right past her in that moment she turned, and I had begun to come, I was coming from all the confluences of my body toward that bud of sweetness I had plucked from her, and for a moment she was making it, she was a move back and surging to overtake me, and then it was gone, she made a mistake, her will ordered all temptings and rhythms to mobilize their march, she drove into the hard stupidities of a marching-band's step, and as I was going off in the best for many a month, she was merely going away, she had lost it again. As I ebbed into what should have been the contentments of a fine after-pleasure, warm and fine, there was one little part of me remaining cold and murderous because she had deprived me, she had fled the domination that was liberty for her, and the rest of the night was bound to be hell.

Her face was ugly. "You're a bastard, do you know that?" she asked of me.

"Let it go. I feel good."

"Of course you feel good. Couldn't you have waited one minute?"

I disliked this kind of thing. My duty was reminding me of how her awakened sweets were souring now in the belly, and her nerves were sharpening into the gone electric of being just nowhere.

"I hate inept men," she said.

"Cool it." She could, at least, be a lady. Because if she didn't stop, I would give her back a word or two.

"You did that on purpose," she nagged at me, and I was struck with the intimacy of her rancor—we might as well have been married for ten years to dislike each other so much at this moment.

"Why," I said, "you talk as if this were something unusual for you."

"It is."

"Come on," I told her, "you never made it in your life."

"How little you know," she said. "This is the first time I've missed in months."

If she had chosen to get my message, I could have been preparing now for a good sleep. Instead I would have to pump myself up again—and as if some ghost of the future laid the squeak of a tickle on my back, I felt an odd dread, not for tonight so much as for some ills of the next ten years whose first life was stirring tonight. But I lay beside her, drew her body against mine, feeling her trapped and irritable heats jangle me as much as they roused me, and while I had no fear that the avenger would remain asleep, still he stirred in pain and in protest, he had supposed his work to be done, and he would claim the wages of overtime from my reserve. That was the way I thought it would go, but Junior from New York University, with her hard body and her passion for proper poetry, gave a lewd angry old grin as her face stared boldly into mine, and with the practical bawdiness of the

Jew she took one straight utilitarian finger, smiled a deceptive girlish pride, and then she jabbed, fingernail and all, into the tight defended core of my clenched buttocks. One wiggle of her knuckle and I threw her off, grunting a sound between rage and surprise, to which she laughed and lay back and waited for me.

Well, she had been right, that finger tipped the balance, and three-quarters with it, and one-quarter hung with the mysteries of sexual ambition, I worked on her like a beaver for forty-odd minutes or more, slapping my tail to build her nest, and she worked along while we made the round of the positions, her breath sobbing the exertions, her body as alive as a charged wire and as far from rest.

I gave her all the Time I had in me and more besides, I was weary of her, and the smell which rose from her had so little of the sea and so much of the armpit that I breathed the stubborn wills of the gymnasium where the tight-muscled search for grace, and it was like that, a hard punishing session with pulley weights, stationary bicycle sprints, and ten breath-seared laps around the track. Yes, when I caught that smell, I knew she would not make it, and so I kept on just long enough to know she was exhausted in body, exhausted beyond the place where a ten-minute rest would have her jabbing that finger into me again, and hating her, hating women who could not take their exercise alone, I lunged up over the hill with my heart pounding past all pleasure, and I came, but with hatred, tight, electric, and empty, the spasms powerful but centered in my heart and not from the hip, the avenger taking its punishment even at the end, jolted clear to the seat of my semen by the succession of rhythmic blows that my heart drummed back to my feet.

For her, getting it from me, it must have been impressive, a convoluted, smashing, and protracted spasm, a hint of the death throe in the animal male that cannot but please the feminine taste for the mortal wound. "Oh, you're lucky," she whispered in my ear as I lay all collapsed beside her, alone in my athlete's absorption upon the whisperings of damage in the unlit complexities of my inner body. I was indeed an athlete, I knew my body was my future, and I had damaged it a bit tonight by most certainly doing it no good. I disliked her for it with the simple dislike we know for the stupid.

"Want a cigarette?" she asked.

I could wait, my heart would have preferred its rest, but there was something tired in her voice beyond the fatigue of what she had done. She too had lost after all. So I came out of my second rest to look at her, and her face had the sad relaxation (and serenity) of a young whore who has finished a hard night's work with the expected lack of issue for herself, content with no more than the money and the professional sense of the hard job dutifully done.

"I'm sorry you didn't make it," I said to her.

She shrugged. There was a Jewish tolerance for the expected failures of the flesh. "Oh, well, I lied to you before," she said.

"You never have been able to, have you?"

"No." She was fingering the muscles of my shoulder, as if in unconscious competition with my strength. "You're pretty good," she said grudgingly.

"Not really inept?" I asked.

"*Sans façons,*" said the poetess in an arch change of mood that irritated me. "Sandy has been illuminating those areas where my habits make for destructive impulses."

"Sandy is Doctor Joyce?" She nodded. "You make him sound like your navigator," I told her.

"Isn't it a little obvious to be hostile to psychoanalysis?"

Three minutes ago we had been belaboring each other in the nightmare of the last round, and now we were close to cozy. I put the sole of my foot on her sharp little knee.

"You know the first one we had?" she asked of me. "Well, I wanted to tell you. I came close—I guess I came as close as I ever came."

"You'll come closer. You're only nineteen."

"Yes, but this evening has been disturbing to me. You see, I get more from you than I get from my lover."

Her lover was twenty-one, a senior at Columbia, also Jewish—which lessened interest, she confessed readily. Besides, Arthur was too passive—"Basically, it's very comprehensible," said the commissar, "an aggressive female and a passive male—we complement one another, and that's no good." Of course it was easy to find satisfaction with Arthur, "via the oral perversions. That's because, vaginally, I'm anaesthetized—a good phallic narcissist like you doesn't do enough for me."

In the absence of learned credentials, she was setting out to bully again. So I thought to surprise her. "Aren't you mixing your language a little?" I began. "The phallic narcissist is one of Wilhelm Reich's categories."

"Therefore?"

"Aren't you a Freudian?"

"It would be presumptuous of me to say," she said like a seminar student working for his pee-aitch-dee. "But Sandy is an eclectic. He accepts a lot of Reich—you see, he's very ambitious, he wants to arrive at his own synthesis." She exhaled some smoke in my face, and gave a nice tough little grin that turned her long serious young witch's face into something indeed less presumptuous. "Besides," she said, "you are a phallic narcissist. There's an element of the sensual that is lacking in you."

"But Arthur possesses it?"

"Yes, he does. And you . . . you're not very juicy."

"I wouldn't know what you mean."

"I mean this." With the rich cruel look of a conquistador finding a new chest of Indian gold, she bent her head and gave one fleeting satiric half-moon of a lick to the conjugation of my balls. "That's what I mean," she said, and was out of bed even as I was recognizing that she was finally not without art. "Come back," I said.

But she was putting her clothes on in a hurry. "Shut up. Just don't give me your goddamned superiority."

I knew what it was: She had been about to gamble the reserves that belonged to Arthur, and the thought of possibly wasting them on a twenty-seven-year-old connoisseur like myself was too infuriating to take the risk.

So I lay in bed and laughed at her while she dressed—I did not really want a go at things again—and besides, the more I laughed, the angrier she would be, but the anger would work to the surface, and beneath it would be resting the pain that the evening had ended on so little.

She took her leisure going to the door, and I got up in time to tell her to wait—I would walk her to the subway. The dawn had come, however, and she wanted to go alone, she had had a bellyful of me, she could tell me that.

My brain was lusting its own private futures of how interesting it would be to have this proud, aggressive, vulgar, tense, stiff, and arrogant Jewess going wild on my bottom—I had turned more than one girl on, but never a one of quite this type. I suppose she had succeeded instead of me; I was ready to see her again and improve the message.

She turned down all dates, but compromised by giving me her address and the number of her telephone. And then glaring at me from the open door, she said, "I owe you a slap in the face."

"Don't go away feeling unequal."

I might have known she would have a natural punch. My jaw felt it for half an hour after she was gone and it took another thirty minutes before I could bring myself back to concluding that she was one funny kid.

All of that added up to the first night with the commissar, and I saw her two more times over this stretch, the last on the night when she finally agreed to sleep over with me, and I came awake in the morning to see her glaring at my head. So often in sex, when the second night wound itself up with nothing better in view than the memory of the first night, I was reminded of Kafka's *Castle*, that tale of the search of a man for his apocalyptic orgasm: In the easy optimism of a young man, he almost captures the castle on the first day, and is never to come so close again. Yes, that was the saga of the nervous system of a man as it was bogged into the defeats, complications, and frustrations of middle age. I still had my future before me of course—the full engagement of my will in some go-for-broke I considered worthy of myself was yet to come, but there were times in that loft when I knew the psychology of an old man, and my second night with Denise—for Denise Gondelman was indeed her name—left me racked for it amounted to so little that we could not even leave it there—the hangover would have been too great for both of us—and so we made a date for a third night. Over and over in those days I used to compare the bed to the bullfight, sometimes seeing myself as the matador and sometimes as the bull, and this second appearance, if it had taken place in the Plaza Mexico, would have been a *fracaso* with kapok seat cushions jeering down on the ring, and a stubborn cowardly bull staying in *querencia* before the doubtful prissy overtures, the gloomy trim technique of a veteran and mediocre *torero* on the worst of days when he is forced to wonder if he has even his *pundonor* to sustain him. It was a gloomy deal. Each of us knew it was possible to be badly worked by the other, and this seemed so likely that neither of us would gamble a finger. Although we got into bed and had a perfunctory ten minutes, it was as long as an hour in a coffee shop when two friends are done with one another.

By the third night we were ready for complexities again—to see a woman three times is to call on the dialectic of an affair. If the waves we were making belonged less to the viper of passion than the worm of inquiry, still it was obvious from the beginning that we had surprises for one another. The second night we had been hoping for more, and so got less; this third night, we each came on with the notion to wind it up, and so got involved in more.

For one thing, Denise called me in the afternoon. There was studying she had to do, and she wondered if it would be all right to come to my place at eleven instead of meeting me for drinks and dinner. Since that would save me ten dollars she saw no reason why I should complain. It was a down conversation. I had been planning to lay siege to her, dispense a bit of elixir from my vast reservoirs of charm, and instead she was going to keep it *in camera*. There was a quality about her I could not locate, something independent—abruptly, right there, I knew what is was. In a year she would have no memory of me, I would not exist for her unless . . . and then it was clear . . . unless I could be the first to carry her stone of no-orgasm up the cliff, all the way, over and out into the sea. That was the kick I could find, that a year from now, five years from now, down all the seasons to the hours of her old age, I would be the one she would be forced to remember, and it would nourish me a little over the years, thinking of that grudged souvenir that could not die in her, my blond hair, my blue eyes, my small broken nose, my clean mouth and chin, my height, my boxer's body, my parts—yes, I was getting excited at the naked image of me in the young-old mind of that sour sexed-up dynamo of black-pussied frustration.

A phallic narcissist she had called me. Well, I was phallic enough, a Village stickman who could muster enough of the divine It on the head of his will to call forth more than one becoming out of the womb of feminine Time, yes a good deal more than one from my fifty new girls a year, and when I failed before various prisons of frigidity, it mattered little. Experience gave the cue that there were ladies who would not be moved an inch by a year of the best, and so I looked for other things in them, but this one, this Den-of-Ease, she was ready, she was entering the time of her Time, and if not me, it would be another—I was sick in advance at the picture of some bearded Negro cat who would score where I had missed and thus cuckold me in spirit, deprive me of those telepathic waves of longing (in which I obviously believed) speeding away to me from her over the years to balm the hours when I was beat, because I had been her psychic bridegroom, had plucked her ideational diddle, had led her down the walk of her real wedding night. Since she did not like me, what a feat to pull it off.

In the hours I waited after dinner, alone, I had the sense—which I always trusted—that tonight this little victory or defeat would be full of leverage, magnified beyond its emotional matter because I had decided to bet on myself that I would win, and a defeat would bring me closer to a general depression, a fog bank of dissatisfaction with myself that I knew could last for months or more. Whereas a victory would add to the panoplies of my ego some peculiar (but for me, valid) ingestion of her arrogance, her stubbornness, and her will—those necessary ingredients of which I could not yet have enough for my own ambition.

When she came in she was wearing a sweater and dungarees, which I had been expecting, but there was a surprise for me. Her braids had been clipped, and a short cropped curled Italian haircut decorated her head, moving her severe young face half across the spectrum from the austerities of a poetess to a hint of all those practical and promiscuous European girls who sold their holy hump to the Germans and had been subsequently punished by shaved heads—how attractive the new hair proved. Once punished, they were now free, free to be wild, the worst had happened and they were still alive with the taste of the first victor's flesh enriching the sensual curl of the mouth.

Did I like her this way? Denise was interested to know. Well, it was a shock, I admitted, a pleasant shock. If it takes you so long to decide, you must be rigid, she let me know. Well, yes, as a matter of fact I was rigid, rigid for her with waiting.

The nun of severity passed a shade over her. She hated men who were uncool, she thought she would tell me.

"Did your analyst tell you it's bad to be uncool?"

She had taken off her coat, but now she gave me a look as if she were ready to put it on again. "No, he did not tell me that." She laughed spitefully. "But he told me a couple of revealing things about you."

"Which you won't repeat."

"Of course not."

"I'll never know," I said, and gave her the first kiss of the evening. Her mouth was heated—it was the best kiss I had received from her, and it brought me on too quickly—"My fruit is ready to be plucked," said the odors of her mouth, betraying that perfume of the ducts that, against her will no doubt, had been plumping for me. She was changed tonight. From the skin of her face and the glen of her neck came a new smell, sweet, sweaty, and tender, the smell of a body that had been used and had enjoyed its uses. It came to me nicely, one of the nicest smells in quite some time, so different from the usual exudations of her dissatisfied salts that it opened a chain of reflexes in me, and I was off in all good speed on what Denise would probably have called the vertical foreplay. I suppose I went at her like a necrophiliac let loose upon a still-warm subject, and as I gripped her, grasped her, groped her, my breath a bellows to blow her into my own flame, her body remained unmoving, only her mouth answering my call, those lips bridling hot adolescent kisses back upon my face, the smell almost carrying me away—such a fine sweet sweat.

Naturally she clipped the rhythm. As I started to slip up her sweater, she got away and said a little huskily, "I'll take my own clothes off." Once again I could have hit her. My third eye, that athlete's inner eye that probed its vision into all the corners, happy and distressed of my body whole, was glumly cautioning the congestion of the spirits in the coils of each teste. They would have to wait, turn rancid, maybe die of delay.

Off came the sweater and the needless brassière—her economical breasts swelled just a trifle tonight, enough to take on the convexities of an Amazon's armor. Open came the belt and the zipper of her dungarees, zipped from the front, which pleased her not a little. Only her ass, a small masterpiece, and her strong thighs justified this theatre. She stood there naked, quite psychically clothed, and lit a cigarette.

If a stiff prick has no conscience, it has also no common sense. I stood there like a clown, trying to coax her to take a ride with me on the bawdy car, she out of her clothes, I in all of mine, a muscular little mermaid to melt on my knee. She laughed, one harsh banker's snort—she was giving no loans on my idiot's collateral.

"You didn't even ask me," Denise thought to say, "of how my studying went tonight."

"What did you study?"

"I didn't. I didn't study." She gave me a lovely smile, girlish and bright. "I just spent the last three hours with Arthur."

"You're a dainty type," I told her.

But she gave me a bad moment. That lovely flesh-spent smell, scent of the well used and the tender, that avatar of the feminine my senses had accepted so greedily, came down now to no more than the rubbings and the sweats of what was probably a very nice guy, passive Arthur with his Jewish bonanzas of mouth-love.

The worst of it was that it quickened me more. I had the selfish wisdom to throw such evidence upon the mercy of my own court. For the smell of Arthur was the smell of love, at least for me, and so from man or woman, it did not matter—the smell of love was always feminine—and if the man in Denise was melted by the woman in Arthur, so Arthur might have flowered that woman in himself from the arts of a real woman, his mother?—it did not matter—that voiceless message which passed from the sword of the man into the cavern of the woman was carried along from body to body, and if it was not the woman in

Denise I was going to find tonight, at least I would be warmed by the previous trace of another.

But that was a tone poem to quiet the toads of my doubt. When Denise—it took five more minutes—finally decided to expose herself on my clumped old mattress, the sight of her black pubic hair, the feel of the foreign but brotherly liquids in her unembarrassed maw, turned me into a jackrabbit of pissy tumescence, the quicks of my excitement beheaded from the resonances of my body, and I wasn't with her a half-minute before I was over, gone, and off. I rode not with the strength to reap the harem of her and her lover, but spit like a pinched little boy up into black forested hills of motherly contempt, a passing picture of the nuns of my childhood to drench my piddle spurtings with failures of gloom. She it was who proved stronger than me, she the he to my silly she.

All considered, Denise was nice about it. Her harsh laugh did not crackle over my head, her hand in passing me the after-cigarette settled for no more than a nudge of my nose, and if it were not for the contempt of her tough grin, I would have been left with no more than the alarm to the sweepers of my brain to sweep this failure away.

"Hasn't happened in years," I said to her, the confession coming out of me with the cost of the hardest cash.

"Oh, shut up. Just rest." And she began to hum a mocking little song. I lay there in a state, parts of me jangled for forty-eight hours to come, and yet not altogether lost to peace. I knew what it was. Years ago in the Air Force, as an enlisted man, I had reached the light-heavyweight finals on my air base. For two weeks I trained for the championship, afraid of the other man all the way because I had seen him fight and felt he was better than me. When my night came, he took me out with a left hook to the liver, which had me conscious on the canvas but unable to move, and as the referee was counting, which I could hear all too clearly, I knew the same kind of peace, a swooning peace, a clue to that kind of death in which an old man slips away— nothing mattered except that my flesh was vulnerable, and I had a dim revery, lying there with the yells of the Air Force crowd in my ears, there was some far-off vision of green fields and me lying in them, giving up all ambition to go back instead to another, younger life of the senses, and I remember at that moment I watered the cup of my boxer's jock, and then I must have slipped into something new, for as they picked me off the canvas the floor seemed to recede from me at a great rate as if I were climbing in an airplane.

A few minutes later, the nauseas of the blow to my liver had me retching into my hands, and the tension of three weeks of preparation for that fight came back. I knew through the fading vistas of my peace, and the oncoming spasms of my nausea, that the worst was yet to come, and it would take me weeks to unwind, and then years, and maybe never to overcome the knowledge that I had failed completely at a moment when I wanted very much to win.

A ghost of this peace, trailing intimations of a new nausea, was passing over me again, and I sat up in bed abruptly, as if to drive these weaknesses back into me. My groin had been simmering for hours waiting for Denise, and it was swollen still, but the avenger was limp, he had deserted my cause, I was in a spot if she did not co-operate.

Co-operate she did. "My God, lie down again, will you," she said, "I was thinking that finally I had seen you relax."

And then I could sense that the woman in her was about to betray her victory. She sat over me, her little breasts budding with their own desire, her short hair alive and flowering, her mouth ready to taste her gentleman's defeat. I had only to raise my hand, and push her body in the direction she wished it to go, and then her face was rooting in me, her angry tongue and voracious mouth going wild finally as I had wished it, and I knew the sadness of sour timing, because this was a prize I could not enjoy as I would have on our first night, and yet it was good enough—not art, not the tease and languor of love on a soft mouth, but therapy, therapy for her, the quick exhaustions of the tension in a harsh throat, the beseechment of an ugly voice going down into the expiation that would be its beauty. Still it was good, practically it was good, my ego could bank the hard cash that this snotty head was searching me, the act served its purpose, anger traveled from her body into mine, the avenger came to attention, cold and furious, indifferent to the trapped doomed pleasure left behind in my body on that initial and grim piddle spurt, and I was ready, not with any joy or softness or warmth or care, but I was ready finally to take her tonight, I was going to beat new Time out of her if beat her I must, I was going to teach her that she was only a child, because if at last I could not take care of a nineteen-year-old, then I was gone indeed. And so I took her with a cold calculation, the rhythms of my body corresponding to no more than a metronome in my mind, tonight the driving mechanical beat would come from me, and blind to nerve-raddlings in my body, and blood pressures in my brain, I worked on her like a riveter, knowing her resistances were made of steel—I threw her a fuck the equivalent of a fifteen-round fight, I wearied her, I brought her back, I drove my fingers into her shoulders and my knees into her hips. I went, and I went, and I went, I bore her high and thumped her hard, I sprinted, I paced, I lay low, eyes all closed, under sexual water, like a submarine listening for the distant sound of her ship's motors, hoping to steal up close and trick her rhythms away.

And she was close. Oh, she was close so much of the time. She was like a child on a merry-go-round. The touch of the colored ring just evaded the tips of her touch, and she heaved and she hurdled, arched and cried, clawed me, kissed me, even gave of a shriek once, and then her sweats running down and her will weak, exhausted even more than me, she felt me leave and lie beside her. Yes, I did that with a tactician's cunning, I let the depression of her failure poison what was left of her will never to let me succeed, I gave her slack to mourn the lost freedoms and hate the final virginity for which she fought, I even allowed her baffled heat to take its rest and attack her nerves once more, and then, just as she was beginning to fret against me in a new and unwilling appeal, I turned her over suddenly on her belly, my avenger wild with the mania of the madman, and giving her no chance, holding her prone against the mattress with the strength of my weight, I drove into the seat of all stubbornness, tight as a vise, and I wounded her, I knew it, she thrashed beneath me like a trapped little animal, making not a sound, but fierce not to allow me this last of the liberties, and yet caught, forced to give up millimeter by millimeter the bridal ground of her symbolic and therefore real vagina. So I made it, I made it all the way—it took ten minutes and maybe more, but as the avenger rode down to his hilt and tunneled the threshold of sexual home all those inches closer into the bypass of the womb, she gave at last a little cry of farewell, and I could feel a new shudder which began as a ripple and rolled into a wave, and then it rolled over her, carrying her along, me hardly moving for fear of damping this quake from her earth, and then it was gone, but she was left alive with a larger one to follow.

So I turned her once again on her back, and moved by impulse to love's first hole. There was an odor coming up, hers at last, the smell of the sea, and none of the armpit or a dirty sock, and I took her mouth and kissed it, but she was away, following the wake of her own waves, which mounted, fell back, and in new momentum mounted higher and should have gone over, and then she was about to hang again, I could feel it, that moment of hesitation between the past and the present, the habit and the adventure, and I said into her ear, "You dirty little Jew."

That whipped her over. A first wave kissed, a second spilled, and a third and a fourth and a fifth came breaking over, and finally she was away, she was loose in the water for the first time in her life, and I would have liked to go with her, but I was blood-throttled and numb, and as she had the first big moment in her life, I was nothing but a set of aching balls and a congested cock, and I rode with her wistfully, looking at the contortion of her face and listening to her sobbing sound of "Oh, Jesus, I made it, oh Jesus, I did."

"Compliments of T. S. Eliot," I whispered to myself, and my head was aching, my body was shot. She curled against me, she kissed my sweat, she nuzzled my eyes and murmured in my ear, and then she was slipping away into the nicest of weary sweet sleep.

"Was it good for you too?" she whispered half-awake, having likewise read the works of The Hemingway, and I said, "Yeah, fine," and after she was asleep, I disengaged myself carefully, and prowled the loft, accepting the hours it would take for my roiled sack to clean its fatigues and know a little sleep. But I had abused myself too far, and it took till dawn and half a fifth of whisky before I dropped into an unblessed stupor. When I awoke, in that moment before I moved to look at her, and saw her glaring at me, I was off on a sluggish masculine debate as to whether the kick of studying this Denise for another few nights—now that I had turned the key—would be worth the danger of deepening into some small real feeling. But through my hangover and the knowledge of the day and the week and the month it would take the different parts of all of me to repair, I was also knowing the taste of a reinforced will—finally, I had won. At no matter what cost, and with what luck, and with a piece of charity from her, I had won nonetheless, and since all real pay came from victory, it was more likely that I would win the next time I gambled my stake on something more appropriate for my ambition.

Then I turned, saw the hatred in her eyes, turned over again, and made believe I was asleep while a dread of the next few minutes weighed a leaden breath over the new skin of my ego.

"You're awake, aren't you?" she said.

I made no answer.

"All right, I'm going then. I'm getting dressed." She whipped out of bed, grabbed her clothes, and began to put them on with all the fury of waiting for me to get the pronouncement. "That was a lousy thing you did last night," she said by way of a start.

In truth she looked better than she ever had. The severe lady and the tough little girl of yesterday's face had put forth the first agreements on what would yet be a bold chick.

"I gave you what you could use," I made the mistake of saying.

"Just didn't you," she said, and was on her way to the door. "Well, cool it. You don't do anything to me." Then she smiled. "You're so impressed with what you think was such a marvelous notch you made in me, listen, Buster, I came here last night thinking of what Sandy Joyce told me about you, and he's right, oh man is he right." Standing in the open doorway, she started to light a cigarette, and then threw the matches to the floor. From thirty feet away I could see the look in her eyes, that unmistakable point for the kill that you find in the eyes of very few bullfighters, and then having created her pause, she came on for her moment of truth by saying, "He told me your whole life is a lie, and you do nothing but run away from the homosexual that is you."

And like a real killer, she did not look back, and was out the door before I could rise to tell her that she was a hero fit for me.

From *Advertisements for Myself* (1959)

# CONVENTION
# TIME

**April–July** **Modene—I**

Thank you for prompt response on queries. Continuation of transcript AURAL-BLUEBEARD, April 12:

MODENE: Actually, I could have kept shopping with Sam instead of rushing back to the Fontainebleau, because it was the longest wait for Jack. When he finally did arrive, I thought he might be on medication. His face was puffed and swollen. He smiled and said, "It's happened. My feet are starting to hurt." "It's all right," I told him, "you still look good to me." But when we kissed, I realized he was in no mood to make love.

WILLIE: That must have set you back.

MODENE: I felt close to him. What a compliment! To keep our date even when he's entirely wrung out. We just had sandwiches and wine. And he started talking again about the desert island.

WILLIE: I wonder if he and his wife will stay together if he doesn't become President.

MODENE: Well, as you can imagine, I've given a little thought to the subject.

WILLIE: Are you building up any expectations?

MODENE: I can only say I never felt closer to Jack. It was evening and we sat in silence. Then he had to go. He told me that it might be our last meeting for a while, since all his effort would be going into West Virginia now, and even if he wins that, there'll be non-stop days and nights of preparation for the convention in July. He seemed to get sad at the thought of how long we'd be apart, and we sat in the room and held hands, and he said, "I don't suppose there has been any time in my life that could have been less propitious for you and me than these madhouse months, but if it's really there for us, we will bear up. We will bear up, won't we?" he said, and I had to do all I could not to cry.

WILLIE: I feel like crying.

MODENE: The trouble is that I don't know what kind of life to go back to. After you've been around people like Frank and Jack, who are you going to date for an encore?

WILLIE: I predict that Sam will take up a large role in the near future.

MODENE: Oh, no. While we were shopping, he told me the name of his girlfriend. It's Phyllis McGuire of the McGuire Sisters. He is off in Las Vegas right now seeing her. I'm all alone by the telephone. (April 12, 1960)

Modene makes occasional calls to Willie in the next two months, and refers to long-distance conversations with Kennedy or with Giancana. It is evident, however, that such communications are becoming infrequent. After the West Virginia primary, however, Jack does phone her.

MODENE: I could hear his political people celebrating in the background. He told me that he didn't think he could be stopped now, and was going to hold a vision—he used exactly that word, *vision*—of our reunion in Los Angeles after he won the nomination. And he invited me to come out for the week of the convention.

AURAL: Are you appropriately thrilled?

BLUEBEARD: I was very happy he said that. And I feel at peace now. I know I can wait these next two months. I'm feeling awfully sure of myself again. (May 11, 1960)

In the second week of July 1960, I discovered that I was not inhabiting the summer so much as I was living in the previous spring, for in my mind, I was following Modene through her travels between Miami, Chicago, and Washington; indeed, I only became fully aware of how removed I was from my own life when I walked into the officers' lounge at Zenith one July evening and there on the television set was John Fitzgerald Kennedy speaking to a press conference at the Democratic Convention. I watched with all the shock of passing through an occult experience. It was as if I had been reading a book and one of the characters had just stepped into my life.

It was then I recognized that Modene was now at the convention in Los Angeles. Such a fact had not held as much reality for me as the account of her earlier activities in April that I had been sending out each night to Hugh Montague.

From *Harlot's Ghost* (1991)

# Superman Comes to the Supermarket—I

Panic was the largest single sentiment in the breast of the collective delegates as they came to convene in Los Angeles. Delegates are not the noblest sons and daughters of the Republic; a man of taste, arrived from Mars, would take one look at a convention floor and leave forever, convinced he had seen one of the drearier squats of Hell. If one still smells the faint living echo of a carnival, it is regurgitated by the senses into the fouler cud of a death gas one must rid oneself of— a cigar-smoking, stale-aired, slack-jawed, butt-littered, foul, bleak, hard-working, bureaucratic death gas of language and faces ("Yes, those *faces*," says the man from Mars: lawyers, judges, ward heelers, *mafiosos,* Southern goons and grandees, grand old ladies, trade unionists, and finks), of pompous words and long pauses that lay like a leaden pain over fever, the fever that one is in, over, or is it that one is just behind history? A legitimate panic for a delegate. A delegate is a man who picks a candidate for the largest office in the land, a President who must live with problems whose borders are in ethics, metaphysics, and now ontology. The delegate is prepared for this office of selection by emptying wastebaskets, toting garbage, and saying yes at the right time for twenty years in the small political machine of some small or large town; his reward, one of them anyway, is that he arrives at an invitation to the convention. An expert on local catch-as-catch-can, a small-time, often mediocre practitioner of small-town political judo, he comes to the big city with nine-tenths of his mind made up, he will follow the orders of the boss who brought him. Yet of course it is not altogether so mean as that: His opinion is listened to—the boss will consider what he has to say as one interesting factor among five hundred, and what is most important to the delegate, he has the illusion of partial freedom. He can, unless he is severely honest with himself—and if he is, why sweat out the low levels of a political machine?—he can have the illusion that he has helped to choose the candidate, he can even worry most sincerely about his choice, flirt with defection from the boss, work out his own small political gains by the road of loyalty or the way of hard bargain. But, even if he is there for no more than the ride, his vote a certainty in the mind of the political boss, able to be thrown here or switched there as the boss decides, still in some peculiar sense he is reality to the boss; the delegate is the great American public, the bar he owns or the law practice, the piece of the union he represents, or the real-estate office, is a part of the political landscape that the boss uses as his own image of how the votes will go and if the people will like the candidate. And if the boss is depressed by what he sees, if the candidate does not feel right to him, if he has a dull intimation that the candidate is not his sort (as, let us say, Harry Truman was his sort, or Symington might be his sort, or Lyndon Johnson), then vote for the candidate the boss will if he must—he cannot be caught on the wrong side, but he does not feel the pleasure of a personal choice. Which is the center of the panic. Because if the boss is depressed, the delegate is doubly depressed, and the emotional fact is that Kennedy is not in focus, not in the old political focus, he is not comfortable; in fact it is a mystery to the boss how Kennedy got to where he is, not a mystery in its structures—Kennedy is rolling in money, Kennedy got the votes in primaries, and, most of all, Kennedy has a jewel of a political machine. It is as good as a crack Notre Dame team, all discipline and savvy and go-go-go, sound, drilled, never dull, quick as a knife, full of the salt of hipper-dipper, a beautiful machine; the boss could adore it if only a sensible candidate were driving it, a Truman, even a Stevenson, please God a Northern Lyndon Johnson, but it is run by a man who looks young enough to be coach of the Freshman team, and that is not comfortable at all. The boss knows political machines, he knows issues, farm parity, Forand health bill, Landrum-Griffin, but this is not all so adequate after all to revolutionaries in Cuba who look like beatniks, competitions in missiles, Negroes looting whites in the Congo, intricacies of nuclear fallout, and NAACP men one does well to call Sir. It is all out of hand, everything important is off the center, foreign affairs is now the lick of the heat, and senators are candidates instead of governors, a disaster to the old family style of political measure, where a political boss knows his governor and knows who his governor knows. So the boss is depressed, profoundly depressed. He comes to this convention resigned to nominating a man he does not understand, or let us say that, so far as he understands the candidate who is to be nominated, he is not happy about the secrets of his appeal, not so far as he divines these secrets; they seem to have too little to do with politics and all too much to do with the private madnesses of the nation. Yes, this candidate for all his record, his good, sound, conventional liberal record, has a patina of that other life, the second American life, the long electric night with the fires of neon leading down the highway to the murmur of jazz.

Not all the roots of American life are uprooted, but almost all, and the spirit of the supermarket, that homogenous extension of stainless surfaces and psychoanalyzed people, packaged commodities, and ranch homes, interchangeable, geographically unrecognizable, that essence of the new postwar SuperAmerica is found nowhere so perfectly as in Los Angeles' ubiquitous acres. One gets the impression that people come to Los Angeles in order to divorce themselves from the past, here to live or try to live in the rootless pleasure world of an adult child. As one travels through the endless repetitions of that city which is the capital of suburbia with its milky pinks, its washed-out oranges, its tainted lime-yellows of pastel on one pretty little architectural monstrosity after another, the colors not intense enough, the styles never pure, and never sufficiently impure to collide on the eye, one conceives the people who live here—they have come out to express themselves, Los Angeles is the home of self-expression, but the artists are middle-class and middling-minded. No passions will calcify here for years in the gloom to be revealed a decade later as the tessellations of a hard and fertile work, no, it is all open, promiscuous, borrowed, half bought, a city without iron, eschewing wood, a kingdom of stucco, the playground for mass men—one has the feeling it was built by television sets giving orders to men. And in this land of the pretty-pretty, the virility is in the barbarisms, the huge billboards, the screamers of the neon lighting, the shouting farm-utensil colors of the gas stations and the monster drugstores, it is in the swing of the sports cars, hot rods, convertibles, Los Angeles is a city to drive in, the boulevards are wide, the traffic is nervous and fast, the radio stations play bouncing, blooping, rippling tunes, one digs the pop in a pop tune, no one of character would make love by it, but the sound is good for swinging a car, electronic guitars, and Hawaiian harps.

So this is the town the Democrats came to, and with their unerring instinct (after being with them a week, one thinks of this party as a crazy, half-rich family, loaded with poor cousins, traveling always in caravans with Cadillacs and Okie Fords, Lincolns and quarter-horse mules, putting up every night in tents to hear the chamber quartet of Great Cousin Eleanor invaded by the Texas-twanging steel-stringing geetarists of Bubber Lyndon, carrying its own mean high-school principal, Doc Symington, chided for its manners by good Uncle Adlai, told the route of march by Navigator Jack, cut off every six months from the rich will of Uncle Jim Farley, never listening to the mechanic of the caravan, Bald Sam Rayburn, who assures them they'll all break down unless Cousin Bubber gets the concession on the garage; it's the Snopes family married to Henry James, with the labor unions thrown in like a Yankee dollar, and yet it's true, in tranquility one recollects them with affection, their instinct is good, crazy family good) and this instinct now led the caravan to pick the Biltmore Hotel in downtown Los Angeles for their family get-together and reunion.

The Biltmore is one of the ugliest hotels in the world. Patterned after the flat roofs of an Italian Renaissance palace, it is eighty-eight times as large, and one-millionth as valuable to the continuation of man, and it would be intolerable if it were not for the presence of Pershing Square, that square block of park with cactus and palm trees, the three-hundred-and-sixty-five-day-a-year convention of every junkie, pot-head, pusher, and queen. For years Pershing Square has been one of the three or four places in America famous to homosexuals, one of the avatars of the good old masturbatory sex, dirty with the crusted sugars of smut, dirty rooming houses around the corner where the score is made, dirty book and photograph stores down the street, old-fashioned out-of-the-Thirties burlesque houses, cruising bars, jukeboxes, movie houses; Pershing Square is the town plaza for all those lonely, respectable, small-town homosexuals who lead a family life, make children, and have the Philbrick psychology (How I Joined the Communist Party and Led Three Lives). Yes, it is the open-air convention hall for the small-town inverts who live like spies, and it sits in the center of Los Angeles, facing the Biltmore, that hotel which is a mausoleum, that Pentagon of traveling salesmen the Party chose to house the headquarters of the Convention.

So here came that family, the delegates dispersed over a run of thirty miles and twenty-seven hotels: the Olympian Motor Hotel, the Ambassador, the Beverly Wilshire, the Santa Ynez Inn, the Mayan, the Commodore, the Mayfair, the Sheraton-West, the Huntington-Sheraton, the Green, the Hayward, the Gates, the Figueroa, the Statler Hilton, the Hollywood Knickerbocker—does one have to be a collector to list such names?—beauties all, with that up-from-the-farm Los Angeles décor, plate-glass windows, patio and terrace, foam-rubber mattress, pastel paints, all of them pretty as an ad in full-page color, all but the Biltmore where everybody gathered every day—the newsmen, the TV, radio, magazine, and foreign newspapermen, the delegates, the politicos, the tourists, the campaign managers, the run-ners, the flunkies, the cousins and aunts, the wives, the grandfathers, the eight-year-old girls, and the twenty-eight-year-old girls in the Kennedy costumes, red and white and blue, the Symingteeners, the Johnson Ladies, the Stevenson Ladies, everybody—and for three days before the convention and four days into it, everybody collected at the Biltmore, in the lobby, in the grill, in the Biltmore Bowl, in the elevators, along the corridors, three hundred deep always outside the Kennedy suite, milling everywhere, every dark-carpeted gray-brown hall of the hotel, but it was in the Gallery of the Biltmore where one first felt the mood which pervaded all proceedings until the conven-tion was almost over, that heavy, thick, witless depression which was to dominate every move as the delegates wandered and gawked and pa-raded and set for a spell, there in the Gallery of the Biltmore, that huge depressing alley with its inimitable hotel color, that faded depth of chiaroscuro which unhappily has no depth, that brown which is not a brown, that gray which has no pearl in it, that color which can be de-scribed only as hotel-color because the beiges, the tans, the walnuts, the mahoganies, the dull blood rugs, the moaning yellows, the sick greens, the grays, and all those dumb browns merge into that lack of color which is an over-large hotel at convention time, with all the small-towners wearing their set, starched faces, that look they get at carnival, all fever and suspicion, and proud to be there, eddying slowly back and forth in that high block-long tunnel of a room with its arched ceiling and square recesses filling every rib of the arch with art work, escutcheons, and blazons and other art, pictures I think, I can-not even remember, there was such a hill of cigar smoke the eye had to travel on its way to the ceiling, and at one end there was galvanized-pipe scaffolding and workmen repairing some part of the ceiling, one of them touching up one of the endless squares of painted plaster in the arch, and another worker, passing by, yelled up to the one who was working on the ceiling: "Hey, Michelangelo!"

Later, of course, it began to emerge and there were portraits one could keep. There was Lyndon Johnson, who had compromised too many contradictions and now the contradictions were in his face: When he smiled, the corners of his mouth squeezed gloom; when he was pious, his eyes twinkled irony; when he spoke in a righteous tone, he looked corrupt; when he jested, the ham in his jowls looked to quiver. He was not convincing.

Stevenson had the patina. He came into the room and the room was different, not stronger perhaps (which is why ultimately he did not win), but warmer. One knew why some adored him—he did not look like other people, not with press lights on his flesh; he looked like a lover, the simple truth, he had the sweet happiness of an adolescent who has just been given his first major kiss. And so he glowed, and one was reminded of Chaplin, not because they were the least alike in features but because Charlie Chaplin was luminous when one met him and Stevenson had something of that light.

There was Eleanor Roosevelt, fine, precise, hand-worked like ivory. Her voice was almost attractive as she explained in the firm, sad tones of the first lady in this small town why she could not admit Mr. Kennedy, who was no doubt a gentleman, into her political house. One had the impression of a lady who was finally becoming a woman, which is to say that she was just a little bitchy about it all—nice bitchy, charming, it had a touch of art to it, but it made one wonder if she were not now satisfying the last passion of them all, which was to become physically attractive, for she was better-looking than she had ever been as she now spurned the possibilities of a young suitor.

Bobby Kennedy, that archetype Bobby Kennedy, looked like a West Point cadet, or, better, one of those unreconstructed Irishmen from Kirkland House one always used to have to face in the line in Harvard house football games. "Hello," you would say to the ones who looked like him as you lined up for the scrimmage after the kick-off, and his type would nod and look away, one rock glint of recognition your due for living across the hall from one another all through Freshman year, and then bang, as the ball was passed back, you'd get a bony king-hell knee in the crotch. He was the kind of man never to put on the gloves with if you wanted to do some social boxing, because after two minutes it would be a war, and ego-bastards last long in a war. And then there was Kennedy, the edge of the mystery. But a sketch will no longer suffice.

The afternoon he arrived at the convention from the airport, there was of course a large crowd on the street outside the Biltmore, and the best way to get a view was to get up on an outdoor balcony of the Biltmore, two flights above the street, and look down on the event. One waited thirty minutes, and then a honking of horns as wild as the getaway after an Italian wedding sounded around the corner, and the Kennedy cortege came into sight, circled Pershing Square, the men in the open and leading convertibles sitting backwards to look at their leader, and finally came to a halt in a space cleared for them by the police in the crowd. The television cameras were out, and a Kennedy band was playing some circus music. One saw him immediately. He had the deep orange-brown suntan of a ski instructor, and when he smiled at the crowd his teeth were amazingly white and clearly visible at a distance of fifty yards. For one moment he saluted Pershing Square, and Pershing Square saluted him back, the prince and the beggars of glamour staring at one another across a city street, and then with a quick move he was out of the car and by choice headed into the crowd instead of the lane cleared for him into the hotel by the police, so that he made his way inside surrounded by a mob, and one expected at any moment to see him lifted to its shoulders like a matador being carried back to the city after a triumph in the plaza. All the while the band kept playing the campaign tunes, sashaying circus music, and one had a moment of clarity, intense as a *déjà vu,* for the scene that had taken place had been glimpsed before in a dozen musical comedies—it was the scene where the hero, the matinee idol, the movie star comes to the palace to claim the princess, or what is the same, and more to our soil, the football hero, the campus king, arrives at the dean's home surrounded by a court of open-singing students to plead with the dean for his daughter's kiss and permission to put on the big musical that night. And suddenly I saw the convention, it came into focus for me, and I understood the mood of depression that had lain over the convention, because finally it was simple: The Democrats were going to nominate a man who, no matter how serious his political dedication might be, was indisputably and willy-nilly going to be seen as a great box-office actor, and the consequences of that were staggering and not at all easy to calculate.

Since the First World War Americans have been leading a double life, and our history has moved on two rivers, one visible, the other underground: There has been the history of politics, which is concrete, factual, practical, and unbelievably dull if not for the consequences of the actions of some of these men; and there is a subterranean river of untapped, ferocious, lonely, and romantic desires, that concentration of ecstasy and violence which is the dream life of the nation.

The twentieth century may yet be seen as that era when civilized man and underprivileged man were melted together into mass man, the iron and steel of the nineteenth century giving way to electronic circuits which communicated their messages into men, the unmistakable tendency of the new century seeming to be the creation of men as interchangeable as commodities, their extremes of personality singed out of existence by the psychic fields of force the communicators would impose.

Nowhere as in America, however, was this fall from individual man to mass man felt so acutely, for America was at once the first and most prolific creator of mass communications, and the most rootless of countries, since almost no American could lay claim to the line of a family that had not once at least severed its roots by migrating here. But, if rootless, it was then the most vulnerable of countries to its own homogenization. Yet America was also the country in which the dynamic myth of the Renaissance—that every man was potentially extraordinary—knew its most passionate persistence. Simply, America was the land where people still believed in heroes: George Washington; Billy the Kid; Lincoln, Jefferson; Mark Twain, Jack London, Hemingway; Joe Louis, Dempsey, Gentleman Jim; America believed in athletes, rum-runners, aviators; even lovers, by the time Valentino died. It was a country that had grown by the leap of one hero past another—is there a county in all of our ground that does not have its legendary figure? And when the West was filled, the expansion turned inward, became part of an agitated, overexcited, superheated dream life. The film studios threw up their searchlights as the frontier was finally sealed, and the romantic possibilities of the old conquest of land turned into a vertical myth, trapped within the skull, of a new kind of heroic life, each choosing his own archetype of a neo-renaissance man, be it Barrymore, Cagney, Flynn, Bogart, Brando, or Sinatra, but it was almost as if there were no peace unless one could fight well, kill well (if always with honor), love well and love many, be cool, be daring, be dashing, be wild, be wily, be resourceful, be a brave gun. And this myth, that each of us was born to be free, to wander, to have adventure,

and to grow on the waves of the violent, the perfumed, and the unexpected, had a force that could not be tamed no matter how the nation's
regulators—politicians, medicos, policemen, professors, priests, rabbis,
ministers, *idéologues,* psychoanalysts, builders, executives, and endless
communicators—would brick-in the modern life with hygiene upon
sanity, and middle-brow homily over platitude; the myth would not
die. Indeed a quarter of the nation's business must have depended
upon its existence. But it stayed alive for more than that—it was as if
the message in the labyrinth of the genes would insist that violence was
locked with creativity, and adventure was the secret of love.

Once, in the Second World War and in the year or two that followed, the underground river returned to earth, and the life of the nation was intense, of the present, electric—as a lady said, "That was the
time when we gave parties which changed people's lives." The Forties
was a decade when the speed with which one's own events occurred
seemed as rapid as the history of the battlefields, and for the mass of
people in America a forced march into a new jungle of emotion was the
result. The surprises, the failures, and the dangers of that life must
have terrified some nerve of awareness in the power and the mass, for,
as if stricken by the orgiastic vistas the myth had carried up from underground, the retreat to a more conservative existence was disor-
derly, the fear of communism spread like an irrational hail of boils. To
anyone who could see, the excessive hysteria of the Red wave was no
preparation to face an enemy but rather a terror of the national self:
free-loving, lust-looting, atheistic, implacable—absurdity beyond absurdity to label communism so, for the moral products of Stalinism
had been Victorian sex and a ponderous machine of ideology. Yes, the
life of politics and the life of the myth had diverged too far. There was
nothing to return them to one another, no common danger, no cause,
no desire, and, most essentially, no hero. It was a hero America
needed, a hero central to his time, a man whose personality might suggest contradictions and mysteries that could reach into the alienated
circuits of the underground, because only a hero can capture the secret
imagination of a people, and so be good for the vitality of his nation—
a hero embodies the fantasy and so allows each private mind the liberty
to consider its fantasy and find a way to grow. Each mind can become
more conscious of its desire and waste less strength in hiding from itself. Roosevelt was such a hero, and Churchill, Lenin, and De Gaulle;
even Hitler, to take the most odious example of this thesis, was a hero,
the hero-as-monster, embodying what had become the monstrous fantasy of a people, but the horror upon which the radical mind and lib-

eral temperament foundered was that he gave outlet to the energies of the Germans and so presented the twentieth century with an index of how horrible had become the secret heart of its desire. Roosevelt is of course a happier example of the hero; from his paralytic leg to the royal elegance of his geniality he seemed to contain the country within himself—everyone from the meanest starving cripple to an ambitious young man could expand into the optimism of an improving future because the man offered an unspoken promise of a future that would be rich. The sexual and the sex-starved, the poor, the hard-working, and the imaginative well-to-do could see themselves in the President, could believe him to be like themselves. So a large part of the country was able to discover its energies because not as much was wasted in feeling that the country was a poisonous nutrient which stifled the day.

Too simple? No doubt. One tries to construct a simple model. The thesis is after all not so mysterious; it would merely nudge the notion that a hero embodies his time and is not so very much better than his time, but he is larger than life and so is capable of giving direction to the time, able to encourage a nation to discover the deepest colors of its character. At bottom the concept of the hero is antagonistic to impersonal social progress, to the belief that social ills can be solved by social legislating, for it sees a country as all-but-trapped in its character until it has a hero who reveals the character of the country to itself. The implication is that without such a hero the nation turns sluggish. Truman for example was not such a hero, he was not sufficiently larger than life, he inspired familiarity without excitement, he was a character but his proportions came from soap opera: Uncle Harry, full of salty common-sense and small-minded certainty, a storekeeping uncle.

Whereas Eisenhower has been the anti-Hero, the regulator. Nations do not necessarily and inevitably seek for heroes. In periods of dull anxiety, one is more likely to look for security than a dramatic confrontation, and Eisenhower could stand as a hero only for that large number of Americans who were most proud of their lack of imagination. In American life, the unspoken war of the century has taken place between the city and the small town: the city, which is dynamic, orgiastic, unsettling, explosive, and accelerating to the psyche; the small town, which is rooted, narrow, cautious, and planted in the life-logic of the family. The need of the city is to accelerate growth; the pride of the small town is to retard it. But since America has been passing through a period of enormous expansion since the war, the double-four years of Dwight Eisenhower could not retard the expansion, it could only denude it of color, character, and the development of novelty. The small-town mind is rooted—it is rooted in the small town—and when it attempts to direct history the results are disastrously colorless because the instrument of world power which is used by the small-town mind is the committee. Committees do not create, they merely proliferate, and the incredible dullness wreaked upon the American landscape in Eisenhower's eight years has been the triumph of the corporation. A tasteless, sexless, odorless sanctity in architecture, manners, modes, styles has been the result. Eisenhower embodied half the needs of the nation, the needs of the timid, the petrified, the sanctimonious, and the sluggish. What was even worse, he did not divide the nation as a hero might (with a dramatic dialogue as the result); he merely excluded one part of the nation from the other.

Some part of these thoughts must have been in one's mind at the moment there was that first glimpse of Kennedy entering the Biltmore Hotel; and in the days that followed, the first mystery—the profound air of depression that hung over the convention—gave way to a second mystery, which can be answered only by history. The depression of the delegates was understandable: No one had too much doubt that Kennedy would be nominated, but if elected he would be not only the youngest President ever to be chosen by voters, he would be the most conventionally attractive young man ever to sit in the White House, and his wife—some would claim it—might be the most beautiful first lady in our history. Of necessity the myth would emerge once more, because America's politics would now be also America's favorite movie, America's first soap opera, America's best-seller. "Well, there's your first hipster," says a writer one knows at the convention, "Sergius O'Shaugnessy born rich," and the temptation is to nod, for it could be true, a war hero, and the heroism is bona-fide, even exceptional, a man who has lived with death, who, crippled in the back, took on an operation that would kill him or restore him to power, who chose to marry a lady whose face might be too imaginative for the taste of a democracy that likes its first ladies to be executives of home-management, a man who courts political suicide by choosing to go all out for a nomination four, eight, or twelve years before his political elders think he is ready, a man who announces a week prior to the convention that the young are better fitted to direct history than the old. Yes, it captures the attention. This is no routine candidate calling every shot by safety's routine book ("Yes," Nixon said, naturally but terribly tired an hour after his nomination, the TV cameras and lights and microphones bringing out a sweat of fatigue on his face, the words coming very slowly from the tired brain, somber, modest, sober, slow, slow enough so that one could touch emphatically the cautions behind each word, "Yes, I want to say," said Nixon, "that whatever abilities I have, I got from my mother." A tired pause . . . dull moment of warning, ". . . and my father." The connection now made, the rest comes easy, ". . . and my school and my church." Such men are capable of anything.)

One had the opportunity to study Kennedy a bit in the days that followed. His style in the press conferences was interesting. Not terribly popular with the reporters (too much a contemporary, and yet too difficult to understand, he received nothing like the rounds of applause given to Eleanor Roosevelt, Stevenson, Humphrey, or even Johnson), he carried himself nonetheless with a cool grace that seemed indifferent to applause, his manner somehow similar to the poise of a fine boxer, quick with his hands, neat in his timing, and two feet away from his corner when the bell ended the round. There was a good lithe wit to his responses, a dry Harvard wit, a keen sense of proportion in disposing of difficult questions—invariably he gave enough of an answer to be formally satisfactory without ever opening himself to a new question that might go further than the first. Asked by a reporter, "Are you for Adlai as vice-president?" the grin came forth and the voice turned very dry, "No, I cannot say we have considered *Adlai* as a vice-president." Yet there was an elusive detachment to everything he did. One did not have the feeling of a man present in the room with all his weight and all his mind. Johnson gave you all of himself, he was a political animal, he breathed like an animal, sweated like one, you knew his mind was entirely absorbed with the compendium of political fact and maneuver; Kennedy seemed at times like a young professor whose manner was adequate for the classroom but whose mind was off in some intricacy of the Ph.D. thesis he was writing. Perhaps one can give a sense of the discrepancy by saying that he was like an actor who had been cast as the candidate, a good actor, but not a great one—you were aware all the time that the role was one thing and the man another— they did not coincide, the actor seemed a touch too aloof (as, let us say, Gregory Peck is usually too aloof) to become the part. Yet one had little sense of whether to value this elusiveness or to beware of it. One could be witnessing the fortitude of a superior sensitivity or the detachment of a man who was not quite real to himself.

From *The Presidential Papers* (1963)

# July                    Modene—II

Hearing Jack Kennedy's reedy voice on TV put me through transformations. Time, I discovered, was no unimpeded river but a medium of valves and locks that had to be negotiated before one could reenter the third week of July. To reenter, however, was hell. Two days before the convention was over, I began to call the Fontainebleau every few hours to see if Modene had returned from L.A. to Miami. When she finally came back to her room on the evening after it ended, her phone was ringing as she came through the door. I am certain she took my voice as an omen and must have concluded that I was gifted with remarkable powers, for she immediately burst into tears.

Shortly after my arrival at her hotel room door, our affair commenced. I had never gone to bed with a girl so beautiful as Modene. If there had been nights I was not likely to forget in the brothels of Montevideo, they had also revealed the trap of commercial pleasure. As my body encountered new sensations, so did the rest of me tear off in a moral panic: To go so far when one cared so little! With Modene, however, it took no more than a night to fall in love. If half of me loved her more than the other half, all of me was moving, nonetheless, in the same direction. I did not know if I would ever have enough of Miss Modene Murphy, and this passion was even larger than my anxiety that I was breaking the first commandment handed over by Harlot. If a sneaky had been planted in her room while she was away, then I was engraving my voice onto the tapes of the FBI and Harlot would eventually acquire them through his special sources. So, even in the middle of our first embrace, I kept telling myself that the FBI must be kept ignorant of the cover name I was using with her. On my race over to her hotel after my call, I had prepared a piece of paper on which was written, "Call me Tom, or call me Dick, but Harry never." Since we embraced as the door clicked shut behind me, and then stopped for breath and kissed again, and she was crying when we finished, so I did not get to hand the note over for the first five minutes, and by then, since she was no longer weeping but laughing as well, she took in the message and laughed some more. "Why?" she whispered.

"Your room has ears," I whispered back.

She nodded. She shivered. A wanton look came over her face. In the midst of loose mascara and smeared lipstick, she was lovely. Her beauty depended on arrogance, and that had just returned. If her room was bugged, she was, at least, a center of attention.

"Tom," she said clearly, "let's fuck."

I would know her better before I would know how seldom she used the word.

On that night, the more Modene and I learned about each other, the more there was to learn. I was not accustomed to being all this insatiable, but then, I had never made love before to the mistress of the man who might yet be President of the United States, nor to the girl who had had an affair with the most popular singer in America, nor to the woman who might be the lover of a brute overlord in crime: All that, and I had not fainted on the doorstep—a monster of resolve was on the prowl in me. I could not have enough of her.

When it was all over and we came down at last to a little sleep in each other's embrace, she whispered to me on awakening at two in the morning, "I'm hungry, Tom, I'm hungry."

In an all-night diner in the southern end of Miami Beach, down in the twenty-four-hour sprawl on Collins Avenue of all-night movie houses and all-night stripper bars, of motels that rented by the hour while their names hissed in their neon signs, we ate sandwiches, drank coffee, and tried to talk. I felt as if I were on a boat, and dead-sweet drunk. I had never been so relaxed in my life. It was only by a last inward tide of duty that I could introduce her to the idea that we needed a private code. She took to it immediately. The urge to conspire lived as brightly as a genie in her. We decided to meet in the bars of hotels near the Fontainebleau, but the name of each hotel would stand for another—if I spoke to her of the Beau Rivage, I would mean the Eden Roc; the Eden Roc would be the Deauville, and mention of the Deauville was a signal to go to the Roney Plaza. An 8:00 P.M. date would be for six in the evening. I worked out the transpositions in duplicate and handed her one of two pieces of paper.

"Am I in danger?" she asked.

"Not yet."

"Not yet?"

I did not know if I wished to come back to any world at all. "Sam worries me," I said at last.

"Sam would not touch my fingernail," she said fondly.

"In that case," I said, "he might touch mine." I regretted the remark instantly.

"You know," she said, "I feel wonderful. My father was a motorcycle racer, and I think his blood is in me tonight. I feel high."

A black pimp at the other end of the diner was trying to catch her eye and in the absence of such contact was leaving his evil cloud on me.

I felt as if I had come into the place I had been expecting to enter all my life.

It would take two weeks before I found out why she had been so distraught on her return. Now that we were lovers, Modene told me less about herself than in our two short meetings for drinks. We could talk about her childhood and mine, about singers and bands, movies and a book or two—she did think *The Great Gatsby* was overrated ("The author doesn't know *anything* about gangsters") and *Gone with the Wind* was a classic, "although it took the movie to convince me of that."

I hardly cared. If we were married, her taste might be a hurdle of the first order, but then it occurred to me that I had never asked myself how much I admired *The Great Gatsby*. One was not supposed to wonder about that. Not at Yale. It was like asking yourself whether you were moved by St. Francis of Assisi.

We agreed, at any rate, on *The Catcher in the Rye*—"Heaven," said Modene, "although not a *great* classic," and that was enough to do with books. We ate and drank well. She knew every good restaurant in southern Florida. Whenever I had a day off, we would go waterskiing or scuba diving in the Keys and spend Saturday night in the bars of Key West. It was amazing I did not get into fights. At bottom, I felt so green in the role of squire to an incredibly lovely girl that I would be on battle-alert whenever anyone looked at her. Hardly confident of my mastery of martial arts—the stint at the Farm had obviously not been enough—I was covertly measuring every conceivable opponent until I came to learn that one seldom got into a fight before one's woman provoked one. Modene forestalled such possibilities. I did not know exactly how she managed, but processing ten thousand or more people a year on an airplane may have had something to do with it. She was pleasant to strange men but not accommodating, and made it clear that I was her date for the evening and she was with me. So, I survived. I prospered. I may even have looked a little more formidable than I felt. I was, in any event, ready to die before I would ever yell, "You can have her, you can have her."

We also drove to Tampa, and to Flamingo in the Everglades. If we would spend a day together as preparation for our night, part of the joy was to be together in a car. She loved convertibles. Soon, I was renting them. I had a principal I could never touch until I was forty that consisted of bonds issued by the City of Bangor in 1922. It had been passed on to me by my paternal grandfather, and I could use the interest, although by family protocol, I was not supposed to. Who knew why our family did what it did? I, at any rate, good Hubbard, always predeposited such interest. Now parsimony would screech at me through each pole vault into the heaven of Modene Murphy. I was beginning to suffer so much from the gap between my richest and stingiest impulses that *Tom* Field began to dip into Harry Hubbard's accumulating interest to splurge on splendid meals and a rented white convertible.

But Tom and Mo loved to drive! Our weather was hot, rainy season was on, and I came to appreciate a South Florida sky. That sky could rest weightless upon you for a splendid morning, its bowl empty and blue over the Everglades like the great empyrean of the American West, but if Florida lands were flat, flat as water level, the sky had its own mountainous topography. Torrents of rain could approach as quickly as sunlit ravines fall into the unforgiving shadow of their cliffs. The changing shape of a cloud was, therefore, never to be ignored or you would not get the top up in time. Some cumulus sailed into one's attention off the spinnaker bellows of a tropical gust; other puffs curled on themselves like hooks prepared to gouge the fabric of the sky. Under a black ceiling of atmospheric wrath, storm clouds massed above one another in ranges and ridge lines that the land below could never offer, and insects were whipped by one's car stream into dark expectorations against the windshield, their small, exploded deaths still pitting the glass after gouts of rain.

How water could fall in southern Florida! One moment I might be close to doubling the speed limit, my highway no more than a long white arrow launched against the horizon; then, clouds would appear like hooded strangers. Ten minutes later, curtains of downpour would force me to the shoulder. A celestial rage, as intimate but almighty as a parent's wrath, would beat upon the metal skin of the car. When the rain ceased, I would drive through southern Florida with her head upon my arm.

We never talked about what had happened in Los Angeles. She did not refer any longer to Jack or to Sam. They seemed to have disappeared, and, given the size of her wound, I was not about to approach such questions. Sorrow and silence were her sensuous companions. I, well used by now to mourning for Kittredge, could ride beside Modene without speaking for an hour at a time. I lived with the lover's optimism that silence brought us nearer. It was not until I began to suspect that her thoughts could wander while making love that I came to realize how much of the beloved candidate remained with us. Sometimes, in the middle of the act, I could sense her mind going far away from me, and I would feel the subtle sense of pall that comes over a party when it has just passed its peak.

From *Harlot's Ghost* (1991)


# Superman Comes
# to the Supermarket—II

So far as the people at the convention had affection for anyone, it was Stevenson, so far as they were able to generate any spontaneous enthusiasm, their cheers were again for Stevenson. Yet it was obvious he never had much chance, because so soon as a chance would present itself he seemed quick to dissipate the opportunity. The day before the nominations, he entered the Sports Arena to take his seat as a delegate—the demonstration was spontaneous, noisy, and prolonged; it was quieted only by Governor Collins' invitation for Stevenson to speak to the delegates. In obedience perhaps to the scruple that a candidate must not appear before the convention until nominations are done, Stevenson said no more than: "I am grateful for this tumultuous and moving welcome. After getting in and out of the Biltmore Hotel and this hall, I have decided I know whom you are going to nominate. It will be the last survivor." This dry reminder of the ruthlessness of politics broke the roar of excitement for his presence. The applause as he left the platform was like the dying fall-and-moan of a baseball crowd when a home run curves foul. The next day, a New York columnist talking about it said bitterly, "If he'd only gone through the motions, if he had just said that now he wanted to run, that he would work hard, and he hoped the delegates would vote for him. Instead he made that lame joke." One wonders. It seems almost as if he did not wish to win unless victory came despite himself, and then was overwhelming. There are men who are not heroes because they are too good for their time, and it is natural that defeats leave them bitter, tired, and doubtful of their right to make new history. If Stevenson had campaigned for a year before the convention, it is possible that he could have stopped Kennedy. At the least, the convention would have been enormously more exciting, and the nominations might have gone through half-a-dozen ballots before a winner was hammered into shape. But then Stevenson might also have shortened his life. One had the impression of a tired man who (for a politician) was sickened unduly by compromise. A year of maneuvering, broken promises, and detestable partners might have gutted him for the election campaign. If elected, it might have ruined him as a President. There is the possibility that he sensed his situation exactly this way, and knew that if he were to run for President, win, and make a good one, he would first have to be restored, as one can indeed be restored, by an exceptional demonstration of love—love, in this case, meaning that the Party had a profound desire to keep him as their leader. The emotional truth of a last-minute victory for Stevenson over the Kennedy machine might have given him new energy; it would certainly have given him new faith in a country and a party whose good motives he was possibly beginning to doubt. Perhaps the fault he saw with his candidacy was that he attracted only the nicest people to himself and there were not enough of them. (One of the private amusements of the convention was to divine some of the qualities of the candidates by the style of the young women who put on hats and clothing and politicked in the colors of one presidential gent or another. Of course, half of them must have been hired models, but someone did the hiring and so it was fair to look for a common denominator. The Johnson girls tended to be plump, pie-faced, dumb sexy Southern; the Symingteeners seemed a touch mulish, stubborn, good-looking pluggers; the Kennedy ladies were the handsomest: healthy, attractive, tough, a little spoiled—they looked like the kind of girls who had gotten all the dances in high school and/or worked for a year as an airline hostess before marrying well. But the Stevenson girls looked to be doing it for no money; they were good sorts, slightly horsy-faced, one had the impression they played field hockey in college.) It was indeed the pure, the saintly, the clean-living, the pacifistic, the vegetarian who seemed most for Stevenson, and the less humorous in the Kennedy camp were heard to remark bitterly that Stevenson had nothing going for him but a bunch of Goddamn Beatniks. This might even have had its sour truth. The demonstrations outside the Sports Arena for Stevenson seemed to have more than a fair proportion of tall, emaciated young men with thin, wry beards and three-string guitars, accompanied (again in undue proportion) by a contingent of ascetic, face-washed young Beat ladies in sweaters and dungarees. Not to mention all the Holden Caulfields one could see from here to the horizon. But of course it is unfair to limit it so, for the Democratic gentry were also committed half en masse for Stevenson. A considerable number of movie stars were as well, Shelley Winters for one: After the convention she remarked sweetly, "Tell me something nice about Kennedy so I can get excited about him."

What was properly astonishing was the way this horde of political half-breeds and amateurs came within distance of turning the convention from its preconceived purpose, and managed at the least to bring the only hour of thoroughgoing excitement the convention could offer.

But then nominating day was the best day of the week, and enough happened to suggest that a convention out of control would be a spectacle as extraordinary in the American scale of spectator values as a close seventh game in the World Series or a tied fourth quarter in a professional-football championship. A political convention is after all not a meeting of a corporation's board of directors; it is a pig-rooting, horse-snorting, band-playing, voice-screaming medieval get-together of greed, practical lust, compromised idealism, career-advancement, meeting, feud, vendetta, conciliation, of rabble-rousers, fist fights (as it used to be), embraces, drunks (again as it used to be), and collective rivers of animal sweat. It is a reminder that no matter how the country might pretend it has grown up and become tidy in its manners, bodiless in its legislative language, hygienic in its separation of high politics from private life, that the roots still come grubby from the soil, and that politics in America is still different from politics anywhere else because the politics has arisen out of the immediate needs, ambitions, and cupidities of the people, that our politics still smell of the bedroom and the kitchen rather than having descended to us from the chill punctilio of aristocratic negotiation. So, on nominating day, there was a whip of anticipation in the air, the seats on the floor were filled, the press section was working, and in the gallery people were sitting in the aisles.

Sam Rayburn had just finished nominating Johnson as one came in, and the rebel yells went up, delegates started filing out of their seats and climbing over seats, and a pullulating dance of bodies and bands began to snake through the aisles, the posters jogging and whirling in time to the music. The dun color of the floor (faces, suits, seats, and floor boards), so monotonous the first two days, now lit up with life as if an iridescent caterpillar had emerged from a fold of wet leaves. It was more vivid than one had expected, it was right, it felt finally like a convention, and from up close when one got down to the floor the nearness to the demonstrators took on high color, that electric vividness one feels on the side lines of a football game when it is necessary to duck back as the ballcarrier goes by, his face tortured in the concentration of the moment, the thwomp of his tackle as acute as if one had been hit oneself.

That was the way the demonstrators looked on the floor. Nearly all had the rapt, private look of a passion or a tension that could only be worked off by one's limbs, three hundred football players, everything from seedy delegates with jowl-sweating shivers to livid models, paid for their work that day, but stomping out their beat on the floor with the hypnotic adulatory grimaces of ladies who had lived for Lyndon these last ten years.

Then from the funereal rostrum, whose color was not so rich as mahogany nor so dead as a cigar, came the last of the requests for the delegates to take their seats. The seconding speeches began, one minute each; they ran for three and four, the minor-league speakers running on the longest as if the electric antenna of television was the lure of the Sirens. Bored cheers applauded their concluding Götter-dämmerungen and the nominations were open again. A favorite son, a modest demonstration, five seconding speeches, tedium.

Next was Kennedy's occasion. Governor Freeman of Minnesota made the speech. Then the demonstration. Well-run, bigger than Johnson's, jazzier, the caliber of the costumes and decorations better chosen: The placards were broad enough, "Let's Back Jack," the floats were garish, particularly a papier-mâché or plastic balloon of Kennedy's head, six feet in diameter, which had nonetheless the slightly shrunken, over-red, rubbery look of a toy for practical jokers in one of those sleazy off–Times Square magic-and-gimmick stores; and the band was suitably corny.

The personnel, however, had something of the Kennedy *élan,* those paper hats designed to look like straw boaters with Kennedy's face on the crown, and small photographs of him on the ribbon, those hats which had come to symbolize the crack speed of the Kennedy team, that Madison Avenue cachet which one finds in bars like P. J. Clarke's, the elegance always giving its subtle echo of the Twenties so that the raccoon coats seem more numerous than their real count, and the colored waistcoats are measured by the charm they would have drawn from Scott Fitzgerald's eye. But there, it occurred to one for the first time that Kennedy's middle name was just that, Fitzgerald, and the tone of his crack lieutenants, the unstated style, was true to Scott. The legend of Fitzgerald had an army at last, formed around the self-image in the mind of every superior Madison Avenue opportunist that he was hard, he was young, he was In, his conversation was lean as wit, and if the work was not always scrupulous, well the style could aspire. If there came a good day . . . he could meet the occasion.

The Kennedy snake dance ran its thirty lively minutes, cheered its seconding speeches, and sat back. They were so sure of winning, there had been so many victories before this one, and this one had been scouted and managed so well, that hysteria could hardly be the mood. Besides, everyone was waiting for the Stevenson barrage, which should be at least diverting. But now came a long tedium. Favorite sons were nominated, fat mayors shook their hips, seconders told the word to constituents back in Ponderwaygot County, treacly demonstrations tried to hold the floor, and the afternoon went by; Symington's hour came and went, a good demonstration, good as Johnson's (for good cause—they had pooled their demonstrators). More favorite sons, Governor Docking of Kansas declared "a genius" by one of his lady speakers in a tense go-back-to-religion voice. The hours went by, two, three, four hours, it seemed forever before they would get to Stevenson. It was evening when Senator Eugene McCarthy of Minnesota got up to nominate him.

The gallery was ready, the floor was responsive, the demonstrators were milling like bulls in their pen waiting for the *toril* to fly open—it would have been hard not to wake the crowd up, not to make a good speech. Gene McCarthy made a great one. Great it was by the measure of convention oratory, and he held the crowd like a matador, timing their *oles!*, building them up, easing them back, correcting any sag in attention, gathering their emotion, discharging it, creating new emotion on the wave of the last, driving his passes tighter and tighter as he readied for the kill. "Do not reject this man who made us all proud to be called Democrats, do not leave this prophet without honor in his own party." One had not heard a speech like this since 1948 when Vito Marcantonio's voice, his harsh, shrill, bitter, street urchin's voice screeched through the loud-speakers at Yankee Stadium and lashed seventy thousand people into an uproar.

"There was only one man who said let's talk sense to the American people," McCarthy went on, his muleta furled for the *naturales*. "There was only one man who said let's talk sense to the American people," he repeated. "He said the promise of America is the promise of greatness. This was his call to greatness. . . . Do not forget this man. . . . Ladies and Gentlemen, I present to you not the favorite son of one state, but the favorite son of the fifty states, the favorite son of every country he has visited, the favorite son of every country which has not seen him but is secretly thrilled by his name." Bedlam. The kill. "Ladies and Gentlemen, I present to you Adlai Stevenson of Illinois." Ears and tail. Hooves and bull. A roar went up like the roar one heard the day Bobby Thomson hit his home run at the Polo Grounds and the Giants won the pennant from the Dodgers in the third playoff game of the 1951 season. The demonstration cascaded onto the floor, the gallery came to its feet, the Sports Arena sounded like the inside of a marching drum. A tidal pulse of hysteria, exaltation, defiance, exhilaration, anger, and roaring desire flooded over the floor. The cry which had gone up on McCarthy's last sentence had not paused for breath in five minutes, and troop after troop of demonstrators jammed the floor (the Stevenson people to be scolded the next day for having collected floor passes and sent them out to bring in new demonstrators) and still the sound mounted. One felt the convention coming apart. There was a Kennedy girl in the seat in front of me, the Kennedy hat on her head, a dimpled healthy brunette; she had sat silently through McCarthy's speech, but now, like a woman paying her respects to the power of natural thrust, she took off her hat and began to clap herself. I saw a writer I knew in the next aisle—he had spent a year studying the Kennedy machine in order to write a book on how a nomination is won. If Stevenson stampeded the convention, his work was lost. Like a reporter at a mine cave-in I inquired the present view of the widow. "Who can think," was the answer, half frantic, half elated, "just watch it, that's all." I found a cool one, a New York reporter, who smiled in rueful respect. "It's the biggest demonstration I've seen since Wendell Willkie's in 1940," he said, and added, "God, if Stevenson takes it, I can wire my wife and move the family on to Hawaii."

"I don't get it."

"Well, every story I wrote said it was locked up for Kennedy."

Still it went on, twenty minutes, thirty minutes, the chairman could hardly be heard, the demonstrators refused to leave. The lights were turned out, giving a sudden theatrical shift to the sense of a crowded church at midnight, and a new roar went up, louder, more passionate than anything heard before. It was the voice, it was the passion, if one insisted to call it that, of everything in America that was defeated, idealistic, innocent, alienated, outside and Beat, it was the potential voice of a new third of the nation whose psyche was ill from cultural malnutrition, it was powerful, it was extraordinary, it was larger than the decent, humorous, finicky, half-noble man who had called it forth, it was a cry from the Thirties when Time was simple, it was a resentment of the slick technique, the oiled gears, and the superior generals of Fitzgerald's Army; but it was also—and for this reason one could not admire it altogether, except with one's excitement—it was also the plea of the bewildered who hunger for simplicity again, it was the adolescent counterpart of the boss's depression before the unpredictable dynamic of Kennedy as President, it was the return to the sentimental dream of Roosevelt rather than the approaching nightmare of history's oncoming night, and it was inspired by a terror of the future as much as a revulsion of the present.

Fitz's Army held. After the demonstration was finally down, the convention languished for ninety minutes while Meyner and others were nominated, a fatal lapse of time because Stevenson had perhaps a chance to stop Kennedy if the voting had begun on the echo of the last cry for him, but in an hour and a half depression crept in again and emotions spent, the delegates who had wavered were rounded into line. When the vote was taken, Stevenson had made no gains. The brunette who had taken off her hat was wearing it again, and she clapped and squealed when Wyoming delivered the duke and Kennedy was in. The air was sheepish, like the mood of a suburban couple who forgive each other for cutting in and out of somebody else's automobile while the country club dance is on. Again, tonight, no miracle would occur. In the morning the papers would be moderate in their description of Stevenson's last charge.

From *The Presidential Papers* (1963)

# First Lady in Waiting

The weather was hectic. It was the Summer of 1960, a few weeks after the Democratic Convention yet before the presidential campaign had formally begun and one was out at Hyannisport, site of the Summer White House. Those of you who know Hyannis ("High-anus," as the natives say,) will know how funny is the title—all those motels and a Summer White House too, the Kennedy compound: An enclosure of three summer homes belonging to Joe Kennedy, Sr., RFK, and JFK, with a modest amount of lawn and beach to share among them. In those historic days the lawn was overrun with journalists, cameramen, magazine writers, politicians, delegations, friends and neighboring gentry, government intellectuals, family, a prince, some Massachusetts state troopers, and red-necked hard-nosed tourists patrolling outside the fence for a glimpse of the boy. He was much in evidence, a bit of everywhere that morning, including the lawn, and particularly handsome at times, looking like a good version of Charles Lindbergh at noon on a hot August day. Well, Jackie Kennedy was inside in her living room sitting around talking with a few of us, Arthur Schlesinger, Jr., Prince Radziwill, Peter Maas, and Pierre Salinger. We were a curious assortment indeed, as oddly assembled in our way as some of the do-gooders and real baddies on the lawn outside. It would have taken a hostess of broad and perhaps dubious gifts, Perle Mesta, no doubt, or Ethel Merman, or Elsa Maxwell, to have woven some mood into this occasion, because pop! were going the flashbulbs out in the crazy August sun on the sun-drenched terrace just beyond the bay window at our back, a politician—a stocky machine type sweating in a dark suit with a white shirt and white silk tie—was having his son, seventeen perhaps, short, chunky, dressed the same way, take a picture of him and his wife, a Mediterranean dish around sixty with a bright, happy, flowered dress. The boy took a picture of father and mother, father took a picture of mother and son—another heeler came along to take a picture of all three—it was a little like a rite surrounding *droit du seigneur*, as if afterward the family could press a locket in your hand and say, "Here, here are contained three hairs from the youth of the Count, discovered by me on my wife next morning." There was something low and greedy about this picture-taking, perhaps the popping of the flashbulbs in the sunlight, as if everything monstrous and overreaching in our insane public land were tamped together in the foolproof act of taking a sun-drenched picture at noon with no shadows and a flashbulb—do we sell insurance to protect our cadavers against the corrosion of the grave?

And I had the impression that Jackie Kennedy was almost suffering in the flesh from their invasion of her house, her terrace, her share of the lands, that if the popping of the flashbulbs went on until midnight on the terrace outside she would have a tic forever in the corner of her eye. Because that was the second impression of her, of a lady with delicate and exacerbated nerves. She was no broad hostess, not at all; broad hostesses are monumental animals turned mellow: hippopotami, rhinoceri, plump lion, sweet gorilla, warm bear. Jackie

Kennedy was a cat, narrow and wild, and her fur was being rubbed every which way. This was the second impression. The first had been simpler. It had been merely of a college girl who was nice. Nice and clean and very merry. I had entered her house perspiring—talk of the politician, I was wearing a black suit myself, a washable, the only one in my closet not completely unpressed that morning, and I had been forced to pick a white shirt with button-down collar: All the white summer shirts were in the laundry. What a set-to I had had with Adele Mailer at breakfast. Food half-digested in anger, sweating like a goat, tense at the pit of my stomach for I would be interviewing Kennedy in a half hour, I was feeling not a little jangled when we were introduced, and we stumbled mutually over a few polite remarks, which was my fault I'm sure more than hers for I must have had a look in my eyes— I remember I felt like a drunk marine who knows in all clarity that if he doesn't have a fight soon it'll be good for his character but terrible for his constitution.

She offered me a cool drink—iced verbena tea with sprig of mint no doubt—but the expression in my face must have been rich because she added, still standing by the screen in the doorway, "We do have something harder of course," and something droll and hard came into her eyes as if she were a very naughty eight-year-old indeed. More than one photograph of Jackie Kennedy had put forward just this saucy regard—it was obviously the life of her charm. But I had not been prepared for another quality, of shyness conceivably. There was something quite remote in her. Not willed, not chilly, not directed at anyone in particular, but distant, detached as the psychologists say, moody and abstracted the novelists used to say. As we sat around the coffee table on summer couches, summer chairs, a pleasant living room in light colors, lemon, white, and gold seeming to predominate, the sort of living room one might expect to find in Cleveland, may it be, at the home of a fairly important young executive whose wife had taste, sitting there, watching people go by, the group I mentioned earlier kept a kind of conversation going. Its center, if it had one, was obviously Jackie Kennedy. There was a natural tendency to look at her and see if she were amused. She did not sit there like a movie star with a ripe olive in each eye for the brain, but in fact gave conversation back, made some of it, laughed often. We had one short conversation about Provincetown, which was pleasant. She remarked that she had been staying no more than fifty miles away for all these summers but had never seen it. She must, I assured her. It was one of the few fishing villages in America that still had beauty. Besides, it was the Wild West of the East. The local police were the Indians and the beatniks were the poor hard-working settlers. Her eyes turned merry. "Oh, I'd love to see it," she said. But how did one go? In three black limousines and fifty police for escort, or in a sports car at 4 A.M. with dark glasses? "I suppose now I'll never get to see it," she said wistfully.

She had a keen sense of laughter, but it revolved around the absurdities of the world. She was probably not altogether unlike a soldier who has been up at the front for two weeks. There was a hint of gone laughter. Soldiers who have had it bad enough can laugh at the fact some trooper got killed crossing an open area because he wanted to change his socks from khaki to green. The front lawn of this house must have been, I suppose, a kind of no-man's-land for a lady. The story I remember her telling was about Stash, Prince Radziwill, her brother-in-law, who had gone into the second-story bathroom that morning to take a shave and discovered, to his lack of complete pleasure, that a crush of tourists was watching him from across the road. Yes, the house had been besieged, and one knew she thought of the sightseers as a mob, a motley of gargoyles, like the horde who riot through the last pages in *The Day of the Locust*.

Since there was an air of self-indulgence about her, subtle but precise, one was certain she liked time to compose herself. While we sat there she must have gotten up a half-dozen times, to go away for two minutes, come back for three. She had the exasperated impatience of a college girl. One expected her to swear mildly. "Oh, Christ!" or "Sugar!" or "Fudge!" And each time she got up, there was a glimpse of her calves, surprisingly thin, not unfeverish. I was reminded of the legs on those adolescent Southern girls who used to go out together and walk up and down the streets of Fayetteville, North Carolina, in the Summer of 1944 at Fort Bragg. In the petulant Southern air of their boredom many of us had found something luminous that summer, a mixture of languor, heat, innocence, and stupidity which was our cocktail vis-à-vis the knowledge we were going soon to Europe or the other war. One mentions this to underline the determinedly romantic aura in which one had chosen to behold Jackie Kennedy. There was a charm this other short Summer of 1960 in the thought a young man with a young attractive wife might soon become President. It offered possibilities and vistas, it brought a touch of life. It was thus more interesting to look at Jackie Kennedy as a woman than as a probable First Lady. Perhaps it was out of some such motive, such a desire for the clean air and tang of unexpected montage, that I spoke about her in just the way I did later that afternoon.

"Do you think she's happy?" asked a lady, an old friend, on the beach at Wellfleet.

"I guess she would rather spend her life on the Riviera."

"What would she do there?"

"End up as the mystery woman, maybe, in a good murder case."

"Wow," said the lady, giving me my reward.

It had been my way of saying I liked Jackie Kennedy, that she was not at all stuffy, that she had perhaps a touch of that artful madness which suggests future drama.

Later (on this day), one had a short session alone with Jack Kennedy, and the next day, another. As one had suspected in advance neither interview was satisfactory, they hardly could have been. The hazards of the campaign make it impossible for a candidate to be as interesting as he might like to be (assuming he has such a desire). One kept advancing the argument that this campaign would be a contest of personalities, and Kennedy kept returning the discussion to politics. After a while one recognized this was an inevitable caution for him. What remained after the interview was a passing remark whose importance was invisible on the scale of politics but proved altogether meaningful to my particular competence. As we sat down for the first time, Kennedy smiled nicely and said that he had read my books. One muttered one's pleasure. "Yes," he said, "I've read . . ." and then there was a short pause that did not last long enough to be embarrassing in which it was yet obvious no title came instantly to his mind, an omission one was not ready to mind altogether since a man in such a position must be obliged to carry a hundred thousand facts and names in his head, but the hesitation lasted no longer than three seconds or four, and then he said, "I've read *The Deer Park* and . . . the others," which startled me, for it was the first time in a hundred similar situations, talking to someone whose knowledge of my work was casual, that the sentence did not come out, "I've read *The Naked and the Dead* . . . and the others." If one is to take the worst and assume that Kennedy was briefed for this interview (which is most doubtful), it still speaks well for the striking instincts of his advisers.

What was retained later is an impression of Kennedy's manners, which were excellent, even artful, better than the formal good manners of Choate and Harvard, almost as if what was creative in the man had been given to the manners. In a room with one or two people, his voice improved, became low-pitched, even pleasant—it seemed obvious that in all these years he had never become a natural public speaker and so his voice was constricted in public, the symptom of all orators who are ambitious, throttled, and determined.

His personal quality had a subtle, not quite describable intensity, a suggestion of dry pent heat perhaps, his eyes large, the pupils gray, the whites prominent, almost shocking, his most forceful feature: He had the eyes of a mountaineer. His appearance changed with his mood, strikingly so, and this made him always more interesting than what he was saying. He would seem at one moment older than his age, forty-eight or fifty, a tall, slim, sunburned professor with a pleasant weathered face, not even particularly handsome; five minutes later, talking to a press conference on his lawn, three microphones before him, a television camera turning, his appearance would have gone through a metamorphosis, he would look again like a movie star, his coloring vivid, his manner rich, his gestures strong and quick, alive with that concentration of vitality a successful actor always seems to radiate. Kennedy had a dozen faces. Although they were not at all similar as people, the quality was reminiscent of someone like Brando, whose expression rarely changes but whose appearance seems to shift from one person into another as the minutes go by, and one bothers with this comparison because, like Brando, Kennedy's most characteristic quality is the remote and private air of a man who has traversed some lonely terrain of experience, of loss and gain, of nearness to death, which leaves him isolated from the mass of others.

> The next day while they waited in vain for rescuers, the wrecked half of the boat turned over in the water and they saw that it would soon sink. The group decided to swim to a small island three miles away. There were other islands bigger and nearer, but the Navy officers knew that they were occupied by the Japanese. On one island, only one mile to the south, they could see a Japanese camp. McMahon, the engineer whose legs were disabled by burns, was unable to swim. Despite his own painfully crippled back, Kennedy swam the three miles with a breast stroke, towing behind him by a life-belt strap that he held between his teeth the helpless McMahon . . . it took Kennedy and the suffering engineer five hours to reach the island.

The quotation is from a book that has for its dedicated unilateral title *The Remarkable Kennedys,* but the prose is by one of the best of the war reporters, the former *Yank* editor Joe McCarthy, and so presumably may be trusted in such details as this. Physical bravery does not, of course, guarantee a man's abilities in the White House—all too often men with physical courage are disappointing in their moral imagination—but the heroism here is remarkable for its tenacity. The above is merely one episode in a continuing saga that went on for five days in and out of the water, and left Kennedy at one point "miraculously saved from drowning (in a storm) by a group of Solomon Island natives who suddenly came up beside him in a large dugout canoe." Afterward, his back still injured (that precise back injury which was to put him on crutches eleven years later, and have him search for "spinal-fusion surgery" despite a warning that his chances of living through the operation were "extremely limited") afterward, he asked to go back on duty and became so bold in the attacks he made with his PT boat "that the crew didn't like to go out with him because he took so many chances."

It is the wisdom of a man who senses death within him and gambles that he can cure it by risking his life. It is the therapy of the instinct, and who is so wise as to call it irrational? Before he went into the Navy, Kennedy had been ailing. Washed out of Freshman year at Princeton by a prolonged trough of yellow jaundice, he was then sick for a year at Harvard. Do his trials suggest the self-hatred of a man whose resentment and ambition are too large for his body? Not everyone can discharge his furies on an analyst's couch, for some angers can be relaxed only by winning power, some rages are sufficiently monumental to demand that one try to become a hero or else fall back into that death which is already within the cells. But if one succeeds, the energy aroused can be exceptional. Talking to a man who had been with Kennedy in Hyannisport the week before the convention, I heard that he was in a state of deep fatigue.

"Well, he didn't look tired at the convention," one commented.

"Oh, he had three days of rest. Three days of rest for him is like six months for us."

One thinks of that three-mile swim with the belt in his mouth and McMahon holding it behind him. There are pestilences which sit in the mouth and rot the teeth—in those five hours how much of the psyche must have been remade, for to give vent to the bite in one's jaws and yet use that rage to save a life: It is not so very many men who have the apocalyptic sense that heroism is the First Doctor.

From *The Presidential Papers* (1963)

# Superman Comes
# to the Supermarket—III

One had not gone to the other convention. It was seen on television, and so too much cannot be said of that. It did however confirm one's earlier bias that the Republican Party was still a party of church ushers, undertakers, choirboys, prison wardens, bank presidents, small-town police chiefs, state troopers, psychiatrists, beauty-parlor operators, corporation executives, Boy Scout leaders, fraternity presidents, tax-board assessors, community leaders, surgeons, Pullman porters, head nurses, and the fat sons of rich fathers. Its candidate would be given the manufactured image of an ordinary man, and his campaign, so far as it was a psychological campaign (and this would be far indeed), would present him as a simple, honest, dependable, hard-working, ready-to-learn, modest, humble, decent, sober young man whose greatest qualification for President was his profound abasement before the glories of the Republic, the stability of the mediocre, and his own unworthiness. The apocalyptic hour of Uriah Heep.

It would then be a campaign unlike the ones that had preceded it. Counting by the full spectrum of complete Right to absolute Left, the political differences would be minor, but what would be not at all minor was the power of each man to radiate his appeal into some fundamental depths of the American character. One would have an inkling at last if the desire of America was for drama or stability, for adventure or monotony. And this, this appeal to the psychic direction America would now choose for itself, was the element most promising about this election, for it gave the possibility that the country might be able finally to rise above the deadening verbiage of its issues, its politics, its jargon, and live again by an image of itself. For in some part of themselves the people might know (since these candidates were not old enough to be revered) that they had chosen one young man for his mystery, for his promise that the country would grow or disintegrate by the unwilling charge he gave to the intensity of the myth, or had chosen another young man for his unstated oath that he would do all in his power to keep the myth buried and so convert the remains of Renaissance man as rapidly as possible into mass man. One might expect them to choose the enigma in preference to the deadening certainty. Yet one must doubt America's bravery. This lurching, unhappy, pompous, and most corrupt nation—could it have the courage finally to take on a new image for itself, was it brave enough to put into office not only one of its ablest men, its most efficient, its most conquistadorial (for Kennedy's capture of the Democratic Party deserves the word), but also one of its more mysterious men (the national psyche must shiver in its sleep at the image of Mickey Mantle–cum-Lindbergh in office, and a First Lady with an eighteenth-century face). Yes, America was at last engaging the fate of its myth, its consciousness about to be accelerated or cruelly depressed in its choice between two young men in their forties who, no matter how close, dull, or indifferent their stated politics might be, were radical poles apart, for one was sober, the apotheosis of opportunistic lead, all radium spent, the other handsome as a prince in the unstated aristocracy of the American dream. So, finally, would come a choice that history had never presented to a nation before—one could vote for glamour or for ugliness, a staggering and most stunning choice: Would the nation be brave enough to enlist the romantic dream of itself, would it vote for the image in the mirror of its unconscious, were the people indeed brave enough to hope for an acceleration of Time, for that new life of drama which would come from choosing a son to lead them who was heir apparent to the psychic loins? One could pause: It might be more difficult to be a President than it ever had before. Nothing less than greatness would do.

Yet if the nation voted to improve its face, what an impetus might come to the arts, to the practices, to the lives, and to the imagination of the American. If the nation so voted. But one knew the unadmitted specter in the minds of the Democratic delegates: that America would go to sleep on election eve with the polls promising Kennedy a victory on the day to come, yet in its sleep some millions of Democrats and Independents would suffer a nightmare before the mystery of uncharted possibilities their man would suggest, and in a terror of all the creativities (and some violences) that mass man might now have to dare again, the undetermined would go out in the morning to vote for the psychic security of Nixon the way a middle-aged man past adventure holds to the stale bread of his marriage. Yes, this election might be fearful enough to betray the polls and no one in America could plan the new direction until the last vote was counted by the last heeler in the last ambivalent ward, no one indeed could know until then what had happened the night before, what had happened at three o'clock in the morning on that long dark night of America's search for a security cheaper than her soul.

From *The Presidential Papers* (1963)

**August**         Modene—III

About this time, a letter came in from my father by way of the Quarters Eye pouch. It is characteristic of him that with the variety of means open for communication within the continental United States— prearranged pay phone to pay phone, Encoder-Decoder, special shunt code line, secure phone, standard Agency phone, and a number of other modes too technical to enumerate—my father employed an old OSS means. He wrote a letter, sealed it in an envelope, girded it about with three-quarter-inch strapping tape (half as strong as steel), stuck it in the daily pouch to wherever it was going, and was done with it. While it might have taken two experts half a week to steam loose such a chastity belt and restore the envelope, there were more brutal methods of interception. The letter called attention to itself and could simply be stolen. Not once in his career, my father would boast, had he ever lost a communication by this means of sending it—no, he would correct himself, once he did; the plane carrying the pouch went down—therefore, he was damned if he was about to give up dispatching his messages without the feel of his hand on a pen sending out his own words directly.

I read:

Dear Son,

I'm going to be in Miami on Sunday, and this abbreviated communication is to say that I would like to spend it with you. Since I don't want to get off on a wrong note, let me issue in advance the unhappy news that wife Mary and I, one year short of our silver wedding anniversary, are now, after six months of separation, entering the process of getting a divorce. The twins, I fear, have lined up on her side. I have assured Roque and Toby that the schism is, under the circumstances, comparatively friendly, but they seem bitter. She is their mother, when all is said.

On Sunday night, after my father flew back to Washington, I had a late date with Modene. She would be returning to Miami on an evening flight, and we would then go to a safe house. She did not like hotels. "Miami Beach is a very small world to its residents, and I am highly noticeable among them," she had told me.

So, we now used a small but elegant place on Key Biscayne that had been leased to the Agency by a wealthy Cuban who would be in Europe for the summer. I had been ready to gamble that it would present no problem for a few meetings. I used to pick her up at the airport in my white convertible and wheel us over Biscayne Bay along Rickenbacker Causeway to the villa off North Mashta Drive. We would spend our nights in the master bedroom, and waken in the morning to a view of royal palms, white habitations, mangrove shore, and pleasure boats in Hurricane Harbor.

I was, of course, balancing a set of lies between Harlot and the safe-house desk at Zenith, but the risk seemed small. Hunt was the only intelligence officer in South Florida who had the right to ask me what I was using the safe house for, and while he would be routinely notified of the fact each time I signed a chit for safe-house use (and Hunt was the man to know a good address by its name—North Mashta Drive would certainly alert his attention), still, I was protected by our procedural restraints. The villa, for purposes of signing out, was merely listed as Property 30G. If I was using it a good deal, Hunt, if curious, would still have to look up its address and owner by way of a classified in-house manual; why bother? Given our hordes of Cubans, we were using safe houses all the time. So, I had little to fear. Once, in a dream, I did awaken long enough to see Hunt's ski jump of a nose peering around the master bedroom door to take in the sight of Modene and myself in carnal clutch, but that was a dream. I was impressed by how little distress I carried compared to what I would have gone through if it had been my first year in the Agency. Perhaps I was beginning to live with Harlot's dictum that in our profession we learn to get along with unstable foundations.

So I could feel pride in my illicit use of La Villa Nevisca. The stucco walls were as white as any edifice on the South Florida shore, and its name in English, House of the Light Snowfall, proved worth repeating to Modene, who exhibited such naïve pleasure in the translation that I began to wonder how long it had taken her father to get accustomed to his money. Sometimes, when her precise way of speaking—the product of years of elocution lessons—began to pall on me, I confess that I began to see all Midwesterners as simple. In defense of such large prejudice, I must say that whenever a building was possessed of charm, or a touch of history, she was too impressed. She liked windows with odd shapes, wood filigree porches, pastel-colored

edifices in general, and romantic names—La Villa Nevisca was perfect! She was even impressed with replicas of Southern mansions in
Key Biscayne. (It became important to me, therefore, not to compare
her in any way to Kittredge.) All the same, I could not keep from en-
visioning Modene's childhood on well-to-do Grand Rapids streets and
concluded that her contempt for my low station in life—"I guess
you're the poorest man I ever dated"—was more than equaled by her
bottomless awe of my attainments: Yale, and a profession I could not
talk to her about. I did not even try to tell her about St. Matthew's.

I am being unfair. She knew what she knew, and her self-
confidence was absolute on certain matters. She loved to dance, for instance. After a couple of evenings in a nightclub, however, we more or
less gave it up. I was adequate on the floor, and she could have been a
professional. If she showed me variants of the samba and the
merengue, the cha-cha and the Madison, if she could go into a triple
lindy off a double lindy, it was only to demonstrate her skill: She had
no desire to raise my abilities through collaboration—it would make
her feel *silly*, she explained. The aristocratic reflex of an artist was in
her rejection: One does not wish to dull one's talent. In preference,
forswear the art.

On the other hand, I came to recognize that my accent fascinated
her. She declared that she could listen to it all night with as much pleasure as if Cary Grant were speaking. I came to recognize that Cary
Grant was her point of reference for people whose minds were occupied with niceties, and I understood then why she would not teach me
how to dance, no, no more than I would spend a part of my life teaching her to speak. She spoke well enough. If it could pall at times on my
ear, well, she had other virtues.

Once she said to me (and I heard echoes of Sally Porringer),
"You're such a snob."

"Do you know," I said, "so is your dear friend Jack Kennedy."
Then I could not resist the cruelty—"Wherever he is."

"He's trying to win an election," she answered, "so how could he
have time for me? Of course, he doesn't."

"Not even for a phone call." My jealousy was scalding my heart as
directly as boiling soup on a tender lap.

"He's not a snob," she said. "He has an intense interest in everyone around him. Unlike you, he's the best listener I ever met."

I was not. She would start to speak and my mind would wander
over to her carnal virtues. I never saw her but in a cloud of sexual intent. I did not have to listen to her—she was so much more than what

she was saying. Soon, we could go to bed, and then I would find her brilliant again, and delicate, deep, and fierce, yes, dear, greedy, generous, warm, and her heart would be ready to melt in sorrow and joy, all this for me on any night when we could transcend each and every annoying impasse of the evening and get to bed. Then I did not have to worry whether I knew how to dance.

Libido may be inner conviction, but libido rampant is megalomania. My mind would tell me that I was the greatest lover she had ever had; somewhat later, libido, by three parts out of four consumed, I became again the man who did not know how to dance. Sinatra knew how. So did Jack. They knew.

"You're mad," she would say to me. "Jack Kennedy has a bad back. He got it in the war. We never danced at all. It didn't matter. I wanted to listen to him when he talked and I loved to talk while he listened."

"And Frank? Frank doesn't dance?"

"It's his profession."

"Dancing?"

"No, but he understands it."

"And I don't?"

"Come here." Lying in bed, she would kiss me, and we would commence again. I would scourge the fourth part of my libido. Next morning, I would be in a towering depression. It would seem to me that I was nothing but a pit stop in the middle of a race. Kennedy would be back; Sinatra might always return, and Giancana was waiting. How crude were my emotions now that they were exposed to myself!

I do not know how well I was prepared, therefore, when a communication came in from Harlot.

SERIAL: J/38,854,256
ROUTING: LINE/ZENITH—OPEN
TO: ROBERT CHARLES
FROM: GLADIOLUS
SUBJECT: BABYLONIAN PARTOUSE
Call me on SEEK.

GLADIOLUS

His conversation was brisk: "Harry, I had one hell of a time collaring this transcript. It's BLUEBEARD-AURAL on July 16th of convention week in Los Angeles. Hoover has kept it not only in Special File, but Select Entry. Still, I plucked it forth. Pressure points pay off."

"How soon," I asked, "can you get it over to me?"

"Will you be at Zenith four o'clock today?"

"I can be."

"Expect my man at your desk on the dot."

"Yessir."

"Are you mermaid-witting yet?"

"No, sir," I lied, "but on the way."

"If it takes too long, it will accomplish less when you get there."

"Sir?"

"Yes?"

"*Partouse.* It's Parisian slang, isn't it?"

"You'll see soon enough."

At 4:00 P.M., a man I recognized as one of the two baboons who had been in Berlin with Harlot four years ago, came into my office, gave a short nod, handed over an envelope, and left without requesting my signature.

"July 17, 1960. AIRTEL TO DIRECTOR FROM FAC SPOON-OVER, subject SELECT, recorded July 16, 7:32 A.M. to 7:48 A.M. Pacific Time."

MODENE: Willie. Please listen. It just blew up with Jack.

WILLIE: It just blew up? It's nine-thirty in the morning here. So it must be seven-thirty L.A. time. What's happened? Not one phone call all week.

MODENE: What I mean is it blew up last night at three in the morning, and I haven't slept since. I'm waiting to get on a plane. I'm at the airport. I didn't sleep.

WILLIE: What did he do?

MODENE: I can't tell you yet. Please! I've got to be orderly about it.

WILLIE: You really are upset.

MODENE: He put me up at the Beverly Hilton all week and said I was his guest, but I felt awfully tucked away. I never knew if I was going to be alone with room service or he would call me out late at night.

WILLIE: Did you go to the convention?

MODENE: Yes. He had me in a box. Only, I think it was the number-four box. There was the Kennedy family in the first one, and more family and friends in another, and then there was a third where I saw a good many important-looking people in the box next to mine, but my box was odd. Some of Frank's friends were installed there, whereas Frank was in the Kennedy family box. My box was second-rate people, I don't know how to describe them. Boston politicians maybe, gold teeth practically, although not that crass. And one or two women I most certainly did not like the look of. Very expensive hair-jobs, like, "Do not ask who I am. I am the mystery woman."

WILLIE: But you did see him?

MODENE: Of course, nearly every night.

WILLIE: How many nights did he miss?

MODENE: Well, three out of seven. I used to wonder if he was with one of the women in my box.

WILLIE: He must have been feeling equal to dynamite.

MODENE: One night he was so tired I just held him. A wonderful glow came off him. So deeply tired, so happy. One night, he was wonderful. Full of energy. His back, which usually bothers him, was feeling absolutely relaxed. Jack Kennedy is one man who should have the right to go around with a healthy back, because it's just right for him.

WILLIE: He probably had a shot of painkiller. I've heard that rumored.

MODENE: It was a consummate night and I had nothing I wanted to keep in reserve for myself. But then I didn't see him for the next couple of nights. Then, the day they chose Lyndon Johnson for Vice President, Jack was very tired and I just held him, but last night . . . (pause) Willie, I don't want to turn the faucet that opens the waterworks.

WILLIE: If you can't cry around me, you are in double-duty trouble.

MODENE: I am in a public place. At a pay phone. Oh, damn, it's the operator.

OPERATOR: Will you deposit seventy-five cents for the next three minutes?

WILLIE: Transfer the call to my number, Operator. It's Charlevoix, Michigan. C-H-A-R-L-E-V-O-I-X, Michigan, 629-9269.

MODENE: On the last night, the parties went on forever. Toward the end, Jack took a group to a friend's suite at the Beverly Hilton and he whispered to me to stay, so I hovered around the edges, and that is an embarrassing position. I stayed as long as I could in the bathroom fixing my hair, until it was down to a few of his top political workers and himself and me, then I drifted into the bedroom, and he came in and sighed, and said, "At last, they are all gone," and I went into the bathroom again to undress. When I came out, he was in bed, and I couldn't believe it—there was also another woman, one of the ones I had seen in the convention box. She was just about out of her clothes.

WILLIE: My God, is he taking lessons from Frank?

MODENE: I went right back into the bathroom and dressed and by the time I came out, the other woman was gone. I couldn't stop shaking. "How did you ever find the time to manage all this?" I asked. I was awfully close to screaming. I couldn't bear it that he was so calm. He said, "It did take a bit of juggling," and I came very near to slapping him. He must have seen the look in my eye because he said he hadn't done it to offend me, he just thought this part of life was an enhancement. "An enhancement," I said. "Yes," he said, "it's an enhancement for those who can appreciate it." Then he told me that he once loved a French woman very much who delighted in such arrangements, even had a name for it—*la partouse*. P-A-R-T-O-U-S-E. If you were ready for it, there was no harm done, he said, although obviously, as he could see by my reaction, he had certainly made an egregious error.

WILLIE: Egregious!

MODENE: Yes, I said, "Jack, how could you? You have everything," and he said, "It's all over so soon, and we do so little with our lives." Can you believe that? He's such an Irishman. Once they get their mind fixed, you need a pickax to break into the concrete. He started to fondle me, and I said, "Let go, or I am going to scream." And I left him there. I went to my room and drank Jack Daniel's until dawn. I didn't answer the phone.

WILLIE: Oh, Modene.

MODENE: I'm not even drunk now. I am cold sober. There is too much adrenaline in me. He had the gall to have eighteen red roses sent up to my room with a bellhop. Just before I checked out. It had a note: "Please forgive the stupidest thing I've ever done!" Well, I want to tell you, I spent well over a hundred dollars and ordered six dozen yellow roses to be delivered to him right away, and signed, Modene. He'll get the message.

WILLIE: Does he know about Sam's yellow roses?

MODENE: Of course he does. I made a point of telling him. I liked to tease him about that.

WILLIE: It sounds to me like you're cooking up a welcoming party for Sam.

MODENE: No, not Sam! Not now! I have to see what kind of mood I'm in when I get back to Miami.

WILLIE: We're going to have some crazy time if this guy gets elected president.

MODENE: Willie, I'm hanging up. I don't want to start crying.

I had an odd reaction. I asked myself whether I would ever try to bring another woman into bed with Modene, and knew I would not, but that was only for fear of losing her. If she ever brought a woman to our bed, well, that I might like very much. There were times, especially lately, when—St. Matthew's be damned—I thought we were here on earth to feel as many extraordinary sensations as we could; perhaps we were supposed to bring such information back to the great Debriefers in the sky.

Soon enough, however, I began to recognize how much real anger I was holding. It seemed to me it was all Sinatra's fault, and I could understand my father's propensity for terminating life with one's bare hands. What a pity that Sinatra would not come through the door of my cubicle at Zenith at this instant—my rage was in my fingers and as palpable as a ball of clay. I muttered to myself, "Modene, how could you have done this to us?" as if she was as responsible for her past as for her present with me.

Yet, time, soon enough, picked up: We pretended Jack Kennedy did not exist. It was almost a viable proposition. I did not know whether she saw me as a dressing station in the great hospital of love's wounded, and I was the pallet on which she could recover, or whether she loved me magically, which is to say, had been struck by love on the night she returned to Miami, and I was her man. She kept speaking of how good-looking I was until I began to peruse my face in the mirror with the critical self-interest of a speculator going over the daily listing of his stocks each morning.

All the while, I was trapped in work and fearful of the day when the baboon would show up at the desk with new transcripts from Harlot and I would learn that she was seeing Jack Kennedy again.

From *Harlot's Ghost* (1991)

# THE SHADOW
# OF THE CRIME

## A Word from the Author

*In November 1960, I stabbed my wife Adele with a pen-knife. The surgeons, looking to stanch the internal bleeding, made an incision from the sternum to the pelvis that left her permanently scarred.*

*Through the years a shadow of the crime would accompany many hours. I could never write about it. Not all woe is kin to prose. It was one matter to be guilty—by inner measure, irredeemably guilty—it was another to present some literary manifest of what was lost and what was wasted, what was given to remorse and what was finally resistant to remorse. Violence is the child of the iron in one's heart, and decomposes by its own laws.*

*In any event, the marriage was lost. It had been a marriage of love and hate, and they had been at war with each other in close to equal proportions. Such marriages move forward with an intimate conviction that they are doomed. Nonetheless, there still remain in all but the most impossible marriages some hours when hope is present and life becomes luminous. Such hope was now destroyed. The damage to our two daughters would be incalculable—not always evident, but over the years incalculable, quietly incalculable. Guilt fed the shadow of the crime.*

*Remorse was soon impaled on another loss. There are paradoxes to comprehending a writer. It will help to recognize that work can become as important as a love affair or an endangered limb. Let it be noted then that earlier in November 1960, before the stabbing, I had written an open letter to Fidel Castro. It is possible that this letter expressed more emotion than anything I had written until then. Perhaps I had not been without hope that this piece of prose might even have its effect on history. Instead, such exaggerated feelings were as strewn and smashed about as the shattered marriage. It will seem bizarre to some, but in counting the loss to one's wife, oneself, one's daughters, one's family, one's friends, it did not seem disproportionate to mourn the impossibility of sending this letter to Castro.*

*In the months that followed, as one tried to put a few parts of life together, the letter to Castro was reread many times. Months later, it was finally published—after the Bay of Pigs.*

*Now that thirty-seven years have passed, let me conclude this section titled "The Shadow of the Crime" with the message to Castro that was never dispatched in time. It may serve to remind us that an act of violence is not only a deed but the echo and the shadow of all the voices and all the acts that do not take place and now never will. That is why murder and its sibling, assault, are the most wanton of the crimes, for they mangle the possibilities and expectations open to others.*

# An Open Letter to Fidel Castro

Dear Fidel Castro:

I have said nothing in public about you or your country since I signed a statement last year in company with Baldwin, Capote, Sartre, and Tynan that we believe in "Fair Play for Cuba." But now I am old enough to believe that one must be ready to be faithful to one's truth. So, Fidel Castro, I announce to the City of New York that you gave all of us who are alone in this country, and usually not speaking to one another, some sense that there were heroes left in the world. One felt life in one's cold overargued blood as one picked up in our newspapers the details of your voyage.

But I go too fast. Since this is an open letter, and thus meant for the people of New York as much as for you, I suppose I must write first of events with which you are more than familiar.

Back in December 1956, you landed near Niquero in the Oriente of Cuba with 82 men and a few arms. Your plan was to ignite an insurrection which would rid Cuba of Batista in a few weeks. Instead, you were to lose all but 12 of these men in the first few days, you were to wander through fields and forests in the dark, without real food or water, living on sugar-cane for five days and five nights. In the depth of this disaster, you were to announce to the few men still with you: "The days of the dictatorship are numbered."

"This man is crazy," one of them admits he said to himself.

It took you more than 20 days to reach the summit of the Pico Turquino, the high peak in Cuba, high in the Sierra Maestra. You reached it on Christmas Eve. There you stayed for two years. For much of that time you were no more than a symbol.

Through Cuba passed the word that 12 men lived on a mountain top, 12 men who had sworn to destroy the tyranny. It was incredible. What that token of resistance came to signify! Day after day, month by month, grew a spirit of rebellion in Cuba.

As the underground developed, so developed Batista's methods of torture, his excesses, his murders, his unrecountable atrocities, at last so open and so foul that he ended by alienating some of the wealthy, the well-born, the best of his own support.

For those two years your army discovered itself; your skill as a military leader developed art, your diplomatic talents untied the complexities of an underground choking with factions and old feuds.

You survived skirmishes, negotiations, and battles; you suffered a major defeat, and recovered quickly enough to hold off 14 battalions of Batista's army with no more than 300 of your own men, you came at last out of the hills to defeat an army of 30,000 professional soldiers. Two years and a month after the disaster of your landing, you were able to enter Havana in triumph.

It was not unheroic. Truth, it was worthy of Cortes.

It was as if the ghost of Cortes had appeared in our century riding Zapata's white horse. You were the first and greatest hero to appear in the world since the Second War.

Better than that, you had a face. One had friends with faces like yours. In silence, many of us gave you our support. In silence. We did not have an organization to address you, we talked very little about you, we said: "Castro, good guy," and let it go, but all the while you were giving us the idea that everything was not hopeless. There has been a new spirit in America since you entered Havana. I think you must be given credit for some part of a new and better mood which has been coming to America.

Now, you did not feel friendly to my country when you had won your war. There was the bitter memory of our Ambassadors, Mr. Gardner and Mr. Smith, and the photographs they took all too often with Batista and his friends; there was the recollection of the American rockets which had been sold to the Cuban government at a time when Batista's Air Force was burning the huts of peasants in your hills; there were the headlines in Cuban newspapers—DULLES TOASTS BATISTA—which appeared the day before Batista held his last false election. You must have wondered why Dulles had chosen that particular day to visit Ambassador Arroyo at the Cuban Embassy in Washington. You may even have wondered why our newspapers chose to print so many of Batista's stories that you were Communist.

Still the situation was not very bad. Much of our press gave you good treatment here, and some of our largest newspapers and magazines welcomed your victory. A general wave of congratulation passed through our mass-media. For a few days, you were popular in America.

Then you had your public executions. I suppose tragedy cannot exist without irony. If Batista's people had just been shot, all 500 of them, shot in their homes, their bars, the automobiles in which they were fleeing, our newspapers would have complained a bit, but it would have been attributed to the excesses of a victorious army, a retaliation in kind upon Batista's assassins.

You, however, were interested in justice, in proclamation, in propaganda—you were saying to the people of Cuba: "I am not a bandit like the ones who come before me, I am the leader of a revolution—I execute the torturers of the past before the eyes of the present."

Our newspapers erupted against you. They used the executions to condemn everything in your regime. One would have thought you were almost a successor to Adolf Hitler the way they excoriated you because 500 Batistas were condemned to death in trials of public spectacle, 500 cut-throats who had maimed the heads, crushed the hearts, and disfigured the genitalia of your men and your women. The worst of our newspapers screamed with rage and terror. As if you were killing them.

*And you were. Like Bolivar, you were sending the wind of new rebellion to our lungs. You were making it possible for us to breathe again. You were aiding our war.*

*But then, I do not know if you can understand our war here.*

*In Cuba, hatred runs over into the love of blood; in America all too few blows are struck into flesh. We kill the spirit here, we are experts at that. We use psychic bullets and kill each other cell by cell.*

*We live in a country very different from Cuba. We have had a tyranny here, but it did not have the features of Batista; it was a tyranny one breathed but could not define; it was felt as no more than a slow deadening of the best of our possibilities, a tension we could not name which was the sum of our frustrations. We all knew that the best of us used up our memories in long nights of drinking, exhausted our vision in secret journeys of the mind; our more stable men and women of some little good will watched the years go by—their idealism sank into apathy. By law we had a free press; almost no one spoke his thoughts. By custom we had a free ballot; was there ever a choice? We were a league of silent defeated men who could not even assent on which were the true battles we lost. In silence we gave you our support. You were aiding us, you were giving us psychic ammunition, you were aiding us in that desperate silent struggle we have been fighting with sick dead hearts against the cold insidious cancer of the power that governs us, you were giving us new blood to fight our mass communications, our police, our secret police, our corporations, our empty politicians, our clergymen, our editors, our cold frightened bewildered bullies who govern a machine made out of people they no longer understand, you were giving us hope they would not always win.*

That is why America persecuted you. That is why our newspapers made their subtle distortions, lied about your accomplishments, put dirt on your name, wrote in a prose of cheap glow that you were sick and would certainly die in a few months, and were even more furious when somehow you did not die, and no power agreeable to America arose in Cuba to steal your power. That is why they mocked your speech at the U.N.

They had reported you were very ill: It did not vouch well for their reliability that now you spoke for four and a half hours. How can anyone talk that long, they say now and giggle nervously. He must be a compulsive, they say. They do not admit to themselves that no one here in this country dares to talk for more than four and a half minutes they are so afraid they will give themselves away.

Now, at the moment, revolted by the cheap muck of the most cess-filled brains in our land, disheartened by the impossibility of receiving a fair report from us, you are obviously getting ready to commit your political fortune to Khrushchev. I do not know the complexities of the situation. Maybe no one does. We hear everything here. We hear that you are committed completely to the Russians, we hear that you are still your own man. The combinations offered are endless. What worries us is that the facts are too many to be able to know what one reads.

I would guess you were not ever a Communist, that you are not now—you have always had too much of a private vision to be Communist—I would speculate of you, sir, that you came to power ready to make a revolution which could give more of what is noble to the people. You were simply bewildered when the American press turned on you. Then it was I would guess that you began to give the Communists your ear. What an argument they had now. "Look," they must have said, "why believe America's lies about the Communists, why believe them when you see how they lie about you?"

Well, we lie about the Communists. They lie as well. We deaden the life of millions by hypocrisy and go on to claim we are the hope of civilization; they liquidate the life of millions and argue they are the imagination of the future.

Of course it may not be agreeable to listen to this now. You have a new friend. He was good to you at a time when my country promulgated its disgrace. You are Latin. Your honor is to be loyal. Still, I must say that as one of your sympathizers I do not trust your new friend. He is a wise peasant bully. Yet an intellectual should not forget that he came to power because of one exceptional ability: He was able to live as a flea in the stumpy tail of a wild old bear named Josef Stalin; this old bear was notorious for eating his tail. At the end Khrushchev was the only flea left who had strength. Perhaps he was the flea closest to the root. Since then he had grown big as a man.

Of course you may not like these words about Khrushchev. At a time when our large newspapers were writing like small-town gossips about the condition in which you left your rooms in one of our New York hotels (what do the same rooms look like after a convention of American salesmen have left, you must have wondered), at a time when you could not make a move in our city without being able to read the next day in the newspapers about it as an act sinister or foolish. Khrushchev had the genius to kiss you on the cheek for our photographers, and so restore your honor.

He has good manners, that man—I suppose a part of you will like him forever because of his embrace that day. But revolutionaries are different from Commissars, and a kiss from one is not the same as a kiss from the other. Khrushchev kissed many before you, and he has signed the papers which removed them forever. He is a Commissar— they like to kiss. But Commissars never made a revolution.

So Khrushchev will never be able to understand that you are serious. He will think he is a realist, and you are an actor. Realists endure, goes the logic of Khrushchev, actors can be replaced. Khrushchev will never understand that when no personal authority exists in a leader, a country sinks into the authority of public relations—it has a vacuum at its center. Khrushchev will never understand that Cuba does not have its strength because the Communists give you arms but because so many of the people still believe in you, they cry out for you to cover yourself when you speak in the rain.

Look! Plain words. I hear from the source of a source that the situation is bad in your country now. I hear Communists control Cuba and shut you into the psychic prison of their encirclement, I hear they manipulate you to say the things which will most irritate our press into striking back in the way which will most irritate you. By every step of this logic you distrust your new friends less, hate America more, and thus begin to prepare yourself for a war you may even begin to desire as a sedative to personal madness, so great is your rage at the monuments of *mierda* laid upon the cross of your expedition down from the peak into the city, so great is your anguish at the filth you must breathe to keep alive the simple idea of the mountain air: One must free the people and give them life. This is what I hear. I do not want to believe it, but I can no longer ignore what I hear, because my private sources are people still sympathetic to Cuba and to you. They go on to declare that the Communists want America to attack. Their hope—so goes the argument of my source—is that America will be incited by you to invade Cuba, create a new Korea, and alienate the people of Latin and South America forever. As a Communist strategy it is excellent. Of course Cuba will lose another 58 years. But the Communists are used to considering small nations expendable—it is part of their pride that they will sacrifice their followers.

It is not so difficult for them. In the other country they do not kill people—they liquidate. Certain people become fascinating, they are too rich in their private time—the State does not care to afford them. They disappear. Friends do not even know if they are dead—one cannot hold a funeral in their memory. One knows just that it is better not to talk about the missing friend. A new shame chases the other. Remembrance of the past turns to fog.

Fidel, is this what you wish for Cuba, for your Cuba which is so alive? I cannot believe it. Your people went through a little too much. They are not statistics. You cannot want them to talk like machines of the state in the new Cuba. You cannot. You must play for power, not commit yourself to it. So do not give up on my country too quickly.

I know it is a bad place, I know well how bad it is, I know millions will be squeezed out of existence here in the center of prosperity, stricken by the deadness of a life which can find no love. Yet one thing will be said for my country. They allow me to speak my mind in a way I never could in the other country. You who are a poet will know this is a freedom some of us do not want to live without.

Besides, in my country, it is possible the people are better than their government: They could come to understand you if you would think of how to speak to us.

I do not expect the way is to listen to your present advisers. You would do better to hire a public-relations man from our Madison Ave. They are corrupt, our men of Madison, so corrupt they will work as well for you as for the corporation. Fact, they will work better. By now, they hate our country more than you could, they know it better.

Bad humor. Forgive it. I have a proposal. Address an open letter in your name to Ernest Hemingway. Many would say—I am one of them—that he has been our greatest writer. It is certain he created my generation—he told us to be brave in a bad world and to be ready to die alone.

Actually he is afraid of our country. He is a very brave old man, I believe, but he does not have a cancer-detector, so he stays away from us, from our smog-ridden, atom-haunted city. He prefers Cuba, as doubtless you know. He has lived there off and on for 20 years. He no longer writes to us. Maybe a letter once in a while. We do not talk about him any longer. Some of us are bitter about him. We feel he has deserted us and produced no work good enough to justify his silence.

There are many of us who will curse his memory if he dies in silence.

So do the old man a favor. Send him an invitation to come back to Cuba, at his own expense or at yours. He may not want to come. He has his work to do, he has a big book on which he has been working for 15 years. If this work is going well it would be an excessive sacrifice for him to interrupt it. But, then, he may not mind an interruption. In the past 15 years he has interrupted his work many times to write about other things. He may come to see that it would not be so very bad to write about you. If he agrees, it is your duty to those of us who care about your fate to let him tell the world whether he likes what is happening with you or not.

Show the world that you will let a Nobel Prize writer who speaks the language of the country travel anywhere in your territory, unmolested, unobstructed, unindoctrinated. Let him come, let him get to know you if he wishes, hope that he will write something about Cuba, a paragraph, a line, a poem, a statement—whatever he says cannot be ignored in my country. The world will read what Hemingway has to say, the world will read it critically, because he will be making a history, he may even be preparing a ground on which you and our new President can meet.

Whether our new President is a good man, I do not know. I had no sense of his moral being the two brief times I talked to him. One had the impression he is a brave man and a complicated man, and he has intelligence. But I thought he had a taint I could not name. It is not an interesting taint, evil, decadent, or extraordinary, it was more a sense that he was dead and dull in little places where some of us are still alive. It is possible he does not understand or is lacking some of the necessary and vital emotions of most people. The question is whether he has a mind deep enough to comprehend the size of the disaster he has inherited here.

If America had a mind and one could stare into it, the landscape of our psyche might be bleak, gutted, scorched by 15 years of mindless government, all nerves withered by the management of men who were moral poltroons. Many of us have hope that Kennedy will help our national mind to see again, but of course one does not know. One does not want to hope too soon. I think Kennedy's statements on Cuba during the election campaign were ugly. They took away the enthusiasm one felt in voting for him. Still, one voted. It was the first time one voted in 12 years. It seemed self-evident he was superior to the other. You could not talk to the other. I think you could talk to our new President, I think he might come to recognize that if a man of Hemingway's age was willing to give up some important moment of his time to write new words about your country, that the culture of the world—that culture existing in every cultivated mind—would be judging Kennedy if he did not respond or react to Hemingway's view (whatever it might be) of your country. And Kennedy wishes to be considered a great man in the cultivated verdicts of history.

So respond to this letter, Fidel. There is value in it for you. If we get no word, it will come to mean that you care no longer about those who want to believe in you, it will come to mean that you have lost interest in all but your hatred of America. So you will then give strength to our enemies here; they will delight in your silence and your hatred.

But I do not know that you will give them such pleasure. You may still believe in that larger part of the world which endures in the possibility that neither the United States nor Russia will triumph, that there is a third way, that futures are not built nor civilizations kept alive by super-states but that it is rather people who make history, people more brave, more talented, or more generous than there was any reason to be. You belong not to the United States nor to the Russians but to We of the Third Force. So long as you exist and belong neither to America nor to Russia, you give a bit of life to the best and most passionate men and women all over the earth, you are the answer to the argument of Commissars and Statesmen that revolutions cannot last, that they turn corrupt or total or eat their own. You are the one who can show the world that a revolutionary belongs to no one, that his actions cannot be predicted because he is possessed by a vision: He knows the world must grow better at a breathless rate or there will be no mankind. Just super-states, endless machines, and empty men who flee the night in all terror of eternity.

Still your brother,
Norman Mailer

From *The Presidential Papers* (1963)

# CUBA

## December 1960    Washington—I

### PREPARING FOR THE BAY OF PIGS

Friday, the Thirteenth

Dear Harry,

That was one good night, last night. Allen had the wit—God, I love that man when he's at his best—to invite all the new Kennedy muckamucks to an evening with a number of us at the Alibi Club. He wanted to put the top new Washington folk into a more gung-ho frame of mind for the Cuban op, and I believe we brought it off. I must say, the Alibi Club was the perfect place for this, just as fusty inside as, let's say, the Somerset Club in Boston. The old menus on the wall set the note, "Turtle Soup, 25 cents," and the martinis are good. It relaxed the young new Kennedy breed, and a few of them are pretty young, I must tell you, and awfully bright, and fitted up with an all-around alert system as to where the next cue is coming from. Bright young top-of-the-Law-Review gents, but instinctive as well. On the other hand, they are certainly in way over their heads. With all due respect to your mother's ancient blood, they do remind me a bit of Phi Beta Kappas (Jewish) at a coming-out party. There was also a contingent of Kennedy's Irish Mafia, just as suspicious as FBI monks, and tough, flinty, ready to strong-arm an issue. However, they are also just ignorant enough to be in over their heads. So the get-together was a good idea. Bissell made a hell of a speech in his gold-plated archbishop's style. Presented himself as paleface of all the palefaces. Took one of his long fingers, poked himself in the chest, and said, "Take a good look at me. I'm the man who eats the sharks in this outfit." That had its impact. A distinguished churchman was talking dirty. It was our way of saying, "Just give us an assignment, brothers, and we will ram it home. We are not afraid of responsibility. We take on high risk. If you want to move mountains, call on us." You could see all the Kennedy people imbibing Bissell's qualifications, Groton, Yale, Ph.D. in economics, and ready to eat sharks. Why, he's even taught at MIT.

I must say, we did feed them good stories. How to steal a country with three hundred men *à la* Guatemala. Cloak-and-dagger has to be the second-oldest profession, Allen told them. And in the course of it, lots of first-rate toasts were exchanged. Then Allen called on me. Damn, the glint in his spectacles was adjuring me in no uncertain terms to recount my now hoary exploits with the secretaries. Back in 1947, in case you never heard, I captured scads of poop on what Truman's Cabinet people were planning because I got to know (in the Biblical sense) a few of the top office girls. Last night, I rounded it off by saying, "Of course, we don't do these things anymore." The Kennedy people loved it. I think the note Allen wished to strike was that we were absolutely the right organization for a roistering jack-in-the-sack like our own President-Elect.

I wasn't going to let myself, however, get stuck in the Department of Legends as one more over-the-hill stunt man, so I went off on a reasonably witty presentation to the effect that we can look forward, White House and CIA, to great times together since we possess in common a liking for the work of Ian Fleming. Let's give a toast to good old Ian Fleming, I said, holding the flagon high. Someone actually did mutter, "His work is such crap!"—I can hear you speaking in that young voice—but I came back with, "Ian Fleming, a stylist for our time." And a few of us on the Agency side, which I suppose comes down to Dulles, Bissell, Montague, Barnes, Helms, and myself, were thinking of those rather Ian Fleming–like toys that have come out of Technical Services, such as the depilatory to take off Fidelito's beard back in 1959 when he visited the UN. At an effectiveness level, it was all pure Dartmouth yahoo crap, but a few of us in the room knew that I was pretending to more, so it was permissible to laugh like hell. We got the idea across. They now understood that we were monkeys with as many tricks in our cage as they had in theirs. We communicated the notion that if you want a quick answer to a knotty problem, CIA is the place to go. Not, repeat, *not* the State Department.

Dean Rusk got a longer and longer face as the evening wore on. I think he was the first to sense what a splendid theatrical grasp Allen has on how-to-make-new-friends in transitional times. Rusk looks constipated. Probably loses half an hour every morning on the evacuation detail.

In any case, I am now on the move again. At least within. Which is what morale is all about.

Your good father,
Big-Bucks Halifax

From *Harlot's Ghost* (1991)

# March 1961         Washington—II

### UNTIL JUST BEFORE THE BAY OF PIGS

Dear Harry,

Last November, not long after the elections—which is, my Lord, almost five months ago—my old friend Polly Galen Smith was at the doorstep. Did I write to you once about her? Polly, as I believe I've told you, has been deliciously unfaithful to Wallace Rideout Smith, her good husband, for years—not in quantity, but she does take abyss-jumper risks. I think it's just as simple as that she enjoys men the way all of you men are supposed to enjoy us.

At any rate, Polly and I get along famously because we are so different. She came to me again about a month before the presidential inauguration to ask "one hell of a favor." Would I let her use the Stable for an hour early Wednesday afternoon while Hugh was away working and I might be shopping? She had a friend who lived two blocks to one side of me in Georgetown, and there was Polly three blocks on the other side. Her friend was the busiest man in Christendom right now, but they had "absolute grabs" for each other. Well, who was he? State secret, she answered. Impossible, I said, there's Christopher to think of, and the maid. Not so, she said. Christopher is still in nursery school at 2:00 P.M., and the maid has Wednesdays off. She had *cased* my situation.

I won't say yes until you let me in on who the man might be, I told her.

Can't be done, she said. In that event, I responded, you and your buddy-buddy will just have to find a motel.

Oh, God, no, Kittredge. Well, why not? Too prominent, the man is too prominent, she kept saying. At last I dragged forth the name. Her beau was none other than her old senatorial pal of two years ago, now our presidential jock-elect, Jack Kennedy. The reason they needed a place just so convenient as mine involved the concerns of the Secret Service. Told in advance, they will remain a discreet half block away. Moreover, Jack can duck out of his house on N Street between meetings, then slip back without raising a stir about sizable gaps in his schedule.

I had one instant of revelation—snobbery, property, propinquity, and good old *droit de seigneur* revealed their trusslike interrelations in me. Harry, I had to say yes. I wanted the President-Elect of the United States infusing my rooms with his carnal presence. I think I became aware at that moment what a slut I could have been with another kind of upbringing.

How I envied Polly. Envy is mean! I found myself insisting on a particular payment. I wasn't going to have Jack Kennedy investing my linens with his spoor when I hadn't even met the man.

Polly protested as if I'd broken a bottle of stink, but she had to give in. So commenced their Wednesdays. They were going to love Wednesdays at the Stable, she said, even if the whole thing was going to take up no more than thirty minutes—an item I was to discover when we arranged how the encounter would take place. I was to pretend to come home unexpectedly, but *on the minute.* "If you're two minutes late, he'll be gone, and if you're five minutes early, you will walk in on the finishing touches." Polly, you can see, is to the point, and that, I comprehended, is exactly why they got together in the first place. I have not met a man who is more to the point than Jack Kennedy, unless it is his brother Bobby. (Of course, their father, I hear, leaves them both in his wake.)

At any rate, I saw him. Even as I turned my key and came through the door to my own parlor, my heart fluttered twice—once for history and once for the person. He is awfully attractive and I think it is because he is not out of measure. I was talking to a man to whom I felt equal, which I must say is bottomlessly agreeable. And he's so direct and sure of himself that it comes off as a natural quality rather than arrogance. He is nice. And so amoral. And so unflappable. Polly was trying to keep from guffawing, which was forgivable—two of her best friends, after all, were meeting, and he—whether or not she had told him—seemed not at all surprised by my supposedly unexpected entrance. (Perhaps she did tell him in advance and he had worked it out with the Secret Service. Indeed, on reflection, they had to have done just that.)

"Do you know," he said for greeting, "you and my wife have a slight resemblance to each other. It's uncanny."

I thought of Jacqueline Kennedy's father, Black Jack Bouvier. Then I had to compare him to my father and I said, "Oh, dear, next to your wife I'm dry-as-dust," and felt shabby suddenly, a most unexpected feeling for me, but it is all genes, isn't it? Folio dust was coming out of my pores by way of my father's pores. Or so I felt! "Dry as dust," I repeated when he just kept smiling, considerably more comfortable in my parlor than I was.

"Oh," he said, "we will see about that," and offered a glint of a very good smile.

"Ho, ho, curfew," said Polly Smith, and Jack gave a small salute and was out the door, leaving Polly behind. "Till next Wednesday," he said.

Polly stayed for tea, and I began to feel disloyal to Hugh. I was so avid to hear about Jack.

By the time Hugh came home, I was in a confessional mode. I said nothing before we went to sleep, and nothing again on the next night, but I was beginning to feel those unruly intimations of dread that I call "the dark wobbles." I knew I had to tell Hugh. He couldn't have taken it worse. "I feel sullied by it," he said. Then he said, and you don't know how much this is out of character for him, "I couldn't feel worse if that fellow Jack Kennedy had buggered me!" Can you conceive of Hugh speaking like that?

"It was Polly, not I," I said to him, "who was in the receiving position."

"That will be the last time she receives in our house," he answered.

"No," I said. "I can't do that to her."

"It pollutes everything here, including the child. Can you make no distinction between the relatively sacred and the wholly profane?"

Well, I was going to strike my colors. He was right, after all, and I knew it; I have also learned, however, that Hugh has no respect for you if he wins too quickly, so I thought I'd hold out till the Tuesday before the next Wednesday and let him think he'd won a major match by the time I struck my flag.

Talk of presidential timing. I'm beginning to see how Jack got where he is. I did not say a word to Polly but on Monday an invitation was delivered by hand. Could Mr. and Mrs. Montague come to dinner on N Street Tuesday night?

I must say that Hugh went through a major stomach upset. I have never known him to throw up in such manner before. And I realized what it was about. He was dying to go to N Street. He wanted to be familiar with Jack Kennedy, oh, how he wanted that. If for nothing else, then for the Agency. But be damned if he was going to have his home tom-catted up. Yet, if Polly were cut off before Wednesday, wouldn't dinner be rescinded for Tuesday? Of course, we could go and then cut the lovers off. No! You didn't do things like that to the President-Elect!

All this is speculation, mind you. Hugh was vomiting so audibly that I would have held his head if I dared, but then he emerged from the loo long enough to say, "It's clear to me. You call Polly now, or I will."

I had to love him even if I couldn't bear the thought of giving up dinner with Jack, but who can deny characterological integrity when it is on that scale? I called Polly. I was able to say no more than, "Hugh's on to the game."

"Oops," she said, "are sirens ringing?"

"No. But cancel your venue for Wednesdays."

Do you know, the dinner invitation was not rescinded, and Hugh, to my surprise, had a hell of a time, and I got along with Jackie Kennedy satisfactorily. Under all that false innocence, she's awfully sensitive to what's wrong in people and she knew there was something just a little off in me vis-à-vis her husband. Still, we got on. She knows a good bit about eighteenth-century Piedmont and Charleston cabinetwork, and had a special little slave tale to tell. It seems one of the greatest furniture makers in Charleston—Charles Egmont—was a former slave whose liberty was given to him by his owner, Charles Cawdill, who set black Charles up in his own shop and they split the profits. She tells such tales with great intimacy, as if with some maidenly pain she is offering you one of her jewels. But, oh, Harry, that's a complex and troubled woman!

Meanwhile, Hugh and Jack were certainly getting along. At one point, Jack confessed to Hugh that it was a pleasure to meet "the mythological Montague." "Mythological?" says Hugh, his mouth all twisted up as if he's being asked to kiss a turkey's tucker.

"Let's say the apocryphal Montague," says Jack.

"I'm only a minor factotum in the Department of Agriculture."

"Come off it. I've heard about you for years."

Well, I could see them cooking up some special understanding. Hugh was brilliant once he got going on Soviet skills at disinformation. To my horror, he started to give the President-Elect and his wife a lecture—to my large pride, he brought it off.

Now, since the inauguration, we get invited back from time to time to the White House. For the more intimate White House dinners, mind you. At the last soirée, Jack chose, while dancing with me, to ask about Polly.

"She pines for you," I said.

"Tell her I'll call one of these days. It's not out of my mind."

"You are awful," I said.

He got that glint in his eye. "Do you know, for a beautiful woman, your dancing is a hint stiff."

I wanted to cream him with my evening bag. Alas, I didn't dare. He's not that splendid a dancer himself, but oh so schooled. Like a rider with a cultivated seat who doesn't really take to horses.

All the same, we get along. I think he's wary enough of Hugh not to entertain notions about me, but we do have the next best thing—promise.

Love, love, love
Kittredge

From *Harlot's Ghost* (1991)

## April 1961          Miami—I

### THE DAY AFTER THE BAY OF PIGS

Allen Dulles came back from Puerto Rico early Thursday morning with a terrible case of gout. To my father, who had gone out to meet him at Andrews Air Force Base, he said, "This is the worst day of my life."

On that same morning, three exiled leaders were flying back from Washington to their families in Miami and I was on board to expedite any problems they might encounter. While it had been deemed discourteous to send our Cubans back alone, none of my superiors wanted the job, so I volunteered one minute before it would have been assigned to me.

It proved a quiet voyage. As heavy as pallbearers, we sat in our Air Force seats, and, on arrival, so soon as I had arranged for transportation, we shook hands gravely to say farewell. It was obvious they had seen enough of the Agency.

Since I was done with this task before noon and could take another Air Force plane back to Washington in the evening, I decided to drive downtown, park the car, and walk about in the April warmth. Crossing NE 2nd Street, I felt an impulse to enter Gesu Catholic Church, a noble armory all of 180 feet wide and not much less than three hundred feet in length, a Miami edifice to be certain, offering pink and green walls and golden-yellow chapels. I had gone there several times over the last ten months to service a dead drop in one of the missal books in the fifth pew of the thirty-second row off the southern aisle.

So, yes, I knew Gesu Catholic Church on NE 2nd Street. I had also dropped in there on my own after bouts of love with Modene, and I do not know why, but the church was balm, I found, for sexual depletions of the spirit. I even used to wonder, if in no serious way (since I understood that I was not the least bit inclined), whether one more High Episcopalian might not be tempted just a little to become a Catholic. As an expression of that random impulse, I had even on one occasion asked Modene to meet me in the back of Gesu at the votive candles, a choice that I suspect irritated her. She had not been inside a Catholic church for over a year, and then it had been for another stewardess's wedding.

Today Gesu was not empty. The last Mass had taken place well over an hour ago, and the next was not due till five in the afternoon, yet the pews were partially filled, and everywhere were women praying. I did not want to look at their faces, since many of them were weeping as well. My ears, keened to the private silence I could always hear within the larger solemnity of a church, became aware at last, in the slow befuddled manner of a drunk who has wandered right up to the edge of the sea, that today there was no silence. Lamentations never ceased. Into them poured, as from many smaller vessels, murmurings of sorrow from the throats of separate men and women, mothers and fathers, brothers and sisters of the lost Brigade, and the dimensions of the loss came over me then with such power that for this one rare time in my life, I had a vision of the suffering of Christ and thought, yes, such suffering was real, and this is how the mourners must have felt as they waited in the shadow of the cross and heard His agony, and feared that some tenderness of spirit was vanishing from the world forever.

That much I felt, and knew the vision was a self-deception. Under my pain was rage. I did not feel tender or loving, but full of the most terrible anger at I knew not what—was it the President, his advisers, the Agency itself? I had the rage of a man who has just lost his arm to the gears of a machine and does not know whether to blame the engine or the finger in some upstairs office which flicked the switch to turn it all on. So I sat alone in church, a stranger to my own lamentations, and knew that the end of the Bay of Pigs would never end for me since I had no real grief to build a tomb for my lost hopes. I was condemned instead to the black, obsessive rings of one oppressive question: Whose fault was it?

At that moment I saw Modene on the other side of the church. She was sitting by herself at the end of a pew with a black lace handkerchief on her head, and she had knelt in prayer.

I saw it as a sign. A sense of happiness as quick as the light on a blade of grass when the wind turns it to the sun came to me, and I stood up and walked to the back of the church and over to her aisle and up to her pew and sat down beside her. When she turned around, I knew that I would see the same light come into her green eyes that I had seen in the long thin palm of the grass blade, and she would whisper, "Oh, Harry."

When the woman turned, however, to look at me, it was not Modene. I was staring at a young Cuban woman who styled her hair in the same manner—that was all.

I had not permitted myself to steal near to any feeling of what I had lost, but now it was there. I had lost Modene. "*Discúlpame,*" I blurted out, and stood up and left the church, only to stop at the first pay phone and call the Fontainebleau. The desk clerk did not react to her name, but merely rang her room. When she answered, I discovered that my voice was near to mutinous. The words almost did not come out.

"God, I love you," I said.

"Oh, Harry."

"Can I come over?"

"All right," she said, "maybe you had better come over."

Her room, when I arrived, proved small enough to suggest she was certainly paying for it herself, and we made love on the carpet on the other side of the door, and from there made our way to bed, and I may have been as happy making love as I had ever been, for when we were done and holding one another, I heard myself say, "Will you marry me?"

It was an amazing remark. I had had no intention of making it, and thought it was desperately wrong so soon as I said it, for she would hate the life of an Agency wife, and, good Lord, she could not even cook, and I had no money unless I broke into the safe of my tightly closed principal and accruing interest—yes, all practical considerations came rushing into my thoughts like travelers arriving too late to catch the train—and were swept away in the big steam and blast of the departure—yes, I wanted to marry her, we would find a way to live together, we were extraordinarily different and wildly connected, we were the very species of cohabitation out of which geniuses are born, and I said again, "Modene, marry me. We'll be happy. I promise you."

To my surprise, she did not throw her arms around me and burst into celebratory tears, but broke out weeping instead with sorrow that came out of so deep a place in herself that she could have been the vehicle for all the grief collected in Gesu Catholic Church on NE 2nd Street.

"Oh, darling," she said, "I can't," and left me waiting for her next words long enough to recognize the true horror that sits like a phantom at the root of every lover's wings. It was coming in on me that the higher I had flown, the more I had been traveling alone, so high on my long-hoarded love that the profound sweet calm in which she received me could have been—now, and much too late, I knew—the whole numb body of grief itself.

"Oh, Harry," she said, "I tried. I wanted to get near to you again, but I can't. I just feel so sorry for Jack."

From *Harlot's Ghost* (1991)

## Summer 1961     Washington—III

### KEEPING UP WITH MODENE

*From a letter to Harry Hubbard from Kittredge Gardiner Montague:*
    . . . I don't want to exaggerate. Relationships, however, do deepen. Between Jack, that is, and myself. Jacqueline Kennedy and I are on a plateau—awfully equal stuff passes back and forth between us, and I respect her because she does not wield rank over me any more than is implicit in the rich-mouse country-mouse syndrome, but, then, that is the price you pay for such entrée. Meanwhile, Hugh

and Jack are off in a corner. You know Hugh—at his best when one on one. And Jack, no matter how furious over the Bay of Pigs, is fascinated with cloak-and-dagger and smart enough to know that Hugh is the *saucier* in that kitchen. And, of course, as laid out above, Jack is chummy with me.

I never realized how much this was disconcerting Hugh until one day this summer, toward the end of July, he suddenly put the BLUE-BEARD dossier in front of me. "Here's another side to one of your friends," he said. I think he expected me to be put off by the contents, but I wasn't; I know Jack's nature: Promiscuity is the price he pays to open the gates to his other skills. Jack Kennedy is like a child that way. Must have his daily reward, and it's in the forbidden jam. Good for him, I say, so long as I'm not part of the private preserve. If he can do a little more good than harm, God will doubtless forgive him for all the girls whose hearts he jiggled and juggled. I'm sure he sees it that way.

Well, I have not only digested your reports, but some later BLUEBEARD transcripts you have not even seen, not yet, and I'm worried, as is Hugh. He's been doing his subtle best to get our young President to recognize what an incubus is J. Edgar Buddha on any administration, especially this one, but in the interim, I don't believe Jack comprehends how many pressure points are being handed over. Hoover could end with a total choke on the Kennedy windpipe. Modene is so fabulously indiscreet. I am not going, as you did, to memorialize her meanderings with her friend Willie, which I find misleading since, under the guise of telling nothing, she tells her friend (and J. Edgar) all, even if it takes too long to find out! I am going to summarize what I have learned and save you some time.

In brief, Modene suffered the lacerations of the abandoned during Jack and Jacqueline's visit to Paris at the end of May. Do you recollect? Our First Lady was a sensational success in Paris. Jack even said, "My real mission in Paris is to escort Jacqueline Kennedy." God, how all that must have been etched into your poor girl's brain. And, of course, our ogrish Sam G. couldn't resist twitting her on the raw nerve. "Are you jealous, Modene?" he kept asking. "Not at all," she kept replying. In recounting it to her stalwart Willie (whom, I must say, I picture as post-deb, blond, and seriously overweight—did you ever obtain a description?) Modene does, however, burst into tears. It comes out that earlier in May, before the trip to Paris, Jack had Modene in bed at the White House. Can you imagine? After a surprisingly dreadful lunch of cold soup and ketchup on the hamburgers—Irish!—Jack took Modene from the family dining room on the second floor to a bedroom, same floor, with a commodious bed. There, they consummated their reunion. She is madly in love again. Or so she will tell Willie that night.

This transcript does happen to be worth offering for flavor.

WILLIE: Wait a minute. The guards just allowed you to walk into the White House?

MODENE: Of course not. I had to go through the gate, and then there was a short, well-built little man named Dave Powers who came down to meet me. He had a twinkle in his eye, permanently, I think. Looked like a troll. The President, he said, was having a swim and would be by soon. Dave Powers kept saying, *"the President"* with a high hush in his voice as if asking you to kneel in church. Of course, he left as soon as Jack came in to lunch. By then Dave Powers had gotten it across to me that he's the fellow who wakes Jack up every morning and tucks him in at night. He certainly makes you feel you are in the White House.

WILLIE: It's not a very sexy place, is it?

MODENE: I would say it is like the inside of a Quaker church, only heavier. Sacred trust sort of feeling. I never wanted a bourbon so much. It was early Saturday afternoon, the place was deserted, and I kept having the feeling I would never get to see Jack. After Powers took me upstairs to the family quarters, though, it was less uncomfortable—I was familiar with all that N Street furniture they had moved over to the second floor.

After lunch, they journey to the bedroom. Following the preliminaries, Jack receives her on his back. Which French king was it who used to greet his mistresses in that manner? Louis XIV, perhaps, given that pampered look. In any event, as Modene explains it, Jack's "lumbar condition" has grown worse. "Cares of office." She is happy to serve the master, but a nugget of discontent remains. "I don't mind which position is chosen. Different positions bring out different sides of me. Only I prefer to get to them on my own."

Mind you, all this while, through a window near the double bed, she can see the Washington Monument.

Dear man, I have to wonder what your reactions must have been while reading the earlier transcripts. I hope I understand you well enough to assume that such perusal spurred you on to greater heights with Modene—or was it faster flats? We do want to shine in the eyes of the Immortal Race Steward.

Oh, Harry, is all this due to the teasing I was never able to give to that younger brother I never had?

I return to the essential. Despite Jackie's triumphs in Paris, Jack does get in touch with Modene again early in June, and all through the summer, on fearfully hot, deserted, dog-day Saturday afternoons in Washington, he keeps bringing her to the same double bed. They used to say of Joe Kennedy that the longer you were in a business deal with the man, the more he took from it, and the less you brought home. Something of that lament creeps into her conversations with Willie. All the same, she finds justifications for Jack. "He is so tired. He does have many concerns to deal with."

It is a most peculiar period for our BLUEBEARD. She is based now in Los Angeles. She is actually sharing an apartment in Brentwood with four other stewardesses. Hardly the Modene you knew! From this base, however, she keeps waiting for the next summons to Washington. Meanwhile the Brentwood apartment is a focus for parties. Actors, marriageable young corporate types, a couple of professional athletes, one or two fringe film executives, and a prodigious amount of drinking. I'm not familiar with evenings of this variety, but gather there's a great deal of dancing and a fair amount of marijuana. Then she's always ready to fly to Chicago or Miami to spend a weekend with that awful Giancana. RAPUNZEL, indeed! Yet—her steadfast claim—there is "no sexual link." I won't bore you with Willie's doubts about this.

What speaks loudly is dissipation. Modene keeps gaining weight, and is drinking so much that she actually goes "as a tourist" to an AA meeting, but is "appalled by the gloom." She is also taking stimulants and depressants. Her hangovers are described as "calamities." A tennis game outside her window sounds "like an antiaircraft barrage." She keeps referring to "a crazy drunken summer." When working, she suffers "as never before." She calls Jack frequently. Apparently, he has given her a special number to reach one of his secretaries. According to Modene's account, Jack does call back when not immediately available. And she has offered hints that last summer she did carry a manila envelope from IOTA to RAPUNZEL. All the same, Jack keeps teasing her. "Don't," says Jack, "let it get too personal with Sammy. He's not a fellow to trust with the collection plate."

Hugh, in one surprising moment of candor, said to me, "I suspect this has to do with Castro. Under it all, your Jack has an IRA mentality. Trust that Mick instinct. He wants to get even. Get even and you can enjoy your old age."

I find the most curious feelings in me. I've always thought of myself as ruefully patriotic, that is, I love America, but it's like having a mate whose gaffes keep you exclaiming, "Oh, my God. He's done it again." I am outraged, however, that this man Castro, who is probably more qualified to be captain of a pirate ship than a head of state, is now gloating over us. It does bother me. And I know it rests like a thorn in the Kennedy heart. With his love of intrigue, it might not be unlike Jack to pick such an outré back channel as Sammy G.

Toward the end of August, our girl is invited once again to lunch on Saturday in the small second-story dining room. This time, however, Dave Powers is invited to eat with them.

MODENE: At the end of the meal, Jack said to me, "Modene, I am picking up a few tales out of school." "Tales?" I asked. For the first time since I knew him, I didn't like his tone. Not at all. He said, "Did you ever say to anyone that I tried to get you to accept another girl to go right in there with us?"

WILLIE: He spoke in such manner right in front of Dave Powers?

MODENE: I think he wanted a henchman there for the record.

WILLIE: Maybe you were being recorded?

MODENE: Don't say that. It's offensive enough already. I certainly had the feeling that he was doing it for Dave Powers' benefit. As if to announce: "Well, here is this unlikely tale, but were you, Modene, malicious enough to go around spreading it?"

WILLIE: You must have been furious.

MODENE: I don't make a habit of swearing, but instinct told me to get downright coarse. So I said: "If you ever tried something so low as hoping to put another girl into the sack with you and me, I sure as hell would be the last one to run around with that story. It's an insult to me."

WILLIE: You did tell him off.

MODENE: He had transgressed the line of privacy.

WILLIE: I appreciate what you are saying.

MODENE: Yes.

WILLIE: Except you did tell it to me.

MODENE: I did? . . . Yes, I did, didn't I? But you don't count.

WILLIE: Did you tell anyone besides me?

MODENE: I may have told Tom. I can't remember. Do you know, I really can't remember. Do you suppose pot and alcohol if taken with sleeping pills might injure a person's memory?

WILLIE: Yes.

MODENE: Well, I do remember telling Sam.

WILLIE: Oh, no.

MODENE: I couldn't stew in it alone.

WILLIE: What happened after you told him off?

MODENE: I kept on the high road. I asked him how he dared to discuss something that personal in front of a third party? Jack must have made some signal then, because Powers left the room. Then Jack tried to make amends. Kept kissing me on the cheek and saying, "I'm awfully sorry. But a story did get back to me." I told him if he didn't like tales out of school, maybe he ought to comport himself in another manner. And then very suddenly I said, "Let's break it off." I couldn't believe I had said it. He tried to get me to stay. I think, after all this, he still wanted to get me in bed. Men are single-minded, aren't they? I finally had to say, "You are insensitive. I want to leave."

WILLIE: You just took off?

MODENE: Oh, no. He wouldn't permit that. Dave Powers had to take me on a tour of the White House.

WILLIE: I'm sure they wanted to check on whether you were under control. All they needed was some mad beauty running out of the White House and ripping off her clothes on Pennsylvania Avenue.

MODENE: You are particularly humorous today.

WILLIE: Sorry.

MODENE: The tour was painful. Dave Powers had done it so many times before that I wanted to scream. I felt as if I were working an all-seats-occupied flight. Dave must have taken forty-five minutes guiding me through the Green Room and the Red Room and the Oval Room and the East Room.

WILLIE: Do you remember any of it?

MODENE: Don't I just? "Elegance is the fruit of rationality."

WILLIE: What?

MODENE: "Elegance is the fruit of rationality." That was in the East Room. Dave Powers kept talking about the noble proportions of the East Room. When we got to the Oval Room, he had to say, "It's traditionally employed for White House weddings." Then he began to describe all the shades of blue that the Oval Room has seen. Originally, under President Monroe, it was crimson and gold, but Van Buren changed it to royal blue, then President Grant made it violet-blue, and Chester Arthur's wife altered it to robin's-egg blue. Mrs. Harrison picked out a cerulean blue.

WILLIE: There is nothing wrong with your memory.

MODENE: Thank you. Mrs. Harrison's cerulean blue was a figured wallpaper.

WILLIE: Thank you.

MODENE: And then Teddy Roosevelt made it steel blue. Harry Truman altered it back to royal blue.

WILLIE: Amazing.

MODENE: I was sick. I wanted to get out of there.

I can feel for Modene. Men don't understand how much importance women attribute to composure when they are feeling nothing but emotional debris. The moment Modene does get back to her hotel, she packs her bags and catches a flight to Chicago.

It is here, I must tell you, that she begins her affair with Sam. However, I don't feel ready to write to you about that today. I would feel more secure if you would answer this letter first.

Yours provisionally,

*Eiskaltblütig*

P.S. Can you believe it? That is one of Hugh's nicknames for me. I, who am as unformed and overheated within as Lava Inchoate can be seen by some as Ice-cold Blood.

From *Harlot's Ghost* (1991)

# 1962            Miami—II

### ARTIME AND CASTRO

January 15, 1963

Dear Kittredge,

This is to announce the reappearance of Howard Hunt. I had not heard from him in fifteen months, but we had dinner a few nights ago. Last seen before this occasion, he was buried in the Domestic Operations Division under Tracy Barnes, either, per his cover, writing spy fiction for New American Library or engaged in more cloak-and-daggered stuff. Wouldn't let on.

I suspect he was dealing in ultra-right-wing Cuban types—I can't be certain. He won't tell. I saw him for no more than our one evening, which came by way of a call saying that he wanted me to join him for dinner with Manuel Artime. So this letter is to impart what I learned from Artime about the Brigade's experience in Cuban prisons.

It was a good night. Do you know, I entered the Agency for adventure, and by now it feels as if, after a day at a desk, most of my excitement has come from dining out? *My Life in Central Intelligence; or, The Hundred Most Memorable Dinners.*

Well, this was one of them. Howard, still stationed in Washington, has obtained for his exclusive Miami use one of our best safe houses, a jewel of a villa out on Key Biscayne called La Nevisca. I used to engage the place occasionally during the pre-Pigs period, but Howard occupies it now, and demonstrates for me that there are amenities to Agency life. We had a corkeroo of a repast, polished off with Château Yquem, served up—I only learn of their existence at this late date— by two contract Agency caterers, who shop for special occasions, chef it forth in haute cuisine, and serve it themselves.

This was five-star. Howard is obviously back in full self-esteem. For all I know, his key passion is to get to just some place like this every night.

At any rate, I felt like an interloper. If Hunt and Artime do not love each other, they are fabulous actors. I do not know that I have ever seen Howard manifest more warmth toward anyone, and thereby was introduced to the untrammeled hyperbole of real Cuban toasts. The art, I discovered, is to raise one's glass as if addressing a hundred folk.

"I drink to a remarkable man," said Howard, "to a Cuban gentleman whose funds of patriotism are inexhaustible. I drink to a man I esteem so highly that, never knowing whether I would see him again, I chose nonetheless to name him, *in absentia,* the godfather of my son, David."

Artime replied in ringing terms—now I know *ringing terms*! He would defend his godson, if need arose, with his life. Do you know, Kittredge, I never heard a man sound more sincere. Artime, if finely drawn from his twenty months in prison, has gained, all the same, in personal impressiveness. Before, in Miami, in the old pre–Bay of Pigs days, he was charming but a hint boyish, and considerably too emotional for my taste. Now, he is more emotional than ever, but his charisma embodies it. You cannot take your eyes off him. You do not know if you are looking at a killer or a saint. He seems endowed with an inner dedication that no human force can overcome. It is far from wholly attractive. My grandmother, Cal's mother, was equally endowed for church work—I do not exaggerate!—and she died at age eighty of cancer of the bowel. One senses the inflexible beast of ideology in such persons. Nonetheless, after spending an evening with Artime, I wished to fight Castro hand to hand.

Let me give you a full presentation of Artime's response to Howard's toast.

"In prison, there were hours," he said, "when despair was the only emotion we could feel. Yet, in the depths of our imprisonment, we were even ready to welcome despair, for that at least is a powerful emotion, and all feelings, whether noble or petty, are but streams and brooks and rivulets"—*riachuelas* was the word he used—"that flow into the universal medium which is love. It was love to which we wished to return. Love for one's fellow man no matter how evil he might be. I wanted to stand in the light of God so that I could regain my strength to fight another day. I was grateful, therefore, for the power of my despair. It enabled me to rise above apathy.

"Yet, despair is spiritual peril. One must rise out of it or lose oneself forever. So one needs stepping-stones, trails to ascend, rungs to a ladder. When one is lost in the black current of limitless misery, the memory of friends can sometimes be the only bridge that leads one back to the higher emotions. While I was in prison, no American friend appeared before my mind with more of a beautiful presence to lift my tortured spirit than you, Don Eduardo, you, *caballero espléndido,* whom I salute tonight in all the honor of feeling myself blessed by the high moral obligation to be the godfather of your son, David."

On they went. I came to recognize that the first good reason for inviting me is that my Spanish is satisfactory, and two grown men cannot speak to each other in such elevated fashion without having at least one witness for audience.

Artime began to talk about prison. Which I certainly wanted to hear about. Much of what he had to say was, however, contradictory. Where the food proved decent in one jail, it was wretched in another; if Brigade leaders were put away in individual cells for a time, they were soon brought back into prison dormitories; when, for a period, treatment turned courteous, it later became ugly. Conditions in one prison bore little relation to the next. They were moved frequently.

This exposition gave me a sense of the turmoil outside the walls. Right now, in Cuba, theories and events must be colliding, for there appeared to be no consistent intent behind the incarceration.

From what he told us, Artime's first hours of imprisonment were his worst. At the dire end of the Bay of Pigs, seeking to avoid capture, he took off with a few men into a trackless swamp called Zapata. He said he had had some idea of reaching the Sierra Escambray, eighty miles off, where he would initiate a guerrilla movement. Two weeks later, his group was rounded up.

Artime was the most important Brigade leader yet captured by Castro's counterintelligence. Since I must assume you are not all that familiar with his background, let me try a quick summary. I hope it was not Samuel Johnson who said, "None but a talentless wretch attempts a sketch." Artime, educated in Jesuit schools as a psychiatrist, was not yet twenty-eight when he joined Castro in the Sierra Maestra: In the first year after victory, however, feeling himself to be "a democratic infiltrator in a Communist government," he set out to build an underground movement. It did not take long for him to become a fugitive hunted by the police. Clothed in the cassock of a priest, and carrying a pistol inside a hollowed-out missal, Artime walked up the steps of the American Embassy in Havana one morning, and was shortly thereafter smuggled out to Tampa on a Honduran freighter. Doubtless, you first heard of him as a leader in the Frente, then in the Brigade. Artime, however, managed to maintain his underground group in Cuba as well. With such tripartite credentials, be certain he received no ordinary interrogation after capture.

Of course, he was in no ordinary condition. The swamp was arid, and choked in thorn bushes. Fresh water was rare. After fourteen days of thirst, no one could speak. They were not able to move their tongues. "I had always thought," said Artime, "that I was one of the people called upon for the liberation of Cuba. God would use me as His sword. After I was captured, however, I came to believe that God must be more in need of my blood, and I had to be prepared to die if Cuba was ever to be liberated.

"Back at Girón, however, as soon as they studied my diary and recognized who I was, one of the counterintelligence said, 'Artime, you have something to pay for all you have done to us. Do you wish to die like a hero, quickly, and by a bullet? Then cooperate. Declare that the Americans betrayed the Brigade. If you fail to help us, you will go out in misery.' "

When Artime would not sign such a declaration, his captors drove him to Havana, where he was brought into a basement room whose walls were lined with old mattresses. There, his shirt removed, his arms and legs strapped to a chair, a spotlight in his eyes, he was questioned for three days.

Not all the voices were angry. Sometimes a man would tell him that the Revolution was prepared to have compassion for his error;

such men were replaced by others with harsh voices. Forced to stare into the spotlight, he never saw any of their faces. The angry voice would say, "Innocent Cubans died for this man's vanity." One interrogator pushed a photograph into his face. He looked at a field of dead men. Corpses from the three-day battle stared back at him.

"I am going to kill you, cocksucker," said the angry voice. Artime felt the barrel of a pistol against his lips. He looked at Hunt and at me. "I was calm. I could not believe it. I said to myself, 'This is how wild horses feel when the bridle goes into their mouth. Yet, this bridle is the exercise of God's will.' Then a man who had a gentle voice said to the man with the angry voice, 'Get yourself out of here. You are making things worse.' 'I won't leave,' said the angry man, 'the Revolution gives me just as much right to be here as it does you.' They kept arguing," said Artime, "until the bad one left. Then the good one said, 'He is in a state of great disturbance because his brother was killed at Girón.'"

"Were you ever close to breaking?" asked Hunt.

"Never," answered Artime. "I did not see how I was going to live, so there was nothing to break." He did nod his head, however. "On the third day, they put me in a cell, and I was visited by a man named Ramiro Valdes, who is Castro's chief of G-2." Valdes seemed concerned with Artime's appearance, particularly the burns received from cigarettes. "Who were your interrogators?" he asked. "We will treat them severely. The Revolution wants revolutionaries, not fanatics. Please describe them to me, Manuel."

"Commander," said Artime, "I never saw their faces. Let us forget about it."

Hunt, in a husky voice, said, "I would have wanted to locate those sons of bitches."

"No," said Artime, "I did not believe Valdes. I knew he wished to establish a good relation with me. Then he would commence conversion. But I was not the proper person for such intentions. My situation as a prisoner was less real to me than my inner psychology. I felt that God was testing Manuel Artime. If I passed His tests, Cuba would become more worthy of liberation."

"Which was the most difficult test?" I asked.

He nodded, as if he liked the question. "Valdes ordered a good dinner to be brought into my cell. There was chicken and rice and black beans. I had forgotten how much I love to eat. No food had ever tasted better, and for a moment I was not ready to die. The beauty that is in life itself received my attention. I began to think of the sweet and simple barnyard life of the chicken who was providing me with this feast. But then, I said to myself, 'No, I am being tested,' and I no longer felt so tender-hearted toward the white meat of the breast. Suddenly I thought, 'I have an immortal soul, and this chicken does not. I am in the devil's hour.' "

A more difficult test came to Artime after he had been a prisoner for a year, had gone to trial, and was awaiting the court's verdict. By then he was accustomed to being alive; so it occurred to him with some force that his refusal to collaborate at the trial was bound to result in a sentence of death for himself.

"At that moment I realized that I would never have a son. To a Cuban, that is a sad thought. When a man feels unfulfilled, he is not ready to meet his end. Therefore, I asked a guard for pencil and paper. I wanted to write out exactly what to say when I was shot. Concentration upon that event might remove the temptation to wish one could stay alive. So, I decided to tell my executioners: 'I forgive you. And I remind you: God exists. His Presence enables me to die while loving you. Long live Christ the King. Long live Cuba Libre.' That took me through the temptation."

Soon after, he was visited by Fidel Castro. By Artime's description, Castro came to the prison at two in the morning six days after the trial and woke up Pepe San Román, who yawned in Castro's face, then stood before him in his underwear.

"What kind of people are you?" asked Castro. "I cannot comprehend. You trust the North Americans. They turn our women into whores and our politicians into gangsters. What would happen if your side had won? The Americans would be here. We would have to live with the hope that if they visit Cuba often enough, we will teach them how to fuck."

"I would rather deal with an American than a Russian," San Román answered.

"I ask you not to waste your life. The Revolution has need of you. We have fought you, so we know how many men in your Brigade have valor."

"Why," asked Pepe San Román, "didn't you say that at the trial? You referred to us as worms. Now you wake me up to tell me that we are brave. Why do you not leave? Enough is enough."

"Enough is enough? My God, man, I wonder if you even want to live."

"We agree on something. I do not want to live. I have been played with by the United States, and now you are playing with me. Kill us, but stop playing."

Castro left. Artime's cell was next. When he saw him in the doorway, Manuel assumed the Maximum Leader was paying this visit in order to execute him. "Do you finally come to see me," asked Artime, "so that you can try to make a fool of me in front of your men?"

"No," said Castro. "The only reason that I did not approach you earlier is I knew you were weak from the swamps. I do not wish you to think that I will make fun of you. In fact, I would ask: How are you now?"

"Very well. Though not as well as you are. You are heavier than you were in the mountains."

Castro smiled. "As yet in our Revolution, not all eat equally. Chico, I am here to ask what you are expecting."

"Death."

"Death? Is this your understanding of the Revolution? To the contrary, we are here to look for the potential in each other. Your side looks to improve the condition of those people who have obtained a good deal already. My side hopes to improve the lot of those who have nothing. My side is more Christian than yours, I would say. What a loss that you are not a Communist."

"What a pity that you are not a democrat."

"Artime, I will demonstrate that you are wrong. You see, we are not going to kill you. Under the circumstances, that is very democratic. We accept the existence of a point of view that wishes to destroy us. Tell me that is not generous. The Revolution is sparing your lives. You may have been sentenced to thirty years in jail, but you will not even have to serve your sentence. Since you are so valuable to the Americans, we are ready to ransom you. In four months, you'll all be gone."

Well, as we know, it took eight.

Toward the end of the evening, Artime shifted the ground of discussion.

"We have yet to commence the true fight," he told Howard and me.

"You can't be ready to go into action this quickly," said Hunt.

"Physically, we still must recover, yes. But we will be ready before long. I feel sorry for any man who believes he will stop us."

"Jack Kennedy can stop you," said Hunt. "He thinks it is obscene not to deal in two directions at once. I will warn you, Manuel, I have heard rumors that the White House is ready to make a deal with Castro."

"The devil," said Artime, "is defined as a man who has his head put on backwards."

Hunt nodded profoundly. "Smiling Jack," he answered.

Hunt has changed, Kittredge. He always had a good deal of anger in him, divided neatly into two parts: half for the Communists, and half for the manner in which his achievements have not been properly recognized. Now, however, his hatred breaks through the skin of what used to be his considerable urbanity. When the crude stuff pops forth, it is strikingly disagreeable. Hunt is not the sort of man who should ever reveal this side of himself.

"Many of us," said Artime, "do not have a clear view on the Kennedys. For example, the brother, Bobby, took me on a ski trip last week. I cannot say I do not like him. When he saw that I do not know how to ski, but was ready to plunge down—you call it the *fall line*—of every slope until I fell, he would laugh and laugh, and then say to me, 'Now I have seen fire on ice.' "

"The Kennedys are adept at charming those they wish to have on their side," said Hunt.

"With all due respect, Don Eduardo, I believe the President's brother is serious about Cuba. He has new plans, he says, and wants me to be a leader in them."

Hunt said: "I would suggest that you develop your own operation. Once you are privately funded and free of the government, I know people who can give you more assistance than if you are directly under Kennedy's nose."

Artime said: "I am not happy with complexity. I heard the President say, 'This flag will be returned some day to a free Havana.' To me, that is an absolute commitment to our cause."

Hunt smiled. Hunt took a sip of his brandy. "I repeat your words: The devil is a man who has his head put on backward."

Artime sighed again. "I cannot pretend that there is no division among my people concerning the subject of the Kennedys."

"I heard that some of you did not want to hand the Brigade flag over to Kennedy?"

"We were divided. That is true. I was uncertain myself," said Artime. "I have to admit that I like the Kennedys better now that Bobby took me skiing."

"Is it true?" asked Hunt. "Was the flag handed over to Jack not the original, but a duplicate?"

Artime looked most unhappy. He threw a glance at me, at which Hunt waved his hand as if to say, "It is all right. He is one of us." That startled me. Hunt is not the kind of enthusiast to put unqualified trust in someone as marginal to his purposes as myself. "Was it a copy?" Hunt persisted.

Artime inclined his head. "We compromised. We made a duplicate flag. It was the forgery that was given to President Kennedy. I am not happy about such a deception. Some of the strength we put into our flag may now drain out of it."

Hunt looked curiously pleased. Writing this, I think I now understand why. Since he was not told the story in confidence, but with myself present, I believe he now feels more free to divulge this item to others. Kittredge, my sentiments about Jack Kennedy are hardly clear-cut, but Hunt's animus makes me frankly uneasy.

Later that night, I had an extraordinary dream in which Fidel Castro and Manuel Artime entered a debate. Artime said: "You, Castro, do not comprehend the character of faith. I am not here to defend the rich. But I must feel compassion for them since God will not be charitable toward their greed. God saves His special mercy for the poor. In Heaven, all injustice is reversed. You, Fidel, claim to work for the poor, but you commit murders in their name. You seal your revolution with blood. You blind the poor with materialism, and thereby remove their vision of God."

"Chico," answered Castro, "it is obvious that we have opposing points of view. One of us has to be wrong. Let me deal with your proposition, therefore, on such a basis. If I am in error, then any human beings that I have injured in this life will most certainly be well received in heaven.

"If, on the other hand, Artime, no God exists to punish the rich and the unjust in the afterlife, what can you say about all of our poor peasants whom your soldiers slaughtered? You killed them on the road to Girón because of your fear that Communism might succeed in Cuba. In that case, your forces will have wasted not only their lives but ours.

"So, Manuel," said Castro, "choose my way. Then, logically speaking, no matter which one of us is correct, you come out better."

Kittredge, that dream concluded in a most curious fashion. Bill Harvey's voice boomed out suddenly: "You are both in error," he shouted. "There is no justice. There is only the Game." Those last two words stayed with me until I woke up.

Yours eternally,
Harry

From *Harlot's Ghost* (1991)

## April 1962        Miami—III

### POISONING CASTRO

Bill Harvey's Cadillac was waiting, motor running, and I reached the vehicle just enough in advance to open the door for him. He grunted and signaled to me to get in first and slide over. While we rode, he did not speak, and the bad mood that came off the bulk of his presence was as palpable as body odor.

Only when we were on the Rickenbacker Causeway to Miami Beach did he speak. "We are going to see a guy named Roselli. You know who he is?"

"Yes."

"All right. When we get there, keep your mouth shut. I will do the talking. Is that clear?"

"Yessir."

"You are not equipped for this job. As you probably know, you have been handed to me. In my opinion, it is a mistake."

"I'll try to make you change your mind."

He belched. "Just pass me that jug of martinis, will you?"

Along Collins Avenue in Miami Beach, he spoke again. "Not only will you keep your mouth shut, but you will not take your eyes off this greaseball. Keep looking at him as if he's a piece of shit and you will wipe him if he moves. Keep thinking that you are capable of splashing acid in his eyes. Don't speak or he'll know it's nothing but cold piss."

"The picture is clear by now," I said.

"Nothing personal. I just don't think you have the makings for this mode of procedure."

Roselli was living in a brand-new houseboat moored on Indian Creek, across Collins Avenue from the Fontainebleau. Lashed next to it was a spanking new thirty-foot power cruiser with a flying bridge. A slim, well-tanned, sharp-featured man about fifty with elegantly combed silver hair was sitting on the deck of the houseboat, and he stood up when he saw the Cadillac come to a stop. Dressed in a white shirt and white slacks, he was barefoot. "Welcome," he said. I noticed that the houseboat was named *Lazy Girl II,* and the power cruiser moored to it, *Streaks III.*

"Can we move out of the sun?" asked Harvey as he came on board.

"Come inside, Mr. O'Brien."

The living room of the houseboat was more than thirty feet long and was decorated in flesh tones like a suite at the Fontainebleau. Puffed-up furniture full of curves undulated along a wall-to-wall carpet. Sitting at a white baby grand piano, with their backs to the keys, were two girls in pink and orange halters, yellow skirts, and white high-heeled shoes. They were blond and suntanned and had baby faces and full lips. Their near-white lipstick gave off a moon-glow as if to say that they were capable of kissing all of you and might not mind since this was exactly what they were good at.

"Meet Terry and Jo-Ann," said Roselli.

"Girls," said Harvey, speaking precisely between recognition and dismissal.

As if by prior agreement, the girls did not look at me; I did not smile at them. I felt that I was going to be surprisingly good at not saying a word. I was still seething, after all, from my boss's evaluation of me.

Harvey gave a small inclination of his chin in the direction of Terry and Jo-Ann.

"Girls," said Roselli, "go up on deck and get some more tan for yourselves, will you?"

The moment they were gone, Harvey lowered himself distrustfully to the edge of one of the large round armchairs, and from his attaché case withdrew a small black box. He switched it on and said, "Let me open our discussion by telling you that I am not here to fart around."

"Totally comprehended," said Roselli.

"If you are wired," said Harvey, "you might as well take it off and get comfortable. If you are operating any installed recording equipment, you are wasting tape. This black box scrambles all reception."

As if in assent, a small unpleasant electronic hum came up from the equipment.

"Now," said Harvey, "I don't care who you dealt with before on this matter, you will at present deal with me and no one else."

"Agreed."

"You agree too quickly. I have a number of questions. If you don't answer them to my satisfaction, I will cut you off the project. If you make noise, I can throw you to the wolves."

"Listen, Mr. O'Brien, do not issue threats. What can you do, kill me? As far as I am concerned, I have visited that place already." He nodded to certify these words and added, "Drinks?"

"Not on duty," said Harvey, "no, thank you. I will repeat: We know why you are in this. You entered the U.S. illegally when you were eight years old and your name was Filippo Sacco. Now you want a citizenship."

"I ought to have one," said Roselli. "I love this country. There are millions of people with citizenship who despise this country, but I, who don't have my passport, love it. I am a patriot."

"There is," said Harvey, "no room to double-cross me, or the people I represent. If you try any tricks, I can have you deported."

"You do not need to talk like a hard-on."

"Would you rather," asked Harvey, "have me say behind your back that I am holding you by the short hairs?"

Roselli laughed. He was all by himself in this merriment but he kept it going for a while.

"I guess, Mr. O'Brien," he said, "you are one total example of a prick."

"Wait until I show you the warts."

"Have a drink," said Roselli.

"Martini. Scotch over the cubes, spill it out, then lay in the gin."

"And you, sir," said Roselli to me, "what would you like?"

I looked at him and did not reply. It was more difficult than I had expected not to offer small courtesies to people I did not know. Besides, I wanted a drink. Roselli shrugged, got up, and went to the bar near the white baby grand piano. Harvey and I sat in silence.

Roselli handed Harvey his martini. He had also mixed a bourbon on the rocks for himself and a Scotch for me which he made a point of setting down on an end table next to my chair, a deft move for Roselli, I decided, since a bit of my attention kept returning to the drink.

"Let's address the positive side of the question," said Roselli. "What if I bring this off? What if the big guy—"

"Rasputin."

"What if he gets hit?"

"In that case," said Harvey, "you get your citizenship approved."

"To success," said Roselli, lifting his drink.

"Now, answer my questions," said Harvey.

"Shoot."

"How did you get into this project in the first place?"

"Classy Bob came to me."

"Why?"

"We know each other."

"What did you do?"

"I went to Sam."

"Why?"

"Because I needed to get to the Saint."

"Why?"

"You know."

"Don't worry about what I know. Answer my questions."

"The Saint is the only man who knows enough Cubans to select the guy who is right for the job."

"What did Sam do?"

"Besides fuck everything up?" asked Roselli.

"Yes."

"He dabbled. He picked a few people. He didn't break a sweat."

"He did, however, get Classy Bob in trouble with the Bureau."

"You are the one who said that."

"You are the one," said Harvey, "who said Sammy fucked everything up."

"I don't know what he did. But I thought we were set to go. Rasputin was supposed to be off the board before the election. Nixon for President. So I ask one question: Did Sam jam the gears?"

"We are referring to October 31 of last year in Las Vegas."

"Yes."

"Sam did it, you say?"

"I," said Roselli, "would rather avoid what I cannot prove."

"Sam," Harvey said, "is bragging that he has worked with some of my associates."

"For a guy with a closed mouth, Sam can open it," said Roselli.

"Why?"

"Vanity."

"Explain that," said Harvey.

"When Sam started out, he was just one more ugly little guy with an ugly little wife. Now, he goes around saying, 'We Italians are the greatest lovers in the world. We can out-do any nigger on his best day. Look at the evidence,' says Sam."

"Who does he say this to?"

"The dummies around him. But word gets out. He brags too much. Vanity. He says, 'Look at the evidence. Two world leaders. Kennedy and Castro.' " Here Roselli stopped. "Forgive me. You mind if I use the names?"

"It's secure," said Harvey, "use them."

"All right," said Roselli, "two guineas like Sammy G. and Frank Fiorini are fucking Kennedy and Castro's broads. Modene may screw Kennedy but she comes back to Sammy, says Sammy, for the real stuff. I would say he has an excessively exaggerated idea of himself. When

I first knew Sam G. he used to wear white socks and black shoes, and the white socks was always falling down. That's what a meatball he used to be."

"Thank you," said Harvey, "you are giving me a clear picture."

"Sam is a big man in the States," said Roselli, "Chicago, Miami, Vegas, L.A.—don't mess with him. Cuba, no. He needs the Saint for Cuba."

"And Maheu?"

"His loyalty is to Howard Hughes."

"Is Hughes interested in Havana?"

"Who isn't? Havana will put Las Vegas back in the desert again."

"This collates," said Harvey. "You are not to deal any longer with Bob and Sammy. Consider them untrustworthy and surplus."

"I hear you. I concur."

"Down the hatch," said Harvey. He held out his martini glass for a refill, and after one good gulp, added: "Let's look at the situation with Santos."

"He is the menu," said Roselli.

"Horseshit," said Harvey. "Trafficante works with us, he works with Castro. How are you to trust him?"

"The Saint works with a lot of people. He used to work with Batista. He is close to some of the Batista people today, Masferrer and Kohly. The Saint has friends in Inter-Pen, in MIRR, Alpha 60, DRE, 30th of November, MDC and CFC. I can name a lot of organizations. Around Miami, half the exiles is taking hits on the other half, but the Saint is friends with all. He is friends with Prio Socarras and Carlos Marcello in New Orleans—a very big friendship—and Sergio Arcacha Smith. With Tony Varona and with Toto Barbaro. With Frank Fiorini. He is friends with Jimmy Hoffa and some of the big oil money in Texas. Why shouldn't he be friends with Castro? Why shouldn't he be friends with you? He will tell Castro what he wants to tell him; he will tell you as much as he feels like telling you. He will do a job for you and do it right, he will do a job for Castro and do it right. His real loyalty—"

"Yes," said Harvey, "the real loyalty?"

"To the holdings in Havana."

"What about Meyer?"

"Santos is also friends with Meyer. He don't worry about Meyer. If Castro goes, Santos will be holding the casinos. That is bigger than being Lansky or Jimmy Hoffa. Santos could become number-one in the mob. That is equal to being the number-two man in America. Right under the President."

"Who taught you to count?" asked Harvey.

"It's a matter of debate. Give me that much."

"If I was Santos," said Harvey, "I would put in with Castro. Castro is there. He can give me the casinos."

"Yes, but then you got to run them for Castro."

"A point," said Harvey.

"Castro will never give the casinos back," said Roselli. "He is keeping them closed. He is a puritan right up the ass. I know Santos. He will come along with us to get Castro."

"Well, I have my hesitations," said Harvey. "There is a little prick with fire coming out of his ears named Bobby Kennedy. He does not cut a deal. Sammy may have helped to bring in Illinois for Jack Kennedy, but the FBI is persecuting Sammy right now. Santos can read that kind of handwriting."

"Santos will take his chances. Once Castro is dead, Santos has a lot of cards to play."

A silence came over both men. "All right," said Harvey, at last, "what are the means?"

"No guns," said Roselli.

"They do the job."

"Yeah," said Roselli, "but the guy who makes the hit would like to live."

"I can get you a high-powered rifle, equipped with a silencer, and accurate at five hundred yards."

Roselli shook his head. "Santos wants pills."

"Pills," said Harvey, "have too many leaks. Castro has always been tipped off."

"Pills. We need delivery next week."

It was Harvey's turn to shrug. "We will produce the product on date specified."

They spent the next few minutes talking about a shipment of weapons for an exile group that Trafficante wanted to supply.

"I will deliver the ordnance myself," said Harvey.

He stood up, packed away the scrambler, and shook hands with Roselli.

"I'd like you," said Harvey, "to answer another question for me."

"Sure," said Roselli.

"Are you any relation to Sacco of Sacco and Vanzetti?"

"Never heard of the cocksucker," Roselli said.

The conscientious effort to look at Roselli as if he were something to wipe off the wall had left me as tired as an artist's model who has been posing in one position for too long. Harvey, who may have been equally tired, did not speak on the ride back, but merely kept filling his glass from the jug of martinis.

As we were getting out of his Cadillac, he said, "When you report to his lordship, tell him to clear Trafficante with Helms. It's rotten meat all the way, and I am not sitting down to this meal alone."

From *Harlot's Ghost* (1991)

# 1962                  New York—I

### WHOM?

We can be grateful that Kennedy did not compound the blunder of the Bay of Pigs by sending a force massive enough to conquer Castro. We would still be occupying Cuba; every day, bodies of American soldiers and Marines would be found ambushed by guerrillas in the hills. All of Latin America and South America would be moving silently and steadily toward the Communists. This way the road was left open for Khrushchev to commit a blunder as large as Kennedy's—when the atomic missiles were sent to Cuba, Khrushchev was returning back to America the fifty years of political advantage Kennedy had given him.

The Bay of Pigs remains a mystery. One can doubt if it will ever be found out how it came to pass, or who in fact was the real force behind it. But there is a tool of investigation for political mysteries. It is Lenin's formula: "Whom?" Whom does this benefit? Who prospers from a particular act?

Well, whom? Kennedy and the liberal center did not gain honor from the Bay of Pigs. Castro most certainly did not gain an advantage, for he was forced now finally to commit his hand altogether to Russia. The Left in America, that fine new Left of Pacifists and beatniks and Negro militants and college students who just knew something was bad—this Left certainly did not benefit from the Bay of Pigs, because they were now divided about Castro even as an earlier generation of Leftists had been divided by the Moscow Trials.

No, the people who benefited from the Bay of Pigs were the people who wanted a serious Communist threat to exist within ninety miles of America's shore. They were the people who had taken the small and often absurd American Communist Party and had tried to exaggerate its menace to the point where the country could be pistol-whipped into silence at the mention of its name. They had infiltrated this party until even the *Saturday Evening Post* offered hints that a large part of the American Communist Party was by now made up of FBI men. These were indeed the people, these secret policemen, who would face an excruciating dilemma if the Communist threat disappeared altogether in America. Because then what would they do? If there were no Communists, the FBI would be required by the logic of their virility to take on the next greatest danger to American life, the Mafia, and how were they ever to do that, how were they to investigate the Mafia without ripping the Republican and Democratic parties up from top to bottom? Because the Republican Party was supported by the Mafia, and the Democratic Party was supported by the Mafia. Through and through. Down at the low level where the little heelers and the small cops got their bite at the local bar, and up at the high level where the monster housing projects were contracted out, and the superhighways, and the real estate grafts. No, it was safer by far that Cuba go Communist. That would be good for the FBI, and it would be good for the Chinese Communists, who wished to increase the pressure on Khrushchev's back. Whom? asked Lenin; who benefits? And the answer is clear: All the totalitarians of the world were benefited by the Bay of Pigs and the missiles that followed.

From *The Presidential Papers* (1963)

# HOLLYWOOD—III

## Marilyn and Arthur Miller

They cannot get free of entanglements. One may as well suppose a law: If the past is full of old complications, the future will grow new ones. They need money. So she is obliged to do another movie before *The Misfits,* and then complications in Gable's schedule force her to begin another. By the time she will finish *Some Like It Hot,* their marriage is in jeopardy; by the end of *Let's Make Love,* they are obliged to hang together like addicts.

What dismantling of hopes! She had believed he would open the life of the mind to her, and came to suspect that her own mind was more interesting than his. "You're like a little boy," says Marilyn's doppelgänger, Maggie, in *After the Fall,* "you don't see the knives people hide." Of course, if Marilyn's unvoiced resentment of him is, after all this, secretly sexual, then who cannot think she might have known better? At no time, certainly, will she live so much on sleeping pills as in her years with Miller, and an insight into the distance between their bodies comes from a story Miller tells of one miserable day when he discovers that the inside of her mouth is covered with open sores. Investigation of the medicine cabinet discloses another horror: She has several dozen bottles of sedatives of all variety. He introduces the cache to a chemist, who informs Miller that the reactions of some pills upon others can be literally poisonous. She is lucky to have gotten away with no more than a sore mouth. Poor pill-taking child. Her chemistry is on this occasion cleared up—that is, Miller succeeds in narrowing her addiction to a few compatible barbiturates—but what a misery of marriage is suggested if he "discovers" her mouth is sore. Is it a week, two weeks, or a month since they have shared a kiss? The episode takes place in Los Angeles and probably occurs in the period just before *Let's Make Love,* when their marriage is again at its worst. But then they are never well suited for one another when she works. We have to attempt to penetrate into her condition at such times. As she begins *Some Like It Hot,* she appears as a monster of will. She is also a fragile shell. If we know her well enough to suspect fragility is her cruelest weapon, and she cannot possibly be as weak as she pretends, in fact we are witness to a debased portion of her strength. She is in the unendurable position of protecting an exquisite sensitivity which has been pricked, tickled, twisted, squashed, and tortured for nearly all of her life. The amount of animal rage in her by these years of her artistic prominence is almost impossible to control by human or chemical means. Yet she has to surmount such tension in order to present herself to the world as that figure of immaculate tenderness, utter bewilderment, and goofy dipsomaniacal sweetness that is Sugar Kane in *Some Like It Hot.* It will yet be her greatest creation and her greatest film. She will take an improbable farce and somehow offer some indefinable sense of promise to every absurd logic in the dumb scheme of things until the movie becomes that rarest of modern art objects, an *affirmation*—the audience is more attracted to the idea of life by the end of two hours. For all of Wilder's skill, and the director may never have been better, for all of first-rate performances by Tony Curtis and Jack Lemmon, and an exhibition of late-mastery by Joe E. Brown, it would have been no more than a very funny film, no more, and gone from the mind so soon as one stepped out of the lobby, if not for Monroe. She brought so good and rare an evocation, it seemed to fit into the very disposition of things, much as if God—having put a few just men on earth in order to hold the universe together—was now also binding the cosmos with a few dim-witted angels as well.

Talking about acting in her last *Life* interview, she says at one point, "You're trying to find the nailhead, not just strike a blow." But what a journey down each day, down to the nailhead. What old emotional mine fields to pass through as she navigates by stimulants out of her chemical stupor into her consciousness. And what bile she must dispense, what poison to her tricks. On the set of *Some Like It Hot* she will drive fellow actors into horrors of repetition. Through forty-two takes, Tony Curtis has to nibble on forty-two chicken legs because Monroe keeps blowing her lines. Repetition kills the soul—Curtis will not touch chicken for many a month. Jack Lemmon and he will stand around in high heels and breast padding, in silk stockings and false hips, for all of a long day's shooting all the while Marilyn is unable to say, "It's me, Sugar." "There were forty-seven takes," as Wilder describes it. "After take thirty, I had the line put on a blackboard. She would say things like, 'It's Sugar, me.' "

Maybe she is searching into nuances of identity. "It's Sugar—the name you know me by, which by my own reference is—*me*." Splendid. She is working out a problem in psychic knots worthy of R. D. Laing. But actors are going mad. When she cannot remember one line, "Where is the bourbon?" as she goes searching through a chest, Wilder finally pastes the line on the inside of the drawer: WHERE IS THE BOURBON? Soon he is pasting the line on every drawer. If she is trying to hit the nail on the head, and get down into that core of herself where the nail meets the nerve, she is also voiding her near to infinite anger at life, men, and the movie-working world. How she exhausts the talents around her. "When I come to cut the film," Wilder says, "I look at the early takes. Curtis looks good on those and Monroe is weak. On the later takes, she is wonderful and he is weak. As a director, I must disregard his best takes . . . and go with Monroe . . . because when Monroe is on the screen, the audience cannot keep their eyes off her."

"Yes," Curtis will tell Paula Strasberg when she weeps after he has said kissing Marilyn is "like kissing Hitler," yes, he will say, "You try acting with her, Paula, and see how you feel." She will be hours late to the set. On a good day she is two hours late; on a bad day, six. The slightest suggestion by Wilder on how to do a scene puts her in a state. She must do it her own way, and once again we learn later that her instinct is right, but she chooses to do it her own way by walking off from him to consult with Paula Strasberg. Shades of Sir Laurence and Ms. Monroe. She is ten years ahead of her time.

Of course, she knows what she protects, knows film is not life or the stage but exists somewhere else. In film, to quote from an essay on *Maidstone,* the actor can

> disobey the director or appear incapable of reacting to his direction, leave the other actors isolated from him and with nothing to react to, he can even get his lines wrong, but if he has film technique, he will look sensational in the rushes, he will bring life to the scene even if he was death on the set. It is not surprising. There is something sinister about film. *Film is a phenomenon whose resemblance to death has been ignored too long.*

And we can wonder at the depth to which she must return each day to be again in contact with Sugar Kane. With what, we can wonder, does Monroe finally make contact?

Is it with some last piece of her own exacerbated nerves, or some place she hovers not alive nor dead and spoiled forever for sleep? Now she spoils the air in which she works. Wilder completes the film in near to total agony. His back is in such misery of muscle spasms that he cannot go to bed at night but instead must try to sleep in a chair.

She will respond by failing to inquire about the state of his back. Since she has an interest in the film, she thinks it is a trick to make her fear the financial consequences if he cannot continue. But then she trusts no director alive. Even Logan in *Bus Stop* has cut out what she feels were her best moments. If she cannot forgive Logan, she will not be light on Wilder. Yet as if to demonstrate that any inability to remember lines is of her own choosing, she will also go through long scenes without an error. Weeks after it is over, Wilder will tell an interviewer he can eat again, sleep again, enjoy life, and finally be able to "look at my wife without wanting to hit her because she is a woman."

It is comic by then, but not very, for Marilyn will see the interview back in New York and excite Miller to send a telegram to inform the director that Marilyn Monroe "is the salt of the earth." Wilder sends his reply: "The salt of the earth told an assistant director to go fuck himself." Soon it is not at all comic. She has discovered she is "pregnant" during *Some Like It Hot,* and her time away from the set has been spent resting in bed. She even takes an ambulance from her hotel to the airport in order not to be jostled on the ride, but the fetus—tubal again? hysterical?—is lost, something in her body or mind is lost by her third month, lost around this time of exchange between Miller and Wilder, and the month of November passes in deep depression, which lingers through the winter. Of course, it is her nature to rally. *Some Like It Hot* opens to her best reviews. She has never looked better at a premiere. Then she receives the David DiDonatello Award for *The Prince and the Showgirl,* and that is at least a small consolation to substitute for that Academy Award for which she has never even been nominated. In June of 1959, she goes into Lenox Hill Hospital for "corrective surgery." She is still trying to have a child.

The summer passes, and the fall of 1959. Presumably, Miller is polishing *The Misfits.* In February, they put up at the Beverly Hills Hotel while she gets ready to do *Let's Make Love.*

Studying the script, there is trouble. She knows the film will not play as well as it reads. It is a fair expression of Twentieth Century-

Fox's comprehension of her film art. Since the new contract was signed, she has made *Bus Stop, The Prince and the Showgirl,* and *Some Like It Hot,* but they give her *Let's Make Love.* Her role is as empty as the memory of an old Zanuck film. So she encourages Miller to build up the part. Once again her talented playwright goes into the lists, tries to add funny dialogue to a film that is not funny. Gregory Peck, supposed to play the male lead, discovers that his part diminishes as hers increases; he resigns the job. It is time for her to walk off as well, but it is possible she would rather work in anything at this point than spend time with Miller in Connecticut or New York. Besides, they still need the money. And then, Yves Montand and Simone Signoret are living across the hall at the Beverly Hills Hotel. Marilyn, who has been in profound depression for months and so deep on sleeping pills (which Miller doles out to her each night) that her eyes will now be incorrigibly bloodshot on color film, comes out of her most terrible moods whenever the Montands are with them. She loves Simone and announces to the press that Yves in his turn . . . but let us give the quote: "Next to my husband and along with Marlon Brando, I think Yves Montand is the most attractive man I've ever met." Miller is next in admiration for Yves. "He and Marilyn are both very vital people. They possess internal engines which emit indescribable rays of energy." Montand, in fact, is part of the perfect prescription for Miller's noble worker, since he comes from peasant stock in Italy, and his father has been a political activist who hated Mussolini enough to emigrate to Marseilles and work on the docks. Montand, who left school in the sixth grade, has worked in his turn since he was eleven. Such details have to rouse Miller. Besides, Montand has played in the Paris production of *The Crucible.* Now Arthur recommends him to replace Gregory Peck.

The ante is up. Montand has been successful in French films. He is a theatrical star of respectable measure on Broadway, where he has done a one-man show—songs, monologues, dances. On the other hand, he is hardly an international household name, no Burton, Chevalier, and certainly no Sinatra, although we can assume he is as ambitious as any Italian peasant with strength and wit who has been working from the age of eleven and been transplanted twice.

Marilyn Monroe is his best ticket to notoriety, since she has been famously faithful to Miller for the three-and-a-half-year run of their marriage. Of course, Miller has had to pay an increasing price—each year she speaks more rudely to him in public. In private we can take a fair idea of how she scourges him from *After the Fall.*

"All you care about is money! Don't shit me!" Maggie tells Quentin.

Two breaths later she will let him know his pants are too tight. "Fags wear pants like that. They attract each other with their asses."

"You calling me a fag now?"

"Just I've known fags and some of them didn't even know themselves . . ." Marilyn is beginning to sound like many another drunken blonde. She is also throwing herself at Montand.

Yet, Miller is grateful. He notes that Marilyn's temper seems to be kept in balance when Yves and Simone are about. "Anyone who could make her smile came as a blessing to me," he was to say later. It is the remark to etch the final lines of marital misery.

Any affair to come seems designed by the gods of purified plot. Signoret is abruptly called back to France for her next film. Worried about the security of her marriage, she induces a friend, Doris Vidor, to look after Montand while she is gone, but in her first conversation with Simone's mate, Mrs. Vidor is told by Yves in all anxiety that Miller is also leaving Los Angeles to see his children in the East. Montand will be left alone with Monroe. "What am I going to do?" he asks. "I'm a vulnerable man." Witness his feelings: "I can't alienate her because I'm dependent upon her good will, and I want to work with her. . . . I'm really in a spot." It is black market talk. Publicity for *Let's Make Love* (which will need it) is going to be obliged to let the world in on the latest hottest name wave in Hollywood, Montand Monroe. Montand Monroe increases each day.

As if in revenge on Miller, Marilyn is docile with Yves. If they are asked to be on time at a party, Montand assures the host, "She'll be anywhere I say on time." He is right. To friends he brags, "She's got so she'll do whatever I ask her to do on the set. Everyone is amazed at her cooperation, and she's constantly looking to me for approval." That is also true. She has never made a movie where she is so agreeable to the director. She has also never made a movie where she is so ordinary. A sad truth is before us again. Art and sex are no more compatible than they care to be. She is wan in the film, and dull. Hollywood looks at *Let's Make Love*. Hollywood offers the verdict: "Fucked-out." Ergo, Twentieth increases all publicity on Montand Monroe. If the film is flat, the love affair must show up at least in the final heats of the year.

All final heats come, however, to an abrupt termination with the end of the film. The picture has been delayed by an actors' strike and so she is obliged to leave for New York and three days of costume fitting for *The Misfits* without even a day's rest. Then, back west again to Reno.

In Reno, Miller is waiting for her. What horrors of the sleeping pill to take up again. Ejected from a love affair of two months' duration (which may or may not be the love of her life—not to mention that she adores Signoret the wife) she is now in the 110-degree July heat of Reno with the remains of an ice-cold marriage. On hand is that husband she will never forgive for giving her away. They are there to stay together to make the film, but she does not know by whom she has been used the most, nor what is the curious state of her womb, awakened again, then left to molder. She is ill as she has never been ill before. Her blessing is that the film will not be made in color and so won't show every wash of bloodshot in the lost white of her eyes.

The world comes to watch the filming. Before they are done, there will be hundreds of press. The word is out. Frank Taylor, the producer, has said to *Time:* "This is an attempt at the ultimate motion picture. . . . Not only the first original screenplay by a major American writer but the best screenplay I have ever read, and we have the best director, John Huston, for it." In turn, Clark Gable thinks it will be the best role he has ever had, and is right if everything else he has done, including Rhett Butler, has suggested a manner rather than a man. It has been perhaps the most successful manner in the history of cinema, but no one has ever seen the actor. Since he has a bad heart and can die in any season of any year, the film is no ordinary venture to him. Nor can it be to Montgomery Clift, who has often been considered the most talented actor in Hollywood but has not had a picture in years to measure this talent. As for Marilyn, she has never had anything written directly for her before. The picture, as we will see, must become nothing less than her canonization. In his turn, Miller has committed everything. He has not had a new play in half a decade, and has written only a few short magazine pieces since their marriage, of which one, published in *Life,* has been nothing more nor less than tribute: "Her beauty shines because her spirit is forever showing itself." *The Misfits* has to be his justification. Five years of drought is next to the loss of limb for a writer.

Only the actors Eli Wallach and Thelma Ritter, ready as always to do their best work, and the director, John Huston, are principals who do not find themselves laying their careers on the line. Huston is, of course, the only celebrated film artist to bear comparison to Hemingway. His life celebrates a style more important to him than film. His movies do not embody his life so much as they seem to emerge out of a pocket of his mind. He will take horses seriously, and hunting, gambling, and serious drinking; he will be famous for a few of the most elaborate practical jokes in the well-documented Hollywood annals— by implication he does his picture work with disdain. It is as if film is an activity good men must not take upon themselves too solemnly. Yet he has made *The Maltese Falcon, The Treasure of the Sierra Madre, The Asphalt Jungle, The Red Badge of Courage, Moulin Rouge, Beat the Devil,* and *The African Queen.* During the making of *The Misfits,* it is possible he will have no hour of greater absorption than the day on which he wins a camel race against Billy Pearson, the ex-jockey.

Huston has been living in Saint Clerans, County Galway, Ireland, where Miller has visited him, and they have had a fund of talk about the script over Irish whisky and a fire. Since Huston has a social life that thinks a great deal of horses and very little about intimate movie gossip, he has not heard too much of Marilyn's problem of getting to the set on time; he has next to no idea of how sick she is. Miller will hardly tell him. Huston remembers Marilyn from *The Asphalt Jungle,* when she was somewhat unresponsive to direction, but then where is the film without an actor's quirks? On her first morning of shooting, however, which Huston has scheduled for ten o'clock rather than nine (out of deference to Miller's suggestion that she can use the sleep), he waits until eleven and there is no leading lady. His crew have their own relation to him. Incompetence is the hard stuff of mockery on a Huston set. As eleven o'clock strikes, so does the crew toll the hour. Miller, trying to camouflage the delay, looks to confer with Huston over the script.

It is a bad start, and in a few days word is out that Marilyn is taking a high count of Nembutals every night—the film promises to move as quickly as a wounded caterpillar. If Huston is furious, it is not in his style to give a sign. He has the contempt of a professional for the unprofessional. Since Miller and Monroe are obliged to make the film of their life in a state of nervous exhaustion, then that happens to be the way they have chosen to play their game and waste their psychic funds. He prefers to waste his substance in other fashion. (He will spend his nights losing a cumulative fifty thousand dollars at the crap tables.) There is the unmistakable possibility that Huston withdraws subtly from the film, which is certainly not to say that he does not work hard, but that he refuses to become involved in any hysteria about making a great film. No, he will do his best to do a good job under the dry hot circumstances of the Reno desert in summer, and the final film has all the tone of a dry distaste for any excess of effort, emotion, or sentiment, as if every pipe of communication in the world were already coated with emotional glop and it was time to clean the pipes. If people were to be moved by *The Misfits* it would be out of a paucity of tricks. The story would deliver what it was good enough to deliver, no more. That is an aesthetic. It is perhaps the most classical of the film aesthetics. But it is not the easiest way to make a major film. If Huston had a problem as a director, it was precisely that he could not come to take his work seriously enough to create a full resonance of atmosphere. Finally, it was as if there were something obscene about moviemaking, some rip-off of emotion that might spoil a finer tissue of subtleties not even to be described. Such as good horseflesh. Precisely because the script of *The Misfits* was so quiet in tone, it may have needed some commitment from the director to push the actors and crew beyond themselves. After one look, however, at Monroe's inability to give of herself in dependable fashion, Huston may have decided that all-out inspiration was going to be directly equal to a loss of face. Dignity for some artists has more worth than art. It is also possible Huston was bored by the miseries of Miller and Monroe. He had been through divorce, and could do without a good seat at this one.

The film settled upon a pattern. They shot with Monroe when available, shot away from her when not. With Miller, Huston worked closely. It was a script so delicate in the drift of its emotions and so taciturn in its story that the daily problem must have been to decide what motive they could offer the actors for a line. It was almost as if the story were too simple: A young divorcee, Roslyn Taber, begins to live in the desert outside Reno with a middle-aged cowboy, Gay Langland, played by Gable, while two other cowboys, Eli Wallach and Monty Clift, begin to find her attractive, flirt with her, and apparently wait for her relation to Langland to end. After a time, the men go out to hunt for mustangs to trap and sell. It is one of the few ways left to earn a living that is "better than wages." Roslyn accompanies them, but is horrified at the cruelty of the capture and the pointless misery of the purpose. If these mustangs were once sold as riding horses for children, now they are canned as dogmeat. "A dog-eat-horse society," Huston will say in comment. So Monroe has a war with Gable that is resolved (1) by his capture of the last mustang as a gesture to himself, plus (2) setting the horse free as a gesture to her. The film ends in such gestures. They drive off together to face a world in which there will be fewer and fewer ways to make a living better than wages. There has been a curious shift in Miller's powers. Values are now vague.

While more can obviously be said in summary, the point is that *The Misfits* is a film, particularly in its first half, that will move on no more powerful hydraulic of plot than the suggestion of one nuance laid like a feather over another—so it is going to be closer to the nature of most emotional relations than other films. But its virtue is also its vulnerability. We see Roslyn and Langland come together, sleep together, set up home together, we feel the other two cowboys perching themselves on the edge of this relation, but no emotional facts are given, no setting of category or foundation, for the plot is never bolted down. We do not know exactly how Roslyn comes to feel for each man, nor how much she feels. The film is even less precise than biography. Unlike in other movies, we have no blueprint to the emotional line of her heart. Instead she seems to shimmer on the screen with many possibilities of reality. When she holds Monty Clift's head on her lap after he has been injured in the rodeo, we do not know whether she is maternal or stirring for him or both—nor is she likely to know what she feels. In life, how would she?

So they are making a movie that is different in *tone* from other films, and she is altogether different from other actresses, even different from her performances of the past. She has no longer anything in common with Lorelei Lee. She is not sensual here but *sensuous,* and by a meaning of the word that can go to the root—she seems to possess no clear outline on screen. She is not so much a woman as a mood, a cloud of drifting senses in the form of Marilyn Monroe—no, never has she been more luminous.

On the other hand, never has Gable been more real. He could be leaning on the fence next door. Finally we have an idea of what Gable is really like. He is not bad! So, scene for scene, as the first rushes are slowly stitched together, it must have been obvious to Huston and Miller that they had a set of cameos which were superb in their understated taste. It was as if some hollow had been created where one could listen for the echo. But would these separate scenes come together into a movie that might work? Speaking of ultimate films, no black and white movie has ever had so high a budget before. So they might also be striking a blow for the economic future of good films to come. But how to know if what they were accomplishing was really good? That was like trying to calculate the final grandeur of a palace from two or three rooms. The question of guiding actors through this plotless plot had therefore to put its full demand upon the playwright and director. In the day-to-day uncertainty of shooting, how were they to know whether an actor was ready with an emotion too rich or too poor, too strident or too vague? In turn, how could the actors know? The man who has become an actor to avoid that hungry hole of the mind that asks "Who am I?" now had to ask "Who are *you*?" of the role he was playing. It was even worse for Miller. In such a delicate shifting script, how could any scene be considered fixed, yet any change of dialogue in one scene might cause its uncalculated bend in another. Poor Miller! His head had to be overloaded with the most subtle literary equations while his life with Monroe was reduced to one livid state: hideous tension! If they had finally and most tragically arrived at the relation of cellmates who have learned over the years to detest each other into the pit of each intimate flaw, he was nonetheless obliged to work each day on scenes that extolled the beauty of her soul.

For Miller had written a lie in *The Misfits*. It was the half-lie that Marilyn was as lovely and vulnerable as Roslyn Taber, and that may have been all right in the beginning—a lie may be the only aesthetic structure available when working up a vehicle for a great movie star (because she can transmute the lie to magic), but Miller's problem was that he had to live in daily union with the lie, then refine it in his writing each night. Each night Monroe rubbed his nose in the other truth. If she had long been obliged when making a film to wrap herself in the psychic greatcoat of full hatred for some man, beginning with Don Murray in *Bus Stop*, then Olivier, then Wilder, and had discovered the cost of having no one to hate in *Let's Make Love*, Miller's suffering presence now became her real leading man. What must have doubled all hostility was that he was there to remind her she had not been superb enough to rise out of the bile of the past. So if Miller was the man who had loved her most, he would now become the man who had to pay the most, and was condemned to be with her in three rooms on the top floor of the Hotel Mapes while traveling down the clock through Reno night after sleepless night. And if the wound of her infidelities with Montand was still glowing, it could only measure the contempt she offered to his heart. Miller suffered. He had the psychology of poverty where the mark of a man is to suffer and endure. So he suffered. And fed her sleeping pills and held them back, and walked the floor, and listened to her abuse, which many another ear in the hotel would also hear, and in the pause between each squall, flopped down for a space, or stared at the script on his desk. Guiles gives a description of the morning after "one such all-night vigil with Marilyn finally asleep while others were getting ready for the day." May Reis, their secretary, and Nan Taylor, the wife of the producer, enter the suite.

> Miller was slumped in a heap on the sofa lapsing at moments into fits of trembling from nervous exhaustion. Nan Taylor . . . had heard that Marilyn had spent an especially bad night, but she was even more distressed to see what it had done to Miller. His hands half covering his face, Miller agonized over his situation. He confessed that he was obviously no help to Marilyn in seeing her through these terrible nights. He wondered if he shouldn't take a room in another hotel. "She needs care at night," he said, and then he seemed to defeat any hope of salvation by crying out, "But I care for her so much."

"I care for her so much." It is the bottomless cry of love. He is face to face with the most unendurable message of all: Love by itself does not conquer hatred. Nor does it heal another heart. It can only climb the walls of its own misery. For love without courage is an insult to those who hate. So he is taken care of in his pain by the two women. "Perhaps we can't solve Marilyn's problem this morning," Nan Taylor will say, "but we can do something about you," and leaves the room, sees someone in the hotel management, and comes back with a key to a spare room on the same floor, where he can work and conceivably sleep.

Each day the picture falls further behind schedule. With Miller a little more removed from her scene, Marilyn begins to firm up future guidelines—she will live with a chosen entourage of technician-friends and social helpers. Paula is always there, and Marilyn can also count on her publicity man, her hair stylist, her makeup man Whitey Snyder, her driver, and Ralph Roberts, an actor big as a professional football player who has been her masseur for many months. She will soon be very sick and go through a crisis that almost ends her participation in the film, but for a few weeks it is almost as if she manages to continue by deriving some strength out of her hatred of Miller. She actually slams a car door in his face one day on location in the desert and tells her driver to leave him behind. (Miller will not share a car with her again.) And then there is the record of an evening when she sat and drank with Roberts and Agnes Flanagan, her hair stylist, while watching brush fires on the horizon of the desert. Power lines have come down in this blaze, and Reno is in blackout. Since Miller's room has a separate generator to provide him illumination by which to write, she asks Roberts to get a little ice from a portable refrigerator in that room, and when Roberts returns—as Guiles reports the dialogue—Marilyn speaks of Miller in the following manner: "I can tell by your face," she says to Roberts, "you saw old Grouchy Grumps. Did you speak to him? I mean did he say *hello*?"

He was lying on the sofa, Roberts tells her.

"He'll go that way until he's too exhausted to move," she remarks without compassion. "From the desk to the sofa and back again." She drops a cube in her glass. "Klunk!" she cries. "At least we got a little ice out of that room." Boom! Next!

Is it possible she is brooding over Montand? A few days later she is in complete collapse. Suffering agonies from a particularly bad menstrual period, she arrives on location at noon with the temperature over 110 degrees, has to be helped out of the car, and, unable to coordinate by herself, is led over to the set. Metty, the cameraman, tells Huston it is hopeless. "Her eyes won't focus."

Huston shuts down. They have to gamble. She is flown to Los Angeles and put in a clinic, where it is hoped she will be able to go on with the picture after ten days (by doctor's estimate) of rest and "medication," which is to say a new poison will perhaps be found to overcome a few effects of the old poison. At her first opportunity, she gets up, sneaks out of the hospital, and looks for Montand at the Beverly Hills Hotel, but he is neither there when she calls nor does he phone back to answer her note. He merely tells friends in Hollywood that she has left a number where she can be reached. Soon a gossip columnist reports that Montand has told her how Marilyn has "a schoolgirl crush on him." It creates bad publicity for Montand and he is obliged to explain himself in more detail: "I think she is an enchanting child and I would like to see her to say good-bye, but I won't." Then he adds, "She has been so kind to me, but she is a simple girl without any guile. Perhaps I was too tender and thought that maybe she was as sophisticated as some of the other ladies I have known. . . ." *Mon Dieu!* "Perhaps she had a schoolgirl crush. If she did, I'm sorry. But nothing will break up my marriage."

Apparently she is not wounded crucially, for she will be in better condition when she comes back to the film. Perhaps she recognizes in the hospital that she can find a way to live without Miller and without marrying again. Perhaps she can even find a substitute for a mate by splicing the rope of her life with the short ends of lovers and friends. In any case, she returns to warm greetings, and for a busy week much is accomplished. Morale, for once, is good. (Huston has just won his camel race.) She does a five-minute non-stop scene with Monty Clift— the longest scene either actor or Huston has ever had to film, and is at her best in a number of crowded bar scenes at Dayton, Nevada. All this is accomplished in one productive week. Like most addicts', her energy is best when she is in transition from one state of drug-life to another, from addiction to abstention, or from abstention back to barbiturates again. It is only a constant state that seems certain to depress her.

In turn, Miller has apparently passed through his own kind of crisis. If their marriage is finally severed, she, of course, will go out of her way to take a walk with him in Reno a night or two after she gets back. In the shooting that day he had delighted her by daring to show Monty Clift the kind of stiff-legged polka he wanted the actor to perform in a particular scene, Miller doing it with Marilyn before the crew. This species of artistic gallantry has touched her. They walk "like everyday people," as Marilyn will say to a reporter in all the bruised sorrow that wells up from an expiring marriage.

Of course, Miller is probably in better shape as a result of the separation. Isolation he can bear, and loss. It is the alternation of love and hate that wears him out. So as he withdraws from Marilyn his working relation to Huston intensifies. Miller may skirt the edge of a breakdown, but like an old prospector he manages to cross these desert lands of the West.

The film proceeds. It is weeks behind schedule and hundreds of thousands of dollars, more than a half million, over budget. (It will cost four million dollars before it is done.) But that reckoning is later. Now the company begins to move out each day to a dry lake perhaps fifty miles from Reno where they will film the climax, a trapping of the wild horses. Now the fundamental conflict of the script, the movie company, the marriage, and even the direction of the picture comes into focus—it is precisely so banal and awe-inspiring as the war between the men and the women, which here becomes the war between Marilyn and her director, her male company of co-stars, and her scriptwriter once a husband. She is at war with each of them to become the center of the film, and if we will conceive of her competitive instincts as equal to a great prizefighter's, we may begin to perceive how so much of the film had to appear to her as a plot where she took on not one antagonist but many. ("You don't see the knives people hide.") Since her orgy of attention in *Gentlemen Prefer Blondes* and her skill in stealing *How to Marry a Millionaire* from Betty Grable and Bacall, she has managed to get past *No Business Like Show Business* and *River of No Return* and gone on to be the center of every production since (except for *Let's Make Love,* which had no center), dominating directors and running away with each film. They have all, in varying degree, become *her* films. Few prizefighters could point to such a string of triumphs. But in *The Misfits* she is up against better opposition than she has ever faced, and it will affect her performance before the film is done. If she is more interesting and extraordinary in the first half of *The Misfits* than she has ever been before, she will yet find herself suffering many a new artistic uncertainty during the long weeks of shooting still to be done after that exciting week back from the hospital. With her suspiciousness of motive, how little can she trust Miller now that they are apart, or for that matter trust Huston with his lifelong absorption in male honor and male corruption. Huston's idea of a good woman is Hepburn in *The African Queen.* How unlimited must be his secret contempt for Marilyn, this converted Jewish princess. The one time Huston and Marilyn play at a crap table in Reno, she wants to know, "What should I ask the dice for, John?"

"Don't think, honey," he replies, "just throw."

Inquiring about the disposition of the dice is the measure of her muddling with magic. No. Huston will have small traffic with such female mystique.

Besides, there is talent in this movie that for once is equal to hers. Clift gives what is possibly the best performance of his life. A recluse from the company, and attached to his thermos of grapefruit juice and vodka (which comes into his veins as regularly as a rubber tube and jar of hospital glucose), he nonetheless impresses Gable altogether with his rushes. "In that scene at the table when he said, 'What was that they put in my arm?' he had a wild look in his eye that could only have come," Gable says, "from morphine . . . *and* booze . . . *and* the steers."

Huston nods. "You can believe Perce has had it all."

When Marilyn, however, did a breakfast scene with Gable that pleased Huston sufficiently for him to embrace her spontaneously (and then hug her again for the photographers) she told one of her staff to save the picture. "I want to have it to show around," she said, "when he begins saying mean things about me." This is hardly uncharacteristic of her distrust of all directors, but there is a difference.

Someone like Billy Wilder might hate her, but in that hatred was help-less adoration. She senses that she is not Huston's favorite, that he does not *react* to her. She has then no secret leverage upon the heart of the director. Pure perfidy of Miller, she begins to discover that the film can always go back to what it was from the beginning, a fine story about three good men whose way of living is almost ready to disap-pear. It was supposed to be her vehicle and yet she is in danger of being incidental to it. Finally she will have to act her utmost in order not to be left in the others' wake. Perhaps she even resorts to a trick. There had been a scene on which she counted much (indeed, she needed every one of her scenes to keep up with the men) and this was the moment when Gay Langland came back to the bed in the morn-ing after their first night together and embraced her. In the script she must have seen it as some high moment of romance, an unforgettable fifty feet of film history—Gable Kisses Monroe. But Huston preferred to maintain his reserve with love scenes—why slide around in the muck after every other director had gone through the old town pipe? So he keeps their lovemaking dry. A middle-aged cowboy and a nice blonde offer a near-documentary style of hello, let's have some eggs, it's morning, wasn't last night fine?

Since she had succeeded, however, in playing the scene with only a sheet to cover her nakedness (which was also fair documentary—how else under such chaste circumstance could the audience know they had slept together?), and since there were two cameras on her, purposefully or inadvertently she let enough of the sheet slip to ex-pose a breast on Take Seven to one of the two cameras, thereby creat-ing a dilemma that would not be settled until the hour of distribution. Should they release the film with the shot of Monroe's nude breast? Monroe, no surprise, is for it. "I love to do the things the censors won't pass. After all, what are we all here for, just to stand around and let it pass us by?" Huston replies, "I've always known that girls have breasts." No, he will not want the aesthetic slant of his film to be nudged by her competitive tit. And the picture, when it finally comes out, has a clear view only of her back. The episode, however, offers its clue to her idea of cinematic balance. She would yet have to compete with Gable the King and Clift the Genius, plus Eli Wallach with his complete set of actor's skills, and she is even convinced that Wallach has formed a conspiracy with Miller to build up his part by giving Roslyn an affair with him. Conspiracy between Miller and Wallach or no, it is true Miller wants to rewrite. Wallach is too good an actor to have nothing to do at the end of the film but rant at Gable and Monroe. If he has even a fair little scene of doing the lindy with Marilyn, she will accuse Wallach of trying to upstage her, since most of the dance takes place with her back to the camera, but then, sharpening the barb, will add, "The audience is going to find my ass more interesting than Eli's face." (She is reported to say "rear," but we know better.) She has been friends with Wallach for five years. Now it is as if in breaking with Miller she is moving from one land to another, for in private she even says to Eli, "You Jewish men don't understand anything."

Is she thinking of the Reform rabbi who told her there is no afterlife? Or of the duplicities in Miller's plot? The concept of this movie is by now three years old. For three years she has lived with the beautiful idea that some day she and Arthur would make a film that would bestow upon her public identity a soul. Her existence as a sex queen will be reincarnated in a woman. It is not that her sex will disappear so much as that the sex queen will become an angel of sex. While she had accomplished something like this already in *Some Like It Hot*, Sugar Kane was a flawed angel—she had no mind. Whereas Marilyn wanted to present herself at her best. Or at least as Miller's early and enraptured idea of her (which we can assume she must alternately have been delighted with and disbelieved), a woman so sensitive and alive, so nubile as flesh and so evanescent as a wisp of vapor, that to present herself in such a way to the world might wipe away all the old killing publicity of the past. It was as if she wanted to become the angel of American life; as if, beneath every remaining timidity and infirmity, she felt that she deserved it. Perhaps she did. Are there ten women's lives so Napoleonic as her own? So she had to hope (with the part of herself not without hope) that the final version of *The Misfits* would be her temple.

Of course, her power to comprehend the relation of the part to the whole was never superb. Actors rarely have such power. When they do, they become directors. Perhaps she never recognized how completely *The Misfits* was a narrative about men. In its original form, it was certainly one of the best short stories about men ever written in a Hemingway tradition. Indeed, much of the prose could pass for Hemingway writing in his quietest manner. It is possibly the best piece of prose Miller ever wrote, and since the subject was a departure for him—he had known next to nothing about cowboys—and he did it in that bold time when he was getting a divorce and embarking on the adventure of his life, a sense of male optimism lives better in that short story than in the film. Miller's strength had always been to write about men. It was just that in *The Misfits* the men were stronger than they had ever been before. And cleaner. (As he may have been in the weeks he wrote it.)

Difficulties were then implicit in bringing Marilyn into the film—not any actress, but Marilyn in a portrait of consummate loveliness. While Roslyn already existed in the short story, she was offstage and merely talked about, an agreeable and attractive middle-aged eastern woman living with Gay Langland (and supporting him). His friends, the other two cowboys, were also attracted to her, powerfully attracted, and Langland did not even know if she was faithful or not. Every movie possibility obviously existed for conflict and drama. But that was opposed to what Marilyn desired. She had no wish to be sleeping with two or three men in *her* film; she wanted respect! It was the cry of her life. Unhappily, she had come to decide no audience would give that accolade to an actress who has carnal knowledge of two or more characters in one film. It is still 1960. So Miller's dramatic choices become limited. She can have a dalliance with Monty Clift and/or Eli Wallach, but only as in a mist. Marilyn wanted her film affair with Gable to be idyllic (exposed breast and all!), and Gable doubtless wanted no less. He was too old and too grand to be seen in some demeaning jealous state—his dignity had been the fuel of his own performances for the last fifteen years. How then is the script to move from celebration of its splendid stars to some obligatory minimum of conflict and plot? Miller is obliged to make the character of Roslyn so tender that the capture of a few wild horses is all of disaster for her, a dramatic bubble that cannot help but burst. It is possible that Marilyn does not begin to assess how unplayable will be her part by the end of *The Misfits* until she is deep into the film—then, too late, she will recognize that her share of the last reel is shrill—a liberal version of "we must stop the locomotive at the pass." So she has to stop Gable, Clift, and Wallach from bringing in the horses, but cinematically what we see is Gable, Clift, and Wallach taking chances, being knocked to the ground under rearing animals or dragged along by runaways, while she screams on the sidelines or dashes in hysteria from one to the other until the movie audience is ready to yell, "Shut that bitch up!"

At the end it is Gable who is canonized. Gay Langland has become the apotheosis of Gable. "Where are you going?" Wallach asks as Clark and Marilyn drive off in a truck at the end.

Miller put in no reply. Gable knew better. "Home," he answers Wallach in his guttiest voice, and the movie screen in every small-town theatre of America would give its little jump. He had finally found his role. Being Clark Gable had also been better than wages. As he drove along with Marilyn through the desert and the last of the film closed down on them, he said, "Just head for that big star. . . ." They were finally done with *The Misfits*. Perhaps it was his best moment since Rhett Butler smiled and said, "Frankly, my dear, I don't give a damn."

Of course, the film company had come down toward the end of their work in something like the bewildered ribald state of an army that has lived off the substance of a town for months and has forgotten the patriotic premise of its war. They had no idea if what they had done was good or ill. It was almost as if filming in Nevada were bound therefore to close with scenes of dust and strife while stuntmen were struck in the head by horses' hooves and Gable was dragged behind a truck on a rope, even as at night social lines were obliged to be drawn to a comic nicety. While Marilyn is losing the biggest bet of her life, Paula Strasberg is giving a party for Marilyn, whose point seems to be that Miller and his intimates are not invited. Strasberg's Revenge—a Balkan *melodrame*! To which in turn Huston gave a party for Miller and Clift to which everybody was invited. There the cameraman, Russell Metty, delivered a valedictory. Of course, only the Cameraman could speak in such a tongue, for he was the altar at which actors' prayers were laid. When the altar speaks, it is in good voice: "Arthur writes scripts," Metty said, "and John shoots ducks. First Arthur screwed up the script and now his wife is screwing it up. Why don't you wish him a happy birthday, Marilyn? Arthur doesn't know whether the horse should be up or down. Marilyn thinks we should keep the scene showing her half-naked in bed. Monty is buying into the Del Monte grapefruit business. . . . This is truly the biggest bunch of misfits I ever saw." Applause.

When the company left Nevada to work in Hollywood on final process shots, more small comedy continued. Looking at the rough cut, an executive from United Artists was unhappy—it did not seem a Huston film where "you put the ingredients in, and he builds up a terrific head of steam." The executive said if he didn't know, he wouldn't have had a clue to who the director might be. Miller agreed that he, too, was disappointed. Huston replied, "These things are missing in the script." Now they played again with the idea of writing new scenes for Wallach until Gable refused, and then, over the next few weeks of editing and adding music, went through the other predictable drama, Huston and Miller, of coming to like each other's work again. They had aid. The film became affecting after all. For Gable had a massive heart attack the day after shooting finished, and would die in the hospital eleven days later. Every scene now could bring to mind half the history of Hollywood's years.

From *Marilyn* (1973)

# FOUND OBJECTS—I

## A Mighty Mother

Marguerite Oswald had begun efforts to find out what happened to Lee. She had written to her Texas congressman, Jim Wright, on March 6, 1960, and a day later to Christian Herter of the State Department:

Dear Sir:

In October 1959 my son (age 20 years) Lee Harvey Oswald (serial no. 1653230) went to Moscow, Russia, three days after his discharge from the Marine Corps . . .

I am very much concerned because I have no contact whatsoever with him now . . .

I am writing to you because I am under the impression that Lee is probably stranded and even if he now realizes he has made a mistake he would have no way of financing his way home. He probably needs help.

I also realize that my son might like Russia. That he might be working and be quite content. In that case, feeling very strongly that he has a right as an individual to make his own decisions, I would in no way want to hinder or influence him in any way.

If it is at all possible to give me any information concerning my son, I would indeed be very grateful.

Thanking you in advance for your kindness in this matter.

I remain
Sincerely,
Mrs. Marguerite Oswald

Confidential memos will go back and forth between State and the American Embassy in Moscow discussing whether the Embassy is in a position to find out from the Soviets where Oswald is located, but the inquiry falls between the cracks.

Bureaucracy is the only form of human organization that can manage to pass a hot potato through a small crack. Ten and one half months will go by before State will hear from Marguerite Oswald again. That lady, however, has been gathering her forces. The next time they hear from her, she is on their doorstep. At the Warren Commission hearings, she will recall the occasion clearly: It is January 21, 1961, the day after President Kennedy's Inauguration.

MARGUERITE OSWALD: . . . I arrived at Washington 8 o'clock in the morning. I took a train and borrowed money on an insurance policy I have, [plus] I had a bank account of $36, which I drew out and bought a pair of shoes. I have all that in proof, sir, the date that I left for the train. I was 3 days and 2 nights on the train, or 2 days and 3 nights. Anyhow, I took a coach and sat up.

I arrived at the station 8 o'clock in the morning and I called the White House. A Negro man was on the switchboard, and he said the offices were not open yet, they did not open until 9 o'clock. He asked if I would leave my number. I asked to speak to the President. And he said the offices were not open yet. I said, "Well, I have just arrived here from Fort Worth, Texas, and I will call back at 9 o'clock."

So I called back at 9 o'clock. Everybody was just gracious to me over the phone. Said that President Kennedy was in a conference, and they would be happy to take any message. I asked to speak with Secretary Rusk and they connected me with that office. And his young lady said he was in a conference, but anything she could do for me. I said, "Yes, I have come to town about a son of mine who is lost in Russia. I do want to speak—I would like personally to speak to Secretary Rusk." So she got off the line a few minutes. Whether she gave him the message or what I do not know. She came back and said, "Mrs. Oswald, Mr. Rusk [said] that you talk to Mr. Boster who is special officer in charge of Soviet Union affairs,"—if I am correct. And Mr. Boster was on the line. I told him who I was. He said, "Yes, I am familiar with the case, Mrs. Oswald." He said, "Will an 11 o'clock appointment be all right with you?" This is 9 o'clock in the morning. So I said—this is quite an interesting story—I said, "Mr. Boster, that would be fine. But I would rather not talk with you." I didn't know who Mr.

Boster was. I said, "I would rather talk with Secretary of State Rusk. However, if I am unsuccessful in talking with him, then I will keep my appointment with you."

So I asked Mr. Boster—I said, "Mr. Boster, would you please recommend a hotel that would be reasonable?" He said, "I don't know how reasonable, Mrs. Oswald, but I recommend the Washington Hotel. It will be near the State Department and convenient to you."

So I went to the Washington Hotel. [And] they asked me if I had a reservation. I said, "No, I didn't but Mr. Boster of the State Department recommended that I come here." So they fixed me up with a room. I took a bath and dressed. I went to the appointment [and] arrived at Mr. Boster's office at 10:30.

But before arriving at Mr. Boster's office, I stopped at a telephone in the corridor and I called Dean Rusk's office again because I didn't want to see Mr. Boster, and I asked to speak to Dean Rusk. And the young lady said, "Mrs. Oswald, talk to Mr. Boster. At least it is a start."

So then I entered around the corridor into Mr. Boster's office [and he] came out and said, "Mrs. Oswald, I am awfully glad you came early because we are going to have a terrible snow storm and we have orders to leave early in order to get home."

So he called [in two other men and] we were in conference. So I showed the papers like I am showing here. And I said, "Now, I know you are not going to answer me, gentlemen, but I am under the impression that my son is an agent." "Do you mean a Russian agent?" I said, "No, working for our Government, a U.S. agent. And I want to say this: That if he is, I don't appreciate it too much, because I am destitute, and just getting over a sickness," on that order.

I had the audacity to say that. I had gone through all of this without medical, without money, without compensation. I am a desperate woman. So I said that.

MR. RANKIN: What did they say to you?

MARGUERITE OSWALD: They did not answer that. I even said to them, "No, you won't tell me." So I didn't expect them to answer that.

THE CHAIRMAN: Did you mean that you were seeking money from them?

MARGUERITE OSWALD: No, sir . . . What I was saying was that I think that my son should be home with me, is really what I implied [but] I didn't come out and say I want my son home. I implied that if he was an agent, that I thought he needed to be home.

MR. RANKIN: Did you say anything about believing your son might know full well what he was doing in trying to defect to the Soviet Union, he might like it better there than he did here?

MARGUERITE OSWALD: I do not remember saying this . . . I said—because I remember this distinctly. I said, "Now, he has been exploited all through the paper as a defector. If he is a defector"—because, as we stated before, I don't know he is an agent, sir—"and if he is a defector, that is his privilege as an individual."

And they said, "Mrs. Oswald, we want you to know that we feel the same way about it." That was their answer.

Still, Marguerite was not about to give up the more interesting alternative. A little later on that day in 1964 when she testified before the Warren Commission about events early in 1961, she would add:

MARGUERITE OSWALD: . . . Approximately 8 weeks later, on March 22, 1961, I received a letter from the State Department informing me . . . that my son wishes to return back to the United States—just 8 weeks after my trip to Washington.

Now, you want to know why I think my son is an agent. And I have been telling you all along.

Here is a very important thing why my son was an agent. . . . On April 30, 1961, he marries a Russian girl—approximately 5 weeks later.

Now, why does a man who wants to come back to the United States, [only] 5 weeks later [decide to] marry a Russian girl? Because I say—and I may be wrong—the U.S. Embassy has ordered him to marry this Russian girl. . . .

MR. RANKIN: Now, was there any time that Marina said anything to you to lead you to believe that she thought your son, Lee, married her because he was an agent?

MARGUERITE OSWALD: No, sir, no, sir. Not at any time at all.

MR. RANKIN: You think she loved him?

MARGUERITE OSWALD: I believe that Marina loved him in a way. But I believe that Marina wanted to come to America. I believe that Lee had talked America to her, and she wanted to come . . .

MR. RANKIN: I am not clear about this being ordered to marry her. You don't mean that your son didn't love her.

MARGUERITE OSWALD: Well, I could mean that—if he is an agent, and he has a girl friend, and it is to the benefit of the country that he marry this girl friend, and the Embassy helped him get this Russian girl out of Russia—let's face it, well, whether he loved her or not, he would take her to America if that would give him contact with Russians, yes, sir.

MR. RANKIN: Is that what you mean?

MARGUERITE OSWALD: I would say that.

MR. RANKIN: And you don't think it was because your son loved her, then?

MARGUERITE OSWALD: I do not know whether my son loved her or not. But I am telling you why he would do this in five weeks' time . . .

MR. RANKIN: . . . I think it is a very serious thing to say about your son, that he would do a thing like that to a girl.

MARGUERITE OSWALD: No, sir, it is not a serious thing. I know a little about the CIA and so on, the U-2, Powers, and things that have been made public. They go through any extreme for their country. I do not think that would be serious for him to marry a Russian girl and bring her here, so he would have contact. I think that is all part of an agent's duty.

MR. RANKIN: You think your son was capable of doing that?

MARGUERITE OSWALD: Yes, sir, I think my son was an agent. I certainly do.

*From Oswald's Tale: An American Mystery* (1995)

# 1961  FOUND OBJECTS—II

## Oswald and Marina in Minsk

From KGB Transcripts
For Object: OLH-2658
For Period: 17 July 1961

[In these transcripts, OLH (Oswald, Lee Harvey) has been changed to LHO. Marina was always referred to as WIFE. Stepan, the KGB officer running the case, underlined those speeches he considered pertinent to his needs, whereas any comments that appear in italics as stage directions were made by the KGB transcriber. That worthy was making his (or her) observations through a peephole in a rented room adjacent to the Oswalds' apartment.]

LHO: I can't tell you what to do. Do what you want to do. If you want, you can go with me.
WIFE: I don't want to.
LHO: Why?
WIFE: I'm simply afraid.
LHO: Of course you're afraid.
WIFE: I don't know America, I only know Russia . . . You can go back to your own people . . . I don't know how things will be there. *Where will you find work?*
LHO: I'll find everything, everything. I'll do everything. That's my job.
WIFE: How will they treat me there?
*(radio drowns out conversation; impossible to get in entirety)*

FROM KGB TRANSCRIPTS
FOR OBJECT: OLH-2658
FOR PERIOD: 19 JULY 1961

WIFE: All you know how to do is torture . . .
*(LHO goes out; yells something from the kitchen)*
WIFE: Go find yourself a girl who knows how to cook . . . I work, I
    don't have time to prepare cutlets for you. You don't want soup,
    you don't want kasha, just tasty tidbits, please!
LHO: I can go eat at a restaurant.
WIFE: Go to hell! When are you ever going to leave me alone? I'll prob-
    ably never live to see the day when you leave me alone.
LHO: But you don't know how to do anything.
WIFE: Leave me alone!

She bumped into Misha Smolsky once on the street, and he asked
her how she was doing with her man, and she answered, "Very difficult." Misha said, "If it is difficult, why did you jump into it?" She said,
"No, he's not a bad guy, but food is very difficult." At that time, in
shops there was a lot to buy, but what do people in Minsk eat, after
all?—potatoes, pork fat, pickled cucumbers, pickled cabbage, beef,
pork, mutton, turkey, goose. She wasn't able to buy food he would
like. For instance, Alik would say, "I want to have corn," and any corn
they grew around there is for livestock. So she said to Misha Smolsky,
"Let's say we have cultural difficulties."

FROM KGB TRANSCRIPTS
FOR OBJECT: OLH-2658
FOR PERIOD: 21 JULY 1961

LHO: Well, why are you crying? *(pause)* I told you crying won't do any
    good.
    *(Wife cries)*
        You know, I never said that I was a very good person.
    *(Wife cries and LHO calms her down)*
WIFE: *(through tears) Why did I get married?* You tricked me.
LHO: . . . You shouldn't cry. I understand, you don't understand your-
    self why.
WIFE: *(through tears)* My friends don't recognize me.
LHO: Well? I've also lost weight, right?

WIFE: (*cries*) *Why did I get married?*

LHO: Well, what am I supposed to do? Is it my fault that you have a lot of work? I mean, you don't ever cook, but other women cook. And I don't say anything about it. I don't yell. You never do anything and you don't want to do the wash. What do you do? The only thing you ever talk about is how tired you are at work.

WIFE: I didn't get any rest.

LHO: Well, what can I do?

(*pause*)

WIFE: Everything was so good, but lately everything has gotten bad. Nothing's right. You can't please *a man like you.*

(*they are silent*)

*Later that night*

LHO: Well, what? This is ridiculous!

WIFE: I want to sleep, don't bother me! . . . *You're so crude!* I'm tired, I swear, I'm tired.

LHO: And what did you do that you're so tired? *You didn't do anything. You didn't cook anything.*

WIFE: The cafeteria's good enough.

LHO: And who's going to wash the shirts, the socks?

WIFE: Everything's already washed, go and take a look. You'll leave and then you'll be unhappy alone, you'll see. So get off my back. What is it you want from me, anyway, what? For God's sake, just don't torture me. Soon enough you won't have me, and that's all there is to it.

(*pause*)

WIFE: You're laughing, but you'll cry later . . . (*pause*) I don't want to now. I'm tired.

LHO: What did you do that you're tired?

WIFE: Don't throw things around . . .

LHO: What can I do? (*mocks Wife*) "I don't want to!" Well, what can I say! We're going to be here four or five months anyway.

WIFE: I'll be here. Let the baby stay by itself.

LHO: Are you crazy!? (*yells*) You should be ashamed! A child without a father! You should be ashamed! (*laughs*) *You're still my wife, you're going!* And if I leave, I'll send you an invitation.

WIFE: You'll leave on your own.

LHO: You should be ashamed! You don't believe yourself what you're saying . . .

WIFE: I'm not going to promise. If I don't go then that's it.

LHO: You're my wife, you're going.

WIFE: No.

LHO: Why?

WIFE: I know why.

LHO: Well, why? You don't know yourself. There, you see. Do you
    know how many foreigners live there?

WIFE: *They won't take me there, and they won't create the conditions for me,*
    *they won't create them. The American Embassy won't look after me.*

LHO: *Why do you think that? I mean, I wrote that I was obligating myself.*
    [Note in left margin: "Obviously, he is obligating himself to pro-
    vide her with everything she needs in United States."] You un-
    derstand that you're my wife and that you're going with me.
    *When I arrived here it was difficult for me too.*

WIFE: That is an entirely different matter.

LHO: *But I'm obligating myself! I'll do everything.*
    *(pause)*

WIFE: You won't convince me.
    *(pause)*

LHO: You're just stubborn.

WIFE: And you're always yelling. *(radio drowns out conversation)*

When Inessa met Lee Oswald, he seemed not exactly unfriendly,
but very suspicious about things. They exchanged a few words and
then he sat down in a chair and became completely occupied with
some comic books his brother had sent him from America. Inessa
spent her time chatting with Marina.

After a few more visits, however, Alik's suspicions began fading
away. Before long, Inessa was eating with them in their kitchen. Indeed, she even liked it that he hadn't become open right away but had
waited and observed. She thinks she probably wouldn't have believed
him if, immediately, he had been too friendly. In fact, she liked him as
a husband for Marina. He did all the man's work around their apartment without needing reminders. Which is not too often true of Russian men.

What she wasn't so comfortable with was that all of a sudden he
would announce what he liked about the Soviet Union and what he
didn't like, and he would do it in the open—never whispering. And
there were other little things. She really couldn't say that she approved of him entirely, even if they were only small things. He would
carry on if dinner wasn't cooked on time, and in her opinion, Marina
didn't fit into his American standards of what a wife should be. When
they had fights, Inessa saw them as children, one more stubborn than

the other. She liked them both and was comfortable with both, and—maybe she was just lucky—in her presence they never had any really big arguments. She does remember that Marina would get irritated when Alik would read his American comic books and begin to laugh loudly. On the other hand, Marina thought he was too pedantic and told Inessa that she was dissatisfied with his mind.

He also had bad habits. Like a worker or a crude soldier. He was always spoiling the air with gases. That was shocking, and he did it as naturally as drinking water.

All the same, Inessa always felt that Alik was more calm than Marina. Outside of those gases, he was very organized. He liked perfection in everything, and Marina used to complain about this trait. Taken all together, Inessa never really thought that Marina was deeply in love with him. She thinks Alik loved her more.

FROM KGB TRANSCRIPTS
FOR OBJECT: OLH-2658
FOR PERIOD: 24 JULY 1961
21:20

WIFE: Alik! Look, I forgot to iron the bedsheets—there's one lying over there. Alik! Look how warm my ears are.
*(they joke around; they laugh)*
LHO: Not bad songs they're singing.
WIFE: There's some festival going on. Everyone's going to Moscow and people can say what they want. Before, you couldn't say anything: not on the street, not on the streetcar, not on the trolley. When Stalin was alive there was a microphone in every house and you couldn't say anything. Nowadays it's a different matter.
LHO: Yes, yes, my sister.

From *Oswald's Tale: An American Mystery* (1995)

# 10,000 WORDS
# A MINUTE

## Journalists

Remember that old joke about three kinds of intelligence: human, animal, and military? Well, if there are three kinds of writers: novelists, poets, and *reporters,* there is certainly a gulf between the poet and the novelist. Quite apart from the kind of living they make, poets invariably seem to be aristocrats, usually spoiled beyond repair; and novelists—even if they make a million, or have large talent—look to have something of the working class about them. Maybe it is the drudgery, the long, obsessive inner life, the day-to-day monotony of applying themselves to the middle of the same continuing job, or perhaps it is the business of being unappreciated at home—has anyone met a novelist who is happy with the rugged care provided by his wife?

Now, of course, I am tempted to round the image out and say reporters belong to the middle class. Only I do not know if I can push the metaphor. Taken one by one, it is true that reporters tend to be hardheaded, objective, and unimaginative. Their intelligence is sound but unexceptional and they have the middle-class penchant for collecting tales, stories, legends, accounts of practical jokes, details of negotiation, bits of memoir—all those capsules of fiction that serve the middle class as a substitute for ethics and/or culture. Reporters, like shopkeepers, tend to be worshipful of the fact that wins and so covers over the other facts. In the middle class, the remark "He made a lot of money" ends the conversation. If you persist, if you try to point out that the money was made by digging through his grandmother's grave to look for oil, you are met with a middle-class shrug. "It's a question of taste whether one should get into the past" is the winning reply.

In his own person there is nobody more practical than a reporter. He exhibits the same avidity for news that a businessman will show for money. No bourgeois will hesitate to pick up a dollar, even if he is not fond of the man with whom he deals: so, a reporter will do a nice story about a type he dislikes, or a bad story about a figure he is fond of. It has nothing to do with his feelings. There is a logic to news—on a given day, with a certain meteorological drift to the winds in the mass media, a story can only ride along certain vectors. To expect a reporter to be true to the precise detail of an event is kin to the sentimentality that asks a fast revolving investor to be faithful to a particular stock in his portfolio when it is going down and his others are going up.

But here we come to the end of our image. When the middle class gather for a club meeting or a social function, the atmosphere is dependably dull, whereas ten reporters come together in a room for a story are slightly hysterical, and two hundred reporters and photographers congregated for a press conference are as void of dignity, even stuffed-up, stodgy, middle-class dignity, as a slew of monkeys tearing through the brush. There is reason for this, much reason: There is always urgency to get some quotation that is usable for their story and, afterward, find a telephone. The habitat of a reporter, at its worst, is identical to spending one's morning, afternoon, and evening transferring from the rush hour of one subway train to the rush hour of another. In time even the best come to remind one of the rush hour. An old fight reporter is a sad sight—he looks like an old prizefight manager, which is to say, he looks like an old cigar butt.

Nor is this true only of sports reporters. They are gifted with charm compared to political reporters, who give off an effluvium which is unadulterated cancer gulch. I do not think I exaggerate. There is an odor to any Press Headquarters that is unmistakable. One may begin by saying it is like the odor in small left-wing meeting halls, except it is worse, far worse, for there is no poverty to put a guilt-free iron into the nose; on the contrary, everybody is getting free drinks, free sandwiches, free news releases. Yet there is the unavoidable smell of flesh burning quietly and slowly in the service of a machine. Have any of you never been through the smoking car of an old coach early in the morning when the smokers sleep and the stale air settles into congelations of gloom? Well, that is a little like the scent of Press

Headquarters. Yet the difference is vast, because Press Headquarters for any big American event is invariably a large room in a large hotel, usually the largest room in the largest hotel in town. Thus it is a commercial room in a commercial hotel. The walls must be pale green or pale pink, dirty by now, subtly dirty like the toe of a silk stocking. (Which is incidentally the smell of the plaster.) One could be meeting bureaucrats from Tashkent in the Palace of the Soviets. One enormous barefaced meeting room, a twenty-foot banner up, a proscenium arch at one end, with high Gothic windows painted within the arch—almost never does a window look out on the open air. (Hotels build banquet rooms on the *inside* of their buildings—it is the best way to fill internal space with revenue.)

This room is in fever. Two hundred, three hundred, I suppose even five hundred, reporters get into some of these rooms, there to talk, there to drink, there to bang away on any one of fifty standard typewriters, provided by the people on Public Relations who have set up this Press Headquarters. It is like being at a vast party in Limbo—there is tremendous excitement, much movement, and no sex at all. Just talk. Talk fed by cigarettes. One thousand to two thousand cigarettes are smoked every hour. The mind must keep functioning fast enough to offer up stories. (Reporters meet as in a marketplace to trade their stories—they barter an anecdote they cannot use about one of the people in the event in order to pick up a different piece that is usable by their paper. It does not matter if the story is true or altogether not true—it must merely be suitable and not too mechanically libelous.) So they char the inside of their bodies in order to scrape up news which can go out to the machine, that enormous machine, that intellectual leviathan which is obliged to eat, each day, tidbits, gristle, gravel, garbage cans, charlotte russe, old rubber tires, T-bone steaks, wet cardboard, dry leaves, apple pie, broken bottles, dog food, shells, roach powder, dry ball-point pens, grapefruit juice. All the trash, all the garbage, all the slop, and a little of the wealth go out each day and night into the belly of that old American goat, our newspapers.

So the reporters smell also of this work, they smell of the dishwasher and the pots, they are flesh burning themselves very quietly and slowly in the service of a machine that feeds goats, that feeds the Goat. One smells this collective odor on the instant one enters their meeting room. It is not a corrupt smell, it does not have enough of the meats, the savory, and the vitality of flesh to smell corrupt and fearful when it is bad, no, it is more the smell of excessive respect for power, the odor of flesh gutted by avidities that are electric and empty. I suppose it is the bleak smell one could find on the inside of one's head during a bad cold, full of fever, badly used, burned out of mood. The physical sensation of a cold often is one of power trapped corrosively inside, coils of strength being liquidated in some center of the self. The reporter hangs in a powerless-power—his voice directly, or via the rewrite desk indirectly, reaches out to millions of readers; the more readers he owns, the less he can say. He is forbidden by a hundred censors, most of them inside himself, to communicate notions that are not conformistically simple, simple like plastic is simple, that is to say, monotonous. Therefore a reporter forms a habit equivalent to lacerating the flesh: He learns to write what he does not naturally believe. Since he did not start, presumably, with the desire to be a bad writer or a dishonest writer, he ends by bludgeoning his brain into believing that something which is half true is in fact—since he creates a fact each time he puts something into a newspaper—nine-tenths true. A psyche is debauched—his own; a false fact is created. For which fact, sooner or later, inevitably, inexorably, the public will pay. A nation that forms detailed opinions on the basis of detailed fact which is askew from the subtle reality becomes a nation of citizens whose psyches are skewed, item by detailed item, away from *any* reality.

So great guilt clings to reporters. They know they help to keep America slightly insane. As a result perhaps they are a shabby-looking crew. The best of them are the shabbiest, which is natural if one thinks about it—a sensitive man suffers from the prosperous life of his lies more than a dull man. In fact the few dudes one finds among reporters tend to be semi-illiterates, or hatchet men, or cynics on two or three payrolls who do restrained public relations in the form of news stories. But this is to make too much of the extremes. Reporters along the middle of the spectrum are shabby, worried, guilty, and suffer each day from the damnable anxiety that they know all sorts of powerful information a half hour to twenty-four hours before anyone else in America knows it, not to mention the time clock ticking away in the vault of all those stories that cannot be printed or will not be printed. It makes for a livid view of existence. It is like an injunction to become hysterical once a day. Then they must write at lightning speed. It may be heavy-fisted but true, it may be slick as a barnyard slide, it may be great, it may be fill—what does it matter? The matter rides out like oats in a conveyor belt, and the unconscious takes a ferocious pounding. Writing is of use to the psyche only if the writer discovers something he did not know he knew in the act itself of writing. That is why a few men will go through hell in order to keep writing—Joyce and

Proust, for example. Being a writer can save one from insanity or cancer; being a bad writer can drive one smack into the center of the plague. Think of the poor reporter, who does not have the leisure of the novelist or the poet to discover what he thinks. The unconscious gives up, buries itself, leaves the writer to his cliché, and saves the truth, or that part of it the reporter is yet privileged to find, for his colleagues and his friends. A good reporter is a man who must still tell you the truth privately; he has bright harsh eyes and can relate ten good stories in a row standing at a bar.

Still, they do not quit. That charge of adrenaline once a day, that hysteria, that sense of powerless-power close to the engines of history—they can do without powerless-power no more than a gentleman junkie on the main line can do without his heroin, Doctor. You see, a reporter is close to the action. He is not *of* the action, but he is close to it, as close as a crab louse to the begetting of a child. One may never be President, but the photographer working for his paper has the power to cock a flashbulb and make the eyes of JFK go blink!

However, it is not just this lead-encased seat near the radiations of power that keeps the reporter hooked on a drug of new news to start new adrenaline; it is also the ride. It is the free ride. When we were children, there were those movies about reporters—they were heroes. While chasing a lead, they used to leap across empty elevator shafts, they would wrestle automatics out of mobsters' hands, and if they were Cary Grant, they would pick up a chair and stick it in the lion's face, since the lion had had the peculiar sense to walk into the editor's office. Next to being a cowboy or a private eye, the most heroic activity in America was to be a reporter. Now it is the welfare state. Every last cigar-smoking fraud of a middle-aged reporter, pale with prison pallor, deep lines in his cheeks, writing daily pietisms for the sheet back home about free enterprise, is himself the first captive of the welfare state. It is the best free ride anyone will find since he left his family's chest. Your room is paid for by the newspaper, your trips to the particular spots attached to the event—in this case, the training camp at Elgin, Illinois, for Patterson, and the empty racetrack at Aurora Downs for Liston—are by chartered limousine. Who but a Soviet bureaucrat, a British businessman, a movie star, or an American reporter would ride in a chartered limousine? (They smell like funeral parlors.) Your typing paper is free if you want it; your seat at the fight, or your ticket to the convention, is right up there, under the ropes; your meals if you get around to eating them are free, free sandwiches only, but then a reporter has a stomach like a shaving mug and a throat like a hog's trough: He couldn't tell steak tartare from *guacamole*. And the drinks—if you are at a big fight—are without charge. If you are at a political convention, there is no free liquor. But you do have a choice between free Pepsi-Cola and free Coca-Cola. The principle seems to be that the reporting of mildly psychotic actions—such as those performed by politicians—should be made in sobriety; whereas a sane estimate of an athlete's chances are neatest on booze. At a fight at Press Headquarters, the drinks are very free, and the mood can even be half convivial. At the Patterson-Liston Press Headquarters there was a head bartender working for Championship Sports whose name was Archie. He was nice. He was a nice man. It was a pleasure to get a drink from him. You remember these things afterward, it's part of the nostalgia. The joy of the free ride is the lack of worry. It's like being in an Army outfit that everyone's forgotten. You get your food, you get your beer, you get your pay, the work is easy, and leave to town is routine. You never had it so good—you're an infant again: You can grow up a second time and improve the job.

That's the half and half of being a reporter. One half is addiction, adrenaline, anecdote-shopping, deadlines, dread, cigar smoke, lung cancer, vomit, feeding the Goat; the other is Aloha, Tahiti, old friends, and the free ride to the eleventh floor of the Sheraton-Chicago, Patterson-Liston Press Headquarters, everything free. Even your news free. If you haven't done your homework, if you drank too late last night and missed the last limousine out to Elgin or Aurora this morning, if there's no poop of your own on Floyd's speed or Sonny's bad mood, you can turn to the handouts given you in the Press Kit, dig, a *Kit*, kiddies, worked up for you by Harold Conrad, who's the Public Relations Director. It's not bad stuff, it's interesting material. No need to do your own research. Look at some of this: There's the tale of the tape for each fighter with as many physical measurements as a tailor in Savile Row might take; there's the complete record of each fighter, how he won, how many rounds, who, the date, so forth; there's the record of how much money they made on each fight, how their KO records compare with the All-Time Knockout Artists, Rocky Marciano with 43 out of 49, batting .878, Joe Louis at .761, Floyd at .725 (29 in 40), and Sonny Liston going with 23 for 34, is down at .676, back of Jim Jeffries, who comes in at .696. There's a column there, there's another if you want to dig into the biographies of each fighter, six single-spaced pages on Patterson, four on Liston. There's a list of each and every fighter who won and lost the Heavyweight Championship, and the year—remember? Remember Jake Kilrain and Marvin Hart (stopped Jack Root at Reno, Nevada, 12 rounds, July 3, 1905). You can win money with Marvin Hart betting in bars. And Tommy Burns. Jack O'Brien. In what year did Ezzard Charles first take Jersey Joe Walcott; in what town? You can see the different columns shaping up. If you got five columns to do on the fight, three can be whipped right up out of Graff/Reiner/Smith Enterprises, Inc. Sports News Release. Marvelous stuff. How Sonny Liston does his roadwork on railroad tracks, what Sonny's best weight is (206–212), what kind of poundages Floyd likes to give away—averages 10 pounds a bout—Floyd's style in boxing, Liston's style in boxing. It's part of the free list, an offering of facts with a little love from the Welfare State.

It is so easy, so much is done for you, that you remember these days with nostalgia. When you do get around to paying for yourself, going into a room like the Camelot Room at the Sheraton-Chicago, with its black-blood three-story mahogany paneling and its high, stained Gothic windows looking out no doubt on an air shaft, it is a joy to buy your own food, an odd smacking sensation to pay for a drink. It is the Welfare State that makes the pleasure possible. When one buys all one's own drinks, the sensation of paying cash is without much joy, but to pay for a drink occasionally—that's near bliss.

And because it is a fight, cancer gulch has its few oases. The Press Headquarters livens up with luminaries, the unhealthiest people in America now meet some of the healthiest, complete self-contained healthy bodies pass modestly through: Ingemar Johansson and Archie Moore, Rocky Marciano, Barney Ross, Cassius Clay, Harold Johnson, Ezzard Charles, Dick Tiger on his way to San Francisco, where he is to fight Gene Fullmer and beat him, Jim Braddock—big, heavy, gray, and guarded, looking as tough as steel drilled into granite, as if he were the toughest night watchman in America, and Joe Louis looking like the largest Chinaman in the world, still sleepy, still sad. That's part of the pleasure of Press Headquarters—the salty crystallized memories that are released from the past, the night ten or eleven years ago when Joe Louis, looking just as sleepy and as sad as he does now, went in to fight Rocky Marciano at the Garden and was knocked out in eight. It was part of a comeback, but Louis was never able to get his fight going at all, he was lethargic that night, and Marciano, fighting a pure Italian street-fighter's style, throwing his punches as if he held a brick in each hand, taking Louis' few good shots with an animal joy, strong enough to eat bricks with his teeth, drove right through Joe Louis and knocked him out hard. Louis went over in a long, very inert fall, as if an old tree or a momentous institution were coming down, perhaps the side of a church wall hovering straight and slow enough in its drop for the onlooker to take a breath in the gulf of the bomb. And it had been a bomb. Louis' leg was draped over the rope. People were crying as they left Madison Square Garden that night. It was a little like the death of Franklin Delano Roosevelt: Something generous had just gone out of the world. And now here was Marciano as well, in the couloirs and coffee shop and lobby of the Sheraton-Chicago, a man looking as different from the young contender he had been on his way to the championship as Louis now looked the same. Louis had turned old in the ring. Marciano retired undefeated, and so aged after he stopped. Now he seemed no longer to be carrying bricks but pillows. He had gotten very plump, his face was round and no longer lumpy, he was half bald, a large gentle monk with a bemused, misty, slightly tricky expression.

# The Mafia

As the fight approached, so did the Mob. That arid atmosphere of reporters alone with reporters gave way to a whiff of the deep. The Mob was like birds and beasts coming in to feed. Heavy types, bouncers, plug-uglies, flatteners, one or two speedy, swishing Negro ex-boxers, for example, now blown up to the size of fat middleweights, slinky in their walk, eyes fulfilling the operative definition of razor slits, murder coming off them like scent comes off a skunk. You could feel death as they passed. It came wafting off. And the rest of the beasts as well—the strong-arm men, the head-kickers, the limb-breakers, the groin-stompers. If a clam had a muscle as large as a man and the muscle grew eyes, you would get the mood. Those were the beasts. They were all orderly, they were all trained, they were dead to humor. They never looked at anyone they did not know, and when they were introduced they stared at the floor while shaking hands, as if their own hand did not belong to them but was merely a stuffed mitten to which their arm was attached.

The orders came from the birds. There were hawks and falcons and crows, Italian dons looking like little old shrunken eagles, gulls, pelicans, condors. The younger birds stood around at modest strategic points in the lobby, came up almost not at all to Press Headquarters, posted themselves out on the street, stood at the head of escalators, near the door of the barbershop, along the elevator strip, by the registration desk. They were all dressed in black gabardine topcoats, black felt hats, and very large dark sunglasses with expensive frames. They wore white scarves or black scarves. A few would carry a black umbrella. They stood there watching everyone who passed. They gave the impression of knowing exactly why they were standing there, what they were waiting to hear, how they were supposed to see, who they were supposed to watch. One had the certainty after a time that they knew the name of every man and woman who walked through the downstairs lobby and went into the Championship Sports office on the ground floor. If a figure said hello to a celebrity he was not supposed to know—at least not in the bird's private handbook—one could sense the new information being filed. Some were tall, some were short, but almost all were thin, their noses were aquiline, their chins were modest, their cheeks were subtly concave. Their aura was succinct. It said, "If you spit on my shoes, you're dead." It was a shock to realize that the Mob, in the flesh, was even more impressive than in the motion pictures.

There were also some fine old *mafiosos* with faces one had seen on the busts of Venetian doges in the Ducal Palace, subtle faces, insidious with the ingrowth of a curious culture built on treachery, dogma, the evil eye, and blood loyalty to clan. They were *don capos,* and did not wear black any longer, black was for subalterns. They were the leaders of the birds, fine old gentlemen in quiet gray suits, quiet intricate dark ties. Some had eyes that contained the humor of a cardinal; others were not so nice. There was an unhealthy dropsical type with pallor, and pink-tinted bifocal glasses—the kind who looked as if they owned a rich mortuary in a poor Italian neighborhood, and ran the local Republican club.

# The Death of Benny Paret

On the afternoon of the night Emile Griffith and Benny Paret were to fight a third time for the welterweight championship, there was murder in both camps. "I hate that kind of guy," Paret had said earlier to

Pete Hamill. "A fighter's got to look and talk and act like a man." One of the Broadway gossip columnists had run an item about Griffith a few days before. His girl friend saw it and said to Griffith, "Emile, I didn't know about you being that way." So Griffith hit her. So he said. Now at the weigh-in that morning, Paret had insulted Griffith irrevocably, touching him on the buttocks, while making a few more remarks about his manhood. They almost had their fight on the scales.

The accusation of homosexuality arouses a major passion in many men; they spend their lives resisting it with a biological force. There is a kind of man who spends every night of his life getting drunk in a bar, he rants, he brawls, he ends in a small rumble on the street. Women say, "For God's sakes, he's homosexual. Why doesn't he just turn queer and get his suffering over with." Yet men protect him. It is because he is choosing not to become homosexual. It was put best by Sartre, who said that a homosexual is a man who practices homosexuality. A man who does not is not homosexual—he is entitled to the dignity of his choice. He is entitled to the fact that he chose not to become homosexual, and is paying presumably his price.

The rage in Emile Griffith was extreme. I was at the fight that night—I had never seen a fight like it. It was scheduled for fifteen rounds, but they fought without stopping from the bell that began the round to the bell which ended it, and then they fought after the bell, sometimes for as much as fifteen seconds before the referee could force them apart.

Paret was a Cuban, a proud club fighter who had become welterweight champion because of his unusual ability to take a punch. His style of fighting was to take three punches to the head in order to give back two. At the end of ten rounds, he would still be bouncing, his opponent would have a headache. But in the last two years, over the fifteen-round fights, he had started to take some maulings.

This fight had its turns. Griffith won most of the early rounds, but Paret knocked Griffith down in the sixth. Griffith had trouble getting up, but made it, came alive, and was dominating Paret again before the round was over. Then Paret began to wilt. In the middle of the eighth round, after a clubbing punch had turned his back to Griffith, Paret walked three disgusted steps away, showing his hindquarters. For a champion, he took much too long to turn back around. It was the first hint of weakness Paret had ever shown, and it must have inspired a particular shame, because he fought the rest of the fight as if he were seeking to demonstrate that he could take more punishment than any man alive. In the twelfth, Griffith caught him. Paret got trapped in a corner, and in the course of trying to slip away, his left arm and his head became tangled on the wrong side of the top rope. Griffith was in like a cat ready to rip the life out of a huge boxed rat. He hit him eighteen right hands in a row, an act that took perhaps three or four seconds, Griffith making a pent-up whimpering sound all the while he attacked, the right hand whipping like a piston rod which has broken through the crankcase, or like a baseball bat demolishing a pumpkin. I was sitting in the second row of that corner—they were not ten feet away from me—and like everybody else, I was hypnotized. I had never seen one man hit another so hard and so many times. Over the referee's face came a look of woe as if some spasm had passed its way through him, and then he leaped on Griffith to pull him away. It was the act of a brave man. Griffith was uncontrollable. His trainer leaped into the ring, his manager, his cut man, there were four people holding Griffith, but he was off on an orgy, he had left the Garden, he was back on a hoodlum's street. If he had been able to break loose from his handlers and the referee, he would have jumped Paret to the floor and whaled on him there.

And Paret? Paret died on his feet. As he took those eighteen punches something happened to everyone who was in psychic range of the event. Some part of his death reached out to us. One felt it hover in the air. He was still standing in the ropes, trapped as he had been before, he gave some little half-smile of regret, as if he were saying, "I didn't know I was going to die just yet," and then, his head leaning back but still erect, his death came to breathe about him. He began to pass away. As he passed, so his limbs descended beneath him, and he sank slowly to the floor. He went down more slowly than any fighter had ever gone down, he went down like a large ship that turns on end and slides second by second into its grave. As he went down, the sound of Griffith's punches echoed in the mind like a heavy ax in the distance chopping into a wet log.

Paret lay on the ground, quivering gently, a small froth on his mouth. The house doctor jumped into the ring. He knelt. He pried Paret's eyelid open. He looked at the eyeball staring out. He let the lid snap shut. He reached into his satchel, took out a needle, jabbed Paret with a stimulant. Paret's back rose in a high arch. He writhed. They were calling him back from death. One wanted to cry out, "Leave the man alone. Let him die." But they saved Paret long enough to take him to a hospital, where he lingered for days. He was in coma. He never came out of it. If he lived, he would have been a vegetable. His brain was smashed. But they held him in life for a week, they fed him chemicals, and made exploratory operations into his skull, and fed details of his condition to the Goat. And the Goat kicked clods of mud all over the place, and spoke harshly of prohibiting boxing. There was shock in the land. Children had seen the fight on television. There were editorials, gloomy forecasts that the Game was dead. The managers and the prizefighters got together. Gently, in thick, depressed hypocrisies, they tried to defend their sport. They did not find it easy to explain that they shared an unstated view of life which was religious.

It was of course not that religion which is called Judeo-Christian. It was an older religion, a more primitive one—a religion of blood, a murderous and sensitive religion that mocks the effort of the understanding to approach it, and scores the lungs of men like D. H. Lawrence, and burns the brain of men like Ernest Hemingway when they explore out into the mystery, searching to discover some part of the secret. It is the view of life that looks upon death as a condition which is more alive than life or unspeakably more deadening. As such it is not a very attractive notion to the Establishment. But then the Establishment has nothing very much of even the Judeo-Christian tradition. It has a respect for legal and administrative aspects of justice, and it is devoted to the idea of compassion for the poor. But the Establishment has no idea of death, no tolerance for Heaven or Hell, no comprehension of bloodshed. It sees no logic in pain. To the Establishment these notions are a detritus from the past.

Like a patient submerged beneath the plastic cover of an oxygen tent, boxing lives on beneath the cool, bored eyes of the Establishment. It would not take too much to finish boxing off. Shut down the oxygen, which is to say, turn that switch in the mass media that still gives sanction to organized pugilism, and the fight game would be dead.

But the patient is permitted to linger for fear the private detectives of the Establishment, the psychiatrists and psychoanalysts, might not be able to neutralize the problem of gang violence. Not so well as the Game. Of course, the moment some piece of diseased turnip capable of being synthesized cheaply might prove to have the property of tranquilizing a violent young man for a year, the Establishment would wipe out boxing. Every time a punk was arrested, the police would prescribe a pill, and violence would walk the street sheathed and numb. Of course the Mob would lose revenue, but then the Mob is also part of the Establishment, it and the labor unions and the colleges and the newspapers and the corporations are all part of the Establishment. The Establishment is never simple. It needs the Mob to grease the chassis on its chariot. Therefore, the Mob would be placated. In a society with strong central government, it is not so difficult to turn up a new source of revenue. What is more difficult is to enter the plea that violence may be an indispensable element of life. This is not the place to have the argument: It is enough to say that if the liberal Establishment is right in its unstated credo that death is a void, and man leads out his life suspended momentarily above that void, why then there is no argument at all. Whatever shortens life is monstrous. We have not the right to shorten life, since life is the only possession of the psyche, and in death we have only nothingness. What then can there be said in defense of sports-car racing, war, or six-ounce gloves?

But if we go from life into a death that is larger than our life has been, or into a death which is small, if death comes to nothing for one man because he swallowed his death in his life, and if for another death is alive with dimension, then the certitudes of the Establishment lose power. A drug that offers peace to a pain may dull the nerve which could have taught the mind how to carry that pain into the death which comes on the next day or in the decades that follow. A tranquilizer gives coma to an anxiety that may later smell of the dungeon beneath the ground. If we are born into life as some living line of intent from an eternity that may have tortured us or nurtured us in death, then we may be obliged to go back to death with more courage and art than we left it. Or face the dim end of going back with less.

That is the existential venture, the unstated religious view of boxers trying to beat each other into unconsciousness or, ultimately, into death. It is the culture of the killer who sickens the air about him if he does not find some half-human way to kill a little in order not to deaden all. It is a defense against the plague that comes from violence converted into the nausea of all that nonviolence which is void of peace. Paret's death was with horror, but not all the horror was in the beating; much was in the way his death was cheated. Which is to say that his death was twice a nightmare. I knew that something in boxing was spoiled forever for me, that there would be a fear in watching a fight now which was like the fear one felt for any *novillero* when he was having an unhappy day, the bull was dangerous, and the crowd was ugly. You knew he would get hurt. There is fascination in seeing that the first time, but it is not as enjoyable as one expects. It is like watching a novelist who has written a decent book get run over by a car.

Something in boxing was spoiled. But not the principle, not the right for one man to try to knock another out in the ring. That was perhaps not a civilized activity, but it belonged to the tradition of the humanist—it was a human activity, it showed a part of what man was like, it belonged to his ability to create art and artful movement on the edge of death or pain or danger or attack, and it had much to say about the subtleties of human style. For there are boxers whose bodies move like a fine brain, and there are others who pound the opposition down with the force of a trade-union leader, there are fools and wits and patient craftsmen among boxers, wild men full of a sense of outrage, and steady oppressive peasants, clever spoilers, dogged infantrymen who walk forward all night, hypnotists (like Liston), dancers, lovers, mothers giving a scolding, horsemen high on their legs. There is knowledge to be found about our nature, and the nature of animals, of big cats, lions, tigers, gorillas, bears, walruses (Archie Moore), birds, elephants, jackals, bulls. No, I was not down on boxing, but I loved it with freedom no longer. It was more like somebody in your family was fighting now. And the feeling one had for a big fight was no longer clear of terror in its excitement. There was awe in the suspense.

All selections from *The Presidential Papers* (1963)

# KENNEDY, CASTRO, AND OSWALD

## November 22 — The Six Time Zones Between Dallas and Paris

Cubela, wearing a tan sport jacket and brown pants, came into the Bistro de la Mairie accompanied by a man in a blue yachting jacket, gray flannels, and horn-rimmed glasses—LYME—who nodded to us and walked out. But for three workingmen standing at the bar by the entrance, we had the place to ourselves, all of the dark floor, dark walls, round bar tables, and one disinterested waiter.

Cubela walked toward us like a heavyweight coming into the ring. My father had described him as tall, but he was heavier than I had expected and his mustache was full, powerful, and pessimistic. He would have been a good-looking man if his face had not been puffy from drink.

"Mr. Scott," said Cubela to my father, who promptly replied, "Señor General, this is Mr. Edgar." I nodded.

Cubela sat down with solemn grace. He would have an Armagnac, he decided. We said no more until the waiter brought it, whereupon Cubela took a taste and asked in a heavy Spanish accent, "*Il n'y a rien de mieux?*" to which our waiter allowed that it was the brand of Armagnac the café served. Cubela nodded in displeasure, and waved him away.

"You have brought the letter?" he asked. Cal nodded. "I would like to see it, Mr. Scott." His English was superior to his French.

The letter was brief, but composed by us with no small care. One of the experts at GHOUL had forged the handwriting on stationery that carried the embossed seal of the Attorney General's office.

November 20, 1963

This is to assure the bearer that in recognition of his successful efforts to bring about a noteworthy and irreversible change in the present government of Cuba, the powers of this office, and all collateral loyalties attendant thereto, will be brought to bear in full support of his high political aims.

Robert F. Kennedy

Cubela read it over, took out a pocket English dictionary, looked up the definition of several words, and frowned. "This letter does not fulfill the understanding arrived at in our last meeting, Mr. Scott."

"I would say it takes care of your specific requests completely, Señor General. You need only contemplate the meaning of 'irreversible change.' "

"Yes," said Cubela, "that addresses half of the fundamental understanding, but where does it say that the older brother of the signatory is well disposed toward me?"

Cal took back the letter and read aloud, " 'The power of this office and *all collateral loyalties attendant thereto . . .*' I think you will find that is a clear reference to the sibling."

"Sibling? Sibling?"

"*El hermano,*" I said.

"It is very abstract. In effect, you ask me to accept your promise on faith."

"Even as we accept your promises," said Cal.

Cubela showed small pleasure in being overtaken. "Whether you trust me or not, you will go back to your home in Washington. For me to trust you, however, means that I must risk my life." He withdrew a magnifying glass from his jacket pocket, and a clipping from a magazine. I could see that it was a printed sample of Robert Kennedy's handwriting.

For several minutes, Cubela compared the script in the letter to the sample in his clipping. "Good," he said at last, and stared carefully at both of us. "I would ask you a question, Mr. Scott. As you know, I once shot a man in a nightclub. In fact, I assassinated him."

"I thought you detest the word."

"I do. And now," he said in Spanish, "I will explain why. It is not because of some fracture of my nervous system that is unable to bear the enunciation of such syllables because that might recall to me the expression on a dying man's face—no, that is what my detractors would claim, but no truth is there. I am a calm man possessed of *pun-*

*donor.* I have depth of resolve. I see myself as the future *comandante* of the tragic island that is my nation. For these reasons, I detest the word. The assassin, you see, not only destroys his victim but the part of himself that contains his larger ambitions. Can you ask me to believe that the President of the United States and his brother are ready to help the political career of a man whom they must talk about during the privacy of their own councils as a half-crazy hired thug?"

"In a time of turmoil," said Cal, "your past will matter less than your heroism. It is your heroic actions in the next few months that will bring you to public view."

"Are you saying that your sponsors will accept me in such circumstances?"

"That is exactly what I am saying."

He sighed heavily. "No," he said, "you are saying that at the summit of the mountain, there are no guarantees."

Cal was silent. After a while, he said, "As a man of intelligence, you know that one cannot control political weather absolutely."

"Yes," said Cubela, "I must be prepared to take all chances. Of necessity. Yes, I am prepared," he said, and let out his breath with such a burst that I realized he was ready to perform the assassination today. "Let us concern ourselves with equipment," he said.

"The telescope is ready," stated my father.

"You are speaking, I presume, of the rifle I have described that has a range of accuracy up to five hundred yards, equipped with a Bausch and Lomb telescopic sight of two-and-one-half times magnification?"

My father, in reflex, tapped on his glass through the length of this speech. Then he reached forward across the table, put his hand on Cubela's arm, and nodded profoundly, although he did not say a word.

"I will accept your concern for precautions," said Cubela. "Forgive me. Now, may I inquire into delivery?"

"Mr. Lyme will service your location."

"I like Mr. Lyme," said Cubela.

"I am pleased to hear that he is likeable," said Cal.

"The telescope will fit into an attaché case?"

"No," said Cal, but added, "do you play pool?"

"Billiards."

"The case we will hand over to you looks like the kind that is used to carry a billiard cue. The kind of cue, of course, that comes in two pieces."

"Excellent," said Cubela. "And the other detail?"

"Yes," said Cal. "The piece of sophisticated equipment. The surprise. I have it on my person."

"May I see it?"

Cal removed a ballpoint pen from his tweed jacket and clicked the button. A hypodermic needle sprang forth. He clicked the button a second time and a thread of liquid darted from the needle like a wall lizard's tongue. "It's only water," said Cal, "but this pen has been designed for use with the common reagent . . ." He removed an index card from his pocket and held it up. It read: BLACKLEAF 40.

"Where do I find such as that?" asked Cubela.

"In any chemical supply house. It is a common reagent employed for insects."

"Of all sizes?"

Cal nodded again. "Most effective."

Cubela took the ballpoint pen and pressed the button several times until all the water had been ejected. "It is a toy," he said with some petulance.

"No," answered Cal, "it is a sophisticated instrument. The needle is so fine that one does not feel it entering the skin."

"You are asking me to walk up to the subject and inject him?"

"The needle is so fine that it causes no pain. It attracts no attention whatsoever."

Cubela looked at both of us with contempt. "Your gift is a device for a woman. She sticks her tongue in the man's mouth and puts the needle in his back. I am not about to use such tactics. It is shameful to eliminate one's enemy in that manner. One does not attack a serious Cuban with a hat pin. I would be subject to ridicule. And rightly so."

He stood up. "I will accept the carrying case with the billiard cue from Mr. Lyme. But this I reject." He was about to depart, then stopped. "No," he said, "I will take reception of it after all," and he put it in his breast pocket.

My father surprised me by his next remark. "For yourself?" he asked.

He nodded. "If the large effort fails, I have no wish to live through the immediate consequences."

"*Cómo no,*" said Cal.

Cubela shook his hand, then mine. His hands were cold. "*Salud!*" he said, and walked out.

"We'll get the billiard cue to him in Veradero," said Cal. "He has a little villa on the beach, three hundred yards away from the beach house that the subject—as he calls him—inhabits on vacation. I hate to say it, but I am getting my hopes up for this fellow. He could deliver a present before Christmas." Cal let out his breath. "Do you mind paying the bill? I need to take a walk." He paused. "We should leave separately in any event."

"All right," I said. "I'll follow you back to the hotel."

Through the café window, I could see the lights on the street. The November evening had long passed, and at 7:00 P.M. it was now dark enough for midnight.

I did not know exactly how I felt, but then I was not in a situation where it was automatic to comprehend one's reactions. In truth, I wanted Rolando Cubela to kill Fidel Castro; I hoped that Helms, Harlot, and Cal were not merely sending out a provocation to the DGI. No, I wanted an execution to be there at the end of the road. I did not begin to have the profound hatred for the Maximum Leader that Hunt or Harlot or Harvey or Helms or Allen Dulles, or Richard Bissell, or Richard Nixon, or, for that matter, my father or Bobby Kennedy contained; no, there was a part of me that kept thinking of Castro as Fidel, yet I was looking for the death of Fidel. I would mourn Fidel if we succeeded, mourn him in just the way a hunter is saddened by the vanished immanence of the slain beast. Yes, one fired a bullet into beautiful animals in order to feel nearer to God: To the extent that we were criminal, we could approach the cosmos only by stealing a piece of the Creation—yes, I understood all of this and wanted Cubela to be an effective assassin rather than a ploy of the DGI whom we, in turn, would use in a superior ploy. A successful assassin was worth a hundred provocations.

I sat at my table alone, finishing the cognac I had not touched during the interview. Then I began to notice that the few workingmen standing at the bar had gathered around the café radio. It had been playing *bal musette* dance music for the last hour, but now a commentator's voice could be heard. I could not discern what was being said. The tone of voice, however, was urgent.

In another minute, the waiter came up to me. "*Monsieur,*" he said, "*vous-êtes américain?*"

"*Mais oui.*"

He was a tired, weary, gray-faced waiter, well over fifty, and wholly unremarkable in appearance, but his eyes looked at me with profound compassion.

"*Monsieur, il y a des mauvaises nouvelles. Des nouvelles étonnants.*" Now, he put his hand gently on mine. "*Votre Président Kennedy a été frappé par un assassin à Dallas, Texas.*"

"Is he alive?" I asked, and then repeated, *"Est-il vivant?"*

The waiter said, *"On ne sait rien de plus, monsieur, sauf qu'il y avait une grande bouleversement."*

From *Harlot's Ghost* (1991)

## November 22        Fort Worth
##                           to Dallas

After the breakfast, Jack Kennedy had gone back to his hotel room for a few minutes of relaxation before he and his entourage would get into *Air Force One* for the brief flight from Fort Worth to Love Field in Dallas. In this passage taken from William Manchester's book *Death of a President,* the First Lady is speaking:

> "Isn't this sweet, Jack?" she said. . . . "They've just stripped their whole museum of all their treasures to brighten this dingy hotel suite." . . . Taking the catalogue, he said, "Let's see who did it." There were several names at the end. The first was Mrs. J. Lee Johnson III. "Why don't we call her?" he suggested. "She must be in the phone book." Thus Ruth Carter Johnson, the wife of a Fort Worth newspaper executive, became the surprised recipient of John Kennedy's last telephone call. She was home nursing a sick daughter. She had watched the ballroom breakfast on WBAP-TV, and when she heard the President's voice she was speechless.

Mrs. J. Lee Johnson III! One has to observe that her married name bears the first initial of J. Edgar Hoover, has Lee in the middle, and ends with the last name of the President who will succeed Jack Kennedy. (As a bonus, her maiden name is Carter.) Perhaps the cosmos likes to strew coincidences around the rim of the funnel into which large events are converging.

*Manchester:* [Kennedy] apologized for not phoning earlier, explaining that they hadn't reached the hotel until midnight. Then Mrs. Kennedy came on. To Mrs. Johnson she sounded thrilled and vivacious. "They're going to have a dreadful time getting me out of here with all these wonderful works of art," she said. "We're both touched—thank you so much."

Ken O'Donnell, the President's assistant, now carried in an unpleasant item. There was a full-page ad in the *Dallas Morning News* with a black border of the sort that accompanies the announcement of a death. It welcomed the President in one breath and then proceeded to accuse him of being a Communist tool. The people who had paid for the ad called themselves "The American Fact-Finding Committee."

Kennedy was not amused by what he read. His face showed as much when he passed the *Dallas Morning News* over to Jackie:

> *Manchester:* Her vivacity disappeared; she felt sick. The President shook his head. In a low voice he asked Ken, "Can you imagine a paper doing a thing like that?" Then, slowly, he said to her, ". . . You know, last night would have been a hell of a night to assassinate a President." . . . He said it casually, and she took it lightly; it was his way of shaking off the ad. . . . "I mean it," he said now . . . "There was the rain, and the night, and we were all getting jostled. Suppose a man had a pistol in a briefcase." He gestured vividly, pointing his rigid index finger at the wall and jerking his thumb twice to show the action of the hammer. "Then he could have dropped the gun and briefcase—" in pantomime he dropped them and whirled in a tense crouch—"and melted away in the crowd."

The flight to Dallas took less than twenty minutes, and Vice-President Johnson was there at Love Field to head up the welcoming committee. The Kennedys got into the rear seat of the presidential limousine and Governor and Mrs. Connally took the jump seats. They would ride to the Trade Mart for a lunch scheduled to begin at twelve-thirty.

From *Oswald's Tale: An American Mystery* (1995)

# November 22          A High-
## Powered Rifle

MR. BAKER: . . . It hit me all at once it was a rifle shot because I had just got back from deer hunting and [so] it sounded to me like it was a high-powered rifle.

MR. BELIN: All right . . . what did you do and what did you see?

MR. BAKER: . . . I immediately kind of looked up, and I had a feeling it came from the building . . . in front of me . . . this Book Depository Building [because] as I was looking, all these pigeons began to fly up . . . and start flying around . . .

MR. BELIN: . . . After the third shot, then, what did you do?

MR. BAKER: Well, I revved that motorcycle up and I went down to the corner which would be approximately 180 to 200 feet from the point where . . . we heard the shots . . . You see, it looked to me like there were maybe 500 or 600 people in this area here [who] started running, you know, every direction, just trying to get back out of the way . . .

MR. BELIN: You then ran into the building, is that correct?

MR. BAKER: That is correct, sir.

MR. BELIN: What did you see and what did you do as you ran into the building?

MR. BAKER: As I entered this building . . . I just spoke out and asked where the stairs or elevator was, and this man, Mr. Truly, spoke up and said, it seems to me like he says, "I am a building manager. Follow me, officer, and I will show you." So . . . we kind of all ran, not real fast but, you know, a good trot, to the back of the building . . . and he was trying to get that service elevator . . . He hollered for it, said, "Bring that elevator down here."

MR. BELIN: How many times did he holler, to the best of your recollection?

MR. BAKER: It seemed like he did it twice . . . I said let's take the stairs . . .

MR. BELIN: . . . what was your intention at that time?

MR. BAKER: . . . to go all the way to the top where I thought the shots had come from, to see if I could find something there . . .

MR. BELIN: And did you go all the way up to the top of the stairs right away?

MR. BAKER: No, sir, we didn't . . . As I came out to the second floor there, Mr. Truly was ahead of me and . . . I caught a glimpse of this man walking away . . . about twenty feet away from me in the lunchroom.

MR. BELIN: What did you do?

MR. BAKER: I hollered at him at that time and said, "Come here." He turned and walked straight back to me . . .

MR. BELIN: He walked back toward you then?

MR. BAKER: Yes, sir . . .

MR. BELIN: Was he carrying anything in his hands?

MR. BAKER: He had nothing at that time.

MR. BELIN: All right. Were you carrying anything in either of your hands?

MR. BAKER: Yes, sir; I was . . . I had my revolver out.

MR. BELIN: When did you take your revolver out?

MR. BAKER: As I was starting up the stairway . . . I assumed that I was suspicious of everybody because I had my pistol out.

REPRESENTATIVE BOGGS: Right.

MR. BAKER: . . . Mr. Truly had come up to my side here, and I turned to Mr. Truly and I says, "Do you know this man? Does he work here?" And he said yes, and I turned immediately and went on out up the stairs . . .

REPRESENTATIVE BOGGS: When you saw him, was he out of breath, did he appear to have been running or what?

MR. BAKER: It didn't appear that to me. He appeared normal, you know.

REPRESENTATIVE BOGGS: Was he calm and collected?

MR. BAKER: Yes, sir. He never did say a word or nothing. In fact, he didn't change his expression one bit.

MR. BELIN: Did he flinch in any way when you put the gun up to his face?

MR. BAKER: No, sir . . .

MR. BELIN: . . . was there any expression after Mr. Truly said he worked there?

MR. BAKER: At that time I never did look back toward him . . . I turned immediately and run on up.


Innocent or guilty, the average man would be bound to flinch looking into the implacable eye of a pistol barrel. Oswald had to be in a remarkable state at this point, a calm beneath agitation, as if at rest in the vibrationless center of a dream. This, of course, assumes that he was the man who shot at Kennedy from the sixth floor. For some, however, there is no greater evidence of his innocence than that he was so cool. How could a man aim and fire three times at a moving target, see that there was impact, and yet have been able to spring up, hide his gun between other cartons in another end of the room, race silently down four flights of stairs, and be standing there in the lunch-room, unwinded, gazing passively at Officer Baker and his gun? For many critics, this seems impossible unless Oswald was not on the sixth floor when the shooting took place. The only reply if one supposes that he did shoot Kennedy is that he had passed through the mighti-est of the psychic barriers—he had killed the king. It was equal psy-chologically to breaking through the sound barrier. All the controls were reversed. If such a transcendent calm was his state facing into Baker's gun, it must have lasted for only a little while. In the following minute, he slipped out of the Texas School Book Depository, and this remarkable if short-lived grasp on such powers of control began to come apart. The next time we see him, and it will be through the eyes of a highly biased witness—his former landlady Mrs. Bledsoe!—he looks demented.

First, however, we must conceive of the impact of Elm Street and Dealey Plaza upon his senses in that instant he steps outside. If he is the killer, then we know enough about him to understand that he has been living within a spiritual caul all morning, and the voices of others have seemed as far away as echoes heard from the other side of a hill. He has been centered on his mission, balanced on his own heartbeat, living in a sense of dread and expectation so intense that it is beyond agitation. He possesses the kind of inner silence some can know when ultimates are coming to a moment of decision: Will he have the courage to fire his rifle and will he shoot well? Everything else, in-cluding the mounting tempo of excitement in the crowds outside the Book Depository, has no more presence for him than the murmur of a passer-by. Stationed within himself, he has now descended to those depths where one waits for final judgment.

He must still have been in such a state when Officer Baker con-fronted him.

Stepping out into Dealey Plaza, therefore, must have been not unlike being hurled through a plate-glass window. Hundreds of peo-ple were milling around in disconnected hysteria. Men and women were weeping. Police sirens from every street and avenue in the area were screaming their way toward Dealey Plaza.

If the act of firing upon Kennedy had taken place as an event staged between himself and his vision of a great and thunderous stroke that would lift him at once from the mediocre to the immortal, this vision would not have included anyone else. Not even the victim.

Now, however, everybody around him is distraught. It is as if, all alone, he has set off an explosion in a mine-shaft. Then, having climbed to the surface, he has come suddenly upon a crowd of the bereaved. It is a scene alien to him. He hurries down the street away from the Book Depository until, several blocks away, he catches a bus.

On it is Mrs. Bledsoe, the same landlady who had cheated him of two dollars in the first week he was back in Dallas after Mexico:

MRS. BLEDSOE: . . . Oswald got on. He looks like a maniac. His sleeve was out here [indicating]. His shirt was undone . . . a hole in it, and he was dirty, and I didn't look at him. I didn't want to know I even seen him, and I just looked off, and then about that time the motorman said the President had been shot.

She may have been recollecting the inner light in Lee's eye when she told him that he would have to leave her rooming house.

The bus moves a block and stops. It is jammed in the gridlock around Dealey Plaza. Oswald goes up to the driver, asks for a transfer and gets off, then walks to the Greyhound bus station, where he can pick up a taxi.

From *Oswald's Tale: An American Mystery* (1995)

# November 23–24      A Visit
# to Lubyanka

Igor Ivanovich was asked, "After the assassination, you must have felt bad?"

And he replied, "Bad? I felt horrible. In fact, it was the worst moment of my life."

When asked if KGB had interrogated any of their prime sources after the assassination, Igor Ivanovich suddenly became emotional. He looked as if he might burst into tears. He did not answer the question. Instead, he cried out: "Everybody blames me for this! It was as if I knew he would shoot." After a minute or two, he added, "We had no data. You could not find one single person from Minsk who would say, 'Yes, Oswald had these intentions to go back to America and cause all this trouble.' "

He and Stepan had tried to consider where they could have failed. Their inner fear: "What if the preparation of this action commenced in Minsk?" They were considering everything.

Then he added, "Quite frankly, we were not worried about public opinion in America. We worried about what Moscow would say once we sent them Oswald's file. Would they consider our job well done or poor? That was what we worried about."

When Stepan Vasilyevich heard the announcement on the radio, his second thoughts, after first saying to himself, "It's impossible!" were more complex. As more news arrived from various broadcasts, he came to a conclusion that Oswald could not have done it alone. Oswald had been sucked into it somehow. Because a single fact was being exploited—that Oswald had been in the Soviet Union. A convenient shield for certain people! "Their mass media started blaming everything on our Soviet Union. My opinion is that it was all sewn together with white threads. To cover their tracks in this crime."

When asked how long it took for word to come from Moscow that they wanted Oswald's file, Stepan's reply was that Moscow Center's request came late on that night of November 22. Igor Ivanovich was given an order, and he told Stepan to take Lee's file to Moscow. Gather it together and leave.

No preparations were necessary. Both men knew Oswald's materials well, and the file had been stored in the archives of their building. So, all Stepan had to do was take it out, put it in a sack, sign for it, and leave. He used a gray mailbag, the kind used for sending quantities of mail, and the file was not large enough to fill it.

Then, Stepan flew to Moscow on November 23, and arrived at Lyubertsy Airport, accompanied by another KGB man from Minsk, who was armed. It was not a regular flight, since Moscow wanted it quickly, but there were two seats open on a military plane.

When asked if he was very nervous, he said, "I don't think so. I didn't feel any guilt. I was pure as crystal. What could I be afraid of? Of course, it was a tragic situation. But being nervous, hands shaking, so forth—why? I was flying to our Center in Moscow with a clean conscience. I didn't have any excessive emotions or anything like that. I just thought about what sort of questions they would ask. And I had only one answer: Oswald did not have any undisclosed relation to our agency. What worried me more was whether official people would be there to meet me at Lyubertsy Airport because, otherwise, how would I get to Moscow on public transport?"

He did not have to worry. Official people greeted him right away, introduced themselves, showed their identification, and they all drove off. It was an overcast day, but no rain, no snow. Gray.

They went to the main building, to Lubyanka, drove directly into the edifice, and were received by higher-ups. Stepan thought it might be the Assistant Director of KGB. He didn't know these high officers personally. It was his first visit to Moscow Center, and this legendary building, Lubyanka, was full of labyrinths. He had to follow closely behind whoever was walking in front of him, down endless narrow halls. A thin red carpet ran the entire length of each long hall.

Later he would go to Lubyanka many times on business trips, so he was able to find his way along some of these halls, but he can't say he ever got it all down. You could go there and go there and still get lost. If he had to get out of that building on his own, he might lose his way. From the exterior, it was a large building of yellow stone, but inside it was strange, with these narrow corridors. In Minsk, their corridors were wide and you could walk more freely.

When he finally was led to the appropriate office, several people were waiting for him in a reasonably large room, but there wasn't anything on their table. He doesn't know if it was in their American Division or some other department, but Stepan merely said, "According to your instructions, our file on Oswald is now delivered." And they said, "Good, just leave it here."

Their first question came: "Did you attempt to recruit Oswald?" He said, "You can cut off my head, but not only did we not try to, this very thought did not even enter our minds. Read these documents. It's very clear in which direction we were working. In accordance with your instructions."

He looked at them and noticed that they practically sighed with relief. He wasn't worried about their believing him, because the documents made it clear what kind of work they had been doing. You couldn't falsify something like that. Of course, Stepan was somewhat disturbed, but he had no large fears. These documents made it clearly visible how they had been conducting their operation.

Afterward, when slanders concerning the Soviet Union kept circulating, he thought maybe Nikita Sergeivich Khrushchev would give these files to the American government. All these American rumors would then burst like a soap bubble. But it didn't happen.

On this day, at this meeting on November 23, 1963, they invited him to sit down; they were polite. He remembers he even tried to stand up, and they said, "Sit down, sit down," but there was nothing on their table, no tea. He doesn't recall whose picture was on the wall, maybe it had been Dzherzhinsky, but no flag—that, he would have noticed. And the room was brightly lit. The last thing they said was, "Leave this file. And thank you. Your mission is over. We'll organize a return ticket for you."

He took a regular night train back to Minsk with the same fellow he had taken off with. Before leaving, they strolled around Moscow and went shopping. He bought something for his children.

On his return trip, Stepan didn't have special thoughts. If Oswald had been CIA, he could not have done any more in Minsk than gather information in a contemplative way, not manifesting anything, not being an active agent. He could have studied Soviet life, and then disclosed such information later in America. Such a version could not be excluded. As much could be said for any foreigner who spent two years in the Soviet Union. "Besides, when Oswald came to Minsk in January 1960, Kennedy wasn't yet elected President. So, Oswald could not have been sent with such a goal in mind."

If Stepan had any troubled thoughts on his return trip, therefore, it was not over his own performance. He explored various scenarios, thoughts came into his head, various versions appeared, but in the end he said to himself, "Ach, it's time to go to bed. Americans cooked it up. Let them figure it out."

When he got home, which was Sunday morning, it was still Saturday night in Dallas, so Oswald would not be ambushed by Ruby for another ten hours; about six in the afternoon on Sunday in Minsk is when Stepan would receive that word. When he returned, therefore, on Sunday morning around eight o'clock, the first thing he did was go to his home to shave. Leaving in such a hurry for Moscow, he had not taken his toilet kit. He washed, then had something to eat and went straight to work, where he reported to his superiors. People, of course, were talking about it in the building. Everyone was listening to radios. Even then, a lot of his colleagues did not know he had worked on this case, but everyone's opinion was stirred up. After all, it was a shadow on Minsk.

People who knew Oswald immediately said Alik couldn't have done it. So said people who knew him.

Even many people who didn't have contact with the fellow didn't believe it: We're getting along with America a little bit better, so now all this business?

They didn't do further analysis. Their file was in Moscow; they didn't have materials. Besides, what could they have analyzed any further? When the file came back from Moscow some twenty-seven years later, nothing had been removed or commented upon; everything was there as he recalled it, certified and signed by him. Stepan was asked why then had Igor Ivanovich reacted so strongly as to say, "Everyone blames me," but Stepan indicated that Igor was a more sensitive person than he was.

*From Oswald's Tale: An American Mystery* (1995)

## November    Terribly Bad Characters

I was to live for a long time with the shock of the assassination in my heart and in my bones, and it was even in the air I breathed at Langley, until time reduced at last my sense of that momentous catastrophe and it blended into the history and whispers of the halls, the weight of the fact now no greater than itself—another impost on the guilt of our lives.

Harlot, however, turned unrelenting in his powers of exaggeration. He knew the seed of consternation that now dwelt in the taproot of many an Agency dream; he memorialized The Day. He ended with a monologue I was to hear more than once, if always with different and most specially chosen associates.

"On that unique Friday afternoon, November 22, 1963," was the way Harlot usually began, "I can tell you that we all congregated in the Director's meeting room on the Seventh Floor for a bit of summitry, all of us, satraps, mandarins, lords paramount, padishahs, maharajahs, grand moguls, kingfish, the lot.

"And we sat there," said Harlot. "It's the only time in all these years that I saw so many brilliant, ambitious, resourceful men—just sitting there. Finally McCone said, 'Who is this Oswald?' And there was a World Series *silence*. The sort you hear when the visiting team has scored *eight runs* in the first inning.

"Let us not try to measure the gloom. We could have been bank directors just informed that a time bomb was ticking away in the vault. Everybody's safety box has to be emptied. But you don't even know at this point how much you have to hide. I began to think of some of the very worst of our people. Bill Harvey over in Rome. Boardman Hubbard in Paris with Cubela. Suppose Fidel produces Cubela? The mind runs amok at such times. Everyone was inhaling everyone else's ghosts. We were waiting for the little details concerning Oswald to commence belaboring our wits. My God, this man Oswald went to Russia after working at Atsugi Air Base in Japan. Isn't that where they tested the U-2? Then this Oswald dares to come back from Russia! Who debriefed him? Which one of us has been into him? Does it even matter? Our common peril may be even more embracing than our individual complicity. Cannot, oh, cannot someone do *something* about Oswald? No one utters the thought aloud. We are too many. We break up our meeting. It has congealed, after all, into silence. We meet all night in twos and threes. Information keeps coming in. Worse and worse. Marina Oswald, the Russian wife—that's how new it all was, we didn't say 'Marina' but 'Marina Oswald, the Russian wife'—has an uncle who is a Lieutenant Colonel in the MVD. Then we hear that George de Mohrenschildt, whom some of us happen to know, a most cultivated contract type, has been Oswald's closest friend in Dallas. My God, George de Mohrenschildt could be earning French money, German money, Cuban money, maybe de Mohrenschildt is earning our money. Who is paying him? Where *did* Oswald hang his hat? None of us goes home for the weekend. We may be enjoying our last hours at Langley. Then comes Sunday afternoon. The news rings around the corridors. Blessed relief. Dead leaves waltz in the garden. A marvelous hoodlum by the gemlike name of Jack Ruby has just killed Oswald. Stocky Jack Ruby can't bear the thought of Jacqueline Kennedy's sufferings at a public trial. We haven't encountered a man so chivalrous since the War of the Roses. The mood on the Seventh Floor is now like the last reel of a film by Lubitsch. We hardly keep back the twinkles. I've always said since: I *like* Jack Ruby. The fellow who paid his debts. The only matter not settled to my absolute satisfaction is whether it was Trafficante or Marcello or Hoffa or Giancana or Roselli who sent the bill.

"In any event, we are home free. There will now be mess enough to smudge the record forever. I remember divining the outcome on that very Sunday night. I asked myself: Who has nothing to fear should the real story come out? That is a list to pursue. The Republicans have to be worried: Their right-wing Texas tycoons could be involved. The liberals must be close to primitive fright. Castro, even if he is innocent, cannot speak for all his Intelligence elements. Helms has the Mafia to contemplate, plus rogue elephants, plus our malcontents at JM/WAVE. By definition, one cannot account for an enclave. Yes, CIA might have much to lose. So might the Pentagon. What if we discover that the Soviets were steering Oswald? One can't have a nuclear war just because an Irish *arriviste* got bumped off by the Reds. And what if it is the anti-Castro Cubans in Miami? A damn good likelihood after all. That will bring us back to the Republicans, to Nixon, the lot. No, not quite the lot. A skilled Vietnamese gunman might be avenging his dead ruler, Diem. The Kennedy gang can't afford exposure on that one, can they? Corrosion of the legend might work its way down to the martyr's bier. And then there is the FBI. How can they allow any of these suppositions to be examined? Each one suggests a conspiracy. It is not to Buddha's interest to advertise to the world that the FBI is singularly incompetent at detecting conspiracies they do not hatch themselves. No, none of this is in the interest of supposedly omniscient, wide-bottom Buddha. Oswald, as the sole killer, is, therefore, in everyone's best service—KGB, FBI, CIA, DGI, Kennedys, Johnsons, Nixons, Mafia, Miami Cubans, Castro Cubans, even the Goldwater gang. What if a John Bircher did it? I can feel the furor in the veins of every conspirator who ever talked about killing Jack Kennedy. They can hardly trust themselves not to have done it even when they know they didn't; after all, how can any one of them vouch for *all* their friends? A broth of disinformation has been on the stove ever since. I knew that we would enter upon a most prestigious investigation that would prove a model of sludge. So, I decided to save myself much untold watching of the pots, and moved right back to serious work where one can make a perceptible dent."

Whether Harlot was actually calling upon his powers of detachment that Sunday night sixty hours after the assassination, or summarizing what he had learned in the months that followed, I, in my turn, was not able to summarize the situation. I was mired in the death. If obsession is a species of mourning for all the fears we bury in unhallowed ground—the unhallowed ground, that is, of our psyche—then I was obsessed. The death of Marilyn Monroe would not leave my mind. If, according to my father, Hoffa could conceive of such a crime in order to leave an unstanchable political wound in both Kennedys, then how many people could I name who might be ready to kill Jack in order to ignite a war against Fidel Castro?

Harlot might have recognized that no pattern can be pulled from such a porridge, but I did not. I lay captive to the velocity of my mind and it raced around the track on many a night. I thought often of Howard Hunt and his deep friendship with Manuel Artime. Hunt had the time, the opportunity—did he have the depth of rage? He might, by way of Artime, have a line into the most violent members of the Brigade. When my mind wore out from asking questions about Hunt, I moved on to brood about Bill Harvey. I went so far as to check on whether he had left Rome on that particular Friday in November. He had not. Then I realized it did not matter. One could run such an operation from Rome. Or could one? And where was Dix Butler? Was he already in Vietnam, or had he stopped over in Dallas? I could not determine that. I also wondered whether Castro, by way of Traffi-cante, had succeeded in one assassination where we had failed in many. There were hours in those sleepless nights when I could not keep from picturing Oswald and his narrow, tortured, working-class face. Oswald had been down to Mexico City in September. Cal showed me a memo. Headquarters at Langley had cabled Mexico Station for the names of all contacts of the two leading KGB men at the Russian Embassy in Mexico City. Station came back with their response. The taps on the Cuban Embassy and the Russian Embassy produced Oswald's name and Rolando Cubela's. Oswald had even made a phone call from the Cuban Embassy to the Soviet Embassy. In a harsh and highly ungrammatical Russian, the man who called himself Oswald had insisted on speaking to "Comrade Kostikov."

"That's dubious," said Cal. "We know that Oswald spoke Russian well."

"And Cubela?"

"Ah, Cubela. He had talks with Comrade Kostikov. We don't know what about. I expect he has contacts with everyone."

"We've dropped him, of course."

"Heavens, yes." Cal shrugged. "In any event, it's over. The FBI is going to tell us that Oswald acted alone."

Had J. Edgar Hoover done it?

My thoughts did not rest. One day, during the hearings of the Warren Commission, Chief Justice Warren inquired of Allen Dulles, "The FBI and the CIA do employ undercover men who are of terrible character?" And Allen Dulles, in all the bonhomie of a good fellow who can summon up the services of a multitude of street ruffians, replied, "Yes, terribly bad characters."

"That has to be one of Allen's better moments," remarked Hugh Montague.

I was at the point where I was ready to believe that Allen Dulles did it. Or Harlot. Or, in the great net of implication, Cal and I might be guilty as well. Thoughts raced. I had not yet approached my first piece of universal wisdom: There are no answers—there are only questions.

Of course, some questions have to be better than others.

From *Harlot's Ghost* (1991)

## November      A Hero to Himself

It was the largest opportunity he had ever been offered.

The assassination of a President would be seismographic in its effect. For Americans, the aftershocks would not cease for the rest of the century or more. Yet he would also be punishing the Russians and the Cubans. They would suffer side effects for decades to come. But then, he was above capitalism and he was above Communism. Both! He had, as he would have seen it, a superior dedication, and the potential of a man like Lenin. If we know that he had none of Lenin's capacity to achieve large goals both philosophically and organizationally, Oswald did hold an equally intense belief in that fabulous end which would justify all his quotidian means. His deepest despair had to arise in those moments when he could not see himself any longer as the key protagonist in forging a new world.

Given his humiliation in Mexico and his lack of stature on weekends in Irving, the odds are that Oswald's political ideology had finally come to rest in the live nerve of nihilism—things had to get vastly worse before they could get better. We can refer ourselves back to that note he wrote on Holland-America Line stationery even as he may have been returning to America:

> I wonder what would happen if someone would stand up and say he was utterly opposed not only to the governments, but to the people, to the entire land and complete foundation of his society.

All the motivation for shooting Kennedy is in that sentence. It may be worth quoting from *Mein Kampf* again:

> Even then I saw that only a twofold road could lead to the goal of improving these conditions:

*The deepest sense of social responsibility for the creation of better foundations for our development coupled with brutal determination in breaking down incurable tumors.* [Hitler's italics]

Kennedy had the ability to give hope to the American ethos. That was, therefore, cause enough to call upon "brutal determination in breaking down incurable tumors." Kennedy was not, as American Presidents went, a bad President; therefore, he was too good. In the profoundest sense, as Oswald saw it, he had located the tumor—it was that Kennedy was too good. The world was in crisis and the social need was to create conditions for recognizing that there had to be a new kind of society. Otherwise, the malignant effects of capitalism, added to the Soviet degradation of Communism, were going to reduce people to the point where they lost all will to create a better world.

An explosion at the heart of the American establishment's complacency would be exactly the shock therapy needed to awaken the world.

It is doubtful that Oswald wanted to debate such a question with himself. He may well have possessed an instinct that told him he had to do something enormous and do it quickly, do it for his own physical well-being. The murderer kills in order to cure himself—which is why murder is properly repudiated. It is the most selfish of acts.

*McMillan:* . . . the uncanny selection of a route that would carry the President right under his window could mean only one thing. Fate had singled him out to do the dangerous but necessary task which had been his destiny all along and which would cause him to go down in history.

Back in March, living on Neely Street, he had said in a letter to Robert Oswald, "It's always better to take advantage of your chances as they come along."

Which may have been Oswald's way of saying that the intent of the universe is ready to reveal itself to us by the chances we are offered. Since the President would pass beneath his Book Depository windows, he did not have the right to violate such a monumental opportunity. Could there be another person in the universe who had been more uniquely designed to take advantage of such a situation, "vouchsafed to *him,*" writes McMillan,

to deal capitalism that final, mortal blow[?] And he would strike it not at the right nor at the left, but, quite simply, at the top. It had become his fate to decapitate the American political process. *He was history's chosen instrument.*

The point absent here from Priscilla Johnson McMillan's interpretation is that after the assassination, Oswald had a choice. He might not only be the instrument but the leading man. That presented a new conflict—to be the instrument of history *or* the leading man? The latter could occur only if he was captured and stood trial. If he succeeded in the act but managed to remain undiscovered, obscurity would be his lot again. He had learned as much from his attempt on Walker.

Capture, however, would guarantee him a very high level of attention. And if he was convicted, he had the temperament to live alone in a cell; he was more than half habituated to that already. He could even view his life up to this point as a preparation for spending many years in prison.

Indeed, it may even have been the thought of his trial that fired him on. What a podium! Such a trial could alter history, stimulate the stupid, rouse the lethargic, confound the powerful. So he had to feel divided between his desire to escape and his recognition that capture, trial, and incarceration might generate a vastly larger destiny.

His personal attitude toward Kennedy had little to do, therefore, with his act. In war, one may execute a man for whom one feels respect or even personal affection; Oswald saw it as an execution. One mighty leader was going to be dispatched by another high and mighty personage—of the future. The future would preempt the present.

If he failed to escape, well, he could tell his story. He could becloud the issue and possibly be acquitted, and if it came to twenty years of prison, he would be able to forge his political agenda—even as Hitler, Stalin, and Lenin had done. Should he face capital punishment, then, at the least, he would be immortal.

What he may never have taken into account is that the furies he set loose would devour him before he could utter one idea. The first element in the loss of an heroic trial became the four shots he fired into Officer Tippit. There can be little doubt that he panicked. As soon as he killed Tippit, the mighty architecture of his ideology, hundreds of levels high and built with no more than the game cards of his political imagination, came tumbling down. He knew Americans well enough to recognize that some might listen to his ideas if he killed a President, but nearly all would be repelled by any gunman who would mow down a cop, a family man—that act was small enough to void interest in every large idea he wished to introduce. By killing Tippit he had wrecked his grand plan to be one of the oracles of history. Now he had to improvise a defense: I'm a patsy.

It might not have occurred to Oswald that the obfuscation and paranoia which followed the assassination of Kennedy would contribute immensely to the sludge and smog of the world's spirit.

Oswald may never have read Emerson, but the following passage from "Heroism" gives us luminous insight into what had to be Oswald's opinion of himself as he sat on the sixth floor waiting for the Kennedy motorcade—he was committing himself to the most heroic deed of which he was capable.

> Self-trust is the essence of heroism. It is the state of the soul at war, and its ultimate objects are the last defiance of falsehood and wrong, and the power to bear all that can be inflicted by evil agents. [Heroism is] scornful of petty calculations and scornful of being scorned. It persists; it is of an undaunted boldness and of a fortitude not to be wearied out. Its jest is the littleness of common life. [Heroism] works in contradiction to the voice of mankind and in contradiction, for a time, to the voice of the great and good. Heroism is obedience to a secret impulse of an individual's character. Now to no other man can wisdom appear as it does to him, for every man must be supposed to see a little farther on his own proper path than anyone else [so] every heroic act measures itself by its contempt of some external good . . .

It would have wounded Oswald to the quick if he had known that history would not see him as a hero but as an anti-hero. He went off to work that last morning, leaving the dregs of instant coffee in a plastic cup, and in two days he ascended to the summit of our national obsessions—he became our First Ghost.

Oswald owned all the properties that belong to a ghost—ambition, deceit, a sense of mission, and the untold frustration of an abrupt death just as a long-held dream of personal prominence is about to unfold. Can there be any American of our century who, having failed to gain stature while he was alive, now haunts us more?

Let us give a word to Lee's brother John, whom he saw so seldom:

MR. PIC: Well, sir, ever since I was born and I was old enough to remember, I always had a feeling that some great tragedy was going to strike Lee in some way or another . . . In fact, on the very day of the assassination I was thinking about it when I was getting ready to go to work . . . and I figured well, when he defected and came back—that was his big tragedy. I found out it wasn't.

From *Oswald's Tale: An American Mystery* (1995)

# The Widow's Elegy

First, Jacqueline Kennedy was a widow, and then Marina. As the second widow, she can no longer know what it is she knows. She has passed through thirty years of interviews, more than a thousand hours of interviews, and the questions never cease. She may be the last living smoker to consume four packs a day. How can it be otherwise? The past is filled with guilt—the future is full of dread. Only the present is clear; she always suspects the motives of the new people to whom she speaks. How innocent can be their motive for approaching? These days she feels that the walls are coming closer. If she starts thinking about what has happened to her, not with pity, she will say, or sorrow for herself, but just hoping to lessen stress, she feels she is choking. She still thinks of the night Lee sat in the dark on their porch in New Orleans and he was weeping. It was such a heavy burden for him. Something, and she does not know what it was.

It is hard for her to remember details. After her Warren Commission testimony, everybody accused her of lying, but she was just a human being and if she was lying, it was honestly—because she was floating through a foggy world. Memories kept coming, going. Maybe it was some self-protective mechanism. To keep her psyche from collapsing. People were saying to her, "You're so strong"—but it was not heroic effort. "It is in every one of us—you just decide not to die, that's all. You dare not to die."

Now that she is fifty-two, Marina would agree that one doesn't need to approach her with such labels as good woman, bad woman, villainess, heroine, someone-who's-been-treated-unfairly, someone-treated-too-well. "You can be all of that in one person," said Marina. "One can be a villain, and next time a hero.

"If we go through Lee's character, I myself would like to find out: Who is he? Was he really that mean of a person?—which I think he was—but it's a hard road for me to take because I do not want to understand him. I have to tell you in advance that, as far as Lee is concerned—I don't like him. I'm mad at him. Very mad at him, yes. When a person dies, people have such anger. They loved their husband or wife for a long time so they say, 'How dare you die on me?' Okay, but that's not my reason. For me, it's, 'How dare you abandon me? In circumstances like that? I mean, *you* die but I'm still here licking my wounds.'

"All the same, I'm definitely sure he didn't do it, even if I'm still mad at him. Because he shouldn't involve a wife and family if he was playing those kinds of games. Yes, I do believe he was on a mission, maybe even when he went to Russia, but first I have to figure out what he was doing here. It wasn't just happening here all of a sudden in America. It was a continuation. In my mind, I'm not trying to convince you or the American public—I have to resolve it for myself. But I think he was sent over to Russia, maybe. I think so. I have no proof. I have nothing. I do think he was more human than has been portrayed. I'm not trying to make an angel out of him, but I was interested in him because he was different, he would broaden my horizon, and all the other men I wanted had been taken or didn't want me."

Every time she watches a film and sees an actor playing Lee, the actor is nothing like him. He turns his head like Lee or waves his hair the same way, but, she says, your American public knows Lee only from a few photographs, and that is what this actor is copying. She sees another Lee, and she does not know the psyche of that fellow. She still has it to discover.

Her interviewers asked how she would have felt if a truck had hit Alik in Minsk—if she had been his widow then, would she have thought of him fondly? She said yes. She would have thought it was just a stormy beginning but they were breaking ground that they would later stand on in their marriage. After all, she took a chance. She had crossed the ocean for him. Of course, she was afraid of him already, even if little by little she had been learning that she did not know, never knew, where she stood. Not with him. But at least you could hope.

She will never forget that on their last night in Irving, he had kept making advances to her until he went to bed, and she had refused. She had said to herself, "No, if I don't teach him this lesson right now, his lying will continue. So, don't butter up to me." She tried to discipline him.

Afterward, she had to think, What if he really wanted to be close to me? What if I put him in a bad mood? It torments her. What if they had made love that last night? But she is the wrong person to talk to about this, she would say, because she is not a sexual person. Sensuous but not sensual. She didn't like sex, she would say. She was not expert, nor could she tell you how grandiose something had been, because she had never experienced that. No Beethoven or Tchaikovsky for her, not in bed, no grand finale.

MARINA: In Texas, sun is very intense for me and very harsh, very bright. I love moon. It's cool and it's shiny and that's my melancholy period. And some people are shining and they are bright and they burn. You know what I mean? I'm not sun. I'm a moon . . .

I look at America, it's all wonderful. But you go to the damn grocery store and it's 200 varieties of cereal. And basically it's only oats, corn, how many things . . . Just so somebody going to make extra million off that. It's so unnecessary. If that's progress, if that's abundance, how stupid for us to want it. 300 bags of poison, maybe only two or three good [well,] that kind of progress I don't think we should strive for . . . Do I make any sense to you? Or I'm just complaining?

INTERVIEWER: No, I agree with you.

After the assassination, there were times when she was close to ending her life. She wondered when her breaking point would come. She had crossed that ocean for nothing. Still, she tried to survive. It was a lonely life. Every day. The worst of the pain was that maybe she loved him more by the end than in their beginning. Maybe grieving was just starting to happen now! Maybe! Because she had never really had such a process. Just numb, with pain always there.

She doesn't know whether they would have stayed married, but still, Lee was the person she would have liked to have been able to make it with. Through life.

The morning when Lee left, Friday morning, November 22, 1963, she did not get up with him when he arose very early. She tried to, but he said, "Don't worry. Go back to sleep." And he left quietly.

She had gone to bed after him the night before. He was already asleep or pretended to be. Then, when she woke up in the middle of the night to check on baby Rachel, she took a look at him. The only illumination was by nightlight, very low. But Lee scared her. She touched him with her foot and he kicked it away. Then he lay so still that it was like he had died. He didn't move for the next hour. She said to herself, "Is he alive?" He looked so still. Absolutely gone. She couldn't hear his breath. She had to bend over very close to feel his breathing—she thought he had died on her. Isn't that funny? For all these years she remembered saying, "Thank goodness he's alive." And he made no sound all night and never moved again.

In the morning, he made himself instant coffee, drank it in a plastic cup, and went off to work.

She sits in a chair, a tiny woman in her early fifties, her thin shoulders hunched forward in such pain of spirit under such a mass of guilt that one would comfort her as one would hug a child. What is left of what was once her beauty are her extraordinary eyes, blue as diamonds, and they blaze with light as if, in divine compensation for the dead weight of all that will not cease to haunt her, she has been granted a spark from the hour of an apocalypse others have not seen. Perhaps it is the light offered to victims who have suffered like the gods.

From *Oswald's Tale: An American Mystery* (1995)

# The Third Widow

MARGUERITE OSWALD: I don't believe this letter belongs with the letters. May I see it, please? Is that a letter from Russia? I don't think so from what I can see from here.

MR. RANKIN: It purports to be, Mrs. Oswald. I hand it to you. Is it Exhibit 198 you are speaking of?

MARGUERITE OSWALD: Yes. I'm sorry. There was another very important letter of this size that I thought maybe had become confused with the Russian letters. You will have to forgive me, Chief Justice Warren, but this is quite a big undertaking.

All day long, throughout her testimony, she has been fumbling through her file of letters, bringing forth "documents, gentlemen," that prove nothing but that she has had her share of lonely nights filled with intolerable scenarios of suspicion. Her letters prove of little use in the lawyerly air of the Warren Commission Hearings. She is wasting their time with trivia, and all the while her possession of these letters remains as important to her as tombstones. Who is moving the tombstones in the family graveyard?

The interlocutors grow testy:

REPRESENTATIVE BOGGS: Why did your son defect to Russia?

MARGUERITE OSWALD: I cannot answer that yes or no sir. I am going to go through the whole story or it is no good. And that is what I have been doing for this Commission all day long—giving a story.

REPRESENTATIVE BOGGS: Suppose you just make it very brief.

MARGUERITE OSWALD: I cannot make it brief. I will say I am unable to make it brief. This is my life and my son's life going down in history.

Marguerite has taken sufficient blame, scorn, and ridicule from other people (including the barely concealed animus of the Warren Commission) that there is no need to depict her in one more unfavorable light—it seems certain at the least that every malformation, or just about, of Lee Harvey Oswald's character had its roots in her. That much granted, it is also difficult not to feel some guarded sympathy for Marguerite Claverie Oswald. As with Lee, the internal workings of her psyche were always condemned to hard labor, and so much of what she tried, and with the best intentions, would fail—especially her obvious desire to receive some love from her sons, enough love at least to match her harsh pride. It is not agreeable to see Marguerite's life through her eyes. The boys are always leaving her as quickly as they can, and their willful wives—willful as she sees them—have no belief in her desire to be a decent mother-in-law. Her sacrifices are many and real—but no love comes back. Merely banishment from her children, and icy silence. And then her favorite is accused of killing the President. In her heart of hearts she has to wonder whether indeed he did it—she knows how far he can go.

Denigrators of Marguerite Oswald will remark on how much she loved the limelight after he was gone, and it is true: His love of attention was equaled by hers—she spoke to large audiences for the first time in her life, and it was a great step forward from that sales job in New York where she was fired because of intractable body odor.

Yet, for all her latter-day notoriety, we have to recall that she died alone and full of a literal cancer to follow upon the bottomless cancer of those endless wounds within personal wounds—no, she had her life, and one would not want it, but somewhere in the bureaucratic corridors of Karmic Reassignment she is probably arguing now with one of the monitors, dissatisfied with the low station, by her lights, of her next placement. "I gave birth to one of the most famous and important Americans who ever lived!" she will tell the clerk-angel who is recording her story.

INTERVIEWER: Do you have any family here at all?

MARGUERITE: I have no family, period. I brought three children into the world, and I have sisters, I have nieces, I have nephews, I have grandchildren, and I'm all alone. That answers that question and I don't want to hear another word about it.

There she stands with her outrageous ego and her self-deceit, her bold loneliness and cold bones, those endless humiliations that burn like sores.

Yet, she is worthy of Dickens. Marguerite Oswald can stand for literary office with Micawber and Uriah Heep. No word she utters will be false to her character; her stamp will be on every phrase. Few people without a literary motive would seek her company for long, but a novelist can esteem Marguerite. She does all his work for him.

Given such modest thoughts, it is time to conclude one's sad tale of a young American who lived abroad and returned to a grave in Texas. Let us, then, say farewell to Lee Harvey Oswald's long and determined dream of political triumph, wifely approbation, and high destiny. Who among us can say that he is in no way related to our own dream? If it had not been for Theodore Dreiser and his last great work, one would like to have used "An American Tragedy" as the title for this journey through Oswald's beleaguered life.

From *Oswald's Tale: An American Mystery* (1995)

# 1963   AN AMERICAN DREAM

But now it wasn't possible to wait in Deborah's room until the police arrived. An anxiety went off in me like the quiver of electricity when there is a short in the line. My body could have been on a subway, it felt as if it *were* the subway, bleak, grinding at high speed; I was jangled with adrenaline.

I went out the bedroom door, down the steps of the duplex, and came up against Ruta in the hall. She was standing there half-dressed, a black skirt, no stockings yet, no shoes, a white blouse not buttoned. Her breasts were bare, no brassiere yet either, and her dyed red hair now uncombed, still mangled by my fingers, stood up like a bush. Dyed, marcelled, lacquered, and then worked over by me, her hair gave off the look of a girl just taken in a police raid. But even at this instant, something relaxed in me. For there was a tough slatternly tenderness in her face, and her prize—those bright little breasts—kept peeking at me through the open shirt. There was an instant between us, an echo of some other night (some other life) when we might have met in the corridor of an Italian whorehouse on an evening when the doors were closed, the party was private, and the girls were moving from bed to bed in one sweet stew.

"I was dreaming," she said, "and you called down the stairs." Suddenly she closed the shirt over her breasts.

"No," and to my surprise, I gave a pure sob. It was an extraordinary sound. "Deborah killed herself. She jumped through the window."

Ruta let out a cry, a thin dirty little cry. Something nasty was being surrendered. Two tears flashed down her cheek. "She was an ingenious woman," Ruta said, and began to weep. There was pain now in the sound, and such a truth in the grief that I knew she was crying not for Deborah, not even quite for herself, but rather for the unmitigatable fact that women who have discovered the power of sex are never far from suicide. And in that sudden burst of mourning, her face took on beauty. A nourishment came off Ruta's limbs. I was in some fargone state: no longer a person, a character, a man of habits, rather a ghost, a cloud of loose emotions which scattered on the wind. I felt as if much of me had gathered like a woman to mourn everything in my lover, that violent brutish tyrant who lived in Deborah. And I groped toward Ruta like a woman seeking another female. We came together, hugged each other. But her breast came out of the open shirt, and slipped into my hand, and that breast was looking for no woman's touch, no, it made its quick pert way toward what was hard and certain in my hand. It was as if I had never felt a breast before (that gift of flesh), for Ruta was still weeping, the sobs were coming now with the fierce rhythm of a child, but her breast was independent of her. That little tit in my hand was nosing like a puppy for its reward, impertinent with its promise of the sly life it could give to me, and so keen to pull in a life for itself that I was taken with a hopeless lust. Hopeless, because I should have been down on the street already, and yet there was no help for it, thirty seconds was all I wanted and thirty seconds I took, one high sniff of the alley coming from her as I took her still weeping right there in the hall, her back against those velvet flowers while I fired one hot fierce streak of fierce bright murder, fierce as the demon in the eyes of a bright golden child.

Something in her leaped to catch that child, I felt some avarice shake its way through; she was beginning as I was done, pinching and squeezing at the back of my neck. She came in ten seconds behind. "Oh," she said, "you are trying to woo me." By which time I was cold as ice, and kissed her mockingly on the nose.

"Now, listen," I said, "take a shower."

"Why?" She shook her head, pretending a half-bewilderment. But those forty seconds had drawn us to focus with each other. I felt as fine and evil as a razor and just as content with myself. There was something further in her I'd needed, some bitter perfect salt, narrow and mean as the eye of a personnel director.

"Because, my pet, the police will be here in five minutes."

"You called them?"

"Of course."

"My God."

"They'll be here in five minutes, and I've got to pretend to be overcome. Which of course I am." And I smiled.

She looked at me in wonder. Was I mad, asked her eyes, or deserving of respect.

"But what," she said like a German, "do you have to explain to them?"

"That I didn't kill Deborah."

"Who says you did?" She was trying to keep up with me, but this last had been a racing turn.

"I didn't like Deborah very much. She detested me. You know that."

"You were not very happy with each other."

"Not very."

"A woman doesn't commit suicide for a man she detests."

"Listen, pet, I have something awful to tell you. She had a sniff of you on me. And then she jumped. Like that. Before my eyes."

"Mr. Rojack, you are hard as nails."

"Hard as nails." I pinched her shoulder a little. "Are you?"

"Yes."

"Let's get out of this together. Then we have fun."

"I'm scared," she said.

"When the police talk to you, tell them the truth. Except for one obvious detail. Obviously, there was nothing between us."

"Nothing between us."

"You let me in tonight. A couple of hours ago. You don't know the time exactly, a couple of hours ago. Then you went to sleep. You heard nothing until I woke you up."

"Yes."

"Don't trust the police. If they say I said we were having an affair, deny it."

"Mr. Rojack, you never laid a hand on me."

"Right." I took her chin between my thumb and forefinger, holding it as if precious. "Now, the second line of defense. If they bring me down to see you, or bring you up to see me, and you hear me say we went to bed tonight, then agree. But only if you hear me say it."

"Will you tell them?"

"Not unless there's evidence. In that case I'll tell the police I wanted to protect our mutual reputation. It'll still be all right."

"Shouldn't we admit it from the start?"

"More natural to conceal the fact." I smiled. "Now, wash yourself. Quickly. If there's time, get dressed. And look—"

"Yes."

"Make yourself plain. Comb out your hair for God's sake."

With that, I quit the apartment. The elevator would take too long, but I rang anyway, five piercing rings to manifest impatience, and then took the stairs. For the second time that night I was on my way down ten flights of stairs, but this time on the run. When I reached the lobby, it was empty, the doorman was doubtless ascending, a bit of good luck or bad luck (I could not keep up with the possibilities any longer), and then I was on the street and running a few steps to the Drive. There was one instant when the open air reached my nose and gave me a perfect fleeting sense of adventure on the wind, of some adventure long gone—a memory: I was eighteen, playing House Football for Harvard. It was a kickoff and the ball was coming to me, I had it, and was running. Off the river came a light breeze with the hint of turf to it. There was a fence lining the East River Drive, but it had no barbed wire on top, I was able to climb up and get over without ripping my pants, and come down the other side. There was now a jump of eight feet further down to a strip of curb, but I dropped—I hated jumping—but I dropped, jarred my ankle, hurt something minor in my groin, some little muscle, and made my way along the southbound traffic whose drivers were crawling by at five miles an hour in the unobstructed lane. Deborah was a hundred feet down the road. I had a glimpse of four or five cars collided into one another, and a gathering of forty or fifty people. A magnesium flare had been lit and it gave off the white intent glare that surrounds workingmen doing serious work at night. Two police cars flanked the scene, their red lights revolving like beacons. In the distance, I could hear the siren of an ambulance, and in the center was that numb mute circle of silence which surrounds a coffin in the center of a room. I could hear a woman weeping hysterically in one of the automobiles. There were the short, rapt, irritable tones of three big men talking to one another, a professional conversation, two police and a detective, I realized, and farther on, an elderly man with dirty gray hair, a large nose, an unhealthy skin, and a pair of pink-tinted glasses was sitting in his car, the door open, holding his temple, and groaning in a whining gurgling sound that betrayed the shoddy state of his internal plumbing.

But I had broken through the crowd and was about to kneel at Deborah's body. An arm in a blue serge sleeve held me back.

"Officer, that's my wife."

The arm went down suddenly. "You better not look, mister."

There was nothing agreeable to see. She must first have struck the pavement, and the nearest car had been almost at a halt before it hit her. Perhaps it pushed the body a few feet. Now her limbs had the used-up look of rope washed limp in the sea, and her head was wedged beneath a tire. There was a man taking photographs, his strobe light going off each time with a mean crackling hiss, and as I knelt, he stepped back and turned to someone else, a doctor with a satchel in his hand, and said, "She's yours."

"All right, move the car back," the doctor said. Two policemen near me pushed on the automobile and retired the front wheels a foot before the car bumped gently into the car behind it. I knelt ahead of the medical examiner and looked at her face. It was filthy with the scrape of asphalt and tire marks. Just half of her was recognizable, for the side of her face that caught the tire was swollen. She looked like a fat young girl. But the back of her head, like a fruit gone rotten and lying in its juices, was the center of a pond of coagulated blood near to a foot in diameter. I stayed between the police photographer who was getting ready to take more pictures and the medical examiner who was opening his satchel and, still on my knees, touched my face to hers, being careful to catch some of the blood on my hands, and even (as I nuzzled her hair with my nose) a streak or two more on my cheeks. "Oh, baby," I said aloud. It might have been good to weep, but nothing of that sort was even near. No, shock and stupor would be the best I could muster. "Deborah," I said, and like an echo from the worst of one's past came a clear sense of doing this before, of making love to some woman who was not attractive to me, of something unpleasant in her scent or dead in her skin, and me saying "Oh, darling, oh, baby," in that rape of one's private existence which manners demand. So, now, the "Oh, darling" came out full of timbre, full of loss. "Oh, Christ, Christ," I repeated dully.

"Are you the husband?" a voice asked in my ear. Without turning around, I had an idea of the man who spoke. He was a detective, and he must be at least six feet tall, big through the shoulder and with the beginning of a gut. It was an Irish voice oiled with a sense of its authority, and in control of a thousand irritations. "Yes," I said, and looked up to meet a man who did not correspond to his voice. He was about five-eight in height, almost slim, with a hard, clean face and the sort of cold blue eyes that live for a contest. So it was like the small shock of meeting somebody after talking on the telephone.

"Your name?"

I told him.

"Mr. Rojack, there's a series of directly unpleasant details to get through."

"All right," I said dumbly, more than careful not to meet his eye.

"My name is Roberts. We have to take your wife to Four Hundred East Twenty-ninth, and we may have to call you down there to identify her again, but for the minute now—if you'd just wait for us."

I was debating whether to say, "My God, right in front of my eyes, she jumped like that!" but that was one duck which would never lift from the lake. I had an uneasy sense of Roberts that was not unlike the uneasy sense I used to have of Deborah.

I wandered down the line of banged-up cars, and discovered that the unpleasant elderly man with the pink-tinted glasses was still moaning. There was a young couple with him, a tall dark good-looking Italian who might have been the man's nephew—he showed a family resemblance. He had a sulky face, a perfect pompadour of black straight hair, and was wearing a dark suit, a white silk shirt, a silver-white silk tie. He was a type I never liked on sight, and I liked him less because of the blond girl he had with him. I caught no more than a glimpse of her, but she had one of those perfect American faces, a small-town girl's face with the sort of perfect clean features that find their way onto every advertisement and every billboard in the land. Yet there was something better about this girl, she had the subtle touch of a most expensive show girl, there was a silvery cunning in her features. And a quiet remote little air. Her nose was a classic. It turned up with just the tough tilt of a speedboat planing through the water.

She must have felt me staring at her, for she turned around—she had been ministering with a certain boredom to the weak gutty sounds of the man in the pink-tinted glasses—and her eyes, which were an astonishing green-golden-yellow in color (the eyes of an ocelot), now looked at me with an open small-town concern. "You poor man, your face is covered with blood," she said. It was a warm, strong, confident, almost masculine voice, a trace of a Southern accent to it, and she took out her handkerchief and dabbed at my cheek.

"It must have been awful," she said. A subtle hard-headed ever-so-guarded maternity lay under the pressure with which she scrubbed the handkerchief at my face.

"Hey, Cherry," said her friend, "go up front, and talk to those cops, and see if we can get Uncle out of here." Studiously, he was avoiding me.

"Let it be, Tony," she said. "Don't look to draw attention."

And the uncle groaned again, as if to begrudge me *my* attention.

"Thank you," I said to her, "you're very kind."

"I know you," she said, looking carefully at my face. "You're on television."

"Yes."

"You have a good program."

"Thank you."

"Mr. Rojack." The detective was calling me.

"What is your name?" I asked her.

"Don't even think about it, Mr. Rojack," she said with a smile, and turned back to Tony.

And now I realized the detective had seen me chatting with nothing less than a blonde.

"Let's go upstairs and talk," he said.

We stepped into a squad car, the siren was opened, and we drove up the Drive to an exit, and then turned back to the apartment. We didn't say a word on the way. That was just as well. Sitting next to me, Roberts gave off the physical communion one usually receives from a woman. He had an awareness of me—it was as if some instinct in him reached into me and I was all too aware of him.

By the time we arrived, there were two more squad cars in the street. Our silence continued as we rode up in the elevator, and when we got to the apartment, a few more detectives and a few more police were standing about. There was a joyless odor in the air now somewhat reminiscent of liquid soap. Two of the police were talking to Ruta. She had not combed out her hair. Instead she had done her best to restore it, and she looked too attractive. The skirt and blouse had been changed for a pink-orange silk wrapper.

But she made up for it by her greeting. "Mr. Rojack, you poor poor man," she said. "Can I make you some coffee?"

I nodded. I wanted a drink as well. Perhaps she would have the sense to put something in the cup.

"All right," said Roberts, "I'd like to go to the room where this happened." He gave a nod to one of the other detectives, a big Irishman with white hair, and the two of them followed me. The second detective was very friendly. He gave a wink of commiseration as we sat down.

"All right, to begin with," said Roberts, "how long have you and your wife been living here?"

"She's been here for six or eight weeks."

"But you haven't?"

"No, we've been separated for a year."

"How many years were you married?"

"Almost nine."

"And since you separated, you've been seeing her often?"

"Perhaps once or twice a week. Tonight was the first time I'd been over in two weeks."

"Now, on the phone you said this was an accident."

"Yes, I think I said it was a frightful accident. I think those were my words."

"An accident in fact?"

"No, Detective. I may as well tell you that it was suicide."

"Why did you say it was an accident?"

"I had some dim hope of protecting my wife's reputation."

"I'm glad you didn't try to go ahead with that story."

"It wasn't until I hung up that I realized I had in effect told the next thing to a lie. I think that took me out of my shock a little. When I called down to the maid, I decided to tell her the truth."

"All right then." He nodded. "It was a suicide. Your wife *jumped* through the window." He was doing his best to make the word inoffensive. "Now, let me get it clear. Your wife got up from bed. Is that correct?"

"Yes."

"Went to the window and opened it?"

"No, I'd opened it a few minutes before. She'd been complaining about the heat and asked me to open the window as wide as I could." I shivered now, for the window was still open, and the room was cold.

"Forgive me for prying," said Roberts, "but suicides are nasty unless they're cleared up quickly. I have some difficult questions to ask you."

"Ask what you wish. I don't think any of this has hit me yet."

"Well, then, if you don't mind, had you been intimate with your wife this evening?"

"No."

"Though there had been some drinking?"

"Quite a bit."

"Was she drunk?"

"She must have had a lot of liquor in her system. However, she wasn't drunk. Deborah could hold her liquor very well."

"But you had a quarrel, perhaps?"

"Not exactly."

"Please explain."

"She was fearfully depressed. She said some ugly things."

"You didn't get angry?"

"I was used to it."

"Would you care to say what she said?"

"What does a wife ever accuse a husband of? She tells him one way or another that he's not man enough for her."

"Some wives," said Roberts, "complain that their husband is running around too much."

"I had my private life. Deborah had hers. People who come from Deborah's background don't feel at ease until their marriage has congealed into a marriage of convenience."

"This sounds sort of peaceful," said Roberts.

"Obviously, it wasn't. Deborah suffered from profound depressions. But she kept them to herself. She was a proud woman. I doubt if even her closest friends were aware of the extent of these depressions. When she felt bad, she would go to bed and stay in bed for a day or two at a time. She would keep to herself. I haven't seen a great deal of her this last year, but you can certainly check with the maid."

"We got a couple of men talking to her right now," said the older detective with a wide happy smile, as if his only desire in the world were to assist me.

"How about the coffee?" I asked.

"Coming up," said Roberts. He went to the door, called down, and came back. "What did she have to be depressed about?" he asked easily.

"She was religious. A very religious Catholic. And I'm not Catholic. I think she felt that to be married to me kept her in mortal sin."

"So as a very religious Catholic," said Roberts, "she decided to save her immortal soul by committing suicide?"

There was just the hint of a pause between us. "Deborah had an unusual mind," I said. "She talked often of suicide to me, particularly when she was in one of her depressions. Particularly in the last few years. She had a miscarriage, you see, and couldn't have any more children." But I had done myself a damage. Not with them—rather with some connection I had to an instinct within me. That instinct sickened suddenly with disgust; the miscarriage, after all, had been my loss as well.

There was of course nothing to do but go on. "I don't think it was the miscarriage so much. Deborah had a sense of something bad inside herself. She felt haunted by demons. Does that mean anything to you?"

"No," said Roberts, "I don't know how to put demons on a police report."

The older detective winked at me again with great joviality.

"Roberts, you don't strike me as the type to commit suicide," I said.

"It's true. I'm not the type."

"Well, then, don't you think a little charity might be in order when you try to understand a suicidal mind?"

"You're not on television, Mr. Rojack," Roberts said.

"Look, I know where I am. I'm doing my best to try to explain something to you. Would you be happier if I were under sedation?"

"I might be more convinced," said Roberts.

"Does that remark indicate suspicion?"

"I didn't hear you."

"Does that remark indicate suspicion?"

"Now, wait a minute, Mr. Rojack, let's get squared away. There must be newspapermen downstairs already. There'll be a mob at the morgue and another mob at the precinct. It can't come as any surprise to you that this will hit the newspapers tomorrow. It may be front page. You can be hurt if there's a hint of irregularity in what is written tomorrow—you can be ruined forever if the coroner's report has any qualifications in it. My duty as a police officer is to find out the facts and communicate them to the proper places."

"Including the press?"

"I work with them every day of the year. I work with you just tonight and maybe tomorrow, and let's hope not any more than that. I want to clear this up. I want to be able to go down and say to those reporters, 'I think she jumped—go easy on that poor bastard in there.' You read me? I don't want to have to suggest, 'This character's a creep—he may have given her a shove.' "

"All right," I said, "fair enough."

"If you wish," he said, "you can answer no questions and just ask for a lawyer."

"I've no desire to ask for a lawyer."

"Oh, you can have one," said Roberts.

"I don't want one. I don't see why I need one."

"Then let's keep talking."

"If you want," I said, "to understand Deborah's suicide—so far as I understand it—you'll have to go along with my comprehension of it."

"You were speaking of demons," Roberts said.

"Yes. Deborah believed they possessed her. She saw herself as evil."

"She was afraid of Hell?"

"Yes."

"We come back to this. A devout Catholic believes she's going to Hell, so she decides to save herself by committing suicide."

"Absolutely," I said.

"Absolutely," said Roberts. "You wouldn't mind repeating this to a priest, would you now?"

"It would be as hard to explain to him as it is to you."

"Better take your chances with me."

"It's not easy to go on," I said. "Could I have that coffee now?"

The big elderly detective got up and left the room. While he was gone, Roberts was silent. Sometimes he would look at me, and sometimes he would look at a photograph of Deborah that stood in a silver frame on the bureau. I lit a cigarette and offered him the pack. "I never smoke," he said.

The other detective was back with the coffee. "You don't mind if I took a sip of it," he said. "The maid put some Irish in." Then he gave his large smile. A sort of fat sweet corruption emanated from him. I gagged on the first swallow of the coffee. "Oh, God, she's dead," I said.

"That's right," said Roberts, "she jumped out the window."

I put out the cigarette and blew my nose, discovering to my misery that a sour stem of vomit had worked its way high up my throat into the base of my nose and had now been flushed through my nostril onto the handkerchief. My nose burned. I took another swallow of coffee and the Irish whiskey sent out a first creamy spill of warmth.

"I don't know if I can explain it to you," I said. "Deborah believed there was special mercy for suicides. She thought it was a frightful thing to do, but that God might forgive you if your soul was in danger of being extinguished."

"Extinguished," Roberts repeated.

"Yes, not lost, but extinguished. Deborah believed that if you went to Hell, you could still resist the Devil there. You see she thought there's something worse than Hell."

"And that is?"

"When the soul dies before the body. If the soul is extinguished in life, nothing passes on into Eternity when you die."

"What does the Church have to say about this?"

"Deborah thought this didn't apply for an ordinary Catholic. But she saw herself as a fallen Catholic. She believed her soul was dying. I think that's why she wanted to commit suicide."

"That's the only explanation you can offer?"

Now I waited for a minute. "I don't know if there's any basis to this, but Deborah believed she was riddled with cancer."

"What do you think?"

"It may have been true."

"Did she go to doctors?"

"Not to my knowledge. She distrusted doctors."

"She didn't take pills," Roberts asked, "just liquor?"

"No pills."

"How about marijuana?"

"Hated it. She'd walk out of a room if she thought somebody was smoking it. She said once that marijuana was the Devil's grace."

"You ever take it?"

"No." I coughed. "Oh, once or twice I might have taken a social puff, but I hardly remember."

"All right," he said, "let's get into this cancer. Why do you believe she had it?"

"She talked about it all the time. She felt that as your soul died, cancer began. She would always say it was a death that was not like other deaths."

The fat detective farted. Abrupt as that. "What is *your* name?" I asked.

"O'Brien." He shifted in his seat, half at his ease, and lit a cigar. The smoke blended easily into the odor of the other fumes. Roberts looked disgusted. I had the feeling I was beginning to convince him for the first time. "My father died of cancer," he said.

"I'm sorry to hear that. I can only say I wasn't very happy to listen to Deborah's theories because my mother passed away from leukemia."

He nodded. "Look, Rojack, I might as well tell you. There'll be an autopsy on your wife. It may or may not show what you're talking about."

"It may show nothing. Deborah could have been in a precancerous stage."

"Sure. But it might be better all around if the cancer shows. Cause there is a correlation between cancer and suicide. I'll grant you that." Then he looked at his watch. "Some practical questions. Did your wife have a lot of money?"

"I don't know. We never talked about her money."

"Her old man's pretty rich if she's the woman I'm thinking of."

"He may have disowned her when we married. I often said to friends that she was ready to give up her share of two hundred million dollars when she married me, but she wasn't ready to cook my breakfast."

"So far as you know, you're not in her will?"

"If she has any money, I don't believe she would have left it to me. It would go to her daughter."

"Well, that's simple enough to find out."

"Yes."

"All right, Mr. Rojack, let's get into tonight. You came to visit her after two weeks. Why?"

"I missed her suddenly. That still happens after you're separated."

"What time did you get here?"

"Several hours ago. Maybe nine o'clock."

"She let you in?"

"The maid did."

"Did you ever give the maid a bang?" asked O'Brien.

"Never."

"Ever want to?"

"The idea might have crossed my mind."

"Why didn't you?" O'Brien went on.

"It would have been disagreeable if Deborah found out."

"That makes sense," said O'Brien.

"All right," said Roberts, "you came into this room, and then what?"

"We talked for hours. We drank and we talked."

"Less than half the bottle is gone. That's not much for two heavy drinkers over three hours."

"Deborah had her share. I only took nips."

"What did you talk about?"

"Everything. We discussed the possibility of getting together again. We agreed it was impossible. Then she cried, which is very rare for Deborah. She told me that she had spent an hour standing by the open window before I came, and that she had been tempted to jump. She felt as if God were asking her. She said she felt a woe afterward as if she'd refused Him. And then she said, 'I didn't have cancer before. But in that hour I stood by the window, it began in me. I didn't jump and so my cells jumped. I know that.' Those were her words. Then she fell asleep for a while."

"What did you do?"

"I just sat in this chair by her bed. I felt pretty low, I can tell you. Then she woke up. She asked me to open the window. When she started to talk, she told me . . . do I really have to go into this?"

"Better if you would."

"She told me my mother had had cancer and I had had it too, and that I gave it to her. She said all the years we were lying in bed as husband and wife I was giving it to her."

"What did you say?"

"Something equally ugly."

"Please go into it," said Roberts.

"I said that was just as well, because she was a parasite and I had work to do. I even said: if her soul was dying, it deserved to—it was vicious."

"What did she do then?"

"She got out of bed and went over to the window, and said, 'If you don't retract that, I'll jump.' I was confident she didn't mean it. Her very use of a word like *retract*. I simply told her, 'Well, then jump. Rid the world of your poison.' I thought I was doing the right thing, that I might be breaking into her madness, into that tyrannical will which had wrecked our marriage. I thought I might win something decisive with her. Instead, she took a step on the ledge, and out she went. And I felt as if something blew back from her as she fell and brushed against my face." I began to shudder—the picture I had given was real to me. "Then I don't know what happened. I think I was half ready to follow her. Obviously I didn't. Instead I called the police, and called down to the maid, and then I must have passed out for a moment because I came to lying on the floor, and thought, 'You're guilty of her death.' So go slow for a while, will you, Roberts. This has not been easy."

"Yeah," said Roberts. "I think I believe you."

"Excuse me," said O'Brien. He got up just a bit heavily and went out.

"There's a few formalities," said Roberts. "If you can take it, I'd like you to come down to Four Hundred East Twenty-ninth for the identification, and then we'll go over to the precinct and check out a few forms."

"I hope I don't have to tell this story too many times."

"Just once more to a police stenographer. You can skip all the details. No Hell, Heaven, cancer, nothing like that. None of the dialogue. Just that you saw her go."

O'Brien came back with another detective, who was introduced as Lieutenant Leznicki. He was Polish. He was about Roberts' height, even thinner than Roberts, and looked to have an angry ulcer, for he moved with short irritable gestures. His eyes were a dull yellow-gray in color, and about the tint of a stale clam. His hair was an iron-gray and his skin was gray. He must have been fifty years old. Just as we were introduced, he sniffed the air with a boxer's quick snort. Then he smiled irritably.

"Why'd you kill her, Rojack?" he asked.

"What's up?" said Roberts.

"Her hyoid bone is broken." Leznicki looked at me. "Why didn't you say you strangled her before you threw her out?"

"I didn't."

"The doctor's evidence shows you strangled her."

"I don't believe it. My wife fell ten stories and then was struck by a car."

Roberts sat back. I looked to him as if he were the first ally and last best friend I had in the world, and he leaned forward and said, "Mr. Rojack, we handle a lot of suicides in a year. They take pills, they cut their wrists, they stick a pistol in their mouth. Sometimes they jump. But in all the years I've been on the Force, I never heard of a woman jumping from an open window while her husband was watching."

"Never," said O'Brien.

"You better get yourself a lawyer, buddy," said Leznicki.

"I don't need one."

"Come on," said Roberts, "let's go over to the precinct."

As they stood up, a mood came from them. It was the smell of hunters sitting in an overheated hut at dawn waiting for the sun to come out, drunk from drinking through the night. I was game to them at this moment. As I stood up, I felt a weakness go through me. No adrenaline followed. I had been taking more punishment than I thought and had the same sense of surprise a fighter knows in the middle of a fight when his legs go mellow and there is nothing left in his arms.

When they took me through the hall, Ruta was nowhere in sight. I could hear voices however in her room.

"The specialists get here yet?" asked Leznicki of the policeman on guard at the door.

"That's them in there," said the cop.

"Tell them I said to give one hundred percent to this job, and one hundred percent to the job upstairs."

Then he rang for the elevator.

"Why don't we take him through the back door," said Roberts.

"No," said Leznicki, "let him meet the Press."

They were downstairs on the street, about eight or ten of them, and they did an odd dance about us, their flashbulbs going off, their questions flying, their faces overcheerful and greedy. They could have been a pack of twelve-year-old beggars in some Italian town, hysterical, almost wild, delighted with the money they might be thrown, and in a whinny of fear they would get nothing. I made no attempt to cover my face—at the moment there seemed no harm worse than to have to look at myself tomorrow in a tabloid with my head humped behind a hat.

"Hey, Leznicki, he do it?" one cried.

Another darted up to me, his face full of welcome, as if to give surety he was the one man on the street I could trust. "Would you care to make a statement, Mr. Rojack?" he asked with concern.

"No, nothing," I said.

Roberts was guiding me into the back seat.

"Hey, Roberts," another cried, "what's the word?"

"Suicide or what?" asked another.

"Routine," said Roberts, "routine."

There was a low undertone of bickering, not unlike the sound an audience gives off when it is announced the understudy will play the part tonight. "Let's get going," said Roberts.

But he sat in front beside the driver, while I was plumped into the back cushions between Leznicki and O'Brien. We were driving now in an unmarked battered sedan, a detective's car, and as we took off from the curb, more flashbulbs went off through the window at me, and I could hear them scrambling for their cars.

"Why'd you do it?" asked Leznicki in my ear.

I didn't answer. I did my best to stare back, as if I were in fact a husband who had watched his wife go out a window and he was no more than some animal barking at me, but my silence must have been livid, because an odor of violence came off him, a kind of clammy odor of rut, and O'Brien, on my other side, who had shown a pronounced smell already, oversweet and very stale, was throwing a new odor, something like the funk a bully emits when he heads for a face-to-face meeting. Their hands twitched in their laps. They wanted to have a go at me. I had a feeling I wouldn't last thirty seconds between them.

"Did you use a stocking to strangle her?" asked Leznicki.

"He used his arm," said O'Brien in a big hollow gloomy voice.

It had started to rain. A light fall, almost a mist, settled in a delicate wash of light over the streets. I could feel my heart beating now like a canary held in my hand. It throbbed with a tender almost exhilarated fatigue. I could have been no more than a drum with a bird's heart trapped inside, and the reverberations seemed to sound outside my body, as if everyone in the car could hear me. There were cars following behind, the photographers and the reporters no doubt, and their headlights gave an odd comfort. Like a bird indeed in a cage in a darkened room, the passing flare of light from outside gave some memory of the forest, and I felt myself soaring out on the beating of my heart as if a climax of fear had begun that might race me through swells of excitement until everything burst, the heart burst, and I flew out to meet my death. The men in the car looked red to me, then green, then red again. I wondered if I was close to fainting. It was suffocating to sit between those men—it was like being a fox in a bog while hounds crooned on either bank. I knew at last the sweet panic of an animal who is being tracked, for if danger was close, if danger came in on the breeze, and one's nostrils had an awareness of the air as close as that first touch of a tongue on your flesh, there was still such a tenderness for the hope one could stay alive. Something came out of the city like the whispering of a forest, and on the March night's message through the open window I had at that instant the first smell of spring, that quiet instant, so like the first moment of love one feels in a woman who has until then given no love.

"Going to marry the maid after you grab your wife's dough?" asked Leznicki.

"You strangled her," O'Brien said in his hollow voice. "Why'd you strangle her?"

"Roberts," I asked, "can you call off these hoodlums?"

There was one instant in which they both came so close to hitting me that I felt a wave of frustration fly out from Leznicki's hand and move across my face with the small impact of a flashlight in the eye. They sat there, their hands on their thighs, shaking, Leznicki with the muscular beat of a piston and O'Brien quivering like a sea-jelly disturbed in its ooze.

"You say that again," said Leznicki, "and I'll give you a pistol-whipping. You've been put on warning now."

"Don't threaten me, friend."

"Let it go," said Roberts to all of us. "Knock it off."

I sat back, feeling the damage I had done. Now the adrenaline was going through them like a mob in a riot.

We went the rest of the way in silence. Their bodies were so heated with anger that my skin felt the kind of burn one knows from staying too long beside an ultraviolet-ray lamp.

We were at the morgue for only a few minutes. There was a walk down a corridor with an attendant unlocking the doors for us, and then the room with sheets over two cadavers lying on stainless-steel tables and a bank of refrigerated bins where the bodies were kept. The light had a color like the underbelly of a whale, that denuded white of fluorescent tubes, and there was now new silence, a dead silence, some stretch of the void with no sense of events beneath, just a silence of the waste. My nostrils hurt from the antiseptic and deodorant and the other smell (that vile pale scent of embalming fluid and fecal waters) insinuated its way through the stricken air. I did not want to look at Deborah this time. I took no more than a glimpse when the sheet was laid back, and caught for that act a clear view of one green eye staring open, hard as marble, dead as the dead eye of a fish, and her poor face swollen, her beauty gone obese.

"Can we get out of here?" I asked.

The attendant put the sheet back with a professional turn of his wrists, casual but slow, not without ceremony. He had the cheerful formal gloom of a men's room attendant. "The doctor'll be here in five minutes. You going to wait?" he asked.

"Tell him to call us at the precinct," said Leznicki.

In a corner, on a desk, at the end of this long room, I could see a very small television set about the size of a table radio. It was turned down low and had gone out of synchronization, for the picture was flaring bright, then dark, then flaring up again, and I had the insane clarity to recognize that it was speaking to the neon tubes and they were answering back. I was close to nausea. When we quit the corridors and left the hospital, I turned to one side and tried to throw up but produced no more than a taste of some bile and the intimate lightning of a photographer taking a picture.

On the way to the precinct, we were silent again. Whatever Deborah would deserve, that morgue was not the place for her. I had a reverie of my own death then, and my soul (some time in the future) was trying to lift and loose itself of the body that had died. It was a long process, as if a membrane trapped in mud were seeking to catch a breeze which would trip it free. In that morgue (for that was where I pictured my own death) the delicate filaments of my soul were also expiring in a paralysis of deodorant while hope withered in the dialogue between the neon tube and the television set. I felt guilty for the first time. It was a crime to have pushed Deborah into the morgue.

There were more photographers and reporters at the entrance to the precinct, and again they were all shouting and talking out at once. "Did he do it?" I heard one yell. "You holding him?" cried another. "What's the pitch, Roberts, what's the pitch?" They came in behind us and then were left as we passed through the Desk Sergeant's room, where a cop was sitting high up on that square raised desk which had always reminded me of a tribunal (but it was only in movies I had ever seen this desk before) and then we passed into a larger room, a very large room, perhaps sixty feet by forty feet, the walls painted a dark institutional green up to the height of one's eyes and then a dirty worn-down institutional tan all the way up to the dirty-white tin plates of the ceiling, those eighteen-inch-square cheap tin plates, each decorated with some nineteenth-century manufacturer's impression of a fleur-de-lis. I saw nothing but desks, twenty desks perhaps, and, beyond, two small rooms. Roberts stopped by the door between the Desk Sergeant's room and this large room, and made a short speech to the reporters. "We're not holding Mr. Rojack for anything. He's just accommodating us by coming here to answer questions." Then he shut the door.

Roberts led me to a desk. We sat down. He took out a folder and wrote in it for a few minutes. Then he looked up. We were alone again. Leznicki and O'Brien had disappeared somewhere. "You're aware," said Roberts, "that I did you a favor out there."

"Yes," I said.

"Well, it was against my better judgment. I don't like the feel of this one. Neither does Leznicki or O'Brien. I'm going to tell you: Leznicki is an animal when it comes to this sort of stuff. He's convinced you killed her. He thinks you broke her hyoid bone with a silk stocking wrapped around her neck. He's hoping you did it a couple of hours before you pushed her out."

"Why?"

"Because, friend, if she was gone for a couple of hours, it could show up in the autopsy."

"If it does, you have a case."

"Oh, we have the beginnings of a case. I have a nose for one thing. I know you were making out with that German maid." His hard blue eyes looked into me. I held the stare until my eyes began to water. Then he looked away. "Rojack, you're lucky nobody got hurt too much in that five-car crack-up. If they had, and we could stick your wife's fall on you, the papers would handle you as Bluebeard, Jr. I mean think if a kid had been killed."

Indeed, I had never considered this until now. It had not been part of my intent after all to telescope five cars on the East River Drive.

"So, look," he went on, "you're not in the worst of spots. But you are at the point where you have to make a decision. If you confess this—forgive your feelings—but if you have any infidelities on your wife's part to bring in as evidence, a smart lawyer could get you off with twenty years. Which as a practical matter is usually about twelve years and can be as little as eight. We'll cooperate to the extent that we'll say your confession was given us of your own free will. I'll have to mark down the time of it, which will mean you didn't confess for the first few hours, but I'll say you were in shock up to then. I won't mention the kind of bullshit you've given us. And I'll stand up for you in court. Whereas if you wait till all the evidence accumulates and then confess, you'll get life. Then, even at best, you won't be out for twenty years. And if you fight it all the way, and we get a lock on the case, you could face the chair, buddy. They'll shave your head and give your soul a charge of voltage. So sit on this, and think. Think of that electric chair. I'm getting some coffee."

"It's way after midnight," I said. "Aren't you supposed to be home by now?"

"I'll bring you a cup."

But I was sorry he was gone. It had been easier somehow when he had been there. Now there was nothing to do but think of what he had said. I was trying to calculate how much time had gone by from that moment I recognized Deborah was dead until she struck the ground on the East River Drive. It could not be less than half an hour. It could be as much as an hour, conceivably an hour and a half. I had had a knowledge of anatomy once, but now I had no idea how long the cells might remain intact, nor how soon they might begin to decompose. While I was sitting here, it was likely they were doing an autopsy on Deborah. A leaden anxiety settled in my stomach—just that sort of bottomless pit I used to feel when I had been away from Deborah for a week or two and was suddenly powerless not to call her. It was difficult to sit still and wait for Roberts to come back, much as if that merciless lack of charity which I had come to depend on in Deborah (as a keel to ballast the empty dread of my stomach) was now provided by the detective. I knew they were probably watching me, and that I should not move too much. I was aware that once I began to walk about, my anxiety would show in every step I took, and yet I did not know if I could expend much more of my will in remaining motionless: I had been firing guns for hours—the armory was near to empty.

Still I forced myself to study the room. There were detectives talking to people at four or five of the desks. An old woman in a shabby coat was busy weeping at the nearest table, and a very bored detective kept tapping his pencil and waiting for her to cease. Further down a big Negro with a badly beaten face was shaking his head in the negative to every question asked him. In the far corner behind a half partition I thought I could hear Ruta's voice.

And then across the room I saw a head with long blond hair. It was Cherry. She was with Uncle and Tony, and her friends were arguing with Lieutenant Leznicki and two detectives I had not seen before. I had been in this room for a quarter of an hour and had been looking at nothing but the expression in Roberts' face. Now I was suddenly aware that there was as much sound as one might find in the dark night ward of a hospital, there was all but a chorus of protests and imprecations, and the leathery pistol-shot insistence of the policemen's voices; I could almost have allowed myself to slip into the anteroom of a dream where we were all swimming about in a sea of mud, calling to each other under the crack of rifles and a dark moon. Voices picked up from one another, the old woman wept louder as our Uncle across the room began to talk in his whining stammering voice, and then Ruta, still out of sight behind the partition, picked up something shrill in tone from the old woman's weeping and the Negro with the smashed-in face was talking faster, nodding his head in rhythm to some beat he had extracted from the sounds. I wondered if I was in fever, for I had the impression now that I was letting go of some grip on my memory of the past, that now I was giving up my loyalty to every good moment I had had with Deborah and surrendering the hard compacted anger of every hour when she had spoiled my need—I felt as if I were even saying goodbye to that night on the hill in Italy with my four Germans under the moon, yes, I felt just as some creature locked by fear to the border between earth and water (its grip the accumulated experience of a thousand generations) might feel on that second when its claw took hold, its body climbed up from the sea, and its impulse took a leap over the edge of mutation so that now and at last it was something new, something better or worse, but never again what it had been on the other side of the instant. I felt as if I had crossed a chasm of time and was some new breed of man. What a fever I must have been in.

A face was looking at me.

"Why'd you kill her?" asked Leznicki.

"I didn't."

But Leznicki seemed happier now. His narrow face was relaxed and the stale clam color of his eyes had a hint of life. "Hey, buddy," he said with an open grin, "you're giving us a hard time."

"All I want is a cup of coffee."

"You think you're kidding. Listen," and he turned a wooden chair around, sitting with its back against his chest, and leaned his face toward me so that I caught the iron fatigue of his breath and his bad teeth, he doing this with no embarrassment the way a race track tout will feed you the good news about the horse with the bad news that rides on the smell of his breath, "listen, do you remember Henry Steels?"

"I think I do."

"Sure you do. We cracked the case right in this precinct, right at that desk over there," and he pointed to a desk that looked to me exactly like all the others. "That poor guy, Steels. Twenty-three years in Dannemora, and when they let him out, he shacks up with a fat broad in Queens. Six weeks later he kills her with a poker. You remember now? By the time we pick him up two weeks later, he's knocked off three queers and two more fat ladies. But we don't know. We just got him for the first job. A patrolman sees him in a hallway in a tenement on Third Avenue, rolls him over, recognizes him, brings him here, and we're just giving him a little cursory questioning to wake him up prior to turning him over to Queens, when he says, 'Give me a pack of Camels, and a pint of sherry, and I'll tell you all about it.' We give him the sherry and he knocks us on our ass. He produces six murders. Fills in half the Unsolveds we had in New York for that two-week period. Phenomenal. I'll never get over it. Just an old con, neat in his habits." Leznicki sucked on a tooth. "So, if you want to talk, I'll give you a bottle of champagne. Maybe you'll give us six murders, too."

We laughed together. I had come to the conclusion a long time ago that all women were killers, but now I was deciding that all men were out of their mind. I liked Leznicki enormously—it was part of the fever.

"Why didn't you tell us," he went on, "that you had a Distinguished Service Cross?"

"I was afraid you'd take it away."

"Believe me, Rojack, I never would have given you that kind of hosing if I'd known. I thought you were just another playboy."

"No hard feelings," I said.

"Good." He looked around the room. "You're on television, right?" I nodded. "Well," he went on, "you ought to get us on a program some night. Assuming the department would approve, I could tell a story or two. Crime has got a logic. You understand me?"

"No."

He coughed with the long phlegmy hacking sound of a gambler who has lost every part of his body but the wire in his brain that tells him when to bet. "A police station, so help me, is a piece of the action. We're like Las Vegas. I know when we're going to have a hot night." He coughed again. "Sometimes I think there's a buried maniac who runs the mind of this city. And he sets up the coincidences. Your wife goes out of a window, for instance. Because of cancer, you say, and five cars smack up on the East River Drive because of her. Who's in one of the cars but little Uncle Ganooch, Eddie Ganucci, you've heard of him."

"In the Mob, isn't he?"

"He's a prince. One of the biggest in the country. And he falls into our lap. We've had a Grand Jury subpoena on him for two years, but he's out in Las Vegas, in Miami, only once or twice a year does he sneak into town. And tonight we got him. Know why? 'Cause he's superstitious. His nephew told him to take a walk, get lost in the crowd. No. He's not leaving the car. There's a dead woman on the road, and she'll curse him if he walks away. He must have had twenty guys killed in his time, he must be worth a hundred million bucks, but he's afraid of a dead dame's curse. It's bad for his cancer, he tells his nephew. Now just look at the connection you could make. Your wife you say had cancer, Uncle Ganooch is swimming in it. There it is." Leznicki laughed as if in apology for the too-rapid workings of his mind. "See why I leaned on you so hard? You can appreciate that the minute I got word Ganucci was our baby tonight, I didn't want to waste time with you."

"What about the girl? Who's she?" I asked.

"A broad. The nephew's got an after-hours spot, and she sings there. A very sick broad. She makes it with spades." He named a Negro singer whose records I had listened to for years. "Yeah, Shago Martin, that's who she makes it with," said Leznicki. "When a dame dyes her straw, she's looking for a big black boogie."

"Beautiful girl," I said. Her hair hardly seemed dyed to me. Perhaps it was tinted a bit.

"I'm getting to like you more and more, Mr. Rojack. I just wish you hadn't killed your wife."

"Well," I said, "here we go again."

"No, look," he said, "do you think I like to exercise my function on a man who's won a Distinguished Service Cross? I just wish I didn't know you did it."

"What if I tried to tell you I didn't."

"If they brought the Good Lord Himself to this room . . ." He stopped. "Nobody ever tells the truth here. It's impossible. Even the molecules in the air are full of lies."

We were silent. The Negro with the beat-up face was the only one talking in the room. "Now, what do I want with that liquor store," he said, "that liquor store is boss, I mean that store is *territory*, man. I don't go near territory."

"The arresting officer," said the detective next to him, "had to subdue you right in that store. You cracked the owner in the face, you emptied the register, and then the patrolman caught you from behind."

"Shee-it. You got me mixed up with some other black man. No cop can tell one nigger from another. You got me mixed up with some other nigger you been beating up on."

"Let's go in the back room."

"I want some coffee."

"You'll get some coffee when you sign."

"Let me think." And they both were silent.

Leznicki put a hand on my arm. "It's beginning to go bad for you," he said. "That German girl is cracking."

"What has she to confess? That I tried to kiss her once in the hall?"

"Rojack, we got her worried. Right now she's thinking about herself. She don't know if you killed your wife, but she admits you could have—that she admitted after we had a matron strip her down. A medical examiner took a smear. That German girl has been in the sack tonight. We can take you out and give you an examination too, and see if you've been working on her tonight. Do you want that?"

"I don't think you have the right."

"There's male body hair in her bed. We can check to see if it's yours or not. That is, if you're willing to cooperate. All we have to do is pull a few out with a tweezer. Do you want that?"

"No."

"Then admit you gave the maid a bang this evening."

"I don't see what the maid had to do with this," I said. "An affair with the maid wouldn't give me cause to murder my wife."

"Forget these petty details," said Leznicki. "I want to propose something. Get one of the best lawyers in town, and you can be on the street in six months." At this moment he looked more like an old thief than a Lieutenant of Detectives. Twenty-five years of muggers and dips, safe men and junkies and bookies and cons had passed before him, and each must have charmed some fine little cell. "Rojack, I know a man, an ex-Marine, whose wife told him she went down on all his friends. He beat in her head with a hammer. They kept him under observation until his trial. His lawyer got him off. Temporary Insanity. He's on the street. And he's in better shape today than you are with your suicide story. Because even if you get out of this, which you won't, nobody will believe you didn't push your wife."

"Why don't you be my lawyer?" I said.

"Think!" said Leznicki. "I'm going over to visit Little Uncle."

I watched him cross the room. The old man stood up to meet him, and they shook hands. Then they put their heads together. One of them must have told a quick joke for they both started to laugh. I saw Cherry look over at me, and on an impulse I waved. She waved back merrily. We could have been Freshmen at a state university catching glimpses of one another at different registration desks.

A policeman came out with a pot of coffee and poured me a cup. Then the Negro shouted to him, "I want a cup, too."

"Keep your voice down," said the cop. But the detective who was sitting with the Negro gave a signal to come over. "This boogie is dead drunk," said the detective, "give him a cup."

"I don't want any coffee now," said the Negro.

"Sure you do."

"No, I don't. It gives me butterflies."

"Take some coffee. Sober up."

"I don't want coffee. I want some tea."

The detective groaned. "Come in the back room," he said.

"I want to stay here."

"Come in the back room and take some coffee."

"I don't need none."

The detective whispered in his ear.

"All right," said the Negro, "I'll go in the back room."

The woman who had been weeping must have signed some paper, for she was gone. There was no one near me now. And I was watching a film of a courtroom. The defense counsel with a dedicated emollient in his voice: "Then, Mr. Rojack, what did your wife say?" "Well, sir, she spoke of her lovers and she said they had made a favorable comparison of her actions in the sexual act with the sexual actions of a plumber—as it is called—in a Mexican brothel." "And would you, Mr. Rojack, tell the court what a 'plumber' is?" "Well, sir, a 'plumber' is the lowest prostitute in a house of prostitution and will commit those acts which other prostitutes for reasons of relative delicacy refuse to perform." "I see, Mr. Rojack. What did you do then?" "I don't know. I don't remember. I had warned my wife of my terrible temper. I have been suffering blackouts ever since the War. I had a blackout then."

A faint nausea, kin to the depression with which one could wake up every morning for years, drifted through my lungs. If one pleaded Temporary Insanity, Leznicki and I would be brothers, we would be present in spirit at each other's funeral, we would march in lock-step through Eternity. Yet, I was tempted. For that emptiness in my chest, that sense of void in my stomach, was back again. I did not have any certainty at all that I could go on. No, they would question me and they would question me; they would tell truths and they would tell lies; they would be friendly, they would be unfriendly; and all the while I would keep breathing the air of this room with its cigarettes and cigars, its coffee that tasted of dirty urns, its distant hint of lavatories and laundries, of junk yards and morgues, I would see dark green walls and dirty-white ceilings, I would listen to subterranean mutterings, I would open my eyes and close them under the blistering light of the electric bulbs, I would live in a subway, I would live for ten or twenty years in a subway, I would lie in a cell at night with nothing to do but walk a stone square floor. I would die through endless stupors and expired plans.

Or I would spend a year of appeals, spend a last year of my life in an iron cage, and walk one morning into a room where ready for nothing, where nothing done, failed, miserable, frightened of what migrations were ready for me, I would go out smashing, jolting, screaming inside, out into the long vertigo of death.

It was then I came very close. I think I would have called Leznicki over and asked him for the name of a lawyer, and stuck my tongue out in some burlesque of him and me and our new contract, and rolled my eyes, and said, "You see, Leznicki, I'm raving mad." I think I really would have done it then, but I did not feel the strength to call across the room, I had a horror of appearing feeble before that young blond girl, and so I sat back and waited for Leznicki to return, experiencing for still one more time tonight what it was like to know the exhaustion and the apathy of those who are very old and very ill. I had never understood before why certain old people, sniffing displeasure in the breath of everyone who stared at them, still held with ferocity to the mediocre tasteless continuation of their days, their compact made with some lesser devil of medicine—"Keep me away from God a little longer." But I understood it now. Because there was a vast cowardice in me which was ready to make any peace at all, ready to pillage in public the memory of that wife I had had for near to nine years, ready to mock the future of my brain by preparing to cry out that I too was insane and my best ideas were poor, warped, distorted, and injurious to others. No, I wanted out, I wanted to get away from this trap I had created for myself, I would have given up if my cowardice had the simple strength to throw my voice across the room. But it didn't, it could only rivet the cheeks of my buttocks to the chair and order me to wait, as if some power had cast a paralysis upon me.

Then the Negro started up in the other room. I could not see him but now I could certainly hear him. "I don't want the coffee," he cried out, "I want some Seagram's Seven. That's what you told me I could have, and that's what I want."

"Drink your coffee, goddamn you," shouted the detective, and through the open door was a glimpse of him walking that big Negro back and forth, and there was a patrolman on the other arm, a hard-faced dull young cop with straight black hair and eyes you see in tabloids on the face of young killers who never miss a Mass until the morning after the night they go berserk, and they were both walking the Negro, they were out of sight now, there was the liquid splattering sound of coffee falling in a large splash and the thump of the mug on the floor, and then there was another splattering sound, the sound of a fist on a face, and the dull thump of a knee in the back, and the Negro groaned, but almost agreeably, as if the beating were his pre-dictable sanity. "Now give me the Seagram's Seven," he cried out, "and I'll sign that paper."

"Drink coffee," shouted the detective. "You can't even see right now."

"Shee-it on that coffee," muttered the Negro, and then came the sound of new beating on him, and all three, all with a stumbling grap-pling hold on each other, went out of view, came into view again, went out again, and more sounds of splattering.

"Goddamn you," cried the detective, "you goddamn stubborn boogie."

And a new detective had taken the seat beside me, a younger man, thirty-five perhaps, with an anonymous face and a somewhat gloomy mouth. "Mr. Rojack," he said, "I just want to tell you that I enjoy your television program very much, and I'm sorry we have to meet under these circumstances."

"Unnh," grunted the Negro, "unnh, unnh, unnh," as the punches went into him, "that's the way, daddy, unnh, unnh, keep moving, you're improving all the time."

"Now, why don't you drink some coffee," shouted the detective who was beating him.

I have to confess that at this instant I put my head down and whispered to myself, "Oh, God, give me a sign," crying it into the deeps of myself as if I possessed all the priorities of a saint, and looked up with conviction and desperation sufficient to command a rainbow, but there was nothing that caught my eye in the room but the long blond hair of Cherry, standing across the floor. She, too, was looking at the room where the beating went on, and there was a clean girl's look on her face as if she had been watching a horse who had broken his leg and was now simply miserable before the proportions of things. I stood up then and started out with some idea of going to the back room, but the dread lifted even as I stood up and once again I felt a force in my body steering away from that back room, and a voice inside me said, "Go to the girl."

So instead I walked across the big room and approached Leznicki and Ganooch and Tony and Cherry and Roberts and O'Brien and even a few others, detectives and lawyers, and stopped near Cherry. I had a good look at her now and she was older than I had expected— she was not eighteen or twenty-one as I had thought on the street but twenty-seven perhaps or twenty-eight, and there were pale green circles of chronic exhaustion beneath her eyes. But I still thought her very nice. She had an elusive silvery air as if once there had been a huge disappointment and now a delicate gaiety had formed to cover the pain. She looked a little like a child who has been anointed by the wing of a magical bird. And she also looked wretched just now.

"Tony, can't you do something about that beating?" she asked.

He shook his head. "Stay out of it, huh?"

Roberts spoke to her. "The boy they got in there tried to beat an old man to death tonight."

"Yes," she said, "but that's not why *they're* beating on him."

"What do *you* want?" said Roberts, looking at me.

"Roberts, I think she's right. I think you ought to call off that detective."

"Planning to talk about it on your program?" asked Leznicki.

"May I invite you when I do?"

"It's better to stop these things," said Uncle Ganooch. "There's too much friction in the world today."

"Hey, Red," Leznicki shouted to the back room, "he's drunk. Stick him in a cell for the night."

"He tried to bite me," Red yelled back.

"Stick him in a cell."

"Now," said Uncle Ganooch, "can we finish our business? I'm a very sick man."

"It's simple," smiled Leznicki, "we just need some assurance you'll show up to honor your subpoena."

"We're going over the old ground," said Ganooch's lawyer, "I will stand manifest for him."

"And what the hell does that mean?" asked Leznicki.

"Let's go back," said Roberts, looking at me. "I want to talk to you."

I nodded. And then moved next to the girl. Her friend Tony was standing on her other side and he gave me a look to quiver in my skin. It was a look that said, "Don't talk to this girl or somebody will break your arm."

But I was thinking I might as well take this girl for a sign—she was the only one in sight. So I said to her, and my voice was easy, "I'd like to come and hear you sing."

"Well, I'd like you to," she said.

"Where is your place?"

"Down in the Village. Just a little place. Just opened up." She looked at Tony, and hesitated, and then gave me the address in a clear voice. Out of the side of my eye I could see the Negro being led out of the big room.

"Let's go, Rojack," said Roberts. "We have something new to talk about."

It must have been three in the morning, but he still looked neat. Once we sat down, he smiled. "There's no use in asking you for a confession, is there?"

"No."

"All right, then. We're going to let you go."

"You are?"

"Yes."

"Is it all over?"

"Oh, no. No. It's not over for you till the coroner brings in a report of suicide."

"When is that?"

He shrugged. "A day, a week. Don't leave town till the coroner is heard from."

"I'm still under suspicion?"

"Oh, come on. We know you did it."

"But you can't hold me?"

"Yeah, we could hold you as a material witness. And we could work on you for seventy-two hours, and you would crack. But you're in luck, you're in great luck. We have to stick with Ganucci this week. We don't have time for you."

"You also have no evidence."

"The maid talked. We know you've been with her."

"Means nothing."

"We have some other evidence, but I don't want to get into it now. We'll see you in a day or two. Stay away from your wife's apartment.

And stay away from the maid. You wouldn't want to tamper with a potential witness."

"No, I wouldn't."

"By the way, no hard feelings."

"Oh, none."

"I mean it. You hold up all right. You're not bad."

"Thank you."

"This may interest you. We got the autopsy report. There's evidence your wife did have cancer. They're going to make some slides to verify it, but it does look good for you."

"I see."

"That's why we're letting you go."

"I see."

"Don't relax too much. The autopsy also showed that your wife's large intestine was in an interesting state."

"What do you mean by that?"

"You'll get your chance to worry later this week." He stood up. "Good night, pal." Then he stopped. "Oh, yes. Forgot to ask you to sign the autopsy papers. Would you sign them now?"

"Your autopsy was illegal?"

"I'd say it was irregular."

"I don't know if I want to sign the papers."

"Suit yourself, pal. If you don't, we can put you in a cell until the coroner brings back his report."

"Beautiful," I said.

"Not that good," said Roberts. "Just a goof. Here, sign here."

Which I did.

"Well," said Roberts, "I'm going home. Can I drop you off?"

"I'll walk," I said.

I did walk. I walked for miles through the long drizzle of the early morning, and close to dawn I found myself in the Village outside the after-hours club where Cherry was singing. I had lived through a night, I had come into a morning. It was morning outside on the street; I could think of the sun coming up. But it would rise into a wintry smog, a wet wan morning gray with mist.

The entrance to the joint was a battered metal door that opened at my knock. "I'm a friend of Tony's," I said to the man in the hall. He shrugged, and let me by. I walked down a corridor and went through another door. The room had once been the rear of a large basement loft but now it was decorated like a bar in Miami, an after-hours box of leatherette, flame-orange stuffing for the booths, the stools, the face of the bar, some dark burnished midnight of black carpet and purple wine ceiling. There was a man playing the piano, and Cherry was singing. She saw me come in and she smiled on the breath she took and made a little sign to indicate that yes she would have a drink with me as soon as her set was done. Well, if Deborah's dying had given me a new life, I must be all of eight hours old by now.

From *An American Dream* (1965)

# CONSERVATISM
# AND LIBERALISM

## From a Debate with William Buckley
## Titled "The Real Meaning
## of the Right Wing in America"

"The minister has preached a superb sermon. It has moved his congregation to lead nobler and more righteous lives. Then the minister says, 'That, of course, was the Lord's side. For the next half hour, to be fair, I'll give equal time to the Devil.' "

Well, ladies and gentlemen, upon me has fallen the unhappy task of following Mr. Buckley. Mr. Buckley was so convincing in his speech that if I had not been forewarned that the Devil cannot know how far he has fallen from Paradise, I would most certainly have decided Mr. Buckley was an angel. A dishonest angel, perhaps, but then which noble speaker is not?

I did not come here, however, to give Mr. Buckley compliments. I appear, presumably, to discuss the real meaning of the Right Wing in America, a phenomenon that is not necessarily real in its meaning, for the Right Wing covers a spectrum of opinion as wide as the peculiarities one encounters on the Left. If we of the Left are a family of anarchists and Communists, socialists, pacifists, nihilists, beatniks, international spies, terrorists, hipsters, and Bowery bums, secret agents, dope addicts, sex maniacs, and scholarly professors, what indeed is one to make of the Right, which includes the president of a corporation or the Anglican headmaster of a preparatory school, intellectually attired in the fine ideas of Edmund Burke, down the road to the Eisenhower-is-a-Communist set of arguments, all the way down the road to an American Nazi like George Lincoln Rockwell, or to the sort of conservatives who attack property with bombs in California. On a vastly more modest and civilized scale, Mr. Buckley may commit a mild mayhem on the American sense of reality when he says Joe Mc-Carthy inaugurated no reign of terror. Perhaps, I say, it was someone else.

But it is easy to mock the Right Wing. I would rather put the best face one can on it. I think there are any number of interesting adolescents and young men and women going to school now who find themselves drawn to the Right. Secretly drawn. Some are drawn to conservatism today much as they might have been attracted to the Left thirty years ago. They are the ones who are curious for freedom, the freedom not only to make money but the freedom to discover their own nature, to discover good and to discover—dare I say it?—evil. At bottom they are ready to go to war with a ready-made world that they feel is stifling them.

I hope it is evident that I do not see the people in the Right Wing as a simple group of fanatics but rather as a contradictory stew of reactionaries and individualists, of fascists and libertarians. It could be said that most Right Wingers don't really know what they want. I would not include Mr. Buckley in this category, but I think it can be said the politics of the Right in America reflects an emotion more than an insight.

I will relate a story told me by a Southerner about his aunt. She lived in a small town in South Carolina. She was a spinster. She came from one of the better families in town. Not surprisingly, the house where she lived had been in the family for a long time. She loved the trees on the walk that bordered each side of the street that ran by her house. They were very old trees.

The City Council passed a bill to cut down those trees. The street had to be widened in order to give access to a new bypass. The reason for the new bypass was to create a new business district: a supermarket, a superpharmacy, a superservice station, a chromium-plated diner, a new cemetery with plastic tombstones, a new armory for the Army Reserve, an auto supply store, a farm implements shop, a store for Venetian blinds, a Laundromat and an information booth for tourists who would miss the town on the new bypass but could read about it in the Chamber of Commerce's literature as they drove on to Florida.

Well, the old lady fought the entrance to the new bypass. To her, it was sacrilege that these trees be cut down. She felt that if there were any value to some older notions of grace and courtesy, courage under duress, and gallantry to ladies, of faith in God and the structure of His ways, that if there were any value at all to chivalry, tradition and manners, the children of the new generations could come to find it more naturally by walking down an avenue of old homes and trees than by reading the *National Review* in front of the picture window under the metal awning of the brand-new town library.

Secretly, the old lady had some radical notions. She seemed to think that the old street and the trees on this old street were the property of everyone in the town, because everyone in the town could have the pleasure of walking down that street. At her gloomiest she even used to think that a new generation of Negroes growing up in the town, strong, hostile, too smart, and just loaded with Northern ideas, would hate the South forever, and never forgive the past once the past was destroyed. If they grew up on the edge of brand-new bypasses in cement-brick homes with asbestos roofs and squatty hothouse bushes in the artificial fertilizer of the front yard, why then, how could they ever come to understand that not everyone in the old South was altogether evil and that there had been many whites who learned much from the Negro and loved him, that it was Negro slaves who had first planted these trees, and that it was Negro love of all that grew well which had set the trunks of these trees growing in so straight a route right into the air.

So the old lady fought the execution of these old trees. She went to see the mayor, she talked to everyone on the City Council, she circulated a petition among her neighbors, she proceeded to be so active in the defense of these trees that many people in town began to think she was just naturally showing her age. Finally, her nephew took her aside. It was impossible to stop the bypass, he explained to her, because there was a man in town who had his heart set on it, and no one in town was powerful enough to stop this man. Not on a matter so special as these trees.

Who was this powerful and villainous man? Who would destroy the beauty of a fine old street? she wanted to know. Was it a Communist? No. Was it the leader for the National Association for the Advancement of Colored People? No. Was it perhaps a Freedom Rider? No. Was it a beatnik or a drug addict? No. Wasn't it one of those New York agitators? No, no, it wasn't even a Cuban. The sad fact of the matter was that the powerful and villainous man was married to the richest woman in the county, came himself from an excellently good family, owned half the real estate around, and was president of the biggest local corporation, which was a large company for making plastic luncheon plates. He was a man who had been received often in the old lady's house. He had even talked to her about joining his organization. He was the leader of the local council of the John Birch Society.

Mr. Buckley may say I am being unfair. The man who puts the new bypass through does not have to be the local leader of the John Birch Society. He can also be a liberal Republican or a Democratic mayor, a white liberal Southerner or—and here Mr. Buckley might tell my story with pleasure—he could be a Federal man. The bypass might be part of a national superhighway. The villain might even be a Federal man who is under scrutiny by the Senate Investigating Committee, the House Un-American Affairs Committee, the FBI, and the CIA. It seems not to matter—a man can be a fellow-traveler or a reactionary—either way those trees get chopped down, and the past is unreasonably destroyed.

The moral well may be that certain distinctions have begun to disappear. The average experience today is to meet few people who are authentic. Our minds belong to one cause, our hands manipulate a machine that works against our cause. We are not our own masters. We suffer from a disease. It is a disease which afflicts almost all of us by now, so prevalent, insidious, and indefinable that I choose to call it a plague.

I think somewhere, at some debatable point in history, it is possible man caught some unspeakable illness of the psyche, that he betrayed some secret of his being and so betrayed the future of his species. I could not begin to trace the beginning of this plague, but whether it began early or late, I think it is accelerating now at the most incredible speed, and I would go so far as to think that many of the men and women who belong to the Right Wing are more sensitive to this disease than virtually any other people in this country. I think it is precisely this sensitivity that gives power to the Right Wing's passions.

Now this plague appears to us as a sickening of our substance, an electrification of our nerves, a deterioration of desire, an apathy about the future, a detestation of the present, an amnesia of the past. Its forms are many, its flavor is unforgettable: It is the disease that destroys flavor. Its symptoms appear everywhere: in architecture, medicine, in the deteriorated quality of labor, the insubstantiality of money, the ravishment of nature, the impoverishment of food, the manipulation of emotion, the emptiness of faith, the displacement of sex, the deterioration of language, the reduction of philosophy, and the alienation of man from the product of his work and the results of his acts.

What a modest list! What a happy century. One could speak for hours on each of the categories of this plague. But we are here tonight to talk about other matters. So I will try to do no more than list the symptoms of this plague.

Even twenty-five years ago architecture, for example, still told one something about a building and what went on within it. Today, who can tell the difference between a modern school and a modern hospital, between a modern hospital and a modern prison, or a prison and a housing project? The airports look like luxury hotels, the luxury hotels are indistinguishable from a modern corporation's home office, and the home office looks like an air-conditioned underground city on the moon.

In medicine, not so long ago, just before the war, there still used to be diseases. Diphtheria, smallpox, German measles, scarlet fever. Today there are allergies, viruses, neuroses, incurable diseases. Surgery may have made some mechanical advances, but sickness is more mysterious than ever. No one knows quite what a virus is, nor an allergy, nor how to begin to comprehend an incurable disease. We have had an avalanche of antibiotics, and now we have a rampage of small epidemics with no name and no distinctive set of symptoms.

Nature is wounded in her fisheries, her forests. Airplanes spray insecticides. Species of insects are removed from the chain of life. Crops are poisoned just slightly. We grow large tomatoes that have no taste. Food is raised in artificial circumstances, with artificial nutrients, full of alien chemicals and foreign bodies.

Our emotions are turned like television dials by men in motivational research. Goods are not advertised to speak to our needs but to our secret itch. Our secondary schools have a curriculum as interesting as the wax paper on breakfast food. Our educational system teaches us not to think but to know the answer. Faith is half-empty. Until the churches can offer an explanation for Buchenwald, or Siberia or Hiroshima, they are only giving solace to the unimaginative. They are neglecting the modern crisis. For all of us live today as divided men. Our hope for the future must be shared with the terror that we may go exploding into the heavens at the same instant 10 million other souls are being exploded beside us. Not surprising, then, if many people no longer look to sex as an act whose final purpose is to continue the race.

Language is drowning in jargons of mud. Philosophy is in danger of becoming obsolescent. Metaphysics disappears, logical positivism arises. The mass of men begin to have respect not for those simple ideas which are mysteries but, on the contrary, for those simple ideas which are certitudes. Soon a discussion of death will be considered a betrayal of philosophy.

Finally, there is a vast alienation of man from responsibility. One hundred years ago Marx was writing about the alienation of man from his tools and the product of his work. Today that alienation has gone deeper. Today we are alienated from our acts. A writer I know interviewed Dr. Teller, "the father of the hydrogen bomb." There was going to be a new test of that bomb soon. "Are you going to see it?" asked the reporter.

"Who is interested in that?" asked Teller. "That is just a big bang."

Face to face with a danger they cannot name, there are still many people on the Right Wing who sense that there seems to be some almost palpable conspiracy to tear life away from its roots. There is a biological rage at the heart of much Right Wing polemic. They feel as if somebody, or some group—in New York no doubt—are trying to poison the very earth, air, and water of their existence. In their mind, this plague is associated with collectivism, and I am not so certain they are wrong. The essence of biology seems to be challenge and response, risk and survival, war and the lessons of war. It may be biologically true that life cannot have beauty without its companion—danger. Collectivism promises security. It spreads security the way a knife spreads margarine. Collectivism may well choke the pores of life.

But there is a contradiction here. Not all of the Right Wing, after all, is individual and strong. Far from it. The Right Wing knows better than I would know how many of them are collectivists in their own hearts, how many detest questions and want answers, loathe paradox, and live with a void inside themselves, a void that fastens upon Communists as equal, one to one, with the Devil. The Right Wing often speaks of freedom when what it desires is iron law, when what it really desires is collectivism managed by itself. If the Right Wing is reacting to the plague, all too many of the powerful people on the Right are helping to disseminate the plague. I do not know if this applies to Senator Goldwater, who may be an honorable and upright man, but I think it can do no harm to take a little time to study the application of his ideas.

As a thoroughgoing conservative, the Senator believes in increasing personal liberty by enlarging economic liberty. He is well known for his views. He would reduce the cost of public welfare and diminish the present power of the unions, he would lower the income tax, dispense with subsidies to the farmer, decentralize the Federal Government and give states' rights back to the states; he would limit the Government's spending, and he would discourage any interference by Washington in the education of the young. It is a complete, comprehensive program. One may agree with it or disagree. But no doubt it is a working program. The reasonableness of this program is attractive. It might even reduce the depredations of the plague. There is just one trouble with it. It does not stop here. Senator Goldwater takes one further step. He would carry the cold war to the Soviet Union, he would recognize, I quote, that:

> . . . If our objective is victory over communism, we must achieve superiority in all of the weapons—military, as well as political and economic—that may be useful in reaching that goal. Such a program costs money, but so long as the money is spent wisely and efficiently, I would spend it. I am not in favor of economizing on the nation's safety.

It is the sort of statement that inspires a novelist's imagination long enough to wonder what might happen to the Senator's program if he were elected President. For we may be certain he is sincere in his desire to achieve superiority in all the weapons, including such ideological weapons as arriving first on the moon. But what of the cost? There is one simple and unforgettable figure. More than sixty cents out of every dollar spent by the Government is spent on military security already. Near to two-thirds of every dollar. And our national budget in 1963 will be in the neighborhood of $90 billion. If we add what will be spent on foreign aid, the figure will come to more than seventy-five cents in every dollar.

Yet these expenditures have not given us a clear superiority to the Soviet Union. On the contrary, Senator Goldwater points out that we must still *achieve* superiority. Presumably, he would increase the amount of money spent on defense. This, I suppose, would not hinder him from reducing the income tax, nor would it force him to borrow further funds. He could regain any monies lost in this reduction by taking the money from welfare and education—that is, he could if he didn't increase our defense efforts by more than 10 percent, for if he did that, we would be spending more already than the money we now spend on welfare. And of course that part of the population which would be most affected by the cessation of welfare, that is, so to speak, the impoverished part of the population, might not be happy. And it is not considered wise to have a portion of the populace unhappy when one is expanding one's ability to go to war, unless one wishes to put them in uniform. Perhaps Goldwater might not reduce the expenditures on welfare during this period. He might conceivably increase them a little in order to show that over the short period, during the crisis, during the arms buildup while we achieve superiority over the Russians, a conservative can take just as good care of the masses as a liberal. Especially since we may assume the Russians would be trying to achieve superiority over us at the same time we are trying to achieve superiority over them, so that an arms and munitions competition would be taking place.

But let me move on to education, where the problem is more simple. To achieve superiority over the Russians there, we simply need more technicians, engineers, and scientists. We also have to build the laboratories in which to teach them. Perhaps, most reluctantly, just for the duration of the crisis, which is to say for the duration of his period in office, President Goldwater might have to increase the Federal budget for education. That would be contrary to his principles. But perhaps he could recover some of those expenditures by asking the farmer to dispense with subsidies. The farmer would not mind if additional Government funds were allocated to education and welfare, and he was not included. The farmer would not mind if the larger corporations of America, General Dynamics and General Motors, General Electric, United States Steel, and A.T.&T., were engaged in rather large new defense contracts. No, the farmer would not mind relinquishing his subsidy. Not at all. Still, to keep him as happy as everyone else, Goldwater might increase his subsidy. Just for the duration of the crisis. Just for the duration of enlightened conservatism in office. It would not matter about the higher income tax, the increased farm subsidies, the enlarged appropriation for welfare, the new magnified role of the Federal Government in education—President Goldwater could still give the states back their rights. He would not have to integrate the schools down South. He could drive the Russians out of the Congo, while the White Councils were closing the white colleges in order not to let a black man in. Yes, he could. For the length of a twenty-minute speech in Phoenix, Arizona, he could. But you know and I know and he knows what he would do—he would do what President Eisenhower did. He would send troops in to integrate the schools of the South. He would do that if he wanted to keep the Russians out of the Congo.

Poor President Goldwater. At least he could cut down on the power of the unions. He could pass a Right-to-Work act. Indeed he could. He could carry the war to the Russians, he could achieve superiority, while the unions of America were giving up their power and agreeing not to strike. Yes. Yes. Of course he could. Poor President

Goldwater. He might have to end by passing a law that would make it illegal ever to pass a Right-to-Work law. Under Goldwater, the American people would never have to be afraid of creeping socialism. They would just have state conservatism, creeping state conservatism. Yes, there are conservatives like the old lady who wished to save the trees and there are conservatives who talk of saving trees in order to get the power to cut down the trees.

So long as there is a cold war, there cannot be a conservative administration in America. There cannot for the simplest reason. Conservatism depends upon a huge reduction in the power and the budget of the central Government. Indeed, so long as there is a cold war, there are no politics of consequence in America. It matters less each year which party holds the power. Before the enormity of defense expenditures, there is no alternative to an ever-increasing welfare state. It can be an interesting welfare state or a dull welfare state. It can even be a totally repressive welfare state like President Goldwater's well might be. But the conservatives would do well to recognize that greater economic liberty is not possible so long as one is building a greater war machine. To pretend that both can be real is hypocritical beyond belief. The conservatives are then merely mouthing impractical ideas that they presume may bring them power. They are sufficiently experienced to know that only liberalism can lead America into total war without popular violence, or an active underground.

There is an alternative. Perhaps it is ill-founded. Perhaps it is impractical. I do not know enough to say. I fear there is no one in this country who knows enough to say. Yet I think the time may be approaching for a great debate on this alternative. I say that at least this alternative is no more evil and no more visionary than Barry Goldwater's promise of a conservative America with superiority in all the weapons. So I say—in modesty and in doubt, I say—the alternative may be to end the cold war. The cold war has been an instrument of megalomaniacal delusion to this country. It is the poison of the Right Wing. It is the poison they feed themselves and it is the poison they feed the nation. Communism may be evil incarnate, but it is a most complex evil that seems less intolerable today than it did under Stalin. I for one do not understand an absolute evil which is able to ameliorate its own evil. I say an evil that has captured some elements of the good is complex. To insist communism is a simple phenomenon can only brutalize the minds of the American people. Already, it has given this country over to the power of every huge corporation and organization in America. It has helped to create an America run by committees. It has stricken us with secret waste and hatred. It has held back the emergence of an America more alive and more fantastic than any America yet created.

So I say: End the cold war. Pull back our boundaries to what we can defend and to what wishes to be defended. There is one dread advantage to atomic war. It enables one powerful nation to be the equal of many nations. We do not have to hold every loose piece of real estate on earth to have security. Let communism come to those countries it will come to. Let us not use up our substance trying to hold on to nations that are poor, underdeveloped, and bound to us only by the depths of their hatred for us. We cannot equal the effort the Communists make in such places. We are not dedicated in that direction. We were not born to do that. We have had our frontier already. We cannot be excited to our core, our historic core, by the efforts of new underdeveloped nations to expand their frontiers. No, we are better engaged in another place; we are engaged in making the destiny of Western man, a destiny that seeks now to explore out beyond the moon and in back into the depths of the soul. With some small fraction of the money we spend now on defense we can truly defend ourselves and Western Europe, we can develop, we can become extraordinary, we can go a little further toward completing the heroic vision of Western man.

So let the true war begin. It is not a war between West and East, between capitalism and communism, or democracy and totalitarianism; it is rather the deep war which has gone on for six centuries in the nature of Western man, it is the war between the conservative and the rebel, between authority and instinct, between the two views of God that collide in the mind of the West, the ceremonious conservative view, which believes that if God allows one man to be born wealthy and another poor, we must not tamper unduly with this conception of place, this form of society created by God, for it is possible the poor man is more fortunate than the rich, since he may be judged less severely on his return to eternity. That is the conservative view and it is not a mean or easy view to deny.

The rebel or the revolutionary might argue, however, that the form of society is not God's creation but a result of the war between God and the Devil, that this form is no more than the line of the battlefield upon which the Devil distributes wealth against God's best intention. So man must serve as God's agent, seeking to shift the wealth of our universe in such a way that the talent, creativity, and strength of the future, dying now by dim dull deaths in every poor man alive, will come to take its first breath, will show us what a mighty renaissance is locked in the unconscious of the dumb. It is the argument which claims that no conservative can ever be certain those imbued with the value of tradition did not give more devotion to their garden, their stable, their kennel, the livery of their servant, and the oratorical style of their clergyman than God intended. Which conservative indeed can be certain that if his class once embodied some desire of the Divine Will, that it has not also now incurred God's displeasure after all these centuries of organized Christianity and enormous Christian greed? Which conservative can swear that it was not his class who gave the world a demonstration of greed so complete, an expropriation and spoilation of backward lands and simple people so avid, so vicious, so insane, a class which finally gave such suck to the Devil, that the most backward primitive in the darkest jungle would sell the grave and soul of his dearest ancestor for a machine with which to fight back?

That is the war which has meaning, that great and mortal debate between rebel and conservative where each would argue the other is an agent of the Devil. That is the war we can welcome, the war we can expect if the cold war will end. It is the war that will take life and power from the Center and give it over to Left and to Right, it is the war that will teach us our meaning, where we will discover ourselves and whether we are good and where we are not, so it is the war which will give the West what is great within it, the war which gives birth to art and furnishes strength to fight the plague. Art, free inquiry, and the liberty to speak may be the only cure against the plague.

But first, I say, first there is another debate America must have. Do we become totalitarian or do we end the cold war? Do we accept the progressive collectivization of our lives that eternal cold war must bring, or do we gamble on the chance that we have armament enough already to be secure and to be free, and do we seek therefore to discover ourselves and, Nature willing, discover the conservative or rebellious temper of these tortured times? And when we are done, will we know truly who has spoken within us, the Lord or the Fallen Prince?

From *The Presidential Papers* (1963)

# My Hope for America: A Review
# of a Book by Lyndon B. Johnson

In twenty years it may be taken for granted that 1964 was the year in which a major party nominated a major pretender to conservatism. It was a loss, and it was conceivably a horror, for 1964 was also a year in which a real conservative still had a great deal to say to the nation. He could have demonstrated with no vast difficulty that America was under the yoke of a monstrous building boom whose architecture gave promise of being the ugliest in the history of man, that our labor unions had watered the value of labor until physical work had become as parasitical as white-collar work, and that our medicine had been overburdened beyond repair by a proliferation of wonder drugs whose side effects (with the notable exception of thalidomide) were still largely unknown—hence a delayed mass poisoning might yet be the fruit of this research. Our fruits, our vegetables, our cattle had lost the opportunity to feed on native soil and organic food; the balance of nature, the fisheries, the economy of marine life, and the insect economies were being disrupted to the root by marinas and insecticides; our old neighborhoods and old homes were being—one could swear it—systematically demolished, and our educational system was glutted by a host of intellectual canapés: art appreciation, domestic economy, sexual efficiency, the modern novel, and so forth.

A real conservative could also have pointed out that the Civil Rights Act, no matter how imperfect and conceivably unconstitutional, was an act to be voted for, since finally there was a matter more important than the protection of property rights—it was spiritual rights: The Negro was entitled to his spiritual rights even if there were hard niggling costs to the rights of the Constitution. Finally, a great conservative could have noted that the expansion of Communism was its misery, that like all top-heavy structures its greatest danger was in its growth. Prosperity was Communism's poison, but attack from capitalism was its transfusion of blood. So the time was open for a great debate. Should we go back to isolationism? Did we not already possess enough nuclear Doomsdays to protect ourselves, was it not perhaps time to recognize that the industrialization of the backward nations was a thankless venture that wise men would avoid? Might it not be best to let the Communists have Asia and Africa after all? Would they not strangle on the meal? Yes, America was perhaps ready to listen to the sophistications of a conservative, if such a man was there to appear in 1964.

But what a conservative came down the pike! Marooned in a hopeless traffic with hate groups and bigots, Southern bullies and oil pirates, offering a program of sinister hints that a Federal police force would protect the young ladies of our land on their walk through our streets at night; reasoning with all the homely assurance of a filthy sock that he would protect the past by destroying the present (as in those remarks about scorching the foliage in Vietnam in order to keep the guerrillas from concealing themselves); wasting the substance of his campaign in pointless technical arguments with the Pentagon; and boring reconciliations and new feuds with the stricken Moderates of his party—the alleged conservative candidate was perhaps no more than a demagogue of the Right with a manly Christian air, a sweet voice, eyeglasses, and total innocence of a sense of contradiction, a spirit so naturally conservative that on the grounds of his home he raised the American flag with an electronic flagpole. Up at dawn, down at dusk, commanded the photoelectric cells in the mast. Well, one couldn't vote for such a man. He pressed the wrong buttons.

The mandate would go therefore to Lyndon Johnson. So most of America had seemed to decide by the eve of election. But it was nonetheless a vote heavy with gloom, and stricken with a sense of possible bad consequence, for there was much about Johnson which appealed not at all, and some of the evidence was intimate. He had written a book. That is intimate evidence. *My Hope for America,* he had called it. Now, of course, a book written by a high official must not be judged by average standards or one would be forced to say, for example, that Jack Kennedy was not a very good writer and that Bobby Kennedy, at last reading, wrote a dead stick's prose—his style almost as bad as J. Edgar Hoover's. But even at its worst, the prose style of Jack Kennedy (and his ghost writers) is to the prose style of L.B.J. (and *his* ghost writers) as de Tocqueville is to Ayn Rand. It is even not impossible that *My Hope for America* is the worst book ever written by any political leader anywhere.

The private personality of L.B.J., as reported by the authority of the best gossip, is different from his public presence. He is, one is told, not too unlike Broderick Crawford in *All the King's Men,* roaring, smarting, bellowing, stabbing fingers on advisers' chests, hugging his daughters, enjoying his food, mean and unforgiving, vindictive, generous, ebullient, vain, suddenly depressed, then roguish, then overbearing, suddenly modest again, only to bellow once more. It is somewhat like the description of an early Renaissance prince, and if one looks hard at the photograph of the President on the cover of *My Hope for America*, a leader of *condottieri* stands forth—hard, greedy, exceptionally intelligent eyes whose cynicism is spiked by a fierce pride, big fleshy inquisitive (and acquisitive) nose, thin curved mouth (a boss mouth), and a slab of round hard jaw, deep dimple on the upper lip, deep dimple on the chin. It is not a bad face altogether; it is sufficiently worldly to inspire a kind of confidence that while no age of high ideals is close at hand, yet no martyrs are to be tortured, for there is small profit in that.

It is a face and a concealed personality that could even, considering the Republican alternative, inspire a touch of happiness, if it were not for the public image—that boundless sea of overweening piety that collects here in this slim volume, this cove of presidential prose whose waters are so brackish that a spoonful is enough to sicken the mind for hours. *My Hope for America* is an abominable, damnable book, and what makes it doubly awful is that nearly all of its ideas are blessed. It is in fact difficult to disagree with almost any one of them.

Who can argue on the side of poverty, or against justice, or against the idea of a Great Society? Let Barry Goldwater argue, not I. No, the ideals in this book are double-barreled, double-ringed, a double end of the cornucopia. More for the poor, more for the rich; more for peace, more for war; dedicatedly opposed to Communism, cautiously conciliatory; out to raise the income of poor nations, out to squash the economy of Cuba; all out for the Negro, all violence to be checked in city streets; all for the Democratic party, all for a party that includes Democrats *and* Republicans. There is even, and it is the achievement of this book, a curious sense of happiness running through its paragraphs. It is that happiness which is found at the end of the vision. It is as if the dream of Rousseau and Condorcet and Bakunin and Herzen and Marx and Lenin and Trotsky and John Dewey and the Webbs and Keynes and Roosevelt, Dreiser, and Darrow—name any of a hundred, any of that long stream of political engineers who dreamed of changing a material world by material means to make all men free and equal—had come down at the end to Little Ol' Lyndon, and hot damn, he had said, discovering Progressive religion in 1964, that's the ticket, that's the liver-eating ticket! And he was off to bring it off. And happy as a clam. That's the happiness which comes off this book. It is like a dream of heaven in a terminal ward.

For beneath this odd disembodied happiness is a prose more sinister than the most pious of Lyndon Johnson's misrepresentations of his own personality; it is a prose that stirs half-heard cries of the death by suffocation of Western Civilization, it is a prose almost so bad and so deadening as the Georgian catechisms Josef Stalin used to hammer out: "Why is the Communist Party the party of the Soviet people? The Communist Party is the party of the Soviet people because . . ." It was enough at the time, reading Stalin, to keep from becoming a Communist. Now, reading Lyndon!—the horror is that one must still vote for him. But what a book is *My Hope for America.*

Examine it: 127 pages, a little more than 200 words to a page, most of the pages half pages or blank pages, so that in bulk there are 17,000 words collected in 13 short chapters; they have titles like "President of All the People," "A President's Faith and Vision," "Building the Atlantic Partnership," "This Developing World," "Creative Federalism." Each page of each chapter is divided into paragraphs. Page 8 has twelve paragraphs; the average page has four or five, with a generous space between each paragraph. This is not because the remarks have the resonant echo of Pascal's *Pensées,* rather—one idea does not lead to another. So the space must be there. It is useful for burying whichever infinitesimal part of the brain died in the gas of the preceding phrase.

Yet every altruistic idea and every well-tuned moderation that Lyndon Johnson's political experience has put together over the years is somehow worked into the organum of his credo. It is impossible to disagree with a single of its humanistic desires ("We know that we can learn from the culture, the arts, and the traditions of other countries"); it is equally impossible to feel the least pleasure at the thought these goods may yet come to be—just so bad and disheartening is the style of this book:

> *Reality rarely matches dream. But only dreams give nobility to purpose. This is the star I hope to follow—which I know most of you have seen, and which I first glimpsed many years ago in the Texas night.*

> *When the helpless call for help—the hearing must hear, the seeing must see, and the able must act.*

> *It is an America where every man has an equal chance for the well-being that is essential to the enjoyment of the freedom that we brag about.*

> *The Gulf of Tonkin may be distant Asian waters, but none can be detached about what happened there.*

High-school students will be writing essays on these paragraphs. One's stomach turns over. It is certain that if Barry Goldwater had written the same book, everyone would be agreed his style was a menace. Still, what is quoted up to here is still English, English more or less. It is in the depth of the real prose articulated by Johnson and his corps of ghost writers that the heart of the darkness resides. For Johnson is not a writer and has no wish to be. He is a communications engineer. He uses words in interlocking aggregates that fence in thoughts like cattle. At bottom, the style consists of nothing but aggregate words—that is, political phrases five words long which are one aggregate word and so should be hyphenated. Example:

*And it is one-of-the-great-tasks-of-Presidential-leadership to make-our-people-aware that they share-a-fundamental-unity-of-interest-and-purpose-and-belief.*

The essence of totalitarian prose is that it does not define, it does not deliver. It oppresses. It obstructs from above. It is profoundly contemptuous of the minds that will receive the message. So it does its best to dull this consciousness with sentences that are nothing but bricked-in power structures. Or, alternately, a totalitarian prose slobbers upon an audience a sentimentality so debauched that admiration for shamelessness is inspired. But then, sentimentality is the emotional promiscuity of those who have no sentiment:

*When I was a child, one of my first memories was hearing the powder go off on an anvil on Armistice Day. I remember the terror that flowed from the* Lusitania. *I remember seeing boys come marching home, and the welcome we gave them at our little schoolhouse. When Pearl Harbor was attacked . . .*

There is one expanding horror in American life. It is that our long odyssey toward liberty, democracy, and freedom-for-all may be achieved in such a way that utopia remains forever closed, and we live in freedom and hell, debased of style, not individual from one another, void of courage, our fear rationalized away. We will all have enough money and we will all have a vote. The money will buy appliances made of plastic, and the money will buy books just as bad as *My Hope for America* or *The Conscience of a Conservative.*

The dream of democracy—that the average man possesses riches within himself worthy of a lord—will evolve into some anomalous electronic shape of human, half genius, half lout, and the liberation of existence will not take place. Only the buildings will continue to be built—bigger housing for all, slum clearance, urban renewal, Edward Durrell Stone, until we will look as if indeed we lost a war, as if we had been bombed to the ground and built ourselves up again just so quickly and cheaply as the barracks could be slapped together.

"In the next forty years," writes Johnson, "we must rebuild the entire urban United States." But who will do it? Whose vision will prevail? Which head of horror may condemn generations not yet born to look at faceless buildings and roofless roofs, the totalitarianism stealing in from without, from the formless forms and imprisoned air of a new society which had lost the clue that a democracy could become equable only if it became great, that finally the world would continue to exist only by an act of courage and a search for style. Democracy flowers with style; without it, there is a rot of wet weeds. Which is why we love the memory so of F.D.R. and J.F.K. For they offered high style to the poor. And that is worth more than a housing project. That is the war against poverty.

Still, Lyndon Johnson must be given a vote. Because *My Hope for America* contains one good sentence, one more than Barry Goldwater could claim. This sentence reads: ". . . the wall between rich and poor is a wall of glass through which all can see." It inspires a corollary that is almost as good—the space between hypocrisy and honest manner may not forever insulate the powerful from the poor.

From *Cannibals and Christians* (1966)

# Excerpt from a Speech at Berkeley on Vietnam Day

One must speak of *alienation,* that intellectual category which would take you through many a turn of the mind in its attempt to explain the particular corrosive sensation so many of us feel in the chest and the gut so much of the time, that sense of the body growing empty within, of the psyche pierced by a wound whose dimensions keep opening, that unendurable conviction that one is hollow, displaced, without a single identity at one's center. I quote Eric Josephson:

It [alienation] has been used to refer to an extraordinary variety of psychosocial disorders, including loss of self, anxiety states, anomie, despair, depersonalization, rootlessness, apathy, social disorganization, loneliness, atomization, powerlessness, meaninglessness, isolation, pessimism and the loss of belief or values. Among the groups . . . described as alienated . . . are women, industrial workers, white-collar workers, migrant workers, artists, suicides, mentally disturbed, addicts, the aged, the young generation as a whole, juvenile delinquents in particular, voters, nonvoters, consumers, audiences of mass media, sex deviates, victims of prejudice and discrimination, the prejudiced, bureaucrats, political radicals, the physically handicapped, immigrants, exiles, vagabonds and recluses.

What a huge and comprehensive list. Is anything to be gained by adding to it the name of Lyndon Johnson? You may still ask—what is he alienated from? The Asian peasant? Of course not. You cannot be alienated unless you wish to participate. Lyndon Johnson does not wish to share a bowl of rice with an Asian peasant.

How then is Lyndon Johnson alienated, and from what? And I say to you in no disrespect and much uneasiness that it is possible he is alienated from his own clear sanity, that his mind has become a consortium of monstrous disproportions. Lyndon Johnson is not alienated from power, he is the most powerful man in the United States, but he is alienated from judgment, he is close to an imbalance that at worst could tip the world from orbit.

The legitimate fear we can feel is vast. Because there was a time when Lyndon Johnson could have gotten out of Vietnam very quietly—the image had been prepared for our departure—we heard of nothing but the corruption of the South Vietnam government and the professional cowardice of the South Vietnamese generals. We read how a Viet Cong army of 40,000 soldiers was whipping a government army of 400,000. We were told in our own newspapers how the Viet Cong armed themselves with American weapons brought to them by deserters or captured in battle with government troops; we knew it was an empty war for our side, Lyndon Johnson made no attempt to hide that from us. He may even have encouraged the press in this direction for a time. Abruptly, he dropped escalation into our daily life.

There is fear we must feel. It was not the action of a rational man but a man driven by need, a gambler who fears that once he stops, once he pulls out of the game, his heart will rupture from tension. You see, Lyndon Johnson is a member of a minority group and so he must have action. But now let me explain. A member of a minority group is—if we are to speak existentially—not a man who is a member of a category, a Negro or a Jew, but rather a man who feels his existence in a particular way. It is in the very form or context of his existence to live with two opposed notions of himself.

What characterizes a member of a minority group is that he is forced to see himself as both exceptional and insignificant, marvelous and awful, good and evil. So far as he listens to the world outside, he is in danger of going insane. The only way he may relieve the unendurable tension that surrounds any sense of his own identity is to define his nature by his own acts; discover his courage or cowardice by actions that engage his courage; discover his judgment by judging; his loyalty by being tested; his originality by creating. A Negro or a Texan or a President is by this definition a member of a minority group if he contains two opposed notions of himself at the same time. What characterizes the sensation of being a member of a minority group is that one's emotions are forever locked in chains of ambivalence—the expression of an emotion forever releasing its opposite—the ego in perpetual transit from the tower to the dungeon and back again. By this definition nearly everyone in America is a member of a minority group, alienated from the self by a double sense of identity and so at the mercy of a self that demands action and more action to define the most rudimentary borders of identity. It is a demand that will either kill a brave man or force him to grow, but when a coward is put in need of such action, he tears the wings off flies.

The great fear that lies upon America is not that Lyndon Johnson is privately close to insanity so much as that he is the expression of the near insanity of most of us, and his need for action is America's need for action—not brave action, but action, any kind of action, any move to get the motors going. A future death of the spirit lies close and heavy upon American life, a cancerous emptiness at the center which calls for a circus.

The country is in disease. It has been in disease for a long time. There has been nothing in our growth that was organic. We never solved our depression, we merely went to war back in 1941, and going to war never won it, not in our own minds, not as men, no, we won it but as sources of supply; we still do not know that we are equal to the Russians. We won a war but we did not really win it, not in the secret of our sleep.

So we have not really had a prosperity, we have had fever. We have grown rich because of one fact with two opposite interpretations: There has been a cold war. It has been a cold war that came because

Communism was indeed a real threat to our freedom, or a cold war that came because capitalism could not survive without an economy geared to war; or is it both—who can know? Who can really know?

The center of our motive is an enigma—is this country extraordinary or accursed? And when we think of Communism, we have to wonder if we are accursed. For we have not even found our Communist threat. We have had a secret police organization and an invisible government large enough by now to occupy the moon, we have hunted Communists from the top of the Time-Life Building to the bottom of the Collier mine; we have not found that many, not that many, and we have looked like Keystone Kops.

We have even had a Negro Revolution in which we did not believe. We have had it, yes we have had it, because (in the true penury of our motive) we could not afford to lose votes in Africa and India, South America and Japan, Vietnam, the Philippines, name any impoverished place: We have been running in a world election against the collective image of the Russ, and so we have had to give the black man his civil rights or Africa was so much nearer to Marx. But there has not been much like love in the civil rights. We have never been too authentic. No.

We have had a hero. He was a young good-looking man with a beautiful wife, and he won the biggest poker game we ever played, the only real one—we lived for a week ready to die in a nuclear war. Whether we liked it or not. But he won. It was our one true victory in all these years, our moment; so the young man began to inspire a subtle kind of love. His strength proved stronger than we knew. Suddenly he was dead, and we were in grief.

But then came a trial that was worse. For the assassin, or the man who had been arrested but was not the assassin—we will never know, not really—was killed before our sight. In the middle of the funeral came an explosion on the porch. Now, we were going mad. It took more to make a nation go mad than any separate man, but we had taken miles too much. Certainties had shattered.

Our country was fearful, half-mad, inauthentic—it needed a war, or it needed a purge. Bile was stirring in the pits of the national conscience and little to oppose it but a lard of guilt cold as the most mediocre of our needs. We took formal public steps toward a great society, that great society of computers and pills, of job aptitudes and bad architecture, of psychoanalysis, superhighways, astronauts, vaccinations, and a Peace Corps, that great society where nothing but frozen corn would be sold in the smallest towns of Iowa, where censorship would disappear but every image would be manipulated from birth to death.

Something in the buried animal of modern life grew bestial at the thought of this Great Society—the most advanced technological nation of the civilized world was the one now closest to blood, to shedding the blood and burning the flesh of Asian peasants it had never seen. The Pentagon had been kept on a leash for close to twenty years. Presidents so mediocre in their talents as Truman and Eisenhower had kept the military from dominating the nation.

But Johnson did not.

Out of the pusillanimities or the madnesses of his secret sleep he came to a decision to listen to the advice of his military machine, that congeries of Joint Forces, War Department, and CIA which had among other noteworthy achievements planned the Bay of Pigs. It was now planning its escalation in Vietnam. And Johnson was in accord. The body of a consummate politician took recognition as it slept that the nation was in disease and its only cure—out where the drums were beating and the fires would not cease—was to introduce us to the first anxieties of a war whose end might be limitless. Miserable nation cursed with a computer for its commander-in-chief, a computer with an ego so vain it could not bear the memory of his predecessor and the power he had had for a week when the world was on the edge of nuclear war.

Yet there still remains the largest question of them all. It is the question of fighting Communism. Look, you may say, is it not possible that with all our diseases admitted, we are still less malignant than the Communists, we are the defense of civilization and they, not us, are the barbarians who would destroy it? If that is true, then—as some of you may argue—the logic must be faced, the Chinese must be stopped, we must bomb their bomb. And I would argue in return that neither capitalism nor Communism is the defense of civilization but that they are both—in their own way—malignancies upon the spirit of honest adventure and open inquiry which developed across the centuries from primitive man to the Renaissance, and that therefore no man alive can say at this point which system will perpetrate the greater harm upon mankind.

But this I do know: An unjust war, an unnatural war, an obscene war brutalizes what is best in a nation and encourages every horror to rise from its sewer.

The Communists could capture every nation on earth but our own and we would still be safe if our intention were clean. Yes. For in the vertiginous terrors of nuclear warfare rests one rock ledge of safety—in future no great power can ever be destroyed without destroying every other power who would attack it. As a corollary, no philosophy of government can occupy nine-tenths of the globe without being altered to its roots. The health of Communism, its secret necessity, is an enemy external to itself; war is indeed the health of the totalitarian state, and peace is its disease. Communism would split and rupture and war upon itself if ever it occupied most of the world, for then it would have to solve the problems of most of the world and those problems are not soluble in the rigidity of a system. Like all top-heavy structures, the greatest danger to Communism lies in its growth. Prosperity is its poison, for without a sense of crisis, Communism cannot discipline its future generations. Attack from capitalism is Communism's transfusion of blood. So our war against Communism, most particularly our war against Communism in Asia, is the death of our future.

Let me repeat what I said in a debate with William Buckley. I say: End the cold war. Pull back our boundaries to what we can defend and to what wishes to be defended. Let Communism come to those countries it will come to. Let us not use up our substance trying to hold on to nations that are poor, underdeveloped, and bound to us only by the depths of their hatred for us. We cannot equal the effort the Communists make in such places. We are not dedicated in that direction. We were not born to do that. We have had our frontier already. We cannot be excited to our core, our historic core, by the efforts of new underdeveloped nations to expand their frontiers.

Let the Communists flounder in the countries they acquire. The more countries they hold, the less supportable will become the contradictions of their ideology, the more bitter will grow the divisions in their internal interest, and the more enormous their desire to avoid a war that could only destroy the economies they will have developed at such vast labor and such vast waste. Let it be their waste, not ours. Our mission may be not to raise the level of minimum subsistence in the world so much as it may be to show the first features and promise of that incalculable renaissance men may someday enter.

I have one set of remarks more to make. They concern practical suggestions. I have been visionary in my demands. For it is visionary in 1965 to ask of America that it return to isolationism. No, this country wishes to have an empire. The grimmest truth may be that half of America at least must be not unwilling to have a war in Vietnam. Otherwise Lyndon Johnson could not have made his move, since

Lyndon Johnson never in his life has dreamed of moving against a majority.

Let us then insist on this—it is equally visionary, but it is at least visionary in a military way and we are talking to militarists—let us say that if we are going to have a war with the Viet Cong, let it be a war of foot soldier against foot soldier. If we wish to take a strange country away from strangers, let us at least be strong enough and brave enough to defeat them on the ground. Our Marines, some would say, are the best soldiers in the world. The counter-argument is that native guerrillas can defeat any force of a major power man to man.

Let us, then, fight on fair grounds. Let us say to Lyndon Johnson, to Monstrous McNamara, and to the generals on the scene—fight like men, go in man to man against the Viet Cong. But first, call off the Air Force. They prove nothing except that America is coterminous with the Mafia. Let us win man to man or lose man to man, but let us cease pulverizing people whose faces we have never seen.

But of course we will not cease. Nor will we ever fight man to man against poor peasants. Their vision of existence might be more ferocious and more determined than our own. No, we would rather go on as the most advanced monsters of civilization pulverizing instinct with our detonations, our State Department experts in their little bow ties, and our bombs.

Only, listen, Lyndon Johnson, you have gone too far this time. You are a bully with an Air Force, and since you will not call off your Air Force, there are young people who will persecute you back. It is a little thing, but it will hound you into nightmares and endless corridors of nights without sleep, it will hound you. For, listen—this is only one of the thousand things they will do. They will print up little pictures of you, Lyndon Johnson, the size of postcards, the size of stamps, and some will glue these pictures to walls and posters and telephone booths and billboards—I do not advise it, I would tell these students not to do it to you, but they will. They will find places to put these pictures. They will want to paste your picture, Lyndon Johnson, on a postcard, and send it to you. Some will send it to your advisers. Some will send these pictures to men and women at other schools. These pictures will be sent everywhere. These pictures will be pasted up everywhere, upside down.

Silently, without a word, the photograph of you, Lyndon Johnson, will start appearing everywhere, upside down. Your head will speak out—even to the peasant in Asia—it will say that not all Americans are unaware of your monstrous vanity, and doubtful motive. It will tell them that we trust our President so little, and think so little of him, that we see his picture everywhere upside down.

You, Lyndon Johnson, will see those pictures up everywhere upside down, four inches high and forty feet high; you, Lyndon Baines Johnson, will be coming up for air everywhere upside down. Everywhere, upside down. Everywhere. Everywhere.

And those little pictures will tell the world what we think of you and your war in Vietnam. Everywhere, upside down. Everywhere, everywhere.

From *Cannibals and Christians* (1966)


# A Happy Solution to Vietnam

Statement by the Editors of *Partisan Review:*

> We do not think that the present or past policies of the United States in Vietnam are good ones, and we lament the increasing and often self-defeating military involvements which those policies require. We have not heard of any alternative policy, however, which would actually lead to a negotiated peace in Vietnam or promote the interests of the people of Southeast Asia. This is not to say that the critics of American actions in Vietnam are therefore required to propose a specific policy. But it is not unfair to ask that their criticism be based on more than the apolitical assumption that power politics, the Cold War, and Communists are merely American inventions. Most of the criticism of Administration policy at the teach-ins and in the various petitions we have been asked to sign has simply taken for granted that everything would be fine if only the Yanks would go home. It is not clear whether these critics think Asia will not go Communist if American troops are withdrawn or whether they don't care. Nor is it clear whether they really care what happens to the people of Southeast Asia so long as America gets out.

The editors ask for a counterpolicy. I offer it. It is to get out of Asia. A Communist bureaucrat is not likely to do any more harm or destroy any more spirit than a wheeler-dealer, a platoon sergeant, or a corporation executive overseas. We have our malignancies, Communism has its own. Whether capitalism or Communism will finally prove more monstrous is out of my capacity, or yours, to guess, but it is perhaps evident to both of us that Communism cannot grow without exploding its own form. If Marx's vision conceivably left room for some minds to remain fertile, Stalin fixed a process of petrifying thought until post-Marxian thought is now an ideology that cannot change remotely so fast as reality and so must be insulated from reality by war. War is the health of Communist ideology, whereas peace and the abrupt *strifeless* acquisition of backward countries are a nightmare to ideology. For backward lands that are not used up by war have wealths of primitive lore with which to mine the foundations of ideology.

Consider—a quiet end to the war in Vietnam by the agency of a quiet victory of the Viet Cong might have given the world one more backward Red nation with still one more tenacious home-grown stubborn little Communist party at odds with China and in intrigue with Russia, thereby dividing world Communism somewhat further. Now, grace of escalation, we have the likelihood that any future alignment between Russia and China will be a little more on China's terms; and for China vis-à-vis North Vietnam (which countries formerly shared the distaste of England and Ireland for one another) we have accelerated a collaboration.

Of course all those Washington Pistols, all those keepers of the chalice, will talk about India falling if we "get out." And there will be tears in Joe Alsop's eyes. Of course. And I, of course, don't know. Maybe if Vietnam falls, so too falls India. So to what? Do we really want India? Do we desire it? Do we desire deeply to die of indigestion? Might it not be simpler if the Communists die of the same disease? But, in fact, might they not hesitate? For, the more Communism grows at a vertiginous rate, the more it must suffer from vertigo. It is like America. So, Communism might even come to recognize that Communism in possession of three-quarters of the world cannot have any world. So Communism might even retreat before the terror of ideology being lost in the jungles and grasslands. What if Communism is not an unstoppable force—but is rather (since we can only approach comprehension of these matters by metaphor) a giant with a specific neurosis that it will awake one morning on the compulsion to eat its own limbs. I say: Throw Asia open to Communism. The meal will not be taken. If it is, we will even live to see the Communists destroy themselves. It is certain we cannot destroy them. We, like them, can only eat upon ourselves—this is after all a century for perverts and Reds.

But, believe me not. Take the alternative: might against might. Our troops against theirs—no, of course we are not serious. Even Barry Goldwater knows that we can't defeat the Communists militarily, not even with atom bombs. How could we occupy what was left? The cost of rebuilding it. The boredom for America's young couples— obliged to live out their early married years in rebuilt cities in Siberia and Mongolia. All the ration stamps. All the ghosts of 900 million atomized corpses. No, we don't really want to defeat Communism militarily. But we do want to stand up man to man, stick to stick. If we cannot stop Communism by the force of our armies, we could of course pitch in to help create a world society of military and bureaucratic behemoths who will nibble at one another forever in small dribbled-out land wars while totalitarian tissues fill up with the waters of political edema, yes, just as our good prophet and saint George Orwell was dying to remind us.

Look to the other side. To absolute isolation. If all the world but America were Communist, America would be militarily in no poor position. We could still fight the rest of the world if we chose to. That is the paradoxical nature of nuclear war. But it is doubtful if Communism would then have the impetus to fight anything. Can anyone conceive of Communism remaining unruptured in its cast-concrete heart on a diet of English lords, French intellectuals, Italian lovers, African drums, Zen, Yoga, pot, the New Wave, Pop art, camp—the prospect invites occupation. "Come on in, honey, this hustler's got enough diseases to keep you dripping all your days."

That, of course, is not programmatic, I would assure you. The world will never go to the Communists because they will never get through Asia, Africa, and South America. They will bog down in the cultural swamps of our imperial wastes; their minds will rupture in the new pressures on their cast-iron formulations. For Communism contends with an impossibility: One cannot bring a modern economy to a backward country in a hurry, bulldozing through a wealth of primitive lore, without manufacturing a horde of mass men. And mass man is equal to the plague. Nihilistic, he is addicted to modern communications. Shakespeare, comic books, motors, electronics, jazz, plastic, fucking, frozen food are all equal grit to his Disposall. He consumes whatever culture is before him and is the secret enemy of any government that presumes to rule him. His secret allegiance is always to the enemy. So let the Communists rather than the Americans do the manufacturing of mass men in backward lands, in order that the secret allegiance of those new mass men be exactly to us.

For there is one way in which the West is superior to the Communists, and without that superiority, mass man cannot live. Mass man is an insatiable man, a malignancy of directionless greed at the mercy of his secret addiction—which is art. No population ever on earth has loved art so much as mass man, for that is the only hope of his deliverance: that he may encounter some great art before he is dead. Only great art can penetrate into the tomb of the modern soul and bring a moment of cease to the backed-up murders of the modern heart. Here, on this violent spit, friends, is the place we are ahead in the Cold War. For our artists are better, our writers are better, our jazz musicians are better, our painters go further, our vision is more fierce, it explores more. It is relentless, we almost dare to think. It may even prevail if we do not burn too many women and children fighting for Christ. Oh, Christ, what assholes be Americans.

Yet it may be too easy to end on this fine proud and strenuous moral note. For the sweet bloody truth is not so neat. If the Lord of the Snopes went to war in Vietnam because finally he didn't have the moral courage to try to solve an impossible mix of Camp, redneck, civil rights, street violence, playboy pornography, and all the glut that bugs our works, if Lyndon Johnson finally decided in his fine brain that only a war was going to get America off the pot (we were that mercilessly screwed to the john by fifty years of smelling our national armpit every time the truth rose up to kiss us), well, what he didn't realize was that the war in Vietnam was not going to serve as cloaca for our worst emotions but instead was going to up the ante and give us more Camp, more redneck, more violence in the streets, more teen-age junkies, more polite society gone ape, more of everything else Lyndon was trying to ship overseas.

Still, with it all, confess it, Mailer, the country is now in good humor. A wild good humor—it has been the wildest summer in years, from Watts to Easthampton; it has been wild. The truth is, maybe we need a war. It may be the last of the tonics. From Lydia Pinkham to Vietnam in sixty years, or bust. We're the greatest country ever lived for speeding up the time. So, let's do it right. Let's cease all serious war, kids. Let's leave Asia to the Asians. Let us, instead, have wars that are like happenings. Let us have them every summer. Let us buy a tract of land in the Amazon, 200 million acres will do, and throw in Marines and Seabees and Air Force, scuba divers for the river bottom, motorcyclists for the mud-races, carrier pilots landing on bounce-all decks in typhoons, invite them all, the Chinks and the Aussies, the Frogs and the Gooks and the Wogs, the Wops and the Russkies, the Yugos, the Israelis, the Hindoos, the Pakistanis. We'll have war games with real bullets and real flame throwers, real hot-wire correspondents on the spot, TV with phone-in audience participation, amateur war movie film contests for the soldiers, discotheques, Playboy Clubs, pictures of the corpses for pay TV, you know what I mean—let's get the hair on the toast for breakfast. So a write-in campaign (all of us) to King Corporation Exec Mr. Pres; let us tell him to get the boys back home by Christmas, back from Vietnam and up the Amazon for summer. Yours—readers—till the next happening.

Unless Vietnam is the happening. Could that be? Could that really be? Little old Vietnam just a happening? 'Cause if it is, Daddy Warbucks, couldn't we have the happening just with the Marines and skip all that indiscriminate roast tit and naked lunch, all those bombed-out civilian ovaries, Mr. J., Mr. L.B.J., Boss Man of Show Biz—I salute you in your White House Oval; I mean America will shoot all over the shithouse wall if this jazz goes on, Jim.

From *Cannibals and Christians* (1966)

# WHY ARE WE
# IN VIETNAM?

Now Rusty was supposed to go originally on an Alaska safari with his opposite number Al Percy Cunningham, the managing director of Tendonex, which is 4C and P's answer to Fiberglas. Rusty and Al Percy C. had reserved an Alaska guide eighteen months in advance, you know the type that is a guide for Charley Wilson or Roger Blough or J. Edgar—I mean, that's who you got to be if you want to get this guide right away, like he wouldn't even take Senators, and you was a Congressman and you wanted Big Luke Fellinka and his assistant Ollie the Indian Water Beaver, forget it, you could lie down on your back and say Big Luke if you consent to be my guide you or Ollie can take one big crap in my mouth just for openers, and Big Luke would yawn. D.J. and Tex read right away the #1 reason all the minions of the Great Plastic Asshole were slobbering over the bear grease on Big Luke's boots. It wasn't just because among Alaska guides he was primus inter pares (you have just had the first and last of D.J.'s Latin), it wasn't cause he got eight clients out of the Brooks Mountains once in a record September blizzard, or fought a grizzly or two bare hand to a kind of draw and had the scars to show it (looked like vines and thorns had grown over an old seam of welding on his back), it wasn't even his rifle work which in offhand shooting could put in 25 one-inch five-shot clusters at one hundred yards, and at two hundred yards in a half-ass clearing of woods could now and then drop a bullet into the eye of an Alaska wolf as directly as you could drop your finger in your own eye—no, what made Big Luke The Man was that he was like the President of General Motors or General Electric, pick one, I don't give a fuck, he had like the same *bottom,* man, I mean D.J.'s here to tell you that if you even a high-grade asshole and had naught but a smidgeon of flunky in you it would still start—you may purchase this in full confidence—it would still start in Big Luke's presence to blow sulfur water, steam, and specks of hopeless diarrhetic matter in your runny little gut, cause he was a *man!* You could hang him, and he'd weigh just as much as Charley Wilson or Robert Bonehead McNamara, I mean you'd get the same intensity of death ray off his dying as you'd get from some fucking Arab sheik who had ten thousand howlers on horses to whoop and scream for the holy hot hour of his departure to Allah. So you can see what a hoedown of a hunting trip it would have been if Al Percy C. alias Kid Tendonex and Rusty had each been burning up that Alaska Brooks Mountain Range brush trying to light a light of love in Big Luke's eye, but Al Percy Cunningham was called off at the last by the Astronaut Program hotline into 4C and P because the real hoedown just that week of departure was between Fiberglas and Tendonex to see who was going to get the contract to put a plastic Univar valve and plug into the bottom of the collapsible built-in space suit chemical toilet in the Gemini (Roman Numeral Unstated) which contract is no superhuge kettle of lobster shit in volume dollars, but just a reasonable 58 million, although Tex and D.J. agree that little Univar plug is First Priority, cause let it malfunction and those astronauts will be swimming in orbits of dehydrated processed food shit (their own— a gritty performance, eh Maurice?). However, it's edge. Does 4C and P, Tendonex Division, or FCA (Fiberglas Corp. of America) get to be the first to fling their product into space; besides there's rumors, Rusty tells us, that smooth plastic in outer space tends to exhibit Independent, Autonomous, Non-pattern-directed Ductile-type Magnification and Expansion Assertions in Non-Operational Gravitational Ultra-Multi-Mach Ellipsoid Program-Oriented Satellite Capsule Negotiations, which is to say that smooth plastic is growing plastic hairs on its palm while in such jerkoff orbit. A big sweat is on. Whose research program has anticipated any of this? "Cunny's sweating this week," Rusty tells the boys. "I told him to load up with Pure Pores once his balls started to get wet, and he just gave me a sick little hunky hunk heh-heh. Probably wanted to haul off and split your dad with an axe."

But Rusty, au fond, is deeply in disappointment, not cause A. P. Cunningham ain't with him, but because the hunting trip is now downgraded. D.J.'s here to tell you that in secret Rusty feels like a movie star who's going out to pump for a weekend with the best new Pumper-head Penis in Cinemaville, and then hears she's missing the opportunity to have a commissary lunch with Prince Philip or Baldy Khrushchev, before Baldy was an ex. Well, you know a movie star, she'd rather have Big K stomp his big shoe jes once in the crack of her ass while he's still Mr. Big than have her cunt stick-tickled into heaven for three days with no one up there in the redwoods to see it except those guests invited to the exhibition like her mother, her father, and her dramatic coach. "Hit high C next time you come, Chérie, we got to get through those vocal locks," says the dramatic coach.

Now D.J. suffers from one great American virtue, or maybe it's a disease or ocular dysfunction—D.J. sees right through shit. There's not a colon in captivity which manufactures a home product that is transparency proof to Dr. Jekyll's X-ray insight. He sees right into the claypots below the duodenum of his father, and any son does that is fit candidate for a maniac, right, T.S.? the point here, Eliot, is that D.J. will never know if Rusty dropped points in the early stages of his contest with Luke because he was dying inside for not being down at the Canaveral table where big power space decisions were being made by his opposite number, Wise-Ass Cunningham, or whether Rusty would have lost in the early stages to Big Luke on the best week he ever had, which is an ambiguity right at the center of D.J.'s message center. But proceed to study the scene.

Give Rusty his straight shot. If Big Al Percy Wise-Ass Cunningham had been there, the set of events would have had to be different. Take away A. P. Cun and what you got—ego status embroilments between numbers, guides, and executives. All right—look into it. You may never get out.

First, Rusty spends no time trying to be the equal of Big Luke head on! He takes Luke's suggestions, is friendly but aloof. When Luke addresses him as Sir, Sir Rutherford Jet-Throne does not say call me Rusty. When Big Luke speaks to Rusty's two accompanying flunkies, Luke naturally picks them up by the handle of their first name, and Rusty, listening, chuckles like poor Clark Gable used to when he was near the end, that is indulgently and wisely, could be worse, man, cause the two flunkies—call them Medium Asshole Pete and Medium Asshole Bill—M.A. Pete (Assistant to Procurement Manager, Pure Pores Filters Company Office of 4C and P) and M.A. Bill (Personnel Director for Production Manager, Pure Pores et cetera Company Office of 4C and P) laugh each of them separately and respectively like Henry Fonda and Jimmy Stewart. Maybe it should be said that they are Medium Assholes with a passing grade of C. Rusty could have done better, but kid you not, it ain't so easy. Talent ain't hanging on meathooks in corporation land, especially when you change plans and invitations at the last minute. Some Americans giving up a lot for the astronauts.

Now, with such for background on personnel, ask yourself Sherlock Onanist Holmes what were Rusty's expectations from this trip, I mean Rusty is corporation, right, that means he's a voice, man, he's a voice, got nothing unexpected ever to say, but he got to say it with quality. These corporation pricks are not there for nothing. They may be dumb and benighted, yeah, and D.J. has wasted his adolescence in their purlieus and company mansions and has eaten off their expense accounts all his days, D.J. knows them asshole to appetite, and can tell you, Horace, they are not all that dumb. Being medium-grade and high-grade asshole, they have high competence in tunnels and channels. They can all swim uphill through shit face first although in fact corporate faces are never seen to move, for they know enough not to try to read each other's corporate fish features when they can read each other's corporate ass voices. Man, they pick up what you're trying to slip by them, they buy nothing that's not tested, not voice-tested. So look at Rusty's problem. He goes on a Class A hunting trip—a Charley Wilson, John Glenn, Arnold Palmer, Gary Cooper kind of trip, next thing in top category you might say to a Jackie Kennedy Bobby Kennedy Ethel and the kids trip—Rusty's stepping up out of category, reaching just a bit, but if he makes out, if he comes back and is able to say, "Well, it was not a record honey-grizzly by any means, it didn't weigh out at more than twelve hundred, but Big Luke thought I got off a fair shot, and was, truth to tell, impressed with the coincidence that George Humphrey dropped one in the same glen just five years ago."

Now, pick up on the potential pitfalls. If Rusty is bird-turding he's got a lot of cabbage verbiage for which he can be faulted on. Take: fair shot. That could mean great shot; could mean piss-ass shot. George Humphrey's name equal to Pope Pius in certain executive Dallas-ass chambers; therefore it's got to be dropped like a feather on velvet. Honey-grizzly has to be enunciated as if you was up tight enough with that variety of bear to tweak his nuts. So on. Mark this, fellow Americans, and file it 2R—Ready Reference—each time Rusty runs into mood-gearings of attention back home in the office, he is going to have to turn to M.A. Pete or M.A. Bill and say, "Isn't that so, Pete? isn't that so, Bill?" and they're going to have to say, "It sure is, Rusty," and say it without a trace of strain, they're yes-men, it is expected of them to be dauntless in their gut yes as they go through the yes ass gears, but perfection breeds perfection, the critical ear gets as sharp as a mad-dragster maniac-type genius listening to two 427 cubic inchers put in tandem—their yes has to have perfection precisioned. Well, even with professional bullshit, and that's the secret of the corporation—it is filled with men who are professional bullshit packers—there is a limit. A yes-man will strain his gut to produce—they are the unsung heroes of America (reason they're unsung is they can't get their tongue out of the boss' ass long enough to sing) but strain a gut as they may they cannot strain it past its own true natural elasticity. Something bona fide has got to happen, they can't just go up to Alaska woods, get drunk for a week, buy a bear skin in Fairbanks or Mc-Grath, take pictures, and slip a suppository up the folks back home, those Texas ears too sharp. There'd be a soupçon of caviar shit in the voice and that would put a rick-tick-tick in the narrator's disc. So Rusty's got to produce something big enough for his boys, M.A. 1 and M.A. 2, to say you're right, Rusty, with an easy harmonious concordium of voice, a choir of Texas ass-purring where the yeah boss you go right ahead and kick my Nigger ass gets a Texas hum. For then corporate power is cooking in Rusty's veins.

So Rusty's problem is simple. He can't begin to consider how to go back without a bear. He got a corporation mind. He don't believe in nature; he puts his trust and distrust in man. Five % trust, 295% distrust. He figures if Big Luke wants him to tag a bear, that's the ball game—if Big Luke don't want him to, then Rusty is left close to being a dead ass this season. He'll be caught stalking around in the brush with a guide who's holding such a rep he can afford to save himself for his major clients and make the minor executives like Rusty do a little work for him. Rusty has taken a full estimate of Big Luke and has this to decide: Man to man, if you put each in the other's job from birth, Rusty could have done everything Luke did except those 25 five-shot one-inch offhand clusters, cause that ain't practice, that's magic, and Rusty is modest about magic, but Big Luke in Rusty's shoes would not have gone as far because he might be, bend your head (in secret), too fucking lazy. First thing, smack off, Luke tells Rusty that it's not the best season this year for bear, and when Rusty, all modesty and politeness, allows as how he'd like to make a push against these poor possibilities, Big Luke, who's coming on one hundred out of one hundred relaxed, kind of smiles, crinkly introductory humor humoring, and says, "They're scarce now. When bear get lonesome they can smell

far." Well, Big Luke got a presence, not much of a face, just a big sunburned mug of a face like a pie with a lot of scars in it, he looks just like
Big Ollie Water Beaver except paler, for Big Ollie is as dark as an old
leather jacket, but Big Luke sends out a wave every time he has a
thought, you can feel it, and around him you can get messages back,
you can feel that one bear out in those woods sending out its message—don't come near, motherfuck—that message transmitted from
the bear to Big Luke and relayed to us, you can tune in on the madness in the air, you now know where a pine tree is rotting and festering somewhere out there, and red ants are having a war in its muck,
and the bear is listening to those little ant screams and smelling that
rotten old pine, and whoong goes his nose into the rot, and he bites
and swallows red ants, slap, bap, pepper on his tongue, he picking up
the bite of death in each ant and the taste of fruit in the pulp, digging
that old rotten tree whose roots tell him where we are, capisce, Luigi?
There's a fucking nervous system running through the earth and air
of this whole State of Alaska, and the bear is tuned in, and Big Luke,
and Ollie and the assistant guide packers, and the ants, and Tex and
D.J., and the air, man, the air is the medium and the medium is the
message, that Alaska air is real message—it says don't bullshit, buster.
And Rusty of course reads this not, cause Big Luke is pouring salt in
his ass. Big Luke is *mean*. "Lot of caribou," Big Luke says. "Think
about starting the week with caribou." Well, Rusty would as soon start
the week with rabbits as caribou deer. D.J. reads this easy—let Rusty
presume to come back from the Brooks Mountain Range of Alaska to
Big D, Texas, air distance 3,247 miles (check not on this detail, for D.J.
has just estimated it—who the mother-butter is going to make such a
small-ass measurement of distance but a hotel lobby type tourist?) let
Rusty travel all that round trip 6,000-plus miles, spending 6,000-plus
dollars on D.J. and himself—not all tax-deductible either, you fuck,
and present himself at 4C and P with a deer's head and no bear. Rusty
and his status (who are as up tight with each other as two plump
yoni—that's Hindu for cunt, son!—doing sixty-nine in the long
Hindu night) can now take a double pine box funeral—they'll never
get off his ass at Combined Consolidated, no, no, the office staff will
wet their little pants waiting for Christmas so they can send him an
anonymous set of antlers off some poor ass spavined Texas buck twice
the antlers in width of measurement and holding four more points
than the one he air-freighted back from Alaska—you know they'll do
that at the office if they got to dig up an old ranch hand's bones and
glue them together for antlers, Rusty knows a piss cutter when it

scratches his scrotum—thank you very much, Mr. Luke Fellinka, but no thanks on that deer.

"Say, Luke," says Rusty, "I sure hope you put the hair on a bear for us cause I'm feeling like the poorest safari victim you've had all year," and Big Luke says, "We, sir, have no safari victims, just happy clients and disappointed clients, and sometimes you can't tell by looking at their face, not by the time they get home."

Well, by the light of the twilight D.J. does a little estimating. There's guides and guides in Alaska, some for scratch-ass hunters, and some for poobahs where the idea is to bring the trophy to the man so that John Foster Dulles types can make the record book without ever getting their cheese wet crossing a brook. By the end of the first night in Fairbanks, while they lolling around getting acquainted in a super deluxe motel bar of a dark chocolate-red velvet interior looks like it was flown up from Seattle (which it was, en route from Hawaii where they imitating the English Pump Room in Threadnelly Gate, London W. 1), D.J. and Tex analyze it out—Big Luke used to be a big hunter, but those grizzly scratches have weakened his Arnold Toynbee coefficient—he interested less in challenge than response—if he caught his share of the three grand a head without having to lead various grades of assholes and tough but untrained adolescents into the brush to look for Mr. Wounded Honey Grizzly holding the head of a magnum in his bear gut and a last dream of murder in his bear eye, well, Big Luke, despite the big man death-guts charisma, may have had his day. Who's to say there is no actors in Alaska?

Listen to the dialogue: "Luke, I'm a stubborn Texas son of a bitch," says Rusty, lifting his bourbon in the Fairbanks, Alaska, motel bar (empty near but for three old couples from Kansas on an airline tour of Anchorage, Fairbanks, Barrow, Nome, and Juneau, with dips into Kotzebue, Unalakleet, and Homer, and a brother and sister at University of Alaska entertaining their ma and pa up to visit from Portland)—this lack of activity may be given total attributability to the vacation-directed personal vector imperatives of the American mind, which shuts up action after Labor Day. This is after Labor Day, early September in Alaska, hence form is more narrative, memory being always more narrative than the tohu-bohu of the present, which is Old Testament Hebrew, cock-sucker, for chaos and void, "Yeah, I'm stubborn," sighs Rusty tenderly, sipping his bourbon like his mother had brought him up on mother's milk and moonshine, "I don't want to carry on about where I've hunted, because I could tell you about going for wild boar in Bavaria, and for elephant in Africa—although I never got the elephant, my gun-buddy Ram Fedderstone got it, I just got a kudu, a snake, an African antelope, and a zebra. I always say I paid five thousand—you count them—bucks for a goddamn convict suit."

"How about that, Pete?" said M.A. Bill, getting in the big chuckle first.

"Shee-it, Rusty," said M.A. Pete, "that's a beautiful set of head and shoulder zebra stripes in the Bomb Shop" (which is what Rusty calls the Jethroe den, the Bomb Shop).

Rusty turns his head, like a maidenhead being told she's pretty, sort of a "It's not for me to say," and then he turns his keen shit hue executive eyes on Big Luke and says, "I even got in on a tiger hunt with the Maharajah of Pandrasore, but that I don't count because I was present in 'semiofficial function,'" a big wink, man, whatever the fuck semiofficial function is CIA supposed to convey, professor, "and we didn't even carry rifles. There was an array of Hindu peons up ahead each with a kris on a bamboo stick, and they did the sticking. The Maharajah's function, it turns out, is to be some variety of the Great White Hunter. The majesty of his attendance on the hunt brings tigers up where there were none before. If there's a tiger this side of Tibet the Maharajah's magnetism will draw him. Sure as bird shit on a parasol, damn if we didn't attract three tigers."

"Maybe I get to learn a couple of new things about hunting from you," says Big Luke F.

"Say, Mr. Fellinka, I may look like a variety of Texas bull, but not that big, I swear. No, no, no. I'm not here to instruct, I'm here to imbibe. At the foot of a master. I just want to make a point, teacher. I want to cut the fiercest mustard you ever tasted with a piece of bear steak, I want to behold Bruin right in his pig red eye so I'll never have to be so scared again, not until I got to face The Big Man. Listen, Luke, here's what I suspect is true—it is that you are the Maharajah of this woods and this range of earth, and so I'm expecting you to make the impossible become directly possible and we're going to carry our stretch of hunting to what I would call a successful termination."

"Was a berry blight in August," says Big Luke, "Now the bear are out digging roots in the brush. That's a little thick there. A little too thick to bring a party in. Get a thorn in your eye, gun gets tangled, you can be looking at the ground about the time Friend Bear is putting an arm over your neck."

"Say, now," says Rusty, "this is a guaranteed bear trophy hunt, now isn't it?"

"Well, sir," says Big Luke's Tour Guide Coordinator, Mr. Kenneth Easterly, who has met the group at the airport, and brought them along Airport Way to the motel, name now forgotten, Alaska Cavalier maybe, or Fairbanks Frontier Arms, some such (Fairbanks being near as flat-ass a city as Dallas has naturally lots of humper-dick in the names), "well, sir," says Kenneth E., who's the olive oil in this operation, "you have a guaranteed bear trophy in the specifications of the safari contract—that's for shit-and-sure," says Easterly, cause people he's addressing are Texans; if they was New York Jew-ass Banker sportsmen, he'd say "certified." Nods his head, as if he's shaking his hand, "Yes-sir, there's a rebate of five hundred per head if we neglect to get you in proper range for a shot at a visible grizzly, although I want to tell you, we've never had to rebate it."

"Everybody who's taken your safari has gotten Mr. Grizzer," asks Rusty, "or had a fair shot?"

"No, sir. Not everybody. Some few do not have that peculiar good fortune. But they don't want the rebate. After they see the way Big Luke and Big Ollie take them around through the Brooks Range— that's *wilderness*, Mr. Jethroe—way they cook for 'em, tote for 'em, skin and pack, they're feeling sufficiently good, they've had the kind of hunting experience the desire for which brought them out here in the first place."

Rusty just shakes his head. "I don't believe I follow you, *boy*."

"Mr. Jethroe," says Kenny E., "we have the best guide in Alaska, and the finest clientele. We're here to take you around and give you *proper* hunting. We're not in competition with the counters. There are counters out in that wilderness, hunters of medium income (and medium ability to stick the muzzles of their rifles into a muddy piece of ground) who have nonetheless saved their pennies to come here— it's the experience of a lifetime for them, and as you know, sir, the experience of a lifetime excites *greed* in the common man and a terror of being cheated. So they are out to get everything they can. They count every last pelt, they'll twist the tape measuring a Dall's horn to get an extra quarter of an inch on the length of it, they'll use handload cartridges make you gasp—it's a wonder simple steel can stand it—they hunt from four in the morning to midnight before they get back to camp, up at four again, they bring out every last piece of meat they can tote, or they don't even cut themselves a steak, just take the head and leave the flesh, imagine! and they maim, Mr. Jethroe, they maim game all over the damn place and then let them suffer. We ain't like that. We have the finest people in America come to us, we wouldn't even know how to advertise—we just hope too many people don't hear about us or the simple fine standard of clientele we possess might be adulterated. Because we offer hunting which is reasonable, decent in its risk, fair to the game, and not utterly deprived of comfort. We do not consider it decadent to have a book or two in the bunkhouse, and if Big Luke knows how to make a mixed drink, well, whiskey sours sweeten the heart after a long day of hunting, I like to claim."

"That's A-OK," says Rusty, "but the bear is the integral part of this expedition."

"Yessir, it is," says Easterly, "provided the bear is in a reasonable state."

"The bear are bad now," says Big Luke.

"What do you mean bad?"

"Changing their habits," Big Luke says. It comes out. All the good news. It seems there's been too much hunting in the Brooks Range. That's the confession of Kenny Easterly. The Moe Henry and Obungekat Safari Group (which is the exclusive George Humphrey special they are on right now) is no longer so alone in bringing its fine people up into that Arctic Circle, all the counter-type safari groups like Hunting, Ltd., and the Sam Sting Safari are pouring in too. The wild game is changing its psychology.

Big Ollie speaks up—his first speech. He talks like a cannibal in a jungle bunny movie. "Brooks Range no wilderness now. Airplane go over the head, animal no wild no more, now crazy."

"Say, friends," says Rusty, "I didn't come to Alaska to debate the merits and vices of technological infiltration."

Big Luke presents the case: "In August, three grizzly been wounded by other safaris in our hunting range. They get told not to move in but they move in. They, like you, sir, thought I'm the one to call the tiger so they hunt near me. They wounded and they neglected to follow up, and they left us three very mean grizzly, right in our own hills and lands up there. Now consider. A mean grizzly has only to smell a man and he is half-crazy. He does not come forward half-nice, half-mean, to take his look, nor does he go the other way—he thinks of how to kill. He circles, he stays downwind from the hunter. He remembers the bullet, that bullet maybe tore his intestine, that is a terrible pain. A bear feeling such pain, sir, is in my opinion, struck as if by lightning and so picking up in certain ways the intelligence of man."

"I see," says Rusty, "you're going to keep us well up above timber so no bear can sneak near on us. We'll have to spend our week climbing rocks just to get a shot at five hundred yards down on some mountain goat across a canyon."

"I'll give the best hunting for conditions," says Luke.

"Let's specify," says Rusty.

A sad-ass show. It flickers off, on, off, for ninety minutes, a muted hot shit hurricane. Finally, Big Luke hints that Rusty can have his rebate now, his deposit, his contract and his week, and that is the end of the first contest, for if there is one thing worse than coming back with no bear, it is coming back a rejectee and rebatee from the Moe Henry and Obungekat Safari Group. If they could satisfy Old General George C. Marshall in his hunting days, who is Sir Jet-Throne to complain? Now he saves face. He compromises, he agrees Luke will give the word on when they go for grizzer. Say. They all go to bed in rooms with a foam-rubber mattress, pink-tile bathrooms, and Venetian blinds, and in the morning, load gear and all ten men into three Piper Apaches with amphibian floats and take off for the Brooks Range, where each plane makes a tasty light water-slap of a landing in a lake, Dolly Ding Bat Lake, where there's an M.H.O.S.G. (for Moe Henry, et cetera) bunkhouse on the shore, which is a pine forest so full of boon in the smell it could make you a religious nut, except D.J. does not dig pine resin out of sight—he likes something a hint more funky if he is entering concupiscent relations with the penumbra of the Lord, ho, ho, but this bunkhouse which is a pâté foie of an Alaska bunkhouse is not theirs for long—they unload the planes, then load up on packhorse, and work up a trail all afternoon, a dog-ass trail which gets dull and then monotonous dull cause it's pine forest and dwarf birch and not spectacular for being up above the Arctic Circle, Rusty is commenting it's just as dull as all of Canada, and then colors start to dim, which gives a hint of some kind of North, cause the rocks have a thin gray, and the bark is gray on the trees and there's a pinched look beginning to appear in the turf, a mossy mean turf like dry bog crusts, the trees get more individual, they have a continuing life story now with the wind. Then timberline. Final timberline, sharp and clean, a little park of grass. They're up high on gray domes looking across to other gray domes, and rising further until even the fold of the canyon is dry of moss, and the packhorses are hawking their breath, and Big Luke finally picks on a shielded-in kind of square saddle between some hunched-up bare knolls, Big Luke calls it a basin, near to a black-ass basin by the time they get there, and put up the tents, Ollie makes the fire, et cetera, roast beef hash with dehydrated pears, good by God! on a white gasoline cookstove. D.J. and Tex exhausted by the dialectic of the night before fall out into dead-ass air mattress sleep with the smell of the North on a September night, a tricky clean smell, like a fine nerve washed in alcohol and lightly powdered to get the rut of flesh off.

Next morning, on a light windless dawn, Tex and D.J. get out of bed, start to brush their teeth in a rill of a stream coming up out of a mountain spring, that water presenting itself to the teeth like sunlight on snow, and Tex saw, just then, a wolf standing and pointing a half mile above the timber, just standing there and studying the dawn in a wolf silence like he had come to some conclusion about the problems of life and occupation, near-relatives, in-laws, phratries, associates, herbs, roots, and grubs. Tex took him down with a shot into the gut and at first he could have been there dead, the animal fell and for an instant the hills clapped together. Down at timberline trees shifted, air moved in the wave which follows a breaking of glass, and then the wolf was up and running, but with a sick-ass lunge like a broken fly, and then slowed, stood still, bore off at a bleeding-ass walk back to the woods, and Tex run after him and got him at two hundred yards; one miss, one hit into the back of the shoulder and the lungs. The look on Big Luke's face was amiable like any boy who could hit a wolf at four hundred yards was not totally undeserving of guided service. Well, he got down and gave us each a cup of blood to drink and that was a taste of fish, odd enough, and salt, near to oyster sauce and then the taste of wild meat like an eye looking at you in the center of a midnight fire, and D.J. was on with the blood, he was half-sick having watched what Tex had done, like his own girl had been fucked in front of him and better, since he had had private plans to show Tex what real shooting might be, and here was Tex, King Front Sight Indian Hunter, Killer of Wolves. D.J. next thing was on his hands and knees, looking into that upper Yukon wolf mouth, those big teeth curved like tusk, and put his nose up close to that mouth, and thought he was looking up the belly of a whale, D.J. was breathing wolf breath, the just dead air from the dead interior, but raucous breath, all the fatigue of the wolf running broken ass to the woods and the life running the other way from him, a crazy breath, wild-ass odor, something rotten from the bottom of the barrel like the stink of that which is unloved, whelp shit smell, wild as wild garlic, bad, but going all the way right back into the guts of things, you could smell the anger in that wolf's heart (fucked again! I'll kill them!) burnt electric wire kind of anger like he'd lived to rip one piece of flesh from another piece, and was going to miss it now, going to miss going deep into that feeling of *release* when the flesh pulls loose from the flesh, and there D.J. was sweating, cause he was ready to get down and wrestle with the wolf, and get his teeth to its throat, his teeth had a glinty little ache where they could think to feel the cord of the jugular, it was all that blood he'd drunk, it was a black shit fuel, D.J. was up tight with the essential animal insanity of things.

That, friends, was the beginning of the hunt. Not so bad. Big Ollie came up, asked Tex if he wanted the wolf for a trophy. Tex gave a blow of breath to his front sight. That's all the tension he was going to show. "I don't want no wolf for a trophy," he said. Ollie then studied the animal, nodded, suddenly dipped his finger in the blood, sucked it with a quick-popping sound of his cheek like a cook testing a cake batter, then took out a knife and cut the wolf's head off, one twisting cut of the knife for the vertebra at the neck, one long sawing swinging cut for the rest. Then he gave the head to the boys for a look. There were two eyes open on El Lobo, both yellow coals of light, but one eye was Signor Lupo, the crazy magician in the wolf, and his eye had the pain of the madman who knows there's a better world but he is excluded, and then the other eye, Willie Wolf, like a fox's eye, full of sunlight and peace, a harvest sun on late afternoon field, shit! it was just an animal eye like the glass they use for an eye in a trophy, no expression, hollow peace maybe, and Big Ollie dug a shallow pan of a hole with his knife in the crust bog tundra, whatever that dry shit moss was, and set the wolf's head in it, muzzle pointing to the north, and covered it over. Then he took a broken twig and laid it in a line with the end of the muzzle, but pointing further north, then got down on his hands and knees and touched his nose to the stick and said nothing for a moment.

"Always remember, boys," said Rusty, who had come up at the end to be part of our blood drinkers' breakfast group and coffee-clutch, "you don't get your proper paganism until you pay these dee-luxe prices."

"What he up to, Mr. J.?" said Tex.

"Well, you're looking at him, Indian to Indian, Tex, and don't forget ah got a drop of the fucking redskin elixir too, he's telling that wolf he respects him and not to spread the word, not to get grizzler turned on. I bet Ollie's telling him not to forget that when he was alive, he and Big Grizzler were not rushing to be asshole buddies, so please don't start a union now."

Well, now here, let's give a rundown on the guns for those good Americans who care. And those who don't, shit, they still get the chance to encounter a lot of meaningless names and numbers that they can then duly repeat at cocktail parties for new name grabbers.

Rusty, well now he's got, well you be sure Rusty is holding, in fact D.J. is now canny to save him for later. So here's Luke and Ollie. Luke got a Model 70 Winchester .375 Magnum restocked (with maple Japanese Shigui finish) and remodeled by Griffin & Howe with a Unertl 2½× scope, and that little rifle and cartridge could knock down anything but an elephant, and if the elephant had just gotten fucked, it would knock him down too. Luke don't need that gun, he could hit and take and flatten anything he wanted in Alaska with his second gun, old Swedish Husqvarna .30-06, restocked and remodeled, also Unertl 2½× scope (Luke was agent for Unertl for a while), which handles a 180-grain bullet on a very flat trajectory, a real 300–400 yard bap of an ice picker, extra high up over 3 thou in velocity delivered at the muzzle. Whereas Ollie has the same gun D.J. has, a factory-bought Remington 721, and both he and D.J. have worked the stock themselves. Ollie has all kinds of ivory totems and taboos inset in his grip and comb, including a profile of wolf head (hot shit and coincidence, Claudia!) and he got a nice Lyman Alaska 2½× scope. D.J. on his side has just done a little stupid-ass inconclusive whittling into his Rem 721 stock—in truth it's a mess—forget it! Scope? He got a nice Stith Bear Cub 2½× scope with Stith mounts.

Tex has a factory-bought Winchester .270 Model 70 with a Weaver K-3 Tilden mount, neat as that. If he was a fink, D.J. would whisper that the first 400-yard shot which hit the wolf, considering it was done with a good .270 like the Winchester 70, was nothing truly spectacular, for Tex had set his Weaver K-3 for 250 yards the day before when they crossed timberline. So, at 400 yards, even with a big 180-grain bullet (and the corresponding big-ass load of powder) he knew he wouldn't drop twenty inches below the cross hair, never, at 400 yards, so it wasn't that hard to put the dot a bit above wolf's back and hit in eight inches or ten inches below his spine. Anyway the whole fucking kill was unaesthetic, cause a 180-grain bullet that lets a wolf walk away after hitting him must hit no closer than a red-hot poker along his ass. Fact, that's what on examination the first shot proved itself to be, for the weight and hard nose of the bullet (bought to penetrate a grizzly hide) went right through the wolf's two legs, breaking only one. Well this fine critique ain't just piss grapes from D.J., because proof is that he is now repeating Tex Hyde's very own critique of his own shot. "If I hadn't been fever ass," says Tex, "I'd have taken the time and got the 100-grain soft nose magazine into Winnie, and I could have torn a hunk of old Wolf right out of his heart so he didn't have to suffer and we didn't have to chase. I can hit *anything* with the hundred grain. That was a fink and fuckup kill, D.J."

Which brings up Rusty, who travels like a big-ass hunter. That Apache looked like it was vomiting big equipment out of its guts, yeah, he got for instance a .404 Jeffrey on a Mauser Magnum action with a Circassian walnut stock, one love of a custom job by Biesen with Zeiss Zielklein 2½× on Griffin & Howe side mount for Gun #1. Gun #2 is Model 70 Winchester rechambered to .300 Weatherly Magnum, Stith Bear Cub scope, birds'-eye maple stock, et cetera, et cetera. Gun #3 is Winslow Regimental Grade 7 mm. Remington Magnum with FN Supreme 400 action and Premium Grade Douglas barrel, ivory and ebony inlays in the stock, basket weave carving on both sides of the forearm and pistol grip, Redfield Jr. mounts, Redfield 2×-7× variable scope.

Gun #4 is Ruger . . .

Gun #5 . . .

Forget it. This account has now come right down to the gnat in the navel of the whole week of hunting which is Sweet Medium Sweet Asshole Pete who don't know about hunting enough to go out and shoot at Texas cactus (which, if you know how to plug it proper, dies with a scream of Pulque blood gushering up and out and an absolutely foul breakwind of Peyote gas), no, Pete has grown up with a nice Savage 99 lever action .250 deer gun, and he runs and freezes his own scared hot shit in a suburban rental frozen food locker when he gets the invitation to Alaska from Rusty, for that means a two- to five-year expediting of his dangerously dull slick as owl shit ascent of the corporation ladder provided he can make it on this Yukon expedition. So he runs out and he borrows a Savage 110 bolt action with Weaver K-4 scope from his deadly daddy (who years ago never thought enough of Pete's shooting to give him the 110, but laid, instead, the 99 lever action on him for Christmas). Well, that takes one nightmare out of Pete's head which is cocking that 99 fuck-your-finger lever while a grizzly, perfectly capable of eating whatever the Savage 99 .250 will throw, ambles and slides and tears across the brush at him. And it warms his heart cockles, cause it's the first treasured thing his daddy ever loaned him. (His daddy's beginning to breathe thin.) Well, Pete now starts hearing about the bolt action 110. It will stop any game, yeah, if the shot is *well placed*. Strangle that little news. Pete ain't looking to make a career of placing his supershots in superb array anywhere but in the office jungle. Don't tell him about 180-grain Core-Lokt or Silver Tipt, he wants a grenade and bullet all in one sweet cartridge package—he wants a bomb that will drop a grizzly if it hits him in the toe. So he what? Better believe! Comedy is the study of the unsound actions of the cowardly under stress, just as tragedy is equal study time of the brave under heroic but enigmatic, reverberating, resonant conditions of loss—yes, professor, you may keep the change, for D.J. is, mean to say, *has* got more than a finger into the cunt of genius, Madame Muse. He has now to tell you that poor Very Low-Grade Medium Asshole Pete is so squash-breathed at the ups and downs of careermanship and sudden death which now confront him that he buys—get in line to look at it—from a white-haired riverboat string-tie type of an ex–oil well promoter, some friend of his wife's shiftless uncle's boss, a third-string Dallas Mafia type (don't even look how that gun got around to there or the Ford Foundation will be up and along for gropes), this gun being a used, indeed banged-up, African rhinoceros-hippo-elephant-soften-the-bullet-for-the-lion double-barreled .600–.577 custom, only-one-of-its-kind-ever-built Jeffrey Nitro Express carrying a 900-grain bullet for Shot #1, a 750-grain for Shot #2, and a recoil guaranteed to knock a grand piano on its ass. Forget about the French walnut and the Jeffrey action, the Hensoldt Zielklein 2¾× scope interchangeable with the Redfield 2×-7× blunt picket post with cross wire variable scope on the Pachmayr Lo-Swing mount or the addition of the Lyman aperture in the 17A front sight on the .577 barrel to be used when the rhinoceros is so close, friends, that the use of a telescopic sight is not indicated (which means, Herbert, that you better put the muzzle in your mouth and blast that rhino horn right back out of your ass). Yeah! This was the gun F. Lap-Ass Medium Asshole Pete brought to Alaska for grizzly. When he saw it, Rusty had a pure shit fit. If it hadn't been a Jeffrey he'd have laughed his nuts off. But, fix on this, Rusty thought he had the only big bore Jeffrey in the State of Texas, and here was his flunky with a bigger, and *double*! . . .

"How'd you get this mother-fuck?" he asked Pete. "I haven't heard of a double Jeff Nite Express since they used it to kill a Swiss dragon who was terrorizing some Tyrolean village in 1921."

"Somebody sold it to me," Pete confesses.

"Well, I hope you didn't pay too much, because the fellow must have stolen it."

In fact, Pete has bought it for 1,000 heart-hurting bucks. A swindle and a crime. The two barrels are thus crooked they could shoot each other. Pore Pete, Be Your Boss Pete, has had already to lay out near to 4,200 bucks for this Brooks Range safari-and-*gun* and has thus had to sell his #2 car, a somewhat used Jag XKE for three big ones plus another thou by converting some Dreyfus Fund into straight cash. He wouldn't dare sell his Pure Pores debentures, no, nor go further into installment debt.

Well, Rusty is in a marching state of perturbation. The very presence of that gun seems enough to shatter the tissue or texture of the spell which hangs over every happy hunter. Up in the basin, by the fire, night before the morning Tex killed the wolf, Big Luke has taken one look at Pete's possession and Rusty knows what he is thinking: This is one extrafine gaggle of goose fat and asshole to contend with for a week. So Rusty attacks. He knows enough to get attention off that Nitro Express! He inquires after Big Ollie's second gun, knowing pure well there is only the Remington 721, Big Ollie is a man for an all-purpose rifle, and when Big Luke says, "Ollie take care of everything with one gun," Rusty says, "Yeah, well why're you carrying a .375?"

"Ollie can back you up just as well with that .30-06."

"You know a .30-06 isn't going to do the job of a .375 Magnum. It wasn't *designed to*," says Rusty, getting a good old Texas range whine like the ricochet of a bullet off a stupid-ass Texas desert rock. He is obviously thinking of Mr. Grizzer. What Big Luke is thinking is not so far from conjecture. He is either (a) carrying a .375 to make his clients happy, since he shoots good enough to stop anything with a .30-06, a #.270, even a .245 if he got to, or (b) he has lost more nerve than Ollie, so he has more power in his fire stick. Either way, he got to protect Ollie and his one gun, he ain't getting in a situation where he might have to tell #2 man what sort of gun said #2 is supposed to sling in order to keep Sir Jet-Throne happy.

Rusty knows all this too, but he hasn't put in the years being a first-line Ranger Commando in 4C and P for zero return, he knows how to keep an expert on the defensive (and remind him of a nightmare or two) by poking in just hard enough to the mysteries between the facts. "Listen," says Rusty, "nobody knows finally what's going to kill big game. Some seem to go over if you put a pin in their butt, others you take right through the heart—they keep running. Running right at you if need be."

"Shoot for the shoulder, not the heart," says Big Luke in a voice like a piece of old oiled gunstock, a voice with a patina—he has said this two thousand times over the years.

"Right," says Rusty, "the shoulder. Break the shoulder bone, and they can't run. Sure. That's where I want my power. Right there. Right then. Maybe a professional hunter takes pride in dropping an animal by picking him off in a vital spot—but I like the feeling that if I miss a vital area I still can count on the big impact knocking them down, killing them by the total impact, shock! it's like aerial bombardment in the last Big War," he said, turning to Tex, D.J., and the Medium Assholes, and dropping his voice as if he were now imparting the flavor of the secret jellies and jams used in black mass of real military lore, "why, face up, gentlemen, the British were right, hear, hear, they were right for once, you don't pinpoint vital areas in a city, you blot it all out, you bury it deep in fire, shit, and fury. Then when the war's over they're glad to see you come in. It's just like if you get in a fight with a fellow, you're well advised to destroy him half to death. If y'get him down, use your shoe on his face, employ your imagination, give him a working-over, hard to believe, but often enough that man is your friend afterward, you've made him sane—maybe he thought before he had the fight with you he could lick whatever was in sight so he was half-crazy, now he knows that is not exactly so. Whereas if you give him a nice clean whipping, you've stimulated him to give you a nice clean whipping back. Of course, the analogy is not perfect, Luke, but I am forced to wonder about the fine difference in ethics between using Ollie's .30-06, and my Special .404, or your .375. Yes, it may be our animals will die a degree more from shock and a hint less from vital execution. But of what final ethical consequence is that, where is the fine difference?"

"Your meat tastes better when you're executed," said Tex.

Big Luke gave a laugh, Rusty gave a look at the undertaker's son. "Let me just tell you," he said into the fire, "I hope I don't have to stand on tiptoe too long waiting for you, Tex, to squeeze a needle out of your .270."

"You won't," said Tex.

Well, M.A. Pete heard all of this and more, he heard from his tentmate M.A. Bill a little later that night, for Bill was a ballistics nut and had spent one full vacation in the ballistics department of the FBI in the Department of Justice building in D.C. (having used the influence of his boss Death-row Jelly-Go Jet-Throne and the friendship of some of the local FBI to be accepted as a guest-visitor and temporary student on the comparative rank basis of police captain so that M.A. Bill got his studying in with visiting foreigners like the head of the Ghana Police Department, and the Mozambique Police Department, and native fuzz from Spokane, Walla Walla, Greensboro—they were all taking the full invitation and orientation course in updated police detection methods, but M.A. Bill was no investigator manqué, rather he was a ballistics nut, and that's where he stayed for two hot blazing summer weeks in the air-conditioned laboratories of the ballistics boys). He'd always gone in for handloading his cartridges, but when he got back, he was abruptly become the cartridge expert in his rifle club cause he could advise you on the FBI selection and use of bullets, primer, case, shot, and powder, he was up on the latest Department of Justice methods of determining chamber pressure, mean effective pressure, hunting loads, reasonable uses for black powder, new powders, flash holes, bullet castings, bullet swaging, etc., he had a spread of loading tools, dies, accessories, components, lathes, and was therefore all equipped to wildcat his own. Some of them were pretty hot. M.A. Bill had been known to come into the office with gunpowder injected in his pores, but a breech had never blown up in his face. Of course, no dentist has love for a doctor, and no wildcatter has a good word for a factory cartridge. M.A. Pete had been ready after Rusty's contumely to bury his Jeffrey Nitro Express and make the trip with the Savage 110 .30-06, but M.A. Bill squared him off on that. He let him in on the secret—factory ammunition was the unspoken scandal of American life, and .30-06, well in M.A. Bill's opinion, they were the worst offenders. The f.p.s. (foot per second, knothead!) variations had been known to go up to 5 percent, and one box in not that very many you'd be surprised had such variations and fluctuations in their max. vel., as tested on the chronograph that trajectories could even be affected. Which meant? Pete wanted to know. Errors in shooting, said M.A. Bill. D.J. is here to tell you that M.A. Pete wished to hear no more, which was error indeed, cause a little cross-examination would have revealed that M.A. Bill was talking about a difference that was not an inch at one hundred yards, not by half. You see, fellow Americans, statistics perverts, and number addicts, the greatest effect of variation in powder loadings speaks up after you go by the sign that says, "You are a rifle bullet passing the three-hundred-yard mark and are bound soon to dip. Keep your nose up!" In fact, M.A. Bill like most ballistics nuts was as nearsighted as an old hound with silver rim lenses so his critique is academic for himself. He's not interested in where the bullet goes, he just wants to stuff it full of the right sort of smokeless. Love, love, the Good Lord may have had no idea how far he cast his seed.

"But your gun is a .30-06," says M.A. Pete.

"Yes, but I've had it rechambered and with a custom barrel. I make my own shell for it. A .311. I wouldn't ever use a .30-06."

"Oh," said Pete, "that .311 must really do the job."

"You can go to sleep on that," said M.A. Bill.

M.A. Pete did not sleep too well. He had visions of a grizzly bearing down on him with a wild cry like a Nigger washerwoman gone ape with a butcher knife, and he had seen himself forced to face such music with the slim pencil of a .30-06. He had had dreams of bringing it off with a .30-06 but that buried scandal of American sporting rifle cartridge ammo f.p.s. discrepancies recounted to him by M.A. Bill had the front sight of his Savage 110 wavering like a fly wing in his mind's eye. If the aim of the bullet could not be trusted, then of what purport the gun? So, fuck if he didn't have his hand on the double Jeffrey all night long and kiss your own ass deep in the heart of Texas if the elephant gun wasn't the tool that M.A. Pete brought with him when he went running down into the valley and the green park of lawn below the black-ass gray basin, down in the sweet green grass right after Tex shot his wolf, that grass green as an English lawn, just where the trees ended and the mountain went up in a gray dome. And standing around, looking at the dead wolf, he looked up, and he, the medium asshole, was the first to see a caribou two hundred yards away through the thin trees, and in the accurate fevered inaccuracy of being awake a night without sleep, he took a sight and the cross hairs on the scope ran a figure eight around the horns, which then plummeted down around the hooves, flew up past the tail into the air, about, and back over the caribou's flanks to a view, all abrupt, honest, naked, and hairy of the buck's testicles magnified 4×, which to M.A. Pete's unprotected eye was equal in force and simple animal revelation to the first sight provided an innocent maiden of a workingman's balls, and then past caribou's deer nuts in a blur as if M.A. Pete was in a movie traveling the curves so it was all a blur, and around came the sights again to the back of the hocks and up and RUMBA! went the Jeffrey and the .600 Nitro Express shot on its way and M.A. Pete took a blow to the shoulder on recoil which canted his vertebrae 3 degrees 21 minutes right then and there, and Wow! came a sound next to him, for the caribou leaped in the air, did a crazy dance, and was off in the woods.

———

D.J., your presumptive philosopher, has not made the grand connection yet between the balls and the ears although he would claim they are related—more of this later, maybe—but the eyes are of course attached to the asshole as beginning is to end: The end is putting something out—the beginning is to see what you are going to have to shit out, and that right here in Brooks Range is easy to know because it will be the recollection of the blood on the cotton white ass of that caribou just hit by M.A. Pete. A liver-vitiating sight, Carter, for the liver goes flat, D.J. would assure you, whenever some scent meets its deodorant, or an herb is fed with aspirin. Pretty literary for adolescent out hunting with Paw? Go fuck, D.J.'s got his purchase on the big thing—genius—and he know this: You deaden a mystery and your liver goes to shit. This chase for a torn-ass caribou revolves around a simple mystery, to wit the ass of the caribou is white, its stumpy tail is white, soft as a white ruffle at Milady Hightits' throat, so D.J. ask you why? Why is the rear view of a thousand head of caribou passing on the tundra like a thousand pops of cotton on the boll? That's a dead-ass question—the ass of your mind go dead trying to answer, yeah, and here was just one caribou, off on a split through the woods. But we all had one look, one crack of a look at something red and hanging bad and loose like a wattle from the white fur. Then we were all walking and jogging down an open aisle of moss-green grass to the spot in the timber two hundred fifty yards below where the deer had plunged in.

Blood for his trail, drops the size of every kind of coin, silver dollars up to florins, even—one the size of a small plate—brown blood already corrupted by a hive of near invisible devourers, insect shitters, chiggers and flies, one big Alaska bumblebee still alive on this cold early September morning, and the sun shining right in the blood with a thousand lights, or so it would look if you had your nose right there on the bloodied leaves close enough to that wet to think you were looking at neon signs, the woods were full of awe, nothing other, the trees standing numb, cowardly spectators, man, watching one of their own take a wasting.

Then the trail of the blood took a bend, beat through dwarf alder, and some nasty kind of brush with too much in the way of catbriers. That took quite a few minutes, then a pine grove, then another aisle between trees, parallel to the one we had come down, but now the caribou trail was rising up to timberline again, and in the distance, up along a thousand yards, was what looked to be the caribou, yes, it was, and through the field glasses Big Luke, watching, shook his head. "You hit him an outside rump shot, Pete."

"Then he'll be all right?"

"No, impact seems to have broke his leg or maybe shocked his spine. He's using only one hind leg. Walking not much faster than us. That's bad. We can't leave him."

"Say," said Pete, trying to shift the rump of the subject, "why'd that buck leave timber?"

"Didn't want to die in those woods. Sometimes you get a buck will cross three open ridgelines to get into the particular woods where he wants to hide or give it up."

"Then he ain't too bad if he can move that much."

"He," said Big Luke, "is bad enough that we got to get him."

It was going to take all day. We were going to spend our first day walking and jogging to chase a wounded caribou, when there were ten thousand head of them in the Brooks Range. All honors due to M.A. Pete's Jeffrey Nitro Express. Well, Luke got the helicopter up. It had been down in Fairbanks for repair the day before, he had not mentioned how near it was to reach, oh no, he did not want to have Rusty on his ear all those hours of the packtrain up the mountain from Dolly Ding Bat Lake, but now he took us up the aisle through the trees till we were above timber again and led us along a shallow canyon and over a saddle into our basin, and there while breakfast was made by one of the flunky packer guide cooks, Ed Smith, an Indian, Big Luke got a big-ass walkie-talkie 3200 RC-1A 16 mile range, and rang down to camp at the lake telling them to come on in, and when they did with a smack of static, he told them to bring the helicopter on up.

That's how they got Kid Caribou. Helicopter pilot was there in five minutes with Buster Bubbletop, a real wasp of a Bell helicopter, and Big Luke got in with M.A. Pete and M.A. Pete's cannon, and they zipped up and over the ridge, and Rusty, and Tex, and D.J. went to the top of a knoll and followed them with Rusty's Hurdle & Reuss 7 × 35 and Tex and D.J.'s own Jap Titan 8 × 35 and Binolux 7 × 35. And, man, this is what they see—half-dead-ass caribou climbing up those rocks, nice head of antlers (look to be fourteen points through the glass) and a bleeding jagged gored red ass, flap of flesh now wide open, and the caribou makes those rocks with lunge and grunt and like then a whimper you could hear almost through the binocs when the sound of the helicopter began to beat on caribou ear with rings of ether just as when you going out on the operating table. Man, that caribou looks as dogged and frantic as a prospector climbing a mountain to get a hill of gold, and then the helicopter is on top of him and hovering and holding him frozen, and it lands not fifty feet away, and the caribou turns his ass and starts to climb up a cliff with a set of deliberate steps like (1) fuck you, (2) go kill, (3) shit on you, each step a pure phrase of the blues—take me away, Mr. Dixieland—and there is M.A. Pete stepping out gingerly from the copter, like, man, he's *close* to the caribou, and got his cannon with him, and just as Old Buck Broken Ass gets to the top of his little cliff, hopping slow on three legs, M.A. Pete sends a Nitro Express up into his gut from the rear, right into the red mask of the old wound and that animal does a Geländesprung right into the air as if his spine is illumined in incandescence, and somersaults in the air, and falls twenty feet from the cliff, smashing one set of antlers off his head (to be wired on later, nothing other) and the .600 900-grain blasted through his intestines, stomach, pancreas, gallbladder, liver, and lungs, and left a hole to put your arm in, all your arm, up to the shoulder if you are not squeamish, entrail swimmer, and then bullet breaking, some of the fragments ripped into the brain and out the head, leaving it scarred to the point where M.A. Pete could claim (and believe) two years later that the scars on the mouth and face of his deer trophy were the fighting marks of a big buck caribou fighter; other fragments sawed through the ribs of the lungs, and deteriorated like buckshot in the forequarter. Big Luke brought that animal back to feed us. Its guts, belly, and lungs were one old jelly flung together by the bullets, one blood pudding of a cocktail vibrated into total promiscuity by the twenty-foot fall down the rocks. Yes, prince, yes, Big Luke got the head off, and rescued the loose antler, and gutted the entrails, dressed the meat to clean fragments, left the hide, which was a mess—clear surprise, yes!—but we had the meat for lunch, and it wasn't exactly gamy, it tasted loud and clear of nothing but fresh venison steeped in bile, shit, and the half-digested contents of a caribou's stomach—it was so bad you were living on the other side of existence, down in poverty and stink wallow with your nose beneath the fever—that was Luke's message to us.

The helicopter was new to him, you read, and for some parties in the last year or so he'd begun to use it, for some not, but he was an American, what the fuck, he had spent his life living up tight with wilderness and that had eaten at him, wilderness was tasty but boredom was his corruption, he had wanted a jolt, so sees it D.J., Big Luke now got his kicks with the helicopter. He was forever enough of a pro not to use it with real hunters, no, man, but he had us, gaggle of goose fat and asshole, killers of bile-soaked venison, so the rest of the hunt, all next seven days he gave what was secretly wanted, which was helicopter heaven, and it was curious shit, all rules and regulations, for of course we did not hunt from the air, no freakmen from TV land us, but rather noble Dallasassians, so we broke open a war between us and the animals, and the hunt hills of the Moe Henry and Obungekat Safari patch rang with ball's ass shooting, the real breeze, hopping to the top of a mountain on copter wings to shoot down on goats, nothing so great as the Alaska mountain goat, yeah, you get up at three A.M. in tent came up high above timber, and you climb, man, on foot above timber, for three hours till dawn, and then climb higher still crabbing up sixty-degree rock slopes, and walking with all heart shit up in your throat along a ledge twelve inches or less, yeah, ooh, making it up, and higher still, *quietly,* and then if you good, you're up there, up above Master Mountain Goat, and when you start to shoot on him, he does a step dance like an old Negro heel-and-toe tap man falling down stairs or flying up them, and the first animal D.J. got in Alaska was a mountain goat at two hundred and fifty yards, and with one shot, animal stood on its nose for one long beast of a second, and then did a running dying dance for fifty yards down the rocks like a fakir sprinting through flaming coals, and when he died, *Wham!* the pain of his exploding heart shot like an arrow into D.J.'s heart, and the animals had gotten him, they were talking all around him now, communicating the unspoken unseen unmeasurable electromagnetism and wave of all the psychic circuits of all the wild of Alaska, and he was only part of them, and part he was of gasoline of Texas, the asshole sulfur smell of money-oil clinging to the helicopter, cause he had not gotten that goat by getting up in the three A.M. of morning and climbing the mountain, no cream not your dear private lace, dear Celia, D.J. had gotten up at seven back in the bunkhouse at Dolly Ding Bat Lake, for once Big Luke had decided this was Helicopter Week for Goose Fat Gaggle, he bundled all souls and A-holes back to the bunkhouse since good old Hail the Cop Turd could take you a day's walk in ten minutes, and he would drop us on spots, top of a mountain, edge of a bull moose pond, across a canyon from Dall ram, near a feeding ground for the grizzer, that copter was dividing us up, carrying us here, there, every which spot, shooting in parties of two and four, guide and guest, or two guides, two guests, and it was a haul of big-ass game getting, for among the five of us safari payers we had a limit of twenty-five assorted grizzly, moose, ram, goat, and caribou, and there was animal steaks being cut and packed all over the place, and trundled out by copter back to Dolly Ding Bat and up again in Super Cub to Fairbanks and freezers, all that hot supersensitive game meat now locked in brown paper and stone ice, paralyzed stiff in a freezer, about to suffer for sins it could not locate, yes, that was how D.J. got his mountain goat, he was flown at seven in the morning up to the top of a spiky ridge not too unlike the moon, set down in a bowl with Tex, Ollie, and Kenny Easterly, and waited, and in two hours had his shot, had his action, climbing down a ravine, and up the other side, a walk of four hundred yards, had his work helping Big Ollie skin, butcher, gut, and package Mr. Goat (being shown by Ollie how to keep the fur away from the meat so the taste would not be tainted— touch of goat skin on raw goat meat smelling as stale and raunchy as overworked whore) and then Big Ollie having radioed the copter, in came the Hail the Cop and let down a line all hovering and they slung the meat packages, and the horns and head onto the lift line, which pulled it up and then pulled them up—that was the kick of the morning, foot in the stirrup, lifting one hundred feet to the Cop Turd which vibrated above like one giant overgrown Hog! its carburetor farting, its motor giving out that family sputter of gasoline being piston-cooked at medium speed, but D.J. never looked at the head of the goat except once, for the goat had a clown's expression in his little-ass red dying eyes, the fires of the heart working to keep custard on the clown's face, it wasn't until that night when he was in the bunkhouse back at Dolly Ding Bat that D.J. relaxed enough to remember that goat picking his way up and down rocks like a slow motion of a skier through slalom, his legs and ass swinging opposite ways, carefree, like take one leg away, I'll do it on the other, and it hit D.J. with a second blow on his heart from the exploding heart of the goat and he sat up in bed, in the bunk, listening to the snores, stole out to the night, got one breath of the sense of that *force* up in the North, of land North North above him and dived back to the bed, his sixteen-year-old heart racing through the first spooks of an encounter with Herr Dread.

What more you want to hear? They got them all, crazy caribou trophy heads, eighteen-point buck for M.A. Bill, M.A. Bill! his handload .311 cartridge did the job, and tore off the ass—D.J. will not dwell on why an asshole is bound to hit the ass, for that is homeopathic magic, man—we got it all, that helicopter made us like a bee pulling honey from flower after flower, moose and goose if there'd been goose, and Dall ram, horns and horns of Dall ram, all five of us in three teams got to blast our own set of horn before one day was done on a herd up in a sink near a pinnacle, and Big Luke's Cop Turd pilot was pushing the rules and regs of Hail Cop hunting, for after he lower us out on the line which had even Rusty close to involuntary defecation (and was the most heroic thing corporation execs have done in many a year), why, we got left set up two hundred yards from old herd of Dall ram, Mr. and Mrs. Beautiful Ibex horn (that's Jew horn, I Beck'n Son, hih, hih) ain't got the curl and spiral of the universe curving out of their brain for nothing, they took up and off, and Mr. Cop Turd went swinging after them like a darning needle after ladybugs and headed the Dall ram off till they started to run back toward us, at which point he cut them off again (by crossing in front of them only thirty feet above—kick hump in this hunting is: be Cop pilot) since unwritten Copt. rules and regs forbid chasing of game into gun, at which point Dall ram leader was like to be very confused and hit out this way and that way, and the Cop just went circling around until the sheep were fixed, shit they were hypnotized, it was pretty to watch, cause Hail Cop was like a bullfighter twisting a bull through the limits of his neck until he just got to stand and wait and let his neck recover, and the copter having the herd of Dall ram finally fixed on a cleft in a ridge across a bare modest draw from us, us hiding in the rocks on the lip of the sink, he pulled up and out, each circle a little bigger than the one before, and now a little higher until the animals shivering from the release of anxiety, in fact all strung out from the sound of air boiling, breaking, roaring, and tearing and the whine— what cry of what beast?—were able to do no more than walk around, hocks trembling, muzzles nuzzling assholes—like get back to that flesh, man! they must have felt they were being born out again.

I got the first shot. Kneeling behind a rock with a moss hummock not larger than the hand for a rest, it all felt good, I had gotten so hypnotized myself, there was no fever looking through the scope, the eye picked on one ram standing on one rock all four legs together and head silhouetted out against a sawtooth ridge maybe five miles behind him, and in the scope I had one look at the prettiest face D.J. has ever seen, almond oval and butter love for eyes, a little black sweet pursed mouth, all quivering now, two nostrils cunning as an old Negro witch smelling gypsy money on a mark, whoo-ee—I got the dot above my reticule in the center of the curl of the horn—those horns went three hundred and sixty degrees around the ear, like holding the mountain in the palm of your hand, they were receptors to hear the curve of the wind in the private cave of the mountains about, they were a coil of horn around the nerve which tunes the herb, and D. Ramses was all horned in on me, hair to the left, hair to the right went his head, we could just as well have been pulling opposite ends. I could not help it, wanting to keep that head intact for a trophy, the scope still would not leave the horn, the dot stayed on the ram brain, one inch above the eye, and feeling like the instant before the jump first time off a garage roof, D.J. pulls his trigger finger, perfect pull, perfect shot, as if all spiral of horn was funnel to pull all of the aim in and the shot went in one inch above the eye and the animal went down like a wall had fallen, best shot D.J. ever made, and Rusty rushed in his shot, cause his sheep took off at D.J.'s shot, Rusty only wounded his beast, got a second blast away too high in the shoulder, off with a third in the hoof—believe it if you want—the hoof later as splattered from the .404 as a wad of tar beaten with a hammer, and finally got him in the shoulder near the heart, the animal not moving hardly now, was Rusty mad. Four .404s for a Dall ram (he not carrying #2 gun or #3, cause who knows where grizzly might be?). If he needed four for the ram, maybe four times four for the bear.

More skinning, more packing, two great trophy heads, and a wait for the helicopter out servicing Tex and M.A.s Pete-Bill. They all had Dall ram that day. Five sets of horns held in the arms of five shit-eating grins standing in semicircle on the banks of Dolly Ding Bat Lake as the pictures were taken, and long careful discussions with Big Luke on taxidermy and where the Moe Henry and Obungekat Safari Group recommended the preservation of the head—any fifty-year guarantee outfits around, or century mounters? "There's no real craftsmen left," says M.A. Pete. "Just embalmers," said Tex.

From *Why Are We in Vietnam?* (1967)

# ON THE ART
# OF THE ABSURD

## Metaphor Versus Science

None of us, scientists first, are equipped to measure the achievements of science. That vast scientific work of the last fifty years has come out of the collective efforts of the twentieth-century laboratories, but the seminal ideas and the culture of science derive from the nineteenth century, the Enlightenment, and the Renaissance. Who may now measure where the creativity was finest? The scientists of the last five centuries were the builders of that foundation from which modern scientists have created a contemporary science. Their ancestors, how-ever, may have been more extraordinary men than our present scien-tists. The scientific ancestors were adventurers, rebels, courtiers, painters, diplomats, churchmen. Our scientists are experts; those of the last decade are dull in person as experts. They write jargon. Their minds are narrow before they are deep. Their knowledge of life is in-carcerated.

The huge industrial developments and scientific advances of the twentieth century—the automobile, antibiotics, radium, flight, the structure of the atom, relativity, the quantum theory, psychoanalysis, the atom bomb, the exploration of space—may speak not so much for the genius of the twentieth century as for the genius of the preceding centuries. For science was founded originally on metaphor, and the twentieth century has shipped metaphor to the ghetto of poets. Con-sider! Science began with the poetic impulse to treat metaphor as equal to equation; the search began at that point where a poet looked for a means (which only later became experiment) to measure the accuracy of his metaphor. The natural assumption was that his discovery had been contained in the metaphor, since good metaphor could only originate in the deepest experience of a man; so science still remained attached to poetic vision, and scientific insight derived from culture—it was not the original desire of science to convert nature, rather to reveal it. Faust was still unborn when Aristotle undertook his pioneer observations.

There is a danger in metaphor, however; the danger that is present in poetry—contradictory meanings collect too easily about the core of meaning. Unconnected meanings tend to connect themselves. So, science sought a methodology through experiment that would be severe, precise, and able to measure the verity of the insight in the metaphor. Experiment was conceived to protect the scientific artist from ambiguity.

Experiment, however, proliferated. As the scientist ceased to be a great amateur and became expert, experiment ran amok, and laboratory men of partial, determined, fanatic brilliance became the scientist's director rather than his assistant. The laboratory evicted the mind; the laboratory declared itself the womb of scientific knowledge; laboratory methodology grew as cumbersome as the labor codes of a theatrical union. Metaphor disappeared.

It was replaced by a rabidity of experiment, a fetishism of experiment. Mediocrity invaded science. Experiment became a faith, experiment replaced the metaphor as a means of inquiry, and technological development pushed far ahead of even the most creative intuition. Penicillin was discovered by accident, as a by-product of experiment—it did not come at the end of a poetic journey of the mind. And by similar mass methods were all the other antibiotics uncovered by observing the bactericidal action of a million molds. Those which gave the best laboratory evidence of success were marketed by drug companies. But the root of the success was not comprehended. There was no general theory to point to a particular mold for a specific disease. No metaphor. Metaphor had been replaced by gross assay.

Metaphor. The word has been used generously. Would an example be welcome? A modern disease, as it is comprehended in a laboratory, is explained to the laboratory technician, the student, and the layman as a phenomenon made up of its own pimples, rash, swelling, and development. The disease is never presented as a creature—real or metaphorical—a creature that might have an existence separate from its description, even as you and I have an existence separate from the fact that we weigh so many pounds and stand so many inches tall. No, the symptom is stripped of its presence. Of course, psycho-analysis made an attempt to say that the root of one disease could be similar to the root of another whose symptoms were different—it was a way of hinting that the metaphor ought to return. Such an approach might have wished ultimately to demonstrate that a malfunction of the liver and an inflammation of the eyes were both connected to de-spair at one's position in society. But psychoanalysis was hungry, and dependent upon the sciences: Like most welfare cases, it was therefore not in a rush for poetry—rather it rushed to advertise the discovery of each new tranquilizer for each disorder in emotion. It was anxious to show itself respectable. So psychiatry became pharmacology.

Let us, however, try to travel in the other direction and look for an extreme metaphor of disease. Let us suppose that each specific ill of the body is not so much a dull evil to be disposed of by any chemi-cal means available but is, rather, a theatrical production presented by some company in oneself to some audience in oneself. To the degree then that our illness is painful, detailed, clear, and with as much edge as a sharply enunciated voice, the particular disease is a *success;* the communion of the body (the statement sent from stage to audience) is deep, is resonant. The audience experiences catharsis. At the end of the drama, the body is tired but enriched. By the logic of our metaphor, that is a good disease. The illness has waged conflict, drama, and distress through the body, and has obliged the body to sit in attention upon it, but now the body knows more. Its experience has become more profound, its intimate knowledge of its own dishar-mony is more acute.

By this reckoning, a disease is the last attempt (*at a particular level of urgency*) to communicate from one part of the body to the other, a last attempt to tell us that if we do not realize how the function before us is now grievously out of harmony, then we will certainly sicken fur-ther. On the other hand, if the disease that presents itself is not ac-cepted, if one's suffering is not suffered, if there are no statements of our suffering enunciated through the caverns of the body, but if in-stead our disease is averted by antibiotic or our pain is silenced by a sedative, then the attempted communication of the illness has failed. The disease, having no other expression, sinks, of necessity, into a lower and less elegant condition. It retreats from a particular pain or conflict into a bog of disharmony. Where one organ or two might have borne the original stress, now ten organs share ubiquitous tension. A clear sense of symptom tends to disappear. Infection begins to be replaced by virus, a way of saying the new diseases are not classifiable—their symptoms reveal no characteristic form. One is close to the plague.

If my metaphor is valid, then drugs to relieve pain, and antibiotics to kill infection, are in fact liquidators of possibility, for they deaden the possibility of any quick dramatic growth. A disease checked by an antibiotic has taught the body nothing—nothing to terminate ambiguity—the body does not know how well it could have cured itself, or even precisely what it had to cure. Yet ambiguity is the seat of disease. Ambiguity demands double communication to achieve a single purpose. It demands we be ready for a particular course of action and yet be ready for its exact opposite. So it demands double readiness or double function for single use, and is, therefore, waste. A man brought back from death by chemicals his own body did not manage to provide cannot know afterward if he should be alive. Small matter, you may argue—he is much alive, is he not? But he has lost biological dignity, he is crucially less alive in a part of his mind and his body. That is one reason metaphors are not encouraged near to science now, for one would then have to say that the patient is alive but his soul has died to a degree.

So the argument would demand that there be metaphors to fit the vaults of modern experience. That is, in fact, the unendurable demand of the middle of this century: to restore the metaphor, and thereby displace the scientist from his center. Would you call for another example? Think of the elaborate architecture in the structure of a protein molecule. The scientist will describe the structure and list the properties of the molecule (and indeed it took technological achievements close to genius to reach that point), but the scientist will not look at the metaphorical meaning of the physical structure, its meaning as an architectural form. He will not ponder what biological or spiritual experience is suggested by the formal structure of the molecule, for metaphor is not to the present interest of science. It is instead the desire of science to be able to find the cause of cancer in some virus; a virus—you may count on it—that will be without metaphor, and thereby will be equal to saying that the heart of the disease of all diseases is empty of meaning, that cancer is caused by a specific virus that has no character or quality and is in fact void of philosophy and bereft of metaphysics. All those who are there to claim that disease and death are void of meaning are there to benefit from such a virus, for next they can move on to say that life is absurd. We are back once again at the enigma surrounding the art of the absurd.

Except now we have hints of the meaning. For if the argument would propose that a future to life depends on creating forms of an intensity that will capture the complexity of modern experience and dignify it, illumine—if you will—its danger, then the art of the absurd reveals the wound in its own heart and the schizophrenia of its impulse, for the art of the absurd wars with one hand against the monotonies of all totalitarian form in politics, medicine, architecture, and media communication and, with the other, trembles and is numb to any human passion and is savage toward discourse.

From *Cannibals and Christians* (1966)

# THE ARMIES OF THE NIGHT

Mailer sighed; like most New Yorkers, he usually felt small in Washington. The capital invariably seemed able to take the measure of men like him.

But as Mailer had come to recognize over the years, the modest everyday fellow of his daily round was servant to a wild man in himself: The gent did not appear so very often, sometimes so rarely as once a month, sometimes not even twice a year, and he sometimes came when Mailer was frightened and furious at the fear, sometimes he came just to get a breath of air. He was indispensable, however, and Mailer was even fond of him, for the wild man was witty in his own wild way and absolutely fearless. He would have been admirable, except that he was an absolute egomaniac, a Beast—no recognition existed of the existence of anything beyond the range of his reach. And when he appeared, it was often with great speed; he gave little warning. Certainly he gave no warning as the Historian checked in at the Hay-Adams, changed his clothes, and prepared to give a few thoughtful remarks a little later that night at the Ambassador Theater on the essential insanity of our venture in Vietnam, such remarks designed presumably to encourage happy participation for Saturday's move to invest the Pentagon.

# The Liberal Party

There was a party first, however, given by an attractive liberal couple. Mailer's heart, never buoyant at best, and once with justice called "sodden" by a critic, now collected into a leaden little ball and sank, not to his feet but his stomach. He was aware for the first time this day of a healthy desire to have a drink, for the party gave every promise of being dreadful. Mailer was a snob of the worst sort. New York had not spoiled him, because it had not chosen to, but New York had certainly wrecked his tolerance for any party but a very good one. Like most snobs he professed to believe in the aristocracy of achieved quality—"Just give me a hovel with a few young artists, bright-eyed and bold"—in fact, a party lacked flavor for him unless someone very rich or social was present. An evening without a wicked lady in the room was like an opera company without a large voice. Of course there were no wicked ladies when he entered this room. Some reasonably attractive wives to be certain, and a couple of young girls, too young for him, they were still in the late stages of some sort of extraordinary progressive school, and were innocent decent-spirited, merry, red-cheeked, idealistic, and utterly lobotomized away from the sense of sin. Mailer would not have known what to do with such young ladies—he had spent the first forty-four years of his life in an intimate dialogue, a veritable dialectic with the swoops, spooks, starts, the masks and snarls, the calm lucid abilities of sin, sin was his favorite fellow, his tonic, his jailer, his horse, his sword, say he was not inclined to flirt for an hour with one bright seventeen-year-old or another when they conceived of lust as no more than the gymnasium of love. Mailer had a diatribe against LSD, hippies, and the generation of love, but he was keeping it to himself. (The young girls, incidentally, had been brought by Ed de Grazia. Not for nothing did de Grazia bear a resemblance to Sinatra.)

But we are back with the wives, and the room has not yet been described. It was the sort of room one can see at many a faculty party in places like Berkeley, the University of Chicago, Columbia—the ground of common being is that the faculty man is a liberal. Conservative professors tend to have a private income, so their homes show the flowering of their taste, the articulation of their hobbies, collections adhere to their cabinets and odd statements of whim stand up in the nooks; but liberal instructors, liberal assistant professors, and liberal associate professors are usually poor and programmatic, so secretly they despise the arts of home adornment. Their houses look one like the other, for the wives gave up herculean careers as doctors, analysts, sociologists, anthropologists, labor relations experts—great servants of the Social Program were lost when the women got married and relinquished all for hubber and kids. So the furnishings are functional, the prevailing hues of wall and carpet and cloth are institutional brown and library gray, the paintings and sculpture are stylized abstract, hopeless imitation I. Rice Pereira, Leonard Baskin, Ben Shahn, but bet your twenty-five dollars to win an assured ten dollars that the artist on the wall is a friend of the host, has the right political ideas, and will talk about literature so well, you might think you were being addressed by Maxim Gorky.

Such were the sour and near to unprintable views of the semi-distinguished and semi-notorious author as he entered the room. His deepest detestation was often reserved for the nicest of liberal academics, as if their lives were his own life but a step escaped. Like the scent of the void that comes off the pages of a Xerox copy, so was he always depressed in such homes by their hint of oversecurity. If the republic was now managing to convert the citizenry to a plastic mass, ready to be attached to any manipulative gung-ho, the author was ready to cast much of the blame for such success into the undernourished lap, the overpsychologized loins, of the liberal academic intelligentsia. They were of course politically opposed to the present programs and movements of the republic in Asian foreign policy, but this political difference seemed no more than a quarrel among engineers. Liberal academics had no root of a real war with technology land itself, no, in all likelihood, they were the natural managers of that future air-conditioned vault where the last of human life would still exist. Their only quarrel with the Great Society was that they thought it temporarily deranged, since the Great Society seemed to be serving as instrument to the Goldwater wing of the Republican party, a course of action so very irrational to these liberal technologues that they were faced with bitter necessity to desert all their hard-earned positions of leverage on real power in the Democratic party, a considerable loss to suffer merely because of an irrational development in the design of the Great Society's supermachine. Well, the liberal technologues were not without character or principle. If their living rooms had little to keep them apart from the look of waiting rooms of doctors with a modern practice, it was exactly because the private loves of the ideologues were attached to no gold standard of the psyche. Those true powers of interior decoration—greed, guilt, compassion, and trust—were hardly the cornerstones of their family furnishings. No, just as money was a concept, no more, to the liberal academic, and needed no ballast of gold to be considered real, for nothing is more real to the intellectual than a concept! so position or power in society was, to the liberal technologue, also a concept, desirable, but always to be relinquished for a better concept. They were servants of that social machine of the future in which all irrational human conflict would be resolved, all conflict of interest negotiated, and nature's resonance condensed into frequencies that could comfortably phase nature in or out as you please. So they were servants of the moon. Their living rooms looked like offices precisely because they were ready to move to the moon and build Utope cities there—Utope being, one may well suppose, the only appropriate name for pilot models of Utopia in Non-Terrestrial Ecologically Sub-Dependent Non-Charged Staging Areas, that's to say dead planets where the food must be flown in, but the chances for good civil rights and all-out social engineering are 100 percent zap!

As is invariably the case with sociological ruminations, the individual guests at this party disproved the general thesis, at least in part. The hostess was small, for example, almost tiny, but vivid, bright-eyed, suggestive of a fiery temper and a childlike glee. It was to pain Mailer later to refuse her cooking (she had prepared a buffet to be eaten before the move to the theater) but he was drinking with some devotion by then, and mixing seemed fair neither to the food nor the bourbon. It was of course directly unfair to the hostess: Mailer priding himself on his good manners precisely because the legend of his bad manners was so prevalent, hated to cause pain to a hostess, but he had learned from years of speaking in public that an entertainer's first duty was to deliver himself to the stage with the maximum of energy, high focus, and wit—a good heavy dinner on half a pint of bourbon was likely to produce torpor, undue search for the functional phrase, and dry-mouthed maunderings after a little spit. So he apologized to the lady, dared the look of rejection in her eye that was almost balanced on a tear—she was indeed surprisingly adorable and childlike to be found in such a liberal academic coven—and tried to cover the general sense of loss by marshaling what he assumed his most radiant look, next assuring her that he would take a rain check on the meal.

"Promise?"

"Next time I'm in Washington," he lied like a psychopath. The arbiter of nicety in him had observed with horror over many a similar occasion that he was absolutely without character for any social situation in which a pause could become the mood's abyss, and so he always filled the moment with the most extravagant amalgams of possibility. Particularly he did this at the home of liberal academics. They were brusque to the world of manners, they had built their hope of heaven on the binary system and the computer, 1 and 0, Yes and No—they had little to do therefore with the spectrum of grace in acceptance and refusal: If you did not do what they wished, you had simply denied them. Now Mailer was often brusque himself, famous for that, but the architecture of his personality bore resemblance to some provincial cathedral that warring orders of the church might have designed separately over several centuries, the particular cathedral falling into the hands of one architect, then his enemy. (Mailer had not been married four times for nothing.) If he was on many an occasion brusque, he was also to himself at least so supersensitive to nuances of manner he sometimes suspected when in no modest mood that Proust had lost a cell mate the day they were born in different bags. (*Bag* is of course used here to specify milieu and not the exceptional character of the mothers, Mme. Proust and Mrs. I. B. Mailer.) At any rate, boldness, attacks of shyness, rude assertion, and circumlocutions tortured as arthritic fingers working at lace all took their turn with him, and these shuttlings of mood became most pronounced in their resemblance to the banging and shunting of freight cars when he was with liberal academics. Since he—you are in on the secret—disapproved of them far more than he could afford to reveal (their enmity could be venomous) he therefore exerted himself to push up a synthetic exaggerated sweetness of manner, and his conversations with liberal ideologues on the consequence consisted almost entirely of overcorrections of the previous error.

"I know a friend of yours," says the ideologue. A nervous voice from the novelist for answer. "Yes? Who?" Now the name is given: It is X.

Mailer: I don't know X.

The ideologue proceeds to specify a conversation that M held with X. M recollects. "Oh, yes!" he says. "Of course! X!" Burbles of conversation about the merits of X, and his great ebullience. Actually X is close to flat seltzer.

There had been just this sort of dialogue with a stranger at the beginning of the party. So Mailer gave up quickly any thought of circulation. Rather, he huddled first with Dwight Macdonald, but Macdonald was the operative definition of the gregarious and could talk with equal facility and equal lack of personal observation to an Eskimo, a collector from the New York Department of Sanitation, or a UN diplomat—therefore was chatting happily with the world fifteen minutes after his entrance. Hence Mailer and Robert Lowell got into what was by all appearances a deep conversation at the dinner table sometime before food was laid out, Mailer thus doubly wounding the hostess with his later refusal.

We find, therefore, Lowell and Mailer ostensibly locked in converse. In fact, out of the thousand separate enclaves of their very separate personalities, they sensed quickly that they now shared one enclave to the hilt: their secret detestation of liberal academic parties to accompany worthy causes. Yes, their snobbery was on this mountainous face close to identical—each had a delight in exactly the other kind of party, a posh evil social affair; they even supported a similar vein of vanity (Lowell with considerably more justice) that if they were doomed to be revolutionaries, rebels, dissenters, anarchists, protesters, and general champions of one Left cause or another, they were also, in private, *grands conservateurs* and, if the truth be told, poor damn émigré princes. They were willing if necessary (probably) to die for the cause—one could hope the cause might finally at the end have an unexpected hint of wit, a touch of the Lord's last grace—but wit or no, grace or grace failing, it was bitter rue to have to root up one's occupations of the day, the week, and the weekend and trot down to Washington for idiot mass manifestations that could only drench one in the most ineradicable kind of mucked-up publicity and have for compensation nothing at this party which might be representative of some of the Devil's better creations. So Robert Lowell and Norman Mailer feigned deep conversation. They turned their heads to one another at the empty table, ignoring the potentially acolytic drinkers at either elbow, they projected their elbows out in fact like flying buttresses or old Republicans, they exuded waves of Interruption Repellent from the posture of their backs, and concentrated on their conversation, for indeed they were the only two men of remotely similar status in the room. (Explanations about the position of Paul Goodman will follow later.)

Lowell, whose personal attractiveness was immense (since his features were at once virile and patrician and his characteristic manner turned up facets of the grim, the gallant, the tender, and the solicitous as if he were the nicest Boston banker one had ever hoped to meet), was not concerned too much about the evening at the theater. "I'm just going to read some poems," he said. "I suppose you're going to speak, Norman."

"Well, I will."

"Yes, you're awfully good at that."

"Not really." Harrumphs, modifications, protestations, and denials of the virtue of the ability to speak.

"I'm no good at all at public speaking," said Lowell in the kindest voice. He had indisputably won the first round. Mailer the younger, presumptive, and self-elected prince was left to his great surprise—for he had been exercised this way many times before—with the unmistakable feeling that there was some faint strain of the second-rate in this ability to speak on your feet.

Then they moved on to talk of what concerned them more. It was the subject first introduced to Mailer by Mitch Goodman. Tomorrow, a group of draft resisters, led by William Sloane Coffin, Jr., Chaplain at Yale, were going to march from their meeting place at a church basement to the Department of Justice, and there a considerable number of draft cards would be deposited in a bag by individual students representing themselves, or their groups at different colleges, at which point Coffin and a selected few would walk into the Department of Justice, turn the cards over to the Attorney General, and await his reply.

"I don't think there'll be much trouble at this, do you?" asked Lowell.

"No, I think it'll be dull, and there'll be a lot of speeches."

"Oh, no," said Lowell with genuine pain, "Coffin's not that kind of fool."

"It's hard to keep people from making speeches."

"Well, you know what they want us to do?" Lowell explained. He had been asked to accompany a draft resister up to the bag in which the draft cards were being dropped. "It seems," said Lowell, with a glint of the oldest Yankee light winging off like a mad laser from his eye, "that they want us to be *big buddy.*"

It was agreed this was unsuitable. No, Lowell suggested, it would be better if they each just made a few remarks. "I mean," said Lowell, beginning to stammer a little, "we could just get up and say we respect their action and support it, just to establish, I suppose, that we're there and behind them and so forth."

Mailer nodded. He felt no ease for any of these suggestions. He did not even know if he truly supported the turning in of draft cards. It seemed to him at times that the students who disliked the war most should perhaps be the first to volunteer for the Army in order that their ideas have currency in the Army as well. Without them, the armed forces could more easily become Glamour State for the more mindless regions of the proletariat if indeed the proletariat was not halfway to Storm Troop Junction already. The military could make an elite corps best when the troops were homogenized. On the other hand, no soldier could go into combat with the secret idea that he would not fire a gun. If nothing else, it was unfair to friends in his outfit; besides it suggested the suicidal. No, the iron of the logic doubtless demanded that if you disapproved of the war too much to shoot Vietcong, then your draft card was for burning. But Mailer arrived at this conclusion somewhat used up as we have learned from the number of decisions he had to make at various moral crossroads en route and so felt no enthusiasm whatsoever for the preliminary demonstration at the Department of Justice tomorrow in which he would take part. To the contrary, he wondered if he would burn or surrender his own draft card if he were young enough to own one, and he did not really know the answer. How then could he advise others to take the action, or even associate his name? Still, he was going to be there.

He started to talk of these doubts with Lowell, but he could hear the sound of his own voice, and it offended him. It seemed weak, plaintive, as if his case were—no less incriminating word—phony, he did not quite know why. So he shut up.

A silence.

"You know, Norman," said Lowell in his fondest voice, "Elizabeth and I really think you're the finest journalist in America."

Mailer knew Lowell thought this—Lowell had even sent him a postcard once to state the enthusiasm. But the novelist had been shrewd enough to judge that Lowell sent many postcards to many people—it did not matter that Lowell was by overwhelming consensus judged to be the best, most talented, and most distinguished poet in America—it was still necessary to keep the defense lines in good working order. A good word on a card could keep many a dangerous recalcitrant in the ranks.

Therefore, this practice annoyed Mailer. The first card he'd ever received from Lowell was on a book of poems, *Deaths for the Ladies (and Other Disasters)* it had been called, and many people had thought the book a joke, which, whatever its endless demerits, it was not. Not to the novice poet at least. When Lowell had written that he liked the book, Mailer next waited for some word in print to canonize his thin tome; of course it never came. If Lowell were to begin to award living

American poets in critical print, two hundred starving worthies could with fairness hold out their bowl before the escaped Novelist would deserve his turn. Still, Mailer was irked. He felt he had been part of a literary game. When the second card came a few years later telling him he was the best journalist in America, he did not answer. Elizabeth Hardwick, Lowell's wife, had just published a review of *An American Dream* in *Partisan Review* that had done its best to disembowel the novel. Lowell's card might have arrived with the best of motives, but its timing suggested to Mailer an exercise in neutralsmanship—neutralize the maximum of possible future risks. Mailer was not critically equipped for the task, but there was always the distant danger that some bright and not unauthoritative voice, irked at Lowell's enduring hegemony, might come along with a long lance and presume to tell America that posterity would judge Allen Ginsberg the greater poet.

This was all doubtless desperately unfair to Lowell who, on the basis of two kind cards, was now judged by Mailer to possess an undue un-Christian talent for literary logrolling. But then Mailer was prickly. Let us hope it was not because he had been beaten a little too often by book reviewers, since the fruit of specific brutality is general suspicion.

Still Lowell now made the mistake of repeating his remark. "Yes, Norman, I really think you are the best journalist in America."

The pen may be mightier than the sword, yet at their best, each belong to extravagant men. "Well, Cal," said Mailer, using Lowell's nickname for the first time, "there are days when I think of myself as being the best writer in America."

The effect was equal to walloping a roundhouse right into the heart of an English boxer who has been hitherto right up on his toes. Consternation, not Britannia, now ruled the waves. Perhaps Lowell had a moment when he wondered who was guilty of declaring war on the minuet. "Oh, Norman, oh, certainly," he said, "I didn't mean to imply, heavens no, it's just I have such *respect* for good journalism."

"Well, I don't know that I do," said Mailer. "It's much harder to write"—the next said with great and false graciousness—"a good poem."

"Yes, of course."

Chuckles. Headmastersmanship.

Chuckles. Fellow headmastersmanship.

They were both now somewhat spoiled for each other. Mailer got up abruptly to get a drink. He was shrewd enough to know that Lowell, like many another aristocrat before him, respected abrupt departures. The pain of unexpected rejection is the last sweet vice left to an aristocrat (unless they should happen to be not aristocrats but secret monarchs—then watch for your head!).

Next, Mailer ran into Paul Goodman at the bar—a short sentence that contains two errors and a misrepresentation. The assumption is that Goodman was drinking alcohol but he was not; by report, Goodman never took a drink. The bar, so-called, was a table with a white tablecloth, set up near the archway between the dining room, where Lowell and Mailer had been talking, and the living room, where most of the party was being enacted—to the tune of ten couples perhaps— so the bar did not qualify as a bar, just a poor table with a cloth to support Mailer's irritated eye. Finally he did not run into Goodman. Goodman and Mailer had no particular love for one another—they tended to slide about each other at a party. In fact, they hardly knew each other.

Their lack of cordiality had begun on the occasion of a piece written by Goodman for *Dissent* that had discussed Washington in the early days of the Kennedy administration. Goodman had found much to displease him then, and kept referring to the "wargasms" of this Kennedy administration, which wargasms he attached with no excessive intellectual jugglery to the existential and Reichian notions of the orgasm that Mailer had promulgated in his piece *The White Negro*. (Goodman was a sexologue—that is, an ideologue about sex. Mailer was then also a sexologue; no war so rich without quarter as the war between two sexologues.) Goodman, at any rate, had scored off Mailer almost at will, something to the general effect that the false prophet of the orgasm was naturally attached to the false hero of Washington who went in for wargasms. Writing for a scholarly Socialist quarterly like *Dissent*, it was hard to miss. The magnetic field of *Dissent*—hostile to Kennedy at the time—bent every wild shot to the target. So Mailer wrote a letter in reply. It was short, sought to be urbane, and was delivered exactly to the jugular, for it began by asserting that he could not judge the merits of Goodman's intellectual points since the other had made a cardinal point of emphasizing Mailer's own incapacity to reason and Goodman was doubtless correct, but Mailer did nonetheless feel competent to comment on the literary experience of encountering Goodman's style and that was not unrelated to the journeys one undertook in the company of a laundry bag . . . Great ferment in scholarly Socialist quarters! A small delegation of the Editors assured Mailer they would print his letter if he insisted, but the hope was that he would not. Mailer had always thought it senseless to undertake an attack unless you made certain it was printed, for otherwise you were left with a determined enemy who was an unmarked man, and therefore able to repay you at leisure and by the lift of an eyebrow. Mailer acceded, however. He was fond of the Editors of *Dissent,* although his private mixture of Marxism, conservatism, nihilism, and large parts of existentialism could no longer produce any polemical gravies for the digestive apparatus of scholarly Socialist minds—nonetheless Mailer had never been asked to leave the Board, and would not have resigned on his own since that would have suggested a public attack on the ideas of people with whom he had no intellectual accord but of whom he was personally fond.

Nonetheless, from that day, Mailer and Goodman slid around one another at parties and waved languid hands in greeting. It was just as well. Each seemed to have the instinct a discussion would use up intellectual ordnance best reserved for articles. Besides, they had each doubtless read very little of the other.

Mailer, of course, was not without respect for Goodman. He thought Goodman had had an enormous influence in the colleges and much of it had been, from his own point of view, very much to the good. Paul Goodman had been the first to talk of the absurd and empty nature of work and education in America, and a generation of college students had formed around the core of his militancy. But, oh, the style! It set Mailer's teeth on edge to read it—he was inclined to think that the body of students who followed Goodman must have something de-animalized to put up with the style, or at least such was Mailer's bigoted view. His fundamental animus to Goodman was still, unhappily, on sex. Goodman's ideas tended to declare in rough that heterosexuality, homosexuality, and onanism were equal valid forms of activity, best denuded of guilt. Mailer, with his neo-Victorianism, thought that if there was anything worse than homosexuality and masturbation, it was putting the two together. The super-hygiene of all this mental prophylaxis offended him profoundly. Super-hygiene impregnated the air with medicated Vaseline—there was nothing dirty in the damn stuff; and sex to Mailer's idea of it was better off dirty, damned, even slavish! than clean, and without guilt. For guilt was the existential edge of sex. Without guilt, sex was meaningless. One advanced into sex against one's sense of guilt, and each time guilt was successfully defied, one had learned a little more about the contractual relation of one's own existence to the unheard thunders of the deep—each time guilt herded one back with its authority, some primitive awe—hence some creative clue to the rages of the deep—was left to brood about. Onanism and homosexuality were not, to

Mailer, light vices—to him it sometimes seemed that much of life and most of society were designed precisely to drive men deep into onanism and homosexuality. One defied such a fate by sweeping up the psychic profit that derived from the existential assertion of one-self—which was a way of saying that nobody was born a man: Manhood was earned provided you were good enough, bold enough.

This most conservative and warlike credo could hardly have meaning to a scientific humanist like Goodman, for whom all obstacles to the good life derived precisely from guilt: guilt, which was invariably so irrational—for it derived from the warped burden of the past. Goodman therefore said hello mildly to Mailer, who answered in as mild a voice, and that was all they had to say. Lowell, following, expressed his condolences to Goodman on the recent death of his son, and Mailer, after depressing the hostess by his refusal to eat, went on to talk to Macdonald.

That was most brief. They were old friends who had a somewhat comic relation, for Macdonald—at least as Mailer saw it—was forever disapproving of the younger author until the moment they came together at one or another party or meeting. Then Macdonald would discover he was glad to see Mailer. In fact, Macdonald could hardly help himself. Of all the younger American writers, Mailer was the one who had probably been influenced most by Macdonald, not so much from the contents of Macdonald's ideas, which were always going in and out of phase with Mailer's, but rather by the style of Macdonald's attack. Macdonald was forever referring the act of writing to his sense of personal standards, which demanded craft, care, devotion, lack of humbug, and simple *a fortiori* honesty of sentiment. All this was a little too simple for Mailer's temper. Nonetheless, Macdonald had given him an essential clue, which was: Look to the feel of the phenomenon. If it feels bad, it *is* bad. Mailer could have learned this as easily from Hemingway, as many another novelist had, but he had begun as a young ideologue—his mind had been militant with positions fixed in concrete—and Macdonald's method had worked like Zen for him—at the least it had helped to get his guns loose. Macdonald had given the hint that the clue to discovery was not in the substance of one's idea but in what was learned from the style of one's attack. (Which was one reason Mailer's style changed for every project.) So, the younger author was unquenchably fond of Macdonald, and it showed. Not a minute would go by before he would be poking Macdonald's massive belly with a finger.

But for now, they were ill at ease. Macdonald was in the process of reviewing Mailer's new novel *Why Are We in Vietnam?* for *The New*

*Yorker*, and there was an empty space in the presence of the mood. Mailer was certain Macdonald did not like the new novel, and was going to do a negative review. He had seemed professionally unfriendly these past few weeks. The Novelist would have liked to assure the Critic that the review could not possibly affect their good feeling for one another, but he did not dare, for such a remark would break a rule, since it would encourage Macdonald to talk about what was in his review, or at worst trick him into an unwilling but revealing reply. Besides, Mailer did not trust himself to speak calmly about the matter. Although Macdonald would not admit it, he was in secret carrying on a passionate love affair with *The New Yorker*—Disraeli on his knees before Victoria. But the Novelist did not share Macdonald's infatuation at all—*The New Yorker* had not printed a line in review of *The Presidential Papers, An American Dream,* or *Cannibals and Christians,* and *that,* Mailer had long ago decided, was an indication of some of the worst things to be said about the magazine. He had once had a correspondence with Lillian Ross, who asked him why he did not do a piece for *The New Yorker.* "Because they would not let me use the word *shit,*" he had written back. Miss Ross suggested that all liberty was his if only he understood where liberty resided. True liberty, Mailer had responded, consisted of his right to say *shit* in *The New Yorker.* So there was old rage behind the arms-length bantering about Dwight's review of Norman's book, and Mailer finally left the conversation. Macdonald was beginning to like him again, and that was dangerous. Macdonald was so full of the very beans of that old-time Wasp integrity that he would certainly bend over much too far backward if for a moment while reviewing the book he might have the thought he was sufficiently fond of Norman to conceivably be giving him too-gentle treatment. No, thought the Novelist, let him keep thinking he disapproves of me until the review is written.

Among his acquaintances at the party, this now left de Grazia. They were old friends of the most superficial sort, which is to say that they hardly knew each other and yet always felt like old friends when they met. Perhaps it was no more than the ability of each man to inspire an odd sense of intimacy. At any rate they never wasted time in needless conversation, since they were each too clever about the other to be penned in position by an evasion.

"How would you like to be the first speaker of the evening?" de Grazia asked.

"There'll be nothing interesting to follow me."

De Grazia's eyes showed pleasure. "Then I thought of starting with Macdonald."

"Dwight is conceivably the world's worst speaker." It was true. Macdonald's authority left him at the entrance to the aura of the podium. In that light he gesticulated awkwardly, squinted at his text, laughed at his own jokes, looked like a giant stork, whinnied, shrilled, and was often inaudible. When he spoke extempore, he was sometimes better, often worse.

"Well," said de Grazia, "I can't start with Lowell."

"No, no, no, you must save him."

"That leaves Goodman."

They nodded wisely. "Yes, let's get rid of Goodman first," said Mailer. But then the thought of that captive audience tuned to their first awareness of the evening by the pious drone of Goodman's voice injured every showman's instinct for the opening. "Who is going to be M.C.?" Mailer asked.

"Unless you want to, I thought I might be."

"I've never been an M.C.," said Mailer, "but maybe I should be. I could warm the audience up before Goodman drops them." De Grazia looked uneasily at Mailer's bourbon. "For Christ's sakes, Ed," said Mailer.

"Well, all right," said de Grazia.

Mailer was already composing his introductory remarks, percolating along on thoughts of the subtle annoyance his role as Master of Ceremonies would cause the other speakers.

# Toward a Theater of Ideas

The guests were beginning to leave the party for the Ambassador, which was two blocks away. Mailer did not know this yet, but the audience there had been waiting almost an hour. They were being entertained by an electronic folk rock guitar group, so presumably the young were more or less happy, and the middle-aged, dim. Mailer was feeling the high sense of clarity that accompanies the light show of the aurora borealis when it is projected upon the inner universe of the chest, the lungs, and the heart. He was happy. On leaving, he had appropriated a coffee mug and filled it with bourbon. The fresh air illumined the bourbon, gave it a cerebrative edge; words entered his brain with the agreeable authority of fresh minted coins. Like all good professionals, he was stimulated by the chance to try a new if related line of work. Just as professional football players love sex because it is so close to football, so he was fond of speaking in public because it was thus near to writing. An extravagant analogy? Consider that a good half of writing consists of being sufficiently sensitive to the moment to reach for the next promise hidden in some word or phrase just a shift to the side of one's conscious intent. (Consciousness, that blunt tool, bucks in the general direction of the truth; instinct plucks the feather. Cheers!) Where public speaking is an exercise from prepared texts to demonstrate how successfully a low order of consciousness can beat upon the back of a collective flesh, public speaking being, therefore, a sullen expression of human possibility metaphorically equal to a bugger on his victim, speaking-in-public (as Mailer liked to describe any speech that was more or less improvised, impromptu, or dangerously written) was an activity like writing—one had to trick or seize or submit to the grace of each moment, which, except for those unexpected and sometimes well-deserved moments when consciousness and grace came together (and one felt on the consequence, heroic), were usually occasions of some mystery. The pleasure of speaking in public was the sensitivity it offered: With every phrase one was better or worse, close or less close to the existential promise of truth, *it feels true,* which hovers on good occasions like a presence between speaker and audience. Sometimes one was better and worse at the same moment; so strategic choices on the continuation of the attack would soon have to be decided, a moment to know the blood of the gambler in oneself.

Intimations of this approaching experience, obviously one of Mailer's preferred pleasures in life, at least when he did it well, were now connected to the professional sense of intrigue at the new task: Tonight he would be both speaker and Master of Ceremonies. The two would conflict, but interestingly. Already he was looking in his mind for kind, even celebrative, remarks about Paul Goodman that would not violate every reservation he had about Goodman's dank glory. But he had it. It would be possible with no violation of truth to begin by saying that the first speaker looked very much like Nelson Algren, because in fact the first speaker was Paul Goodman, and both Nelson Algren and Paul Goodman looked like old cons. Ladies and Gentlemen, without further ado let me introduce one of young America's favorite old cons, Paul Goodman! (It would not be necessary to add that where Nelson Algren looked like the sort of skinny old con who was in on every make in the joint and would sign away Grandma's farm to stay in the game, Goodman looked like the sort of old con who had first gotten into trouble in the YMCA and hadn't spoken to anyone since.)

All this while, Mailer had in clutch *Why Are We in Vietnam?* He had neglected to bring his own copy to Washington and so had borrowed the book from his hostess on the promise he would inscribe it. (Later he was actually to lose it—working apparently on the principle that if you cannot make a hostess happy, the next best charity is to be so evil that the hostess may dine out on tales of your misconduct.) But the copy of the book is now noted because Mailer, holding it in one hand and the mug of whiskey in the other, was obliged to notice on entering the Ambassador Theater that he had an overwhelming urge to micturate. The impulse to pass urine, being for some reason more difficult to restrain when both hands are occupied, there was no thought in the Master of Ceremonies' mind about the alternatives—he would have to find The Room before he went on stage.

That was not so immediately simple as one would have thought. The twenty guests from the party, looking a fair piece subdued under the fluorescent lights, had therefore the not unhaggard look of people who have arrived an hour late at the theater. No matter that the theater was by every evidence sleazy, no matter the guests had the uneasiness of very late arrivals. Apologetic, they were therefore in haste for the speakers to begin.

Mailer did not know this. He was off already in search of The Room, which, it developed, was up on the balcony floor. Imbued with the importance of his first gig as Master of Ceremonies, he felt such incandescence of purpose that he could not quite conceive it necessary to notify de Grazia he would be gone for a minute. Incandescence is the *satori* of the Romantic spirit, which spirit would assume that everyone understands exactly what he is about to do, therefore waste not a moment by stopping to tell them.

Flush with his incandescence, happy in all the anticipations of liberty this Götterdämmerung of a urination was soon to provide, Mailer did not know, but he had already metamorphosed into the Beast. Wait and see!

He was met on the stairs by a young man from *Time* magazine, a stringer presumably, for the young man lacked that I-am-damned look in the eye and rep tie of those whose work for *Time* has become a life addiction. The young man had a somewhat ill-dressed look, a map showed on his skin of an old adolescent acne, and he gave off the unhappy furtive presence of a fraternity member on probation for the wrong thing, some grievous mis-deposit of vomit, some hanky panky with frat-house tickets.

But the Beast was in a great good mood. He was soon to speak; that was food for all. So the Beast greeted the *Time* man with the geniality of a surrogate Hemingway unbending for the Luce-ites (Loosights was the pun), made some genial cryptic remark or two about finding Herr John, said cheerfully in answer to why he was in Washington that he had come to protest the war in Vietnam, and, taking a sip of bourbon from the mug he kept to keep all fires idling right, stepped off into the darkness of the top balcony floor, went through a door into a pitch-black men's room, and was alone with his need. No chance to find the light switch for he had no matches, he did not smoke. It was therefore a matter of locating what's what with the probing of his toes. He found something finally that seemed appropriate, and pleased with the precision of these generally unused senses in his feet, took aim between them at a point twelve inches ahead, and heard in the darkness the sound of his water striking the floor. Some damn mistake had been made, an assault from the side doubtless instead of the front, the bowl was relocated now, and Master of Ceremonies breathed deep of the great reveries of this utterly non-Sisyphian release—at last!—and thoroughly enjoyed the next forty-five seconds, being left on the aftermath not a note depressed by the condition of the premises. No, he was off on the Romantic's great military dream, which is: Seize defeat, convert it to triumph. Of course, pissing on the floor was bad—very bad; the attendant would probably gossip to the police (if the *Time* man did not sniff it out first) and The Uniformed in turn would report it to The Press, who were sure to write about the scandalous condition in which this meeting had left the toilets. And all of this contretemps merely because the management was now so pocked and stingy they doused the lights. (Out of such stuff is a novelist's brain.)

Well, he could convert this deficiency to an asset. From gap to gain is very American. He would confess straight out to all aloud that he was the one who wet the floor in the men's room, he alone! While the audience was recovering from the existential anxiety of encountering an orator who confessed to such a crime, he would be able—their attention now riveted—to bring them up to a contemplation of deeper problems, of, indeed, the deepest problems, the most chilling alternatives, and would from there seek to bring them back to a restorative view of man. Man might be a fool who peed in the wrong pot, man was also a scrupulous servant of the self-damaging admission—man was therefore a philosopher who possessed the magic stone. He could turn loss to philosophical gain, and so illumine the deeps, find the poles, and eventually learn to cultivate his most special fool's garden: *satori,* incandescence, and the hard gemlike flame of bourbon burning in the furnaces of metabolism.

Thus composed, illumined by these first stages of Emersonian transcendence, Mailer left the men's room, descended the stairs, entered the back of the orchestra, all opening remarks held close file in his mind like troops ranked in order before the parade, and then suddenly, most suddenly saw, with a cancerous swoop of albatross wings, that de Grazia was on the stage, was acting as M.C., was—no calling it back—launched into the conclusion of a gentle stammering stumbling—small orator, de Grazia!—introduction of Paul Goodman. All lost! The magnificent opening remarks about the forces gathered here to assemble on Saturday before the Pentagon, this historic occasion, let us hold it in our mind and focus on a puddle of passed water on the floor above and see if we assembled here can as leftists and proud dissenters contain within our minds the grandeur of the two—all lost!—no chance to do more than pick up later—later! after de Grazia and Goodman had finished dead-assing the crowd. Traitor de Grazia! Sicilian de Grazia!

As Mailer picked his way between people sitting on the stone floor (orchestra seats had been removed—the movie house was a dance hall now with a stage) he made a considerable stir in the orchestra. Mailer had been entering theaters for years, mounting stages—now that he had put on weight, it would probably have been fair to say that he came to the rostrum like a poor man's version of Orson Welles, some minor note of the same contemplative presence. A titter and rise of expectation followed him. He could not resist its appeal. As he passed de Grazia, he scowled, threw a look from Lower Shakespearia "Et tu Brute," and proceeded to slap the back of his hand against de Grazia's solar plexus. It was not a heavy blow, but then de Grazia was not a heavy man; he wilted some hint of an inch. And the audience pinched off a howl, squeaked on their squeal. It was not certain to them what had taken place.

Picture the scene two minutes later from the orchestra floor. Paul Goodman, now up at the microphone with no podium or rostrum, is reading the following lines:

> *. . . these days my contempt*
> *for the misrulers of my country*
> *is icy and my indignation raucous.*

It is impossible to tell what he is reading. Off at the wing of the stage where the others are collected—stout Macdonald, noble Lowell, beleaguered de Grazia, and Mailer, Prince of Bourbon—the acoustics are atrocious. One cannot hear a word the speaker is saying. Nor are there enough seats. If de Grazia and Macdonald are sitting in folding chairs, Mailer is squatting on his haunches, or kneeling on one knee like a player about to go back into the ball game. Lowell has the expression on his face of a dues payer who is just about keeping up with the interest on some enormous debt. As he sits on the floor with his long arms clasped mournfully about his long Yankee legs, "I am here," says his expression, "but I do not have to pretend I like what I see." The hollows in his cheeks give a hint of the hanging judge. Lowell is of a good weight, not too heavy, not too light, but the hollows speak of the great Puritan gloom in which the country was founded—man was simply not good enough for God.

At this moment, it is hard not to agree with Lowell. The cavern of the theater seems to resonate behind the glare of the footlights, but this is no resonance of a fine bass voice—it is rather electronics on the march. The public address system hisses, then rings in a random chorus of electronic music, sounds of cerebral mastication from some horror machine of Outer Space (where all that electricity doubtless comes from, child!), then a hum like the squeak in the hinges of the gates of Hell—we are in the penumbra of psychedelic netherworlds, ghostodysseys from the dead brain cells of adolescent trysts with LSD, some ultrapurple spotlight from the balcony (not ultraviolet—ultrapurple, deepest purple one could conceive) there out in the dark like some neon eye of the night, the media is the message, and the message is purple, speaks of the monarchies of Heaven, madnesses of God, and clamvaults of people on a stone floor. Mailer's senses are now tuned to absolute pitch or sheer error—he marks a ballot for absolute pitch—he is certain there is a profound pall in the audience. Yes, they sit there, stricken, inert, in terror of what Saturday will bring, and so are unable to rise to a word the speaker is offering them. It will take dynamite to bring life. The shroud of burned-out psychedelic dreams is in this audience, Cancer Gulch with open maw—and Mailer thinks of the vigor and the light (from marijuana?) in the eyes of those American soldiers in Vietnam who have been picked by the newsreel cameras to say their piece, and the happy healthy never unintelligent faces of all those professional football players he studies so assiduously on television come Sunday (he has neglected to put his bets in this week) and wonders how they would poll out on sentiment for the war.

HAWKS 95    DOVES 6

NFL FOOTBALLERS APPROVE VIETNAM WAR

Doubtless. All the healthy Marines, state troopers, professional athletes, movie stars, rednecks, sensuous life-loving Mafia, cops, mill workers, city officials, nice healthy-looking easy-grafting politicians full of the light (from marijuana?) in their eye of a life they enjoy—yes, they would be for the war in Vietnam. Arrayed against them as hard-core troops: an elite! the Freud-ridden embers of Marxism, good old American anxiety strata—the urban middle class with their proliferated monumental adenoidal resentments, their secret slavish love for the oncoming hegemony of the computer and the suburb, yes, they and their children, by the sheer ironies, the sheer ineptitude, the *kinks* of history, were now being compressed into more and more militant stands, their resistance to the war some hopeless melange, somehow firmed, of Pacifism and closet Communism. And their children—on a freak-out from the suburbs to a love-in on the Pentagon wall.

It was the children in whom Mailer had some hope, a gloomy hope. These mad middle-class children with their lobotomies from sin, their nihilistic embezzlement of all middle-class moral funds, their innocence, their lust for apocalypse, their unbelievable indifference to waste: twenty generations of buried hopes perhaps engraved in their chromosomes, and now conceivably burning like faggots in the secret inquisitional fires of LSD. It was a devil's drug—designed by the Devil to consume the love of the best, and leave them liver-wasted, weeds of the big city. If there had been a player piano, Mailer might have put in a quarter to hear "In the Heart of the City Which Has No Heart."

Yes, these were the troops: middle-class cancer-pushers and drug-gutted flower children. And Paul Goodman to lead them. Was he now reading this?

*Once American faces*
*were beautiful to me*
*but now they look cruel*
*and as if they had narrow thoughts.*

Not much poetry, but well-put prose. And yet there was always Goodman's damnable tolerance for all the varieties of sex. Did he know nothing of evil or entropy? Sex was the superhighway to your own soul's entropy if it was used without a constant sharpening of the taste. And orgies? What did Goodman know of orgies, real ones, not lib-lab college orgies to carry out the higher program of the Great Society, but real ones with murder in the air and witches on the shoulder? The collected Tory in Mailer came roaring to the surface like a cocked hat in a royal coach.

"When Goodman finishes, I'm going to take over as M.C.," he whispered to de Grazia. (The revery we have just attended took no more in fact than a second. Mailer's melancholy assessment of the forces now mounting in America took place between two consecutive lines of Goodman's poem—not because Mailer cerebrated that instantly, but because he had had the revery many a time before—he had to do no more than sense the audience, whisper Cancer Gulch to himself, and the revery went by with a mental ch-ch-ch Click! reviewed again.) In truth, Mailer was now in a state. He had been prepared to open the evening with apocalyptic salvos to announce the real gravity of the situation, and the intensely peculiar American aspect of it—which is that the urban and suburban middle class were to be offered on Saturday an opportunity for glory—what other nation could boast of such option for its middle class? Instead—lost. The benignity and good humor of his planned opening remarks now subjugated to the electronic hawking and squabbling and *hum* of the P.A., the maniacal necessity to *wait* was on this hiatus transformed into a violent concentration of purpose, all intentions reversed. He glared at de Grazia. "How could you do this?" he whispered to his ear.

De Grazia looked somewhat confused at the intensity. Meetings to de Grazia were obviously just meetings, assemblages of people who coughed up for large admissions or kicked in for the pitch; at best, some meetings were less boring than others. De Grazia was much too wise and guilty-spirited to brood on apocalypse. "I couldn't find you," he whispered back.

"You didn't trust me long enough to wait one minute?"

"We were over an hour late," de Grazia whispered again. "We had to begin."

Mailer was all for having the conversation right then on stage: to hell with reciprocal rights and polite incline of the ear to the speaker. The Beast was ready to grapple with the world. "Did you think I wouldn't show up?" he asked de Grazia.

"Well, I was wondering."

In what sort of mumbo-jumbo of promise and betrayal did de Grazia live? How could de Grazia ever suppose he would not show up? He had spent his life showing up at the most boring and onerous places. He gave a blast of his eyes to de Grazia. But Macdonald gave a look at Mailer, as if to say, "You're creating disturbance."

Now Goodman was done.

Mailer walked to the stage. He did not have any idea any longer of what he would say, his mind was empty, but in a fine calm, taking for these five instants a total rest. While there was no danger of Mailer ever becoming a demagogue, since if the first idea he offered could appeal to a mob, the second in compensation would be sure to enrage them, he might nonetheless have made a fair country orator, for he loved to speak, he loved in fact to holler, and liked to hear a crowd holler back. (Of how many New York intellectuals may that be said?)

"I'm here as your original M.C., temporarily displaced owing to a contretemps"—which was pronounced purposefully as contretempse— "in the men's room," he said into the microphone for opening, but the gentle high-strung beast of a device, pushed into a panic by the electric presence of a real Beast, let loose a squeal that shook the welds in the old foundation of the Ambassador. Mailer immediately decided he had had enough of public address systems, electronic fields of phase, impedance, and spooks in the circuitry. A hex on collaborating with Cancer Gulch. He pushed the microphone away, squared off before the audience. "Can you hear me?" he bellowed.

"Yes."

"Can you hear me in the balcony?"

"Yes."

"Then let's do away with electronics," he called out.

Cries of laughter came back. A very small pattern of applause. (Not too many on his side for electrocuting the public address system, or so his orator's ear recorded the vote.)

"Now I missed the beginning of this occasion or I would have been here to introduce Paul Goodman, for which we're all sorry, right?"

Confused titters. Small reaction.

"What are you, dead-heads?" he bellowed at the audience. "Or are you all"—here he put on his false Irish accent—"in the nature of becoming dead ahsses?" Small laughs. A whistle or two. "No," he said, replying to the whistles, "I invoke these dead asses as part of the gravity of the occasion. The middle class plus one hippie surrealistic symbolic absolutely insane March on the Pentagon, bless us all," beginning of a big applause that offended Mailer for it came on "bless" and that was too cheap a way to win votes, "bless us all—shit!" he shouted. "I'm trying to say the middle class plus shit, I mean plus revolution, is equal to one big collective dead ass." Some yells of approval, but much shocked curious rather stricken silence. He had broken the shank of his oratorical charge. Now he would have to sweep the audience together again. (Perhaps he felt like a surgeon delivering a difficult breech—nothing to do but plunge to the elbows again.)

"To resume our exposition," a good warm titter, then a ripple of laughter, not unsympathetic to his ear; the humor had been unwitting, but what was the life of an orator without some bonus? "To resume this orderly marshalling of concepts"—a conscious attempt at humor that worked less well; he was beginning to recognize for the first time that bellowing without a mike demanded a more forthright style—"I shall now *engage* in confession." More Irish accent. (He blessed Brendan Behan for what he had learned from him.) "A public speaker may offer you two opportunities. Instruction or confession." Laughter now. "Well, you're all college heads, so my instruction would be as pearls before—I dare not say it." Laughs. Boos. A voice from the balcony: "Come on, Norman, say something!"

"Is there a black man in the house?" asked Mailer. He strode up and down the stage pretending to peer at the audience. But in fact they were illumined just well enough to emphasize one sad discovery—if black faces there were, they were certainly not in plenty. "Well ah'll just have to be the *impromptu* Black Power for tonight. Woo-eeeeee! Woo-eeeeee! HMmmmmmm." He grunted with some partial success, showing hints of Cassius Clay. "Get your white butts moving."

"The confession. The confession!" screamed some adolescents from up front.

He came to a stop, shifted his voice. Now he spoke in a relaxed tone. "The confession, yeah!" Well, at least the audience was awake. He felt as if he had driven away some sepulchral phantoms. Now to charge the center of vested spookery.

"Say," he called out into the semidarkness with the ultrapurple light coming off the psychedelic lamp on the rail of the balcony, and the spotlights blaring against his eyes, "say," all happiness again, "I think of Saturday, and that March, and do you know, fellow carriers of the holy unendurable grail, for the first time in my life I don't know whether I have the piss or the shit scared out of me most." It was an interesting concept, thought Mailer, for there was a difference between the two kinds of fear—pursue the thought, he would, in quieter times—"we are up, face this, all of you, against an existential situation—we do not know how it is going to turn out, and what is even more inspiring of dread is that the government doesn't know either."

Beginning of a real hand, a couple of rebel yells. "We're going to try to stick it up the government's ass," he shouted, "right into the sphincter of the Pentagon." Wild yells and chills of silence from different reaches of the crowd. Yeah, he was cooking now. "Will reporters please get every word accurately," he called out dryly to warm the chill.

But humor may have been too late. *The New Yorker* did not have strictures against the use of sh*t for nothing—nor did Dwight Macdonald love *The New Yorker* for nothing; he also had strictures against sh*t's metaphorical associations. Mailer looked to his right to see Macdonald approaching, a book in his hands, arms at his sides, a sorrowing look of concern in his face. "Norman," said Macdonald quietly, "I can't possibly follow you after all this. Please introduce me, and get it over with."

Mailer was near to stricken. On the one hand interrupted on a flight; on the other, he had fulfilled no duty whatsoever as M.C. He threw a look at Macdonald that said: Give me this. I'll owe you one.

But de Grazia was there as well. "Norman, let me be M.C. now," he said.

They were being monstrous unfair, thought Mailer. They didn't understand what he had been doing, how good he had been, what he would do next. Fatal to walk off now—the verdict would claim he was unbalanced. Still, he could not hold the stage by force. That was unthinkably worse.

For the virtuous, however, deliverance (like buttercups) pops up everywhere. Mailer now took the microphone and turned to the audience. He was careful to speak in a relaxed voice. "We are having a disagreement about the value of the proceedings. Some think de Grazia should resume his post as Master of Ceremonies. I would like to keep the position. It is an existential moment. We do not know how it will turn out. So let us vote on it." Happy laughter from the audience at these comic effects. Actually Mailer did not believe it was an existential situation any longer. He reckoned the vote would be well in his favor. "Will those," he asked, "who are in favor of Mr. de Grazia succeeding me as Master of Ceremonies please say aye."

A good sound number said aye.

Now for the ovation. "Will those opposed to this, please say no." The no's to Mailer's lack of pleasure were no greater in volume. "It seems the ayes and no's are about equal," said Mailer. (He was thinking to himself that he had posed the issue all wrong—the ayes should have been reserved for those who would keep him in office.) "Under the circumstances," he announced, "I will keep the chair." Laughter at this easy cheek. He stepped into the middle of such laughter. "You have all just learned an invaluable political lesson." He waved the microphone at the audience. "In the absence of a definitive vote, the man who holds the power, keeps it."

"Hey, de Grazia," someone yelled from the audience, "why do you let him have it?"

Mailer extended the microphone to de Grazia, who smiled sweetly into it. "Because if I don't," he said in a gentle voice, "he'll beat the shit out of me." The dread word had been used again.

"Please, Norman," said Macdonald, retreating.

So Mailer gave his introduction to Macdonald. It was less than he would have attempted if the flight had not been grounded, but it was certainly respectable. Under the military circumstances, it was a decent cleanup operation. For about a minute he proceeded to introduce Macdonald as a man with whom one might seldom agree but could never disrespect because he always told the truth as he saw the truth, a man therefore of the most incorruptible integrity. "Pray heaven, I am right," said Mailer to himself, and walked past Macdonald, who was on his way to the mike. Both men nodded coolly to each other.

In the wing, visible to the audience, Paul Goodman sat on a chair clearly avoiding any contaminatory encounter with The Existentialist. De Grazia gave his "It's tough all over" smile. Lowell sat in a mournful hunch on the floor, his eyes peering over his glasses to scrutinize the metaphysical substance of his boot, now hide? now machine? now, where the joining and to what? foot to boot, boot to earth—cease all speculations as to what was in Lowell's head. "The one mind a novelist cannot enter is the mind of a novelist superior to himself," said once to Mailer by Jean Malaquais. So, by corollary, the one mind a minor poet may not enter . . .

Lowell looked most unhappy. Mailer, minor poet, had often observed that Lowell had the most disconcerting mixture of strength and weakness in his presence, a blending so dramatic in its visible sign of conflict that one had to assume he would be sensationally attractive to women. He had something untouchable, all insane in its force; one felt immediately there were any number of causes for which the man would be ready to die, and for some he would fight, with an axe in his hand and a Cromwellian light in his eye. It was even possible that physically he was very strong—one couldn't tell at all—he might be fragile, he might have the sort of farm mechanic's strength that could manhandle the rear axle and differential off a car and into the back of a pickup. But physical strength or no, his nerves were all too apparently delicate. Obviously spoiled by everyone for years, he seemed nonetheless to need the spoiling. These nerves—the nerves of a consummate poet—were not tuned to any battering. The squalls of the mike, now riding up a storm on the erratic piping breath of Macdonald's voice, seemed to tear along Lowell's back like a gale. He detested tumult—obviously. And therefore saw everything that was hopeless in a rife situation: the dank middle-class depths of the audience, the strident squalor of the mike, the absurdity of talent gathered to raise money—for what, dear God? who could finally know what this March might convey or, worse, purvey, and worst of all—to be associated now with Mailer's butcher boy attack. Lowell's eyes looked up from the shoe, and passed one withering glance by the novelist, saying much, saying, "Every single bad thing I have ever heard about you is not exaggerated."

Mailer, looking back, thought bitter words he would not say: "You, Lowell, beloved poet of many, what do you know of the dirt and the dark deliveries of the necessary? What do you know of dignity hard-achieved, and dignity lost through innocence, and dignity lost by sacrifice for a cause one cannot name. What do you know about getting fat against your will, and turning into a clown of an arriviste baron when you would rather be an eagle or a count or, rarest of all, some natural aristocrat from these damned democratic states. No, the only subject we share, you and I, is that species of perception which shows that if we are not very loyal to our unendurable and most exigent inner light, then some day we may burn. How dare you condemn me! You know the diseases that inhabit the audience in this accursed psychedelic house. How dare you scorn the explosive I employ?"

And Lowell with a look of the greatest sorrow as if all this *mess* were finally too shapeless for the hard Protestant smith of his own brain, which would indeed burst if it could not forge his experience into the iron edge of the very best words and the most unsinkable relation of words, now threw up his eyes like an epileptic as if turned out of orbit by a turn of the vision—and fell backward, his head striking the floor with no last instant hesitation to cushion the blow, but like a baby, downright sudden, savagely to himself, as if from the height of a foot he had taken a pumpkin and dropped it splat on the floor. "There, much-regarded, much-protected brain, you have finally taken a blow," Lowell might have said to himself, for he proceeded to lie there, resting quietly, while Macdonald went on reading from "The

White Man's Burden," Lowell seeming as content as if he had just tested the back of his cranium against a policeman's club. What a royal head they had all to lose!

# A Transfer of Power

The evening went on. It was in fact far from climax. Lowell, resting in the wing on the floor of the stage, Lowell recuperating from the crack he had given his head, was a dreamy figure of peace in the corner of the proscenium, a reclining shepherd contemplating his flute, although a Washington newspaper was to condemn him on Saturday in company with Mailer for "slobbish behavior" at this unseemly lounging.

Now Macdonald finished. What with the delays, the unmanageable public address system, and the choppy waters of the audience at his commencement, for Mailer had obviously done him no good, Macdonald had been somewhat less impressive than ever. A few people had shown audible boredom with him. (Old-line Communists perhaps. Dwight was by now one of the oldest anti-Communists in America.)

> *Take up the White Man's burden—*
> *Ye dare not stoop to less—*
> *Nor call too loud on Freedom*
> *To cloak your weariness;*
> *By all ye cry or whisper,*
> *By all ye leave or do,*
> *The silent, sullen peoples*
> *Shall weigh your Gods and you.*

read Macdonald from Kipling's poem, and the wit was in the selection, never the presentation.

He was done. He walked back to the wings with an air of no great satisfaction in himself, at most the sense of an obligation accomplished. Lowell's turn had arrived. Mailer stood up to introduce him.

The novelist gave a fulsome welcome to the poet. He did not speak of his poetry (with which he was not conspicuously familiar) nor of his prose, which he thought excellent—Mailer told instead of why he had respect for Lowell as a man. A couple of years ago, the poet had refused an invitation from President Johnson to attend a garden party for artists and intellectuals, and it had attracted much attention at the time for it was one of the first dramatic acts of protest against the war in Vietnam, and Lowell was the only invited artist of first rank who had refused. Saul Bellow, for example, had attended the garden party. Lowell's refusal could not have been easy, the novelist suggested, because artists were attracted to formal afternoons of such elevated kind since that kind of experience was often stimulating to new perception and new work. So, an honorific occasion in full panoply was not easy for the mature artist to eschew. Capital! Lowell had therefore bypassed the most direct sort of literary capital. Ergo, Mailer respected him—he could not be certain he would have done the same himself, although, of course, he assured the audience, he would not probably have ever had the opportunity to refuse. (Hints of merriment in the crowd at the thought of Mailer on the White House lawn.)

If the presentation had been formal up to here, it had also been somewhat graceless. On the consequence, our audience's amusement tipped the slumbering Beast. Mailer now cranked up a vaudeville clown for finale to Lowell's introduction. "Ladies and gentlemen, if novelists come from the middle class, poets tend to derive from the bottom and the top. We all know good poets at the bot'—ladies and gentlemen, here is a poet from the top, Mr. Robert Lowell." A large vigorous hand of applause, genuine enthusiasm for Lowell, some standing ovation.

But Mailer was depressed. He had betrayed himself again. The end of the introduction belonged in a burlesque house—he worked his own worst veins, like a man on the edge of bankruptcy trying to collect hopeless debts. He was fatally vulgar! Lowell passing him on the stage had recovered sufficiently to cast him a nullifying look. At this moment, they were obviously far from friends.

Lowell's shoulders had a slump, his modest stomach was pushed forward a hint, his chin was dropped to his chest as he stood at the microphone, pondering for a moment. One did not achieve the languid grandeurs of that slouch in one generation—the grandsons of the first sons had best go through the best troughs in the best eating clubs at Harvard before anyone in the family could try for such elegant note. It was now apparent to Mailer that Lowell would move by instinct, ability, and certainly by choice, in the direction most opposite from himself.

"Well," said Lowell softly to the audience, his voice dry and gentle as any New England executioner might ever hope to be, "this has been a zany evening." Laughter came back, perhaps a little too much. It was as if Lowell wished to reprove Mailer, not humiliate him. So he shifted, and talked a bit uneasily for perhaps a minute about very little. Perhaps it was too little. Some of the audience, encouraged by earlier examples, now whistled. "We can't hear you," they shouted, "speak louder."

Lowell was annoyed. "I'll bellow," he said, "but it won't do any good." His firmness, his distaste for the occasion, communicated some subtle but impressive sense of his superiority. Audiences are moved by many cues, but the most satisfactory to them is probably the voice of their abdomen. There are speakers who give a sense of security to the abdomen, and they always elicit the warmest kind of applause. Mailer was not this sort of speaker; Lowell was. The hand of applause that followed this remark was fortifying. Lowell now proceeded to read some poetry.

He was not a splendid reader, merely decent to his own lines, and he read from that slouch, that personification of ivy climbing a column, he was even diffident, he looked a trifle helpless under the lights. Still, he made no effort to win the audience, seduce them, dominate them, bully them, amuse them, no, they were there for him, to please *him,* a sounding board for the plucked string of his poetic line, and so he endeared himself to them. They adored him—for his talent, his modesty, his superiority, his melancholy, his petulance, his weakness, his painful, almost stammering shyness, his noble strength—*there* was the string behind other strings.

> *O to break loose, like the chinook*
> *salmon jumping and falling back,*
> *nosing up to the impossible*
> *stone and bone-crushing waterfall—*
> *raw-jawed, weak-fleshed there, stopped by ten*
> *steps of the roaring ladder, and then*
> *to clear the top on the last try,*
> *alive enough to spawn and die.*

Mailer discovered he was jealous. Not of the talent. Lowell's talent was very large, but then Mailer was a bulldog about the value of his own talent. No, Mailer was jealous because he had worked for this audience, and Lowell without effort seemed to have stolen them: Mailer did not know if he was contemptuous of Lowell for playing *grand maître* or admiring of his ability to do it. Mailer knew his own version of *grand maître* did not compare. Of course no one would be there to accept his version either. The pain of bad reviews was not in the sting but in the subsequent pressure that, like water on a joint, collected over the decade. People who had not read your books in fifteen years were certain they were missing nothing of merit. A buried sorrow, not very attractive (for bile was in it, and the bitterness of unrequited literary injustice), released itself from some ducts of the heart, and Mailer felt hot anger at how Lowell was loved and he was not, a pure and surprising recognition of how much emotion, how much simple and childlike bitter sorrowing emotion, had been concealed from himself for years under the manhole cover of his contempt for bad reviews.

> *Pity the planet, all joy gone*
> *from this sweet volcanic cone;*
> *peace to our children when they fall*
> *in small war on the heels of small*
> *war—until the end of time*
> *to police the earth, a ghost*
> *orbiting forever lost*
> *in our monotonous sublime.*

They gave Lowell a good standing ovation, much heartiness in it, much obvious pleasure that they were there on a night in Washington when Robert Lowell had read from his work—it was as nice as that—and then Lowell walked back to the wings, and Mailer walked forward. Lowell did not seem particularly triumphant. He looked still modest, still depressed, as if he had been applauded too much for too little and so the reservoir of guilt was still untapped.

Nonetheless, to Mailer it was now *mano a mano*. Once, on a vastly larger scale of applause, perhaps people had reacted to Manolete not unlike the way they reacted to Lowell, so stirred by the deeps of sorrow in the man that the smallest move produced the largest emotion. If there was any value to the comparison then Mailer was kin to the young Dominguin, taking raucous chances, spitting in the eye of the bull, an excess of variety in his passes. But probably there was no parallel at all. He may have felt like a matador in the flush of full competition, going out to do his work after the other torero has had a triumph, but for fact he was probably less close in essence now to the bullfighter than the bull. We must not forget the Beast. He had been sipping the last of the bourbon out of the mug. He had been delayed, piqued, twisted from his purpose, and without anything to eat in close to ten hours. He was on the hunt. For what, he hardly knew. It is possible the hunt existed long before the victim was ever conceived.

"Now, you may wonder who I am," he said to the audience, or bellowed to them, for again he was not using the mike, "and you may wonder why I'm talking in a Southern accent which is phony"—the Southern accent, as it sounded to him in his throat, was actually not too bad at this moment—"and the reason is that I want to make a presentation to you." He did not have a notion of what he would say next, but it never occurred to him something would not come. His impatience, his sorrow, his jealousy were gone, he just wanted to live on the edge of that rhetorical sword he would soon try to run through the heart of the audience. "We are gathered here"—shades of Lincoln in hippieland—"to make a move on Saturday to invest the Pentagon and halt and slow down its workings, and this will be at once a symbolic act and a real act"—he was roaring—"for real heads may possibly get hurt, and soldiers will be there to hold us back, and some of us may be arrested"—how, wondered the wise voice at the rear of this roaring voice, could one ever leave Washington now without going to jail?— "some blood conceivably will be shed. If I were the man in the government responsible for controlling this March, I would not know what to do." Sonorously—"I would not wish to arrest too many or hurt anyone for fear the repercussions in the world would be too large for my bureaucrat's heart to bear—it's so full of shit." Roars and chills from the audience again. He was off into obscenity. It gave a heartiness like the blood of beef tea to his associations. There was no villainy in obscenity for him, just—paradoxically, characteristically—his love for America: He had first come to love America when he served in the U.S. Army, not the America of course of the flag, the patriotic unendurable fix of the television programs, and the newspapers, no, long before he was ever aware of the institutional oleo of the most suffocating American ideas he had come to love what editorial writers were fond of calling the democratic principle, with its faith in the common man. He found that principle and that man in the Army, but what none of the editorial writers ever mentioned was that the noble common man was obscene as an old goat, and his obscenity was what saved him. The sanity of said common democratic man was in his humor, his humor was in his obscenity. And his philosophy as well—a reductive philosophy that looked to restore the hard edge of proportion to the overblown values overhanging each small military existence—viz.: being forced to salute an overconscientious officer with your back stiffened into an exaggerated posture. "That Lieutenant is chickenshit," would be the platoon verdict, and a blow had somehow been struck for democracy and the sanity of good temper. Mailer once heard a private end an argument about the merits of a general by saying, "His spit don't smell like ice cream either," only the private was not speaking of spit. Mailer thought enough of the line to put it into *The Naked and the Dead,* along with a good many other such lines the characters in his mind and his memory of the Army had begun to offer him. The common discovery of America was probably that Americans were the first people on earth to live for their humor—nothing was so important to Americans as humor. In Brooklyn, he had taken this for granted, at Harvard he had thought it was a by-product of being at Harvard, but in the Army he discovered that the humor was probably in the veins and the roots of the local history of every state and county in America—the truth of the way it really felt over the years passed on a river of obscenity from small-town story-teller to storyteller there down below the bankers and the books and the educators and the legislators—so Mailer never felt more like an American than when he was naturally obscene—all the gifts of the American language came out in the happy play of obscenity upon concept, which enabled one to go back to concept again. What was magnificent about the word *shit* is that it enabled you to use the word *noble:* a skinny Southern cracker with a beatific smile on his face saying in the dawn in a Filipino rice paddy, "Man, I just managed to take me a noble shit." Yeah, that was Mailer's America. If he was going to love something in the country, he would love that. So after years of keeping obscene language off to one corner of his work, as if to prove after *The Naked and the Dead* that he had many an arrow in his literary quiver, he had come back to obscenity again in the last year—he had kicked goodbye in his novel *Why Are We in Vietnam?* to the old literary corset of good taste, letting his sense of language play on obscenity as freely as it wished, so discovering that everything he knew about the American language (with its incommensurable resources) went flying in and out of the line of his prose with the happiest beating of wings—it was the first time his style seemed at once very American to him and very literary in the best way, at least as he saw the best way. But the reception of the book had been disappointing. Not because many of the reviews were bad (he had learned, despite all sudden discoveries of sorrow, to live with that as one lived with smog), no, what was disappointing was the crankiness across the country. Where fusty conservative old critics had once defended the obscenity in *The Naked and the Dead,* they, or their sons, now condemned it in the new book, and that *was* disappointing. The country was not growing up so much as getting a premature case of arthritis.

At any rate, he had come to the point where he liked to use a little obscenity in his public speaking. Once people got over the shock, they were sometimes able to discover that the humor it provided was not less powerful than the damage of the pain. Of course he did not do it often and he tried not to do it unless he was in good voice— Mailer was under no illusion that public speaking was equal to candid conversation; an obscenity uttered in a voice too weak for its freight was obscene, since obscenity probably resides in the quick conversion of excitement to nausea—which is why Lyndon Johnson's speeches are called obscene by some. The excitement of listening to the American President alters abruptly into the nausea of wandering down the blind alleys of his voice.

This has been a considerable defense of the point, but then the point was at the center of his argument and it could be put thus: The American corporation executive, who was after all the foremost representative of Man in the world today, was perfectly capable of burning unseen women and children in the Vietnamese jungles yet felt a large displeasure and fairly final disapproval at the generous use of obscenity in literature and in public.

The apology may now be well taken, but what in fact did Mailer say on the stage of the Ambassador before the evening was out? Well, not so very much, just about enough to be the stuff of which footnotes are made, for he did his best to imitate a most high and executive voice.

"I had an experience as I came to the theater to speak to all of you, which is that before appearing on this stage I went upstairs to the men's room as a prelude to beginning this oratory so beneficial to all"—laughs and catcalls—"and it was dark, so—ahem—I missed the bowl—all men will know what I mean. Forgiveness might reign. But tomorrow, they will blame that puddle of water on Communists, which is the way we do things here in Amurrica, anyone of you pinko poos want to object, lemme tell ya, the reason nobody was in the men's room, and it so dark, is that if there been a light they'd had to put a CIA man in there and the hippies would grope him silly, see here, you know who I am, why it just came to me, ah'm so phony, I'm as full of shit as Lyndon Johnson. Why, man, I'm nothing but his little old alter ego. That's what you got right here working for you, Lyndon Johnson's little old *dwarf* alter ego. How you like him? How you like him?" (Shades of Cassius Clay again.)

And in the privacy of his brain, quiet in the glare of all that sound and spotlight, Mailer thought quietly, My God, that is probably exactly what you are at this moment, Lyndon Johnson with all his sores, sorrows, and vanity, squeezed down to five foot eight, and Mailer felt for the instant possessed, as if he had seized some of the President's secret soul, or the President seized some of his—the bourbon was as luminous as moonshine to the spores of insanity in the flesh of his brain, a smoke of menace swished in the air, and something felt real, almost as if he had caught Lyndon Johnson by the toe and now indeed, bugger the rhyme, should never let him go.

"Publicity hound," shouted someone from the upper balcony.

"Fuck you," cried Mailer back with absolute delight, all the force of the Texas presidency in his being. Or was it Lucifer's fire? But let us use asterisks for these obscenities to emphasize how happily he used the words, they went off like fireworks in his orator's heart, and asterisks look like rocket-bursts and the orbs from Roman candles ***. F*ck you he said to the heckler but with such gusto the vowel was doubled. F*-*ck you! was more like it. So, doubtless, had the President disposed of all opposition in private session. Well, Mailer was here to bring the presidency to the public.

"This yere dwarf alter ego has been telling you about his imbroglio with the p*ssarooney up on the top floor, and will all the reporters please note that I did not talk about defecation commonly known as sheeee-it!"—full imitation of LBJ was attempted there— "but to the contrary, speak of you-rye-nation! I p*ssed on the floor. Hoo-ee! Hoo-ee! How's that for Black Power full of white p*ss? You just know all those reporters are going to say it was sh*t tomorrow. F*ck them. F*ck all of them. Reporters, will you stand up and be counted?"

A wail of delight from the students in the audience. What would the reporters do? Would they stand?

One lone figure arose.

"Where are *you* from?" asked Mailer.

"Washington *Free Press.*" A roar of delight from the crowd. It was obviously some student or hippie paper.

"Ah want *The Washington Post,*" said Mailer in his best Texas tones, "and the *Star.* Ah know there's a *Time* magazine man here for one, and twenty more like him no doubt." But no one stood. So Mailer went into a diatribe. "Yeah, people," he said, "watch the reporting that follows. Yeah, these reporters will kiss Lyndon Johnson's *ss and Dean Rusk's *ss and Man Mountain McNamara's *ss, they will rush to kiss it, but will they stand up in public? No! Because they are the silent assassins of the Republic. They alone have done more to destroy this nation than any force in it." They will certainly destroy me in the morning, he was thinking. But it was for this moment worth it, as if two very different rivers, one external, one subjective, had come together; the frustrated bile, piss, pus, and poison he had felt at the progressive contamination of all American life in the abscess of Vietnam, all of that, all heaped in lighted coals of brimstone on the press' collective ear, represented one river, and the other was the frustrated actor in Mailer—ever since seeing *All the King's Men* years ago he had wanted to come on in public as a Southern demagogue.

The speech went on, and a few fine things possibly were said next to a few equally obscene words, and then Mailer thought in passing of reading a passage from *Why Are We in Vietnam?* But the passage was full of plays of repetition on the most famous four-letter word of them all, and Mailer thought that was conceivably redundant now and so he ended modestly with a final "See you on Saturday!"

The applause was fair. Not weak, but empty of large demonstration. No standing ovation for certain. He felt cool, and in a quiet, pleasant, slightly depressed mood. Since there was not much conversation between Macdonald, Lowell, and himself, he turned after a moment, left the stage, and walked along the floor where the audience had sat. A few people gathered about him, thanked him, shook his hand. He was quiet and reserved now, with genial slightly muted attempts to be cordial. He had noticed this shift in mood before, even after readings or lectures that had been less eventful. There was a mutual embarrassment between speaker and audience once the speaker had left the stage and walked through the crowd. It was due no doubt to the intimacy—that most special intimacy—that can live between a speaker and the people he has addressed, yes they had been so intimate then that the encounter now, afterward, was like the eye-to-the-side maneuvers of client and whore once the act is over and dressing is done.

Mailer went on from there to a party of more liberal academics, and drank a good bit more and joked with Macdonald about the superiority of the introduction he had given to Lowell over the introduction Dwight had received.

"Next time don't interrupt me," he teased Macdonald, "and I'll give you a better introduction."

"Goodness, I couldn't hear a word you said," said Macdonald, "you just sounded awful. Do you know, Norman, the acoustics were terrible on the wing. I don't think any of us heard anything anyone else said."

Some time in the early morning, or not so early, Mailer got to bed at the Hay-Adams and fell asleep to dream no doubt of fancy parties in Georgetown when the Federal period in architecture was young. Of course if this were a novel, Mailer would spend the rest of the night with a lady. But it is history, and so the Novelist is for once blissfully removed from any description of the hump-your-backs of sex. Rather he can leave such matters to the happy or unhappy imagination of the reader.

# The Marshal and the Nazi

They put him in the rear seat of a Volkswagen camper and he welcomed the opportunity to relax. Soon they would drive him, he guessed, to some nearby place where he would be arraigned.

Now a new man entered the Volkswagen. Mailer took him at first for a Marshal or an official, since he was wearing a dark suit and a white motorcycle helmet, and had a clean-cut stubborn face with short features. But he was carrying something that looked like a rolled-up movie screen over five feet long, and he smiled in the friendliest fashion, sat down next to Mailer, and took off his helmet. Mailer thought he was about to be interrogated and he looked forward to that with this friendly man, no less! (of course the prisoner often looks forward to his interrogation) but then another man carrying a clipboard came up to them and, leaning through the wide double door of the camper, asked questions of them both. When Mailer gave his name, the man with the clipboard acted as if he had never heard of him, or at least pretended never to have heard of him, the second possibility seeming possible since word traveled quickly from reporters.

"How do you spell it?"

"M.A.I.L.E.R."

"Why were you arrested, Mr. Miller?"

"For transgressing a police line as a protest against the war in Vietnam."

The Clipboard then asked a question of the man sitting next to him. "And why were *you* arrested?"

"As an act of solidarity with oppressed forces fighting for liberty against this country in Southeast Asia."

The Clipboard nodded dryly, as if to say, "Yeah, we're all crazy here." Then he asked, pointing to the object that looked like a rolled-up movie screen, "You want that with you?"

"Yessir," said the man next to Mailer. "I'd like to take it along."

The Clipboard gave a short nod, and walked off. Mailer would never see him again. If the History has therefore spent a pointless exchange with him, it is to emphasize that the first few minutes of an arrest such as this are without particular precedent, and so Mailer, like a visitor from Mars, or an adolescent entering polite society, had no idea of what might be important next and what might not. This condition of innocence was not, however, particularly disagreeable since it forced him to watch everything with the attention, let us say, of a man like William Buckley spending his first hour in a Harlem bar—no, come! things are far safer for Mailer at the Pentagon.

He chatted with his fellow prisoner, Teague, Walter Teague was the name, who had been in the vanguard of the charge Mailer had seen from the parking lot. But before any confused impressions were to be sorted, they were interrupted by the insertion of the next prisoner put into the Volkswagen, a young man with straight blond hair and a Nazi armband on his sleeve. He was installed in the rear, with a table between, but Mailer was not happy, for his eyes and the Nazi's bounced off each other like two heads colliding—the novelist discovered he was now in a hurry for them to get this stage of the booking completed. He was also privately indignant at the U.S. Army (like a private citizen, let us say, who writes a letter to his small-town newspaper) at the incredible stupidity of putting a Nazi in the same Volkswagen camper with Pentagon demonstrators—there were two or three other cars available, at least!—next came the suspicion that this was not an accident but a provocation in the making. If the Nazi started trouble, and there was a fight, the newspaper accounts would doubtless state that Norman Mailer had gotten into an altercation five minutes after his arrest. (Of course, they would not say with whom.) This is all doubtless most paranoid of Mailer, but then he had had nearly twenty years of misreporting about himself, and the seed of paranoia is the arrival of the conviction that the truth about oneself is never told. (Mailer might have done better to pity the American populace—receiving misinformation in systematic form tends to create mass schizophrenia: Poor America—Eddie and Debbie are True Love.)

Now they were moved out of the camper and over to an Army truck. There was Teague, and the novelist, and another arrestee—a tall Hungarian, who quickly told Mailer how much he liked his books and in much the same breath that he was a Freedom Fighter—there was also a new U.S. Marshal, and the Nazi. The prisoners climbed one by one over the high tailgate, Mailer finding it a touch awkward, for he did not wish to dirty his dark blue pinstripe suit, and then they stood in the rear of the truck, a still familiar 2½-ton 6-by of a sort that the novelist hadn't been in for twenty-one years, not since his Army discharge.

Standing in the truck, a few feet apart from each other, all prisoners regarding one another, the Nazi fixed on Mailer. Their eyes locked like magnets coming into line, and for perhaps twenty seconds they stared at each other. Mailer looked into a pair of yellow eyes so compressed with hate that back of his own eyes he could feel the echo of such hatred ringing. The Nazi, taller than Mailer, well-knit, and with neatly formed features and a shock of blond hair, would have been handsome but for the ferocity of his yellow eyes, which were sunk deep in their sockets. Those eyes made him look like an eagle.

Yet Mailer had first advantage in this eye-staring contest. Because he had been prepared for it. He had been getting into such confrontations for years, and rarely lost them, even though he sometimes thought they were costing him eyesight. Still, some developed instinct had made him ready an instant before the Nazi. Every bit of intensity he possessed—with the tremors of the March and the Marshal's arm still pent in him—glared forth into the other's eyes. He was nonetheless aghast at what he saw. The American Nazis were all fanatics, yes, poor mad tormented fanatics, their psyches twisted like burning leaves in the fire of their hatreds, yes, indeed! but this man's conviction stood in his eyes as if his soul had been focused to a single point of light. Mailer could feel violence behind violence rocking through his head. If the two of them were ever alone in an alley, one of them might kill the other in a fight—it was not unlike holding an electric wire in the hand. And the worst of it was that he was not even feeling violent himself—whatever violence he possessed had gone to his eyes—by that route had he projected himself on the Nazi.

After the first five seconds of the shock had passed, he realized he might be able to win—the Nazi must have taken too many easy contests, and had been too complacent in the first moment, yes it was like wrestlers throwing themselves on each other: one knuckle of one finger a little better able to be worked on a grip could make the difference—now he could feel the hint of force ebbing in the other's eyes, and could wonder at his own necessity to win. He did not hate the Nazi nearly so much as he was curious about him, yet the thought of losing had been intolerable as if he had been *obliged* not to lose, as if the duty of his life at this particular moment must have been to look into that Nazi's eye and say with his own, "You claim you have a philosophical system that comprehends all—you know nothing! My eyes encompass yours. My philosophy contains yours. You have met the wrong man!" And the Nazi looked away, and was hysterical with fury on the instant.

"You Jew bastard," he shouted. "Dirty Jew with kinky hair."

They didn't speak that way. It was too corny. Yet he could only answer, "You filthy Kraut."

"Dirty Jew."

"Kraut pig."

A part of his mind could actually be amused at this choice—he didn't even hate Germans any more. Indeed Germans fascinated him now. Why, they liked his books more than Americans did. Yet here he could think of nothing better to return than "Kraut pig."

"I'm not a Kraut," said the Nazi, "I'm a Norwegian." And then as if the pride of his birth had tricked him into communication with an infidel, thus into sacrilege, the Nazi added quickly, "Jew bastard red," then cocked his fists. "Come here, you coward," he said to Mailer, "I'll kill you."

"Throw the first punch, baby," said Mailer, "you'll get it all."

They were both absolutely right. They had a perfect sense of the other. Mailer was certainly not brave enough to advance on the Nazi—it would be like springing an avalanche on himself. But he also knew that if the Nazi jumped him, one blond youth was very likely to get massacred. In retrospect, it would appear not uncomic—two philosophical monomaniacs with the same flaw—they could not help it, they were counterpunchers.

"Jew coward! Red bastard!"

"Go fuck yourself, Nazi baby."

But now a tall U.S. Marshal who had the body and insane look of a very good rangy defensive end in professional football—that same hard high-muscled build, same coiled spring of wrath, same livid conviction that everything opposing the team must be wrecked, sod, turf, grass, uniforms, helmets, bodies, yes even bite the football if it will help—now leaped into the truck and jumped between them. "Shut up," he said, "or I'll wreck both of you." He had a long craggy face somewhere in the physiognomical land between Steve McQueen and Robert Mitchum, but he would never have made Hollywood, for his skin was pocked with the big boiling craters of a red lunar acne, and his eyes in Cinemascope would have blazed an audience off their seat, for such gray-green flame could only have issued from a blowtorch. Under his white Marshal's helmet, he was one impressive piece of gathered wrath.

Speaking to the Marshal at this point would have been dangerous. The Marshal's emotions had obviously been marinating for a week in the very special bile waters American Patriotism reserves for its need. His feelings were now caustic as a whip—too gentle the simile!—he was in agonies of frustration because the honor of his profession kept him from battering every prisoner's head to a Communist pulp. Mailer looked him over covertly to see what he could try if the Marshal went to work on him. All reports: negative. He would not stand a chance with this Marshal—there seemed no place to hit him where he'd be vulnerable; stone larynx, leather testicles, ice cubes for eyes. And he had his Marshal's club in his hand as well. Brother! Bring back the Nazi!

Whether the Marshal had been once in the Marine Corps or in Vietnam, or if half his family was now in Vietnam, or if he just hated the sheer Jew York presumption of that slovenly, drug-ridden weak contaminating America-hating army of termites outside this fortress' walls, he was certainly any upstanding demonstrator's nightmare. Because he was full of American rectitude and was fearless, and savage, savage as the exhaust left in the wake of a motorcycle club, gasoline and cheap perfume were one end of his spectrum, yeah, this Marshal loved action, but he was also in that no man's land between the old frontier and the new ranch home—as they, yes *they*—the enemies of the Marshal—tried to pass bills to limit the purchase of hunting rifles, so did *they* try to kill America, inch by inch, all the forces of evil, disorder, mess, and chaos in the world, and *cowardice*! and city ways, and slick shit, and despoliation of national resources, all the subtle invisible creeping paralyses of Communism that were changing America from a land where blood was red to a land where water was foul—yes in this Marshal's mind—no lesser explanation could suffice for the Knight of God light in the flame of his eye—the evil was without, America was threatened by a foreign disease, and the Marshal was threatened to the core of his sanity by any one of the first fifty of

Mailer's ideas which would insist that the evil was within, that the best in America was being destroyed by what in itself seemed next best, yes American heroism corrupted by American know-how—no wonder murder stood out in his face as he looked at the novelist—for the Marshal to lose his sanity was no passing psychiatric affair: Think rather of a rifleman on a tower in Texas and a score of his dead on the street.

But now the Nazi began to play out the deepest of ceremonies. The truck standing still, another Marshal at the other end of the van (the one indeed who had arrested Mailer), and Teague and the Hungarian to different sides, everyone had their eyes on the Norwegian. He now glared again at Mailer, but then whipped away his eyes before a second contest could begin, and said, "All right, Jew, come over here if you want a fight."

The Marshal took the Nazi and threw him against the side-wall of the truck. As he bounced off, the Marshal gave him a rap below the collarbone with the butt of his club. "I told you to shut up. Now, just shut up." His rage was intense. The Nazi looked back at him sullenly, leaned on the butt of the club almost defiantly as if the Marshal didn't know what foolish danger he was in to treat the Nazi so, the Nazi had a proud curved hint of a smile, as if he were recording the features of this Marshal forever in the history of his mind, the Nazi's eyes seemed to say to the Marshal, "You are really on my side although you do not admit it—you would like to beat me now because in the future you know you will yet kiss my boots!" And the Marshal, traveling a high edge of temper, began to slam the Nazi against the wall of the truck with moderate force, but rhythmically, as if he would pacify them both by this act, bang, and bang, step by step, the imaginary dialogue of the Marshal to the Nazi now sounding in Mailer's ear somewhat like this, "Listen, Nazi, you're nothing but a rat fart who makes my job harder, and gives the scum around me room to breathe, 'cause they look at you and feel righteous. You just keep me diverted from the real danger."

And the Nazi looked back with a full sullen pouting defiance as if from deep in himself he was all unconsciously saying to the Marshal, "You know I am beautiful, and you are frightened of me. I have a cause, and I am ready to die for it, and you are just ready to die for a uniform. Join me where the real war is. Already the strongest and wildest men in America wear our symbol on their motorcycle helmets."

And the Marshal, glaring back at the Nazi, butt of his club transfixing him against the wall of the van, gave a contemptuous look, as if to drop him with the final unspoken word. "Next to strong wild men, you're nothing but a bitch."

Then the truck began to move, and the Marshal, calmer now, stood silently between Mailer and the Nazi; and the Nazi, also quiet now, stood in place looking neither at the Marshal nor Mailer. Some small storm of hysteria seemed to have worked itself out of the van.

From *The Armies of the Night* (1968)

# 1968

# MIAMI
# AND THE SIEGE
# OF CHICAGO

**May–June**     **Bobby Kennedy**

The reporter met Bobby Kennedy just once. It was on an afternoon in May in New York just after a victory in the Indiana primary and it had not been a famous meeting, even if it began well. The Senator came in from a conference (for the reporter was being granted an audience) and said quickly with a grin, "Mr. Mailer, you're a mean man with a word." He had answered, "On the contrary, Senator, I like to think of myself as a gracious writer."

"Oh," said Kennedy, with a wave of his hand, "that too, that too!"

So it had begun well enough, and the reporter had been taken with Kennedy's appearance. He was slimmer even than one would have thought, not strong, not weak, somewhere between a blade of grass and a blade of steel, fine, finely drawn, finely honed, a fine flush of color in his cheeks, two very white front teeth, prominent as the two upper teeth of a rabbit, so his mouth had no hint of the cruelty or calculation of a politician who weighs counties, cities, and states but was rather a mouth ready to nip at anything that attracted its contempt or endangered its ideas. Then there were his eyes. They were most unusual. His brother Teddy Kennedy spoke of those who "followed him, honored him, lived in his mild and magnificent eye," and that was fair description, for he had very large blue eyes, the iris wide in diameter, near to twice the width of the average eye, and the blue was a milky blue like a marble so that his eyes, while prominent, did not show the separate steps and slopes of light some bright eyes show but rather were gentle, indeed beautiful—one was tempted to speak of velvety eyes—their surface seemed made of velvet as if one could touch them, and the surface would not be repelled.

He was as attractive as a movie star. Not attractive like his brother had been, for Jack Kennedy had looked like the sort of vital leading man who would steal the girl from Ronald Reagan every time, no, Bobby Kennedy had looked more like a phenomenon of a movie star—he could have filled some magical empty space between Mickey Rooney and James Dean, they would have cast him sooner or later in some remake of *Mr. Smith Goes to Washington,* and everyone would have said, "Impossible casting! He's too young." And he was too young. Too young for Senator, too young for President—it felt strange in his presence thinking of him as President, as if the country would be giddy, like the whirl of one's stomach in the drop of an elevator or jokes about an adolescent falling in love, it was incredible to think of him as President, and yet marvelous, as if only a marvelous country would finally dare to have him.

That was the best of the meeting—meeting him! The reporter spent the rest of his valuable thirty minutes arguing with the Senator about Senator McCarthy. He begged him to arrange some sort of truce or liaison, but made a large mistake from the outset. He went on in a fatuous voice, sensing error too late to pull back, about how effective two Irish Catholics would be on the same ticket, for if there were conservative Irishmen who could vote against one of them, where was the Irish Catholic in America who could vote against two? and Kennedy had looked at him with disgust, as if offended by the presumption in this calculation; his upper lip had come down severely over his two front white teeth, and he had snapped, "I don't want those votes." How indeed did the reporter presume to tell him stories about the benightedness of such people when he knew them only too well. So the joke had been a lame joke and worse, and they got into a dull argument about McCarthy, Kennedy having little that was good to say, and the reporter arguing doggedly in the face of such remarks as "He doesn't even begin to campaign until twelve."

They got nowhere. Kennedy's mind was altogether political on this afternoon. It did not deal with ideas except insofar as ideas were attached to the name of bills, or speeches, or platforms, or specific debates in specific places, and the reporter, always hard put to remember such details, was forced therefore to hammer harder and harder on the virtues of McCarthy's gamble in entering the New Hampshire primary until Kennedy said, "I wonder why you don't support Senator McCarthy. He seems more like your sort of guy, Mr. Mailer," and in answer, oddly moved, he had said in a husky voice, "No, I'm supporting you. I know it wasn't easy for you to go in." And even began to mutter a few remarks about how he understood that powerful politicians would not have trusted Kennedy if he had moved too quickly, for his holding was large, and men with large holdings were not supportable if they leaped too soon. "I know that," he said, looking into the Senator's mild and magnificent eye, and Kennedy nodded, and in return a little later Kennedy sighed, and exhaled his breath, looked sad for an instant, and said, "Who knows? Who knows? Perhaps I should have gone in earlier." A few minutes later they said good-bye, not unpleasantly. That was the last he saw of him.

Of course, the reporter had been partisan to Bobby Kennedy, excited by precisely his admixture of idealism plus willingness to traffic with demons, ogres, and overloads of corruption. This had characterized the political style of the Kennedys more than once. The Kennedys had seemed magical because they were a little better than they should have been, and so gave promise of making America a little better than it ought to be. The reporter respected McCarthy, he respected him enormously for trying the vengeance of Lyndon Johnson, his heart had been given a bit of life by the success of the New Hampshire primary campaign. If there had then been little to make him glad in the abrupt and unhappy timing of Bobby Kennedy's immediate entrance into the race for nomination, he had, nonetheless, remained Kennedy's man—he saw the battle between the two as tragic; he had hardly enjoyed the Kennedy-McCarthy debate on television before the California primary; he had not taken pleasure in rooting for Kennedy and being thereby forced to condemn McCarthy's deadness of manner, blankness of affect, and suggestion of weakness in each deep pouch beneath each eye. The pouches spoke of clichés—eyes sitting in sagging brassieres of flesh, such stuff. He knew that McCarthy partisans would find equal fault somewhere in Kennedy.

A few nights after this debate, the reporter was awakened from a particularly oppressive nightmare by the ringing of a bell. He heard the voice of an old drinking friend he had not seen in two years. "Cox," he shouted into the phone, "are you out of your skull? What do you mean calling at three A.M.?"

"Look," said the friend, "get the television on. I think you ought to see it. Bobby Kennedy has just been shot."

"No," he bellowed, "No! No! No!" his voice railing with an ugliness and pain reminiscent to his ear of the wild grunts of a wounded pig. (Where he had heard that cry he did not at the moment remember.) He felt as if he were being despoiled of a vital part of himself, and in the middle of this horror noted that he screamed like a pig, not a lion, nor a bear. The reporter had gone for years on the premise that one must balance every moment between the angel in oneself and the swine—the sound of his own voice shocked him therefore profoundly. The balance was not what he thought it to be. He watched television for the next hours in a state that drifted rudderless between two horrors. Then, knowing no good answer could come for days, if at all, on the possible recovery of Bobby Kennedy, he went back to bed and lay in a sweat of complicity, as if his own lack of moral *witness* (to the subtle heroism of Bobby Kennedy's attempt to run for President) could be found in the dance of evasions his taste for a merry life and a married one had become, as if this precise lack had contributed (in the vast architectonics of the cathedral of history) to one less piton of mooring for Senator Kennedy in his lonely ascent of those vaulted walls, as if finally the efforts of brave men depended in part on the protection of other men who saw themselves as at least provisionally brave, or sometimes brave, or at the least—if not brave—balanced at least on a stability between selflessness and appetite and therefore—by practical purposes—decent. But he was close to having become too much of appetite—he had spent the afternoon preceding this night of assassination in enjoying a dalliance—let us leave it at that—a not uncharacteristic way to have spent his time, and lying next to his wife now, TV news pictures of the assassination rocketing all over the bruised stone of his skull, he hated his wife for having ever allowed such a condition to come to be, hated her subtle complicity in driving him out, and then apart, and knew from the other side of his love that he must confess this afternoon now, as if that would be a warrant of magic to aid Senator Kennedy on the long voyage through the depth of the exploded excavations in his brain, and did not have the simple courage to confess, stopped in his mental steps as if confronting a bully in an alley and altogether unable to go on—the bully in the alley no less than his wife's illimitable funds of untempered redneck wrath. So he did what all men who are overweight must do—he prayed the Lord to take the price of his own poor mortal self (since he had flesh in surfeit to offer), he begged that God spare Senator Kennedy's life, and he would give up something, give up what?—give up some of the magic he could bring to bear on some one or another of the women, yes, give that up if the life would be saved, and fell back into the horror of trying to rest with the sense that his offer might have been given too late and by the wrong vein—confession to his wife was what the moral pressure had first demanded—and so fell asleep with some gnawing sense of the Devil there to snatch his offering after the angel had moved on in disgust.

Kennedy dead, he was doubly in gloom, passionate gloom for the loss of that fine valuable light—like everyone else he loved Bobby Kennedy by five times more in death than life—a few lives have the value to illumine themselves in their death. But he was also dull in dejection at what he might have given away that other night. For he believed a universe in which at stricken moments one could speak quietly to whichever manifest of God or Devil was near, had to be as reasonable a philosophical proposition as any assumption that such dialogues were deluded. So it was possible he had given something away, and for nothing: The massive irreversible damage to the Senator's brain had occurred before the spring of his own generosity had ever been wet. Indeed! Who knew what in reality might have been granted if he had worked for the first impulse and dared offer confession on a connubial bed. A good could have come to another man and by another route.

The closest he was to come again to Bobby Kennedy was to stand in vigil for fifteen minutes as a member of the honor guard about his coffin in St. Patrick's. Lines filed by. People had waited in line for hours, five hours, six hours, more, inching forward through the day and through the police lines on the street in order to take one last look at the closed coffin.

The poorest part of the working class of New York had turned out, poor Negro men and women, Puerto Ricans, Irish washerwomen, old Jewish ladies who looked like they ran grubby little newsstands, children, adolescents, families, men with hands thick and lined and horny as oyster shells, calluses like barnacles, came filing by to bob a look at that coffin covered by a flag. Some women walked by praying, and knelt and touched the coffin with their fingertips as they passed, and after a time the flag would slip from the pressure of their fingers and an usher detailed for the purpose would readjust it. The straightest line between two points is the truth of an event, no matter how long it takes or far it winds, and if it had taken these poor people six hours of waiting in line to reach that coffin, then the truth was in the hours. A river of working-class people came down to march past Kennedy's coffin, and this endless line of people had really loved him, loved Bobby Kennedy like no political figure in years had been loved.

The organ played somewhere in the nave and the line moved forward under the vast—this day—tragic vaults of the cathedral so high overhead and he felt love for the figure in the coffin and tragedy for the nation in the years ahead, the future of the nation seemed as dark and tortured, as wrenched out of shape, as the contorted blood-spattered painted sculpture of that garish Christ one could find in every dark little Mexican church. The horror of dried blood was now part of the air, and became part of the air of the funeral next day. That funeral was not nearly so beautiful; the poor people who had waited on line on Friday were now gone, and the mighty were in their place, the President and members of the Congress, and the Establishment, and the Secret Service, and the power of Wall Street; the inside of St. Patrick's for the length of the service was dank with the breath of the over-ambitious offering reverence—there is no gloom so deep unless it is the scent of the upholstery in a mortician's limousine, or the smell of morning in a closed Pullman after executives have talked through the night.

## June      Gene McCarthy in Cambridge

He met Senator McCarthy at a cocktail party in Cambridge not a week after the assassination. McCarthy was in a depression as well.

At this party, McCarthy looked weary beyond belief, his skin a used-up yellow, his tall body serving for no more than to keep his head up above the crowd at the cocktail party. Like feeder fish, smaller people were nibbling on his reluctant hulk with questions, idiotic questions, petulant inquiries he had heard a thousand times. "Why?" asked a young woman, college instructor, horn-rimmed glasses, "why don't we get out of Vietnam?" her voice near hysterical, ringing with the harsh electronics of cancer gulch, and McCarthy looked near to flinching with the question and the liverish demand on him to answer. "Well," he said in his determinedly mild and quiet voice, last drop of humor never voided—for if on occasion he might be surrounded by dolts, volts, and empty circuits, then nothing to do but send remarks up to the angel of laughter. "Well," said Senator McCarthy, "there seem to be a few obstacles in the way."

But his pale green eyes had that look somewhere between humor and misery that the Creation might offer when faced with the bulldozers of boredom.

Years ago, in 1960, the reporter had had two glimpses of Eugene McCarthy. At the Democratic convention in Los Angeles that nominated John F. Kennedy, McCarthy had made a speech for another candidate. It was the best nominating speech the reporter had ever heard. He had written about it with the metaphor of a bullfight:

> . . . he held the crowd like a matador . . . gathering their emotion, discharging it, creating new emotion on the wave of the last, driving his passes tighter and tighter as he readied for the kill. "Do not reject this man who made us all proud to be called Democrats, do not leave this prophet without honor in his own party." McCarthy went on, his muleta furled for the *naturales.* "There was only one man who said let's talk sense to the American people. He said, the promise of America is the promise of greatness. This was his call to greatness . . . Do not forget this man . . . Ladies and gentlemen, I present to you not the favorite son of one state, but the favorite son of the fifty states, the favorite son of every country he has visited, the favorite son of every country which has not seen him but is secretly thrilled by his name." Bedlam. The kill. "Ladies and gentlemen, I present to you Adlai Stevenson of Illinois." Ears and tail. Hooves and bull. A roar went up like the roar one heard the day Bobby Thomson hit his home run at the Polo Grounds and the Giants won the pennant from the Dodgers in the third playoff game of the 1951 season. The demonstration cascaded onto the floor, the gallery came to its feet, the sports arena sounded like the inside of a marching drum.

Perhaps three months later, just after his piece on that convention had appeared, and election time was near, he had met Senator McCarthy at another cocktail party on Central Park West to raise money for the campaign of Mark Lane, then running for State Assemblyman in New York. The reporter had made a speech himself that day. Having decided, on the excitements of the Kennedy candidacy and other excitements (much marijuana for one), to run for Mayor of New York the following year, he gave his maiden address at that party, a curious, certainly a unique political speech, private, personal, tortured in metaphor, sublimely indifferent to issues, platform, or any recognizable paraphernalia of the political process, and delivered in much too rapid a voice to the assembled bewilderment of his audience, a collective (and by the end very numb) stiff clavicle of Jewish Central Park West matrons. The featured speaker, Senator McCarthy, was to follow, and climbing up on the makeshift dais as he stepped down, the Senator gave him a big genial wide-as-the-open-plains Midwestern grin.

"Better learn how to breathe, boy," he whispered out of the corner of his mouth, and proceeded to entertain the audience for the next few minutes with a mixture of urbanity, professional elegance, and political savvy. That was eight years ago.

But now, near to eight years later, the hour was different, the audience at this cocktail party in Cambridge with their interminable questions and advice, their over-familiarity yet excessive reverence, their desire to touch McCarthy, prod him, *galvanize* him, seemed to do no more than drive him deeper into the insulations of his fatigue, his very disenchantment—so his pores seemed to speak—with the democratic process. He was not a mixer. Or if he had ever been a mixer, as he must have been years ago, he had had too much of it since, certainly too much since primaries in New Hampshire, Wisconsin, Indiana, Oregon, and California—he had become, or he had always been, too private a man for the damnable political mechanics of mixing, fixing, shaking the hands, answering the same questions that had already answered themselves by being asked. And now the threat of assassination over all, that too, that his death might come like the turn of a card, and could a man be ready? The gloomy, empty tomb-like reverberations of the last shot shaking rough waves doubtless through his own dreams, for his eyes, sensitive, friendly, and remote as the yellow eyes of an upper primate in a cage, spoke out of the weary, sagging face, up above the sagging pouches, seeming to say, "Yes, try to rescue me—but as you see, it's not quite possible." And the reporter, looking to perform the errand of rescue, went in to talk about the speech of 1960 in Los Angeles, and how it was the second best political speech he had ever heard.

"Oh," said McCarthy, "tell me, what was the best?"

And another questioner jostled the circle about McCarthy to ask another question, the Secret Service man in the gray suit at McCarthy's elbow stiffening at the impact. But McCarthy held the questioner at a distance by saying, "No, I'd like to listen for a while." It had obviously become his pleasure to listen to others. So the reporter told a story about Vito Marcantonio making a speech in Yankee Stadium in 1948, and the Senator listened carefully, almost sadly, as if remembering other hours of oratory.

On the way out the door, in the press of guests and local party workers up to shake his hand before he was gone, a tall bearded fellow, massive chin, broad brow for broad horn-rimmed glasses, spoke out in a resonant voice marred only by the complacency of certain nasal intrigues. "Senator, I'm a graduate student in English, and I like your politics very much, but I must tell you, I think your poetry stinks."

McCarthy took it like a fighter being slapped by the referee across the forearms. "You see what it is, running for President," said the laughter in his eyes. If he worshipped at a shrine, it was near the saint of good humor.

"Give my regards to Robert Lowell," said the reporter. "Say to him that I read 'The Drunken Fisherman' just the other day."

McCarthy looked like the victim in the snow when the St. Bernard comes up with the rum. His eyes came alight at the name of the poem . . . "I will catch Christ with a greased worm," might have been the line he remembered. He gave a little wave, was out the door.

Yet the reporter was depressed after the meeting. McCarthy did not look nor feel like a President, not that tall tired man with his bright subtle eyes which could sharpen the razor's edge of a nuance, no, he seemed more like the dean of the finest English department in the land. There wasn't that sense of a man with vast ambition and sufficient character to make it luminous, so there was not that charisma which leaves no argument about the nature of the attempt.

# Miami Beach, August 2–8

### BURG-JUNGLE

They snipped the ribbon in 1915, they popped the cork, Miami Beach was born. A modest burg they called a city, nine-tenths jungle. An island. It ran along a coastal barrier the other side of Biscayne Bay from young Miami—in 1868 when Henry Lum, a California 'forty-niner, first glimpsed the island from a schooner, you may be certain it was jungle, coconut palms on the sand, mangrove swamp and palmetto thicket ten feet off the beach. But by 1915, they were working the vein. John S. Collins, a New Jersey nurseryman (after whom Collins Avenue is kindly named), brought in bean fields and avocado groves; a gent named Fisher, Carl G., a Hoosier—he invented Prestolite, a millionaire—bought up acres from Collins, brought in a work-load of machinery, men, even two elephants, and jungle was cleared, swamps were filled, small residential islands were made out of baybottom mud, dredged, then relocated, somewhat larger natural islands adjacent to the barrier island found themselves improved, streets were paved, sidewalks put in with other amenities—by 1968, one hundred years after Lum first glommed the beach, large areas of the original coastal strip were covered over altogether with macadam, white condominium, white luxury hotel, and white stucco flea-bag. Over hundreds, then thousands, of acres, white sidewalks, streets and white buildings covered the earth where the jungle had been. Is it so dissimilar from covering your poor pubic hair with adhesive tape for fifty years? The vegetal memories of that excised jungle haunted Miami Beach in a steam-pot of miasmas. Ghosts of expunged flora, the never-born groaning in vegetative chancery beneath the asphalt came up with a tropical curse, an equatorial leaden wet sweat of air that rose from the earth itself, rose right up through the baked asphalt and into the heated air which entered the lungs like a hand slipping into a rubber glove.

The temperature was not that insane. It hung around 87 day after day, at night it went down to 82, back to the same 87 in the A.M.—the claims of the News Bureau for Miami Beach promised that in 1967 temperature exceeded 90 degrees only four times. (Which the Island of Manhattan could never begin to say.) But of course Miami Beach did not have to go that high, for its humidity was up to 87 as well—it was, on any and every day of the Republican Convention of 1968, one of the hottest cities in the world. Crawling through 5 P.M. Miami Beach traffic in the pure miserable fortune of catching an old taxi without air conditioning, dressed in shirt and tie and jacket—formal and implicitly demanded uniform of political journalists—the sensation of breathing, then living, was not unlike being obliged to make love to a 300-pound woman who has decided to get on top. Got it? You could not dominate a thing. That uprooted jungle had to be screaming beneath.

Of course it could have been the air conditioning. They say that in Miami Beach the air conditioning is pushed to that icy point where women may wear fur coats over their diamonds in the tropics. For ten miles, from the Diplomat to the Di Lido, above Hallandale Beach Boulevard down to Lincoln Mall, all the white refrigerators stood, piles of white refrigerators six and eight and twelve stories high, twenty stories high, shaped like sugar cubes and ice-cube trays on edge, like mosques and palaces, shaped like matched white luggage and portable radios, stereos, plastic compacts and plastic rings, Moorish castles shaped like waffle irons, shaped like the baffle plates on white plastic electric heaters, and cylinders like Waring blenders, buildings looking like giant op art and pop art paintings, and sweet wedding cakes, cottons of kitsch and piles of dirty cotton stucco, yes, for ten miles the hotels for the delegates stood on the beach side of Collins Avenue: the Eden Roc and the Fontainebleau (Press Headquarters), the Di Lido and the De Lano, the Ivanhoe, Deauville, Sherry Frontenac and the Monte Carlo, the Cadillac, Caribbean and the Balmoral, the Lucerne, Hilton Plaza, Doral Beach, the Sorrento, Marco Polo, Casablanca, and Atlantis, the Hilyard Manor, Sans Souci, Algiers, Carillon, Seville, the Gaylord, the Shore Club, the Nautilus, Montmartre, and the Promenade, the Bal Harbour on North Bay Causeway, and the Twelve Caesars, the Regency and the Americana, the Diplomat, Versailles, Coronado, Sovereign, the Beau Rivage, the Crown Hotel, even Holiday Inn, all oases for technological man. Deep air conditioning down to 68 degrees, ice-palaces to chill the fevered brain—when the air-conditioning worked. And their furnishings were monumentally materialistic. Not all of them: The cheaper downtown hotels like the Di Lido and the Nautilus were bare and mean, with vinyl coverings on the sofas and the glare of plastic off the rugs and tables and tiles, inexpensive hotel colors of pale brown and buff and dingy cream, sodden gray, but the diadems like the Fontainebleau and the Eden Roc, the Doral Beach, the Hilton Plaza (Headquarters for Nixon), the Deauville (Hq for Reagan), or the Americana—Rockefeller and the New York State delegation's own ground—were lavish with interlockings, curves, vaults, and runs of furnishings as intertwined as serpents in the roots of a mangrove tree. All the rivers of the very worst taste twisted down to the delta of each lobby in each grand Miami Beach hotel—rare was the central room that did not look like the lobby of a movie palace, imitation of late-Renaissance imitations of Greek and Roman statues, imitations of baroque and rococo and brothel Victorian and Art Nouveau and Bauhaus with gold grapes and cornucopias welded to the modern bronze tubing of the chair, golden moldings that ran like ivy from room to room, chandeliers complex as the armature of dynamos, and curvilinear steps in the shape of amoebas and palettes, cocktail lounge bars in deep rose or maroon with spun-sugar white tubes of plaster decor to twist around the ceiling. There was every color of iridescence, rainbows of vulgarity, aureoles of gorgeous taste, opium den of a middle-class dollar, materialistic as meat, sweat, and the cigar. It is said that people born under Taurus and Capricorn are the most materialistic of us all. Take a sample of the residents in the census of Miami B.—does Taurus predominate more than one-twelfth of its share? It must, or astrology is done, for the Republicans, Grand Old Party with a philosophy rather than a program, had chosen what must certainly be the materialistic capital of the world for their convention. Las Vegas might offer competition, but Las Vegas was materialism in the service of electricity—fortunes could be lost in the spark of the dice. Miami was materialism baking in the sun, then stepping back to air-conditioned caverns where ice could nestle in the fur. It was the first of a hundred curiosities—that in a year when the Republic hovered on the edge of revolution, nihilism, and lines of police on file to the horizon, visions of future Vietnams in our own cities upon us, the party of conservatism and principle, of corporate wealth and personal frugality, the party of cleanliness, hygiene, and balanced budget, should have set itself down on a sultan's strip.

That was the first of a hundred curiosities, but there were mysteries as well. The reporter had moved through the convention quietly, as anonymously as possible, wan, depressed, troubled. Something profoundly unclassifiable was going on among the Republicans and he did not know if it was conceivably good or a concealment of something bad—which was the first time a major social phenomenon like a convention had confused him so. The Republican assembly in Miami Beach in 1968 was a different affair—one could not tell if nothing much was going on, or to the contrary, nothing much was going on near the surface but everything was shifting down below. So dialogue with other journalists merely depressed him—the complaints were unanimous that this was the dullest convention anyone could remember. Complaints took his mind away from the slow brooding infusion he desired in the enigmas of conservatism and/or Republicanism, and any hope of perspective on the problem beyond. The country was in a throe, a species of eschatological heave. John Updike, after the assassination of Robert F. Kennedy, had made the remark that God might have withdrawn His blessing from America. It was a thought that could not be forgotten, for it gave insight to the perspectives of the Devil and his political pincers: Left-wing demons, white and Black, working to inflame the conservative heart of America, while Right-wing devils exacerbated Blacks and drove the mind of the New Left and liberal middle class into prides of hopeless position. And the country roaring like a bull in its wounds, coughing like a sick lung in the smog, turning over in sleep at the sound of motorcycles, shivering at its need for new phalanxes of order. Where were the new phalanxes one could trust? The reporter had seen the faces of too many police to balm his dreams with the sleep they promised. Even the drinks tasted bad in Miami in the fever and the chill.


## ROCKEFELLER

The Rockefeller plane, an American Airlines 727 jet that had carried the candidate 65,000 miles into forty-five states during the campaign, was landing, for security reasons, at the Coast Guard Airport.

Perhaps a hundred or 150 newsmen, TV cameras, and still photographers were out at the main hangar with the Press bus, way out in the quiet empty reaches of the all but deserted airdrome, and overhead, light planes and helicopters patrolled the near sky, and four or five police cars were parked in uneasy relation to the crowd. The reporter had to show no identification to enter the gate, and needed none now; a potential assassin, tipped to Rockefeller's entrance at Opa Locka, could have packed a piece to within a yard of him—of course, afterward, he could never have escaped. If he managed to shoot past the twenty-odd cops in the direct vicinity, the helicopters would have followed his car all the way to Miami, maybe nailed him on Arthur Godfrey Causeway from the sky. Like pieces of flesh fragmented from the explosion of a grenade, echoes of the horror of Bobby Kennedy's assassination were thus everywhere: helicopters riding overhead like roller coasters, state troopers with magnums on their hip and crash helmets, squad cars, motorcycles, yet no real security, just powers of retaliation. It forced one to cherish major politicians—no matter how colorless, they all had hints of charisma now that they were obviously more vulnerable to sudden death than bullfighters, and so they were surrounded with a suggestion of the awe peasants reserve for the visit of the bishop—some rushed to touch them, others looked ready to drop to their knees. Thus, at least, for Rockefeller and the Press. He was surrounded almost immediately after he came down the landing ramp, and never left alone, surrounded by Press and cameramen five deep, the photographers by long practice holding their cameras and even their movie cameras up over their heads, aiming down by skillful guess, so that from a distance one could always tell exactly where the candidate was situated, for a semicircle of cameras crooned in from above like bulbs of seaweed breaking surface at high tide, or were they more like praying mantises on the heads of tall grass?—a bazaar of metaphor was obviously offered.

Rocky had come off the plane with his entourage and his wife. She was surprisingly attractive, with a marvelous high color that made her vastly better looking than her photographs, and Rocky looked like much less than his photographs, gray beyond gray in the flesh, gray as New York City pavements, gray as an old con—the sun could not have touched him in a month or else all the fighting blood of the heart was somewhere deep inside the brain, working through the anxiety-ridden calculations with which he must have come to Miami, for Nixon with his six-hundred-plus votes now almost secure was a handful or a score or at best not fifty votes from the first ballot nomination.

Yet, by the enthusiasm that greeted him, Rockefeller was obviously the near-unanimous choice of the Press, and above all, the television—a mating of high chemical potentials existed between the media and the man as if they had been each conceived for the other. Except for his complexion, Rocky had an all but perfect face for President, virile, friendly, rough-hewn, of the common man, yet uncommon—Spencer Tracy's younger brother gone into politics. He had only one flaw—an odd and unpleasant mouth, a catfish mouth, wide, unnaturally wide, with very thin lips. In the center of the mouth there seemed almost another mouth that did the speaking, somewhat thicker lips that pursed, opened, deliberated—all the while the slit-thin corners of the mouth seemed off on their own, not really moving with the center. So he gave the impression of a man to whom expert instruction had disclosed what he might be expected to say—therefore only the middle of the mouth would be on call.

The rain, which had begun to come down and then providentially stopped, was coming on again. So the candidate was able to slip out of the tight ring of interviewers locked about him after answering fifty more of the million political questions he would reply to in his life, and now the press bus and the private cars were off in a race across Miami to the 72nd Street public beach in Miami Beach maybe ten miles away where a big rally was scheduled. The helicopters rode lead and flank cowhand overhead, the cavalcade sped from Opa Locka. Not thirty minutes later, band playing, cymbals smashing, Rocky walked a half-block through a crowd on 72nd Street and Collins Avenue, accepting the mob, walking through them to partial deliriums of excitement, a crazy mob for politicking, dressed in bathing suits, bikinis, bathrobes, surfers' trunks, paper dresses, terry cloth shirts, they jammed the pavement in bare feet, sandals, clodhoppers, bathers screaming, calling out, falling in line around the free Pepsi-Cola wagon, good-natured but never super-excited—the rally was on the edge of the beach after all, and a leaden milky-green sea was pounding an erratic, nervous foam of surf onto the water's-edge of the beach not fifty yards away.

As Rocky moved forward in his brown-gray business suit, murmurs went up everywhere—"There goes the next President of the United States." But the crowd was somehow not huge enough to amplify this sentiment—they looked more like tourists than Republicans—all those votes he would get some day if ever he would capture the nomination. And as he moved forward through the crowd, shaking hands, saying, "Hiya, hiya," big grin on his face at the shouts of "We want Rocky," so also at that instant a tall skinny Negro maybe thirty years old leaped in front to shake hands and with the other hand, looking for a souvenir, he flipped Rocky's purple handkerchief out of his breast pocket. But Rockefeller showed true Republican blood. A look of consternation for one stricken gap of an instant—*was this an attempt?*—until, seeing the handkerchief in the man's hand, the situation was recovered: Rocky strode forward, pulled the handkerchief back, gave an admonishing look, as if to say, "Come on, fellow!" and immediately had some cardboard sunglasses pilfered from the same breast pocket by a heated happy hysterical lady tourist with whom he could not wrestle. Kerchief recovered, sunglasses offered up in tribute, he made the speaker's stand—the flatbed of a truck—and the meeting began. *The New York Times* was to report 3,000 people there; perhaps it was half—they cheered everything he said, those who could hear him. The acoustics varied from punko to atrocious, and the reporter circling the crowd heard one plain buxom girl with long brown hair—hippie hints of trinket and dungarees, girl formed out of the very mold of Rockefeller supporters—turn nonetheless sadly to her friend and say, "I can't hear a thing—bye bye." Next step, a sixty-year-old blonde in a bikini with half of a good figure left (breast and buttocks) the flesh around her navel unhappily equal to the flesh around her neck, wearing orange plastic bracelets, gold charm necklace, rings, rhinestone sunglasses, wedgies, painted toes, red hot momma kisser lips, a transistor radio giving rock, and she—whatever she was hearing—beating out the rhythm on one of her two consorts, the one younger than herself; the older, a husband? had a cigar, a paunch, and that benign cool which speaks of holding property out in Flatbush in Brooklyn, and putting up with a live-wire wife.

But indeed it must have been reminiscent to Rocky of campaigning on beaches in Brooklyn and Queens; the crowd had the same

646 THE TIME OF OUR TIME

propinquity, same raucous cheery wise hard middle-class New York smarts—take the measure of everything and still give your cheer because you are there, Murray. Even the smells were the same—orgiastic onions in red hot dog and knish grease, dirty yellow sand—Rocky had to recognize it all, for when he introduced Claude Kirk, "the young alive Governor of Florida" (sole vote for him in the Florida delegation), a smattering of applause came up, a spattering of comment, and one or two spit-spraying lip blats—it was obvious the crowd didn't know Kirk from a Mafia dance-contest winner. So Rocky shifted gears. "It's a thrill for us from New York to be here, in Florida," he said, "and half of you must be here from New York." The laugh told him he was right. A delicate gloom began to come in equal to the first tendrils of mist over a full moon; God would know what his advisers had been telling him about the possible power of this open street rally on the 72nd Street beach—with luck and a mass turnout massive enough to break all records in category, he could be on his way—a people's candidate must ride a tidal wave. This was not even a bona fide breaker. Half of his audience was from New York. Well, he was no weak campaigner. He kept it going, hitting the hard spots, "The Republican Party must become again a national party, the voice of the poor and the oppressed." Great cheers for the size of the crowd. In the background, Miami Mummers wearing pink and orange and yellow and white and sky-blue satin outfits with net wings and white feathers, Miami Beach angels playing triangles and glockenspiels piped up tinklings and cracklings of sweet sound. Oompah went the oompah drum. "I offer," said Rocky, "a choice. It is . . . victory in November . . . victory for four years." He held up both hands in V-for-Victory signs.

"Eight years," shouted someone from the crowd.

"I won't quibble," said Rocky with a grin. But then, defeat licking at the center of this projected huge turnout that was finally not half huge enough, he added drily, "The gentleman who just spoke must be from New York."

The rally ended, and a black sky mopped out the sun for ten minutes, hid the cumulus. Rain came in tropical force, water trying to work through that asphalt, reach the jungle beneath. Everyone scattered, those who were dressed not quite in time. The rain hit with a squall. And the luminaries on the flatbed truck went off with Rocky.

### WASPS IN MIAMI

On the night before the convention was to begin, the Republicans had their Grand Gala at the Fountainebleau, no Press admitted, and the reporter by a piece of luck was nearly the first to get in. The affair was strict in its security, for some of the most important Republican notables would be there, but strolling through the large crowd in the lobby the reporter discovered himself in the immediate wake of Governor Reagan's passage along a channel of security officers through the mob to the doors of the Gala. It was assumed by the people who gave way to the Governor that the reporter must be one of the plainclothesmen assigned to His Excellency's rear, and with a frown here, judicious tightening of his mouth there, look of concern for the Governor's welfare squeezed onto his map, offering a security officer's look superior to the absence of any ticket, he went right in through the ticket-takers, having found time in that passage to observe Governor Reagan and his Lady, who were formally dressed to the hilt of the occasion, now smiling, now shaking hands, eager, tense, birdlike, genial, not quite habituated to eminence, seeking to make brisk but not rude progress through the crowd, and obviously uneasy in the crowd (like most political figures) since a night in June in Los Angeles. It was an expected observation, but Mr. and Mrs. Reagan looked very much like an actor and actress playing Governor and Wife. Still, Reagan held himself sort of uneasily about the middle, as if his solar plexus were fragile and a clout would leave him like a fish on the floor.

Once inside the ballroom, however, the reporter discovered that the Governor had been among the first guests to enter. His own position was therefore not comfortable. Since there were no other guests among whom to mix (nothing but 240 empty tables with settings for 2,000 people, all still to come in) and no cover to conceal him but small potted trees with oranges attached by green wire, since Security might be furious to the point of cop-mania catching him thus early, there was no choice but to take up a stand twenty feet from the door, his legs at parade rest, his arms clasped behind, while he scrutinized the entrance of everybody who came in. Any security officer studying him might therefore be forced to conclude that he belonged to *other* Security. Suffice it, he was not approached in his position near the entrance, and for the next thirty minutes looked at some thousand Republicans coming through the gate, the other thousand entering out of view by an adjacent door.

It was not a crowd totally representative of the power of the Republican Party. Some poor delegates may have been there as guests, and a few other delegates might have chosen to give their annual contribution of $1,000 for husband and wife here ($500 a plate) rather than to some other evening of fund-raising for the party, indeed an air of sobriety and quiet dress was on many of the Republicans who entered. There were women who looked like librarians and schoolteachers, there were middle-aged men who looked like they might be out for their one night of the year. The Eastern Establishment was of course present in degree, and powers from the South, West, Midwest, but it was not a gang one could hold up in comparative glitter to an opening at the Met. No, it was modesty that hung over these well-bred subscribers to the Gala.

Still, exceptions noted, they were in large part composed of a thousand of the wealthiest Republicans in the land, the corporate and social power of America was here in legions of interconnection he could not even begin to trace. Of necessity, a measure of his own ignorance came over him, for among those thousand, except for candidates, politicians, and faces in the news, there were not ten people he recognized. Yet here they were, the economic power of America (so far as economic power was still private, not public), the family power (so far as position in society was still a passion to average and ambitious Americans), the military power (to the extent that important sword-rattlers and/or patriots were among the company, as well as cadres of corporations not unmarried to the Pentagon), yes, even the spiritual power of America (just so far as Puritanism, Calvinism, conservatism, and golf still gave the Wasp an American faith more intense than the faith of cosmopolitans, one-worlders, trade-unionists, Black militants, New Leftists, acid-heads, tribunes of the gay, families of Mafia, political machinists, fixers, swingers, Democratic lobbyists, members of the Grange, and government workers, not to include the *Weltanschauung* of every partisan in every minority group). No, so far as there was an American faith, a belief, a mystique that America was more than the sum of its constituencies, its trillions of dollars and billions of acres, its constellation of factories, empyrean of communications, mountain transcendant of finance, and heroic of sport, transports of medicine, hygiene, and church, so long as belief persisted that America, finally more than all this, was the world's ultimate reserve of rectitude, final garden of the Lord, so far as this mystique could survive in every American family of Christian substance, so then were the people entering this Gala willy-nilly the leaders of this faith, never articulated by any of them except in the most absurd and taste-curdling jargons of patriotism mixed with religion, but the faith existed in those crossroads between the psyche and the heart where love, hate, the cognition of grace, the all but lost sense of the root, and adoration of America congregated for them.

Their own value was in this faith, the workings of their seed from one generation into the next, their link to the sense of what might be life-force was in the faith. Yes, primitive life was there, and ancestral life, health concealed in their own flesh from towns occupied and once well-settled, from farms that prospered, and frontiers they had—through ancestors—dared to pass. They believed in America as they believed in God—they could not really ever expect that America might collapse and God yet survive, no, they had even gone so far as to think that America was the savior of the world, food and medicine by one hand, sword in the other, highest of high faith in a nation that would bow the knee before no problem since God's own strength was in the die. It was a faith which had flared so high in San Francisco in 1964 that staid old Republicans had come near to frothing while they danced in the aisle, there to nominate Barry. But their hero had gone down to a catastrophe of defeat, blind in politics, impolite in tactics, a sorehead, a fool, a disaster. And if his policies had prevailed to some degree, to the degree of escalating the war in Vietnam, so had that policy depressed some part of America's optimism to the bottom of the decade, for the country had learned an almost unendurable lesson—its history in Asia was next to done, and there was not any real desire to hold armies on that land. Worse, the country had begun to wear away inside, and the specter of Vietnam in every American city would haunt the suburb, the terror of a dollar cut loose from every standard of economic anchor was in the news, and some of the best of the youth were mad demented dogs with teeth in the flesh of the deepest Republican faith.

They were a chastened collocation these days. The high fire of hard Republican faith was more modest now, the vision of America had diminished. The claims on Empire had met limits. But it was nonetheless uncommon, yes bizarre, for the reporter to stand like an agent of their security as these leaders of the last American faith came through to the Gala, for, repeat: They were in the main not impressive, no, not by the hard eye of New York. Most of them were ill-proportioned in some part of their physique. Half must have been, of course, men and women over fifty and their bodies reflected the pull of their character. The dowager's hump was common, and many a man had a flaccid paunch, but the collective tension was rather in the shoulders, in the girdling of the shoulders against anticipated lashings on the back, in the thrust forward of the neck, in the maintenance of the muscles of the mouth forever locked in readiness to bite the tough meat of resistance, in a posture forward from the hip since the small of the back was dependably stiff, loins and mind cut away from each other by some abyss between navel and hip.

More than half of the men wore eyeglasses, young with old—the reporter made his count, close as a professional basketball game, and gave up by the time his score was up to Glasses 87, No Glasses 83. You could not picture a Gala Republican who was not clean-shaven by 8 A.M. Coming to power, they could only conceive of trying to clean up every situation in sight. And so many of the women seemed victims of the higher hygiene. Even a large part of the young seemed to have faces whose cheeks had been injected with Novocain.

Yet he felt himself unaccountably filled with a mild sorrow. He did not detest these people, he did not feel so superior as to pity them, it was rather he felt a sad sorrowful respect. In their immaculate cleanliness, in the somewhat antiseptic odors of their astringent toilet water and perfume, in the abnegation of their walks, in the heavy sturdy moves so many demonstrated of bodies in life's harness, there was the muted tragedy of the Wasp—they were not on earth to enjoy or even perhaps to love so very much, they were here to serve, and serve they had in public functions and public charities (while recipients of their charity might vomit in rage and laugh in scorn), served on opera committees, and served in long hours of duty at the piano, served as the sentinel in concert halls and the pews on the aisle in church, at the desk in schools, had served for culture, served for finance, served for salvation, served for America—and so much of America did not wish them to serve any longer, and so many of them doubted themselves, doubted that the force of their faith could illumine their path in these new modern horror-head times. On and on they came through the door, the clean, the well-bred, the extraordinarily prosperous, and, for the most astonishing part, the almost entirely proper. Yes, in San Francisco in '64 they had been able to be insane for a little while, but now they were subdued, now they were modest, now they were looking for a leader to bring America back to them, their lost America, Jesus-land.

## NIXON

Nixon had come in earlier that day. A modestly large crowd, perhaps six hundred at the entrance to the Miami Hilton, two bands playing "Nixon's the One," and the Nixonettes and the Nixonaires, good clean blond- and brown-haired Christian faces, two Negresses, a cluster of 2,000 balloons going up in the air, flings of color, thin dots of color, and Nixon himself finally in partial view at the center of the semicircle of cameras held overhead. Just a glimpse: He has a sunburn—his forehead is bright pink. Then he has made it into the hotel, pushed from behind, hands in hand-shakes from the front, hair recognizable—it is curlier than most and combed in roller coaster waves.

The crowd had been enthusiastic without real hurly-burly or hint of pandemonium. More in a state of respectful enthusiasm, and the hot patriotic cupidity to get near the man who is probably going to be the next American President. The office, not the man, is moving them. And Nixon passes through them with the odd sticklike motions that are so much a characteristic of his presence. He is like an actor with good voice and hordes of potential but the despair of his dramatic coach (again it is High School). "Dick, you just got to learn how to move." There is something almost touching in the way he does it, as if sensitive flesh winces at the way he must expose his lack of heart for being warm and really winning in crowds, and yet he is all heart to perform his task, as if the total unstinting exercise of the will must finally deliver every last grace, yes, he is like a missionary handing out Bibles among the Urdu. Christ, they are filthy fellows, but deserving of the *book*. No, it is not so much that he is a bad actor (for Nixon in a street crowd is *radiant* with emotion to reach across the prison pen of his own artificial moves and deadly reputation and show that he is sincere), it is rather that he grew up in the worst set of schools for actors in the world—white gloves and church usher, debating team, Young Republicanism, captive of Ike's forensic style—as an actor, Nixon thinks his work is to signify. So if he wants to show someone that he likes them, he must smile; if he wishes to show disapproval of Communism, he frowns; America must be strong, out goes his chest. Prisoner of old habit or unwitting of a new kind of move, he has not come remotely near any modern moves, he would not be ready to see that young people love McCarthy because he plays forever against his line. "If I'm nominated, I can't see how I'd possibly fail to win," says McCarthy in a gloomy modest mild little voice, then his eyes twinkle at the myriad of consequences to follow: raps in the newspaper about his arrogance, the sheer delicious zaniness of any man making any claim about his candidacy—yes, many people love McCarthy because his wan wit is telling them, "We straddle ultimates: spitballs and eternals."

Nixon has never learned this. He is in for the straight sell.

But the reporter is obsessed with him. He has never written anything nice about Nixon. Over the years he has saved some of his sharpest comments for him, he has disliked him intimately ever since his Checkers speech in 1952—the kind of man who was ready to plough sentimentality in such a bog was the kind of man who would press any button to manipulate the masses—and there was large fear in those days of buttons that might ignite atomic wars. Nixon's presence on television had inspired emotions close to nausea. There had been a gap between the man who spoke and the man who lived behind the speaker which offered every clue of schizophrenia in the American public if they failed to recognize the void within the presentation. Worse. There was unity only in the way the complacency of the voice matched the complacency of the ideas. It was as if Richard Nixon were proving that a man who had never spent an instant inquiring whether family, state, church, and flag were ever wrong could go on in secure steps, denuded of risk, from office to office until he was President.

In 1962 the reporter had given a small celebration for the collapse of Nixon after his defeat in the election for Governor of California. To the Press: "Well, gentlemen," the defeated man had said, "you won't have Nixon to kick any more." It had seemed the absolute end of a career. Self-pity in public was as irreversible as suicide. In 1964, Nixon had stood about in the wings while Barry was nominated. Now, in 1968, he was on the edge of becoming the nominee. It was obvious something was wrong with the reporter's picture. In his previous conception of Richard Nixon's character there had been no room for a comeback. Either the man had changed or one had failed to recognize some part of his character from the beginning. So there was interest, even impatience, to hear him speak.

He was not having a press conference, however, on the day of his arrival. That would wait until the next morning at 8:15. Then, he would face the Press.

The room filled slowly. By the time Nixon began, it was apparent that 500 seats had been an excessive estimate. Perhaps half of them were filled, certainly no more than two-thirds. It was nonetheless a large press conference. Nixon came in wearing a quiet blue-gray suit, white shirt, black and blue close-figured tie, black shoes, and no handkerchief for the breast pocket. He stepped up on the dais diffidently, not certain whether applause would be coming or not. There was none. He stood there, looked quietly and warily at the audience, and then said that he was ready for questions.

This would be his sole press conference before the nomination. He was of course famous for his lack of sparkling good relation with the Press, he had in fact kept his publicity to a functional minimum these past few months. The work of collecting delegates had been done over the last four years, particularly over the last two. Their allegiance had been confirmed the last six months in his primary victories. He had no longer anything much to gain from good interviews, not at least until his nomination was secured; he had everything to lose from a bad interview. A delegate who was slipping could slide further because of an ill-chosen remark.

To the extent that the Press was not Republican, and certainly more than half, privately, were not, he would have few friends and more than a few determined enemies. Even among the Republicans he could expect a better share of the Press to go to Rockefeller. Even worse, for the mood of this conference, he did not, in comparison with other political candidates, have many reporters who were his personal friends. He was not reputed to smoke or drink, so he did not have drinking buddies as Johnson once had, and Goldwater, and Bill Miller, and Humphrey; no brothel legends attached to him, and no outsize admiration to accompany them—no, the Press was a necessary tool to him, a tool he had been obliged to employ for more than twenty years, but he could not pretend to be comfortable in his use of the tool, and the tool (since it was composed of men) resented its employment.

Probably Nixon had agreed to this conference only to avoid the excess of bad feeling that no meeting with the Press would be likely to cause. Still, this was an operation where his best hope was to minimize the loss. So he had taken the wise step of scheduling the conference at 8:15 in the morning, a time when his worst enemies, presumably the heavy drinkers, free lovers, and free spenders on the Reagan Right and Far Left of the press corps, would probably be asleep in bed or here asleep on their feet.

Nonetheless his posture on the stage, hands to his side or clasped before him, gave him the attentive guarded look of an old ball player—like Rabbit Maranville, let us say, or even an old con up before Parole Board. There was something in his carefully shaven face—the dark jowls already showing the first overtones of thin gloomy blue at this early hour—some worry that gave promise of never leaving him, some hint of inner debate about his value before eternity which spoke of precisely the sort of improvement that comes upon a man when he shifts in appearance from looking like an undertaker's assistant to looking like an old con seriously determined to go respectable. The Old Nixon, which is to say the young Nixon, used to look, on clasping his hands in front of him, like a church usher (of the variety who would twist a boy's ear after removing him from church). The older Nixon before the Press now—the *new* Nixon—had finally acquired some of the dignity of the old athlete and the old con—he had taken punishment, that was on his face now, he knew the detailed schedule of pain in a real loss, there was an attentiveness in his eyes that gave offer of some knowledge of the abyss, even the kind of gentleness which ex-drunkards attain after years in AA. As he answered questions, fielding them with the sure modest moves of an old shortstop who hits few homers but supports the team on his fielding (what sorrow in the faces of such middle-aged shortstops!) so now his modesty was not without real dignity. In Eisenhower days his attempts at modesty had been as offensive as a rich boy's arrogance, for he had been so transparently contemptuous of the ability of his audience to *witness* him. Now, the modesty was the product of a man who, at worst, had grown from a bad actor to a surprisingly good actor, or from an unpleasant self-made man—outrageously rewarded with luck—to a man who had risen and fallen and been able to rise again, and so conceivably had learned something about patience and the compassion of others.

When the reporter was younger, he might have said, "Nixon did not rise again; they raised him; if a new Nixon did not exist, they would have had to invent him." But the reporter was older now—presumably he knew more about the limits of the ruling class for inventing what they needed; he had learned how little talent or patience they had. Yes, at a certain point they might have decided, some of them at any rate, to dress Richard Nixon for the part again, but no one but Nixon had been able to get himself up from the political deathbed to which his failure in California had consigned him. He was here, then, answering questions in a voice that was probably closer to his own than it had ever been.

And some of the answers were not so bad. Much was Old Nixon, extraordinarily adroit at working both sides of a question so that both halves of his audience might be afterward convinced he was one of them. ("While homosexuality is a perversion punishable by law, and an intolerable offense to a law-abiding community, it is life-giving to many of those who are in need of it," he might have said if ever he had addressed a combined meeting of the Policemen's Benevolent Association and the Mattachine Society.) So he worked into the problem of Vietnam by starting at A and also by starting at Z, which he called a "two-pronged approach." He was for a negotiated settlement, he was for maintaining military strength because that would be the only way to "reach negotiated settlement of the war on an honorable basis." Later he was to talk of negotiations with "the next superpower, Communist China." He spoke patiently, with clarity, gently, not badly but for an unfortunate half-smile pasted to his face. The question would come, and he would back-hand it with his glove or trap it; like all politicians he had a considered answer for every question, but he gave structure to his answers, even a certain relish for their dialectical complexity. Where once he had pretended to think in sentimentalities and slogans, now he held the question up, worked over it, deployed it, amplified it, corrected its tendency, offered an aside (usually an attempt to be humorous), revealed its contradiction, and then declared a statement. With it all, a sensitivity almost palpable to the reservations of the Press about his character, his motive, and his good intention. He still had no natural touch with them, his half-smile while he listened was unhappy, for it had nowhere to go but into a full smile and his full smile was as false as false teeth, a pure exercise of will. You could all but see the signal pass from his brain to his jaw. "SMILE," said the signal, and so he flashed teeth in a painful kind of joyous grimace that spoke of some shrinkage in the liver, or the gut, which he would have to repair afterward by other medicine than good-fellowship. (By winning the Presidency, perhaps.) He had always had the ability to violate his own nature absolutely if that happened to be necessary to his will—there had never been anyone in American life so resolutely phony as Richard Nixon, nor anyone so transcendentally successful by such means—small wonder half the electorate had regarded him for years as equal to a disease. But he was less phony now, *that was the miracle,* he had moved from a position of total ambition and total alienation from his own person (at the time of Checkers the dog speech) to a place now where he was halfway conciliated with his own self. As he spoke, he kept going in and out of focus, true one instant, phony the next, then quietly correcting the false step.

Question from the Press: *You emphasized the change in the country and abroad. Has this led you to change your thinking in any shape or form specifically?*

Answer: *It certainly has.* (But he was too eager. Old Nixon was always ready to please with good straight American boyhood enthusiasm. So he tacked back, his voice throttled down.) *As the facts change, any intelligent man* (firm but self-deprecatory, he is including the Press with himself) *does change his approaches to the problems.* (Now sharp awareness of the next Press attitude.) *It does not mean that he is an opportunist.* (Now modestly, reasonably.) *It means only that he is a pragmatist, a realist, applying principles to the new situations.* (Now he will deploy some of the resources of his answer.) *For example . . . in preparing the acceptance speech I hope to give next Thursday, I was reading over my acceptance speech in 1960, and I thought then it was, frankly, quite a good speech. But I realize how irrelevant much of what I said in 1960 in foreign affairs was to the problems of today.* (The admission was startling. The Old Nixon was never wrong. Now, he exploited the shift in a move to his political left, pure New Nixon.) *Then the Communist world was a monolithic world. Today it is a split world, schizophrenic, with . . . great diversity . . . in Eastern Europe* (a wholesome admission for anyone who had labored in John Foster Dulles' world.) *. . . after an era of confrontation . . . we now enter an era of negotiations with the Soviet Union.*

While he was never in trouble with the questions, growing surer and surer of himself as he went on, the tension still persisted between his actual presence as a man not altogether alien to the abyss of a real problem and the political practitioner of his youth, that snake-oil salesman who was never back of any idea he sold but always off to the side, where he might observe its effect on the sucker. The New Nixon groped and searched for the common touch he had once been able to slip into the old folks with the ease of an incubus on a spinster. Now he tried to use slang, put quotes around it with a touching, almost pathetic, reminder of Nice-Nellyism, the inhibition of the good clean church upbringing of his youth insisting on exhibiting itself, as if he were saying with a YMCA slick snicker, "After we break into slang, there's always the danger of the party getting *rough*." It was that fatal prissiness which must have driven him years ago into all the militaristic muscle-bending witch-hunting foam-rubber virilities of the young Senator and the young Vice President. So now he talked self-consciously of how the members of his staff, counting delegates, were "playing what we call 'the strong game.' " SMILE said his brain. FLASH went the teeth. But his voice seemed to give away that whatever they called it, they probably didn't call it "the strong game," or if they did, *he* didn't. So he framed little phrases. Like "a leg-up." Or "my intuition, my 'gut feelings,' so to speak." Deferential air followed by SMILE—FLASH. Was it possible that one of the secrets of Old Nixon was that his psyche had been trapped in rock-formations, nay, geological strata of Sunday School inhibitions? Was it even possible that he was a good man, not a bad man, a good man who had been trapped by an early milieu whose habits had left him with such innocence about three-quarters of the world's experience that he had become an absolute monster of opportunism about the quarter he comprehended all too well? Listening to Nixon now, studying his new modesty, it was impossible to tell whether he was a serious man on the path of returning to his own true seriousness, out to unite the nation again as he promised with every remark—"Reconciliation of the races is a primary objective of the United States"—or whether the young devil had reconstituted himself into a more consummate devil, Old Scratch as a modern Abe Lincoln of modesty.

Question from the Press: *A little less than six years ago, after your defeat for the Governorship of California, you announced at the ensuing press conference that that was going to be your last news conference. Could you recall for us this morning two or three of the most important points in your own thinking which made you reverse that statement and now reach for political office on the highest level?*

Answer: *Had there not been the division of the Republican Party in 1964 and had there not been the vacuum of leadership that was created by that division and by that defeat, I would not be here today. . . . I believe that my travels around the country and the world in this period of contemplation and this period of withdrawal from the political scene* (some dark light of happiness now in his eye, as if withdrawal and contemplation had given him the first deep pleasures, or perhaps the first real religious pleasures of his life), *in which I have had a chance to observe not only the United States but the world, has led me to the conclusion that returning to the arena was something that I should do* (said almost as if he had heard a voice in some visitation of the night)—*not that I consider myself to be an indispensable man.* (Said agreeably in a relaxed tone, as if he had thought indeed to the bottom of this and had found the relaxation of knowing he was not indispensable an absurd vanity if one stares at Nixon from without, but he had been Vice President before he was forty, and so had had to see himself early, perhaps much too early, as a man of destiny. Now, reservation underlined, he could continue.) *But something that I should do* (go for the Presidency) *because this is the time I think when the man and the moment in history come together.* (An extraordinary admission for a Republican, with their Protestant detestation of philosophical deeps or any personification of history. With one remark, Nixon had walked into the oceans of Marx, Spengler, Heidegger, and Tolstoy; and Dostoevski and Kierkegaard were in the wings. Yes, Richard Nixon's mind had entered the torture chambers of the modern consciousness!)

*I have always felt that a man cannot seek the Presidency and get it simply because he wants it. I think that he can seek the Presidency and obtain it only when the Presidency requires what he may have to offer* (the Presidency was then a mystical seat, mystical as the choice of a woman's womb) *and I have had the feeling* (comfortably pleasant and modest again—no phony Nixon here) *and it may be a presumptuous feeling, that because of the vacuum of leadership in the Republican Party, because of the need for leadership particularly qualified in foreign affairs, because I have known not only the country, but the world as a result of my travels, that now time* (historical-time—the very beast of the mystic!) *requires that I re-enter the arena.* (Then he brought out some humor. It was not great humor, but for Nixon it was curious and not indelicate.) *And incidentally, I have been very willing to do so.* (Re-enter the arena.) *I am not being drafted. I want to make that very clear. I am very willing to do so. There has never been a draft in Miami in August anyway.* (Nice laughter from the Press—he has won them by a degree. Now he is on to finish the point.) . . . *I believe that if my judgment—and my intuition, my "gut feelings" so to speak, about America and American political tradition—is right, this is the year that I will win.*

The speech had come in the middle of the conference and he kept fielding questions afterward, never wholly at ease, never caught in trouble, mild, firm, reasonable, highly disciplined—it was possible he was one of the most disciplined men in America. After it was over, he walked down the aisle, and interviewers gathered around him, although not in great number. The reporter stood within two feet of Nixon at one point but had not really a question to ask that could be answered abruptly. "What, sir, would you say is the state of your familiarity with the works of Edmund Burke?" No, it was more to get a sense of the candidate's presence, and it was a modest presence, no more formidable before the immediate Press in its physical aura than a floorwalker in a department store, which is what Old Nixon had often been called, or worse—Assistant Mortician. It was probable that bodies did not appeal to him in inordinate measure, and a sense of the shyness of the man also appeared—shy after all these years!—but Nixon must have been habituated to loneliness after all those agonies in the circus skin of Tricky Dick. Had he really improved? The reporter caught himself hoping that Nixon had. If his physical presence inspired here no great joy nor even distrust, it gave the sense of a man still entrenched in toils of isolation, as if only the office of the Presidency could be equal (in the specific density of its importance) to the labyrinthine delivery of the natural man to himself. Then and only then might he know the strength of his own hand and his own moral desire. It might even be a measure of the not-entirely-dead promise of America if a man as opportunistic as the early Nixon could grow in reach and comprehension and stature to become a leader. For if that were possible in these bad years, then all was still possible, and the country not stripped of its blessing. New and marvelously complex improvement of a devil, or angel-in-chrysalis, or both—good and evil now at war in the man, Nixon was at least, beneath the near to hermetic boredom of his old presence, the most interesting figure at the convention, or at least so the reporter had decided by the end of the press conference that Tuesday in the morning.

### RONALD REAGAN IN 1968

For years in the movies he had played the good guy and been proud of it. If he didn't get the girl, it was because he was too good a guy to be overwhelmingly attractive. That was all right. He would grit his teeth and get the girl next time out. Since this was conceivably the inner sex drama of half of respectable America, he was wildly popular with Republicans. For a party that prided itself on its common sense, they were curiously, even outrageously, sentimental.

On Tuesday the reporter had found Reagan at the Di Lido in downtown Miami Beach, where the Alabama and Louisiana delegations were housed. In with Louisiana in a caucus, the Governor came out later to give a quick press conference, pleading ignorance of his situation. Listening to him, it was hard to believe he was fifty-seven, two years older than Nixon, for he had a boy's face, no gray in his head—he was reputed to dye his hair—and his make-up (about which one could hear many a whisper) was too excellent, if applied, to be detected.

Still, unlike Nixon, Reagan was altogether at ease with the Press. They had been good to him, they would be good again—he had the confidence of the elected governor of a big state, precisely what Nixon had always lacked; besides, Reagan had long ago incorporated the confidence of an actor who knows he is popular with interviewers. In fact, he had a public manner which was so natural that his discrepancies appeared only slightly surrealistic: At the age of fifty-seven, he had the presence of a man of thirty, the deferential enthusiasm, the bright but dependably unoriginal mind of a sales manager promoted for his ability over men older than himself. He also had the neatness, and slim economy of move, of a man not massive enough to be President, in the way one might hesitate, let us say, ever to consider a gentleman like Mr. Johnny Carson of television—whatever his fine intelligence—as Chief Executive of a Heavyweight Empire. It was that way with Reagan. He was somehow too light, a lightweight six feet one inch tall—whatever could he do but stick-and-move? Well, he could try to make Generals happy in order to show how heavy he really might be, which gave no heart to consideration of his politics. Besides, darkening shades of the surreal, he had a second personality that was younger than the first, very young, boyish, maybe thirteen or fourteen, freckles, cowlick, I-tripped-on-my-sneaker-lace aw shucks variety of confusion. For back on Tuesday afternoon they had been firing questions at him on the order of how well he was doing at prying delegates loose from Nixon, and he could only say over and over, "I don't know. I just don't know. I've been moving around so quickly talking to so many delegations in caucus that I haven't had time to read a paper."

"Well, what do the delegations say, Governor?"

"Well, I don't know. They listen to me very pleasantly and politely, and then I leave and they discuss what I've said. But I can't tell you if we're gaining. I think we are, but I don't know, I don't know. I honestly don't know, gentlemen," and he broke out into a grin, "I just don't know," exactly like a thirteen-year-old, as if indeed gentlemen he *really* didn't know, and the Press and the delegates listening laughed with him as if there were no harm in Ronald Reagan, not unless the lightning struck.

# Chicago, August 24–29

Chicago is the great American city. New York is one of the capitals of the world, but Chicago is a great American city. Perhaps it is the last of the great American cities.

The reporter was sentimental about the town. Since he had grown up in Brooklyn, it took him no time to recognize, whenever he was in Chicago again, that the urbanites here were like the good people of Brooklyn—they were simple, strong, warm-spirited, sly, rough, compassionate, jostling, tricky, and extraordinarily good-natured because they had sex in their pockets, muscles on their back, hot eats around the corner, neighborhoods that dripped with the sauce of local legend, and real city architecture, brownstones with different windows on every floor, vistas for miles of red-brick, and two-family wood-frame houses with balconies and porches, runty stunted trees rich as farmland in their promise of tenderness the first city evenings of spring, streets where kids played stick-ball and roller-hockey, lots of smoke and iron twilight. The clangor of the late nineteenth century, the very hope of greed, was in these streets. London one hundred years ago could not have looked much better.

Brooklyn, however, beautiful Brooklyn, grew beneath the sky-scrapers of Manhattan, so it never became a great city, merely an asphalt herbarium for talent destined to cross the river. Chicago did not have Manhattan to preempt top branches, so it grew up from the savory of its neighborhoods to some of the best high-rise architecture in the world, and because its people were Poles and Ukrainians and Czechs as well as Irish and the rest, the city had Byzantine corners worthy of Prague or Moscow, odd tortured attractive drawbridges over the Chicago River, huge Gothic spires like the skyscraper that held the *Chicago Tribune,* curves and abutments and balconies in cylindrical structures thirty stories high twisting in and out of the curves of the river, and fine balustrades in its parks. Chicago had a North Side on Lake Shore Drive, where the most elegant apartment buildings in the world could be found—Sutton Place in New York betrayed the cost analyst in the eye of the architect next to these palaces of glass and charcoal colored steel. In superb back streets behind the towers on the lake were brownstones that spoke of ironies, cupidities, and intricate ambition in the fists of the robber barons who commissioned them—substantiality, hard work, heavy drinking, carnal meats of pleasure, and a Midwestern sense of how to arrive at upper-class decorum were also in the American grandeur of these few streets. If there was a fine American aristocracy of deportment, it was probably in the clean tough keen-eyed ladies of Chicago one saw on the streets off Lake Shore Drive on the near North Side of Chicago.

Not here for a travelogue—no need then to detail the Loop, in death like the center of every other American city, but what a dying! Old department stores, old burlesque houses, avenues, dirty avenues, the El with its nineteenth-century dialogue of iron screeching against iron about a turn, and caverns of shadow on the pavement beneath, the grand hotels with their massive lobbies, baroque ceilings, resplendent as Roman bordellos, names like Sheraton-Blackstone, Palmer

House, red fields of carpet, a golden cage for elevator, the unheard crash of giant mills stamping new shapes on large and obdurate materials is always pounding in one's inner ear—Dreiser had not written about Chicago for nothing.

To the West of the Lake were factories and Ciceros, Mafia-lands and immigrant lands; to the North, the suburbs, the Evanstons; to the South were Negro ghettos of the South Side—belts of Black men amplifying each the resonance of the other's cause—the Black belt had the Blackstone Rangers, the largest gang of juvenile delinquents on earth, two thousand by some count—one could be certain the gang had leaders as large in potential as Hannibal or Attila the Hun—how else account for the strength and wit of a stud who would try to rise so high in the Blackstone Rangers?

Further South and West were enclaves for the University of Chicago, more factories, more neighborhoods for Poles, some measure of more good hotels on the lake, and endless neighborhoods— white neighborhoods that went for miles of ubiquitous dingy wood houses with back yards, neighborhoods to hint of Eastern Europe, Ireland, Tennessee, a gathering of all the clans of the Midwest, the Indians and Scotch-Irish, Swedes, some Germans, Italians, Hungarians, Rumanians, Finns, Slovaks, Slovenes—it was only the French who did not travel. In the Midwest, land spread out; not five miles from the Loop were areas as empty, deserted, enormous, and mournful by night as the outer freight yards of Omaha. Some industrial desert or marsh would lie low on the horizon, an area squalling by day, deserted by night, except for the hulking Midwestern names of the boxcars and the low sheds, the warehouse buildings, the wire fences that went along the side of unpaved roads for thousands of yards.

The stockyards were like this, the famous stockyards of Chicago were at night as empty as the railroad sidings of the moon. Long before the Democratic Convention of 1968 came to the Chicago Amphitheatre, indeed eighteen years ago, when the reporter had paid his only previous visit, the area was even then deserted at night, empty as the mudholes on a battlefield after a war has passed. West of the Amphitheatre, railroad sidings seemed to continue on for miles, accompanied by those same massive low sheds larger than armories, with pens for tens of thousands of frantic beasts, cattle, sheep, and pigs, animals in an orgy of gorging and dropping and waiting and smelling blood. In the slaughterhouses, during the day, a carnage worthy of the Disasters of War took place each morning and afternoon. Endless files of animals were led through pens to be stunned on the head by hammers, and then hind legs trussed, be hoisted up on hooks to hang head down, and ride along head down on an overhead trolley which brought them to Negroes or whites, usually huge, the whites most often Polish or Hunkies (hence the etymology of Honkie—a Chicago word) the Negroes up from the South, huge men built for the shock of the work, slash of a knife on the neck of the beast and gouts of blood to bathe their torso (stripped of necessity to the waist) and blood to splash their legs. The animals passed a psychic current back along the overhead trolley—each cut throat released its scream of death into the throat not yet cut and just behind, and that penultimate throat would push the voltage up, drive the current back and further back into the screams of every animal upside down and hanging from that clanking overhead trolley, bare electric bulbs screaming into the animal eye and brain, gurglings and awesome hollows of sound coming back from the open plumbing ahead of the cut jugular as if death were indeed a rapids along some underground river, and the fear and absolute anguish of beasts dying upside down further ahead passed back along the line, back all the way to the corrals and the pens, back even to the siding with the animals still in boxcars, back, who knew—so high might be the psychic voltage of the beast—back to the farm where first they were pushed into the truck that would take them into the train. What an awful odor the fear of absolute and unavoidable death gave to the stool and stuffing and pure vomitous shit of the beasts waiting in the pens in the stockyard, what a sweat of hell-leather, and yet the odor, no, the titanic stench, that rose from the yards was not so simple as the collective diarrhetics of an hysterical army of beasts, no, for after the throats were cut and the blood ran in rich gutters, red light on the sweating back of the red throat-cutters, the dying and some just-dead animals clanked along the overhead, arterial blood spurting like the nip-ups of a little boy urinating in public, the red-hot carcass quickly encountered another Black or Hunkie with a long knife on a long stick who would cut the belly from chest to groin and a stew and a stink of two hundred pounds of stomach, lungs, intestines, mucosities, spleen, exploded cowflop and pigshit, blood, silver lining, liver, mother-of-pearl tissue, and general gag-all would flop and slither over the floor, the man with the knife getting a good blood-splatting as he dug and twisted with his blade to liberate the roots of the organ, intestine and impedimenta still integrated into the meat and bone of the excavated existence he was working on.

Well, the smell of the entrails and that agonized blood electrified by all the outer neons of ultimate fear got right into the grit of the stockyard stench. Let us pass over into the carving and the slicing, the boiling and scraping, annealing and curing of the flesh in sugars and honeys and smoke, the cooking of the cow carcass, stamp of the inspector, singeing of the hair, boiling of hooves, grinding of gristle, the wax-papering and the packaging, the foiling and the canning, the burning of the residue, and the last slobber of the last unusable guts as it went into the stockyard furnace, and up as stockyard smoke, burnt blood and burnt bone and burnt hair to add their properties of specific stench to fresh blood, fresh entrails, fresh fecalities already all over the air. It is the smell of the stockyards, all of it taken together, a smell so bad one must go down to visit the killing of the animals or never eat meat again. Watching the animals be slaughtered, one knows the human case—no matter how close to angel we may come, the butcher is equally there. So be it. Chicago makes for hard minds. On any given night, the smell may go anywhere—down to Gary to fight with the smog and the coke, out to Cicero to quiet the gangs with their dreams of gung ho and mop-up, North to Evanston to remind the polite that *inter faeces et urinam* are we born, and East on out to Lake Michigan, where the super felicities in the stench of such earthbound miseries and corruptions might cheer the fish with the clean spermy deep waters of their fate.

Yes, Chicago was a town where nobody could ever forget how the money was made. It was picked up from floors still slippery with blood, and if one did not protest and take a vow of vegetables, one knew at least that life was hard, life was in the flesh and in the massacre of the flesh—one breathed the last agonies of beasts. So something of the entrails and the secrets of the gut got into the faces of native Chicagoans. A great city, a strong city with faces tough as leather hide and pavement, it was also a city where the faces took on the broad beastiness of ears that were dull enough to ignore the bleatings of the doomed, noses battered enough to smell no more the stench of every unhappy end, mouths—fat mouths or slit mouths— ready to taste the gravies that were the reward of every massacre, and eyes, simple pig eyes, which could look the pig truth in the face. In any other city, they would have found technologies to silence the beasts with needles, quarter them with machines, lull them with Muzak, and have stainless steel for floors, aluminum beds to take over the old overhead trolley—animals would be given a shot of vitamin-enrichment before they took the last ride. But in Chicago, they did it straight, they cut the animals right out of their hearts—which is why it was the last of the great American cities, and people had great faces, carnal as blood, greedy, direct, too impatient for hypocrisy, in love with honest plunder. They were big and human and their brother in heaven was the slaughtered pig—they did not ignore him. If the yowls and moans of his extinction was the broth of their strength, still they had honest guts to smell him to the end—they did not flush the city with Odorono or Pinex or No-Scent, they swilled the beer and assigned the hits and gave America its last chance at straight-out drama. Only a great city provides honest spectacle, for that is the salvation of the schizophrenic soul. Chicago may have beasts on the street, it may have a giant of fortitude for Mayor who grew into a beast—a man with the very face of Chicago—but it is an honest town, it does not look to incubate psychotics along an air-conditioned corridor with a vinyl floor.

## McCARTHY IN CHICAGO

There were differences now by the end of August. McCarthy, at Midway Airport to greet his followers, looked big in his presidential candidate's suit this sunny afternoon, no longer tired, happy apparently with the crowd and the air of his reception. He went down the aisle of friends and reporters who had managed to get ahead of the restraining rope for the crowd and shook hands, gave a confident wink or good twinkle there, "Whatever are you doing *here,* Norman?" he said with a grin, quick as a jab, and made his way up to the platform, where a clump of microphones on spikes garnished the podium. But the microphones were dead. Which set McCarthy to laughing. Meanwhile posters waved out in the crowd: AMERICA'S PRIMARY HOPE; LUCIDITY, NOT LUNACY; MAKE MINE MCCARTHY. He scanned the home-made posters, as if his sense of such language, after a decade and more, had become sufficiently encyclopedic to treasure every rare departure, and he laughed from time to time as he saw something he liked.

Finally, he called out to the crowd, "*They* cut the power line. *We're* trying to fix it." Great college moans at the depravity of the opposition—wise laughter at the good cheer of the situation. "Let's sing," said Gene McCarthy; a shout from the crowd. His standard was theirs: Good wit could always support small horror. So they sang, This land is your land, this land is my land, and McCarthy moved along to another mike, much shifting of position in his entourage to be near him, then gave up and came back to the first mike. Things were now fixed. He introduced Senator Yarborough from Texas, who would in turn introduce him. Yarborough looked like a florid genial iron-ribbed barrel of a British Conservative M.P., and spoke with a modest Texas accent; he told the audience that McCarthy had "won this campaign in the hearts of the American people." While he spoke, McCarthy sat next to his wife, Abigail, a warm-colored woman with a pleasant face full of the arch curves of a most critical lady of the gentry. Something in her expression spoke of uncharitable wit, but she was elegant—one could see her as First Lady. Indeed! One could almost see him now as President. He had size, he had humor. He looked strong. When he got up to speak, he was in easy form. Having laughed at a poster that said, WELCOME TO FORT DALEY, he began by paying his respects to the Mayor of Chicago who is "watching over all of us."

"Big Brother," shouted a powerhouse in the crowd.

McCarthy talked for six or seven minutes. The audience was looking for a bust-out-of-the-corrals speech, but the Senator was not giving it. He talked mildly, with his throwaway wit, his almost diffident assertion—"We can build a new society and a new world," said he at one point in the mildest tones of his mild register, and then added as if to take the curse off such intellectual presumption, "We're not asking for too much—just a modest use of intelligence."

"Too much," murmured a news-service man admiringly.

A good yell came up. Even a modest use of intelligence would forbid Vietnam.

McCarthy drew one more big cheer by declaring he was not interested in being Vice President. "I'm not here to compromise what we've all worked for," he said to cheers, and shortly after, to the crowd's disappointment, was done. The band played—Warren King's Brass Impact, four trombones, two guitars, drums, six trumpets, one tenor sax, two Negroes not very black among the musicians.

Yes, he had compromised nothing, not even the musicians. If he was at heart a conservative, and no great man for the Blacks, then damned if he would encourage harmoniums and avalanches of soul music. No, he had done it his way up to now, cutting out everyone from his councils who was interested in politicking at the old trough, no, his campaign had begun by being educational, and educational had he left it—he had not compromised an inch, nor played the demagogue for a moment, and it had given him strength, not strength enough perhaps to win, certainly not enough to win, but rectitude had laid the keel, and in that air of a campaign run at last for intelligent men, and give no alms to whores, he left.

# Property

Lyndon Johnson was first preceptor of the key that politics-is-property so you never give something away for nothing. Convention politics is not the art of the possible so much as the art of what is possible when you are dealing with property holders. A delegate's vote is his holding—he will give it up without return no more than a man will sign over his house entire to a worthy cause.

The true property-holder is never ambivalent about his land, he does not mock it or see adjacent estates as more deserving than his own—so a professional in politics without pride in his holding is a defector. The meanest ward-heeler in the cheapest block of Chicago has his piece—he cannot be dislodged without leaving his curse nor the knotty untangling of his relations with a hundred job-holders in the area; he gives up tithes in the umbilical act of loyalty to his boss, he receives protection for his holding in return.

Such property relations are to be witnessed for every political sinecure in the land—judgeships, jobs, contracts, promises—it comes down to chairs in offices, and words negotiable like bonds: All of that is politics as simple property. Everybody in the game has a piece, and that piece is workable, it is equivalent to capital, it can be used to accrue interest by being invested in such sound conservative enterprises as decades of loyalty to the same Machine. So long as the system progresses, so will one's property be blessed with dividends. But such property can also be used as outright risk capital—one can support an insurgent movement in one's party, even risk the loss of one's primary holding in return for the possibility of acquiring much more.

This, of course, is still politics at city hall, county, or state house, this is the politics of the party regular, politics as simple property, which is to say politics as concrete negotiable power—the value of their engagement in politics is at any moment just about directly convertible to cash.

Politics at national level can still be comprehended by politics-as-property provided one remembers that moral integrity (or the public impression of such) in a high politician is also property, since it brings power and/or emoluments to him. Indeed a very high politician—which is to say a statesman or leader—has no political substance unless he is the servant of ideological institutions or interests and the available moral passions of the electorate, so serving, he is the agent of the political power they bestow on him, which power is certainly a property. Being a leading anti-Communist used to be an invaluable property for which there was much competition—Richard Nixon had once gotten in early on the equivalent of an Oklahoma landgrab by staking out whole territories of that property. "End the war in Vietnam" is a property to some, "Let no American blood be shed in vain" is obviously another. A politician picks and chooses among moral properties. If he is quick-witted, unscrupulous, and does not mind a life of constant anxiety, he will hasten—there is a great competition for things valuable in politics—to pick up properties wherever he can, even if they are rival holdings. To the extent a politician is his own man, attached to his own search for his own spiritual truth—which is to say willing to end in any unpalatable position to which the character of his truth could lead him—then he is ill-equipped for the game of politics. Politics is property. You pick up as much as you can, pay the minimum for the holding, extract the maximum, and combine where you may— small geniuses like Humphrey saw, for example, that devout trade-unionism and devout anti-Communism might once have faced each other across no-man's-land but right after the Second World War were ready to enrich each other into the tenfold of national respectability.

There is no need to underline Lyndon Johnson's ability to comprehend these matters. Johnson understood that so far as a man was a political animal (and therefore not searching for some private truth that might be independent of politics), he was then, if deprived of his properties, close to being a dead man. So the true political animal is cautious—he never, except in the most revolutionary times, permits himself to get into a position where he will have to dare his political stake on one issue, one bet, no, to avoid that, he will even give up small pieces of his stuff for nothing, he will pay tribute.

The pearl in the oyster of this proposition is that there is only one political job in America which has no real property attached to it, except for the fantastical property of promotion by tragedy, and that, of course, is the Vice Presidency. It is the only high office to which all the secondary characteristics of political property may adhere—comprehensive public awareness of the name, attention in the press to one's speeches, honorary emoluments in the Senate, intimacy (of varying degree) with the President, junkets abroad. If you are very active as Vice President, everyone in America knows your name. But that is your only property. It is not the same thing as real power—more like being a movie star. Taken in proportion to the size of the office, the Vice President has less real holding than the ward-heeler in his anteroom chair. The Vice President can promise many things, but can be certain of delivering on nothing. So he can never be certain of getting anything back. It is not a job for a politician but a philosopher.

It is the thesis of this argument that Lyndon Johnson, having recognized that he could not win the election in 1968 (and could win the nomination for a candidate of his choice only by exploding his own party into two or more fragments), nonetheless set out to make the party vindicate him. The last property of political property is ego, ego intact, ego burnished by institutional and reverential flame. Not all men wish statues of themselves on their tomb, but it is hard to think of LBJ with a plain stone—"Here lies a simple fellow with many victories and one catastrophic mistake"—Lyndon would carry his emoluments into the debating chambers of Hell. He had had to live after all through March and April and May with the possibility of Bobby Kennedy winning the nomination, winning the election, the laughter of the Kennedys playing echoes off the walls of his own bad dreams; Lyndon had learned during the propertyless period of his own Vice Presidential days how rapid could be the slide of your holdings, how soluble the proud salts of your ego. How quickly might come his deterioration if a Kennedy were again in office—his own bleak death in such a case may have spoken to him already. Men whose lives are built on ego can die of any painful disease but one—they cannot endure the dissolution of their own ego, for then nothing is left with which to face emotion, nothing but the urge to grovel at the enemy's feet. It is the primitive price one pays for holding on to property that possesses no moral value. How much Johnson must have been ready to offer in March and April and May in order that Bobby Kennedy be stopped. Perhaps even his own vindication might have been sacrificed.

After the Senator's assassination, however, nomination for Humphrey was empty for Johnson. If Humphrey wished to win the election, his interest was to separate himself from the President. Since this was counter to Johnson's interest, the torture of Hubert Humphrey began.

Mark it: Politics is the hard dealing of hard men over properties; their strength is in dealing and their virility. Back of each negotiator is the magic of his collected properties—the real contention of the negotiation is: Whose properties possess the more potent magic? A good politician then can deal with every kind of property-holder but a fanatic, because the fanatic is disembodied from his property. He conceives of his property—his noble ideal!—as existing just as well without him. His magic partakes of the surreal. That is why Lyndon Johnson could never deal with Ho Chi Minh, and why he could manipulate Hubert Humphrey with absolute confidence. Humphrey had had to live for four years with no basic property, and nobody knew better than the President what that could do to an animal as drenched in politics as Hubert. Humphrey could never make his move. Deprived for four years of his seat as Senator, deprived of constituency and the power to trade votes, the small intricate nourishing marrow of being able to measure the profit or loss of concrete favors traded for concrete favors, the exchange of political affections based on solid property-giving, property-acquiring negotiations, forced to offer influence he now might or might not possess, Humphrey never knew where to locate himself in negotiations spoken or unspoken with Lyndon Johnson. So his feet kept slipping. Against the crusades of law and order building on the Right, his hope was to build a crusade on the Left, not to divide the Left. But to do that, he would have had to dare the enmity of Lyndon Johnson, have had to dare the real chance that he might lose the nomination, and that was the one chance he could not take, for that would be the hollowest death of them all. He would be lost in retirement, his idle flesh would witness with horror the decomposition of his ego. A politician in such trouble can give away the last of his soul in order not to be forced to witness how much he has given away already.

Hubert Humphrey was the small genius of American politics—his horror was that he was wed to Lyndon Johnson, the domestic genius of us all. Humphrey could not find sufficient pride in his liver to ask for divorce. His liver turned to dread. He came to Chicago with nobody to greet him at the airport except a handful of the faithful—the Vice President's own poor property—those men whose salary he paid, and they were not many. Later, a group of a few hundred met him at the Sherman House, the boys and the Humphrey girls were out. In 1964 some of the Goldwater girls had looked like hookers on horses, now in '68, some of the women for Humphrey looked like hookers. The Mafia loved Humphrey; they always loved a political leader who kept a well-oiled pair of peanuts in his pants, and there was big money behind Humphrey, $800,000 had been raised for him in one night in New York. He would be the perfect President—for a time—for every speculator who liked a government contract to anchor his line while he got off that touchdown pass. So Humphrey money was there in Chicago for convention frolics, and a special nightclub or cabaret in the Hilton called the Hubaret where you needed a scorecard to separate the trade-union leaders from the Maf, and the women—let us not insult women. Suffice it that the beehives were out, and every girl named Marie had a coif like Marie Antoinette. Every Negro on the take was there as well—some of the slickest, roundest, blackest swingers ever to have contacts in with everyone from Mayor Daley to the Blackstone Rangers. There was action at the Hubaret, and cheer for every late-night drinker. If Hubie got in, the after-hours joints would prosper; the politics of joy would never demand that all the bars be dead by four—who could argue with that?

Negroes in general had never been charmed with McCarthy. If he was the epitome of Whitey at his best, that meant Whitey at ten removes, dry wit, stiff back, two and a half centuries of Augustan culture and their distillate—the ironic manners of the tightest country gentry; the Blacks did not want Whitey at his best and boniest in a year when they were out to find every justification (they were not hard to find) to hate the Honkie. But if the Black militant and the Black workingman would find no comfort or attraction in McCarthy, think then of how the Black mixer-dixer was going to look on Clean Gene. He wasn't about to make a pilgrimage up to some Catholic rectory in the Minnesota North Woods where they passed one bean through the hot water for bean soup, no, he wanted some fatback in his hands. You couldn't take the kind of hard and sanctified little goat turds McCarthy was passing out for political marbles back to the Black homefolk when they were looking for you to spread the gravy around. So Hubie Humphrey came into Chicago with nine-tenths of the organized Democratic Party—Black support, labor support, Mafia support, Southern delegates support, and you could find it all at the Hubaret if you were looking, as well as a wet wash of delegates with buttons for Humphrey, the big bold **HHH.**

There were 1,400 to 1,500 delegates secured for Hubert Humphrey on the day he came to town—such was the hard estimate of the hardest heads on his staff, Larry O'Brien, Norman Sherman, Bill Connell; the figure was low, they were not counting on the favorite sons of the South, nor on the small reserve of uncommitted delegates. Still there were rumors up of gale warnings, and much anxiety—Mayor Daley had led the Illinois delegation into caucus on Sunday, and led them out again without committing a single one of the state's 118 votes to a single delegate and there were stories Daley wanted Teddy Kennedy.

Either the convention was sewed up for Humphrey or the convention was soft. No one really knew. Usually it was enough to come to conventions with less than a first ballot victory, even two hundred votes less, and you were certain of winning. The panic among delegates to get on the winning side at the last minute is always a stampede. It is as though your land will double in value. Humphrey came in with one hundred to two hundred votes more than he needed, yet he was not without his own panic; he took care to announce on *Meet the Press* before taking the plane to Chicago that he supported President Johnson's Vietnam policies because they were "basically sound." For two months he had been vacillating, giving hints one day that he was not far from the doves, rushing back the next to be close in tone to the Administration. It could be said, of course, that it was part of his political skill to keep the McCarthyites uncertain of his position; once convinced that he would take a line close to Lyndon Johnson on the war in Vietnam, they might look—McCarthy included—to induce Teddy Kennedy to run. So Humphrey played at being a dove as a way of holding the youngest Kennedy in Hyannis. But what was he to gain besides the approval of Lyndon Johnson? A liaison with McCarthy could even give him a chance for victory in November. Yet Humphrey engaged in massive safe play after massive safe play, paying court to the South, paying court to LBJ, to Daley, to Meany, to Connally; even then, he came to Chicago with his nomination insecure. He had 1,500 votes, but if something went wrong he did not know if he could count on a single one of them—they could all wash away in the night. Humphrey was staying at the Conrad Hilton, but his first act after landing at O'Hare was to proceed to the Sherman House to visit the Illinois delegation. Daley was working to induce Teddy Kennedy to run—once Teddy Kennedy ran and lost, he might have to accept a draft as Vice President. At the same time, once running, he might show huge strength—Daley would then be able to claim he stole the nomination from Humphrey and got it over to Kennedy. Daley could not lose. All the while he was encouraging Kennedy to run, Humphrey was promising Daley more and more treasures, obliged—since he had no political property of his own just yet—to mortgage future property. He was assigning future and double substance to Daley, to the unions, to the South, to business interests. His holding operations, his safe plays to guarantee the nomination once the nomination was already secure, became exorbitantly expensive. A joke made the rounds of the convention:

"What was Hubert able to keep?"

"Well, he was able to keep Muriel."

His dangers were absurdly small. McCarthy, three times unpopular with the delegates, for being right, for being proud that he was right, and for dealing only in moral property, had no chance whatsoever. Moreover, he was disliked intensely by the Kennedyites. If Bobby Kennedy and Gene McCarthy had been in the Sinn Fein together they would have carried their guns in holsters under opposite shoulders—they embodied the ultimate war of the Irish. McCarthy was reputed to carry volumes of Augustine and Aquinas in his suitcase; it is possible Bobby Kennedy thought one of the penalties of being Irish is that you could get lost in the *Summa Theologica*.

But Hubert Humphrey carried no gun and no tome. Finally he was a hawk not a dove for the most visceral of reasons—his viscera were not firm enough to face the collective wrath of that military-industrial establishment he knew so well in Washington, that rifleman's schizophrenia one could see in the eyes of the clerks at the Pentagon; yes, his fear went beyond political common sense and a real chance to win, it went even beyond slavery to LBJ (because LBJ finally had also been afraid of the Pentagon), it came down to the simple fear that he was not ready to tell the generals that they were wrong. Peace they might yet accept, but not the recognition that they were somewhat insane—as quickly tell dragons to shift their nest.

### McCARTHY'S RESIGNATION DINNER

Early in the evening, McCarthy went into a meeting with Steve Smith, Teddy Kennedy's brother-in-law, and told him that he was willing to withdraw from the race if Kennedy would enter, and that he would instruct his delegates that they were free; further, he would suggest that they give their support to Kennedy.

Would there be anything he desired in return?

No, he was not asking for anything in victory or defeat. (McCarthy was obviously a fanatic—he was seeking to destroy politics-is-property.)

Smith thanked him, told him he would relay his message to Teddy Kennedy, made some comment on the munificence of the offer, perhaps thinking to himself that it came a little late, and left.

Perhaps two hours after this, the reporter encountered McCarthy by chance in a Chicago restaurant on the North Side.

The Senator, sitting at a long table in the corner of the main dining room, a modest room (for the restaurant was situated in a brownstone), had his back comfortably to the wall, and was chatting over the coffee with his guests. The atmosphere was sufficiently relaxed for the reporter and his friend, another reporter who had been doing a story on McCarthy for *Look,* to come up past the Secret Service without great strain and greet the Senator. Neither of the reporters was to know anything about the meeting with Steve Smith until some days later, but it was likely McCarthy had come to some decision—at the least, he was more relaxed than at any other time the reporter had seen him in Chicago. Perhaps it was the friends he was with, big Irishmen like himself for the most part, a couple of them present with their wives, or at least such was the reporter's impression, for he was introduced to more than a half-dozen people in the aftermath of meeting the Senator and some were big genial Irishmen with horn-rimmed glasses and some were lean Irishmen with craggy faces and one was an Irishman from Limerick with a Dublin face, one-third poet, one-third warrior, one-third clerk. Perhaps it was the company, but the reporter had never seen McCarthy in such a mood. The benign personality of the public meetings, agreeable but never compelling, was gone; the personality which suggested that serious activity had something absurd about it—gone. The manner which declared, "I'm a nice guy, and look what I got into"—gone!

Speaking with the license a man has when his dinner is interrupted, McCarthy struck back to the conversation twelve weeks earlier in a living room in Cambridge, "Still waiting for me to repeat that 1960 speech?"

"Well, Senator," said the reporter—he was trying to become sufficiently presumptuous to say, "If you could make a speech like that on the war in Vietnam tonight when the peace plank is debated . . ."

But McCarthy cut him off. "That was then. We don't retain all our abilities necessarily. Once the ability leaves you, how do you regain it?" It was impossible to tell if he was mocking the reporter or mocking himself. "I used to be angry then," he said across the table with an evil look of amusement, as if recording these remarks for posterity as well, his yellow eyes gleaming in the light, "but I can't seem to get angry again. It's a gift to get angry when you wish to get angry, Mailer."

"A grace I would say, sir."

If the table had been laughing at McCarthy's sallies, they chuckled now with his. The Senator's friends looked tough and were tough-minded, but they were obviously open to wit from any corner.

"Then you also want to ask yourself if you should get people angry." McCarthy went on in a voice of the hardest-tempered irony. "Once you get them angry, you've got to get them quieted down.

That's not so easy. Lyndon, for instance, has never understood the problem. He thinks politicians are cattle, whereas in fact most politicians are pigs. Now, Norman, there's a little difference between cattle and pigs which most people don't know. Lyndon doesn't know it. You see, to get cattle started, you make just a little noise, and then when they begin to run, you have to make more noise, and then you keep driving them with more and more noise. But pigs are different. You have to start pigs running with a great deal of noise, in fact the best way to start them is by reciting Latin, very loudly, that'll get them running—then you have to quiet your voice bit by bit and they'll keep moving. Lyndon has never understood this."

These gnomic remarks now concluded, the reporter had no idea precisely what the Senator was talking about. He had been expanding a metaphor, and images of the stockyards, the convention, the war on the streets, the expression on the face of Humphrey delegates and McCarthy delegates, and some tidal wave of contempt at the filthy polluted plumbing of things was in the remark. In the laughter that followed, the reporter was silent.

"It's a funny thing about pigs," McCarthy went on. "They have an odd way of keeping warm in winter if they find themselves outside. You see, pigs don't know if they're cold, provided their nose is warm. So they stand around in a circle with their nose between the hind legs of the pig in front of them. Wouldn't you call that a curious relationship?"

"Oh, Senator, I would call that a Satanic relationship."

McCarthy joined in the laughter. Hard was his face, hard as the bones and scourged flesh of incorruptibility, hard as the cold stone floor of a monastery in the North Woods at five in the morning. The reporter leaned forward to talk into his ear.

"You see, sir," he said, "the tragedy of the whole business is that you should never have had to run for President. You would have been perfect for the Cabinet." A keen look back from McCarthy's eye gave the sanction to continue. "Yessir," said the reporter, "you'd have made a perfect chief for the F.B.I!" and they looked at each other and McCarthy smiled and said, "Of course, you're absolutely right."

The reporter looked across the table into one of the hardest, cleanest expressions he had ever seen, all the subtle hints of puffiness and doubt sometimes visible in the Senator's expression now gone—no, the face that looked back belonged to a tough man, tough as the harder alloys of steel, a merciless face and very just, the sort of black Irish face that could have belonged to one of the hanging judges in a true court of Heaven, or to the proper commissioner of a police force too honest ever to have existed.

The reporter left. But the memory of McCarthy at this table persisted. And the memory of his presence, harder than the hardest alloys of steel. But not unjust. What iron it must have taken to be annealed in Lyndon's volcanic breath. Yes, the reporter had met many candidates, but McCarthy was the first who felt like a President, or at least felt like a President in that hard hour after he had relinquished the very last of his hopes, and so was enjoying his dinner.

### LINCOLN PARK

A moment:

The following is a remark by Dino Valente, an electric guitarist. It ran as the headline in an advertisement in the *East Village Other* for an album of his records.

> You take this electrical power out of the wall and you send it through the guitar and you bend it and shape it and make it into something, like songs for people and that power is a wonderful thing.

Yes, the Yippies were the militant wing of the Hippies, Youth International Party, and the movement was built on juice, not alcoholic juice, which comes out of the mystery of fermentation—why, dear God, as fruits and grains begin to rot, does some distillate of this art of the earth now in decomposition have the power to inflame consciousness and give us purchase on visions of Heaven and Hell?—no, rather, we are speaking of the juice that comes from another mystery, the passage of a metallic wire across a field of magnetism. That serves to birth the beast of all modern technology, electricity itself. The Hippies founded their temple in that junction where LSD crosses the throb of an electric guitar at full volume in the ear, solar plexus, belly, and loins. A tribal unity had passed through the youth of America (and half the nations of the world), a far-out vision of orgiastic revels stripped of violence or even the differentiation of sex. In the oceanic stew of a non-violent, tribal ball on drugs, nipples, arms, phalluses, mouths, wombs, armpits, short-hairs, navels, breasts, and cheeks, incense of odor, flower, and funk went humping into Breakthrough Freak-out Road together, and children on acid saw Valhalla, Ne-

penthe, and the Taj Mahal. Some went out forever, some went screaming down the alleys of the mad, where cockroaches drive like Volks-
wagens on the oilcloth of the moon, gluttons found vertigo in
centrifuges of consciousness, vomitoriums of ingestion; others found
love, some manifest of love, in light, in shards of Nirvana, sparks of
satori—they came back to the world a twentieth-century tribe wearing
celebration bells and filthy garments. Used-up livers gave their com-
plexions a sickly pale, and hair grew on their faces like weeds. Yet they
had seen some incontestable vision of the good—the universe was not
absurd to them; like pilgrims, they looked at society with the eyes of
children: Society was absurd. Every emperor who went down the path
was naked, and they handed flowers to policemen.

It could hardly last. The slum in which they chose to live—for they
were refugees in the main from the suburbs of the middle class—fretted against them, fretted against their filth, their easy casual cohabiting, their selflessness (which is always the greatest insult to the ghetto,
for selflessness is a luxury to the poor, it beckons to the spineless, the
undifferentiated, the inept, the derelict, the drowning—a poor man is
nothing without the fierce thorns of his ego). So the Hippies collided
with the slums, and were beaten and robbed, fleeced and lashed and
buried and imprisoned, and here and there murdered, and here and
there successful, for there was scattered liaison with bikers and Panthers and Puerto Ricans on the East Coast and Mexicans on the West.
There came a point when, like most tribes, they divided. Some of the
weakest and some of the least attached went back to the suburbs or
moved up into commerce or communications; others sought gentler
homes, where the sun was kind and the flowers plentiful; others hardened and, like all pilgrims with their own vision of a promised land,
began to learn how to work for it, and finally, how to fight for it. So the
Yippies came out of the Hippies, ex-Hippies, diggers, bikers, dropouts from college, hipsters up from the South. They made a community of sorts, for their principles were simple—everybody, obviously,
must be allowed to do (no way around the next three words) his own
thing, provided he hurt no one doing it—they were yet to learn that
society is built on many people hurting many people, it is just who does
the hurting that is forever in dispute. They did not necessarily understand how much their simple presence hurt many good citizens in the
secret velvet of the heart—the Hippies and probably the Yippies did
not quite recognize the depth of that schizophrenia on which society is
built. We call it hypocrisy, but it is schizophrenia, a modest ranch-
house life with Draconian military adventures; a land of equal oppor-

tunity where a white culture sits upon a Black; a horizontal community of Christian love and a vertical hierarchy of churches—the cross was well-designed! a land of family, a land of illicit heat; a politics of principle, a politics of property; nation of mental hygiene with movies and TV reminiscent of a mental pigpen; patriots with a detestation of obscenity who pollute their rivers; citizens with a detestation of government control who cannot bear any situation not controlled. The list must be endless, the comic profits are finally small—the society was able to stagger on like a four-hundred-pound policeman walking uphill because living in such an unappreciated and obese state it did not at least have to explode in schizophrenia—life went on. Boys could go patiently to church at home and wait their turn to burn villages in Vietnam. What the Yippies did not recognize is that their demand for all-accelerated entrance into twentieth-century Utopia (where modern mass man would have all opportunities before him at once and could thus create and despoil with equal conscience—up against the wall mother-fucker, let me kiss your feet), whether a vision to be desired or abhorred, was nonetheless equal to straight madness for the Average Good American, since his liberated expression might not be an outpouring of love but the burning of his neighbor's barn. Or, since we are in Chicago, smashing good neighbor's skull with a brick from his own back yard. Yippies, even McCarthyites, represented nothing less by their presence than the destruction of every saving hypocrisy with consequent collision for oneself—it is not so easy to live every day of your life holding up the wall of your own sanity. Small wonder the neighborhood whites of Chicago, like many small-town whites in other places, loved Georgie Wallace—he came in like cavalry, a restorer of every last breech in the fort.

Somber thoughts for a stroll through Lincoln Park on a Sunday afternoon in summer, but the traffic of the tourists and the curious was great; one had to leave the car six blocks away. Curiosity was contained, however, in the family automobile: The burghers did not come to the park. Young tourists and cruisers were there in number, tough kids, Polish and Irish (not all plainclothesmen) circulating around the edges of the crowd, and in the center of the southern part of Lincoln Park where the Yippies had chosen to assemble on an innocuous greensward undistinguished from similar meadows in many another park, a folk-rock group was playing. It was an orderly crowd. Somewhere between one and two thousand kids and young adults sat on the grass and listened, and another thousand or two thousand, just arrived, or too restless to sit, milled through an outer ring, or worked forward to get a better look. There was no stage—the entrance of a flatbed truck from which the entertainers could have played had not been permitted, so the musicians were half hidden, the public address system—could it work off batteries?—was not particularly clear. For one of the next acts it hardly mattered—a young white singer with a cherubic face, perhaps eighteen, maybe twenty-eight, his hair in one huge puff ball teased out six to nine inches from his head, was taking off on an interplanetary, then galactic, flight of song, halfway between the space music of Sun Ra and "The Flight of the Bumblebee," the singer's head shaking at the climb like the blur of a buzzing fly, his sound an electric caterwauling of power come out of the wall (or the line in the grass, or the wet plates in the batteries) and the singer not bending it but whirling it, burning it, flashing it down some arc of consciousness, the sound screaming up to a climax of vibrations like one rocket blasting out of itself, the force of the noise a vertigo in the cauldrons of inner space—it was the roar of the beast in all nihilism, electric bass and drum driving behind out of their own non-stop to the end of mind. And the reporter, caught in the din—had the horns of the Huns ever had noise to compare?—knew this was some variety of true song for the Hippies and adolescents in the house, in this enclave of grass and open air (luxury apartments of Lake Shore Drive not five football fields away), crescendos of sound as harsh on his ear, ear of a generation that had danced to "Star Dust," as to drive him completely out of the sound, these painted dirty under-twenties were monsters, and yet, still clinging to recognition in the experience, he knew they were a generation that lived in the sound of destruction of all order as he had known it, and worlds of other decomposition as well; there was the sound of mountains crashing in this holocaust of the decibels, hearts bursting, literally bursting, as if this were the sound of death by explosion within, the drums of physiological climax when the mind was blown, and forces of the future, powerful, characterless, as insane and scalding as waves of lava, came flushing through the urn of all acquired culture and sent the brain like a foundered carcass smashing down a rapids, revolving through a whirl of demons, pool of uproar, discords vibrating, electric crescendo screaming as if at the electromechanical climax of the age, and these children like filthy Christians sitting quietly in the grass, applauding politely, whistles and cries of mild approval when the song was done, and the reporter as affected by the sound (as affected by the recognition of what nihilisms were calmly encountered in such musical storm) as if he had heard it in a room at midnight with painted bodies and kaleidoscopic sights, had a certainty that went through gangs and groups and rabble, tourists and consecrated saints, vestal virgins with finger bells, through the sight of Negroes calmly digging Honkie soul, sullen Negroes showing not impressed, but digging, cool on their fringe (reports to the South Side might later be made) through even the hint of menace in the bikers, some beaks alien to this music, come to scoff, now watching, half turned on by noise so near to the transcendencies of some of their own noise when the whine of the gears cohabited with the pot to hang them out there on the highway singing with steel and gasoline, yeah, steel and gasoline exactly equal to flesh plus hate, and blood plus hate; equations were pure while riding the balance of a machine, yes, even the tourists and the college boys who would not necessarily be back contributed nonetheless to the certainty of his mood. There was a mock charade going on, a continuation of that celebration of the Yippie Convention yet to come, when Pigasus, a literal pig, would be put in nomination. VOTE PIG IN '68, said the Yippie placards, and now up at the stage, music done, they announced another candidate to a ripple of mild gone laughter across the grass, Humphrey Dumpty was the name, and a Yippie clown marched through the crowd, a painted egg with legs, "the next President of the United States," and in suite came a march of the delegates through an impromptu aisle from the stage to the rear of the crowd. A clown dressed like a Colorado miner in a fun house came first; followed Miss America with hideous lip-sticked plastic tits, stars of rouge on her cheeks; Mayor Daley's political machine—a clown with a big box horizontal to his torso, big infant's spoon at the trough on top of the box, and a green light that went on and off was next; then the featured delegate, the Green Beret, a clown with a toy machine gun, soot, and red grease on his face, an Australian bush hat on his head. Some sort of wax vomit pop art work crowned the crown. Yes, the certainty was doubled. Just as he had known for one instant at the Republican Gala in Miami Beach that Nelson Rockefeller had no chance of getting the nomination, so he knew now on this cool gray Sunday afternoon in August, chill in the air like the chill of the pale and the bird of fear beginning to nest in the throat, that trouble was coming, serious trouble. The air of Lincoln Park came into the nose with that tender concern which air seemed always ready to offer when danger announced its presence. The reporter took an unhappy look around. Were these odd unkempt children the sort of troops with whom one wished to enter battle?

## MILITANTS IN GRANT PARK

They were young men who were not going to Vietnam. So they would show every lover of war in Vietnam that the reason they did not go was not for lack of the courage to fight; no, they would carry the fight over every street in Old Town and the Loop where the opportunity presented itself. If they had been gassed and beaten, their leaders arrested on fake charges (Hayden, picked up while sitting under a tree in daylight in Lincoln Park, naturally protested; the resulting charge was "resisting arrest"), they were going to demonstrate that they would not give up, that they were the stuff out of which the very best soldiers were made. Sunday, they had been driven out of the park, Monday as well, now Tuesday. The centers where they slept in bedrolls on the floor near Lincoln Park had been broken into by the police, informers and provocateurs were everywhere; tonight tear-gas trucks had been used. They were still not ready to give up. Indeed their militancy may have increased. They took care of the worst of their injured and headed for the Loop, picking up fellow demonstrators as they went. Perhaps the tear gas was a kind of catharsis for some of them, a letting of tears, a purging of old middle-class weakness. Some were turning from college boys to revolutionaries. It seemed as if the more they were beaten and tear-gassed, the more they rallied back. Now, with the facility for underground communication that seemed so instinctive a tool in their generation's equipment, they were on their way to Grant Park, en masse, a thousand of them, two thousand of them; there were conceivably as many as five thousand boys and girls massed in Grant Park at three in the morning, listening to speakers, cheering, chanting, calling across Michigan Avenue to the huge brooding façade of the Hilton, a block wide, over twenty-five stories high, with huge wings and deep courts. The lights were on in hundreds of bedrooms in the Hilton, indeed people were sleeping and dreaming all over the hotel with the sound of young orators declaiming in the night below, voices rising twenty, twenty-five stories high, the voices clear in the spell of sound that hung over the Hilton. The Humphrey headquarters were here, and the McCarthy headquarters. Half the Press was quartered here, and Marvin Watson as well. Postmaster General and Presidential troubleshooter, he had come to bring some of Johnson's messages to Humphrey. His suite had a view of the park. Indeed two-thirds of the principals at the convention must have had a view early this morning, two and three and four A.M. of this Tuesday night, no, this Wednesday morning, of Grant Park filled across the street with a revolutionary army of dissenters and demonstrators and college children and McCarthy workers and tourists ready to take a crack on the head, all night they could hear the demonstrators chanting, "Join us, join us," and the college bellow of utter contempt, "Dump the Hump! Dump the Hump!" all the fury of the beatings and the tear-gassings, all the bitter disappointments of that recently elapsed bright spring when the only critical problem was who would make a better President, Kennedy or McCarthy (now all the dread of a future with Humphrey or Nixon). There was also the sense that police had now entered their lives, become an element pervasive as drugs and books and sex and music and family. So they shouted up to the windows of the Hilton, to the delegates and the campaign workers who were sleeping, or shuddering by the side of their bed, or cheering by their open window; they called up through the night on a stage as vast and towering as one of Wagner's visions, and the screams of police cars joined them, pulling up, gliding away, blue lights revolving, lines of police hundreds long in their sky-blue shirts and sky-blue crash helmets, penning the demonstrators back of barriers across Michigan Avenue from the Hilton, and other lines of police and police fences on the Hilton's side of the street. The police had obviously been given orders not to attack the demonstrators here, not in front of the Hilton with half the Democratic Party watching them, not now at three in the morning—would anyone ever discover for certain what was to change their mind in sixteen hours?

Now, a great cheer went up. The police were being relieved by the National Guard. The Guard was being brought in! It was like a certificate of merit for the demonstrators to see the police march off and new hundreds of Guardsmen in khaki uniforms, helmets, and rifles take up post in place, army trucks coughing and barking and filing back and forth on Michigan Avenue, and on the side streets now surrounding the Hilton, evil-looking jeeps with barbed-wire gratings in front of their bumpers drove forward in echelons, and parked behind the crowd. Portable barbed-wire fences were now riding on jeeps.

Earlier in the week, it had been relatively simple to get into the Hilton. Mobs of McCarthy workers and excited adolescents had jammed the stairs and the main entrance room of the lobby, chanting all day, singing campaign songs, mocking every Humphrey worker they could recognize, holding station for hours in the hope, or on the rumor, that McCarthy would be passing through, and the cheers had the good nature and concerted rhythmic steam of a football rally. That had been Saturday and Sunday and Monday, but the police finally had barricaded the kids out of the lobby, and now at night covered the entrances to the Hilton, and demanded press passes, and room keys, as warrants of entry. The Hilton heaved and staggered through a variety of attacks and breakdowns. Like an old fort, like the old fort of the old Democratic Party, about to fall forever beneath the ministrations of its high shaman, its excruciated warlock, derided by the young, held in contempt by its own soldiers—the very delegates who would be loyal to Humphrey in the nomination and loyal to nothing in their heart—this spiritual fort of the Democratic Party was now housed in the literal fort of the Hilton staggering in place, all boilers working, all motors vibrating, yet seeming to come apart from the pressures on the street outside, as if the old Hilton had become artifact of the party and the nation.

Nothing worked well in the hotel, and much didn't work at all. There was no laundry because of the bus strike, and the house phones usually did not function; the room phones were tapped so completely, and the devices so over-adjacent, that separate conversations lapped upon one another in the same earpiece, or went jolting by in all directions like three handballs at play at once in a four-wall handball court. Sometimes the phone was dead, sometimes it emitted hideous squawks, or squeals, or the harsh electronic displeasure of a steady well-pulsed static. Sometimes one got long distance by taking it through the operator, sometimes one got an outside line only by ringing the desk and demanding it, sometimes one could get the hotel operator only by dialing the outside line. All the while, a photograph of Mayor Daley the size of a postage stamp was pasted on the cradle of the phone. "Welcome to the 1968 National Democratic Convention," it said. Often, one could not even extract a whimper from the room phone. It had succumbed. Sometimes the phone stayed dead for hours. Success in a convention is reduced to success in communications, as the reporter was yet to learn; communications in the headquarters of the largest party in the nation most renowned for the technology of its communications was breaking apart under strikes, pressure, sabotage, security, security over-check, overdevelopment, and insufficient testing of advanced technical devices: at the base of the pyramid, sheer human inefficiencies before the combined onslaught of pressure and street war.

The elevators worked abominably. On certain floors the signal did not seem to ring. One could wait a half hour for an elevator to stop on the way down. After a time everybody went up to the top in order to be able to go down. Yet one could not use the stairs, for Secret Servicemen were guarding them. It could, at worst, demand an hour to go to one's room and go down again. So it might have been better to live in a hotel across the Loop; but then there were traffic jams and police lines and demonstrators every night, demonstrators marching along with handkerchiefs to their noses.

This night with the demonstrators up and aroused in Grant Park, tear gas was blowing right into the hotel. The police had tried to gas the kids out of the park when they first arrived in numbers from Lincoln Park, but the wind blew the wrong way, blew the tears across the street into the air-conditioning of the Hilton lobby, and delegates and Press and officials walked about with smarting eyes, burning throats, and the presentiment that they were going to catch a cold. The lobby stunk. Not from the tear gas but from stink bombs, or some advanced variety of them, for the source of the odor was either mysterious, or unremovable, or had gotten into the very entrails of the air-conditioning since it got worse from day to day and drenched the coffee shop and the bars and the lobby with a stench not easily forgettable, rather like a truly atrocious body odor that spoke of the potential for sour vomit in every joint of a bad piece of psychic work. So personal relations were curious. One met attractive men or women, shook hands with them, chatted for a time, said good-bye. One's memory of the occasion was how awful it had smelled. Delegates, powerful political figures, old friends, and strangers all smelled awful.

So nothing worked well in the hotel, and everything stank, and crowds—those who could get in—milled about, and police guarded the entrance, and across the street, as the reporter moved through the tight press of children sitting packed together on the grass, cheering the speakers, chanting "Join us! Join us!" and "Dump the Hump," the smell of the stink bombs was still present but different now, equally evil and vomitous but from a faded odor of Mace. The nation divided was going to war with stinks: Each side would inflict a stink upon the other. The years of sabotage were ahead—a fearful perspective: They would be giving engineering students tests in loyalty before they were done; the F.B.I. would come to question whoever took a mail order course in radio. It was possible that one was at the edge of that watershed year from which the country might never function well again, and service in American hotels would yet be reminiscent of service in

Mexican motels. Whatever! the children were alive with revolutionary fire on this fine Tuesday night, this early Wednesday morning, and the National Guard policing them was wide-awake as well. Incidents occurred. Flare-ups. A small Negro soldier started pushing a demonstrator with his rifle, pushing him in sudden fury as at the wild kickoff of a wild street fight; the demonstrator—who looked to be a kindly divinity student—aghast at what he had set off; he had not comprehended the Negro wished no special conversation from him. And a National Guard officer came running up to pull the Negro back. (On the next night, there would be no Negroes in the line of National Guards.)

The kids were singing. There were two old standards that were sung all the time. An hour could not go by without both songs. So they sang "We Shall Overcome" and they sang "This Land Is Your Land," and a speaker cried up to the twenty-five stories of the Hilton, "We have the votes, you have the guns," a reference to the polls that had shown McCarthy to be more popular than Hubert Humphrey (yes, if only Rockefeller had run for the Democrats and McCarthy for the Republicans this would have been an ideal contest between a spender and a conservative), and then another speaker, referring to the projected march on the Amphitheatre next day, shouted, "We're going to march without a permit—the Russians demand a permit to have a meeting in Prague," and the crowd cheered this. They cheered with wild enthusiasm when one speaker, a delegate, had the inspiration to call out to the delegates and workers listening in the hundreds of rooms at the Hilton with a view of the park, "Turn on your lights, and blink them if you are with us. If you are with us, if you are sympathetic to us, blink your lights, blink your lights." And to the delight of the crowd, lights began to blink in the Hilton, ten, then twenty, perhaps so many as fifty lights were blinking at once, and a whole bank of lights on the fifteenth floor and the twenty-third floor went off and on at once, off and on at once. The McCarthy headquarters on the fifteenth and the twenty-third were blinking, and the crowd cheered. Now they had become an audience to watch the actors in the hotel. So two audiences regarded each other, like ships signaling across a gulf of water in the night, and delegates came down from the hotel; a mood of new beauty was in the air, there present through all the dirty bandaged kids, the sour vomit odor of the Mace, the sighing and whining of the army trucks moving in and out all the time, the adenoids, larynxes, wheezes, and growls of the speakers, the blinking of lights in the Hilton, yes, there was the breath of this incredible crusade where fear was in every breath you took, and so breath was tender, it came into the lungs as a manifest of value, as a gift, and the children's faces were shining in the glow of the headlights of the National Guard trucks and the searchlights of the police in front of the Hilton across Michigan Avenue. And the Hilton, sinking in its foundations, twinkled like a birthday cake. Horrors were coming tomorrow. No, it is today. It is Wednesday already.

# A Massacre
# on Michigan Boulevard

"Here, I read it to you—these are not my words, these are the words of General Abrams: 'If the bombing in North Vietnam now authorized were to be suspended unilaterally, the enemy in ten days to two weeks could develop a capability in the DMZ area in terms of scale, intensity, and duration of combat on the order of five times what he now has.'

"I cannot agree. I cannot agree to place our forces at the risk which the enemy's capability would then pose. That, my friends, concludes our debate." (Hale Boggs was the hawk's own tern.)

The Administration was taking no chances on birds. A confidential White House briefing had been thrown into the shot-load for this debate, and by the time the last speaker had his word, the military was concluding the debate, that same military which had been giving expert guesses for years on just how many troops and just how many bombs would be necessary to guarantee victory in exactly so many weeks or exactly so many months; the party was still buying just such expert advice. "Scale, intensity, and duration of combat on the order of five times." The Texas delegation up front cheered. Put a big man in a big uniform, let him recite big figures, and they would take the word of no priest or pope. In America the uniform always finished first, the production expert second, and Christ was welcome to come in third. So the vote came out as 1,567¾ to 1,041½—the majority plank was passed. Lyndon Johnson was vindicated by the same poor arguments that had originally implicated him. Politics was property, and the gravitational power of massive holdings was sufficient to pull you out of your own soup.

But the floor would not rest. The New York and California delegations began to sing "We Shall Overcome." Quickly, the Platform was passed; still the New York delegation sang. Now Wisconsin stood on its seats. The rear of the floor booed the front of the floor. A few hundred posters, STOP THE WAR, quickly printed a couple of hours earlier for this occasion, were held up. Defeated delegates yelled, "Stop the War," in the fierce frustration of knowing that the plank was Lyndon Johnson's and the party was still his. The convention recessed. Still the New York delegation sang "We Shall Overcome," standing on their seats. The convention band across the way tried to drown them out. It played in ever-increasing volume "We Got a Lot of Living to Do."

The managers of the convention turned the New York microphones down, and amplified the public address system for the band. So on the floor of the convention the doves were drowned in hostile sound, but on the television sets the reception was opposite, for the networks had put their own microphones under the voices of the delegates, and they sang in force across the continent. Thus a few thousand people on the floor and the gallery heard little of the doves—all the rest of America heard them well. Politics-is-property had come to the point of fission. He who controlled the floor no longer controlled the power of public opinion. Small wonder the old party hands hated the networks—it was agitating to have mastered the locks and keys in the house of politics and discover that there was a new door they could not quite shut. In disgust the hawk delegations left the floor. The doves continued to sing "We Shall Overcome." Now, the orchestra played "Happy Days Are Here Again."

The demonstrators chanted, "We want peace! We want peace!" "I'm Looking Over a Four-Leaf Clover," the orchestra offered, then rejected, then switched over to "If You Knew Suzy," then they gave up. The demonstrators began to sing the "Battle Hymn of the Republic." New York, California, Oregon, Wisconsin, South Dakota, and other delegations marched around the empty floor. Still they sang. It had been a long war to lose.

Meanwhile, a mass meeting was taking place about the bandshell in Grant Park, perhaps a quarter of a mile east of Michigan Avenue and the Conrad Hilton. The meeting was under the auspices of the Mobilization, and a crowd of ten or fifteen thousand appeared. The Mayor had granted a permit to assemble but had refused to allow a march. Since the Mobilization had announced that it would attempt, no matter how, the march to the Amphitheatre that was the first purpose of their visit to Chicago, the police were out in force to surround the meeting.

An episode occurred during the speeches. Three demonstrators climbed a flag pole to cut down the American flag and put up a rebel flag. A squad of police charged to beat them up, but got into trouble themselves, for when they threw tear gas, the demonstrators lobbed the canisters back, and the police, choking on their own gas, had to fight their way clear through a barrage of rocks. Then came a much larger force of police charging the area, overturning benches, busting up members of the audience, then heading for Rennie Davis at the bullhorn. He was one of the coordinators of the Mobilization, his face was known, he had been fingered and fingered again by plainclothesmen. Now urging the crowd to sit down and be calm, he was attacked from behind by the police, his head laid open in a three-inch cut, and he was unconscious for a period. Furious at the attack, Tom Hayden, who had been in disguise these last two days to avoid any more arrests for himself, spoke to the crowd, said he was leaving to perform certain special tasks, and suggested that others break up into small groups and go out into the streets of the Loop "to do what they have to do." A few left with him; the majority remained. While it was a People's Army and therefore utterly unorganized by uniform or unity, it had a variety of special troops and regular troops; everything from a few qualified Kamikaze who were ready to charge police lines in a Japanese snake dance and dare on the consequence, some vicious beatings, to various kinds of small saboteurs, rock-throwers, gauntlet-runners—some of the speediest of the kids were adept at taunting cops while keeping barely out of range of their clubs—not altogether alien to running the bulls at Pamplona. Many of those who remained, however, were still nominally pacifists, protesters, Gandhians—they believed in non-violence, in the mystical interposition of their body to the attack, as if the violence of the enemy might be drained by the spiritual act of passive resistance over the years, over the thousands, tens of thousands, hundreds of thousands of beatings over the years. So Allen Ginsberg was speaking now to them.

The police looking through the Plexiglas face shields they had flipped down from their helmets were then obliged to watch the poet, with his bald head, soft eyes magnified by horn-rimmed eyeglasses, and massive dark beard, utter his words in a croaking speech. He had been gassed Monday night and Tuesday night, and had gone to the beach at dawn to read Hindu Tantras to some of the Yippies, the combination of the chants and the gassings had all but burned out his voice, his beautiful speaking voice, one of the most powerful and hypnotic instruments of the Western world was down to the scrapings of the throat now, raw as flesh after a curettage.

"The best strategy for you," said Ginsberg, "in cases of hysteria, overexcitement, or fear, is still to chant OM together. It helps to quell flutterings of butterflies in the belly. Join me now as I try to lead you."

The crowd chanted with Ginsberg. They were of a generation that would try every idea, every drug, every action—it was even possible a few of them had made out with freaky kicks on tear gas these last few days—so they would chant OM. There were Hindu fanatics in the crowd, children who loved India and scorned everything in the West; there were cynics who thought the best thing to be said for a country which allowed its excess population to die by the millions in famine-ridden fields was that it would not be ready soon to try to dominate the rest of the world. There were also militants who were ready to march. And the police there to prevent them, busy now in communication with other detachments of police, by way of radios whose aerials were attached to their helmets, thereby giving them the look of giant insects.

A confused hour began. Lincoln Park was irregular in shape, with curving foot walks; but Grant Park was indeed not so much a park as a set of belts of greenery cut into files by major parallel avenues between Michigan Avenue and Lake Michigan half a mile away. Since there were also cross streets cutting the belts of green perpendicularly, a variety of bridges and pedestrian overpasses gave egress to the city. The park was in this sense an alternation of lawn with superhighways. So the police were able to pen the crowd. But not completely. There were too many bridges, too many choices, in effect, for the police to anticipate. To this confusion was added the fact that every confrontation of demonstrators with police, now buttressed by the National Guard, attracted hundreds of newsmen. The demonstrators finally tried to force a bridge and get back to the city. Repelled by tear gas, they went to other bridges, still other bridges, finally found a bridge lightly guarded, broke through a passage, and were loose in the city at six-thirty in the evening. They milled about in the Loop for a few minutes, only to encounter the mules and three wagons of the Poor People's Campaign. City officials, afraid of provoking the Negroes on the South Side, had given a permit to the Reverend Abernathy, and he was going to march the mules and wagons down Michigan Avenue and over to the convention. An impromptu march of the demonstrators formed behind the wagons immediately on encountering them, and ranks of marchers, sixty, eighty, a hundred in line across the width of Michigan Avenue, began to move forward in the gray early twilight of 7 P.M.; Michigan Avenue was now suddenly jammed with people in the march, perhaps so many as four or five thousand people, including onlookers on the sidewalk, who jumped in. The streets of the Loop were also reeking with tear gas—the wind had blown some of the gas west over Michigan Avenue from the drops on the bridges, some gas still was penetrated into the clothing of the marchers. In broken ranks, half a march, half a happy mob, eyes red from gas, faces excited by the tension of the afternoon, and the excitement of the escape from Grant Park, now pushing down Michigan Avenue toward the Hilton Hotel with dreams of a march on to the Amphitheatre four miles beyond, and in the full pleasure of being led by the wagons of the Poor People's March, the demonstrators shouted to everyone on the sidewalk, "Join us, join us, join us," and the sidewalk kept disgorging more people ready to march.

But at Balbo Avenue, just before Michigan Avenue reached the Hilton, the marchers were halted by the police. It was a long halt. Perhaps thirty minutes. Time for people who had been walking on the sidewalk to join the march, proceed for a few steps, halt with the others, wait, get bored, and leave. It was time for someone in command of the hundreds of police in the neighborhood to communicate with his headquarters, explain the problem, time for the dilemma to be relayed, alternatives examined, and orders conceivably sent back to attack and disperse the crowd. If so, a trap was first set. The mules were allowed to cross Balbo Avenue, then were separated by a line of police from the marchers, who now, several thousand compressed in this one place, filled the intersection of Michigan Avenue and Balbo. There, dammed by police on three sides, and cut off from the wagons of the Poor People's March, there, right beneath the windows of the Hilton, which looked down on Grant Park and Michigan Avenue, the stationary march was abruptly attacked. The police attacked with tear gas, with Mace, and with clubs, they attacked like a chain saw cutting into wood, the teeth of the saw the edge of their clubs, they attacked like a scythe through grass, lines of twenty and thirty policemen striking out in an arc, their clubs beating, demonstrators fleeing. Seen from overhead, from the nineteenth floor, it was like a wind blowing dust, or the edge of waves riding foam on the shore.

The police cut through the crowd one way, then cut through them another. They chased people into the park, ran them down, beat them up; they cut through the intersection at Michigan and Balbo like a razor cutting a channel through a head of hair, and then drove columns of new police into the channel who in turn pushed out, clubs flailing, on each side, to cut new channels, and new ones again. As demonstrators ran, they re-formed in new groups only to be chased by the police again. The action went on for ten minutes, fifteen minutes, with the absolute ferocity of a tropical storm. Watching it from a window on the nineteenth floor was like studying a storm at evening through a glass. The light was a lovely gray-blue, the police had uniforms of sky-blue, even the ferocity had an abstract elemental play of forces of nature at battle with other forces, as if sheets of tropical rain were driving across the street in patterns, in curving patterns that curved upon each other again. Police cars rolled up, prisoners were beaten, shoved into wagons, driven away. The rain of police, maddened by the uncoiling of their own storm, pushed against their own barricades of tourists pressed on the street against the Hilton Hotel, then pressed them so hard—but here is a quotation from J. Anthony Lukas in *The New York Times:*

> Even elderly bystanders were caught in the police onslaught. At one point, the police turned on several dozen persons standing quietly behind police barriers in front of the Conrad Hilton Hotel watching the demonstrators across the street.
>
> For no reason that could be immediately determined, the blue-helmeted policemen charged the barriers, crushing the spectators against the windows of the Haymarket Inn, a restaurant in the hotel. Finally the window gave way, sending screaming middle-aged women and children backward through the broken shards of glass.
>
> The police then ran into the restaurant and beat some of the victims who had fallen through the windows and arrested them.

Now another quote from Steve Lerner in *The Village Voice:*

> When the charge came, there was a stampede toward the sidelines. People piled into each other, humped over each other's bodies like coupling dogs. To fall down in the crush was just

as terrifying as facing the police. Suddenly I realized my feet weren't touching the ground as the crowd pushed up onto the sidewalk. I was grabbing at the army jacket of the boy in front of me; the girl behind me had a stranglehold on my neck and was screaming incoherently in my ear.

Now, a longer quotation from Jack Newfield in *The Village Voice*. (The accounts in the *Voice* of September 5 were superior to any others encountered that week.)

At the southwest entrance to the Hilton, a skinny, long-haired kid of about seventeen skidded down on the sidewalk, and four over-weight cops leaped on him, chopping strokes on his head. His hair flew from the force of the blows. A dozen small rivulets of blood began to cascade down the kid's temple and onto the sidewalk. He was not crying or screaming, but crawling in a stupor toward the gutter. When he saw a photographer take a picture, he made a V sign with his fingers.

A doctor in a white uniform and Red Cross arm band began to run toward the kid, but two other cops caught him from behind and knocked him down. One of them jammed his knee into the doctor's throat and began clubbing his rib cage. The doctor squirmed away, but the cops followed him, swinging hard, sometimes missing.

A few feet away a phalanx of police charged into a group of women, reporters, and young McCarthy activists standing idly against the window of the Hilton Hotel's Haymarket Inn. The terrified people began to go down under the unexpected police charge when the plate glass window shattered, and the people tumbled backward through the glass. The police then climbed through the broken window and began to beat people, some of whom had been drinking quietly in the hotel bar.

Let us escape. The reporter, watching in safety from the nineteenth floor, could understand now how Mussolini's son-in-law had once been able to find the bombs he dropped from his airplane beautiful as they burst, yes, children and youths and middle-aged men and women were being pounded and clubbed and gassed and beaten, hunted and driven, sent scattering in all directions by teams of policemen who had exploded out of their restraints like the bursting of a boil, and nonetheless he felt a sense of calm and beauty, void even of the desire to be down there, as if in years to come there would be beatings enough, some chosen, some from nowhere, but it was as if the war had finally begun, and this was therefore a great and solemn moment, as if indeed even the gods of history had come together from each side to choose the very front of the Hilton Hotel before the television cameras of the world and the eyes of the campaign workers and the delegates' wives, yes, there before the eyes of half the principals at the convention was this drama played, as if the military spine of a great liberal party had finally separated itself from the skin, as if, no metaphor large enough to suffice, the Democratic Party had here broken in two before the eyes of a nation like Melville's whale charging right out of the sea.

A great stillness rose up from the street through all the small noise of clubbing and cries, small sirens, sigh of loaded arrest vans as off they pulled, shouts of police as they wheeled in larger circles, the intersection clearing further, then further, a stillness rose through the steel and stone of the hotel, congregating in the shocked centers of every room where delegates and wives and Press and campaign workers innocent until now of the intimate working of social force, looked down now into the murderous paradigm of Vietnam there beneath them at this huge intersection of this great city. Look—a boy was running through the park, and a cop was chasing. There he caught him on the back of the neck with his club! There! The cop is returning to his own! And the boy stumbling to his feet is helped off the ground by a girl who has come running up.

Yes, it could only have happened in a meeting of the Gods, that history for once should take place not on some back street, or some inaccessible grand room, not in some laboratory indistinguishable from others, or in the sly undiscoverable hypocrisies of a committee of experts, but rather on the center of the stage, as if each side had said, "Here we will have our battle. Here we will win."

The demonstrators were afterward delighted to have been manhandled before the public eye, delighted to have pushed and prodded, antagonized and provoked the cops over these days with rocks and bottles and cries of "Pig" to the point where police had charged in a blind rage and made a stage at the one place in the city where audience, actors, and cameras could all convene, yes, the rebels thought they had had a great victory, and perhaps they did; but the reporter wondered, even as he saw it, if the police in that half hour of waiting had not had time to receive instructions from the power of the city, perhaps the power of the land, and the power had decided, "No, do not let them march another ten blocks and there disperse them on some quiet street, no, let it happen before all the land, let everybody see that their dissent will soon be equal to their own blood; let them realize that the power is implacable, and will beat and crush and imprison and yet kill before it will ever relinquish the power. So let them see before their own eyes what it will cost to continue to mock us, defy us, and resist. There are more millions behind us than behind them, more millions who wish to weed out, poison, gas, and obliterate every flower whose power they do not comprehend than heroes for their side who will view our brute determination and still be ready to resist. There are more cowards alive than the brave. Otherwise we would not be where we are," said the Prince of Greed.

Who knew. One could thank the city of Chicago, where drama was still a property of the open stage. It was quiet now, there was nothing to stare down on but the mules, and the police guarding them. The mules had not moved through the entire fray. Isolated from the battle, they had stood there in harness waiting to be told to go on. Only once in a while did they turn their heads. Their role as actors in the Poor People's March was to wait and to serve. Finally they moved on. The night had come. It was dark. The intersection was now empty. Shoes, ladies' handbags, and pieces of clothing lay on the street outside the hotel.

There have been few studies on the psychological differences between police and criminals, and the reason is not difficult to discover. The studies based on the usual psychological tests fail to detect a significant difference. Perhaps they are not sufficiently sensitive.

If civilization has made modern man a natural schizophrenic (since he does not know at the very center of his deliberations whether to trust his machines or the imperfect impressions still afforded him by his distorted senses and the more or less tortured messages passed along by polluted water, overfertilized ground, and poisonously irritating air) the average man is a suicide in relation to his schizophrenia. He will suppress his impulses and die eventually of cancer, overt madness, nicotine poisoning, heart attack, or the complications of a chest cold. It is that minority—cop and crook—which seeks issue for violence who now attracts our attention. The criminal attempts to reduce the tension within himself by expressing in the direct language of action whatever is most violent and outraged in his depths; to the extent he is not a powerful man, his violence is merely antisocial, like self-exposure, embezzlement, or passing bad checks. The cop tries to solve his violence by blanketing it with a uniform. That is virtually a commonplace, but it explains why cops will put up with poor salary, public dislike, uncomfortable working conditions, and a general sense of bad conscience. They know they are lucky; they know they are getting away with a successful solution to the criminality they can taste in their blood. This taste is practically in the forefront of a cop's brain; he is in a stink of perspiration whenever he goes into action; he can tolerate little in the way of insult, and virtually no contradiction; he lies with a simplicity and quick confidence that will stifle the breath of any upright citizen who encounters it innocently for the first time. The difference between a good cop and a bad cop is that the good cop will at least do no more than give his own salted version of events—the bad cop will make up his version. That is why the police arrested the pedestrians they pushed through the window of the Haymarket Inn at the Conrad Hilton: The guiltier the situation in which a policeman finds himself, the more will he attack the victim of his guilt.

There are—it is another commonplace—decent policemen. A few are works of art. And some police, violent when they are young, mellow into modestly corrupt, humorous, and decently efficient officials. Every public figure with power, every city official, high politician, or prominent government worker, knows in his unspoken sentiments that the police are an essentially criminal force restrained by their guilt, their covert awareness that they are imposters, and by a sprinkling of career men whose education, rectitude, athletic ability, and religious dedication make them work for a balance between justice and authority. These men, who frighten the average corrupt cop as much as a priest frightens a choirboy, are the thin restraining edge of civilization for a police force. That, and the average corrupt cop's sense that he is not wanted that much by anyone.

What staggered the delegates who witnessed the attack—more accurate to call it the massacre, since it was sudden, unprovoked, and total—on Michigan Avenue was that it opened the specter of what it might mean for the police to take over society. They might comport themselves in such a case not as a force of law and order, not even as a force of repression upon civil disorder, but as a true criminal force, chaotic, improvisational, undisciplined, and finally—sufficiently aroused—uncontrollable.

Society was held together by bonds no more powerful proportionately than spider's silk; no one knew this better than the men who administered a society. So images of the massacre opened a nightmare. The more there was disorder in the future, the more there would be need for larger numbers of police and more the need to indulge them. Once they were indulged, however, it might not take long for their own criminality to dominate their relation to society. Which spoke then of martial law to replace them. But if the Army became the punitive force of society, then the Pentagon would become the only meaningful authority in the land.

So an air of outrage, hysteria, panic, wild rumor, unruly outburst, fury, madness, gallows humor, and gloom would hang over nominating night at the convention.

# Convention's End

Let us look rather at the last night of the convention. Two hours before the final evening session the Progress Printing Company near the stockyards finished a rush order of small posters, perhaps two feet high, which said: CHICAGO LOVES MAYOR DALEY. They were ready to be handed out when the crowds arrived tonight; thousands of workers for the city administration were packed into the spectators' gallery, then the sections reserved for radio, TV, and periodicals. The crowd fortified with plastic tickets cut to the size of Diner's Club cards, and therefore cut to the size of the admission pass one had to insert in the signal box to enter, had flooded all available seats with their posters and their good Chicago lungs-for-Daley. The radio, television, and periodical men wandered about the outer environs of the Amphitheatre and were forced to watch most of the convention this night from the halls, the ends of the tunnels, the television studios.

Daley had known how to do it. If he had been booed and jeered the first two nights and openly insulted from the podium on Wednesday, despite a gallery already packed in his favor, he was not going to tolerate anything less than a built-in majesty for tonight.

Shortly after convening, the convention showed a movie thirty-two minutes long, entitled *Robert Kennedy Remembered,* and while it went on, through the hall, over the floor, and out across the country on television, a kind of unity came over everyone who was watching, at least for a little while. Idealism rarely moved politicians—it had too little to do with property. But emotion did. It was closer to the land. Somewhere between sorrow and the blind sword of patriotism was the fulcrum of reasonable politics, and as the film progressed, and one saw scene after scene of Bobby Kennedy growing older, a kind of happiness came back from the image, for something in his face grew young over the years—he looked more like a boy on the day of his death, a nice boy, nicer than the kid with the sharp rocky glint in his eye who had gone to work for Joe McCarthy in his early twenties, and had then known everything there was to know about getting ahead in politics. He had grown modest as he grew older, and his wit had grown with him—he had become a funny man as the picture took care to show, wry, simple for one instant, shy and off to the side on the next, but with a sort of marvelous boy's wisdom, as if he knew the world was very bad and knew the intimate style of how it was bad, as only boys can sometimes know (for they feel it in their parents and their schoolteachers and their friends). Yet he had confidence he was going to fix it—the picture had this sweet simple view of him that no one could resent for somehow it was not untrue. Since his brother's death, a subtle sadness had come to live in his tone of confidence, as though he were confident he would win—if he did not lose. That could also happen, and that could happen quickly. He had come into that world where people live with the recognition of tragedy, and so are often afraid of happiness, for they know that one is never in so much danger as when victorious and/or happy—that is when the devils seem to have their hour, and hawks seize something living from the gambol on the field.

The movie came to an end. Even dead, and on film, he was better and more moving than anything that had happened in their convention, and people were crying. An ovation began. Delegates came to their feet, and applauded an empty screen—it was as if the center of American life were now passing the age where it could still look forward; now people looked back into memory, into the past of the nation—was that possible? They applauded the presence of a memory. Bobby Kennedy had now become a beloved property of the party.

Minutes went by and the ovation continued. People stood on their chairs and clapped their hands. Cries broke out. Signs were lifted. Small hand-lettered signs that said, BOBBY, BE WITH US, and one enormous sign eight feet high, sorrowful as rue in the throat— BOBBY, WE MISS YOU, it said.

Now the ovation had gone on long enough—for certain people. So signals went back and forth between floor and podium and phone, and Carl Albert stepped forward and banged the gavel for the ovation to end, and asked for order. This party, which had come together for five minutes (after five days and five months and five years of festering discord), was now immediately divided again. The New York and California delegations began to sing the "Battle Hymn of the Republic," and the floor heard, and delegations everywhere began to sing, Humphrey delegations as quick as the rest. In every convention there is a steamroller, and a moment when the flattened exhale their steam, and "Mine eyes have seen the glory of the coming of the Lord!" was the cry of the oppressed at this convention, even those unwittingly oppressed in their mind, and not even knowing it in their heart until this instant, now they were defying the Chair, clapping their hands, singing, stamping their feet to mock the chairman's gavel.

Carl Albert brought up Dorothy Bush to read an appreciation the convention would offer for the work of certain delegates. The convention did not wish to hear. Mrs. Bush began to read in a thin mean voice, quivering with the hatreds of an occasion like this, and the crowd sang on, "Glory, Glory, Hallelujah, his truth goes marching on," and they stamped their feet and clapped their hands, and were loose finally and having their day as they sang the song that once, originally, had commemorated a man who preached civil disorder, then mutiny, and attacked a fort in his madness and was executed, John Brown was also being celebrated here, and the Texas and Illinois delegations were now silent, clapping no longer, sitting on their seats, looking bored. Every delegate on the floor who had hated the Kennedys was now looking bored, and the ones who had loved them were now noisier than ever. Once again the party was polarized. Signs waved all over the floor: BOBBY, WE'LL REMEMBER YOU; BOBBY, WE'LL SEEK YOUR NEWER WORLD; and the ever-present BOBBY, WE MISS YOU. Yes they did, missed him as the loving spirit, the tender *germ* in the living plasma of the party. Nothing was going to make them stop—this offering of applause was more valuable to them than any nutrients to be found in the oratorical vitamin pills Hubert would yet be there to offer. The demonstration went on for twenty minutes and gave no sign of stopping at all. Dorothy Bush had long ago given up. Carl Albert, even smaller than Georgie Wallace, was now as furious as only a tiny man can be when his hard-earned authority has turned to wax— he glared across the floor at the New York delegation like a little boy who smells something bad.

However did they stop the demonstration? Well, convention mechanics can be as perfect as the muscle in a good play when professionals have worked their football for a season. Mayor Daley, old lover
of the Kennedys, and politically enough of an enigma six months ago
for Bobby to have said in his bloodwise political wisdom, "Daley is the
ballgame," Mayor Daley, still flirting with the Kennedys these last
three days in his desire for Teddy as Vice President, now had come to
the end of this political string, and like a good politician he pulled it.
He gave the signal. The gallery began to chant, "We love Daley." All
his goons and clerks and beef-eaters and healthy parochial school students began to yell and scream and clap, "We love Daley," and the
power of their lungs, the power of the freshest and the largest force in
this Amphitheatre, soon drowned out the Kennedy demonstrators,
stuffed their larynxes with larger sound. The Daley demonstration
was bona fide too—his people had suffered with their Mayor, so they
screamed for him now and clapped their hands, and Mayor Daley
clapped his hands too, for he also loved Mayor Daley. Simple narcissism gives the power of beasts to politicians, professional wrestlers,
and female movie stars.

At the height of the Daley demonstration, it was abruptly cut off.
By a signal. "Shut your yaps" was an old button, no matter how the
signal came. In the momentary silence, Carl Albert got his tongue in,
and put Ralph Metcalfe (Daley's Black Man), who was up on the
podium already, into voice on the mike, and Metcalfe announced a
minute of silence for the memory of Martin Luther King. So New
York and California were naturally obliged to be silent with the rest,
the floor was silent, the gallery was silent, and before the minute was
up, Carl Albert had slipped Dorothy Bush in again, and she was reading the appreciation of the convention for certain delegates. Business
had been resumed. The last night proceeded.

At length, the moment came for Humphrey's acceptance speech.
Tonight, he looked good—which is to say he looked good for Humphrey. Indeed if a man could not look good on the night he accepted
the nomination of his party for President, then his prospects of lon-
gevity must certainly be odd. Humphrey, of course, had been looking terrible for years. His defeat in West Virginia in 1960 by Jack
Kennedy seemed to have done something of a permanent nature,
perhaps had dissolved some last core of idealism—it was a cruel campaign: If one would dislike the Kennedys, West Virginia was the place
to look. Since then, Humphrey had had a face that was as dependent
upon cosmetics as the protagonist of a coffin. The results were about

as dynamic. Make-up on Hubert's face somehow suggested that the flesh beneath was the color of putty—it gave him the shaky put-together look of a sales manager in a small corporation who takes a drink to get up in the morning and another drink after he has made his intercom calls: the sort of man who is not proud of drinking, and so in the coffee break, he goes to the john and throws a Sen-Sen down his throat. All day he exudes odors all over; Sen-Sen, limewater, pomade, bay rum, deodorant, talcum, garlic, a whiff of the medicinal, the odor of Scotch on a nervous tum, rubbing alcohol! This resemblance Hubert had to a sales manager probably appeared most on those average days when he was making political commercials to be run as spots all over the land—in such hours he must have felt like a pure case of the hollows, a disease reserved usually for semi-retired leading men. They have been actors so long they must be filled with something—lines of a script, a surprise bouquet of attention, a recitation of Shakespeare, a bottle of booze, an interview. Something! Don't leave them alone. They're hollow. That was how Humphrey must have looked on average days, if his commercials were evidence.

Tonight, however, he was not hollow but full. He had a large audience, and his actor's gifts for believing a role. Tonight he was the bachelor uncle who would take over a family (left him by Great-Uncle Baines), and through kindness, simple courtesy, funds of true emotional compassion, and stimulating sternness upon occasion of the sort only a bachelor uncle could comprehend—". . . rioting, burning, sniping, mugging, traffic in narcotics, and disregard for law are the advance guard of anarchy, and they must and they will be stopped . . ." he would bring back that old-fashioned harmony to his ravaged folks. Since he was now up on the podium, the crowd was cheering, and the gallery on signal from Daley roared like a touchdown just scored. Hubert Humphrey was warm; he could believe in victory in the fall. He smiled and waved his hands and beamed, and the delegates, loosened by the film on Bobby Kennedy (their treachery spent in revolt against the Chair), demonstrated for Humphrey. The twenty years in Washington had become this night property to harvest; politicians who didn't even like him could think fondly of Hubert at this instant, he was part of their memory of genteel glamour at Washington parties, part of the dividend of having done their exercise in politics with him for twenty years, for having talked to him ten times, shaken his hand forty, corresponded personally twice, got drunk with him once—small property glows in memory, our burning glass! These Humphrey politicians and delegates, two-thirds of all this convention, had lived their lives in the shadow of Washington's Establishment, that eminence of Perle Mesta parties and Democratic high science, they had lived with nibbles of society, and gossip about it, clumps of grass from Hubert's own grounds; but it was their life, or a big part of it, and it was leaving now—they all sensed that. The grand Establishment of the Democratic Party and its society life in Washington would soon be shattered—the world was shattering it. So they rose to cheer Humphrey. He was the end of the line, a sweet guy in personal relations so far as he was able—and besides, the acceptance speech at a convention was pure rite. In such ceremonies you were required to feel love even if you didn't like him. Politicians, being property holders, could feel requisite emotions at proper ceremonies. Now they gave proper love to Humphrey, two-thirds of them did. They would only have to give it for an hour. Everybody knew he would lose. The poor abstract bugger.

He gave his speech out of that bolt of cloth he had been weaving for all his life, that springless rhetoric so suited to the organ pipes of his sweet voice, for it enabled him to hold any note on any word, and he could cut from the sorrows of a sigh to the injunctions of a wheeze. He was a holy Harry Truman. Let us not quote him except where we must, for the ideas in his speech have already entered the boundless deep of yesterday's Fourth of July, and ". . . once again we give our testament to America . . . each and every one of us in our own way should once again reaffirm to ourselves and our posterity that we love this nation, we love America!" If sentiment made the voter vote, and it did! and sentiment was a button one could still prick by a word, then Humphrey was still in property business because he had pushed "Testament" for button, "America" for button, "each and every one of us in our own way"—*in our own way*—what a sweet button is that! and "reaffirm"—pure compost for any man's rhetoric, "our posterity," speaks to old emotion from the land of the covered loins, "we love this nation"—pure constipation is now relieved—"we love America." The last was not exactly property but rather a reminder to pay the dues. Not every last bit of politics was property—some portion consisted of dunning the ghost-haunted property of others. Nobody had to tell **HHH.** One could deduce the emotional holdings and debts of the most mediocre Americans by studying **HHH** in the art of political speaking—he showed you how to catalogue your possessions: Franklin Roosevelt, Harry Truman, winner! John F. Kennedy, Lyndon Johnson—there were sudden boos. Lyndon Johnson, he repeated, and got the cheers from the medicine balls and gallery ding-dongs for Daley. "And tonight to you, Mr. President, I say thank you. Thank you, Mr. President." His presumption was that Lyndon Johnson was necessarily listening.

Then he called for Peace in Vietnam, and the crowd roared and the band offered florid *dianas* as if he had made a glorious pass. Peace in Vietnam was now the property of all politicians; Peace in Vietnam was the girl who had gone to bed with a thousand different guys but always took a bath, and so was virgin. Hubert felt like a virgin every time he talked of Peace in Vietnam. He spoke with the innocent satisfaction of a drop of oil sliding down a scallion.

Of course, Hubert was no vegetable. He was the drugstore liberal. You had better believe it. He knew who had asthma and who had crabs. It is important to locate him in the pharmacopoeia. Back of that drop of oil, he was an emollifacient, a fifty-gallon drum of lanolin—"We are and we must be one nation, united by liberty and justice for all, one nation, under God, indivisible, with liberty and justice for all. This is our America." He was like honey from which the sugar had been removed and the saccharine added, he was a bar of margarine the color of make-up. He had the voice of a weeper, a sob in every arch corner and cavern of his sweet, his oversweet heart; he was pious with a crooning invocation of all the property of sentiment, he was all the bad faith of twenty years of the Democratic Party's promises and gravy and evasion and empty hollers. He was the hog caller of the mountain and the pigs had put him in—he would promise pig pie in the sky. ". . . With the help of that vast, unfrightened, dedicated, faithful majority of Americans, I say to this great convention tonight, and to this great nation of ours, I am ready to lead our country!" And he ended, and the rite of love went up to its conclusion, and the band played, and the simple common people, and the villainous faces, and the whores with beehive head-dresses in on passes, and the boys and the Southern pols stomped around and were happy, because their man was in, which meant they had won this game, this game, anyway, and happiness consisted of thinking of no future. And Hubert looked shining up on the stage, and made jokes with photographers, and jumped in the air to be tall as Edmund Muskie for one still shot—Humphrey would be a sport at a party— and McGovern came up to the podium and Hubert took him in, and his eyes were bright with light and love and tears. It is not every man who can run for President after four long years as towel boy in Unca Baines' old haw-house with Madame Rusk. He turned to greet others, and from the back had the look of a squat little Mafioso of middle rank, a guy who might run a bookie shop and be scared of many things, but big with his barber, and the manicurist would have Miami hots for him. Let us give the day to Hubert. He had always seen himself as such a long shot and out.

All selections from *Miami and the Siege of Chicago* (1968)

# OF A FIRE
# ON THE MOON

## The Psychology of Astronauts

Well, let us make an approach to the astronauts. Aquarius sees them for the first time on the fifth of July, eleven days before the launch. They are in a modern movie theater with orange seats and a dark furrowed ceiling overhead, much like marcelled waves in a head of hair, a plastic ceiling built doubtless to the plans of one of the best sound engineers in the country. Sound is considerably ahead of smell as a fit province for scientific work, but since the excellence of acoustics in large and small concert chambers seems to bear more relation to old wood and the blessings of monarchs and bishops than to the latest development of the technical art, the sound system in this movie theater (seats six hundred) is dependably intolerable most of the time. The public address system squeals and squeaks (it is apparently easier to have communication with men one-quarter of a million miles away) and one never gets a fair test of the aural accommodations. The walls and overhead are of plastic composition, and so far as one can tell, the tone is a hint sepulchral, then brightened electronically, finally harsh and punishing to that unnamed fine nerve which runs from the anus to the eardrum. As the sound engineers became more developed, the plastic materials provided for their practice by corporations grew acoustically more precise and spiritually more flattening—it was the law of the century. One was forever adjusting to public voices through the subtlest vale of pain.

Still this movie theater was the nearest approach to a diadem in the Manned Spacecraft Center. The theater was part of the visitors' center, where tourists could go through the space museum, a relatively modest affair of satellites, capsules, dioramas, posters, and relics, now closed and given over to the installation of monitors and cables for the television networks, even as the gallery to the rear of the theater was now being converted into the Apollo News Center and would consist finally of endless aisles of desks, telephones, and typewriters, plus one giant Buddha of a coffee urn. (Coffee is the closest the press ever comes to *satori*.)

In the theater, perhaps eight rows back of the front seats, was a raised platform on which television cameras and crews were mounted. From the stage they must have looked not unrelated to artillery pieces on the battlement of a fort—in the front row were fifty photographers, which is to say fifty sets of torsos and limbs each squeezed around its own large round glass eye. Little flares of lightning flashed out of bulbs near their heads. The astronauts did not really have to travel to the moon—life from another planet was before them already. In the middle ranks, between the front row and the barricade of television cameras, were seated several hundred newspaper men and women come to Houston for the conference this morning. They were a curious mixture of high competence and near imbecility; some assigned to Space for years seemed to know as much as NASA engineers; others, innocents in for the big play on the moon shot, still were not just certain where laxatives ended and physics began. It was as if research students from the Institute of Advanced Studies at Princeton had been put in with a group of fine young fellows from an Army class in remedial reading. Out of such a bag would questions come to the astronauts. Wait! There will be samples.

The astronauts entered from the wings wearing gas masks, gray snout-nosed covers that projected out from their mouths and gave their profiles the intent tusk-ready slouch of razorback hogs. They were aware of this—it was apparent in the good humor with which they came in. In fact, a joke of some dimensions had been flickering for a few days—the Press had talked of greeting them with white hospital masks. In the attempt to protect the astronauts as much as possible from preflight infection they were being kept in a species of limited quarantine—their contacts with nonessential personnel were restricted. Since journalists fit this category, today's press conference had installed Armstrong, Aldrin, and Collins up on the stage in a plastic box about twelve feet wide, ten feet deep, and ten feet high. Blowers within this three-walled plastic room blew air from behind them out into the audience—thereby, the breath of the astronauts could enter the theater, but the airborne germs of journalists would not blow back. It made a kind of sense. Of course the cause of the common cold was still unknown, but gross studies of infection would surmise a partial quarantine might be effective partially. However, the instrumentation of this premise was not happy. The astronauts looked a bit absurd in their plastic box, and the few journalists who had actually fleshed their joke by putting on masks caused the astronauts to grin broadly as though to dissociate themselves from the pyramids of precaution they were in fact obeying.

Once they sat down, their manner changed. They were seated behind a walnut-brown desk on a pale blue base that displayed two painted medallions in circles—NASA and Apollo 11. Behind them at the rear of the plastic booth stood an American flag; the Press actually jeered when somebody brought it onstage in advance of the astronauts. Aquarius could not remember a press conference where Old Glory had ever been mocked before, but it had no great significance, suggesting rather a splash of derision at the thought that the show was already sufficiently American enough. In fact, between the steady reporters who worked out of Houston and the astronauts there was that kind of easy needling humor which is the measure of professional respect to be found among teams and trainers.

So the entrance went well. The astronauts walked with the easy saunter of athletes. They were comfortable in motion. As men being scrutinized by other men they had little to worry about. Still, they did not strut. Like all good professional athletes, they had the modesty of knowing you could be good and still lose. Therefore they looked to enjoy the snouts they were wearing, they waved at reporter friends they recognized, they grinned. A reporter called back to Collins, "Now, you look good." It all had that characteristically American air which suggests that men who are successful in their profession do best to take their honors lightly.

Once they sat down, however, the mood shifted. Now they were there to answer questions about a phenomenon that even ten years ago would have been considered material unfit for serious discussion. Grown men, perfectly normal-looking, were now going to talk about their trip to the moon. It made everyone uncomfortable. For the relation of everyone to each other and to the event was not quite real. It was as if a man had died and been brought back from death. What if on questioning he turned out to be an ordinary fellow? "Well, you see," he might say, "having visited death, I come back with the following conclusions . . ." What if he had a droning voice? There was something of this in the polite unreality of the questioning. The century was like a youth who made love to the loveliest courtesan in Cathay. Afterward he was asked what he thought and scratched his head and said, "I don't know. Sex is kind of overrated." So now people were going to ask questions of three heroes about their oncoming voyage, which on its face must be in contention for the greatest adventure of man. Yet it all felt as if three young junior executives were announcing their corporation's newest subdivision.

Perhaps for this reason, the quiet gaiety of their entrance had deserted them as they sat behind the desk in the plastic booth. Now it was as if they did not know if they were athletes, test pilots, engineers, corporation executives, some new kind of priest, or sheepish American boys caught in a position of outlandish prominence—my God, how did they ever get into this? It was as if after months in simulators with knowing technicians geared to the same code languages, they were now debouched into the open intellectual void of this theater, obliged to look into the uncomprehending spirits of several hundred media tools (human) all perplexed and worried at their journalistic ability to grasp more than the bare narrative of what was coming up. Yaws abounded. Vacuums in the magnetism of the mood. Something close to boredom. The astronauts were going to the moon, but everybody was a little frustrated—the Press because the Press did not know how to push into nitty-gritty for the questions, the astronauts because they were not certain how to begin to explain the complexity of their technique. Worse, as if they did not really wish to explain but were obliged out of duty to the program, even if their privacy was invaded.

So the conference dragged on. While the focus of attention was naturally on Armstrong for commanding the flight, he seemed in the beginning to be the least at ease. He spoke with long pauses, he searched for words. When the words came out, their ordinary content made the wait seem excessive. He minted no phrases. "We are here" . . . a pause . . . "to be able to talk about this attempt" . . . a real pause, as if the next experience were ineffable but with patience would yet be captured . . . "because of the success of four previous Apollo command flights" . . . pause, as if to pick up something he had left out . . . "and a number of unmanned flights." A shy smile. "Each of those flights"—he was more wooden than young Robert Taylor, young Don Ameche, young Randolph Scott—"contributed in a great way" . . . deprecatory smile . . . "to this flight." As a speaker he was all but limp—still it did not leave him unremarkable. Certainly the knowledge he was an astronaut restored his stature, yet even if he had been a junior executive accepting an award, Armstrong would have presented a quality that was arresting, for he was extraordinarily remote. He was simply not like other men. He would have been more extraordinary in fact if he had been just a salesman making a modest inept dull little speech, for then one would have been forced to wonder how he had ever gotten his job, how he could sell even one item, how in fact he got out of bed in the morning. Something particularly innocent or subtly sinister was in the gentle remote air. If he had been a young boy selling subscriptions at the door, one grandmother might have warned her granddaughter never to let him in the house; another would have commented, "That boy will go very far." He was apparently in communion with some string in the universe others did not think to play.

Collins and Aldrin followed with their opening remarks, and they had personalities that were more comfortable to grasp. Aldrin, all meat and stone, was a man of solid presentation, dependable as a tractor, but suggesting the strength of a tank, dull, almost ponderous, yet with the hint of unpredictability, as if, eighteen drinks in him, his eyes would turn red, he would arm-wrestle a gorilla or invite you to join him in jumping out a third-story window in order to see who could do the better somersault on the follow-through out of the landing. This streak was radium and encased within fifty psychical and institutional caskings of lead, but it was there, Aquarius thought, perhaps a clue in the way he dressed—very dressy for an astronaut—a green luminous silk suit, a white shirt, a green luminous tie. It clashed with the stolid presentation of his language. Aldrin spoke in a deep slow comfortingly nasal tone—a mighty voice box—his face was strong and grim. The movie director in Aquarius would have cast him on the spot for Major in Tank Cavalry. He had big features and light brown hair, almost gold. His eyes took a turn down like samurai eyes, the corners of his lips took a right-angle turn down—it gave him the expression of a serious man at home on a field of carnage, as if he were forever saying, "This is serious stuff, fellows, there's lots of blood around." So Aldrin also looked like the kind of jock who could be headmaster of a prep school. He had all the locker-room heartiness and solemnity of a team man. Although he had been a pole-vaulter at West Point, it would have been easy to mistake him for a shot-putter, a lacrosse player, or a baseball catcher. In football he would have probably been a linebacker. For this last, he was actually not big enough (since the astronauts were required to be no more than five feet eleven inches tall and could hardly be overweight), but he was one of those men who looked larger than his size, for his condition was excellent—every discipline of his moves spoke of grim devoted unrelenting support given to all his body-world of muscle. From the back of the neck to the joints of the toes, from the pectorals to the hamstrings, the deltoids to the abdominals, he was a life given over to good physical condition, a form of grace, since the agony of the lungs when straining is not alien to the agony of the soul. Leave it that Aldrin was so strong he had a physical presence that was bigger than his bulk.

He talked like a hardworking drill. He had the reputation of being the best physicist and engineer among the astronauts—he had written a valuable thesis on Orbital Rendezvous Techniques at MIT, but he put no humor into his presentation, he was selling no soap. If you did not read technologese, you might as well forget every last remark, for his words did not translate, not unless you were ready to jog along with him on technology road. Here is the way he gave himself to the Press: "We do have a few items on the Lem side of the house on this particular mission. We'll be picking up where Apollo 10 left off when they did their phasing maneuver. And at this point after departing the Command Module, coming down in the descent orbit, we'll be igniting the descent engine for the first time under a long burn condition when it is not docked with the Command Module. And executing this burn under control of a computer, being directed towards the various targets that are fed into the computer will be new on this flight. Also we'll be making use of the landing radar and its inputs into the computer. Inputs in terms of altitude and velocity updates which will bring us down in the prescribed conditions as we approach the surface of the moon."

He went on to talk of star sightings and the powered ascent from the moon—that moment when, having landed successfully and reconnoitered the moon ground, they would be back in the Lem and ready to ascend—would the motor ignite or did the moon have a curse? Aldrin spoke of this as a "new item," then of rendezvous with the Command Module, which would return them to earth, of "various contingencies that can develop," of "a wider variety of trajectory conditions"—he was talking about not being able to join up, wandering through space, lost forever to life in that short eternity before they expired of hunger and thirst. Small hint of that in these verbal formulations. Even as the Nazis and the Communists had used to speak of mass murder as liquidation, so the astronauts spoke of possible personal disasters as "contingency." The heart of astronaut talk, like the heart of all bureaucratic talk, was a jargon that could be easily converted to computer programming. Anti-dread formulations were the center of it, as if words like pills were there to suppress emotional symptoms. Yet Aldrin, powerful as a small bull, deep as his grasp of Celestial Mechanics, gave off in his air of unassailable solemnity some incommunicable speech about the depth of men's souls and that razor's edge between the hero's endeavor and vainglory. Vainglory looked real to him, one might assume, real as true peril—he had the deep gloomy clumsy dignity of a man who had been face to face in some stricken hour with the depths of his own nature, more complex than he had hitherto known.

Collins, in contrast, moved easily; Collins was cool. Collins was the man nearly everybody was glad to see at a party, for he was the living spirit of good and graceful manners. Where Armstrong referred to Wapakoneta, Ohio, as his hometown, and showed a faint but ineradicable suspicion of anyone from a burg larger than his own, where Aldrin protected himself from conversation with the insulations of a suburban boyhood and encapsulement among his incommunicable fields of competency, Collins had been born in a well-set-up apartment off the Borghese Gardens in Rome. His father, General James L. Collins, was military attaché (and could conceivably have been having a drink around the corner in the bar at the Hassler to celebrate the birth of his son). Since the year was 1930, Dick Diver could have been getting his going-over from the Fascisti police in the basement of *Tender Is the Night*. No surprise then if Collins had a manner. It was in part the manner of Irish elegance—a man must be caught dead before he takes himself seriously. It was as if Collins were playing a fine woodwind that had the merriment and the sadness (now that the madness was gone) of those American expatriates for whom culture began in the Year One of *The Sun Also Rises*. Indeed, if Collins was later to grow a mustache on the trip back, an act that increased his slight but definite resemblance to the young Hemingway, he had a personal style that owed more to Fitzgerald. It was Fitzgerald, after all, who first suggested that you could become the nicest man in the world. So Collins had that friendliness which promises it would be sacrilege to give offense in a social situation. It was apparently as unnatural for him not to make a small joke as it would have been offensive to Aldrin not to take on a matter in its full seriousness. Yet Collins had little opportunity to show his humor. It existed mainly in the fine light smiling presence he bestowed on the interview while the others were asked all the questions. Collins was the only one of the three not landing on the moon. So he would obviously be the one whose remarks would go into the last paragraph, where the layout man would probably lop them off. Therefore nobody had bothered to direct a question to him through all the interview.

Toward the end of the press conference, somebody asked of the astronauts at large, "Two questions. Firstly, what precautions have been taken at your own homes to prevent you from catching germs from your own family? And secondly, is this the last period that you will spend at home here with your families?" The Public Affairs Officer, Brian Duff, was quick to say, "Take a crack at that, Mike."

It could not have been easy to have waited so long for so little. But Collins came up smiling, and said, "My wife and children have signed a statement that they have no germs and—and yes this will be the last weekend that we will be home with our families." It was not much of a joke but the press conference had not been much of a joke either, and the Press brightened, they laughed. Collins, quick not to offend the man who had asked the question, now added, "Seriously, there are no special precautions being taken."

His conversational manner was easy. It was apparent that of the three, he was the only one you could drink with comfortably. Since the ability to drink with your material is as important to a journalist as the heft of his hammer to a carpenter, a sense of dismay passed through the press corps—why hadn't NASA had the simple sense of press relations to put Collins in command? What a joy it could have been to cover this moon landing with a man who gave neat quotes, instead of having to contend with Armstrong, who surrendered words about as happily as a hound allowed meat to be pulled out of his teeth. Collins would have been perfect. He looked to be the kind of man who would be at ease with a martini, but he also had the trim build, the bald forehead, and economical features of a college boxer, or a short-stop, or a quarterback. (In fact he was the best handball player among the astronauts and had been captain of his wrestling team at St. Albans.) He looked like copy, he talked like copy, and Armstrong had the sad lonely mien of a cross-country runner.

The story resided, however, with the two men who would land on the moon—it could reside nowhere else—but since Collins with a few smiles and a remark or two had become the favorite, a question and then another came his way at the end of the interview. Finally, the real question came.

"Colonel Collins, to people who are not astronauts, you would appear to have the most frustrating job on the mission, not going all the way. How do you feel about that?" The contradiction implicit in being an astronaut was here on this point—it was skewered right here.

If they were astronauts, they were men who worked for the team, but no man became an astronaut who was not sufficiently exceptional to suspect at times that he might be the best of all. Nobody wins at hand-ball who is not determined to win.

He answered quickly. "I don't feel in the slightest bit frustrated. I'm going 99.9 percent of the way there, and that suits me just fine." Growing up in Rome, Puerto Rico, Baltimore and Washington, Texas and Oklahoma, son of one of the more cultivated purlieus of the mil-itary grace, the code would be to keep your cool. The only real guide to aristocracy in American life was to see who could keep his cool under the most searing conditions of unrest, envy, ambition, jealousy, and heat. So not a quiver showed. "I couldn't be happier right where I am," he concluded, and the voice was not hollow, it did not offer a cousin to a squeak. Still, nobody believed him. Somewhere in the room was the leached-out air of a passion submitted to a discipline. For a moment Collins was damnably like an actor who plays a good guy.

Armstrong came in quickly. "I'd like to say in that regard that the man in the Command Module" . . . pause . . . "of course by him-self" . . . another pause . . . "has a giant-sized job." When Armstrong paused and looked for the next phrase he sometimes made a sound like the open crackling of static on a pilot's voice band with the control tower. One did not have the impression that the static came from him so much as that he had listened to so much static in his life, suffered so much of it, that his flesh, his cells, like it or not, were impregnated with the very cracklings of static. "He has to run Buzz's job and my job" . . . static . . . "along with his own job simultaneously" . . . sta-tic . . . "in addition act as relay to the ground" . . . pause and static. . . . "It's at least a three-man job and"—he murmured a few words— "Michael is certainly not lacking for something to do while he's cir-cling around." Then Armstrong flashed a smile. One of his own jokes came. His humor was pleasant and small-town, not without a taste of the tart. "And if he can't think of anything else, he can always look out the window and admire the view."

Now came a question from a reporter who was new on the job: "From your previous experience in the two and a half hours or so that you're atop the rocket before actual blast-off, is this a period of maxi-mum tension, rather like being in a dentist's waiting room?"

A temporary inability to understand the question was finally re-placed by this speech. "It's one of the phases that we have a very high confidence in," Armstrong answered with his characteristic mixture of modesty and technical arrogance, of apology and tight-lipped superiority. "It's nothing new. It's the thing that's been done before," now static while he searched for the appropriate addition, "and done very well on a number of occasions, and we're quite sure this girl will go," he said solemnly, pleasantly, lightly, carefully, sadly, sweetly. He was a presence in the room, as much a spirit as a man. One hardly knew if he was the spirit of the high thermal currents or that spirit of neutrality which rises to the top in bureaucratic situations, or both, both of course—why should Armstrong have a soul less divided than the unruly world of some billions of men? Indeed contradictions lay subtly upon him—it was not unlike looking at a bewildering nest of leaves: Some are autumn fallings, some the green of early spring. So Armstrong seemed of all the astronauts the man nearest to being saintly, yet there was something as hard, small-town, and used in his face as the look of a cashier over pennies. When he stopped to think, six tired parallel lines stood out on his forehead, and his hair was very straight, small-town hair-colored humorless straight, his pupils were very small, hardly larger than buckshot, you could believe he flew seventy-eight combat missions off the *Essex* near Korea. He was very thin-mouthed, almost as thin and wide a mouth as Joe E. Brown, yet with no comic spirit, or better, or worse, the spirit of comedy gave orders to the mouth most of the time. Much like President Nixon, he would smile on command. Then a very useful smile appeared—the smile of an enterprising small-town boy. He could be an angel, he could be the town's devil. Who knew? You could not penetrate the flash of the smile—all of America's bounty was in it. Readiness to serve, innocence, competence, modesty, sly humor, and all ambition was muzzled. He spoke with the unendurably slow and triple caution of a responsibility-laden politician who was being desperately careful to make no error of fact, give no needless offense to enemies, and cross no conflicting zones of loyalty among friends. At communicating he was as tight as a cramped muscle.

Perversely, it became his most impressive quality, as if what was best in the man was most removed from the surface, so valuable that it must be protected by a hundred reservations, a thousand cautions, as if finally he had such huge respect for words that they were like tangible omens and portents, zephyrs and beasts of psychic presence, as if finally something deep, delicate, and primitive would restrain him from uttering a single word of fear for fear of materializing his dread. So, once, men had been afraid to utter the name of the Lord, or even to write it in such a way as to suggest the sound, for that might be enough to summon some genie of God's displeasure at so disrupting the heavens. Armstrong of course did not brandish an ego one could perceive on meeting; where Aldrin gave off the stolid confidence of the man who knows that problems can be solved if properly formulated and appropriately attacked (which is to say attacked in good condition!) and where Collins offered the wiry graceful tension of a man who will quietly die to maintain his style, Armstrong could seem more like a modest animal than a man—tracer hints of every forest apprehension from the puma to the deer to the miseries of the hyena seemed to stalk at the edge of that small-town clearing he had cut into his psyche so that he might offer the world a person. But his thoughts seemed to be looking for a way to drift clear of any room like this where he was trapped with psyche-eaters, psyche-gorgers, and the duty of responding to questions heard some hundreds of times.

On the other hand, he was a professional and had learned how to contend in a practical way with the necessary language. Indeed, how his choice of language protected him!

"Mr. Armstrong, at the time you are down on the moon, what will be your overriding consideration and what will be your main concern?"

"Well," said Armstrong, "immediately upon touchdown our concern is the integrity of the Lunar Module itself" . . . nnnnnnnhr went the sound of the static. . . . "For the first two hours after touchdown we have a very busy time verifying the integrity of the Lunar Module and all of its systems" . . . nnnnhr. . . . "A great deal of technical discussion . . . between spacecraft and ground during a time period when most people will be wondering, well what does it look like out there? . . . We will be eager to comment" . . . nnnnhr . . . "but reluctant to do so in the face of these more important considerations on which . . . the entire rest of the lunar mission depends."

Aldrin, the formalist, had said just previously, "I think the most critical portion of the EVA will be our ability to anticipate and to interpret things that appear not to be as we expected them to be, because if we don't interpret them correctly then they will become difficult." It was the credo of the rationalist. Phenomena are only possessed of menace when they do not accommodate themselves to language-controls. Or, better, to initial-controls. EVA stood for Extravehicular Activity, that is, for action taken outside their vehicle, the Lem. EVA therefore referred to their walk on the moon; but the sound of the letters E, V, A might inspire less perturbation than the frank admission that men would now dare to walk on an ancient and alien terrain where no life breathed and beneath the ground no bodies were dead.

It was, of course, a style of language all the astronauts had learned. There were speeches where you could not tell who was putting the words together—the phrases were impersonal, interlocking. One man could have finished a sentence for another. "Our order of priorities was carefully integrated into the flight plan . . . there is no requirement on the specific objectives that we're meeting on the surface to go great distances from the spacecraft, and to do so would only utilize time that we now have programmed doing things in the specific mission objectives." Sell newspapers with that kind of stuff! The quote could belong to any one of a dozen astronauts. In this case it happened to be not Aldrin but Armstrong.

Only on occasion did the language reveal its inability to blanket all situations. Mainly on personal matters. There came a question from one of the remedial readers. "Tell us very briefly how your families have reacted to the fact that you're taking this historic mission."

"Well," Aldrin deliberated, "I think in my particular case, my family has had five years now to become accustomed to this eventuality, and over six months to face it very closely. I think they look on this as a tremendous challenge for me. They look upon it also as an invasion somewhat of their privacy and removing of my presence away from the family for a considerable period of time." He spoke glumly, probably thinking at this moment neither of his family nor himself— rather whether his ability to anticipate and interpret had been correctly employed in the cathexis-loaded dynamic shift vector area of changed field domestic situations (which translates as: attractive wife and kids playing second fiddle to astronaut number two sometimes blow group stack). Aldrin was a man of such powerful potentialities and iron disciplines that the dull weight of appropriately massed jargon was no mean gift to him. He obviously liked it to work. It kept explosives in their package. When his laboriously acquired speech failed to mop up the discharge of a question, he got as glum as a fastidious housewife who cannot keep the shine on her floor.

They could not, of course, restrain the questions that looked for ultimate blood. "James Gunn, BBC. You had mentioned that your flight, like all others, contains very many risks. What, in view of that, will your plans be"—a British courtesy in passing—"in the extremely unlikely event that the Lunar Module does not come up off the lunar surface?"

Armstrong smiled. His detestation of answering questions in public had been given its justification. Journalists would even ask a man to comment on the emotions of his oncoming death. "Well," said Armstrong, "that's an unpleasant thing to think about." If, as was quite possible, he had been closer to death than anyone in the room, and more than once, more than once, that did not mean the chalice of such findings was there to be fingered by fifty. "We've chosen not to think about that up to the present time. We don't think that's at all a likely situation. It's simply a possible one." He had, however, not answered the question. If he put in twelve and more hours a day in simulators, if there were weeks when they worked seventy and eighty hours a week at the abrasive grind of laying in still more hierarchies of numbers and banks of ratio in their heads, well, they were accustomed to hard work. So the grind today of being interviewed in full press conference, then by the wire services, then by magazine writers, and finally for the television networks, a fourteen-hour day before it would all be done, and of the worst sort of work for them—objects on display to be chipped at by some of the worst word-sculptors ever assembled in southeastern Texas—well, that would still be work they must perform to the best of their duty. Being an astronaut was a mission. Since the political and power transactions of the age on which NASA's future was—put no nice word on it—hung were not in spirit religious, the astronauts did not emphasize their sense of vocation. But being an astronaut was a mission and therefore you were obliged to perform every aspect of your work as well as you could. At a press conference you answered questions. So Armstrong now finally said in answer to what they would do if the Lunar Module did not come up off the lunar surface, "At the present time we're left without recourse should that occur."

It was the answer Aquarius thought about after the conference was done, for that was the nearest anyone had come to saying that a man could get killed in the pits of this venture. And yes, they did think about it. A man who was in training for six months to go to the moon would be obliged to think about his death. Yet, if to contemplate the failure of the ascent stage of the Lunar Module to rise off the moon was unpleasant for Armstrong to think about, did that derive automatically and simply because it would mean death, or was it, bottomless taint of the unpleasant, a derivation deep out of the incommensurable fact that the moon ground would be the place where his body must rest in death? People who had nearly died from wounds spoke of the near death as offering a sensation that one was rising out of one's body. So had spoken Hemingway long ago, writing in Paris, writing in Spain, probably writing in apartments off the Borghese Gardens near where Collins had been born. Now was there to be a future science of death, or did death (like smell and sound and time—like the theory of the dream) resist all scientists, navigators, nomenclature, and charts and reside in the realm of such unanswerables as whether the cause of cancer was a malfunction of the dream? *Did* the souls of the dead choose to rise? Was the thought of expiring on the moon an abyss of unpleasantness because the soul must rest in the tombless vacuums of a torso dead on the moon and therefore not able to voyage toward its star? A vertigo of impressions, but Aquarius had been living at the edge of such thoughts for years. It was possible there was nothing more important in a man's life than the hour and the route and the power of his death, yes, certainly if his death were to launch him into another kind of life. And the astronauts—of this he was convinced—would think this way, or at least would have that vein of imagination in some inviolate and noncommunicatory circuit of their brain; somewhere, far below the language of their communication, they must suspect that the gamble of a trip to the moon and back again, if carried off in all success, might give thrust for some transpostmortal insertion to the stars. Varoom! Last of all over the years had Aquarius learned how to control the rapid acceleration of his brain. Perhaps as a result, he was almost—in these first few days of covering the astronauts in Houston—fond of the banality of their speech and the anodyne of technologese, yes, from their conscious mind to their unconscious depth, what a spectrum could be covered! Yes, Aquarius thought, astronauts have learned not only to live with opposites, but it was conceivable that the contradictions in their nature were so located in the very impetus of the age that their personality might begin to speak, for better or worse, of some new psychological constitution to man. For it was true—astronauts had come to live with adventures in space so vast one thought of the infinities of a dream, yet their time on the ground was conventional, practical, technical, hardworking, and in the center of the suburban middle class. If they engaged the deepest primitive taboos, they all but parodied the conventional in public manner; they embarked on odysseys whose success or failure was so far from being entirely in their own control that they must be therefore fatalistic, yet the effort was enterprising beyond the limits of the imagination. They were patriots, but they were moonmen. They lived with absolute lack of pri-

vacy, their obvious pleasure was to be alone in the sky. They were sufficiently selfless to be prepared to die for their mission, their team,
their corporate NASA, their nation, yet they were willy-nilly narcissistic as movie stars. "Sugar, I tried and couldn't make doo-doo," says
Lulu Meyers in *The Deer Park*. The heart pressure, the brain waves, the
bowel movements of astronauts were of national interest. They were
virile men, but they were prodded, probed, tapped into, poked,
flexed, tested, subjected to a pharmacology of stimulants, depressants,
diuretics, laxatives, retentives, tranquilizers, motion sickness pills, antibiotics, vitamins, and food that was designed to control the character
of their feces. They were virile, but they were done to, they were done
to like no healthy man alive. So again their activity was hazardous, far-
flung, bold, demanding of considerable physical strength, yet the
work and physical condition called for the ability to live in cramped
conditions with passive bodies, the patience to remain mentally alert
and physically inactive for days. They lived, it was evident, with no ordinary opposites in their mind and brain. On the one hand to dwell in
the very center of technological reality (which is to say that world
where every question must have answers and procedures, or technique cannot itself progress) yet to inhabit—if only in one's dreams—
that other world where death, metaphysics, and the unanswerable
questions of eternity must reside, was to suggest natures so divided
that they could have been the most miserable and unbalanced of men
if they did not contain in their huge contradictions some of the profound and accelerating opposites of the century itself. The century
would seek to dominate nature as it had never been dominated,
would attack the idea of war, poverty, and natural catastrophe as
never before. The century would create death, devastation, and pollution as never before. Yet the century was now attached to the idea
that man must take his conception of life out to the stars. It was the
most soul-destroying and apocalyptic of centuries. So in their turn the
astronauts had personalities of unequaled banality and apocalyptic
dignity. So they suggested in their contradictions the power of the
century to live with its own incredible contradictions and yet release
some of the untold energies of the earth. A century devoted to the rationality of technique was also a century so irrational as to open in
every mind the real possibility of global destruction. It was the first
century in history which presented to sane and sober minds the fair
chance that the century might not reach the end of its span. It was a
world half convinced of the future death of our species yet half
aroused by the apocalyptic notion that an exceptional future still lay

before us. So it was a century which moved with the most magnificent display of power into directions it could not comprehend. The itch was to accelerate—the metaphysical direction unknown.

# Wernher Von Braun

Since the formal title of Wernher Von Braun is Center Director of George C. Marshall Space Center at Huntsville, Alabama, he can hardly be the Boss of NASA, but to the public sense of these affairs, to the Press, and to a corps of space workers, he is the real engineer, the spiritual leader, the inventor, the force, the philosopher, the genius! of America's Space Program. Such is his legend in the street. That is the positive side of his reputation—it is enormous; say, rather it is immense. Yet he has that variety of glamour usually described as fascinating, which is to say the evocation of his name is attractive and repellent at once, because no one forgets for an instant that he worked on the V-2 rockets at the German Rocket Research Center at Peenemünde, second only to General Dornberger, and so was implicated on one occasion by giving an orientation lecture to the Leader himself, who stood and stared and did not say a word when rockets were later fired for him on test stands. It was expected that Hitler with his love of the cosmic, the primitive, the apocalyptic, and the more audible wars of Hell and Heaven would be enthusiastic about the extraordinary sound of rocket motors. The future of the rocket program at Peenemünde was indeed even dependent in 1939 upon just such hopes as Hitler's ecstatic reaction. But the Führer did not say a word until lunch, when he stated, "*Es war doch gevaltig,*" which may be translated as "That was sensational." (Göring, who visited a week later, was openly enchanted. Rocket propulsion for railroad and passenger cars, airplanes, airships! and ocean liners! was what he saw next.)

Then in 1943, after an audience with Hitler, Von Braun was granted the very high honor of a titular professorship. That much was ineradicable from Von Braun's record, but he had also had the opposite honor of being arrested and jailed for two weeks in an SS prison by Heinrich Himmler himself. One of the accusations: Von Braun was not really interested in rockets for war so much as for space exploration. It took General Dornberger's intercession with Hitler to spring Von Braun from Stettin Prison. Without Von Braun, said Dornberger to Hitler, there would be no V-2. Then in 1945 Von Braun had managed with considerable skill to move about five thousand employees and their families, and some of their papers, documents, and drawings, to the Harz Mountains, in the south of Germany, where they could be captured by Americans rather than Russians.

Von Braun had not been out of higher headquarters since. While the U.S. Army test-fired V-2's at the White Sands Proving Grounds in New Mexico, he served as adviser. Five years later, still working for the Army, he directed the development of the Redstone and Jupiter missiles. For NASA he had created the launch vehicle for the Apollo program, the famous, the monumental, the incomparable three-stage Saturn V, that launch vehicle we have already glimpsed at the VAB, a booster the size and weight of a full Navy destroyer, a rocket to deliver seven and a half million pounds of thrust at blast-off, Saturn V, 281 feet long, 33 feet wide, designed to put—we may be Germanic in metaphor here—designed to put its *little brother,* the 82-foot Apollo spacecraft implanted on top of it, into Trans-Lunar Injection, which is to say: on its way to the moon. In terms of size, the Apollo spacecraft was no more than a witch's hat perched on Saturn V's Instrument Unit of a head!

Yet since this launch vehicle in all its three stages did not have fuel to burn for even eighteen minutes, all six million pounds of fuel consumed in bursts of two and a half minutes and six and a half minutes, then two minutes and six minutes, near to five million pounds of fuel being burned in the first 150 seconds, whereas, in contrast, the Command Module would be in flight for eight days. Since Saturn V in relation to the complexity of the electronic vitals and conceptions on the Command Module was relatively simple in design, Saturn V hardly more by the severest measure than a mighty mortar of a firework to blast an electric brain into space, why then was Von Braun so worshiped, why, if the true technology, the vertiginous complexity of the engineering feat, of putting a man on the moon and back belonged rather in sum of work and intimate invention to echelons of electronic engineers out at MSC, North American, and Grumman and too many other places to name? Well, the brute but inescapable answer if one studies the morphology of rockets is that man worships his phallus in preference to a drop of his seed. Yeah and yea. Saturn V was guts and grease, plumbing and superpipes, Lucifer or the Archangel grinding the valves. Saturn V was a furnace, a chariot of fire. One could witness some incandescent entrance to the heavens. But Apollo 11 was Command Module and therefore not to be seen. It spoke out of a crackling of static, or rolled like a soup can, a commercial in a sea of television, a cootie in a zoo of oscillating dots.

We may, then, absorb the lesson: Electricity is an avatar of hate that gives pain to the senses, emits static, electronic hum, neon flicker, light glare, shock, heat radiation. Whereas thoughts of the sun and royal spectacle are in the mystery of a flame. So Von Braun was the heat in rocketry, the animal in the program. By public estimate he had been a Nazi—that was glamour enough. Who could begin to measure the secret appeal of the Nazis by now? It was a fit subject for Aquarius to begin to brood upon: America was this day mighty but headless, America was torn by the specter of civil war, and many a patriot and many a big industrialist—they were so often the same!—saw the cities and the universities as a collective pit of Black heathen, Jewish revolutionaries, a minority polyglot hirsute scum of nihilists, hippies, sex maniacs, drug addicts, liberal apologists, and freaks. Crime pushed the American public to give birth to dreams of order. Fantasies of order had to give way to lusts for new order. Order was restraint, but new order would call for a mighty vault, an exceptional effort, a unifying dream. Was the conquest of space then a potential chariot of Satan, the unique and grand avenue for the new totalitarian? Aquarius was not certain. It was possible that neo-Nazism and technology were finally inimical to each other, but it was all to be considered again and again. It was complex. At this instant, he would not have minded the return of his ego.

Meanwhile, here was Von Braun for study. Yes, he had come in by helicopter to the Royal Oak Country Club in Titusville. The roads were crowded and it was incontestable that on this night, this night above all, hours before the mightiest launching of his life, Von Braun's hours were of value to him and to others. Still, the impression had to arise that he would have arrived by helicopter in any case. The helicopter had become the vehicle of status of that Praetorian Guard now forming of generals, state troopers, admirals, Republican congressmen with wives-on-junket, governors from he-man states, he-man senators, law-and-order mayors, traffic-crisis monitors, and VIPs on state visits to troublesome cities. The helicopter was there to signify: A man engaged in *flag* activity was dropping in on the *spot*. So the helicopter was a status symbol as special as a Junior League Ball. Not everybody who was moderately rich and powerful in American life would necessarily want to go to the ball or ride in the bubble, but for that matter not everybody who was thus rich and powerful was welcome at either.

Under whose auspices, then, had Von Braun descended? We can pretend to investigate. A large publishing corporation long associated with the Space Program had invited corporation presidents of important firms to voyage out for a few days on a trip to Houston to meet astronauts, then on to Kennedy to see the launching. A private speech by Von Braun was one of the features of the junket, and they waited for him now in a hexagonal banquet room finished in varieties of walnut-colored wood, a fit meeting place for American gods and cousins of the gods, since the shape of the chamber gave an echo of clans meeting in a wooded glen. Talismans in the form of intricate hex signs were inlaid in the wood of the walls around the room below the ceiling. Yet the walls, as though aware the gods were American, their powers corporate, were finished pale in stain, and therefore not excitative to the bottled emotions of business leaders. In any case, the golf course abutted the premises, and some of the guests left the bar and waited for the helicopter outside, standing in the steamy air of evening on that stiff rubbery thick-bladed Florida grass so much an overnight product of hyperfertilizer, turf-planting, and the tropics, that it felt like plastic underfoot.

It was a not untypical American gathering. Doubtless, equivalent Soviet meetings were similar. It did not matter how high or prominent these people had become, how far some of them had traveled from their beginnings. There was still the same awkward, embarrassed, well-scrubbed air of a church social. Americans might yet run the world, they were certainly first on the way to the stars, and yet they had never filled the spaces between. Americans were still as raw as an unboiled potato. It hardly mattered if Americans were rich or poor. When they got together, they did not know what to say to each other. It is part of the double life of Americans, the unequal development of the lobes in the national schizophrenia. Men whose minds worked with an admirable depth of reference and experience in their business or occupation were less interesting in a social gathering, at least in this social gathering, where they were plucked up from a more familiar core of small talk and deposited on the rubber-mat turf of the Royal Oak. It was almost a reflection of the national belief that a man who worked thoroughly at his job was given dispensation from the obligation to have a good time. So conversation took overloaded steps over successive hills, and that was all right, the point of the evening was that they would hear Von Braun and be able to refer to it afterward. The American family travels to strange states and places in order to take photographs and bring them back, as if the photographs will serve in future years as data-points, crystals of memory to give emotional resonance to experience that was originally without any. The data-point will give warmth in old age. So Von Braun would be a data-point tonight. It would not matter if a good time was not otherwise had. Aquarius' mind, brooding through these familiar thoughts, was brought up short with the radically new idea that perhaps some instinct in American life had been working all these decades to keep the country innocent, keep it raw, keep it crude as a lout, have it indeed ready to govern the universe without an agreeable culture to call its own—for then, virgin ore, steadfastly undeveloped in all the hinterworld of the national psyche, a single idea could still electrify the land. Culture was insulation against a single idea, and America was like a rawboned lover gangling into middle age, still looking for his mission.

Since Aquarius on evenings like this would look for the nutrient in liquor the way a hound needles out marrow from a bone, he was nose-deep into his second drink, and hardly saw the helicopter come in. A sense of presence overhead, fore and aft lights whirruping like crickets in the dusk, a beating of rotors in a wheat-flattened gust, and it was down, a creature. Nothing inspired so fine a patriotic cocktail of mild awe, mild respect, and uncorrupted envy as the sight of Praetorians emerging from an insect the size of an elephant which *they* commanded.

The guests immediately made their way inside. Von Braun, dressed in a silver-gray suit, white shirt, and black tie, looked more impressive tonight than the day before at a press conference. That had taken place in front of several hundred correspondents with movie cameras, television, and ushers in the audience holding portable microphones to amplify and record all questions the Press might ask for posterity. Von Braun had been on a panel with Dr. Mueller, Dr. Debus, Dr. Gilruth, and a director from Langley, but half the questions had gone to Von Braun. He seemed sensitive to the fact that the Press made jokes about his past. There was one tale every reporter had heard—"Tell me, Dr. Von Braun," a correspondent said, "what is there to keep Saturn V from landing on London?" Von Braun walked out of the room. But the story was doubtless apocryphal; it smacked of reporters' bile. Journalists were often vicious in their prior comments about VIPs they were going to interview, as if to compensate for the uxorious tone of the restrained questions they would finally ask. Aquarius had been with a small pack who had gone to talk to Dr. Debus, director of all launching operations at Kennedy and a former colleague of Von Braun's. "Just give the Nazi salute and he'll holler, 'Heil Hitler!' " they all promised each other, but Debus to their consternation proved out a pleasant Junker gentleman with dueling scars on his mouth and bags under his eyes—the sort of aristocratic face and gracious if saturnine manner that belongs to an unhappy German prince from a small principality. The questions of the Press were predictably unctuous, and trading notes afterward, they quoted Debus respectfully. He had given them the best of lines; when asked if he was planning a celebration while the astronauts were on the moon surface, he had smiled and cleared his throat with a cultivated sound. "No," he had said, "no champagne in the refrigerator." Debus was not afraid of the Press.

But Von Braun was too prominent, and had—although his official position was nominally no more elevated than his countryman's—much too much to lose. A press conference, no matter how many he had had, was a putative den of menace. So his eyes flew left and right as he answered a question, flicking back and forth in their attention with the speed of eyes watching a Ping-Pong game, and his mouth moved from a straight line to a smile, but the smile was no more than a significator, a tooth-filled rectangle. Words were being mouthed like signal flags.

Since he had, in contrast to his delivery, a big burly squared-off bulk of a body that gave hint of methodical ruthlessness, his relatively small voice, darting eyes, and semaphoric presentations of lip made it obvious he was a man of opposites. He revealed a confusing aura of strength and vulnerability, of calm and agitation, cruelty and concern, phlegm and sensitivity, which would have given fine play to the talents of so virtuoso an actor as Mr. Rod Steiger. Von Braun had in fact something of Steiger's soft voice, that play of force and weakness which speaks of consecration and vanity, dedication and indulgence, steel and fat.

Still, he did not do badly at his press conference. If he had started nervously, there was an exchange where he encountered his opposition. A correspondent from East Berlin asked him in German to answer a question. There had been a silence. For an instant Von Braun had not known exactly what to do, had in fact stolen a look at Mueller. NASA was sensitive about origins. Two of the three directors in the center of the Manned Spacecraft Program were, after all, German. And there was no joy in emphasizing this, since those few liberal congressmen who were sympathetic to the needs of the space budget would only find their way harder if Von Braun and Debus were too prominent.

Von Braun fielded the difficulty as follows: He translated the question into English. Then he gave a long detailed answer in English (which succeeded in boring the Press). Then, taking an equally long time, he translated his answer back to German. Finally, he took a nimble step away from this now somnolent situation by remarking, "I must warn the hundred and thirty-four Japanese correspondents here at Cape Kennedy that I cannot do the same in Japanese." The remark drew the largest laugh of the afternoon, and thereby enabled him to prosper. The contest in press conferences is to utter the remark that will be used as the lead quotation in wire-service stories, and Dr. George Mueller, anxious to establish his centrality on this panel, and his eminence over his directors, answered every question helpfully, giving facts, figures, prognostications of future activity. He was a one-man mine of pieces of one-line information with follow-up suitable for heads, leads, paragraph leads, and bottom-of-the-page slugs, but Von Braun picked up the marbles. In fact he had the subtle look of a fat boy who has gathered the shooters in many a game.

When asked how he evaluated the importance of the act of putting a man on the moon, Von Braun answered, "I think it is equal in importance to that moment in evolution when aquatic life came crawling up on the land." It drew a hand of applause. It would get the headline. Some of the Press literally stood up.

Thus, he was sound, sensible, and quick as mercury. Yet his appearance had been not as impressive then as now tonight at the Royal Oak. Then he had been somehow not forceful enough for the public image, small-voiced, almost squeaky for a man with so massive a frame. Whereas, here at the Country Club, shaking hands, he had obvious funds of charisma.

Yes, Von Braun most definitely was not like others. Curiously shifty, as if to show his eyes in full would give away much too much, he offered the impression of a man who wheeled whole complexes of caution into every gesture—he was after all an engineer who put massive explosives into adjoining tanks and then was obliged to worry about leaks. Indeed, what is plumbing but the prevention of treachery in closed systems? So he would never give anything away he did not have to, but the secrets he held, the tensions he held, the very philosophical explosives he contained under such supercompression, gave him an air of magic. He was a rocketeer. He had lived his life with the obsession of reaching other planets. It is no small impulse. Immediate reflection must tell you that a man who wishes to reach heavenly bodies is an agent of the Lord or Mephisto. In fact, Von Braun, with his handsome spoiled face, massive chin, and long and highly articulated nose, had a fair resemblance to Goethe. (Albeit none of the fine weatherings of the Old Master's head.) But brood on it: The impulse to explore the universe seems all but to suppose a divine will or a divine displeasure, or—our impurities matched only by our corruptions—some mixture of the two. What went on in Von Braun's mind during a dream? "Yes," he said with a smile to Aquarius, "we are in trouble. You must help us give a shove to the program."

"Who are you kidding?" said Aquarius, the good American. "You're going to get everything you want."

Whether the intimacy was too abrupt, or Von Braun's reaction disclosed too much—his eyes gleamed with sudden funds of pleasure at the remark—he quickly looked discomposed, and as quickly left the conversation by failing to forward a remark in return. Then he waved some ambiguous good-bye and moved quickly across the room. If his sense of friend and foe was good—a reasonable assumption to make about a man like Von Braun—it was obvious he did not think Aquarius would make such a good friend.

The banquet was roast beef. Ice creams and sauces for dessert. Coffee. The spoon on the glass. When Von Braun stood up to speak, a particularly hearty and enthusiastic hand of applause swelled into a standing ovation. Nearly everybody stood up. Aquarius, who finally cast his vote by remaining seated, felt pressure not unrelated to refusing to stand for "The Star-Spangled Banner." It was as if the crowd with true American enthusiasm had finally declared, "Ah don' care if he is some kind of ex-Nazi, he's a good loyal patriotic American."

Von Braun was. If patriotism is the ability to improve a nation's morale, then Von Braun was a patriot. It was plain that some of these corporation executives loved him. In fact, they revered him. He was the high priest of their precise art—manufacture. If many too many an American product was accelerating into shoddy these years since the war, if planned obsolescence had often become a euphemism for sloppy workmanship, cynical cost-cutting, swollen advertising budgets, inefficiency, and general indifference, then in one place at least, and for certain, America could be proud of a product. It was high as a castle and tooled more finely than an exquisite watch.

Now the real and true tasty beef of capitalism got up to speak, the grease and guts of it, the veritable brawn, and spoke with fulsome language in his small and well-considered voice. He was with friends this occasion, and so a savory, a gravy of redolence, came into his tone; his voice was not unmusical, it had overtones that hinted of angelic superpossibilities one could not otherwise lay on the line. He was when all was said like the head waiter of the largest hofbrau house in Heaven. "Honored guests, ladies and gentlemen," Von Braun began, "it is with a great deal of respect tonight that I meet you, the leaders and the captains of the mainstream of American industry and life. Without your success in building and maintaining the economic foundations of this nation, the resources for mounting tomorrow's expedition to the moon would never have been committed. . . . Tomorrow's historic launch belongs to you and to the men and women who sit behind the desks and administer your companies' activities, to the men who sweep the floors in your office buildings and to every American who walks the street of this productive land. It is an American triumph. Many times I have thanked God for allowing me to be a part of the history that will be made here today and tomorrow and in the next few days. Tonight I want to offer my gratitude to you and all Americans who have created the most fantastically progressive nation yet conceived and developed." He went on to talk of space as "the key to our future on earth," and echoes of his vision drifted through the stale tropical air of a banquet room after coffee—perhaps he was hinting at the discords and nihilism traveling in bands of brigands across the earth. "The key to our future on earth. I think we should see clearly from this statement that the Apollo 11 moon trip even from its inception was not intended as a one-time trip that would rest alone on the merits of a single journey. If our intention had been merely to bring back a handful of soil and rocks from the lunar gravel pit and then forget the whole thing"—he spoke almost with contempt of the meager resources of the moon—"we would certainly be history's biggest fools. But that is not our intention now—it never will be. What we are seeking in tomorrow's trip is indeed that key to our future on earth. We are expanding the mind of man. We are extending this God-given brain and these God-given hands to their outermost limits and in so doing all mankind will benefit. All mankind will reap the harvest. . . . What we will have attained when Neil Armstrong steps down upon the moon is a completely new step in the evolution of man."

He was almost done with his formal remarks. Out of his big bulk and his small voice he would offer miracles. That was his knowledge of America, no mean knowledge. Prosperity satisfies those who are rich in culture. But in lands where the geography like the people is filled with empty space, then faith in miracles is the staple of the future.

"Every man achieves his own greatness by reaching out beyond himself, and so it is with nations. When a nation believes in itself as Athenians did in their Golden Age, as Italians did in the Renaissance, that nation can perform miracles. Only when a nation means some-thing to itself can it mean something to others. We are truly faced with the brightest prospects of any age of man. Knowing this, we can watch the launch tomorrow with a new dimension of hope. We can cheer the beginning of a new age of discovery and the new attainment that spans the space distances and brings us nearer to the heavens."

When applause subsided, the publisher cried out in his cheerful voice, "I have a question. Will you be fired if you don't get on that he-licopter and greet the senators and Cabinet members who are wait-ing?" Von Braun made a point of staying for two questions, then took his departure. The sound of helicopters rose over the room.

Aquarius would have thought the evening concluded, but as he was learning again, he would never understand Americans. Another speaker, a representative of American business, rose and gave a hu-morous introduction to a man as massive and slow-speaking as Lyn-don Johnson, who proceeded to get up and tell jokes in an absolutely assured drawl. The audience seemed happy with them. "I was in an airport not long ago and sitting next to a woman smoking a cigar. I asked her how long she'd been smoking cigars. And she said ever since her husband had come home and found one in her ashtray in the bedroom."

The couple in front of Aquarius, young, stingy, ambitious, and very respectable, were laughing. The husband scowled at the wife and said with existential humor, "I wouldn't laugh at that joke if I was you."

"Why not?" responded the wife with the serenity of total practi-cality. "I've never done it."

Yes, they were all good Americans and they would listen to jokes and be a little relieved Von Braun was gone (although they would treasure the experience), and as new jokes came along, Aquarius began to look again into his drink and brood on Von Braun's remarks. He had declared that reaching the moon would be the greatest event in history since aquatic life had moved up onto land, and that was a remark! for it passed without pause over the birth and death of Christ. Indeed Von Braun had said even more in a newspaper interview. "Through a closer look at Creation, we ought to gain a better knowl-edge of the Creator." Man was voyaging to the planets in order to look for God. Or was it to destroy Him? Was the Space Program admirable or abominable? Did God voyage out for NASA, or was the Devil our line of sight to the stars?

NASA. The word had derived from NACA—National Advisory Committee for Aeronautics, which became the National Aeronautics and Space Administration, or NASA. It was an unhappy sound. Just

think of NASA-ism. NASA would have no deliberate relation whatsoever to Nazi. But we are not a schizophrenic land for nothing. Deep in
the unconscious where each sound leaves first its murmur and then its
roar at a combustion of hitherto unconnected meanings, NASA had to
stand for something. You bet.

Listening to the jokes, Aquarius was still brooding about Nazism.
For the philosophy of the Folk, detesting civilization, claiming to be in
love with the primitive, had nonetheless killed millions in the most orderly technological fashion yet devised. Nazism had been not one philosophy but two—and each philosophy was utterly opposed to the
other. It was primitive, it was vertiginously advanced. It gave brave
men a sense of nobility in their hearts—it had been utterly heartless.
It spoke of clean futures and buried Germany (for a time!) in vomit
and slime and swill. Now its ghosts were pacing on every battlement of
every surviving palace, now its ghosts were bubbling in the tubes of
every laboratory, burning in the wires. Nazism had been an assault
upon the cosmos—why think of it as less? That is why it moved as the
specter behind every civilized transaction. For it had said: Civilization
will stifle man unless man is delivered onto a new plane. Was space its
amputated limb, its philosophy in orbit?

Now the speaker was telling a joke about a Texan in Alaska who
had mixed up his respective missions with a woman and a bear. Big
was the laugh from the audience. And out on the beaches and the
causeways and riverbanks, another audience was waiting for the
launch. America like a lazy beast in the hot dark was waiting for a hint
in the ringing of the night.

# Red and Mollie

Saturn V would take off from a plain of gray-green moor and marsh,
no factory or habitation within three and a half miles. Saturn V had almost six million pounds of fuel. So it would take the equivalent of
thirty thousand strong men to raise it an inch. It would take liquid
oxygen, liquid hydrogen, and a very high grade of kerosene called
RP-1. It had hydrazine, unsymmetrical dimethylhydrazine, and nitro-
gen tetroxide in the Service Module. It was in effect a bomb, thirty-
three feet wide—the length of a long living room. Corporation

executives earning $50,000 a year just begin to think of a thirty-three-foot living room for themselves. And it was the height of a football field set on end. Sometimes they described it as a thirty-six-story building (ten feet to a floor) but a football field was clear measure of size, and this bomb, 363 feet high, 33 feet wide at the base, would blow if it blew with a force kin to one million pounds of TNT. That was like an old-fashioned bombing raid in World War II—one thousand planes, each carrying one thousand pounds of bombs. So Saturn V would devastate an area if ever it went. Flight Control, the Press Site, and the VIP stands were located therefore three and a half empty miles away across barren moors that, having been built by dredging fill into marshland, looked as if a bomb had gone off on them already.

On the night before the launch of Apollo 11, in the heart of Brevard County, in that stretch which runs from Melbourne through Eau Gallie, and Cocoa, to Titusville, on the coastal strip from Patrick Air Force Base through Cocoa Beach and Cape Canaveral to the Cape Kennedy Air Force Station and above to the Space Center and Launch Pad 39, through all that several hundred square miles of town and water and flat swampy waste of wilderness, through cultivated tropical gardens, and back roads by rivers lined with palms, through all the evening din of crickets, cicadas, beetles, bees, mosquitoes, grasshoppers, and wasps, some portion of a million people began to foregather on all the beaches and available islands and causeways and bridges and promontories that would give clear view of the flight from six miles and ten miles and fifteen miles away. Tomorrow most of them would need field glasses to follow the flight up from the pad and out of sight over the sea down a chain of Caribbean isles, but they would have a view—they knew tonight that if the skies were clear they would have their view, because they were encamped only where the line of sight was unimpeded to Launch Pad 39 on the horizon. There one could certainly see Apollo 11 on her Saturn V, see her for seven, nine, eleven miles away; she was lit up. A play of giant arc lights, as voluminous in candlepower as the lights for an old-fashioned Hollywood premiere, was directed on the spaceship from every side. On U.S. 1 in Titusville, eleven miles from Cape Kennedy across Merritt Island and the Banana and Indian rivers, all that clear shot across the evening waters, at an artillery range of twenty thousand yards, two hundred football fields away, by an encampment of tourists up from southern Florida, Everglades, Miami, and the Keys; in from Tampa, and Orlando; down from Daytona, St. Augustine, Gainesville, and Jacksonville; come from Fort Myers and Fort Lauderdale, from Sarasota, St. Petersburg, Lakeland, Ocala, and Tallahassee, come from all the towns of Georgia and points farther north and west as well as every itinerant camper in the area from all of the ambulatory camping-out families of the fifty states, and tourists down on economy flights for a week in cheap hot summer Florida and now slung out in the back seats of rented cars, on U.S. 1 in Titusville, in an encampment of every variety of camper, was a view of the spaceship across flat land and waters, and she looked like a shrine with the lights upon her. In the distance she glowed for all the world like some white stone Madonna in the mountains, welcoming footsore travelers at dusk. Perhaps it was an unforeseen game of the lighting, but America had not had its movie premieres for nothing, nor its Rockettes in Radio City and fifty million squares tooling the tourist miles over the years to Big Town to buy a ticket to spectacle and back home again. If you were going to have a Hollywood premiere and arc lights, a million out to watch and a spaceship that looked across the evening flutter like the light on the Shrine of Our Lady outside any church in South Brooklyn or Bay Ridge, then by God you might just as well have this spectacle on the premiere trip to the moon. That deserved a searchlight or two! And the campers stared across the waters in their bivouac off Route 1 in Titusville, campers sat on the banks of the Indian River at twilight and waited for the tropical night to pass its hold on the hours.

There were new industries in America these years. After five decades of suspense movies, and movies of the Wild West, after the adventures of several generations of men in two world wars and Korea and Vietnam, after sixteen years of *Playboy* and American iconization of the gravity-defying breast and the sun-ripened buttock, after ten years of the greatest professional football, after a hundred years and more of a tradition that the frontier was open and would never close, and after twenty more perplexing technological years when prosperity came to nearly every White pocket, and technology put out its plastic, its superhighways, its supermarkets, its appliances, its suburbs, its smog, and its intimation that the frontier was damn shut, shut like a boulder on a rabbit burrow, America had erupted from this pressure between its love of adventure and its fear that adventure was not completely shut down; America had spewed out on the road. The country had become a nation of campers, of cars toting trailers, of cars pulling tent-trailers, of truck-campers, top-of-car tent packs, Volkswagen buses converted to ambulatory bedrooms, jeeps with Chic Sale houses built on the back, Land-Rovers with bunks, Broncos with more bunks—any way a man could get out of the house with his buddies or his family or his grandmother, and take to the road and find some ten-by-twenty feet of parking grass not posted, not tenanted, and not too muddy; he would camp. All over America in the summer the night fields were now filled with Americans sleeping on air mattresses that reposed on plastic cloth floors of plastic cloth tents—what a sweet smell of Corporate Chemical, what a vat and void to mix with all the balmy ferny chlorophylls and pollens of nature! America the Sanitary and America the Wild went out to sleep in the woods, Sanitary-Lobe and Wild-Lobe nesting together neatly, schizophrenic twins in the skull case of the good family American.

So they were out tonight, some portion of a million, all drawn on the lines of sight in Brevard County, and on every highway and causeway in the area the ground was covered with cars and campers, the shelter-roof extension of one family's tent near to topping the picnic blanket spread out behind the tailgate of the next station wagon, and the open trunk lid of a twelve- or fifteen-year-old Dodge convertible (rusty, top all rent, peeling friction tape and dirty white adhesive tape chasing a flap of a patch) stood next to both, part of the family sleeping in the trunk, the others with their good dirty feet out the windows. It was hardly just middle-class America here tonight, rather every echo of hard trade-union beer-binge paunch-gut-and-muscle, and lean whippy redneck honky-tonk clans out to bird-watch in the morning with redeye in the shot glass. There were tourists and not inelegant campers that spoke of peanut butter and jelly, watercress, and cucumber—suburban campers—but there was also the raw gasoline of expectation in the air, and families of poor Okies. One felt the whole South stirring on this night. Quiet pious Baptists, out somewhere on their porches (kin to some of the redneck and Okie—Okie for Okeechobee!—and working class here) seemed to be waiting over an arc of a thousand miles, certainly all the way from Cape Kennedy across Florida along the Gulf of Mexico to Houston and the Manned Spacecraft Center and back again, all across that belt of Fundamentalist piety, hot dry tempers burning like closed-up balefire against the humidity of the swamps, religion, and lust to work their combat in the tropical nights, yes all over the South they had to be praying, yes even more than everywhere for the safety of this shot, the astronauts part of that family of concern which White Southerners could share with each other out of the sweet deep wells of their Christian hearts, what was left of them. It was not hard to have a vision of mothers and grandmothers looking like spinsters, silver-rimmed glasses to shield your skin from their eyes of burning faith, predictable turkey wattles on the neck: They would be praying for America tonight—thoughts of America served to replace the tender sense of the Virgin in Protestant hearts. And out here on the campgrounds of Brevard County, out on all the scorched shoulders and oil-coated grass of the available highway, were men getting ready to drink with their wives, middle-aged, green-eyed Southern mill workers with sunburned freckled skin, reddish hair, hard mechanic's muscles in their forearms, wife a trinity of worrying mother, fattening slattern, and give-me-a-drink-and-I'll-holler-happy sort of bitch. Dutiful work, devotion to family and property, their sloven property! mingy propriety, real raucous bust-outs—that sort of South, married out of high school, oats half-sown like three-quarters of all America over thirty, and their boys on the hunt through the encampment looking for opposite numbers, other boys or—Gods of fornication with them!—girls without bank locks on their bloomers. You can expect nothing less on a night so filled with heat, human meat, bubbles of fear, prayer soft as love, and tropical sex in every sauce. And that mill worker with red hair and gray-green eyes, red sunburn, red peeling skin on his knotty forearms—he could be an astronaut in another life. He looks like an older version of Neil Armstrong, maybe, he looks like some of them, like Gordon Cooper for sure, or Deke Slayton, or Walt Cunningham of Apollo 7, yeah, the mill worker is tonight an American all drenched in pride and fear and sorrow—his wild rebel yell guaranteed to diminish each year, is riding the range with awe tonight. He has worked with machines all his life, he has tooled cars to the point where he has felt them respond to his care, he has known them and slept beside them as trustingly as if they were hunting dogs, he knows a thousand things about the collaboration between a man and a machine, and he knows what can go wrong. Machines—all the old machines he has known—are as unreasonable as people. And here, tomorrow, going up three men of whom he could have been one if he had a) not been a drunken fool half his life b) not married young c) had an education d) had twice as many guts and e) been full of real luck rather than cursed family luck, could have been going up with them in a machine with millions of parts, 80 percent electronics which he does not put his hand to, no grease, nut, wrench, and arm in electronics. Yes, could have been going up in a machine no man could ever sleep next to, or trust, not a machine with millions of parts, and ten million fingers worked on them—how much evil, error, and deception in millions of fingers?—he is thinking of his wife, why she alone when drunk and in full lunatic cohabitation with the all-out rays of the full moon was a hundred thousand fingers of evil herself! and his bowels come near to dropping out of him with awe at the daring of the act in the morning. He has spent his life with machines, they are all he has ever trusted with affectionate trust, for he has had a nose for their treacheries (more than he can say for women), and now, twelve hours from now, in the full light of nine-thirty in the morning, that Apollo-Saturn is going to go up. He will see a world begin where machines are king and he does not know whether to cry from pride or the all-out ache that he does not really comprehend the new machinery.

And the wife sipping the booze, hot and much too funky is her flesh on this hot night, listening to transistor radio Red has bought her, is moony and full of tears at the heroism of male craziness tomorrow. She wishes—floodgates of middle-age sorrow—some crack of that holy lightning in her womb: too late now! and trying to love up a warmth for Red, married all these nineteen years, she rears up on the very pinpoint of spite. She has powers, her family has powers, there's Indian blood in both her grandmas, and bruises, sorrows, slights, and nights of the loveliest now lost in the disappearing wahoo of studs she will never see again, our redneck Molly abloom in this encampment, she thinks on that pinpoint of spite of a curse she could put and will not on the launch tomorrow. For if Saturn were ever to burst and explode—she sees the flames across the sky: All witch and bitch on a holiday, such pictures encourage the lapping of gentle waters in her. Whereas putting wax on the tip of the needle, and capping the curse, leaves dull lead in her chest. Not to mention the future woman troubles of her gut. She stoppers the bottle and looks on a slant at Red—there'll be an angle soon by which to pick a fight.

And men and women, tired from work and travel, sat in their cars and sat outside their cars on aluminum pipe and plastic-webbing folding chairs, and fanned themselves, and looked across the miles at the shrine. Out a car window projected the sole of a dirty foot. The big toe pointed straight up to Heaven in parallel to Saturn V.

# Lift-off

*This is Apollo-Saturn Launch Control. We've passed the eleven-minute mark. Now T minus 10 minutes 54 seconds on our countdown for Apollo 11.*

Aquarius began to look for a place from which to watch. The grandstand had a roof that would obstruct the view once the rocket was high in the air. But standing on the field, he felt a hint too low. Finally he took up a careful position a few steps from the ground in a wing of additional bleachers. He was still not properly ready for the spectacle. Yes, the future spoke of a human species that would live on diets and occasional feasts, and would travel to spectacles to feel extraordinary sensations. They might even look at photographs of starving Black faces in order to generate some of their deepest thoughts.

But he knew now why he was so irritated with everything and why he could not feel a thing. It was simple masculine envy: He too wanted to go up in the bird.

*This is Apollo-Saturn Launch Control. Now 5 minutes 52 seconds and counting. Spacecraft Test Conductor Skip Chauvin now has completed the status check of his personnel in the control room. All report they are GO for the mission. Launch Operations Manager Paul Donnelly reports GO for launch. Launch Director Rocco Petrone gives a GO. We're 5 minutes 20 seconds and counting. The swing-arm now coming back to its fully retracted position as our countdown continues. T minus 4 minutes 50 seconds and counting.*

Nobody was talking a great deal. If something went wrong, they would all be implicated. Who would know which evil had entered the ripe oven of space technology? Aquarius took note of himself. Yes, his throat was dry.

*We're now passing the four-minute 30-second mark in the countdown— still GO at this time. Four minutes 15 seconds—the Test Supervisor now has informed Launch-Vehicle Test Conductor Norm Carlson you are GO for launch. We're now hitting the four-minute mark. Four minutes and counting. Launch Operations Manager Paul Donnelly wished the crew on behalf of the launch team "Good luck and Godspeed." Three minutes 25 seconds and counting. We're still GO at this time. All still GO at this time. Neil Armstrong reported back when he received the good wishes, "Thank you very much. We know it will be a good flight." Firing command coming in now. We are on the automatic sequence. We're approaching the three-minute mark in the count. T minus 3 minutes and counting. T minus 3—we are GO with all elements of the mission at this time.*

He had his binoculars to his eyes. A tiny part of him was like a penitent who had prayed in the wilderness for sixteen days and was now expecting a sign. Would the sign reveal much or little?

*. . . Just passed the two-minute mark in the countdown. T minus 1 minute 54 seconds and counting. Our status board indicates that the oxidizer tanks*

*in the second and third stages now have pressurized. T minus 1 minute 35 seconds on the Apollo mission, the flight that will land the first man on the moon. All indications coming in to the Control Center at this time indicate we are GO. One minute 25 seconds and counting. Eighty-second mark has now been passed. We'll go on full internal power at the fifty-second mark in the countdown. Fifty-five seconds and counting. Neil Armstrong just reported back, "It's been a real smooth countdown." We have passed the fifty-second mark. Forty seconds away from the Apollo 11 lift-off. All the second-stage tanks now pressurized. Thirty-five seconds and counting. We are still GO with Apollo 11. Thirty seconds and counting. Astronauts reported, "Feels good." T minus 25 seconds. Twenty seconds and counting. T minus 15 seconds, guidance is internal, 12, 11, 10, 9, ignition sequence start, 6, 5, 4, 3, 2, 1, zero, all engines running, LIFT-OFF. We have a lift-off, 32 minutes past the hour. Lift-off on Apollo 11.*

But nobody watching the launch from the Press Site ever listened to the last few words. For at 8.9 seconds before lift-off, the motors of Apollo-Saturn leaped into ignition, and two horns of orange fire burst like genies from the base of the rocket. Aquarius never had to worry again about whether the experience would be appropriate to his measure. Because of the distance, no one at the Press Site was to hear the sound of the motors until fifteen seconds after they had started. Although the rocket was restrained on its pad for nine seconds in order for the motors to multiply up to full thrust, still the rocket began to rise a full six seconds before its motors could be heard. Therefore the lift-off itself seemed to partake more of a miracle than a mechanical phenomenon, as if all of huge Saturn itself had begun silently to levitate, and was then pursued by flames.

No, it was more dramatic than that. For the flames were enormous. No one could be prepared for that. Flames flew in cataract against the cusp of the flame shield, and then sluiced along the paved ground down two opposite channels in the concrete, two underground rivers of flame which poured into the air on either side a hundred feet away, then flew a hundred feet further. Two mighty torches of flame like the wings of a yellow bird of fire flew over a field, covered a field with brilliant yellow bloomings of flame, and in the midst of it, white as a ghost, white as the white of Melville's Moby Dick, white as the shrine of the Madonna in half the churches of the world, this slim angelic mysterious ship of stages rose without sound out of its incarnation of flame and began to ascend slowly into the sky, slow as Melville's Leviathan might swim, slowly as we might swim upward in a dream looking for the air. And still no sound.

Then it came, like a crackling of wood twigs over the ridge, came with the sharp and furious bark of a million drops of oil crackling suddenly into combustion, a cacophony of barks louder and louder as Apollo-Saturn fifteen seconds ahead of its own sound cleared the lift tower to a cheer which could have been a cry of anguish from that near-audience watching; then came the earsplitting bark of a thousand machine guns firing at once, and Aquarius shook through his feet at the fury of this combat assault, and heard the thunderous murmur of Niagaras of flame roaring conceivably louder than the loudest thunders he had ever heard and the earth began to shake and would not stop, it quivered through his feet standing on the wood of the bleachers, an apocalyptic fury of sound equal to some conception of the sound of your death in the roar of a drowning hour, a nightmare of sound, and he heard himself saying, "Oh, my God! oh, my God! oh, my God! oh, my God! oh, my God! oh, my God!" and the sound of the rocket beat with the true blood of fear in his ears, hot in all the intimacy of a forming of heat, as if one's ear were in the cauldron of a vast burning of air, heavens of oxygen being born and consumed in this ascension of the rocket, and a poor moment of vertigo at the thought that man now had something with which to speak to God—the fire was white as a torch and long as the rocket itself, a tail of fire, a face, yes now the rocket looked like a thin and pointed witch's hat, and the flames from its base were the blazing eyes of the witch. Forked like saw teeth was the base of the flame which quivered through the lens of the binoculars. Upward. As the rocket keened over and went up and out to sea, one could no longer watch its stage, only the flame from its base. Now it seemed to rise like a ball of fire, like a new sun mounting the sky, a flame elevating itself.

Many thousands of feet up it went through haze and the fire feathered the haze in a long trailing caress, intimate as the wake which follows the path of a fingerling in inches of water. Trailings of cloud parted like lips. Then a heavier cloud was punched through with sudden cruelty. Then two long spumes of wake, like two large fish following our first fish—one's heart took little falls at the changes. "Ahhh," the crowd went, "Ahhh," as at the most beautiful of fireworks, for the sky was alive, one instant a pond and at the next a womb of new turns: "Ahhh," went the crowd, "Ahhh!"

Now, through the public address system, came the sound of Armstrong talking to Launch Control. He was quieter than anyone else. "Inboard cutoff," he said with calm in his voice.

Far in the distance, almost out of sight, like an all-but-transparent fish suddenly breaking into head and tail, the first stage at the rear of the rocket fell off from the rest, fell off and was now like a man, like a sky diver suddenly small. A new burst of motors started up, some far-off glimpse of newborn fires that looked pale as streams of water, pale were the flames in the far distance. Then the abandoned empty stage of the booster began to fall away, a relay runner, baton just passed, who slips back, slips back. Then it began to tumble, but with the slow tender dignity of a thin slice of soap slicing and wavering, dipping and gliding on its way to the floor of the tub. Then mighty Saturn of the first stage, empty, fuel-voided, burned out, gave a puff, a whiff and was lost to sight behind a cloud. And the rocket with Apollo 11 and the last two stages of Saturn V was finally out of sight and on its way to an orbit about the earth. Like the others he stayed and listened to the voices of the astronauts and the Capcom through the P.A. system.

PUBLIC AFFAIRS OFFICER: *At 3 minutes, downrange 70 miles, 43 miles high, velocity 9,300 feet per second.*
ARMSTRONG: *We've got skirts up.*
CAPSULE COMMUNICATOR: *Roger, we confirm. Skirts up.*
ARMSTRONG: *Tower is gone.*
CAPCOM: *Roger, tower.*
PAO: *Neil Armstrong confirming separation and the launch escape tower separation.*
ARMSTRONG: *Houston be advised the visual is GO today.*

On the way back to Cocoa Beach there was a monumental traffic jam, and Aquarius had time to look at objects by the road. There was a parked trailer with a twelve-foot inflated rubber rocket—it looked like a condom with a painted tip. Down its length ran a legend.

GOOD
LUCK
A
P
O
L
L
O
11
Montg.
Ala.

The radio was playing in the car. Fred Something-or-other from the Titusville Chamber of Commerce was talking fast. "And when the folks who were visiting this launch here go home, I want them to tell everybody how beautiful it was from Titusville."

"Folks," said an announcer, "get in on the Apollo 11 Blast-off Sale." The radio had lost no time.

America—his country. An empty country filled with wonders.

Aquarius did not know how he felt. He was happy all afternoon and went surfboarding for the first time, not even displeased that it was harder than he thought to stand up.

In the evening he left Cocoa Beach to fly back to Houston, where he would cover the trip to the moon and back. On the flight, everybody was drunk, and the hostesses were flip and hippy and could have been drinking themselves. The Southern businessmen were beaming.

In the late edition he brought with him, Aquarius read that the Reverend Abernathy together with a few poor families had watched the launching from the VIP area, after making a request of Dr. Thomas O. Paine, Administrator of NASA, for special badges. "If it were possible for us not to push the button tomorrow and solve the problems with which you are concerned, we would not push the button," Dr. Paine said.

Answered the Reverend Abernathy after the launch, "This is really holy ground. And it will be more holy once we feed the hungry, care for the sick, and provide for those who do not have houses."

Aquarius thought more than once of how powerful the vision of Apollo-Saturn must have been for the leader of the Poor People's Crusade. Doubtless he too had discovered that his feet were forced to shake. However, Aquarius was not yet ready to call this hallowed ground. For all he knew, Apollo-Saturn was still a child of the Devil. Yet if it was, then all philosophers flaming in orbit, the Devil was beautiful indeed. Or rather, was the Devil so beautiful because all of them, Johnsons, Goldwaters, Paines, Abernathys, press grubs, and grubby Aquarius, were nothing but devils themselves. For the notion that man voyaged out to fulfill the desire of God was either the heart of the vision or anathema to that true angel in Heaven they would violate by the fires of their ascent. A ship of flames was on its way to the moon.

# The Greatest Week

If lift-off had just provided him with sensations not unlike the very mania of apocalypse, the ensuing flat heat of Houston on his return, the oppression of Nassau Bay off NASA Highway 1, came into his lungs with the smell of a burnt-out tire. He plummeted into a profound depression. Everything was wrong. In the avalanche of reporters and corporation representatives who descended on the Texas plain near Manned Spacecraft Center to be near the collective brain that would pilot the flight, he, miserable sophisticate from the East, had somehow suffered a missed accommodation—as agreeable under the circumstances as a slipped disc—and was forced to camp out in the boondocks: in this case, a buried little basement apartment, one-room-with-kitchenette, furnished in convalescent spaced-out colors of dead gray, dull brown, dishwater white, and bargain-furniture green. Dingy Venetian blinds, plastic of course. Each time he tilted the slats to a new angle of admission of light, the blinds gave an *oooong* sound that went without pause into the Graves Registration Department of his depressed psyche. Still he kept working the slats. At least it gave him power over some dimension of his environment.

It was one thing to be without ego, quite another to indulge this new modesty in mean quarters. Like many men who had lived comfortably for years, he had always taken it for granted that he was superior to his surroundings and could dwell anywhere. Well, maybe one could still dwell anywhere with love, but loveless this week he was obliged to recognize that his basement apartment installed in an interlocking layout of ranch-style apartments, inner patios, and underground garages was no place for him to thrive. Not on this job. If he had become a little obsessed with the meanings of a trip to the moon—going on now full attraction into its first night and second day and second night while he languished in his dun coop—if he had come to recognize that the more one brooded on this trip, the more fantastic it became, there was still the thundering and most depressing fact that it was a cancer bud for a journalist to cover. There were assignments that could make a reporter happy—he sometimes thought it would be impossible for a good quick-working novelist to be unable to write a decent piece about a political convention or a well-organized anarchy of the modern young. Give Aquarius a great heavyweight championship fight, and he would give you a two-volume work. There was so much to say. One's senses threatened to sear one's brain with excess of perception. The people at the center of such events nourished you with the tragicomedy of the traps they entered and sometimes escaped. But in NASA-land, the only thing open was the technology—the participants were so overcome by the magnitude of their venture they seemed to consider personal motivation as somewhat obscene. He had never before encountered as many people whose modest purr of efficiency apparently derived from being cogs in a machine—was this the perspective of the century to come or was this the end of a long and insane road?

He did not know, and the fact that he did not know depressed him further. Usually when one did a journalistic piece, the events fit in advance into some part of one's picture of the world. Most interesting about such events was the way they obliged you to make modest or delightful adjustments in the picture. Or even grim adjustments. But you did not have to contemplate throwing the picture away. Aquarius, now plucked up from the circus bonanzas and flaming cathedrals of lift-off, was in Houston dropped smack into the fact that the best way to do the rest of this damnable story was probably to go home and cover the works by television. He simply did not feel himself coming closer in Houston to the value or horror of the oncoming achievement; he did not see that there was any way to come closer. Occasionally, which is to say five or six times a day, he would drive over to the Press Center at MSC on the other side of the highway, and skulk around the movie theater with the marcelled ceiling. When there was no press conference on—and usually there wasn't—he would look at a blank screen and listen to talk on the squawk box go back and forth between the Capcom and the spacecraft, the astronauts' voices wiped as clean of emotion as a corncob shucked of kernels. In the interim, distances increased. When he got back to Houston that first night, they were fourteen hours out, so their journey had already covered 66,000 nautical miles! All that while he had been surf-boarding, celebrating, and then flying back from Melbourne, Florida, to Intercontinental Airport at Houston. Indeed the astronauts even covered another 5,000 miles in the hour it took Aquarius to drive his rented car the fifty-odd miles from the airport through Houston, to Nassau Bay on the other side of town. Next afternoon, thirty hours into their flight, they were over 120,000 land miles out, and their speed had reduced to 3,500 miles an hour. Their voices were of course the same. It did not matter whether they spoke from 3,000 miles away or 133,000 miles away, the hard peasant facts upon which Aquarius' education had been built, the consciousness that numbers were real units, hard as hours of work and miles one walked, now had to be discarded into some waste-nexus of the mind, some stink of the unusable like the Jersey flats. The real fact was that distance was now an abstract concept; men performing brave and heroic acts were communing over radio whatever the distance. The absence of simple human witness was the fact, not the distance. Sitting in the movie theater, he realized he would find out nothing he desired to know. Yet back of the movie theater was the Newsroom, now jammed with men, rows of desks fifty feet long, hundreds of typewriters, hundreds of phones, hundreds of soft-links in shirt-sleeves transmitting the information that came in at one end of the communication belt from all the publicity pipes in NASA and would soon go out on the other end after all the news-transmitters (human) had retyped the words. Milling through this matrix were forty or fifty men with portable tape recorders and microphones with radio call letters which looked like branding irons. They were always shoving these branding irons in your face, Australian blokes, Swiss blokes, Italian jokers, Japanese gentlemen, Norwegian asthma sufferers, French dudes, Swedish students, even Texas local radio station apprentices. They wanted to interview Aquarius. Aquarius, three weeks habituated to his new uncomfortable racket! Aquarius, Doctor of Rocketry! He said no. He, who had once thought he had only to get on all the radio and television available and he would be able to change the world, now wished only to flee this room with its hundreds of journalists, some so bored and aimless they even wished to interview him, he who now had nothing to say. The latest in the quintessential ironies of his life is that he had become a celebrity at precisely the hour when he ceased to desire it. Oh, what a depression!

Events kept passing him by. In fact he could not forgive the astronauts their resolute avoidance of a heroic posture. It was somehow improper for a hero to be without flamboyance as if such modesty deprived his supporters of any large pleasure in his victories. What joy might be found in a world that could have no hope of a Hemingway? Or, nearest matters first, of a Joe Namath, or Cassius Clay, Jimmy Dean, Dominguin?—it was as if the astronauts were there to demonstrate that heroism's previous relation to romance had been highly improper—it was technology and the absence of emotion that were the only fit mates for the brave. Yesterday, or one of the days that had already become interleaved in the passage of time at Dun Cove, he had read a newspaper story where Armstrong's wife, Jan, had been quoted: "What we can't understand, we fear." Even the ladies of brave men spoke like corporation executives on this job. His heart went dull at the thought of the total take-over implicit in the remark, so neat, so ambitious, so world-vaulting in its assumption that sooner or later everything would be understood—"I paid a trip to death, and death is a pleasant place and ready for us to come in and renovate it." Abruptly Aquarius realized that for years he had thought of death as located in the milieu of the moon, as if our souls, those of us who died with one, might lift and rise, be free of the law of gravity and on trajectory to the satellite of the craters. Yes, wouldn't it be in the purview of the Wasp, damn corporate Wasp, to disturb the purlieus of the dead? He did not know. His thoughts were always furthest out when he was most depressed, as though like a bird half drowned, the only way to lift was by the wildest beating of wings.

The real heroism, he thought, was to understand, and, because one understood, be even more full of fear at the enormity of what one understood, yet at that moment continue to be ready for the feat one had decided it was essential to perform. So Julien Sorel had been brave when he kissed Madame de Rênal, and Jimmy Dean been brave in *Rebel Without a Cause,* and Namath when he mocked the Baltimore Colts knowing the only visions he would arouse in his enemy were visions of murder. So had Cassius Clay been brave—to dare to be rude to Liston—and Floyd Patterson brave to come back to boxing after terrible humiliation, and Hemingway conceivably brave to continue to write in short sentences after being exposed to the lividities of the literary world.

But the astronauts, brave men, proceeded on the paradoxical principle that fear once deposed by knowledge would make bravery redundant. It was in the complacent assumption that the universe was no majestic mansion of architectonics out there between evil and nobility, or strife on a darkling plain, but rather an ultimately benign field of investigation that left Aquarius in the worst of his temper.

Next morning came the news of Teddy Kennedy's accident at Chappaquiddick. Dead was the young lady who had been driving with him. How subtle was the voice of the moon. Aquarius remembered a speech Kennedy had given two months earlier at Clark University in Worcester. Mrs. Robert H. Goddard, widow of the father of American rocketry, had been there, and Buzz Aldrin as well. Kennedy had urged that future space funds be moved over to such problems as poverty, hunger, pollution, and housing. The chill that came back from NASA was as cold as the architecture at the Manned Spacecraft Center. "We won't be including this item in the daily news reports we send up to the Apollo 10 astronauts on their voyage to the moon," Thomas O. Paine, administrator of NASA had said. Now the reverberations of this accident at Chappaquiddick went off in Aquarius' brain. As happens so often when a motive is buried, Aquarius felt excitement around the hollows of his depression. For if the blow to the fortunes of the Kennedys was also a blow to one hundred interesting possibilities in American life, if the accident was of such benefit to Richard Nixon that the Devil himself if he had designed the mishap (which is what every liberal Democrat must secretly believe) could have awarded himself a medal for the artistry, yet there was at least a suggestion that the moon had thought to speak. Perhaps that was why there was still a trace of stimulation in the gloom—magic might not be altogether dead.

The day went by, a cloudy day in southeastern Texas. From time to time, Aquarius checked in at the Press Center. Excitement was now divided between Kennedy and the moon. Or was Kennedy even more interesting? The separate phases of the preparation for landing were certainly without high tension. Indeed the Lem even undocked from the Command Module while both were behind the moon. When they came around and signal was picked up again, the voice of Armstrong came over the squawk box. "The Eagle has wings," he said, or was it Aldrin who said it?—there was discussion on this for the remark was universally quotable. Yet the happy buzz of conversation among the reporters at the thought of an oncoming climax was dampened considerably by the dialogue that followed:

CAPCOM: . . . *Coming at you with a DOI pad. 101361-407981 minus 00758 plus all balls plus 00098 plus corrections 00572 perigee plus 00085 00764 030000293 986 minus 00759 plus all balls plus 00090 rest of the pad is NA. Stand by on your read-back. If you are ready to copy the PDI data, I have it for you. Over.*

ALDRIN: . . . *Go ahead with the PDI.*

CAPCOM: *Roger. PDI pad, PIG 102330436 0950 minus 00021 182287000 plus 56919—*

So one got ready for the climax of "the greatest week since Christ was born." An hour and twenty minutes later, the Lem having flown around the moon and gone behind it again, the braking burn for the

Descent Orbit Initiation would be begun in radio silence. An hour later the final ignition for the final descent would commence. Aquarius, bereft of personal radar or gyroscope, bereft even of the sniff-sensors of his poor journalistic nose, wandered from point to point in the Press Center, rushed back to Dun Cove to look at color television—there were no color sets in the Press Room—then, bored with listening to commentators, and finally incapable of witnessing the event alone, went back to the movie theater and settled in with about a hundred other reporters for the last half hour.

Phrases came through the general static of the public address system. "Eagle looking great. You're go," came through, and statements of altitude. "You're go for landing, over!" "Roger, understand. Go for landing. 3,000 feet." "We're go, hang tight, we're go. 2,000 feet." So the voices came out of the box. Somewhere a quarter of a million miles away, ten years of engineering and training, a thousand processes and a million parts, a huge swatch out of twenty-five billion dollars and a hovering of machinery were preparing to go through the funnel of a historical event whose significance might yet be next to death itself, and the reporters who would interpret this information for the newsprint readers of the world were now stirring in polite if mounting absorption with the calm cryptic technological voices that came droning out of the box. Was it like this as one was waiting to be born? Did one wait in a modern room with strangers while numbers were announced—"Soul 77-48-16—you are on call. Proceed to Staging Area CX—at 16:04 you will be conceived."

So the words came. And the moon came nearer. "3½ down, 220 feet, 13 forward, 11 forward, coming down nicely. 200 feet, 4½ down. 5½ down. 160, 6½ down. 5½ down. 9 forward. 5 percent. Quantity light. 75 feet. Things looking good. Down a half. 6 forward."

"Sixty seconds," said another voice.

Was that a reference to fuel? Had that been the Capcom? Or was it Aldrin or Armstrong? Who was speaking now? The static was a presence. The voice was almost dreamy. Only the thinnest reed of excitement quivered in the voice.

"Lights on. Down 2½. Forward. Forward. Good. 40 feet. Down 2½. Picking up some dust. 30 feet, 2½ down. Faint shadow. 4 forward. 4 forward. Drifting to the right a little. 6 . . . down a half."

Another voice said, "Thirty seconds." Was that thirty seconds of fuel? A modest stirring of anticipation came up from the audience.

"Drifting right. Contact light. Okay," said the voice as even as before, "engine stop. ACA out of detente. Modes control both auto, descent engine command override, off. Engine arm, off. 413 is in."

A cry went up, half jubilant, half confused. Had they actually landed?

The Capcom spoke: "We copy you down, Eagle." But it was a question.

"Houston, Tranquility Base here. The Eagle has landed." It was Armstrong's voice, the quiet voice of the best boy in town, the one who pulls you drowning from the sea and walks off before you can offer a reward. The Eagle has landed—it reached the Press. They burst into applause. It was the kind of applause you used to hear in the packed film houses of the Thirties when the movie came over the hill of the last reel and you heard the doctor say the star would live after the operation. Now, a small bedlam of actions began, some of the Press sprinting from the room—could they pretend it was necessary to phone the City Desk?—others talking to each other in babble, others still listening to the squawk box as technology took up again. A few minutes later: "Eagle. Houston. You loaded R2 wrong. We want 10254."

"Roger—that is V horizontal 5515.2."

"That's affirmative."

Aquarius discovered he was happy. There was a man on the moon. There were two men on the moon. It was a new feeling, absolutely without focus for him. If he felt a faint graveling on the surface of this sentiment, a curdle of emotional skin which formed from his effort to advance heroes he could not find altogether admirable, still he knew he had been dislocated as profoundly by the experience as the moment he learned in the fathers' waiting room at the hospital that his first child had indeed and actually just been born. "Well, think of that," he had said. What a new fact! Real as the presence of immanence and yet not located at all, not yet, not in the comfortable quarters one afforded for the true and real facts of life.

"Let's go interview the wives," someone suggested. And Aquarius, grateful for an opportunity to try a few journalistic tools, was happily off and away from the reign of the Capcom, the squawk box, and the abstract incubated existence of brand-new Tranquility Base.


The Armstrong house was modest, with a high-pitched roof of brown shingles. It was like half a million other houses in suburbs combining modern and brand-new traditional style. It had hints of an English country inn, for it was a dark-colored warren with small windows and long eaves. Yet the house was situated on a street whose curve had come from no meandering cow but from favorable indices on graphs that showed the relation of income to cost for planned curved-development streets as opposed to planned straight-development streets. El Lago—the name of this suburb—like those others named Kingston and Timber Cove and Nassau Bay—was a soft checkerboard of carefully bent little avenues that ran at reasonable approximations of right angles into other paved prospects, a street occasionally dead-ending, a street just as occasionally completing a full circle. The realty layout-computer in its wisdom for random play in home-road curvature had designed the layout logic so comprehensively, so ready to take into account the variety of desire-factors expressed by consumer dweller-groups oriented in at these precise income-purchase levels, that the effect—what a blow to the goodwill of the progressive designer who had doubtless opted for just once let's have something better!—was as agreeable and sterile to the eye as a model department store living room for brides on a medium-high budget layaway.

What a curious scene then! This moderately undulated street of angled plots and recently constructed private homes, this curved asphalt bordered by trees of the same year of growth, with vista of cars parked in garages, air conditioners, lawn mowers, sprinklers, and bicycles, a street in which five children and two adults on foot might be seen on any average hour of the day, what a shock down the block to the habituated eye to see that gaggle of Press all straining at a rope, TV men and still photographers in their customary war for position with word-men—the crush now fortified by the more curious neighbors, Texas grandmothers in the main with gray-greenish eyes, tight not unintelligent mouths, small-town grits in the anticipation, and a real Texas bone-and-leather use of elbows to fight their leading toe in for position against this invasion of hippie journalist gogglers and foreigners with cameras, beards, sideburns, Nehru jackets, turtlenecks, love beads, medallions, shades, tape recorders, and foreign tongues, Japs talking to Japs, Germans to Germans, an Italian to other Italians and all the Scandinavians come to NASA-land in El Lago. "I'm an American!" cried out one full vigor of a gray-haired Texas female being pushed off the frontier by one ham-hock and handlebar of an English ruddy.

There would have been small mayhem, but Jan Armstrong came out then, escorted by an official who treated her with the kind of gravity reserved for the Pope's sister. She was laughing and smiling, she was obviously very happy as she stepped on a raised platform behind the rope. The platform was about a yard square and a foot high, set out for her probably by the television men, and it may have been the color of its candy-pink carpet reflecting pink and violet and delicate rose hues to her healthy skin, but she was an attractive sight on this overcast Sunday afternoon. She was a woman one would not normally have thought of as beautiful, her hair was almost gray and close-cropped, her mouth while full and strong was without coquetry or that hint of duplicity so attractive in a woman for the implicit sugges-tion that only a real man could ever set her straight. No, her mouth spoke of the stubborn and the steadfast, and she was dressed in no re-markable fashion, she had on a white blouse buttoned at the neck and an orange-red skirt. She had a Scotch nose, strong, not small, not del-icate in nostril, the wings cut with determination, the tip showing a hint of two lobes, she had in all the sort of face one sees in the best of small-town schoolteachers or librarians, that complete statement in the features of deep and dedicated strength. So she possessed in this hour a beautiful face, it was radiant—the word could finally be em-ployed—the face was utterly separated from the planned street and the media men surrounding her with their microphones, the face lifted up to that moment in the past when she had directed her strength and her will to one goal, and the goal was now fulfilled—few faces are more beautiful than the dedicated when their deepest hour is in, when the plan utters its first word aloud, and the word is "yes." So no question could bother her at this instant. If she had a reputation for being shy, grim, a swimming instructor, a phys ed teacher, a churchgoer, a conformist, a humorless embodiment of the space fron-tier in female form, she was now on top of it all, she was in rollicking good humor from the release of that safe landing.

"Will you let the children stay up and watch the moon walk tonight?" asked a journalist.

A devil came into her eye. "I don't care for what they do," she said with happy idiom, a grammar from the universal interior of the na-tion, not Midwestern, not Texan, by now from anywhere in there.

The questions went on. She laughed happily at their absurdity. She could not make a mistake. "Is this the greatest moment of your life?" asked one of the voices.

"No, sir," said her shining face, "when I was married, it was the greatest moment of my life."

They had known each other for three years before they had their first date, they had lived soon after their marriage in a cabin in the mountains with no plumbing, he would wave the wings of the test planes he flew as he burned through the sky over their house. It was a marriage of piano duets and long solo flights in gliders; the death of their only daughter, age three, came from a tumor of the brain. Aquarius hated to comprehend marriages by such contradictory details picked up on the fly, but these details promised to fit, they spoke of the serious physician's daughter from Illinois and the dream-absorbed boy with the lonely face of early photographs, the boy whose family moved a dozen times when he was young in Ohio. He had worked for a pharmacy at forty cents an hour to earn the nine dollars an hour for flying lessons. Would the relation of husband and wife to each other be so very different from Armstrong's relation to the sky? Everything about Armstrong suggested that he would be happiest in the sky, that surf of space where intimations of a language few could speak might hover on the changing of a cloud.

"Are you pleased with the Sea of Tranquility as a place to land?" asked a questioner.

She liked Tranquility Base. It was obvious the word was agreeable. For those who have been living in dread, tranquility is grace, the very decency of ecstasy.

"What are you having for dinner tonight? Space food?"

She threw back her head like a mare so happy with the day she can support any rider. "No, sir," she said and left it there, proper for NASA and the team, but the glint in her eye had its own look. "We ain't quite so square as you think us, Mister Reporter," said the unvoiced look.

Another few questions and the NASA representative at her elbow returned her to the house. The Press was off to cars and TV vans, the ride was on to find the Collins home and the Aldrin house, each a block from the other, but back in Nassau Bay itself, back in another soft checkerboard of curves at right angles to the interesection of other curves, a suburb built even closer to men's occupations in buildings with windowless walls.

Pat Collins was another woman in another state. She was conventionally good-looking, with the sort of attractive and competent features one finds in secretaries to important executives or in the woman who is supervisor of hostesses for an airline. She had black hair pinned up high and green-blue eyes bright as the lights in a valuable stone. Her arms and legs were very slim, and she smiled a lot as she talked to the Press. She seemed flustered, and not unravaged by the tension of the last few days. Her remarks were polite, enthusiastic, hardworking. She said that by the time they touched down on the moon, she was cheering, but in fact she had the glitter of an actress who is loyal to the company and loyal to the production, and so will mouth the lines clearly even if the theater is half-empty, the play is falling apart, and the cast will be given their notice in another night. She was loyal to what was demanded of her, but the strain was show-ing—of the three wives, she had had the most difficult relation to the event. She was obliged to suffer with the other wives as an equal among equals, share the agonies and the jubilation of the landing with them, yet in fact her husband was not landing, he was up in the air all alone, he would be alone for another day or more, sometimes alone on the back side of the moon while the others explored ground no liv-ing man had stepped upon. She had a face that was obviously not without ambition, one of those faces that exhibit no outrageous vice but nonetheless want the best for themselves, not ruthless so much as ready to commit oneself to the partner and work all the way to go all the way. Now her husband had gone 99.9 percent of the way. If it was secretly hard on him, it would have to be twice as hard on her. What a role to play! The interviewers asked her again and again, "Do you mind that your husband is not landing with the others?" And again and again in a voice which was using the reserves of her good looks she kept replying in a tone determinedly bright (and so bumped over to the edge of the haggard) that she didn't mind a bit and knew Mike didn't either. The laws of propriety at NASA went as deep as the reg-ulations at a hospital—woe to any astronaut or wife who uttered in public any sentiment that would fail to bore the expectations of fifty million viewers. There was a true and proper standard of behavior for every public situation in which they might find themselves. A clear rule of measure: Do not under any circumstance say anything more interesting than Richard Nixon would say in the same situation. That was the clubhouse rule; Pat Collins was obeying it. Since she also had the look of a woman who must have real flashes of Irish beauty when relaxed, the expostulations of complete happiness made her remarks so ordinary that Aquarius discovered afterward he had not worked to take a note.

Down the block was the Aldrin house, a structure of pale orange brick with another steep roof. There was a wait for Mrs. Aldrin. It had begun to rain out of an uneven lead-colored hesitant sky—a few drops would tattoo the big Texas leaves of the modest suburban trees and then halt, then rain a little harder, stop again. It was thought at first that the delay was due to uncertainty whether to begin the interview under such conditions—after a while a rumor circulated that Mrs.

Aldrin was primping for the Press. It made sense to Aquarius. She had wanted to be an actress—she had worked at having a career for a period, had made the rounds against the objections of her father. Having been married to three women who were actresses at one time or another, one of them even a modest movie star who had her career much interrupted for such marrying, Aquarius was able to make broken-hearted jokes about the woes of any man so foolish as to smash into the devotions of an acting career by an act of marriage. As a consequence he was naturally interested in Mrs. Aldrin. She, like Jan Armstrong, had had a long courtship. He was obliged to recognize on looking at a newspaper photo that she looked much like her husband, as indeed Jan Armstrong looked like her mate, and Pat Collins like Mike Collins. He did not understand these marriages of people who looked alike and courted each other for years—he did not know if the delay of proper people who looked alike came from deep respect for marriage or was rather excessive caution to make certain one's narcissism would find the cleanest mirror. He did not know. It seemed to him he had always gotten married in a hurry to women who were remarkably different, except for his final inability to get along with them. Gloomy as the weather was Aquarius. From time to time, like the memory of a telegram whose news was so awful one kept circling the fact of it, came back the simple unalterable fact that Teddy Kennedy had been in a bad accident and a girl had drowned and the senator had not reported it until morning.

Joan Aldrin had blond hair, she was a big woman with generous features, nose, teeth, mouth, there, all there, but finally she was all eyes. They were the large expressive soulful instruments of a woman who had a real and intense awareness of her stage, which is to say a sense of the air she offered, the way it was received, the space between. She made a good entrance beneath an umbrella thoughtfully held over her by the man who served as guide from the house to a roped-off space between the trees; she was a lady who transmitted palpable gratitudes for courtesies rendered, she had the ability to exercise the air, but not as a flirt or a sexual provocation, rather as a tragedienne one instant, a comedienne the next, she had the quick-changing vital bounce of a woman who might have made a reasonable career in musical comedy—she had as she spoke the slightly slow withheld timing, the meaningless but tasty syncopation that women who belt out a song give to a dull line. So, as she spoke, it was fun to listen.

"What were you doing when they landed?"

"Well, I was holding on to the wall. I was praying," she said in a loud and syncopated whisper.

She was at once utterly serious, and camping it up. A part of her had been in agonies of suspense that went right into the agonies and deepest attachments of her marriage—another part of her, droll as the humor of her full nose, had been obliged to see herself—"Here you are, big girl, holding on to the wall at a time like this!"

The interview went on. Aquarius monitored it with a mild part of his brain. There was talk about one activity, then another—what the plans were for watching the moon walk—would the children stay up, so forth. The mood was sluggish. The Press had interviewed two wives already.

She was too much of a performer to come in third in a three-horse race. "Listen," she cried out suddenly in a big voice, waking up the Press. "Aren't you all excited?" She looked around coquettishly, carefully, as if to measure what employment could be made of an audience as super-sophisticated and sodden as this. Then it came over her, as it had come over everyone else from time to time. There were men on the moon.

"They did it!" she shrieked happily. "They did it!"

After she had gone back inside, there was a vacuum. Her vitality was gone. One wouldn't have minded more of her.

Aquarius was left with his gloom. It was finally a dubious male occupation to interview the wives of men who were heroes for the day. He was depressed as he walked away thinking of his own wife, and his own marriage, now deteriorating—what work to be obliged to look in on other marriages in their hour of triumph!

That night, the walk on the moon had been scheduled to begin long after midnight, so plans had been laid for late moon-watching parties. But the astronauts, to no one's surprise, were in no mood to sleep, and the moon walk was rescheduled for eight in the evening. Yet, this once, the astronauts were not on time.

Waiting in the movie theater, the Press was in a curious state of mingled celebration and irritation. It was hard not to feel like a fool. They were journalists, not movie critics, and tonight they would be taking notes on events that transpired upon a video screen. Of course, the climax of days of the most difficult kind of reporting was finally at hand, but it was a little as if one's nervous system had been appropriated and the final shake would take place in somebody else's room.

The psychology of journalists is not easy to comprehend—they scurry around like peons, they have the confidence of God. Over the years they develop an extraordinary sense of where the next victory is located. If a man gives a press conference and is not surrounded by reporters when it is over, he need not wonder how his fortunes are moving—the reporters have already told him. It is for this reason journalists pick up the confidence that they shape events—in fact they are only sensors in the currents of the churn, Venturi tubes to give you the speed of the history that passes. Nonetheless, there is no psychological reality like a man's idea of himself. Even if a writer has lost the best reaches of his talent by putting out facts for years which have been stripped of their nuance—writing newspaper stories, in short— still he retains an idea of himself: it is that his eye on an event may be critical to correct reportage of it. Now put five hundred reporters in a room to report on the climax of an event "equal in importance to that moment in evolution when aquatic life came crawling up on the land," and put a movie screen in front of them, and a television transmission on that screen which is not only a pioneer effort in communication from a satellite one good quarter of a million miles away, but is also, you may be sure, wildly out of focus. Reporters wear eyeglasses in order not to miss the small print—bad focus on the screen puts a new injury right inside the wound of the previous injury. Something in them reverted. Watching the mooncast, they were like college kids on Friday night in the town movie house—one never knew what would make their laughter stir next, but their sense of the absurd was quick and furious. Like college students who roar with disgust because by God they were being trained to run a supposedly reasonable world with highly reasonable skills, and yet the fools who made this movie had the real power, so the Press took the mooncast on its own literal terms of spectacle—where it was good as spectacle they loved it, where it was poor they mocked.

But let us take it from the start. The screen was dark when the voices began, and since it stayed without image for many minutes while one heard the voices of the astronauts working to get ready, a strain developed in the audience. Would the picture ever come on tonight, or had something gone wrong?

Then one learned from the Public Affairs Officer that the Portable Life Support Systems were working—the astronauts were now connected by umbilical tubes to the big white box on their back, that box which could cool them, clear the fog from their helmets, give them oxygen to breathe, and absorb the wastes of their exhalation. But the minutes went by. There was no image on the screen. Oxygen was being used. They had only a few hours of Life Support in the system—would they be obliged to use it overcoming the difficulties of opening the hatch? Hoots and a hum of restlessness worked through the theater. The journalists were nervous. That rare hysteria which is generated by an inability to distinguish between the apocalyptic and the absurd was generating. What if—assuming they could actually see something—what if Armstrong were to take a step on the moon and simply disappear? Whatever would one do in this theater? The event would be a horror to watch if tragedy occurred; yet it would be a humiliation if it all went on schedule.

A cheer not unmixed with mockery came at the announcement at 9:40 in the evening that the hatch was open. Still no image on the screen. Now followed long incomprehensible instructions back and forth, talk of window clanks and water valves, high-gain antenna and glycol pumps. Out of all this, quiet exhortations from Aldrin to Armstrong. Through the words emerged the realization that Armstrong, made twice bulky by his space suit and the Portable Life Support System on his back, was trying to push through the open hatch of the Lem out onto the small metal porch that led to the ladder which in turn he could descend to the moon ground. It was obviously a very tight fit to get through the hatch. As Aldrin gave instructions there was an inevitable suggestion of the kind of dialogue one hears between an obstetrician and a patient in the last minutes before birth.

ALDRIN: *Your back is up against the (garbled.) All right, now it's on top of the DSKY. Forward and up, now you've got them, over toward me, straight down, relax a little bit.*

ARMSTRONG: *(Garbled)*

ALDRIN: *Neil, you're lined up nicely. Toward me a little bit, okay down, okay, made it clear.*

ARMSTRONG: *To what edge?*

ALDRIN: *Move. Here roll to the left. Okay, now you're clear. You're lined up on the platform. Put your left foot to the right a little bit. Okay that's good. Roll left.*

The Press was giggling. Sanctimony at NASA was a tight seal. A new church, it had been born as a high church. No one took liberties.

Now, two of the heroes of NASA were engaged in an inevitably comic dialogue—one big man giving minute adjustments of position to another. The Press giggled.

Armstrong spoke out suddenly. "Okay, Houston, I'm on the porch."

The audience broke into applause. There was mockery, as if the cavalry had just come galloping down the ridge.

A few minutes went by. Impatience hung in the air. Then a loud bright cheer as a picture came on the screen. It was a picture upside-down, blinding in contrast, and incomprehensible, perhaps just such a kaleidoscope of shadow and light as a baby might see in the first instants before silver nitrate blinds its eyes. Then, twists and turns of image followed, a huge black cloud resolved itself into the bulk of Armstrong descending the ladder, a view of confusions of objects, some rough-hewn vision of a troglodyte with a huge hump on his back and voices—Armstrong, Aldrin, and Capcom—details were being offered of the descent down the ladder. Armstrong stepped off the pad. No one quite heard him say, "That's one small step for a man, one giant leap for mankind," nor did anyone quite see him take the step—the TV image on the movie screen was beautiful, but still as marvelously abstract as the branches of a tree, or a painting by Franz Kline of black beams on a white background. Nonetheless, a cheer went up, and a ripple of extraordinary awareness. It was as if the audience felt an unexpected empathy with the sepulchral, as if a man were descending step by step, heartbeat by diminishing heartbeat into the reign of the kingdom of death itself and he was reporting, inch by inch, what his senses disclosed. Everybody listened in profound silence. Irritation was now gone as Armstrong described the fine and powdery substance of the surface: "I can see the footprints of my boots and the treads in the fine sandy particles." Every disclosure for these first few minutes would be a wonder. If it would have been more extraordinary to hear that the moon had taken no imprint in soft powder, or the powder was phosphorescent, still it was also a wonder that the powder of the moon reacted like powder on earth. A question was at least being answered. If the answer was ordinary, still there was one less question in the lonely spaces of the human mind. Aquarius had an instant when he glimpsed space expanding like the widening pool of an unanswered question. Was that the power behind the force which made technology triumphant in this century?—that technology was at least a force which attempted to bring back answers from questions that had been considered to be without answers?

The image was becoming more decipherable. As Armstrong moved away from the ladder in a hesitant loping gait, not unlike the first staggering steps of a just-born calf, he called back to Mission Control, "No trouble to walk around," but as if that were too great a liberty to take with the feelings of the moon, he came loping back to the ladder.

Activities went on. There were photographs to take, descriptions of the appearance of the rocks, of the character of the sun glare. One of Armstrong's first jobs was to pick up a sample of rock and put it in his pocket. Thus if something unforeseen were to occur, if the unmentionable yak or the Abominable Snowman were to emerge from a crater, if the ground began to rumble, if for any reason they had to reenter the Lem and take off abruptly, they would then have the chance to return to earth with at least one rock. This first scoop of moon stone and moon dust was called the contingency sample, and it was one of Armstrong's first tasks, but he seemed to have forgotten it. The Capcom reminded him subtly, so did Aldrin. The Capcom came back again: "Neil, this is Houston. Did you copy about the contingency sample? Over?"

"Rog," said Armstrong, "I'm going to get to that just as soon as I finish this picture series."

Aldrin had probably not heard. "Okay," he asked, "going to get the contingency sample now, Neil?"

"Right!" Armstrong snapped. The irritability was so evident that the audience roared with laughter—don't we laugh when we glimpse a fine truth and immediately conceal it? What a truth! Nagging was nagging, even on the moon.

The television image was improving. It was never clear, never did it look any better in quality than a print of the earliest silent movies, but it was eloquent. Ghosts beckoned to ghosts, and the surface of the moon looked like a ski slope at night. Fields of a dazzling pale ran into caverns of black, and through this field moved the ghost of Armstrong. There were moments when one had the impression it was possible to see through him. His image was transparent.

Aldrin descended the ladder, then jumped back on the lowest rung to test his ability to return to the Lem. The abruptness of the action broke the audience into guffaws again, the superior guffaw a sophisticate gives to a chair creaking too crudely in a horror movie. Now two ghosts paraded about, jogging forward and back, exchanging happy comments on the new nature of hopping and walking, moving faster than a walk but like much-padded toddlers, or over-swathed beginners on skis. Sometimes they looked like heavy elderly gentlemen dancing with verve, sometimes the sight of their boots or their gloves, the bend of their backs setting up equipment or reaching for more rocks gave them the look of beasts on hindquarters learning to think, sometimes the image went over into negative so that they looked black in their suits on a black moon with white hollows, sometimes the image was solarized and became positive and negative at once, images yawing in and out of focus, so the figures seemed to squirt about like one-celled animals beneath a slide—all the while, images of the Lem would appear in the background, an odd battered object like some Tartar cooking pot left on a trivet in a Siberian field. It all had the look of the oldest photographs of expeditions to the North Pole—there was something bizarre, touching, splendid, and ridiculous all at once, for the feat was immense, but the astronauts looked silly, and their functional conversations seemed farcical in the circumstances.

"What did you say, Buzz?"

"I say the rocks are rather slippery."

Huge guffaws from the audience. When the flag was set up on the moon, the Press applauded. The applause continued, grew larger— soon they would be giving the image of the flag a standing ovation. It was perhaps a way of apologizing for the laughter before, and the laughter they knew would come again, but the experience was still out of register. A reductive society was witnessing the irreducible. But the irreducible was being presented with faulty technique. At that they could laugh. And did again and again. There were moments when Armstrong and Aldrin might just as well have been Laurel and Hardy in space suits.

The voice of Collins came into the public address system. He had been out of radio contact for almost an hour during his trip around the back of the moon, so he did not know how the Extra Vehicular Activity was proceeding. He had left communication before Armstrong had reached the lunar surface. Now he asked, "How's it going?"

CAPCOM: *Roger. The EVA is progressing beautifully. I believe they are setting up the flag now.*

COLLINS: *Great.*

The audience laughed at this hard pea of envy beneath twenty mattresses of NASA manners.

CAPCOM: *I guess you're about the only person around that doesn't have TV coverage of the scene.*
COLLINS: *That's right. That's all right. I don't mind a bit.*

Now, the Press roared.

COLLINS: *How is the quality of the TV?*
CAPCOM: *Oh, it's beautiful, Mike. Really is.*
COLLINS: *Oh, gee, that's great.*

The video continued, the astronauts worked on styles of gait, ordinary walking, half-run, kangaroo hops. There was a sense of the astronauts' happiness as they loped about, and now a delicate envy, almost tender in its sensibility, went to them from the crowd. There was finally something marvelous. This old-fashioned indistinct movie of comedians in old-fashioned suits was in fact but a cover upon the curious happiness everyone was feeling. It was the happiness that comes from a wound. For with the pain, and there was pain in the thought of the moon—so private a body to the poet buried in every head—the moon being now invaded, there was also the happiness that accompanies the pain, for the landing was a straight-out wound to every stable disposition of the mind. So the world was watching the loping bumbling skittering low-gravity movements of these men with the kind of concentration we offer to the study of our own wound. Something in the firmament was being operated upon.

Well, the flag was up. The Capcom spoke. He asked the astronauts to stand in view of the camera, then announced that the President of the United States wanted to say a few words.

ARMSTRONG: *That would be an honor.*
CAPCOM: *Go ahead, Mr. President, this is Houston. Out.*

It had been announced in advance that the President would speak to the astronauts, but the liberal portion of the Press groaned, to be answered by a pattering of stiff hands from the patriots in the room.

PRESIDENT NIXON: *Neil and Buzz, I am talking to you by telephone from the Oval Room at the White House. And this certainly has to be the most historic telephone call ever made.*

Large jeers from the audience. The most expensive telephone call ever made! Stentorian hand clapping in counter-response.

PRESIDENT NIXON: *I just can't tell you how proud we all are of you. For every American this has to be the proudest day of our lives. And for people all over the world, I am sure they too join with Americans in recognizing what a feat this is. Because of what you have done, the heavens have become a part of man's world. And as you talk to us from the Sea of Tranquility, it inspires us to double our efforts to bring peace and tranquility to earth. For one priceless moment in the whole history of man, all the people on this earth are truly one. One in their pride in what you have done. And one in our prayers that you will return safely to earth.*

Every word had its function. It could be said that the psychology of machines begins where humans are more machinelike in their actions than the machines they employ.

"Thank you, Mr. President," answered Armstrong in a voice not altogether in control. What a moment for Richard Nixon if the first tears shed on the moon flowed on the consequence of his words! "It's a great honor and a privilege," Armstrong went on, "to be representing not only the United States but men of peace of all nations." When he finished, he saluted.

Some of the crowd jeered again. The image of Nixon faded on home TV screens, his voice was gone from the theater. The moon walk continued. In fact, it was not half done, but the early excitement had ebbed in this last play of rhetoric—the minds of the Press had gone on to the question of whether Nixon was considering it politically advantageous to support a future program of space. As the astronauts continued to walk, to hop, to flit, and to skip from one vale of moon ground to another, as the experiments were set out and the rocks picked up, so the temper of the audience shifted. It was a Twentieth Century audience when all was said. By an hour and a half of the moon walk they were bored—some were actually slipping out. All over the room was felt the ubiquitous desire of journalists for the rescue of a drink. Boredom deepened. Now the mood was equal to the fourth quarter of a much anticipated football game whose result had proved lopsided. Now it looked as if rookies were out on the chill field running fumbles back and forth. More and more reporters departed. Even Aquarius left before the end.

—

It was the event of his lifetime, and yet it had been a dull event. The language that would now sing of this extraordinary vault promised to be as flat as an unstrung harp. The century had unstrung any melody of words. Besides—the event was obdurate on the surface and a mystery beneath. It was not at all easy to comprehend. Like an adolescent married before he could vote, the congratulation "You're a married man" had no reality to the brand-new groom. So America and the world would be in a round of congratulations—we had landed a man on the moon. The event was so removed, however, so unreal, that no objective correlative existed to prove it had not conceivably been an event staged in a television studio—the greatest con of the century— and indeed a good mind, product of the iniquities, treacheries, gold, passion, invention, deception, and rich worldly stink of the Renaissance could hardly deny that the event if bogus was as great a creation in mass hoodwinking, deception, and legerdemain as the true ascent was in discipline and technology. Indeed, conceive of the genius of such a conspiracy. It would take criminals and confidence men mightier, more trustworthy, and more resourceful than anything in this century or the ones before. Merely to conceive of such men was the surest way to know the event was not staged. Yes, the century was a giant and a cretin. Man had become a Herculean embodiment of the Vision, but the brain on top of the head was as small as a transistorized fist, and the chambers of the heart had shrunk to the dry hard seeds of some hybrid future.

To make sense of Apollo 11 on the moon, to rise above the verbiage that covered the event, was to embark on a project which would not satisfy his own eye unless it could reduce a conceptual city of technologese to one simplicity—was the venture worthwhile or evil?

If Marx had done his best to gut the past of every attachment to the primitive, the sacramental, and the magical, if the Marxian formula that history was a reflection of the state of productive relations had thereby elevated reason to that vertiginous even insane eminence out of which technology had been born, then the task now appeared in reverse: One was obliged to make a first reconnaissance into the possibility of restoring magic, psyche, and the spirits of the underworld to the spookiest venture in history, a landing on the moon, an event whose technologese had been so complete that the word "spook" probably did not appear in twenty million words of NASA prose.

# A Dream of the Future's Face

Early on the afternoon of July 21, the Lunar Module fired its ascent motor, lifted off Tranquility Base, and in a few hours docked with Columbia. Shortly after, the astronauts passed back into the Command Module and Eagle was jettisoned. It would drift off on a trajectory to the sun. A little before midnight, out of communication for the last time with Mission Control, traveling for the final orbit around the back of the moon, Apollo 11 ignited the Service Module engine and accelerated its speed from 3,600 miles to 5,900 miles per hour. Its momentum was now great enough to lift it out of the moon's pull of gravity and back into the attractions of the earth—the spacecraft was therefore on its way home. Since the trip would take sixty hours, a quiet two and a half days were in store and Aquarius decided to get out of Nassau Bay and visit some friends.

His host and hostess were wealthy Europeans with activities that kept them much of the time in Texas. Since they were art collectors of distinction, invariably served a good meal, and had always been kind to him, the invitation was welcome. To go from the arid tablelands of NASA Highway 1 to these forested grounds now damp after the rain of a summer evening was like encountering a taste of French ice in the flats of the desert. Even the trees about the house were very high, taller than the tallest elms he had seen in New England—"Wild pigs used to forage in this part of Houston," said his host, as if in explanation, and on the lawn, now twice-green in the luminous golden green of a murky twilight, smaller tropical trees with rubbery trunks twisted about a large sculpture by Jean Tinguely which waved metal scarecrow arms when a switch was thrown and blew spinning faucets of water through wild stuttering sweeps, a piece of sculpture reminiscent of the flying machines of La Belle Epoque, a hybrid of dragon and hornet that offered a shade of the time when technology had been belts and clanking gears, and culture was a fruit to be picked from a favored tree.

The mansion was modern—it had been one of the first modern homes in Houston and was designed by one of the more ascetic modern architects. With the best will, how could Aquarius like it? But the severity of the design was concealed by the variety of the furniture, the intensity of the art, the presence of the sculpture, and the happy design in fact of a portion of the house: The living room shared a wall with a glassed-in atrium of exotics in bloom. So the surgical intent of the architect was partially overcome by the wealth of the art and by the tropical pressure of the garden whose plants and interior tree, illumined with spotlights, possessed something of that same silence that comes over audience and cast when there is a moment of theater and everything ceases, everything depends on—one cannot say—it is just that no one thinks to cough.

There had been another such moment when he entered the house. In the foyer was a painting by Magritte, a startling image of a room with an immense rock situated in the center of the floor. The instant of time suggested by the canvas was comparable to the mood of a landscape in the instant just before something awful is about to happen, or just after, one could not tell. The silences of the canvas spoke of Apollo 11 still circling the moon: The painting could have been photographed for the front page—it hung from the wall like a severed head. As Aquarius met the other guests, gave greetings, took a drink, his thoughts were not free of the painting. He did not know when it had been done—he assumed it was finished many years ago—he was certain without even thinking about it that there had been no intention by the artist to talk of the moon or projects in space, no, Aquarius would assume the painter had awakened with a vision of the canvas and that vision had he delineated. Something in the acrid breath of the city he inhabited, some avidity emitted by a passing machine, some tar in the residue of a nightmare, some ash from the memory of a cremation had gone into the painting of that gray stone—it was as if Magritte had listened to the ending of one world with its comfortable chairs in the parlor, and heard the intrusion of a new world, silent as the windowless stone which grew in the room, and knowing not quite what he had painted, had painted his warning nonetheless. Now the world of the future was a dead rock, and the rock was in the room.

There was also a Negro in his host's living room, a man perhaps thirty-five, a big and handsome Black man with an Afro haircut of short length, the moderation of the cut there to hint that he still lived in a White man's clearing, even if it was on the very edge of the clearing. He was not undistinguished, this Negro, he was a professor at an Ivy League college; Aquarius had met him one night the previous year after visiting the campus. The Negro had been much admired in the college. He had an impressive voice and the deliberate manner of a leader. How could the admiration of faculty wives be restrained? But this Black professor was also a focus of definition for Black students in the college—they took some of the measure of their militancy from his advice. It was a responsible position. The students were in the college on one of those specific programs which had begun in many a university that year—students from slum backgrounds, students without full qualification were being accepted on the reasonable if much embattled assumption that boys from slums were easily bright enough to be salvaged for academic life if special pains were taken. Aquarius had met enough of such students to think the program was modest. The education of the streets gave substantial polish in Black ghettos— some of the boys had knowledge at seventeen Aquarius would not be certain of acquiring by seventy. They had the toughness of fiber of the twenty-times tested. This night on the campus, having a simple discussion back and forth, needling back and forth, even to even—so Aquarius had thought—a Black student suddenly said to him, "You're an old man. Your hair is gray. An old man like you wants to keep talking like that, you may have to go outside with me." The student gave an evil smile. "You're too old to keep up with me. I'll whomp your ass."

It had been a glum moment for Aquarius. It was late at night, he was tired, he had been drinking with students for hours. As usual he was overweight. The boy was smaller than him but not at all overweight, fast. Over the years Aquarius had lost more standards than he cared to remember. But he still held on to the medieval stricture that one should never back out of a direct invitation to fight. So he said with no happiness, "Well, there are so many waiting on line, it might as well be you," and he stood up.

The Black boy had been playing with him. The Black boy grinned. He assured Aquarius there was no need to go outside. They could talk now. And did. But what actors were the Blacks! What a sense of honor! What a sense of the gulch! Seeing the Black professor in this living room in Houston brought back the memory of the student who had decided to run a simulation through the character of Aquarius' nerve. It was in the handshake of both men as they looked at each other now, Aquarius still feeling the rash of the encounter, the other still amused at the memory. God knows how the student had imitated his rise from the chair. There had been a sly curl in the Black man's voice whenever they came across each other at a New York party.

Tonight, however, was different. He almost did not recognize the professor. The large eyes were bloodshot, and his slow deliberate speech had become twice-heavy, almost sluggish. Aquarius realized the man had been drinking. It was not a matter of a few shots before this evening, no, there was a sense of somebody pickling himself through three days of booze, four days of booze, five, not even drunk, just the heavy taking of the heaviest medicine, a direct search for thickening, as if he were looking to coagulate some floor between the pit of his feelings at boil and the grave courtesies of his heavy Black manner. By now it showed. He was normally so elegant a man that it was impossible to conceive of how he would make a crude move— now, you could know. Something raucous and jeering was still withheld, but the sourness of his stomach had gotten into the sourness of his face. His collar was a hint wilted.

He had a woman with him, a sweet and wispy blonde, half plain, still half attractive, for she emitted a distant echo of Marilyn Monroe long gone. But she was not his equal, not in size, presence, qualifications—by the cruel European measure of this richly endowed room, she was simply not an adequate woman for a man of his ambitions. At least that was the measure Aquarius took. It was hard not to recognize that whatever had brought them together, very little was now sustaining the project. The Black man was obviously tired of her, and she was still obviously in love with him. Since they were here enforcedly together, that was enough to keep a man drinking for more than a day. Besides—if he was a comfortable house guest of these fine Europeans, he might nonetheless not wish to leave the grounds. Being seen with her on Houston streets would not calm his nerves.

But there were other reasons for drinking as well. America had put two White men on the moon, and lifted them off. A triumph of White men was being celebrated in the streets of this city. It was even worse than that. For the developed abilities of these White men, their production, their flight skills, their engineering feats, were the most successful part of that White superstructure which had been strangling the possibilities of his own Black people for years. The professor was an academic with no mean knowledge of colonial struggles of colored peoples. He was also a militant. If the degree of his militancy was not precisely defined, still its presence was not denied. His skin was dark. If he were to say "Black is beautiful" with a cultivated smile, nonetheless he was still saying it. Aquarius had never been invited to enter this Black man's vision, but it was no great mystery the Black believed his people were possessed of a potential genius that was greater than Whites'. Kept in incubation for two millennia, they would be all the more powerful when they prevailed. It was nothing less than a great civilization they were prepared to create. Aquarius could not picture the details of that civilization in the Black professor's mind, but they had talked enough to know they agreed that this potential greatness of the Black people was not to be found in technology. Whites might need the radio to become tribal but Blacks would have another communion. From the depth of one consciousness they could be ready to speak to the depth of another; by telepathy might they send their word. That was the logic implicit in CPT. If CPT was one of the jokes by which Blacks admitted Whites to the threshold of their view, it was a relief to learn that CPT stood for Colored People's Time. When a Black friend said he would arrive at 8 P.M. and came after midnight, there was still logic in his move. He was traveling on CPT. The vibrations he received at 8 P.M. were not sufficiently interesting to make him travel toward you—all that was hurt were the host's undue expectations. The real logic of CPT was that when there was trouble or happiness the brothers would come on the wave.

Well, White technology was not built on telepathy, it was built on electromagnetic circuits of transmission and reception, it was built on factory workers pressing their button or monitoring their function according to firm and bound stations of the clock. The time of a rocket mission was Ground Elasped Time, GET. Every sequence of the flight was tied into the pure numbers of the timeline. So the flight to the moon was a victory for GET, and the first heats of the triumph suggested that the fundamental notion of Black superiority might be incorrect: In this hour, it would no longer be as easy for a militant Black to say that Whitey had built a palace on numbers, and numbers killed a man, and numbers would kill Whitey's civilization before all was through. Yesterday, Whitey with his numbers had taken a first step to the stars, taken it ahead of Black men. How that had to burn in the ducts of this Black man's stomach, in the vats of his liver. Aquarius thought again of the lunar air of technologists. Like the moon, they traveled without a personal atmosphere. No wonder Blacks had distaste for numbers, and found trouble studying. It was not because they came—as liberals necessarily would have it—from wrecked homes and slum conditions, from drug-pushing streets, no, that kind of violence and disruption could be the pain of a people so rich in awareness they could not bear the deadening jolts of civilization on each of their senses. Blacks had distaste for numbers not because they were stupid or deprived but because numbers were abstracted from the senses, numbers made you ignore the taste of the apple for the amount in the box, and so the use of numbers shrunk the protective envelope of human atmosphere, eroded that extrasensory aura which gave awareness, grace, the ability to move one's body and excel at sports and dance and war, or be able to travel on an inner space of sound. Blacks were not the only ones who hated numbers—how many attractive women could not bear to add a column or calculate a cost? Numbers were a pestilence to beauty.

Of course this particular Black man, this professor, was in torture, for he lived half in the world of numbers and half in the wrappings of the aura. So did Aquarius. It was just that Aquarius was White and the other Black—so Aquarius could not conceal altogether his pleasure in the feat. A little part of him, indefatigably White, felt as mean as a Wasp. There was something to be said after all for arriving on time. CPT was excellent for the nervous system if you were the one to amble in at midnight, but Aquarius had played the host too often.

"You know," said the professor, "there are no Black astronauts."

"Of course not."

"Any Jewish astronauts?"

"I doubt it."

The Black man grunted. They would not need to mention Mexicans or Puerto Ricans. Say, there might not even be any Italians.

"Did you want them," asked Aquarius, "to send a Protestant, a Catholic, and a Jew to the moon?"

"Look," said the Black professor, "do they have any awareness of how the money they spent could have been used?"

"They have a very good argument: They say if you stopped space tomorrow, only a token of the funds would go to poverty."

"I'd like to be in a position to argue about that," said the Black. He sipped at his drink. It trickled into his system like the inching of glucose from a bottle down a rubber tube. "Damn," he said, "are they still on the moon?"

"They took off already," said Aquarius.

"No trouble?"

"None."

If the Blacks yet built a civilization, magic would be at its heart. For they lived with the wonders of magic as the Whites lived with technology. How many Blacks had made a move or inhibited it because the emanations of the full moon might affect their cause? Now Whitey had walked the moon, put his feet on it. The moon presumably had not spoken. Or had it, and Richard Nixon received the favor and Teddy Kennedy the curse? Was there no magic to combat technology? Then the strength of Black culture was stricken. There would not be a future Black civilization, merely an adjunct to the White. What lava in the raw membranes of the belly. The Black professor had cause to drink. The moon shot had smashed more than one oncoming superiority of the Black.

That night Aquarius had trouble falling asleep, as if the unrest of the Black professor at the passage of men's steps on the moon had now passed over to him. Nothing in the future might ever be the same— that was cause for unrest—nor could the future even be seen until one could answer the obsessive question: Was our venture into space noble or insane, was it part of a search for the good, or the agent of diabolisms yet unglimpsed? It was as if we had begun to turn the pocket of the universe inside out.

He had had at the end a curious discussion with the Black professor. "It's all in the remission of sin," the Black man had said. "Technology begins when men are ready to believe that the sins of the fathers are not visited on the sons. Remission of sin—that's what it's all about," he said in his Black slow voice.

Yes, if the sons were not punished, then the father might dare, as no primitive father had dared, to smash through a taboo. If the father was in error, or if he failed, the sons would be spared. Only the father would suffer. So men were thereby more ready to dare the gods. From that love on the cross which had requested that the sons not pay for the sins of the fathers had opened a hairline split that would finally crack the walls of taboo. And the windowless walls of technology had come through the gap. Back to Sören the Dane. You could not know if you were a monster or a saint of the deep.

In the Nineteenth Century, they had ignored Kierkegaard. A middle-class White man living on the rise of Nineteenth Century technology was able to feel his society as an eminence from which he could make expeditions, if he wished, into the depths. He would know all the while that his security was still up on the surface, a ship—if you will—to which he was attached by a line. In the Twentieth Century, the White man had suddenly learned what the Black man might have told him—that there was no ship unless it was a slave ship. There was no security. There was no guide. Anyone could lose his soul. That recognition offered a sensation best described as bottomless.

Lying there, unable to sleep, lost in the caverns of questions whose answers never came (Mr. Answer Man, what is the existential equivalent of infinity?—Why insomnia, Sandy, good old insomnia), Aquarius knew for the first time in years that he no longer had the remotest idea of what he knew. It was the end of the decade, and the fashion was rising in New York literary lakes to inquire after the nature of the decade to come. He had been a poor prophet of the Sixties, but it was not a century for prophets—poor as he had been, he had still been one of the few who had some sense of what was coming. He had known that marijuana was on its way, and Hip, and the Kennedys, and a time of upheaval, and in the center of the Establishment: loss of belief. Now they asked him what he thought of the Seventies. He did not know. He thought of the Seventies and a blank like the windowless walls of the computer city came over his vision. When he conducted interviews with himself on the subject, it was not despair he felt, or fear—it was anesthesia. He had no intimations of what was to come, and that was conceivably worse than any sentiment of dread, for a sense of the future, no matter how melancholy, was preferable to none—it spoke of some sense of continuation in the projects of one's life. He was adrift. If he tried to conceive of a likely perspective in the decade before him, he saw not one structure to society but two: If the social world did not break down into revolutions and counter-revolutions, into police and military rules of order with sabotage, guerrilla war and enclaves of resistance, if none of this occurred, then there would certainly be a society of reason, but its reason would be the logic of the computer. In that society, legally accepted drugs would become a necessity for accelerated cerebration, there would be inchings toward nuclear installation, a monotony of architectures, a pollution of nature that would arouse technologies of decontamination odious as deodorants, and transplanted hearts monitored like spaceships. In the society of computer-logic, the atmosphere would obviously be plastic, air-conditioned, sealed in bubble-domes below the smog, a prelude to living in space stations. People would die in such societies like fish expiring on a vinyl floor. So of course there would be another society, an irrational society of the dropouts, the saintly, the mad, the militant, and the young. There the art of the absurd would reign in defiance against the computer.

Aquarius got out of bed. He was a disciplinarian about insomnia. Having suffered from it years before, he had learned how to live with an occasional bad night. He took no pill, he took no drink, he looked to ride it out. Sometimes he indulged in a game of formal optimism, carrying over from artillery training the injunction to bracket a target. So now if his sense of the future was too pessimistic—he could only hope it was too dark!—he would look for the formal opposite: try to regard science as reasonable. But he could not regard science apart from technology.

But the mood of space which remained with Aquarius, that mood elegant and austere as the perfect laws of physical principle, was still a force for disruption. Sitting in the spaced-out colors of Dun Cove, he had the thought that the moon shot was conceivably the first voyage of the very cancer of the world, for indeed the first journeys of the cancer cell in a body, taken from the point of view of the cancer cell, were certainly bold and dangerous. Not by little effort did a cell leave its own organ and learn how to survive in another. Cancer cells, seen in relation to ordinary cells, were often extraordinary in the variety of their form, as different as a view of Las Vegas at night is different from a village in the Bluegrass, or as different as the internal works of Apollo were in comparison to the works of the family car. Did that account for the curious depression, the sobriety mixed in so many faces with the pride of the achievement? Aquarius did not know.

What if space were not benign? What if we did not act upon space, explore into space, but space rather drew us toward her dispositions, her plans for us, her intent upon human life, what if we thought we moved up but were drawn up, what if the moon was as quiet as the fisherman when he lays the fly on the water . . .

Having journeyed to the center of his gloom, Aquarius went to sleep. In his dreams a country doctor he had known for years murmured, "I don't know about all of this. Recognize that the moon could be some kind of catchall simple as the tonsils to protect us here on earth. Maybe those craters come from catching all the cess." In his dream Aquarius answered back, "It depends on your idea of God, that's what it must depend on." Out into sleep he went again, ringings of ether in his ear.

In the morning after breakfast, he found himself rereading a transcript of the postlaunch briefing, a curious activity, but he was like a
man on the cusp of a clue. To fall asleep in pursuit of the answer to a
mystery was to awaken with the fire in a new place. It had burned beneath the ground while he was sleeping.

What if one recognized that to believe in progress and believe in
God as well might make it necessary to conceive of our Lord as a vision of existence who conceivably was obliged to compete with other
visions of existence in the universe, other conceptions of how life
should be. But this had brought him to the heart of the question. He
was, after all, quick to hunt for reason in absurdity.

To believe in God and to believe in progress—what could that
mean but that the desire for progress existed in the very creation of
man, as if man were designed from the outset to labor as God's agent,
to carry God's vision of existence across the stars. If this were true
then the intent of the Lord could hardly be to reveal His goodness to
us; rather He must employ us to reveal His vision of existence *out
there,* somewhere out there where His hegemony came to an end and
other divine conceptions began to exist, or indeed were opposed to
us. If God finally was the embodiment of a vision that might cease to
exist in the hostilities of the larger universe, a vision which indeed
might be *obliged* to prevail or would certainly cease to exist, then it was
legitimate to see all of human history as a cradle which had nurtured
a baby that had now taken its first step. Intended by divine will to
travel across the heavens, we were now at least on our way to the
moon, and who could know if we were ahead or behind of some
schedule the Lord had presented us, a schedule which presumably
each man and woman alive would keep in the depths of their unconscious along with everything else most vital for the preservation of life.
A large and uncomfortable thought, for if it was so, then the flight of
Apollo 11 was a first revelation of the real intent of History. So this
much, anyway, had been revealed: One could not make a judgment
on the value or absurdity of devoting such effort to go to the moon
unless one was ready to recognize that eschatology had conceivably
been turned on its head. For if eschatology, that science of "the four
last things: death, judgment, heaven and hell," was now to be considered in the light of God's need for supermen to negotiate His passage
quickly through the heavens, then how much more value might He

give to courage than to charity, how much harsh judgment to justice itself if the act to be considered was not expeditious but merely just, yes if speed were of the essence then Hell's Angels were possibly nearer to God than the war against poverty.

This last suggested a step Aquarius was not prepared to take—the idea was as disruptive to a liberal philosophical system as tartar emetic and mustard to a glutton. For it offered a reason why the heroes of the time were technologists, not poets, and the art was obliged to be in the exceptional engineering, while human communication had become the routine function. It was because the Power guiding us had desired nothing less. He was looking to the day when all of mankind would yet be part of one machine, with mechanical circuits, social flesh circuits, and combined electromagnetic and thought-transponder circuits, an instrument of divine endeavor put together by a Father to whom one might no longer be able to pray since the ardors of His embattled voyage could have driven Him mad.

Sweet thoughts for Aquarius to have as a sequel to the ascent, but the questions were grand at least; they could occupy the consciousness of the century. It was somehow superior to see the astronauts and the flight of Apollo 11 as the instrument of such celestial or satanic endeavors than as a species of sublimation for the profoundly unmanageable violence of man, a meaningless journey to a dead arena in order that men could engage in the irrational activity of designing machines that would give birth to other machines which would travel to meaningless places as if they were engaged in these collective acts of hugely organized but ultimately pointless activity because they had not the wit, goodness, or charity to solve their real problems and so would certainly destroy themselves if they did not have a game of gargantuan dimensions for diversion, a devilish entertainment, a spend-spree of resources, a sublimation, yes, the very word, a sublimation of aggressive and intolerably inhuman desires, as if like a beast enraged with the passion of gorging nature, we looked now to make incisions into the platinum satellite of our lunacy, our love, and our dreams.

Aquarius would have given much to find a truly revealing face at NASA, for that could have given a clue to these questions, but it was in the logic of such endeavor that no answers be apparent on the surface. If it would take the rest of the century to begin to disclose the real intent of the act, no lightning raid on the evidence, no single happy disclosure, could possibly offer a reply.

Still, Aquarius preferred the first assumption, that we were the indispensable instruments of a monumental vision with whom we had begun a trip. On that conclusion he would rest his thoughts. Having come back at last to earth from the orbits of the dream with such a hypothesis in his pocket, Aquarius was a little more ready to head for home, the writing of a book and conceivably the pouring of a drink. The study of more than one technical manual awaited him.

All selections from *Of a Fire on the Moon* (1971)

# The Raging Affair:
# Kate Millett and Henry Miller

By any major literary perspective, the land of Millett is a barren and mediocre terrain, its flora reminiscent of a Ph.D. tract, its roads a narrow argument and its horizon low. Still, there is a story they tell of Kate Millett when the winds blow and lamps gutter with a last stirring of the flame. Then, as the skirts of witches go whipping around the wick, they tell how Kate went up to discuss the thesis at her college and a learned professor took issue with her declaration that the wife of the hero Rojack in a work called *An American Dream* had practiced sodomy with husband and lovers.

"No, no," cried the professor. "I know the author, I know him well, I have discussed the scene with him more than once and it is not sodomy she practices but analingus. It is for that she is killed, since it is a vastly more deranging offense in the mind's eye!"

It is said that Kate turned pale and showed cold sweat upon her skin. But she was not a future leader of millions for nothing; her argument depended on sodomy, and the art of argument was to ignore forever what did not fit—her work appeared with this good passage:

> . . . Here is where one must depend on the forceful role of sodomy in the book, she admits that she has been enjoying this very activity with her new lovers. Now sodomy is a specialty in which our hero takes personal pride. Though he boasts to her face that his mistresses far excel her in this activity, the notion that

his wife is committing sodomous adultery is evidently too severe a trial on his patience . . . he promptly retaliates by strangling the upstart. As Mrs. Rojack is one of those Celtic sporting women, it is not easy work . . .

Well, it could be said for Kate that she was nothing if not a pug-nosed wit, and that was good, since in literary matters she had not much else. Her lack of fidelity to the material she read was going to be equaled only by her authority in characterizing it—analingus was yes as sodomy—and the yaws of her distortion were nicely hidden by the smudge pots of her indignation. So her land was a foul and dreary place to cross, a stingy country whose treacherous inhabitants (were they the very verbs and phrases of her book?) jeered at difficulties that were often the heart of the matter, the food served at every inn was a can of ideological lard, a grit and granite of thesis-factories turned out aggregates of concept-jargon on every ridge, stacks of such clauses fed the sky with smoke, and musical instruments full of the spirit of non-violence emitted the sound of flaws and blats. Bile and bubbles of intellectual flatulence coursed in the river, and the bloody ground steamed with the limbs of every amputated quote. Everywhere were signs that men were guilty and women must win.

What then has happened to her promise of a varied terrain of mountains and jungles, of explorations into the work of novelists known for their preoccupation with the needs of men? Has it disappeared altogether, or is it that any trek across this bog of flatland, swamp, and grinding sands of prose is no more than a skitter across a rhetorical skin, a steamy literary webbing whose underneath, once upturned, reveals another world, a circus of subterranean attractions that can be viewed only by digging up each quotation buried in her book? For each corpse was so crudely assassinated, then so unceremoniously dumped, that the poor fellows are now as martyrs beneath the sod, and every shroud is become a phosphorescence of literary lights, a landscape of metaphorical temples. Yet if we are able to find such a literary world, when entrance requires no less than the resurrection of the corpses in her graves, what is to be said of her method? Can she be an honor student in some occult school of thuggee (now open to the ladies via the pressures of Women's Liberation)? It is possible. For Kate is the perfect gun. It is as if she does not know why she kills, just senses that here the job is ready to be done, and there the job must be done. It is almost as if some higher tyrant has fingered the quotes, has said, "They are getting too close to a little divine sense here—bury 'em deep in shit, Kate-baby."

Kate-baby nods, goes out. A sawed-off shotgun is her tool. What a blast at Henry Miller:

> As all Americans know, the commercial world is a battlefield. When executives are "fucked" by the company, they can retaliate by "fucking" their secretaries. Miller's is "part-nigger" and "so damned pleased to have someone fuck her without blushing," that she can be shared out to the boss's pal Curley. She commits suicide eventually, but in business, "it's fuck or be fucked," Miller observes, providing some splendid insight into the many meanings we attach to the word.

"It's fuck or be fucked," writes Millett, quoting Miller. Except it is not Miller she is quoting—even if she gives him words and puts them in quotation marks. Did an editor discover a discrepancy? There is a footnote: "This is the sense of the passage." But it is not the sense. Miller writes: "We were a merry crew, united in our desire to fuck the company at all costs. And while fucking the company we fucked everything in sight that we could get hold of . . ."—a merry observation, not a bitter one. But Kate's version works more effectively to slip a reader the assumption that Miller is a racist who jeers at his secretary's death: "She commits suicide eventually, but in business, 'it's fuck or be fucked,' Miller observes," although now we know this has not been his observation. In fact, the suicide isn't even mentioned at that point in *Tropic of Capricorn*—it's mentioned twenty-eight pages later in an opposite context, where Miller, discovering that the secretary is about to be fired because one of his superiors doesn't want a Negro in the company, comes to her defense, describes her indeed to his superiors as "extremely intelligent and extremely capable." To himself, he thinks, "when she was angry she was magnificent . . ." Miller has begun to fall in love with her. But we may as well enjoy the passage.

> *I told her quietly that if she were fired I would quit too. She pretended not to believe it at first. I said I meant it, that I didn't care what happened. She seemed to be unduly impressed; she took me by the two hands and she held them very gently, the tears rolling down her cheeks.*
>
> *That was the beginning of things. I think it was the very next day that I slipped her a note saying that I was crazy about her. She read the note sitting opposite me and when she was through she looked me square in the eye and said she didn't believe it. But we went to dinner again that night and we had more to drink and we danced and while we were dancing she pressed herself against me lasciviously. It was just the time, as luck*

*would have it, that my wife was getting ready to have another abortion. I was telling Valeska about it as we danced. On the way home she suddenly said—"Why don't you let me lend you a hundred dollars?" The next night I brought her home to dinner and I let her hand the wife the hundred dollars. I was amazed how well the two of them got along. Before the evening was over it was agreed upon that Valeska would come to the house the day of the abortion and take care of the kid. The day came and I gave Valeska the afternoon off. About an hour after she had left I suddenly decided that I would take the afternoon off also. I started toward the burlesque on Fourteenth Street. When I was about a block from the theater I suddenly changed my mind. It was just the thought that if anything happened—if the wife were to kick off—I wouldn't feel so damned good having spent the afternoon at the burlesque. I walked around a bit, in and out of the penny arcades, and then I started homeward.*

*It's strange how things turn out. Trying to amuse the kid I suddenly remembered a trick my grandfather had shown me when I was a child. You take the dominoes and you make tall battleships out of them; then you gently pull the tablecloth on which the battleships are floating until they come to the edge of the table when suddenly you give a brisk tug and they fall onto the floor. We tried it over and over again, the three of us, until the kid got so sleepy that she toddled off to the next room and fell asleep. The dominoes were lying all over the floor and the tablecloth was on the floor too. Suddenly Valeska was leaning against the table, her tongue halfway down my throat, my hand between her legs. As I laid her back on the table she twined her legs around me. I could feel one of the dominoes under my feet—part of the fleet that we had destroyed a dozen times or more.*

At this point, Miller goes off into a reverie about his grandfather and his boyhood (which is his way of protracting the act). A nostalgic reverie follows with memories of photographs in boyhood books, Teddy Roosevelt, San Juan Hill, the *Maine*, Admiral Dewey, Schley and Sampson. Then he writes:

*. . . We had hardly finished when the bell rang and it was my wife coming home from the slaughterhouse. I was still buttoning my fly as I went through the hall to open the gate. She was as white as flour. She looked as though she'd never be able to go through another one. We put her to bed and then we gathered up the dominoes and put the tablecloth back on the table.*

Well, he has certainly fucked her, and fucked her while his wife is having an abortion, and left us with an image of a white man making love to a black woman while thinking of San Juan Hill, and one hundred twenty-one pages later he has not so much loaned her as lost her to his friend Curley, but the sense we have been given by Millett of a boss using his black secretary shamelessly, and jeering at her suicide, is warped. "She was so damned pleased to have someone fuck her without blushing" is in context the bitter and painful remark of a man who felt some love for a woman who when alive "was picked clean too, by the human worms who have no respect for anything which has a different tint, a different odor."

That last note is, of course, vintage. Only a comic liberal would speak today of respect for people with different tints, but *Tropic of Capricorn* came out in 1939 and is about the Twenties, when it was still radical to believe whites and blacks could make love together; the work of Miller is in fact a Baedeker to the remarkable sexuality of the Twenties, and one would expect in a book called *Sexual Politics,* which contains a part titled "The Sexual Revolution, First Phase: 1830–1930," that much would be made of the Twenties, and the work of Miller in relation to it. But "Sexual Revolution, First Phase: 1830–1930," while it includes nothing less than a brief history of feminism plus a view of nineteenth-century attitudes toward women in the work of the Brontës, Mill, Ruskin, Meredith, Hardy, Wilde, and Engels, is egregiously mistitled, since there is nothing in it from 1900 to 1930, nothing of the First World War and the Twenties, nothing of Fitzgerald, Aleister Crowley, and Caresse Crosby, nothing of Prohibition, surrealism, Daisy Buchanan, Brett Ashley, Hollywood, jazz, or the Charleston, not a word from 1920 to 1930, a decade conceivably as interesting in the emancipation of women as any other ten years since the decline of Rome. But such an inclusion might have called for another hundred pages, which conceivably Millett didn't have in her head. The Twenties are a thicket for any thesis-monger with an ax. That may be why Millett never once looks at Miller as some wandering troubadour of the Twenties who carried the sexual revolution through the cities of the New World and the Old, no, Miller has been labeled a "counterrevolutionary sexual politician," he belongs to that tidy part of her thesis which will neatly see 1930 to 1960 as a time of sexual counterrevolution. She would hardly be ready, plans drawn, subdivisions staked and sold, to put up with the thundering horror that Miller is an archetype of the man of the Twenties, is indeed the true sexual revolutionary if we are willing to grant that any equivalent figure of the Renaissance would by that measure also be a revolutionary, since no revolution ever picks up momentum without a profound change in the established consciousness of the time. Just as the Renaissance was a period in which men dared, as perhaps never before in history, to allow themselves to pursue the line of their thought and embark on exploration with the idea that such activities were good and valid in themselves and so did not have to be initiated with external blessing or forced to scurry under the shadow of inviolable taboo, but rather the world was a theater, and nature a laboratory open to the adventurer with an inquiring mind—so the Twenties were a species of sexual renaissance where man emerged from the long medieval night of Victorian sex, with its perversions, hypocrisies, and brothel dispensations, and set out to explore not the world but himself, not man of Victorian reason with his buried sexual pocket but man as himself, Henry Miller, with his brain and his balls in the intimate and continuing dialogue of his daily life, which meant that one followed the line of one's sexual impulse without a backward look at what was moral, responsible, or remotely desirable for society, that one set out to feed one's cock (as man from the Renaissance had set out to feed his brain), and since the effort was pioneer in the very real way that no literary man with the power to shift consciousness had ever given that much attention before to the vagaries and outright contradictions of a stiff prick without a modicum of conscience, no one had ever dared to assume that such a life might be as happy and amusing as the next, that the paganism of a big-city fucker had its own balance, and such a man could therefore wage an all-out war to storm the mysteries with his phallus as a searchlight because all sexual experience was valid if one looked at it clearly and no fuck was in vain, well, it was a sexual renaissance sure enough, and it depended on a rigorous even a delighted honesty in portraying the detail of one's faults, in writing without shit, which is to say writing with the closest examination of one's own. Miller was a true American spirit. He knew that in a nation of transplants and weeds the best was always next to the worst, and right after shit comes Shinola. It was all equal to him because he understood that it is never equal—in the midst of heaven a hole, and out of the slimy coruscated ridiculous comes a pearl; he is a demon at writing about bad fucks with all the gusto he gives to good ones, no fuck is in vain—the air may prove most transcendent at the edge of the vomit, or if not, then the nausea it produces can give birth to an otherwise undiscovered project as the mind clears out of its vertigo. So he dives into the sordid, portrays men and women as they have hardly been painted before, a girl having her period in the middle of an orgy, cock, balls, knees, thighs, cunt, and belly in a basting of blood, then soap and towels, a round of good-byes—a phrase or two later he is off on the beginning of a ten-page description of how he makes love to his wife that goes through many a mood, he will go right down to the depths, no cellar has maggots or rats big enough to frighten him, he can even write about the whipped-out flayed heel-ground end of his own desire, about fucking when too exhausted to fuck, and come up with a major metaphor. Let it be introduced by Kate Millett:

> One memorable example of sex as a war of attrition waged upon economic grounds is the fifteen-franc whore whom Miller and his friend Van Norden hire in the Paris night and from whom, despite their own utter lack of appetite and her exhaustion from hunger, it is still necessary to extort the price.

Let us see what Millett is talking about. She seems to have price confused with product. Here is Miller.

> *And then she commences a hard luck story, about the hospital and the back rent and the baby in the country. But she doesn't overdo it. She knows that our ears are stopped; but the misery is there inside her, like a stone, and there's no room for any other thoughts. She isn't trying to make an appeal to our sympathies—she's just shifting this big weight inside her from one place to another. I rather like her. I hope to Christ she hasn't got a disease.*
>
> *In the room she goes about her preparations mechanically. "There isn't a crust of bread about by any chance?" she inquires, as she squats over the* bidet. *Van Norden laughs at this. "Here, take a drink," he says, shoving a bottle at her. She doesn't want anything to drink; her stomach's already on the bum, she complains.*
>
> *"That's just a line with her," says Van Norden. "Don't let her work on your sympathies. Just the same, I wish she'd talk about something else. How the hell can you get up any passion when you've got a starving cunt on your hands?"*

Up to this point, Kate's description has been a reasonable summary. Now she goes on with:

> As sex, or rather "cunt," is not only merchandise but a monetary specie, Miller's adventures read like so many victories for sharp practice, carry the excitement of a full ledger, and operate on the flat premise that quantity is quality.

"How the hell can you get up any passion when you have a starving cunt on your hands?" We are installed on the heights of chivalry. Can any author ever recover from this point? But Miller is following the logic where it leads—out of the deepest dungeons will the logic of cock lead him to the towers of metaphor.

*Precisely! We haven't any passion either of us. And as for her, one might as well expect her to produce a diamond necklace as to show a spark of passion. But there's the fifteen francs and something has to be done about it. It's like a state of war: the moment the condition is precipitated nobody thinks about anything but peace, about getting it over with. And yet nobody has the courage to lay down his arms, to say, "I'm fed up with it . . . I'm through." No, there's fifteen francs somewhere, which nobody gives a damn about any more and which nobody is going to get in the end anyhow, but the fifteen francs is like the primal cause of things and rather than listen to one's own voice, rather than walk out on the primal cause, one surrenders to the situation, one goes on butchering and butchering and the more cowardly one feels the more heroically does he behave . . .*

*It's exactly like a state of war—I can't get it out of my head. The way she works over me, to blow a spark of passion into me, makes me think what a damned poor soldier I'd be if I was ever silly enough to be trapped like this and dragged to the front. I know for my part that I'd surrender everything, honor included, in order to get out of the mess. I haven't any stomach for it, and that's all there is to it. But she's got her mind set on the fifteen francs and if I don't want to fight about it she's going to make me fight. But you can't put fight into a man's guts if he hasn't any fight in him.*

Victories for sharp practice? Excitement of a full ledger?

*Van Norden seems to have a more normal attitude about it. He doesn't care a rap about the fifteen francs either now; it's the situation itself which intrigues him. It seems to call for a show of mettle—his manhood is involved. The fifteen francs are lost, whether we succeed or not. There's something more involved—not just manhood perhaps, but will. It's like a man in the trenches again: he doesn't know any more why he should go on living, because if he escapes now he'll only be caught later, but he goes on just the same, and even though he has the soul of a cockroach and has admitted as much to himself, give him a gun or a knife or even just his bare nails, and he'll go on slaughtering and slaughtering, he'd slaughter a million men rather than stop and ask himself why.*

*As I watch Van Norden tackle her, it seems to me that I'm looking at a machine whose cogs have slipped. Left to themselves, they could go on this way forever, grinding and slipping, without ever anything happening. Until a hand shuts the motor off. The sight of them coupled like a pair of goats without the least spark of passion, grinding and grinding away for no reason except the fifteen francs, washes away every bit of feeling I have except the inhuman one of satisfying my curiosity. The girl is lying on the edge of the bed and Van Norden is bent over her like a satyr with his two feet solidly planted on the floor. I am sitting on a chair behind him, watching their movements with a cool, scientific detachment; it doesn't matter to me if it should last forever. It's like watching one of those crazy machines which throw the newspaper out, millions and billions and trillions of them with their meaningless headlines. The machine seems more sensible, crazy as it is, and more fascinating to watch, than the human beings and the events which produced it. My interest in Van Norden and the girl is nil; if I could sit like this and watch every single performance going on at this minute all over the world my interest would be even less than nil. I wouldn't be able to differentiate between this phenomenon and the rain falling or a volcano erupting. As long as that spark of passion is missing there is no human significance in the performance. The machine is better to watch. And these two are like a machine which has slipped its cogs. It needs the touch of a human hand to set it right. It needs a mechanic.*

*I get down on my knees behind Van Norden and I examine the machine more attentively. The girl throws her head on one side and gives me a despairing look. "It's no use," she says. "It's impossible." Upon which Van Norden sets to work with renewed energy, just like an old billy goat. He's such an obstinate cuss that he'll break his horns rather than give up. And he's getting sore now because I'm tickling him in the rump.*

*"For God's sake, Joe, give it up! You'll kill the poor girl."*

*"Leave me alone," he grunts. "I almost got it in that time."*

But it is just this last fillip of male humor, that fat tone of the farmer working his bull into the calf, the pride of men able to get their hands in the short hair that enrages Millett most, blinds her with such anger that she misses the point Miller will make in another few lines—the quintessential point that lust when it fails is a machine.

*You can get over a cunt and work away like a billy goat until eternity; you can go to the trenches and be blown to bits; nothing will create that spark of passion if there isn't the intervention of a human hand. Somebody has*

*to put his hand into the machine and let it be wrenched off if the cogs are*
*to mesh again. Somebody has to do this without hope of reward, without*
*concern over the fifteen francs . . .*

But again, what sort of victory is this for sharp practice? The only
sharp practice is in her assessment of the passage. Literary lawyers
cannot do criticism, they can only write briefs, and Kate holds court in
the land of Millett. Poor Henry. He has spent his literary life exploring the watershed of sex from that uncharted side that goes by the
name of lust and it is an epic work for any man; over the centuries,
most of the poets of the world have spent their years on the other side;
they wrote of love. But lust is a world of bewildering dimensions, for
it is that power to take over creation and convert it to a force. Curious
force. Lust exhibits all the attributes of junk. It dominates the mind
and other habits, it appropriates loyalties, generalizes character,
leaches character out, rides on the fuel of almost any emotional gas—
whether hatred, affection, curiosity, even the pressures of boredom—
yet it is never definable because it can alter to love or be as suddenly
sealed from love, indeed the more intense lust becomes, the more it is
indefinable, the line of the ridge between lust and love is where the
light is first luminous, then blinding, and the ground remains unknown. Henry, a hairy prospector, red eye full of lust, has wandered
these ridge lines for the years of his literary life, getting to know the
mosquitoes by name down in every swamp and calling to the ozones
of the highest lust on many a cloud-covered precipice. While cunts are
merely watering places for that lust, boscage, fodder, they are also, no
matter how despised—it is the private little knowledge of lust—that
indispensable step closer to the beyond, so old Priapus the ram admits, "perhaps a cunt, smelly though it may be, is one of the prime
symbols for the connection between all things."

He has slipped the clue across. Here is a motive to the lust that
drives a man to scour his balls and his back until he is ready to die
from the cannonading he has given his organs, the deaths through
which he has dragged some futures of his soul, it is a clue which all but
says that somewhere in the insane passions of all men is a huge desire
to drive forward into the seat of creation, grab some part of that creation in the hands, sink the cock to the hilt, sink it into as many hilts
as will hold it; for man is alienated from the nature that brought him
forth, he is not like woman in possession of an inner space that gives
her link to the future, so he must drive to possess it, he must if necessary come close to blowing his head off that he may possess it. "Per-

haps a cunt, smelly though it may be, is one of the prime symbols for the connection between all things."

Of course Kate will put it in somewhat less commendatory fashion:

> In the case of the two actual women . . . who appear in Miller's world amidst its thousand floozie caricatures, personality and sexual behavior is so completely unrelated that, in the sexual episodes where they appear, any other names might have been conveniently substituted. For the purpose of every bout is the same: a demonstration of the hero's self-conscious detachment before the manifestations of a lower order of life. During an epic encounter with Mara, the only woman he ever loved, Miller is as clinical as he was toward Ida; Mara just as grotesque:

> > *"And on this bright and slippery gadget Mara twisted like an eel. She wasn't any longer a woman in heat, she wasn't even a woman; she was just a mass of indefinable contours wriggling and squirming like a piece of fresh bait seen upside down through a convex mirror in a rough sea.*

> > *"I had long ceased to be interested in her contortions; except for the part of me that was in her I was cool as a cucumber and remote as the Dog Star . . .*

> > *"Towards dawn, Eastern Standard Time, I saw by the frozen condensed-milk expression about the jaw that it was happening. Her face went through all the metamorphoses of early uterine life, only in reverse. With the last dying spark it collapsed like a punctured bag, the eyes and nostrils smoking like toasted acorns in a slightly wrinkled lake of pale skin."*

Mouthpiece for a corporate body of ideas, Kate has neglected to state that it is another of Miller's descriptions of the worst of fucks, of a marathon of lust-fuck in which he is fixed, which he loathes. It is, precisely, not typical of the act with Mara, but then here is what he wrote just before the passage she quotes:

> *When I returned to resume the ordeal my cock felt as if it were made of old rubber bands. I had absolutely no more feeling at that end; it was like pushing a piece of stiff suet down a drain-pipe. What's more, there wasn't another charge left in the battery; if anything was to happen now it would be in the nature of gall and leathery worms or a drop of pus in a solution of thin pot cheese. What surprised me was that it continued to stand up*

*like a hammer; it had lost all the appearance of a sexual implement; it looked disgustingly like a cheap gadget from the five and ten cent store, like a bright-colored piece of fishing tackle minus the bait. And on this bright and slippery gadget Mara twisted like an eel.*

It is curious that she will find these extraordinary descriptions of the horrors of near-dead ice-cold bang-it-out fucking to be odious, as if she is the Battling Annie of some new prudery, yet Kate is still the clarion call for that single permissive sexual standard where a man's asshole is the democratic taxpaying equivalent of any vagina. Of course, it is denigration of woman she protests, the reduction of woman to object, to meat for the cock, woman as a creature who can tune the prick and allow man to adjust his selfish antenna toward the connection of all things, it is the lack of Miller's regard for woman as a person that she claims to abhor, yet in another part of the land of Millett, on page 117 of *Sexual Politics,* Kate is all but invoking praise for Masters and Johnson because they "prove that the female sexual cycle is capable of multiple orgasms in quick succession, each of which is analogous to the detumescence, tumescence, ejaculation, and loss of erection in the male. With proper stimulation, a woman is capable of multiple orgasms in quick succession," she repeats, hardly able to contain herself, and goes on to sing of the clitoris as "the organ specific to sexuality in the human female," yes, the red-hot button of lust gets its good marks here, even as she approves by implication of the methods used to make the Masters and Johnson study, yes, those vibrators and plastic dildoes are honorable adjuncts of sexo-scientific endeavor as opposed to the foul woman-hating billy-goat bulb of old Henry. What a scum of hypocrisy on the surface of her thought, bold sexual revolutionary who will not grant that such a revolution if it comes will have more to do with unmanageable metamorphoses between love and lust than some civilized version of girls-may-hold-hands-in-the-suburbs. It is the horror of lust, and yet its justification, that wild as a blind maniac it still drives toward the creation, it witnesses such profound significations as "Her face went through all the metamorphoses of early uterine life, only in reverse." And the clue again is upon us of that moment of transcendence when the soul stands in the vault of the act and the coming is its mirror. Yes, even fifty clitoral comes in white-hot vibrating laboratory lust is a mirror (if only of the outer galaxies of nausea) but it is not love but lust, good old scientific lust, pure as the lust in the first fierce fart of the satyr.

How Kate hates old Henry for this: that he dares to be an energetic scientist but is without a smock, that he does his lab work out of the lab and yet is so scientific that his amours are as case histories. "Personality and sexual behavior is so completely unrelated that . . . any other names might have been conveniently substituted." How she bangs away at him! "Miller is a compendium of American sexual neuroses," says lab assistant Kate; Miller articulates "the disgust, the contempt, the hostility, the violence, and the sense of filth with which our . . . masculine sensibility surrounds sexuality." "Sheer fantasy . . . exploitative character . . . juvenile egotism . . . brutalized adolescence . . . anxiety and contempt . . . masturbatory revery . . . utter impersonality . . . cruelty and contempt . . . humiliating and degrading . . . sadistic will . . . gratified egotism . . . total abstraction . . . arrested adolescence . . . cultural homosexuality . . . compulsive heterosexual activity . . . authoritarian arrangements . . . absolute license . . . truly obscene ruthlessness . . . virulent sexism . . . a childish fantasy of power . . ." Conceive of these items of abuse, alive as nerves. They twitch in every paragraph for twenty pages. What an apostle for nonviolence is the lady.

Yet the irony is that a case can be brought against Miller. He is so completely an Old Master at his best (he is, in fact, the only Old Master we have) that the failure of the later works to surpass the early ones is a loss everywhere, to Miller, to literature, to us, to all of us. For he captured something in the sexuality of men as it had never been seen before, precisely that it was man's sense of awe before woman, his dread of her position one step closer to eternity (for in that step were her powers), which made men detest women, revile them, humiliate them, defecate symbolically upon them, do everything to reduce them so one might dare to enter them and take pleasure of them. "His shit don't smell like ice cream either," says a private of a general in a novel, and it is the cry of an enlisted man whose ego needs equality to breathe. So do men look to destroy every quality in a woman that will give her the powers of a male, for she is in their eyes already armed with the power that she brought them forth, and that is a power beyond measure—the earliest etchings of memory go back to that woman between whose legs they were conceived, nurtured, and near strangled in the hours of birth. And if women were also born of woman, that could only compound the awe, for out of that process by which they had come in, so would something of the same come out of them; they were installed in the boxes-within-boxes of the universe, and man was only a box, all detached. So it is not unnatural that men, perhaps a majority of men, go through the years of their sex with women in some compound detachment of lust which will enable them to be as fierce as any female awash in the great ocean of the fuck, for as it can appear to the man, great forces beyond his measure seem to be calling to the woman then.

That was what Miller saw, and it is what he brought back to us: that there were mysteries in trying to explain the extraordinary fascination of an act we can abuse, debase, inundate, and drool upon, yet the act repeats an interest—it draws us toward obsession, as if it is the mirror of how we approach God through our imperfections, *Hot*, full of the shittiest lust. In all of his faceless characterless pullulating broads, in all those cunts which undulate with the movements of eels, in all those clearly described broths of soup and grease and marrow and wine that are all he will give us of them—their cunts are always closer than their faces—in all the indignities of position, the humiliation of situation, and the endless revelations of women as pure artifacts of farce, asses all up in the air, still he screams his barbaric yawp of utter adoration for the power and the glory and the grandeur of the female in the universe, and it is his genius to show us that this power can survive any context or any abuse.

Let us relax a moment on the moralisms of Millett.

They are not only pushovers, they are puppets. Speaking boy to boy about another "fuck," Miller remarks, "I moved her around like one of those legless toys which illustrate the principle of gravity." Total victory is gratuitous insult; the pleasure of humiliating the sexual object appears to be far more intoxicating than sex itself. Miller's protégé, Curley, is an expert at inflicting this sort of punishment, in this instance, on a woman whom both men regard as criminally overambitious, disgracefully unaware she is only cunt:

> "He took pleasure in degrading her. I could scarcely blame him for it, she was such a prim, priggish bitch in her street clothes. You'd swear she didn't own a cunt the way she carried herself in the street. Naturally, when he got her alone, he made her pay for her highfalutin' ways. He went at it cold-bloodedly. 'Fish it out!' he'd say, opening his fly a little. 'Fish it out with your tongue!' . . . once she got the taste of it in her mouth, you could do anything with her. Sometimes he'd stand her on her hands and push her around the room that way, like a wheelbarrow. Or else he'd do it dog fashion, and while she groaned and squirmed he'd nonchalantly light a cigarette and blow the smoke between her legs. Once he played her a dirty trick doing it that way. He had worked her up to such a state that she was beside herself. Anyway, after he had almost polished the ass off her with his

*back-scuttling he pulled out for a second, as though to cool his cock off . . . and shoved a big long carrot up her twat."*

The last sentence was supposed to read: "He pulled out for a second, as though to cool his cock off, and then very slowly and gently he shoved a big long carrot up her twat." Millett obviously had not wished to weaken her indictment by qualifying the force of the shove—that was where she once again lost Miller. His work dances on the line of his dialectic. But Millett hates every evidence of the dialectic. She has a mind like a flatiron, which is to say a totally masculine mind. A hard-hat has more curves in his head. Look how the hideousness of the description as Millett has excerpted it is given other nuances by what immediately follows.

*. . . Very slowly and gently he shoved a big long carrot up her twat. "That, Miss Abercrombie," he said, "is a sort of Doppelgänger to my regular cock," and with that he unhitches himself and yanks up his pants. Cousin Abercrombie was so bewildered by it all that she let out a tremendous fart and out tumbled the carrot. At least, that's how Curley related it to me. He was an outrageous liar, to be sure, and there may not be a grain of truth in the yarn, but there's no denying that he had a flair for such tricks. As for Miss Abercrombie and her high-tone Narragansett ways, well, with a cunt like that one can always imagine the worst.*

A page later, the dialectic has whipped him clear over to a description of the "best fuck" he ever had, and here the statement of the case is pure Henry, for the girl "was a deaf-mute who had lost her memory, and with the loss of memory she had lost her frigidaire, her curling irons, her tweezers and handbag. She was even more naked than a fish . . . and she was even slipperier. . . . It was dubious at times whether I was in her or she in me." He is in heaven. A cornucopia of encomiums inundate us. Never has he stated his case better.

*She just stood there quietly and as I slid my hand up her legs she moved one foot a little to open her crotch a bit more. I don't think I ever put my hand into such a juicy crotch in all my life. It was like paste running down her legs, and if there had been any billboards handy I could have plastered up a dozen or more. After a few moments, just as naturally as a cow lowering its head to graze, she bent over and put it in her mouth. I had my whole four fingers inside her, whipping it up to a froth. Her mouth was stuffed full and the juice pouring down her legs. Not a word out of us, as I say. Just a couple of quiet maniacs working away in the dark like gravediggers. It was a fucking Paradise and I knew it, and I was ready and willing to fuck my brains away if necessary. She was probably the best fuck I ever had. She never once opened her trap—not that night, nor the next night, nor any night. She'd steal down like that in the dark, soon as she smelled me there alone, and plaster her cunt all over me. It was an enormous cunt, too, when I think back on it. A dark, subterranean labyrinth fitted up with divans and cosy corners and rubber teeth and syringas and soft nestles and eiderdown and mulberry leaves. I used to nose in like the solitary worm and bury myself in a little cranny where it was absolutely silent, and so soft and restful that I lay like a dolphin on the oyster banks. A slight twitch and I'd be in the Pullman reading a newspaper or else up an impasse where there were mossy round cobblestones and little wicker gates which opened and shut automatically. Sometimes it was like riding the shoot-the-shoots, a steep plunge and then a spray of tingling sea crabs, the bulrushes swaying feverishly and the gills of tiny fishes lapping against me like harmonica stops. In the immense black grotto there was a silk-and-soap organ playing a predaceous black music. When she pitched herself high, when she turned the juice on full, it made a violaceous purple, a deep mulberry stain like twilight, a ventriloqual twilight such as dwarfs and cretins enjoy when they menstruate. It made me think of cannibals chewing flowers, of Bantus running amuck, of wild unicorns rutting in rhododendron beds. . . . It was one cunt out of a million, a regular Pearl of the Antilles. . . . In the broad Pacific of sex she lay, a gleaming silver reef surrounded with human anemones, human starfish, human madrepores.*

But Henry won't be allowed to rest for long. Squirt-bomb at the ready, Millett is laying for him. Something in the fling of the imagination is odious as a water bug to her.

Throughout the description one not only observes a vulgar opportunistic use of Lawrence's hocus pocus about blanking out in the mind in order to attain "blood consciousness," but one also intuits how both versions of the idea are haunted by a pathological fear of having to deal with another and complete human personality. . . . One is made very aware here that in the author's scheme the male is represented not only by his telepathic instrument, but by mind, whereas the perfect female is a floating metonomy, pure cunt, completely unsullied by human mentality.

But why is Kate now so prim? Doesn't the single permissive sexual standard offer depersonalization via the wallop-and-suck of the orgy? Kate is reminiscent of one of those nice-nellie scourges who used to tyrannize the back pages of *The New York Times Book Review,* yes, it is as if Miller deprives her of the right to have a mind by so splendiferous a description of the cunt, yes, just as any hardworking intellectual in the 1950s was livid at the intimation that some blacks might have more genital orientation than Freud had prescribed for the human lot, so is Millett now properly incensed. Stretched with every adrenaline of overkill, her mind next to rigid with fear that women might have some secret but fundamental accommodation to Miller's lust that brings them into just such absurd positions, she is therefore always missing the point of her case, she is always pushing into that enforced domain of equality where the sexes, she would declaim, "are inherently in everything alike, save reproductive systems, secondary sexual characteristics, orgasmic capacity and genetic and morphological structure. Perhaps the only thing they can uniquely exchange is semen and transudate." Good laboratory assistant Kate. She is a technologist who drains all the swamps only to discover that the ecological balance has been savaged. She is also one of those minds, totalitarian to the core, which go over to hysteria, abuse (and liquidation at the end of the road) whenever they are forced to build their mind on anything more than a single premise. The real case against Miller is not that he is all wrong, and cocks and cunts are no more than biological details on human beings so that we are even unable to distinguish semen from transudate when suffering from a cold, no, the real case is that Miller is right, yet Ibsen's Nora is also right when she says, "I have another duty, just as sacred. . . . My duty to myself. . . . I believe that before everything else I'm a human being—just as much as you are . . . or at any rate, I shall try to become one." What have we not lost in his novels that there will be never a character like Nora to stand against his men? For it is our modern experience that men filled with every appreciation of sex and women's rights encounter women with an equal appreciation, and the war still continues with what new permutations only a novelist can begin to explore, since the novelist is the only philosopher who works with emotions that are at the very edge of the word system, and so is out beyond the scientists, doctors, psychologists, even—if he is good enough—the best of his contemporaries who work at philosophy itself. If it is easy to mock him when, like Miller, he comes close to stumbling off the end of the word system, we know his best and wildest ideas will become the ones most quickly attacked by literary technologists like Millett since such ideas lend themselves to confetti-making in ideological mincers. Miller, a hero twice, to take up writing late and to take it up by writing books he could think no one would ever publish, a writer with the individuality of a giant, was still so lacerated by the loneliness of his midnight concepts that his later works often thin out into subtle parodies of the earlier ones, and he finally hooks his moon-anchor onto what has become for us the same old literary fields of flesh and cunt. The knowledge of our age is different. Those fields are an endless treasure to him, but we have the problem of our contemporary love, and so can only tip our hat, we are looking for an accommodation of the sexes, whereas he calls out for an antagonism—"the eternal battle with woman sharpens our resistance, develops our strength, enlarges the scope of our cultural achievements." Yes, he cries out to us, "the loss of sex polarity is part and parcel of the larger disintegration, the reflex of the soul's death and coincident with the disappearance of great men, great causes, great wars." The ram wandering the ridges has come back as a prophet, and the tablets are in his hands. "Put woman back in her rightful place."

But the men moving silently in all retreat pass the prophet by. It is too late to know if he is right or wrong. The women have breached an enormous hole in the line, and the question is only how far back the men must go before they are ready to establish a front. Confusion is at the crossroads. Will D. H. Lawrence have to be surrendered as well?

*From A Prisoner of Sex (1971)*

# Millett and D. H. Lawrence

Of course, Kate Millett was not without her own kind of political genius in perceiving that any technologizing of the sexes into twin-unit living teams complete with detachable subunits (kids) might yet have to contend with the work of D. H. Lawrence. Not, of course, for any love of children, it would not be until his last book that one of Lawrence's romances would end with the heroine pregnant, tranquil, and fulfilled, no, Lawrence's love affairs were more likely to come in like winds off Wuthering Heights—but never had a male novelist written more intimately about women—heart, contradiction, and soul; never had a novelist loved them more, been so comfortable in the tides of their sentiment, and so ready to see them murdered. His work held, on the consequence, huge fascination for women. Since by the end he was also the sacramental poet of a sacramental act, for he believed nothing human had such significance as the tender majesties of a man and woman fucking with love, he was also the most appalling subversive to the single permissive sexual standard: The orgy, homosexuality, and the inevitable promiscuity attached to a sexual search repelled him, and might yet repel many of the young as they become bored with the similarity of the sexes.

Indeed, which case-hardened guerrilla of Women's Liberation might not shed a private tear at the following passage:

> And if you're in Scotland and I'm in the Midlands, and I can't put my arms round you, and wrap my legs round you, yet I've got something of you. My soul softly flaps in the little pentecost flame with you, like the peace of fucking. We fucked a flame into being. Even the flowers are fucked into being between the sun and the earth. But it's a delicate thing, and takes patience and the long pause.
>
> So I love chastity now, because it is the peace that comes of fucking. I love being chaste now. I love it as snowdrops love the snow. I love this chastity, which is the pause of peace of our fucking, between us now like a snowdrop of forked white fire. And when the real spring comes, when the drawing together comes, then we can fuck the little flame brilliant and yellow . . .

Yes, which stout partisan of Female Liberation would read such words and not go soft for the memory of some bitter bridge of love she had burned behind. Lawrence was dangerous. So delicate and indestructible an enemy to the cause of Liberation that to expunge him one would have to look for Millett herself. If she is more careful with Lawrence than with Miller, acting less like some literary Molotov, if her disrespect for quotation is in this place more guarded, if she even functions as a critic and so gives us a clue to the meaning of Lawrence's life and work, she has become twice adroit at hiding the real evidence. It is crucial to her case that Lawrence be the "counter-revolutionary sexual politician" she terms him, but since women love his work, and remember it, she is obliged to bring in the evidence more or less fairly, and only distort it by small moves, brief elisions in the quotation, the suppression of passing contradictions, in short bring in all the evidence on one side of the case and harangue the jury but a little further. Since she has a great deal of evidence, only a careful defense can overthrow her case. For Lawrence can be hung as a counterrevolutionary sexual politician out of his own words and speeches. There is a plethora of evidence—in his worst books. And in all his books there are unmistakable tendencies toward the absolute domination of women by men, mystical worship of the male will, detestation of democracy. There is a stretch in the middle of his work, out in such unread tracts as *Aaron's Rod* and *Kangaroo*, when the uneasy feeling arrives that perhaps it was just as well Lawrence died when he did, for he could have been the literary adviser to Oswald Mosley about the time Hitler came in, one can even ingest a comprehension of the appeal of fascism to Pound and Wyndham Lewis, for the death of nature lived already in the air of the contract between corporate democracy and technology, and who was then to know that the marriage of fascism and technology would be even worse, would accelerate that death. Still, such fear for the end of Lawrence is superficial. He was perhaps a great writer, certainly flawed, and abominably pedestrian in his language when the ducts of experience burned dry, he was unendurably didactic then, he was a pill and, at his worst, a humorless nag; he is pathetic in all those places he suggests that men should follow the will of a stronger man, a purer man, a man conceivably not unlike himself, for one senses in his petulance and in the spoiled airs of his impatient disdain at what he could not intellectually dominate that he was a mama's boy, spoiled rotten, and could not have commanded two infantrymen to follow him, yet he was still a great writer, for he contained a cauldron of boiling opposites—he was on the one hand a Hitler in a teapot, on the other he was the blessed breast of tender love, he knew what it was to love a woman from her hair to her toes, he lived with all the sensibility of a female burning with tender love—and these incompatibles, enough to break a less extraordinary man, were squared in their difficulty by the fact that he had intellectual ambition sufficient to desire the overthrow of European civilization; his themes were nothing if not immense—in *The Plumed Serpent* he would even look to the founding of a new religion based on the virtues of the phallus and the submission of women to the wisdom of that principle. But he was also the son of a miner, he came from hard practical small-minded people, stock descended conceivably from the Druids, but how many centuries had hammered the reductive wisdom of pounds and pennies into the genes? So a part of Lawrence was like a little tobacconist from the English Midlands who would sniff the smoke of his wildest ideas—notions, we may be certain, that ran completely off the end of anybody's word system—and hack out an irritable cough at the intimate intricate knobby knotty contradictions of his ideas when they were embodied in people. For if we can feel how consumed he was by the dictatorial pressure to ram his sentiments into each idiot throat, he never forgets that he is writing novels, and so his ideas cannot simply triumph, they have to be tried and heated and forged, and finally be beaten into shapelessness against the anvil of his profound British skepticism, which would not buy his ideas, not outright, for even his own characters seem to wear out in them. Kate Leslie, the heroine of *The Plumed Serpent,* a proud sophisticated Irish lady, falls in love with one of the Mexican leaders of a new party, a new faith, a new ritual, gives herself to the new religion, believes in her submission—but not entirely! At the end she is still attached to the ambivalence of the European mind. Lilly, the hero of *Aaron's Rod,* finally preaches "deep fathomless submission to the heroic soul in a greater man" and the greater man is Lilly, but he is a slim small somewhat ridiculous figure, a bigger man for example strikes him in front of his wife and he is reduced to regaining his breath without showing he is hurt, he is a small hard-shelled nut of contradictions, much like Lawrence himself, but the grandeur of the ideas sounds ridiculous in the little cracked shell. Of course, Lawrence was not only trying to sell dictatorial theorems, he was also trying to rid himself of them. We can see by the literary line of his life that he moves from the adoration of his mother in *Sons and Lovers* and from close to literal adoration of the womb in *The Rainbow* to worship of the phallus and the male will in his later books. In fact, Millett can be quoted to good effect, for her criticism is here close to objective, which is to say not totally at odds with the defense:

> *Aaron's Rod, Kangaroo,* and *The Plumed Serpent* are rather neglected novels, and perhaps justly so. They are unquestionably strident, and unpleasant for a number of reasons, principally a rasping protofascist tone, an increasing fondness of force, a personal arrogance, and innumerable racial, class, and religious bigotries. In these novels one sees how terribly Lawrence strained after triumph in the "man's world" of formal politics, war, priestcraft, art and finance. Thinking of *Lady Chatterley* or the early novels, readers often equate Lawrence with the personal life which generally concerns the novelist, the relations of men and women—for whether he played a woman's man or a man's man,

Lawrence was generally doing so before an audience of women, who found it difficult to associate him with the public life of male authority. After *Women in Love,* having solved, or failed to solve, the problem of mastering the female, Lawrence became more ambitious. Yet he never failed to take his sexual politics with him, and with an astonishing consistency of motive, made it the foundation of all his other social and political beliefs.

It is fair analysis as far as it goes, but it fails to underline the heroism of his achievement, which is that he was able finally to leave off his quest for power in the male world and go back to what he started with, go back after every bitterness and frustration to his first knowledge that the physical love of men and women, insofar as it was untainted by civilization, was the salvation of us all, there was no other. And in fact he had never ceased believing that, he had merely lost hope it could be achieved.

Millett's critical misdemeanor is to conceal the pilgrimage, hide the life, cover over that emotional odyssey that took him from adoration of the woman to outright lust for her murder, then took him back to worship her beauty, even her procreative beauty. Millett avoids the sympathy this might arouse in her female readers (which dead lover is more to be cherished after all than the one who returned at the end?), yes, avoids such huge potential sympathy by two simple critical stratagems: She writes about his last book first, which enables her to end her very long chapter on Lawrence with an analysis of his story "The Woman Who Rode Away." Since it may be the most savage of his stories, and concludes with the ritual sacrifice of a white woman by natives, Millett can close on Lawrence with the comment, "Probably it is the perversion of sexuality into slaughter, indeed, the story's very travesty and denial of sexuality, which accounts for its monstrous, even demented air." Not every female reader will remind herself that Lawrence, having purged his blood of murder, would now go on to write *Lady Chatterley.* But then Millett is not interested in the dialectic by which writers deliver their themes to themselves; she is more interested in hiding the process, and so her second way of concealing how much Lawrence has still to tell us about men and women is simply to distort the complexity of his brain into snarling maxims, take him at his worst and make him even worse, take him at his best and bring pinking shears to his context. Like a true species of literary Mafia, Millett works always for points and the shading of points. If she can't steal a full point, she'll cop a half.

Examples abound, but it is necessary to quote Lawrence in some fullness; a defense of his works rests naturally on presenting him in uninterrupted lines, which indeed will be no hardship to read. Besides, the clearest exposure of the malignant literary habits of the prosecutor is to quote her first and thereby give everyone an opportunity to see how little she shows, how much she ignores, in her desire to steal the verdict.

> "You lie there," he orders. She accedes with a "queer obedience"—Lawrence never uses the word female in the novel without prefacing it with the adjectives "weird" or "queer": this is presumably done to persuade the reader that woman is a dim prehistoric creature operating out of primeval impulse. Mellors concedes one kiss on the navel and then gets to business:
> "And he had to come into her at once, to enter the peace on earth of that soft quiescent body. It was the moment of pure peace for him, the entry into the body of a woman. She lay still, in a kind of sleep, always in a kind of sleep. The activity, the orgasm was all his, all his; she could strive for herself no more."

This is the passage from which she has drawn her quotation:

> *"You lie there," he said softly, and he shut the door, so that it was dark, quite dark.*
>
> *With a queer obedience, she lay down on the blanket. Then she felt the soft, groping, helplessly desirous hand touching her body, feeling for her face. The hand stroked her face softly, softly, with infinite soothing and assurance, and at last there was the soft touch of a kiss on her cheek.*
>
> *She lay quite still, in a sort of sleep, in a sort of dream. Then she quivered as she felt his hand groping softly, yet with queer thwarted clumsiness among her clothing. Yet the hand knew, too, how to unclothe her where it wanted. He drew down the thin silk sheath, slowly, carefully, right down and over her feet. Then with a quiver of exquisite pleasure he touched the warm soft body, and touched her navel for a moment in a kiss. And he had to come into her at once, to enter the peace on earth of her soft, quiescent body. It was the moment of pure peace for him, the entry into the body of a woman.*
>
> *She lay still, in a kind of sleep, always in a kind of sleep. The activity, the orgasm was his, all his; she could strive for herself no more. Even the tightness of his arms round her, even the intense movement of his body, and the springing seed in her, was a kind of sleep, from which she did not*

*begin to rouse till he had finished and lay softly panting against her breast.*

It is a modest example, but then it is a modest act and Constance Chatterley is exhausted with the deaths of the world she is carrying within—since they will make other kinds of love later, the prosecutor will have cause enough to be further enraged, but the example can show how the tone of Lawrence's prose is poisoned by the acids of inappropriate comment. "Mellors concedes one kiss on the navel and then gets to business." Indeed! Take off your business suit, Comrade Millett.

But it is hardly the time for a recess. We will want to look at another exhibit. The quoted lines up for indictment are from *Women in Love:*

> Having begun by informing Ursula he will not love her, as he is interested in going beyond love to "something much more impersonal and harder," he goes on to state his terms: "I've seen plenty of women, I'm sick of seeing them. I want a woman I don't see . . . I don't want your good looks, and I don't want your womanly feelings, and I don't want your thoughts nor opinions nor your ideas." The "new" relationship, while posing as an affirmation of the primal unconscious sexual being, to adopt Lawrence's jargon, is in effect a denial of personality in the woman.

Or is it Millett's denial of personality in Lawrence? Witness how our literary commissar will void the strength of Lawrence's style by cutting off our acquaintance with the marrow of his sensibility, the air of his senses. For Lawrence is always alert to the quiet ringing of the ether, the quick retreat of a mood, the awe of the thought about to be said, then left unsaid, then said after all. But his remarks cannot be chopped out of their setting. A bruised apple at the foot of a tree is another reality from a bruised apple in the Frigidaire.

> *There was silence for some moments.*
>
> *"No," he said. "It isn't that. Only—if we are going to make a relationship, even of friendship, there must be something final and irrevocable about it."*
>
> *There was a clang of mistrust and almost anger in his voice. She did not answer. Her heart was too much contracted. She could not have spoken.*

*Seeing she was not going to reply, he continued, almost bitterly, giving himself away:*

*"I can't say it is love I have to offer—and it isn't love I want. It is something much more impersonal and harder—and rarer."*

*There was a silence, out of which she said:*

*"You mean you don't love me?"*

*She suffered furiously, saying that.*

*"Yes, if you like to put it like that. Though perhaps that isn't true. I don't know. At any rate, I don't feel the emotion of love for you—no, and I don't want to. Because it gives out in the last issues . . ."*

How different is all this from "going beyond love to 'something much more impersonal and harder,'" how much in fact we have the feeling they are in love.

*"If there is no love, what is there?" she cried, almost jeering.*

*"Something," he said, looking at her, battling with his soul, with all his might.*

*"What?"*

*He was silent for a long time, unable to be in communication with her while she was in this state of opposition.*

*"There is," he said, in a voice of pure abstraction, "a final me which is stark and impersonal and beyond responsibility. So there is a final you, and it is there I would want to meet you—not in the emotional, loving plane—but there beyond, where there is no speech and no terms of agreement. There we are two stark, unknown beings, two utterly strange creatures, I would want to approach you, and you me. And there could be no obligation, because there is no standard for action there, because no understanding has been reaped from that plane. It is quite inhuman—so there can be no calling to book, in any form whatsoever—because one is outside the pale of all that is accepted, and nothing known applies. One can only follow the impulse, taking that which lies in front, and responsible for nothing, asking for nothing, giving nothing, only each taking according to the primal desire."*

*Ursula listened to this speech, her mind dumb and almost senseless, what he said was so unexpected and so untoward.*

*"It is just purely selfish," she said.*

*"If it is pure, yes. But it isn't selfish at all. Because I don't know what I want of you. I deliver* myself *over to the unknown, in coming to you, I am without reserves or defenses, stripped entirely, into the unknown.*

*Only there needs the pledge between us, that we will both cast off every-*
*thing, cast off ourselves even, and cease to be, so that that which is per-*
*fectly ourselves can take place in us."*

As we shall soon see, Lawrence will go further than this, he will
come to believe that a woman must submit—a most blood-enriching
submission, bet on it—yet in that book where such submission takes
place, in *The Plumed Serpent* where Kate Leslie has her most profound
sex with a man who insists on remaining a stranger and an Indian,
the moral emerges that he wants her by the end, wants Kate Leslie
just so deeply as she desires him. Lawrence's point, which he refines
over and over, is that the deepest messages of sex cannot be heard by
taking a stance on the side of the bank, announcing one is in love,
and then proceeding to fish in the waters of love with a breadbasket
full of ego. No, he is saying again and again, people can win at love
only when they are ready to lose everything they bring to it of ego,
position, or identity—love is more stern than war—and men and
women can survive only if they reach the depths of their own sex
down within themselves. They have to deliver themselves "over to
the unknown." No more existential statement of love exists, for it is a
way of saying we do not know how the love will turn out. What message more odious to the technologist? So Millett will accuse him endlessly of patriarchal male-dominated sex. But the domination of men
over women was only a way station on the line of Lawrence's ideas—
what he started to say early and ended saying late was that sex could
heal, sex was the only nostrum which could heal, all other medicines
were part of the lung-scarring smoke of factories and healed nothing,
were poison, but sex could heal only when one was without "reserves
or defenses." And so men and women received what they deserved of
one another. Since Women's Lib has presented itself with the clear
difficulty of giving modern woman a full hard efficient ego,
Lawrence's ideas could not be more directly in the way. Still, it is
painful to think that, quickly as men are losing any sense of fair play,
women—if Millett can model for her sex—are utterly without it.
Maybe Millett is not so much Molotov as Vishinsky. What a foul exhibit must now be displayed!

Passive as she is, Connie fares better than the heroine of *The*
*Plumed Serpent,* from whom Lawrentian man, Don Cipriano, deliberately withdraws as she nears orgasm, in a calculated and
sadistic denial of her pleasure:

*"By a swift dark instinct, Cipriano drew away from this in her. When, in their love, it came back on her, the seething electric female ecstasy, which knows such spasms of delirium, he recoiled from her. . . . By a dark and powerful instinct he drew away from her as soon as this desire rose again in her, for the white ecstasy of frictional satisfaction, the throes of Aphrodite of the foam. She could see that to him, it was repulsive. He just removed himself, dark and unchangeable, away from her."*

The passage restored will be of interest to any jury looking for further evidence on the virtues or deterrents of the clitoral come:

*She realised, almost with wonder, the death in her of the Aphrodite of the foam: the seething, frictional, ecstatic Aphrodite. By a swift dark instinct, Cipriano drew away from this in her. When, in their love, it came back on her, the seething electric female ecstasy, which knows such spasms of delirium, he recoiled from her. It was what she used to call her "satisfaction." She had loved Joachim for this, that again, and again, and again he could give her this orgiastic "satisfaction," in spasms that made her cry aloud.*

*But Cipriano would not. By a dark and powerful instinct he drew away from her as soon as this desire rose again in her, for the white ecstasy of frictional satisfaction, the throes of Aphrodite of the foam. She could see that to him, it was repulsive. He just removed himself, dark and unchangeable, away from her.*

*And she, as she lay, would realise the worthlessness of this foam-effervescence, its strange externality to her. It seemed to come upon her from without, not from within. And succeeding the first moment of disappointment, when this sort of "satisfaction" was denied her, came the knowledge that she did not really want it, that it was really nauseous to her.*

*And he, in his dark, hot silence, would bring her back to the new, soft, heavy, hot flow, when she was like a fountain gushing noiseless and with urgent softness from the volcanic deeps. Then she was open to him soft and hot, yet gushing with a noiseless soft power. And there was no such thing as conscious "satisfaction." What happened was dark and untellable. So different from the friction which flares out in circles of phosphorescent ecstasy, to the last wild spasm which utters the involuntary cry, like a death-cry, the final love-cry. This she had known, and known to the end, with Joachim. And now this too was removed from her. What she had with Cipriano was curiously beyond her knowing: so deep and hot and flowing, as it were subterranean. She had to yield before it. She could not grip it into one final spasm of white ecstasy which was like sheer knowing.*

*And as it was in the love-act, so it was with him. She could not* know *him. When she tried to know him, something went slack in her, and she had to leave off. She had to let be. She had to leave him, dark and hot and potent, along with the things that* are, *but are not known. The presence. And the stranger. This he was always to her.*

Yes, sex was the presence of grace and the introduction of the stranger into oneself. That was the only medicine for the lividities of the will. So Lawrence would preach, but he was a man in torture. If Millett had wished to get around Lawrence in the easiest way for the advance of the Liberation, she would have done better to have built a monument to him, and a bridge over his work, rather than making the mean calculation she could bury him by meretricious quotation. For Lawrence is an inspiration, but few can do more than respect him on the fly (the way a Soviet official might duck into an Orthodox church to smell the incense). The world has been technologized and technologized twice again in the forty years since his death, the citizens are technologized as well. Who will go looking for the "new, soft, heavy, hot flow" or the "urgent softness from the volcanic deeps" when the air of cities smells of lava and the mood of the streets is like the bowels turned inside out? What he was asking for had been too hard for him, it is more than hard for us; his life was, yes, a torture, and we draw back in fear, for we would not know how to try to burn by such a light.

Yet, he was a man more beautiful perhaps than we can guess, and it is worth the attempt to try to perceive the logic of his life, for he illumines the passion to be masculine as no other writer, he reminds us of the beauty of desiring to be a man, for he was not much of a man himself, a son despised by his father, beloved of his mother, a boy and young man and prematurely aging writer with the soul of a beautiful woman. It is not only that no other man writes so well about women, but indeed is there a woman who can? Useless for Millett to answer that here is a case of one man commending another man for his ability to understand women—what a vain and pompous assumption, she will hasten to jeer, but such words will be the ground meat of a dull cow. The confidence is that some of Lawrence's passages have a ring—perhaps it is an echo of that great bell which may toll whenever the literary miracle occurs and a writer sets down words to resonate with that sense of peace and proportion it is tempting to call truth. Yet whoever believes that such a leap is not possible across the gap, that a man cannot write of a woman's soul, or a white man of a black man, does not believe in literature itself. So, yes, Lawrence understood women as they had never been understood before, understood them with all the tortured fever of a man who had the soul of a beautiful, imperious, and passionate woman, yet he was locked into the body of a middling male physique, not physically strong, of reasonable good looks, a pleasant to somewhat seedy-looking man, no stud. What a nightmare to balance that soul! to take the man in himself, locked from youth into every need for profound female companionship, a man almost wholly oriented toward the company of women, and attempt to go out into the world of men, indeed even dominate the world of men so that he might find balance. For his mind was possessed of that intolerable masculine pressure to command which develops in sons outrageously beloved by their mothers—to be the equal of a woman at twelve or six or any early age that reaches equilibrium between the will of the son and the will of the mother, strong love to strong love, is all but to guarantee the making of a future tyrant, for the sense of where to find one's inner health has been generated by the early years of that equilibrium—its substitute will not be easy to create in maturity. What can then be large enough to serve as proper balance to a man who was equal to a strong woman in emotional confidence at the age of eight? Hitlers develop out of such balance derived from imbalance, and great generals and great novelists (for what is a novelist but a general who sends his troops across fields of paper?).

So we must conceive then of Lawrence arrogant with mother love and therefore possessed of a mind that did not believe any man on earth had a mind more important than his own. What a responsibility then to bring his message to the world, unique message that might yet save the world! We must conceive of that ego equal already to the will of a strong woman while he was still a child—what long steps had it taken since within the skull! He needed an extraordinary woman for a mate, and he had the luck to find his Frieda. She was an aristocrat and he was a miner's son, she was large and beautiful, she was passionate, and he stole her away from her husband and children—they could set out together to win the world and educate it into ways to live, do that, do all of that out of the exuberance of finding one another.

But she was a strong woman, she was individual, she loved him but she did not worship him. She was independent. If he had been a stronger man, he could perhaps have enjoyed such personal force, but he had become a man by an act of will, he was bone and blood of the classic family stuff out of which homosexuals are made, he had lifted himself out of his natural destiny, which was probably to have the sexual life of a woman, had diverted the virility of his brain down into some indispensable minimum of phallic force—no wonder he worshiped the phallus, he above all men knew what an achievement was its rise from the root, its assertion to stand proud on a delicate base. His mother had adored him. Since his first sense of himself as a male had been in the tender air of her total concern—now, and always, his strength would depend upon just such outsize admiration. Dominance over women was not tyranny to him but equality, for dominance was the indispensable elevator which would raise his phallus to that height from which it might seek transcendence. And sexual transcendence, some ecstasy where he could lose his ego for a moment, and his sense of self and his will, was life to him—he could not live without sexual transcendence. If he had had an outrageously unequal development— all fury to be a man and all the senses of a woman—there was a direct price to pay: He was not healthy. His lungs were poor, and he lived with the knowledge that he would likely have an early death. Each time he failed to reach a woman, each time he failed particularly to reach his own woman, he was dying a little. It is hopeless to read his books and try to understand the quirky changeable fury-ridden relationships of his men and women without comprehending that Lawrence saw every serious love affair as fundamental do-or-die: He knew he literally died a little more each time he missed transcendence in the act. It was why he saw lust as hopeless. Lust was meaningless fucking and that was the privilege of the healthy. He was ill, and his wife was literally killing him each time she failed to worship his most proud and delicate cock. Which may be why he invariably wrote on the edge of cliché—we speak in simples as experience approaches the enormous, and Lawrence lived with the monumental gloom that his death was already in him, and sex—some transcendental variety of sex—was his only hope, and his wife was too robust to recognize such tragic facts.

By the time of writing *Women in Love*, his view of women would not be far from the sinister. One of the two heroines would succeed in driving her man to his death. His rage against the will of women turns immense, and his bile explodes on the human race, or is it the majority of the races?—these are the years when he will have a character in *Aaron's Rod*, Lilly, his mouthpiece, say:

> *I can't do with folk who teem by the billion, like the Chinese and Japs and Orientals altogether. Only vermin teem by the billion. Higher types breed*

*slower. I would have loved the Aztecs and the Red Indians. I know they hold the element in life which I am looking for—they had living pride. Not like the flea-bitten Asiatics. Even niggers are better than Asiatics, though they are wallowers. The American races—and the South Sea Islanders—the Marquesans, the Maori blood. That was true blood. It wasn't frightened. All the rest are craven . . .*

It is the spleen of a man whose organs are rotting in parts and so, owner of a world-ego, he will see the world rotting in parts.

These are the years when he flirts with homosexuality but is secretly, we may assume, obsessed with it. For he is still in need of that restorative sex he can no longer find, and since his psyche was originally shaped to be homosexual, homosexuality could yet be his peace. Except it could not, not likely, for his mind could hardly give up the lust to dominate. Homosexuality becomes a double irony—he must now seek to dominate men physically more powerful than himself. The paradoxes of this position result in the book *Aaron's Rod*, which is about a male love affair (which never quite takes place) between a big man and a little man. The little man does the housework, plays nursemaid to the big man when he is ill, and ends by dominating him, enough to offer the last speech in the book.

> *All men say, they want a leader. Then let them in their souls* submit *to some greater soul than theirs . . . You, Aaron, you too have the need to submit. You, too, have the need livingly to yield to a more heroic soul, to give yourself. You know you have [but] . . . perhaps you'd rather die than yield. And so, die you must. It is your affair.*

He has separated the theme from himself and reversed the roles, but he will die rather than yield, even though earlier in the book he was ready to demonstrate that platonic homosexuality saves. It is the clear suggestion that Aaron recovers only because Lilly anoints his naked body, lays on hands after doctors and medicines had failed.

> *Quickly he uncovered the blond lower body of his patient, and began to rub the abdomen with oil, using a slow, rhythmic, circulating motion, a sort of massage. For a long time he rubbed finely and steadily, then went over the whole of the lower body, mindless, as if in a sort of incantation. He rubbed every speck of the man's lower body—the abdomen, the buttocks, the thighs and knees, down to his feet, rubbed it all warm and glowing with camphorated oil, every bit of it, chafing the toes swiftly, till he was almost ex-*

*hausted. Then Aaron was covered up again, and Lilly sat down in fatigue to look at his patient.*

*He saw a change. The spark had come back into the sick eyes, and the faint trace of a smile, faintly luminous, into the face. Aaron was regaining himself. But Lilly said nothing. He watched his patient fall into a proper sleep.*

Another of his heroes, Birkin, weeps in strangled tones before the coffin of Gerald. It is an earlier period in Lawrence's years of homosexual temptation; the pain is sharper, the passion is stronger. "He should have loved me," he said. "I offered him." And his wife is repelled, "recoiled aghast from him as he sat . . . making a strange, horrible sound of tears." They are the sickly sounds of a man who feels ready to die in some part of himself because the other man would never yield.

But homosexuality would have been the abdication of Lawrence as a philosopher-king. Conceive how he must have struggled against it! In all those middle years he moves slowly from the man who is sickened because the other did not yield to the man who will die because he himself will not yield. But he is bitter, and with a rage that could burn half the world. It is burning his lungs.

Then it is too late. He is into his last years. He is into the five last years of his dying. He has been a victim of love, and will die for lack of the full depth of a woman's love for him—what a near to infinite love he had needed. So he has never gotten to that place where he could deliver himself to the unknown, be "without reserves or defenses . . . cast off everything . . . and cease to be, so that that which is perfectly ourselves can take place in us," no, he was never able to go that far. By the time he began *Lady Chatterley,* he must have known the fight was done; he had never been able to break out of the trap of his lungs, nor out of the cage of his fashioning. He had burned too many holes in too many organs trying to reach into more manhood than the course of his nerves could carry, he was done; but he was a lover, he wrote *Lady Chatterley,* he forgave, he wrote his way a little further toward death, and sang of the wonders of creation and the glory of men and women in the rut and lovely of a loving fuck.

*"When a woman gets absolutely possessed by her own will, her own will set against everything, then it's fearful, and she should be shot at last."*

*"And shouldn't men be shot at last, if they get possessed by their own will?"*

*"Ay!—the same!"*

The remark is muttered, the gamekeeper rushes on immediately to talk of other matters, but it has been made, Lawrence has closed the circle, the man and the woman are joined, separate and joined.

From *A Prisoner of Sex (1971)*

# Brooding over Abortion

During the Democratic Convention in Miami in the summer of 1972, there had been a Women's Caucus, and behind the speaker's podium a large hand-lettered banner declaring WOMEN POWER was attached to the curtain. Viewed from his angle off to the side, Aquarius first read it as OMEN POWER, a tribute to witchcraft in the new political cosmos.

When McGovern addressed OMEN POWER, an incident occurred. The speaker who introduced him said that one reason they were able to attend the convention in large numbers was because of McGovern's efforts to open the party to women.

McGovern rose, and said with modest humor, "The credit for that must go to Adam."

He was booed. "Should I have said Adam and Eve?" asked McGovern. But the laughter was tight-lipped. A humorless friction was in the air. Hisses continued. This cold reception was due warning. Not since militant Blacks arrived on the American scene had a political group appeared who were as threatening. But there had been a legitimacy to the ugliest Black demands, obviously still was—every injustice against a Black man poisoned the root of America's existence. Whereas every injustice against a lady in Women's Liberation gave every promise of poisoning her husband's existence. But just this was the intolerable disproportion of Women's Liberation—they pretended to a suffering as profound as the Blacks, when their anguish came out of nothing more intolerable than the intolerable pointlessness of middle-class life. (Which of course was as intolerable for the men.) So Women's Liberation might be a totalitarian movement, yes, more totalitarian than not was its style. It appeared to speak for a volcano of legitimate furies, but its rage was more likely to derive from boundless seas of monotony.

No surprise, then, if they booed McGovern for giving the credit

to Eve. She was a comic book creation of the male chauvinist pig Jehovah; Eve was acquiescent nature with tits to pop for *Playboy* and a
sea-smelling cunt. Whereas the pride of Women's Liberation was that
cunts had the right to smell as bad as any man's half-dead cigar. There
was the total twentieth-century proposition! Of course, Aquarius' real
opinion was that at the bottom of Women's Liberation was all the explosive of alienated will, a will now so detached from any of the old female functions, and hence so autocratic, that insanity, cancer, or
suicidal collapse might have to be the penalty if the will did not acquire huge social power. Totalitarian power. What a fund of scientific
jargon was their ideology. They spoke of the nonexistence of the vaginal orgasm (which was a way of certifying that they had never had
one), since it was indeed most likely that the vaginal orgasm involved
some temporary surrender of the will to something else, whether
man, god, nature, or some portion of the cosmos termed "It." So the
best operative definition of a female in Women's Liberation might be
that she had so little notion of vaginal orgasm she was convinced it did
not exist and thereby was fortified in her contention that the clitoris
was the last station on the line. But the liberator was wrong. Suicide
was the terminal station. For people of outrageous and buried will, the
failure to attain power is suicide. The liberator is first a woman of
murderous will, but then many a suicide is an absolute murderer who
is finally reduced to the absolute humiliation of killing himself.

Now, if this was his own prejudice (all because the women booed
McGovern for invoking Eve), still one had to recognize that the best
was usually bent like a line to the worst. So Aquarius had to contend
more than once with a recurring recognition that Women's Liberation
had given birth to some revolutionary ideas that he had to respect:
The first was their view on abortion. If he had supported the legal
right to abortion for as long as he could remember, even took an unadmitted intellectual pleasure in the way the problem buttressed his
political philosophy as a left conservative, it was because he found
himself in favor of abortion but opposed to contraception; even, by his
logic, more opposed to the pill than the pharmacological reek of the
diaphragm. The latter offered, at least, a choice each night, whereas
the pill removed the dignity of such choice, and so invaded the unde-
clared rights of the fuck whose romantic imperative is to prevail—
against all odds! Something had to be lost when there was no last
possibility for lovers to declare, "This fuck is becoming apocalyptic—
why else reach in, remove the plug, and try to have a child?" Yes,
upon such remote and unendurably sentimental possibilities did any
larger dignity of a fuck depend, for the act of love which discharged

into chemical fences of the pill bore the same relation to capital punishment as the old California gas chamber, whereas the apocalyptic fuck owed a little at least to the early Christian who survived the lions.

Of course, abortion, in its turn, was a classical curb against excesses of the romantic spirit. Embryos extinguished by abortion were more likely to be the product of extraordinary fucks than the legal infant who saw the first light in a hospital—all too often embryos who were to be aborted had been conceived in the first place by too many good things happening not to conceive them. Since it is hard to imagine an optimistic view of human nature which would not assume that those who are born out of apocalyptic fucks are more likely to be rich in potential than those conceived from a dribble, abortion is tragic. (In clear opposition, it is exactly the logical premise of the technological society that artificial insemination is the perfect equal of any great fuck, so much so that readers can recognize themselves as advocates of a technological society if they believe such a proposition.)

Seen by this perspective, there was the real possibility then that abortion killed off more than an average proportion of superb babies: If so, advocates of the Right To Live had a powerful argument. Aquarius, nonetheless, would remain in favor of abortion; he thought the argument had only been raised to a higher level. For if at its most tragic abortion is the decision to kill the memory of an extraordinary night, and so can be cruel and unendurable, close on occasion to creating insanity in the woman, still abortion is the objective correlative of sanity. Even in the abysmal condition of much love lost, it always speaks, it says: "My nature is divided between the maximum of my romantic moments and the minimum of my daily self-calculation, too divided to permit this child to live. Finally I prefer to be loyal to my working habits rather than to the recollection of magic." Abortion is therefore an act of self-recognition (which is a step to sanity) even as the decision not to have an abortion is another kind of sanity, which states, "I am committed to the best moments I have known and take my truth from that." (Which is why the pill like all other technological concepts is an insulation against sanity, for it inhibits the possibility of those confrontations which might reveal a woman to herself.)

The real argument to be presented then to advocates of the Right To Live is that if a woman had the ability to begin an extraordinary conception, she had also the right to terminate it. Who could be certain that a more virulent pollution was not given to existence every time a child was born with remarkable potential and failed to fulfill it than when a soul of such potential was murdered in the womb? Nobody had a deeper sense of what could be provided for a future child than the woman who carried it. If she knew she was not ready to devote herself to such a creation, then why not assume she was in her right to deny the life? For who could ever calculate the violation left on life by the loveless development of souls who had been conceived in love? So he thought abortion of even the most apocalyptic fuck was still the measure of a woman's right. Therefore, when it came to the question of abortion for conceptions that had never been wanted (creations emerging out of such resolute mediocrity of impulse as to shatter every romantic idea that conception was a serious product of human state), well then Aquarius could find no argument against abortion at all, not when the world was in danger of being overpopulated with a new wad who promised to be as uninteresting as the mass architecture that would house them, no, better to let abortion have its legal status and become still another social hypocrisy that it was not murder even if, indeed, it was.

The women of the liberation had come up, however, with an idea that went further than his own, and he admired it. Abortion legislation would of course be equal to giving women a new right to control what went on within their bodies. The extension of that principle was wondrous! It might give patients the right to die in peace when doctors were determined to extend, stupefy, and therefore shift their last meditations before death. It might even open the idea that soldiers had first rights over their own bodies and need not go out on patrol if in their opinion there was an unreasonable or foolish chance that they might die. That was equivalent to saying soldiers could demand the right to military actions in which their death would not be in vain, an altogether stimulating idea, for in nations of one hundred million men would there then be ten thousand willing to die in an army? What a fine inhibition upon the power of mammoth countries to wage mammoth war if this became a principle of the world, which of course it would (just so soon as the Age of Aquarius arrived).

So one did not quit the thought in a hurry.

From *St. George and the Godfather* (1972)

# Togetherness

My flesh must smell like an old tire
my sex is bitter and gone
my days are leafless and all sleep
   said the housewife
   going to the specialist
one knows what kind

but in the waiting room
she was racked by a plague
from the pots of the American
     miasma—our magazines,
     and so lady murmured
       too quietly
even for her mind to hear:

Reader's Digest, please save *your* soul
and leave mine free to contemplate
eternity which must be more
    than I glimpse for myself now
    an endless promenade
across a field of baked old beans
    a cataract of dishwater
    regurgitated by the memory
of champagne I never drank
    and kings I never kissed

From *Death for the Ladies (and Other Disasters)* (1962)

# 1971 THE CAVETT SHOW WITH GORE VIDAL AND JANET FLANNER

From a letter to *Women's Wear Daily:*

Sirs:

It has come to my attention that Gore Vidal has been speaking in your pages of my hatred of women. Let me present the following items.

| | | |
|---|---|---|
| Number of times married: | Mailer 5 | Vidal 0 |
| Number of children: | Mailer 7 | Vidal 0 |
| Number of daughters: | Mailer 5 | Vidal 0 |

These statistics of course prove nothing unless it is to suggest that the reason Vidal may have married no lady and fathered no child is due perhaps to his love of women and his reluctance therefore to injure their tender flesh with his sharp tongue.

Yours sincerely,
Norman Mailer

Until this letter, Vidal and Mailer had managed to keep a public peace for years. They had each decided long ago there were more profitable wars in the literary world, and so maintained the professional pact not to speak ill of each other for too little.

Probably this peace had exacted its small price. It is difficult for certain authors not to say terrible and/or accurate things about each other in print. Mailer might hear occasionally of a nasty remark Vidal had made in private, but ignored it on the assumption that Gore, tuning up for a little writing, was once again confusing malice for precision.

Still, Mailer knew his own career had become too popular for the pact to continue. Sometime after *The Armies of the Night* won a couple of prizes, Vidal began to sour in public. Condescending and somewhat righteous references to Mailer began to appear in Vidal's interviews. That was a clue to the temper of the time. Vidal was one literary politician with an impeccable nose for ripe liberal issues, and he was now rushing into the most useful denunciations, politically speaking, against machismo, and was quick to attach to this theme the-hatred-of-Norman-Mailer-for-women as if that were a well-established fact known to most of the citizenry.

Since Mailer was fond of repeating that there were four stages to comprehending a woman's character, and you could not claim to know her until you had passed through the four, that is, living together, being married, having children, and going through divorce, he thought (as we can see by his letter to *Women's Wear Daily*) that it was kind of gross of Gore to declare that Mailer hated women when (to be downright crass about it) it was not Vidal, dig! who had spent his life in the collective arms of the powerhouse.

Of course, in compensation, Gore had taken up a seat in the power of print. If people saw something in a magazine, they liked to believe it. That much, Vidal knew. Stupid people! So, some time after his letter to *Woman's Wear Daily,* Mailer picked up *The New York Review of Books* one summer day and read a review by Vidal of a book by an author named Eva Figes in which the young-old critic stopped long enough to say, "There has been from Henry Miller to Norman Mailer to Charles Manson a logical progression. The Miller-Mailer-Manson man, or M3 for short, has been conditioned to think of women as, at best, breeders of sons, at worst, objects to be poked, humiliated, killed. . . ." Vidal, going on from here to speak of M3 as if the case were made—well, in truth, even as Mailer knew that Vidal was looking for just such a result, just so did something blow in his brain.

"Why," asked Mailer in his mind of Vidal, "didn't you have the simple literary decency to say, 'This literary progression, extreme as it may sound at first, will engage my best efforts to show that there are startling and frightening similarities between Manson and Miller and Mailer'?"

Instead, this arrogance! Vidal, with his insensitivity to nuance, would not even make a suitable valet for Henry Miller.

And then, there was himself! He had not been writing for thirty years to be called M3. Mailer could hardly wait to catch up with Gore Vidal.

Yet the opportunity, when it came, did not give good anticipation. Indeed, he hardly knew whether the meeting would take place. He had been invited to appear on Cavett, then he heard Vidal had also been invited, then was told Vidal had dropped off the show. Finally he was informed Vidal was back again. It seemed Cavett would now have one more guest: Janet Flanner. The assistant producer who offered this piece of news said she was formidable.

Mailer had never met Janet Flanner but was used to seeing her pen name, Genêt, in *The New Yorker*. She had been doing a column on Paris for as long as he could remember (for decades it seemed before the real Genet came along), a firm gossipy *feuilleton*. It is the kind of writing whose merit is not easy to evaluate unless you know as much about the subject as the author; ergo, he had been less impressed with Janet Flanner's literary abilities than by her power to keep a job for a lifetime.

"I assume she's Gore's friend," Mailer said.

"It's more like he's her doll," replied the assistant producer.

"Thank you very much," said Mailer.

It did not bother him. Formidable people were often not formidable under video. Indeed, there was never a reason any longer to be bothered with what was awaiting you. By just so much had Mailer's opinion of television's importance changed. By now, he saw no point in being splendid on a TV show—it did not contribute to the sort of meaningful career where every step was on the staircase, in fact one rarely had an idea of when one was good and when terrible. Mailer had appeared on shows where he felt splendid and full of energy, yet looked uncomfortable to himself, even agitated, when he watched it afterward; conversely, he had come into many a studio feeling lifeless and later looked a model of cool deportment. The secret on TV, if there was a secret, was not to do too much.

Yet it could never be as simple as that. Sitting next to Johnny Carson, for example, was like setting up camp next to an ant-hill. Carson never stopped fidgeting. None of his nervousness, however, passed through the tube. Finally, one was at the mercy, Mailer expected, of this as yet undiscovered psycho-electronic valve that filtered vices out of certain people only to distort enthusiasm into the appearance of hysteria for others.

Of course, if you could not control how you would appear, if it was up to the valve, then there was no point to getting charged-up for a show. Mailer had come to believe in the old Hindu saw: Do not spend time worrying about matters you cannot affect.

So he made other appearances that day, other radio or TV—he could no longer remember—he may have been making some kind of effort on *The Prisoner of Sex*—was it for the hardcover or the paperback? and had, in any case, done a show already, and gone to a cocktail party where he enjoyed three or four drinks to the hilt. Mailer had the operative definition of *to the hilt:* It was the state where a carelessly lit match sent you up in flames.

When he arrived at the studio, they rushed him to makeup. Vidal had been supposed to go on first, but hadn't arrived. Would Mailer object to taking his place? He had hardly given his assent before he was informed that Vidal had arrived after all. Would he now mind if Mr. Vidal went on as originally planned? Since Mailer had formed the little vice, when appearing on Cavett, of comporting himself as the star, he could not pretend to happiness at finding himself on the shuttle. Still, he kept his mouth shut. He did not wish to jostle his liquor.

At this moment, alone in the Green Room, he felt a tender and caressing hand on the back of his neck. It was Vidal. Vidal had never touched him before, but now had the tender smile of a man who might be ready to claim that it hardly matters, old sport, what we say about each other—it's just pleasant to see an old friend.

Mailer answered with an open-handed tap across the cheek. It was not a slap, neither was it a punch, just a stiff tap.

To his amazement, Vidal slapped him back.

Norman smiled. He leaned forward and looked pleasantly at Gore. He put his hand to the back of Gore's neck. Then he butted him hard in the head.

Vidal asked him if he was crazy.

"Shut up," said Mailer.

Vidal now declared that Mailer was absolutely mad and *violent!*

"I'll see you on the show," Mailer replied quietly.

He was, after Vidal left (and that was quickly enough), obliged to pace about. Other people came into the Green Room, saw him, and went away. It was obvious; he did not feel like speaking.

The show began. Cavett did his monologue, and it was a good one. "A lot of critics knock television. They have a kind of snobbish attitude towards TV and they think it lacks culture," he said with a smile. He had the only smile that came through the valves of video looking wicked and angelic at once.

"Tonight," continued Cavett, "I have three people on who are important in writing; they've done other things too, but they're all well-known writers. Just to prove to them that television has figured in the thoughts and writings of people of some stature among the literary profession, I asked my research department to come up with a few things that have been written about this program from some prominent figures. In a couple of cases I have a tendency to do it in the voice of the well-known person. This is from an unpublished work of William F. Buckley, Jr., entitled, 'A Felicitous Discourse on Epistemological Incunabula,' subtitled, 'God: The Man and The Myth.' " The audience applauded his smile with laughter. "The quote is: 'One of the less onerous duties incumbent upon a quondam political journalist is the occasional appearance on sundry quotidian chat programs that proliferate these days like Liberals at a hundred dollar a plate dinner for the poor. Not the least in stature, though clearly the least in stature actually, is a jovial dwarf named Cavett,' "—they roared—" 'who fortnightly forays into—or nightly actually—all fields of erudition and these forays are unblemished by the slightest knowledge of any of them.' That's old Bill." There was laughter.

"Here," Cavett went on, "is a paragraph by women's liberationist Kate Millett entitled 'Little Pig, Big Mouth.' " (Laughter) " 'Let's look at the facts. In the past year, sexist talk-show host Dick Cavett has welcomed several hundred guests on his show. Why have these not included one woman Supreme Court justice, one woman admiral, one woman pro-football player,' "—he stopped for the laughter—" 'one woman-father, husband, king or rapist? I'll tell you, sisters. Because Mr. Cavett, like all arrogant, ignorant, hypocritical, selfserving, pompous, rotten male chauvinist pigs, is simply . . .' and then she goes on to become slightly insulting." The audience adored him. "I don't," said Cavett with his finest smile, "want to read that part to you."

A question period with the audience followed, and he was asked "Do you dye your hair?"

"No," Cavett replied, "I tint my body a little to set it off."

Vidal now came out, and was as sluggish as a club-fighter who is looking for his mother.

VIDAL: You're looking very well. Do you tint your body? (*laughter*)
CAVETT: Funny, that was going to be my first question to you.
VIDAL: That was it exactly, yeah.

CAVETT: You heard all that?

VIDAL: I was overhearing the audience, yeah.

CAVETT: The audience was giving me a bit of time there, as we say in America.

VIDAL: As you say in America. Well . . . love it or leave it.

Vidal, however, was not a professional for too little. After the commercial, he began to rally; indeed Mailer was finally obliged to admire how Gore was able (wonder of wonders) to recover from the head-butting. Having been taught this informal martial art by a retired black Light-Heavyweight named John Bates, who worked for a spell in the late Fifties as a bouncer in the Cafe Riviera on Sheridan Square—Bates' head felt like a cannonball!—Mailer knew the aftermath; nausea, and an ongoing vacuum in the brain.

Still, Gore was only showing a few bad effects. Of course, his head had been somewhat harder than expected—writers' heads tended to be more rock-like, for example, than actors', who suffered disproportionately from even a tap: Head-butting may be ultimately a question of how heavy an identity (authentic or false) one is able to support— but, even so! Mailer knew how hard he had hit him. (Between half- and three-quarter throttle.) Of course, Gore had given his television routines on so many shows that he could probably recite the same lines, with the same wit, same timing, and same turn of delivery, under sodium pentothal. Moreover, Vidal was not one to forget an effective remark—he never used a new thought so long as the old one could still seem new; it was obvious he had no respect for Mailer's long-held belief that repetition kills the soul. On the contrary, if such a law were in force, Gore would decide it was best not to have a soul. The soul was most famous, after all, for getting in your way—this much cynicism had Vidal absorbed from world literature!

Therefore, the only evidence, at present, that young Gore had passed through a contretemps in the Green Room—that is, had his head smashed—was his gesture, repeated somewhat frequently, of bringing up several fingertips to gently massage the skin of his forehead, same fingers indeed that had so recently offered to caress the back of Mailer's stiff neck. Other than that, Mr. Vidal was getting around to presenting a first-rate picture of himself.

He was speaking of his friendship with Mrs. Roosevelt. He and she had interests in common, including the protection of the Hudson River from further pollution. For Cavett's liberal audience, there was no name, Mailer decided gloomily, more calculated than Eleanor

Roosevelt's to give the wholly satisfactory sensation of having one's buttocks stroked with velvet. To be given intimate glimpses of the lady! Even though he sneered at such crowd-pleasing tactics, Mailer was as taken as anyone in the audience. His only contact, after all, with Mrs. Roosevelt had been at long distance in the Fifties, when he saw her printed reaction to a statement he had made in Lyle Stuart's *Exposé* that white Southerners did not wish to give the Negro his equality because—he had been quick to explain—Southern Whites felt they had their social superiority and Negroes had their sexual superiority, and that—thought Southern Whites—was fair enough. Eleanor Roosevelt's short statement read: "I think Mr. Mailer's remarks are horrible and unnecessary."

Vidal's life with Mrs. Roosevelt transpired, however, on less troubled waters. He spoke of their first meeting with tender éclat. "I drove down," he told Cavett's audience, "to Val-Kill Cottage, where she lived. It was a summer afternoon. The place was absolutely empty. Front door was open, walked in, nobody there. 'Anybody home?' She was a little deaf. No answer. So I went to the—the nearest door was half open, so I opened the door and there to my horror was Eleanor Roosevelt—very tall woman—standing in front of the toilet bowl. And I thought, 'Oh, my God.' And she gave a terrible cry, and then she turned around and she said, 'Well, I suppose you'd better know everything.' And she had some gladiolas in the toilet bowl, which she was arranging. She said, 'It keeps them fresh.'" The audience laughed happily. "So we began with perfect intimacy, Mrs. Roosevelt and I. I knew everything from then on that was in the bathroom."

Clever Vidal! Out of the twenty-eight routines suitable for an appearance on Cavett, Gore had chosen to disclose Eleanor Roosevelt's watercloset. How could the audience not believe they had divine relations?

VIDAL: (*ruminatively*) What I liked about her was there was nothing human that she felt human ingenuity wouldn't sense and right action could fix it, and she really believed that, and many people found her very boring because of it. I found her very inspiring. Gosh, I've been with her four in the morning in Schenectady trying to get a bus someplace when we were out campaigning, and on and on she would go, this old woman, quite sick, because she felt it was worth doing. And what's gone wrong in the world now, I think a great many of us feel that things are now irreversible, you know. They're never going to make the rivers clear and clean again, they're not going to save the land, they're not going to do

anything about Detroit, the American empire is not going to liquidate itself. And there's beginning a sense of despair. You cannot
turn it back, and Eleanor was the last person really who said,
"Oh, we can, and we must."

Janet Flanner now came on. She was not a large woman, but she
was old and grand and had an air of giving short measure to fools. By
the manner in which she sat down next to Vidal and laid her white-
gloved hand on his arm, it was also apparent that she was authorita-
tively fond of him.

Cavett began to say that the last time he had had Janet Flanner
on his program, she had told of finding Ernest Hemingway in her
bathtub.

"He was stealing my warm water, that's what he was doing. Sheer
theft is what I called it," said Janet Flanner.

She had a nice crust to her personality. It was like the crust on
good bread that lets out agreeable sounds when a piece is broken off
for you. The audience was tittering to show their approval. It hardly
mattered how much she said since she could give you a lesson in deportment by the clearing of her throat.

Cavett asked: "Can you bury once and for all the tired old myth
of the Frenchman being the sexual marvelous athlete of all time? . . ."
And she replied: "Well, I've only buried a few, so I can't tell about all
the rest of them." In the midst of the applause, it was now obvious
that Cavett, in his turn, was certainly fond of her. His manner seemed
to suggest that the only reason he had ever wanted to have his own
show in the first place was for the honor of introducing a lady so
splendid as herself. He was actually laughing with happiness at her
remarks.

For that matter, Mailer was obliged to admit all three were getting
on very well:

VIDAL: Did you know that George Washington used to take his false
    teeth at night and put them in a bowl of Madeira wine?
CAVETT: No.
VIDAL: I thought you would like to know that, Dick.
FLANNER: As they were made of wood they must have been quite tasty
    by breakfast. (*laughter*)
VIDAL: It was his brunch that he would put in the next morning.
CAVETT: Madeira wine. Why? What's the effect of that on the false teeth?
VIDAL: I think he liked the taste and they were made out of elephant
    bone and wood.

FLANNER: And out of bone. The elephant bone is a new trick to me.

CAVETT: I thought they were always wood. I always wondered—I pictured his dentist saying, "I have bad news for you—termites," or something. (*laughter*)

FLANNER: Oh, you're a wicked boy. (*laughter*)

CAVETT: Am I? (*laughs*) Where are we going?

In the Green Room, Mailer—like that general he could never become—was contemplating the military chances for entering an ambush of such delicacy connected to such strength. The only answer was attack. Shatter all prepared positions. Go out, he said to himself, and smash that fucking tea-house.

Those watching would see Norman Mailer emerge on the screen in a dark and disheveled suit, bow heavily to Janet Flanner, shake hands with Cavett, and pointedly not shake hands with Vidal. People in the studio audience would comment audibly at this display of discourtesy. Mailer would glare at them. Cavett would ask why he did not shake hands. Mailer would reply that he did not approve of Vidal, and thought him shameless in intellectual argument.

The camera would cut to Vidal's face. He would look composed on occasion, less composed on other occasions. Occasionally, Janet Flanner would touch his arm in reassurance, as if to signify that she would protect him from ruffians. Vidal was obliged to simper at that. It takes real machismo to look stern when your protection is seventy years old.

Under these loads, the next minutes progressed unevenly. Mailer was wound-up, and Vidal was silent. Cavett did not seem to know whether to put lanolin on a rash, or pull cocks' feathers. Given this sort of prompting, Norman managed to get in a few words he had written about Vidal in *The Prisoner of Sex*.

MAILER: I said that the need of the magazine reader for a remark he could repeat at dinner was best satisfied by writers with names like Gore Vidal.

FLANNER: All those writers called Gore Vidal.

VIDAL: I know. There are thousands of them, yeah.

CAVETT: Writers with names like Gore Vidal.

MAILER: There are two or three, you see.

CAVETT: Who are some of the others?

MAILER: I don't know.

CAVETT: Who wants to host the rest of this show for me? (*laughter*)

Who had butted who in the head? Mailer now asked himself. After this exchange, his ability to mount a sustained argument, never impressive at best, was hardly robust in the face of Cavett's wit and Flanner's deft interruptions. In short time, the audience turned unmistakably against him. When he said that the contents of Vidal's stomach were "no more interesting than the contents of an intellectual cow," they began to boo. He turned to them, and said, "You boo before you know what the man has done." They booed him again. He knew that he must move the conversation over to how Vidal had characterized Miller, Mailer, and Manson as M3, but there was nothing routine about scoring a point when you were debating one on three, or, since Gore was so silent, one on two-and-a-half. During each commercial, Mailer would sit heavily in his seat, staring with a dead eye at Vidal, but this time—air-time certainly racing away—he handed Cavett a page he had torn out of *The New York Review of Books* with Vidal's review, and asked him to pass it over to be read aloud. As the show proceeded, however, Vidal did not read it. Norman began to upbraid him further.

"You go in for intellectual adulteration," he said to Vidal, and then with no great display of coherence added that Vidal was welcome to rip apart any piece of his writing. "By God," Mailer vowed, "I may be writing on the floor, but if you taught me something about writing, I'd look up and I'd love you for having taught me something about writing. But when you only teach me something about the tricks of adulteration," Mailer shook his head. "You say the rivers will never be clean again and you pollute the intellectual rivers . . ."

"I wasn't," Vidal drawled, "setting myself up as the Famous Writers School, you know." He drew the chortles he must have anticipated for that.

MAILER: Why don't you try to talk just once, Gore, without yuks? Why not just talk to me instead of talking to the audience?

VIDAL: Well, by a curious thing we have not found ourselves in a friendly neighborhood bar, but both, by election, are sitting here with an audience, so therefore it would be dishonest of us to pretend otherwise. (*applause*)

MAILER: All right, Gore, look. We are here with an audience by choice, but let us at least—let us at least—

He wanted to grapple with him in argument, get him to read his own words. In the confusion of trying to get to Vidal with one hand

and keep Cavett and Flanner off with the other, he was planning to say, "At least, read your own words," when Flanner whispered half-audibly to Gore.

MAILER: Hey, Miss Flanner. Are you workin' as the referee or as Mr. Vidal's manager? (*laughter*) I'm perfectly willing to accept you in either role . . .

CAVETT: Can we afford you both talking?

MAILER: But my mind is fragile and I find it very hard to think and if you're muttering in the background it's difficult.

FLANNER: I made only the slightest mutter. (*laughter*) You must be very easily put off center.

MAILER: It's true, you made only the slightest mutter.

FLANNER: A tiny mutter.

MAILER: Yes, yes. But I listen to you spellbound—

FLANNER: I won't bother you anymore.

Norman was beginning to wonder if anything would work. He made a small vow never to drink again before going on TV. That valuable paper with Vidal's invaluable comments on Manson, Miller, and Mailer was now in Vidal's pocket, oh that fine review with such plums as "M3 is on the defensive, shouting names; he thinks that to scream dyke is enough to make the girls burst into tears. . . ." "It was in those years that M3 was born, emigrated to America, killed Indians, killed blacks, conned women. . . ." "Miller-Mailer-Manson. Women, beware. Righteous murder stalks the land. . . ."

In the absence of any substance to Mailer's attack, Vidal was taking on strength. The show was past the three-quarter mark and Gore was coming alive. Yes, Gore was now saying avuncularly, the good thing about Norman "is his constant metamorphosis. He does rebear himself like the phoenix, and what the next reincarnation will be, I don't know."

MAILER: You seem to have figured out that the next reincarnation for me is going to be Charles Manson.

VIDAL: Well, you left yourself—

MAILER: Why don't you read what you wrote?

VIDAL: You let yourself in for it, and I will tell you—I'll give you a little background here—that Mailer has—

MAILER: We all know that I stabbed my wife years ago, we do know that, Gore. You were playing on that.

VIDAL: Let's just forget about it.

MAILER: You don't want to forget about it. You're a liar and a hypocrite. You were playing on it.

VIDAL: But that wasn't a lie or a hypocrisy.

MAILER: The fact of the matter is that people who read *The New York Review of Books* know perfectly well—they know all about it and it's your subtle little way of doing it . . .

VIDAL: Oh, I'm beginning to see what bothers you, now. Okay, I'm getting to the point.

MAILER: Are you ready to apologize?

VIDAL: I would apologize if—if it hurts your feelings, of course I would.

MAILER: No, it hurts my sense of intellectual pollution.

VIDAL: Well, I must say, as an expert you should know about such things. (*laughter*)

MAILER: Yes, well, I've had to smell your works from time to time and that has helped me to become an expert on intellectual pollution, yes.

VIDAL: Yeah, well . . . let's—I was going to say, I—

FLANNER: Not only do you insult each other, not only in public, but you act as if you were in private. That's the odd way—

MAILER: It's the art of television, isn't it?

FLANNER: It's very odd that you act so—you act as if you were the only people here.

MAILER: Aren't we?

FLANNER: They're here, he's here. *I'm* here, and I'm becoming very, very bored. (*laughter, applause*)

MAILER: You still haven't told me whether you're Gore's manager or the referee.

CAVETT: If you make history here by punching a lady . . . (*laughter*)

FLANNER: I won't have it! I won't have it!

MAILER: Now, look, you see the sort of thing that goes on. Now you say I make history by punching a lady. You know perfectly well—you know perfectly well that I'm the gentlest of the four people here. (*laughter*)

CAVETT: I just hope it lasts through the next whatever we have left. (*laughter*)

MAILER: I guarantee you I wouldn't hit any of the people here because they're smaller.

CAVETT: In what ways? (*laughter*)

MAILER: Intellectually smaller.

CAVETT: Let me turn my chair and join these three. (*laughter, applause as he moves his place*) Perhaps you'd like two more chairs to contain your giant intellect. (*laughter, applause*)

MAILER: I'll take the two chairs if you will all accept fingerbowls.

This remark was sufficiently gnomic for Cavett to chew it and get to no witty place.

CAVETT: Who wants to grab this on our team? (*laughter*) I nearly have it, it means something to me. Fingerbowls. Fingerbowls. Things you dip your fingers in after you've gotten them filthy from eating. Am I on the right track? Am I warm?

MAILER: Why don't you look at your question sheet and ask a question.

CAVETT: Why don't you fold it five ways and put it where the moon don't shine.

It was received as the remark of the evening. Boborygimous was the laughter. Mailer sat there, contemplating a region in the depth of his rectum. "Mr. Cavett," he said, "on your word of honor, did you just make that up or have you had it canned for years and were you waiting for the best moment to use it?"

"I have to tell you a quote from Tolstoy," said Cavett, and the laughter continued.

Mailer turned his chair away from the guests and toward the theater. "I want to ask all of you something," he said to the audience. "Are you all really truly idiots or is it me?"

The audience replied, "YOU!"

"Oh, that was an easy answer," said Cavett. The music came up. Another intermission was on them.

CAVETT: I just wonder what the people at home think happened during the break. The four of us sat here in stony silence and—

VIDAL: No, somebody in the audience shouted, "Your argument is immature," to all four of us.

CAVETT: To all four of us. Oh. So we can each take as much—

FLANNER: We can each take a bow.

CAVETT: —as we feel we deserve. I'm sorry, Norman, I did interrupt you, and you were talking to the assembled audience.

MAILER: Yes, I was going to ask the audience what I was doing that was making them cheer every time the other side connected with a pass from one to the other of my three opponents.

MAN IN AUDIENCE: You're rude.

WOMAN IN AUDIENCE: You're a snot.

MAILER: That's fair. Someone said I'm rude and someone said I'm being a snot.

WOMAN IN AUDIENCE: You're a pig.

MAILER: Ohhh, the joint is loaded with libbies, ohhh. (*applause*) Gore, my God, it wasn't enough to trundle Janet Flanner along, the most formidable presence in the history of television, but you had to load the balcony with your libbies, your little libbies.

CAVETT: Well, now, wait a minute. There was only one lady's voice that rang out. Do you consider that loaded?

MAILER: It was the voice of legions. (*laughter*)

WOMAN IN AUDIENCE: Why do you have to argue so negatively and insulting to your guests?

MAILER: They're not my guests. They're not my guests any more than they're your guests.

CAVETT: It seems it's your show now.

WOMAN IN AUDIENCE: Why do you have to answer them with insults and nasty statements and they're answering you maturely and with dignity? (*applause*)

MAILER: That's because they're mature and full of dignity and they'd cut my throat in any alley and I answer rudely because I'm crude and a lout and a clod, that's why. (*applause*) Now have we progressed at all? Can I reach you, can I talk to any of you, or is it hopeless? I mean, if you care to listen, I do have a thing or two to say, believe it or not.

MAN IN AUDIENCE: Why are you bellyaching so much?

MAILER: Well, I'm bored with being misrepresented, you see. I've been misrepresented, by my own paranoid lights, for twenty-five years in this country, something like that, and to find an older litterateur like Gore Vidal, who knows his way around, you know . . . knows the ropes, and then suddenly, after all these years, he's suddenly developed a particularly dirty literary game. Well, it inflames me, you know. I've been so bold as to pretend to be the presumptive literary champ, you know, whether I deserve to be or not. The reason people always talk about me in relation to Hemingway is just that Hemingway at a certain point said to himself with his huge paranoia, "They're going to kill me for this but I'm going to be the champ, it's all I care about." And he shifted the course of American letters because up to that point people who wrote books were men of letters, they were gentlemen, they wrote books, and Hemingway said, in effect, "No, people who write books take as much punishment as prizefighters and one of them has to be a champion." Now, we've had a time that has not been interesting in terms of champions. In Hemingway's time there were great writers: There was Faulkner, there was Hemingway, and there were many other writers like Steinbeck and Farrell and Dos Passos and Thomas Wolfe, many, many really wonderful writers. Our time has been much more complicated and there hasn't been that many really extraordinary writers around, and I have presumed with all my extraordinary arrogance and loutishness and crudeness to step forth and say, "I'm going to be the champ until one of you knocks me off." Well, fine, but, you know, they don't knock you off because they're too damned simply yellow, and they kick me in the nuts, and I don't like it.

That was perhaps the most impassioned speech he had ever delivered on television. It said little but it was full of feeling, and it contained the cardinal virtue of television (for any ambitious performer), which is that it kept attention on himself. It suggested that his closeup in the scheme of things would demand more minutes than the others'. The audience, obedient to these conditioned reflexes of television, actually gave him a hand, a powerful hand of applause. But, of course, he was hardly finished.

The time had now come to give his peroration on Women's Liberation. He was not opposed to it, he wished to tell the world, he even honored it. It would free the best of women to discover how brave they were; a world in which women were maintained systematically in cowardice had to be a bad world. But, look, he wanted to say, as in all revolutions, the worst are running with the best, and there is an evil loose in Women's Liberation. It is the idea that the male search for bravery is mean and ridiculous, and that it is easier to be a man than a woman. Destroy the difference in the sexes, he would tell this audience, and a world of asexual human units, ready to fit the computers of a future totalitarianism, would also be prepared; these were the questions Vidal was polluting with his use of M3.

It might have been worth giving, but the commercial came before he was half-launched, and what he had to say was unsaid.

During the intermission, they argued on how to proceed. Vidal now wanted time to reply. Cavett indicated that it was Cavett's place to decide; he decided Vidal was entitled to equal time. Mailer offered to accept if Vidal would at least read from his review. With nothing agreed, the music came up.

CAVETT: Gore, the aim narrowed down to you and we have three and a half minutes left. I insist that you get them.

VIDAL: Well, I'll begin to answer Norman's charge about what a bad person I am. The attack on him, really, if you want to know, Norman, is simply what I detest in you—and I like many things in you, as you know, I'm a constant friend despite this—but your violence, your love of murder, your celebration of rage, of hate . . . *American Dream*—what was the dream? A man murders his wife and then buggers this woman afterwards to celebrate an American man's dream. This violence, this knocking people down, this carrying on, is a terrible thing. Now, it may make you a great artist—

MAILER: I demand one minute at the end—

VIDAL: It may make you a great artist—

MAILER: I'll listen, but I demand one minute at the end . . .

VIDAL: It may make you an interesting artist, I don't say that, but to the extent that one is interested in the way the society is going, there is quite enough of this stress, quite enough of this violence, without what I think are your celebrations of it, your attitude towards women in this thing, which I thought really horrible, and you said I compared you to Charles Manson. I said Henry Miller in his way, Norman in his, and Manson in his far out mad way, are each reflecting a hatred of women and a hatred of place.

One person was applauding loudly. At that moment, Norman got up from his chair, took a few steps over to Vidal's chair, flipped the review from *The New York Review of Books* out of his hand (for Vidal had been waving it as he spoke), and then returned to his seat. Vidal had been in the thick of saying, "And frankly if I may say so," when he saw Norman's bulk looming above, and he flinched. Vidal flinched discernibly: a monumentally high number of electrons were thereby shifted in millions of TV sets.

Back in his seat, Mailer began to read from Gore Vidal's review:

MAILER: "There has been from Henry Miller to Norman Mailer to Charles Manson a logical progression." Period. "The Miller-Mailer-Manson man, or M3 for short, has been conditioned to think of women as, at best, breeders of sons, at worst, objects to be poked, humiliated, killed," and from there on in the piece you speak of Miller, the great writer Henry Miller, the greatest writer alive in America—if we're going to talk like muckers, I'll talk too like a mucker—Henry Miller, the greatest writer alive in America, and myself, and Charles Manson, a hugely complex and contradictory figure, are spoken of, lumped together as M3, and if you call that good intellect working, to lump together three people as curious as Henry Miller, Norman Mailer, and Charles Manson?

VIDAL: Well, you must read the piece. You can't—

MAILER: I read it.

VIDAL: You happened to read it, but the audience has not. You are selecting this one passage as representative of the whole. I made my case very carefully. But I will say, giving you a few minutes more on the program, you will prove my point. So, it is—I come back to what I said. I detest this violence in you. You have actually written that "murder is never nonsexual."

MAILER: Well, is it ever nonsexual?

VIDAL: Well, I'm—

MAILER: Don't you know, Gore?

VIDAL: Not having murdered anybody lately, no, I don't know.

MAILER: You bragged about what you did to Jack Kerouac, after all.

VIDAL: He didn't die.

MAILER: Well, he did.

VIDAL: Oh, come on.

MAILER: Don't you remember the stories you used to tell about him—

VIDAL: I'm going to give you a line that Degas said to Whistler—two celebrated painters—and Whistler was a great performer, like Norman, and Degas said, "You know, Whistler, you act as if you had no talent." You represent yourself as though you really had no talent at all and, of course, you are one of our best writers.

MAILER: I read it in the same place you read it, which is Edmund Wilson's answer to Vladimir Nabokov in last week's *Times*.

VIDAL: So what? What's that got to do with it?

MAILER: I thought it was marvelous.

VIDAL: Good. I'm happy that we both agree that the sentiment is correct.

MAILER: The difference is that I savor the remark and you throw it into the battle.

VIDAL: Oh, Norman.

MAILER: Now, may I have my one minute for rebuttal?

CAVETT: There is one minute remaining.

MAILER: There is one minute. All right. He speaks of a character in a book of mine murdering his wife and then buggering a woman as a celebration of American manhood. Now I throw myself upon your court, hanging judge. I say that's intellectual muckerism of the worst sort, because the character I have there was a particularly complex character and, in fact, he did not simply bugger a woman, he entered her the other way as well and there was a particularly complicated—

FLANNER: Oh, goodness sake. (*laughter*)

MAILER: I know you've lived in France for many years, but believe me, Janet, it's possible to enter a woman another way as well.

FLANNER: So I've heard. (*laughter*)

CAVETT: On that classy note . . . (*laughter*)

FLANNER: I don't think it's restricted to French information, dear.

CAVETT: She said she doesn't think that's restricted to the French.

FLANNER: Practically international.

MAILER: Are we quitting on that classy note?

CAVETT: On that classy note, we have a brief message from our local stations and we will be back.

Cavett and Mailer were not looking at each other. Vidal was looking off into space. Flanner was grinning at Mailer as if he were a most curious fellow. What a way to use his last minute!

The music came up.

CAVETT: Well, this has been an interesting evening around the old table and, Miss Flanner, I'm glad to see you got that box of cookies that you wanted. And you other two fellows—

FLANNER: It's the only solace.

CAVETT: Yeah. (*laughter*) Could you two come back New Year's Eve and maybe we can— (*laughter*)

MAILER: That's the night.

CAVETT: Christmas Eve. Well, let us know who you think won. That'll be interesting, and we'll see you next time we're on the air. If. (*laughter, applause*)

The goodbyes were short. Mailer turned around and Vidal was gone.

From *Pieces and Pontifications* (1982)

**1972**    **FOUR MORE YEARS**

## St. George

Having come down now to the final minutes of the convention week, with the speeches done and the huge hall closed, the convention's aisles finally empty as if the echo of the chairman asking the delegates and Press to clear the floor had finally taken ghostly effect, having returned down Collins Avenue in the early morning for the last time, and having come in the final hour before dawn to the entrance of the Doral where hordes of the young, half-dressed in the heats of a late Southern night again gave an exotic sense of disarray while they lounged on the steps of the hotel (as if one were transported beyond Bombay to some future where Americans to come would sit half-naked in Lotus position before the gates of the American palaces), and having ascended the elevator to a private party in some roof garden of the Doral where McGovern was accepting the congratulations of some of the people of means who had helped to finance his campaign, Aquarius was able to take up position at last before the nominee and live in the charisma (or lack of it) his presence might convey. If there was all the warmth of a quiet and winning mood, and the sense of a vast relaxation as McGovern chatted for a few words with first a friend and then a sponsor, his tall body planted on legs that must have felt like posts of concrete after these two long years of campaigning, and these tense days of dealing and refusing to deal in Miami, the wealth of fatigue which came off McGovern now was as happy and compassionate as the last rose-colored velvets of evening before the night was in, and it occurred to Aquarius that if he had stood next to many politicians over the years, he had not ever before had such a splendid sense that he was standing near a man who had a heart which could conceivably be full of love—something awfully nice came off McGovern—and that was an extraordinary gift for a politician to give. It clearly returned Aquarius to the events of the convention and restored a knowledge of why these days had been so agreeable and so boring, and why the faces of the delegates massed in ranks on the floor had been like no faces any political observer had ever seen before, not in a convention hall, for they were in majority the faces of men and women who had come to have a good and serious time, like the faces of a crowd who have gone to the most important basketball game of the year in their home state, and so felt honored to have the ticket of admission, and happy, and there to squeeze the goodness in their will and determination out across the air and into the bodies of their players—a sense of *innocence* lived in more than half these faces as if they had yet to learn of the deaths within compromise and calculation. One had to be partial to a man whose delegates had the fair and average and open faces of an army of citizenry, as opposed to an army of the pols, and Aquarius knew then why the convention was obliged to be boring. There was insufficient evil in the room. With all the evil he had seen, all the lies and deals and evasions and cracks of the open door, with the betrayals of planks and the voids of promises, still there had been so little of real evil in the room.

So one could know none of the fascination one found at other conventions, when a walk on the floor was a promenade through vales of malignity or a passage through corridors of vested bile, and a study of faces was equal to a study of American corporations and crime. There, in those old conventions, the posture of political fixes came out in the set of the hips when a deal was in, and the skill with which it was once possible to read the moves of a convention (because the faces of the leaders and the gargoyle heads of the minions had been as dead and carved and fixed and ornamented forever as the pieces in a set of chess), such skill was lost. There was now no leader to follow as he put a finger to his nose to tip the vote to the leader across the aisle. The spell of drama when an evil piece of political property was traded for a more or less equal piece of profitable position was also gone, all gone except for a delegation here and there, as old in appearance with their baffled old-pol stone-set faces as the portraits of another century, and of course one was ready to laugh as one walked down the aisle because the count was already in—there were more live faces than dead ones on the floor—so McGovern was in, simple as that, and how different a sensation and how less compelling than in the days of other conventions when it was one dead face against another, and which of the candidates for nomination was best equipped to enter the sinuosities of negotiation with evil, for evil was the law of politics and the provender of the floor.

Now there was a convention where delegates had come to work. How diffident they were at parties and how good at work—it was as if the animation of being at a party came to them on the floor—their politics was their pleasure, and the tide of those faces returning to him as he stood near McGovern now, there came to him as well the first strains of that simple epiphany which had eluded him through these days, and he realized it, and it was simple, but he thought it true. In America, the country was the religion. And all the religions of the land were fed from that first religion which was the country itself, and if the other religions were now full of mutation and staggering across deserts of faith, it was because the country had been false and ill and corrupt for years, corrupt not in the age-old human proportions of failure and evil, but corrupt to the point of terminal disease, like a great religion foundering.

So the political parties of America might be the true churches of America, and our political leaders the popes and prelates, the bishops and ministers and warring clergymen of ideologies that were founded upon the spiritual rock of America as much as any dogma, and so there was a way now to comprehend McGovern and enter the loneliness which lived in his mood, for he inhabited that religious space where men dwell when they are part of the powers of a church and wish to alter that church to its roots. For yes, the American faith might even say that God was in the people. And if this new religion, not two hundred years old, was either the best or the worst idea ever to shake the mansions of eschatology in the world beyond, one knew at least how to begin to think of McGovern; if he had started as a minister in the faith of his father, he had left that ministry to look for one larger. When it came Aquarius' turn to speak to the new candidate of the Democratic party he felt content to say no more than that he had liked all three speeches at the end of the night. Eagleton, Kennedy, and the speech of the candidate himself, which was the best he had ever heard him give. And McGovern listened with that charisma which was finally and indisputably his own—which was to listen—for if his voice had no flaming tongue of fire, his power to listen surrounded everyone who spoke in his presence, and so had the depth to capture many a loyalty before he was done. Then the words of the speech came back to Aquarius:

"From secrecy and deception in high places—come home, America. From military spending so wasteful that it weakens our nation—come home, America. From the entrenchment of special privilege and tax favoritism—come home, America. From the waste of idle hands to the joy of useful labor—come home, America. From the prejudice of race and sex—come home, America. From the loneliness of the aging poor and the despair of the neglected sick—come home, America. Come home to the affirmation that we have a dream. Come home to the conviction that we can move our country forward. Come home to the belief that we can seek a newer world. May God grant us the wisdom to cherish this good land to meet the great challenge that beckons us home."

"I thought Ted Kennedy gave a very fine speech," McGovern said.

"He did. All the speeches were good. It was a fine mood, it was strong and tender," and McGovern nodded (as if it might be his own observation as well) and it was only after they had talked for another minute and Aquarius stepped back to listen to McGovern talk to others again that he realized he had used the word "tender" in speaking to a presidential candidate and felt no remorse and, agog on this realization, headed slowly for the exit with the rueful admission to himself that for the days left in which to write his piece he must leave out much in order to be able to put this little in, and thought McGovern was the first tall minister he had ever really liked, and so must have a chance to win the election. He kept his good mood until getting in the elevator, when it happened that a dreamy McGovern kid started to approach the car ahead of a Secret Service man, who gave the practiced equivalent of a karate chop with a small quick blow of his shoulder—for nothing!—and the kid bounced off to the side and the Service man, carrying his drink in his hand, went in first and stared morosely into his glass as though those waters went all the way back to the raw seed of the hurricane. And if Aquarius had been a man to pray, he might have thought of the embattled God he discovered years ago. But then who had the right to ask the Lord to let America have one election that went all the way down the rails without a wreck? He shivered. The idea next to the unexorcised nomenclatures of Oswald and Sirhan left a discomfort on his back.

# Candidate Emeritus

Interviewing Eagleton on the afternoon of the morning of his resignation as vice-presidential candidate, Aquarius finds him changed from the diffident politician who perspired before the television cameras on the night of his nomination and looked too furtive, too nervous, too quick, too quick-tongued, too bright, too unsure of himself, and finally too modest to be Vice-President. Now in the two weeks and more that had elapsed since nomination and through the last seven days of disclosure, the nightmare of his most secret life has blazoned every breakfast table, as well as the political shame of his treatment in a mental hospital for electric shock, not once but then and again, 1960, 1964, 1966, all kept so secretly by the family and skillfully over the years that even the worst of the whispering campaigns against him hinted at drink as a serious problem—an excusable vice in a politician. But never shock. Shock spoke of incarceration, not treatment, of manacled hands and the possibility of a blasted mind. For there was the public prejudice and who to refute it? A man who drank too much could be wrestling for his soul and losing it—implicit was the idea he might yet regain it. A heavy drinker could still carry on a political life—the impost of booze spoke of a war against too much of some powerful quality in oneself, too much perhaps of passion, talent, or pain. But shock treatment spoke of the irrevocable. Cures derived from a machine, when the cure itself was not comprehended, left an aversion. Nobody could argue that the cure had not come from blinding the innermost eye of the soul—so went the unspoken weight of public prejudice, and who to refute it? Not Eagleton when it was obvious he had made the choice to let rumors of drinking hang him first. (His disappearance into the Mayo Clinic had even been once announced as a visit to Hopkins for gastric disturbance.)

Now, in the last week, the secret of his life disgorged, he sat behind his desk in the New Senate Office Building, with a change in his looks. He was bigger today, heavier, stronger, and more relaxed, somehow not unreminiscent of a quick and nervous boxer who has finally gotten into a punchout, been hit hard for ten rounds, and now sits around in the next week with lumps on his head, welts on his face, even a certain thickening of his wits, but manhood has come to him. He has a new kind of calm. So sat Eagleton. Yesterday, after a week of desperate campaigning to win public approval of his candidacy, after a week in which half of America took Eagleton to its heart like a wounded puppy, while half of the top brass in the Democratic party threatened to boycott the election if he wasn't dropped from the ticket, and campaign money went dry, McGovern had the fell political embarrassment of asking him to withdraw, this after making the needless remark at the first height of the disclosure that he was behind Eagleton "1,000 percent," a phrase which entered the language so quickly that 1,000 percent might yet live as the conclusive way to let someone know they must certainly not count on your word. A whole disaster for McGovern that had not been helped by Eagleton's unwillingness to withdraw—anyone familiar with politics had to know that McGovern was counting, if it came to it, on just such a voluntary withdrawal to safeguard that 1,000 percent. But Eagleton had been riding with all the energy of his cyst being lanced, a buried horror released and himself still alive, crowds cheered him, strangers (from states other than Missouri) grabbed his hand, he was a national figure for the first time in his life, and with a brand-new constituency—all of that Wallace folk who liked a candidate with a flaw they could recognize, something homey and down to rights, a skeleton in the closet at which they had had a peek, what pleasure! That threw a cunning shadow into the soap-opera light. Just as the folk loved Wallace because Lurleen had made the sacrifice to run for governor knowing it could not help her dread disease, and folk loved Wallace again for recovering from her loss and marrying a young woman—renewal was the precise salvation of which the soap opera sang—so now Wallace folk loved Eagleton because he was a rich boy with a bad secret who was going through a crisis and not giving up. (If Aquarius had any doubt of this last hypothesis, it was demonstrated to the detail while he sat in Eagleton's outer office waiting for the interview, and a file of tourists kept coming by to pay their respects to the Senator, murmuring in intense throat-filled voices to the receptionist that they sure were sorry the Senator wouldn't be running and didn't know if they wanted to express their feelings about George McGovern but leave it that they sure wouldn't vote for him now—Wallace faces, every last one of them, clear in their election plumage to a face-watcher like Aquarius, equal after such years of practice to many a bird-watcher.) Eagleton had lived in politics all his life, could smell the turn of one's luck in the sweat of the work. So he knew better than anyone else that he had become a species of new political dynamite, and he didn't want to quit— how could he? But the less he wished to withdraw, the more livid and enormous became the wrath of the party at the caper he had pulled.

"Get that motherfucker out," had to be the sweetest message on the hour to McGovern from all the boss and divergent forces in the party he was trying to unite. By refusing to withdraw, Eagleton had the largest play of his life available to him—but the odds against him were huge, and the bulk of his own party would treat him like a leper. So he met with McGovern, and they came out, Eagleton's arm on McGovern's shoulder, using the old senatorial wedge as they drove into a press conference, and Eagleton announced he would withdraw, and did this morning, and now sat back on his chair, his legs on his desk, and talked in a deep politician's voice which still vibrated with the pain of loss and the pleasure of relaxation. Of course, he was far from wholly relaxed as yet, soon jumping to his feet to read aloud an item from the *St. Louis Post-Dispatch* that had just come in, and read (in the loud throw-it-away tones of an actor picking up new lines just handed him) that McGovern was "spineless."

"Spineless," Eagleton repeated. "A little too extreme, don't you think?" he said, but he was obviously enjoying himself.

"Oh, oh," he added with mock pain as he picked up another paper, "they're still misspelling my name. My God, they've called me everything and I don't mean dog catcher, I mean Eggleston, Eaglesworth, Eggnog, you call it." His secretary now handing him a take-out menu from the Senate cafeteria; he groaned at the familiar items. "Darn it, I'd like something more glamorous than cherry pie," he complained, as if finding his stomach convalescent.

Back again behind the desk, Eagleton replied to the quick question, "Do you play chess?" with the answer, "No, I wish I did, why do you ask?"

"Sometimes in chess games between masters, a move comes up which is so unprecedented and therefore so good or so bad that the people who annotate the game put both an exclamation and a question mark after the move. And I thought if you had not withdrawn, it would have been such a situation."

"I see what you mean," he said heartily. "No, I must say I never learned chess, but I wish now that I might have gone in for it." It was a politician's response. Complimented the questioner but did not answer him; took pains to praise what might be a hobby. A hobby commended is usually worth a vote.

"Granted this may not be the day to ask such a question, but wouldn't you say that on balance you're still in pretty good position? The nation is aware of you, and there are new friends . . ."

"Oh," he rumbled, "I'm not bitter. Hell, we could say it was the cheapest campaign I ever ran. They gave me a free charge for my batteries. Think of it. All that publicity, and I didn't have to spend a cent."

It was an interview that so far had persisted in remaining out of focus. Not twenty-four hours ago, Eagleton had still been running; now with the proper politician's love for a meaty role (even the role of a loser done well is fertilizer for future votes) he was already working out the tone of new lines, but it was the first day, he was probably a slow study after all this pounding, and so he had to sound a fraction off on every reading. The problem was to work out how much he could speak against McGovern—which would be tonic for his blood— and how much he should support him, a professional decision that might take weeks to work out. So now he chose to get away from any suggestion of bile, and also gave up the forced and hearty gallantry he had been exhibiting of a man who is being good about his pain. Instead, he said in the voice of an absolute good guy, "I'm really not bitter—George McGovern was wonderfully decent to me last night." This line was delivered with no more or less conviction than the others. The new role was going to take work.

"Senator, could I ask a question which might be a little presumptuous?"

"After what I've been asked these last seven days, you could bounce the worst insult off my head, and I wouldn't even know I'd been hit."

Well, one thing did confuse him, the questioner admitted. He had read the reports of Eagleton waiting for hours on the last day of the convention to find out if McGovern would pick him for Vice-President. The former candidate nodded. And it had also been reported that as he waited, his good mood naturally began to go down. Eagleton nodded again. "Well, Senator, forgive me for entering your head, but didn't there come a moment when you said to yourself, 'They're turning me down because of that electro-shock business.' "

Eagleton looked thoughtful. "Earlier in the week when my name first came up as a possibility, and there were still twenty names in the hopper, I talked about the shock treatments with my wife, and we felt it was over and done with. I don't know if you'll believe this, but I then forgot about it."

"You didn't think about it once all that long day of waiting?"

"While I can't vouch for my unconscious, it was not an element of calculation in my conscious head, no sir, strange as that may now sound."

It was preferable to believe he told the truth, that somehow it had not been in his mind when Mankiewicz asked him if there were skeletons in the closet. But who could know what was in Eagleton's mind? Probably he did not know himself. When our motive is imperfect, the flaw is whipped like a pea from mental shell to shell. We smuggle our honesty just out of our reach while keeping an eye on the other man's game. Maybe Eagleton had built so many reflexes on his ability to whip a miserable recollection from shell to shell that he had lost the power to think of the hospital episode when questions were asked, just as a murderer living in a respectable world must manage to forget his murder and feel as much indignation as anyone else at the thrashing of a cat.

Leaving, Aquarius asked, "Anyone ever told you about a resemblance to Scott Fitzgerald?" He was thinking of photographs in those late years when Fitzgerald was handsome still but growing heavy.

"I've been compared to Jack Lemmon, but never Fitzgerald." He smiled. "Do I want to look like Fitzgerald? Didn't he have a drinking problem after all? I'm in enough trouble without being told I remind people of a drunk."

"Not just a drunk. A fine Irish poet."

"Well," said Eagleton, "*The Great Gatsby* is one of my favorite books."

If he was not telling the truth now, there was a fair chance good George McGovern had just disengaged himself from a congenital teller of the worst fibs.

Walking down the hall, Aquarius felt as if he had been talking to a nice friendly reasonably hardworking good-drinking congressman who in another term would be ready to run for senator. No matter how many times it happened, it was unnerving to meet men who had been near to high office and recognize they were no more magnificent than yourself. Perhaps there were mysteries to charisma he would yet do well to ponder.


# A Visit to Dr. Kissinger

Since it was an interview that had been scheduled weeks in advance and confirmed the day before, with all option given to meet at Sans Souci for lunch or the White House, he had naturally picked the White House. How often did such opportunities arise? Still, it took fifteen long minutes and then five more to pass through the special police at the gate. Interrogating him through a microphone in a plate-glass facade, they claimed at first to have no record of his appointment, and then informed him he had been due at nine in the morning, only to discover they were looking through the schedule of the resident White House physician, Dr. Tkach. Kissinger! now that was better! but before they could announce him, he would have to complete a questionnaire. There was something as reductive as a steam bath in this colloquy through the glass. Already he was perspiring at the minutes being lost for the interview.

Once admitted to the kiosk, however, he was freezing in the air conditioning and fuming at the questionnaire. When he handed it back, the Sergeant who conducted the inquiry through the window, scolded him. "I told you not to use abbreviations, didn't I?"

"Why don't you have a form that gives you space to write out the full word?" he snapped back, and was apparently accepted at last by the Sergeant as a man of sufficient self-importance to visit the White House, for he was invited to take a chair.

Still, he had to wait while they phoned for clearance. In the meantime, he listened to the Sergeant and his assistant, a bright-eyed and wiry Southerner, who said, "I just reduced crime in my neighborhood by forty percent."

The Sergeant jeered; the other policeman, a young Black with a ramrod posture, smiled uneasily.

"Hell, yeah. The other night I talked my wife out of hitting me on the side of the head with a skillet. That's forty percent right there. But when it comes to armed robbery I'm helpless. I come home at the end of the week with my pay check and she holds me up for all fifty-one cents."

"Why," said the Sergeant, "don't you study the life of George Washington and stop telling so many fucking lies?"

"There's an example. George Washington cut down the cherry tree and they gave him ten thousand dollars a year. Why, way back then he was making more money than I am right now."

"What are you complaining about?" asked the Sergeant. "He was the first President of the U.S. What was you ever the shit first of?"

But a young Secret Service man had now come up to the kiosk, and conducted him across the North Lawn. Inside the West Lobby a receptionist apologized politely for the delay. Ushered through a door into a hallway, he was met by Kissinger, who gave the greatest of broad smiles, pumped his hand, and said in a deep and gutty German accent, "Today must be my day for masochism since I dare to be inter-viewed by you."

Almost immediately, they were in his office, large and full of lights. "We have a momentous decision to make instantly," said Kissinger. "It is: where shall we eat? I can offer you respectable food if you wish the interview here, not exciting but respectable, and we won't be interrupted. Or we can go to a restaurant just around the corner where the food will be very good and we will be interrupted a little although not very much."

Similar in height and build, it was probable they would not wish to miss a good lunch. So in much less time than it took him to enter, he left the White House (that most placid of mansions!) with Kissinger, hardly noticing the same Secret Service man who unobtrusively—it was the word!—had stopped the traffic on Pennsylvania Avenue while they crossed. If not for just such a rare American pomp, he could have had the impression that he knew Kissinger over the years. For as they walked along, chatting with no pain, it was much as if the learned doc-tor had been an editor of some good and distinguished quarterly and they were promenading to lunch in order to talk over a piece.

In fact, that was the first topic—his piece. "We must, from the be-ginning," said Kissinger, "establish ground rules. We may make them whatever you wish, but we have to keep them. I can speak frankly with you, or not so frankly. But if I am frank, then you have to allow me the right to see what you put into my mouth. It is not because of vanity, or because of anything you may say about me, you may say anything you wish about me, in fact"—with the slyest grin—"you will probably hurt my position more if you say good things than bad, but I have, when all is said, a position I must be responsible to. Now, if you don't wish to agree to such a procedure, we can do the interview at arm's length, which of course I'm used to and you need show me nothing. Either method is agreeable, provided we establish the rules."

They had by now reached Sans Souci, and Kissinger's advance to his table was not without ceremony. Since he was hardly back twenty-four hours from Paris and some talks with the North Vietnamese, the headwaiter teased him over the pains of quitting Parisian cuisine. Passing by the table of Larry O'Brien there were jokes about Water-gate.

"That was good luck, Henry, to get away just before it hit the fan," said O'Brien.

"Ah, what a pity," said Kissinger. "You could have had me for the villain of the sixth floor."

And a friend intercepted him before he could take his seat. "Henry, what truth to the rumor that McGovern is picking you for Vice-President?"

Kissinger chuckled. "Twenty-two thousand people in the State Department will be very happy." He was animated with the pleasure these greetings had given him. While not a handsome man, he was obviously more attractive to women now than when he had been young, for he enjoyed what he received, and he was a sensuous man with a small mouth and plump lips, a Hapsburg mouth; it was not hard to see his resemblance to many a portrait of many an Austrian archduke and prince. Since he gave also every sign of the vanity and vulnerability and ruddy substance of a middle-aged man with a tendency to corpulence—the temptation to eat too much had to be his private war!—his weaknesses would probably be as amenable to women as his powers, and that German voice, deep, fortified with an accent that promised emoluments, savories, even meat gravies of culture at the tip of one's tongue—what European wealth!—produced an impression altogether more agreeable than his photographs. So one mystery was answered—Kissinger's reputation as a ladies' man. And a difficulty was commenced—Aquarius' work might have been simplified if he liked the Doctor less. A hint of some sinister mentality would have been a recognizable aid.

Yet even the demand for ground rules was reasonable. The meal ordered, Kissinger returned to the subject—he repeated: He would obviously expect the rules to be clarified before he could go further. Nor was there much impulse to resist him with argument. Secretly, he respected Kissinger for giving the interview—there was indeed not a great deal the Doctor could gain, and the perils were plentiful, including the central risk that Kissinger would have to trust him to keep his side of the bargain. Since his position not only as Assistant to the President on National Security Affairs but as court favorite must excite the ten thousand furies of bureaucracy—"this man who can't speak English that they keep hidden in the White House" being a not uncommon remark—the medium of this interview was not without its underlying message: Kissinger, in some part of himself at least, must be willing to function as a cultural ambassador across the space of mind between the constellations of the White House and the island galaxies of New York intellectual life. So Aquarius made his own speech. Like a virgin descending the steps of sexual congress, he said that he had never done this before, but since he was not unsympathetic to Kissinger's labors and had no wish to jeopardize his position, which he would agree was delicate . . . so forth. They set up some ground rules.

"Now what should we talk about?" asked Kissinger.

Well, they might talk about the huge contradiction between the President's actions in Russia and China as opposed to Vietnam. "You know, if not for the bombing I might have to think about voting for Nixon. Certainly no Democrat would have been able to look for peace with Russia and China. The Republicans would never have let him. So Nixon's achievement is, on the one hand, immense, and on the other ghastly." Kissinger nodded, not without a hint of weariness to show his familiarity with the argument.

"If I reply to you by emphasizing the difference in our styles of negotiation in each country, it is not to pretend that these negotiations preempt moral questions, but rather that I'm not so certain we can engage such questions properly if they're altogether stripped of context. For instance, it would be impossible to discuss the kind of progress we made with China and Russia unless I were to give you the flavor of those negotiations for they were absolutely characteristic and altogether different. For instance, I was not unfamiliar with Russian matters, but my ignorance about China was immense on the first secret visit, and I had no idea of how they would receive me"—a hint of the loneliness of his solitary position now passes across the table at Sans Souci—"nor even what we necessarily would be able to talk about. In the beginning I made the mistake of assuming that they negotiate like the Russians, and they don't. Not at all. With the Russians you always know where you stand. If, for example, you are hammering out a joint statement, you can be certain that if you ask them to remove a comma in one place, depend on it they will ask you for a comma in return. Whereas the character of men like Chou must emerge to a great degree from experiences like the Long March, and so I discovered—and not immediately—that you always had to deal with them on the real substance of the question. I remember when the President visited China, and I was working with Chou on the joint statement we would issue describing our areas of agreement and difference, I asked if a certain point the Chinese had brought up could be dropped because the wording would be difficult for us in America. In return I would give up a point to them. Chou said 'Explain to me why this point causes you difficulty, and if your explanation makes sense I will cede it to you. If it doesn't convince me, however, then nothing can make me give it up. But I don't need or want your point. You can only give your points back to *your* President, you cannot give them to us.' So he shamed me," Kissinger finished.

"And the Vietnamese?"

"They could hardly be more different. The problem is to convince them we really want peace."

"Don't you think a million tons of bombs a year makes it hard for them to believe?"

"No. I know this has to sound unendurably callous to you, but the North Vietnamese are inconceivably tough people, and they've never known peace in their lives. So to them the war is part of the given. They are able to live with it almost as a condition of nature. But when it comes to negotiation, they refuse to trust us on the most absurd little points. Let them feel if they will that we are not to be relied on in the larger scheme of things—that is not my point of view, but an argument can obviously be advanced—it is just that they refuse to trust us on the pettiest points where it would not even be to our interest to cheat them. So they are not easy to comprehend. On the one hand they have a fortitude you cannot help but admire; on the other, they are near to little lawyers who are terrified of the larger processes of the law—and so cling to the most picayune items. That is one difficulty in dealing with the North Vietnamese. The other is their compulsion to the legalistic, which bears no relation to reality, nor to the possibility of reality. In effect they expect us to win their war for them for they want us to write up into the peace agreement their literal investiture of the government of South Vietnam. And that obviously we can't do. There's nothing we want more than for the war to end, but they must take their chances too. They have to win their own war."

"When they began their offensive in April, why then didn't the President just let them drive ahead and solve the problem for you? Why, just at that point, did he choose to escalate the bombing?"

Kissinger did not reply. The difficulty in continuing the discussion was that they would now be obliged to talk about the character of Richard Nixon rather than the nature of the North Vietnamese; given Kissinger's position, that was hardly possible—so the character of the interview changed. If it was easy for Aquarius to have the idea that Nixon and Kissinger were more in accord on Russia and China than on Vietnam, there was no evidence for it. Kissinger took pains to express his respect. "The President is a very complex man," he said, "perhaps more complex than anyone I've known, and different from the public view of him. He has great political courage for instance."

"Yes. It was no ordinary gamble to go to China."

"And he made moves in Russia which would take too long to explain now, but believe me he showed extraordinary decisiveness."

"Still, don't you think it's a vice that he has a personality which is of no use to the country?"

"Nixon is wary of exhibiting anything personal in himself. You have to consider the possibility it's for very good cause considering the way he has been treated by the Media."

"Still his wariness creates contempt."

"And a spirit of debunking which I don't find very happy. It was like that in the Weimar Republic. Just the kind of wholesale debunking that may yet lead to totalitarianism." Kissinger shrugs. "I wonder if people recognize how much Nixon may be a bulwark against that totalitarianism."

"Can he be?"

"I'm not certain I know what you mean."

"As people grow up, don't they form their characters to some extent on the idea a President gives of his person to the public. Nixon may give too little."

"Is it your point of view then that in the presidency one needs to have a man it is worth being like?"

"Yes. Nixon offers nothing authentic of himself."

"You would argue that he is not primarily a moral leader. I do not wish to agree. But perhaps you go along with me that he has political genius," Kissinger said.

"Absolutely."

It was indeed Aquarius' opinion. Still, that was a thought he could return to. Their lunch broke up with the passing of their table by Art Buchwald, who announced to Kissinger that Dobrinin was coming to his house one night soon to play chess, and schedules permitting, he thought, granting Dobrinin's status as a chess player, that they should make a date to team up against the Ambassador. Kissinger agreed.

On the way back to the White House, they talked companionably of the hazards of working life, of jet-lag and fatigue. "How much sleep do you get?" asked Aquarius.

"I am happy if I can average five hours."

"Is it enough?"

"I always thought my mind would develop in a high position. But fatigue becomes a factor. The mind is always working so hard that you learn little. Instead, you tend to work with what you learned in previous years."

They said good-bye in the white office in the White House with its blue sofas, its Oriental rugs, and its painting by Olitsky, a large canvas

in blue-purple, a wash of dark transparencies with a collection of pigment near the center as if to speak of revery and focus. "I've only
come to like modern art in the last few years," Kissinger remarked.

Aquarius was to think again of focus. Because Kissinger opened
to him a painful question on the value of the act of witness: Lunch had
been agreeable. Yet how could one pretend that Kissinger was a man
whose nature could be assessed by such a meeting; in this sense, he
was not knowable—one did not get messages from his presence of
good or evil, rather of intelligence, and the warm courtesy of Establishment, yes, Kissinger was the essence of Establishment, his charm
and his presence even depending perhaps on just such emoluments of
position as the happiness he obtained in the best restaurants. If there
was a final social need for Establishment, then Kissinger was a man
born to be part of it and so automatically installed in the moral schizophrenia of Establishment, a part of the culture of moral concealment, and yet never was the problem so perfect, for the schizophrenia
had become Aquarius' own. Kissinger was a man he liked, and in effect was ready to protect—he would even provide him with his own
comments back to read. So Aquarius wondered if he had come into
that world of the unendurably complex where one gave parts of one's
allegiance to men who worked in the evil gears and bowels and blood
left by the moral schizophrenia of Establishment, but still worked
there, as one saw it, for good more than ill. It was a question to beat
upon every focus of the brain, and he prepared with something near
to bewilderment to go down to Miami again and see if there were
moral objects still to be delineated in the ongrowing blur of his surest
perceptions.

# Pat Nixon

After her arrival at the Fontainebleau, Aquarius watches Pat Nixon do
her work, goes twice that afternoon to see her, once at her planned
spontaneous tumultuous entrance with Secret Service men who quietly, gently, steadily, *politically*, forced an aisle for her up the steps and
for a few hundred feet along the lobby to an elevator up to a private
room in the Fontainebleau Towers while the band played (a trip which
must have consumed a half hour) and there after a bath presumably—

how much desire for still another shower did such waves of human flesh arouse in a First Lady?—she had changed and came down again with her daughters to plunge into an orgy of hand-shaking and autographing as she proceeded along a six-foot-wide roped-off aisle to a banquet room of the Fontainebleau where a reception party was being given for Pat Nixon, her girls, and the Young Voters for the President.

What a rich opportunity then to study Pat Nixon, first with her entrance to the hotel in a pink dress, then her immersion later into the reception crowd with a royal-blue dress, long-sleeved, straight-skirted, a light soft material vulnerable to crowds, she was able to demonstrate that particular leathery hard-riding sense of grace she possessed which spoke of stamina first, for she could knee and elbow her own defense through a crowd and somehow never involve the dress, that was one of the straight-out tools of her trade and she knew how to employ it—that material was not going to get snagged on some dolt's ragged elbow or *ripped* any more than a seaman would get his feet caught in a rope he was coiling in a storm.

So, for instance, had she managed her passage through the lobby for the reception, pointing her head at an angle up to the glare of the Media lights poised like flaming swords over her way, the ears inured to the sound of another brass combo (with one black trumpeter, trombone, banjo, other trumpet, and drums), still she moves a little to it, just a flash, as though to demonstrate that dancing is one of the hundred and sixty-eight light occupations she can muster.

Earlier Clark MacGregor has come down the steps with his wife, he stands close, he is proud of her like a college kid with one smash of a keen steady! Indeed there are older people all through the lobby waiting with love in their eyes for Pat—she has worked hard and she is better off for it—they are ready to revere her for caulking the hull of the ship so well (it is their ship, too—the presidency residing somewhere in the awesome fall between one's god and one's parents) and the crowd is orderly, not pushing, the YVPers all stashed in the reception room, but Pat is still going slowly down the aisle through the older folks in the lobby, tarrying to say hello, and before her comes Julie, committed, determined to do a good job in a green top and white-skirted dress, black belt, and Tricia in a white and pink dress with her husband, Ed Cox, who looks gracious, as if he takes considerate care of her, which she might need for she is near to beautiful and tiny, wearing perhaps a size 5 dress, with blond hair all pulled back and sprayed into an immaculate pale-gold mass, but her dark eyes, nymphlike and lost, suggest the vacant remote and yet flirtatious look of a princess who has been told about life outside the castle. Then comes Pat. There are liver spots to perceive on her hands, and her teeth must be capped, she has obviously pinched and pushed and tightened her presentation of herself all her life, but she had ridden the beast of such discipline, she looks better now than when she entered politics. No, she has emerged as a pro, such a pro indeed with such a pride in having mastered every side of her occupation that one did not ask oneself if she liked shaking hands. Possibly the question did not exist for her, since it was a matter of indifference whether she liked it or not—she was not on earth to like things but to do them!

Still, for a politician, the love of shaking hands is equal to a writer's love of language. Ultimately that is the material with which a politician must work, yet not all politicians love shaking hands, nor with everyone, any more than Ernest Hemingway loved every word in the English language. Certain words like "gorgeous" brought out Papa's snobbery—perhaps he was in this sense equivalent to a Republican politician who preferred to grasp the hand of the clean, the neat, the precise, and the well-laundered. (Hubert Humphrey, to the contrary, was a veritable Thomas Wolfe of a politician; just as no word was too mean or out-size splendiferous for the man who could write *Of Time and the River,* so Hubert would kiss Queens and scrofula victims with the same warmth.) Now, if Pat Nixon had been a writer, she would have gravitated to the commonest words that everyone used or the most functional words—she would have wanted to reach the largest audiences with ideas they could comprehend on first reading—that was how she shook hands. In the way that a *Reader's Digest* editor attacked a paragraph. She loved to work with the wad. Give her the plainest dullest face, no spark, no flair, just the urgency to get what it wants—her autograph, her handshake. She gave them out equally, like the bills and smiles of a bank teller. There are faces to greet, currency to handle, stay on top of the job!

In his own mayoralty campaign, Aquarius ended up by shaking hands wherever he could, had in fact to his surprise ended up liking that act more than anything else in politics, at least once he comprehended that the only way to do it was to offer as much of himself as was present with every greeting. The phenomenon was that energy came back, and the hand did not get tired. It was as if in shaking a thousand hands, six hundred may have returned a little more energy than they took, as if the generosity of a mass of people might be larger than their greed, a belief that was as it should be if one wanted to become a politician, for it gave, on balance, some confidence to the thought of working for others.

But Pat Nixon had obviously come from folds of human endeavor which believed the reward for service was not to be found in the act but afterward. Naturally she gave energy and she took energy, impossible not to, and was somewhat wilted if with a glow when she was done, but it was the muscles of her arm that worked, and the muscles in her smile, her soul was the foreman of the act, and so did not reside in her muscles, but off to the side and vigilant as she worked the machine. She no longer saw faces, no, she was a heavy worker on an assembly line, and bodies came her way, there were touches and taps, a gloved rhythm to keep—she moved in some parallel perhaps to the burden of a slim tight-mouthed Negress with heavy family worries on a heavy assembly line for whom the pay was good and so she was in it until death or double overtime. So, too, would Pat Nixon have no inner guilt before trade unionists or Blacks—she had worked as hard as any of them—in her own way, she moved as well. Afterward, her fixed expression stayed in memory, for she had the features of a woman athlete or the heroine of some insurmountable disease that she has succeeded in surmounting.

A man getting an autograph from her asks, "How do you stay so young?"

She smiles carefully. "With hard work," she says.


# Nixon Comes to Miami

At the foot of the plane he embraces his wife and kisses his daughters, but with appropriate reserve—they are being watched after all. The embrace is suggestive of five million similar such greetings each evening as commuters get off at a suburban stop and go through the revelation, and the guard they throw up against revelation, of their carnal nitty-gritty. A good game for a face-watcher, and Nixon's is not different from many another man who pecks a kiss in public. But as he walks toward the Young Voters for the President and salutes and smiles and grins, preparing to stop before them and raise both his arms (for they are now no longer just cheering him as the principal, but are off on all the autoerotics of thrusting their own arms in the air four fingers up while screaming "Four more years, four more years"), so Nixon promenading toward them exhibits again that characteristic gait that is his alone and might have provided thought for analysis in even so profound a student of body movements as Wilhelm Reich, for Nixon has character-armor, hordes of it! He handles his body like an adolescent suffering excruciations of self-consciousness with every move. After all these years! It is as if his incredible facility of brain, which manages to capture every contradiction in every question put to him and never fails to reply with the maximum advantage for himself in a language that is resolutely without experiment, is, facile and incredible brain, off on a journey of inquiry into the stubborn refusal of the body to obey it. He must be obsessed with the powers he could employ if his body could also function intimately as an instrument of his will, as intimate perhaps as his intelligence (which has become so free of the *distortions* of serious moral motivation), but his body refuses. Like a recalcitrant hound, it refuses. So he is still trying out a half dozen separate gestures with each step, a turn of his neck to say one thing, a folding of his wrist to show another, a sprightly step up with one leg, a hint of a drag with the other, and all the movements are immediately restrained, pulled back to zero revelation as quickly as possible by a brain which is more afraid of what the body will reveal than of what it can discover by just once making an authentic move that gets authentic audience response.

Yet when he begins to talk to the crowd, this muted rebellion of his activities comes to a halt. Now, hands clasped behind him, Nixon begins. "I was under some illusion that the convention was downtown," he says.

It takes a while for the kids to get it. YVPers are not the sort of hogs who grab the high I.Q.'s. But when they realize he is not only complimenting them for the size of their numbers but on their importance, they come back with all the fervor of that arm in the air and the four fingers up in the double V. Up go the double horns of the kids. "Four more years." Now, the signs painted by the YVPers all begin to wave, these Young Voters for the President who in the eyes of the liberal Press will yet look like ears of goldenrod to hayfever sufferers. Somebody has provided all YVPers with the paint, no dark secret, Republican money can be spent for Republican posters and paint, but the kids have done the work themselves and the signs say "We stand for Pat"; "We Love Julie"; "Trish You're a dish"; "Miami loves the 1st family"—there is just a hint of the slovenly in the uncertain use of capital letters. "Welcome back, Pat"; "Agnew for peace"; "Vote for a WIN-

NER"; "Nixon gives a damn"—here is one—"Nixon is For Love."
Now kids are chanting "Four more years," "Hey, hey, whateya say,
Nixon, Nixon, all the way." They are not the most attractive faces he
has seen. Hundreds of young faces and not one is a beauty, neither by
natural good looks nor by the fine-tuning of features through vitality
or wit—the children in this crowd remind him of other crowds he
knows well, and does not like. Of course!—they are the faces of the
wad!—all those blobs of faces who line up outside TV theaters and
wait for hours that they may get in to see the show live, yes, the show
will be more alive than their faces. The genius of Nixon! Has he selected this gaggle of mildly stunted minds from photograph files? Or
had they been handed applications as they left the theaters after the
live shows? Aquarius remembers the look of the television set in his
room at the Fontainebleau. It was up on a small pickled-white dais
and looked like some kind of altar for a medico-religious event. Nixon
may have drawn the deep significance from such a sight twenty years
ago—how valuable must be the insights he could pass on to McLuhan,
well, Aquarius was frothing again.

One thing can be said for the presidency—it gives every sign of
curing incurable malaise. Nixon is genial! Now, he jokes with the
crowd. "I think I'm going to be nominated tonight. I *think* so," he says
charmingly. It is the first time he has ever spoken with italics in public. "And so is Vice-President Agnew," he adds. "He's going to be nominated too." They cheer. Ever since they arrived on Saturday, the
YVPers have been cheering, on the street, at receptions in the gallery,
in the lobby of each hotel they visit, and here at the airport they exhibit all the inner confidence of a Fail-Safe. When in doubt, cheer.

Once again Aquarius is depressed at the sight of their faces. It is
not only that all those kids seem to exist at the same level of intelligence—which is probably not quite high enough to become Army officers—but they also seem to thrive on the same level of expression.
They have the feverish look of children who are up playing beyond
the hour of going to sleep; their eyes are determined, disoriented,
happy, and bewildered. So they shriek. With hysteria. The gleam in
their eye speaks of no desire to go beyond the spirit they have already
been given. Rather, they want more of what they've got. It is unhappy
but true. They are young pigs for the President.

"I've been watching the convention on television," Nixon says
through the microphone. "I want to thank you for the tribute you
paid my wife." Now for the first time he puffs his chest up, which—
given the mating dance he performs whenever addressing a crowd—
has to signify that a remark of portent is on its way. "Based on what

I've seen on television, and based on what I have seen here today,"—
Four more years!—"those who predict the other side is going to win
the young voters are simply wrong." Deep breath. Solemn stare. Now
comes the low voice that backs the personality with the presidential
bond of integrity: "We're going to win the young voters." Shrieks.
Squeals. Cheers. Four more years! They are the respectable youth and
they are going to triumph over fucked-up youth.

Back at the convention, the delegates are watching this arrival on
the three huge screens above the podium—it is being televised live
both to the convention and to America. Only the galleries are empty
this afternoon, but that is because the YVPers are not present to fill
their seats—they are here!

Nixon takes them into his confidence. He knows they are interested in politics or they would not be in Miami, he says. And maybe
one of them someday will be President, "Maybe one of your faces that
I now am looking at will be President. It is possible. One thing I want
you to know. That is that we want to work with the trust and faith and
idealism of young people. You want to participate in government and
you're going to." Cheers. He smiles genially. "However, let me give
you a bit of advice. To succeed in politics, the first thing you want to
do, is to marry above yourself."

They do not begin to comprehend the seismographic profundity
of this advice. They only yell, "We want Pat. We want Pat."

"Well, you can't have her," Nixon says. "I want to keep her."

Yes, he had wanted her and he had wanted to keep her. Back in
Whittier, before they were married, he would drive her to Los Angeles when she had a date with another man. Then he would pick her
up and drive her back to Whittier when the date was done. That is not
an ordinary masochism. It is the near to bottomless bowl in which the
fortitude of a future political genius is being compounded. It had
made him the loser who did not lose.

But how many years and decades it must have taken before he
recognized that in a face-off with another man, he would be the second most attractive. Once he had made the mistake of fighting
Kennedy man to man, and wife to wife. Jack had beaten Dick, and
Jackie had certainly taken Pat. But now he had learned that the
movies were wrong and the second most attractive man was the one to
pick up the marbles, since losers (by the laws of existential economy)
had to be more numerous than winners.

"Some public men," he had said in an interview, "are destined to
be loved, and other public men are destined to be disliked, but the
most important thing about a public man is not whether he's loved or

disliked, but whether he's respected. So I hope to restore respect to the presidency at all levels of my conduct.

"My strong point, if I have a strong point, is performance. I always do more than I say. I always produce more than I promise."

And now here was this nice man talking to children, this nice man who has the reputation of being considerate about small things to the people who work for him, this family man married so many years to the same wife, possessor of two daughters who are almost beautiful and very obedient. He is a genius. Who would know?

Yes, the loser stands talking to all of his gang of adolescent losers who are so proud to have chosen stupidity as a way of life, and they are going to win. Smog lies over the heart. Freud is obsolete. To explain Nixon, nothing less than a new theory of personality can suffice.

All selections from *St. George and the Godfather* (1972)

# WATERGATE

## Into the Credibility Gap

Clark MacGregor gave a press conference just one hour after his arrival in Miami for the Republican Convention. A big man with straight sandy hair and dark horn-rimmed glasses, a big friendly nose, his manner is there to suggest that if only there were no Blacks, no Latins, and no slaughter in Vietnam, then America could be a country where Republicans administer government for other Republicans, and they would be superb at it. MacGregor's presence gives off that necessary aura of confidence, good management, and impersonal courtesy which the managers of successful corporations are also able to convey. Of course MacGregor is no corporation executive but a former congressman from Minnesota appointed recently by Nixon to run the Committee for Reelection of the President after John Mitchell has resigned, and in fact he dresses with just a little too much hint of the lost Square to work for an *Eastern* corporation, he is wearing a gray suit, baggy from travel, a pale-blue shirt *and* a black tie with little red diamonds, but these are unworthy items—what Clark MacGregor promotes is the geniality of high confidence. Behind him are charts. "Rate of Inflation Is Down," they say; "Real Earnings Are Up"; "Total Civilian Employment Is Up While Armed Forces Man Power Is Down!" and they stand in front of the powder-blue curtain (TV-blue), while underfoot is a blue-green carpet and gold-painted chairs for the Press. Mermaids and sea horses look down on MacGregor from the ornate ceiling of the Mediterranean Room as he is asked if there is any way the Republicans can lose the election.

"No," he says. A smile. "Although I think it will get closer. Let me say that we are gearing up for a close fight, and absolutely on the watch against overconfidence."

"But you think the polls are good?"

"In Minnesota, my home state, 96 percent of the Republicans are for Nixon, and that's an incredible figure if you know anything about party breakdowns."

"What about Watergate?" comes the first voice. "Will that hurt you?"

He is unflappable. "I am absolutely satisfied that the so-called Watergate caper will have absolutely no effect on the election of Richard Nixon." His doughty air suggests that he could be hired equally well as a sales manager or a police commissioner.

"In relation to Watergate," says another reporter, "is it possible you've set up your tight security in this hotel because you expect the Democrats to bug it?" There is mocking laughter, for the Press is much irritated. A security tight enough to guard the President has been installed at the Doral, yet the President won't even stay here!

To get to see even a minor Republican official, it is necessary to obtain a special folder and look up his room, then get the official's permission by telephone for an interview, then look to obtain a pass in the downstairs lobby in order to set foot on the elevator. A woman reporter cries out that the Republicans call themselves the Open-Door party. "Will you please open the door of the Doral a little?"

Now the conference is moving to its point. If there is a single flaw in any Republican presentation of themselves, it is to be found in Watergate. What a mess. Five men have been caught trying to remove the bugging devices they have installed (by breaking and entering) in Democractic Headquarters in Washington, and the two leaders not only have had links to the CIA but to the Committee to Reelect the President, indeed have worked for a more important team with the modest name of "plumbers" who were set up to investigate White House leaks to the Media: The "plumbers" include members of the White House staff, and a former Assistant Attorney General, are even connected to a special counsel to Nixon. One of the plumbers, E. Howard Hunt, formerly a high official in the CIA and White House consultant, has temporarily disappeared. Yes, what a mess. MacGregor has now replaced Mitchell as the head of the Committee to Reelect the President and now can dodge the worst of the questions by saying that he has only been on his new job since July 1. So he has no first-hand knowledge of what has gone on before, "although, I am convinced, let me say, that no one in the White House, or in high responsible position on the Committee to Reelect the President, has any prior knowledge of, or gave sanction to the operation generally known as the so-called Watergate caper. I will say," MacGregor stated solemnly, pushing his glasses up on his large nose, "that I have talked to the White House principals in this affair, and Mr. Stans, Mr. Mitchell, and Mr. Colson have all assured me that they were not involved, and I am convinced that they are men of honor. I can only say that they have satisfied me."

"Will you agree that if any of them were lying, there was no way you could know?"

"No, I cannot agree. The word of men of honor is good enough for me. More than that, I cannot say. We have been warned by Judge Richey to employ all necessary discretion against impinging on the rights of the defendants by making disclosures which would then hurt the government's case."

"But since you were not there before July 1, you have only the word of these high officials to go on?"

MacGregor has a temper, and he is containing it now. The straight sandy hair suggests some fire at the root, for his face is getting red. "I have endeavored to be as forthright as I can, given my lack of knowledge before July 1 of the activities of the Committee to Reelect the President."

No one quite dares to suggest he is saying that he knows but he doesn't know. "In public life," MacGregor says, "you have to learn when to trust the word of other people." But what he can't know is when an honorable man has an overpowering motive to lie. MacGregor gulps and reddens and his temper singes his hair, his glasses slide down his nose and are pushed up once more, the sea horses and mermaids look down on him, the Press looks up from their golden chairs and he does not move. He doesn't know and he does know, but he is a man who has been picked to weather more than one storm, and it will be no trick at all, here today, to ride this out. The Judge, he repeats, wishes to restrain them from talking of the case. ". . . necessary discretion . . . you fellows are trying to get me to impinge . . . rights of the defendants. . . ."

From *St. George and the Godfather* (1972)

# Interview with Ehrlichman

During the five days and thirty cumulative hours John Ehrlichman testified in the Caucus Room of the Old Senate Office Building before the Senate Watergate Committee in late July 1973, he was a formidable witness for the Nixon administration. Douglas Kneeland, writing for *The New York Times,* described him as "a combative cocky defender of the faith," and indeed Ehrlichman had something of the look on those room-packed occasions of an Irish or German middleweight with black eyebrows and a balding head, able to hit hard with either hand. Ehrlichman had a boxer's confidence. Kneeland went on to say, "Not that the tanned and muscular-looking former chief domestic affairs adviser to the President didn't smile now and then. But the smiles were those of a man who enjoys a good scrap—and he came out fighting . . . Mr. Ehrlichman was a new kind of witness for the Committee, a tough, unapologetic Nixon stalwart who obviously felt that a good offense was the best defense."

After a string of deferential or obviously frightened witnesses like Jeb Magruder, Hugh Sloan, Herbert Porter, Robert Odle, Gordon Strachan, and Richard Moore, Ehrlichman seemed to show by contrast a lack of ultimate respect for the good motives of the Committee: implicit in his attitude was the suggestion that politics and morality were not noted for their propinquity, and a political confrontation might be nearer to a football game than a religious convocation. If you played for a team, you did your best to play very well, but there was something obscene, said his attitude, in starting to think there was more moral worth to Michigan than Ohio State. So he looked sardonically, keenly, contemptuously, and on occasion subtly into the moral gravity of the Ervin committee as if all the while he were saying in effect, "Gentlemen, I wouldn't trust you with the collection plate."

Ehrlichman was one man who loved the sting of good English.

SAM DASH: So there came a time when you were administering an investigative unit?
EHRLICHMAN: Yes. In a literal sense, that is true.
DASH: Literal sense?
EHRLICHMAN: Yessir.

DASH: Not in an actual sense?

EHRLICHMAN: Well, here I am dueling with a professor.

There is a liberal eschatology whose first law is: Respect our latest hero or Hell awaits. Since liberal ideology is oriented toward a blood-less society, and imbibes its anti-machismo in daily doses, there is more need in the liberal firmament for heroes. They are less easy to find. Little in liberal ideology is conducive to hero-worship, yet the average liberal still wants to get a charge out of his liberal politics. The media, therefore, have a tendency to keep the Liberal-Hero-of-the-Month Club well stocked. In the summer of 1972, it was Henry Kissinger. In the fall of 1973, it would be Archibald Cox. In July '73, the Liberal-Hero-of-the-Month was that old Southern conservative Sam Ervin. His ideology took nothing from his qualifications—maybe it added to them. He had a fine theatrical presence, spoke like an old Shake-spearean actor, and was willing to serve as an instrument that might chop down Richard Nixon. Remarks, therefore, like Ehrlichman's reply to Sam Ervin, "The Chairman has the delightful trial room practice of interrupting something you don't want to hear," were as offensive as brimstone to liberal devotions. In that pious summer when hopes collected like in-held breath for the final impalement of Richard Nixon, a day of bad news for Nixon meant the millennium was nearer. So Ehrlichman's unrepentant defense made him stand out like a warlock.

SENATOR ERVIN: . . . your testimony is that John Dean told an untruth.

EHRLICHMAN: Yessir, twice. Once in the out-of-town tryout, once here.

SENATOR ERVIN: . . . you made some suggestions about disposing of the papers that were in [Hunt's] briefcase. My recollection is that you advised Mr. Dean to "deep six" these papers.

EHRLICHMAN: . . . it would have been folly for me . . . to suggest that the briefcase be thrown into the flood tide of the Potomac. . . . As I said, we have a great disposal system at the White House. If you really want to get rid of a document, you put it in a burn bag and you seal it up and it's never found again. It goes into a furnace and that is the end of it.

The gallery in the Caucus Room hated Ehrlichman. The Hero-of-the-Month may live only for a month but in those thirty days he is to be treated like Eleanor Roosevelt. One wasn't required to talk back to Sam Ervin.

Just as Conservatives prove good at weeding gardens and/or administering capital punishment but can be powerfully insensitive to the anguish of minorities who have lost their culture and their roots, so the liberal has his Christly sentiments (not wholly false) for the pain of that multitude who live on the edge of decent existence. Liberals want to believe they keep the weak alive. It is just that the liberal spirit, with its emphasis on administrative compassion and its detestation of violence, gets a touch hysterical when it comes to killing its enemies. Richard Nixon is one of the great American villains, but that is *not* because he tried to cover up a scandal. Rather he is a villain by way of the twenty-five years he did his best to murder the English language with a margarine of pieties—he is a villain because he had a negative charisma. He sucked the hope and heart out of American wit and creativity to the very limit of his personal ability. He was the apotheosis of Uriah Heep. He would yet be the only American President whose political career would die in the unwinding of his own excrement—he would end politically by suffocating himself. He was awful—with a force larger than himself. And yet he was the true test for liberal compassion. The liberals failed it miserably. Liberals were always saying: Love the odious, the crippled, and the weak. Love the cancer-ridden and the leprous. Build the hospitals and the schools. All bodies are salvageable, all organs interchangeable, all hearts redeemable; surgery and education are sacraments and grace.

The liberals failed. If Richard Nixon had been standing alone on the street and a thousand nonviolent liberals had been standing around him with flails, they would have beaten each other to death in their rush to get at him. They would have drowned in each other's slobber in the fury to beat him to a pulp. Richard Nixon had intensified the demonic lust-to-destroy in all those good compassionate Judeo-Christian liberal atheists. He had scorched reason a little further out of existence.

Civilization was in the Caucus Room on the days Ehrlichman testified. Civilization was nonviolent. But to the people in the Caucus Room, and the majority of people watching through the hot mornings and hotter July afternoons on television, John Ehrlichman was baiting the Hero-of-the-Month, good Sam Ervin, as powerful to the media for those thirty days as a newly elected Pope, and suppressed violence ran like a virus through liberal veins. Ehrlichman was unendurable. He acted as if he were proud to be on the side he was on; his pride was what could not be suffered. For it spoke of a world whose real complexity could savage a liberal brain. Liberals could certainly live with the hot idea they were fighting Mephisto's own Nixon, but they couldn't support the Kierkegaardian complexity that the good guys might be right next to the bad guys on the same team. Ehrlichman came forward as if he were one of the Good Guys, born knowing it. Implicit in everything he did in that Caucus Room was an attitude: Gentlemen, detest Richard Nixon and sneer at me, but do not pretend these Watergate peccadilloes are serious matters when we all know politics is a business as dirty as the rest of life, and we are only players choosing and re-choosing sides in a game whose rules are never honored. Gentlemen, I come to you in the firm tradition of high shenanigans and illegal Presidential practice long and well practiced by John F. Kennedy and Lyndon Johnson.

So Ehrlichman was his own man for five days and took a cannonading of cross-examination and never looked worried, and the liberals never forgave him, because he had tried to deny them a clean-cut holy war by suggesting that the end of Richard Nixon did not end a single one of the world's ongoing fevers.

After pride comes attrition. After the adrenaline that is found in advocacy comes the anemia of protracted legal defense, of convictions and appeals, and the costs of law firms charging for thousands of hours of work. It is not the legal process that breaks a man's confidence but the cost of paying for it. Ehrlichman was found guilty in a Washington, D.C., court (before a black jury to whom he brought a black lawyer) on charges of conspiracy, obstruction of justice, and lying under oath. In another trial, Ehrlichman was convicted of lying to a grand jury on the Ellsberg break-in. He was sentenced to prison for twenty months to five years, the terms to run concurrently. There was a view of him on a TV newscast just after one of these trials, and the power of his presence before the Watergate committee was gone. Now he looked like a skilled professional middleweight who had had some internal organs surgically removed. Punishment lived on his face. His cheeks looked soft, as if self-pity would convert them before long into jowls; his small (well-curved) mouth was fighting petulance. It was obvious he thought he had been given a very bad decision. Some elasticity had gone out of his body, some joy in combat. His appearances before the Watergate committee took on, in retrospect, their own kind of luster. He had had such confidence then in the value of spirited advocacy itself, as if his secret faith had been that something in the scheme of things approved of men who found happiness in the midst of battle. That kind of belief now looked to be gone. Maybe there is no moral shock so profound as the idea that the brave and cowardly are ground up equally on the grindstone. Looking at Ehrlichman now aroused compassion, a surprising emotion considering how little was held in common with his politics. In the Sixties, after revolution on the campuses, marches on Washington, and the war in Vietnam, Ehrlichman was not a man to sit down with, not comfortably. Politics had been teleological in the Sixties—in the distance was a barricade; one would fight on one side of it, or the other. But in the Seventies it was not political teleology that offered the obsession, but entropy. Were the forms disappearing and the energies descending? Was America hearing the gurgle of historical waters going down the drain? In bland times, a man's clear-cut manner could seem more significant to the life of things than his politics. Witness the pleasure one could take in Ehrlichman before the Watergate committee. Something valuable had been lost in the shadow of self-pity that had now come over him.

It is possible that our sense of our own identity is no more than the self-esteem we put into our psychic account—a punched-out haunted look is the true equivalent of psychic bankruptcy. It is agonizing to give up a powerful personality. In many an organized psyche the perquisites of the ego are the nearest one can come to sensual bliss.

There was evidence, however, in the years after his trials and convictions that Ehrlichman must have given up one identity to take on another. Reported in the press was a separation from his wife. He was living in Santa Fe in a four-room adobe house on a hill up a dirt road. "Inside, nubby fabrics and earthenware, a fire lit against morning chill, a window flat of kale and corn seedlings for the little vegetable bed out back." (*Village Voice*, S. J. Diamond, June 7, 1976.) Suspended from the federal and the California bars, he had decided he might as well disbar himself in Washington state to save "pain and embarrassment," and so he was living now on no income other than his advances as a novelist, a new novelist! Why, indeed, was he writing novels?

But then Ehrlichman, in the midst of appealing two convictions, may not have wished to confuse his legal situation by writing too directly of his own experiences. That might oblige him to deal with facts whose disclosure could affect the legal appeals. Besides, he had a thesis he could not prove: Ehrlichman's novel, *The Company*, was ready to suggest that the real account of the break-in and cover-up could best be told by the CIA.

It is a tour-de-force of a novel for the word *Watergate* does not appear in its pages. We have instead a book about a CIA man named

Martin who orders the death of a militant priest in an unsuccessful Bay-of-Pigs-type invasion of a Caribbean republic, we learn that Martin has been given these assassination orders by the President of the United States (who, it is suggested, is trying to satisfy some pre-arranged balance of power with the Russians). A secret CIA report is made on this murder, the Primula Report, and only one copy exists.

Years later, Martin has worked up the echelons of the CIA to the post of CIA director. He has labored under three Presidents, and is now in trouble again from the old affair. The new President of the United States, Richard Monckton, is hostile to the CIA, wishes to reduce the Agency's power, and is on the track of the Primula Report. If Martin is obliged to surrender it, his own career will be destroyed, and the CIA grievously damaged. So Martin devises a situation where some Presidential agents working out of the White House are encouraged to undertake the burglary of a prominent gossip columnist's house. It is a set-up, however. Martin has these agents secretly photographed in the act, and shows the photographs to the President, thereby enabling Martin to make a deal for himself. The Primula Report is destroyed and the President gives up on his war with the CIA. The point of the novel is clear. Watergate, the White House "horrors," and the consecutive panics of the cover-up are offered their back-lighting. The CIA was holding the flashlight.

Given the explosion in Ehrlichman's own life—from the second most powerful administrator in Washington out to a disbarred lawyer living on a dirt road in the New Mexico hills—the restraint of the novel, its intricate clockwork of plot, and its lack of overt rage speak a full volume of the passions Ehrlichman chose to contain within himself. We can only guess at his mastery over the chaos implicit in such a state. To have power and lose it through one's own errors can induce self-pity or self-examination, but to have power and lose it because one was set up is to be marooned in obsession, paranoia, and impotent fury. The absence of passion and the lucidity of Ehrlichman's novel offer therefore a spiritual credential—it is a virtuoso if ironic act to write sympathetically, even intimately, about the problems of one's enemies as they are plotting to destroy your power. *The Company*, as a result, has to be one of the most curious novels ever published in America.

Certainly, its author, arriving for a conversation about his novel, seemed to have traveled one full identity away from the man seen in the Caucus Room of the Old Senate Office Building. Now, he had a beard that was turning gray and he had a paunch. It was not the fat which comes from overeating—more the slacking of abdominal muscles that enters men in their fifties when they have taken a great deal of punishment. Since he also had the easy and agreeable manner of a man who has been through an experience bad enough not to fear smaller experiences, he may have seemed representative again of what he had been originally—an American from the Far West. With his beard, his casual clothes, and the character of the calm he presented—that sense of peace we offer when we have relinquished something valuable in ourselves—he was not unlike a cross between a gray-bearded prospector and some hippie professor from a Western college, the radical on the faculty, champion of *Whole Earth Catalogue,* soft-voiced, gentle, equable, open to conferences with campus friends—yes, the first professor on the faculty to smoke pot openly with his students, and not much on sports anymore. Something of these qualities was now in his style. It took a wrench of the mood to insist that he had ever been one of the Prussian twins of the Nixon administration, no, it was more like talking to an old classmate across the years who had been, yeah, teaching in this rather agreeable cow college out at the edge of desert country, yes, and the minds were separate but not that far apart. The Seventies were proving different from the Sixties.

MAILER: I picked up *The Company* to read yesterday about four in the afternoon, and I finished it at eleven in the evening.

EHRLICHMAN: Which is cruel and unusual punishment.

MAILER: It's fast for me because I read slowly, but I heard we could do this interview today and there wouldn't be another opportunity for weeks, so I rushed. I offer this actually as a compliment, because I don't get through too many books from beginning to end.

EHRLICHMAN: I don't either.

MAILER: But there was something about *The Company.* I think both its virtue and vice as a novel is that it reads as much like a brief as a novel. There is a clarity of argument in it from beginning to end—a point being made. You were arguing a hypothetical brief, how the CIA could have implicated a President of the United States in such a way as to have power over him, a special power to be able to make him do their bidding. If you will, it is the reverse of Watergate, where the situation broke loose and got unruly.

EHRLICHMAN: I started out to write a penny melodrama about the CIA rigging of Presidential elections. An awful lot of my experience has been in campaigns, and I thought that it would be something that I could do realistically. As I got into the outlining of the story, it became what it is, quite another story, the one that you described.

MAILER: Well, I was fascinated with your novel, fascinated with the brief. I've felt for a long time that Watergate began as a mystery and has ended as a larger mystery than it seemed to be in the beginning. In fact, I am all but convinced that to a great extent, if not entirely, Watergate was a CIA operation.

EHRLICHMAN: Have you seen Fred Thompson's book called *At That Point in Time?*

MAILER: No.

EHRLICHMAN: He was the minority counsel on the Watergate committee, you know, that Ervin committee. He devotes about the last third of his book to his efforts and Howard Baker's efforts to find out whether that assertion you just made is true or not. And he obviously leaves the reader with one hundred questions unanswered, and paints a picture of the CIA totally in command, totally able to frustrate a Senator's inquiry, totally able to frustrate the Senate Committees' staff inquiry. I think he makes a case of probable cause.

MAILER: In the White House, during Watergate, was it generally the assumption that the CIA had a lot to do with the break-in?

EHRLICHMAN: No, I don't think so. Bear in mind, I left quite early in that whole episode, and when I left, after a month or two, I was pretty effectively cut off, so that I haven't been able to derive very much information at all from the White House after about spring '73.

MAILER: Well, I know, but we can go back to June '72 . . . [laugh] . . . when it all happened. After all, there were some *fairly* intelligent people [Mailer chuckles] in that place, there had to be a number of speculations, and it seems, on the face of whatever little evidence we can trust, that the first speculation was: Of course it was a CIA operation, and the CIA will probably take care of it very neatly, because they are more embarrassed than we are. Wasn't that virtually the attitude?

EHRLICHMAN: It was obviously something that occurred to Richard Nixon in June '72, as some of us have since discovered.

MAILER: Didn't General Walters say at one point, "We've looked into our files, and it is not one of our operations," and didn't Haldeman answer at that point, "We have reason to believe it *is* CIA"?

EHRLICHMAN: Yeah, but I don't know how much Haldeman believed that. His response may have been pure baloney.

MAILER: Poker.

EHRLICHMAN: Exactly, exactly.

MAILER: Anybody who knows anything about the CIA has to admit Haldeman had a legitimate and workable response. I said poker advisedly. Because at that point Walters couldn't know whether Haldeman was bluffing or not. Walters knew enough about his agency to know that of course the CIA could have done it, and very well might have, and Haldeman could be in possession of more information than he, Walters, given the cellular nature of the CIA that you point out in *The Company*.

EHRLICHMAN: I think you are probably right, that those "little did he know that I knew" kind of things were what was going on.

MAILER: I would take it a step further, I think the situation had to be Kafkan for people in the Nixon administration. It seems to me, just speculating about Haldeman, that Haldeman himself, while he didn't know precisely what had happened, could well believe he had a case—that is, he could bluff with the assurance that his hand might well be stronger than the other man's hand.

EHRLICHMAN: Well, I think the bluff worked to a point.

MAILER: To a point?

EHRLICHMAN: I suspect that around that time the CIA got all its in-house stories straight, they went around and picked up or destroyed McCord's papers, and did all those housekeeping things Fred Thompson talks about. I think there *was* a certain amount of doubt in the minds of both Helms and Walters on June 23 as to just how much involvement the CIA had had, at least from the answers that we were being given. I think Helms and Walters went back to Langley and got a lot of people around the table, and asked, "Well, what really did happen here? Was Martinez on the payroll of the CIA at the time of the break-in? He was! . . . Well, *who else!* Let's tote it all up, let's see just how deep we are in this, and who gave what orders."

MAILER: Do you think they then came out with a feeling it was not one of their own operations?

EHRLICHMAN: I don't know, I really don't know.

MAILER: You see, I have always been a firm believer in the enclave theory of the CIA, to wit that no one who directs the CIA can ever be certain, and very often can't even be fairly certain whether the CIA is implicated in a caper.

EHRLICHMAN: That is why I think they had to go back and do some checking.

MAILER: But can they really find out?

EHRLICHMAN: I doubt it.

MAILER: There must be enclaves not amenable to that kind of checking out.

EHRLICHMAN: Particularly when something goes wrong.

MAILER: Yeah. It seemed to me that if I had been the head of the CIA, facing Nixon's continuing desire to take over some of the functions and powers of the CIA, it would have been to my interest to infiltrate CREEP. There must have been people in CREEP who were CIA agents.

EHRLICHMAN: The Joint Chiefs had a guy stealing stuff left and right . . .

MAILER: That was Yeoman Radford.

EHRLICHMAN: The guy would walk through Henry Kissinger's paper mill like a cafeteria. Take one of these, one of those, he helped himself as he went around and made Xeroxes of whatever he wanted, then put it all back. If he could do it, certainly others could.

MAILER: I guess the point I am leading toward is that if I were the head of the CIA, I would very much want to implicate CREEP in much the same way the FBI used to get the Black Panthers implicated. Indeed, the worst things the Black Panthers ever did were done by black FBI men posing as Panthers. In fact I sometimes think the history of the left through the Sixties . . .

EHRLICHMAN: There was none, you are about to say?

MAILER: Well, two-thirds of it may have been made by America's secret police. That is staggering. You know, in the Sixties, I was very much a man of the left, and I used to walk around in a state of shock wondering how our people could be so idiotic. I can't tell you what some of the excessive infantile militancy of the left did to my morale as a leftist. That goddamned FBI! They really blunted my point. I am less of a leftist today, and one of the reasons is because those bastards were working away full-time committing their supposedly leftist atrocities. It made me despair then about the militancy of the left. It was so adolescent, and ridiculous and unbalanced, finally frightening. And the FBI was doing it. How much they did, we still don't know—it keeps being uncovered—but they contributed a lot to the freakiest parts of the history of the left in that period. Now, the CIA had to be aware of how effective the FBI had been. If I am a CIA patriot, working for the CIA and devoted to it, and I am terribly distrustful of the Nixon administration and am afraid they want to take over the agency's powers, precisely the situation you lay out in *The Company*, then, in effect, I'm wrestling with them for power, and naturally want to get a better grip.

EHRLICHMAN: The only problem that I see with that is CREEP was less important than it is given credit for, certainly as a way to get at Nixon. In an emergency, it was detachable. A whole bunch of people could have been put over the side in June '72 without really touching Nixon.

MAILER: Was it Nixon who held on to CREEP?

EHRLICHMAN: I would say it was. There were a lot of knee-jerk reactions by a lot of people who tended to defend people at CREEP on the false premise that if Mitchell and Magruder and folks of that rank were criticized or penalized, it would, in some way or other, reflect directly on the President. In fact, it wouldn't have, it was detachable.

MAILER: Well it may have been detachable, but in June '72, McGovern had a lot of momentum.

EHRLICHMAN: Sure.

MAILER: There had to be a panic that Watergate could give McGovern the election.

EHRLICHMAN: Well, yeah, I run into people all the time that say, why in the world did they go in there, we don't understand it, he won by 60-some percent. Nixon was a sure thing, why in the world was CREEP doing all this stuff? The fact is, you are right, at that time I don't think there was any sense of confidence in the White House that Nixon was surely going to be re-elected, but—and I am using great hindsight—it would have been possible to cut that problem out at CREEP without hurting the President as such. My argument is that our somebody in the CIA would have thought it better to have his fellow in the White House committing an atrocity than in CREEP. For instance, I think something overlooked today is the Schlesinger study. Jim Schlesinger did a study of the intelligence community in 1970 or 1971 when he was still in the Office of Management of the Budget, and the CIA had to know about the existence of that study. It called for a major overhaul of them, virtually a disestablishment of some of the existing intelligence apparatus. Of all the threats to the CIA that existed, I think that study was probably considered the foremost threat by the core management of the CIA. Only that kind of bureaucratic concern to protect themselves suggests, to me at least, an infiltration of the White House itself rather than CREEP if the alternatives were being considered.

MAILER: In secret police work one tries to get an agent wherever one can. One has not only the A plan but the B plan, the C plan. The A plan may be to infiltrate the White House, but maybe the CIA got further into CREEP because it was easier to infiltrate. Operatives don't wait for the master plan to unfold. They seize at tactical advantages, creating their particular mischief as they go. It may be that elements of the CIA, having infiltrated CREEP, were relatively on their own. Helms may not have been sending the word down every day. Helms may not even have known about it.

EHRLICHMAN: If you put a termite in a block of wood, you expect him to do his job without a lot of supervision.

MAILER: Perfect. I think the intent may have been, if there was intent as such, may have been to get some kind of grip on the Nixon administration one way or another. If CREEP could be implicated in wiretapping, the President would be not exactly implicated, but tarnished sufficiently to wish to keep the matter quiet—thus, a bargaining point could be gained. Then, for all we know, a double-cross might have occurred. Two opposed wings of the CIA, as personified by Hunt and McCord, could have been working at cross-purposes. Or, the FBI could have decided to trip the CIA. Watergate could have been a setup where the police were tipped off by one of the agents. There is no telling what went on. All we know is that we have no explanation. Watergate is more of a mystery today.

EHRLICHMAN: I totally agree, I totally agree.

MAILER: The element I find most mysterious to me now is what happened afterwards. If we keep using this metaphor of the wrestler's grip, if the CIA wanted to get a punishing grip on the Nixon administration to improve the balance for themselves, still the first interest of the intelligence establishment must have been to keep Nixon in, bad as he was for them, rather than have to deal with McGovern. So it was important to them that Nixon win the election. The establishment of the CIA may have been as worried about the consequences of Watergate as Nixon, especially if it was an operation that was supposed to get CREEP implicated in the power plays of the invisible government but not exposed in the public media. After the election, however, things began to change. Something in the power structure of the country began to shift. Some of the very people and corporations who had made Nixon in the first place and supported him and who drew their notion of stable government and society from Nixon began to turn on him.

EHRLICHMAN: The thing began to deteriorate after the Ervin hearing. That display was brilliant politics. It seems to me underrated at the present time. A lot of people in the administration and establishment were either personally disaffected or they reacted to what seemed to be an overwhelming national reaction. Things began to flake away. Substantial respectable business and academic support which Nixon had enjoyed began to shut up and stay at home. I think those televised hearings were the major contributors to that.

MAILER: One other thing I have never understood is why the Nixon administration did not in general use a tougher defense. I remember the day Helms testified. Cross-examination of him, even by Republicans, was benign. The timidity with which the Senators approached Helms was impressive in reverse by what it suggested of his powers.

EHRLICHMAN: That is the problem with congressional oversight over the CIA. It is possible for the CIA to cultivate and coopt the Congress to an extent that even J. Edgar Hoover didn't equal. I don't know what goes into that mix, but there were two oversight committees, Senate and House, and I appeared at both those committees in the course of investigation of the CIA relationship to the White House. The CIA had both of those committees totally psyched. There was not anybody on any of them who would seriously question anything that a representative of the CIA told them. That is the product of years of work on the part of the CIA. Early on, they had identified the congressional flank . . . as potentially very troublesome and no lengths were too great for the CIA in terms of cultivating particular members of Congress. So that attitude on Helms' part was totally natural, because this is his vineyard. Those were his grapes sitting up there.

From *Chic* (December 1976)

# A Harlot High and Low

The nature of the difficulty begins to disclose itself. We cannot construct an explanation. We do not know which of our facts are bricks and which are papier-mâché painted to look like bricks. We can only watch the way the bricks are handled.

It is painful, nonetheless, to relinquish one's hope for a narrative, to admit that study of the CIA may not lead to the exposure of facts so much as to the epistemology of facts. We will not get the goods so quickly as we will learn how to construct a model which will tell us why we cannot get the goods. Of course, that will never be enough—willy-nilly, the habit will persist to look for a new narrative (and damn the papier-mâché bricks).

In the meantime, however, a short course:

Epistemological Model I:

If half the pieces in a jigsaw puzzle are missing, the likelihood is that something can still be put together. Despite its gaps, the picture may be more or less visible. Even if most of the pieces are gone, a loose mosaic can be arranged of isolated elements. The possibility of the real picture being glimpsed under such circumstances is small but not altogether lost.[1] It is just that one would like to know if the few pieces left belong to the same set.[2]

Epistemological Model II:

Maybe it is the splinters of a mirror rather than the scattered pieces of a jigsaw puzzle that provide a superior ground for the metaphor. We are dealing not with reality, after all, but that image of reality which reaches the surface through the cracked looking glass of the media.

Epistemological Model III:

What is most crucial is that we do not forget that we are interpreting curious actions. Men who seem to be honest are offering cover. We are obliged to remind ourselves that a life lived under cover produces a chronic state of mind which is not unlike those peculiar moments when staring in the mirror too long we come to recognize that the face looking back at us must—inescapably—be our own. Yet it is not. Our vicissitudes (but not our souls) stand revealed in the mirror; or, given another day, and another mirror, there we are, feeling wretched, looking splendid.

Epistemological Model IV:

Doubtless the difficulty is analogous to writing a poem with nothing but names, numbers, facts, conjecture, gossip, trial balloons, leaks, and other assorted pieces of prose.

[1]Larry Rivers has taught us as much.
[2]Is this what Robert Rauschenberg is up to?

For example:

When we interviewed him in my office on December 10, 1973, he struck all of us as a highly intelligent, highly motivated person. . . . Finally I asked him, "Mr. Martinez, if in fact you were a CIA plant on the Watergate team and were reporting back to the Agency, would you tell us?" He broke into a broad smile, looked around the room, and laughed. He never answered the question; no answer was necessary.

*—At That Point in Time*

Let us go back to the facts, to the false facts, distorted facts, concealed facts, empty facts, secretly rich facts, and unverifiable speculations of our narrative.

In this connection, nothing we have read about Gordon Liddy explains his long silence in jail so well as the supposition that he is an agent of real caliber. Of his biography we know he was in the FBI in the early Sixties, an assistant district attorney in Dutchess County, ran for Congress on the Conservative party ticket, and got a job with the Treasury Department high up in a Customs Bureau drug campaign called Operation Intercept. It was not a position to leave him alien to certain intimacies of the CIA, the Mafia, and the flow of profits in the drug trade. Liddy came to the White House to work for Egil Krogh, who was trying to organize the Nixon administration's war on drugs with a projected team of CIA men, FBI men, narcs, and private detectives, an undertaking some would see darkly as a most ambitious cover for Nixon's real intent, which was to commence his own Intelligence on a competitive level with the CIA and the FBI. It is worth mentioning that during this period, Liddy wrote a memo for Nixon in criticism of the FBI, which Nixon described to Krogh as "the most brilliant memorandum" to come his way "in a long time."[3] It is with this background that Liddy comes to CREEP. There is nothing in these details to suggest he could not be a career agent.

We read of how he burns his hand in a flame to impress a girl and threatens to kill Magruder if Jeb touches him on the shoulder again. John Dean describes to us how Liddy offers to commit suicide if that will protect the administration. Liddy offers a lecture on how to kill a man with a finely sharpened pencil. There is nothing in these details to suggest he could not be a career agent.

[3]These details are given in a book impressively researched by Edward Jay Epstein, *An American Coup D'Etat* (Putnam's).

"The master who instructed me in the deadliest of the Oriental martial arts taught me that the outcome of a battle is decided in the minds of the opponents before the first blow is struck."

—G. Gordon Liddy[4]

We have the habit to look on the Watergate burglars as ignorant Cubans led by clowns. Being scorned as ridiculous is, of course, a cover in itself; the CIA can count on such a disguise being provided by the wire services. Simple declarative sentences make curious actions appear automatically absurd.

Under examination, the burglars look better. Gonzales had been a bodyguard for Batista, and fought in the Bay of Pigs. Martinez had been a CIA boat captain and made 354 illegal runs to Cuba. Barker was a member of Batista's secret police, and an FBI contact in Cuba, then an informer against Castro. By Hunt's own description, Barker became his "principal assistant" during the Bay of Pigs, and Hunt was chief of political action.

The fourth Cuban happens to be Italian—Frank Sturgis, an ex-Marine born Frank Angelo Fiorini. He served with Castro in the Sierra Maestra—and would later claim he was already an agent for the Company. In any case, he was good enough to be working as Fidel's personal supervisor in the Havana casinos until the day gambling was eliminated. Then Sturgis decided to defect. To the Mafia and to the CIA. (Or is it simpler to say the Mafia wing of the CIA?) It is a not inconsiderable defection.

Before the Bay of Pigs, Sturgis would act as contact for Santo Trafficante, who with his son Santo, Jr., "controlled much of Havana's tourist industry," and was alleged to have received "bulk shipments of heroin from Europe and forwarded them through Florida to New York."[5] During this period, Sturgis joined a CIA unit called Operation Forty, which had been set up to kill Castro and a number of important Fidelistas. Involved in this training were Trafficante and E. Howard Hunt,[6] Frank Sturgis,[7] and Robert Maheu. Maheu and Sturgis must

---

[4]As quoted in *Nightmare.*
[5]Alfred W. McCoy et al., *The Politics of Heroin in Southeast Asia.*
[6]"Strange Bedfellows."
[7]In *Undercover,* Hunt mentions in passing that he did not meet Sturgis until shortly before Watergate. Of course, he also does not mention that there was a plot to assassinate Castro. Nor does he bother to inform us that Hank Sturgis is the name of a character in Hunt's early novel, *Bimini Run,* which Frank Angelo Fiorini liked well enough to modify into an alias.

have been reasonably well met, since Sturgis is still pivotal enough eleven years later to be chatting with Jack Anderson in the lobby of Washington National Airport on the morning he arrives from Miami with Barker, Martinez, and Gonzales for the last break-in at Watergate, but then it would be difficult to name an investigative reporter in America more pivotal than Anderson.

> "I don't know if I told you before," Sturgis wrote to his wife [while in jail], "but William F. Buckley used to work for CIA and I don't know if he still does. When he found out that Howard (Hunt) was going to work in the White House, he told Howard it was good that he could be so close to the President but Howard told him that he was there to take orders and not to influence anyone. That was a good answer!"
>
> ... Buckley frankly admitted he was a "deep cover agent" for the CIA from July, 1951, to March, 1952, but said he had not worked for them since.
>
> —Jack Anderson, September 18, 1973

> It was apparent from the documents that in November 1971, a month after he took part in the Fielding break-in, Martinez mentioned his association with Hunt to his case officer who, in turn, took Martinez to the CIA's chief of station in Miami.
>
> We immediately requested that the chief of station be brought from Florida for an interview. The chief, a heavyset man who appeared rather nervous, told us that in March 1972, Martinez had asked him if he "really knew all about the Agency activities in the Miami area." Martinez had dropped hints about Hunt's activities, the chief said, which had concerned him so much that he wrote a letter to CIA headquarters inquiring about Hunt's status. The answer, we were told, was that the chief should "cool it" and not concern himself with Hunt's affairs.
>
> —*At That Point in Time*

One does better not to rely on that comfortable picture we have of E. Howard Hunt as an unhinged undercover man in a wild red wig impotently badgering Dita Beard on her hospital bed—the wig may have been chosen to make him startling to a fearful woman.

By the rank of the posts he occupied in his career, it is obvious that Hunt, for a long time at least, was well regarded in the Agency.

For that matter, he has so many credentials we can wonder how close he came in his own mind to becoming director of the CIA. In his auto-biography, *Undercover,* he remarks, "Obviously I was never going to be director of Central Intelligence, nor did I particularly want to be," but the year is 1966 and he says it after more than fifteen years of service and such prime positions as deputy chief of station in Mexico (which is where William F. Buckley, Jr., worked for him); chief of covert op-erations for southeastern Europe—Albania, Yugoslavia, Bulgaria, Greece, and Turkey; chief of political action for the Guatemala opera-tion that overthrew Arbenz; chief of covert operations for the north Asia command—China, Korea, Japan; chief of station in Uruguay; chief of political action for the Bay of Pigs; chief of Domestic Opera-tions Division (the United States); and chief of covert action for West-ern Europe.

Before joining the CIA Hunt had been an English major at Brown, served in the Navy, the OSS, had been a war correspondent for *Life,* published novels, worked in Hollywood, had a Guggenheim Fellowship for one of his novels, and was in Europe for the ECA under Averell Harriman. Later, within the CIA, he collaborated with Allen Dulles in the writing of *The Craft of Intelligence.* He also worked closely with Frank Wisner, Allen Dulles, Dick Helms, Richard Bissell, Tracy Barnes, Tom Karamessines—there are no larger names in the CIA. If his autobiography fails to mention Cord Meyer or James Angleton there is no reason we cannot speculate on his concealed relations with them, particularly from 1966 to 1970, when Hunt neglects to describe what he is doing for the Company, and the assumption, since he is sta-tioned in America, is capers, domestic capers.

> A Dutch manufacturer of electronic gadgetry was demonstrating some ultrasophisticated electronic "sneakies." The Dutch sales-man announced that over twenty items of gadgetry had been hid-den in the exhibition room and invited his CIA guests to find them. Then the Dutchman set about to uncover them, and *he* couldn't find them. Jim McCord had sneaked into the room be-fore the demonstration, found them all, and removed them. "Jim is one fine operator," said Helms. . . .
>
> —Miles Copeland, *National Review.*
> September 14, 1973

McCord was in the CIA for twenty years but he seems like nothing so much as an FBI man. A devout Methodist, he was abstemious and soft-voiced in his right-wing opinions. His personality speaks of law and order rather than espionage or counterespionage. With the CIA from the first years of its inception (those years when it was raiding the FBI, and Hoover did not like it, and may for all we know have been casting about for a career agent who could infiltrate the CIA for the rest of his working life), McCord worked for the Company from 1951 to 1970 and became chief of the Physical Security Division of the Office of Security.

As we know, his work had in part to do with finding concealed bugs and dealing with advanced eavesdropping equipment. He was good enough to receive a Distinguished Service Award from Helms, and Allen Dulles once referred to him as "my top man."[8] We do not know what he was top man in, but it is not mean praise.

His performance during the Watergate break-in is on the consequence fascinating for its incompetence. McCord, according to Hunt's account, bought only four walkie-talkies where six had been needed. He delayed charging the batteries. He neglected to disconnect a burglar-alarm system. In the course of the first break-in, he removed his men from the Democratic National Committee offices before the job was done. Then for several days he was unable to process the two rolls of film the Cubans did manage to take because McCord's "man" was out of town. In addition, according to Liddy, McCord "bugged the wrong telephone line. He was supposed to tap O'Brien's."[9] So a second attempt was necessary. On the next try, two of McCord's walkie-talkies had uncharged batteries. McCord retaped the locks after the guard had removed the tapes. He then insisted to Liddy on going ahead with the operation. He also retaped the locks horizontally instead of vertically; the tape was therefore visible at a glance. Hunt would finally decide that McCord was a double agent for the Democrats. A double agent he may have been—for the CIA—and a triple agent for the FBI, but a Democrat? McCord?

Whoever he was, McCord broke the Watergate case by his letter in March 1973 to Judge Sirica: "There was political pressure applied to the defendants to plead guilty and remain silent. Perjury occurred during the trial. . . ."

He also said, "The Watergate Operation was not a CIA operation. . . . I know for a fact that it was not." It is a retired CIA operative speaking, which is to say a man who may or may not be retired.

[8]Lewis Chester et al., *Watergate.*
[9]*Undercover.*

Authoritative disclaimers by CIA officials bear the same relation to fact that the square root of minus one bears to a real number. The net effect of McCord's remark, therefore, is to make us more suspicious of the CIA. The possibility that he is an FBI man thereby increases an iota.

The second break-in took place in order that the tap on Larry O'Brien's phone that McCord had not put in well enough to function after the first break-in should now be put in again. Hunt thought the project was odd. "O'Brien's in Miami," he said to Liddy. "Why in hell should we tap the phone in his Washington office? . . . What's the rationale? As a friend, colleague and fellow professional, I'm asking you to go back to Mitchell, Dean, and Magruder and reargue the case."[10] Liddy replied, "Okay, I'll try again, but I hate to do it. They look to me to get things done, not argue against them."

Since Liddy is the conspirator who has remained silent, we do not know his "principal," that is, we do not know who told him to break into Democratic headquarters the first time, nor—it may be more interesting—who insisted on a second time when Hunt thought the only logic was to call it off. It is not impossible that Magruder, Mitchell—or could it be Dean?—had an undisclosed relation to the CIA. Let us spur on the vertigo of that thought.

> Mr. Haldeman said he had never understood why Alexander P. Butterfield, the aide who disclosed the existence of the White House tapes to the Senate Watergate committee, wanted to join the White House staff. . . .
>
> "He was soon to become an Air Force General. I have never understood why he insisted, against my advice, on dropping his commission or why he suddenly wanted to be part of the Nixon team.
>
> "In view of his subsequent role," Mr. Haldeman went on, "these actions seem even more curious today. Was Butterfield a CIA agent? Maybe. I just don't know."
>
> —*The New York Times,* June 23, 1976

> In the early Sixties he [Haig] ran a CIA-financed Bay of Pigs rehabilitation program, preceding Alexander Butterfield in the job.
> —"Strange Bedfellows"

[10]Quoting from Hunt is biting the bullet. Still, it is tempting to quote. From *Undercover.*

Colson complained to Bast that the President was always on the verge of coming down hard on the CIA. But, Colson groused, Nixon was talked out of it by presidential staff chief, Al Haig, who feared it would "take down the whole intelligence community."

—Jack Anderson, July 15, 1974

Haig told us there was "no way" he was working for the CIA.

—Jack Anderson, July 15, 1974

[Leon] Jaworski had been . . . a director of a private foundation that laundered funds for the CIA.

—"Strange Bedfellows"

We also learned that Paul O'Brien, who had served as counsel to the Committee to Re-elect the President after the Watergate break-in, was a former CIA operative.

—*At That Point in Time*

Among the officers of OSS Detachment 101 was Clark MacGregor, later a Congressman, a White House staffer, and, after the Watergate break-in, the replacement for John Mitchell as head of the Committee for the Re-Election of the President.

—*Compulsive Spy*

At one point, Colson would say in pain, "Every story that Woodward won the Pulitzer Prize for was fed to him by the CIA."

An observer of the Company, hearing of this, shook his head. "Deep Throat is a cover in itself. Where is the casual reader who will argue with so agreeable a story—one man's revelation pulling down the entire Nixon administration? If Deep Throat told all, it was only because the information had already been neatly collected for Deep Throat to tell." The observer shook his head. "Learn the law of reversal. The victims can be the agents in these affairs. There is as much need to remain suspicious of Colson as to feel sorry for him, since in attacking the CIA, Colson creates good cover for them. The reaction of the newspaper reader who dislikes old Chuck is to think, 'Even if it is true, I won't believe the story if it comes from Colson.' The Bast interview, you see, bothers me. Colson visits Bast, a private investigator, sits down by the pool next to the shrubbery and never wonders if he is being taped? Colson? Pit-bull Colson?

"By the same guideline, the heroes can be the villains. Beware of the heroes of Watergate. I look at the Washington *Post* and think, 'Isn't it a brave paper? Isn't that a heroic editor who dares what no editor of no other major paper will dare? Isn't that right in the vein of major newspaper editors as we have come to know them?' "

On publication of this piece, the editor of *The Washington Post* emphatically denied that he had ever been, or was now, a member of the CIA.

"Never allow yourself," the observer says, "to think you have a fixed platform from which to measure these motions. We're out in the stars with Einstein, I assure you. For instance, you speak of McCord as being inefficient when what you relate is no more than Hunt's description of how McCord acted in the break-in. Hunt's book could have been written by an enclave."

"Were they wishing to suggest that McCord was dealing with the Democrats?"

"Never look for the answer. Pursue the question into the next question. The answer is invariably smudged, but the questions are beautiful. There is the rapture of the depths descending into the questions."

Of course, the CIA had infiltrated the FBI, and the FBI had unknown men working for it in the CIA. We must assume both had agents in the Bureau of Narcotics and Dangerous Drugs, the IRS, the National Security Council, the 40 Committee, the Atomic Energy Commission, the Special Operations Division, Naval Intelligence, Air Force Intelligence, the Defense Intelligence Agency, the National Security Agency, the Council on Foreign Relations, HUGHES, plus a number of private intelligence companies whose work extended from military-industrial security to private detectives' offices. In turn, these companies, bureaus, groups, and agencies had to the best of their ability infiltrated the CIA and the FBI. Since the CIA, the FBI, and other major intelligence also had had their authority infiltrated by their own unknown enclaves, it is, in certain circumstances, meaningless to speak of the CIA as a way of differentiating it from the AIA, the DIA, the NSC, HUGHES, or the SOD—let us use the initials CIA therefore like a mathematical symbol that will, depending on the context in which it is employed, usually offer specific reference to a CIA located physically in Langley, Virginia, with near to eighteen thousand employees, understanding that under other circumstances the CIA may be no more than a general locus signifying an unknown factor whose function is intelligence and whose field is the invisible government.

Students of Einstein's work on tensor calculus may find it comfortable to deal with these varieties of unknowns. In the world of social theory, however, we are at the point where a special and general theory of relative identity in social relations would be of inestimable use, since the only situation for which there can be no cover is *anguish,* and the operation of the twentieth century may be to alienate us from that emotion in preparation for the ultimate destruction of the human soul as opposed to the oncoming hegemony of the technological person.

Generally, his enemies and friends agreed that Nixon was a fool not to destroy the tapes. They may not have understood the depth of the pot in which he was boiling. There was reason to believe there were copies of the tapes. If Butterfield would reveal their existence, he could be an agent; if one agent was near those tapes, then more than one. What reason to assume duplicates of the damaging tapes were not being systematically prepared all the while he was being set up? Impeachment was certain if he burned the evidence and a copy appeared.

"You do not understand. This man stood at the threshold of his own idea of greatness. He was going to write the peace with Communism. He was going to be immortal. Now, as he loses respect, it is slipping away from him inch by inch." Kissinger smiles sadly over his salad. Across the city, the Ervin committee is holding a hearing in the hot summer afternoon. "People criticize Nixon for being irresolute about Watergate. Why does he not confess what is wrong and end it? they ask. They do not understand that he cannot make a move, because he is not in possession of all the facts. He does not know what is going to happen next. He does not know what is going to break upon him next." Kissinger sighs. "Nobody will ever know how close that man was to getting the foreign situation he wanted."

Nixon is not only a Shakespearean protagonist in the hour of his downfall, but Macbeth believing that Birnam Wood will never come to Dunsinane.

Epistemological Model V

There is hardly an episode in Watergate which was not presented to us in a way that makes it seem more stupid than it ought to have been. Or, is it closer to say that what we hope to perceive is more brilliant than the level at which we have been encouraged to perceive it?

The tapes, for example. If a tape can be made, a copy can be made. Until we brood upon the matter, it is natural to assume the copy is equal to the original. We do not stop to think that the poor tapes we thought were the originals could in fact have been inferior copies. The remarkably bad quality of the tapes might have been produced by design. There are advantages to a tape that can hardly be heard: The affair is downgraded, and seems less sinister. No cover is more comfortable to a clandestine operation than the appearance of ineffectuality. Let us remind ourselves of how inept the Secret Service seemed in its taping operation. Possessing all that White House power, all those funds, all that available electronic equipment—yet the product sounds as if it was recorded in the glove compartment of a moving car. Admittedly, there were technical difficulties to the taping, but the product still seems inadequate. Nixon must have suffered another turn of the screw. Since he cannot know if the tapes he hears are the unique, original, and only tapes or a debased copy prepared by his enemies, he cannot even be certain whether it is a trap to encourage him to take advantage of the garbled sound and rephrase the transcripts in his favor. He takes the plunge. But his emendations are discovered later by the House Judiciary Committee. A corrected transcript is presented to America. How can Nixon not wonder whether somebody substituted a subtly clearer version of the tapes to John Doar's staff?

All the while, Nixon has to confront another question. If he evades every snare, pit, impressment, and delusion, if he even manages to work his way through the Senate to the edge of being declared not guilty in the impeachment, how can he be certain that in the last minute after the very last of all these abominably unexpected breaches in his cover-up, the missing eighteen minutes will still not appear? Then he can envision how America will spank the horse, and he will twist forever in the wind.

From *Pieces and Pontifications* (1982)

# Nixon's Fall

Nixon's crime is his inability to rise above admiration for the corporation. Throughout the transcripts, he is acting like the good, tough, even-minded, cool-tempered, and tastefully foul-mouthed president of a huge corporation—an automobile man, let us say, who has just discovered that his good assistants have somehow, God knows how, allowed more than a trace of tin to get into the molybdenum. Now they have the choice of calling back one hundred thousand cars with faulty bearings or letting a few pile up at the traffic lights. The press and the politicians scream that he has no moral values. He has no more and no less sense of value than any big corporation president in the land. Who, after all, polluted America in the first place? Now we're having an Aztec ceremony to clean up the mess. We won't be happy until we cut Richard Nixon's heart out and hold it high on the summit of the Presidential pyramid while an ooh goes up from the crowd. But his crime, moral insensitivity, is the one with which he began, prospered, lost, despaired, and finally succeeded in the passion of Richard Nixon. Good old American moral inanition. Was Lyndon Johnson less disgusting in Vietnam, or Jack Kennedy less cynical in some of the conversations he had—doubtless had—about the little workings of the CIA? Poor Nixon. He makes the peace with Russia and China by pitching the political equivalent of a shutout on his own right-wing Murderers' Row (which no Democrat ever had the nerve to do). Then he slips on the dugout steps. One could pity him, if not for having been shamed by his presence as the Uriah Heep of the Indo-Chinese war—all those years when one had to listen to Nixon speak of the enemy as he ordered the carnage and bombardment. For that, Nixon will never be forgiven, but these are schizophrenic years—the separate parts of ourselves hardly communicate—and so one is even tempted to admire the final release of these unreleasable transcripts. What a boon to historians, what a blow to ambiguity. How much easier it might have been for Nixon to resign and cry foul for the rest of his life, thereby to muddy the last washes of Watergate. Instead, he takes the gamble, he rages "against the dying of the light." Yet as he takes this last desperate step, he nonetheless repeats the theme of his life—he cannot take the step with all of himself in the same place. Expletive deleted. He lacks the simple New York smarts to keep the obscenities in. All his life he has been trying to tell us he is a man, a real man, and we keep replying he ain't. A real man knows how to swear. Now he finally has the stuff to show it. Better, he flings himself on the final court of public opinion. Yet we still do not know if he even swears well. He could have had the bars of America laughing with his prejudices, saying, Hey, the guy is no good and he can prove it, but he's one funny guy, he'll make you laugh. Instead, our Richard squirts deodorant at the smell in the room, and we all feel the pall. I'm beginning to think he is doomed. The stubbornest man in America, and doomed. With all his congealed and unadmitted boldness, with all his transcendent hypocrisy (the gas of his false pieties enters the very spirit of anti-matter), still he has always been, in the final crisis, the fool of small-town caution. So, in the grand boiling of the pots of American opinion, our National Yardbird goes into the broth without his feathers, and all salts withheld. We will be a great nation on the day we come to see that his ability to poach in his own juice is the American disease of us all. For the flavor of his moral invention, as he cooks himself, is saccharin, preservative, and gobs of super-burger. Bile in the stomach, canker on the tongue, and woe in the pit. What if his horror is the same as ours when we say at 3 A.M. *we are not so bad as they think we are,* and writhe in the thought that God may not agree? Let someone say, at any rate, that if ever a human was obliged to drink the cup of his own excretions, then the last or the next-to-last of the classic American Presidents has been that man. What a curiosity is our Democracy, what a mystery. No novelist unwinds a narrative so well.

From *The New Yorker* (May 20, 1974)

**1974**  # THE FAITH OF GRAFFITI

**1.**

Journalism is chores. Journalism is bondage unless you can see yourself as a private eye inquiring into the mysteries of a new phenomenon. Then you may even become an Aesthetic Investigator ready to
take up your role in the twentieth-century mystery play. Aesthetic Investigator! Make the name A-I for this is about graffiti.

A-I is talking to CAY 161. That is the famous Cay from 161st
Street, there at the beginning with TAKI 183 and JUNIOR 161, as famous in the world of wall and subway graffiti. Cay has the power of his
own belief. If the modern mind has moved from Giotto, who could
find the beginnings of perspective in the flight of angels across the
bowl of a golden sky, if we have mounted the high road of the Renaissance into Raphael's celebration of the True, the Good, and the Beautiful in each succulent three-dimensionality of the gluteus maximus,
why so, too, have we also moved from the celebration to the name,
traveled from men and women who wrested a degree of independence from Church and God down now to the twentieth-century certainty that life is an image.

A couple of stories:

The first is a Jewish joke. Perhaps it is *the* Jewish joke. Two grandmothers meet. One is pushing a baby carriage. "Oh," says the other,
"what a beautiful grandchild you have." "That's nothing," says the
first, reaching for her pocketbook. "Wait'll I show you her picture!"

The second seems apocryphal. Willem de Kooning gives a pastel to Robert Rauschenberg, who takes it home and promptly erases it. Next he signs his name to the erasure. Then he sells it. Can it be that Rauschenberg is saying, "The artist has as much right to print money as the financier?" Yes, Rauschenberg is giving us small art right here and much instruction. Authority imprinted upon emptiness is money. And the ego is capital convertible to currency by the use of the name. For six and a half centuries we have been moving from the discovery of humanity into the circulation of the name, advancing out of some primitive obeisance to dread so complete that painting once lay inert on the field of two dimensions (as if the medieval eye was not ready to wander). Then art dared to rise into that Renaissance liberation from anxiety. The painterly capacity entered the space-perspective of volume and depth. Now, with graffiti, we are back in the prison of two dimensions once more. Or is it the one dimension of the name—the art-form screaming through space on a unilinear subway line?

Something of all this is in the mind of our Aesthetic Investigator as he sits in a bedroom on West 161st Street in Washington Heights and talks to CAY 161 and JUNIOR 161 and LI'L FLAME and LURK. They talk about the name. He has agreed to do a centerpiece for a book of photographs on graffiti by Jon Naar, has agreed to do it on the instant (in a Los Angeles hotel room) that he has seen it. The splendid pictures and his undiscovered thoughts on the subject leap together. There is something to find in these pictures, thinks A-I, some process he can all but name. The intellectual hedonism of an elusive theme is laid out before him. So, yes, he accepts. And discovers weeks later that his book has already been given a title. It is *Watching My Name Go By*. He explains to the pained but sympathetic ears of his collaborators that an author needs his own title.

Besides, there is a practical reason. Certain literary men cannot afford titles like *Watching My Name Go By*. Norman Mailer may be first in such a category. One should not be able to conceive of one's bad reviews before writing a word.

But then he also does not like *Watching My Name Go By* for its own forthright meaning. These young graffiti writers do not use their own name. They adopt one. It is like a logo. Moxie or Socono, Tang, Whirlpool, Duz. The kids bear a not quite definable relation to their product. It is not MY NAME but THE NAME. Watching The Name Go By. He still does not like it. Yet every graffiti writer refers to the word. Even in newspaper accounts, it is the term heard most often. "I have put my name," says Super Kool to David Shirey of the *Times*, "all over the place. There ain't nowhere I go I can't see it. I sometimes go on Sunday to Seventh Avenue 86th Street and just spend the whole day"—yes, he literally says it—"watching my name go by." But then they all use it. JAPAN I, being interviewed by Jon Naar and A-I in a subway, grins as a station cop passes and scrutinizes him. He is clean. There is no spray can on him today. Otherwise he would run, not grin. Japan says, with full evaluation of his work, "You have to put in the hours to add up the names. You have to get your name around." Since he is small and could hardly oppose too many who might choose to borrow his own immortal JAPAN I, he merely snorts in answer to the question of what he would do if someone else took up his name and used it. "I would still get the class," he remarks.

Whether it is one's own interviews or others, the word that prevails is always the name. MIKE 171 informs *New York* magazine, "There are kids all over town with bags of paint waiting to *hit* their names." A bona-fide clue. An object is hit with your name, yes, and in the ghetto, a hit equals a kill. "You must kill a thing," said D. H. Lawrence once, "to know it satisfactorily." (But then who else could have said it?) You hit your name and maybe something in the whole scheme of the system gives a death rattle. For now your name is over their name, over the subway manufacturer, the Transit Authority, the city administration. Your presence is on their presence, your alias hangs over their scene. There is a pleasurable sense of depth to the elusiveness of the meaning.

So he sits with Cay and Junior and the others in the bedroom of Junior's parents and asks them about the name. It is a sweet meeting. He has been traveling for all of a wet and icy snowbound Sunday afternoon through the monumental drabs of South Bronx and Washington Heights, so much like the old gray apartment house ranks of Eastern Parkway in Brooklyn near where he grew up, a trip back across three generations. The Puerto Ricans in this apartment may not be so different from the poor ambitious families of relatives his mother would speak of visiting on the Lower East Side when she came as a child up from the Jersey shore to visit. So little has changed. Still the-smell-of-cooking-in-the-walls, a single word, and the black-pocked green stucco of the halls, those dark pits in the plaster speaking of the very acne of apartment house poverty. In the apartment, entering by the kitchen, down through the small living room and past the dark bedrooms in a file off the hall, all the shades drawn, a glimpse has been had of the television working like a votive light in some poor slum church chapel (one damp fire in the rainforest) while the father in shorts sleeps on the sofa, and the women congregate—the kitchen is near. The windows are stained glass, sheets of red and yellow plastic pasted to the glass—the view must be on an air shaft. No light in this gray and late winter day. It is all the darkness of that gloom which sits in the very center of slum existence, that amalgam of worry and dread, heavy as buckets of oil, the true wages of the working class, with all that attendant fever for the attractions of crime, the grinding entrapments of having lost to the law—lawyers' fees, bondsmen, probation officers, all of it.

Yet now there is also a sense of protection in the air. The mood is not without its reverence: CAY 161 has the face of a martyr. He looks as if he has been flung face first against a wall, as if indeed a mighty hand has picked him up and hurled him through the side of a stone house. He is big, seventeen, and almost six feet tall, once good-looking and may yet be good-looking again, but now it is as if he has been drawn by a comic strip artist, for his features express the stars, comets, exclamation points, and straight-out dislocation of eyes and nose and mouth that accompanies any hero in a comic strip when he runs into a collision. SOCK! ZAM! POW! CAY 161, driving a stolen van, fleeing the cops in an old-fashioned New York street chase, has gone off the road on a turn, "and right on 161st Street where he was born and raised, he hit a hydrant, turned over a few times, and wound up inside a furniture store. . . . When the police looked inside the car,"—description by José Torres in the N.Y. *Post*—"Cay lay motionless in the driver's seat, and another youth, a passenger, sprawled unconscious outside, hurled from the car by the impact." The friend had a broken leg, and Cay had part of his brain taken out in a seven-hour operation. The doctor gave warning. He might survive. As a vegetable. For two months he did not make a move. Now, six months later, Cay is able to talk, he can move. His lips are controlled on one side of his face but slack on the other—he speaks as if he has had a stroke. He moves in the same fashion. Certain gestures are agile, others come up half-paralyzed and top-heavy, as if he will fall on his face at the first false step. So his friends are his witness. They surround him, offer the whole reverence of their whole alertness to every move he makes. There is all the elegance of good manners in the way they try to conceal that he is different from the others.

But Cay is happy now. He is in Junior's house, JUNIOR 161, his best friend. They used to go out writing together for years, both tall, a twin legend—when one stands on the other's shoulders, the name goes up higher on the wall than for anyone else. True bond of friendship: They will each write the other's name, a sacramental interchange. Junior has a lean body, that indolent ghetto languor which speaks of presence. "I move slow, man," says the body, "and that is why you watch me. Because when I move fast, you got to watch out." He is well dressed, ghetto style—a white turtleneck sweater, white pants, a white felt hat, white sneakers, nothing more. Later he will step out like this into the winter streets. You got to meet the eye of the beholder with class. Freezing is for plants.

A-I interviews them. Yes, they started three years ago and would hit four or five names a day. Junior liked to work at least an hour a day. So go the questions: Cay liked to use red marker; Junior, blue. Hundreds of masterpieces to their credit. Yes, Junior's greatest masterpiece is in the tunnel where the track descends from 125th Street to 116th Street. There, high on the wall, is JUNIOR 161 in letters six feet high. "You want to get your name in a place where people don't know how you could do it, how you could get up to there. You got to make them think." It is the peril of the position that calls. Junior frowns on the later artists who have come after Cay and himself. The talk these days is of SLY and STAY HIGH, PHASE 2, BAMA, SNAKE, and STITCH. The article by Richard Goldstein in *New York* (March 26, 1973) has offered a nomenclature for the styles, Broadway, Brooklyn, and Bronx, disquisitions on bubble and platform letters. Perhaps his source is BAMA, who has said to another reporter in his full articulate speaking style, "Bronx style is bubble letters, and Brooklyn style is script with lots of flourishes and arrows. It's a style all by itself. Broadway style, these long slim letters, was brought here from Philadelphia by a guy named Topcat. Queens style is very difficult, very hard to read."

Junior is contemptuous of this. The new forms have wiped out respect for the old utilitarian lettering. If Cay likes the work of STAY HIGH, Junior is impressed by none. "That's just fanciness," he says of the new. "How're you going to get your name around doing all that fancy stuff?"

Cay speaks into this with his deep, strangled, and wholly existential voice—he cannot be certain any sound he utters will come out as he thinks. "Everybody tries to catch up to us," he says.

"You have to put in the hours?"

A profound nod.

Of course, he is not doing it any longer. Nor is Junior. Even before the accident, both had lost interest. On the one hand, the police were getting tough, the beatings when you were caught were worse, the legal penalties higher, the supplies of paint getting to be monitored, and on the other hand something had happened to the process itself. Too many names had grown—a jungle of ego creepers.

A-I queries them about the prominence of the name. He hesitates how to pose the question—he fears confidence will be lost if he asks straight-out. "What is the meaning of the name?" but, indeed, he does not have to—Cay speaks up on what it means to watch the name go by. "The name," says Cay, in a full voice, Delphic in its unexpected resonance—as if the idol of a temple had just chosen to break into sound—"the name," says Cay, "is the *faith* of graffiti."

It is quite a remark. He wonders if Cay knows what he has said. "The name," repeats Cay, "is the *faith*." He is in no doubt of the depth of what he has said. His eyes fix on A-I, his look is severe. Abruptly, he declares that the proper title is "The Faith of Graffiti." So it is.

A Sunday afternoon has come to its end. A-I walks downstairs with Junior, Cay, Lurk, and Li'l Flame, and is shown modest examples of their writing on the apartment house walls. Cay has also used another name. At times he has called himself THE PRAYER 161. They say goodbye in the hall. Cay shows A-I the latest 161st Street sequence of thumb-up finger-curled handshakes. The pistol-pointed forefinger and upraised thumb of one man touch the thumb and forefinger of the other in a quick little cat's cradle. Cay's fingers are surprisingly deft. Then he and Junior spar a bit, half-comic for he lurches, but with the incisive tenderness of the ghetto, as if his moves also say, "Size don't come in packages. A cripple keeps the menace." It is agreeable to watch. As he attempts to spar, Cay is actually moving better than he has all day.

The name is the faith of graffiti. Was it true that the only writing which did not gut one's health lay in those questions whose answers were not known from the start? A-I still had no more than a clue to graffiti. Were the answers to be found in the long war of the will against the power of taboo? Who could know when one of the gods would turn in sleep as images were drawn? Was that a thought in the head of the first savage to put the silhouette of an animal on the wall of a cave? If so, the earliest painting had been not two dimensions but one—one, like graffiti—the hand pushing forward into the terror of future punishment. Only later would come an easier faith that the Lord might be on the side of the artist.

## 2.

No, size doesn't come in packages, and the graffiti writers had been all heights and all shapes, even all the ages from twelve to twenty-four.

They had written masterpieces in letters six feet high on the side of walls and subway cars, and had scribbled furtive little toys, which is to say small names without style, sometimes just initials. There was panic in the act for you wrote with an eye over your shoulder for oncoming authority. The Transit Authority cops would beat you if they caught you, or drag you to court, or both. The judge, donning the robes of Solomon, would condemn the early prisoners to clean the cars and subway stations of the names. HITLER 2 (reputed to be so innocent of his predecessor that he only knew Hitler 1 had a very big rep!) was caught, and passed on the word of his humiliation. Cleaning the cars, he had been obliged to erase the work of others. All proportions kept, it may in simple pain of heart have been not altogether unequal to condemning Cézanne to wipe out the works of Van Gogh.

So there was real fear of being caught. Pain and humiliation were implacable dues, and not all graffiti artists showed equal grace under such pressure. Some wrote like cowards, timidly, furtively, jerkily. "Man," was the condemnation of the peers, "you got a messed-up handwriting." Others laid one cool flowering of paint upon another, and this was only after having passed through all the existential stations of the criminal act, even to first *inventing* the paint, which was of course the word for stealing the stuff from the stores. But then, an invention is the creation of something that did not exist before—like a working spray can in your hand. (Indeed, if Plato's Ideal exists, and the universe is first a set of forms, then what is any invention but a theft from the given universal Ideal?)

There was always art in a criminal act—no crime could ever be as automatic as a production process—but graffiti writers were opposite to criminals, since they were living through the stages of the crime in order to commit an artistic act—what a doubling of intensity when the artist not only steals the cans but tries for the colors he wants, not only the marker and the color, but steals them in double amounts so you don't run out in the middle of a masterpiece. What a knowledge of cops' habits is called for when any Black or Puerto Rican adolescent with a big paper bag is bound to be examined by a Transit cop if he goes into the wrong station. So after his paint has been invented a writer has to decide by which subway entrance it is to be transported, and once his trip is completed back to the station that is the capital of his turf, he still has to find the nook where he can warehouse his goods for a few hours. To attempt to take the paint out of the station is to get caught. To try to bring it back to the station is worse. Six or seven kids entering a subway in Harlem, Washington Heights, or the

South Bronx are going to be searched by Transit cops for cans. So they stash it, mill around the station for a time painting nothing, they are, after all, often in the subways—to the degree they are not chased, it is a natural clubhouse, virtually a country club for the sociability of it all—and when the cops are out of sight, and a train is coming in, they whip out their stash of paint from its hiding place, conceal it on their bodies, and in all the wrappings of oversize ragamuffin fatigues, get on the cars to ride to the end of the line where in some deserted midnight yard they will find their natural canvas which is of course that metal wall of a subway car ready to reverberate into all the egos on all the metal of New York.

But it is hardly so quick or automatic as that. If they are to leave the station at the end of the line, there is foreign turf to traverse which guarantees no safe passage, and always the problem of finding your way into the yards.

In the A-train yard at 207th Street, the unofficial entrance was around a fence that projected out over a cliff and dropped into the water of the Harlem River. You went out one side of that fence on a narrow ledge, out over the water, and back the other side of the fence into the yards "where the wagons," writes Richard Goldstein, "are sitting like silent whales."

We may pick our behemoth—whales and dinosaurs, elephants folded in sleep. At night, the walls of cars sit there possessed of soul—you are not just writing your name but trafficking with the iron spirit of the vehicle now resting. What a presence. What a consecutive set of iron sleeping beasts down all the corrals of the yard, and the graffiti writers stealthy as the near-to-silent sound of their movements working up and down the line of cars, some darting in to squiggle a little toy of a name on twenty cars—their nerve has no larger surge—others embarking on their first or their hundred-and-first masterpiece, daring the full enterprise of an hour of living with this tension after all the other hours of waiting (once they had come into the yard) for the telepathic disturbance of their entrance to settle, waiting for the guards patrolling the lines of track to grow somnolent and descend into the early morning pall of the watchman. Sometimes the graffiti writers would set out from their own turf at dark, yet not begin to paint until two in the morning, hiding for hours in the surest corners of the yard or in and under the trains. What a quintessential marriage of cool and style to write your name in giant separate living letters, large as animals, lithe as snakes, mysterious as Arabic and Chinese curls of alphabet, and to do it in the heart of a winter night when the hands are frozen and only the heart is hot with fear. No wonder the best of the graffiti writers, those mountains of heavy masterpiece production, STAY HIGH, PHASE 2, STAR III, get the respect, call it the glory, that they are known, famous and luminous as a rock star. It is their year. Nothing automatic about writing a masterpiece on a subway car. "I was scared," said Japan, "all the time I did it." And sitting in the station at 158th and St. Nicholas Avenue, watching the trains go by, talking between each wave of subway sound, he is tiny in size, his dark eyes as alert as any small and hungry animal who eats in a garden at night and does not know where the householder with his varmint gun may be waiting.

Now, as Japan speaks, his eyes never failing to miss the collection of names, hieroglyphs, symbols, stars, crowns, ribbons, masterpieces, and toys on every passing car, there is a sadness in his mood. The city has mounted a massive campaign. There was a period in the middle when it looked as if graffiti would take over the world, when a movement that began as the expression of tropical peoples living in a monotonous iron-gray and dull brown brick environment, surrounded by asphalt, concrete, and clangor, had erupted to save the sensuous flesh of their inheritance from a macadamization of the psyche, save the blank city wall of their unfed brain by painting the wall over with the giant trees and petty plants of a tropical rain-forest. Like such a jungle, every plant, large and small, spoke to one another, lived in the profusion *and* harmony of a forest. No one wrote over another name, no one was obscene—for that would have smashed the harmony. A communion took place over the city in this plant growth of names until every institutional wall, fixed or moving, every modern new school that looked like a new factory, every old slum warehouse, every standing billboard, every huckstering poster, and the halls of every high-rise low-rent housing project that looked like a prison (and all did) were covered by a foliage of graffiti that grew seven or eight feet tall, even twelve feet high in those choice places worth the effort for one to stand on another, ah, if it had gone on, this entire city of blank architectural high-rise horrors would have been covered with paint. Graffiti writers might have become mountaineers with pitons for the ascent of high-rise high-cost swinger-single apartments in the East Sixties and Seventies. The look of New York, and then the world, might have been transformed, and the interlapping of names and colors, those wavelets of ego forever reverberating upon one another, could have risen like a flood to cover the monstrosities of abstract empty twentieth-century walls where no design ever predominated over the most profitable (and ergo most monotonous) construction ratio implicit in a twenty-million-dollar bill.

The kids painted with less than this in view, no doubt. Sufficient in the graffiti-proliferating years of the early Seventies to paint the front door of every subway car they could find. The ecstasy of the roller coaster would dive down their chest if they were ever waiting in a station when a twelve-car train came stampeding in and their name, HONDO, WILDCAT, SABU, or LOLLIPOP, was on the *front*! Yes, the graffiti had not only the feel and all the super-powered whoosh and impact of all the bubble letters in all the mad comic strips, but the *zoom,* the *aghr,* and the *ahhr* of screeching rails, the fast motion of subways roaring into stations, the comic strips come to life. So it was probably not a movement designed to cover the world so much as the excrescence of an excrescence. Slum populations chilled on one side by the bleakness of modern design, and brain-cooked on the other by comic strips and TV ads with zooming letters, even brain-cooked by politicians whose ego is a virtue—I am here to help my nation—brained by the big beautiful numbers on the yard markers on football fields, by the whip of the capital letters in the names of the products, and gut-picked by the sound of rock and soul screaming up into the voodoo of the firmament with the shriek of the performer's insides coiling like neon letters in the blue satanic light, yes, all the excrescence of the highways and the fluorescent wonderlands of every Las Vegas sign frying through the Iowa and New Jersey night, all the stomach-tightening nitty-gritty of trying to learn how to spell was in the writing, every assault on the psyche as the trains came slamming in. Maybe it was no more than a movement that looked to take some of the excrescence left within and paint it out upon the world, no more than a species of collective therapy of grace exhibited under pressure in which they never dreamed of painting over the blank and empty modern world, but the authority of the city reacted as if the city itself might be in greater peril from graffiti than from drugs, and a war had gone on, more and more implacable on the side of the authority with every legal and psychological weedkiller on full employ until the graffiti of New York was defoliated, cicatrized, Vietnamized. Now, as A-I sat in the station with Jon Naar and Japan and they watched the trains go by, aesthetic blight was on the cars. Few masterpieces remained. The windows were gray and smeared. The cars looked dull red or tarnished aluminum—their recent coat of paint remover having also stripped all polish from the manufacturer's surface. New subway cars looked like old cars. Only the ghost-outline of former masterpieces still remained. The kids were broken. The movement seemed over. Even the paint could no longer be invented. Now the cans set out for display were empty, the misdemeanors were being upped to felony, the fines were severe, the mood was vindictive. Two hideous accidents had occurred. One boy had been killed beneath a subway car, and another had been close to fatally burned by an inflammable spray can catching a spark, yes, a horror was on the movement and transit patrols moved through the yards and plugged the entrances. The white monoliths of the high-rise were safe. And the subways were dingier than they had ever been. The impulse of the jungle to cover the walled tombs of technology had been broken. Was there a clue to graffiti in the opposite passion to look upon monotony and call it health? As A-I walked the streets with Jon Naar, they passed a sign: DON'T POLLUTE—KEEP THE CITY CLEAN. "That sign," the photographer murmured, "is a form of pollution itself."

### 3.

Since the metaphor of plant life had climbed all over his discussion of graffiti he went with profit to the Museum of Modern Art for it confirmed the botanical notion with which he began: that if subway graffiti had not come into existence, some artist might have found it necessary to invent, for it was in the chain of such evolution. Art had been rolling down the fall-line from Cézanne to Frank Stella, from Gauguin to Mathieu. On such a map, subway graffiti was an alluvial delta, the mud-caked mouth of a hundred painterly streams. If the obvious objection was that you might interview a thousand Black and Puerto Rican kids who rushed to write their name without having ever seen a modern painting, the answer, not quite as obvious, was that plants spoke to plants.

Famous plant-man Backster, attaching the electrodes of his polygraph to a philodendron one night, wonders in the wake of this passing impulse how to test the plant for some emotional reaction. Abruptly, a current courses through the philodendron at the horror of this thought. (When Backster cuts or burns the leaf, however, the polygraph registers little: now, the plant is numb. Its sensitivity seems to be its life, its suffering an abstention from life.) By the new logic of the experiment, plants must be a natural species of wireless. (What, indeed, did Picasso teach us if not that every form offers up its own scream when it is torn?) Radio is then no more than a prosthetic leg of communication, whereas plants speak to plants, and are aware of the death of animals on the other side of the hill. Some artists might even swear they have known this from the beginning, for they would see themselves as stimulants who inject perception into the blind vision of the century.

Still, when it comes to a matter of who might influence the writers of graffiti, one is not obliged to speak only of neon signs, comic strips, and TV products, one has the other right to think the kids are enriched by all art that offers the eye a resemblance to graffiti. Which might enable us then to talk of Jackson Pollock and the abstract graffiti of his confluences and meanderings, of Stuart Davis' dramatization of print as a presence that grows in swollen proportion to its size, even include Hans Hofmann's *Memoria in Aeternum,* where those red and yellow rectangles float like statements of a name over indistinct washes beneath, or Matisse's blue and green *Dance.* (Matisse's limbs wind onto one another like the ivy-creeper calligraphies of New York graffiti.) So might one refer to work that speaks of ghetto emotion in any place, of Siqueiros' *Echo of a Scream,* or Van Gogh's *Starry Night.* If the family histories of the most messed-up families have all the garbage-can chaos of de Kooning's *Woman,* no wonder the subway writers prided themselves on style and eclat—"you got a messed-up handwriting" being the final term of critical kill.

But on reflection, was A-I trying to slip in some old piety on the distribution of art down from the museums through media to the masses?—these subway children may never have seen *Memoria in Aeternum* at the head of the stairs at MOMA, but it filtered through to them by way of advertising artists. Fell crap! Rather say art begot art, and the migrations were no one's business. For if plants were telepathic, then humans lived in a psychic sea where all the forms of art also passed through the marketplace of the dreamer in his sleep, and every part of society spoke to every other part, if only with a curse.

So he had the happy thought during his visit to MOMA to decide that some paintings might be, by whatever measure, *on the air*—leave it to the engineers of some future techno-coven to try to determine the precise migrations of Miró's *Plate 8 from Series One, 1953, "The Family"* into the head of an espontaneo with a spray can looking over his shoulder for the black mother in a uniform who will beat his own black blue.

### 4.

Like a good reporter he goes to see the Mayor. It is ten days to Christmas and the last two weeks of the Lindsay administration. On that Saturday morning, A-I has his appointment to visit, nearly a week from the previous Sunday, when he talked to Junior and Cay. Again the weather is iron-gray and cold. At Gracie Mansion, the wind is driving in from the East River, and the front porch looks across its modest private lawn to the Triboro Bridge in the north. (To the west, apartment houses rise like the sheer face of Yosemite.) It is not a large lawn in front of the Mayor's residence nor even a large house. Old white Gracie Mansion might be no exceptional residence on any wealthy road in Portland, Oregon, or Portland, Maine—there is even a basketball hoop on a backboard not far from the front door, a political touch dating from recent years, when the Knicks became the most consistently successful team in New York—yet with all its limited grandeur, Gracie Mansion is still one fine Federalist of a house (built in 1799) and if the spirit of an age could have been captured by a ratio, then where better to measure this magic mean if not in the proportions of the Mansion's living room and dining room? They speak in their harmony of some perfect period of Arcadian balance between the early frontier being settled to the West and the new sense of democratic government forging itself in the state capitals of the East. How better to characterize the decorum, substance, grace, and calm center of such architecture if not to think that the spirit and style of the *prose* of the American Constitution is also in it (even to the hint of boredom in prose and buildings both), yet why not precisely these high ceilings, paucity of curves, and all the implicit checks and balances of the right angle? Lindsay, it may be said, is at home in such surroundings. They seem built to his frame. Only a tall lean man could look well-proportioned in so *enlightened* a set of rooms. Nothing like a Gothic arch is present to suggest any mad irreconcilable opposites of God and man, no Corinthian columns to resonate with praetorian tyrannies (and orgies at the top), nor any small and slanted ceilings to speak of craft and husbandry, just government here in Federal style without the intervention of Satan or Jehovah (and next to nothing of Christ), just a fundament of Wasp genius, a building style to state that man could live without faith if things were calm enough. Perhaps the economy of balance is the true god of the Wasp.

His appointment is at eleven, but it is an unusual morning for the Lindsay family, since they have been up until five the night before at a farewell party given the Mayor to honor the eight years of his administration. Lindsay has worked as hard as any man in New York for eight years, and can afford the luxury of being hungover before a reporter this Saturday morning. What a nice relaxation. Lindsay chuckles at the memory of each unexpected rejoinder of party dialogue and laughs at the expression on Tom Morgan's face, press secretary to the Mayor, a tall man with a dark brush mustache who recapitulates in the sardonic gloom of his hungover eyes the incandescence of all those good drinks at that good party. Watching them all, studying Lindsay's face with its patrician features so endowed with every purchase on the meaning of handsome that he could be not only a movie star but there at the front, right ahead of Burt Lancaster and Steve McQueen, on a par with Robert Redford, and hardly a millimeter of profile behind Paul Newman, it occurs indeed that no movie star could be more convincing than Lindsay if it came to playing some very important American politician in the quiet American years from 1800 to 1825. Even his eroded teeth—Lindsay's one failing feature—speak with authenticity of the bad teeth of those English who became the American ruling classes in that Federalist era one hundred and seventy years ago. So sitting in such a dining room, and a little later adjourned to a living room with Lindsay and Morgan to bring up the subject of his interview, he is thinking that Gracie Mansion never had a Mayor nearly so perfectly suited to itself. If there were some divine renting agency in the halls of karma, then come soon or late the post of Mayor of New York would have had to be found for John Vliet Lindsay or the house would feel unfulfilled.

For Lindsay, however, the question may have been whether an ambitious man had ever come to power at a time less promising for himself. He had labored in his two terms, innovated and negotiated, explored, tinkered, tampered, and shifted the base of every municipal machine of government upon which he could work his cadres. He had built a constituency in the ghetto. Mailer-Breslin running for the mayoralty in '69 also ran into one argument over and over in Bedford-Stuyvesant, Harlem, and the South Bronx. It was, "What do we want with you? Lindsay's our man." Lindsay had walked the streets in summer riots, and held some kind of line for decontrol, which is to say, local control, in the ghetto schools. That had taken political courage. Yet make him no saint! He had also worked with the most powerful real estate interests in the city. No question that in his eight years, the ugliest architecture in the history of New York had also gone up. The new flat tops of the skyline now left New York as undistinguished in much of its appearance as Cleveland or Dallas. It is possible Lindsay had bought ghetto relief at the price of aesthetic stultification. Call it desecration. The view of New York's offices and high-rise apartments proved sacrilegious to the mood of any living eye—Wasp balance had done it again.

Still, with all this effort, New Yorkers hated him. For every intolerable reason, first of which was his defense of the ghettos. "If I wanted a nigger for Mayor, I'd have voted for a nigger," said every archetype of a cab driver to any tourist who would listen. And yet this Federalist movie star, this hard-working mayor for ghetto rights, had been the first and most implacable enemy of subway graffiti. So there was a feather falling through the mood when he told Lindsay and Morgan why he had come.

But A-I had his speech. If he thought the Mayor had done an honorable job, and was prepared to say so, he still could not comprehend how a man who worked so hard to enter the spirit of ghetto conditions had been nonetheless so implacable in his reaction to graffiti. "Insecure cowards," Lindsay had called the kids. "A dirty shame." Others in his administration offered civic blasts: "graffiti pigs"; "thoughtless and irresponsible behavior." It was surprising. While the management of a city required you to keep it clean—where would a mayor hide if he could not get the garbage out?—there was a difference between political necessity and the fury of this reaction. How could he call the kids cowards? Why the venom? It seemed personal.

Lindsay grinned. He had heard enough preambles from reporters to know when an interview was manageable. "Well, yes," he said, "I did get hot under the collar, and I suppose if we had to go through it again, I would hope to lose my temper a little less, but you have no idea what a blow that graffiti was to us." He shook his head at the memory. "You see, we had gone to such work, such ends, to get those new subway cars in. It meant so much to people here in the city to get a ride for instance in one of the new air-conditioned cars. On a hot summer day their mood would pick up when they had the luck to catch one. And, you know, that was work. It's hard to get anything done here. You stretch budgets, and try to reason people into activities they don't necessarily want to take up on their own. We were proud of those subway cars. It took a lot of talking to a lot of committees to get that accomplished."

Morgan nodded. "And then," Lindsay said, "the kids started to deface them."

A-I put his demurrer. "Deface," after all, was the core of the argument. Some people might think subway graffiti was art. He suggested in passing Claes Oldenburg's classic remark ". . . You're standing there in the station, everything is gray and gloomy and all of a sudden one of those graffiti trains slides in and brightens the place like a big bouquet from Latin America."

Lindsay smiled as if recalling the screams, moans, epithets, and agonized squawks of every bright college intellectual on his staff when Oldenburg's quote first came riding in. Grand division in the Establishment! Aesthetic schism! "Yes, we remember that quote," Lindsay's grin seemed to say. He had the most curious quality of personality. One did not know if he was secretly more or less decent than his personality. While the personality itself was decent enough, it was also patently not the man, nor, unhappily for him, characteristic at all of New York. He seemed now like a Westerner, full of probity, rawhide, and something buried in the personality, a man you might not get to know at all even after a night of drinking together. He wasn't in the least like Richard Nixon except to share one quality. Lindsay was out of focus. He had always been out of focus. Part of his political trouble.

Well, Lindsay suggested, they had never really wondered whether it was anything but defacement. "People would come into new cars and suddenly they'd see them all marked up, covered inside and out, and it depressed people terribly. You know, we have to be a kind of nerve center to the city. Reports came in from everywhere. This graffiti was profoundly depressing—it truly hurt people's moods. The life would go out of everybody when they saw the cars defaced, they felt it was defacement, no question of that. And we kept hearing one request over and over, 'Can't you do something about it?' Then, too, we had our own pride in these matters. You know, you get to feel after you've put through a new municipal building that it's yours in some way. As Mayor I'd get as angry when a city building got marked up as if I owned it personally. Oh, it's easier to talk about it now, but I must say it was hard at times not to blow up."

"Actually," Morgan observed, "the Mayor would go around calming some of us down. 'Remember,' he would tell us, 'they're only kids.'"

Yes, in the framework of that time in the Summer of '71 and the Winter and Spring of '72 when Lindsay was looking to get the Democratic nomination for President, what an upset to his fortunes, what a vermin of catastrophe that these writings had sprouted like weeds all over the misery of Fun City, a new monkey of unmanageables to sit on Lindsay's overloaded political back. He must have sensed the presidency draining away from him as the months went by, the graffiti grew, and the millions of tourists who passed through the city brought the word out to the rest of the nation: "Filth is sprouting on the walls."

Of course, where was the tourist who could distinguish between men's-room and subway graffiti? Who was going to dare to look long enough to see that it was a name and not an obscene thought in the writing. Today, just before he had come to Gracie Mansion, he had stopped in the lavatory of a York Avenue bar for a minute, and there on the john wall was drawn a pure old-fashioned piece of smut graffiti. A balloon of dialogue issued out of a girl's mouth. No art in the lettering, no style. "Did you know," said her balloon, "that your clit is in your ass?" Some lost shred of fecal communion now nailed to the wall. Was there a public comfort station in America that did not have a dozen such insights—"Suck me," "Fuck you"? That was what people expected to see on the subways. They assumed the full mad explosive shithouse of America was now erupting in their faces. So they did not look but rode in the cars with their heads down, and brought the news out to the rest of America that Lindsay could not keep the city clean. No wonder he called it a dirty shame. And labeled the aplomb of the graffiti writers cowardice. That was his attempt to soothe the terror in the heart of every subway citizen who looked at the graffiti and put his head down so his eye would not meet any eye that might be connected to the hand which held a knife, yes, that was one side of the fear, and the other was fear of the insane graffiti writer in one's own self. For what filth would burst out of every civilized office worker in New York if ever *they* started to write on moving public walls, my God, the feces to spread and the blood to spray, yes, the good voting citizen of New York would know that the violent ward at Bellevue was opening its door to him on the day he would take a spray can to a subway. So, New York citizenry saw all the children as mad—and therefore saw madness, instability, and horror in the New York Transit. No wonder Lindsay had gone to war against graffiti. The city would tolerate junk, graft, insanities of traffic, mugging, every petty crime of the street, and every major pollution, but it could not accept a towering rainforest of graffiti on all the forty-story walls. Yes, build a wall and balance a disease. For the blank wall of the new architecture was a deadening agent above to balance the growing violence beneath. (Could it be said that the monotony of modern architecture increased all over the world in direct relation to the volcanic disturbances of each society it would contain?)

In the face of such questions the interview was effectively over. They chatted for a while, and got up to say goodbye. On the way out, A-I noticed there was a Rauschenberg on the wall.

Lindsay, in his courtesy, walked with him to the gate. Wearing a blue windbreaker, he looked in the gray outdoor light like a veteran big league ballplayer, tall, weathered, knowledgeable. They took leave not uncordially, and he complimented the Mayor on eight good years, even meant it.

"I wish I had the talent to write," Lindsay said in parting. Was that a politician's gift? A-I pulled back the reply that he wished he could have been Mayor.

Outside the fence, a policeman was standing with a drawn gun. It was a simple measure of the times: Be forever ready at the Gracie gate.

And indeed a ten-year-old boy on roller skates cried aloud, "That's him, that's him, that's the Mayor," and promptly took out a cap pistol and fired a number of bang-bangs at the back of John Lindsay going back into his house.

For a while, A-I walked, and had a little fantasy of how impossible it would have proved if the miracle worked and he had been elected in the campaign of 1969. What would he have done about graffiti? Would he have tried to explain its virtues to the people of New York— and laughed in all the pain of absolute political failure? The answer was simple—nobody like himself would ever be elected Mayor until the people agreed bad architecture was as poisonous as bad food. No, graffiti as a political phenomenon had small hope for life. His faith in the value of the question would have to explore in another place. Did the final difficulty lie in the meaning of graffiti as art? There the inquiry might become as incomprehensible as the motives of the most advanced artists. On then to the rim of the enigma, to the Sea of Vortices, where the meanings whirl with no meaning.

### 5.

Years ago, so much as twenty years ago, A-I had conceived of a story he was finally not to write, for he lost his comprehension of it. A rich young artist in New York in the early Fifties, bursting to go beyond Abstract Expressionism, began to rent billboards on which he sketched huge, ill-defined (never say they were sloppy) works in paint that had been chosen to run easily and flake quickly. The rains distorted the lines, made gullies of the forms, automobile exhausts laid down a patina, and comets of flying birds crusted the disappearing surface with their impasto. By the time fifty such billboards had been finished—a prodigious year for the painter—the vogue was on. His show was an event. They transported the billboards by trailer-truck and broke the front wall of the gallery to get the art objects inside. It was the biggest one-man exhibition in New York that year. At its conclusion, two art critics were arguing whether such species of work still belonged to art.

"You're mad," cried one, "it is not art, it is never art."

"No," said the other, "I think it's valid."

So would the story end. Its title, Validity. But before he had written a word he made the mistake of telling it to a young Abstract Expressionist whose work he liked. "Of course it's valid," said the painter, eyes shining with the project. "I'd do it myself if I could afford the billboards."

The story was never written. He had assumed he was proposing a satire, but it was evident he had no insight into how painters were ready to think. Some process had entered art and he could not discern it out.

Let us go back to the pastel by de Kooning that Rauschenberg erased. The details, when further inquiry is made, are less impromptu. Rauschenberg first informed de Kooning of what he would do, and de Kooning agreed. The work, when sold, bore the inscription "A drawing from Willem de Kooning erased by Robert Rauschenberg." Both artists are now proposing something more than that the artist has the same right as the financier to print money; they may even be saying that the meat and marrow of art, the painterly core, the life of the pigment, and the world of technique with which hands lay on that pigment are convertible to something other. The ambiguity of meaning in the twentieth century, the hollow in the heart of faith, has become such an obsessional hole that art may have to be converted into intellectual transactions. It is as if we are looking for stuff, any stuff with which to stuff the hole, and will convert every value into packing for this purpose. For there is no doubt that in erasing the pastel and selling it, art has been diminished, but our knowledge of society is certainly enriched. An aesthetic artifact has been converted into a sociological artifact. It is not the painting that intrigues us now but the lividities of art fashion which made the transaction possible in the first place. Something rabid is loose in the century. Maybe we are not converting art into some comprehension of social process but rather are using art to choke the hole, as if society has become so hopeless, which is to say so twisted in knots of faithless ideological spaghetti, that the glee is in strangling the victims.

But take the example further. Let us imagine a show at the Guggenheim. It will be like many we have seen. Let us make it a plausible modern one-man show. Nothing will be exhibited but computer read-out sheets from a statistical operation. Hundreds of such sheets tacked to the wall. Somewhat irregularly. Attempts at neatness will be contradicted by a confusion in the style of placing them on the wall of the Guggenheim as it spirals up the ramp. Checkerboards alternate with ascending bands, then cul-de-sacs, paper stapled up every way.

We try to digest the aesthetic experience. Of what do the computer read-out sheets consist? What is the subject of their inquiry? we ask. And what is the motive of the artist? Is he telling us something about the order and disorder of the mind in relation to a technological world? Has he presented us with an ongoing composition of exceptional cunning? Is it possible he even has set the problem for the computer himself? Maybe the endless numbers on these computer sheets reflect some analogue to the tension of major themes in his brain. Do we then have here an arithmetical display whose relation to art is as complex as *Finnegans Wake* to literature?

Bullshit, responds the painter. The computer sheets were selected at random. Because the artist did not even wish to bear an unconscious responsibility for the selection, he chose an acquaintance with whom he shared no great psychic identity to pick up the computer sheets for him. Neither he nor the acquaintance ever inquired into the subject of the statistical problem, and he never took a look at what was brought back. Rather, he spoke to the janitor at the Guggenheim by telephone and told him to tack up the pages any way at all. The checkerboards and bands and cul-de-sacs of stapled paper were merely a reflection of the personnel—the janitor worked with two assistants. One was neat, the other drunk. And the painter never came to see the show. The show was the fact that people came, studied the walls, lived for an uncertain hour in the Guggenheim, and went out again, their minds exercised by a question that not only had no answer but may not even have been a question. The artist had done his best to have no intent. Not unless his intent was to demonstrate that most of the experience of viewing a painting is the context of the museum itself. We are next to one of John Cage's compositions in silence. Art has been saying with more and more intensity that the nature of the painting has become less interesting than the relation of painting to society—we can even erase Rauschenberg's erasure. Get the artist out of it altogether, and it is still art. The world is turning inside out.

What step is left to take? Only one. A show that offers no object at all. The last reference to painting or sculpture is the wall on which something can be hung, or the floor on which a piece can sit. That must now disappear. The art-piece enters the artist: The work can only be experienced within his psyche.

From *The New York Times,* September 2, 1973, by Peter Plagens:

a marksman-friend shot Chris Burden in the upper left arm with a .22 long-jacket before an audience of 12 intimates. He (Burden) figured on a graze wound with a Band-Aid slapped on afterward, but it "felt like a truck hit my arm at 80 miles per hour"; he went to the hospital, nauseous, and filed the requisite police report ("accident").

Plagens goes on to describe other "pieces." Burden chooses situations for their possibility of danger, pain, humiliation, or boredom. There is:

"Movie on the Way Down," in which Burden, hanging by his heels, nude, six feet off a gym floor with a movie camera in his hands, is summarily chopped loose.

The movie is presumably taken on the way down (is it filmed in slow motion?) and he ends with a cut lip. There are other pieces where he rockets flaming matches "at his nude supine wife" or sets ablaze two 16-foot wooden crosses on Laguna Canyon Road at 2 A.M.— "the intended audience for that piece," says Burden, "was the one guy driving down the road who saw it first." Ah, Los Angeles! For "Endurance/real time," he 1) stays in a locker for five days; 2) does 1,600 tours of a gallery on his bicycle; and 3) remains in bed for three weeks and a day. He also pretends to be a dead man lying under a tarpaulin on the street and is arrested by the police for creating a traffic hazard. He gets a hung jury at his trial and the case is dismissed but "one of the nine votes for conviction, a stewardess, told Burden if she ever saw him under a tarp again, she'd run over him herself." He even does a study in the shift of identity. For "I Became a Secret Hippie," Burden cuts his hair short and dresses in FBI clothes. "If you want to be a heavy artist nowadays," Plagens, reporting on Burden, concludes, "you have to do something unpleasant to your body, because every-thing *else* has been done. . . . [Burden] may be a product of art-world art history—backed into some untenable masochistic corner because all the other novelty territory has been claimed."

At the least, Burden is fulfilling the dictum of Jean Malaquais that once there are enough artists in the world, the work of art will become the artist himself. Burden is refining his personality. Through existential tests. Burden is not exploring his technique but his vibrations. The situations he chooses are, as Plagens describes, "edgy." They have nothing remotely resembling a boundary until they are done. In "Movie on the Way Down," Burden can hardly know if he will cut his lip or break his neck, feel a live instant on the descent or some dull anxiety. When he shoots lighted matches at his nude wife the areas defined are empty before the action begins. Given every variable from Women's Liberation to the sadomasochistic tales of Wilhelm Stekel, Burden can know in advance only that a psycho-dramatic enterprise will be commenced. But where it may end, and what everybody might feel—will the matches burn her skin?—will the marriage be fortified or scorched?—no, there is no confidence which question is going to offer an answer. Perhaps he is not refining his personality so much as attempting to clear a space in his psyche free of dread. But isn't that the fundamental operation of the primitive at the dawn of civilization, the establishment of the ego? For what is the human ego but a clearing in the forest of the psyche free of dread? Money, held in one's hand, is free of time. Cash has no past; its future is assignable. It is powerful and empty. So, too, is the ego. It bears the same relation to the psyche as cash bears to the security or comfort of the body. The ego is virtually separate from the psyche even as money is still separate from every organic communicating logic of nature.

We are back to the cave man and his cave painting. His hand draws the outline of the animal in defiance of those gods who watch him. Burden is smashing his nose on the floor or displaying his wife in defiance of the last gods of conventional art. They are that audience remnant of a once-leviathan bourgeois culture. They still trickle out to see Happenings for the desire of the middle class is to preserve its last religion—the world of the artist, palette, museum, and gallery wall. Middle-class passion is to appreciate the work of art.

But art may be the little ball rolling off the table. Perhaps art now signifies some unheard reverberation from the subterranean obsession of us all: Is civilization coming to an end? Is society burning? Is the day of the cave man returning? Has our search for ego which was once so routine—a useful (somewhat heartless) ego to be fashioned for a useful (if heartless) society—now gone past the measure of our experience so that we no longer try to construct a control center at the core of the mind, but plunge instead into absurdities which offer us that curious calm we find in the art of the absurd, even as the cave man, defying his gods, discovered he was not always dead on the next day?

But we are at the possible end of civilization, and tribal impulses start up across the world. The descending line of the isolated artist goes down from Michelangelo all the way to Shoot. But Chris Burden is finally more comfortable to us than the writers of graffiti. For Burden is the last insult from the hippie children of the middle class to the bourgeois art-patron who is their spiritual parent, but graffiti speaks of a new civilization where barbarism is stirring at the roots.

If, at the beginning of Western painting, man was small and God was large; if, in the Renaissance, man was mysteriously large in his relation to God; now, in our times man has disappeared into God. He is mass-man without identity, and he is God. He is all the schizophrenia of the powerless and all-powerful in one psyche.

As we lose our senses in the static of the oncoming universal machine, so does our need to exercise the ego take on elephantiastical proportions. Graffiti is the expression of a ghetto that is near to the plague, for civilization is now closed off from the ghetto. Too huge are the obstacles to any natural development of a civilized man. In the ghetto it is almost impossible to find some quiet identity. No, in the environment of the slum, the courage to display yourself is your only capital, and in the streets crime is the only productive process that converts such capital to the modern powers of the world, ego and money. Art is not peace but war, and form is the record of that war.

Yet there is a mystery still. From which combat came these curious letters of graffiti, with their Chinese and Arabic calligraphies? Out of what connection to the past did these lights and touches of flame become so much like the Hebrew alphabet, where the form of the letter itself was worshipped as a manifest of the Lord? No, it is not enough to think of the childlike desire to see one's name ride by in letters large enough to scream your ego across the city, no, it is almost as if we must go back into some more primeval sense of existence. If our name is enormous to us, it is also not real—as if we have come from other places than the name, and lived in other lives.

Perhaps that is the unheard echo of graffiti, the vibration of that profound discomfort it arouses. Can the unheard music of its proclamation and/or its mess, the rapt intent seething of its foliage, be the herald of some oncoming apocalypse less and less far away? For graffiti lingers on our subway door as a memento of all the lives ever lived, sounding now like the bugles of gathering armies across the unseen ridge.

From *The Faith of Graffiti* (1974)

**THE FIGHT**

## Bantu Philosophy

Months ago, a story had gotten into the newspapers about a novel he was writing. His publishers were going to pay him a million dollars sight unseen for the book. If his candles had been burning low in the literary cathedral these last few years, the news story went its way to hastening their extinction. He knew that his much-publicized novel (still nine-tenths to be written) would now have to be twice as good as before to overcome such financial news. Good literary men were not supposed to pick up *sums*. Small apples for him to protest in every banlieu and literary purlieu that his Boston publisher had not been laid low with a degenerative disease of the cortex but that the million was to be paid out as he wrote five to seven hundred thousand words, the equivalent of five novels. Since he was being rewarded only as he delivered the work, and had debts and a sizable advance already spent and five wives and seven children, plus a financial nut at present larger than his head, so the sum was not as large as it seemed, he explained—the million, you see, was nominal.

Well, the literary world was built on bad cess. For good cause. If no one would be in a hurry to forgive him unless his novel proved immense, then maybe that would force his work closer to such scope. He might have time, at least to parse it out.

Here in Africa, however, it was another tale. Since the word of his million had hit the wire services, his name throughout the Black community had been *underlined*. No'min Million was a man who could make it by using his head. No rough stuff! He did not have to get hit in the head, nor hit on the side of *your* head. This man had to be the literary champ. To make a million without taking chances—show respect! To sign for a sum that Heavyweight champs had not been able to make until Muhammad Ali came along—why, the optimistic element of the Black community, looking now at every commercial horizon in America, began to gaze at writing. Hang around this man, went the word. Something might rub off!

Once, he would have been miserable at being able to prosper from such values. But his love affair with the Black soul, a sentimental orgy at its worst, had been given a drubbing through the seasons of Black Power. He no longer knew whether he loved Blacks or secretly disliked them, which had to be the dirtiest secret in his American life. Part of the woe of the first trip to Africa, part of that irrationally intense detestation of Mobutu—even a photo of the President in his plump cheeks and horn-rimmed eyeglasses igniting invective adequate to a Harvard professor looking at an icon of Nixon—must be a cover for the rage he was feeling toward Blacks, any Blacks. Walking the streets of Kinshasa on that first trip while the Black crowds moved about him with an indifference to his presence that succeeded in niggering him, he knew what it was to be looked upon as invisible. He was also approaching, if not careful, the terminal animosity of a Senior Citizen. How his hatred seethed in search of a justifiable excuse. When the sheer evidence of Africa finally overcame these newly bigoted senses (when a drive over miles of highway showed thousands of slim and probably hungry Zairois running like new slum inhabitants for overcrowded buses, and yet, in some absolute statement of aesthetic, some imprimatur of the holy and final statement of the line of the human body, these Blacks could still show in silhouette, while standing in line for the bus, almost every one of those thousand slim dark Africans, an incorruptible loneliness, a stone mute dignity, some African dignity he had never seen on South Americans, Europeans, or Asiatics, some tragic magnetic sense of self as if each alone and all were carrying the continent like a halo of sorrow about their head), then it became impossible not to feel the unique life of Africa—even if Kinshasa was to the rain forest as Hoboken to Big Sur—yes, impossible not to sense what everyone had been trying to say about Africa for a hundred years, big Papa first on line: The place was so fucking sensitive! No horror failed to stir its echo a thousand miles away, no sneeze was ever free of the leaf that fell on the other side of the hill. Then he could no longer hate the Zairois or even be certain of his condemnation of their own Black oppressors, then his animosity switched a continent over to Black Americans with their arrogance, jive, ethnic put-down costumes, caterwauling soul, their thump-your-testicle organ sound, and black new vomitous egos like the slag of all of alienated sewage-compacted heap U.S.A.; then he knew that he had not only come to report on a fight but to look a little more into his own outsized feelings of love and—could it be?—sheer hate for the existence of Black on earth.

Then Foreman's eye was cut in training. It would take six weeks to heal. Norman went back to America. He was, however, not surprised when his illness flared on return to the States, and he went through a week and then ten days of total detestation of himself, a fever without fantasies, an illness without terror, for he felt as if his soul had expired or, worse, slipped away. It was enough of a warning to lay a message on him. He got up from bed with the determination to learn a little about Africa before his return, a healthy impulse that brought him luck (but then, do we not gamble with the unrecognized thought that a return of our luck signifies a return of our health?). After inquiries, he went to the University Place Book Shop in New York, an operative definition of the word *warren,* up on the eighth or ninth floor of a wheezing old office building below Fourteenth Street—the smell of the catacombs in its stones—to find at exit from the elevator a stack and excelsior of books, cartons, and dust where a big blond clerk with scraggly sideburns working alone assured the new customer that he could certainly afford these many books being laid on him, since he had after all been given the million, hadn't he, a worthless excursion to describe if not for the fact that the clerk picked the books, the titles all unfamiliar. Would there be one paragraph of radium in all this geographical, political, historical sludge? His luck came in—not a paragraph but a book: *Bantu Philosophy,* by Father Tempels, a Dutch priest who had worked as missionary in the Belgian Congo and extracted the philosophy from the language of the tribes he lived among.

Given a few of his own ideas, Norman's excitement was not small as he read *Bantu Philosophy.* For he discovered that the instinctive philosophy of African tribesmen happened to be close to his own. Bantu philosophy, he soon learned, saw humans as forces, not beings. Without putting it into words, he had always believed that. It gave a powerful shift to his thoughts. By such logic, men or women were more than the parts of themselves, which is to say more than the result of their heredity and experience. A man was not only what he contained, not only his desires, his memory, and his personality, but also the forces that came to inhabit him at any moment from all things living and dead. So a man was not only himself but the karma of all the generations past that still lived in him, not only a human with his own psyche but a part of the resonance, sympathetic or unsympathetic, of every root and thing (and witch) about him. He would take his balance, his quivering place, in a field of all the forces of the living and the dead. So the meaning of one's life was never hard to find. One did one's best to live in the pull of these forces in such a way as to increase one's own force. Ideally, one would do it in harmony with the play of all forces, but the beginning of wisdom was to enrich oneself, enrich the *muntu* that was the amount of life in oneself, the size of the human being in oneself. Crazy. We are returned to the Calvinism of the chosen, where the man with most possessions is chosen, the man of force and wealth. We are certainly in the ghetto, where you do not invade another turf. We are allied to every pride of property and self-enrichment. Back to the primitive sinews of capitalism! Bantu philosophy, however, is not so primitive. It may offer a more sinister vision—maybe it is nobler. For if we are our own force, we are also a servant of the forces of the dead. So we have to be bold enough to live with all the magical forces at loose between the living and the dead. That is never free of dread. It takes bravery to live with beauty or wealth if we think of them as an existence connected to the messages, the curses, and the loyalties of the dead.

In the presence of a woman who is finely dressed, an African might do more than salute the increase of power that accrues to the woman with her elaborate gown. To his eye, she would also have taken on the force that lives in the gown itself, the *kuntu* of the gown. That has its own existence. It, too, is a force in the universe of forces. The gown is like the increment in power an actor feels when he enters his role, when he senses the separate existence of the role as it comes up to him, much as if it had been *out there* waiting for him in the dark. Then, it is as if he takes on some marrow of the forgotten caves. It is why certain actors must act or go mad—they can hardly live without the clarity of that moment when the role returns—yes, every word will have its relation to the primeval elements of the universe. "The word," says a Dogon sage named Ogotemmêli, "is water and heat. The force that carries the word comes out of the mouth in a water vapor which is both water and word." Nommo is at once the name of the word and the spirit of water. So Nommo lives everywhere—in the vapor of the air and the pores of the earth. Since the word is equal to water, all things are effected by Nommo, the word. Even the ear becomes an organ of sex when Nommo enters: "The good word, as soon as it is received by the ear, goes directly to the sex organ where it rolls in the uterus. . . ."

What exhilaration! This small fine book, *Bantu Philosophy*, and then a larger work bursting with intellectual sweetmeats, *Muntu, the New African Culture*, by Janheinz Jahn, is illumining his last hours in New York, his flight on the plane—a night and a day!—his second impressions of Kinshasa. It has brought him back to a recognition of his old love for Blacks—as if the deepest ideas that ever entered his mind were there because Black existed. It has also brought back all the old fear. The mysterious genius of these rude, disruptive, and—down to it!—altogether indigestible Blacks. What noise they still made to the remains of his literary mind, what hooting, screaming, and shrieking, what promise of oblivion on the turn of a card.

How his prejudices were loose. So much resentment had developed for Black style, Black snobbery, Black rhetoric, Black pimps, superfly, and all that virtuoso handling of the ho. The pride Blacks took in their skill as pimps! A wrath at the mismanagement of his own sensual existence now sat on him, a sorrow at how the generosity of his mind seemed determined to contract as he grew older. He could not really bring himself to applaud the emergence of a powerful people into the center of American life—he was envious. They had the good fortune to be born Black. And felt a private fury at the professional complacency of Black self-pity, a whole rage at the rhythmic power of those hectoring voices, a resentment at last of their values, of that eternal emphasis on centrality—"I am the real rooster on this block, the most terrible cock, the baddest fist. I'm a *down* dude. You motherfuckers better know it."

Yet even as he indulged this envy, he felt a curious relief. For he had come to a useful recognition. When the American Black was torn out of Africa, he was ripped out of his philosophy as well. So his violence and his arrogance could be a fair subject for comprehension once more. One had only to think of the torture. Everything in African philosophy was of the root, but the philosophy had been uprooted. What a clipped and overstimulated transplant was the American Negro. His view of life came not only from his livid experience in America but from the fragments of his lost African beliefs. So he was alienated not from one culture but from two. What idea could an Afro-American retain, then, of his heritage if not that each man seeks the maximum of force for himself? Since he lived in a field of human forces that were forever changing, and changing dramatically, even as the people he knew were killed or arrested or fell out on junk, so he had to assert himself. How else could he find life? The loss of vital force was pure loss, equal to less ego, less status, less purchase on the availability of beauty. By comparison to the American Black, a white Judeo-Christian could live through a loss of vital force and feel moral, unselfish, even saintly, and an African could feel himself in balance among traditional forces. An African could support the weight of his obligation to his father because his father was one step nearer in the chain to God—that unbroken chain of lives going back to the source of creation. But the American Black was sociologically famous for the loss of his father.

No wonder their voices called attention to themselves! They spoke of a vital (if tense) force. A poor and uneducated man was nothing without that force. To the degree it lived inside him, he was full of capital, ego capital, and that was what he possessed. That was the capitalism of the poor American Black trying to accumulate more of the only wealth he could find, respect on his turf, the respect of local flunkies for the power of his soul. What a raw, searching, hustling, competitive capitalism. What a lack of profit. The establishment offered massive restraint for such massive fevers of the ego. No surprise if tribal life in America began to live among stone walls and drugs. The drug gave magnification of the sentiment that a mighty force was still inside oneself, and the penitentiary restored the old idea that man was a force in a field of forces. If the social contract of the African restraint had been tradition, the American Black with a political ideal was obliged instead to live with revolutionary discipline. As he endured in his stone walls it became a discipline as pulverizing to the soul as the search for condition of a boxer.

# King of the Flunkies

Like many a hustler he was *sweet*. He could cry like a child—indeed he cried whenever Ali boxed with beauty, cried at the bounty of the Lord to provide such athletic bliss—and his eyes beamed with love at any remark that excited his own powers of metaphor. Then his big round face would show the simple happiness of Aunt Jemima, his big husky voice would croon in admiration at such wonders of wisdom. That was half of him; Bundini was just as proud of his other soul. If he was all emotion, he could show his ice; if he had class, he could be without class—he'd give his life for a friend and you might believe him, but "he would," said a critic, "take the dimes off a dead man's eyes and put nickels back." Small surprise if he had a build like nobody else. Over six feet, with a big crystal ball for a head, he had small shoulders, a small protruding stomach that seemed to center its melon on his diaphragm, and spindles for legs—it was the body of a spaceman who grew up in a capsule. Yet he had fought in Navy competitions as an adolescent; even now nobody would take Bundini on for too little (except Ali, who slapped him at will as though dealing with an unregenerate child). Bundini was plain as a mouthful of gold teeth and handsome as black velvet. If he called his young wife Mother, he had been about as fatherly in his day as any other player: A magazine story once spoke of his desire to be a "marketable pimp." But then he sold interviews of himself that told it all, and gave metaphors away for nothing. He could not spell a word, and had a dozen movie scripts he was trying to sell, his own, he claimed. Recall us to "Float like a butterfly, sting like a bee." Bundini was the walking definition of the idea that each human is born with two souls—two distinct persons to inhabit each body. If Africans did not have the concept, one would have to invent it. All that spirit, all that prick. The two never came together. After a while, Norman and he were no longer friends and did not speak for years. But the fight game shakes old prejudices like castanets. Since he and Bundini kept being thrown together at fights, and since Bundini kept helping him in little ways whether he wished it or not, they finally began to talk a little, if more than a little on guard. For years they talked to each other just a little.

This fight, Bundini was shifting the terms. One afternoon, just as Norman was walking down the bank of the Zaïre after a visit with Ali, he heard a voice shout to him from a neighboring villa.

"Hey, No'min, come here."

The tone was not pleasant, but he was curious who was calling. Somewhat too late, he realized he was approaching Bundini, who stood in the vestibule of the villa surrounded by a group of Black friends. He had been drinking. Straight out, he was drunk. It was easy to tell with Bundini. The whites of his eyes turned egg-yolk yellow and blooded with webs of red. His breath smelled of the vats.

"I learned," he declared to Norman, "the meaning of my name in African today. I've been blessed. What you been blessed with?"

"Meeting you."

"You talking like I'm still a nigger. Niggers is yesterday. I've been blessed with the root. I'm in harmony. What you been blessed with?" he asked once more. Bundini was warming up to play the dozens. "Show me your blessing," he said, "show me your blessing." The dozens, no mistake. Other Blacks were grinning with the possibilities.

"I'm blessed with listening to you beat your gums." Hardly a good reply. Points were already accumulating to Bundini.

"My black gums are dark with the misery and the wonder. The jewels of oppression are shining in my black gums, motherfucker."

No smiles from the audience. Bundini was treating him like a stranger. "I learned my black name today," he said, "I learned what Bundini means."

"What does it mean?" The answer was weak. You did not parley the dozens for that encouraged an onslaught.

"Bundini means I'm back in the blood of my people. I'm the steeple. I'm the point of it all. My black heart is beautiful. Bundini! *Something like dark* is what they say Bundini means. *Something like dark,*" said Bundini, going back over the translation with relish.

"*Not quite dark* is what it means." For the first time the Blacks around Bundini laughed a little.

"You're just envious," said Bundini, "because you don't have a name in African, motherfucker. You have none of the Black juice. The berries in your belly are pale. Your blood is in jail, motherfucker. As you shit, you mumble, you're afraid of the jungle. You're afraid of the jungle, motherfucker!"

"I just wish my mother was here," Norman managed to say, "because if she was, she would give you a whupping!"

Maybe his voice caught something of Ali's tone, or maybe it had just gone on long enough, but everybody burst into laughter, and Bundini smote his hand as if he were now Honorary Black. On the round of good feeling this had to offer, Norman also felt some large part of unforgiveness to Bundini begin to lift. Only afterward did it occur to him that drunk in the middle of the afternoon, Bundini was still wise enough to choose the dozens as a way of reestablishing relations, certainly wise enough to thrust victory upon him.

So this night, passing the table where Bundini sat with his Jewish wife, Shere, it was impossible to refuse his offer of a drink. Before too long, Norman accepted his invitation to dinner. Bundini asked about

Ali's mood and they talked about that for a while, since Norman had spent the afternoon with Ali at Nsele. It had been a curious Sunday. Ali's voice had left him. Ali could offer no more than a hoarse whisper, a frightening prospect for the fight if his voice was the measure of his strength. But he certainly seemed happy enough. At twilight, he took a walk on the banks of the river, and was surrounded by hundreds of Zairois men, women, and children. He kissed babies and had his picture taken with numbers of Black and jubilant housewives in African Sunday dress, and with shy adolescent girls, and little boys who glared at the camera with machismo equal to the significance of these historic events. All the while Ali kissed babies with deliberation, slowly, savoring their skin, as if he could divine which infants would grow up healthy. He was one politician who would love kissing babies.

Bundini, having listened to Norman's account, now nodded somberly, and said across the table, "Jesus has no fear."

"Do you mean Allah has no fear?"

"It all comes out of God. Whatever you call Him. My man is right there with Jesus, Allah, Jehovah. He's got it all."

Slowly, the motive for Bundini's invitation to dinner emerged. He wanted Norman to look at his scripts and advise him.

"But I thought you can't read or write."

"I can't. But I can talk. People took down my words. I want you to take down some of my words."

"Drew—why don't you learn to write? You can do it. It's time."

Bundini looked serious and very sad. "I'm afraid to," he said. "I learned what I learned not knowing how to read, not knowing how to write. My strength is in the same place as Samson's hair. Reading and writing is Delilah to me. I don't want to lose the magic God alone gave me. I got to fight for my boy," he said. "He's in there to fight. I got to be there too." He offered one fine confidence. "I'm sharpening the spike. I'm going to give Foreman's people the needle tonight."

"How do you do that?"

"Oh, I'm going up to them to put some money on Ali. But I won't ask for three to one. I'm going to give two thousand dollars against their three. That got to worry them. They be wondering where I get the confidence. It go right back to George Foreman."

"You have a real two thousand dollars?"

"Better be real!"

They laughed.

And so in the middle of the lobby, having attracted some of Foreman's people, the sparring partner Stan Ward among them, Bundini began to jeer. "I don't want three to one, I don't need three to one. *My* man is three to one."

"Then give *us* three to one," said Stan Ward.

"I would. If God was here, I would. But He ain't. He don't associate with flunkies who work for George Foreman, that big man, that big white man. I don't give you three to one because I don't give no advantage to people who work for the White Man."

"Then why you asking three to two instead of three to one," someone said suspiciously.

"Because you the bullies. Anybody works for the White Man is a bully. A bully needs advantage. I'm giving you advantage. You go out in the casinos and try to get your bet. You have to lay three to get one. You people are too fucking scared to do that. 'Cause you know the White Man upstairs. You know his faults. You know you going to lose."

"Foreman ain't going to lose," said Stan Ward.

"Give me *your* bet," said Bundini.

"How much you laying?"

"My two thousand dollars is in my hands," said Bundini, pulling out a roll. "Now show me, nigger, where your three thousand dollars is."

"I can't get it right away," said Ward. "But I'll have it in the morning. I'll meet you here at eleven in the morning."

"Yeah, if the White Man tells you to go ahead and pee, then you can piss," said Bundini.

"He ain't the White Man."

"Shit, he ain't. There he is in the Olympics, a big fat fool dancing around with an eentsy American flag in his big dumb fist. He don't know what to do with a fist. My man does. My man got his fist in the air when he wins. Power to the People! That's my man. Millions follow him. Who follows your man? He's got nobody to follow him," said Bundini, "that's why he keeps a *dog*." The followers of Foreman suddenly roared with happiness. The *kuntu* was audacity and they paid their respects to the spirit of audacity embodied in Bundini. "What are you ready to die for?" asked Bundini. He answered them, "Nothing. You ain't ready for nothing. But I'm ready to die for Muhammad. I put my bread on the line. I don't have to consult and come back here at eleven in the morning with my dick in my hand, permission to piss. I put my bread on the line. If I got no bread, I'm dead. If I got no loaves, I'm cold stone in the oven," crooned Bundini. "That's what it's all about. Muhammad Ali has Bundini ready to die, and what does the White Man have? Twenty-two niggers and a dog."

Foreman's people roared with all the happiness of knowing that Foreman would win and that the spirit of audacity was nonetheless not dead. A very heavyset Negro with a cane for his game leg and heavy horn-rimmed glasses for his game eyes gave a peal of shrill laughter high as a spurt of water shooting up, and held out his palm.

Bundini struck it, showed his own palm, the man struck it back. Happiness. If words were blows, Bundini was champ of the kingdom of flunkies. Long live Nommo, spirit of words.

# The Run

He could go back to the Inter-Continental, eat early, and try to get some sleep before the run, but sleep was not likely between eight in the evening and midnight—besides, there was no question of keeping up with Muhammad. His conscience, however (now on the side of good journalism), was telling him that the better his own condition, the more he would be able to discern about Ali's. What a pity he had not been jogging since the summer. Up in Maine he had done two miles every other day, but jogging was one discipline he could not maintain. At five feet eight inches and one hundred and seventy pounds, Norman was simply too heavy to enjoy running. He could jog at a reasonable gait—fifteen minutes for two miles was good time for him—and if pushed, he could jog three miles, conceivably four, but he hated it. Jogging disturbed the character of one's day. He did not feel refreshed afterward but overstimulated and irritable. The truth of jogging was it only felt good when you stopped. And he would remind himself that with the exception of Erich Segal and George Gilder, he had never heard of a writer who liked to run—who wanted the brilliance of the mind discharged through the ankles?

Back in Kinshasa, he decided to have drinks and a good meal after all, and during dinner there was amusement at the thought he would accompany Ali on the road. "You know you have to do it," said John Vinocur of the AP. "I know," said Mailer, in full gloom. "Ali isn't expecting me to show up, but he won't forgive it if I don't." "That's right, that's right," said Vinocur, "I offered to run with Foreman once, and when I didn't get there, he never let me forget. He brings it up every time I see him."

"Plimpton, you've got to come with me," said Mailer.

George Plimpton wasn't sure he would. Mailer knew he wouldn't. Plimpton had too much to lose. With his tall thin track man's body and his quietly buried competitive passion (large as Vesuvius, if smokeless), Plimpton would have to keep on some kind of close terms with Ali or pay a disproportionate price in humiliation. Whereas it was easy for Mailer. If he didn't get a leg cramp in the first five hundred yards, he could pick the half-mile mark to take his bow. He just hoped Ali didn't run too fast. That would be jogger's hell. At the thought of being wiped out from the start, a little bile rose from the drinks and the rich food. It was now only nine in the evening, but his stomach felt as if the forces of digestion were in stupor.

Still, it was a good meal. They were eating in the open air with the funky grandeur of a dilapidated grand hotel for backdrop. The Palace Hotel. It was now an apartment house and offered its miasma—there was from time to time an operative whiff of what Victorians used to call *the smell of drains*. The toilet in the restroom was rimless, a needless even excrementitious detail if not for the fact that our man of wisdom was hoping to move himself properly before going out to run, but the sight of the bowl, the missing seat, and the indescribable condition closed off his chances. Worse may have been glimpsed in many an American gas station, but never so settled in. SANICONGO was the brand name of the toilet, and it looked to have been installed in time for the coronation of King Leopold. Maybe the bowl even had its *kuntu,* for when he got back to the table, Horst Fass was telling stories about Vietnam, and they were in the mode of SANICONGO. Fass worked with Vinocur, and had the job—no casual responsibility—of making certain the communications of the AP would get out for the fight, a nightmare of telephones, teletypes, Telexes, Telstars, and hysterical assistants. He was a cool and cheerful young German with all the confidence of his trades—not only a top technician but a reporter, a cameraman. He had been the AP man in many a war, many a port, and many an international conference—not surprising that he also had a journalist's eye for the fine stories that cannot be used. So Mailer and Plimpton learned for the first time—be certain their mouths were open—that certain Americans in Nam had volunteered to be undertakers because they were connoisseurs of necrophilia and enjoyed making love to parts of a human body rather than the predictable dead whole. Fass told this with the expression of a man who has seen everything and so will never again be shocked but is nonetheless attached to the detail because it is an example of the extreme. As if this story, however, had been entree of wild boar and one needed sherbet for dessert, Fass offered a touching tale about the brothels managed by the U.S. Army, a preventive measure against the special virulence of Vietnamese V.D.: There in the military brothels, the girls wore yellow and red badges, one color underwriting disease-free copulation and the other holding them in temporary chastity. Nonetheless, they could still work. At a lower rate. They were on hand for men who just wished to talk to a girl. "They did good business," said Fass. "A lot of the GIs just wanted to talk."

A little later, they all went to a Casino and played Black Jack. The thought that he would run with Ali was beginning to offer its agreeable tension, a sensation equal to the way he felt when he was going to win at Black Jack. Gambling had its own libido. Just as one was ill-advised to make love when libido was dim, so was that a way to lose money in gambling. Whenever he felt empty, he dropped his stake; when full of himself, he often won. Every gambler was familiar with the principle—it was visceral, after all—few failed to disobey it in one fashion or another. But never had he felt its application so powerfully as in Africa. It was almost as if one could make a living in Kinshasa provided one gambled only when one's blood was up.

Naturally, he drank a little. He had friends at this Casino. The manager was a young American not yet twenty-one and in love with the taste of his life in Africa; the croupiers and dealers were English girls, sharp as birds in their accents—the keen vibrating intelligence of the London working class was in their quick voices. He was getting *mal d'Afrique,* the sweet infection that forbids you to get out of Africa (in your mind, at least) once you have visited it. What intoxication to gamble and know in advance whether one would win or lose. Even orange juice and vodka gave its good thump. He was loving everything about the evening but the sluggishness of his digestion. Pocketing his money, he went back to the hotel to put on a T-shirt and exercise pants.

The long drive to Nsele, forty-five minutes and more, confirmed him in the first flaw of his life. He was a monster of bad timing. Why had he not paced himself so that the glow he was feeling at the Casino would be with him when he ran? Now his fighting spirit was fading with the drinks. By the time they hit the road, he would have to work off the beginnings of a hangover. And his stomach, that invariably reliable organ, had this night simply not digested his food. My God. A thick fish chowder and a pepper steak were floating down the Congo of his inner universe like pads of hyacinth in the clotted Zaïre. My God, add ice cream, rum and tonic, vodka and orange juice. Still, he did not feel sick, just turgid—a normal state for his fifty-one years, his heavy meals, and this hour.

It was close to three in the morning as he reached Nsele, and he would have preferred to go to sleep. He was even ready to consider turning around without seeing Ali. By now, however, that was hardly a serious alternative.

But the villa was dark. Maybe Ali would not run tonight. A couple of soldiers, polite but somewhat confused by the sight of visitors at this hour—Bob Drew, a cameraman from the AP, was also waiting—asked them not to knock on the door. So they all sat in the dark for a quarter of an hour, and then a few lights went on in the villa, and Howard Bingham, a young Black from *Sports Illustrated* who had virtually become Ali's private photographer, came by and brought them in. Ali was still sleepy. He had gone to bed at nine and just awakened, the longest stretch of sleep he would take over twenty-four hours. Later, after running, he might nap again, but sleep never seemed as pervasive a concern to him as to other fighters.

"You did come," he said with surprise, and then seemed to pay no further attention. He was doing some stretching exercises to wake up and had the surliness of any infantryman awakened in the middle of the night. They would make four for the run. Bingham was coming along and Pat Patterson, Ali's personal bodyguard, a Chicago cop, no darker than Ali, with the solemn even stolid expression of a man who has gone through a number of doors in his life without the absolute certainty that he would walk out again. By day, he always carried a pistol; by night—what a pity not to remember if he strapped a holster over his running gear.

Ali looked sour. The expression on his face was not difficult to read. Who wanted to run? He gave an order to one of the two vans that would accompany them, telling it to be certain to stay well behind so that its fumes would not bother them. The other had Bob Drew inside to take photographs, and it was allowed to stay even.

Norman may have hoped the fighter would want to walk for a while, but Ali right away took off at a slow jogger's gait, and the others fell in. They trotted across the grass of the villas set parallel to the river and, when they came to the end of the block, took a turn toward the highway two miles off and kept trotting at the same slow pace past smaller villas, a species of motel row where some of the press was housed. It was like running in the middle of the night across suburban lawns on some undistinguished back street of Beverly Hills, an occasional light still on in a room here and there, one's eyes straining to pick up the driveways one would have to cross, the curbings, and the places where little wire fences protected the plantings. Ali served as a guide, pointing to holes in the ground, sudden dips, and slippery spots where hoses had watered the grass too long. And they went on at the same slow steady pace. It was, in fact, surprisingly slow, certainly no faster than his own rate when jogging by himself, and Norman felt, everything considered, in fairly good condition. His stomach was already a full soul of heated lead, and it was not going to get better, but to his surprise, it was not getting worse—it seemed to have settled in as one of the firm discontents he would have on this run.

After they had gone perhaps half a mile, Ali said, "You're in pretty good shape, Norm."

"Not good enough to talk," he answered through closed teeth.

Jogging was an act of balance. You had to get to the point where your legs and your lungs worked together in some equal state of exertion. They could each be close to overexertion, but if one was not more fatigued than the other, they offered some searing and hardworking equivalent of the tireless, to wit, you would feel no more abominable after a mile than after the first half mile. The trick was to reach this disagreeable state without having to favor the legs or the lungs. Then, if no hills were there to squander one's small reserve, and one did not lose stride or have to stop, if one did not stumble and one did not speak, that steady progressive churning could continue, thoroughgoing, raw to one's middle-aged insides, but virtuous—one felt like the motors of an old freighter.

After a few weeks of steady running, one could take the engines of the old freighter through longer and longer storms, one could manage hills, one could even talk (and how well one could ski later in the year with the legs built up!), but now his body has been docked for two months and he was performing a new kind of balancing act. It was not only his legs and his lungs but the gauges on the bile in his stomach he had to watch, and the pressure on his heart. If he had always run before breakfast, and so was unaccustomed to jogging with food in his stomach, he was having an education in that phenomenon now. It was a third factor, hot, bilious, and working like a bellows in reverse, for it kept pushing up a pressure on his lungs, yet, to his surprise, not nauseating, just heavy pressure, so that he knew he could not keep up with this faster pace much longer. Soon his stomach would be engorging his heart.

Still, they had covered what must be three-quarters of a mile by now and were long past the villas and formal arrangement of Nsele's buildings, and just padded along on a back road with the surprisingly disagreeable exhaust of the lead van choking their nostrils. What a surprising impediment to add to the run—it had to be worse than cigar smoke at ringside, and to this pollution of air came an intermittent freaking of a photographic flash pack from Bob Drew's camera.

Still, he had acquired his balance. What with food, drink, and lack of condition, it was one of the most unpleasant runs he had ever made, certainly the most caustic in its preview of hell, but he had found his balance. He kept on running with the others, the gait most happily not stepped up, and came to recognize after a while that Ali was not a bad guy to run with. He kept making encouraging comments, "Hey, you're doin' fine, Norm," and, a little later, "Say, you're in good condition," to which the physical specimen could only grunt for reply—mainly it was the continuing sense of a perfect pace to Ali's legs that helped the run, as if his own legs were somehow being tuned to pick their own best rate, yes, something easy and uncompetitive came off Ali's good stride.

"How old are you, Norm?"

He answered in two bursts, "Fifty—one."

"Say, when I'm fifty-one, I won't be strong enough to run to the corner," said Ali. "I'm feeling tired already."

They jogged. Wherever possible, Ali ran on the turf. Pat Patterson, used to pounding concrete, ran on the paving of the road, and Bingham alternated. Norman stayed on the turf. It was generally easier on the feet and harder on the lungs to jog over grass, and his lungs so close to the pressure of his stomach were more in need than his legs, but he could not keep the feel of Ali's easy rhythm if he left the turf.

On they went. Now they were passing through a small forest, and by his measure, they had come a little more than a mile. He was beginning to think it was remotely possible that he could cover the entire distance—was it scheduled for three miles?—but even as he was contemplating the heroics of this horror they entered on a long slow grade uphill, and something in the added burden told him that he was not going to make it without a breakdown in the engines. His heart had now made him prisoner—it sat in an iron collar around his neck, and as they chugged up the long slow grade, the collar tightened every fifty feet. He was breathing now as noisily as he had ever breathed, and recognized that he was near to the end of his run.

"Champ," he said, "I'm going—to stop—pretty soon," a speech in three throttled bursts. "I'm just—holding you—back," and realized it was true—except how could Ali put up with too slow a gait when the fight was just four nights away? "Anyway—have good run," he said, like the man in the water waving in martyred serenity at the companions to whom he has just offered his spot in the lifeboat. "I'll see you— back there."

And he returned alone. Later, when he measured it by the indicator on his car, he found that he had run with them for a mile and a half, not too unrespectable. And enjoyed his walk. Actually, he was a little surprised at how slow the pace had been. It seemed unfitting that he had been able to keep up as long as he had. If Ali was going to run for fifteen rounds, there should, he thought, be something more kin to a restlessness in his legs tonight. Of course, Ali was not wearing sneakers but heavy working shoes. Still. The leisureliness of the pace made him uneasy.

There is no need to follow Norman back on his walk, except that we are about to discover a secret to the motivation of writers who achieve a bit of prominence in their own time. As the road continued through the forest, dark as Africa is ever supposed to be, he was enjoying for the first time a sense of what it meant to be out alone in the African night, and occasionally, when the forest thinned, knew what it might also mean to be alone under an African sky. The clarity of the stars! The size of the bowl of heaven! Truth, thoughts after running are dependably banal. Yet what a teeming of cricket life and locusts in the brush about him, that nervous endless vibration seeming to shake the earth. It was one of the final questions: Were insects a part of the cosmos or the termites of the cosmos?

Just then, he heard a lion roar. It was no small sound, more like thunder, and it opened an unfolding wave of wrath across the sky and through the fields. Did the sound originate a mile away, or less? He had come out of the forest, but the lights of Nsele were also close to a mile away, and there was all of this deserted road between. He could never reach those lights before the lion would run him down. Then his next thought was that the lion, if it chose, could certainly race up on him silently, might even be on his way now.

Once, sailing in Provincetown harbor on nothing larger than a Sailfish, he had passed a whale. Or rather the whale passed him. A frolicsome whale that cavorted in its passage and was later to charm half the terrified boats in its path. He had recognized at the moment that there was nothing he could ever do if the whale chose to swallow him with his boat. Yet he felt singularly cool. What a perfect way to go. His place in American literature would be forever secure. They would seat him at Melville's feet. Melville and Mailer, ah, the consanguinity of the M's and the L's—how critics would love Mailer's now discovered preoccupations (see Croft on the mountain in *The Naked and the Dead*) with Ahab's Moby Dick.

Something of this tonic sangfroid was with him now. To be eaten by a lion on the banks of the Congo—who could fail to notice that it was Hemingway's own lion waiting down these years for the flesh of Ernest until an appropriate substitute had at last arrived?

They laughed back at Ali's villa when he told them about the roar. He had forgotten Nsele had a zoo and lions might as well be in it.

Ali looked tired. He had run another mile and a half, he would estimate, three miles in all, and had sprinted uphill for the last part, throwing punches, running backward, then all-out forward again, and was very tired now. "That running," he said, "takes more out of me than anything I ever felt in the ring. It's even worse than the fifteenth round, and that's as bad as you can get."

Like an overheated animal, Ali was lying on the steps of his villa, cooling his body against the stone, and Bingham, Patterson, and Ali did not talk too much for a while. It was only 4 A.M. but the horizon was beginning to lighten—the dawn seemed to come in for hours across the African sky. Predictably, Ali was the one to pick up conversation again. His voice was surprisingly hoarse: He sounded as if a cold were coming on. That was all Ali needed—a chest cold for the fight! Pat Patterson, hovering over him like a truculent nurse, brought a bottle of orange juice and scolded him for lying on the stone, but Ali did not move. He was feeling sad from the rigors of the workout and talked of Jurgin Blin and Blue Lewis and Rudi Lubbers. "Nobody ever heard of them," he said, "until they fought me. But they trained to fight me and fought their best fights. They were good fighters against me," he said almost with wonder. (Wonder was as close as he ever came to doubt.) "Look at Bugner—his greatest fight was against me. Of course, I didn't train for any of them the way they trained for me. I couldn't. If I trained for every fight the way I did for this, I'd be dead. I'm glad I left myself a little bit for this one." He shook his head in a blank sort of self-pity, as if some joy that once resided in his juices had been expended forever. "I'm going to get one million three hundred thousand for this fight, but I would give one million of that up gladly if I could just buy my present condition without the work."

Yet his present condition was so full of exhaustion. As if anxiety about the fight stirred in the hour before dawn, a litany began. It was the same speech he had made a day and a half ago to the press, the speech in which he listed each of Foreman's opponents and counted the number who were nobodies and the inability of Foreman to knock his opponents out cold. Patterson and Bingham nodded in the sad patience of men who worked for him and loved him and put up with this phase of his conditioning while Ali gave the speech the way a patient with a threatening heart will take a nitroglycerin pill. And Norman, with his food still undigested and his bowels hard packed from the shock of the jogging, was blank himself when he tried to think of amusing conversation to divert Ali's mood. It proved up to Ali to change the tone and by the dawn he did. After showering and dressing he showed a magic trick and then another, long cylinders popping out of his hands to become handkerchiefs, and, indeed, next day at training, still haranguing the press, Ali ended by saying, "Foreman will never catch me. When I meet George Foreman, I'll be free as a bird," and he held up his hand and opened it. A bird flew out. To the vast delight of the press. Ali was writing the last line of their daily piece from Kinshasa today. Nor did it take them long to discover the source. Bundini had captured the bird earlier in the day and slipped it to Ali when the time came. Invaluable Bundini, improvisatory Bundini.

Still, as Norman drove home to the Inter-Continental and breakfast, he measured Ali's run. He had finished by the Chinese pagoda. That was two and a half miles, not three! Ali had run very slowly for the first mile and a half. With an empty stomach and the fair condition of the summer in Maine, he thought he could probably have kept up with Ali until the sprint at the end. It was no way for a man fighting for a Heavyweight title to do roadwork. Norman did not see how Ali could win. Defeat was in the air. Ali alone seemed to refuse to breathe the fear of the people close to him.

# The Impresario

King had magical eyes. Until one met him, it was hard to understand how he could possibly have managed to bring the fighters together, for he had few financial resources to match an event of this scope. Don King had, however, the ability to take all his true love (which given his substantial Black presence was not necessarily small), plus all of his false love, and pour them out together through his eyes, his lambent eyes. Mailer had never believed in the real existence out in the field of the word *lambent* but then he had never looked before into a pair of eyes as full of love. "You are a genius in tune with the higher consciousness," King offered as the first compliment on meeting, "yet an instinctive exponent of the untiring search for aspiration in the warm earth-embracing potential of exploited peoples." Norman had once known a Rumanian doctor with just such a mouth-filling taste for rhetoric and pastrami. Don King was a cross between a Negro Heavyweight large as Ernie Terrell and that Jewish Rumanian doctor, nay, King was even B'nai Brith-ical. He could not say *ecstatic* if you did not let him add *with delight*. Occasions were never joyous if they could be *very joyous*. After a while Mailer realized that the description of himself offered with such generosity by King was in fact a way of letting you in on King's view of himself—"a genius in tune with the higher consciousness," et cetera.

Say, it would be hard to prove King was not a genius. A former nightclub owner and numbers king of Cleveland with four years in jail for killing a man in a street fight, he had approached Ali and Foreman with the splendid credentials of a fight manager whose two best fighters, Earnie Shavers and Jeff Merritt, had just both been knocked out in the first round. Still, he offered to promote Ali-Foreman. Each fighter would get five million dollars, he said. Those eyes of true love must have made the sum believable, for they glowed doubtless with the cool delights of lemonade, the fantasies of Pernod, and the golden kernels of corn—somehow, those eyes took him through barriers—he convinced Herbert Muhammad that he could produce this fight. "I reminded him of the teaching of his father, Elijah Muhammad, that every qualified Black man should be given a chance by his fellow Black men." Of course, the more cynical were quick to point out that Herbert Muhammad had little to lose—King was quickly locked into a contract where he had to pay $100,000 a month every month until a letter of credit for the $10 million was in the bank for both fighters, and King, to everybody's surprise, managed to hang on long enough to raise the money through John Daly of Helmdale Leisure Corp, and Risnailia, a Swiss corporation whose heart belonged, it was said, to Sese Seko Kuku Ngbendu Wa Za Banga, our own Mobutu. What skills. Quantity changes quality, Engels said once, and a hustler of dimensions is a financier. How King could talk. He was a tall man, but his graying hair stood up four inches from his head, straight up, straight up—he was one Black whose Afro was electrified by a perpetually falling elevator—*whoosh* went the hair up from his head. Down came his words. King wore diamonds and pleated shirts, dashikis with gold pendants, powder-blue tuxedos and suits of lipstick-red; the cummerbunds of a sultan were about his waist, and the pearls of the Orient in the cloth he wore. How he could talk. He was the *kuntu* of full dialogue, and no verbal situation could be foreign to him. Once when one of his lesser-known fighters hinted that a contract was unsatisfactory and King could get hurt, Don leaned forward—fond was he of telling this story—and said, "Let us not bullshit each other. You can leave here, make a call, and have me killed in half an hour. I can pick up the phone as you leave and have you offed in five minutes." That was expression appropriate to the point, but King could cut a wider path. "The fight," he said, "will draw a trillion fans, because Ali is Russian, Ali is Oriental, Ali is Arabic, Ali is Jewish, Ali is everything that one could conceive with the human mind. He appeals to all segments of our world. Some polarize themselves with hostility and affection, but regardless he stimulates—and this is the most significant part—Ali motivates even the dead." Yes, even the dead who were dying of thirst and waiting for beer at the altar. "The dead tremble in their graves" was what King said as Leonard Gardner reported it in Caracas on the night Foreman annihilated Norton and the last impediment to Ali-Foreman was gone. King had been happy that night, and he was happy this night with the weigh-in staged and the television satellite tested and proved. He was a man who obviously placed serious investments of faith in formal ceremony, and that brought tears to King's eyes as he spoke of it. "Tonight has been a culmination," he said. "Tonight the history of our problems on this fight become converted to the history of our hardworking triumphs. I had a vision tonight of the event to come and it leaves me ebullient for I see an encounter that will be without compare in the relentless power of its tenacity and fury. Therefore it occasions in me the emotion that I am an instrument of eternal forces."

Once you became accustomed to the stately seesaw of his rhetoric it gave nourishment to your ear the way a Cossack's horse in full stride would give drumbeats to the steppes. Still, it became evident after a while that King whipped his tongue for rhetoric when he did not have a finer reply. (As Shaw once assured Sam Goldwyn, poetry was there to write when he did not feel inspired for prose.) So King shifted gears whenever the beginnings of a small distance were sensed between himself and the person to whom he spoke; when he rapped, however, ah, then King became the other man in himself.

He liked to talk about his four years in prison and his five unsuccessful appearances before a parole board. "My past was jamming me with those people, you see. I had to put in the years, had to learn how to rechannel myself, and be able to meditate in a room full of violent men. No easy task. It was sheer hell just to go to the hole. You could wake up in the middle of the night and have to take a leak. What a sight in the urinals. Prisoners sucking guards. Guards going down on prisoners. One man taking another's ass. Hell, man, you got to get your head in order."

At the next table, Hunter Thompson leaned over to John Vinocur and said, "Bad Genet."

"I decided to study," said King. "I got myself a list. Got my education in prison. Read Freud. He almost blew my mind. Breast, penis, anus. Powerful stuff. Then Masters and Johnson, Kinsey, and . . ." He hesitated. "Knee's itch, I read a lot of him."

"Who?"

"Knee's itch. Nigh zith."

"Nietzsche?"

"Yeah." But the error had him jiving for embarrassment. "Yeah, cerebrum and cerebellum, you got to use them, that's what I learned from that man."

"Who else did you read?"

"Kant—*The Critique of Pure Reason*. That helped my head. And I read Sartre—fascinating!—and then the guy who wrote the book on Hitler, Shirer, I read him. And Marx, I read Karl Marx, a cold motherfucker, Marx. I learned a lot from him. Hitler and Marx—I think of them in relation to some of the things they're doing here, you know, the country is the family. Concentrate on the young."

At the next table, Hunter Thompson, having finished his drink, said, "Very bad Genet."

But King did not hear him. Why should King care? He had probably read Genet. The fatigue and happiness of the thousand perils of successfully promoting this fight sat in kindly weight upon his back. "Yes," he said, "I look upon tonight as a classically satisfying experience."

# The Dressing Room

It was a grim dressing room. Perhaps it looked like a comfort station in a Moscow subway. Big, with round pillars tiled in white, even the wallpaper was white. So it also looked like an operating room. In this morgue all groans were damped. White tile was everywhere. What a place to get ready!

The men gathered had no more cheer than the decor. Dundee, Pacheco, Plimpton, Mailer, Walter Youngblood, Pat Patterson, Howard Bingham, Ali's brother Rachman, his manager, Herbert Muhammad, his business manager, Gene Kilroy, Bundini, a small fat Turk named Hassan, and Roy Williams, his sparring partner, were in the room and no one had anything to say. "What's going on here," said Ali as he entered. "Why is everybody so scared? What's the matter with you?" He began to peel off his clothes, and wearing no more than a jockstrap was soon prancing around the room, shadowboxing with the air.

"We're going to dance," cried Ali as he flew around, enjoying each near collision with the pillars at his back. Like a child, he had a sense of objects behind him, as if the circle of his sensations did not end at his skin. "Ah, yes," he shouted out, "we're going to stick him," and he threw jabs at the air.

He was the only cheerful presence. "I think I'm more scared than you are," said Norman as Ali came to rest.

"Nothing to be scared about," said the fighter. "It's just another day in the dramatic life of Muhammad Ali. Just one more workout in the gym to me." He turned to Plimpton and added, "I'm afraid of horror films and thunderstorms. Jet planes shake me up. But there is no need to be afraid of anything you can control with your skill. That is why Allah is the only One who terrifies me. Allah is the only One of whom the meeting is independent of your will. He is One, and has no associates." Ali's voice was building in volume and piety. As though to protect himself against too much strength being discharged into a sermon, he went on quietly, "There's nothing to be scared of. Elijah Muhammad has been through things that make this night nothing. And in a small way, I have been through such things. Getting into the ring with Liston the first time beats anything George Foreman ever had to do, or I have had to do again. Except for living with threats against my life after the death of Malcolm X. Real death threats. No, I have no fear of tonight." He darted away from the writers as if his minute in the corner was up and shadowboxed some more, teasing a few friends with quick lancing shots that once more stopped an inch from their eyes. As he went by Hassan, the fat little Turk, he extended his long thumb and long forefinger to pinch him in the ass.

Yet for all this fine effort, the mood of the room hardly improved. It was like a corner in a hospital where relatives wait for word of the operation. Now Ali stopped dancing and took out the robe he would wear into the ring and put it on. It was a long white silk robe with an intricate black pattern, and his first comment was, "It's a real African robe." He said this to Bundini, who gave him the full look of a child just denied a reward that has been promised for a week.

"All right," Ali said at last. "Let's see your robe."

Now Bundini displayed the garment that he had brought for Ali to wear. It was also white but had green, red, and black piping along its edges, the national colors of Zaïre. A green, red, and black map of the country was stitched over the heart. Bundini wore a white jacket of the same material and decoration. Ali tried on Bundini's robe, looked in the mirror, took it off, handed it back. He put on the first robe again. "This one's more beautiful," he said. "It's really prettier than the one you brought. Take a look in the mirror, Drew, it's really better." It was. Bundini's robe looked a suspicion shopworn.

But Bundini did not look in the mirror. Instead he fixed his look on Ali. He glared at him. For a full minute they scalded one another's eyes. *Look!* said Bundini's expression, *don't mess with the wisdom of your man. I brought a robe that matches my jacket. Your strength and my strength are linked. Weaken me, and you weaken yourself. Wear the colors I have chosen.* Something of that strength had to be in his eyes. Some unspoken threat as well, doubtless, for Ali suddenly slapped him, sharp as the crack of a rifle. "Don't you ever dare do that again," he cried out at Bundini. "Now take a look at me in the mirror," Ali commanded. But Bundini refused to look. Ali slapped him again.

The second slap was so ritual that one had to wonder if something like this was a well-worked ceremony, even an exorcism. It was hard to tell. Bundini seemed too furious to speak. His expression clearly said: *Beat me to death, but I will not look in the mirror. The robe you describe as beautiful is not the one.* Ali finally walked away from him.

It was time to decide on the trunks. He tried several. One pair was all white with no decoration at all, as pure and silver a white as the priestly robes of Islam. "Take this one, Ali," his brother Rachman cried, "take this white one, it's nice, Ali, take it." But Ali after much deliberation before the mirror decided to wear white trunks with a vertical black stripe (and indeed in the photographs one would see later of the fight, there is the black stripe articulating each movement from his torso down to his legs).

Now Ali sat on a rubbing table near the middle of the room, and put on his long white boxing shoes and held each foot in the air while Dundee scraped the soles with a knife to roughen them. The fighter took a comb someone handed him, the Y-shaped comb with steel teeth that Blacks use for an Afro, and worked with deliberation on his hair while his shoes were being scraped. At a signal of his finger, somebody brought him a magazine, a Zaïre periodical in French, which gave the complete list of Foreman's fights and Ali's. He read the names aloud to Plimpton and Mailer, and once again contrasted the number of nobodies Foreman had fought with the number of notables he had met. It was as if he had to take still one more look at the marrow of his life. For the first time in all these months, he seemed to want to offer a public showing of the fear that must come to him in a dream. He began to chatter as though no one were in the room and he were talking in his sleep, "Float like a butterfly, sting like a bee, you can't hit what you can't see," he repeated several times, as though the words were long gone, and then he murmured, "I been up and I been down. You know, I been around." He shook his head. "It must be dark when you get knocked out," he said, contemplating the ogre of midnight. "Why, I never been knocked out," he said. "I been knocked down, but never *out*." Like a dreamer awakening to the knowledge that the dream is only a net above one's death, he cried out, "That's *strange* . . . being stopped." Again, he shook his head. "Yeah," he said, "that's a bad feeling waiting for night to choke up on you," and he looked at the two writers with the blank eyes of a patient who has encountered some reality in the coils of his condition no doctor will ever comprehend.

Then he must have come to the end of this confrontation with feelings that moved in on him like fog, for he used a phrase he had not employed in months, not since he had last given great woe to every high official in Zaïre, "Yes," he said to the room at large, "let's get ready for the rumble in the jungle," and he began to call to people across the room.

"Hey, Bundini," he cried out, "are we gonna dance?"

But Bundini did not reply. A sorrow was in the room.

"Does anybody hear me?" cried Ali. "Are we going to the dance?"

"We're going to dance and dance," said Gene Kilroy sadly.

"We're going to dance," said Ali, "We're going to da-ance."

Dundee came up to tape his hands. The observer from Foreman's dressing room, Doc Broadus, now moved up to study the operation.

Ali stared at him hard, and Broadus shifted his feet. He was shy with Ali. Maybe he had admired his career for too many years to be able to confront him easily now.

"Tell your man," Ali said confidentially, "he better get ready to dance."

Again, Broadus shifted uncomfortably.

Now Ali started talking to Bundini. "Say, Bundini, we gonna dance?" he asked. Bundini would not reply.

"I said, are we going to dance?"

Silence.

"Drew, why don't you speak to me?" Ali said in a big voice, as if exaggeration were the best means to take Bundini out of his mood. "Bundini, ain't we going to dance?" he asked again, and in a droll tender voice, added, "You know I can't dance without Bundini."

"You turned down my robe," Bundini said in his deepest, huskiest, and most emotional voice.

"Oh man," said Ali, "I'm the Champ. You got to allow me to do something on my own. You got to give me the right to pick my robe or how will I ever be Champ again? You going to tell me what to eat? You going to tell me how to go? Bundini, I am blue. I never seen a time like this when *you* don't cheer me up."

Bundini fought it, but a smile began to tickle his lips.

"Bundini, are we going to dance?" asked Ali.

"All night long," said Bundini.

"Yes, we're going to dance," said Ali, "we're going to dance and dance."

"What are we going to do?" he asked of Bundini and Dundee and Kilroy. "We're going to dance," said Gene Kilroy with a sad loving smile, "we're going to dance all night long."

"Yes, we're going to da-ance," cried Ali, and said again to Broadus, "You tell him to get ready."

"I'm not telling him nothing," muttered Broadus.

"Tell him he better know how to dance."

"He don't dance," Broadus managed to say as if to warn: My man has heavier things to do.

"He don't what?" asked Ali.

"He don't dance," said Broadus.

"George Foreman's man," cried Ali, "says George can't dance. George can't come to the da-ance!"

"Five minutes," somebody yelled out, and Youngblood handed the fighter a bottle of orange juice. Ali took a swig of it, half a glass worth, and stared with amusement at Broadus. "Tell him to hit me in the belly," he said.

## Right Hand Leads

Now the word came down the line from the stadium outside. "Ali in the ring, Ali in the ring."

Solemnly, Bundini handed Ali the white African robe that the fighter had selected. Then everybody in the dressing room was on their way, a long file of twenty men, who pushed and were hustled through a platoon of soldiers standing outside the door and then in a gang's rush in a full company of other soldiers were racing through the gray cement-brick corridors with their long-gone echoes of rifle shots and death. They emerged into open air, into the surrealistic bliss and green air of stadium grass under electric lights, and a cheer of no vast volume went up at the sight of Ali, but then the crowd had been waiting through an empty hour with no semifinal to watch, just an empty ring, and hours gone by before that with dancers to watch, more dancers, then more tribal dancers, a long count of the minutes from midnight to four. The nation of Zaïre had been awaiting this event for three months, now they were here, some sixty thousand, in a great oval of seats far from that ring in the center of the soccer field. They must be disappointed. Watching the fighters would prove kin to sitting in a room in a housing project studying people through a window in another housing project on the other side of a twelve-lane freeway. The fighters would work under a big corrugated tin shed roof with girders to protect the ring and the twenty-five hundred ringside seats from tropical downpour, which might come at any minute on this night so advanced already into the rainy season. Heavy rains were overdue by two weeks and more. Light rain had come almost every afternoon and dark portentous skies hung overhead. In America that would speak of quick summer storms, but the clouds in Africa were patient as the people and a black whirling smoky sky could shift overhead for days before more than a drop would fall.

Something of the weight of this oncoming rain was in the air. The early night had been full of oppression, and it was hot for so early in the morning, eighty degrees and a little more. Thoughts, however, of the oncoming fight left Norman closer to feeling chill. He was sitting next to Plimpton in the second row from the ring, a seat worth traveling thousands of miles to obtain (although counting two round trips, the figure might yet be twenty-five thousand miles—a barrel of jet lag for the soul). In front of them was a row of wire service reporters and photographers leaning on the apron of the ring; inside the ropes was Ali checking the resin against his shoes, and offering flashes of his shuffle to the study of the crowd, whirling away once in a while to throw a kaleidoscope-dozen of punches at the air in two seconds, no more—one-Mississippi, two-Mississippi—twelve punches had gone by. Screams from the crowd at the blur of the gloves. He was all alone in the ring, the Challenger on call for the Champion, the Prince waiting for the Pretender, and unlike other fighters who wilt in the long minutes before the titleholder will appear, Ali seemed to be taking royal pleasure in his undisputed possession of the space. He looked unafraid and almost on the edge of happiness, as if the discipline of having carried himself through the two thousand nights of sleeping without his title after it had been taken from him without ever losing a contest—a frustration for a fighter doubtless equal in impact to writing *A Farewell to Arms* and then being unable to publish it—must have been a biblical seven years of trial through which he had come with the crucial part of his honor, his talent, and his desire for greatness still intact, and light came off him at this instant. His body had a shine like the flanks of a thoroughbred. He looked fully ready to fight the strongest meanest man to come along in Heavyweight circles in many years, maybe the worst big man of all, and while the Prince stood alone in his ring, and waited out the minutes for the Champion to arrive and had his thoughts, whatever they were, and his private communion with Allah, however that might feel, while he stood and while he shuffled and while he shadowboxed the air, the Lord Privy Seal, Angelo Dundee from Miami, went methodically from ring post to ring post and there in full view of ringside and the stadium just as methodically loosened each of the four turnbuckles on each post that held the tension of each of the four ropes, and did it with a spoke and a wrench he must have put in his little carrying bag back at Nsele and transported on the bus and carried from the dressing room to this ring. And when the ropes were slack to his taste, loose enough for his fighter to lean way back, he left the ring and returned to the corner. Nobody had paid any particular attention to him.

Foreman was still in his dressing room. Later Plimpton learned a detail from his old friend Archie Moore. "Just before going out to the ring, Foreman joined hands with his boxing trust—Dick Sadler, Sandy Saddler, and Archie—in a sort of prayer ritual they had practiced (for every fight) since Foreman became Champion in Jamaica," Plimpton wrote. "Now they were holding hands again in Zaïre, and Archie Moore, who had his head bowed, found himself thinking that he should pray for Muhammad Ali's safety. Here's what he said: 'I was praying, and in great sincerity, that George wouldn't *kill* Ali. I really felt that was a possibility.' " So did others.

Foreman arrived in the ring. He was wearing red velvet trunks with a white stripe and a blue waistband. The colors of the American flag girded his middle and his shoes were white. He looked solemn, even sheepish, like a big boy who, as Archie said, "truly doesn't know his own strength." The letters GF stood out in embossed white cloth from the red velvet of his trunks. GF—Great Fighter.

The referee, Zack Clayton, Black and much respected in his profession, had been waiting. George had time to reach his corner, shuffle his feet, huddle with the trust, get the soles of his shoes in resin, and the fighters were meeting in the center of the ring to get instructions. It was the time for each man to extort a measure of fear from the other. Liston had done it to all his opponents until he met Ali, who, then Cassius Clay at the age of twenty-two, glared back at him with all the imperative of his high-destiny guts. Foreman, in turn, had done it to Frazier and then to Norton. A big look, heavy as death, oppressive as the closing of the door of one's tomb.

To Foreman, Ali now said (as everybody was later informed), "You have heard of me since you were young. You've been following me since you were a little boy. Now, you must meet me, your master!"—words the press could not hear at the time, but Ali's mouth was moving, his head was twelve inches from Foreman's, his eyes were on the other. Foreman blinked, Foreman looked surprised, as if he had been impressed just a little more than he expected. He tapped Ali's glove in a move equal to saying, "That's *your* round. Now *we* start."

The fighters went back to their corners. Ali pressed his elbows to his side, closed his eyes, and offered a prayer. Foreman turned his back. In the thirty seconds before the fight began, he grasped the ropes in his corner and bent over from the waist so that his big and powerful buttocks were presented to Ali. He flexed in this position so long it took on a kind of derision as though to declare: "My farts to you." He was still in such a pose when the bell rang.

The bell! Through a long unheard sigh of collective release, Ali charged across the ring. He looked as big and determined as Foreman, so he held himself, as if *he* possessed the true threat. They collided without meeting, their bodies still five feet apart. Each veered backward like similar magnetic poles repelling one another forcibly. Then Ali came forward again, Foreman came forward, they circled, they feinted, they moved in an electric ring, and Ali threw the first punch, a tentative left. It came up short. Then he drove a lightning-strong right straight as a pole into the stunned center of Foreman's head, the unmistakable thwomp of a high-powered punch. A cry went up. Whatever else happened, Foreman had been hit. No opponent had cracked George this hard in years and no sparring partner had dared to.

Foreman charged in rage. Ali compounded the insult. He grabbed the Champion around the neck and pushed his head down, wrestled it down crudely and decisively to show Foreman he was considerably rougher than anybody warned, and relations had commenced. They circled again. They feinted. They started in on one another and drew back. It was as if each held a gun. If one fired and missed, the other was certain to hit. If you threw a punch, and your opponent was ready, your own head would take his punch. What a shock. It is like seizing a high-voltage line. Suddenly you are on the floor.

Ali was not dancing. Rather he was bouncing from side to side looking for an opportunity to attack. So was Foreman. Maybe fifteen seconds went by. Suddenly Ali hit him again. It was again a right hand. Again it was hard. The sound of a bat thunking into a water-melon was heard around the ring. Once more Foreman charged after the blow, and once more Ali took him around the neck with his right arm, then stuck his left glove in Foreman's right armpit. Foreman could not start to swing. It was a nimble part of the advanced course for tying up a fighter. The referee broke the clinch. Again they moved through invisible reaches of attraction and repulsion, darting forward, sliding to the side, cocking their heads, each trying to strike an itch to panic in the other, two big men fast as pumas, charged as tigers—unseen sparks came off their moves. Ali hit him again, straight left, then a straight right. Foreman responded like a bull. He roared forward. A dangerous bull. His gloves were out like horns. No room for Ali to dance to the side, stick him, and move, hit him and move. Ali went back, feinted, went back again, was on the ropes. Foreman had cut him off. The fight was thirty seconds old, and Foreman had driven him to the ropes. Ali had not even tried to get around those out-stretched gloves so ready to cuff him, rough him, break his grace, no, retreating, Ali collected his toll. He hit Foreman with another left and another right.

Still a wail went up from the crowd. They saw Ali on the ropes. Who had talked of anything but how long Ali could keep away? Now he was trapped, so soon. Yet Foreman was off his aim. Ali's last left and right had checked him. Foreman's punches were not ready and Ali parried, Ali blocked. They clinched. The referee broke it. Ali was off the ropes with ease.

To celebrate, he hit Foreman another straight right. Up and down the press rows, one exclamation was leaping, "He's hitting him with *rights*." Ali had not punched with such authority in seven years. Champions do not hit other champions with right-hand leads. Not in the first round. It is the most difficult and dangerous punch. Difficult to deliver and dangerous to oneself. In nearly all positions, the right hand has longer to travel, a foot more at least than the left. Boxers deal with inches and half-inches. In the time it takes a right hand to travel that extra space, alarms are ringing in the opponent, counter-attacks are beginning. He will duck under the right and take off your head with a left. So good fighters do not often lead with their right against another good fighter. Not in the first round. They wait. They keep the right hand. It is one's authority, and ready to punish a left that comes too slowly. One throws one's right over a jab; one can block the left hook with a right forearm and chop back a right in return. Classic maxims of boxing. All fight writers know them. Off these principles they take their interpretation. They are good engineers at Indianapolis but Ali is on his way to the moon. Right-hand leads! My God!

In the next minute, Ali proceeded to hit Foreman with a combination rare as plutonium: a straight right hand followed by a long left hook. Spring-zing! went those punches, bolt to the head, bolt to the head—each time Foreman would rush forward in murderous rage and be caught by the neck and turned. His menace became more impressive each time he was struck. If the punches maddened him, they did not weaken him. Another fighter would be staggering by now. Foreman merely looked more destructive. His hands lost no speed, his hands looked as fast as Ali's (except when he got hit), and his face was developing a murderous appetite. He had not been treated so disrespectfully in years. Lost was genial George of the press conferences. His life was clear. He was going to dismember Ali. As he kept getting hit and grabbed, hit and grabbed, a new fear came over the rows at ringside. Foreman was awesome. Ali had now hit him about fifteen good punches to the head and not been caught once in return. What would happen when Foreman finally hit Ali? No Heavyweight could keep up the speed of these moves, not for fourteen more rounds.

But then the first was not even over. In the last minute, Foreman forced Ali to the ropes, was in on him, broke loose, and smashed a right uppercut through Ali's gloves, then another. The second went like a spear through the top of Ali's skull. His eyes flew up in consternation, and he grabbed Foreman's right arm with his left, squeezed it, clung to it. Foreman, his arm being held, was still in a mood to throw the good right again, and did. Four heavy half-smothered rights, concussive as blows to the heavy bag, went up to the head, then two down to the body, whaling on Ali even as he was held, and it was apparent these punches hurt. Ali came off the ropes in the most determined embrace of his life, both gloves locked around the back of Foreman's neck. The whites of Ali's eyes showed the glaze of a combat soldier who has just seen a dismembered arm go flying across the sky after an explosion. What kind of monster was he encountering?

Foreman threw a wild left. Then a left, a right, a left, a left, and a right. Some to the head, some to the body, some got blocked, some missed, one collided with Ali's floating ribs, brutal punches, jarring and imprecise as a collision at slow speed in a truck.

With everybody screaming, Ali now hit Foreman with a right. Foreman hit him back with a left and a right. Now they each landed blows. Everybody was shaking his head at the bell. What a round!

Now the press rows began to ring with comment on those right-hand leads. How does Ali dare? A magnificent round. Norman has few vanities left, but thinks he knows something about boxing. He is ready to serve as engineer on Ali's trip to the moon. For Ali is one artist who does not box by right counter to left hook. He fights the entirety of the other person. He lives in fields of concentration where he can detect the smallest flicker of lack of concentration. Foreman has shown himself a lack of quiver flat to the possibility of a right. Who before this had dared after all to hit Foreman with a right? Of late his opponents were afraid to flick him with a jab. Fast were Foreman's hands, but held a flat spot of complacency before the right. He was not ready for a man to come into the ring unafraid of him. That offered its beauty. But frightening. Ali cannot fight every round like this. Such a pace will kill him in five. Indeed he could be worried as he sits in the corner. It has been his round, but what a force to Foreman's punches. It is true. Foreman hits harder than other fighters. And takes a very good punch. Ali looks thoughtful.

Somewhere in the middle of the second round, Ali must have made a decision on how to shape the rest of the fight. He did not seem able to hurt Foreman critically with those right-hand leads. Nor was he stronger than Foreman except when wrestling on his neck, and certainly he could not afford any more of those episodes where he held on to Foreman even as George was hitting him. It was costly in points, painful, and won nothing. On the other hand, it was too soon to dance. Too rapid would be the drain on his stamina. So the time had come to see if he could outbox Foreman while lying on the ropes. It had been his option from the beginning and it was the most dangerous option he had. For so long as Foreman had strength, the ropes would prove about as safe as riding a unicycle on a parapet. Still what is genius but balance on the edge of the impossible? Ali introduced his grand theme. He lay back on the ropes in the middle of the second round, and from that position he would work for the rest of the fight, reclining at an angle of ten and twenty degrees from the vertical and sometimes even further, a cramped near-tortured angle from which to box.

Of course Ali had been preparing for just this hour over the last ten years. For ten years he had been practicing to fight powerful sluggers who beat on your belly while you lay on the ropes. So he took up his station with confidence, shoulders parallel to the edge of the ring. In this posture, his right would have no more impact than a straight left but he could find himself in position to cover his head with both gloves, and his belly with his elbows, he could rock and sway, lean so far back Foreman must fall on him. Should Foreman pause from the fatigue of throwing punches, Ali could bounce off the ropes and sting him, jolt him, make him look clumsy, mock him, rouse his anger, which might yet wear Foreman out more than anything else. In this position, Ali could even hurt him. A jab hurts if you run into it, and Foreman is always coming in. Still, Ali is in the position of a man bowing and ducking in a doorway while another man comes at him with two clubs. Foreman comes on with his two clubs. In the first exchange he hits Ali about six times while Ali is returning only one blow. Yet the punches to Ali's head seem not to bother him; he is swallowing the impact with his entire body. He is like a spring on the ropes. Blows seem to pass through him as if he is indeed a leaf spring built to take shock. None of his spirit is congested in his joints. Encouraged by the recognition that he can live with these blows, he begins to taunt Foreman. "Can you hit?" he calls out. "You can't hit. You push!" Since his head has been in range of Foreman's gloves, Foreman lunges at him. Back goes Ali's head like the carnival boy ducking baseballs. Wham to you, goes Ali, catapulting back. Bing and sting! Now Foreman is missing and Ali is hitting.

It is becoming a way to fight and even a way to live, but for Ali's corner it is a terror to watch. In the last thirty seconds of this second round, Ali hits out with straight rights from the ropes fast as jabs. Foreman's head must feel like a rivet under a riveting gun. With just a few seconds left, Foreman throws his biggest punch of the night, an express train of a left hook, which leaves a spasm for the night in its passing. It has been a little too slow. Ali lets it go by in the languid unhurried fashion of Archie Moore watching a roundhouse miss his chin by a quarter of an inch. In the void of the effort, Foreman is so off-balance that Ali could throw him through the ropes. "Nothing," says Ali through his mouthpiece. "You have no aim." The bell rings and Foreman looks depressed. There has been premature desperation in that left. Ali shakes his head in derision. Of course that is one of Ali's basic tricks. All through his first fight with Frazier he kept signaling to the crowd that Joe failed to impress him. All the while Ali was finding himself in more trouble.

# The Man in the Rigging

It seems like eight rounds have passed yet we only finished two. Is it because we are trying to watch with the fighters' sense of time? Before fatigue brings boxers to the boiler rooms of the damned, they live at a height of consciousness and with a sense of detail they encounter nowhere else. In no other place is their intelligence so full, nor their sense of time able to contain so much of itself, as in the long internal effort of the ring. Thirty minutes go by like three hours. Let us undertake the chance, then, that our description of the fight may be longer to read than the fight itself. We can assure ourselves: It was even longer for the fighters.

Contemplate them as they sit in their corners between the second and third rounds. The outcome of the fight is not yet determined. Not for either. Ali has an enormous problem, equal to his enormous confidence. Everybody has wondered whether Ali can get through the first few rounds and take Foreman's punch. Now the problem has been refined: Can he dismantle Foreman's strength before he uses up his own wit?

Foreman has another problem—he may not be as aware of it as his corner. There is no fear in his mind that he will fail to win the fight. He does not think about that any more than a lion supposes it will be unable to destroy a cheetah; no, it is just a question of catching Ali, a maddening frustration. Still the insult to his rage has to worry his corner. They can hardly tell him not to be angry. It is Foreman's rage after all that has led him to knock out so many fighters. To cut it off is to leave him cowlike. Nonetheless he must contain his anger until he catches Ali. Otherwise he is going to wear himself out.

So Sadler works on him, rubs his breasts and belly, Sadler sends his fingers into all the places where rage has congested, into the meat of the pectorals and the muscle plating beneath Foreman's chest, Sadler's touch has all the wisdom of thirty-five years of Black fingers elucidating comforts for Black flesh, sensual are his fingers as he plucks and shapes and shakes and balms, his silver bracelet shining on his Black wrist. When Sadler feels the fighter is soothed, he begins to speak, and Foreman takes on the expression of a man whose head is working slowly. He has too much to think about. He spits into the bowl held before him and nods respectfully. He looks as if he is listening to his dentist.

In Ali's corner, Dundee, with the quiet concern of a sommelier, is bringing the mouth of the adhesive-taped water bottle to Ali's lips, and does it with a forefinger under the neck so the bottle will not pour too much as he tips it up. Ali rinses and spits with his eyes off on the serious calculation of a man weighing grim but necessary alternatives.

The bell. Once more Ali comes out of the corner with a big and threatening face, as if this round for certain he will bring the attack to Foreman and once again sees something wrong in the idea, profoundly wrong, shifts his plan instantly, backs up, and begins to play the ropes. On comes Foreman. The fight has taken its formal pattern. Ali will go by choice to the ropes and Foreman will chase him. Now in each round Ali will work for thirty or forty seconds or for so much even as a minute with his back no more than a foot or two from the top rope, and he is on the rope as often as not. When the strength of the mood or the logic of the clinch suggests that the virtue of one set of ropes has been used up, he will back off across the ring to use another set. He will spend on an average one-quarter of each round on each of the four sides of the ring. He might just as well be drawing conscious strength from the burial gods of the North, the West, the East, and the South. Never has a major fight been so locked into one pattern of movement. It appears designed by a choreographer who knows nothing about the workings of legs and is endlessly inventive about arms. The fight goes on in exactly this fashion round after round, and yet it is hardly boring, for Ali appears in constant danger, and is, and is not. He is turning the pockets of the boxing world inside out. He is demonstrating that what for other fighters is a weakness can be for him a strength. Foreman has been trained to cut instinctively from side to side in such a way as to spoil Ali's ability to circle, Foreman has learned how to force retreat to the ropes. But Ali makes no effort to get away. He does not circle, neither does he reverse his circle. Instead he backs up. Foreman's outstretched arms become a liability. Unable to cuff at a dancing target, he must probe forward. As he does, Ali keeps popping him with straight lefts and rights fast as karate strokes.

Sooner or later, however, Foreman is always on him, leaning on him, banging him, belting away with all the fury George knows how to bring to the heavy bag. Ali uses the ropes to absorb the bludgeoning. Standing on one's feet, it is painful to absorb a heavy body punch even when blocked with one's arms. The torso, the legs, and the spine take the shock. One has to absorb the brunt of the punch. Leaning on the ropes, however, Ali can pass it along—the ropes will receive the strain. If he cannot catch Foreman's punches with his gloves, or deflect them, or bend Foreman's shoulder to spoil his move, or lean away with his head, slip to the side, or loom up to hug Foreman's head, if finally there is nothing to do but take the punch, then Ali tightens his body and conducts the shock out along the ropes, so that Foreman must feel as if he is beating on a tree trunk that is oscillating against ropes. Foreman's power seems to travel right down the line and rattle the ring posts. It fortifies Ali's sense of relaxation—he has always the last resort of composing himself for the punch. When, occasionally, a blow does hurt, he sticks Foreman back, mean and salty, using his left and right as jabs. Since his shoulders are against the ropes, he jabs as often with his right as his left. With his timing it is a great jab. He has a gift for hitting Foreman as Foreman comes in. That doubles or triples the force. Besides, he is using so many right jabs Foreman must start to wonder whether he is fighting a southpaw. Then comes the left jab again. A converted southpaw? It has something of the shift of locus that comes from making love to a brunette when she is wearing a blond wig. Of course, Ali has red wigs too. At the end of the round, Ali hits Foreman with some of the hardest punches of the fight. A right, a left, and a right startle Foreman in their combination. He may not have seen such a combination since his last street fight. Ali gives a look of contempt and they wrestle for a few seconds until the bell. For the few extra seconds it takes Foreman to go to his corner, his legs now have the look of a bedridden man's. He has almost stumbled on the way to his stool.

Nonetheless, he looked lively as he came out for the bell. He came right across the middle of the ring to show Ali a new kind of feint, a long pawing movement of his hands accompanied by short moves of his head. It was to a different rhythm, as if to say, "I haven't begun to show what I know."

He looked jaunty, but he was holding his right hand down by the waist. Fatigue must have lent carelessness to what he did, for Ali immediately answered with an insulting stiff right, an accelerating hook, and another right so heavy to Foreman's head that he grabbed for a clinch, first time in the fight. There, holding on to Ali while vertigo collided with nausea, and bile scalded his breath, he must have been delivered into a new awareness, for George immediately started to look better. He began to get to Ali on the ropes and hit him occasionally, and for the first time in a while was not getting hit as much himself. He was even beginning to jam a number of Ali's rhythms. Up to now, whenever Ali took a punch, he was certain to come off the ropes and hit Foreman back. A couple of times in this round, however, even as Ali started his move, George would jam his forearm into Ali's neck, or wrestle him to a standstill.

All the while Ali was talking. "Come on, George, show me something," he would say. "Can't you fight harder? That ain't hard. I thought you was the Champion, I thought you had punches," and Foreman working like a bricklayer running up a pyramid to set his bricks would snort and lance his arms in sudden unexpected directions and try to catch Ali bouncing on the rope, Ali who was becoming more confirmed every minute in the sinecure of the rope, but at the end of the round, Foreman caught him with the best punch he had thrown in many a minute, landing just before the bell, and as he turned to leave Ali, he said clearly, "How's that?"

It must have encouraged him, for in the fifth round he tried to knock Ali out. Even as Ali was becoming more confident on the ropes, Foreman grew convinced he could break Ali's defense. Confidence on both sides makes for war. The round would go down in history as one of the great rounds in Heavyweight boxing; indeed it was so good it forged its own frame as they battled. One could see it outlined forever in lights: *The Great Fifth Round of the Ali-Foreman fight!*

Foreman came out in the fifth with the conviction that if force had not prevailed against Ali up to now, more force was the answer, considerably more force than Ali had ever seen. If Foreman's face was battered to lumps and his legs were moving like wheels with a piece chipped out of the rim, if his arms were beginning to sear in the lava of exhaustion and his breath come roaring to his lungs like the blast from a bed of fire, still he was a prodigy of strength, he was *the* prodigy, he could live through states of torture and hurl his cannon-ade when others could not lift their arms, he had been trained for en-durance even more than execution and back in Pendleton when first working for this fight had once boxed fifteen rounds with half a dozen sparring partners coming on in two-round shifts while Foreman was permitted only thirty seconds of rest between each round. He could go, he could go and go, he was tireless in the arms, yes, could knock down a forest, take it down all by himself, and he set out now to chop Ali down.

They sparred inconclusively for the first half-minute. Then the barrage began. With Ali braced on the ropes, as far back on the ropes as a deep-sea fisherman is braced back in his chair when setting the hook on a big strike, so Ali got ready and Foreman came on to blast him out. A shelling reminiscent of artillery battles in World War I began. Neither man moved more than a few feet in the next minute and a half. Across that embattled short space Foreman threw punches in barrages of four and six and eight and nine, heavy maniacal slam-ming punches, heavy as the boom of oaken doors, bombs to the body, bolts to the head, punching until he could not breathe, backing off to breathe again and come in again, bomb again, blast again, drive and steam and slam the torso in front of him, wreck him in the arms, break through those arms, get to his ribs, dig him out, dig him out, put the dynamite in the earth, lift him, punch him, punch him up to heaven, take him out, stagger him—great earthmover, he must have sobbed to himself, kill this mad and bouncing goat.

And Ali, gloves to his head, elbows to his ribs, stood and swayed and was rattled and banged and shaken like a grasshopper at the top of a reed when the wind whips, and the ropes shook and swung like sheets in a storm, and Foreman would lunge with his right at Ali's chin and Ali go flying back out of reach by a half-inch, and half out of the ring, and back in to push at Foreman's elbow and hug his own ribs and sway, and sway just further, and lean back and come forward from the ropes and slide off a punch and fall back into the ropes with all the calm of a man swinging in the rigging. All the while, he used his eyes. They looked like stars, and he feinted Foreman out with his eyes, flashing white eyeballs that pulled Foreman through into lurching after him on a wrong move, Ali darting his expression in one direction while cocking his head in another, then staring at Foreman expression to expression, holding him in the eye, soul to soul, muntu to muntu, hugging his head, peeking through gloves, jamming his armpit, then taunting him on the edge of the ropes, then flying back as Foreman dove forward, tantalizing him, maddening him, looking for all the world as cool as if he were sparring in his bathrobe, now banishing Foreman's head with the turn of a matador sending away a bull after five fine passes were made, and once when he seemed to hesitate just a little too long, teasing Foreman just a little too long, something stirred in George like that across-the-arena knowledge of a bull when it is ready at last to gore the matador rather than the cloth, and like a member of a cuadrilla, somebody in Ali's corner screamed, "Careful! Careful! Careful!" and Ali flew back and just in time, for as he bounced on the ropes Foreman threw six of his most powerful left hooks in a row and then a right, it was the center of his fight and the heart of his best charge, a left to the belly, a left to the head, a left to the belly, a left to the head, a left to the belly, another to the belly and Ali blocked them all, elbow for the belly, glove for the head, and the ropes flew like snakes. Ali was ready for the lefts. He was not prepared for the right that followed. Foreman hit him a powerful punch. The ringbolts screamed. Ali shouted, "Didn't hurt a bit." Was it the best punch he took all night? He had to ride through ten more after that. Foreman kept flashing his muscles up out of that cup of desperation boiling in all determination, punches that came toward the end of what may have been as many as forty or fifty in a minute, any one strong enough to send water from the spine to the knees. Something may have finally begun to go from Foreman's n'golo, some departure of the essence of absolute rage, and Ali reaching over the barrage would give a prod now and again to Foreman's neck like a housewife sticking a toothpick in a cake to see if it is ready. The punches got weaker and weaker, and Ali finally came off the ropes and in the last thirty seconds of the round threw his own punches, twenty at least. Almost all hit. Some of the hardest punches of the night were driven in. Four rights, a left hook, and a right came in one stupendous combination. One punch turned Foreman's head through ninety degrees, a right cross of glove and forearm that slammed into the side of the jaw; double contact had to be felt—once from the glove, then from the bare arm, stunning and jarring. Walls must begin to crack inside the brain. Foreman staggered and lurched and glared at Ali and got hit again, zing-bing! two more. When it was all over, Ali caught Foreman by the neck like a big brother chastising an enormous and stupid kid brother, and looked out to someone in the audience, some enemy or was it some spiteful friend who said Foreman would win, for Ali, holding George around the neck, now stuck out one long white-coated tongue.

# A Long Collapsing Two Seconds

Not often was there a better end to a second act than Foreman's failure to destroy Ali on the ropes. But the last scenes would present another problem. How was the final curtain to be found? For if Foreman was exhausted, Ali was weary. He had hit Foreman harder than he had ever hit anyone. He had hit him often. Foreman's head must by now be equal to a piece of vulcanized rubber. Conceivably you could beat on him all night and nothing more would happen. There is a threshold to the knockout. When it comes close but is not crossed, then a man can stagger around the ring forever. He has received his terrible message and he is still standing. No more of the same woe can destroy him. He is like the victim in a dreadful marriage that no one knows how to end. So Ali was obliged to produce still one more surprise. If not, the unhappiest threat would present itself as he and Foreman stumbled through the remaining rounds. There is agony to elucidate even a small sense of the aesthetic out of boxing. Wanton waste for an artist like Ali to lose the perfection of this fight by wandering down a monotonous half hour to a dreary unanimous decision.

A fine ending to the fight would live in legend, but a dull victory, anticlimactic by the end, could leave him in half a legend—overblown in reputation by his friends and contested by his enemies—precisely the state that afflicted most heroes. So Ali had to dispose of Foreman in the next few rounds and do it well, a formidable problem. He was like a torero after a great faena who must still face the drear potential of a protracted inept and disappointing kill. Since no pleasure is greater among athletes than to overtake the style of their opponent, Ali would look to steal Foreman's last pride. George was an executioner. But how do you execute the executioner?

The problem was revealed in all its sluggish intricacies over the next three rounds. Foreman came out for the sixth looking like an alley cat with chewed-up brows. Lumps and swellings were all over his face, his skin equal to tar that has baked in the sun. When the bell rang, however, he looked dangerous again, no longer a cat but a bull. He lowered his head and charged across the ring. He was a total demonstration of the power of one idea even when the idea no longer works. And was immediately seized and strangled around the neck by Ali for a few valuable and pacifying seconds until Zack Clayton broke them. Afterward, Foreman moved in to throw more punches. His power, however, seemed gone. The punches were slow and tentative. They did not reach Ali. Foreman was growing glove-shy. His fastest moves were now in a nervous defense that kept knocking Ali's punches away from his own face. The next two minutes turned into the slowest two minutes of the fight. Foreman kept pushing Ali to the ropes out of habit, a dogged forward motion that enabled George to rest in his fashion, the only way he still knew, which was to lean on the opponent. Ali was by now so delighted with the advantages of the ropes that he fell back on them like a man returning home in quiet triumph, yes, settled in with the weary pleasure of a working man getting back into bed after a long day to be treated to a little of God's joy by his hardworking wife. He was almost tender with Foreman's laboring advance, holding him softly and kindly by the neck. Then he stung him with right and left karate shots from the shoulder. Foreman was now so arm-weary he could begin a punch only by lurching forward until his momentum encouraged a movement of the arm. He looked like a drunk, or rather a somnambulist, in a dance marathon. It would be wise to get him through the kill without ever waking him up. While it ought to be a simple matter to knock him down, there might not be enough violence left in the spirit of this ring to knock him out. So the shock of finding himself on the floor could prove a stimulant. His ego might reappear: Once on the floor, he was a champion in dramatic danger of losing his title—that is an unmeasurable source of energy. Ali was now taking in the reactions of Foreman's head the way a bullfighter lines up a bull before going in over the horns for the kill. He bent to his left and, still crouched, passed his body to the right under Foreman's fists, all the while studying George's head and neck and shoulders. Since Foreman charged the move, a fair conclusion was that the bull still had an access of strength too great for the kill.

Foreman looked ready to float as he came to his corner. In his corner Ali looked thoughtful, and stood up abstractedly before the bell and abstractedly led a cheer in the stadium, his arm to the sky.

The seventh was a slow round, almost as slow as the sixth. Foreman had no speed, and in return Ali boxed no faster than he had to, but kept shifting more rapidly than before from one set of ropes to another. Foreman was proving too sluggish to work with. Of course, Foreman was not wholly without hope. He still worked with the idea that one punch could catch Ali. And with less than a minute left, he managed to drive a left hook into Ali's belly, a blow that indeed made Ali gasp. Then Foreman racked him with a right uppercut strong enough for Ali to hold on in a clinch, no, Foreman was not going to give up. Now he leaned on Ali with one extended arm and tried to whale him with the other. He looked like he was beating a rug. Foreman had begun to show the clumsiness of a street fighter at the end of a long rumble. He was reverting. It happened to all but the most cultivated fighters toward the exhausted end of a long and terrible fight. Slowly they descended from the elegance of their best style down to the knee in the groin and the overhead punch (with a rock in the fist) of forgotten street fights.

Ali, half as tired at least, was not wasting himself. He was still graceful in every move. By the end of the round he was holding Foreman's head tenderly once more in his glove. Foreman was becoming reminiscent of the computer Hal in *2001* as his units were removed one by one, malfunctions were showing, and spastic lapses, and he looked as a man walking up a hill of pillows, he was reminiscent of the slow and curving motions of a linebacker coiling around a runner with his hands and arms in the slow-motion replay—the boxing had shifted from speed and impact to an intimacy of movement. Delicately Ali would cradle Foreman's head with his left before he smashed it with his right. Foreman looked ready to fall over from exhaustion. His face had the soft scrubbed look of a child's, but then they both had that gentle look boxers get when they are very tired and have fought each other very hard.

Back in the corner, Moore's hands were massaging Foreman's shoulders. Sandy Saddler was working on his legs. Dick Sadler was talking to him. And two rounds had gone by. The two dullest rounds of the fight. The night was hot. Now the air would become more tropical with every round. In his corner, Ali looked to be in pain as he breathed. Was it his kidneys or his ribs? Dundee was talking to him and Ali was shaking his head in disagreement. In contrast to Foreman's, his expression was keen. His eyes looked as quick as the eyes, indeed, of a squirrel. The bell rang for the eighth round.

Working slowly, deliberately, backing up still one more time, he hit Foreman carefully, spacing the punches, taking aim, six good punches, lefts and rights. It was as if he had a reserve of good punches, a numbered amount like a soldier in a siege who counts his bullets, and so each punch had to carry a predetermined portion of the work.

Foreman's legs were now hitched into an ungainly prance, like a horse high-stepping along a road full of rocks. Stung for the hundredth time with a cruel blow, his response was to hurl back a left hook that proved so wild he almost catapulted through the ropes. But the wild punch seemed to have refreshed him by its promise that some of his power was back. If his biggest punches were missing, at least they were big. Once again he might be his own prodigy of strength. Now there were flurries on the ropes that had an echo of the great bombardment in the fifth round. And still Ali taunted him, still the dialogue went on. "Fight hard," said Ali, "I thought you had some punches. You're a weak man. You're all used up." After a while, Foreman's punches were whistling less than his breath. For the eighteenth time Ali's corner was screaming, "Get off the ropes. Knock him out. Take him home!" Foreman had used up the store of force he transported from the seventh to the eighth. He pawed at Ali like an infant six feet tall waving its uncoordinated battle arm.

With twenty seconds left to the round, Ali attacked. By his own measure, by that measure of twenty years of boxing, with the knowledge of all he had learned of what could and could not be done at any instant in the ring, he chose this as the occasion and, lying on the ropes, he hit Foreman with a right and left, then came off the ropes to hit him with a left and a right. Into this last right hand he put his glove and his forearm again, a head-stupefying punch that sent Foreman reeling forward. As he went by, Ali hit him on the side of the jaw with a right, and darted away from the ropes in such a way as to put Foreman next to them. For the first time in the entire fight he had cut off the ring on Foreman. Now Ali struck him a combination of punches fast as the punches of the first round, but harder and more consecutive, three capital rights in a row struck Foreman, then a left, and for an instant on Foreman's face appeared the knowledge that he was in danger and must start to look to his last protection. His opponent was attacking, and there were no ropes behind the opponent. What a dislocation: The axes of his existence were reversed! He was the man on the ropes! Then a big projectile exactly the size of a fist in a glove drove into the middle of Foreman's mind, the best punch of the startled night, the blow Ali saved for a career. Foreman's arms flew out to the side. In a doubled-over position he tried to wander out to the center of the ring. All the while his eyes were on Ali and he looked up with no anger, as if Ali, indeed, were the man he knew best in the world and would see him on his dying day. Vertigo took George Foreman and revolved him. Still bowing from the waist in this uncomprehending position, eyes on Muhammad Ali all the way, he started to tumble and topple and fall even as he did not wish to go down. His mind was held with magnets high as his championship and his body was seeking the ground. He went over like a six-foot sixty-year-old butler who has just heard tragic news, yes, fell over all of a long collapsing two seconds, down came the Champion in sections and Ali revolved with him in a close circle, hand primed to hit him one more time, and never the need, a wholly intimate escort to the floor.

The referee took Ali to a corner. He stood there, he seemed lost in thought. Now he raced his feet in a quick but restrained shuffle as if to apologize for never asking his legs to dance, and looked on while Foreman tried to rouse himself.

Like a drunk hoping to get out of bed to go to work, Foreman rolled over, Foreman started the slow head-agonizing lift of all that foundered bulk God somehow gave him and, whether he heard the count or no, was on his feet a fraction after the count of ten and whipped, for when Zack Clayton guided him with a hand at his back, he walked in docile steps to his corner and did not resist. Moore received him. Sadler received him. Later, one learned the conversation.

"Feel all right?"

"Yeah," said Foreman.

"Well, don't worry. It's history now."

"Yeah."

"You're all right," said Sadler, "the rest will take càre of itself."

In the ring Ali was seized by Rachman, by Gene Kilroy, by Bundini, by a host of Black friends old, new, and very new, who charged up the aisles, leaped on the apron, sprang through the ropes, and jumped near to touch him. Norman said to Plimpton, in a tone of wonder, like a dim parent who realizes suddenly his child is indeed and indubitably married, "My God, he's Champion again!" as if one had trained oneself for years not to expect news so good as that.

In the ring Ali fainted.

It occurred suddenly and without warning and almost no one saw it. Angelo Dundee circling the ropes to shout happy words at reporters was unaware of what had happened. So were all the smiling faces. It was only the eight or ten men immediately around him who knew. Those eight or ten mouths that had just been open in celebration now turned to grimaces of horror. Bundini went from laughing to weeping in five seconds.

Why Ali fainted, nobody might ever know. Whether it was a warning against excessive pride in years to come—one private bolt from Allah—or whether the weakness of sudden exhaustion, who could know? Maybe it was even the spasm of a reflex he must have refined unconsciously for months—the ability to recover in seconds from total oblivion. Had he been obliged to try it out at least once on this night? He was in any case too much of a champion to allow an episode to arise, and was back on his feet before ten seconds were up. His handlers, having been lifted, chastened, terrified, and uplifted again, looked at him with faces of triumph and knockdown, the upturned mask of comedy and the howling mouth of tragedy next to each other in that instant in the African ring.

David Frost was crying out: "Muhammad Ali has done it. The great man has done it. This is the most joyous scene ever seen in the history of boxing. This is an incredible scene. The place is going wild. Muhammad Ali has won." And because the announcer before him had picked the count up late and was two seconds behind the referee and so counting eight when Clayton said ten, it looked on all the closed circuit screens of the world as if Foreman had gotten up before the count was done, and confusion was everywhere. How could it be other? The media would always sprout the seed of confusion. "Muhammad Ali has won. By a knockdown," said Frost in good faith. "By a knockdown."

Back in America everybody was already yelling that the fight was fixed. Yes. So was *The Night Watch,* and *Portrait of the Artist as a Young Man.*

All selections from *The Fight* (1975)

**PORTRAIT—III**

## Christ, Satan, and the Presidential Candidate: A Visit to Jimmy Carter in Plains

Plains was different from what one expected. Maybe it was the name, but anticipation had been of a dry and dusty town with barren vistas, ramshackle warehouses, and timeless, fly-buzzing, sun-baked afternoons. Instead, Plains was green. As one approached, the fields were green and the trees were tall. The heat of southern Georgia was as hot in summertime as it promised to be, but there was shade under the elms, the pecan trees, and the oaks, and if the streets were wide, the foliage was rich enough to come together overhead. A surprising number of houses were big and white and wooden and looked to be fifty years old or more. Some were a hundred years old. They had porches and trees in the front yard, and lawns ran a good distance from the front door to the sidewalk while the grass to the rear of the house meandered leisurely into the back yard of the house on the street behind. Some homes might be newly painted, and some were shabby, but the town was pleasant and spread out for a population of 683 inhabitants. By comparison with meaner-looking places with a gas station, barbecue shack, general store, junkyard, empty lots and spilled gasoline, a redneck redolence of dried ketchup and hamburger napkins splayed around thin-shanked, dusty trees, Plains felt peaceful and prosperous. It had the sweet deep green of an old-fashioned town that America has all but lost to the Interstates and the ranch houses, the mobile homes and the condominiums, the neon strips of hotted-up truck stops and the static pall of shopping centers.

Plains had an antique store on the main street that must have been a hundred feet deep, and it was owned by Alton Carter, Jimmy Carter's uncle; Plains had a railroad running through the middle of the main street and a depot that was not more than twice as long as a tinker's wagon: Plains had an arcade one block long (the length of the main street), and all the stores were in the shade under the arcade, including a brand-new restaurant called The Back Porch with white tin ceilings fifteen feet high, four-blade propeller fan turning overhead, and chicken-salad sandwiches with a touch of pineapple and a touch of pepper—tasty. Plains was that part of America which hitherto had been separate from the media, the part that offered a fundamental clue to the nature of establishment itself. One could pass through a hundred small towns in a state, and twenty or thirty might be part of a taproot for the establishment of its capital to draw upon. A place like Plains could be modest by the measure of its income and yet offer an unmistakable well-ordered patina, a promise that the mysterious gentility of American life was present, that there were still people interested in running things without showing the traces, that the small-town establishment remained a factor to be taken account of among all the other factors like exhaust roar and sewage slick and those plastic toylands stretching to the American horizon.

Maybe it was the architecture of the leading church in each town that gave the clue. Plains Baptist Church, now famous for the Sunday Bible classes for men conducted once a month (in his turn) by Jimmy Carter, had a fine architecture within. Painted white, with a ceiling of gracious wooden eaves and two splendid old chairs with red velvet seats on either side of the pulpit, it was an elegant church for a very small town, and its architect, whoever he had been—one could hope it was the town carpenter—must have lived a life that dwelt with ease in the proportions and needs of ecclesiastical space. The choir sang the hymns and the congregation sang with them, the words full of Christian exaltation, their sword of love quivering in the air, that secret in the strength of Christianity where the steel is smelted from the tears. "I will sing the wondrous story of the Christ who died for me," went the words, "how He left His home in glory for the cross of Calvary." When they came to sing, "Bringing in the sheaves," or may it have been, "When the roll is called up yonder, I'll be there," a member of the choir took out his harmonica and played it with feeling pure enough to take one back to the last campfires of a Confederate Army 111 years gone, the harmonica stirring old river reeds out of the tendrils of the past. It was a fine church service, and it gave the visitor from the North a little too much to think about, especially since he had spent a bemused hour in the basement of Plains Baptist Church somewhat earlier the same Sunday morning taking in Men's Bible Class 10 to 11 A.M. The basement, a schoolroom with institutional pale green walls, gray floor, gray metal seats, a blackboard, and a metal table up front for the deacons where Jimmy Carter sat, even an open window on the other side of which a ladder was leaning, had been relatively filled this Sunday with curious visitors, some press and two women from the media who had been allowed, as a political point (in the ongoing epic of women's liberation), to be admitted. They must have wondered what they were seeing. There was a devotion in the dry little voice, drier than gunpowder, of the deacon who interpreted the scripture, a farmer or a shopkeeper, thin as jerky dried in the sun, a dry, late-middle-aged man with eyeglasses, hollow cheeks, and an ingrown devotion that resided in the dungeon clamor of his lungs. He spoke in a wispy Georgia snuffle, very hard to hear, and his piety being as close to him as the body of one young beloved clasping the body of another through the night, it was not the place to pull out a pad and start taking notes.

In the second row of seats, the first row being all but empty, sat the real stalwarts of the Bible class, seven or eight big Georgia farmers, pleased by the crowd of visitors in the class, bemused in their own right that the church, the town, the county was a center suddenly of all the buzzing, insectlike instruments of the media and the peculiar pale faces of the media people. The second row owned the basement. They nudged each other in the ribs as they sat down next to one another. "Didn't see you sneak in here," they said to each other. They were the meat and mind of the South. They looked as if they had been coming here fifty Sundays a year for twenty years, here to think whatever thoughts they had on such occasions—one might be better situated to read the minds of Martians—and they were impressive in their mixture of hard-working bodies and hard-working hands, red necks with work-wrinkle lines three-sixteenths of an inch deep, and the classic ears of Southern farmers, big ears with large flappy chewed-out lobes as if they had been pulled on like old dugs over the ten thousand problems of their years. Men's Bible Class was teaching that Christian love was unselfish devotion to the highest good of others, and up front Jimmy Carter sat silently at the metal table with a couple of other deacons, his face calm, his mind attentive to one knew not necessarily what, dressed in a gray-blue suit and harmonious tie, and the hour passed and it was time to go upstairs to eleven o'clock service.

Somewhere the yeast must have been working in the religious call, for in the early afternoon, a couple of hours after church, when his private interview with Jimmy Carter took place, it proved to be the oddest professional hour Norman Mailer ever spent with a politician—it must have seemed twice as odd to Carter. In retrospect, it quickly proved mortifying (no lesser word will do), since to his embarrassment, Mailer did too much of the talking. Perhaps he had hoped to prime Carter to the point where they could have a conversation, but the subject he chose to bring up was religion, and that was ill-chosen. A man running for President could comment about Christ, he could comment a little, but he could hardly afford to be too enthusiastic. Religion had become as indecent a topic to many a contemporary American as sex must have been in the nineteenth century. If half the middle-class people in the Victorian period held almost no conscious thoughts about sex, the same could now be said of religion, except it might be even more costly to talk about than sex, because religious conversations invariably sound insane when recounted to men or women who never feel such sentiments. Since it was a safe assumption that half of America lived at present in the nineteenth century and half in the twentieth, a journalist who had any respect for the candidate he was talking to would not ask an opinion on sex or religion. Still, Mailer persisted. He was excited about Carter's theological convictions. He wanted to hear more of them. He had read the transcript of Bill Moyers' one-hour TV interview with Carter ("People and Politics," May 6, 10:00 P.M., Public Broadcasting Service) and had been impressed with a few of Carter's remarks, particularly his reply to Moyers's question "What drives you?"

After a long silence Carter had said, "I don't know . . . exactly how to express it . . . I feel I have one life to live. I feel that God wants me to do the best I can with it. And that's quite often my major prayer. Let me live my life so that it will be meaningful." A little later he would add, "When I have a sense of peace and self-assurance . . . that what I'm doing is the right thing, I assume, maybe in an unwarranted way, that that's doing God's will."

These were hardly historic remarks, and yet on reflection they were certainly remarkable. There was a maw of practicality that engulfed Presidents and presidential candidates alike. They lived in all those supermarkets of the mind where facts are stacked like cans; whether good men or bad, they were hardly likely to be part of that quintessential elevation of mind that can allow a man to say, "Let me live my life so that it will be meaningful." It was in the nature of politicians to look for *programs* to be meaningful, not the psychic substance of their lives. Reading the Moyers interview shortly before leaving for Plains must therefore have excited a last-minute excess of curiosity about Carter, and that was last-minute to be certain. Through all of the political spring when candidates came and went, Mailer had not gone near the primary campaigns. Working on a novel, he had made the whole decision not to get close to any of it. One didn't try to write seriously about two things at once. Besides, it was hard to tell much about Carter. Mailer thought the media had an inbuilt deflection that kept them from perceiving what was truly interesting in any new phenomeon. Since he rarely watched television any longer, he did not even know what Carter's voice was like, and photographs proved subtly anonymous. Still, he kept reading about Carter. In answer to the people who would ask, "What do you think of *him*?" Mailer would be quick to reply, "I suspect he's a political genius." It was all he knew about Carter, but he knew that much.

He also had to admit he enjoyed Carter's reaction to meeting Nixon and Agnew, McGovern and Henry Jackson, Hubert Humphrey, George Wallace, Ronald Reagan, Nelson Rockefeller, Ed Muskie. Carter confessed he had not been impressed sufficiently to think these men were better qualified to run the country than himself. Mailer understood such arrogance. He had, after all, felt enough of the same on meeting famous politicians to also think himself equipped for office, and had been brash enough to run for Mayor of New York in a Democratic primary. Mailer had always assumed he would be sensational as a political candidate; he learned, however, that campaign work ran eighteen hours a day, seven days a week, and after a while it was not yourself who was the candidate but 50 percent of yourself. Before it was over, his belly was drooping—one's gut is the first to revolt against giving the same speech eight times a day. He came in fourth in a field of five, and was left with a respect for successful politicians. They were at least entitled to the same regard one would offer a professional athlete for his stamina. Later, brooding on the size of a conceit that had let him hope he could steal an election from veteran Democrats, Mailer would summarize his experience with the wise remark, "a freshman doesn't get elected president of the fraternity."

But Carter had. Carter must be a political genius. Nonetheless, Mailer felt a surprising lack of curiosity. Genius in politics did not interest him that much. He thought politics was a dance where you need not do more than move from right to left and left to right while evading the full focus of the media. The skill was in the timing. You tried to move to the left at that moment when you would lose the least on the right; to the right, when the damage would be smallest on the left. You had to know how to steer in and out of other news stories. It was a difficult skill, but hardly possessed of that upper esthetic which would insist skill be illumined by a higher principle—whether elegance, courage, compassion, taste, or the eminence of wit. Politics called for some of the same skills you needed in inventing a new plastic. Politics called to that promiscuous material in the personality which could flow into many a form. Sometimes Mailer suspected that the flesh of the true politician would yet prove nonbiodegradable and fail to molder in the grave!

Still, there was no question in his mind that he would vote for Carter. In 1976 he was ready to vote for many a Democrat. It was not that Mailer could not ever necessarily vote for a Republican, but after eight years of Nixon and Ford, he thought the country could use a Democratic administration again. It was not that Ford was unendurable. Like a moderately dull marriage, Ford was endlessly endurable—one could even get fond of him in a sour way. Jerry Ford, after all, provided the clue to how America had moved in fifty years from George Babbitt to Jerry Ford. He even offered the peculiar security of having been shaped by forces larger than himself. Maybe that was why Ford's face suggested he would do the best he could with each problem as he perceived it: "Don't worry about me," said his face, "I'm not the least bit dialectical."

Of course, the President was only a handmaiden to the corporate spirit. The real question was whether the White House could afford another four years of the corporate spirit, that immeasurably self-satisfied public spirit whose natural impulse was to cheat on the environment and enrich the rich.

It was certainly time for the Democrats. He would probably vote for any Democrat who got the nomination. Nonetheless, it was irritating to have so incomplete an idea of Carter, to be so empty of any thesis as to whether he might be deemed ruthless, a computer, or saintly.

A day earlier, on the press plane to Albany, Georgia, he had felt—what with a few drinks inside him—that he was coming closer to what he wanted to discuss with Carter in the interview that would be granted next day. The sexual revolution had come out of a profound rejection of the American family—it had been a way of saying to the parents, "If you say sex is dirty, then it has to be good, because your lives are false!" But Carter would restore the family. Faithful, by public admission, to his wife for thirty years, he was in every way a sexual conservative. Since his economic proposals would appeal to progressives, he might be undertaking the Napoleonic proposition of outflanking two armies, Republicans and Democrats, from the right and the left. Yes, there was much to talk about with Carter. Even on the airplane, Mailer could feel his head getting overcompressed with themes of conversation arriving too early.

Jimmy Carter's home was on a side street, and you approached it through a barricade the Secret Service had erected. It was possible this was as unobtrusive a small-town street as the Secret Service had ever converted into an electronic compound with walkie-talkies, sentries, and lines-of-sight. The house was in a grove of trees, and the ground was hard-put to keep its grass, what with pine needles, pecan leaves, and the clay of the soil itself, which gave off a sandy-rose hue in the shade.

The rambling suburban ranch house in those trees spoke of California ancestry for its architecture, and a cost of construction between $50,000 and $100,000, depending on how recently it was built. The inside of the house was neither lavish nor underfurnished, not sumptuous or mean—a house that spoke of comfort more than taste. The colors laid next to one another were in no way brilliant, yet neither did their palette of soft shades depress the eye, for they were cool in the Georgia summer. Carter's study was large and dark with books, and there were busts of Kennedy and Lincoln, and his eight-year-old daughter Amy's comic book (starring Blondie) was on the floor. It was the only spot of red in all the room. Over his desk was a fluorescent light.

Maybe Carter was one of the few people in the world who could look good under fluorescent light. Wearing a pale blue button-down shirt open at the neck—pale blue was certainly his color—Carter had a quintessential American cleanliness, that silvery light of a finely tuned and supple rectitude that produces our best ministers and best generals alike, responsible for both the bogs of Vietnam and the vision of a nobler justice.

Now, sitting across the desk from Carter, he was struck by a quiet difference in Carter this Sunday afternoon. Maybe it was the result of church, or maybe the peril implicit for a politician in any interview—since one maladroit phrase can ruin a hundred good ones—but Carter seemed less generous than he had expected. Of course, Mailer soon knew to his horror that he was close to making a fool of himself, if indeed he had not done it already, because with his first question taking five minutes to pose, and then ten, he had already given a speech rather than a question. What anguish this caused, that he—known as criminally egomaniacal by common reputation, and therefore for years as careful as a reformed criminal to counteract the public expectation of him—was haranguing a future President of the United States. He had a quick recollection of the days when he ran for Mayor and some fool or other, often an overly educated European newspaperman, would ask questions that consisted of nothing but long-suppressed monologues. To make matters worse, Carter was hardly being responsive in his answer—how could he be? Mailer's exposition dwelt in the bowels of that limitless schism in Protestantism—between the fundamental simplicities of good moral life as exemplified a few hours ago in Bible class and the insuperable complexities of moral examination opened by Kierkegaard, whose work, Mailer now told Carter with enthusiasm, looked to demonstrate that we cannot know the moral role we enact. We can feel saintly and yet be evil in the eyes of God, feel we are evil (on the other hand) and yet be more saintly than we expect; equally, we may do good even as we are feeling good, or be bad exactly when we expect we are bad. Man is alienated from his capacity to decide his moral worth. Maybe, Mailer suggested, he had sailed on such a quick theological course because Carter had quoted Kierkegaard on the second page of his autobiography. "Every man is an exception," Kierkegaard had written.

But it was obvious by the smile on Carter's face—a well of encouragement to elicit the point of this extended question—that Carter was not necessarily one of America's leading authorities on Kierkegaard. How foolish of Mailer to expect it of him—as if Norman in his turn had never quoted an author he had not lived with thoroughly.

Having failed with the solemnity of this exposition, but his voice nonetheless going on, beginning to wonder what his question might be—did he really have one, did he really enter this dialogue with the clean journalistic belief that ultimate questions were to be answered by presidential candidates?—he now began to shift about for some political phrasing he could offer Carter as a way out of these extensive hypotheses. The sexual revolution, Mailer said hopefully, the sexual revolution might be a case in point. And he now gave the lecture he had prepared the night before—that the family, the very nuclear family whose security Carter would look to restore, was seen as the enemy by a large fraction of Americans. "For instance," said Mailer, clutching at inspiration, "there are a lot of people in New York who don't trust you. The joke making the rounds among some of my friends is 'How can you put confidence in a man who's been faithful to the same woman for thirty years?' "

Carter's smile showed real amusement, as if he knew something others might not necessarily know. Of course, whether he was smiling to the left or right of this issue was another matter. Curiously encouraged by the ambiguous fiber of the smile, Mailer went on toward asking his first question. He had presented the joke, he suggested, to show the gulf of moral differences that awaited a Carter presidency—for instance, to talk of the drug problem just a moment, statistics reexamined showed that addicts deprived of heroin, or methadone, did not commit more crimes to get scarce heroin but instead took speed or barbiturates or pot, or even went to bourbon. The implication of this, Mailer said, is that there's a chasm in the soul that might have to be filled, a need precisely not to be oneself but rather to give oneself over to the Other, to give oneself to some presence outside oneself; the real answer to drug addiction might not be in social programs but in coming to grips with the possibility that Satanism was loose in the twentieth century. One question he would like to ask in line with this was whether Carter thought much about the hegemony of Satan, or did he—yes, this unasked question was now being silently answered by Carter's eyes, yes, Carter's concern was not with Satan but with Christ. On and on went Mailer with considerable fever, looking, for instance, to propose that one difference between Carter's religious point of view as he, Mailer, presumed to comprehend it, and his own might be that he had a notion of God as not clearly omnipotent but rather as a powerful God at war with other opposed visions in the universe—a ridiculous picture of God to present to Carter, Mailer told the candidate, except that going back to the Moyers interview, where Carter had certainly said that he felt he might be doing God's will when he felt a sense of peace and self-assurance—did it ever bother Carter, keeping Kierkegaard's Principle of Uncertainty in mind, if he, Mailer, could, heh heh, steal a title from Heisenberg—did it ever bother him that God might be in anguish or rage at what He had not accomplished across the heavens? For instance, there was the Hasidic tale of Rabbi Zusya, who begged God to reveal himself in reward for Zusya's devotions to him, and God finally replied by revealing Himself, and Zusya crawled under the bed and howled in fear like a dog, and said, "O God, please do not reveal yourself to me." Did that story, that image of God, strike any chord in Carter, was there any recognition that God, close to losing, could live in wrath and horror? Christ, when all was said, had died on the Cross, on a mission He believed would succeed and had failed.

Mailer ground down into silence, furious with himself for scattering prodigious questions like buckshot. He looked across at Carter. He was realizing all over again that the only insanity still left in his head was this insane expectation he had of men in public places.

Carter nodded sadly. He looked a little concerned. He had every right to be. However would such an interview appear in *The New York Times*?

Well, answered Carter soberly, thoughtfully, he was not certain that he could reply to everything that had been raised since their points of view were not the same in many respects. He was not, for instance, as devout and as prayerful as the press had perhaps made him out to be. Religion was something he certainly did and would live with, but he didn't spend as much time as people might expect exploring into the depths of these questions; perhaps—he suggested politely—he ought to be more concerned, but in truth, he did not think his personal beliefs were to be carried out by the government; there were limits to what government could do, yet in those limits, he thought much more could be done than was now being done. For example, he would recognize that there is little that government could do directly to restore the family. Welfare payments might, for example, be revised in such a way that fathers would not be directly encouraged to desert their families, as they were most ironically now encouraged to do, but he would admit that this, of course, was to the side of the question. He supposed, Carter said, that the answer, as he saw it, was in turning government around so that it would be more of a model. There was a yearning in this country for the restoration of something precious. "There's been a loss of pride in this country that I find catastrophic." The deterioration of family values was linked, Carter thought, to that loss of pride. It would be his hope that if he could get the actual workings of the government turned around, so that government was at once more efficient and more *sensitive,* then perhaps it could begin to serve as more of a model to counteract the fundamental distrust of people in relation to government, that is, their feeling they won't find justice. "The real answer is to get those of us who are running the government going right." You see, Carter went on to say, he was not looking to restore the family by telling people how to live; he did not wish to be President in order to judge them. "I don't care," he said in his quiet decent voice, as if the next words, while not wholly comfortable, had nonetheless to be said, "I don't care if people say—," and he actually said the famous four-letter word that the *Times* has not printed in the 125 years of its publishing life.

He got it out without a backing-up of phlegm or a hitch in his rhythm (it was, after all, not the easiest word to say to a stranger), but it was said from duty, from the quiet decent demands of duty, as if he, too, had to present his credentials to that part of the twentieth century personified by his interviewer.

No, Carter went on, his function was not to be a religious leader but to bring the human factor back into economics. The same economic formula, he suggested, would work or not work depending on the morale of the people who were doing the work.

Mailer nodded. He believed as much himself. But he was still dissatisfied with his lack of contact on questions more fundamental to himself. Like a child who returns to the profitless point (out of obscure but certain sense of need), Mailer looked to return their conversation to Kierkegaardian ambiguities and so spoke of marijuana, for it was on marijuana, he told Carter, that he had had the first religious experience he had ever known—indeed, marijuana might even pose the paradox of arriving at mystical states for too little. One began to feel the vulnerability of God about the time one recognized a little more clearly in the unwinding of the centers of one's consciousness that one was consuming one's karma, possibly stripping—for no more than the pleasure of the experience—some of the resources of one's future lives. He asked Carter then if he had any belief in reincarnation, in the reincarnation of karma as our purgatory here on earth? And Carter said no, Carter said he believed we had our one life and our judgment. And then with that gentle seductiveness all good politicians have, Carter mentioned that his understanding was not wholly alien to drugs, his sons had experimented with marijuana a few years ago, and had later done some work in the rehabilitation of addicts. He felt as if their experiences had helped them in such work.

Mailer was thinking morosely of the meeting of Sam Goldwyn and George Bernard Shaw to discuss making a film. Goldwyn had spoken of his admiration for Shaw's work, of his love of fine dramatic subjects, of the pleasures of esthetics, and Shaw had finally replied, "Mr. Goldwyn, the difficulty is that you care only about art, and I am interested only in money." He had certainly been playing Goldwyn to Jimmy Carter's George Bernard Shaw—no, worse!

Mailer was finally beginning to feel the essential frustration of trying to talk about religion with Carter on equal terms. Carter had more troops, which is to say he had more habits. If you go to church every Sunday for most of your life, then you end with certain habits. You live in a dependable school of perception. In the case of Baptists, it might be living with the idea that if you were good enough and plucky and lucky and not hating your neighbor for too little, Christ was quietly with you. Certainly, if you had the feeling He was with you at all, He was with you in church on Sunday. So you could form the habit over the years of thinking about Him in a comfortable way.

Maybe Carter saw God in the little continuing revelations churchgoing offered on the personalities of one's friends. It was like enjoying a film or a best-selling novel. Cause and effect lived in a framework you could perceive. A good man had his character written on his face.

Whereas Mailer's love of God (we must assume he has some) owed too much to Kierkegaard, who could have said that a good man would have his character written on his face unless he wasn't a good man but an exceptional bad man with a good face—Mailer saw no reason why the Devil could not be the most beautiful creature God ever made. Yet, equally, a man could develop an evil face and a loving heart. There was the difference. Carter might be able to see hints of God in his neighbor; Mailer was forever studying old photographs of Gurdjieff and Rasputin.

They had come to the end of their hour. The author was feeling a dull relief that he would have, at least, another hour tomorrow. How fortunate that that had been scheduled in advance. He started to apologize in some roundabout form for how the first hour had gone, and Carter replied with his gracious smile: it was all right, he said, they had needed the first hour to loosen up, to become acquainted. Mailer left with the twice dull sense that he liked Carter more than Carter had any reason to like him.

From *The New York Times Magazine* (September 26, 1976)

# THE
# EXECUTIONER'S
# SONG

## April      Brenda, Johnny, and Gary

They pulled up to the island that ran parallel to the main entrance of the terminal building. So soon as she got out of the car, there was Johnny over on the driver's side, trying to tuck his shirttail in. That annoyed Brenda no end.

She could see Gary leaning against the building. "There he is," Brenda cried, but Johnny said, "Wait, I have to zip my pants."

"Who gives a shit about your shirttail?" said Brenda. "I'm going."

As she crossed the street between the parking island and the main door, Gary saw her and picked up his satchel. Pretty soon they were running toward each other. As they met, Gary dropped his bag, looked at her, then encircled her so hard she could have been hugged by a bear. Even Johnny had never gripped Brenda that hard.

When Gary put her down on the ground again, she stood back and looked at him. She had to take him all in. She said, "My God, you're tall."

He started to laugh. "What did you expect, a midget?"

"I don't know what I expected," she said, "but, thank God, you're tall."

Johnny was just standing there with his big good face going, um, um, um.

———

"Hey, coz," said Gary, "it's fine to see you." He shook hands with Johnny.

"By the way, Gary," said Brenda demurely, "this is my husband."

Gary said, "I assumed that's who it was."

Johnny said, "Have you got everything with you?"

Gary picked up his flight bag—it was pathetically small, thought Brenda—and said, "This is it. This is all I have." He said it without humor and without self-pity. Material things were obviously no big transaction to him.

Now she noticed his clothes. He had a black trench coat slung on his arm and was wearing a maroon blazer over—could you believe it?—a yellow and green striped shirt. Then a pair of beige polyester trousers that were badly hemmed. Plus a pair of black plastic shoes. She paid attention to people's footwear because of her father's trade, and she thought, Wow, that's really cheap. They didn't even give him a pair of leather shoes to go home in.

"Come on," said Gary, "let's get the hell out of here."

She could see then he'd had something to drink. He wasn't plastered, but he sure was tipped. Made a point of putting his arm around her when they walked to the car.

When they got in, Brenda sat in the middle and Johnny drove. Gary said, "Hey, this is kind of a cute car. What is it?"

"A yellow Maverick," she told him. "My little lemon."

They drove. The first silence came in.

"Are you tired?" asked Brenda.

"A little tired, but then I'm a little drunk too." Gary grinned. "I took advantage of the champagne flight. I don't know if it was the altitude, or not having good liquor for a long time, but, boy, I got tore up on that plane. I was happier than hell."

Brenda laughed. "I guess you're entitled to be snockered."

The prison sure cut his hair short. It would, Brenda judged, be heavy handsome brown hair when it grew out, but for now it stuck up hick style in the back. He kept pushing it down.

No matter, she liked his looks. In the half-light that came into the car as they drove through Salt Lake on the Interstate, the city sleeping on both sides of them, she decided that Gary was everything she expected in that department. A long, fine nose, good chin, thin well-shaped lips. He had character about his face.

"Want to go for a cup of coffee?" Johnny asked.

Brenda felt Gary tighten. It was as if even the thought of walking into a strange place got him edgy. "Come on," Brenda said, "we'll give the ten-cent tour."

They picked Jean's Cafe. It was the only place south of Salt Lake open at 3 A.M., but it was Friday night and people were sporting their finery. Once installed in their booth, Gary said, "I guess I got to get some clothes."

Johnny encouraged him to eat, but he wasn't hungry. Obviously too excited. Brenda felt as if she could pick up the quiver in each bright color that Gary was studying on the jukebox. He looked close to being dazzled by the revolving red, blue, and gold light show on the electronic screen of the cigarette console. He was so involved it drew her into his mood. When a couple of cute girls walked in, and Gary mumbled, "Not bad," Brenda laughed. There was something so real about the way he said it.

Couples kept coming from parties and leaving, and the sound of cars parking and taking off didn't stop. Still Brenda was not looking at the door. Her best friend could have walked in, but she would have been all alone with Gary. She couldn't remember when somebody had absorbed her attention this much. She didn't mean to be rude to Johnny, but she did kind of forget he was there.

Gary, however, looked across the table and said, "Hey, man, thanks. I appreciate how you went along with Brenda to get me out." They shook hands again. This time Gary did it thumbs up.

Over the coffee, he asked Brenda about her folks, her sis, her kids, and Johnny's job.

Johnny did maintenance at the Pacific State Cast Iron and Pipe. While he was blacksmithing now, he used to make iron pipe, fire it, cast it, sometimes do the mold work.

The conversation died. Gary had no clue what to ask Johnny next. He knows nothing about us, Brenda thought, and I know so little about his life.

———

Gary spoke of a couple of prison friends and what good men they were. Then he said apologetically, Well, you don't want to hear about prison, it's not very pleasant.

Johnny said they were only tiptoeing around because they didn't want to offend him. "We're curious," said Johnny, "but, you know, we don't want to ask: What's it like in there? What do they do to you?"

Gary smiled. They were silent again.

Brenda knew she was making Gary nervous as hell. She kept staring at him constantly, but she couldn't get enough of his face. There were so many corners in it.

"God," she kept saying, "it's good to have you here."

"It's good to get back."

"Wait till you get to know this country," she said. She was dying to tell him about the kind of fun they could have on Utah Lake, and the camper trips they would take in the canyons. The desert was just as gray and brown and grim as desert anywhere, but the mountains went up to twelve thousand feet, and the canyons were green with beautiful forests and super drinking parties with friends. They could teach him how to hunt with bow and arrow, she was about ready to tell him, when all of a sudden she got a good look at Gary in the light. Speak of all the staring she had done, it was as if she hadn't studied him at all yet. Now she felt a strong sense of woe. He was marked up much more than she had expected.

She reached out to touch his cheek at the place where he had a very bad scar, and Gary said, "Nice-looking, isn't it?"

Brenda said, "I'm sorry, Gary, I didn't mean to embarrass you."

This set up such a pause that Johnny finally asked, "How'd it happen?"

"A guard hit me," said Gary. He smiled. "They had me tied down for a shot of Prolixin—and I managed to spit in the doctor's face. Then I got clobbered."

"How," asked Brenda, "would you like to take that guard who hit you, and get ahold of him?"

"Don't pick my brain," said Gary.

"Okay," said Brenda, "but do you hate him?"

"God, yeah," said Gary, "wouldn't you?"

"Yeah, I would," said Brenda. "Just checking."

—

Half an hour later, driving home, they went by Point of the Mountain. Off to the left of the Interstate a long hill came out of the mountains and its ridge was like the limb of a beast whose paw just reached the highway. On the other side, in the desert to the right, was Utah State Prison. There were only a few lights in its buildings now. They made jokes about Utah State Prison.

Back in her living room, drinking beer, Gary began to unwind. He liked beer, he confessed. In prison, they knew how to make a watery brew out of bread. Called it Pruno. In fact, both Brenda and Johnny were observing that Gary could put brew away as fast as anyone they knew.

Johnny soon got tired and went to sleep. Now Gary and Brenda really began to talk. A few prison stories came out of him. To Brenda, each seemed wilder than the one before. Probably they were half true, half full of beer. He had to be reciting out of his hind end.

It was only when she looked out the window and saw the night was over that she realized how long they had been talking. They stepped through the door to look at the sun coming up over the back of her ranch house and all her neighbors' ranch houses, and standing there, on her plot of lawn, in a heap of strewn-about toys, wet with cold spring dew, Gary looked at the sky and took a deep breath.

"I feel like jogging," he said.

"You've got to be nuts, tired as you are," she said.

He just stretched and breathed deep, and a big smile came over his face. "Hey, man," he said, "I'm really out."

In the mountains, the snow was iron gray and purple in the hollows, and glowed like gold on every slope that faced the sun. The clouds over the mountains were lifting with the light. Brenda took a good look into his eyes and felt full of sadness again. His eyes had the expression of rabbits she had flushed, scared-rabbit was the common expression, but she had looked into those eyes of scared rabbits and they were calm and tender and kind of curious. They did not know what would happen next.

Brenda put Gary on the foldout couch in the TV room. When she began to make the bed, he stood there smiling.

"What gives you that impish little grin?" she said after a pause.

"Do you know how long it's been since I slept on a sheet?"

He took a blanket but no pillow. Then she went to her room. She never knew if he fell asleep. She had the feeling he lay down and rested and never took off his polyesters, just his shirt. When she got up a few hours later, he was up and around.

They were still having coffee when Toni came over to visit, and Gary gave her a big hug, and stood back, and framed her face with his hands and said, "I finally get to meet the kid sister. Man, I've looked at your photographs. What a foxy lady you are."

"You're going to make me blush," said Toni.

She certainly looked like Brenda. Same popping black eyes, black hair, same sassy look. It was just that Brenda was on the voluptuous side and Toni was slim enough to model. Take your pick.

When they sat down, Gary kept reaching over and putting his arm around Toni, or taking hold of her hand. "I wish you weren't my cousin," he said, "and married to such a big tall dude."

Later, Toni would tell Brenda how good and wise Howard had been for saying, "Go over and meet Gary without me." She went on to describe how warm Gary made her feel, not sexy, but more like a brother. He had amazed her with how much he knew of her life. Like that Howard was six foot six. Brenda kept herself from remarking that he had not learned it from any letters Toni had written, since Toni had never written a line.

Before Brenda took Gary over to meet Vern and Ida, Johnny showed a test of strength. He took the bathroom scale and squeezed it between his hands until the needle went up to 250 pounds.

Gary tried and reached 120. He went crazy and squeezed the scales until he was shaking. The needle went to 150.

"Yeah," said Johnny, "you're improving."

"What's the highest you've gone?" asked Gary.

"Oh," said Johnny, "the scale stops at 280, but I've taken it past there. I suppose 300."

———

On the drive to the shoe shop, Brenda told Gary a little more about her father. Vern, she explained, might be the strongest man she knew.

Stronger than Johnny?

Well, Brenda explained, nobody could top Johnny at squeezing the scales, but she didn't know who had ever beaten Vern Damico at arm wrestling.

Vern, said Brenda, was strong enough to be gentle all the time. "I don't think my father ever gave me a spanking except once in my whole life and I truly asked for that. It was only one pat on the hind end, but that hand of his could cover your whole body."

The mountains had been gold and purple at dawn, but now in the morning they were big and brown and bald and had gray rain-soaked snow on the ridges. It got into their mood. The distance from the north side of Orem, where she lived, to Vern's store in the center of Provo was six miles, but going along State Street, it took a while. There were shopping malls and quick-eat palaces, used-car dealers, chain clothing stores and gas stops, appliance stores and highway signs and fruit stands. There were banks and real estate firms in one-story office compounds and rows of condominiums with sawed-off mansard roofs. There hardly seemed a building that was not painted in a nursery color: pastel yellow, pastel orange, pastel tan, pastel blue. Only a few faded two-story wooden houses looked as if they had been built even thirty years ago. On State Street, going the six miles from Orem to Provo, those houses looked as old as frontier saloons.

"It sure has changed," said Gary.

Overhead was the immense blue of the strong sky of the American West. That had not changed.

At the foot of the mountains, on the boundary between Orem and Provo, was Brigham Young University. It was also new and looked like it had been built from prefabricated toy kits. Twenty years ago, BYU had a few thousand students. Now the enrollment was close to thirty thousand, Brenda told him. As Notre Dame to good Catholics, so BYU to good Mormons.

"I better tell you a little more about Vern," Brenda said. "You have to understand when Dad is joking and when he is not. That can be a little hard to figure out because Dad does not always smile when he is joking."

She did not tell him that her father had been born with a harelip, but then she assumed he knew. Vern had a full palate, so his speech was not affected, but the mark was right out there. His mustache didn't pretend to hide it. When he first went to school it didn't take him long to become one of the toughest kids. Any boy who wanted to kid Vern about his lip, said Brenda, got a belt in the snout.

It made Vern's personality. To this day, when children came into the shoe shop and saw him for the first time, Vern did not have to hear what the child was saying when the mother said, Hush. He was used to that. It didn't bother him now. Over the years, however, he had had to do a lot to overcome it. Not only did it leave him strong, but frank. He might be gentle in his manner, Brenda said, but he usually came out and said what he thought. That could be abrasive.

Yet when Gary met Vern, Brenda decided she had prepared him too much. He was a little nervous when he said hello, and looked around, and acted surprised at the size of the shoe shop, as if he hadn't expected a big cave of a place. Vern commented that it was a lot of room to walk around in when customers weren't there, and they got on from that to his osteoarthritis. Vern had a powerfully painful accumulation in his knee that had frozen the joint. Just hearing about it seemed to get Gary concerned. It didn't seem phony, Brenda thought. She could almost feel the pain of Vern's knee pass right into Gary's scrotum.

Vern thought Gary ought to move in with Ida and himself right away, but shouldn't plan to go to work for a few days. A fellow needed time to get acquainted with his freedom, Vern observed. After all, Gary had come into a strange town, didn't know where the library was, didn't know where to buy a cup of coffee. So he talked to Gary real slow. Brenda was accustomed to men taking quite a while to say anything to each other, but if you were impatient, it could drive you crazy.

When she and Gary went over to the house, however, Ida was thrilled. "Bessie was my special big sister, and I was always her favorite," Ida told him. She was getting a little plump, but with her red-brown hair and her bright-colored dress, Ida looked like an attractive gypsy lady.

She and Gary began talking right away about how when he was a little boy, he used to visit Grandma and Grandpa Brown. "I loved them days," Gary said to her. "I was as happy then as I've ever been in my life."

Together, Gary and Ida made a sight in that small living room. Although Vern's shoulders could fill a doorway, and any one of his fingers was as wide as anyone else's two fingers, he was not that tall, and Ida was short. They wouldn't be bothered by a low ceiling.

It was a living room with a lot of stuffed furniture in bright autumn colors and bright rugs and color-filled pictures in gold frames and there was a ceramic statue of a black stable boy with a red jacket standing by the fireplace. Chinese end tables and big colored hassocks took up space on the floor.

Having lived among steel bars, reinforced concrete, and cement-block walls, Gary would now be spending a lot of his time in this living room.

Back at her house, on the pretext of helping him pack, Brenda got a peek at the contents of his tote bag. It held a can of shaving cream, a razor, a toothbrush, a comb, some snapshots, his parole papers, a few letters, and no change of underwear.

Vern slipped him some underclothes, some tan slacks, a shirt, and twenty bucks.

Gary said, "I can't pay you back right now."

"I'm giving you the money," Vern said. "If you need more, see me. I don't have a lot, but I'll give you what I can."

Brenda would have understood her father's reasoning: A man without money in his pocket can get into trouble.

Monday morning, Gary broke the twenty-dollar bill Vern had given him, and bought a pair of gym shoes. That week, he would wake up every day around six and go out to run. He would take off from Vern's house in a fast long stride down to Fifth West, go around the park, and back—more than ten blocks in four minutes, good time. Vern, with his bad knee, thought Gary was a fantastic runner.

In the beginning, Gary didn't know exactly what he could do in the house. On his first evening alone with Vern and Ida, he asked if he could get a glass of water.

"This is your home," Vern said. "You don't have to ask permission."

Gary came back from the kitchen with the glass in his hand. "I'm beginning to get onto this," he said to Vern. "It's pretty good."

"Yeah," said Vern, "come and go as you want. Within reason."

Gary didn't like television. Maybe he'd seen too much in prison, but in the evening, once Vern went to bed, Gary and Ida would sit and talk.

Ida reminisced about Bessie's skill with makeup. "She was so clever that way," said Ida, "and so tasteful. She knew how to make herself look beautiful all the time. She had the same elegance about her as our mother, who is French and always had aristocratic traits." Her mother, said Ida, had a breeding that she gave to her children. The table was always set properly, not to the stiffest standards—they were just poor Mormons—but a tablecloth, always a tablecloth, and enough silverware to do the job.

Bessie, Gary told Ida, was now so arthritic she could hardly move, and the little trailer in which she lived was all plastic. Considering the climate in Portland, that trailer had to be damp. When he got a little money together, he would try to improve matters. One night Gary actually called his mother and talked for a long time. Ida heard him say he loved her and was going to bring her back to Provo to live.

It was a warm week for April, and pleasant talking through the evenings, planning for the summer to come.

About the third night, they got to talking about Vern's driveway. It wasn't wide enough to take more than one car, but Vern had a strip of lawn beside it that could offer space for another car provided he could remove the concrete curb that separated the grass from the paving. That curb ran for thirty-five feet from the sidewalk to the garage. It was about six inches high, eight inches wide, and would take a lot of work to be chopped out. Because of his bad leg, Vern had been holding off.

"I'll do it," said Gary.

Sure enough, next morning at 6 A.M., Vern was awakened by the sound of Gary taking a sledgehammer to the job. Sound slammed through the neighborhood in the dawn. Vern winced for the people in the City Center Motel, next door, who would be awakened by the reverberation. All day Gary worked, cracking the curbing with overhead blows, then prying chunks out, inch by inch, with the crowbar. Before long, Vern had to buy a new one.

Those thirty-five feet of curbing took one day and part of the next. Vern offered to help, but Gary wouldn't allow it. "I know a lot about pounding rocks," he told Vern with a grin.

"What can I do for you?" asked Vern.

"Well, it's thirsty work," said Gary. "Just keep me in beer."

It went like that. He drank a lot of beer and worked real hard and they were happy with the job. When he was done, he had open blisters on his hand as large as Vern's fingernails. Ida insisted on bandaging his palms, but Gary was acting like a kid—a man don't wear bandages—and took them off real quick.

Doing the work, however, had loosened him up. He was ready to do his first exploring around town.

Provo was laid out in a checkerboard. It had very wide streets and a few buildings that were four stories high. It had three movie theaters. Two were on Center Street, the main shopping street, and the other was on University Avenue, the other shopping street. In Provo, the equivalent of Times Square was where the two streets crossed. There was a park next to a church on one corner and diagonally across was an extra-large drugstore.

During the day, Gary would walk around town. If he came by the shoe shop around lunchtime, Vern would take him to the Provo Cafe, or to Joe's Spic and Span, which had the best coffee in town. It was just a box of a joint, with twenty seats. At lunchtime, however, people would be waiting on the street to get in. Of course, Vern told him, Provo was not famous for restaurants.

"What is it famous for?" asked Gary.

"Darned if I know," said Vern. "Maybe it's the low crime rate."

Looking around, Gary decided to get out of his polyesters and buy some Levi's. He borrowed a few more bucks from Vern, and Brenda took him to a shopping mall.

He told her that he had never been to anything like this before. It was mind-stopping. He couldn't keep his eyes off the girls. Right in the middle of goggling at them, Gary walked into the ledge of a fountain. If Brenda hadn't grabbed his sleeve, he'd have been in. "You certainly haven't lost your eye," she told him. He had only been gawking at the most beautiful girls. He was nearly all wet, but he had very good taste.

In the Levi's department at Penney's, Gary just stood there. After a while, he said, "Hey, I don't know how to go about this. Are you supposed to take the pants off the shelf, or does somebody issue them to you?"

Brenda really felt sorry for him. "Find the ones you want," she said, "and tell the clerk. If you want to try them on, you can."

"Without paying for them?"

"Oh, yeah, you can try them on first," she said.

## May        Gary and Nicole

Gary called up Brenda. He would be getting his first pay that night. His first check from Spence McGrath. "Hey, I want to treat you guys," he told her.

They decided to go to a movie. It was a flick he had seen before. *One Flew Over the Cuckoo's Nest.* He had watched them film it down the road from the penitentiary, watched it right from his cell window. Besides, he told her, he had even been sent over to that very mental institution a couple of times from the prison. Just like Jack Nicholson in the film. Brought him in the same way, with handcuffs and leg irons.

Since the movie was at the Una Theatre in Provo, Brenda and Johnny drove over from Orem and by the time they picked him up at Vern and Ida's, Gary had had about four or five beers to celebrate his paycheck.

In the truck, he smoked a joint. Made him happier than hell. By the time they covered the few blocks to the theatre he was giggling. Brenda said to herself: This is going to be a disastrous evening.

Soon as the movie went on, Gary started to give a running commentary. He said, "You see that broad? She really works in the hospital. But the guy next to her is a phony. Just an actor. Hey!" Gary told the movie theatre at large.

After a while, his language got to be God forbid! "Look at that fucker over there," he said. "I know that fucker."

Brenda could have died. No pain. "Gary—there are people trying to hear the show. Will you shut up?"

"Am I offensive?"

"You're *loud*."

He spun around in his seat and asked the people behind, "Am I being loud? Am I bothering you folks?"

Brenda slammed her elbow into his ribs.

Johnny got up and moved over a space or two.

"Where's Johnny going?" asked Gary. "Does he have to take a piss?" More people started to move.

Johnny slid down in his seat until no one could see his head. Gary's narration of *One Flew Over the Cuckoo's Nest* continued. "Son of a bitch," he shouted, "that's just the way it was."

From the rear rows, people were saying, "Down in front. Shhh!" Brenda grabbed him by the shirttail. "You're obnoxious."

"I'm sorry." In a big whisper, he said, "I'll hold it down." But his voice came out in a roar.

"Gary, all kidding aside, you're really making me feel like a turd sitting here."

"All right, I'll be good." He put his feet up on the back of the chair in front and started rocking it. The woman who was sitting there had probably been holding out on every impulse to change her seat, but now she gave up, and moved away.

"What'd you do that for?"

"My God, Brenda, do you have to ride herd all the time?"

"You made that poor lady move."

"Her hair was in my way."

"Then sit up straighter."

"Not comfortable sitting up straight."

Going back to Vern's, Gary looked pretty smug. Brenda and Johnny didn't go in with him.

"What's the matter?" asked Gary. "Don't you like me anymore?"

"Right now? I think you are the most insensitive human being I've ever known."

"Brenda, I am not insensitive," said Gary, "to being called insensitive."

He whistled all the way up the steps.

At breakfast, his mood was fine. He saw Vern watching him eat and said, "I guess you think I gobble like a pig, kinda quick."

Vern said, "Yeah, I noticed that."

Gary said, "Well, in prison you learn to eat in a hurry. You've got fifteen minutes to get your food, sit down and swallow it. Sometimes you just don't get it."

"Did *you* manage to get it?" asked Vern.

"Yeah, I worked in the kitchen for a while. My job was to make the salad. Took five hours to make that much salad. I can't touch the stuff now."

"That's fine," said Vern, "you don't need to eat it."


"You're a pretty strong fellow, Vern, aren't you?"

"Just the champ."

"Let's arm wrestle," said Gary.

Vern shook his head, but Ida said, "Go ahead, arm wrestle him."

"Yeah, come on," said Gary. He squinted at Vern: "You think you can take me?"

Vern said, "I don't have to think. I can take you."

"Well, I feel pretty strong today, Vern. What makes you think you can beat me?"

"I'm gonna make up my mind," Vern said, "and I think I can do it."

"Try it."

"Well," Vern said, "you eat your breakfast first."


They got into it before the table was cleared. Vern kept eating his breakfast with his left hand, and arm wrestled with the other.

"Son of a bitch," Gary said, "for an old bastard you're pretty strong."

Vern said, "You're doing pitiful. It's a good thing you finished your breakfast. I wouldn't even give it to you now."


When he got Gary's arm halfway over, Vern set down his fork, picked up a few toothpicks, and held them in his left hand. He said,

"Okay, my friend, any time you want to say uncle, just quit. If you don't, I'm going to jam your hand right on these toothpicks."

Gary was straining with every muscle. He started giving karate yells. He even got half out of his seat, but it didn't make much difference. Vern got him down on the point of the toothpicks. Gary quit.

"One thing I want to know, Vern. Would you really have stuck me if I hadn't hollered uncle?"

"Yep, I told you I would, didn't I?"

"Son of a gun." Gary shook his hand.

A little later, Gary wanted to wrestle with the left arm. He lost again.

Then he tried finger wrestling. No one beat Vern at that.

"You know," Gary said, "I don't usually take a whipping very kindly."

When Vern didn't look away, Gary said, "Vern, you're all right."

Vern wasn't so sure how he felt about the whole thing.

Spencer McGrath had developed a few novel techniques in his field. He was able, for instance, to take old newspapers and produce high-quality insulation for homes and commercial buildings. At present, he was working on a plan to take in all the county garbage for recycling. He had been trying to interest people in such projects for twenty years. Now, the field had begun to open up. Just two and a half years ago, Devon Industries in Orem arranged with Spencer McGrath to transfer his operation from Vancouver, Washington, to Utah County.

Spencer had fifteen people in his employ. They were engaged in building the machinery he would need to fulfill his contract with Devon Industries. It was a large contract and McGrath was working very hard. He knew it had become one of those times in a man's life when he could advance his career and his finances ten years in two years. Or he could fail, and have gained very little beyond the knowledge of how hard he could work.

So his social activities were minimal. Seven days a week, he worked from seven in the morning into the night. Once in a while, in the late spring, he would go water-skiing in Utah Lake, or have friends over for a barbecue, but for days in a row he wouldn't even get home in time to see the ten o'clock news on TV.

Maybe he could have gotten away with less work, but it was Spencer's idea that you gave the time that was necessary to each person who came before you in the day. So it was natural that he not only kept an eye on Gilmore after he hired him, but talked to him quite a bit, and so far as he could see, nobody was trying to downgrade him in any way. The men knew, of course, that he was an ex-con—Spencer thought it was only fair to them (and to Gary for that matter) to have it known—but they were a good crew. If anything, this kind of knowledge could work in Gilmore's favor.

Yet it was all of a week before Spencer McGrath learned that Gary was walking to work whenever he couldn't hitch a ride, and he only found out because there had been some snow that morning and Gilmore came in late. It had taken him longer to walk all the way.

That got to Spencer. Gilmore had never told a soul. Such pride was the makings of decent stuff. McGrath made sure he had a ride home that night.

Later that day, they had a little talk. Gilmore wasn't real anxious to get into the fact that he didn't have a car while most people did. That got to Spencer too. He thought that with another paycheck or two, he could take Gary to Val J. Conlin, a used-car dealer he knew. Conlin sold cars for a little down and small weekly payments thereafter. Gilmore seemed to be appreciative of this conversation.

Next day, Gary asked Spencer if he was serious about the car. He wanted to know if they could go down that afternoon and look at one.

At V. J. Motors, there was a 6-cylinder '66 Mustang that seemed to be pretty clean. The tires were fair, the body was good. Spencer thought it was a reasonable proposition. The car sat on the lot for $795, but the dealer said he would move it at five and a half for Spence. It beat walking.

So that Friday when Gary got paid, Spencer took him back to the car lot and it was arranged that Gary would put up $50, Spencer McGrath would add another $50 against future salary, and Val Conlin would carry the rest of it in bi-weekly $50 payments. Since Gary was getting $140 a week and taking home $95 of that, the deal could be considered functional.

Wednesday, he picked up the Mustang after work. That night, to celebrate, he had an arm-wrestling contest with Rikki Baker at Sterling's house. Rikki tried pretty hard, but Gary won and kept bragging it up through the poker game.

Rikki felt embarrassed at losing and stayed away. When, a few days later, he dropped in again, it was to hear that his sister Nicole had gone to visit Sterling one evening, and Gary had been there. Nicole and Gary ended up with each other that night. Now, they were staying out in Spanish Fork. His sister Nicole, who always had to go her own way, was living with Gary Gilmore.

Rikki didn't like the news one bit. Nicole was the best thing in his family as far as he was concerned. He told Sterling that if Gary did anything to hurt her, he would kill him.

Yet when Rikki saw them together, he realized that Nicole liked the guy a lot. Gary came over to Rikki and said, "Man, you've got the most beautiful sister in the world. She's just the best person I ever met." Gary and Nicole held hands like they were locked together at the wrist. It was all different from what Rikki had expected.

Sunday morning, Gary brought Nicole over to meet Spencer and Marie McGrath. Spencer saw a very good-looking girl, hell of a figure, not too tall, with a full mouth, a small nose, and nice long brown hair. She must have been nineteen or twenty and looked full of her own thoughts. She was wearing Levi's that had been cut off at the thigh, a T-shirt, and no shoes. It sounded like a baby was crying in her car, but she made no move to go back.

Gary was immensely proud of her. He acted as if he had just walked in with Marilyn Monroe. They were sure getting along in supergood shape. "Look at my girl!" Gary was all but saying. "Isn't she fabulous?"

When they left, Spencer said to Marie, "That's just about what Gary needs. A girl friend with a baby to feed. It doesn't look like she'll be too much of an asset to him." He squinted after their car. "My God, did he paint his Mustang blue? I thought it was white."

"Maybe it's her car."

"Same year and model?"

"Wouldn't surprise me a bit," said Marie.

Brenda wasn't too happy when he brought Nicole to her house. Oh, God, Brenda said to herself, Gary *would* end up with a space cadet.

Nicole just sat there and looked at her. She had a little girl by the arm and didn't seem to know the arm was there. The child, a tough-looking four-year-old, looked to be living in one world and Nicole in another.

Brenda asked, "Where are you staying?"

Nicole roused herself. "Yeah." She roused herself again. "Down the road," she said in a soft and somewhat muffled voice.

Brenda must have been on radar. "Springville?" she asked. "Spanish Fork?"

Nicole gave an angelic smile. "Hey, Spanish Fork, she got it," she said to Gary as if little wonders grew like flowers on the highway of life.

"Don't you love her looks?" Gary said.

"Yeah," said Brenda, "you got yourself a looker."

Yeah, thought Brenda, another girl who pops a kid before she's fifteen and lives on the government ever after. One more poverty-stricken welfare witch. Except she had to admit it. Nicole *was* a looker. Star quality for these parts.

My God, she and Gary were in a trance with each other. Could sit and google at one another for the entire day. Don't bother to visit. Brenda was ready to ask the fire department to put out the burn.

"She's nineteen, you know," Gary said the moment Nicole stepped away.

"You don't say," said Brenda.

"Do you think she is too old for me?" he asked. At the look on his cousin's face, he began to laugh.

"No," said Brenda, "quite frankly I think you are both of the same intellectual and mental level of maturity. Good God, Gary, she's young enough to be your daughter. How can you mess around with a kid?"

"I feel nineteen," he told her.

"Why don't you try growing up before you get too old?"

"Hey, coz, you're blunt," said Gary.

"Don't you agree it's the truth?"

"Probably," he said. He muttered it.

They were sitting on the patio blinking their eyes in the sun when Nicole came back. Just as if nothing had been said in her absence, Gary pointed tenderly to the tattoo of a heart on his forearm.

When he had stepped out of Marion, a month ago, he said, it had been a blank heart. Now the space was filled with Nicole's name. He had tried to match the blue-black color of the old tattoo, but her name appeared in blue-green. "Like it?" he asked Brenda.

"Looks better than having a blank," she said.

"Well," said Gary, "I was just waiting to fill it in. But first I had to find me a lady like this."

Nicole also had a tattoo. On her ankle. GARY, it said.

"How do you like it?" he asked.

Johnny replied, "I don't."

Nicole was grinning from ear to ear. It was as if the best way to ring her bell was to tell the truth. Something about the sound set off chimes in her. "Oh," she said, extending her ankle for all the world to see the curve of her calf and the meat of her thigh, "I think it looks kinda nice."

"Well, it's done," said Brenda, "with a nice steady touch. But a tattoo on a woman's ankle looks like she stepped in shit."

"I dig it," said Gary.

"Okay," said Brenda, "I'll give you my good opinion. I like that tattoo about as much as I like that silly-ass hat you wear."

"Don't you like my lid?"

"Gary, when it comes to hats, you've got the rottenest taste I've ever seen." She was so mad she was ready to cry.

Less than a week ago, he had come over to apologize for how he had acted in the movie theatre, came over all decked out in beige slacks and a nice tan shirt, but wearing a white Panama hat with a wide rainbow band. That hat wouldn't even have looked happy on a black pimp, and Gary wore it with the brim tilted down in front and up in back like the Godfather might wear it. He'd stood outside on her mat, his body slouched, his hands in his pockets, and kicked the base of the door.

"Why don't you just lift the latch?" Brenda had asked in greeting.

"I can't," he'd said, "my hands are in my pockets," and waited for her to applaud the effect.

"It's a pretty hat," Brenda said, "but it doesn't fit your personality. Not unless you've turned into a procurer."

"Brenda, you're rotten," he'd said, "you're really ignorant." His whole posture was gone.

She had done it to him again. It didn't strike him well that she didn't like Nicole's tattoo any more than his hats. He got up to leave then, and Brenda walked them to the door. Coming outside, she was also surprised by the sight of the pale blue Mustang.

That was enough to restore him. Didn't it have to be fantastic, he told her. He and Nicole had both bought exactly the identical model and year. It was a sign.

She was in all wrong sorts the rest of the day. Kept thinking of the tattoo on Nicole's ankle. Every time she did, her uneasiness returned.

One day he came home with water skis and that bothered Nicole. It just wasn't worth the risk. He was stealing something he probably couldn't sell for more than $25, yet the price tag was over $100. That meant they could get you for felony. Nicole hated such dumb habits. He would take a chance on all they had for twenty-five bucks. It came over her that this was the first time she ever disliked him.

As if he sensed it, he then told her the worst story she ever heard. It was supergross. Years ago, while still a kid, he pulled off a robbery with a guy who was a true sadist. The manager of the supermarket was there alone after closing and wouldn't give the combination to the safe. So his friend took the guy upstairs, heated a curling iron, and rammed it.

She couldn't help herself. She laughed. The story got way in. She had a picture of that fat supermarket manager trying to hold on to the money and the poker going up his ass. Her laughter reached to the place where she hated people who had a lot of things and acted hot shit about it.

—

For the first time she had a day when she thought she shouldn't be living with Gary so much. A part of her simply didn't like staying that close to a man for so long a stretch, but as soon as she realized how she felt, Nicole knew she couldn't tell him. He expected their souls to breathe together. More and more, however, an old ugly feeling was coming back. It was the way she got when she had to fit herself to somebody. You could put that off only so long. She still felt better with Gary than with anyone else, but that wasn't going to change the fact that when she got into a bad mood, it was like she had two souls, and one of them loved Gary a lot less than the other. Of course, maybe a part of him was the same way. He couldn't be loving her that much when they got into one of those five-hour deals.

This night, from seven to midnight, Nicole and Gary argued first about the water skis, then everything else. Finally she convinced Gary she wasn't going to fuck him. He had gone too far on uppers, downers, and around-ers. If she had a gift, Gary was not exactly bringing it out. Not with his demands to do this, do that. Suck him now. She looked at Gary across their bodies and said, "I hate sucking cock."

The Fiorinal had put a glaze on his eyes, but her words still hit. He took off. Left at midnight and didn't come back until 2 A.M. He was hardly through the door when he was asking her to suck him all over again.

Why? she asked. Like a dunce. Do it because I want you to, he said. It was as bad as the first night. They didn't get to sleep till five. At five-thirty, Gary was up like a maniac, ready for work.

Between midnight and two, Gary had been to see Spencer and Marie. When McGrath opened the door, Gary asked if he and Marie would like to play three-hand poker.

Marie was already in bed, but she got up and made a cup of coffee. The McGraths, however, did not want to play poker. Not after midnight. Spencer kept himself from saying, "It's a little rude to come by this late."

Next morning, before they were even straightened out on the

job, Gary was asking if anybody'd like to buy a pair of water skis. One fellow came up to Spence to inquire if Gary might have stolen them. Spence asked, "Are they brand-new?" Couldn't believe Gary had ripped off water skis. A man might slip cufflinks or a watch into his pocket, but how did you steal those big slats right out of a store?

Spencer looked upon himself as a real simple character, but he was beginning to wonder if Gary was taking marijuana on the job or something. He sure looked awful this morning.

"Gary," Spence said, "let's get down to something basic. Every week you're broke. Why don't you take the money you spend on beer and save it?" Gary said, "I don't pay for beer." "Well, then who in hell gives it to you?" Gary said, "I just walk in a store and take a six-pack."

Spence said, "Nobody catches you, huh?" "No." "How long you been doing that?" "Weeks." Spencer said, "Steal a six-pack of beer every day and never been caught?" Gary said, "Never." Spencer said, "I don't know. How come people get caught and you don't?" Gary said, "I'm better than they are."

"I think you're pulling my leg," said Spencer.

Gary proceeded to tell about the black convict he had stabbed fifty-seven times. Now Spencer thought Gary was trying to impress him with how tough he was, see if he would scare. "Come on, Gary," he said, "fifty-seven times sounds like a variety of soup."

After they finished laughing, Gary broke it to Spence. He'd like to get off early on Friday.

"I don't know if you've noticed," said Spence, "but the other fellows don't take off. They work all day, and take care of things after hours. That's how it's normally done."

Still, he gave him the time. One more time. Spence felt a little uneasy. After all, the government, with the ex-convicts' program, was paying half of Gary's $3.50 an hour. It could account for why Gary was giving him half an hour on the hour.

Gary dropped in on Val Conlin. The beer he brought was ice cold. After a run-in for not paying on time, Gary made a practice of bringing a six-pack when he went by. Val was appreciative.

—

Gary had his eye on a truck. The one on the lot that was painted white.

"Buddy," said Val, "pay off the Mustang and I'll get you something better."

"I got to have that truck."

"No can do without mucho mazuma," said Val. The truck was up for sale at $1,700. "Listen, pardner, unless you come back with a co-signer, it's too good a truck for you."

Gary thought he could. Maybe his Uncle Vern.

"I know Vern," said Val, "and I don't think he's in shape for this kind of credit. But, if you want, have him fill out the application. We can always see what we can do."

"Okay," said Gary, "okay." He hesitated. "Val," he said, "that Mustang is no good. I had to put a new battery in, and an alternator. It came to fifty dollars."

"What do you want me to do?"

"Well, if I buy the truck, I think you could allow for what I had to lay out on the Mustang."

"Gary, you buy the truck, and we'll knock that fifty dollars off. No problem. Just get a co-signer."

"Val, I don't need a co-signer. I can make the payments."

"No co-signer, no truck. Pardner, let's keep it simple."

"The goddamn Mustang isn't any good."

"Gary, I'm doing you the favor. If you don't want the Mustang, leave the son of a bitch right out there."

"I want the truck."

"The only way you get the truck is by putting a lot of money on the front end of the loan. Or come in with a co-signer. Here, take this credit application to Vern."

Gary sat across the desk, looking out the window at the white truck on the end of the line. It was as white as the snow you could still see on the peak of the mountains.

"Gary, fill out the application and bring it back."

Val knew it. Gary was madder than hell. He didn't say a word, just took the application, got up, walked out the door, wadded it up, and threw it on the ground.

Harper, Val's salesman, said, "Boy, he's hot."

"I don't give a shit," said Val. Around him, people got hot. That was run of the mill. Just his hell-of-a-success-story boiling away.

———

In the middle of making love that night, Gary called Nicole, Pardner. She took it wrong. Thought he was jiving at her. But as he tried to explain later, he often called men and women alike by Buddy or Pal, Pardner, things like that.

In the morning, it was the Mustang. His car would not start. It was as if something in Gary's makeup killed off the electrical system every morning.

Kathryne was getting quite an impression of Gary. It began one day around lunchtime when he came knocking on her door. It startled her. He was so covered with insulating material that he looked like a man who had clawed his way out of the earth.

He had dropped by, he told her, to take a look at the room she wanted done. Kathryne just about remembered that the time Nicole had brought him over to meet her, there was a conversation about insulating the back room. Fine, Kathryne told him now, fine. She wanted to get rid of Gary fast.

Well, he took the look and said he'd have to talk to a boy who worked with him. Then they'd give the estimate. Kathryne said that was real nice. Sure enough, he was back that same afternoon with a kid of eighteen, who figured the job at $60. She said she'd think about it.

Three days later, at lunchtime, there was Gary in the doorway again. Talking fast. Said, I thought I'd come and have a beer with you. Got some beer? Gee, she didn't, said Kathryne, just coffee. Well, he told her, I'll come in anyway. Got something to eat?

She said she could make him a sandwich. That was okay. He would run down and get a six-pack. Kathryne just looked at her kid sister, Kathy.

Ten minutes later, he was back with the beer. While she fixed the sandwiches, he started talking. What a conversation. If the first time he came to her house he never opened his mouth, now, right off, he told Kathryne and Kathy that he had stolen the six-pack. Wanted to know if they might need cigarettes. No, she said, she had plenty. How about beer? he inquired. Seldom drink it, very seldom.

The day before he had gone in the store, he said, picked up a case, walked out, and was setting it in his trunk when a kid not old enough to drink asked if Gary would buy him a case, and handed over five bucks. Gary started to laugh. "I walked in, picked up the kid's beer, walked out, gave it to him, and took off with the cash."

They were careful to laugh. Weren't you afraid? they asked. No, said Gary, act like you own the place.

He started telling stories. One after another. They couldn't believe him. Told of a fellow he hit over the head with a hammer, and he stabbed a nigger fifty-seven times. He'd look at them carefully, say, Now did you understand that? His voice got gruff.

They would put on a smile. Gary, the ladies would say, that's something else, you know. They got themselves to laugh. Kathryne didn't know if she was more afraid for Nicole or herself. About the time he'd stayed an hour and a half, she asked if he wouldn't be late getting back to work.

To hell with the job, said Gary. If they didn't like it over at the job, they knew what they could do. Then he told about a friend of his who gave it to the manager of a supermarket with a hot curling iron.

All the while, he watched them real close. He had to see their reaction. They felt they better have a reaction.

Weren't you afraid, Gary? they would ask. Didn't you think somebody would catch you?

He did a lot of boasting. Sounded like he was banging along in a boat from rock to rock. When he left, he thanked them for being so sociable.

—

Nicole heard about the lunch. There was a piece of him, she decided, that liked to tell crazy stories to grown-ups. It must have gotten locked in at the age of eight.

—

Then she wondered if he was a magnet to evil spirits. Maybe he had to act that nasty to keep things off. The idea didn't cheer her. He could get meaner and meaner if that was the truth.

Around midnight, Nicole was feeling awfully cooped up with Gary. She found herself thinking of other guys. It kept working away in her.

All the while she was having these thoughts, Gary had been sitting at her feet. Now he had to pick this moment to look up with all the light of love shining in his eyes. "Baby," he said, "I really love you all the way and forever." She looked back. "Yeah," she said, "and so do seven other motherfuckers."

Gary hit her. It was the first time, and he hit her hard. She didn't feel the pain so much as the shock and then the disappointment. It always ended the same way. They hit you when they felt like it.

Soon enough, he apologized. He kept apologizing. But it did no good. She had been hit so fucking many times. The kids were in bed, and she looked at Gary and said, "I want to die." It was how she felt. He kept trying to make up. Finally, she told him that she had felt like dying before but never did anything about it. Tonight, she wouldn't mind.

Gary got a knife and held the point to her stomach. He asked her if she still wanted to die.

It was frightening that she wasn't more afraid. After a few minutes, she finally said, "No, I don't," but she had been tempted. After he put the knife away, she even felt trapped. She couldn't believe the size of the bad feeling that came down on her then.

They had one more marathon. Up all night about whether to fuck. In the middle, around midnight, he took off. Not too long later, he came in with a bunch of boxes. There was a pistol in every box.

She got over it a little. She had to. The guns hung around.

Sterling Baker had a birthday party the last Sunday afternoon in June, and the party went on in Sterling's apartment and out in the backyard, fifteen or twenty good people. A lot brought bottles. Nicole had cut-offs on, and a halter top, and knew she was looking good. Gary was sure showing her off. A couple of dudes began to tell Gary what a hot lady he had. Gary would say, "Know it," and grab her by both breasts, or pull her into his lap.

Well, it was Sterling's birthday, and Nicole still had this little crush on her cousin. So Nicole started kidding him about a birthday kiss and Sterling said he'd take her up on it. She asked Gary if it was okay. He gave her a look, but she went and sat on Sterling's lap anyway. Gave him a long kiss that would tell a lot about her.

When she opened her eyes, Gary was sitting with no expression on his face. He said, "Had enough?"

They were keeping a keg of beer out in the back. The fellow upstairs had also invited his friends, and one of them was a guy called Jimmy, a Chicano. He picked up a pair of sunglasses that Sterling had laid on the roof of a broken-down old car out in the back lot while he was tapping a keg. Nicole figured maybe Jimmy didn't know. Just picked them up. Only thing, the glasses were a present from Gary to Sterling.

Gary came on strong. "I want them glasses back," he told Jimmy, "they're mine." Jimmy got kind of upset and left. Nicole started shrieking. "You're fucking up the party," she shouted at Gary. "All this horseshit over a stupid pair of glasses."

Jimmy came back to the party with a couple of friends. As soon as he walked in the yard, Gary was on his feet and heading toward him. They were throwing fists before you could stop it.

Maybe Gary was too drunk, but Jimmy split his eye with the first punch. Blood was running all over Gary's face. He got hit again and went down to his knees, got back up and started swinging.

About that time, everybody broke the fight up. Sterling walked Jimmy around the front of the house and got him to leave. Just as Jimmy was walking off, Gary came up holding a gear knob that he'd taken off the beat-up car in the backyard. Sterling stepped in front of him. "Gary, you're through with that, you're not going to hit him," he said. Just talking in a normal tone of voice. But he had a big fellow standing next to him to back what was said. Nicole got Gary out and took him home.

She hated to see her man have his ass whipped. Especially when he started it. She thought he was a fool all the way.

He wanted to go back and find Jimmy. By keeping her mouth shut about how disappointed she was in his fighting, she managed to get him to Spanish Fork. She had hardly ever known a guy who hated to lose a rumble as much as Gary. That softened her feelings somewhat. After all, he had taken a beating from a very tough dude, and hadn't quit.

After she washed him off, Nicole discovered that the cut was bad. So she took him next door to her neighbor Elaine, who had just gotten through taking this emergency course on being an ambulance driver, and Elaine said he definitely needed stitches. Nicole started to worry. She had heard that oxygen in the air could enter a cut near the eye, go right to the brain, and kill you. So she did take him to the doctor. Through the rest of the night she kept ice packs on his face and babied him, and kind of enjoyed it, considering how things had been lately. In the morning, when he tried to blow his nose, his cheeks blew up right around his glands and sinuses.

Spencer said, "Gary, it doesn't make much sense putting your body up to be abused."

"They can't hurt me," said Gary.

"Oh, no? Your eye is cut and it's turning black, and you've got a lump on your forehead and he gave you a good one on the nose. Don't stand there and put that stuff on me, Gary. I just can't believe you keep getting the best of these deals."

Gary said, "I sure did, you know."

Spencer said, "What's going to happen one night is some little guy about five foot six"—which was around Spencer's height—"is going to stuff a mudhole right in the middle of your face. Because that's what happens. A guy doesn't have to be seven feet tall to be mean."

"I'm Gary Gilmore," Gilmore said, "and they can't hurt me."

In the evening, driving around with Nicole and Sunny and Peabody, he stopped at V. J. Motors to talk to Val Conlin about the truck. Even got to take it out for an hour. Gary was that happy up high behind the wheel with something like a real motor in front of them. All the while she could feel him thinking of the guns. They were shining like $$$ in his eyes.

When he got back, he talked to Val about the size of a down payment. Nicole was hardly listening. It was boring to sit in the showroom with all the freaks and deadbeats who were waiting to get some piece of a car. One girl was wearing a turban and had a big swipe of eyeshadow under each eye, and her blouse just about pulling out of her belt. She said to Nicole, "You have very beautiful eyes." "Thank you," said Nicole.

Gary kept repeating himself like a record with a scratch. "I don't want that Mustang," he said to Val.

"Then let's get closer to the truck, buddy. We're not near it. Come in with a co-signer or with money."

Gary stalked away. Nicole hardly had time to gather the kids and follow. Outside the showroom, Gary was swearing like Val had never heard him swear before. Through the showroom window Val could see the Mustang, and it wouldn't start. Gary sat there pounding the wheel as hard as he could.

"Jesus," said Harper, "this time, he is really hot."

"I don't give a shit," said Val, and walked through the people sitting around with their debts on different cars. Yeah, I'm right on top of the mountain, thought Val, and went outside and said to Gary, "What's the matter?"

"This son of a bitch," said Gary, "this goddamn car."

"Well, now, hold it. Let's get some jumper cables, we'll get it started," and, of course Val did, just needed the boost, and Gary took off in a spray of gravel like he had a switch to his hind end.

By the following night, Gary had a guy who would sell the guns. But they had to meet him. That meant carrying the guns in the car. Gary didn't have a license and her Mustang still had last year's license plates. Both cars had the crappy kind of look a State Trooper would pull over for nothing. So they had quite an argument before they finally put the pistols in her trunk and started out. They brought the kids along. The kids might be insurance against a State Trooper waving them over for too little.

On the other hand, Sunny and Jeremy made her awfully aware of his driving tonight. That definitely got Nicole nervous. He finally swung into the Long Horn Cafe, a taco joint between Orem and Pleasant Grove, to make a phone call. Only he couldn't get ahold of the guy who was to peddle the guns. Gary was getting more and more upset. It looked like the evening was going to get totally squandered. A sweet early summer night.

He came back out of the Long Horn and looked in the car for another phone number, then started tearing pages out of the book. By the time he finally found the number, his guy was out. Sunny and Jeremy were beginning to make a lot of noise. Next thing she knew, Gary spun out of the Long Horn and headed back toward Orem. He was going 80. She was petrified for the kids. Told him to pull over.

He slammed to the shoulder. A screeching halt. He turned around, and started spanking the kids. They hadn't even been making a sound the last minute. Too scared of the speed.

She started hitting Gary right there, hit him with her fists as hard as she could, hollered for him to let her out of the car. He grabbed her hands to hold her down, and then the kids started screaming. Gary wouldn't let her out. Then this really dumb-looking guy walked by. She must have sounded as if Gary was killing her, but the fucker just stopped and said, "Anything wrong?" Then walked on.

Nicole wouldn't stop hollering. Gary finally wedged her into the space between the bucket seats and got his hand over her mouth. She was trying not to pass out. He had his other hand on her throat to hold her down. She couldn't breathe. He told her then that he would let her go if she promised to be quiet and go home. Nicole mumbled, Okay. It was the best she could get out. The moment he let go, she started yelling. When his hand came back to her mouth, she bit real hard into the flesh near his thumb. Tasted the blood.

Somehow, she didn't know how, she got out of the car. She couldn't remember later if he let her go, or if she just got away. Maybe he let her go. She ran across the street to the middle of the highway divider, a kid in each hand, and started walking. She would hitchhike.

Gary began to follow on foot. At first he let her try to bum a ride, but a car almost stopped for her, and so Gary tried to pull her back to the Mustang. She wouldn't budge. He got smart and tried to yank one of the kids away. She wouldn't let loose, hung on with all she had. Between them, it must have been stretching the kids. Finally a pickup truck pulled over and a couple of guys came over with a chick.

The girl happened to be an old friend Nicole hadn't seen in a year. Pepper, her first girl friend ever. Yet, Nicole couldn't even think of the last name, she was that upset.

Gary said, "Get out of here, this is a family matter." Pepper looked at Gary, just as tall as she could be, and said, "We know Nicole, and you ain't family." That was all of it. Gary let go and walked up the street toward her car. Nicole got the kids into the truck with Pepper, and they took off. The moment she remembered how once she had wanted everything to be good for Gary, she started crying. Nicole couldn't help it. She cried.

Nicole spent the night at her great-grandmother's house, where he would never think of looking for her. In the morning, she went back to her mother's, and Gary called not long after, and said he was coming over. Nicole was scared. She put in a call to the police, and, in fact, was talking to the dispatcher when Gary walked in. So she said into the phone, "Man, get them out here as fast as you can."

She didn't know if Gary had come to drag her away. But he just stood at the kitchen sink. She told him to go away and leave her alone, and he just kept looking at her. He had a look as if everything inside him hurt, man, really hurt. Then he said, "You fight as good as you fuck."

She was trying hard not to smile, but, in fact, it made her a little less afraid of him. He came over and put his hands on her shoulders. Again, she told him to leave. To her surprise, he turned around and went. He practically passed the cops as they were coming in.

By afternoon, she regretted not letting him stay. She was really afraid he would not come back. A voice in her head kept sounding like an echo in a tunnel. It said, "I love him, I love him."

He showed up after work with a carton of cigarettes and a rose. She couldn't help but smile. She went on the porch to meet him, and he handed her a letter.

*Dear Nicole,*
*I don't know why I did this to myself. You are the most beautiful thing I've ever seen and touched . . .*
*You just loved me and touched my soul with a wondrous tenderness and you treated me so kindly.*
*I just couldn't handle that. There's no bullshit or meanness about you and I couldn't deal with an honest spirit like yours that didn't want to hurt me . . .*

After she read the letter, they sat on the porch for a while. Didn't say too much. Then Nicole went in and got the kids, picked up their diapers, and left with him.


# June          The Guns

Gary had gone drinking at Fred's Lounge with a couple of heavies in the Sundowners and now he was talking of getting a motorcycle. Told them he was going to rip one off. Then he looked kind of sheepishly at Nicole. Admitted they had almost laughed out loud at him. The one thing, they explained, a cop always looked over was a *motorcycle!* A hot motorcycle lasted about as long as an ice cube in your ass. Still, they were real dudes—equal to himself. He looked forward, he said, to doing business with them.

He was like a nineteen-year-old kid. Into bikes. Happy that bikers liked him. It softened her enough for things to get sweet again. So they started to get it on. Then Gary had a time getting it up. She couldn't think of how she had once been so sure it would improve.

Gary always put the blame on prison. All those years he had to get his rocks off on nude pictures instead of learning on a real woman.

She got mad enough tonight to tell him it was bullshit. He was drinking too much, using Fiorinal too much. Gary defended the Fiorinal. "I don't want to make love with a headache," he said. "I have headaches all the time, and Fiorinal relieves it."

She sat there with her anger pushed in like a spring. Dead and wet, he was going to give it a go. Don't start what you can't finish, she told him. Be straight.

The work began. Now they wouldn't get to bed till four, and he'd be up at six. Then he took some speed, and it took effect. He got hard as a horn and wanted to fuck. She was so tired she could only think of sleep. But they were doing it. On and on. He couldn't come.

Lying there, she said it clearly to herself, "He's a bad package." She could feel a lot of ugliness collecting in her.

Next day, she was able to let some of it out. Since she didn't always have money for diapers or laundry soap and there wasn't always clean underwear, she liked to let the kids play naked in the summer. Some of the neighbors must have gotten uptight.

On this day, while Jeremy was on the grass of somebody's lawn, and the rest of the kids were sitting on the edge of the ditch between the sidewalk and the street, their feet in the water, a cop car pulled up and hollered something. Nicole couldn't believe what she was seeing. The cop drove no faster than a walking pace right up to her house, and came to her door, and started laying down some unbelievable shit, like you know, your kids are in danger of their lives playing in the ditch down there. Your little boy could drown. Nicole said, "Mister, you don't know what you're talking about. My little boy wasn't anywhere near that water. He doesn't have one drop on his body." He didn't.

The cop started to say the neighbors had been phoning in complaints about her not taking proper care of the kids. "Get off my property," said Nicole, "get your fucking ass down the road."

She knew she could say anything so long as she stayed in her house. The cop stood outside making threats about welfare, and she shut the door in his face. He hollered, I better not see those kids outside. She swung the door open again.

Nicole said, "Those kids are going to play outside all the god-damn day, and you better not touch them, or I'll shoot you."

The cop looked at her. He had an expression like, "Now what do I do?" In the middle of her anger, she could see his side—it was such a crazy situation for a cop. Threatened by a lady. Then she closed the door, and he drove off, and Gary got up from bed. These hot days the bed had been moved up right by the living-room window.

Suddenly she realized what those last couple of minutes must have done to him. She had completely forgotten about the guns. The sight of that cop stopping at their house was going to add up to a lot more beer and Fiorinal.

Next morning, he was over at Kathryne's house. She thought he was real abrupt. "Come outside," he said. Kathryne felt scared. "Can't you tell me here?" "No," he said, "outside."

She didn't like the way he was acting, but it was daylight. So she went out and Gary said, "I've got something in my car I want to leave here for a little while," and he went over to the Mustang and took a di-aper bag out of the trunk and moved it over to the back of her car. Kathryne said, "What have you got, Gary?" and he answered, "Guns."

"Guns?" she said. "Yes," he said, "guns." She asked where he got them. "Where do you think? I stole them." Kathryne just said, "Oh." Right there on the back deck of her car he started bringing them out for examination. "I'd like," said Gary, "to leave them here." "My God, Gary," said Kathryne, "I don't think you better. I can't keep them here."

"I'll be back," Gary said, "when I get off work. I just want to leave them in a safe place for a little while."

She couldn't believe the way he had set them out on the trunk of the car. If any of the neighbors looked through the window, they wouldn't believe what they were seeing.

Deliberately, he took each gun and described it to her like it was a rare beauty. One was a .357 Magnum this-or-that, another was a .22

Automatic Browning, then a Dan Weston .38 something-or-other. Kathryne just said, "Gary, I don't know much about guns."

"How do you like this one?" he asked.

"Oh, they're nice, they're all nice, you know." She said, "What are you going to do with them, Gary?"

"A couple of dudes are going to buy them," he said.

By now, all the guns were unwrapped. He said, "I gave Nicole one to protect herself. Pretty little over-and-under Derringer. I want you to have this one."

"I don't need it, Gary. I really don't want it."

"I want you to," he said. "You're Nicole's mother."

"God, Gary," said Kathryne, "I've already got a gun."

"Well," he said, "I want you to have this Special. It's just not safe for two women living out here alone like you and your sister."

She tried to explain that she already had her husband's Magnum. But Gary said, "That's too big a gun. You shouldn't even attempt to shoot it."

Now he laid the guns in her car trunk. Kathryne let him know that she definitely didn't want to be driving around with them. So he said, "Let me leave them in the house." Told her he'd return at five o'clock. Well, she declared, she wouldn't be home then.

That was all right, he'd just come and get them. With that, he carried the diaper bag into the house, and put the guns behind the couch, all seven or eight of them. Then he wrapped the Special in an old cloth, and put it under her bedroom mattress.

That evening when she and Kathy got home, they ran to look behind the couch and yes, the guns were gone.

Gary came home in a sloppy old windbreaker with the sleeves cut off. His pants were a mess, and he was half drunk. He told her to go over with him to Val Conlin's to examine the truck. She asked him to get cleaned up first. She didn't really want to be seen with him. He looked as if he had slept out in the yard.

Gary kept talking to that man Conlin as if he had the money. It was a real irritant. Then on the way back, Gary started to tee off on Val

Conlin for making him wait on the truck. "I'll wreck the place and a couple of his cars too," he said. "I'm going to kick them windows in." It was like opening a bottle that smelled awful.

Then, darn if the Mustang didn't stall again. Gary got so pissed he broke the windshield.

Simply reared back with his feet and kicked the windshield. It cracked.

That got the kids upset. Nicole didn't say two words. She got out and helped him push the car to get it started. It still didn't go. Then somebody came along to give them a shove. They drove in silence for a couple hundred yards.

For a week she had been trying to say that they could live in separate places and see each other time to time. Now, when it came to it, Gary spoke. "I'm taking you to your mother's house," he said, "I don't want to ever see your face again."

He dropped her off with the kids as easily as going down to the grocery for a six-pack. She thought she'd be glad, but she wasn't. It didn't feel like it was over in the right way.

In twelve hours, Gary showed up at Kathryne's house. Just ahead of lunch. He wanted Nicole to come back. He was drunk even as he asked her. She said she wouldn't. She said, I want to think about it awhile.

He didn't want her to think. He wanted her to agree. Still, it amazed her. He didn't force a thing. After he left, though, she decided it had been too easy. By tomorrow he would be coming over every few hours. So she called her ex-husband, Barrett, and asked if she could stay at his pad. Nicole made it clear she didn't want to hang in. Just wanted a bed for a couple of days.

If she was going to disappear from Gary, there had to be better places than Barrett's. She went looking for an apartment. The next day, Barrett found one in Springville. Hardly anyone knew the address, and she made him swear to keep it secret.

———

Now she was living five miles away from the house in Spanish Fork. If Gary took the back highway to Provo instead of the Interstate, he would pass two streets from her place.

Barrett wanted them to try one more time. One more trip of the mind. When she was young and used to read animal stories, Kathryne had told her about reincarnation. Made it sound like a fairy tale. That was when Nicole made the choice to come back as a little white bird. Now she thought that if she didn't straighten out the way she lived with men, she was going to come back ugly and no man would ever want to look at her.

# June                     Back in Jail

Nielsen brought along a briefcase on which you could flip the handle, and a tape recorder inside would start functioning unseen. He didn't dare take it, however, into the cell. Gilmore would have the right to inquire what was in that briefcase, and whether he was being recorded. Nielsen would then have to open it up. That would destroy all confidence Gilmore might have in him. So he left it turned on in the hall just on the other side of the bars. It would pick up what it could.

The county jail had to be one of the oldest buildings in Utah County. By July, it was hot enough inside to offer a free ticket to hell. With its windows open, you had to breathe the exhausts of the freeway. The prison sat on the edge of the desert in a flat field of cinders midway between the ramp that came off the freeway and the one that went up to it. The sound of traffic was loud, therefore. Since a spur of railroad track also went by, boxcars rumbled through the interview. When Nielsen tried listening to the tape recorder in his office, the sound of traffic on a hot summer evening was the clearest statement he could hear.

The detective had hopes for the interview. He felt Gilmore would talk ever since the moment right after the capture in Pleasant Grove when Gary asked for him. Nielsen had a strong feeling then that there would be a chance to get his confession. So he moved quickly and not at all unnaturally, into the role of the old friend and the good cop.

In police work, you had to play a part from time to time. Nielsen liked that. The thing is, for this role, he was supposed to show compassion. From past experience, he knew it wouldn't be altogether a role. Sooner or later, he would really feel compassion. That was all right. That was one of the more interesting sides of police work.

He had had his experiences. Years ago, when he was a patrolman, Nielsen did some undercover work in narcotics. There was a working agreement then with the Salt Lake City Police. Because Orem was still small, its police were well known to the locals. To get any effective undercover work, they had to import officers from Salt Lake City. In turn, Orem paid back the debt by sending a few of their own cops. That was how Nielsen first got into it.

His personal appearance, however, presented a problem. He had been a scoutmaster for seven or eight years and looked it. His substantial build, his early baldness, his eyeglasses and red-gold hair gave him the appearance of a businessman rather than a fellow who might be dealing in drugs. For cover, therefore, he had pretended to be a Safeway meat-cutter, a job he knew something about, since he had done a little of that while working his way through BYU. He even had a union card.

In Salt Lake City he became known for a time as the meat-cutter who was always looking for dope on the weekend. That worked. A lot of meat-cutters weren't known as the straightest people. Nielsen even used to wear working clothes that showed bloodstains on the chest of his white smock, and below the knees of his white slacks where the apron gave no protection.

On this hot July evening, Nielsen began by saying that Gilmore's story, unhappily, was full of holes. They were checking it out, but it did not add up. So he wanted to know if it would be all right if they talked. Gilmore said, "I've been charged with a capital offense, and I'm innocent, and you're all screwing up my life."

———

"Gary, I know things are serious," Nielsen said, "but I'm not screwing with anybody's life. You don't have to talk to me if you don't want to, you know that."

Gary walked away and then came back a little later and said, "I don't mind talking."

Nielsen was with Gilmore about an hour and a half. There, in a Maximum Security cell, the two of them locked in together, they spoke. Nielsen came on very light at first. "Have you seen your attorney?" he asked, and Gilmore said he had. Then Nielsen asked him how he was feeling. "How's the arm?" Gilmore said, "Hey, I'm really hurting. They only give me one pain pill, and the doctor said I was supposed to have two."

"Well," Nielsen said, "I'll tell them I heard the doctor say two."

Nielsen tried to be as easygoing as he could. He inquired if Gary liked to fish, and Gilmore answered that with the time he'd spent in jail, there just hadn't been much fishing. Nielsen began to talk a little about fly casting and Gilmore showed interest at the idea that you had to get good enough to guess under different circumstances what a trout was likely to accept in the way of a fly. The detective told him of taking overnight camping trips with his family up in the canyons.

Gilmore, in turn, talked about a few of his experiences in prison. Told of the fat girl who died, and the time they gave him too much Prolixin, and he swelled up, and couldn't move. Spoke of how prison demanded you be a man every step of the way. Then he asked a little more about Nielsen's background. He seemed interested that Nielsen had a wife and five children.

Was his wife a good Mormon? Gilmore asked. Oh, yes. He had met her at BYU where she had gone to get away from Idaho. What did she major in? asked Gilmore, as if he were truly fascinated. Nielsen shrugged. "She majored in home economics," he said. Then he grinned at Gilmore. "Her interest was to—you know, maybe, you know, kind of find a husband." Now they both laughed. Yes, said Nielsen, they had met in freshman year and were married the next summer. Well, said Gilmore, that was interesting. How did Nielsen become a cop? He didn't seem much like a cop. Well, actually, Gerald explained, he had planned on being a science and mathematics teacher when he went up to Brigham Young University from the family ranch at St. John's, Arizona, but he was an active Mormon and in his church work he met a detective on the police force whom he liked and so got interested and took a job as a patrolman.

Now he was a lieutenant, Gilmore remarked. Yes, in a little more than ten years he'd risen to be a detective, then a sergeant, now a lieutenant. He didn't say that he'd taken courses at the FBI Academy at Quantico, Virginia.

Well, that was interesting, said Gilmore. His mother had been a Mormon, too. Then he paused and shook his head. "It's going to kill my mother when she finds out." Again, he shook his head. "You know, she's crippled," said Gilmore, "and I haven't seen her for a long time."
"Gary," said Nielsen, "why did you kill those guys?"
Gilmore looked him right back in the eye. Nielsen was used to seeing hatred in a suspect's eyes, or remorse, or the kind of indifference that could lay a chill on your heart, but Gilmore had a way of looking into his eyes that made Nielsen shift inside. It was as if the man was staring all the way to the bottom of your worth. It was hard to keep the gaze.

"Hey," said Gilmore, "I don't know. I don't have a reason." He was calm when he said it, and sad. Looked like he was close to crying. Nielsen felt the sorrow of the man; felt him fill with sorrow at this moment.

"Gary," said Nielsen, "I can understand a lot of things. I can understand killing a guy who's turned on you, or killing a guy who hassles you. I can understand those kind of things, you know." He paused. He was trying to keep in command of his voice. They were close, and he wanted to keep it just there. "But I just can't understand, you know, killing these guys for almost no reason."

Nielsen knew he was taking a great many chances. If it ever came to it, he was cutting the corners on the Miranda close enough to send the whole thing up on appeal, and he was also making a mistake to keep talking about "those guys" or "why did you kill those guys?" If any of this was going to be worth a nickel in court, he should say, "Mr. Bushnell in Provo," and, "Why did you kill Max Jensen in Orem?" You couldn't send a guy to trial for killing two men on two separate nights in separate towns if you put both cases into one phrase. Legally speaking, the killings had to be separated.

Nielsen, however, was sure it would be nonproductive to question him in any more correct way. That would cut it off. So he asked, "Was it because they were going to bear witness against you?" Gilmore said, "No, I really don't know why."

"Gary," said Nielsen, "I have to think like a good policeman doing a good job. You know, if I can prevent these kinds of things from happening, that makes me successful in my work. And I would like to understand—why would you hit those places? Why did you hit the motel in Provo or the service station? Why those particular places?" "Well," said Gilmore, "the motel just happened to be next to my uncle Vern's place. I just happened on it."

"But the service station?" said Nielsen. "Why that service station in the middle of nowhere?"

"I don't know," said Gilmore. "It was there." He looked for a moment like he wished to help Nielsen. "Now you take the place where I hid that thing," he said, "after the motel." Nielsen realized he was speaking of the money tray lifted from Benny Bushnell's counter. "Well, I put the thing in that particular bush," he said, "because when I was a kid I used to mow the lawn right there for an old lady."

Nielsen was trying to think of a few Court decisions that might apply to a situation like this. A confession obtained in an interview that was conducted without the express permission of the man's attorney would not be legal. On the other hand, the suspect himself could initiate the confession. Nielsen was ready to claim that Gilmore had done just this today. After all, he had asked Gary in their first interview today at 5 A.M. if he could come back and talk to him after the story was checked out. Gilmore had not said no. With the present Supreme Court, Nielsen had the idea a confession like this might hold up.

Nevertheless, Nielsen wasn't forgetting the Supreme Court decision on the Williams case. A ten-year-old girl in Iowa had been raped and murdered by a mental patient named Williams, who had been picked up in Des Moines and taken back to the place where he was to be charged. Williams' attorney in Des Moines told the detectives trans-porting him, "Don't question him out of my presence," then told his client, "Don't make any statements to policemen." All the same, on the way back, one of the detectives accompanying the suspect started playing Williams on his Christian side. The old boy was deeply reli-gious and so the detective said: "Here we are, just a few days before Christmas, and the family of that little girl doesn't know where the body is. It sure would be nice if we could find the body and give the little girl a good Christian burial before Christmas. The family could at least have that much peace." He went on in such a low-key way that the old guy finally told them where the corpse could be found, and got convicted. The Supreme Court, however, had just overruled. They said once a guy has an attorney, the police could not interview him without permission.

Yet here he was talking to Gilmore while his attorneys were not aware of it. Still, a couple of technicalities could be argued. Gilmore had already, out on the road, in Nielsen's presence, been read his Mi-randa rights. Also, the attorneys had been appointed for the Provo case, not for Orem. He might still be, therefore, on legal ground. Be-sides, the key thing was not to get a confession but a conviction.

What would be good about a confession, even if they couldn't use it, was that it would produce information they could then employ to dig up further evidence against the guy, and get a good solid case. If they never used the confession in Court, they would have no trouble with the Miranda.

Besides, it would be good for morale. Once the police knew their man was guilty, they could feel more incentive to keep plugging hard on detail work. It would also avoid any power conflict with officers who wanted to work other leads. The confession would integrate the case, make it a psychological success.

They went through the cycle again. Nielsen talked about the Church of Jesus Christ of the Latter-Day Saints and what his kids con-tributed on family night each week. Gilmore was interested in the de-tails, and mentioned again that not only was his mother a Mormon, but all of her folks, and he talked about his father, who had been a Catholic and drank like hell, and they stayed off the real subject as if they had earned a rest.

———

Then they would get back to it. Nielsen would ask one question, then a couple of questions. So soon as Gilmore began to assume a look that said, "No more questions," Nielsen would talk of other things.

Jensen's coin changer had been missing from the service station, and the police had spent much of yesterday going through garbage at the Holiday Inn with no results. Casually, Nielsen now asked about that. Gilmore stared at him for a long time, as if to say, "I don't know whether to answer you or not. I don't know if I can trust you." Finally he muttered, "I really don't remember. I threw it out the window of the truck, but I can't recollect if it was in the drive-in or on the road." He paused as if searching into his recollection of a movie and he said, "I honestly don't remember. It could have been at the drive-in."

"Would Nicole's sister know?" Nielsen asked.

"Don't worry about April," Gilmore said. "She didn't see a thing." He shook his head. "For all practical purposes, she wasn't there."

When Nielsen began to wonder whether April had any idea of the murder, Gary repeated, "Don't worry, she didn't see a thing. In her head, that little girl was never there."

He gave a turn to his mouth that was almost a smile. "You know," he said, "if I'd been thinking as straight the last couple of nights as I am today, you guys would not have caught me. When I was a kid I used to pull off robberies . . ." He had a look on his face like a pimp bragging of the number of women who worked for him over the years. "I guess," he said, "I must have pulled off fifty or seventy, maybe even a hundred successful robberies. I knew how to plan something and do it right."

Nielsen then asked him if he would have gone on killing if he hadn't been caught. Gilmore nodded. He thought he probably would have. He sat there for a minute and looked amazed. Not amazed, but certainly surprised, and said, "God, I don't know what the hell I'm doing. I've never confessed to a cop before." Nielsen thought he probably hadn't. His record was certainly hard-core all the way. Egotistically speaking, Nielsen felt bolstered. He had gotten a confession out of a hard-core criminal.

"How many guns did you steal?" Nielsen asked. "Nine," Gilmore told him. "Where did they come from?" "Spanish Fork." "Then we've recovered all but three." That left three unaccounted for. Where might they be? "They're gone," said Gilmore. Nielsen didn't bother to follow up. The way Gilmore said that made it obvious they had been sold, and he would never tell who he sold them to. "I'm responsible," said Gilmore. "Don't blame other people."

Then he asked, "Did Nicole tell you about her gun?" "No," Nielsen said, "I asked her." Gary said, "I don't want her to get in any trouble about those guns." Nielsen assured him.

Nielsen tried to get a few more facts about the homicides themselves. Gilmore would give details up to the point where he entered the service station and then he would talk of everything after he left. But he did not wish to describe the crime itself.

Nielsen was trying to determine what went on during the act. Gilmore had asked Jensen to lie on the floor. He must then have told him to put his arms beneath his body. No one would ever be found lying face down in such an uncomfortable position of their own choice. Next Gilmore had fired the shots right into Jensen's head. First with the pistol two inches away, then with the pistol touching. It was the surest way to kill a man and cause him no suffering. On the other hand, ordering those arms to stay under the body was the surest way to be certain the victim didn't grab your leg as you were putting the muzzle to his head. He could not, however, get Gilmore to talk about this.

"Why'd you do it, Gary?" Nielsen asked again quietly.
"I don't know," Gary said.
"Are you sure?"
"I'm not going to talk about that," Gilmore said. He shook his head delicately, and looked at Nielsen, and said, "I can't keep up with life."

Then he asked, "What do you think they'll do to me?"
Nielsen said, "I don't know. It is very serious."

"I'd like to be able to talk to Nicole," Gilmore said. "I've been looking for her and I'd really like to talk to her."
"Hey," Nielsen said, "I'll do anything I can to get her here." They shook hands.

—

About five o'clock that afternoon, while Nielsen was talking to Gary, April came home. She had heard about the murders on the radio and said it wasn't true. Gary hadn't done it. She also said she wasn't going to no police station.

Charley Baker had come in from Toelle when Kathryne phoned to say April was missing. Now, so soon as April saw them together, she got hostile and began shouting that if they tried to take her to the police station by force she would call on her protection to stop them. Then, all of a sudden, she seemed to give in. Said she would go.

## July 21, 1976

NIELSEN: What time did he get gas?

APRIL: When we were at the service station in Pleasant Grove.

NIELSEN: Was it after dark?

APRIL: It was dark, it was past sundown.

NIELSEN: After that did you drive around for a while?

APRIL: He said he was taking me home and he wasn't going to put up with any of my smart-ass crap telling him where to go and he said he wanted a classy place like the Holiday Inn, so we went there and I was going to go to sleep because I was really tired. I didn't really know why, I felt like I was running from somebody—ever since somebody broke the windows in our bathroom at home, and I can't really sleep well since then.

NIELSEN: And then you stayed there for that night until what time the next morning?

APRIL: About 8:30 or 9:00.

NIELSEN: I don't mean to imply anything or to pry into your personal life, but did you sleep with him that night?

APRIL: I almost did, but I changed my mind.

NIELSEN: Did he get mad at you then?

APRIL: He was mad at me for acting like a kid half the time, but I just lost my love for him, only I never did sleep with him or anything.

NIELSEN: Did you tell your mom that?

APRIL: She didn't ask me because she knows I have my private life and if I wanted to blow it, I could . . .

NIELSEN: April, Gary is in very serious trouble. I know that, I have talked to him about it, and there is no question about it. He already told me you were with him at the time and so I know that you know about it. I am not interested in you telling me so that I can charge you. I don't intend to charge you with it, but I do intend to see that you tell the truth.

APRIL: I am a split personality. I am controlling it pretty good today. A lot of time I like to just let go and let the other person creep on out . . .

NIELSEN: Where did you go last night when you left home?

APRIL: I went riding around with a couple of friends.

NIELSEN: Did they know him?

APRIL: No.

NIELSEN: Do you mind telling me who they were?

APRIL: One is Grant and one is Joe.

NIELSEN: Where did you stay last night?

APRIL: I didn't sleep all night, rode to Wyoming, and just went in the mountains and down this road and came home.

NIELSEN: What time did you get home?

APRIL: 4:30 or 5:00.

NIELSEN: Don't you worry about your mom worrying about you?

APRIL: I don't think she worries about me. I'm not afraid of no guns and I am not afraid of no dudes with knives. They don't scare me. I have learned self-defense.

NIELSEN: I want to ask you one more time about the service station. April, I think it would be best if you tell me what you know.

APRIL: I don't remember the service station in Orem.

NIELSEN: Do you remember seeing him pull a gun at the service station?

APRIL: We went into a service station right before we went to the Holiday Inn and I am sure there were no guns attached. They may have been carrying them, but that's all.

NIELSEN: Who are "they"?

APRIL: Any of the dudes that were around.

NIELSEN: Do you know any of them?

APRIL: I recognize all of them, but I don't know some of their names. One of them works with him at the insulation place.

NIELSEN: Insulation?

APRIL: Where he works at the Ideal Insulation. I am pretty sure it was the friend we visited.

NIELSEN: At the cafe?

APRIL: It may not have been.

NIELSEN: Are you about ready to go back home?

APRIL: Yes. I am wondering why I am here.
NIELSEN: I will be glad to help you if I can.

When April came out of the interview, she said, "Mama, they told me Gary killed two men. Do you believe that?"

Kathryne said, "Well, April, I guess he must have."

"Gary couldn't kill someone, Mama."

"Well, April," Kathryne said, "I think Gary told them he did."

Next morning, Gilmore was brought from Provo to Orem, and Nielsen saw him in his office, and apologized about the crowd outside. There were TV lights and a lot of reporters and city employees in the hall, but what really embarrassed Nielsen was that half the police force including off-duty officers had also come out. People were even standing on chairs to get a look.

Nielsen had his secretary bring a cup of coffee. Then he said, "Lieutenant Skinner is going to sign a complaint charging you with the homicide of Max Jensen." After a short pause, Gary said, "Hey, I really feel bad about those two guys. I read one of their obituaries in the paper last night. He was a young man and had a kid and he was a missionary. Makes me really feel bad."

"Gary, I feel bad too. I can't understand taking a life for the amount of money you got."

Gary replied, "I don't know how much I got. What was there?"

Nielsen said, "It was $125, and in Provo, approximately the same amount." Gary began to cry. He didn't weep with any noise but there were tears in his eyes. He said, "I hope they execute me for it. I ought to die for what I did."

"Gary, are you ready to?" Nielsen asked. "It doesn't scare you?"

"Would you like to die?"

"Criminy," said Nielsen, "no."

"Me neither," said Gilmore, "but I ought to be executed for it."

"I don't know," said Nielsen; "there's got to be forgiveness somewhere along the line."

A little later, Gary made a private call to Brenda.

Brenda said, "Gary, you're going to go down hard this time. You're going to ride this one clear to the bottom."

He said, "Man, how do you know I'm not innocent?"

"Gary, what's the matter with your head?"

"I don't know," Gary said, "I must have been insane."

Brenda asked, "What about your mother? What do you want me to tell her?"

He was quiet for a while. Then he said, "Tell her it's true."

Brenda said, "Okay. Anything else?"

"Just tell her I love her."

Nicole was in Springville with Barrett when the police came. They didn't phone or anything. Just a cop to ask her to get ready. A little later, Lieutenant Nielsen was there in a car. He would drive her over to see Gary.

She didn't know how she felt, and she didn't know if she cared how she felt. It had been a real hang-up listening to Barrett. The last couple of days he had been coming on as the wise man. Her judgment, he kept saying, was so goofy. Like she had picked a middle-aged murderer for herself.

On the way, Lieutenant Nielsen was nice and polite, and he laid it out. They were going to let Nicole talk to Gary, but she had to ask if he had done the murders. Nicole was about to get mad at the suggestion, except she figured out Nielsen needed a reason to justify bringing her over. She was sure he wasn't so dumb as to think Gary was going to answer her question while a bunch of cops was listening.

That was how it turned out. Nicole walked into this funky one-story jail, went down a couple of short corridors, passed a bunch of inmates who looked like beer bums, then a couple of dudes who whistled as she went by, twirled their mustaches, showed a bicep, generally acted like the cat's ass. Two cops and Detective Nielsen were right behind her, and she came to a big cell with a table in the middle of it, four bunks she could see, and thick prison bars in front of her.

Then she saw Gary come toward her from the back of the cell. His left hand was in a cast. It was only three days from the night she had seen him arrested and lying on the ground, but she could feel the difference. He said, "Hello, baby," and, at first, she didn't even want to look at him.

With her head down, she muttered, "Did you do this?"

She was really whispering, as if should he say yes, maybe the cops wouldn't hear the question. He said, "Nicole, don't ask me that."

Now, she looked up. She couldn't get over how clear his eyes were. There was a minute where they didn't say any more. Then he put one arm through the bars. She wanted to touch him, but didn't. However, she kept feeling the impulse. More and more she had this desire to touch him.

It was close to a spooky experience. Nicole didn't know what she was feeling. She certainly wasn't feeling sorry for him. She wasn't feeling sorry for herself. Rather, she couldn't breathe. She could hardly believe it, but she was ready to faint. That was the moment when she knew that it didn't matter what she had said about him these last couple of weeks. She had been in love with him from the moment she met him and she would love him forever.

It wasn't an emotion so much as a physical sensation. A magnet could have been pulling her to the bars. She reached out to put a hand on the arm he extended through, and one of the officers stepped forward and said, "No physical contact."

She stepped back, and Gary looked good. He looked surprisingly good. His eyes were more blue than they had ever been. All that fog from the Fiorinal was gone. His eyes looked into her as if he was returning from all the way back and something ugly had passed through completely and was gone. All through these last couple of bad weeks, it was like he had been looking a year older every day. Now he looked fine. "I love you," he said as they said good-bye. "I love you," she said.

In the same hour that Nicole was going to and from the jail, April went berserk. She began to scream that someone was trying to blow her head off. Kathryne could do nothing. First she had to call the police and then she decided to commit her to the hospital. It was horrible. April had flipped out completely. Kathryne even had to keep the children out of the house all those hours while it was being decided.

———

The Sheriff, Ken Cahoon, was a tall man with an easygoing manner and white hair. He wore metal-rimmed glasses, had a large nose, a small mouth, a small chin, and a little potbelly. He liked to believe he ran a reasonably good jail. His main tank had bunks for thirty men, but he never went over twenty if he could help it. That kept the fights down. The trustees who worked in the kitchen were given a cell to themselves, and there was also Maximum Detention, with room for six. That was the tank where Gary now sat by himself. Plus another cell for six down the same hall to hold prisoners on work release. Altogether, Cahoon's jail could carry forty people without busting the seams of anyone's patience.

A while after Nicole left, Cahoon decided to look back in on Gilmore.

"I have blisters on my feet," Gilmore told him.

"From doing what?" asked Cahoon.

"Why," said Gilmore, "I've been jogging in place."

"Well, dummy, quit jogging in place."

"No," said Gilmore, "give me some Band-Aids. I'll put them on, and I can jog some more."

Next day, he asked the same thing. Said he wanted Band-Aids because his feet were sore. "Why, let's see," said Cahoon, "if you got an infection."

Gilmore said, "Just give me some Band-Aids. It's not that bad."

"No," said Cahoon, "if you got blisters, I want to see them."

"Oh, hell," said Gilmore, "forget it."

Cahoon decided he was pulling a bluff. There was no telling what he might use the Band-Aids for, unless it was to tape contraband to the bottom of the bedsprings or something.

Next morning, Gilmore said to a guard, "I want out of here today. I've got a Writ of Habeas Corpus. Let me see the head man of the jail."

Cahoon decided Gilmore must have the opinion they were backwoodsy in this little old humble place. Now Gary said to Cahoon in a nice confidential voice, "Look, I'm in for five days. I'm not being held for nothing but a traffic violation. So I would like out of here right now. You see," he said, "I've got to be under a doctor's care. As you may know, I came in with this cast on, and things of this nature want attention. I'd like to be taken to the hospital. The hand has to have its medication, and if you can't get me out, you see, there could be complications."

Cahoon thought Gilmore was a pretty good con man, considering the odds, and he didn't exactly laugh at the idea that Gilmore might get loose in some simple but crazy way. A while back, they'd had a man in the tank named Dennis Howell, and another prisoner happened to come in also named Dennis Howell. The same day, word came to release the first Dennis. So the jailer on duty who was new on the job went down the list, went back and said to the new arrival, "Howell, your wife is outside, you can go now." The wrong Dennis walked out the door, trotted right past the woman, took off like a whistle.

Gilmore sure kept trying. A little later, he wanted to get ahold of his attorney. Said he was going to sue the jail for not giving attention to his hand. He was really in sympathy with himself over that hand.

After it all failed, Gary said, "I know Utah County is poor in spirit, and full of hard feelings toward me, but, Sheriff, you can let me go home now. I'm not mad anymore."

That was a pretty good sense of humor, Cahoon decided.

It made it easier for him to put up with Gilmore decorating the walls. Cahoon liked to eliminate any drawing of obscenity pictures, but Gary was not doing that. Pictures he drew were nice pictures. They were also something you could erase. One day he'd do a drawing, and next day wipe it out, do another, so Cahoon never made an issue of it.

They really got along all right until Gilmore learned that they wouldn't allow him to see Nicole on visits. It seemed she wasn't family. That left Gary not speaking to anybody.

About the second time that Brenda went down to the jail, which was on Sunday, a week and a half after his arrest, Nicole had also shown up. When Gary heard she was outside, the expression on his face, Brenda had to admit, was beautiful. "Oh, God," he said, "she promised to come back and she did."

However, he explained, it didn't mean he could visit with her. She wasn't allowed on his list just yet. Brenda said, "Let me see what I can do." She went up to a big tough Indian guard at the door, a confident-looking fellow, and said, "Alex, could you put Nicole Barrett in for the last five minutes of my time?" "Well, now," he said, "we really shouldn't break the rules." "Bullshit," said Brenda, "what's the difference if it's me or Nicole? He ain't going to go nowhere! Why, Alex Hunt, you mean to tell me," she asked, "you can't take care of this poor man with a busted-up hand? What's he going to do with one hand? Tear you apart?" "Well," said Alex, "I think we can handle Gilmore."

While Nicole was visiting, Brenda walked over to Nicole's sister-in-law, who had also come. It was hot that day, and Sue Baker was holding her newborn baby and perspiring in volumes. "How is Nicole doing?" asked Brenda.

The sun didn't stir on the black cinder gravel back of the jail.

"She's pretty broke up," said Sue.

Brenda said, "Gary's not going to get out of this one. If Nicole gets all hung up, it's going to ruin her."

"She won't quit," said Sue, "we already tried."

"Well," said Brenda, "she's in for a lot of hurt."

When Nicole came out, she was weeping. Brenda put her arms around her and said, "Nicole, we both love him."

Then Brenda said: "Nicole, why don't you think a little about giving up the ship? Gary is never going to get out. You'll spend the rest of your life visiting this guy. That's all the future you're going to have." Now Brenda began to cry. "Tuck those beautiful memories in your heart," she said, "tuck them away."

Nicole muttered, "I'll stick."

She was feeling an animosity toward Brenda she didn't even understand. Nicole heard herself thinking, "As if I owe her a million dollars for giving me five minutes of her visiting time."

There was a Preliminary Hearing on August 3 in Provo, and Noall Wootton was determined to ram it through as hard and fast as he could. He had a lot of witnesses so his problem was to keep the case intact. When the defense asked for delay, Wootton objected.

He was reasonably confident of the conviction, or to put it more precisely, he was confident that if he did not get a conviction, it would be his own fault. He was, however, not at all sure of getting the death penalty. So he was feeling the usual tension he had before a case began. His stomach was right with him that morning.

At the Preliminary Hearing, Gilmore didn't take the stand, but Wootton did talk face to face with him in the recess. They got on well. They even joked. Wootton was impressed with his intelligence. Gilmore told Wootton that the prison system was not doing what it was designed to achieve, that is, rehabilitate. In his opinion, it was a complete failure.

Of course, they avoided talking about the crimes themselves, but Noall did detect that Gilmore was doing his best to soften him up. Gary certainly kept flattering him about what a fair and efficient prosecutor he was, what a basic sense of fairness he had. Said he'd never seen another prosecutor with that kind of fairness.

Not every con knew enough to run that line. Wootton expected Gilmore was working up to a deal. He must have heard they were going for the death penalty, and thought if he was nice enough, Wootton might feel encouraged to return from so far out a stand, far out at least from the defendant's point of view.

Sure enough, Gilmore got around asking what Wootton thought would happen. Noall looked him in the eye and said, "They might come back with the death penalty." Gilmore said, "I know, but what are they really going to do?" Wootton repeated, "They might execute you." He had the impression that took Gilmore aback.

Snyder also approached Noall, and suggested they plead guilty to Murder One, and accept a life top. Wootton kind of dismissed it. "No way," he said.

He had made up his mind to go for Death after looking at Gilmore's record. It showed violence in prison, a history of escape, and unsuccessful efforts made at rehabilitation. Wootton could only conclude that, one: Gilmore would be looking to escape; two: he would be a hazard to other inmates and guards; and, three: rehabilitation was hopeless. Couple this to a damned cold-blooded set of crimes.

Nicole drove down to the Preliminary Hearing in Provo on August 3, but they let her visit with Gary for only a moment. It made her dizzy to see him in leg shackles. Then they only gave her time for one hug and a tremendous kiss before pulling him away. She was left in the hall of the court with the world rocketing around her. Outside, in the summer light, the horseflies were mean as insanity itself.

On the drive back to Springville, she was dreaming away and got in a wreck. Nobody was hurt but the car. After that, all the way home, her Mustang sounded like it was breaking up in pain. She couldn't shift out of second.

It became a crazy trip. She kept having an urge to cross the divider, and bang into oncoming traffic. Next day, when the mail came, there was a very long letter from Gary that he had begun to write as soon as they took him back to jail from the hearing. So she realized he had been saying these words to her at the same time she had been driving along with the urge to smash into every car going the other way.

Now she read Gary's letter over and over. She must have read it five times and the words went in and out of her head like a wind blowing off the top of the world.

*August 3*

*Nothing in my experience, prepared me for the kind of honest open love you gave me. I'm so used to bullshit and hostility, deceit and pettiness, evil and hatred. Those things are my natural habitat. They have shaped me. I look at the world through eyes that suspect, doubt, fear, hate, cheat, mock, are selfish and vain. All things unacceptable, I see them as natural and have even come to accept them as such. I look around the ugly vile cell and know that I truly belong in a place this dank and dirty, for where else should I be? There's water all over the floor from the fucking toilet that don't flush right. The shower is filthy and the thin mattress they gave me is almost black, it's so old. I have no pillow. There are dead cockroaches in the corners. At nite there are mosquitoes and the lite is very dim. I'm alone here with my thoughts and I can feel the oldness. Remember I told you about The Oldness? and you told me how ugly it was—the oldness, the oldness. I can hear the tumbrel wheels creak. So fucking ugly and coming so close to me. When I was a child . . . I had a nightmare about being beheaded. But it was more than just a dream. More like a memory. It brought me right out of the bed. And it was sort of a turning point in my life. . . . Recently it has begun to make a little sense. I owe a debt, from a long time ago. Nicole, this must depress you. I've never told anybody of this thing, except my mother the nite I had that nitemare and she came in to comfort me but we never spoke of it after that. And I started to tell you one nite and I told you quite a bit of it before it became plain to me that you didn't want to hear it. There have been years when I haven't even thought much of it at all and then something (a picture of a guillotine, a headmans block, or a broad ax, or even a rope) will bring it all back and for days it will seem I'm on the verge of knowing something very personal, something about myself. Something that somehow wasn't completed and makes me different. Something I owe, I guess. Wish I knew.*

*Once you asked me if I was the devil, remember? I'm not. The devil would be far more clever than I, would operate on a much larger scale and of course would feel no remorse. So I'm not Beelzebub. And I know the devil can't feel love. But I might be further from God than I am from the devil. Which is not a good thing. It seems that I know evil more intimately than I know goodness and that's not a good thing either. I want to get even, to be made even, whole, my debts paid (whatever it may take!) to have no blemish, no reason to feel guilt or fear. I hope this ain't corny, but I'd like to stand in the sight of God. To know that I'm just and right and clean. When you're this way you know it. And when you're not, you know that too. It's all inside of us, each of us—but I guess I ran from it and when I did try to approach it, I went about it wrong, became discouraged, bored, lazy, and finally unacceptable. But what do I do now? I don't know. Hang myself?*

*I've thought about that for years, I may do that. Hope that the state executes me? That's more acceptable and easier than suicide. But they haven't executed anybody here since 1963 (just about the last year for legal executions anywhere). What do I do, rot in prison? growing old and bitter and eventually work this around in my mind to where it reads that I'm the one who's getting fucked around, that I'm just an innocent victim of society's bullshit? What do I do? Spend a life in prison searching for the God I've wanted to know for such a long time? Resume my painting? Write poetry? Play handball? Eat my heart out for the wondrous love you gave me that I threw away Monday nite because I was so spoiled and couldn't immediately have a white pickup truck I wanted? What do I do? We always have a choice, don't we?*

*I'm not asking you to answer these questions for me, Angel, please don't think that I am. I have to make my own choice. But anything you want to comment on or suggest, or say, is always welcome.*

*God, I love you, Nicole.*

## August      Gilmore and Gibbs

Gary was so quiet over the next few days that it got ominous. Cahoon decided he was too morbid and needed company, so he moved over a prisoner named Gibbs from the main tank. They had both done so much time, they might get along.

Cahoon noticed that soon as he shut the bars, they started a conversation in jail talk. It was that gibberish talk. Use a word like figger to say nigger. Show the other fellow how many years you put in by carrying on a whole conversation. Cahoon didn't try to get it all. If they said lady from Bristol, that meant pistol, and he would have to get concerned, but Gilmore was talking of ones and twos, and those were shoes. "Yeah," said Gilmore to Gibbs, "A nice pair to go with my fleas and ants."

"You still got to think," said Gibbs, "of your bunny and boat."

"Fuck the goat," said Gilmore, "let me stroll in with a dickery dick."

"That's right, it could juice the chick."

Cahoon left. They were just doing time. He thought they made a cute couple. Both had Fu Manchu goatees. It was just that Gilmore was a lot bigger than Gibbs. Like cat and mouse. Hell, like cat and rat.

There were only three things in the world Gibbs could honestly say he had any feeling for: children, kittens, and money. Been on his own since he was fourteen. When seventeen, he wrote and cashed $17,000 worth of checks in a month and bought himself a new car. Always had new cars.

By the time he was fourteen, Gilmore said, he'd broken into fifty houses. Maybe more.

———

First time Gibbs went to prison out here, he was behind a 2½-million-dollar forgery. He took, Gibbs said, twenty-one counts. Next time he went back was when he blew up a cop's car in Salt Lake. Captain Haywood's car.

Gave him fifteen years when he was twenty-two, Gilmore said. Did them at Oregon and Marion. Gibbs nodded. Marion had the credentials. Flattened eleven years consecutively, Gilmore told him. Probably four years altogether in Solitary. Gilmore showed real pedigree.

He was in for rubber rafts, Gibbs told him. Stole forty of them in two weeks out of J.C. Penney's in Utah Valley, Salt Lake Valley, $139 apiece. Chain saws same way. Made two or three hundred bucks a day. Just couldn't manage his money, that's all.

My problem, too, allowed Gilmore. He had also done a little boosting at J.C. Penney's.

"Yeah," said Gibbs, "the only difference between you and me is when I do it, I have two shoulder men to run interference. If they come after, my big boys say, 'What are you chasing this guy for?' "

Gibbs could recognize that Gilmore didn't know any heavies out of Salt Lake. Didn't know the Barbaro brothers, Len Rails, Ron Clout, Mardu, or Gus Latagapolos. "You're talking heavies, then," said Gibbs.

Gilmore spoke of the Aryan Brotherhood and his connections there. Gibbs could recognize some heavy names out of Oregon and Atlanta, Leavenworth and Marion. Not legends, but still heavies. Gilmore carried himself like he was well regarded. Of course, Murder One gives a man standing. When they ask you, "What do you get for killing?" the answer is "self-satisfaction." Clears the mind.

His ring, Gibbs told Gilmore, had done outboard motors, inboard motors, house trailers, and trailer homes. Don't get nervous when they see you carrying the stuff. They had a laugh over this. "Half a million dollars' worth," said Gibbs, "going right down the Interstate."

———

"If you get out before me," said Gilmore, "can you bring back some hacksaw blades?"

"Anybody would, I probably would," said Gibbs. In fact, thought Gibbs, he might. He had as much loyalty in one direction as in the other. He was the man in the old saying "You got blue eyes, one blew north, one blew south." Except it was Gilmore had the blue eyes. He liked Gilmore. A lot of class.

"Hey," said Gilmore, "if you could figure a way to get me out of here, I'd pull any job you want. Just keep enough money for me and my old lady to leave the country, and I'll give you the rest."

"If I wanted out of this jail," said Gibbs, "I'd have people come take me out."

"Well, around here, I don't know people," said Gilmore.

"If anybody would, I would," repeated Gibbs.

The cell they were in was divided into two parts, a small dining area with a table and benches, and to the back, away from the bars, a toilet, a sink, a shower, and six bunks. On the other side of the bars was a corridor that led to the next tank. That was used as the women's cell. When no women were there, it was the pen for drunks. Their first night, they had a drunk next door who kept yelling.

Gilmore answered as if he were the jailer. "What do you want?" he bellowed. The drunk said he had to make a phone call. Had to get bond. Gilmore told him no Judge would give it. Why, the little boy he had hit in the trailer court died. What little boy, said the drunk? Those are your charges: drunk driving, auto homicide, hit and run. Gibbs loved it. The drunk believed Gilmore. Spent the rest of the night crying to himself instead of yelling for the jailer.

Gilmore began to do his exercises. That was something, he told Gibbs, he did every night. Had to, in order to tire himself out enough to get a little sleep.

He did a hundred sit-ups, took a break, then did jumping jacks, clapping his hands over his head. Gibbs lay on his bunk and smoked and lost count. Gilmore must have done two or three hundred. Then he took another break and tried push-ups but could only get to twenty-five. His left hand was still weak, he explained.

Then he stood on his head for ten minutes. What's the purpose of that, asked Gibbs. Oh, said Gilmore, it gets the blood circulating in your head, good for your hair. He wanted, Gilmore added, to try to keep as much youthfulness in appearance as possible. Gibbs nodded. Every con he knew, including himself, had a complex about age. What the hell, the youthful years were all lost. "My personal opinion," Gibbs said, "is that you are a young-looking person for thirty-five years old. I am five years younger, and look five years older than you."

"It's your coffin nails," said Gilmore, sniffing the smoke. He had picked a top bunk as far away as possible from Gibbs, who was sleeping in the bottom bed across.

"You don't smoke?" said Gibbs.

"I don't believe in supporting any habit you have to pay for," said Gary. "Not if you spend your time in lockup. They had a cell in Isolation named after me."

The drunk in the next tank was whimpering piteously. Gilmore said, "Yeah, the Gary M. Gilmore Room," and they both laughed. Listening to the drunk cry was as comfortable as lying in bed on a summer night hearing trees rustle. Yes, Gilmore told him, he had put in so much time in Segregation that he almost never earned money from a prison job. And there sure wasn't money coming from outside. Any luxuries allowed in the can, he had learned to do without. "Besides," he said, "smoking is bad for your health. Of course, speaking of health . . ." He looked at Gibbs.

Speaking of health, he expected the death sentence.

"A good lawyer could get you Second Degree. They parole Second Degree in Utah in six years. Six years, you're on the street."

"I can't afford a good lawyer," said Gilmore. "The State pays for my lawyers." He looked down at Gibbs from his bunk and said, "My lawyers work for the same people that are going to sentence me."

"They keep taking me," said Gilmore, "to be interviewed by psychiatrists. Shit, they come up with the stupidest questions. Why, they ask, did I park my car to the side of the gas station? 'If I parked in front,'

I said to them, 'you'd ask me why I didn't park to the side.' " He snorted at that. "I could put on an act, have them saying, 'Yeah, he's crazy,' but I won't."

Gibbs understood. That offended a true man's idea of himself.

"I am telling them that the killings were unreal. That I saw everything through a veil of water." Now they could hear the drunk moaning again. " 'It was like I was in a movie,' I say to them, 'and I couldn't stop the movie.' "

"Is that how it came down?" asked Gibbs.

"Shit, no," said Gilmore. "I walked in on Benny Bushnell and I said to that fat son of a bitch, 'Your money, son, *and* your life.' "

They both cracked. It was funny as hell. Right there in the middle of the night, in this hot fucking two-bit asshole jail, with the drunk slobbering in his shit and counting his sins, they couldn't stop laughing. "Pipe down in there," said Gilmore to the drunk. "Save your crying for the Judge." The drunk was one wet sorrow. Like a puppy first night in a new house. "Hell," said Gilmore, "the morning after I killed Jensen, I called up the gas station and asked them if they had any job openings." Again they cracked.

Gilmore, tonight, would break off his arm if he could make a good joke. Cut off his head and hand it to you, if his mouth would spit nails. "What's your last best request when they're hanging you?" he asked, and answered, "Use a rubber rope." Pretended to be bouncing on the end, he put his face in a scowl, and said, "Guess I'll be hanging around for a while."

Gibbs thought he'd piss his pants. "What," asked Gilmore, "is your last request when they put you in the gas chamber?" He waited. Gibbs wheezed. "Why," Gilmore said, "ask them for laughing gas."

"That is enough," said Gibbs, "to choke you up."

For that matter, he was almost strangling on his own phlegm. Smoking gave him a dozen oysters every meal. The kid with the phlegm-pot. Gilmore asked, "What do you say to the firing squad?"

"I," said Gibbs, "ask them for a bullet-proof vest." They laughed back and forth like an animal going in circles and getting weak. "Yeah," said Gibbs, "I heard that one."

Gilmore had a quality Gibbs could recognize. He accommodated. Gibbs believed he, himself, could always get near somebody—just use the side that was like them. Gilmore did the same. Around each other tonight, they were like boiler-plated farts. Filthy devils.

No sooner did he think this than Gilmore got serious. "Hey," he said to Gibbs, "they're figuring to give me the death penalty, but I have an answer for them. I'm going to check into the State of Utah's hole card. I'm going to make them do it. Then we'll see if they have as many guts as I do."

Gibbs couldn't decide if the guy was a bullshitter. He couldn't visualize doing something like that.

"Yes," said Gilmore, "I'll tell them to do it without a hood. Do it at night if it's outside, or in a dark room with tracer bullets. That way I can see those babies coming!"

The drunk was screaming, "I didn't mean to kill the little boy, oh Judge, I'll never drive again."

"Knock it off," shouted Gilmore.

Yeah, he said to Gibbs, the only legitimate fear a man in his position could have while facing the firing squad was that one of the marksmen might be a friend or relative of one of the victims. "Then," said Gilmore, "they might shoot at my head. I don't like that. I have perfect twenty-twenty, and I want to donate my eyes."

This guy was a roulette wheel, decided Gibbs. Just depended which number came up. "I've made a lot of mistakes in my life," said Gilmore from the upper bunk, "and a great many errors in judgment the last couple of months, but this I will say, Gibbs. I am in my element now. I have never misjudged a person who has done time."

"I hope you have a favorable impression of me."

"I believe you are a good convict," said Gilmore.

On that high praise, no higher praise, they went to sleep. It was three in the morning. They would bullshit until three every morning.

*September 9*
*I'm not a weak man. I've never been a punk, I've never been a rat, I've always fought—I ain't the toughest son of a bitch around but I've always stood up and been counted among the men. I've done a few things that would make a lot of motherfuckers tremble and I've endured some shit that nobody should have to go thru. But what I want you to understand, little girl, is that you hold my heart*

*and along with my heart I guess you have the power to crush me or destroy me. Please don't. I have no defense for what I feel for you.*

*I can't share you with any other man or men Nicole. I'd rather be dead and burning in some hell than have any other man be with you.*

*I can't share you—I want all of you—*

*I have to go without fucking, you can too. Sorry to be crude but that's true. We love each other and belong to each other let's don't ever hurt each other Nicole let's don't ever hurt each other.*

*This pain paralyzes me. I keep thinking of you being with somebody. I can't help it. I have to chase the ugly pictures out of my mind. I don't want anybody to kiss you or hold you or fuck you. You're mine I love you.*

*You said on the last page of your letter that I will not have reason to hurt that way ever again—I'm 35 fucking years old been locked up more than half my life. I should be a tough son of a bitch, all the things that have happened to me.*

*But I can't take being away from you—I miss you every minute.*

*And I cannot stand the thought of some man holding your naked body and watching your eyes roll back sleeping in your arms.*

*I can't share you—I won't. You've got to be all mine. I don't care that you say you have this crazy heart that won't let you refuse any request to make another happy. I have a crazy heart too. And my crazy heart makes a request of your crazy heart—don't refuse my request to be only mine in heart mind soul and body. Let me be the next and only man to have you.*

*God I want you baby baby baby*

*fuck only me*

*don't fuck anybody else dont dont it kills me dont kill me*

*Am I demanding too much??*

*Write and tell me—*

TELL ME                     TELL ME

GODDAMN IT

                            TELL ME

*Fuck shit piss God Nicole*

*Tell me.*

*Wednesday and Sunday are too far apart———why don't you write me more!?*

*Nicole don't be with anybody else dont dont dont dont*

    *dont*

*I'm really fucking this letter up*

*I've got to come to a conclusion and this is it. I've got to hava <u>all</u> of you! With nobody can I share you. I love you.*

I LOVE YOU                    I LOVE YOU                    I LOVE YOU
                             *I LOVE YOU*

*No, I ain't drunk or loaded or nothing this is just me writing this letter
that lacks beauty—just me Gary Gilmore thief and murderer. Crazy Gary. Who
will one day have a dream that he was a guy named GARY in 20th century
America and that there was something very wrong . . . but what was it and is it
why things are so super shitty, to the max, as they used to say in 20th century
Spanish Fork. And he'll remember that there was something very beautiful too
in that long ago Mormon mountain Empire and he'll begin to dream of a dark
red haired sort of green eyed elfin fox whose eyes rolled back and could swallow
all of his cock and who laughed and cried with him and didn't care that his
teeth were fucked up forever and who taught him how to fuck girls again instead of his hand and pictures in Playboy.*

Next night, they put a girl in the same tank where the drunk had
been. She was also crying and Gary hollered over, Hey, sister, it can't
be all that bad. She immediately quieted down.

Gary found out her name was Connie, and when she inquired if
he had a cigarette, Gibbs slid a pack down the hallway to her cell and
Connie thanked them.

They kept trying to talk but you had to holler loud, so Gary wrote
a note and slid it over. Told her he was rather handsome, liked young
girls, western music, and yodeling. Especially, he liked to yodel. She
wrote back that she'd seen his picture in the newspaper and agreed he
was good-looking. Thanked him for being kind and asked if he would
yodel.

"Well, Tex," said Gibbs, "crank up." Gary could no more yodel
than Gibbs could knit. So Gary just hollered over shucks he was lying,
couldn't oo-lay, oo-lay-oo to save his butt. All three began to laugh.
They had a good night sending notes back and forth. In the morning,
she got out. Gary's depression was back.

*September 11*
*I could not sleep for the third nite running. Somethings happening to me.
I dozed briefly last nite and awoke in the middle of a dream about a severed*

head. I can hear the tumbrel wheels creaking again and the swift slide of the blade—in my dream I was being interviewed by a female parole officeress or whatever, dreams take their own course, and pretty soon a doctor, or somebody, came back.

I've told you that I haven't slept lately—the ghosts have descended and set upon me with a force I didn't believe they possessed. I smack 'em down but they sneak back and climb in my ear and demons that they are tell me foul jokes, they want to sap my will, drink my strength, drain my hope leave me derelict bereft of hope lost empty alone foul demon motherfuckers with dirty furry bodies whispering vile things in the nite chortling and laughing with a hideous glee to see me toss sleepless in durance truly vile they plan to pounce on me in a shrieking mad fury when I leave with their hideous yellow long toe and finger claws teeth dripping with rank saliva and mucous thick yellow green. Dirty inhuman beasts jackals hyena rumor monger plague ridden unhappy lost ghostly foul ungodly things unacceptable creeping crawling red eyed bat eared soulless beasts.

They won't let the ol' boy have a nites sleep. God-damned lost motherfuckers. I need our silver sword against them. They're slippery motherfuckers.

The demon ghosts

All selections from *The Executioner's Song* (1979)

# 1000 B.C.  THE EMBALMING

A hook went into my nose, battered through the gate at the roof of the nostril, and plunged into my brain. Pieces, gobbets, and whole parts of the dead flesh of my mind were now brought out through one aperture of my nose, then the other.

Yet for all it hurt, I could have been made of small rocks and roots. I ached no more than the earth when a weed is pulled and comes up with its hairs tearing away from the clods of the soil. Pain is present, but as the small cry of the uprooted plant. So did the hooks, narrow in their curve, go up the nose, enter the head, and poke like blind fingers in a burrow to catch stuffs of the brain and pull them away. Now I felt like a rock wall at the base of which rakes are ripping, and was warm curiously as though sunlight were baking, but it was only the breath of the first embalmer, hot with wine and figs—how clear was the sense of smell!

Still, an enigma remained. How could my mind continue to think while they pulled my brain apart? They were certainly scooping chunks of material as lively as dry sponge through the dry tunnels of my nose, and I realized—for there was a flash in my cranium when the hook first entered—that one of my lights in the Land of the Dead had certainly stirred. Was it the Ba, the Khaibit or the Ka that was now helping me to think? And I gagged as a particularly caustic drug, some wretched mixture of lime and ash, was poured in by the embalmers to dissolve whatever might still be stuck to the inside of my skull.

How long they worked I do not know, how long they allowed that liquid to dwell in the vault of my emptied head is but one more question. From time to time they lifted my feet, held me upside down, then set me back. Once they even turned me on my stomach to slosh the fluids, and let the caustic eat out my eyes. Two flowers could have been plucked when those eyes were gone.

At night my body would go cold; by midday it was close to warm. Of course I could not see, but I could smell, and got to know the embalmers. One wore perfume yet his body always carried the unmistakable pungency of a cat in heat; the other was a heavy fellow with a heavy odor not altogether bad—he was the one with breath of wine and figs. He smelled as well of fields and mud, and rich food was usually in him—a meat-eater, his sweat was strong yet not unpleasant—something loyal came out of the gravies of his flesh. Because I could smell them as they approached, I knew it was daylight so soon as the embalmers arrived, and I could count the hours. (Their scent altered with the heat of the air in this place.) From midday to three, every redolence, good and bad, of the hot banks of the Nile was also near. After a time I came to realize I must be in a tent. There was often the crack of sailcloth flapping overhead, and gusts would clap at my hair, a sensation as definite in impression as a hoof stepping on grass. My hearing had begun to return but by a curious route. For I had no interest in what was said. I was aware of the voices of others, but felt no desire to comprehend the words. They were not even like the cry of animals so much as the lolling of surf or the skittering of wind. Yet my mind felt capable of surpassing clarity.

Once I think my mother came to visit, or since it is likely the tent was on family grounds, it is possible she strolled through the gardens and stopped to look in. Certainly I caught her scent. It was Hathfertiti, certain enough; she gave one sob, as if belief in the mortal end of her son had finally come, and left immediately.

Somewhere in those first few days they made an incision in the side of my belly with a sharp flint knife—I know how sharp for even with the few senses my Remains could still employ, a sense of sharpness went through me like a plow breaking ground, but sharper, as if I were a snake cut in two by a chariot wheel, and then began the most detailed searching. It is hard to describe, for it did not hurt, but I was ready in those hours to think of the inside of my torso as common to a forest in a grove, and one by one trees were removed, their roots disturbing veins of rock, their leaves murmuring. I had dreams of cities drifting down the Nile like floating islands. Yet when the work was done, I felt larger, as if my senses now lived in a larger space. Was it that my heart and lungs had been placed in one jar, and my stomach and small intestines in another? Leave it that my organs were spread out in different places, floating in different fluids and spices, yet still existing about me, a village. Eventually, their allegiance would be lost. Wrapped and placed in the Canopic jars, what they knew of my life would then be offered to their own God.

How I brooded over what they would know of me once my organs were in Their jars. The God Qebhsenuf would dwell in my liver and know of all the days when my liver's juices had been brave; as well would Qebhsenuf know of the hours when the liver, like me, lived in the fog of a long fear. A simple example, the liver, but more agreeable to contemplate than my lungs. For, with all my lungs knew of my passions would they still be loyal once they moved into the jar of the jackal Tuamutef, and lived in the domain of that God, that scavenger? I did not know. So long, at least, as my organs remained unwrapped, and therefore in a manner still belonged to me, I could understand how, once embalmed and in their jar, I would lose them. No matter how scattered my parts might be over all the tables of this tent, there still remained the sense of family among us—the vessel of my empty corpse comfortably surrounded by old fleshly islands of endeavor, these lungs, liver, stomach, and big and little guts all attached to the same memories of my life (if with their own separate and fiercely prejudiced view—how different, after all, had my life seemed to my liver and to my heart). So, not at all, therefore, was this embalming tent as I had expected, no, no bloody abattoir like a butcher's stall, more like an herb kitchen. Certainly the odors encouraged the same long flights of fancy you could find in a spice shop. Merely figure the vertigos of my nose when the empty cavity of my body (so much emptier than the belly of a woman who has just given birth) was now washed, soothed, and stimulated, cleansed, peppered, herbified, and left with a resonance through which no hint of the body's corruption could breathe. They scoured the bloody inside with palm wine, and left the memories of my flesh in ferment. They pounded in spices and peppers, and rare sage from the limestone foundations to the West; then came leaves of thyme and the honey of bees who had fed on thyme, the oil of orange was rubbed into the cavity of the ribs, and the oil of lemon balmed the inside of my lower back to free it of the stubborn redolence of the viscera. Cedar chips, essence of jasmine, and branchlets of myrrh were crushed—I could hear the cries of the plants being broken more clearly than the sound of human voices. The myrrh even made its clarion call. A powerful aromatic (as powerful in the kingdom of herbs as the Pharaoh's voice) was the myrrh laid into the open shell of my body. Next came cinnamon leaves, stem, and cinnamon bark to sweeten the myrrh. Like rare powders added to the sweetmeats in the stuffing of a pigeon were these bewildering atmospheres they laid into me. Dizzy was I with their beauty. When done, they sewed up the long cut in the side of my body, and I seemed to rise through high vales of fever while something of memory, intoxicated by these tendrils of the earth, began to dance and the oldest of my friends was young while the children of my mistresses grew old. I was like a royal barge lifted into the air under the ministrations of a rare Vizier.

Cleaned, stuffed, and trussed, I was deposited in a bath of natron—that salt which dries the meat to stone—and there I lay with weights to keep me down. Slowly, over the endless days that followed, as the waters of my own body were given up to the thirst of the salt (which drank at my flesh like caravans arriving at an oasis) so all moisture, with its insatiable desire to liquefy my meats, had to leave my limbs. Bathed in natron, I became hard as the wood of a hull, then hard as the rock of the earth, and felt the last of me depart to join my Ka, my Ba, and my fearsome Khaibit. And the shell of my body entered the stone of ten thousand years. If there was nothing I could smell any longer (no more than a stone can be aware of a scent), still the hardened flesh of my body became like one of those spiraled chambers of the sea that are thrown up on the beach yet contain the roar of waters when you hold them to your ear. I became not unlike that roar of waters, for I was close to hearing old voices that passed across the sands—if now I could not smell, I could certainly hear—and like the dolphin whose ears are reputed able to pick up echoes from the other end of the sea, so I sank into the bath of natron, and my body passed farther and farther away. Like a stone washed by fog, baked by sun, and given the flavor of the water on the bank, I was entering that universe of the dumb where it was part of our gift to hear the story told by every wind to every stone.

Yet even as I was carried on these voyages, I must have stirred in sleep, or gone through a space in the travels of sleep. I felt my body descend, breath by breath, into the case of the mummy, yes, sink into it as if the hard case were only a soft and receiving earth, yes, was laid into the case of the mummy. Once more I felt the ministrations of the embalmers, and lived through the hours when they washed the natron from my hardened body with the liquor of a vase that held no less than ten perfumes, "O sweet-smelling soul of the Great God," they intoned, "You contain such a sweet odor that Your face will never change or perish," words I did not hear, but their cadence had been heard before, I understood what was said, and never had to sniff the unguent with which they rubbed my skin and smeared my feet, laid my back in holy oil, and gilded my nails and my toes. They laid special bandages upon my head, put the bandage of Nekheb on my brow, and Hathor for my face, Thoth was the bandage over my ears, and folded pieces within the mouth and a cloth over the chin and back of the neck, twenty-two pieces to the right of my face were laid in, and twenty-two to the left. They offered up prayers that I might be able to see and hear in the Land of the Dead, and they rubbed my calves and thighs with blackstone oil and holy oil. My toes were wrapped in linen whose every piece had a drawing of the jackal, and my hands were bandaged in another linen on which were images of Isis and Hep and Ra and Amset. Ebony gum-water was washed over me. They laid in amulets as they wrapped, figures of turquoise and gold, of silver and lapis-lazuli, crystal and carnelian, and a ring was slipped over one gold-painted finger, its seal filled with a drop of each of the thirty-six substances of the embalmer. Then they laid on flowers of the *ankham* plant, and widths and windings of linen, narrow strips longer than the length of a royal barge, and folded linens to fill my cavities. I heard the sound of prayers, and the soft breath of the artists as they painted my burial case and sang to one another in the hot tent beneath the moving sun, and on a day I came to know at last the sounds of paving stones thundering beneath a sledge while I was dragged with all the weight of my case to the tomb where I would be put away in my enclosing coffins, and I could hear the quiet sobbing of the women, delicate as the far-off cry of gulls and the invocation of the priest: "The God Horus advances with His Ka." The coffin case bumped on the steps of the tomb. Then hours passed—was it hours?—in a ceremony I could neither hear nor smell, but for the grating of vessels of food and the knocking of small instruments and the sound of liquors being poured upon the floor, but that resounded through the stone of me like an underground river in a cavernous fall, and then the blow of a rock fell on my head and was followed by the grinding of chains, but it was only the scratch of an instrument upon my face. Then I felt a great force opening my stone jaws, and many words flowed into my mouth. I heard a roaring of the waters of my conception, and sobs of heartbreak—my own? I did not know. Rivers of air came to me like a new life—and the forgotten first instant of death also came and was gone as quickly. Then was my Ka born, which is to say I was born again, and was it a day, a year, or not for the passing of ten Kings? But I was up and myself again apart from Meni and his poor body in the coffin.

Yes, I was separate, I was aware of myself, but I was ready to weep. For now I knew why Meni was my dearest friend and his death an agony to me, yes, my dim memory of his life was now nothing but the dim memory of my own life. For now I knew who I was, and that was no better than a ghost in a panic for food. I was nothing but the poor Ka of Menenhetet Two, yes, the Ka, the most improperly buried and fearful Ka who now must live in this tomb, oh, where was I now that I knew where I was? And the thought of the Land of the Dead opened to me with all the recognition that I was but a seventh part of what had been once the lights, faculties, and powers of a living soul, once my living soul. Now I was no more than the Double of the dead man, and what was left of him was no more than the corpse of his wrapped body, and me.

From *Ancient Evenings* (1983)

# AMATEURS—I

### Excerpts from
### *Tough Guys Don't Dance*

And again I knew that peace comes from contemplating the love, no matter how pinched, that one holds for a parent. Since I had poured myself a drink as the one legitimate sedative I could call upon this morning and had gone to my *querencia,* the study on the third floor where I used to work looking out on the bay, so did I go back to the legend of Dougy "Big Mac" Madden and meditate on its great cost to him, and to my mother, and to me. Because for all his height and bulk we never had enough of him. A good deal of my father, I can tell you, was lost before he ever met my mother. That much knowledge I had already gained in childhood listening to the talk of his old friends.

I remember that they used to come out to our house on Long Island to visit him for an afternoon before they all went over to his bar, and since they were longshoremen and former longshoremen like himself, and almost as large, my mother's modest living room would look, so soon as they all stood up, like an overloaded boat ready to capsize. How much I liked those occasions. I would already have heard, over and over, the story of my father's great hour.

Years later I was told by a lawyer that if separate accounts given by two witnesses agree in every detail, you are listening to a lie. In that case, my father's legend must have had a good deal of truth in it. All the versions varied. They could, however, agree this much: On a day back in the late thirties, at a time when the Italians were driving the Irish out of the leadership in the longshoremen's union, my father—

one of the leaders in the ILA—was parking his car on a side street in Greenwich Village when a man darted out of a doorway and took six shots at him with a .45. (I also heard it was a .38.) How many struck him, I do not know. It is hard to believe, but most of the stories said six, and I could count four gunshot wounds on his torso when he showered.

He was renowned in those days for his strength. A strong man among longshoremen had to be a phenomenon, but he must have been as powerful as a Kodiak bear on this occasion, because he looked at his assailant and took a step forward. The gunman (whose .45, I assume, was now empty) saw that his victim did not drop. So he began to run. I find it hard to believe, but my father chased him. For six blocks along Seventh Avenue in Greenwich Village he ran after his assailant (some say eight blocks, some say five, some say four), but it took all of such a distance before Dougy recognized that he could not catch him and came to a stop. Only then did he see blood oozing from his shoes and realize that he was dizzy. He turned around just before the street began to turn around on him and saw that he was outside the emergency entrance of St. Vincent's Hospital. So he knew he was in bad shape. He hated doctors and he hated hospitals, but he was going in.

The attendant at the desk must have decided the new arrival was a drunk. A huge distraught man with a considerable amount of blood on his clothing was teetering over the table.

"Please sit down," said the orderly. "Wait your turn."

While my father normally did no more than nod or frown as friends told the story, here he would sometimes speak up himself. When I was a child, the look of absolute murderous certainty that came into his eyes was so thrilling to my keyed-up young interior that once or twice I wet my pants a drop. (Although before such manly company, I kept the secret to myself.)

My father, in telling it, would seize an imaginary orderly by the shirt, his arm extended stiffly, his fingers clutching the collar as if his strength might be all but expired, yet what remained was enough to throw this specimen of unfeeling humanity through a wall.

"Take care of me," Dougy Madden said in a low, deadly voice in my mother's living room. "I'm hurt."

He was. They kept him in St. Vincent's for three months. When he came out, his hair was white, and he was done with the union. I don't know whether lying in bed for so long a time took away a part of his massive nerve or whether the Irish leaders had lost. Maybe, by now, his mind was in another place, that far-off place, full of unspoken sorrow, where he lived for the rest of his life. In this sense, he retired before I was born. Maybe he was mourning no more than his lost eminence, for he was a labor leader no longer, merely a barrel of a man. In any event, he borrowed money from his relatives, opened a bar on the Sunrise Highway forty miles out on the South Shore, and for eighteen years was the proprietor of a place that did not prosper and did not fail.

Most bars, given this description, figure to be managed with economy, since they are usually empty. My father, however, had a bar that was like himself, large, full of generosity and only half managed, even if Big Mac did look like the bartender out of whom the mold was made.

He was there for eighteen years in his white apron and his prematurely white hair, his blue eyes measuring the drinkers when they got obstreperous, and his skin so red from the steady inflow of drink ("It's my only medicine," he would tell my mother) that he looked an angrier man than he was, fierce as a lobster making one last lunge out of the pot.

He got a fair daily crowd, a good Saturday crowd, albeit beer drinkers, and a heavy summer crowd, full of weekend lovers out on Long Island and fishermen going or coming. He would have been a prosperous man, but he drank a bit of the profits, gave back more across the bar, sent scuds of them across on free drinks to the farthest reaches of the room, let people run up a tab so large they could have paid the funeral expenses of their fathers and mothers and uncles and aunts, and he loaned money at no interest and didn't always get it back, and gave it away, and gambled it away—so as the Irish say (or is it the Jews?), "It was a living."

Everyone loved him but my mother. She came to love him less over the years. I used to wonder how they ever got married and finally decided she had to be a virgin when they met. I would suspect that their short and most loving affair (for long after they divorced, my mother's voice would still be tremulous when she spoke of their first weeks together) was stimulated not only by how different they were but because she was also a liberal and wished to defy the prejudices of her parents against the Irish, the working classes, and the smell of beer in bars. So they married. She was a small, modest, pleasant-looking woman, a schoolteacher from a nice town in Connecticut, as delicate as he was large, and she had nice manners and was a lady to him. I think she always remained a lady to him, and while he would never admit that his own great secret prejudice was just for that, for the high elegant splendor of a lady's hand in a long glove, nonetheless, he adored her. He was terribly impressed that he had married such a woman. Alas, they remained a sad couple. To use his expression, neither could move the other a cunt-hair to the left. If not for my presence, they would soon have foundered in frustration and boredom. I was there, however, and their marriage lasted through my fifteenth year.

Maybe it would have gone all the way, but my mother made one error. She won a fundamental argument with my father and got him to move from our floor-through apartment above his bar, to a town called Atlantic Lanes, and that was a quiet catastrophe. The shift proved equal, doubtless, to the shock his grandfather took on leaving Ireland. The one major concession given my mother was the one he should never have agreed to. Dougy distrusted Atlantic Lanes on sight. Although it sounds, I know, like a bowling alley, the developers bestowed the name on their brand-new town because we were no more than two miles from the ocean, and our streets had been designed to show a few bends. (Lanes.) The shape of our twisting roads came from the draftsmen laying it out on drawing paper with French curves. Since the land was as flat as a parking lot, our S-turns served no purpose I could see except to make it easier not to have to look at your neighbor's ranch house which was exactly like your own. It's a joke, but Dougy could not find his way back when drunk. It was no joke. Something was leached out of all of us who grew up there. I cannot name it, although in the eyes of my father, we kids were awfully civilized. We didn't hang out on a street corner—no right angles in Atlantic Lanes—we didn't run in gangs (we had best friends instead) and once when I was having a fist fight, my disputant said in the middle of it, "Okay, I quit." We stopped and shook hands. My mother was not displeased that (1) I won, since she had learned over the years that would make my father happy and (2) I had acted like a gentleman. I had shaken hands nicely. My father was intrigued. It was truly the suburbs. You could get into a fight and say "I quit," and the winner would not celebrate by banging your head on the pavement. "Boy, where I grew up," he told me (it happened to be Forty-eighth Street west of Tenth Avenue) "you never quit. You might just as well say 'I die!'"

Once, a few years before the end of their marriage, I overheard my mother and father in the living room on a rare night when he was home from the bar. I was trying not to listen, in fact was staying away by doing my homework in the kitchen. When, on these rare occasions, they would find themselves together, they could sit for hours without speaking, and their mutual gloom often got so intense that even the audio on the TV seemed to quaver. On this night, however, they may have been close, for I heard my mother say in a gentle voice, "Douglas, you never say that you love me."

That was true enough. For years I had hardly ever seen him give her a kiss and then only like a miser pulling out the one ducat he will spend this year. My poor mother. She was so affectionate she would kiss me all the time. (Out of his sight.) She never wanted him to think my habits were unmanly.

"Not once, Douglas," she now repeated, "do you ever say you love me."

He did not reply for a minute, but then he answered in an Irish street voice—it was his declaration of love—"I'm here, ain't I?"

Of course, he was famous among his friends for such an ascetic view. In longshoreman days, he had earned another legend for the number of women he could attract and the powerful number of times he could do it in a night. All the same, it was his manly pride that he was never obliged to kiss the girl. Who knows what ice room of the heart my skinny Irish grandmother raised him in? He never kissed. Once, not long after I was kicked out of Exeter, I went drinking with Dougy and his oldest buddies, and he was meat for the roast on this matter of a kiss. His friends might be scarred and half toothless and in their fifties, and since I was twenty, they looked ancient to me, but, God, they were filthy-minded. When they talked, they rolled around in sex like it was stuck to their pants.

My father was, by then, not only divorced from my mother, but had, in the general waste that followed, lost his bar. He lived in a rented room, had a lady friend once in a while, worked in a barroom for wages, and saw a lot of his old friends.

Every one of these old friends, I soon discovered, had a quirk, and the rule of the game was to kick your old buddy on the quirk. Some were tight with a dollar, some had foolish habits like betting long shots, one of them always threw up when he was drunk ("I have a sensitive stomach," he would complain. "Yeah, we have sensitive noses," they would reply) and my father always got it about kissing.

"Oh, Dougy," his old friend Dynamite Heffernon would say, "last night I was with a nineteen-year-old who had the juiciest, sweetest, plumpest, loveliest mouth you ever saw. Could she kiss! Oh, the moist breath of her fine smile. Do you have any idea of what you're missing?"

"Yeah, Dougy," another would cry out, "give it a try. Break down. Give the broad a kiss!"

My father would sit there. It was the game, and he would suffer it, but his thin lips showed no pleasure.

Francis Frelagh, a.k.a. Frankie Freeload, took his swipes at the ball. "I had one widow with a tongue last week," he told us. "She put that tongue in my ears, down my mout', she licked my t'roat. If I let her, she would have swiped my nostrils."

At the look of disgust on my father's face, they laughed like choir boys, high-pitched and shrill, Irish tenors kicking Dougy Madden's quirk.

He took it all. When they were done, he shook his head. He did not like to be performed on while I was there—that was the measure of his fallen state—so he said, "I think you're all full of shit. None of you has been laid in the last ten years." When they whooped at his anger, he stuck out his palm. "I'll give you," he said, "the benefit of the doubt. Let's say you know a couple of girls. And they like to kiss. Maybe they even go down on you. All right. That's been known to happen. Only, ask yourself: The broad is taking care of you now, but whose joint did she cop last night? Where was her mouth then? Ask yourself that, you cocksuckers. Cause if she's able to kiss you, she can eat dog turds."

This speech put his old gang in heaven. "I wonder who's kissing her now," they would croon in Dougy's ear.

Tough guys don't dance. On that curious proposition my memory, like a boat coming around a buoy into harbor, returned to my adolescence and I could feel myself dwelling again in the year I turned sixteen and went into the Golden Gloves. I started to smile. For, at sixteen, I always pictured myself as tough. I had, after all, the toughest father on the block. While I knew, even then, that I would never be his equal, still I told myself that I was enough like him to make my high school football varsity by my sophomore year. That was a feat! And I remember how that winter, once football was over, I used to feel a mean and proud hostility toward the world that I could hardly control. (It was the year of my parents' divorce.) I started to go to a boxing gym near my father's bar. It was inevitable. Being Dougy Madden's son, I had to sign up for the Golden Gloves.

A Jewish boy I knew told me once that the year before he turned thirteen was the worst in his life. He spent it getting ready for his Bar Mitzvah, and never knew if on a given night he could fall asleep or would be wide awake reciting the speech he had to give next winter in the synagogue to two hundred friends of his family.

That wasn't as bad, I suggested to him, as your first night in the Gloves. "For one thing," I said, "you walk in half naked, and nobody has prepared you for that. Five hundred people are there. Some of them don't like you. They're for the other guy. They're very critical when they stare at you. Then you see your opponent. He looks like dynamite."

"What made you do it?" my friend asked.

I told him the truth. "I wanted to make my father happy."

For a boy with such a good purpose, I had, all the same, a nervous stomach in the dressing room. (I was sharing it with fifteen other fighters.) They, like me, were to be in the blue corner. On the other side of a partition was a dressing room with fifteen contenders from the red corner. Every ten minutes or so, one of us on each side would go out to the auditorium and another would come back. There is nothing like the danger of humiliation to build fast alliances. We didn't know each other, but we kept wishing each guy luck. Devoutly. Every ten minutes, as I say, one kid would go out, and soon after, the previous kid would return. He would be ecstatic if he won, and in misery if he lost, but at least it was over. One kid was carried in, and they sent for an ambulance. He had been knocked out by a black puncher with a big rep. In that minute I considered forfeiting my match. Only the thought of my father sitting in the first row kept me from speaking up. "Okay, Dad," I said to myself, "my death is for you."

Once the fight started, I discovered that boxing, like other cultures, takes years to acquire, and, immediately, I lost the little culture I had. I was so scared I never stopped throwing punches. My opponent, who was fat and black, was just as frightened and never stopped either. At the bell, neither of us could move. My heart felt ready to explode. By the second round, we could not do a thing. We stood still, we glowered, we used our heads to block punches because we were too tired to duck—it cost less to get hit than to move. We must have looked like longshoremen too drunk to fight. Both of us were bleeding from the nose and I could smell his blood. I learned on this night that blood has a scent as intimate as body odor. It was an horrendous round. When I got to my corner, I felt equal to an overraced engine whose parts were ready to seize.

"You got to do better, or we don't win," said the trainer. He was a friend of my father's.

When I could catch my voice, I said as formally as I could—you would have thought I was already in prep school—"If you want to terminate the fight, I will abide by that."

The look in his eye told me that he would repeat my remark for the rest of his life.

"Kid, just go beat the shit out of him," my trainer said.

The bell rang. He gave me my mouthpiece and a shove toward the center of the ring.

Now I fought with desperation. I had to eat the entrails of my remark. My father was shouting so loudly, I even thought I was going to win. Boom! I ran into a bomb. The side of my head could just as well have stopped the full swing of a baseball bat. I suppose that I careened around the ring because I only saw the other boxer in jump cuts. I was in one place, then I was in the next place.

New adrenaline must have been shaken loose by the punch. My legs were shocked full of life. I began to circle and to jab. I ran and I ducked and I jabbed (which is what I should have done from the beginning). At last I could recognize the given: my opponent knew less about boxing than me! Just as I was measuring him for a hook (since I had now discovered that he lowered his right each time I feinted with my left to the belly) why, the bell rang. Fight was over. They lifted his hand.

Afterward, when the well-wishers were gone and I was sitting alone with my father in a coffee shop, a second wave of pain just commencing, Big Mac muttered, "You should have won."

"I thought I did. Everybody says I did."

"That's friends." He shook his head. "You lost it in the last round."

No, now that it was over and I had lost, I thought I had won. "Everybody said it was beautiful the way I took that punch and kept moving."

"Friends." He said it in so lugubrious a voice that you would have thought it was friends, not drink, that was the bane of the Irish.

I never felt more argumentative with my father. There is no surliness like sitting around, half dislodged in every vale of your mind, torso and limbs, your organs hot and full of lead, your heart loaded with consternation that maybe you did lose the fight your friends say was stolen from you. So I said out of my own puffed mouth, and I probably never sounded cockier to him, "My mistake was that I didn't dance. I should have come out fast at the bell and stuck him. I should have gone: Stick! Stick! Slide," I said, moving my hands, "and circled away. Then back with the jab, dance out of range, circle and dance, stick him! Stick him!" I nodded at this fine war plan. "When he was ready, I could have dropped the bum."

My father's face was without expression. "Do you remember Frank Costello?" he asked.

"Top of the mob," I said with admiration.

"One night Frank Costello was sitting in a night club with his blonde, a nice broad, and at the table he's also got Rocky Marciano, Tony Canzoneri and Two-ton Tony Galento. It's a guinea party," my father said. "The orchestra is playing. So Frank says to Galento, 'Hey, Two-ton, I want you to dance with Gloria.' That makes Galento nervous. Who wants to dance with the big man's girl? What if she likes him? 'Hey, Mr. Costello,' says Two-ton Tony, 'you know I'm no dancer.' 'Put down your beer,' says Frank, 'and get out there and move. You'll be very good.' So Two-ton Tony gets up and trots Gloria around the floor at arm's length, and when he comes back, Costello tells the same thing to Canzoneri, and he has to take Gloria out. Then it's Rocky's turn. Marciano believes he's big enough in his own right to call Costello by his first name, so he says, 'Mr. Frank, we heavyweights are not much on a ballroom floor.' 'Go do some footwork,' says Costello. While Rocky is out there, Gloria takes the occasion to whisper in his ear, 'Champ, do me a favor. See if you can get Uncle Frank to do a step with me.'

"Well, when the number is over, Rocky leads her back. He's feeling better and the others got their nerve up too. They start to rib the big man, very careful, you understand, just a little tasteful chaffing. 'Hey, Mr. Costello,' they say, 'Mr. C., come on, why don't you give your lady a dance?'

" 'Will you,' Gloria asks, 'please!'

" 'It's your turn, Mr. Frank,' they say.

"Costello," my father told me, "shakes his head. 'Tough guys,' he says, 'don't dance.' "

Now, my father had about five such remarks and he never dropped them on you until he did. "*Inter faeces et urinam nascimur*" became the last and the unhappiest, even as "Don't talk—you'll spill the wind out of the sails" was always the happiest, but through my adolescence, it used to be: "Tough guys don't dance."

At sixteen, a half-Mick from Long Island, I did not know about Zen masters and their koans, but if I had, I would have said the remark was a koan, since I didn't understand it, yet it stayed with me, and the older I became, the more meaning it offered.

We had not seen each other in quite a while, but I cannot say that either of us was cheered a good deal by how the other looked. My father was making instant coffee, yet at his first sight of me, he put down the jar and whistled softly.

I nodded. I had come downstairs with a swollen foot, a left arm I could not raise above my head, and a bucket of ice water inside my chest. Who knows what circles were beneath my eyes.

Dougy was the greater shock, however. There was almost no hair left on his head and he had lost a lot of weight. High on his cheeks was a fierce pink flush that reminded me of a fire in a wind-swept place.

The recognition came like a touch of the crud itself. He must be on chemotherapy.

I guess he had become accustomed to the quick wipe from people's eyes of the initial aversion, for he said, "Yeah, I got it."

"Where's it situated?"

He made a gesture to indicate that was neither here nor there.

"Thanks for sending a telegram," I said.

"Kid, when there's nothing anybody can do about your story, keep it to yourself."

He looked weak, which is to say he did not look all-powerful. I couldn't tell, however, if he was in discomfort.

"Are you on chemotherapy?" I asked.

"I quit it a couple of days ago. The nausea is a disgrace." He walked forward and gave me a little hug, not too close, as if he felt in-fectious.

"I heard a joke," he said. "This Jewish family is waiting in the hospital lobby. The doctor comes up to them. He's a prosperous son of a bitch with a peppy voice. He choips like a boid." My father liked on occasion to remind me, as he used to remind my mother, that the roots were back in Hell's Kitchen and be damned to you. His snob-bery remained unflaggingly inverse, so he would go out of his way to say "boid" for "bird."

Now he could proceed with his joke. " 'I have,' says the doctor, 'good news *and* bad news for you. The bad news is that your father's disease is incurable. The good news is that it is not cancer.' The family says, 'Thank God.' "

We laughed together. When we were done, he handed me his un-touched cup of instant coffee and started to spoon himself out an-other. "Here we have bad news," he said.

"It's incurable?"

"Tim, who the fuck can say? Sometimes I think I know the mo-ment I got it. If I'm that close to the source, maybe I can find my cure.

I tell you, I hate those pills the doctors push. I hate myself for taking them."

"How do you sleep?"

"I never been a famous sleeper," he said. Then he nodded. "Kid, I can handle anything but the middle of the night." That was quite a speech for him. He cut it off. "What happened to you?" he asked.

I found myself telling him about the fight, and how I had won it.

"Somebody raised you right," he said.

We stayed in the kitchen all morning. After I made some eggs, we tried the living room, but Patty's furniture was not for an old long-shoreman. Soon we were back in the kitchen. Outside it was another gray day, and looking through the window, he shivered.

"What do you like about this godforsaken place?" he said. "It's like the back coast of Ireland in winter."

"No, I love it," I told him.

"Yeah?"

"The first time I came here was after being kicked out of Exeter. Remember we got drunk?"

"I sure do." It was a pleasure to see him smile.

"Well, in the morning you went back to New York, and I decided to come here for the summer. I'd heard of this town. I liked it right off, and then when I was here a week, I went to a dance joint out near the highway one night. There was a good-looking girl I kept watching, but I didn't go near her. She was with her crowd and dancing. I just kept observing. At closing, I took a shot at it. I went up to her on the dance floor, looked in her eyes, she looked in mine, and we went out the door together. Screw the dudes she was with. They didn't do a thing. So the girl and I crossed the road, went into the woods, lay down, and, Dougy, I was in her. I figure it took six minutes from the time I walked up to her till I was in. That impressed me more about myself than anything I'd done till that day."

He enjoyed my story a good deal. His hand reached out in an old reflex for his tumbler of bourbon and then he realized it wasn't there. "So this place is your luck," he said.

"To a degree."

"Are you all right?" he asked. "For a guy who's just beaten up a hood who was swinging a tire iron, you don't look too happy. Are you afraid he'll return?" What a look of happiness came into my father's eyes at the thought that Stoodie might decide to come back.

"There's a lot to talk about," I said, "but I don't know if I'm ready to tell you."

"Have to do with your wife?"

"Some."

"Say, if I was going to be around for another ten years, I wouldn't say a word, but since I won't, I'll tell you. I believe you married the wrong broad. It should have been Madeleine. She may be a vindictive guinea, but I liked her. She had class. She was subtle."

"Is this your blessing?"

"I kept my mouth shut on too many things for too many years. Maybe it started to rot inside. One of the causes of cancer, says the choipy boids, is a harsh environment."

"What do you want to tell me?"

"A guy who marries a rich woman deserves every last thing he gets."

"I thought you liked Patty." They had loved to drink together.

"I liked her guts. If all the other rednecks was as macho as her, they'd be running the world. But I didn't like what she was doing to you. Certain dames ought to wear a T-shirt that says: 'Hang around. I'll make a cocksucker out of you.' "

"Thanks."

"Hey, Tim—it's a figure of speech. Nothing personal."

"You were always worried about me, weren't you?"

"Well, your mother was delicate. She spoiled you a lot. Yeah," he said, looking at me out of his ice-blue eyes, "I worried about you."

"Maybe you didn't have to. I took my three years in the slammer without a fall. They called me Iron Jaw. I wouldn't take cock."

"Good for you. I always wondered."

"Hey, Dougy," I said, "what's the virtue? You think I feel like a man most of the time? I don't. What was I protecting? You're an old-line fanatic. You'd put all the faggots in concentration camps including your own son if he ever slipped. Just cause you were lucky enough to be born with tiger's balls."

"Let's have a drink. You're off your feed."

"Should you have a drink?"

He made a move with his hands again. "It's an occasion."

I got two glasses and put bourbon in them. He added a considerable amount of water to his. If nothing else, that was enough to tell me he was ill.

"You have me wrong," he said. "Do you think I've been living alone for twenty-five years in a furnished room, and I do no thinking? I try to keep up. In my day, if you were queer, you were damned. Don't even ask. You were an agent of hell. Now, they got Gay Liberation. I watch them. There's faggots everywhere."

"Yeah, I know," I said.

"Ha, ha," he said and pointed a finger at me. The early liquor was obviously doing angel's work on his spirits. "My son wins the round."

"Good at dancing," I said.

"I remember," he said. "Costello, right?"

"Right."

"I'm not sure I know what that means anymore," he said. "Six months ago they told me to stop drinking or I was dead. So I stopped. Now, when I go to sleep, the spirits come out of the woodwork and make a circle around my bed. Then they make me dance all night." He gave a cough filled with all the hollows of his lungs. It had been an attempt to laugh. " 'Tough guys don't dance,' I tell them. 'Hey, you bigot,' the spirits answer, 'keep dancing.' " He looked into the lights of the bourbon as if their kin could be found there, and sighed. "My illness makes me less of a bigot," he said. "I think about faggots and you know what I believe? For half of them, it's brave. For the wimps, it takes more guts to be queer than not. For the wimps. Otherwise they marry some little mouse who's too timid to be a dyke and they both become psychologists and raise whiz kids to play electronic games. Turn queer, I say, if you're a wimp. Have a coming-out party. It's the others I condemn. The ones who ought to be men but couldn't show the moxie. You were supposed to be a man, Tim. You came from me. You had advantages."

"I never heard you talk so much before. Not once in my life."

"That's cause you and I are strangers."

"Well, you look like a stranger today," I said. It was true. His large head was no longer crowned by his rich white hair, white with the corrupt splendors of ivory and cream. Now he just had an enormous bald head. He looked more like a Prussian general than the model of an Irish bartender.

"I want to talk to you now," he said. "I may be acting thick, but it came over me at Frankie Freeload's funeral: Tim is all I got."

I was moved. Sometimes a couple of months would go by, sometimes a half-year, before one of us called. Still, it seemed all right. I had always hoped so. Now he confirmed it.

"Yes," he said, "I got up early this morning, borrowed the widow's car, and told myself all the way here that this time we speak it out face to face. I don't want to die without you knowing of my regard for you."

I was embarrassed. Therefore, I leaped on the way he said "the widow's car." "Did you have any hanky-panky with Freeload's wife?" I asked.

Not often did I see my father look sheepish. "Not lately," he said.

"How could you? With a friend's wife!"

"For the last ten years, Frankie was pickled in booze. He couldn't find his tool or the pot."

"A friend's wife?" I gave him the family laugh. High tenor.

"It was only once or twice. She needed it. An act of mercy."

I laughed until the tears came. " 'I wonder who's kissing her now,' " I sang. It was wonderful to have your father at his own wake. Suddenly I felt like crying.

"You're right, kid," he said. "I hope and pray Frankie never knew." He looked at the wall for an instant. "You get older and you begin to feel as if something is wrong. You're in a box, and the sides keep coming closer. So you do things you didn't do before."

"How long have you known you were sick?"

"Ever since I went into St. Vincent's forty-five years ago."

"That's quite a while to have cancer and never show it."

"None of the doctors have a feel for the subject," he said. "The way I see the matter, it's a circuit of illness with two switches."

"What are you saying?"

"Two terrible things have to happen before the crud can get its start. The first cocks the trigger. The other fires it. I've been walking around with the trigger cocked for forty-five years."

"Because you couldn't recover from all those hits you took?"

"No. Cause I lost my balls."

"You? What are you talking about?"

"Tim, I stopped, and I felt the blood in my shoes, and there was St. Vincent's in front of me. I should have kept chasing the bastard who did the shooting. But I lost my nerve when I saw the hospital."

"Hell, you had already gone after him for six blocks."

"Not enough. I was built to be that good anyway. The test came when I stopped. I didn't have the nerve to go on and catch him. Cause I could have. Something in the scheme of things might have made him trip. I didn't push my luck. Instead, I stopped. Then I heard a voice clearly in my head. It's the only time I would say that God or someone *highly superior* was speaking to me. This voice said, 'You're out of gas, kid. It's your true test. Do it.' But I went into St. Vincent's and grabbed the orderly by the collar, and just at the moment when I got tough with that punk in the white jacket was when I felt the first switch get thrown in the cancer."

"What threw the second switch?"

"It never got thrown. It corroded. Cumulative effects. Forty-five years of living with no respect for myself."

"You're crazy."

He took a big belt of his watered bourbon. "I wish I was. Then I wouldn't have cancer. I've studied this, I tell you. There's buried statistics if you look for them. Schizophrenics in looney bins only get cancer half as often as the average population. I figure it this way: Either your body goes crazy, or your mind. Cancer is the cure for schizophrenia. Schizophrenia is the cure for cancer. Most people don't know how tough it is out there. I was brought up to know. I got no excuse."

I was silent. I stopped arguing with him. It is not easy to sort out what effect his words were having. Was I coming to understand for the first time why the warmth he had for me always seemed to cross a glacial field? I may once have been a seed in Douglas Madden's body but only after that body was no longer held by him in high esteem. I was, to a degree, defective. Agitation had to be stirring in all my old wounds, well-buried and long-resigned. No wonder my father had taken no great joy in me. Intimations came how in years ahead—if I lived—the memory of this conversation might make me shake with rage.

Yet, I also felt compassion for my father. Damnable compassion. He had cast a long shadow across my understanding of him.

From *Tough Guys Don't Dance* (1984)

# AMATEURS—II

## The Best Move
## Lies Close to the Worst

One morning at the Gramercy Gym on East Fourteenth Street in New York, a friend of one of our regulars came along to join us for the Saturday-morning workout. He had never put on gloves before, but he was quietly confident. Having finished the New York City Marathon in close to three hours, he was even ready to get in the ring on his first day, and that was notable, since it usually took a couple of months to build up to such a moment. Of course, the marathoner was in superb shape.

He sparred for three minutes with his friend and by the end of that round was too used up to go another. The answer was to be found in the special nature of boxing. If our visitor had been playing baskets one-on-one for the first time, or running after a tennis ball, he might have felt talentless, even foolish, but he would not have been wholly winded in three minutes.

Boxing, however, is not like other tests in sport between one athlete and another; it arouses two of the deepest anxieties we contain. There is not only the fear of getting hurt, which is profound in more men than will admit to it, but there is the opposite panic, equally unadmitted, of hurting others. Part of this second fear rests, of course, on the well-comprehended equation that the harder you hit your opponent, the more he is going to feel free to bang back on you, but it goes a long way beyond that. To be born into that middle class, which is two-thirds of America by now, is to be brought up not to strike others. Probably it is worth noting that General S.L.A. Marshall's classic study of infantrymen in battle for World War II, *Men Against Fire*, came to the conclusion that the large majority of soldiers in combat for the first time could not bring themselves to fire their rifles.

No surprise then if it is difficult to deliver a good punch. It not only requires about as much coordination as to throw a football in a spiral for thirty yards, but, in addition, the punch must find some inner sanction. You have to feel justified. The marathoner wore out because two wholly opposed anxiety systems had been working at full thrust in him. It is one thing to be frightened—some part of yourself can sometimes pull you through. When your cowardice and aggression are both in a flurry, however, quick exhaustion is the consequence.

Be it said that for professionals such opposed fears still exist—it is just that the ante has gone up. Now, you can kill a man in the ring or be killed yourself.

Muhammad Ali once paid a press-inspired visit to Floyd Patterson's training camp in the Catskills a few weeks before their championship match in Las Vegas, and on arrival proceeded to savage Floyd. "You're nothing but a rabbit," Ali told Patterson in front of the reporters, and then decamped in high operatic disgust. Patterson managed to throttle his visible perturbation down to a wry grin. "Well," he said, "I won't have to worry about motivation with that guy, will I?"

One can take one's pass at Ali's premise: For a man like Patterson, an overload of sanction could prove disastrous. He would feel too murderous. On the night that the bout took place in Vegas, Floyd was so tense that his lower back went out on him in the second round. He managed to keep on his feet, fighting from one contorted position after another until the contest was stopped in the twelfth round, but he never had a chance. Ali was a genius.

In the ring, genius is transcendent moxie—the audacity to know that what usually does not work, or is too dangerous to attempt, can, in a special case, prove the winning move. Maybe that is why attempts are made from time to time to compare boxing with chess—the best move can lie very close to the worst move. At Ali's level, you had to be ready to die, then, for your best ideas.

For our pugilistic fold, however, out there on Saturday morning in the gray, grimy, now-closed Gramercy Gym, where even the ropes and the canvas were gray, and the windows, summer or winter, were a greasy patina of dishrag gray, it was enough that we were ready to show up, each at our own private frequency—some regularly once a week, some once a month, and all variations between—were, yes, ready to wake up on Saturday morning with the knowledge that no legitimate excuse was there on this occasion to get us out of it. We were not hung over, had had enough sleep, yes, we would have to show up. Nonetheless, it was also true that once there, one did not have to box; one could merely work out, hit the speed bag, the heavy bag, do situps, jump rope, shadowbox, or even less—there were no rules, and no obvious rewards, and virtually no shame for doing too little, other than a faint and subtle queasiness concerning macho matters.

Or, one could get into the ring. Sometimes there were weeks in a row when you went one or, better, two three-minute rounds on every Saturday. It varied. No one judged anyone else. Given our separate lives, we were nonetheless not that unalike when it came to our guts and our skill. Most of us did not have a great deal of the latter. We were there to make delicate adjustments on our ongoing workaday ego. Sparring honestly for several weeks in a row, just that once-a-week submersion into three minutes or six minutes of high-speed (for us) boxing, did wonders for the self-esteem one could bring back to one's social life.

Of course, most of us went our separate ways outside. We had among us a cabdriver, a bearded editor of a porny magazine, a high school English teacher who suffered a broken jaw one Saturday morning, an actor who worked nights as a dealer in a gambling joint and purchased headgear with a vertical bridge to protect his handsome nose—which we all found ludicrous until he went on to become a star in a TV crime series.

We also had a couple of young writers and one Golden Gloves aspirant who lost his first and only bout, and we had an established older writer, myself. For the record, I didn't hang up my fourteen-ounce gloves until I was fifty-eight, but by then my knees were gone, I had beaten them half to death jogging on sidewalks, and if you cannot do a little running for the requisite three times a week, you certainly don't have the wind to box on Saturday. It does not matter then how much you know about boxing's systems of anxiety—the fact is that when you have no wind, you cannot be any kind of pugilist unless you are as sly as Archie Moore or as wise as George Foreman. For an average man to go into the ring without wind is equal to going in without blood. So I gave it up, I eased out of it, and have never felt as virtuous since.

We had others who came on Saturday morning, transients. A criminal lawyer was there for a few weeks, and a Greek fencer who could never come up with a way to convert fencing to boxing, although he did muster a kind of long left jab. The friends of friends showed up for short periods, and there was one year when we had an instructor, a fast Puerto Rican bantamweight professional, who was too small and too good to impart anything to us that was not in slow motion. He had been brought in by José Torres, our resident dean, who used to enjoy sparring with all of us despite the fact that he had been light-heavyweight champion of the world. Torres won his title from Willie Pastrano in 1965 by a TKO in the ninth round at Madison Square Garden and, after several successful defenses, lost it to Dick Tiger in 1966 in fifteen rounds in the same place in a very close fight.

Why Torres enjoyed getting in the ring with us, I never quite understood. It bore comparison to the bemused pleasure Colin Powell might take in teaching close-order drill to recruits. On the other hand, we all enjoyed being able to say we had been in with a former light-heavyweight champion. He was impossible to hit and that was an interesting experience—you felt as if you were sharing the ring with a puma. Be it understood, part of his honor was not to hurt anyone. When you made a mistake, he would tap you. If you repeated the error, he would tap you harder. Defensive reflexes developed in the student. One's offense, however, had to fend for itself. Over ten years of boxing with José Torres I was able to catch him with a good right hand lead twice, and the first occasion was an event. He ran around the ring with his arms high in triumph, crying out, "He hit me with a right—he hit me with a right!" unconscionably proud that day of his pupil.

It was thanks to José that we had the use of the gym. The management had provided him with the keys. When he did not show up on an occasional Saturday, a poet who lived in a fourth-floor loft above the third-story gym would let us in by opening his begrimed window long enough to drop a key down to us in a rolled-up sock, and when we climbed the stairs, the premises still reeked of the serious sweat of the professional and Golden Gloves aspirants who had trained there from Monday to Friday.

Such was our club. But for one or two clear exceptions, we were all more or less equal, and we went at it like club members. There were few wars, and most of us went out to eat and drink together afterward. We worked on what we considered most lacking, a better left hook, a sharper jab, a hook off the jab, a heavier or faster right hand. Some of us even ventured into combinations, but never too far. Mediocre condition was the scythe that cut into the rate of one's improvement. It is hard to describe how tired you can get in a three-minute round when you are forced to labor at your utmost. Two-minute rounds, the duration employed in the Golden Gloves for subnovices, would have been a considerably more satisfactory interval for us, but at the Gramercy, our bell was set on a three-minute professional interval, with only that quick sixty seconds of rest before it rang again. So we worked through three-minute rounds, and paid the price: The last thirty seconds of a three-minute round can get to feel as long as the first two and a half minutes. Going a couple of such rounds in a row (which total of six minutes is equal to a three-round subnovice bout), you often got tired enough to find it considerably easier to take the other's arm-weary punch to your head rather than to raise your own bone-dead arms in defense.

Ryan O'Neal came to join us, however, and our Saturdays were altered. Ryan was making a movie in New York that season, and José Torres was his friend—José had worked as a boxing adviser on *The Main Event,* a comedy O'Neal had made with Barbra Streisand. Now, each Saturday morning, after five days of shooting on his film, O'Neal would come into the Gramercy.

He was good enough to have been a ring professional. When they boxed, Torres could not play with him, and once Ryan even managed to catch José with a shot to the mouth that drew a little blood. That was equal to sacrilege. Torres nodded curtly, and stepped out of the ring. It was a sizable rebuke. The retaliation he had chosen not to express was as palpable as the air in summer before a storm, and O'Neal looked sheepish, like a man who is too far from home to be caught without a raincoat.

After that, he and José did not box too frequently, and when they did, all the parameters were kept in place. O'Neal began to work out instead with whoever was there. By our measure, he was in impressive condition. He would take us on serially, each of us going for a round or two, depending on our ability to continue, and by the end of his workout he had boxed his way through eight to ten rounds against such easy opposition. Then he would go off to play racquetball with Farrah Fawcett.

Getting in the ring with Ryan O'Neal became not only the focus of each Saturday but the point to what some of us had been half-looking to do for years, that is, get extended a little in the ring. Ryan could be mean as cat piss. Even when he was carrying a man, he would punish him, and when he had dislikes, he liked to take them out on the opponent. In spite of every love affair in his private life, public fodder for more than a decade to the gossip columns, Ryan had his dry spot—the puritanism of the Irish. He took a secret dislike to the bearded editor of the porny magazine, who happened to be not much of a boxer. The editor was awkward in the ring, so it was not hard to play tricks on him. He had surprising stamina, however. Until Ryan came along, the pornographer had, in fact, the most notable stamina of any of us. Maybe Ryan equated that ability to sexual prowess and disapproved of its presence in so unworthy a vessel, maybe he just disliked hirsute New York lumpen intelligentsia, but in any case, he all but disemboweled the man, throwing cruel left hooks to the stomach until the editor collapsed, still conscious, in the middle of the second round, wholly unable to go on. What made it worse was that the pornographer's lady love, a good-looking girl who worked in a massage parlor, was witnessing it all at ringside. Something in their love—and it was, after all, *their* love—was lost that day.

I happened to be next in the ring with Ryan, which proved to be my good luck. After every discharge of mean feelings, Ryan would turn angelic. A little ashamed, I expect, of what he had just done to the pornographer, he was not now boxing like a movie star—he certainly did not protect his face. Since the man he had hurt happened to be a sweet guy, extraordinarily optimistic about life (which is probably how he had gotten into pornography in the first place), I liked the editor. When I saw him take this beating, I recognized that I saw him as a friend. If this seems something of a digression, let me say that it helps to carry the auctorial voice around the embarrassment of declaring that I boxed better on that day than I ever did before, or since. I was in a rare mean mood myself, mean enough not to be afraid of Ryan, and—it is very hard to do any kind of good boxing against a superior without some premise to carry you—I was feeling like an avenger. And here was Ryan boxing with his face. It was hard not to hit him straight rights, and he reacted with all the happiness of seeing a beloved senior relative get up from a sickbed. In our first clinch, he whispered, "You punch sharper than anyone here."

"Go fuck yourself," I told him.

We fell into a mutually pleasing pattern. He would give me his face for a target, I would bop it, and he would counterpunch. He hit harder than anyone in the club, but that was the day when my two systems of anxiety were in quiet balance, and I never enjoyed boxing as much.

Following that Saturday, Ryan and I took up predictable weekly behavior. I would invariably be the first to box with him (mainly, I think, so I could enjoy watching the others now that I was done), and he would continue to spar with his hands low, daring me to catch him. I would, often enough, and he would counterpunch. How much he took off his blows I do not know—at whatever level he gunned down his motors for me, his punches still took your head half-around, or left a space in your gut, and I, in turn, reduced my punches very little for him. Whatever the equilibrium, we had found it, and it was as close as it ever came for me to gain some knowledge of how a professional might feel in a real bout for money with a hard-hearted crowd out there and the spirit of electricity in the ring lights. Damn, it was exciting. I even came to understand what it was to feel love for the man you were fighting because he had forced you to go a little beyond yourself, and I never took as many good punches or threw as many as in those one or two rounds each Saturday with Ryan O'Neal.

Life, in the form of Luce publications, caught up with this romance. Ryan, having produced my Saturday illumination, would then box with another three or four of us, and kept to his habit—I always thought it was penance for having become a movie star—of showing that good-looking open face, so relatively easy to score upon.

There came a day when I popped him in the left eye a few times running and the boxers who came after me did approximately as much in the same place, and when he was done, he had a mouse. That little animal got into the papers. One of the gossip columns recounted how Norman Mailer had given Ryan O'Neal a shiner.

*People* magazine called up. They were ready to do a story. The dangers were obvious. We would all be famous for too little. So I turned the reporter from *People* over to José Torres. José would know how to protect Ryan.

He did. For my money, he protected him too well. "Ryan could have easily beaten Norman up," said Torres for publication—which was exactly true. I understood that it was true with all the hard objective core of my pride in being a writer who would always look into the eye of the truth, that severe gray lady, gray as the Gramercy Gym, but, José, José, I whispered within, how about a little transcendence?

Torres was much too agile, however, to sacrifice one friend altogether in order to protect another. So, for *People* magazine, he added: "Norman could whip Sly Stallone in one round."

"Yes," I said later to José, "and what happens when I run into Stallone?"

José shrugged. More immediate problems were usually waiting for him around any corner.

I do not recall if it was one year or two or three before I encountered Sylvester Stallone, but it did happen one night in a particularly dark disco with a raked floor.

"I understand," said Stallone, "that you're the guy who can beat me in one round."

He had never looked in finer shape.

"Yeah," I said, applying all the thickener I could muster to my voice, "I remember when José said that, I said to him, 'Yeah, swell, but what happens if I don't knock Stallone out in one round?' and José said, 'Oh, then he will *keel* you.' "

Stallone gave his sad, sleepy-eyed smile. "Mr. Mailer, I can assure you, I don't go around killing people."

It was gracious. One could only respond in kind. "Mr. Stallone," I said, "I don't go around getting in the ring with people who can do one-arm push-ups."

"Ah," he said sadly, "I can't do them anymore. I hurt my arm."

We grinned at each other, we shook hands. I think we were in silent league (for the modest good it could do) against the long reductive reach of the media.

Afterward, I would smile at the cost of such knowledge. It had taken me ten years of boxing to come up with a glimmer of pugilist's wit—what if I don't knock him out in the first round?—yes, one boxed for the better footing it could offer in the social world, and one could even believe, yes, absolutely, that boxing was one of the sixty things a man should learn if he is to get along in this accelerating world, so, farewell, Gramercy Gym, gray lady of my late middle age, I will always be loyal to you.

From *Esquire* (October 1993)

# 1985  HUCKLEBERRY FINN—ALIVE AT 100

Is there a sweeter tonic for the doldrums than old reviews of great novels? In nineteenth-century Russia, *Anna Karenina* was received with the following: "Vronsky's passion for his horse runs parallel to his passion for Anna" . . . "Sentimental rubbish" . . . "Show me one page," says *The Odessa Courier,* "that contains an idea." *Moby-Dick* was incinerated: "Graphic descriptions of a dreariness such as we do not remember to have met with before in marine literature" . . . "Sheer moonstruck lunacy" . . . "Sad stuff. Mr. Melville's Quakers are wretched dolts and drivellers and his mad captain is a monstrous bore."

By this measure, *Huckleberry Finn* gets off lightly. *The Springfield Republican* judged it to be no worse than "a gross trifling with every fine feeling . . . Mr. Clemens has no reliable sense of propriety," and the public library in Concord, Massachusetts, was confident enough to ban it: "the veriest trash." *The Boston Transcript* reported that "other members of the Library Committee characterize the work as rough, coarse, and inelegant, the whole book being more suited to the slums than to intelligent, respectable people."

All the same, the novel was not too unpleasantly regarded. There were no large critical hurrahs, but the reviews were, on the whole, friendly. A good tale, went the consensus. There was no sense that a great American novel had landed on the literary world of 1885. The critical climate could hardly anticipate T. S. Eliot and Ernest Hemingway's encomiums fifty years later. In the preface to the English edition, Eliot would speak of "a masterpiece . . . Twain's genius is completely realized," and Ernest went further. In *Green Hills of Africa*, after disposing of Emerson, Hawthorne, and Thoreau, and paying off Henry James and Stephen Crane with a friendly nod, he proceeded to declare, "All modern American literature comes from one book by Mark Twain called *Huckleberry Finn*. . . . It's the best book we've had. All American writing comes from that. There was nothing before. There has been nothing as good since."

Hemingway, with his nonpareil gift for nosing out the perfect *vin du pays* for an ineluctable afternoon, was more like other novelists in one dire respect: He was never at a loss to advance himself with his literary judgments. Assessing the writing of others, he used the working author's rule of thumb: If I give this book a good mark, does it help appreciation of my work? Obviously, *Huckleberry Finn* has passed the test.

A suspicion immediately arises. Mark Twain is doing the kind of writing only Hemingway can do better. Evidently, we must take a look. May I say it helps to have read *Huckleberry Finn* so long ago that it feels brand-new on picking it up again. Perhaps I was eleven when I saw it last, maybe thirteen, but now I only remember that I came to it after *Tom Sawyer* and was disappointed. I couldn't really follow *The Adventures of Huckleberry Finn*. The character of Tom Sawyer whom I had liked so much in the first book was altered, and did not seem nice anymore. Huckleberry Finn was altogether beyond me. Later, I recollect being surprised by the high regard nearly everyone who taught American Lit. lavished upon the text, but that didn't bring me back to it. Obviously, I was waiting for an assignment from *The New York Times*.

Let me offer assurances. It may have been worth the wait. I suppose I am the ten millionth reader to say that *Huckleberry Finn* is an extraordinary work. Indeed, for all I know, it is a great novel. Flawed, quirky, uneven, not above taking cheap shots and cashing far too many checks (it is rarely above milking its humor)—all the same, what a book we have here! I had the most curious sense of excitement. After a while, I understood my peculiar frame of attention. The book was so up-to-date! I was not reading a classic author so much as looking at a new work sent to me in galleys by a publisher. It was as if it had arrived with one of those rare letters that says, "We won't make this claim often, but do think we have an extraordinary first novel to send out." So it was like reading *From Here to Eternity* in galleys, back in 1950, or *Lie Down in Darkness, Catch-22*, or *The World According to Garp* (which reads like a fabulous first novel). You kept being alternately delighted, surprised, annoyed, competitive, critical, and, finally, excited. A new writer had moved onto the block. He could be a potential friend or enemy, but he most certainly was talented.

That was how it felt to read *Huckleberry Finn* a second time. I kept resisting the context until I finally surrendered. One always does surrender sooner or later to a book with a strong magnetic field. I felt as if I held the work of a young writer about thirty or thirty-five, a prodigiously talented fellow from the Midwest, from Missouri probably, who had had the audacity to write a historical novel about the Mississippi as it might have been a century and a half ago, and this young writer had managed to give us a circus of fictional virtuosities. In nearly every chapter new and remarkable characters bounded out from the printed page as if it were a tarmac on which they could perform their leaps. The author's confidence seemed so complete that he could deal with every kind of man or woman God ever gave to the middle of America. Jail-house drunks like Huck Finn's father take their bow, full of the raunchy violence that even gets into the smell of clothing. Gentlemen and river rats, young, attractive girls full of grit and "sand," and strong old ladies with aphorisms clicking like knitting needles, fools and confidence men—what a cornucopia of rabble and gentry inhabit the author's river banks.

It would be superb stuff if only the writer did not keep giving away the fact that he was a modern young American working in 1984. His anachronisms were not so much in the historical facts—those seemed accurate enough—but the point of view was too contemporary. The scenes might succeed—say it again, this young writer was talented!—but he kept betraying his literary influences. The author of *The Adventures of Huckleberry Finn* had obviously been taught a lot by such major writers as Sinclair Lewis, John Dos Passos, and John Steinbeck; he had certainly lifted from Faulkner and the mad tone Faulkner could achieve when writing about maniacal men feuding in deep swamps; he had also absorbed much of what Vonnegut and Heller could teach about the resilience of irony. If he had a surer feel for the picaresque than Saul Bellow in *Augie March*, still he felt derivative of that work. In places one could swear he had memorized *The Catcher in the Rye*, and he probably dipped into *Deliverance* and *Why Are We in Vietnam?* He might even have studied the mannerisms of movie stars. You could feel traces of John Wayne, Victor McLaglen, and Burt Reynolds in his pages. The author had doubtless digested many a Hollywood comedy on small-town life. His instinct for life in hamlets on the Mississippi before the Civil War was as sharp as it was farcical, and couldn't be more commercial.

No matter. With a talent as large as this, one could forgive the obvious eye for success. Many a large talent has to go through large borrowings in order to find his own style, and a lust for popular success while dangerous to serious writing is not necessarily fatal. Yes, one could accept the pilferings from other writers, given the scope of his work, the brilliance of the concept—to catch rural America by a trip on a raft down a great river! One could even marvel uneasily at the depth of the instinct for fiction in the author. With the boy Huckleberry Finn, this new novelist had managed to give us a character of no comfortable, measurable dimension. It is easy for characters in modern novels to seem more vivid than figures in the classics but, even so, Huckleberry Finn appeared to be more alive than Don Quixote and Julian Sorel, as naturally near to his own mind as we are to ours. But how often does a hero who is so absolutely natural on the page also succeed in acquiring convincing moral stature as his adventures develop?

It is to be repeated. In the attractive grip of this talent, one is ready to forgive the author of *Huckleberry Finn* for every influence he has so promiscuously absorbed. He has made such fertile use of his borrowings. One could even cheer his appearance on our jaded literary scene if not for the single transgression that goes too far. These are passages that do more than borrow an author's style—they copy it! Influence is mental, but theft is physical. Who can declare to a certainty that a large part of the prose in *Huckleberry Finn* is not lifted directly from Hemingway? We know that we are not reading Ernest only because the author, obviously fearful that his tone is getting too near, is careful to sprinkle his text with "a-clutterings" and "warn'ts" and "anywheres" and "t'others." But we have read Hemingway—and so we see through it—we know we are reading pure Hemingway disguised:

> We cut young cottonwoods and willows, and hid the raft with them. Then we set out the lines. Next we slid into the river and had a swim . . . then we set down on the sandy bottom where the river was knee-deep and watched the daylight come. Not a sound anywheres . . . the first thing to see, looking away over the water, was a kind of dull line—that was the woods on t'other side; you couldn't make nothing else out; then a pale place in the sky; then more paleness spreading around; then the river softened up away off, and warn't black any more . . . by and by you could see a streak on the water which you know by the look of the streak

that there's a snag there in a swift current which breaks on it and makes that streak look that way; and you see the mist curl up off the water and the east reddens up and the river.

Up to now I have conveyed, I expect, the pleasure of reading this book today. It is the finest compliment I can offer. We use an unspoken standard of relative judgment on picking up a classic. Secretly, we expect less reward from it than from a good contemporary novel. The average intelligent modern reader would probably, under torture, admit that *Heartburn* was more fun to read, minute for minute, than *Madame Bovary,* and maybe one even learned more. That is not to say that the first will be superior to the second a hundred years from now but that a classic novel is like a fine horse carrying an exorbitant impost. Classics suffer by their distance from our day-to-day gossip. The mark of how good *Huckleberry Finn* has to be is that one can compare it to a number of our best modern American novels and it stands up page for page, awkward here, sensational there—absolutely the equal of one of those rare incredible first novels that come along once or twice in a decade. So I have spoken of it as kin to a first novel because it is so young and so fresh and so all-out silly in some of the chances it takes and even wins. A wiser older novelist would never play that far out when the work was already well along and so neatly in hand, but Twain does.

For the sake of literary propriety, let me not, however, lose sight of the actual context. *The Adventures of Huckleberry Finn* is a novel of the nineteenth century and its grand claims to literary magnitude are also to be remarked upon. So I will say that the first measure of a great novel may be that it presents—like a human of palpable charisma—an all but visible aura. Few works of literature can be so luminous without the presence of some majestic symbol. In *Huckleberry Finn* we are presented (given the possible exception of Anna Livia Plurabelle) with the best river ever to flow through a novel, our own Mississippi, and in the voyage down those waters of Huck Finn and a runaway slave on their raft, we are held in the thrall of the river. Larger than a character, the river is a manifest presence, a demiurge to support the man and the boy, a deity to betray them, feed them, all but drown them, fling them apart, float them back together. The river winds like a fugue through the marrow of the true narrative, which is nothing less than the ongoing relation between Huck and the runaway slave, this Nigger Jim whose name embodies the very stuff of the slave system itself—his name is not Jim but Nigger Jim. The growth of love and knowledge between the runaway white and the runaway black is a relation equal to the relation of the men to the river, for it is also full of betrayal and nourishment, separation and return. So it manages to touch that last fine nerve of the heart where compassion and irony speak to one another and thereby give a good turn to our most protected emotions.

Reading *Huckleberry Finn,* one comes to realize all over again that the near burned-out, throttled, hate-filled dying affair between whites and blacks is still our great national love affair, and woe to us if it ends in detestation and mutual misery. Riding the current of this novel, we are back in the happy time when the love affair was new and all seemed possible. How rich is the recollection of that emotion! What else is greatness but the indestructible wealth it leaves in the mind's recollection after hope has soured and passions are spent? It is always the hope of democracy that our wealth will be there to spend again, and the ongoing treasure of *Huckleberry Finn* is that it frees us to think of democracy and its sublime, terrifying premise: Let the passions and cupidities and dreams and kinks and ideals and greed and hopes and foul corruptions of all men and women have their day and the world will still be better off, for there is more good than bad in the sum of us and our workings. Mark Twain, whole embodiment of that democratic human, understood the premise in every turn of his pen, and how he tested it, how he twisted and tantalized and tested it until we are weak all over again with our love for the idea.

From *The New York Times Book Review* (December 9, 1984)

# 1989 A FOLLY REPEATED

## A Speech on Salman Rushdie

By my limited comprehension of the Muslim religion, martyrdom is implicit in the faith. While all faiths sooner or later suggest that a true believer may have to be ready to die for the governing god, it is possible that the Muslims, of all religions, have always been the most dedicated to this stern test. Now it seems as if the spiritual corruption of the twentieth century has entered Islam's ranks as well. Any Muslim who succeeds in assassinating Salman Rushdie will be rewarded with the munificent sum of $5 million. This must be the largest hit contract in history. Islam, with all its mighty virtues and vices, equal at the least to the virtues and vices of every other major religion, has now introduced a novel element into the history of theology. It has added the logic of the syndicate. One does not even have to belong to the family to collect. One has only to be the hit man. Of course, the novelist in me insists on thinking how I would hate to be that hit man trying to collect $5 million. Now that the deed was done, I might be looked upon as an infidel. "Oh, you see," my Iranian paymaster might say, "we really cannot afford the five million. We lost so many men in the war with Iraq. There are so many widows in need of alms, and we have our orphans, and our veterans who are now missing a limb. Tell you, kind killer, we think you might wish to make your charitable contribution."

This is but a novelist's speculation. That is what we are here for—to speculate on human possibilities, to engage in those fantasies, cynicisms, satires, criticisms, and explorations of human vanity, desire, and courage that the blank walls of mighty corporations like to conceal from us. We are scribblers who try to explore what is left to look at in the interstices. Sometimes we make mistakes and injure innocent victims by our words. Sometimes we get lucky and make people with undue worldly power a bit uncomfortable for a short time. Usually, we spend our days injuring each other. We are, after all, a fragile resource, an endangered species. It is not untypical of the weak and endangered to chew each other up a little on the way down. But now the Ayatollah Khomeini has offered us an opportunity to regain our frail religion, which happens to be faith in the power of words and our willingness to suffer for them. He awakens us to the great rage we feel when our liberty to say what we wish, wise or foolish, kind or cruel, well-advised or ill-advised, is endangered. We discover that, yes, maybe we are willing to suffer for our idea. Maybe we are even willing, ultimately, to die for the idea that serious literature, in a world of dwindling certainties and choked-up ecologies, is the absolute we must defend.

We have had the example of our largest corporate chain of booksellers in America, Waldenbooks, withdrawing *The Satanic Verses* from its bookshelves in order to secure the safety of their employees. Immediately, they were followed by B. Dalton. Both had honest motives, doubtless. What is the use of being upwardly mobile in one's job in a massive corporate chain if security cannot be guaranteed? Get killed selling a book? The end of the world has come. Worse! One could get killed buying a book. Who would ever forgive the corporate chain? Of course, the option of assessing such danger calmly, and informing employees and customers of the real odds was never engaged—though both chains did eventually change their stance. In Russian roulette, using the classic revolver, there is one chance in six you will kill yourself each time you pull the trigger. I am happy to say I have never played Russian roulette, but if I had, I am certain the odds would have felt much more like even money. I would have needed one part of my brain to explain to the other, over and over, that the odds were really 5 to 1 in my favor.

Waldenbooks has something like a thousand outlets. In one working week from Monday to Saturday, if one terrorist succeeded in making one successful attack on one store, the odds that it would not be the store you worked in would be 6,000 to 1 in your favor. If, as a customer, you spent half an hour in any one of these thousand stores, while it was in the course of being open for eight hours a day for six days, the odds in your favor would increase to 16 times 6,000, or close to 100,000 to 1 on your side. I think such odds, if loudly promulgated, would have brought in as many prospective customers looking for the spice of a very small risk as would have been frightened away; for the employees, a 10 percent increase for temporary combat pay could have been instituted. What are contingency funds for?

No, the answer to why Waldenbooks shut down *The Satanic Verses* is that they sell their product like soup cans. Only the homeless will ever endanger themselves over a can of soup. The largest purveyors of our books do not care about literature, whether serious, half-serious, or failed. The purveyors see books as a commodity that rots into the very spirit of the circulation of money if the books stay too long on the shelf. So they hire clerks who tend to reflect their own mores. If Saul Bellow were to purchase one of his own novels in a chain where he did not normally shop and paid for it with his own credit card, the odds that the clerk would recognize his name are about the same as the odds in Russian roulette—1 in 6. Saul Bellow could walk in and out of a chain bookstore like a ghost. So could I. So could any other established serious writer who has been around thirty or forty years. Tom Wolfe might be recognized, but then Tom, for this year anyway, is the fastest selling can of soup around.

No surprise, therefore, if retail chains of American booksellers seem to have more respect for terrorists than for culture. How, then, can they not help to accelerate the latest mega-farce down the media road?

A serious book that may or may not have been irresponsible in part, as most serious books are—I cannot pretend to define the issue more closely since I, I fear, in company with the people issuing the death threats, have not yet read it, although I certainly intend to—yes, this serious yet possibly irresponsible contribution to serious literature, if it had been treated like other serious novels, which are almost always in part sacrilegious, blasphemous, and secretly against the state, would, if it had encountered no formal outrage, have suffered the fate of other serious books. It would have received good, even hearteningly good, but still modest sales, it would have been discussed and taken its small place on the shelf of serious works to be picked up again by a few devoted readers. Islam might have been injured by one part in one hundred thousand. Now, Islam is injured vastly more. Oceans of publicity have been given to the sacrilege. I say the act of attracting such attention to a book despised was a willful chosen act by the Muslim leaders. The wise men of Iran know that the Western moral conscience is dulled, and no one in our monotonous Yuppie overlay of skillful surface floating above incalculable horrors such as drug wars and acute poverty is ready to die for any idea, other, conceivably, than receiving a big payoff in cash. So the Ayatollah may have wished to show the great length of the whip he can crack, the whip whose secret name is found in our bottomless pit of terrorism. If we believe in nothing, how can we bear to die? The wise men of Islam know that about us.

One would have to respect the incisiveness of such understanding if not for the fact that the wise men of Iran are also wholly indifferent to the fate of our literature, and are savagely opposed to those freedoms of expression we wish to believe we hold dear.

In this period of turmoil, we can now envision a fearful time in the future when fundamentalist groups in America, stealing their page from this international episode, will know how to apply the same methods to American writers and bookstores. If they ever succeed, it will be due to the fact that we never found an honest resistance to the terrorization of Salman Rushdie.

I would suggest, therefore, that it is our duty to form ranks behind him, and our duty to state to the world that if he is ever assassinated, it will then become our obligation to stand in his place. If he is ever killed for a folly, we must be killed for the same folly, and we may indeed be, since we will then vow to do our best to open all literary meetings with a reading of the critical pages in *The Satanic Verses*. A folly repeated is no longer a folly but a statement of intent. If what Salman Rushdie wrote was grave folly, then by killing him you will be obliging us to immortalize that same grave folly. For if one writer can be killed on a hit contract and all concerned get away with it, then we may be better off being hit each of us, one by one, in future contracts, until our chiefs in the Western world may be finally aroused by the shocking spectacle of our willingness, even though we are selfish creative artists, to be nonetheless martyred.

I will not, however, put my name on such a list alone. Like others, I have my family, my projects, my life to see through to its conclusion. Join with me, rather, ten good American authors, male and female, or twenty, or a hundred in such a vow, and we are relatively safe. At least, we are safer to a considerable degree, and can feel honorable to ourselves. We will have struck a real blow for freedom. For the wise men of Iran will know then that we possess our spiritual wisdom, too. Certain acts count for more than others in the defense of freedom, and the willingness to embrace an idea at perilous cost to our inner calm may be at the center of what the Western World is all about. If we would ask bookstore clerks to stand and serve, then we must demand more than that of ourselves.

From *The Rushdie Letters: Freedom to Speak, Freedom to Write* (1989)

# THE BEST OF
# ABBIE HOFFMAN

Abbie was one of the smartest—let us say, one of the quickest—people I ever met, and he was probably one of the bravest. In the land from which he originated, Worcester, Mass., they call it moxie. He had tons of moxie. He was also one of the funniest people I ever met. He was also one of the most appealing if you ask for little order in personality. Abbie had a charisma that must have come out of an immaculate conception between Fidel Castro and Groucho Marx. They went into his soul and he came out looking like an ethnic milkshake—Jewish revolutionary, Puerto Rican lord, Italian street kid, Black Panther with the old Afro haircut, even a glint of Irish gunman in the mad green eyes. I remember them as yellow-green, like Joe Namath's gypsy green eyes. Abbie was one of the most incredible-looking people I ever met. In fact, he wasn't Twentieth Century but Nineteenth. Might just as well have emerged out of *Oliver Twist*. You could say he used to look like a chimney sweep. In fact, I don't know what chimney sweeps looked like, but I always imagined them as having a manic integrity that glared out of their eyes through all the soot and darked-up skin. It was the knowledge that they were doing an essential job that no one else would do. Without them, everybody in the house would slowly, over the years, suffocate from the smoke.

If Abbie was a reincarnation, then chimney sweep is one of his past lives. It stands out in his karma. It helps to account for why he was a crazy maniac of a revolutionary, and why, therefore, we can say that this book is a document, is indeed the autobiography of a bona fide American revolutionary. In fact, as I went through it, large parts of the sixties lit up like areas of a stage grand enough to hold an opera company. Of course, we all think we know the sixties. To people of my generation, and the generation after us, the sixties is a private decade, a good relative of a decade, the one we believe we know the way we believe we know Humphrey Bogart. I always feel as if I can speak with authority on the sixties, and I never knew anybody my age who didn't feel the same way (whereas try to find someone who gets a light in their eyes when they speak of the seventies). Yet reading this work, I came to decide that my piece of the sixties wasn't as large as I thought. If we were going to get into comparisons, Abbie lived it, I observed it; Abbie committed his life, I merely loved the sixties because they gave life to my work.

So I enjoyed reading these pages. I learned from them, as a great many readers will. It filled empty spaces in what I thought was solid knowledge. And it left me with more respect for Abbie. I had tended to think of him as a clown. A tragic clown after his cocaine bust, and something like a ballsy wonder of a clown in the days when he was making raids on the media, but I never gave him whole credit for being serious. Reading this book lets you in on it. I began to think of Dustin Hoffman's brilliant portrait of Lenny Bruce, where, at the end, broken by the courts, we realize that Lenny is enough of a closet believer in the system to throw himself on the fundamental charity of the court—he will try to make the judge believe that under it all, Lenny, too, is a good American, he, too, is doing it for patriotic reasons. So, too, goes the tone of this unique autobiography. Comrades, Abbie is saying, "under my hustle beats a hot Socialist heart. I am really not a nihilist. I am one of you—a believer in progress."

He was serious. Abbie was serious. His thousand jokes were to conceal how serious he was. It makes us uneasy. Under his satire beat a somewhat hysterical heart. It could not be otherwise. Given his life, given his immersion in a profound lack of security, in a set of identity crises that would splat most of us like cantaloupes thrown off a truck, it is prodigious how long he resisted madness and death. He had to have a monumental will. Yet it is part of our civilized trap that an incredible life is not enough. The survivor must rise to heights of irony as well. This was not Abbie's forte. His heart beat too fiercely. He cared too much. He loved himself too much. All the same, we need not quibble. In an age of contracting horizons, we do well to count our blessings. How odd that now, Abbie is one of them. Our own holy ghost of the Left. Salud!

From *The Best of Abbie Hoffman* (1989)

# CHILDREN OF THE
# PIED PIPER

## A Review of *American Psycho*

"The Communists," says someone at a literary party, "at least had the decency to pack it in after seventy years. Capitalism is going to last seven hundred, and before it's done, there will be nothing left."

If there is reality to *American Psycho,* by Bret Easton Ellis—if, that is, the book offers any insight into a spiritual plague—then capitalism is not likely to approach its septicentennial, for this novel reverses the values of *The Bonfire of the Vanities.* Where *Bonfire* owed some part of its success to the reassurance it offered the rich—"You may be silly," Wolfe was saying in effect, "but, brother, the people down at the bottom are unspeakably worse"—Ellis' novel inverts the equation. I cannot recall a piece of fiction by an American writer that depicts so odious a ruling class—worse, a young ruling class of Wall Street princelings ready, presumably, by the next century to manage the mighty if surrealistic levers of our economy. Nowhere in American literature can one point to an inhumanity of the moneyed upon the afflicted equal to the following description. I think it is best to present it uncut from the original manuscript:

> "Listen, what's your name?" I ask.
> "Al," he says.
> "*Speak* up," I tell him. "Come on."
> "Al," he says, louder.
> "Get a goddamn job, *Al,*" I say, earnestly. "You've got a neg-ative attitude. That's what's stopping you. You've got to get your act together. *I'll* help you."

"You're so kind mister. You're kind. You're a kind man," he blubbers. "I can tell."

"Ssshhh," I whisper. "It's okay." I start petting the dog.

"Please," he says, grabbing my wrist, but lightly, with kindness. "I don't know what to do. I'm so cold."

I ask him, "Do you know how bad you smell?" I whisper this soothingly, stroking his face. "The *stench*. My god . . ."

"I can't . . ." he chokes, then swallows, shaking. "I can't find a shelter."

"You *reek*," I tell him again. "You *reek* of . . . *shit* . . ." I'm still petting the dog, its eyes wide and wet and grateful. "Do you know that? Goddamnit Al, look at me and stop crying like some kind of *faggot*," I shout. My rage builds then subsides and I close my eyes, bringing my hand up to the bridge of my nose which I squeeze tightly, then sigh, "Al . . . I'm sorry. It's just that . . . I don't know, I don't have anything in common with you."

The bum's not listening. He's crying so hard he's incapable of a coherent answer. I put the bill slowly back into the other pocket of my Luciano Soprani jacket and with the other hand stop petting the dog and reach into the other pocket. The bum stops sobbing abruptly and sits up, looking for the fiver or, I presume, his bottle of Thunderbird. I reach out and touch his face gently, once more with compassion and whisper, "Do you know what a fucking loser you are?" He starts nodding helplessly and I pull out a long thin knife with a serrated edge and being very careful not to kill the bum push maybe half-an-inch of the blade into his right eye, flicking the handle up, instantly popping the retina and blinding him.

The bum is too surprised to say anything. He only opens his mouth in shock and moves a grubby, mittened hand slowly up to his face. I yank his pants down and in the passing headlights of a taxi can make out his flabby black thighs, rashed because of constant urinating in his pant-suit, the stench of shit rises quickly into my face and breathing through my mouth, on my haunches, I start stabbing him below the stomach, lightly, in the dense matted patch of pubic hair. This sobers him up somewhat and instinctively he tries to cover himself with his hands and the dog starts barking, yipping really, furiously, but it doesn't attack, and I keep stabbing at the bum now in between his fingers, stabbing the back of his hands. His eye, burst open, hangs out of its socket and runs down his face and he keeps blinking which causes what's left of it inside the wound to pour out, like red, veiny egg yolk. I grab his head with the one hand and push it back and then with my thumb and forefinger hold the other eye open and bring the knife up and push the tip of it into the socket, first breaking the protective film so the socket fills with blood, then slitting the eyeball open sideways and he finally starts screaming once I slit his nose in two, spraying me, the dog with blood, Gizmo blinking trying to get the blood out of his eyes. I quickly wipe the blade clean across his face, breaking open the muscle above his cheek. Still kneeling I throw a quarter in his face, which is slick and shiny with blood, both sockets hollowed out, what's left of his eyes literally oozing over his lips, creating thick, webby strands when stretched across his screaming open mouth. I whisper calmly, "There's a quarter. Go buy some *gum* you crazy fucking *nigger*." Then I turn my attention to the barking dog and when I get up, stomp on its front paws while it's crouched down ready to jump at me, its fangs bared, and immediately crunch the bones in both its legs and it falls on its side squealing in pain, its front paws sticking up in the air at an obscene, satisfying angle. I can't help but start laughing and I linger at the scene, amused by this tableaux. When I spot an approaching taxi, I slowly walk away.

Afterwards, two blocks west, I feel heady, ravenous, pumped-up, as if I've just worked out heavily, endorphins flooding my nervous system, my ears buzzing, my body tuning in, embracing that first line of cocaine, inhaling the first puff of a fine cigar, sipping that first glass of Cristal.

Obviously, we have a radioactive pile on our hands. Canceled by Simon and Schuster two months before publication at an immediate cost to the publisher of a $300,000 advance, picked up almost at once by Vintage Books, and commented upon all over the media map in anticipation of Christmas, although the book will now not come out much before Easter, we are waiting for a work with not one, not two, but twenty or thirty scenes of unmitigated torture. Yet the writer may have enough talent to be taken seriously. How one wishes he were without talent! One does not want to be caught defending *American Psycho*. The advance word is a tidal wave of bad cess.

The Sunday *New York Times Book Review* took the unprecedented step of printing a review, months in advance, on December 16. In the form of an editorial titled "Snuff This Book! Will Bret Easton Ellis Get

Away with Murder?" it is by Roger Rosenblatt, a "columnist for *Life* magazine and an essayist for 'The MacNeil/Lehrer Newshour,' " who writes in a style to remind one of the critical bastinadoes with which *Time* magazine used to flog the ingenuous asses of talented young writers forty years ago.

> "American Psycho" is the journal Dorian Gray would have written had he been a high school sophomore. But that is unfair to sophomores. So pointless, so themeless, so everythingless is this novel, except in stupefying details about expensive clothing, food and bath products, that were it not the most loathsome offering of the season, it certainly would be the funniest. . . . Patrick Bateman . . . is a Harvard graduate, 26 years old, is single, lives on Manhattan's Upper West Side, nurtures his appearance obsessively, frequents health clubs by day and restaurants by night and, in his spare time, plucks out the eyes of street beggars, slits the throats of children and does things to the bodies of women not unlike things that Mr. Ellis does to prose. . . .
>
> But his true inner satisfaction comes when he has a woman in his clutches and can entertain her with a nail gun or a power drill or Mace, or can cut off her head or chop off her arms or bite off breasts or dispatch a starving rat up her vagina.
>
> The context of these high jinks is young, wealthy, hair-slicked-back, narcissistic, decadent New York, of which, one only assumes, Mr. Ellis disapproves. It's a bit hard to tell what Mr. Ellis intends exactly, because he languishes so comfortably in the swamp he purports to condemn.

The indictment becomes more personal in *Spy*, December 1990, by a young—I assume he is young—man who calls himself Todd Stiles:

> [Ellis] couldn't actually write a book that would earn attention on its merits, so he chose a course that will inevitably cause controversy and get him lots of press and allow him to pontificate, kind of like the novelist and critic Leo Tolstoi, on the question What is Art? *I am purposely exaggerating the way yuppie men treat women. That's the point*, he will say. *I meant to convey the madness of the consumerist eighties.* Not much could be more sickening than the misogynistic barbarism of this novel, but almost as repellent will be Ellis's callow cynicism as he justifies it.

In fact, Ellis has given a few indications that he is ready to justify it. For the "Arts & Leisure" section of the Sunday *Times*, December 2, 1990, he wrote a piece called "The Twentysomethings, Adrift in a Pop Landscape."

> We're basically unshockable. . . . This generation has been wooed with visions of violence, both fictive and real, since childhood.
>
> If violence in films, literature and in some heavy-metal and rap music is so extreme . . . it may reflect the need to be terrified in a time when the sharpness of horror-film tricks seems blunted by repetition on the nightly news.

It is obvious. Ellis wants to break through steel walls. He will set out to shock the unshockable. And *Spy* writer Todd Stiles is right—we are face-to-face once more with the old curmudgeon "novelist and critic Leo Tolstoi" (who not so long ago used to be known as Tolstoy). We have to ask the question once more: What is art? The clue presented by Bret Easton Ellis is his odd remark on "the need to be terrified."

Let me take us through my reading of the book, even though the manuscript I read was close to 200,000 words; the Vintage edition is bound to be shorter, for the novel is needlessly long—in fact, the first fifty pages are close to unendurable. There is no violence yet, certainly not if the signature of violence is blood, but the brain receives a myriad of dull returns. No one who enters the book has features, only clothing. We will learn in a while that we are in the mind of our serial killer, Patrick Bateman, but from the second page on, we are assaulted by such sentences as this: "Price is wearing a six-button wool-and-silk suit by Ermenegildo Zegna, a cotton shirt with French cuffs by Ike Behar, a Ralph Lauren silk tie, and leather wing-tips by Fratelli Rossetti." On page 5, "Courtney opens the door and she's wearing a Krizia cream silk blouse, a Krizia rust tweed skirt and silk satin D'Orsay pumps from Manolo Blahnik."

By page 12, Price is "lying on a late 18th century French Aubusson carpet drinking espresso from a cerelane coffee cup on the floor of Evelyn's room. I'm lying on Evelyn's bed holding a tapestry pillow from Jenny B. Goode nursing a cranberry and Absolut."

Bateman's apartment has "a long, white down-filled sofa and a 30-inch digital TV set from Toshiba; it's a high-contrast highly defined model . . . a high-tech tube combination from NEC with a picture-in-picture digital effects system (plus freeze-frame); the audio includes built-in MTS and a five watt-per-channel on-board amp." We progress through Super Hi-Band Beta units, three-week eight-event timers, four hurricane halogen lamps, a "glass-top coffee table with oak legs by Turchin," "crystal ashtrays from Fortunoff," a Wurlitzer jukebox, a black ebony Baldwin concert grand, a desk and magazine rack by Gio Ponti, and on to the bathroom, which presents twenty-two name products in its inventory. One has to keep reminding oneself that on reading Beckett for the first time it was hard not to bellow with fury at the monotony of the language. We are being asphyxiated with state-of-the-art commodities.

Ditto the victuals. Every trendy restaurant that has succeeded in warping the parameters of the human palate is visited by the Wall Street yuppies of this book. For tens of thousands of words, we make our way through "cold corn chowder lemon bisque with peanuts and dill . . . swordfish meatloaf with kiwi mustard."

Themes will alternate in small variations. We pass from meetings at the office (where business is never transacted) to free-weight work-outs in the gym, to Nell's, to taxi rides, to more descriptions of cloth-ing, furnishings, accessories, cosmetics, to conference calls to expedite restaurant reservations, to acquaintances who keep mistaking each other's names, to video rentals and TV shows. We are almost a third of the way through an unending primer on the artifacts of life in New York, a species of dream where one is inhaling not quite enough air and the narrative never stirs because there is no narrative. New York life in these pages is circular, one's errands footsteps in the caged route of the prison bull pen. Bateman is living in a hell where no hell is external to ourselves and so all of existence is hell. The advertise-ments have emerged like sewer creatures from the greed-holes of the urban cosmos. One reads on addicted to a vice that offers no pleasure whatsoever. One would like to throw the book away. It is boring and it is intolerable—these are the worst and dullest characters a talented author has put before us in a long time, but we cannot get around to quitting. The work is obsessive—the question cannot be answered, at least not yet: Is *American Psycho* with or without art? One has to keep reading to find out. The novel is not written so well that the art be-comes palpable, declares itself against all odds, but then, it is not writ-ten so badly that one can reject it with clear conscience. For the first third of its narrativeless narrative it gives off a mood not dissimilar to living through an unrelenting August in New York when the sky is never clear and rain never comes.

Then the murders begin. They are not dramatic. They are episodic. Bateman kills man, woman, child, or dog, and disposes of the body by any variety of casual means. He has penetrated to the core of indifference in New York. Humor commences; movie audiences will laugh with all the hysteria in their plumbing as Bateman puts a body in a sleeping bag, drags it past his doorman, heaves it into a cab, stops at a tenement apartment he keeps as his private boneyard, hefts it up four flights of stairs, and drops the cadaver in a bathtub full of lime. Smaller body parts are allowed to molder in the other apartment with the concert grand and the ashtrays from Fortunoff. To visitors, he explains away the close air by suggesting that he cannot find just where the rat has died. He gets blood on his clothing and brings this soiled package to a Chinese laundry. A few days later, he will curse them out for failing to clean his suit immaculately. The proprietors know the immutable spots are blood, but who is to debate the point? If you argue with a stranger in New York, he may kill you.

So, Bateman's murders are episodic: Nothing follows from them. His life goes on. He works out in the gym with dedication, he orders shad roe and pickled rabbit's kidney with cilantro mousse, he consumes bottles of Cristal with friends, and in discos he scores cocaine. Over one summer, he has an idyll in the Hamptons with Evelyn, the girl he may marry, and succeeds in restraining himself from murdering her; he masturbates over porny videos, he tells a friend in the middle of an acrimonious meal that if friend does not button his lip, he will be obliged to splatter friend's blood all over the blond bitch at the next table, and, of course, the speech is heard but not taken in. Not over all that restaurant gabble, not in all that designer din. When tension builds, Bateman kills in the same state of loneliness with which he masturbates; for relief, he hires two escort girls and tortures them to death before going off to the office next morning to instruct his secretary on who he will be available to on the telephone, and who not.

The murders begin to take their place with the carambola sorbet, the Quilted Giraffe, the Casio QD-150 Quick-Dialer, the Manolo Blahnik shoes, the baby soft-shell crabs with grape jelly. Not differentiated in their prose from all the other descriptions, an odd aesthetic terror is on the loose. The destruction of the beggar is small beer by now. A boy who strays a short distance from his mother at the Central Park Zoo is killed without a backward look. A starving rat is indeed introduced into the vagina of a half-slaughtered woman. Is Bateman the monster or Bret Easton Ellis? At best, what is to be said of such an imagination? The book is disturbing in a way to remind us that attempts to create art can be as intolerable as foul manners. One finishes with an uneasy impulse not to answer the question but to bury it. Of course, the question can come back to haunt us. A novel has been written that is bound to rest in unhallowed ground if it is executed without serious trial.

So the question returns, what is art? What can be so important about art that we may have to put up with a book like this? And the answer leads us to the notion that without serious art the universe is doomed.

These are large sentiments, but then, we live in a world which, by spiritual measure, if we could measure it, might be worse than any of the worlds preceding it. Atrocities, injustice, and the rape of nature have always been with us, but they used to be accompanied by whole architectures of faith that gave some vision to our sense of horror at what we are. Most of us could believe in Catholicism, or Marxism, or Baptism, or science, or the American family, or Allah, or Utopia, or trade-unionism, or the synagogue, or the goodness of the American president. By now, we all know that some indefinable piece of the whole is not amenable to analysis, reason, legislative manipulation, committees, expertise, precedent, hard-earned rule of thumb, or even effective political corruption. We sense all too clearly that the old methods no longer suffice, if they ever did. The colloquies of the managers (which can be heard on any given TV night and twice on Sunday morning) are now a restricted ideology, a jargon that does not come close to covering our experience, particularly our spiritual experience—our suspicion that the lashings have broken loose in the hold.

In such a world, art becomes the remaining link to the unknown. We are far beyond those eras when the English could enjoy the spoils of child labor during the week and read Jane Austen on the weekend. Art is no longer the great love who is wise, witty, strengthening, tender, wholesomely passionate, secure, life-giving—no, Jane Austen is no longer among us to offer a good deal more than she will disrupt, nor can Tolstoy still provide us (at least in the early and middle work) with some illusion that life is well proportioned and one cannot cheat it, no, we are far beyond that moral universe—art has now become our need to be terrified. We live in the fear that we are destroying the universe, even as we mine deeper into its secrets. So art may be needed now to provide us with just those fearful insights that the uneasy complacencies of our leaders do their best to avoid. It is art that has to take the leap into all the truths that our media society is insulated against. Since the stakes are higher, art may be more important to us now than ever before.

Splendid, you may say, but where is *American Psycho* in all this? Is the claim being advanced that it is art?

I am going to try an answer on these lines: Art serves us best precisely at that point where it can shift our sense of what is possible, when we now know more than we knew before, when we feel we have—by some manner of leap—encountered the truth. That, by the logic of art, is always worth the pain. If, then, our lives are dominated by our fears, the fear of violence dominates our lives. Yet we know next to nothing about violence, no matter how much of it we look at and live with. Violence in movies tells us nothing. We know it is special effects.

All the more valuable then might be a novel about a serial killer, provided we could learn something we did not know before. Fiction can serve as our reconnaissance into all those jungles and up those precipices of human behavior that psychiatry, history, theology, and sociology are too intellectually encumbered to try. Fiction is indeed supposed to bring it back alive—all that forbidden and/or unavailable experience. Fiction can conceive of a woman's or a man's last thoughts where medicine would offer a terminal sedative. So Ellis' novel cannot be disqualified solely by a bare description of its contents, no matter how hideous are the extracts. The good is the enemy of the great, and good taste is certainly the most entrenched foe of literature. Ellis has an implicit literary right, obtained by the achievements of every important and adventurous novelist before him, to write on any subject, but the more he risks, the more he must bring back or he will leach out the only capital we have, which is our literary freedom.

We have to take, then, the measure of this book of horrors. It has a thesis: *American Psycho* is saying that the eighties were spiritually disgusting and the author's presentation is the crystallization of such horror. When an entire new class thrives on the ability to make money out of the manipulation of money, and becomes altogether obsessed with the surface of things—that is, with luxury commodities, food, and appearance—then, in effect, says Ellis, we have entered a period of the absolute manipulation of humans by humans: The objective correlative of total manipulation is coldcock murder. Murder is now a lumbermill where humans can be treated with the same lack of respect as trees. (And scream commensurately—Bateman's main tools of dispatch are knives, chain saws, nail guns.)

Such a massive thesis does not sit well on underdeveloped legs—nothing less than a great novel can support a great, if monstrous, thesis. A good novel with too major a theme can only be crushed by the weight of what it is carrying. The test of *American Psycho* is whether we can ever believe the tale. Of course, it is a black comedy—that all-purpose cop-out!—but even black comedies demand an internal logic.

If we can accept the idea that the political air turned flatulent after eight years with the hornpipe wheezes of the Pied Piper, we must also entertain the thesis that the unbridled manipulations of the money-decade subverted the young sufficiently to produce wholly aimless lives for a generation of Wall Street yuppies. But was it crowned by the ultimate expression of all these meaningless lives—one total monster, a Patrick Bateman? Can he emerge entirely out of no more than vapidity, cupidity, and social meaninglessness? It does not matter whether a man like him does, in fact, exist; for all we know there might be a crew of Patrick Batemans at large in New York right now.

The demand is not that Bateman be factual but that he be acceptable as fiction. Do we read these pages believing that the same man who makes his rounds of restaurants and pretends to work in an office, this feverish snob with a presence so ordinary that most of his casual acquaintances keep mistaking him at parties and discos for other yuppies who look somewhat like him, can also be the most demented killer ever to appear in the pages of a serious American novel? The mundane activity and the supersensational are required to meet.

Bret Easton Ellis enters into acute difficulties with this bicameral demand. He is a writer whose sense of style is built on the literary conviction (self-serving for many a limited talent) that there must not be one false note. In consequence, there are often not enough notes. Even with writers as splendidly precise as Donald Barthelme, as resonant with recollected sorrow as Raymond Carver, or as fine-edged as Ann Beattie, there are often not enough notes. A book can survive as a classic even when it offers much too little—*The Great Gatsby* is the prime example forever—but then Fitzgerald was writing about the slowest murders of them all, social exclusion, whereas Ellis believes he is close enough to Dostoyevsky's ground to quote him in the epigraph. Since we are going to have a monstrous book with a monstrous thesis, the author must rise to the occasion by having a murderer with enough inner life for us to comprehend him. We pay a terrible price for reading about intimate violence—our fears are stirred, and buried savageries we do not wish to meet again in ourselves stir uneasily in the tombs to which we have consigned them. We cannot go out on such a trip unless we believe we will end up knowing more about extreme acts of violence, know a little more, that is, of the real inner life of the murderer.

Bateman, however, remains a cipher. His mother and brother appear briefly in the book and are, like all the other characters, faceless—we are less close to Bateman's roots than to his meals. Exeter and

Harvard are named as parts of his past but in the manner of Manolo Blahnik and Ermenegildo Zegna—names in a serial sequence. Bateman is driven, we gather, but we never learn from what. It is not enough to ascribe it to the vast social rip-off of the eighties. The abstract ought to meet the particular. In these pages, however, the murders begin to read like a pornographic description of sex. Bateman is empty of inner reaction and no hang-ups occur. It may be less simple to kill humans and dispose of them than is presented here, even as real sex has more turns than the soulless high-energy pump-outs of the pornographic. Bateman, as presented, is soulless, and because we cannot begin to feel some instant of pity for him, so the writing about his acts of violence is obliged to become more hideous externally and more affectless within until we cease believing that Ellis is taking any brave leap into truths that are not his own—which happens to be one of the transcendent demands of great fiction. No, he is merely working out some ugly little corners of himself.

Of course, no one could write if art were entirely selfless. Some of the worst in us has also to be smuggled out or we would use up our substance before any book was done. All the same, a line is always in place between art and therapy. Half of the outrage against this book is going to come from our suspicion that Ellis is not creating Bateman so much as he is cleaning out pest nests in himself. No reader ever forgives a writer who uses him for therapy.

If the extracts of *American Psycho* are horrendous, therefore, when taken out of context, that is Ellis' fault. They are, for the most part, simply not written well enough. If one is embarked on a novel that hopes to shake American society to the core, one has to have something new to say about the outer limits of the deranged—one cannot simply keep piling on more and more acts of machicolated butchery.

The suspicion creeps in that much of what the author knows about violence does not come from his imagination (which in a great writer can need no more than the suspicion of real experience to give us the whole beast) but out of what he has picked up from *Son* and *Grandson of Texas Chainsaw Massacre* and the rest of the filmic Jukes and Kallikaks. We are being given horror-shop plastic. We won't know anything about extreme acts of violence (which we do seek to know if for no less good reason than to explain the nature of humankind in the wake of the Holocaust) until some author makes such acts intimately believable, that is, believable not as acts of description (for that is easy enough) but as intimate personal states so intimate that we enter them. That is why we are likely never to know: Where is the author ready to bear the onus of suggesting that he or she truly understands the inner logic of violence?

To create a character intimately, particularly in the first person, is to convince the reader that the author is the character. In extreme violence, it becomes more comfortable to approach from outside, as Bret Easton Ellis either chose to do, or could do no better. The failure of this book, which promises to rise occasionally to the level of the very good (when it desperately needs to be great), is that by the end we know no more about Bateman's need to dismember others than we know about the inner workings in the mind of a wooden-faced actor who swings a broadax in an exploitation film. It's grunts all the way down. So, the first novel to come along in years that takes on deep and Dostoyevskian themes is written by only a half-competent and narcissistic young pen.

Nonetheless, he is showing older authors where the hands have come to on the clock. So one may have to answer the question: What would you do if you happened to find yourself the unhappy publisher who discovered this book on his list two months before publication?

I am not sure of the answer. The move that appeals most in retrospect is to have delayed publication long enough to send the manuscript to ten or twelve of the most respected novelists in America *for an emergency reading*. Presumably, a number would respond. If a majority were clearly on the side of publication, I would feel the sanction to go ahead. To my knowledge, that possibility was never contemplated. A pity. Literature is a guild, and in a crisis, it would be good if the artisan as well as the merchants could be there to ponder the decision.

This is, of course, fanciful. No corporate publisher would ever call on an author, not even his favorite author, on such a matter, and perhaps it is just as well. A lot of serious literary talent could have passed through a crisis of conscience. How to vote on such a book? The costs of saying "Yes, you must publish" are fearful. The reaction of certain women's groups to *American Psycho* has been full of unmitigated outrage.

Indeed, an extract from one of the most hideous passages in the novel was read aloud by Tammy Bruce, president of the Los Angeles chapter of the National Organization for Women, on a telephone hot line. The work is described as a "how-to novel on the torture and dismemberment of women . . . bringing torture of women and the mutilation deaths of women into an art form. We are here to say that we will not be silent victims anymore."

While it is certainly true that the fears women have of male violence are not going to find any alleviation in this work, nonetheless I dare to suspect that the book will have a counter-effect to these dread-filled expectations. The female victims in *American Psycho* are tortured so hideously that men with the liveliest hostility toward women will, if still sane, draw back in horror. "Is that the logical extension of my impulse to inflict cruelty?" such men will have to ask themselves, even as after World War II millions of habitual anti-Semites drew back in similar horror from the mirror of unrestrained anti-Semitism that the Nazis had offered the world.

No, the greater horror, the real intellectual damage this novel may cause is that it will reinforce Hannah Arendt's thesis on the banality of evil. It is the banality of Patrick Bateman that creates his hold over the reader and gives this ugly work its force. For if Hannah Arendt is correct and evil is banal, then that is vastly worse than the opposed possibility that evil is satanic. The extension of Arendt's thesis is that we are absurd, and God and the Devil do not wage war with each other over the human outcome. I would rather believe that the Holocaust was the worst defeat God ever suffered at the hands of the Devil. That thought offers more life than to assume that many of us are nothing but dangerous, distorted, and no damn good.

So I cannot forgive Bret Easton Ellis. If I, in effect, defend the author by treating him at this length, it is because he has forced us to look at intolerable material, and so few novels try for that much any more. On this basis, if I had been one of the authors consulted by a publisher, I would have had to say, yes, publish the book, it not only is repellent but will repel more crimes than it will excite. This is not necessarily the function of literature, but it is an obvious factor here.

What a deranging work! It is too much of a void, humanly speaking, to be termed evil, but it does raise the ante so high that one can no longer measure the size of the bet. Blind gambling is a hollow activity and this novel spins into the center of that empty space.

From *Vanity Fair* (March 1991)

# 1991    **CREATIONISM REVISITED**

In the I-J-K-L, standing there in the dark, looking across the inter-
vening distance between himself and the next building, in a lighted
office across the court, Harlot saw one of his colleagues kissing a secretary. He promptly dialed that office, and as he watched, the man
separated himself from the embrace long enough to pick up his
phone.

"Aren't you appalled by yourself?" Harlot asked.

"Who is this?"

"God," said Harlot, and hung up.

The last time Hugh Montague had spoken to me about God was
the last time I had taken the trip from Langley to his farmhouse on
the eyebrow of the four-lane truck road. He had expatiated that afternoon on the theory of Creationism, his brilliance, one can certify,
not at all diminished.

"Would you say, Harry," he inquired, "that two such words as 'sophisticated fundamentalist' make one oxymoron?"

"Can't see how it wouldn't," I told him.

"Intellectual snobbery," replied Harlot, "is your short suit. You
would do better to ponder the meanings that can be extracted from
apparent folly."

As so often, a flick into the eye of your ego was the price you paid
for obtaining the products of his mind.

"Yes," he said, "Creationists rush to tell us that the world, according to the Bible, was commenced five thousand and some hundreds of

years ago. It makes for merriment, don't it? Fundamentalists are such whole fools. Yet I said to myself once, 'What would I do if I were Jehovah about to conceive of this creature, man, who, as soon as I create him, will be hell-bent—given the equal opportunity I have offered Satan—to discover My nature. How can that not become man's passion? I have created him, after all, in My image, so he will wish to discover My nature in order to seize My throne. Would I ever have permitted such a contract in the first place, therefore, if I had not taken the wise precaution to fashion a cover story?' "

"A cover story?" I did not wish to repeat his words, but I did.

"A majestic cover story. Nothing vulgar or small. Absolutely detailed, fabulously complete. Just suppose that in the moment of striking that agreement with Satan, God brought forth the world complete. Five thousand and some hundreds of years ago, we were given an absolutely realized presentation of the world. God created it *ex nihilo*. Gave it to us complete. Everyone began to live at the same instant of Creation. Yet all were given a highly individual background. All had been put together, of course, from nothingness infused with divine genius. The creation of this imaginary past was God's artwork. All who lived, all men, women, and children of all varying tribes and climates, the eighty-year-old, the forty-five-year-old, the young lovers, and the two-year-old were all created at the same instant that He placed the half-cooked food on the stone-hearth fire. All of it appeared at once, the animals in their habitat just so much as the humans, each creature possessing its separate memory, the plants in command of their necessary instincts, the earth bountiful here and unfulfilled there, some crops even ready to go to harvest. All the fossil remains were carefully set in the rock. God gave us a world able to present all the material clues that Darwin would need fifty-odd centuries later to conceive of evolution. The geological strata had all been put in place. The solar system was in the heavens. Everything had been set moving at rates of orbit to encourage astronomers to declare five thousand and more years later that the age of the earth was approximately five billion years. I like this notion immensely," said Harlot. "You can say the universe is a splendidly worked-up system of disinformation calculated to make us believe in evolution and so divert us away from God. Yes, that is exactly what I would do if I were the Lord and could not trust My own creation."

From *Harlot's Ghost* (1991)

**1991**     # HOW THE WIMP
# WON THE WAR

On August 2, 1990, it could be said that George Bush's media prospects were dire. The budget, prisons, drugs, inner cities, AIDS, crack, crime, and the homeless were exhibiting an obdurate, malicious, even perverse inclination to resist all solution.

There was also the $500 billion S&L scandal. While one could not yet speak of it as a cancer upon the presidency—no, not so bad as Watergate—still, it was a damn chancre at the least. The media would not be media if they did not have the instincts of a lynch mob. George Bush knew that well enough. He had spent eight years in the advanced course in media manipulation under Ronald Reagan, and you could hardly not learn a lot from Ronald Reagan, who worked on the notion that most Americans would rather be told they were healthy than be healthy.

Since this condition can inspire a good deal of free-floating anxiety, Reagan also recognized that the media had acquired the power of a shadow government, ready to cater to all the dread in American life. If a widow encountered an ax murderer in her bedroom, the lady's blood went onto the television screens that night, and the blood was sometimes as red as the ketchup in the commercial that followed. Ronald Reagan, the survivor of more than fifty B-movies, understood that TV was the spirit of interruption—we were in the age of postmodernism, where anything could be connected to anything and sometimes gave you an interesting—that is, a new—sensation. Ronald

Reagan was ready to apply postmodernism to history and its retinue of facts. Henry Ford, who struggled with the concept when it was new, had said, "History is bunk," and was ridiculed; Reagan took the notion out of the swamps. History was not bunk but chosen statements.

If you were President, you could tell stories that were not true, yet they, too, could become facts inasmuch as denial of the statement didn't carry one-quarter the heft of the initial declaration. It came down to knowing how to feed the media. The media were a valve installed in the governing heart of the nation, and they decided which stories would receive prominence. Reagan recognized that one had to become the valve within the valve. Otherwise, certain catastrophes could produce headlines equal to spurting arteries. They could pump away the plasma of your reputation. When 241 Marines were killed in Beirut by one bomb carried in one truck by one Arab terrorist on October 23, 1983, Reagan gave the order two days later to invade Grenada. A catastrophe must immediately be replaced by another act so bold that it, too, may end in catastrophe—that takes moxie!

Grenada worked, however. Nineteen hundred Marines conquered something like half their number of Cuban construction workers, and the media were banned from reporting events firsthand for the three days of the campaign. Then America celebrated the victory. A phenomenon ensued. The American public reacted as if the victory in Grenada had removed the shame of Vietnam.

Only a political genius can turn a debacle into a media success, and George Bush had studied Ronald Reagan with all the intensity of an unwanted child for eight hard years, taken his snubs, suffered the nitty-twit positions Reagan left him in, and the wimp slanders prevalent in the press. George Bush was keen, lean, competitive, and wanted the presidency as much as any vice president before him. Without it, he had nothing to anticipate but an enduring reputation as the ex–vice presidential wimp. Male pride is insufficiently appreciated. It can approach earthquake force. George Bush was not to be stopped by the likes of Dole or Dukakis; George Bush knew that you win elections by kissing the great American electorate on the mouth—"I want a kinder, gentler nation"—and by kicking the opposition in the nuts.

Grenada may have demonstrated that the need for pride in one's patriotism was the largest unsatisfied love in American life, but the most feared nightmare in American life (now that the Evil Empire was benign) had to be the black criminal avenger whom good liberals were blind enough to let out of jail long enough to rape a white, doubtless Christian, female person. The case of Willie Horton was a real shitkicker's stomp, and the creative author, Lee Atwater, who happened to be an aficionado of black music, would subsequently develop a tumor in his head and die. Who can say how much he felt inwardly condemned for conceiving and carrying out such a caper on a people whose music he loved?

George Bush cut his thin thread of congressional liaison to the Democratic Party with Willie Horton (and that would cost him later, since Democrats do control Congress), but then, he did not know at the time that Michael Dukakis would prove leadfooted as a candidate. Bush saw the immediate world head-on. Win the presidency. Do not debate the efficacy of overkill. Swear allegiance to the first precept of Ronald Reagan: *Be as shallow as spit on a rock and you will prevail.* Bush prevailed and entered the postmodern American presidency of crack, crime, AIDS—we have the list.

On August 2, 1990, however, the Iraqis invaded Kuwait, and Saddam Hussein entered American life.

We will assume for the purposes of this reconnoiter through recent history that it was no more than George Bush's good luck for Saddam Hussein to misread a few signs en route to gobbling the Kuwaitis. That sort of error would not have been difficult to make. Saddam was endangered at home by problems as deep as the need of other people to see him dead, and he was surrounded by sycophants, a condition that is tonic for a leader's vanity, but does feed elephantiasis of the ego.

In addition, Saddam was a poet. "The mother of all battles" is a metaphor primeval enough to reach into the nightmares of every infantryman arrayed against him. No poet ever believes he or she is incapable of world-shaking moves. When you know the power of the word, you depend on it.

To strengthen this mix, the president of Iraq was a degenerate gambler. He had played all his life with table stakes larger than he could afford. That was his strength. Few men gain a sense of personal power greater than does a degenerate gambler who has not been destroyed by his vice. One tends to believe that God, or Providence, or some mysterious demiurge like Lady Luck, is enraptured with your presence on earth.

Hitler held to such beliefs; there may be no other explanation for him. So, by an extrapolation of his imagination, George Bush was able to speak of Saddam Hussein as Hitler, and that was certainly a page taken from the gnomic maxims of Ronald Reagan—a Muslim Hitler who comes to the stage as your foe can do a lot to save the American presidency.

Now, Saddam could conceivably have become as monstrous as Hitler. For that, however, he would have had to acquire Saudi Arabia, Jordan, and the Emirates, then Iran and Syria (two formidably indigestible items), plus Israel—a major war—and Egypt, and North Africa. There may not be the rudiments of enough administrative ability in all of Islam to take care of such an empire, temperamentally supercharged, technologically Third World, oil-rich, and revolution-rife; yes, if you can conquer all of that in a decade, when Saudi Arabia alone is one-quarter the size of the United States, then you are the equal of Adolf Hitler and would doubtless exhibit the same cavernous disregard for the deaths of whole millions of people; yes, putting Saddam Hussein into the equation with Hitler was also a metaphor, but then, George Bush was even competitive about that. Saddam Hussein was Hitler, Q.E.D., and there would be no Munichs for George.

On a stripped budget, Hussein could have been stopped, probably, from moving into Saudi Arabia by sending over a division of Marines with naval and air support. The troops could have been kept—as they were, in fact, for months—hundreds of miles south of the Kuwait border. It would have been effective militarily if one wanted to avoid war; it would have drawn, precisely, a line in the sand.

George Bush, however, needed war. It would take no less than that to dig into the macho meat of B-movie sentiments. As Ronald Reagan had delineated, this was the real emotional broth of a majority of voting Americans—they had, after all, put in their time growing up on the narrative reflexes of B-movies, plus all the A-movies that happened to be no more elevated in sentimental vision than the B-movies. George Bush could avoid war by keeping a token force in Saudi Arabia—and who but the Kuwaitis would grieve for Kuwait?—but the prognosis suggested poor media potential; the action could downgrade itself into one headline blight after another. A task force underwriting such a limited peace in the Middle East would hardly be large enough to accomplish dramatic results. Incidents were bound to occur. Carousing soldiers would sooner or later be killed by Saudi policemen (which, in the absence of other news, would loom as large as a tank battle). Governing America in company with the media is like spending a honeymoon with your mother-in-law's ear to the door. George Bush's aim was hardly going to focus, therefore, on something as minimal as avoiding a war; his goal was to save his presidency. For that, nothing less than a major campaign would do.

Many a political leader has the ability to bear comparison to Napoleon for a season. Maggie Thatcher had the Falklands in 1982, and it gave her eight and a half more years of political life. The President, abetted by the skills of his secretary of state, had a few such weeks in August of 1990: Showing precisely the sort of competence Michael Dukakis had advertised as his own first virtue, Bush and Baker succeeded between them in establishing UN sanctions against Iraq. Twenty-eight countries joined the coalition. A mighty and magnetic movement toward war got under way in America against an outraged liberal defense: "No blood for oil."

The liberals had the commonsense logic, the good ethics, the good morals, the anti-war pieties, the slogans, the demonstrations, and the inner conviction that they were on the side of the angels, but they were entering a trap larger and deeper than any of the moats ablaze with burning oil that Saddam Hussein had promised American troops. Intellectually speaking, liberal ideology had become about as stimulating as motel furniture. You could get through a night with it provided you didn't have to hang around in the morning. Liberalism was opposed to war, poverty, hunger, AIDS, drugs, corruption in high places, crowded prisons, budget cuts, sexism, racism, and opposition to gay liberation, but it had not had an idea in twenty-five years for solving any of those problems.

George Bush, however, had heard the music of the Pied Piper. He knew that Ronald Reagan had launched America on a fiduciary way of life once practiced by Marie Antoinette and various members of the French, British, and Russian aristocracy. One spent lavishly for one's pleasures, and looked for entertainments that would offer new zest for life to the populace watching outside. Reagan established the principle: You cannot be a good President unless you keep the populace entertained. Reagan understood what hard workers like Lyndon Johnson, Richard Nixon, and Jimmy Carter did not—he saw that the President of the United States was the leading soap-opera figure in the great American drama, and one had better possess star value. The President did not have to have executive ability nearly as much as an interesting personality. A touch of the selfish or the unscrupulous— just a touch!—might be necessary to keep a hero interesting.

Ronnie, of course, was perfect—the nicest movie actor ever to serve up his young manhood to losing the girl to the handsome guy who might not deserve her quite as much. His presidency was delivered from that hint of insipidity, however, by the presence of Nancy. She suggested more than a few touches of the cruel, the narrow, and the exclusive. So, they were interesting. You followed them. You kept waiting over eight years, like the rest of the American public, to see one small crack in the surface of their marriage. You never succeeded, but then, the rock-bottom aesthetic of the long-running soap opera is to keep the same anticipation alive.

George Bush, as the central figure in the new series, had a totally different problem. His wife was strong, decent, gracious, and an obvious helpmate, but George had to prove he was worthy of her. Overcoming the wimp burden could then prove a narrative asset. Given such parameters, he was not about to look for a draw with Saddam Hussein. Only wimps were eager to endure the headaches and the dull obsessional arguments that follow in the wake of a contest that ends without decision.

George Bush, in it for the win, knew that sanctions, now that he had them, were not likely to work. How was one to keep Saddam Hussein encysted within the embargo for the two long years, or three, that starving him out was going to take? There were already trouble spots in the UN firmament—Syria, then the Soviet Union, Morocco, Germany, and Japan. And what of such uncommitted or barely committed nations as Iran, Afghanistan, Cuba, and China? Constant vigilance would be required to accomplish, yes, what? Hussein would flood the world press with pictures of starving Iraqi children. Any Red Cross food that entered the country would feed his Republican Guard. Hussein could tolerate famine in large parts of Iraq—he would be busy making certain that it was his internal enemies who were suffering the hunger. Meanwhile, he could play upon the passions of the Palestinians, and provoke the Israelis. For that matter, when the time was propitious, what would ever keep him from starting a war with Israel? Every Muslim leader in the coalition would then have to hold down his own people. From George Bush's point of view, maintaining sanctions would be about as sensible as going into a brothel to announce, "I'll be in town for the next year. I want you girls to promise that during this period you won't pick up a venereal disease." No, the sanctions had to be seen as an instrument, a staging area from which to prepare the shooting war.

Bush, undeniably adroit at such a game, managed to maneuver the Security Council of the UN into agreement: If Saddam did not agree to pull out of Kuwait by January 15, 1991, then the allied armies, ultimately 750,000 strong, were authorized by the UN to engage in combat with Iraq. A vote of approval still had to be taken in Congress, however, and was on January 12, 1991.

During the TV hours of watching that debate in the House and Senate, our writer was to discover surprising sentiments in himself. He was on the side of war.

He could not believe it, but he felt a lifting of his spirit. A few days later, the sentiment was confirmed by a whole sense of excitement that the war had actually begun. For a man who disliked news shows, he now listened to generals with as much as half an open ear. He knew that if he felt himself viscerally allied with this combat, then nearly all of America would be gung ho over it.

It had gone beyond morality. Some cures can be found only in the art of the binge. Was this the phenomenon at work now? Did the country need a war?

Well, it had also needed Ronald Reagan, and Grenada, and Panama, and our writer had been opposed to all three. Where, now, was the difference? Perhaps it was that the country kept getting worse and worse. All the American revolutions seemed to have degenerated into enclaves of jargoneers who were not even capable of debate if their opponent did not employ their jargon. No, it was worse than that. When one forced oneself to contemplate the phalanxes of the left, one by one, it could be seen that no effective left remained in the country. The trade unions were bureaucratic when they were not corrupt; the sexual left was confounded, fragmented, bewildered, and AIDS was a catastrophe; little power groups fought over the remains of gay liberation. The thought began to intrude itself into the mind of many an American that no matter how tragic individual cases might be, not everyone who came down with AIDS was necessarily entitled to a medal. Women's liberation, contributing to no cause but its own, had grown tiresome. Their agenda was sexist: Women were good, and men were no damn good.

Then there were the blacks. The Black Power movement of the sixties, intended to give blacks a more powerful sense of identity, had, in the absence of real social improvement, succeeded merely in moving whites and blacks even further away from each other. Encapsulated among themselves (in direct relation to how poor they were), the blacks were now divided between a bare majority who worked and a socially unassimilable minority who did not. Legions of black youth were marooned in hopelessness, rage at how the rich grew obscenely rich during the eighties, and self-pity. If there was a fair possibility that black people were more sensual than white people, then the corollary was that they suffered poverty more. Sensual people who are poor can drown in self-pity as they dream of how much real pleasure they could enjoy if they had money. It is a point of view that will draw you to the luminous inner life of drugs. Afterward, the luminosity used up, the habit keeps one chasing the high through crime, for crime is not only quick money but the heady rewards of risk, at least when risk is successful. Prison, the unsuccessful consequence, comes to be seen as a species of higher education. It is a way of life for young blacks that does not gear into the working black community, and it has nothing whatever to do with the working white community. The Democratic Party had a hole in its flank from the spearhead of this problem, and the Republican Party had a hole in its head. Republican thoughts on the subject had run out long ago. Given the essential austerity of the Christian ethic, the Republican Party was never wholly comfortable with the idea that Americans like themselves ought to be that rich. They grew more and more choleric about the blacks. Their unspoken solution became the righteous prescription: If those drug bastards won't work, throw them in jail.

Of course, the jails were another disaster system. The best of them were overcrowded, and there were no budgets for new prisons. If avalanches of new prisoners came along, the only place for them would be camps, guarded by the military.

This was merely a scenario, no more than one more doomsday scenario as long as the economy held. Money could still soothe some crucial margin of every American's exacerbated feelings. Let the river of money go dry, however, and what would hold the country together? There might be revolts in the ghetto, curfews in the inner cities, and martial law.

It was hard to believe that Bush or any other Republican or Democrat could offer a solution to the real problem, which was that standards of craftsmanship were deteriorating among the American work force. Our consumer products were not as good as they used to be. The Germans and the Japanese made better cars and better toasters. Their best engineers were working in consumer industries, while ours were being hired by the military-industrial complex. Given the shoddy show, one could blame corporate packaging, advertising, and TV—one could blame hedonism and its hangovers; one could blame drugs, blacks, labor unions; one could blame the Pied Piper. It did not matter whom you blamed. It was multiple choice, and all of the answers might be correct. The fact was that America was mired in grievances, miseries, miscalculations, slave history, and obsessions; the economy was reflecting it.

In fact, Mailer was surprised by himself. Something deep in him—which is to say no longer censorable—was now saying: "The country needs a purge, a fling, some sacrifice of blood, some waste of the blood of others, some colossal event, a triumph. We need an extravaganza to take us out of ourselves. We are Romans, finally, and there is no moral force left among our citizens to countermand that fact. So this war will be a crucial vacation from the morose state of American affairs. If it succeeds, the country may even be able to face a few real problems again."

It was, at least, a perspective. A nation's ego might be not unlike the human ego: When its view of itself was able to lift, there was more human energy available; yes, energy liberated itself best under the aegis of a happy ego. By that logic, America needed to win a war.

On the night in early March when George Bush delivered his victory speech to Congress, he was welcomed with an ovation that rivaled any outpouring of approval Ronald Reagan had received in the same Capitol building—which is no small remark. He had not only won the war but accomplished it with an astonishingly small loss of American life—a double victory for Bush. When it came to the sacrifice of one's own countrymen, the President was also a liberal. He had merely altered the slogan to "Virtually no blood for oil," and there was no more talk of tens of thousands of body bags having been ordered by the Pentagon.

Of course, there were ironies. A war without ironies searing enough to brand one's moral flesh is not a real war. The triumph in the Gulf may in time be characterized by military historians as a brilliant military plan that encountered no more than a desert horizon of prisoners who had been waiting for weeks to surrender. A technological Leviathan had overcome a magician of metaphors.

Other ironies followed. It had taken seven months of sleeping through nightmares for young American soldiers to find a balance between their morale and their fears. The stiffening of their resolve to be ready to die had turned out in the end to be no more than a gargantuan poker bluff. The Gulf soldiers were now going to live with obsession: What would I have been like in combat if it had turned out to be as bad as the minefields, the burning ditches, the barbed wire, and the fields of fire that I contemplated in my dreams?

That was an obsession to live with for the rest of one's life. After all, many of these American soldiers had been obliged to put the will to fight together out of no more than a tautology of truisms: We've got to get the job done so we can all go home. If they found any higher moral sanction, it doubtless came from admiring the will to work under excruciating conditions that characterizes line play in the National Football League.

Of course, the soldiers seen on television had been carefully chosen for blandness of affect. This was one campaign the military was not going to lose to the press. So the most interesting war in two decades for Americans was obliged to wag along on TV with talking heads and zoom-aways of fighter planes taking off into the wild-rose yonder of the desert at evening. The Pentagon was the producer of this entertainment, and its ranks were composed of solemn people. They were no part of that consumer economy, now as subtly sleazy as all the half-rented suburban malls—no, the military had not acquired most of the best engineering minds for the last two decades, and then brooded like serious men upon their own faults and shortcomings in Vietnam (first of which was that they had been too obliging to the press), to make the same mistakes again; no, the consumer economy might not show the happiest comparison with the Germans and the Japanese, but the military was prepared to prove that it was now, by far, the finest fighting force on earth.

Military men live within life-missions of pride. Since their activities take place inside the enclaves of national security, part of their ethic is to suffer in silence. Silently, the Pentagon had undergone the ravages of congressional investigation into why it spent $600 on a toilet seat for one airplane and $1,600 on a wrench for another; the military had had to live with the general public cognition that the B-2 Stealth bomber was a monumentally expensive disappointment. All the while, the generals were obliged to keep silent with the knowledge that if all else in America might be getting worse, they were getting better.

How could George Bush not turn them loose? They were what we had to show for the Reagan years. From 1980 to 1988, the Pied Piper had spent $2.1 trillion on the military—which is four times the amount of the S&L scandal. Maybe we couldn't make cars and toasters any more, but we had forced the Russians to spend, over these same eight years, $2.3 trillion, $200 billion more than ourselves, and the Soviets couldn't afford it at all. They couldn't even make decent soap.

The military, wounded by the shame of Vietnam and fortified by the budget, had become a superior fighting force as a corollary to the main Reagan strategy, which had been to wreck the Russians economically. In that, we succeeded, but at the cost of handing over economic hegemony in the world to Germany and Japan while we enlarged the list of our unsolvable crises in the cities.

Now that the Soviet Union had folded as a foe, all we had to show was the state-of-the-art strengths of our forces. So George Bush used them the first chance he had. The technological display was full of stardust. The F-117A Stealth fighter with its laser-guided bombs hit

95 percent of its targets. In numbers, it was only 2.5 percent of the U.S. aircraft, but it managed to account for 31 percent of the successful hits on its first day. Endless nuggets of such sparkling statistics were now floating about in the vitreous fluid of the media. Yes, the air war, ignoring all lack of opposition, had been a massive success; the deep, if natural, fear of the Bush administration and the Pentagon that the ground troops might not be well motivated enough to fight the Iraqis did not have to be tested. George Bush had gone up to the great dentist in the sky, but none of his teeth had been pulled. We had probably dumped some amount like 200 million pounds of explosive on Iraq and Kuwait, and that came down to ten pounds virtually per person for all of 21 million people. Of course, the bombs and rockets had not been directed against people, but all the same, the Pentagon was not releasing the figures. Those tonnages could yet take on the long shadows of overkill. The country preferred instead to enjoy the victory.

In an appearance before state legislators at the White House in March, George Bush went so far as to suggest that the ghosts of Vietnam had been exorcised and the shame of the past had been overcome. The misery of losing a war to a Third World power could be forgotten. Our great win in the Gulf could replace our obsession with Southeast Asia.

George Bush, however, might encounter some subtle troubles with his thesis in time to come. If the nation was going to enjoy the fruits of victory, which is to say a strengthening of the national ego that, one hoped, would be able to produce a new vigor for tackling our problems, then maybe the war in Vietnam ought not to be exorcised so quickly. The President was, after all, getting into the same slough of muddy reasoning as the liberals. They had decided in advance that the Gulf War was a repetition of Vietnam, and that had been a perfect example of American thinking at its most simplistic. Now the Bush administration was going to run with the same errors around the other end of the ideological line. When you got down to it, the only similarity between the two wars was that America had been in both of them. One, after all, had been combat waged in the jungle, and the canopy offered concealment of ground troops from planes and much-restricted access to tanks. Soldiers encountered one another face-to-face in deep shadows. In the Gulf, war had been fought in the open vistas of the desert against a mad poet who was hated by all too many of his own troops. In Vietnam, we were allied against a people ready to die for a leader who not only looked like a saint but embodied the travails of a long-delayed liberation. He offered the idea that their deaths would not be in vain, and that a more humane world would follow for their children. The Democrats had kept the war in Southeast Asia going eight years beyond its time, and then Nixon kept it going for another six, and by the time we left Saigon, two million Vietnamese had been killed.

Of course, we had a bad conscience concerning Vietnam. It was part of the national honor to remind ourselves that we, a great and democratic nation, had been capable of monstrous deeds. It revealed to us that America might never come to maturity, nor develop a culture rich enough and sufficiently resonant to counterbalance our technology. No, we might end as computer hacks and body louts—the last superlouts in the history of the world—but if we had a national conscience, and it would yet prevail, then we were obliged to live with Vietnam and keep measuring the cost. Bury the ghosts of that war too soon, and the last irony of the desert sands would be released. That great news machine, which eats our history as fast as it is created, might even move so fast that our power to enjoy the success of the war in the Gulf could also be covered over prematurely and we could lose whatever good it was going to do our long-bruised view of ourselves. While it was a war that might yet make a difference for good or for ill in the tangled nests of the Middle East, it might also turn out to be no more than its own weight, a military exercise on a colossal level, panoramas of technical virtuosity in a moral thicket, and if that was all it was, then the news machine would damn sure eat it. The memory of Vietnam, however, is not going to disappear. Vietnam is embedded in our moral history.

From *Esquire* (May 1991)

# BY HEAVEN
# INSPIRED

Once an agreeable Texas town, Houston had expanded so prodigiously since the Second World War that one could now think of it as a gargantuan humanoid in a special effects movie (after the humanoid has been dismembered by a magnum ray-gun). Modern Houston sprawls over the nappy carpet of Texas soil in shreds, bones, nerves, and holes, a charred skeleton with an eye retained here, and there a prosthetic hand still smoking.

The megacity is, of course, not burned out; rather, it is not yet built. Except in parts. The parts are often called edge-cities, clusters of modern office buildings thirty or forty stories high with nothing much around them. Five miles away, like an amputated elbow of the humanoid, one can find another cluster of tall corporate structures in mirrored glass. Between one edge-city and another there are, occasionally, funky streets of old cottages or middle-aged ranch houses to remind one of the more modest homeowner passions that once belonged to the West; often these streets come to an end by polluted creeks, or peter out on a country road that will cross a rail track to run eventually next to one or another elevated highway that races on into another edge-city. Thirty-six by thirty-eight miles in dimension, fourth largest urban center in the United States (never crowded except on superhighways), its pride is its absence of form. You can virtually find a nose on the hip bone, an ear on the navel, and all the eyes you would ever want in the blue-gray and gray-green mirrored walls of all those edge-city thirty-story glass phalluses with their corporate hubris pointing up into the muggy Texas sky. So it was a city fit for Republicans in August, since, like the GOP mind, it had never had any other sense of the whole than how to win elections.

This convention year, however, the Republicans could hardly take in what had happened to them. Under Reagan and Bush, they had, by their lights, produced gouts of great and phenomenal history, had ended the threat of nuclear war; now all too many Americans did not seem to care about such achievement, and lately their political vanity had been trashed by the Democrats. In consequence, they were as mad as a hive of bees just kicked over.

It was an odd morning. The floor of a convention offers intensities of mood comparable to the stirring of a beast, but in these first hours, the animal looked too comatose to stir. It was an opportunity, therefore, to study the 2,000-plus delegates and 2,000-plus alternates at 10 A.M., hung over and/or depressed, their faces formed in the main (given much anal and oral rectitude) around the power to bite. Leading an honest hard-working responsible life, at work from 9 to 5 over the middle decades of one's life, can pinch the mouth into bitterness at the laziness and license of others. If one had been a convict up for parole, one would not be happy encountering these faces across the table. Imagination had long surrendered its ghost to principles, determined and predetermined principles.

On the other hand, who had ever said that parole board officers were ideally equipped to run the country? Republicans sitting in their orderly rows of folding chairs, the aisles considerably wider than the cramped turns on the floor of Madison Square Garden (where the Democrats had held their convention), the Astrodome ceiling much higher, the vast floor lavishly carpeted, were, nonetheless, a sullen, slow-to-settle audience. They did not listen to the minor speakers— one rarely did unless he was from one's home state—but they applauded moderately on cue, and tried to contemplate the problems of the change that might be in the air. The only speaker to wake them up all morning was Alan Keyes, a dynamic black man running for the Senate in Maryland. The Democrats, he asserted, had brought the poor to a pass where they were "trapped in welfare slavery. It does what the old slavery never could. It kills the spirit." So Keyes received a standing ovation, but it was a lonely event in a congealed opening morning void of other excitement.

By the time of the evening session, however, the mood had altered completely. Two events had intervened. George Bush had come to town that afternoon, and earlier there had been a jam-packed meeting at a "God and Country" rally at the Sheraton Astrodome across the street from the convention arena. Inside, in the Sam Houston Ballroom of the Sheraton, a medium-sized hotel chamber with no significant decorations other than a very large American flag, a small stage, and a podium, a crowd of delegates, evangelists, and fundamentalist congregations estimated as high as 2,000 people were standing with a remarkable display of patience as various speakers came up to promise the appearance of other speakers, and singers performed, notably Pat Boone, wearing a cream-colored suit.

The assembled were healthy-looking people in the main, with a tendency, given the augmentations of marriage, to put on weight, and a great many young fathers and mothers were holding infants in their arms, the parents cleanly dressed, with domiciled haircuts, fresh-washed faces perspiring now, not a bad-looking group except for the intellectual torpor that weighed on the enthusiasm of the room. The assembled bore resemblance to those faces one sees among daytime TV audiences, the minds graceless, the eyes blank, the process of thought as slack-jawed as chewing gum before the complexity of things. If they were pro-life, and they were, it was because, whatever valid and sincere reasons were present, they were also being furnished with an intellectual *rock*. God—as the Republican platform they had participated in shaping now told them—was present in every pregnancy. "We believe the unborn child has a fundamental individual right to life which cannot be infringed. We therefore reaffirm our support for a human life amendment to the Constitution, and we endorse legislation to make clear that the Fourteenth Amendment's protections apply to unborn children." Pregnancy was an aspect of God's will and every embryo was therefore a divine soul. A mighty certainty resided in this one notion, enough to make abortion illegal again; indeed, they called for a constitutional amendment to codify it as a crime of murder. The consequences, if carried to legal conclusion, could conceivably jail 1.5 million women a year, since such was the number of abortions a year, but then the prohibitive logic of these numbers could never prevail against their *other* knowledge.

"I think," said Sylvia Hellman, a member of the Christian Coalition from Dallas, to David Von Drehle of *The Washington Post,* "that the media are actually good people who want to do good, but they go at it from the human perspective, not God's."

She was a lady who could still present a hint of lavender from that lost era before deodorant, dungarees, air conditioning, and parking-lot asphalt malls had come to America, and she added, "In the Bible, which conservative Christians take literally, there are rules to live by. Sometimes the rules demand that we do things that don't make sense to us, but we find out later they are best."

It would have taken a brutal turn of intellect to suggest to her faith that there were men and women who thought the devil might have as much purchase on the sexual act as God, and, if so, then many a young girl with an unwanted pregnancy might feel that she possessed a devil in her heart, or was it the devil she was bearing in her womb? By such livid light, the murder of an ogre within one might seem less unholy than encouraging such a presence to appear and deaden others in small measure daily by words and ugly deeds. The calculus of gestation is as much a moral labyrinth as the food chains of nature, but that is not a thought to propose to those who have found their piece of the eternal parchment. As Richard Bond, the Republican National Committee chairman (once George Bush's job), said to Maria Shriver, "We are America. These other people are not America."

Since nearly all 2,000 people in the Sam Houston Ballroom were obliged to stand, not only visibility was limited at the rear, but audibility as well. One could hardly hear the Reverend Pat Robertson, presidential candidate in the Republican primaries of 1988, as he introduced Dan Quayle, but some words were more distinct than others, and the vice president, despite the towering religiosity of the hundreds of heads between, was heard to say, "It is a pleasure to be with people who are the real America." No need to describe the cheers. "I don't care what the media say. I don't care what the critics say. I will never back down." He would repeat that sentiment several times in days to come, and was always clean-shaven as he said it. Dan Quayle might have his slips of tongue and occasional misalignment of facts or letters, but one could not conceive of him ever missing a single hair when he shaved.

"Well," Pat Robertson had remarked earlier, "this is a resurrection here today," and it is true that nearly all of God's minions had been on their feet and unable to move for close to two hours: That had proved more impressive than the rhetoric. Robertson was, by now, quietly celebrated among the liberal media for the appearance of a fund-raising letter in which he had declared that the feminist movement "encourages women to leave their husbands, kill their children, practice witchcraft, destroy capitalism, and become lesbians." He had a cherubic face, and he beamed forth a good, warm non-sexual Christian vitality with every smile and gesture. Perhaps he did not realize that his abusive language was calculated to drive feminists a little further into the precise roles he had catalogued.

George Bush arrived in Houston a little later and hastened to the American Spirit Pavilion, now the name for the born-again Astro-arena, a ministadium and shopping center on one of the flanks of the Astrodome. There, before a crowd of 15,000 media, delegates, Astro-arena mall-shoppers, and assorted guests, he laid into his problems with a squire's wrath. This was no longer the George Bush who vomited at a Japanese state dinner, or suffered a paucity of thyroid from Graves Disease, or was loved by Americans less than they loved his wife—not at all the George Bush who failed to knock out old Sad-damn after all, or had to patty-cake with the religious right and be bollixed by abortion and AIDS and have to listen to the interminable inner-party debates whether to deep-six Dan Quayle; certainly not the George Bush who was asked to solve the economy when none of his economists had a clue how to begin. Put it that he had one problem larger than all the others: The cold war was over. Could one begin to measure how much George Bush owed the cold war?

These were endemic concerns. But George Bush was not the man to sink into the natural pessimism of his condition. He did stand up for one idea, after all, and it was named George Bush. Neither the spirit of wisdom nor of insight, he was the soul of Waspitude, one man of the gentry born to fight. He could hear the clash of armor when crusaders met Saracens; he had his own taproot into the universe of guts, a soldier's bowels, a knight of embattlement. Of all the misperceptions of the liberal media (and they were legion!), none was so unfounded as the still-prevailing notion that he was a wimp.

Problems passed, worries ceased. Combat was the medicine beneath all other prescriptions. If George Bush stood for one political idea other than himself, it was that America loved a fighter, and if you could maneuver the other elements, why, brother, the electorate would vote for the warrior every time.

So George Bush came to the podium of the American Spirit Pavilion, and in that auditorium, with 15,000 supporters there to listen and whoop, he started with the reinstallation of Dan Quayle.

It was part of his strategy. Perhaps it was the most honorable part. If every poll had shown that Quayle was a liability fast approaching the drag of a sea anchor, if most of George's advisers had all but begged him to take on a new dynamite vice president like Jack Kemp or Jim Baker or Cheney or Powell or Schwarzkopf, or even Bill Bennett if you had to keep your conservatives happy, Bush consulted his own psychology. All things being more or less equal, Americans not only loved a battler, but they adored a warrior faithful to his own troops. If he was to overcome the foe, how much more happiness he would find in victory, and how much more virtue (an indispensable companion was virtue) if he kept Quayle with him. The essence of noblesse oblige (which God knows you could not lose sight of no matter what other options had to be picked up) was to do it the hard way.

So he filled the sound of the word "Quayle" with whalebone.

Four years ago, Dan Quayle and I teamed up and I told him then, speaking from some personal experience, that the job of vice president was a real character builder, and I was not exaggerating. But look, this guy stood there and in the face of those unfair critics he never wavered. And he simply told the truth and let the chips fall where they may. And he said we need families to stick together and fathers to stick around, and he is right.

This was George right off the cuff, and his minutes at the podium turned into an event. The convention came to life. This was the George who could win any battle against any Democratic foe any time because he knew the American people and what they cared about and what they laughed about. It was auto-intoxication for sure, but then mountains are climbed by just these will-to-win guys.

I couldn't help but notice an interview my opponent gave to the *USA Today* last week. It was absolutely incredible. . . . He's already planning his transition, figuring out who should be deputy assistant undersecretary in every Washington agency . . . and I half expected, when I went over to the Oval Office, to find him over there measuring the drapes. Well, let me say as the first shot out of the barrel, I have a message for him. Put those drapes on hold; it is going to be curtain time for that ticket. And I mean it.

Yes, curtains. The other guy played the saxophone, and everyone knows what that instrument is attempting to convey. It's just a blither-blather of illicit sex and farts.

The first large event was on Monday night in the Astrodome—Pat Buchanan's speech. Trounced repeatedly in the Republican primaries by Bush, having to contend with the full weight of the Republican establishment in state after state, and succeeding nowhere after the early good showing in New Hampshire, Buchanan had managed nonetheless to amass 3 million votes. Half of them must have been as hard-core in their conservatism as Buchanan himself. Since he had also brought a heart attack on himself following such expenditures of energy, Buchanan could speak with the *gravitas* gained from reconnoitering early mortality.

Unlike the majority of speakers who strode up to the pale and massive podium of the Astrodome only to be overwhelmed by the caverns and hollows of volume in that huge and amplified space, he did not get into the trap of bellowing out his lines. Most speakers had a tendency to exercise hortatory rights—to yell louder as one lost more and more of one's audience. So they sounded cranky as their applause lines failed to elicit large response. All bad orations, whether by actors or politicians, have this in common: the speaker becomes exactly equal to his text—There is no human space between, no subtext to give resonance to the difference between the person and what he is saying.

Buchanan possessed a good deal of subtext. He was pleasant-faced and, in the beginning, mild-voiced, and no audience can fail to hang on every word of a killer speaker when he is pleasant-faced. So they took in each phrase and cheered with happiness at nearly every applause line. Patrick Buchanan was off to a fine start.

> Like many of you last month, I watched that giant masquerade ball at Madison Square Garden where 20,000 radicals and liberals came dressed up as moderates and centrists—in the greatest single exhibition of cross-dressing in American political history. . . .

Buchanan, having paused for the cheers he received, went on with the attack. He had inner sanction. He laid down a gauntlet:

> My friends, this election is about much more than who gets what. It is about what we believe, what we stand for as Americans. There is a religious war going on for the soul of America. It is a cultural war, as critical to the kind of nation we will one day be— as was the cold war itself. . . .
>   We must take back our cities, and take back our culture, and take back our country.

Buchanan was drawing his own line in the sand. If it took martial law, barbed wire, camps of detention, and Pentagon management of the media, then, by God, fellow Republicans, is that not a comfortable price to pay for walking carefree again on the street? The temptation would go deep for many an American. Would one care to see the results of a confidential poll on just this point? Inner-city unrest, however, would hardly be solved by his solution. For a religious man, Buchanan did not seem to comprehend that freedom which is obtained for a majority by amputating the rights of a minority offers no more balance to heaven than to the streets.

Next on Monday night would come Ronald Reagan. With a few cuts, his text could have been delivered by many a senior Democratic statesman. It was as if Reagan was looking to attain the eminence that is above politics.

> In my life's journey over these past eight decades, I have seen the human race through a period of unparalleled tumult and triumph. I have seen the birth of communism and the death of communism. I have witnessed the bloody futility of two world wars, Korea, Vietnam, and the Persian Gulf. I have seen television grow from a parlor novelty to become the most powerful vehicle of communication in history. As a boy I saw streets filled with model-Ts; as a man I have met men who walked on the moon. . . .
>
> Yet tonight is not a time to look backward. For while I take inspiration from the past, like most Americans I live for the future. So this evening, for just a few minutes, I hope you will let me talk about a country that is forever young. . . .

So it went. He gave credit to the Republicans for ending the cold war; he chided the Democrats. "Our liberal friends," he called them. What got liberals most upset were "two simple words: Evil Empire."

Though Reagan's popularity was great in this hall, it was smaller outside. He had spoken of the "Evil Empire" too often, and now we were left with the bill. Part of the profound confusion that hung over the political atmosphere of America this election year is that we had gotten ourselves in so much debt under Ronald Reagan. If he had come into office promising to cut taxes, balance the budget, and beef up the military so that it could defeat the Evil Empire, the dire fact was that our debt had expanded from $1 trillion in the time of Jimmy Carter to 4 trillion now (4 trillion, we can remind ourselves, is 4 million separate sums of $1 million each); yes, the truth was he had spent it not to fight but to bankrupt the Russians. We did not wage a holy war so much as a battle of U.S. versus Soviet military disbursements, and it had been needless. Once, under Stalin, the USSR had been a charnel house for human rights, but the monstrosities of the Fifties had ebbed by the Seventies into a dull and daily oppression, a moribund economy, a corrupt bureaucracy, a cynical leadership, and no capacity whatever, no matter how large the vastly inefficient Soviet armies, to succeed at world conquest. By 1980, when Ronald Reagan came to presidential office, the Evil Empire had been reduced to an immense Third World collection of backward nations incapable of defeating even one other Third World country like Afghanistan. So we had spent our trillions in the holy crusade of a Pentagon build-up against an enemy whose psychic and economic wherewithal was already collapsed within, and had pursued communism into little countries, and wrecked their jerry-built tropical economies even as we were wearing out what was left of the Soviets', but it all cost us twenty times more than it had to. Our grandchildren would pay the bill.

The American public, however, had been as attracted to Reagan's scenarios as he was. So our vision of an Evil Empire did not vanish altogether until the fall of communism itself. Then the fraud was out. Evil Empires, like dragons, slaughter millions in their last throes, but Eastern Europe and the Soviet Union went over to capitalism peacefully. Blood did not run in the streets. Caught in the middle of a long sleep, the American mind began to ask itself: Were we taken? Had there been, for a long time, something phony about the cold war? It might be that Ronald Reagan was the last person in America to realize that he had not won such a conflict, but had merely extended it.

With the conclusion of Reagan's speech, the first convention evening came to a close, and Bush's strategy could begin to be seen. Clinton had been attacked scores of times, the nation had been celebrated, the Bush administration had been glorified, pro-life had been affirmed, and legal abortion denied. That conservative movement which had sought to get the government off the backs of the American people had now put its foot into the womb of the American woman. Yet, with all the rhetoric, not a new word, nor a new idea, had been brought forth on the economy. The overall strategy was clear. In court, if you have a weak case and can argue neither the facts nor the law, dedicate yourself to arousing the emotions of the jury.

If Clinton was going to base his campaign on improving the weak state of the economy, which certainly handed him the facts, then Bush would look to dig deep into the mother lode of American politics—patriotism. Since the Republicans had been mining such ore since the Second World War, the question was whether the vein had been played out. All the same, Bush could only try. What with his hardest campaign workers coming from the religious right, he could hardly debate in the center; his would have to be the war between the Patriots and the Bureaucratic Managers, between the warriors and the hedonists (read: faggots, feminists, lawyers, media).

Nonetheless, the strategy worked but minimally on the second night. Jack Kemp spoke with reasonable effectiveness and Phil Gramm put his audience to sleep with the keynote speech. The theme for the third day, Wednesday, was Family Values, and it was introduced in the Republican Gala at noon. Four thousand wealthy Republicans, paying $1,000 each, came to lunch at the George Brown Convention Center in Downtown Houston (largest edge-city of them all), and in the huge main room, as large as a football field, and therefore commodious enough for 400 tables, the gentry of Texas and a few country clubs beyond had congregated in support of the president and first lady, who, after notables had been seated at the dais, entered the festivities in a mock railroad train called the American Eagle Express, a black and gold behemoth of a toy locomotive about the size of a large stagecoach. On the rear platform of the observation car it pulled were standing the Bushes and Quayles, and in their wake walked the Secret Service, as alert on this occasion as attack dogs. All considered, it was a hairy maneuver: The facsimile of a train choo-chooed and whistled gaily as it trundled through the aisles along the luncheon floor, but it left the president and his wife wholly exposed as they smiled and nodded and occasionally reached out to shake hands with friends on either side.

Standing near the locomotive as it crawled by, one had a fair look at Barbara Bush, who was immensely animated and appeared capable of taking in a formidable amount of information at once. Her eyes scanned every face within ten feet of her, and she did not miss a dear acquaintance or those who were at this hour somewhat less than friends, the smallest movements of her eyes and lips indicating a welcome across the gap, or a small reminder that things between were not altogether in order. To bestow warmth or display rectification in one's greetings suggests command of that spectrum of recognition that usually belongs to royals. On reflection, that was no surprise. Barbara Bush did not look like a first lady so much as like a woman who could be Queen of England, and that did little for George, standing beside her, since his absolute trimness of figure, reminiscent of

George VI, could also bring to mind King George's older brother, the former Prince of Wales, Edward, the old dear haunted poof who married Wallis Simpson, although George Bush, God knows, was no way a poof, but possessed the genuine steel (no matter how he might be cursed with that mild face and mild voice, and—said the Democrats—his mild brain!). Nonetheless, it was a moment to recall—Barbara Bush as the Queen of America, or, better yet, our queen mother.

Entered the chow in chuck wagons, pushed along by teenagers in cowhand and cowgirl outfits, the boys leaning on the heavy wagons with all their strength, while the girls, obviously not liberated, were taking it easy. And the gathering of 4,000, whose least costly denominator when it came to dress was the Neiman-Marcus boutique, was delighted by such campy re-creation of chuck-wagon roots, but of course, as was true so often of Republican promises, the wagons were but symbols for the food to come—the real grub came out later, carried by other files of cowhands and cowgirls toting stacks of round plastic plates and plastic covers with fried chicken and fritters within.

Bush came to the podium as a very large American flag was unrolled behind him, and he flattered his people:

> This is our last big convention, the last time—you might say—around the track. It is great to come back home to Texas, come home to where it really began for us in the political sense. The friends we made here and throughout our lives are the friends who are in this room.

There was a photographers' platform erected fifteen feet above the floor and a hundred feet from the podium, and it was jammed with echelons of TV cameras, perhaps so many as forty or fifty; crowded in was a second host of still cameras. Out of this intensely compressed work force, a voice shouted, "*Bullshit!*"

Later, the heckler was reported as saying, "What are you going to do about AIDS?" but that was later. The first muffled sound was "Bullshit," and everyone at the lunch froze for an instant, as if everyone belonged again to one American family and was passing through the hour when Jack and Bobby Kennedy and Martin Luther King had been killed, and Ronald Reagan and Gerald Ford wounded. Like all families who put together a fragile composure after the death of someone who inhabited the center of the home and circle, it was as if the air went pale.

"*Bullshit,*" came another voice, "What are you going to do about AIDS?" and by then, security was up on the platform manhandling the malefactors, who proved to be two wan young men with the tell-tale pallor of the disease, their hair cut in a punk-rock clump, and sores on their faces; now they were hustled down the stairs from the photographers' platform and out the exit.

Bush picked up his discourse, but he was shaken—how could he not be? The moment one will be assassinated must become one of the hundred entrenched expectations in every public leader's life—unlike other crises, there is not much to prepare for; the angle of attack is never known. In the aftermath, Bush started to make a sour joke—with all else, he felt sour—"This is a crazy year when they can get credentials for this," he muttered, but other voices started up on the photographers' platform ("What are you going to do about AIDS?"), and now several of the new hecklers—second wave of the plan—waved condoms at the boutique crowd there for lunch, and security whammed and slammed the second group of hecklers down from the platform and out of the room, while Bush came up fast with a few figures on what his administration was spending on AIDS—one cannot be a major politician without having a statistics tape in one's head—and then he added, the room now feeling at last restored, "In my line of work lately, this seems normal. . . . If anyone else has anything they would like to say while we are all standing . . ."

It was the presence of AIDS that would build in the Astrodome that night, however. Mary Fisher, a slim, blond, and undeniably lovely young lady with a delicacy of feature and a poignancy of manner, proceeded to give the Republican address on AIDS not long after the prime time commenced. If a casting director had searched for a fine actress unlikely ever to have contact with the virus, he would have selected Mary Fisher if she had been an actress, but she was not. She was in a rare category, a Republican princess; her father, Max Fisher, eighty-four years old and reputedly worth hundreds of millions of dollars, had been a major fund-raiser for the party since the early days of Richard Nixon. Mary Fisher could speak of Georgette and Robert Mosbacher and Gerald and Betty Ford as her friends; indeed, the women were weeping and the men were wiping their eyes as she spoke. Before she was done, the Astrodome floor would be awash. She was not only lovely but innocent, after all; she had caught the disease from her ex-husband before they separated. Now, presumably, she would die and have to say farewell to her sons, Max and Zachary, four and two. If, at the Democratic convention, there had been accusations that not enough had been done by the Bush administration to fight against AIDS, Bill Clinton had declared that such a fight would be one of the central issues in his campaign.

Mary Fisher was the Republican answer, and she was effective beyond measure. Outside their gates, across the bordering street beyond the Astrodome, in a weed-filled vacant lot now named the Astrodomain and renamed Queer Village by the protesters themselves, there had been a riot on Monday night. A half-dozen arrests and a number of beatings had been handed out "professionally" by the police after a few of the 1,000 protesters had put up effigies of George Bush, set them afire, and then had begun smashing wooden police barricades to feast the fire. The police had charged in on horse and foot and a helicopter shook the sky overhead as chants of doggerel came up from the protesters. "150,000 dead," they began, "Off with George Bush's head!" and "Burn, baby, burn!" They cried to the effigy, "We're queer and we're here." One protester announced, "This shows how far we mean to take our anger," but then the anger was as bottomless as the rage that victims feel against hurricanes and earthquakes. "We're all innocent. Do you want to see me die?" had shouted one AIDS activist to Senator Alfonse D'Amato in a Houston church when D'Amato made the mistake of remarking on the tragedy of AIDS when it took the lives of innocent children. "What about us?" someone shouted back. "We're also innocent and we're going to die."

Well, they were innocent or they were guilty. It was the intolerable and unspoken question at the heart of AIDS. Many a Republican was harboring ugly thoughts. AIDS, went the whisper, stood for Anal Injection—Dirty Sex! Out in Oregon a movement was commencing against the gay nation. The Oregon Citizens' Alliance had sent out mass mailings that said, "Homosexual men on average ingest the fecal material of twenty-three different men per year," which, if a particularly roto-rooter way of stating that the average homosexual had twenty-three lovers a year, also posed the riddle of how the Oregon Citizens' Alliance ever obtained their statistic. But the anxiety of homosexuals, borne in private for who knows how many centuries, was now inflamed by the enigma of nature. Was excrement a side-product of nature, offensive to some, as the Democrats would doubtless have argued, or was Satan in everyone's shit? Which, in turn, was a way of saying that the devil was present more often in homosexual than in heterosexual encounters—exactly the question that blazed in the divide. We are dying, said the victims of AIDS, and you have no mercy. Are you cold to our pain because we are the devil's spawn?—beware, then, for we will haunt you. That was the question. Was the gay nation guilty or innocent, victims or devils, damned by Jehovah or to be comforted by Christ? Were such acts shameful or natural? The wheel of obsessive and unanswerable questions went round and round, and gay rage came up from the bottomless funnels of the vortex. Was their illness for cause in a world of immutable principles? Or was it the absurdity of a badly designed natural system that had not provided for safe sex short of the damnable deadhead odor of a condom?

What had happened to American politics? Like Mr. Magoo, it teetered on the lip of ultimate peril—which is to say ultimate questions—and all the while a blood rage had been building in the nation. "If I am young and dying of AIDS," went the credo that was forming, "then I might as well go down in flames." Yes, the riots were building, and the forces of the right, equally inflamed by the more and more vivid presence of the gay nation, were out to extirpate—so went the secret agenda—all human flesh that carried such a virus. Scenarios were germinating on the other side of that hill of time which is ten years away. Scenarios, we know, are rarely put into production by the cosmic forces who make the real films of our lives, but let us contemplate the Republicans in this pass—an enormous congregation of the conservative-minded, who can be enumerated as the greedy, the spiteful, the mean-spirited, in party congress with the sincere, the godly, the principled, and the tidy, all philosophically unsuited to contemplate the nightmare of a disease that is not amenable to medical science and may or may not have the deepest moral roots; yes, the Republicans were paralyzed before the obscene enigma of AIDS, and so when Mary Fisher spoke like an angel that night, the floor was in tears, and conceivably the nation as well, for instead of the Evil Empire, so nicely manipulable by American might—we always held the aces—now we lived on the edge of uncontrollables we did not know how to stir against—drugs, crime, abortion, race, disease. How much, nearly half of the nation at least, must have longed for Buchananite solutions—how bewildered was each angry soul of the right that there was no retaking of the disease of AIDS block by city block.

Into this stew of choked passions and muffled fears (where a city was now defined as a place you would not enter until you knew where you would be able to park your car and ascend by elevator to your event), into this ongoing panic, came Mary Fisher with a message so old that the coruscated souls of the Republicans, nine-tenths barnacled by now in greed and wealth, cant and bad conscience, fury and fear, began to weep in longing for the old memory of Christ kissing the feet of the poor. How contradictory are our conventions! At this one, the most moving message of the four days came from a Republican princess

who had the Republicans bawling their hearts out at sentiments usually characterized by the L-word.

> Less than three months ago, at Platform Hearings in Salt Lake
> City, I asked the Republican Party to lift the shroud of silence
> which has been draped over the issue of HIV/AIDS. I have come
> tonight to bring our silence to an end.
>
> I bear a message of challenge, not self-congratulation. I want
> your attention, not your applause. I would never have asked to
> be HIV-positive. But I believe that in *all* things there is a purpose,
> and I stand before you and before the nation gladly.
>
> Tonight I represent an AIDS community whose members
> have been reluctantly drafted from every segment of American
> society. Though I am white and a mother, I am one with a black
> infant struggling with tubes in a Philadelphia hospital. Though I
> am female, and contracted this disease in marriage, and enjoy
> the warm support of my family, I am one with the lonely gay man
> sheltering a flickering candle from the cold wind of his family's
> rejection. . . . We may take refuge in our stereotypes but we can-
> not hide there long. Because HIV asks *only one thing* of those it at-
> tacks: Are you *human*? And this is the right question. *Are* you
> human? Because people with HIV have not entered some alien
> state of being. They are *human*.
>
> I want my children to know that their mother was not a vic-
> tim. She was a messenger. I do not want them to think, as I once
> did, that courage is the absence of fear; I want them to know that
> courage is the strength to act wisely when most we are afraid . . .

Marilyn Quayle came next. Had the coordinators been wholly un-
ready for the impact of Mary Fisher's speech and so had not foreseen
what a powerful effect it would produce upon the mean-spirited not to
be mean-spirited for a little while? Or did the convention organizers
possess the wisdom to know that Marilyn Quayle was ready to appear
at the podium after anyone—Gorbachev, St. Peter, Madonna—she
would not be cowed by those who came before. She had, after all, the
insularity of a duchess, an insensitivity to her surroundings so monumental that it was almost attractive—one of a kind!

So she gave her little speech with absolute composure, the only
sign that not everyone in herself was right there at home and listening
came from her logo—that is, her horsey smile—that peculiarly self-
intoxicated stretch of lips and protrusion of teeth that came and went

to a rhythm that had next to nothing to do with what she said. Her words might be pious or reflective, or she might even attempt to be funny, "If only Murphy Brown could meet Major Dad—what a story," but then the smile would come, on the beat, off the beat; it was like the reflex learned in childhood to hold off tears when one is being scolded.

Her language, however, was always correct. When it came to being politically correct—as a Bush Republican, that is—who could approach her? Her speech was seamless, and her espousal of Republican womanhood could not be improved, nor injured; it was there, flat as Indiana. "Watching and helping my children as they grow into good and loving teenagers is a source of daily joy for me."

On the other hand, she was not a duchess for too little. She had a nasal voice that could drill into clay, and given her disconnected smile, she could have been the president of a garden society, bird-like for all her horsiness, elevated above dross, and spacey as a space station. Let us say farewell while listening to her encomiums to the royal couple:

> Because leadership has everything to do with character and unwavering commitment to principle, Dan and I have been deeply honored to serve these four years with President and Mrs. Bush. America loves Barbara Bush because she exemplified our ideal of a strong and generous woman, dedicated to her husband, her children, and her nation. She is a model for all generations, a woman I am proud to call a friend and our nation is proud to call first lady.

Barbara Bush was the major gamble of the Bush strategy. The economy was going to remain a problem antipathetic to solution. One might as well roll the dice then with Barbara Bush, and pump up the advantage the Republicans held in family values. It was certainly a gamble. If America reacted with the cry—jobs, not happy hearths—then the election could be lost. On the other hand, Barbara Bush was the only exceptional card they had to play, and one could find a logic to the bet—patriotism, the flag, and the family were, after all, the values taught in elementary schools (even if they were public schools), whereas politics only commenced (if it did) with high school civics. So, family values were gut-bets. Unless the economy got so bad that people had to vote with their minds, patriotism, the flag, and the family had a real chance to hit. George could take care of the patriotism, but Barbara could demolish every Clinton position when it came to family values, and you wouldn't even see the smoke. The beauty of it all was that she was also an ameliorative and corrective force. If the good ship GOP was tilted ten degrees further over to the right than it cared to be, with every attendant impediment to responsive steering, Barbara could ballast it back a little to the left. The pro-lifers had kept cutting too hellish a swath in Houston that week, blockading abortion clinics so violently that forty-one of their *religiosos* got arrested on Monday, and then were so bad in court that they called the judge, who was a mother and a Catholic named O'Neill, nothing less than "anti-Christ"—Jesus, it was enough to make you swear. Ultra-religious Americans were not paying heed to the effect on the electoral result. After Judge O'Neill ordered Operation Rescue to keep one hundred feet away from Planned Parenthood clinics, one preacher even started praying for the judge to repent or she would "be stricken from the face of the earth." Somebody else left a stink bomb at Planned Parenthood. Besides, you couldn't have a crazy-looking father, holding his kid, scared frozen, by one hand, while he swings a seven-month fetus (still reeking of formaldehyde) with the other. Republican women were going to leave the party in droves. George understood female psychology. You don't allow something as ugly as a fetus to be waved in public—women do not like to advertise the disagreeableness of some personal and private functions. Damnit, the Party needed amelioration concerning pro-life.

Family values was the epoxy, then, to keep the party together, and Barbara could handle any press conference or podium assignment. Trust her every time. In with reporters from *The Boston Globe* and *The Washington Post* just a week ago, why, she blocked every thrust, and these were top-flight journalists, true hard-ons, *honed!*

*BOSTON GLOBE:* On abortion, I have to ask you something. Why is it so many of your friends think you are pro-choice?

BARBARA BUSH: I have no idea. I have no idea.

*BOSTON GLOBE:* Because you never expressed it to them? Never talked about it?

BARBARA BUSH: I've always felt that if I ran for President, George Bush would back me 100 percent. That's the best I can do. [So] we can't return to that. I've given my answer.

*WASHINGTON POST:* Well, I'm returning to it and I want you to tell me how the Republican Party which . . .

BARBARA BUSH: I don't know the answer.

*WASHINGTON POST:* . . . which wants less government in our lives . . .

BARBARA BUSH: I don't know the answer to your question and so, in all honesty, don't ask it. I don't know the answer to your question.

Pro or con. I just don't want to get into abortion. I've had it with abortion.

She could front any confrontation. The day before she had said, "It's a personal choice. . . . The personal things should be left out of . . . platform and conventions." She had said that during a televised interview in a simple setting. The only picture in the room was on the end table next to her, and it was a framed photograph (signed, presumably) of Pope John Paul II. She could offer every indication to Republican women that she was their advocate for choice in the land while reassuring the religious right by dint of her close respect for John Paul II—no champion of abortion was he!

Speak of presumption, let us hack away at the matter on our own. Concerning abortion, Barbara Bush is leaving just the kind of mixed message that only a monarch can dare to send out. Mixed messages are the prerogative of kings and queens; they are supposed to represent the entirety of the populace.

That was just what she did in her speech on Family Values. It was no rhetorical gem. On the page, it read like one of those decaffeinated pieces of prose that used to blanket the old *Reader's Digest,* affirmative, highly simplified, and emotionally available to anyone whose IQ had managed to stay below 100. But the GOP, we can assume, was profoundly aware, along with Barbara Bush, that most of the electorate was right there, right under that magic number.

Virtually at her commencement, she paid lip service to other orators, but it was evident that despite her protestations, she was an exceptionally good speaker, and this because of one virtuous ability—she could address tens of thousands of people as if they were not more than two or three individuals sitting across from her on a couch. This faculty is available to few, and it suggests she had managed some personal transcendence—a woman once sensitive about her stocky build and much-lined face, her dumpy presence, had undergone so many rites of passage that she was now possessed of a consummate ease in public. So she gave her audience in the Astrodome a satisfaction they had found nowhere else—a wholly comfortable, social, witty, and reigning queen in their midst; yes, Barbara Bush was politics in the deepest sense, even as is monarchy. Her confidence suggested that one thing at least was right in the world—herself! We vote for what looks right.

So the royal presence that the Reagans had imperfectly commenced, the Bushes had now developed. The presidency had become a monarchy. In place of landed estates or thousand-year-old families, we had endowed symbols. Intrinsic to us was our heraldry, our American West, our Cavalry, the Marines, the Air Corps, the spirit-of-the-fourth-quarter, Notre Dame, and the kind of family values that had come down to us from Queen Victoria and been brought over by boat-loads of immigrants, a sense of propriety brought up to the mark now by Queen Mother Barbara, and our own not wholly overpowering King George, a fantasy of rich national theatre. However, since Mr. and Mrs. Bush partook of it as only Wasp gentry and Wasp vigor can settle into a set of roles they are able to spend their lives living out, a sublim-inal nourishment was there for that part of America that could hardly survive without the certainty of a single powerful and uplifting idea, the unvoiced sense that Barbara Bush was, for all effects, our Queen and so could underwrite the religion beneath all other American reli-gions—America itself. Well, thought the Republicans, we'll win by an avalanche if we can only keep the focus on Hillary versus Barbara, Hillary with her feminist intelligence and her hairband.

The Republicans in the Astrodome were delirious. They could believe in victory for the first time. Clinton's lead was vanishing even as the first lady spoke. For there was depth to this gambit. It would ap-peal not only to all who were happy and fierce about their family, but one could probably add a host of those loners bereft of family, plus the unhappy families that wished to be happy so much that their hearts tugged at the thought that it might still be possible. Family values was bound to exert some force on 75 percent of the vote—all the people who were in favor of Barbara.

> You may be exhausted from working a job . . . or two jobs and taking care of your children, or you may have put your career on hold. Either way, you may wonder, as I did every now and then, am I really doing the right thing? . . . Yes, you are . . . from the bottom of my heart I'm here to tell you that you are doing the right thing and God bless you for it.

Tonight, with seventeen children and grandchildren surrounding Barbara and George, the story about Woody Allen, Mia Farrow, and Soon-Yi was circulating happily among the Republicans. William Kris-tol, an able servant in the development of the Republican mind—he was Dan Quayle's chief of staff—was heard to remark at a press brief-ing, "I'm tempted to say Woody Allen is a good Democrat and leave it at that." Newt Gingrich looked to rake in the pot. "Woody Allen having non-incest with a non-daughter to whom he was a non-father because they were a non-family fits the Democratic platform perfectly."

On the following night, Thursday, last session of the convention, came Dan Quayle's speech. No routine task. One would have needed the light forged by inner contests with one's rage and anguish, and Quayle, from the day he had been chosen by Bush in 1988, had been unable to take in one breath that was not predeterminedly partisan. Embattled, ridiculed, in liege to a wife who seemed twice as strong as he was and eight times more opinionated, he had had a full term of skirmishing with the media, and now, four years later, his petulance still leaked through. After a bow to the greatness of George Bush, he said:

> I know my critics wish I were not standing here tonight. They don't like our values. They look down on our beliefs. They're afraid of our ideas. And they know the American people stand on our side. That is why, when someone confronts them, they will stop at nothing to destroy him. To them I say: You have failed. I stand before you, and before the American people—unbowed, unbroken, and ready to keep fighting for our beliefs.

Quayle might speak with defiance, but he still seemed not so much unfinished as uncommenced. "It is not just a difference between conservative and liberal," said Quayle, speaking with the sanctimoniousness that no politician in America seemed to have in greater supply, "It is a difference between fighting for what is right and refusing to see what is wrong." That is probably why he inspired such hostility in the media. A young, rich, good-looking man does well not to be pious—piety, we sense, is not convincing unless it is based on tragedy and dread. Even as he threw down the gauntlet, he lacked dimension, a mediocre actor reciting a line more powerful than the true register of his experience.

Besides, he lacked taste. He mashed tuna salad onto blueberry muffins.

> We have taught our children to respect single parents and their challenges—challenges that faced my grandmother many years ago and my own sister today. And we have taught our children about the tragedy of diseases like breast cancer—which took the life of Marilyn's mother. Marilyn and I have hosted an annual event called the Race for the Cure of Breast Cancer. Two months

ago, 20,000 runners, men and women, young and old, joined us in the nation's capitol to race for the cure.

Enter George Bush. Once again, as in 1988, he would have to give the speech of his life. Or so it was generally agreed. The feeling among Republicans was that Family Values had taken a full bite out of the Democrats' lead in the polls, and if George could deliver on this occasion, parity might be near.

Bush had fretted over the need to prove himself one more time. It was as if he could not overcome his resentment that he, the conqueror of the Persian Gulf, was still obliged to seek victory through oratorical splendor. Whatever his desires, he had ended as the focus of narrative interest for this four-day convention. Would he or would he not startle and encourage the nation with new ideas and new policies? Or, would he fail to?

Thursday morning at an ecumenical prayer breakfast, he had said, "Tonight, I give my acceptance speech—and if it catches fire, it may give a whole new meaning to the burning Bush." A humorous remark, but a vain hope. He was too angry within: The delegates were treated instead to the smoldering Bush. If Clinton had failed to deliver a great speech and took fifty-four minutes to prove it, the same sentence could now be employed for George Bush except that he ate up fifty-eight minutes. One reason was that the president, having no new themes, provided a hundred applause lines. In the beginning, response came quickly and frenetically, his audience steamed up to hysteria. Ergo George Bush had difficulties handling the din. His first estimated ten minutes must have consumed twenty. But his text read like a committee production, and by the end, a quiet pall was on the Astrodome.

It is pointless to do more than give a most restricted sampling of what he offered. He had, after all, said it before, and would say it again. The speech, like his ideas, was in bits and pieces, a Broadway comedy that cashed laugh after laugh and left its audience muttering, "What an empty show!" The philosophical content was the one protagonist who never appeared.

Here, then, is Bush's climactic speech presented in snippets that will prove less injurious to him than the complete text.

This convention is the first at which an American president can say—the cold war is over, and freedom finished first. . . . What about the leader of the Arkansas National Guard—the man who hopes to be commander in chief? Well, while I bit the bullet, he bit his nails. . . . Sounds to me like his policy can be summed up by a road sign he's probably seen on his bus tour, "Slippery when Wet." . . .

Listening carefully in one of the VIP boxes above the floor was Jim Baker. Studying his expression, one could only decide that he was not the fellow to play poker with—by his expression you could not tell whether Baker was enthralled, appalled, or bored. As Bush went on, Baker proceeded to study the text of the speech with the concentration others might give to a musical score. Was he noting which lines produced more genuine response or less than he had anticipated?

> Now, I know Americans are tired of the blame game, tired of people in Washington acting like they are candidates for the next episode of American Gladiators. I don't like it either. Neither should you. But the truth is the truth. Our policies haven't failed; they haven't even been tried.

It was a long exercise in the use of the larynx to come from a man whose voice was sixty-eight years old, and he was beginning to whine.

He was near the end, however. It was time to produce a new sound.

> I believe that America will always have a special place in God's heart, as long as He has a special place in ours. And maybe that's why I've always believed that patriotism is not just another point of view. . . . Tonight I appeal to that unyielding spirit. . . . Tonight I say to you—join me in our new crusade—to reap the rewards of our golden victory—to win the peace—so that we may make America safer and stronger. . . .

The last 100,000 of a quarter-million balloons floated down with the conclusion of his speech, and golden confetti gave an effulgence as it fell, a heavenly light to outline the podium as the singer offered "God Bless America."

Yes, God bless us—we need it. If fascism comes from the rotting away of a nation's virtue until words like *trust* mean "corrupt," then yes, we are going to need it.

From *The New Republic* (October 12, 1992)

**PORTRAIT—IV**

## Madonna

Conceive of a Hispanic novelist with exceptional powers whose name is Jesus Ramirez. He has the conviction, given in part by his first name, that he is here on earth to make a great change in the way people perceive themselves, and so he signs his books with his first name only: *Transcendence*, by Jesus; *Vertigo*, by Jesus; *Shadow of War*—Jesus. He is renowned around the world. He lives with his one name, Jesus.

What goes on in Madonna Ciccone's head every time she happens to think of the single name she now carries—the immutable Madonna? She is either among us for extraordinary reasons or is a pint-size Italian American with a heart she hopes is built out of the cast-iron balls of the *paisans* in generations before her. She knows that she doesn't know the answer. Who could? There is nothing comparable to living with a phenomenon when the phenomenon is you and you observe yourself with a cool intelligence, your own, and yet are trapped in the cruelest pit of the narcissist—you not only are more interested in yourself than in anyone else alive, but suffer from the likely suspicion that this may be justified. You could be more interesting than anyone you've encountered.

Well, we can try to get into one or two small corners of Madonna's mind, although the secret may be not to try too hard. It is going to be no easy exploration. Her views and her philosophy are in deeds, not words. Her words give but an indication of where the dark stuff is stored.

Probably it is most comfortable to start our trip in company with David Letterman. He offers the most certitude. She was on his program, *Late Show with David Letterman,* on March 31, and the results produced a two-day Kristallnacht in the media. Madonna, once again, was being called sick, sordid, depraved, unbalanced, out of control, offensive, outrageous, and stupid. So wrote all the boozers, cokeheads, and solid suburbanites who do the TV columns, and their language frothed with enough effervescence to bring in the wire services and even the respectable daily press. Madonna, having said *fuck* thirteen times on the show, also had, with the aid of CBS' precise workmanship, been bleeped every time, and that was enough to light up the media machine guns. Outraged propriety! Defense of home and flag! The first requirement of a news story, after all, is to excise everything that gets in the way of a dramatic judgment. Madonna was a slut.

Actually, she and Letterman had been perfect foils for each other. If Madonna shows a predominant vice, it is that she always stands for something. It is usually rich enough, or by her detractors' estimate, gamy enough, to be on the very edge of the public's digestive powers. Letterman, on the other hand, stands for nothing at all. It is his number-one asset in our parlous time. During periods of lassitude and confusion, it is reassuring to listen to someone who is absolutely at home in the idle sounds of drift. At 11:30, when his audience is ready for a mild pleasure before bed, Letterman serves as their Ovaltine—a little flavor, a lot of pablum—and the implicit promise that nothing serious is going to take place. He will not even be too funny. That could stir the blood and inspire thoughts of going out for a drink. Johnny Carson, mean as his own minted embodiment of Waspitude, used, at least, to give audiences his sharp sense—whether you agreed with him or not—of what constituted proper social deportment. Letterman, on an average night, would not be caught dead offering one indication of how to conduct your life. Keep it meaningless and we'll all get along. To be meaningless in a meaningless time is to be the Buddha of the befuddled.

Well, you don't attack Buddha for too little—as Madonna discovered. It is worth excerpting a few moments from their evening.

Madonna came out dressed in black, her hair dark, her manner demure—but for her combat boots, she looked like a socialite stepping out for a charity dinner. Unfortunately, Letterman, at the conclusion of his introduction, did remark that Madonna had "slept with some of the biggest names in the entertainment industry," to which his bandleader exclaimed in real or simulated horror, "She's your guest!"

"Just relax," said David. "Everything's fine. We're just trying to have fun."

All the same, no visitor in the history of late-night television had ever received a comparable greeting. Soon enough, Madonna said, "Why are you so obsessed with my sex life?"

"Well," said David, "I have none of my own," to which Madonna would shortly reply, "David, you are a sick fuck."

The audience laughter was long. They had heard it. The rest of America would be bleeped, but they had waited on line to get tickets and they had heard Madonna say *fuck.* "You realize this is being broadcast?" David asked. "Well," he added, "you can't go on talking like that."

Madonna reminded him of a pair of her panties that were, presumably, in his desk drawer. "Aren't you going to smell them?" she asked. He said to the audience: "I'll tell you what—we're going to do a commercial and we're going to wash her mouth out with soap."

MADONNA: And he's going to smell my underwear . . .

DAVID: And we'll be right back.

>*They broke for the commercial. When they came on again, Madonna was smoking a huge cigar.*

MADONNA: You know, you've really changed since the last time I was on the show. . . . Life's made you soft.

DAVID: You think so? . . . In what sense?

MADONNA: Because you kiss up to everybody on your show. . . . I see you kissing up to, like, all these movie stars come on here—you used to give people a hard time.

DAVID: I can suspend that behavior tonight, if you like.

>*Heavy clapping followed. It inspired Letterman.*

DAVID: You can't—you can't be coming on here—this is American television; you can't talk like that.

MADONNA: Why?

DAVID: Because people don't want that in their own homes at 11:30 at night.

>*Now there was long applause in support of his sentiment: Away with filth at 11:30 P.M.*

MADONNA: Wait a minute, wait a minute—people don't want to hear the word *fuck?*

DAVID: Oh, stop it! Will you stop? Ladies and gentlemen, turn down your volume! Turn it down immediately! She can't be stopped! There's something wrong with her.

MADONNA: There's definitely something wrong with me—I'm sitting here!

DAVID: I think you're a decent, nice person, and I'm happy you could come by tonight and gross us all out. . . .

MADONNA: Did you know it's good if you pee in the shower?

DAVID [*to the audience*]: I'm sorry. . . .

MADONNA: Don't fuck with me . . . peeing in the shower is really good; it fights athlete's foot. [*Uneasy audience laughter.*] I'm serious. Urine is like an antiseptic. It all has to do with the enzymes in your body.

DAVID: Don't you know a good pharmacist? Get yourself some Desenex. . . .

The air went out of the bout. Right there. Buddha had just blown his cool. He might have spent his working hours dribbling on the brains of Americans, but he could not bear a little dithering over his toes. His voice was so petulant that it all became clear: David worked for the corporation; David believed that cures came in bottles. If he was overseer to all that was meaningless, it was because he had no poetry. He did not believe in a god who would be witty enough to put the cure for athlete's foot into the patient's urine.

So begins our modest story. Norman Mailer had been sufficiently taken with the manner in which Madonna disposed of David Letterman to mention it to Liz Smith. Friends of twenty years' standing, they were happy to talk to each other at parties, and only occasionally was he concerned that an indiscreet remark would slip into one of her columns.

On this occasion, however, he could not pretend that he was unhappy at being quoted. Stick it to Letterman, by all means! What he did not expect were the consequences. His agent was asked the next day whether Mailer would write a substantial piece on Madonna for *Esquire*. That gave him pause (for twenty-four hours) while Andrew Wylie, agent, and Ed Kosner, editor, came to terms. Nor could he pretend that he was overjoyed at the assignment: Madonna, on the face of it, had to have an ego even larger than his own.

Still, he had liked the woman who was on the Letterman show. What the news stories had failed to convey was how ladylike she had been all the while that she was setting network records at the number of times Outstanding Guest was being bleeped per minute. It is not easy to keep uttering *fuck* with style to millions of Americans you cannot see.

So, at the least, Mailer had that much interest. Moreover, *Esquire* had agreed to an offer too decent to refuse. Mailer was a great believer in taking on jobs that simultaneously satisfied both your best and worst motives; a challenging assignment on fields of green was always an inducement to opening that vault where the bullion of extra energy is stored. Since Madonna would obviously be witting to such a principle—had she done anything in her life that did not engage her best and worst sides at once?—they would have for commencement that much in common.

A few days later, he was asked most politely by the magazine whether he would consider being photographed in black tie with Madonna while she was in evening gown. It was the kind of request he usually took pleasure in rejecting: He hated abetting photographic stunts in magazines, but on this occasion, he accepted. He would be going to a black-tie party that night, and the photographic session could be scheduled to take place an hour earlier. Photographer, Wayne Maser; place, a loft in SoHo. It might be more interesting to meet Madonna in such manner than to drop in at her apartment with a tape recorder.

Let us not, however, pretend that he saw it as a wholly happy solution to the magazine's need to have a picture of the principals taken together. Mailer was now seventy-one years old and, in consequence of the shrinkage that visits a senior citizen, was not quite five feet seven inches tall. He weighed two hundred pounds. Since he pumped modest amounts of iron from time to time, he looked (at his best) like a barrel. How can a barrel find pleasure in having itself commemorated in a dinner jacket, even a good dinner jacket? He would look like a barrel wrapped in velvet.

The shoot, of course, turned all too quickly into a prepared scenario. Which is to say that Wayne Maser had his own ideas or instructions on where to go with it. Mailer had barely had time to say hello to Madonna, who was wearing a green evening dress and a black blindfold as she stood in front of a white canvas drop, before the blindfold was off and the photographer had stepped forward long enough to pull down the left strap of her gown, so exposing her breast, doing it, mind you, with about as much ceremony as a furniture mover flips a throw cloth off an armchair. Now we had portly Norman Mailer standing next to diminutive Madonna, in a green gown, one breast showing, a small nose ring in her left nostril. When she saw the stricken look with which he gazed upon her breast, she covered the gap in her gown with a dainty hand.

He had been stricken for the best of reasons. Mailer, like many an upstart before him, maintained a secret gentleman in a closet—the nice part of himself, so to speak. This Edwardian was puffed with outrage by the imposition on Madonna. It was not that her breast had been exposed—Mailer, along with much of America, had seen her bare breasts looking splendid more than a hundred times in film, video, magazines, and books. It was just that this was not the time for Madonna to be seen. If a man wished to present his naked genitals to the public, he would choose an occasion when his erection was noble. Much the same can be said of the female breast. It is full of moods. A breast can be as proud as the prow of a racing boat, or it can droop, pallid and sad. Madonna, by this purview, was obviously depressed, or so said her poor breast, and our stout Edwardian was outraged that he should be assisting at such a dim revelation. They had been photographing her for hours before he arrived, and, of course, she was tired; of course her breasts would be the first part of her to express such physical discontent, even as any good fellow's penis would shrivel when he was low in spirit. Still, how could her breast droop so at the sight of him!

Nonetheless, they were able to chat. She was easy to talk to. He looked, Madonna informed Mailer, like her former father-in-law, and after a moment, the connection was clear—she was referring to Sean Penn's father. "Well," he said, "that's not surprising," and went on to explain that on meeting Sean Penn two years ago, he had been struck with the actor's resemblance to himself in his youth, except, of course, that Sean Penn was better-looking. A reasonable exchange. Their only difficulty was that they wished to talk, not to take pictures, and Wayne Maser had his job and proceeded to pose them. Pretty soon, he had Madonna sitting on Norman Mailer's lap. The evening strap was up in place over her shoulder again, and her waist certainly felt agreeable, but a shoulder strap that could go up could as easily come down again, and Mailer knew that *Esquire,* with all its new influx of editorial talent, could hardly keep from printing such a picture. He, Norman Mailer, would be famous for much too little.

So Mailer interrupted the proceedings. If he was going to be photographed, he told everyone, it would be side by side, standing up, head shots only. What a dim prospect for the photographer's craft! Maser kept trying to reinstitute a stunt. Finally, Mailer said to him: "I respect your intelligence. Can't you respect mine?"

Wayne Maser gave up. He could recognize a battle-scarred veteran of the photographic wars, and so a half-dozen more restrained shutter clicks ended the session. Madonna and Mailer agreed to meet a couple of times over the next few days for intensive interviews.

He was depressed by the place in which she lived. It was a duplex on Central Park West in a classic apartment house of the West Sixties. The ceilings were high, and the rooms were gloomy by afternoon. Central Park West speaks of upper-middle-class lives, the decorum of prescribed responses, slow, successful professions, and solid family life with few excesses of love. The stairwells in such buildings are as downhearted as slum tenements. Actors also live on Central Park West, but architecture is more powerful than personality, and all the stars of stage and screen whom Mailer had ever visited on Central park West seemed to have succumbed to the gloom.

Madonna, if anything, had augmented it. The upstairs living room, in which they met for interviews, had white walls, a dark-maroon carpet, and but three massive, dark stuffed chairs without arms.

For two of the four walls, there was only a Picasso of Dora Maar and a Léger, a third wall had windows on the park, and to the rear, a full bar of mirrors, chromium, glass, and black trim—a formidably cold room.

One might find its equivalent in the best hotel suites of the most dictatorial countries in South America: Black, brown, and white are hues to emphasize that power also has its color scheme. Mailer could not help but think that Mussolini would have been happy in a room like this.

Of course, he did catch a glimpse down a long hall of other rooms with hints of pink and rose, but not the upstairs living room! How it all contrasted with the fine, rich colors of her music videos!

Mailer had been greeted by Madonna's assistant, Carisse, pronounced *Careese,* a small, jovial girl who escorted him up the spiral stairway, offered him a drink, and left. Fifteen minutes later, Madonna joined him. Not five minutes after, as if unrecorded preliminaries might waste good dialogue, he was invited to turn on his tape, and hours of questions and answers commenced.

If her apartment belonged to a dictatorial spirit, her candor, in contrast, proved agreeable. Never had he met a celebrity who could speak so openly about herself.

He was not altogether surprised. When one is talented enough to become a phenomenon, the sensation that the psyche is divided into two halves (with which all of us are more or less familiar) becomes so pronounced that one lives with it as a condition of existence.

MADONNA: When I'm onstage performing, or even when I was on the David Letterman show, I detach from myself. I have no control over that person. Though I know it's connected to my psyche and my soul, there's really nothing I can do about it.

MAILER: Well, the artist is a separate person from the one who does all the daily things. Each tells the other, "I will permit you, under these terms and conditions . . ." And the other side says, "Let me do my thing, and I won't bother you most of the time."

MADONNA: Exactly. That's interesting.

MAILER: As one gets older, the halves come together.

MADONNA: Really? I'm looking forward to getting together with myself.

Even before Mailer came with his tape recorder, he had arrived at some sense of how to do his story. It would not be necessary to interview her family, her friends, or those who worked for her. They would understand her less well than she could comprehend herself. Besides, they were all on record. As part of the effort Madonna was always making to explore into the profound enigma of herself—how indeed had this girl from a lower-middle-class family in Detroit emerged as a supernova of celebrity?—of course she would study herself. So had Picasso. Secretive as a bivalve in the mud about his private life, he nonetheless dated every drawing he made; if he did twenty drawings in a day, their sequence was numbered. It was a scientific matter as far as Picasso was concerned. By his own reckoning, he was a prodigious talent and so should be available for close study by the art critics and scientists of the future— nature might be expressing herself through him.

Similarly, Madonna was dedicated to examining herself. He was bemused by the essential confidence of her speaking voice, for it contrasted with the subtle depression he had encountered on their first meeting, a depression, he felt, that was still present today, although it might be no more than a reaction to how she had been trashed over *Letterman*.

MADONNA: The funny thing is, David Letterman's been asking me to do the show—forever. I kept saying, "I don't have anything to promote; what's the point?" And he said, "Just come on the show and we'll have a good time, just be silly and have fun." And I said, "Oh, what the hell," just the kind of mood I was in. Before I went on the show, all his writers were coming in my dressing room, giving me tons of stuff they wanted me to say, and it was all insulting. Rag on this, make fun of his hair, and this and that. They gave me a list of insults, basically. So in my mind, he knew that that's what the game plan was, that we were going to fuck with each other on TV. I told some of the writers I was going to swear, and they went, "Oh, great, do it, we'll bleep it and it'll be hysterical." I just had the best time, and I actually thought he was having a good time, too. But he's kind of like a yuppie version of Beavis and Butt-head, you know, "*Oooooooooh,* gross." I don't think he knew what he was getting into, but once he realized how the show went, the next day, instead of just saying, "We had a good time; it was all good fun and completely consensual," maybe the networks freaked out and he didn't want to fall from grace with them, so he went with the gestalt of the media and said, "Yeah, it was really disgusting and, yes, she really behaved badly," and turned it into something to save face.

MAILER: And how do you feel about that?

MADONNA: I don't think there's anything someone could say that would hurt me or shock me. Everyone already thinks I'm insane.

MAILER: Well, my idea for this interview is to prove that if you have a fault, it's that you're so levelheaded.

MADONNA: Oh. Oh, dear . . .

MAILER: At least the half of yourself that you bring to this interview.

MADONNA: Well, I suppose I am. I'm extremely sort of regimented and anal in my thinking.

MAILER: Actually, if I didn't know anything about you, I would think, She's a lady . . .

MADONNA: What do you mean by *lady*?

MAILER: One of the things I hate most about female liberationists is their expropriation of the language. *Lady* is a wonderful word. A lady is a woman who will do everything other women will do but with a little more style.

MADONNA: Okay, that's nice.

MAILER: Yes. And the word is going out of existence.

MADONNA: That's important. Having manners can be terribly important.

MAILER: Sometimes it's the only way we can offer some warmth to another human being.

MADONNA: I agree.

MAILER: Anyway, if I saw you under those circumstances, I would say, "That's a lonely lady"—

MADONNA: Why do you say I'm lonely?

MAILER: Just an air about you, an air of privacy.

MADONNA: But no one will believe that. They think I've revealed everything.

They were still talking, however, at arm's length—marvelously polite, but he wished to push the interview.

MAILER: You've withstood attack. But now you're living in a culture that is suffused with all the hatred that used to be funneled out into the cold war.

MADONNA: Right. We've turned it in on ourselves.

MAILER: And you go in and say, "Fuck you. I don't care if you hate me."

MADONNA: Well, I've certainly had enough time to think about the ins and outs of being famous and lots of time to analyze people's reactions to me. As a celebrity, or an unbelievably famous person, you are, in this country certainly, allowed to operate with everyone's approval for a certain amount of time. People do live vicariously through you. But it can never last, because several things need to happen: You need to disappear, run out of steam, run out of ideas. You need to get married, have a lot of children, get fat or something. You need to have a drinking or a drug problem. You have to go in and out of rehabs so people can feel sorry for you. The fact is that none of those things have happened to me, and people go around making all these pronouncements. "Oh, her career's over, she's finished now, she's a failure." It just sounds like so much wishful thinking.

MAILER: The people who have power in the media now, there's only one thing they really care about, other than obtaining a little more power. It's not money or sex or good food or pleasure, but their acumen. They are opinion makers. So their acumen is their hard-on. When they're wrong, it's like they're losing an erection. They hate you because you prove them wrong.

MADONNA: Since the David Letterman show, the news is that I've lost my mind.

MAILER: You're also tilting with a huge social machine that no longer knows where it's going and is afraid that it's going to crash sometime in the next twenty or thirty years.

MADONNA: Yes. It's frightening.

There was only one way, he recognized, that he could take this interview further. He would have to sacrifice a bit of himself. Confessions—in good society—breed confessions.

MAILER: Certain people cannot live without promiscuity. There have been years of my life when I was young when that was absolutely true. I had this feeling that something was near death in me ... that something was trapped, and it was symbolized by the word *cancer*. To break out of this trap, I had to take on many roles, because every time you make love with someone else, you are in a new role, you're a new person.

When she was not immediately forthcoming, he suggested that thirty years ago, his ego would have been on an elevator while talking to her. How was the Sex Queen of America relating to him? Up or down?

MADONNA: The Sex Queen of America—what a great title. [*Laughs.*] We couldn't be talking about me.

MAILER: Well, there you are, and every time you feel empty inside, you say to yourself, "Sex Queen of America! Oh, brother, they should only know!"

MADONNA: Exactly. If they only knew.

MAILER: Yes, we pay a hell of a price for giving out, giving out. . . . Emptiness is the largest single factor in my life. I just work, work, work, and sometimes it's all going out and nothing's coming back.

MADONNA: Oh, absolutely. I mean, you really feel that when you perform and there's a hundred thousand people in a stadium, and they're all there because of you, and the responsibility of entertaining that many people in two hours is daunting and exhausting—there's no way to describe it, but that's the only word I can come up with now. Then you go up to your hotel room, and you can't go out because you're too famous to go out without everyone following you and twenty bodyguards, so you sit in your room while everyone else has fun being anonymous, and you sit there and feel the most unbelievable loneliness. Yes, everyone adores you in a kind of mass-energy way, but then you're absolutely separated from humanity. It's the most bizarre irony, don't you think? In *Truth or Dare,* for instance, we worked for six months and we went around the world, and I saw the world and I would sit in my room all the time while everybody else was out, the dancers, the musicians, the bodyguards, and using me to get laid—you know, "I work with Madonna," that type of thing. I thought it was sort of unfair, you know, because everyone else was out having fun but me.

He had learned how to listen with full attention. It was an indispensable virtue for a decent interview. But now there seemed a spot to the side of his vision, a flaw in his concentration. Then he realized what was causing it.

MAILER: This is just a personal question, but I am curious. I don't understand nostril earrings.

MADONNA: It's just another adornment.

MAILER: Don't you have practical problems? Don't you need special makeup for that little red spot where it's pierced?

MADONNA: No. You take it out and your nose heals really quickly. So I'm not worried about that.

MAILER: On my stuffy side, I thought: If I had a ring in my nose, it would take me two minutes to get it all cleaned out.

MADONNA: It doesn't take me two minutes. I just have to blow my nose carefully. It's nice to have to think about something you take for granted.

MAILER: But in kissing, you could get injured—slightly, but enough to shift the given.

MADONNA: That's the beauty of it. You have to be careful. It's like, well, someone could hurt my nose. It's like riding a motorcycle without a helmet. It's just a risk. In the most simplistic way, it's just another way to take a chance.

He had the feeling that the cork was now out of the bottle, that they could talk about more.

MAILER: In one of your shows, you had these huge cones for breasts—

MADONNA: The Blonde Ambition tour.

MAILER: And I saw them and I said, "Why?"

MADONNA: Don't look too far for any meaning.

MAILER: They're ugly.

MADONNA: Well, I didn't think so. There's something kind of medieval and interesting about them. I asked Gaultier, who's a French clothes designer, to do the costumes for my tour, and he already had these designs in one of his collections, but now I had two male dancers coming out in them. It's very camp. Women used to wear those cones on their heads, but now they've become like a bra. The idea is to take something meant for one part of the body and place it on another part. Also, they're pointed. So there's something slightly dangerous about them. If you bump into them, you'll cut yourself. Plus the idea that the men were wearing them, not the women. I was singing "Like a Virgin," lying on this red velvet bed, and I reversed the whole Playboy Bunny thing, just two Playboy Bunnies in some costume that pushes their bodies into some unnatural shape, but now it's the men.

MAILER: A woman with her breasts undulating over a man is very close to loveliness. Those cones smash expectation.

MADONNA: The idea behind it is that breasts are these soft things that men rely on to some extent, so it's a way of saying, "Fuck off."

MAILER: But if the women truly succeed in telling men to fuck off and they truly do, then the human race is going to come to an end.

MADONNA [*laughing*]: No, not fuck off forever and ever; just think of my breasts in another way, that's all, not something soft you can fall into. Believe me, I love to have my breasts touched by a man that I care for—I wouldn't want it any other way—but it's really important to me—don't ask me why—that people look at life a different way, seeing that women can seduce and women can have sexual fantasies. Imagine Hugh Hefner with two Playboy Bunnies. I was having an inverted fantasy of that in my show . . . just another way of getting people to look at it.

MAILER: What I would argue back is that women have become so obsessed with the idea of not being taken for granted that I think they are in danger of losing sight of their real power over men, which they have always had, an extraordinary power women have over men. What it comes down to is males know, no matter what they've done to women, no matter how they abuse them, no matter how they've tyrannized them, men know that they are not indispensable to human existence. If women ever take over everything, as they well may—now, you're trying to keep from grinning at the thought—

MADONNA [*laughs*]: I think it's inevitable, too. Every dog has his day, you know?

MAILER: But if they do take over, and you get the equivalent of a Stalin or a Hitler among the women (and having had some contact with a few of the early women's liberationists, I can easily conceive of such a female), I see a day when a hundred male slaves will be kept alive and milked every day and the stuff will be put in semen banks to keep the race going. No more than a hundred men will have to be maintained alive at any time. Men have a very deep fear of women as a result. It isn't that men think, "Oh, there's a breast, I'll lay my head on it; it'll cost me nothing." Rather, what they know is that in that tender breast there are chill zones of feeling, icy areas, zones of detestation, and if they have any sense at all of women, they know that approaching a woman is quite equal to climbing a rock face.

MADONNA: Yes, but you're an evolved man.

MAILER: Not everyone thinks the same way I think, but men feel it instinctively, I'd argue. You're talking for all women, after all.

MADONNA: No, I'm not talking for all women. I've been accused for years and years, especially at the beginning of my career, of setting the women's movement back because I was being sexual in a traditional way, with my corsets and push-up bras and garter belts and this and that, and feminists were beating the fuck out of me: "What are you doing? You're sending out all the wrong messages to young girls. They should be using their heads, not their tits and their asses." My whole thing is you use all you have, *all* you have, your sexuality, your femininity, your—any testosterone you have inside of you, your intellect—use whatever you have and use bits and pieces wherever it's good. I'm not saying you have to break down every last thing, but . . .

MAILER: Very well said. But in the name of what?

MADONNA: In the name of what?

MAILER: Well, you're a revolutionary. What will this revolution be in the name of?

MADONNA: In the name of human beings relating to human beings. And treating each other with compassion.

MAILER: And for that, you feel that the stereotyped male notions of how to treat women have to be broken down.

MADONNA: Yes.

MAILER: Destroyed.

MADONNA: Yes.

MAILER: What about female attitudes about men?

MADONNA: That, too.

MAILER: But the female movement offers almost no compromise with men.

MADONNA: Well, that's a problem, but you've got to start somewhere.

MAILER: I don't argue with what you're doing from your point of view, but I am saying you could come to a dead end: The women could win and have nothing.

MADONNA: I hope that doesn't happen. Once you reach a certain amount of understanding, knowledge doesn't end. There's more to learn about everything.

MAILER: Don't you feel a certain danger in the women's movement? That the real desire is not for greater compassion and understanding of both sexes but for power over men?

MADONNA: I don't know about the women's movement—it's not my goal, it's not my intention. This is not about me being a woman but about me being a human being.

MAILER: So you wear pointed cones to remind men . . .

MADONNA: It's to wake women up, too—there's a lot of women oppressing other women; it's not just men.

Of course, she had not really answered him. He just gave up on the pointed cones. He could recognize, even as he had earlier, that with her, one had to keep raising the ante.

MAILER: As you know, I'm not in love with your book, *Sex.*

MADONNA: I didn't know.

MAILER: I told you the other day that I thought the metal covers were tacky, and the spiral binding kept jamming when you tried to open and close the thing.

MADONNA: You're talking about the way it was packaged. I'm saying: Look beyond, read the text. You're telling me you don't like the book because it has metal covers.

MAILER: No, I *started* to tell you . . .

MADONNA: And I rudely interrupted you. . . . Go on with your list. I'm curious.

MAILER: Well, let me begin with smaller things and work toward larger ones. I thought your text, while it was funny, was either too much or not enough. There could have been more, and that would have balanced the photographs. Or there should have been less. But the way it was, turned out arch and cute. Besides, the book was a misery to hold.

MADONNA: That's part of it. It was meant to be a piece of pop art.

MAILER: Yes, but I have the idea—correct me if I'm wrong—that the idea of metal covers did not come from you.

MADONNA: It absolutely came from me. What we originally wanted was something completely encased in metal with a lock you couldn't get into. . . .

MAILER: Now, that's an idea . . .

MADONNA: We couldn't manufacture it because it was too costly. The best thing we could come up with as a compromise was that.

MAILER: Well, there you go. Once you have to compromise an idea, maybe it's better to do without it. I thought if you were going to say, as you did in *Sex,* "I'm not interested in porno movies because everybody is ugly and faking it and it's just silly," and yet you were going to attempt to shock people, then you should have had a beaver shot of yourself. Given the number of nude and semi-nude pictures of you in costume, I thought that was an evasion, as if you or your advisers were saying, "Beaver shots could hurt us commercially. What we want is soft porn." So, the fact that *Sex* was designedly commercial got a lot of people's backs up. They felt you were promoting yourself without large enough commitment. This sets up a dismissal of the reader.

MADONNA: Then why did everyone buy it?

MAILER: That's not the measure. People bought it because of everything you'd done up to then. You were saying, "You've seen me in my music videos, you've seen me suggesting aspects of nudity, now you're really going to see something." But if Richard Avedon had ever been able to take a picture of Ronald Reagan's Cabinet while they were all mooning, and put it in book form, that would have sold out, too.

MADONNA [*laughs*]: I see your point.

MAILER: So I think the sales are irrelevant. But the way you pay for it is in the crap you're running into now.

MADONNA: Right.

He had been married six times, and this was the first occasion on which he had won an argument with an intelligent lady. It was enough to contemplate becoming a Madonna fan.

MAILER: In *Sex,* you say, "Condoms are not only necessary but mandatory." I really want to talk about that. The only thing you can depend on with condoms is that they will take 20 to 50 percent off your fuck. Safe sex is part of the insanity of this country. We are always looking for one simple tool or program with which to solve a serious problem.

MADONNA: A Band-Aid. You don't think they're useful?

MAILER: They're terrible.

MADONNA: I'll agree with you, they feel terrible; but you don't think their usefulness is valid in terms of preventing sexually transmitted diseases?

MAILER: That they keep some people from getting AIDS? Yes. But that's the short haul. In the long term, sex is difficult enough for most people. Now, with the shadow of AIDS hanging over homosexuals, it's horrendous.

MADONNA: The shadow of AIDS isn't hanging just over homosexuals. It's hanging over all of us. There are a lot of bisexual people in the world who don't cop to their past. So it's hard to say, "I'll never sleep with anyone who's gay." You just never know.

MAILER: What the condom does is make you give up most of the joy of entrance. The insight you get into the other person is diminished. Maybe it would be better to give up instead the idea of penetration, and do all the things you can do without it. Then, if you really love that person, you might say, "Fuck it, I'll take a chance. If I die, I die. I'll die for love."

MADONNA: If you love that person.

MAILER: But what condoms are saying is, "Never die for love or anything remotely resembling it." Probably the single hardest thing emotionally is to distinguish between lust that has enough personal warmth to feel like love, and love itself. The two are very close, yet different for one's karma. So it helps if you don't use a condom, because then at least you can say to yourself, "I lust so much for this person that I'll dare death," or, "I love this person enough to dare it."

MADONNA: Yes, but as you said, most people have a hard time distinguishing between the two. So how do you know at the time if you're lusting for death or loving?

MAILER: You don't know. What you do know is the intensity of your feelings. Once your lust is pretty well satisfied, then you will know whether it's love—or anger or power or all the things that go into lust. But at least you know more about yourself. What I hate about condoms is that you end up knowing less. And that aggravates one's need for power. It's like those cigarettes that have filters on them and contain less nicotine, and so people draw more deeply and take in the same amount of nicotine. People with condoms have more sexual contacts because they're less satisfying.

MADONNA: Well, to a certain extent, I subscribe to what you're saying. When you get to know somebody and you get to love them, you do say, "I'm willing to take a chance for this." I've been there. I'm not going to sit here and say that from the time I found out about AIDS, I've always had intercourse with a man with a condom on. That would be a lie. And I do think you get to a point with a person that you say, "I love this person or care for them enough that I'm willing to take a chance."

MAILER: And you say that's happened to you.

MADONNA: Yes. Absolutely.

MAILER: And there might have been a chance of AIDS?

MADONNA: I didn't even question that. I just said, "I instinctively know that this is the right thing to do." But I would never do that in the beginning, not knowing somebody. And, yes, it is harder to know somebody when—in the physical sense, with a condom on—it's a nightmare. But I guess there are other things you can do—you can meet someone and sleep with them for a month with condoms on, and it's not great sex as far as intercourse is concerned, but then you go and get AIDS tests together. That's happened to me, too. "Our tests are both negative, so let's do it without a condom." Now, we could find out in ten years we're both sick and it didn't come out in the test, so I guess that's the chance you take.

MAILER: Well, condoms are one element in a vast, unconscious conspiracy to make everyone part of the social machine. Then we lose whatever little private spirit we've kept.

MADONNA: On the flip side, couldn't you say: If it makes everybody stop and question who they're sleeping with, then isn't that a good thing, too? You don't just blindly and madly go ahead. Maybe it's a way of getting people to think how much they care about this person they're sleeping with. You know what I mean?

MAILER: You see, I think sex has always been dangerous. In the Middle Ages, before modern medicine or contraception, a woman had to love a man, or feel huge lust, in order to have intercourse with him, because if she got pregnant, she could die. Very easy to die—something like one in ten women died in childbirth. That meant your lover could be your executioner. Maybe that's the way it was meant to be. Take sex seriously. Don't believe it's there to be violated.

MADONNA: I've never thought of it that way.

MAILER: Well, in your work, you do daring things with sex and have fun with it, but you never mock the seriousness of it. What you're saying to your audience is, "Look, you're nervous because I'm taking more chances than you are. That's why you hate me."

In *Truth or Dare*, there is a moment when Warren Beatty upbraids Madonna: "She doesn't want to live off-camera," he says to the camera, and turns to her. "Why would you say something," he asks, "if it's off-camera? Tomorrow, if they're not here, what's the point of existing?"

Beatty had said it. Would she give of herself unless it could be recorded? Such a stance is repellent in elected officials, but that is because they offer the part of themselves that is good for their case.

Madonna, however, offers all of herself to the occasion: her best, her worst, her middling whimsies, her snarls, her whines, even her fascination with evil. What had impressed Mailer almost as much as her music videos were her last two films. In *Body of Evidence,* she had been absolutely convincing as a murderess. In *Dangerous Game,* she had been equally believable as an actress who is playing a whimpering misery of a half-destroyed slut. It had been a bad, hysterical, messed-up film, but she had given a double characterization: She was an actress, and she was also the same actress playing the slut, two effective performances in the midst of much mess, considering that the story has her being abused by a pimp of a husband who puts her out to graze in home-video porn-and-orgy fields of cash. Then he beats her up with all the intensity of violence building on its own violence. (He doesn't know whether he is enraged because his wife is a slut or because she wishes to cease being one.) For an actress, the role bore resemblance to going over Niagara Falls in a barrel.

Madonna was, then, a rarity, a world celebrity who did not select roles to buttress her status. If she would consent faster than any other star on earth to an existence in which every movement, every sigh, every sound of love, digestion, and sleep could be recorded, if she was as interesting to herself at her worst as at her best, that might be because she always had to learn more about herself.

We could take leave of her here, but do we have a full sense of the poisonous spirit of the world in which she succeeded? One does not speak of the money-wheel or the billion-dollar record moguls but of the world in which all of us have lived.

By the late middle of the twentieth century, human contempt for itself had reached epidemic proportions. The recognition had come that we might be a species ready to finish ourselves off by way of nuclear apocalypse. It was possible. Even without the atom bomb, the Second World War had left as a legacy the shadow of the concentration camps, and that darkened all belief that humankind was evolving into a more humane future. Then the cold war proceeded to erode those institutions of marriage, family, and property that for two hundred years had kept society—or so society believed—relatively stable but for peculiar times of armed conflict. That happy view of humankind had washed out to sea by the late Fifties, and in the Sixties, nothing made more sense to the average young man or woman than a prodigious absorption in oneself. That usually meant: Explore sex. The search for meaning translated into a search for pleasure. For if death was likely to present itself as nuclear termination arriving without warning, then everyone would be destroyed more or less simultaneously, no grave, no ancestors, no heirs, no roots. Madonna, born in 1958, was part of this horde of walking wounded. If nuclear fission would be the mortician to preside over her last rites, then, indeed, she would explore sex, and with an instinctive rebellion against all large hypocrisies. One did not have to be political to sense the vast fraud of the cold war—we had all been adjured to triumph over an Evil Empire that had turned out to be no more than a Sad Morass, a giant Third World quagmire buried in inefficiencies, bereft of desire for world domination. Our political leaders had converted language into cant, and our young—particularly those with good ears—reacted to the false note.

Yet if Madonna spoke to her generation, she was still condemned to explore herself. The explorations were chilling to some. In all the multimillion-dollar crops of her popularity, she was still without that hyperbolic popularity Marilyn Monroe gained in her own lifetime. Madonna was admired, but she was not loved. Not like Marilyn.

Our love for Marilyn is not complex. She was our movie star of the Fifties, but Marilyn spoke of a simpler time, the Thirties. It was to the Thirties that she belonged. She was three and a half years old at the end of 1929, and a young adolescent by the time 1940 arrived. Her smile goes back to such archetypes in our sentimental loyalties as the songs of the Thirties. She would be valiant and loyal through our sorrows—so said the sweet welcome of her face. Marilyn's horrors were kept within, and we mourn her because she gave it all to us and sacrificed herself until she was ridden with inner lividities and died.

Madonna is not only a survivor but has chosen, perhaps out of the necessity to survive, to take her kinks to the public: "You want to be with me, then come along for the fucking cure." She offers no balm to sweet, sore places; she is the stern instructor who shows us how difficult it all is, especially sex. Yet she gives us something Marilyn never could, something less attractive but equally valuable—she dramatizes for us how dangerous is any human's truth once we dare to explore it; she reminds us that the joys of life bed down on broken glass. She is not a lapsed Catholic for too little. *Inter faeces et urinam, nascimur,* she is always telling us, even if she never heard of Saint Odon of Cluny, but indeed it is true. "Between piss and shit are we born," and the road to heaven, if you would find it, lies between the two. Madonna comes to us as a bastard descendant of the void, but how she seeks to fill that empty space!

The music videos she had made over the last ten years had employed the services of countless directors and cameramen, but just about all of them and particularly the best-known ones—"Like a Virgin," "Like a Prayer," "Justify My Love," "Borderline," "Material Girl," "Papa Don't Preach," "True Blue," "Bad Girl," "Rain," "Erotica"—had belonged to Madonna. There had been a discernment in the style, a characteristic irony, a sensuous sorrow, a wicked rebuttal of expectation, a hoydenish intimacy—one can go on with such a list; appreciations bear resemblance to the plucking of flower petals—but the summary fact was that watching Madonna on music video was to encounter a high intelligence in an artist. There could be no question. She not only made the best music videos of them all, but they transcended personality. She was the premier artist of music video, and it might be the only new popular art form in American life.

If one wished to measure her stature, it was interesting to compare her work with the videos of Michael Jackson. His productions were virtuoso—they depended on his person—a product of his physical gifts, his speed, his agility, his voice, his astonishing looks, whereas Madonna had transcended her own limitations to create visualizations in sound equal to fine poems; one could measure their worth by the resonance they offered. Her best videos would prove richer on each viewing; one could not perhaps say as much about Michael Jackson.

MAILER: I've come to the conclusion that you are a great artist. [*Madonna gasps slightly.*] It's on record now.
MADONNA: Okay.
MAILER: That will be the theme of this piece, that what we have among us is our greatest living female artist.
MADONNA: Thank you.

Most people, no matter how brilliant, are vessels. Once you come to the end of what is interesting in them, you can touch the side of the jar. There will be nothing afterward but repetition of what you have learned already. It might take a night, a year, or half a lifetime, but once you can reach the side of the vessel, a good part of the larger feeling is gone.

So it was agreeable talking to Madonna. She had not settled yet on any of her boundaries. Perhaps she never would.

MAILER: Did anyone ever say that you have a resemblance to Princess Diana?

MADONNA: Get out of here! No one has ever said that. That's hysterical. . . . I guess I could do worse.

MAILER: A lot worse.

MADONNA: Poor Princess Diana.

From *Esquire* (August 1994)

# PORTRAIT—V:
# CLINTON AND DOLE

**Summer**

## The War of the Oxymorons

**Oxymoron—n. [Greek *oxymoron*, fr. neut of *oxymoros*, *oxy*- sharp, keen + *moros* dull, foolish]; a figure of speech in which opposite or contradictory ideas are combined (e.g., thunderous silence, sweet sorrow, purple yellow)**

They were the same age—which might be about all they had in common. Still, Norman did remember their one meeting. It had only lasted a couple of minutes, but sometime in the early Nineties, as one of the perks after a Folger Library gala, he was ushered with a couple of authors into Dole's Senate office, a predictable domain. It could boast of a gracious chamber, large windows, a commodious balcony. On the instant of their meeting, he had, however, been surprised. Expecting an encounter with a stern and somewhat wooden figure—the senator certainly looked no less on television—he was taken aback. When they said hello, Dole's eyes danced with private humor, as if he were ready to say: "You don't know the first thing about me, Mailer." It worked.

Novelists live for the moment when their imaginations come alive, since such a moment can feel as good as a match being struck in the dark. Afterward, he never discounted Dole. There had been too much light in the eye.

So he was not startled when surprises popped up in the last week before the San Diego convention. Indeed, he blessed the gods for having made him a writer of fiction. It might be that only a novelist could hope to understand this particular Republican candidate.

His confidence was that he was ready to make a few guesses concerning that inscrutable inner life Dole would hardly bring to an interview. Did one desire to comprehend the senator's motives? That seemed an effort worthy in itself. Be brave enough to divine him. What else, after all, was the domain of the novelist? So, he would write about Dole as if he understood him well.

All right, then. A plunge. One night in the mind of Bob Dole as he approaches San Diego in July 1996 to accept the nomination for President of the Republican party.

They kept saying, "Character. Bring up the issue of character." Win on character? Didn't think you could. Didn't like politicians who looked to impress with character. Grated on him. Besides, certain things—damned if he would discuss them. Nitty-gritty of nursing. Being nursed. Pretty degrading.

Wounds of war come down to being helpless. Couldn't take care of himself for close to three years. Why talk about that? Shipped home in a body cast, lost one kidney, lost more than seventy pounds, lost control of this and that, whatever. Didn't look into a mirror those years. Hell of a cadaver looked back. Thirty-nine months to put hospitals behind him. His right arm would never move well. Never again. Had to keep a black pen clutched in his right fist so you wouldn't try to shake hands. Everybody knew that. Except they didn't. Always trying to shake hands.

Somebody told him of a writer named Ernest Hemingway who said, "Don't talk about it." He wouldn't. Keep what virtue you can retain. Don't put it on the air. Certainly nothing good. A man lies wounded. In real pain. Gets to know the air. All the air around him. Knows that forever. Air is as alive as you and me. So, keep what you have learned. Don't put it on the air. Keep that secret chamber. If no one knows your next move, your surprises can pick up some smack. But what surprises? Problems do not guarantee a solution. Still, the idea of Clinton beating him. That would be awful. Sweet Billy Clinton didn't have enough ethics to worry that he was betraying his ethics. Trouble was, Billy had one positive quality: His heart was in the right place. And it was big. Big as a field of cowflop. Hang around him, you take off your shoes, you put on boots. Billy could cry for others as quickly as another man zips up his pants. Of course, Billy's butt was owned by fat cats. Probably why his other part got inflamed so often.

Heart and the other part were all that was left to him. Corporate suits owned Clinton's nuts. Dole was sure he could do better. Had lived with the big boys for a long time, and they didn't own his testicles. Just held a mortgage on them.

Unkind thoughts about Billy weren't going to get him anywhere, however. Not with people these days. They want you softhearted. Back to first principles. It's basic. Use an oxymoron. Put opposites together. Art of politics. Use every oxymoron you can get away with. Marry incompatibles. Get twice as many votes. Speak of family and freedom as if they are one. The virtues of the family are many, particularly at Christmastime. What isn't said: Family happiness is obtained by losing a considerable amount of your freedom. Of course, there never was a dictator who failed to talk up the virtues of the family. But then fascists were emperors—emperors of the oxymoron.

Trying to copy Clinton might be an infectious disease, but he had caught Billy's bug. The kind of light you get from fever, he had it now. Wanted to win. Could do it if he played a good game. Had to keep telling himself: Think it through.

After all, Republicans had one real achievement: They had made it impossible for that old Democratic party to survive. Survive, that is, as their old Democratic party. Reagan had run the debt up. Then Bush. Now it had gotten to where every Democrat who got in had to work to reduce debt. Had to dismantle their Great Society. Couldn't afford it anymore. Law of reversal. Now, a strong Republican could get away with running up a new deficit. Could claim it was the Democrats' fault. After all, wasn't it always Democrats who went to war? Then it took Republicans to make peace. Couldn't be otherwise. No Democrat can end a war. How could he? Republicans would beat him to death for lack of patriotism. For cowardice. By contrast, no Republican President could go to war without half of America getting full of distrust. Democrats, anyway. Look at Bush's trouble getting into war with Iraq. So, there's an edge. Only a Republican can run up a new deficit. Could be his surprise. Get elected on tax cuts. Extra money is as valuable to the American people as elixir of libido. Great stuff, elixir of libido.

Of course, they would say he was helping to bring about breakdowns in family values. Extra money could certainly lead to more infidelity. Well, you get elected and that gives you a bully pulpit. Try to undo the damage done getting elected. First things first.

Daring idea. But feasible. Larger your oxymoron, more chance it has. Cut taxes. Insist you can balance your budget. Brings the two halves of the Republican party together. Certainly has to stimulate curiosity. People will ask, Does Dole succeed or fail on this promise? People want to know what happens next.

Of course, you don't want to get into details. Can't speak of cuts in Social Security or Medicare. Equal to being dead in the water. Only other real solution: End corporate welfare. Something to consider. It would take Dole to do it. Just like Nixon was the one to make peace with China. But you can't mention corporate welfare. Just say: I have the will. I have the will to do it. Trust me. When the debates come, look Clinton in the eye. The fat boy might melt. Nothing lost for trying. Will try it.

Well, tried it, announced it. Didn't work. No credibility. Not even for Dole. War wounds worth less these days. Credibility has to be reinforced. Buttressed. Consider it. Jack Kemp for running mate. Will guarantee credibility on your tax cut. Kemp's been talking about it for years. So, Dole-Kemp could wake this convention up. Tantamount to Mae West strolling down center aisle stark naked.

Dole-Kemp will do it. The trick is to keep telling yourself: An election campaign is not cut in stone. Not like legislation. For the Senate, you have to respect legislation. How can a nation survive all the bad bills that get passed if there aren't a few good ones? Keel of government. Underline that. As a legislator, you have to be responsible. Some of the time.

As a presidential candidate, it's opposite. Be ready to get away with what you can. Look at Reagan. Easier to catch a fly with your thumb and forefinger than to corner Reagan on a weak point. Emulate Ronnie. Don't look back. Most voters are not living in Kansas. So stop treating them as if they are smart enough to read character. Failing memory is the fastest-growing disease of the twentieth century. People do not wish to have to recall what was said five days ago.

All the same, don't go off half-cocked. Calculate media cost. They'll bring up those jokes. What were they? How long ago was that? He had said, "If Jack Kemp were smart, he would corner the market on hair spray instead of undergoing all that personal expense." Something like that. Kemp had an answer. Not a bad one. Talked about poor Bob Dole. Said how sad it was that this fire burned down Dole's house. However, Dole's library was saved. Both of his books were intact. That was nice, because Dole hadn't yet finished his coloring book.

Well, he couldn't laugh all the way home, not over that one. Kemp had upped the ante. Ergo, do unto others as they do unto you. Our good news, Dole had said, is that Jack Kemp and some of his supply-siders were in a bus crash. The bad news is that three of the seats were empty.

You could say he had gone too far. Had to watch that streak. Dark, Dole, dark. The media would swarm over those jokes. Still, it would keep everybody paying attention to Dole-Kemp. Do those two guys get along? Do they not? Will produce narrative interest. And Kemp will be loyal. For the next couple of months, anyway. Had to. Would want to be elected vice president. And no need to worry about a change of life in office. It's all in an old Italian saying. Heard it in Italy: Revenge is a dish that people of taste eat cold. He could live with the joke about the coloring book.

Would Kemp accept his offer? Would Neil Armstrong refuse to take a first step for mankind? Dole knew political figures when they were making policy on the inside. Knew them when they were pushed outside. He had installed some fellows in good places. Had maneuvered a few gentlemen out. Been inside and outside himself. At one point, Nixon had turned chilly. That hurt. Practically speaking, you could call it one big crisis of identity. Left you feeling small.

Now Kemp had been out for a while. Called it living in his "wilderness years." But he was going to call Kemp back to the fray. That would do it. How could Kemp not love him? All the same, he couldn't approve of Kemp altogether. Talked too much. Very little Kemp wouldn't put on the air. Nonetheless! Dole-Kemp. A Mac-Whopper of an oxymoron.

He was hearing it all over the place. An enthusiastic crowd was waiting for them. Good for warming the bones. In front of the courthouse in Russell, he introduced Kemp to a large group—all home folks. Called him an "American original." Of course, you could say that Dole was an American original. For that matter, so was Sweet Billy Clinton. Whatever. And Jack Kemp, when he got up to talk to the folks in Russell, mentioned that at lunch he had asked Bob Dole how long he wanted him to speak, and Dole had answered, "Kemp, you can speak as long as you want, but we're only going to be here for five more minutes. . . ."

We must prepare for a shock. We are going to move over to Jesse Jackson giving a speech on August 27 at the Democratic convention. Jesse Jackson may be our greatest orator, but his voice is sometimes muffled by all his withheld sounds—rage of frustration, clamped-down sobs of exasperation, the dark vibration of this year's patience compressed upon last year's patience. Sometimes you can hardly hear him. Truth, there are many whites who would not wish to hear him, a majority doubtless. Still, he said it on Tuesday night, August 27, 1996, in Chicago, like no one else happened to be saying it these days. Let us put up his words as a benchmark by which we can measure both conventions by their resolute inability to look into the eye of the issues, the few real issues:

"One-tenth of all American children will go to bed in poverty tonight. Half of all America's African-American children grow up amidst broken sidewalks, broken hearts, broken cities, and broken dreams. The Number One growth industry in urban America: jail. Half of all public housing built to last ten years. Jails. The top 1 percent wealthiest Americans own as much as the bottom 95 percent. . . . We must seek a new moral center."

The ghostly tone of the Democratic convention in Chicago can more easily be found, however, in the following speech: "We Democrats believe that the family, fueled by values, must be restored to the central place in American life if we are to keep the dream alive. Yet, families cannot thrive and pass on these beliefs if parents cannot bring home a decent, living wage for a hard day's work. . . . In this richest nation on earth, we still have not solved the problems of poverty . . . which tear away at the roots of strong families. . . . We have to make sure that reduced government spending does not single out just the poor and the middle class. Corporate welfare and welfare for the wealthy must be the first in line for elimination. . . . It is the entitlement state that must be reformed and not just the welfare state. And we must do it in a way that does not paint all of government as the enemy.

"We are a big enough party—and big enough people—to disagree on individual issues and still work together for our common goal: restoring the American Dream. I am a Democrat because I believe in that dream, and I believe we are the ones to keep it alive."

A liberty has been taken. Two words were changed. "Republicans" and "Republican" were altered to "Democrats" and "Democrat." The speaker was not in Chicago but in San Diego on Monday, August 12, and he was Colin Powell.

Given his remarks on corporate welfare, he is, in fact, to the left of the Democratic party. Powell was, of course, to the left of the Republican party as well—there was no other luminary in the GOP who spoke out against corporate welfare at the convention. A year earlier, that had not been so. John Kasich, head of the House Budget Committee, had been looking to wipe out the deficit by the year 2002. He also had to find no less than $200 billion to pay for the tax breaks promised in the Contract with America. For a time, he thought corporate welfare might even be the place to do it. Kasich said in an interview, "I think it is an absolute outrage that some of this crap is still in this budget, and it just infuriates me every day when I think about it."

It is not the sentiments of men that make history but their actions. Kasich came down from the mountain of $200 billion to $25 billion. Didn't get anywhere with that, either. By the time he stood at the podium in San Diego, he did not mention corporate welfare. Rather, he spoke of "reattaching our souls to one another," and "sending a clear message to God that He is being invited back into American life."

God, who is reputed to mark the fall of every sparrow, might not need an invitation.

Of course, the numbers involving corporate welfare are, to put matters in the politest form, full of discomfort. Stephen Moore of the right-wing Cato Institute has said, if we were able to get rid of all the corporate welfare spending programs, "we could cut our budget deficit in half . . ."

We can also take a quote from a signally good article on corporate welfare in the *Boston Globe* on July 9, 1996: " 'Clinton initially wanted to make a strong statement on corporate welfare, but backed away,' an administration source said. He eschewed the words 'corporate welfare' in public, the source said, adding: 'He uses the phrase in private and cabinet meetings, but the phrase is too combative for him.' "

Shall we call it corpfare from now on? Corpfare the rich child; welfare the hungry child. We need not be surprised that the Democratic convention was close to an overlay of the Republican convention.

The American political body had evolved into a highly controlled and powerfully manipulated democracy overseen by a new species of aristocracy formed at the junction of four royal families—the ten-thousand-dollar suits of the mega-corporations, the titans of the media, the high ogres of Congress, and the upper lords of the White House. The inner disputes of a court with four such elements are not easy to follow, but their accords are clear.

Both parties were linked on balancing the budget, increasing the sentences on drug dealers, upgrading the best armed forces in the world and downsizing government (as if the two had no relation to each other!). Both parties would change welfare as we know it. No one asked whether anyone writing the specifications for those changes had any intimate knowledge about what life might be like on welfare.

There were, it is true, a few points of dispute: The Democrats, for example, were tougher on cigarette smoking among adolescents than were the Republicans, and the Democrats were certainly pro-choice. Family values would prevail in both parties except for those special cases where family values might interfere with mega-size profits. There, in the realm of film, music, and health management organizations, family values could take a walk.

Given these similarities, we do not have to catalogue the Democratic Convention activities either. Details are interesting when a dramatic turn in one event produces an unforeseen shift in another. None of that occurred. No riots, demonstrations, or protests offered enough impact to be closely followed by the media. Both conventions had been prepared so thoroughly for TV that an irony intervened. Except for the last night, the major networks refused to show more than an hour of convention time. The largest question for the media became: Who will win a larger share of the TV public during the prime-time hours on the first night of each convention?

The Republicans brought the deaf, the wounded, the victim of rape to testify to the honor and compassion of Bob Dole; on their initial network hour, the Democrats did not discuss politics at all. What a stroke! The genius of Dick Morris was once more confirmed. Focus groups had given him an ideal speaker for the first night, a nonpolitical person with immense TV impact, none other than Superman, Christopher Reeve, who had broken his neck taking his horse over a jump. In his *20/20* appearance with Barbara Walters last year, he had generated an enormous response. The Democrats, having no one available for their first night with status comparable to Colin Powell, chose Reeve, and he gave one of the best speeches of both conventions. Because everyone knew that he could not move his limbs, the stern small shifts of his lips as he intoned his hard-earned sentiments of compassion occasioned real oratorical intensity. He stirred large emotional depths in the audience, and much of that was in relation to how handsome he was, and how immobile. He was not unlike a mythic idol, human, but made of stone. As he spoke of the need for research, one could see that it was the plainest women who were weeping most. His voice, transmitted through a larynx mike, was stirring precisely because it was small and necessarily measured: "We don't need to raise taxes; we just need to raise our expectations.

"We found nothing is impossible. That should be our motto. It's not a Democratic motto nor a Republican motto. It's an American motto. It's something we will have to do together. America is stronger when all of us take care of all of us."

At the end of Reeve's ovation, Clinton came in on the big TV screen. He was speaking from Columbus, Ohio, and looked as large as a big-time football coach at a Friday night rally. His mojo was working. Thanks to Christopher Reeve, the returns for the Democrats' first night had done almost as well as the Republicans' first night had with Powell and Nancy Reagan.

It is a true change of scene to go from Christopher Reeve to Barbara Boxer, for the senator from California was tiny and peppy, and she wore very high heels. She talked a great deal about children. She was so devoted to their welfare that one wondered why she seemed 1 percent phony. Later, one learned that she and Dianne Feinstein, the other senator from California, voted on the side of corpfare. It was, however, no evil deed. The bill to take a whack at corporate welfare had been voted down 74 to 25. So, Boxer and Feinstein were just 2 of 74 senators defending the nest where the big birds hatched their eggs.

On Monday afternoon in the Sheraton Ball Room, Barbara Boxer, at the podium, turned to Hillary Clinton on the dais and said, "We're going to take back the Hill because of you." She saluted her. She added, "To my favorite first lady of all time." Barbara Boxer was the only one wearing red on the speaker's platform, a primary red that gave a bounce to her black hair and red lipstick. If you're tiny, flaunt it. It was also likely that she dieted with major passion. She was older than the new generation but nonetheless had the look of the New Woman. She was the instrument of her own will. She would make herself into what she chose to be. It was possible that she did not understand that one virtue we cannot acquire by an act of will is to improve our minds in such a manner that we can improve the minds of others. Acts of will, on the contrary, tend to produce abilities that oppress others. Piety, for example.

But we have strayed, we have moralized! (We are moralizing among the moralizers.) And we have hardly declared where we are, nor why. Hillary was having a session at Chicago's grandest new hotel, where she was staying and where Bill would join her. More than 1,500 people were present, 85 percent of whom were well-dressed women. When she came forward to speak, Senator Carol Moseley-Braun even waved her right arm in the air like a prize fighter. But then their subject was the empowerment of women.

Hillary's speech soon followed. It was so easy for her. She had only to touch a button and the women would cheer and rise to their feet. "Doesn't it feel good to have a President who stood up against the National Rifle Association?" she asked. Cheers. Sound bites, one after the other. But then there were a great many TV people there. A sizable stand had been erected for them. Now, no matter how the TV would cut her remarks, there would always be a selling point. "I have listened to our women senators, and I say to myself, 'Go, girl, go!' "

To the huge roar that came up on this last, she added, "We are applauding women who ran for office to help affect the lives of men, women and children." If she had asked them to march all the way to the convention center, they might have sprouted a bouquet of blisters in their high heels, but they would have followed her. If she had asked them to bare their breasts, they would have shucked their blouses and their bras. They might be corporate ladies, but they were loyal troops. Command me—I am yours!

How the Republicans were enraged by St. Hillary's army, so militant, so sure of themselves. Republicans had often been left with dry, hard-edged specimens of women or obese cuties with beehive hairdos, but then the GOP had been giving it all to the men for a century—giving it to their tycoons, to their military heroes, their white athletes, their independent-minded riflemen who believed in freedom (while relinquishing more of it every day to the spiritual depredations of the corporation). What depredations? Why, to list a few—plastic, highrises, fluorescent lighting, and sealed windows in expensive hotels.

That was Monday afternoon. On Tuesday night when Hillary spoke at the convention, she was wearing a knit dress somewhere in hue between baby blue and royal blue. A perfect color for television, it reached out for your eye but did not burn it. Her hair was coiffed for the kind of dinner party only doyennes give in New York. Immaculate yet subtle was her hair, and well colored. In two decades, Hillary had moved half the distance from bottle-lens Rodham—the angry formidable dark-haired no-nonsense Yale Law School grind and soon young wife of young Governor Clinton—all the way over to a modest copy of Sharon Stone. Hillary had become a blond actress. She was not yet a very good one, but she was certainly better than the average ingenue.

At the convention on Tuesday night, the delegates were expecting a powerful speech to burn out the power of the impression Liddy Dole had left at the Republican Convention. But Hillary was not competitive, not, at least, on this night. She had a quiet, caring, interested-in-your-doings family chat prepared, and she was not going to stray. She did her best to fulfill the role. But she was not all that compassionate. Ice blondes can hide a variety of faults—they cannot convince you of their loving care, however, when they are not feeling it.

"I want to talk about what matters most in our lives and in our nation—children and families. I wish we could be sitting around a kitchen table, just us, talking about our hopes and fears, and our children's futures. For Bill and me, family has been the center of our lives. . . .

"Of course, parents, first and foremost, are responsible for their children. . . . Just think about what many parents are responsible for on any given day: packing lunches, dropping the kids off at school, going to work, checking to make sure the kids get home from school safely, shopping for groceries, making dinner, doing the laundry, helping with homework, paying the bills, and I didn't even mention taking the dog to the vet."

One could see why so many Americans disliked her. She was decompressing the presidency. She was pretending to be near to the people, but the nature of her position made that impossible. We laugh at the English royals when they pay their visits to factory workers, but at least they remain royal. Hillary was pretending that she was one of us, and it was hardly true. One wanted political leaders who were full of passion for the people but were also noble and a touch aloof: FDR and Eleanor set the standard. That was easier to trust than someone who pretended to know which laundry detergent to use, or, even worse, was not pretending. She did know. What a waste of the upper faculties.

During the half hour she spoke, there were more than seventy references to children, to mother and father, to family. It no longer had anything to do with politics. There she was, absolutely in place, ice-blond, a saint to her gender even as she proceeded to talk about PTA solutions to profound problems. None of the real questions came into her purview, nothing about the sleazy quality of so many American products advertised to the hilt, nothing trenchant about the waste of the ghettos, the paucity of good wages among working people, the fever of global capitalism to send the profits to the top rather than sharing some of the wealth with those who worked to make the stuff.

To her credit, Hillary had succeeded in weathering the 400 blows aimed at her over the last four years. A weaker woman would have been in a sanitarium by now. She became stronger. We all know: If it does not kill you, it will make you stronger. Yet she had not become a nicer woman. Her ice-blond presence now offered the unhappy suggestion that acts of transcendence do not always lead us to the light. Saint Hillary and her Knights Templar were a force to emblazon one another, but they might not be exactly what the country needed. They were too eager to show that they could be the equal of any man in the corporation or the government. Probably they could. And so what? Women are as ugly as men when personal power is their life cause, their only real life cause.

If black people are often seen by some fearful whites as the wildest people in America, it is not as easily recognized that they can also be the most disciplined men and women. If that helps to explain why a million black people can march on Washington without one act of violence, it can also account for the genial affect with which they came to Chicago and stayed there through the week, never breaking their own good mood, even if aspects of the Clinton overdrive—all that moderate Republicanism—had to be heartbreaking to the majority of them. Many of the welfare women and children, who would soon be having cruel and heartless dealings with the local authorities in their states, might be friends of the delegates, or their neighbors, or even poor members of their own families. The word was out, however, among the brothers and sisters—we are here to celebrate how good our relations are with white Democrats.

And they were. One had to go back to the Fifties to recall a time when liberal whites and blacks had been so ready to have a good time together. Whatever Clinton's faults, political omissions, and betrayals, there was this to his credit—relations between blacks and whites, in the Democratic party at least, were on the mend. Blacks knew the figures. At the Dole convention, about 3 percent of the delegates were black. In Chicago, the figure was about 19 percent. Now, however, blacks also knew that they were the Democrats' best chance for recapturing the House and the Senate. It could be done if they came out to vote in force.

So, Clinton had gambled that blacks would accept his signing of the welfare bill. Many Democrats were unhappy that he signed, but they were certainly not mutinous. Where was there to go? They hoped, and some believed, that Clinton would fix the worst parts of the new welfare machine (not even yet designed) if he were re-elected with a Democratic Congress. No voice, but for Jesse Jackson, rose in real wrath to declare: If welfare is to be cleansed at the bottom, why not have it fumigated at the top? Corpfare!

Silence prevailed. Since the fire was out of the Democratic party, geniality took its place. Many of the black delegates liked Clinton. He was warm, he was good-hearted, he had tears in his eyes before the pain of others—he had been there to commiserate with black congregations after their churches were burned. If he was a sinner, he was also a churchgoer. (As you should be after you have sinned.) Of course, he was also sufficiently active as a sinner to salivate at the sight of a hotel room in a strange town, or, for that matter, in his own town.

He was okay. He was alive, he was American, he had his good side, he had his bad side.

So the mood was genial. It was not a time to brood on the low state of the party. The Democratic party, after all, had been in an unhealthy condition for years. In 1968 it had been torn in half by Vietnam. The slash of the wound still ran across the face of the party. And of late, its soul had been bruised. Inanition bruises the soul.

The years from 1992 to 1994 were a terrible time for the Democrats. A wholly quixotic effort to get gays into the military was followed by a year-long sludge-filled effort to arrive at a medical health plan. It failed altogether. Did one have to go back to the Civil War to find battles where so much had been committed and so little gained?

After two years in the White House, it was clear that Clinton's past was a puddle and he was sitting in it. In consequence, the Democratic party had been without a general. There was no one to lead them back to ground where they could fight the Republican party. Instead, they all but joined it. The Democrats remained weak before the righteousness of the Republicans, whose blitzkrieg in 1994 had been underwritten by a fundamental public anger: There were too many indulgent poor people being supported on the taxes of the hardworking. Of course, the hardworking were often not too bright, especially the white men who had been brought up to succeed and believed, therefore, that to be hardworking was virtuous. It was, but it was not as virtuous as they thought. The top was taking more from the middle than the bottom was taking. The failure to recognize this (or the resolute cowardice not to recognize it) was also a failure of virtue.

On Thursday night, President William Jefferson Clinton came to the podium to present his acceptance speech. Rarely had he looked better or spoken with more vigor. His energy never waned. He had the charisma on that Thursday night to give a great speech and indeed he would have—if he had had a speech. But he didn't. He had a list of items, political items, most of them modest. He had, in effect, the kind of speech that a man running for mayor in a small city might give to the locals.

The wonder of it all, however, was that it took something like half the speech, a full thirty minutes, for the emptiness of the offering to become apparent. Clinton had risen in his person so completely above his text that he stood before the TV cameras of the world—tall, ruddy, handsome, vigorous, confident, even proud. His manner provided the assertion: He was going to do wonderful things for the country. But his text was offering less than any President had promised in a long time.

There is no need to quote at length from what he said. It is all pretty much the same, a demonstration of the inner life of political sin. Clinton's punishment for his sins was that he had become intellectually dull: "We must require that our students pass tough tests to keep moving up in school. A diploma has to mean something when they get out (*applause*). We should reward teachers who are doing a good job, remove those who don't measure up. But in every case, never forget that none of us would be here tonight if it weren't for our teachers. I know I wouldn't. We ought to lift them up, not tear them down (*cheers*). With all respect, we do not need to build a bridge to the past, we need to build a bridge to the future, and this is what I commit to you to do (*cheers, applause*).

"So tonight, let us resolve to build that bridge to the twenty-first century, to meet our challenges and protect our values. Let us build a bridge to help our parents raise their children, to help young people and adults get the education and training they need, to make our streets safer, to help Americans succeed at home and at work, to break the cycle of poverty and dependence, to protect our environment for generations to come, and to maintain our world leadership for peace and freedom. Let us resolve to build that bridge (*applause, cheers*). . . ."

He mentioned that bridge more that fifteen times in the hour. It was his metaphor.

How good he looked! It did not matter what he said. He never lost his vigor. Still! Excitement began to ooze out of the occasion. The delegates had heard too many other speakers go on this week about children and the family. One felt at last as if one were trapped in one of the old (by now classic) MGM films, one of those well-made dung heaps of sentimentality. We were receiving the world view of the long-gone Hollywood studio lot with its L. B. Mayer star and starlet system.

In an interview Clinton had done for *USA Today*, he had listed the books that had been "sources of real inspiration." He had shaped his values by those books. They were *The Meditations of Marcus Aurelius;* and *The Imitation of Christ* by Thomas à Kempis. Christians should, Clinton said, "tend to their own soul's health before all else." There was *Moral Man & Immoral Society* by Reinhold Niebuhr, and that had influenced Clinton about "how you can deal with the question of personal integrity in public life." There was "Politics as a Vocation" by Max Weber. "If you have power over other people," suggested Clinton, "we risk our soul in the exercise of that power. It's a great call for humility."

Finally, there was his weekly reading of the Bible. He quoted Saint Paul: "It is the very thing I would not do that I do; the very thing that I would do that I do not." Romans 7:15.

He was so bright. He was worthy of becoming a great character in a novel. It wasn't what he had done but what he had failed to do. Gogol would have enshrined him. He was perfect for *Dead Souls*. He had failed to go to the root of any problem. He had a mind that wonked and wonked, and none of the vehicles of thought that his reading brought to him had been able to make a real stir in his political world, not Marcus Aurelius, Thomas à Kempis, Reinhold Niebuhr, Max Weber, St. Paul, Jesus, or Jehovah. If only just once he would say, "Look, I'm no good and I can prove it, but for a bad guy working in a very bad town, maybe I am entitled to say, 'I have accomplished one thing. I never gave up. I take a good punch. You can't keep me down.' "

Would he be ready to listen to a reply from someone else who was no good and could prove it? The words would go like this: "If you screw around a lot, it may do a great many things for you (increase your experience, expand your ego, and/or reduce your chances of getting cancer). It will certainly make you more knowing in the art of seducing the electorate, but in most cases, you cannot pretend that it is particularly good for the kids."

If Clinton beat Dole—and he certainly would, provided creatures from the President's past did not rise up out of the black lagoon—the credit could go to the last forty years of television. For a majority of TV-watching Americans, it was likely that Clinton was by now the most fascinating character to come along since J.R. That large share of America's viewers would not wish the Clintons to go off the air. For this is a TV entertainment with the potential to rise above all the video heights of the past, and even the Simpson case could pale before the future adventures of Bill and Hillary.

From *George* (November 1996)

# Fall

# How the Pharaoh
# Beat Bogey

He had never taken an assignment as a reporter without looking to give himself a name. A new role demanded a novel tag. Now, he had two, Dean and Neophyte. He decided, of course, on Dean. He was, after all, the dean of political correspondents on every plane—always the oldest man aboard. Yet when it came to knowledge of how to cover a presidential campaign, it was fair to call him a neophyte. He had been close to a major election campaign only once before, and that was for *The Mail on Sunday,* back in 1983. It turned out to be a one-sided battle for prime minister between Maggie Thatcher and Michael Foot.

Foot had been a decent man and honorable, but soon grew cranky that the Labour campaign was going nowhere. Maggie Thatcher provided the bonus. You could learn a lot observing Maggie. She would have made a mighty actress.

In Edinburgh, speaking to the gentry at a Conservative party dinner, she played a country lady with an old name. On a visit to a small factory in the Midlands, she wore a shawl around her head and managed to look plain as a pudding while conversing with middle-aged factory women. "She's not as bad as I thought," one of them said.

But at a press conference in London, Thatcher turned into Queen Elizabeth (of the sixteenth century). In answer to a penetrating question from a prestigious journalist, she replied, "Mr. Kingsby, I don't think you've done your homework."

"Oh, I have," said Mr. Kingsby. "No, no, no," said Maggie. "I'm going to send you a batch of our papers, and you can sharpen up."

She was beautiful in profile. Bette Davis would have picked up a few nuggets from the manner. Of course, Thatcher may have been cribbing from Davis. The dean was left with a useful rule. You know nothing about political candidates, the precept would declare, until you perceive what kind of actor they would make.

It took a while, however, to recognize that Dole was a leading man, whereas Clinton was star material, a category usually reserved for great athletes. Michael Jordan, Dennis Rodman, Charles Barkley, Deion Sanders, and Muhammad Ali come to mind. Or entertainers like Madonna and Elvis Presley. Or movie actors like Jack Nicholson, Sylvester Stallone, Warren Beatty, Marilyn Monroe, and Elizabeth Taylor. Few thespians, however, become stars, and when they do, they are no longer like other actors. A new kind of entity arises, not yet a king but as difficult to comprehend.

Let us, however, get down to business: The debates were the doldrums. The dean remembered them with the same distaste one reserves for those social occasions where one invests much and receives little. He had watched all three carefully and got back nothing but carefully machined nuts and bolts delivered by Clinton and Gore, and old Republican assertions from Dole and Kemp. The debate's opening remarks summarize much of what they would say the first evening.

CLINTON: We passed Family and Medical Leave; now let's expand it so more people can succeed as parents and in the workforce. We passed 100,000 police, the assault weapons ban, the Brady bill. Now, let's keep going by finishing the work of putting the police on the street and tackling juvenile gangs. We passed welfare reform; now let's move a million people from welfare to work. And most important, let's make education our highest priority. . . .

DOLE: America's the greatest place on the face of the earth. Now, I know millions of you still have anxieties. You work harder and harder to make ends meet and put food on the table. You worry about the quality and the safety of your children and the quality of education. But even more importantly, you worry about the future and will they have the same opportunities that you and I have had. . . . I'll try to address your concerns and not try to exploit them. It's a tall order, but I've been running against the odds for a long time.

Of course, it had barely been a debate. The names of bills passed and vetoed, dates, imprecations ("Liberal!") and buzz phrases ("bridge to the 21st century") all spewed forth at a great rate of speed. The determination one was obliged to make was which spew gave better splat. Such events, the dean decided, were by now a part of the ongoing American disease. Neither candidate had gone anywhere near the real problems. Real problems bite back. If we had had such a debate, the argument might have gone, *Resolved: It is neither seemly nor healthy for a great democracy to maintain a condition where the very rich get richer and the very poor grow poorer.* Clinton and Dole were no more ready to cross such a divide than an average suburbanite would walk into the inner city on Saturday night.

The next debate was three days later, on October 9, in St. Petersburg, Florida. If the new question was whether Jack Kemp would go on the attack against Gore, such speculation was ended by Kemp's reply to the moderator's first question.

JIM LEHRER: Mr. Kemp, some supporters of Senator Dole have expressed disappointment over his unwillingness in Hartford Sunday night to draw personal and ethical differences between him and President Clinton. How do you feel about it?

KEMP: Bob Dole and myself do not see Al Gore and Bill Clinton as our enemy. We see them as our opponents. . . .

It was the kind of remark you make if you have a comfortable lead in the polls, but it made few Republicans happy. Most of them had only one political passion this year: to dismember Bill Clinton. Dole had failed them. Now, given the opportunity, Kemp had whiffed.

He would soon have other troubles. Jack was not a debater. He did not live for structured discussion but for the exposition of his own ideas; he had a hearty, manly, cheerful style, full of enthusiasm. These ninety-, sixty-, and thirty-second responses were totally unsuitable for him. He was more like a fellow in a bar who has an idea and will harangue everyone with it.

All through the debate Jack kept coming back to the same theme—small business was great and big business was great. All you had to do was remove the stultifying effects of heavy taxation. Bring the freedom to be a capitalist right into the ghetto. Empower the poor. Empower the rich.

Whether Kemp's argument did or did not have merit, it was too large to be summarized in a debate without sounding like a high wind. Besides, there was Al Gore to confront and Al was looking as principled as a parson who has just sniffed a dog turd in the vestry.

Al Gore had been doing his homework for four years. He could memorize squadrons of statistics and reduce them to talking points: "10.5 million new jobs in the last four years . . . 105 empowerment zones and enterprise communities."

Jack, however, kept trying. "The single greatest problem, in our opinion, in the domestic economy," he said, "is that this tax code—83 years old, a relic of the Cold War and hot war, inflation and depression, 7.5 million words long—overtaxes capital, overtaxes working men and women and families. Clearly the Gordian knot needs to be broken in one fell swoop. . . . Dana Crist of Lancaster said the day [a new] tax bill is passed in Congress, she will open a new factory with 40 or 50 or 60 employees. . . . He [Gore] will call that trickle-down. I call it Niagara Falls."

GORE: The problem with this version of Niagara Falls is that Senator Dole and Mr. Kemp would put the American economy in a barrel and send it over the falls. [*Laughter*]

In boxing there is the term "a manager's punch." In the dressing room, your manager tells you: "Before he throws his right, he clears his throat. When you hear the phlegm, duck and take him out with your left hook." Kemp had been using his line about Niagara Falls for years and Gore was more than ready. The only knockdown of the evening.

Kemp's only hope had been to attack Clinton. And there would have been ways. You did not have to get ugly. The dean had heard a story that Al Gore and Jack Kemp had gone to lunch together before their debate and Kemp said: "Al, you're the loyalest vice president there ever was. No vice president was ever more loyal to his boss. Why, you went over and became a Republican just like Bill Clinton. Just for him."

Apocryphal or not, the clue was there. In the debate, Kemp could have said, "You're a decent man, Al, but you work for a fellow who has betrayed everything his party ever stood for. He is now a Republican, and we welcome him to our side. But he would worry us. He is too much like a hermit crab. He changes his shell every time he finds a better one."

That would have opened the debate. Kemp might have gone on to say: "Clinton is the kind of Republican who likes to hobnob with bankers and big boys. We in Dole-Kemp stand for bringing opportunity to the poor." Of course, it would have been hyperbole—a veritable whoopee cushion of party gas. The only real race that the Republicans and Democrats were in was to see who could pick up the richest corporate support here and abroad. But this was a debate—you were supposed to win it, not look for an honorable draw.

Kemp lost. You do not beat the brightest boy in the class when he has had four years to prepare and you have no new strategy.

Coming up soon were Dole's difficulties with the format of the last debate. The small, elegant theater at the University of San Diego where the two candidates would meet had seats for only three hundred audience members, most of whom were Southern Californians of such prosperous substance that an old hand like Dole could tell with one hawk-eye sweep that propriety of manners was going to count for much too much with this gang.

Shortly after the selected 113 questioners were seated in a semicircle on the stage, Liddy Dole, dressed in good Republican pale green, came out from the wings with her stepdaughter, Robin Dole, and they were warmly applauded. But the Clintons were handling the event like a heavyweight bout, where the idea is to keep the contender waiting in the ring for the champion. So Hillary Clinton did not show. After five minutes, the soft-throated stir of the audience grew noticeable.

Now, Hillary entered. She was dressed in a silvery-cream gown. It was luminous. It confirmed the impact of her royal appearance at the Democratic convention last August. The audience, supposedly balanced, broke into applause at her entrance, more than they had offered to Liddy Dole. Bill and Bob now came out, and the last debate began.

It became no great event. The true drain of the occasion came out of the recognition that if we are a great nation, which we are always being told every day and in every way, why then must we, like spoiled children, keep hearing these endless repetitions of our worth when our real need may be to comprehend that greatness is not a stable condition of existence but rather, like love, has to be re-created over and over.

In any event, if we are a great nation, there was little evidence of it on this night. The two principals kept offering up incense to the idol of the voracious American ego. "This is the most religious—great country in history," said Clinton and had the minimal good taste to add, "including the freedom not to believe." (After all, he could hardly insult Thomas Jefferson.) And Dole, never one to hesitate before a patriotic encomium, had already said, "I think anybody who wears the uniform is a great American."

Ah, well. Dole was in trouble from the start. He had to sound like a nice man and, being 20 points down in the polls, he had to attack. Meanwhile, political questions from the onstage group of "undecideds" kept being presented to him with all the dead-ass of a civics class. "I'm a beginning educator in this country," said the first questioner, "and I really think it's important what children have to say. They're still very idealistic. . . . A sixth grader says, 'If I were President, I would think about Abraham Lincoln and George Washington and what they did to make our country great. We should unite the white and black people and people of all cultures. Democrats and Republi-

cans should unite also. . . . I believe that when we are able to come together and stop fighting amongst ourselves, we will get along a lot
better.' "

So had spoken the sixth-grade child. The teacher who quoted the
boy now asked, "If you are our President, how will you begin to practice what we are preaching to our children, the future of our nation?"

DOLE: Well, I'd like to say, first of all, I think it's a very good question. . . . There's no doubt about it that many American people
have lost their faith in government. They see scandals almost on
a daily basis. They see ethical problems in the White House today.
They see 900 FBI files, private person, being gathered up by
somebody in the White House. Nobody knows who hired this
man. So, there's a great deal of cynicism out there. But I've always tried in whatever I've done to bring people together. . . . I
think we have a real obligation. . . . Young people are looking to
us. They're looking to us for leadership. They are watching what
we do, what we say, what we promise, and what we finally deliver.
And I would think, it seems to me, that there are opportunities
here. When I am president of the United States, I will keep my
word. My word is my bond.

As the debate went on, Clinton remained mild, modest, informa-
tive. Indeed, he had begun by saying, "I'll do my best to make this a
discussion of ideas and issues and not insults." He sounded young and
presidential as he said it, happy, sensual, successful—like the president of the best fraternity on campus. It was his kind of evening.

The questions were so serviceable. Just civics. Had there ever been
a brighter civics student in high school than Bill Clinton must have
been? Meanwhile, Dole kept flailing away at points that only made
sense to those who knew congressional politics from the nitty to the
gritty. He seemed oblivious to the possibility that millions of voters
might surf into the debate and soon surf out again with no more impression than that the President seemed to know what he was talking
about. One piety that issued from Clinton is likely to be quoted for a
century to come. It was another manager's punch: "No attack ever created a job or educated a child or helped a family make ends meet. No
insult ever cleaned up a toxic waste dump or helped an elderly person."

Ten minutes before the end, Dole could only come up with
"honor, duty, country—that's what America is all about." Another
entry for the book *Great Sayings by Great Americans.*

At conclusion, the audience applauded generously. Having been present at a historic occasion, they were delighted with themselves.

The dean left the theater and walked over to the building where the spin-meisters of both parties were holding forth. The room was jammed with media and politicians. Everyone was talking. Everybody was sweating. If not for the phalanxes of fluorescent tubes overhead and the bare white walls, you could say it was an Arab bazaar. Certainly as noisy. The pols and the media had coalesced into one family. Everyone looked sickly under the fluorescent lights.

The Democrats, however, looked not only sickly but happy. Christopher Dodd was sitting in the corner, and he was beaming. When one met his eye, he winked. He knew the score. Clinton was still 15 to 20 points ahead.

Tomorrow, the dean would be on the road for three days. He would join the press contingent that traveled with Dole. Perhaps he would come a little closer to the enigma of the campaign. Why were the Republicans so inept? Why had all the proposed solutions become so superficial? There was a good deal to meditate upon.

Dole left San Diego with about a hundred reporters, staff, and TV cameramen in two large planes, each the size of a New York—Boston shuttle. Dole bunkered in up front, and the press, sequestered in back, even entered and departed from the tail. But that was fair. Dropping in on three states a day, Dole was up by six in the morning and rarely in bed before midnight—he spoke to more than half a dozen groups a day and exchanged greetings with mothers and fathers and two-year-olds and ten-year-olds waiting behind a rope, a fence, or a chain-mesh barricade. Then, back to his plane and the aerie up front.

The tour, however, was agreeable. There were times when it was not unlike working with a movie company on location. One was in a different place every few hours and kept moving from vans to buses to airplanes and back to buses. Half the assembled crew looked like recent retirees from Hell's Angels. Some of them probably were. The equipment toted for TV was heavy, and the raised platforms on which the cameramen worked gave no more sense of permanent stability than a motorcycle between your legs.

One slept in a different place every night, in carpet-stained old motels and in scientifically designed, mid-priced motor inns with sealed windows. Comparable to life in a movie company, one could eat, if one wished, six, eight, or ten times a day. Food was everywhere.

Breakfast at the motel, breakfast on the plane, lunch and dinner on the plane, candy in dishes, tortilla chips in dishes, cold cuts, pickles, and another set of meals with dessert at every stop.

There was lots of chatter. As on a movie set, everyone talked, and all day long. Rookies listened to veterans, middle-aged correspondents exchanged war stories, and the candidate was analyzed—often in kindly terms. Some of the press had been on his campaign for months. If there was nothing new to write about on any given day, still there had to be something, some ripple in the seamless fabric of campaign speeches forever repeated, some minor turn of event that might yet be a major turn by tomorrow. When a Dole staff member came back to the rear of the plane from his sanctum up front, the press gathered about him like family members around a doctor looking to obtain a little more news of the operation.

Seen up close, Dole looked tall and spare like a movie man, a leading man. Cowboy roles. Not Randolph Scott, exactly, not Gary Cooper or Clint Eastwood, but a casting director would put him in the file that said: HUMPHREY BOGART ON A HORSE. He was, all said, much better looking than he appeared on TV, and yet one could see how he did not appeal to women. But for the clenched right fist, as untouchable as a small wild animal, there was no other sign of vulnerability.

At the first stop, in San Bernardino, Dole went over to shake hands with a score of followers standing on the tarmac behind the rope line. In the main, they were middle-aged men in work clothes, and they had a similarity of expression around their mouths as if to say, "Life is full of surprises, sour surprises." They would take pleasure in sour news; it would confirm their acumen.

Dole shook each hand, said a word or two, then was off with his caravan—a dozen police cars, many motorcycles, staff cars, his limousine, and a press bus. The Mission Inn, where the candidate spoke first, was an old hotel with dark wood decor, and the crowd whooped and hollered with upraised arms. Dole talked to these Republicans as if they were children. "Yes," he told them, "you're going to get the tax cut. It's not a Wall Street tax cut; it's a Main Street tax cut."

The debates were behind him and he could cut loose on Clinton. "Just remember," he said, "it's not his money he's giving away for political purposes; it's your money." His daughter, Robin Dole, standing beside him, a head shorter, kept nodding wisely at her father's remarks.

A little later, on the street outside the Mission Inn, there was another rally, not unlike a village block party with a loud band. Never before had one been so aware of Dole's voice, his Plains voice. "The big difference between Bill Clinton and myself is that he trusts government and I trust you."

He liked to speak in spurts—stop—and off to the next spurt. He was like a roulette wheel. He had about thirty-two subjects, all one- and two-liners, and what he said next in a speech usually had no more to do with what went before than the successive drops of the ball.

"President Clinton never got a tax bill he didn't like." Stop. "The Democrats have so much money coming in that they have their own laundromat." Stop. At the whoop that went up, he added, "And I'm gonna get tough. I'm gonna put in tough, strict, conservative judges. Liberals need not apply." Stop. "Harry Truman said, 'I'm not gonna give them hell. I'm gonna tell them the truth. The truth is hell.' We're gonna fight for the soul of America."

Most of the people at another rally in a plaza outside the Mission Inn were young and there for a good time. It hardly mattered what Dole said. The kids and young marrieds were there to see real TV luminaries. Like Dole. In Glendale, next on the tour (after a twenty-minute flight), the rally was outside city hall, and it was more of the same. A large banner greeted the occasion: DOLE'S GOLDEN RULE: YOU EARN IT, YOU KEEP IT.

There were black-on-yellow round signs, about eighteen inches in diameter, saying 15%, and half of the street crowd seemed to be holding them. The band was playing "This Land Is Your Land." A good many high school kids had turned out, and on cue they yelled, "Dole! Dole! Dole!" Which soon became "Go, Go, Go." When he spoke of putting extra money in their pockets, the kids started chanting, "Rent. Car. Money. Rent. Car. Money."

At the New Mexico rally Friday morning, a Dole functionary told the crowd, "Didn't Bob Dole do a great job in the debate?" They cheered, but it was a little empty. A lot of them obviously had missed the encounter. However there were many signs in the park: WE WOMEN DIG DOLE. DOLE MEANS GOOD MORALS. HONEST BOB. SOCCER MOMS 4 DOLE. CHARACTER—IT DOES COUNT.

Governor Gary Johnson got up. "What do I say in two minutes to get you to vote for Bob Dole?" he asked.

But he knew what he would tell them: "When Clinton was here, he went out and played golf. Said he shot an 83. I asked everyone, Democrats and Republicans. None of them thought he shot an 83. With Bob Dole, you could bet the farm that Bob Dole would give you an honest score."

Dole said, "I don't know if he shot an 83, a 283, a 483. With this guy, you never know." Stop. "This is an election about basic values." Stop. "Bring back integrity and common sense to the presidency." Stop. "I will be a President for all the people. You ought to be able to trust your President." Stop. "He can't cut taxes. He can only raise taxes."

The next rally was at the Place Middle School, in Denver, for sixth, seventh, and eighth graders, and Dole was flat. He was good at bringing out the child in adults, but it didn't work as well in reverse. "President Clinton," he said, "wants to increase spending up to 20 percent over the next four years. I would increase it by 14 percent. That's 6 percent for you. It's your money. Remember, it's your money." That made him a little happier. He always seemed most happy when talking about money. It had to be those Kansas farmers of his boyhood. They had taught him: Cash was the crop of crops. Your harvest. You deserve to keep your harvest. Not for too little had they made the American dollar green. "If elected, we will not sell access to the White House," he said.

The older Republicans all cheered. You did not need a scorecard to distinguish between Democrats and Republicans. The faces were there to demonstrate the difference between polymorphous-perverse and anus-rictus. But if you had any doubt, you had only to listen to the heavy sounds of approval that came up from the Republican crowd each time Dole told them, "It's *your* money. It's *your* money."

Finally he got going. A few sentences came together. "Here is a President who often talks about a bridge to the future. [I think] it's a bridge to wealthy political donors. It goes through a laundromat, takes a left at the Democratic National Committee, and then rolls all the way down to the Oval Office." Later, in Wichita, the pool (Blaine Harden and Judy Keen) would ask, "Do you really believe there is a money laundering operation going on in the White House?"

"In the White House? I didn't say in the White House. But something is going on somewhere. I didn't say in the White House, did I?"

Nelson Warfield, Dole's press secretary, tall, pale, with straight sandy hair, pale-rimmed glasses, and the gloomy mien of a responsible aide—a bright young Republican if ever there was one—said, "I think he is speaking metaphorically. If they want to see where the laundromat is, we want to see where the bridge is."

By the time the first press plane got to Wichita, it was late afternoon, and the rally was in an airplane hangar. A crowd of about a thousand was gathered, and they kept yelling for Bob. At the appointed moment, the long hangar doors opened. Outside, it was early twilight. The loudspeaker system came on with *Also Sprach Zarathustra,* the theme music for *2001,* and the white 727 saying BOB DOLE FOR PRESIDENT 1996 taxied up and wheeled around on the tarmac in full close view of the wide-open hangar doors. It was a nice piece of Republican theatricality, but later, the cameramen would complain. No one had told them. They had set their exposures for the artificial lighting of the hangar and so were not ready for a beautiful, cold October twilight, the last of the sun luminous on the white skin of the plane.

Dole soon got going on Clinton. "He is invited to retire right here in Kansas." Stop. "I believe the American people are looking for strong leadership, strong leadership." Stop. "Robin has been a godsend. I appreciate her a good deal." Stop. The crowd shouted after each sally. "No more years," they repeated, "no more years." A handlettered sign read: PISS ON THE POLLS. VOTE FOR DOLE.

It was evening by the time this speech ended, and it had been a full day. Albuquerque, Denver, Wichita, and on with the plane to Kentucky to be ready for the morning rally. Before he left Wichita, Dole worked the line at the airport. "The apparition of these faces in the crowd," Ezra Pound had written. "Petals on a wet, black bough." The faces had hands that kept reaching out to Dole's good left hand. They had gathered at every fence to watch and wait for the candidate. Sooner or later he might come by and greet them. Afterward, they would be able to say that he had said hello.

Standing near the candidate, the dean saw another face on Dole. It was old and concentrated and fragile. Distracted by the unexpected presence of a couple of unfamiliar reporters, his eyes were as bleak and empty of warmth as an eagle startled in its nest. Yes, it had been a long day. With each hour, the returns on the debate, now forty-eight hours old, must have settled in. One indigestible core of woe in the old eagle's gut.

That night on the airplane trip to Kentucky, one of the veterans began to talk of how much fun there had been on the Reagan campaign plane in 1980. One particularly powerful TV grip who sat at the back of the plane would try against all the force of gravity (as the plane went into its first steep climb after take-off) to roll an orange up the aisle like a bowling ball. Nancy Reagan got into the spirit and would answer with an orange from the front of the plane. By the time it reached the TV crew, it was traveling with major-league speed. If they couldn't stop it, the fruit would pulp itself on the back bulkhead.

Much yodeling after a catch, groans from a wipeout. That had to be 1980. In 1984, Ronnie was running for re-election and *Air Force One* didn't have an aisle. Nothing but compartments.

The rally on Saturday morning was in Somerset, Kentucky, a beautiful town that did not look to have changed since the 1930s. There were no high-rise buildings in sight. It was too small a town for the powerful if aesthetically deprived hand of the corporation. You could even hear leaves rustle.

Somerset was, of course, a Republican stronghold, full of small-town virtues and small-town nastiness. The first speaker, another sparse-haired worthy, made a reference to Hillary Clinton. Called her "Hilarious." Even in a Republican town, that was going too far. But small-town wisdom is to attack when it turns uncomfortable. He adjured the crowd: "Get off your duff and vote. Send a message to the bureaucrats in Washington."

More speakers: "I can say, Bob Dole, this is the kind of country you came from. We believe in our nation, and we are going to fight for it. We need a president you can trust, like Abraham Lincoln, born here in Kentucky."

Dole came on: "The one bill we need to veto is Bill Clinton. He can't cut taxes and balance the budget, but we can." Stop. "This is a fight for the heart and soul of America." Stop. "When everything else fails, try a little common sense. That's a Kansas saying." Stop.

The last rally on Saturday was in Norfolk, Virginia. The dean had seen it once, fifty-five years ago, while hitchhiking from New Jersey to North Carolina. Norfolk had been one tough town. All seaport. None of the buildings were tall then, and most of them were weathered gray. You could feel the mood. It was not altogether agreeable, but then not all moods are. A good many offer some sense, rather, of the complexity of good and evil. In those years, Norfolk was full of mood. Lots of prostitutes (and where is the prostitute who is not a mood standing on high heels?) and lots of commerce of the sea. He remembered Norfolk. It had been like a good many songs of the Depression—"Let's have another cup of coffee, and let's have another piece of pie."

Now, it had the typical skyline of a medium-sized burg, that half-finished and never-to-be-finished corporate skyline. Ugly vertical box-shaped buildings stood up like isolated iron plugs on the baseplate of a machine that once upon a time was actually being put together.

The rally took place in the National Maritime Center. Dole spoke with his back to the harbor. By this hour, middle of the afternoon, the water behind him looked a dark gray. A storm was coming in, and Dole was wearing some sort of ill-fitting windbreaker, a hospital white with black lapels. It was the only time in three days that he did not look well dressed, but then the Norfolk rally was equally out of kilter for the occasion. The crowd gave forth an angry sound, reminiscent of the low, bull roar you can hear at a European soccer match, before the violence breaks out.

Like all Dole's rallies, this one was inconclusive. Whether charming or ugly at the podium, Dole was never signally lucid. The dean had by now concluded that something was drastically wrong with the Republican party, and he would have hours to meditate on the matter, for the storm hovering at Norfolk had delayed commercial flights in Washington, and the dean didn't get to bed until early in the morning.

One point was awfully clear. Dole could hardly wish for insight on his real political situation. Such analysis would be equal to taking poison. Dole just had to keep campaigning. But, oh, how the Republicans were spoiled, intellectually spoiled. For years they had had need of no new ideas. The Cold War provided all their philosophical fuel. America, being wonderful, was duty-bound to defeat the USSR. Since the liberals shared the shadow of an idea with the Soviets—that the government should take responsibility for poor people—the liberals were always on the defensive.

Meanwhile, the conservatives drew converts. They were on the march. They succeeded in getting the average American to believe conservatism was a well-integrated philosophical house that could offer spiritual security to all who would approach.

In fact, it was a schizophrenic set of beliefs. At one end, it was the libertarianism of the free market, a philosophy that was not ready to face the very real possibility that the quest for money might succeed in closing out all other values. It has yet to be proven that a search for profit is equal to the expansion of human possibility. Who can guarantee that the growth will not be full of anomaly, spiritual entropy, and a billion obsolescent sneakers?

That was one half of American conservatism—the free market. On the other half was the political terrain that belonged to Pat Buchanan in the first primaries of 1996. It called for pro-life and rigorous morality. Yet family values, if truly pursued, call for strict restrictions on personal liberty. Such conservatives distrust big business and see the free market as an encouragement to crime, drugs, drive-by shootings.

Marxism had accommodated—unsuccessfully!—a huge division within itself: social idealism versus party oppression. Ultimately, conservatism might develop as large a divide. Inflammatory were the differences between rich Republicans (free market) and poor ones (pro-life).

Dole was the victim of this divide. He had made his attempt to bind the two sides of the party—accepted pro-life (in which he probably did not believe) and touted the 15 percent tax cut (in which, probably, he also did not believe). Noble. He had given his body to one faction and his soul to the other. If he wanted to be President (and one side of him had to be cynical about that, too—dark humor doth not good Presidents make), he had gotten himself into a most unhealthy condition—he was so divided that he could speak only by way of a new disease: sound bite-itis.

Well, Dole could tell himself: He was certain of one thing—Bill Clinton was a very bad influence for the country, a free marketer with the family values of a Turkish sultan. A true Rockefeller Republican. Ready to get government into everything. Yes, try waking up each morning to hear that Clinton was still 20 points up.

Dole didn't really want to look into his problems. They were like Chinese boxes. One inside another. Polls had shown that values bothered people more than the economy. But what had destroyed the values? He might think privately that we had carried on the Cold War for too long. But how could he tell people that? Say that the Russians had not been in any way a real enemy for twenty years. Maybe thirty years. It would be political suicide to say that excessive use of patriotism as a political tool is debilitating to national intelligence. Or, take advertising. Has to corrupt values. Has to be manipulative, meretricious, mendacious. Fastest way to dull a child's brain. Yes, just keep shattering your child's attention. Every ten to twelve minutes. Do it with a TV commercial. Yes, fine things for him to say. Well, Dole could begin to feel sorry for himself. How do you restore those old American values? Two lonely fellows on the highway of life—Dole and his sound bite.

Over the next five days, everything got worse. Dole went to New Hampshire on Sunday, and the storm was so bad that all the oxygen masks tumbled out of their receptacles as the 727 slammed down in its landing. Only a small crowd was waiting to see him. New Hampshire. Dole's old Vale. Vale of Defeat. The *New York Times*/CBS News Poll had Clinton up by 22 points. In Michigan, Dole said, "I'm going to win whether you like it or not." His fatigue was beginning to show. Worst kind: brain fatigue. "I'm running for President of the United States because I believe that—with strong leadership—America's days will always lie ahead of us. Just as they are now."

On October 24, Dole asked Perot to quit. Perot responded. Called the request "weird and totally inconsequential." In New Orleans, same day, Dole said, "This country is going to hell in a handbasket." In Montgomery, Alabama, same day, October 24, Dole said, "It's coming from Indonesia, it's coming from India! All over the world, money's coming into America right into the President's coffers!" Stop.

In Pensacola, Dole said, "Something's wrong in America. . . . I wonder . . . if people are thinking at all. Wake up, America!" Stop. "When will the American people have had enough?" Stop. "Don't inflict this on America for four more years. We can't take it."

Then he hit full stride. "You probably heard about the drug dealer in Miami who got invited to the White House. We will not have drug dealers eating at the White House in a Dole administration. This is a disgrace. This is a disgrace. . . . Bill Clinton ought to be voted out of office in a landslide. . . . To him, this is all a power game. It's a game! It's a game! It's a game!"

Next day in Houston, Dole was asked about a report in the New York *Daily News*. It stated that he had a long affair with an Australian woman, which had begun close to four years before the end of his first marriage. From *The Washington Post*, October 26: "Dole looked disbelievingly at the questioner, waved his arms dismissively and said, 'You're worse than they are.' "

From the *New York Post*, same day: "Dole asked, 'Where is the outrage?' seven times. At one point he lowered his voice to say it softly, as if he was saddened as well as frustrated. 'If it wasn't for the media, I could have won this election two weeks ago. . . .' At Southern Methodist University, Dole said, 'Don't read that stuff! Don't watch television! Don't let them make up your mind for you.' "

On Friday, October 25, at a rally in Atlanta, one of Clinton's supporters, Mayor Bill Campbell, told the crowd, "Bob Dole is out of touch, out of steam, and out of time."

By then, the dean had been with the Clinton campaign for two days. The differences were large. Now, one was following the camp of an engineer who planned superhighways. They might not get past the state line—but no one knew that yet, not even the engineer. He was ready to build a road around the world.

One matter was not in doubt. Clinton was going to win the election. That had seemed almost certain after the debates, but if any trace of reservation remained, it was gone by the time the dean followed

Clinton through Alabama, Louisiana, and Georgia. The impact was equal to watching a prodigiously powerful football team come out on the field against a school with a modest athletic department. The Clintons had it all: the size of the crowd—always three to five times the count of Dole's audiences—the throw of the loudspeaker system, the attention given to every item of his program. Dole's campaign grew in charm as one recalled its carnival atmosphere, a one-ring circus next to these five rings. Naturally, the big tent was not as much fun. Too little went wrong. But the dean came to understand one more cliché—the power of the incumbency. To be near the man, to see him pass, conceivably to touch his hand, to raise your offspring on your shoulder so that the child could see the President clearly was to endow your family, for years to come, with a recollection of strength. You had gained some instinctively felt relation to the immortal. In city after city, they would praise the President because he had been good enough to visit them. Clinton could not have been happier with the office.

In Bantu philosophy, there is a belief in *kuntu*. It is an individual spirit that adheres to concepts and to objects. A beautiful woman who puts on a beautiful dress has her beauty magnified more than the combination of the woman and the dress, provided the *kuntu* of each is in harmony. (High fashion would be hard-pressed to exist without the instinctive belief of society women that something of this sort is true.)

The *kuntu* of the presidency fit Clinton. There in Birmingham, Alabama, again in Louisiana and Georgia, he looked prodigiously like a President. One was sharing a city square with nothing less than a celestial oxymoron—part rogue, part god. What other man in America has ever had as many vices catalogued? Yet, to the crowd, he was all but luminous. One had to go back to the pharaohs to comprehend such worship. The dean recollected a story of how Ramses II, at the climax of the year's largest religious festival in Thebes circa 1250 B.C., lifted his short white robe to reveal to 300,000 Egyptians a mighty phallus. It was erect. Ramses II is probably the star of all time. Those 300,000 souls cheered. Their pharaoh was mighty; Egypt would prosper.

We are civilized, even corporatized, but our enthusiasm may still go back to that root. Seeing Clinton at work with a partisan crowd was to recognize that he might have as many personalities as Bob Dole (or Maggie Thatcher). Unlike Dole, he would not offer three or four of them in fifteen minutes. On the campaign trail, Clinton remained one man, but that man was not the guarded, near-diffident, reasonable, self-protective, and uneasy candidate of the debates. Now, his confidence was immense, his comfort was complete, and his energy did not flag. He loved the crowd and they loved him. He was with those who knew he was the Man. It was balmier than sweet sleep. A young crowd, always a young crowd, they hardly cared what he had done to get where he was. Power had its own signature.

Let us, however, not ignore all the details. No matter how well things had been arranged by Clinton's advance men, a few things did go wrong. A school band was playing the music in the Academic Quadrangle at Birmingham-Southern College, and when they were asked to produce the "Star-Spangled Banner," they did not have the sheet music. Who would sell that sheet music down in Alabama? Ask them rather to play the fight song of the U of A. So there was an embarrassed silence, perhaps one extended minute before someone was inspired enough to suggest they sing it, whereupon the band, much abashed, all heartfelt trumpets dented, sang away slowly. Some of the audience even joined in.

Senator Howell Heflin got up to speak, but could not make the last step up to the podium. Now retiring from the U.S. Senate, Heflin is a grand old man with horn-rimmed glasses, a full underhang of double chin, and a prodigious belly in graceful concert with that double chin. But Heflin was too fat to occupy the small riser at the base of the podium. His belly kept pushing him back. The crowd laughed and he laughed, and he stayed where he was and just spoke a little louder. "Radical far-right pachyderms," he told the crowd, "have been raising their snouts to fling their mud and vicious slander."

"Give it to them, Howell," yelled the crowd.

"You, Mr. President, however, have conducted yourself in a disciplined, gentlemanly Southern manner." High applause from the crowd.

Clinton was next and began by saying, "Hello, Alabama. (*Prodigious cheers.*) I met Howell Heflin 21 years ago, when he was the chief justice of the Alabama Supreme Court, and I was a former candidate for Congress—and a loser, I might add. He came in the law school at the university, and I thought that he was the darndest fella I ever met in my life. He had a wonderful sense of humor, a great sense of compassion, a fine mind and a lot of country common-sense wisdom. . . .

"Folks, we are on the verge of a new century. . . . This is the last election for President of the twentieth century and the first election for President of the twenty-first century. And you have to decide. Many of you young people in this audience, in a few years, you will be doing jobs that haven't been invented yet. Some of you will be doing work that has not even been imagined yet. And you have to decide: What kind of America do you want? . . . For me the answer is simple but profound. I dream of an America in the twenty-first century where every person—without regard to race or region or income or religion or gender or background—who is responsible enough to work for it, can have a shot at the American Dream." [*Applause*]

That evening, outside of New Orleans, in Marrero, a town that had had its troubles with crime, Clinton had seventeen prize cops lined up in front of the backdrop on the dais. The focus proved to be the SPAR program: Surveillance, Policing, Arresting, and Rejuvenation. "The job they are doing," said Clinton, pointing to the police, "is a job second to none."

"Thank you, President Clinton," said one of the speakers, "for a peaceful night's rest." Marrero, obviously, was one bad town.

Half of the principals that night were black, as indeed had been true in Birmingham. The proportion would be kept the next day in Atlanta. Clinton would engage in a conference call with more than six hundred black ministers during a late lunch at Paschal's restaurant, and he had materials to lay on them. He was for blacks and he was for women, middle-class blacks and middle-class women. Had any American President understood as well as Clinton those who aspire to the middle class?

Here he was on the conference call: "One reason I try to make sure every person would be guaranteed at least two years of education after high school is that I think our country ought to work more the way these community colleges do. . . . They're not bureaucratic; they're flexible, they're changing all the time. They have to meet high standards of performance or they go broke. Everybody that graduates from them gets hired. And they're open to everybody, and everybody is treated the same. That's what I'm trying to do for America. So I'm proud of the results we've achieved . . . the biggest decline in inequality among working people in twenty-seven years, the biggest drop in child poverty in twenty years, the biggest drop in poverty among female heads of households in thirty years, and the lowest overall poverty rate among African-Americans and American senior citizens ever recorded. . . . I'm sure most of you on this phone call know, we have appointed more African-Americans to important positions in the cabinet and the White House, in the administration, on the federal bench, than any other administration in history [and] though there have been more women and minority appointments, by far, than any previous administration, the American Bar Association has given higher ratings to my federal judges than any other President since the rating system began. Which proves that we can have excellence and diversity. Which proves you can have affirmative action and equal opportunity and high standards."

How could those black clergymen listening over the phone not warm to him? They understood human complexity better than their white counterparts. They knew all too well how much goodness was to be found in a bad man and how much evil was secreted in someone nominally good. So Clinton's morals would not bother them. He was comfortable with black people. They were comfortable with him. They could see him as the kind of car salesman whose clients would trust him even after he had palmed off a lemon. (Like the end of welfare!)

"Friend, I feel for you," he might say, "and I want to make you feel better. You just fix your heart and vision on the law of averages. Because that's going to reward you in the future. I certify that the next car you buy from me will be top of the line."

How were you going to desert a fellow like that? Hell, his uncle, Raymond Clinton, a huge influence on his life, had owned a Buick dealership in Hot Springs, the old mobster hangout. Yes, Clinton was full of pain for your car's bad performance.

For that matter, he said to the clergymen, "Atlanta is one of the urban centers of the world, because forty years ago, it became the city too busy to hate." A beautiful sentiment. Like everything he uttered, it was half true. One didn't have to be in Atlanta long to recognize that it was one more corporate town. The vitality of Atlanta was there, and thousands of blacks and whites, well dressed, mingled in the crowd with little tension, but Atlanta looked like all the other new American skylines. Coming into a large American city no longer offered much excitement unless you were arriving on business. Then, you might thrive within the spiritual blockade of forty-story offices and hotels, but the truth was that Atlanta was about as unattractive as any of the other new and major corporate monoliths that offered no mood other than the emptiness of the mood they projected upon the skyline. They were without resonance, sentimental memory, surprise, or hope for a little fresh air in one's existence. So, they were invariably reinforced with security. They had to be. They were minimum-security prisons for our good American character. What was there about America that no politician or civic leader ever raised an objection to how we kept building these corporate blockhouses of the soul?

In Woodruff Park, a green surrounded by corporate architecture, Clinton held his morning rally. The young trees were still not tall enough to hide the surroundings, and so to set a mood, the band played loudly for the thousands assembled. A lot of electric power was in the sound. Kids with enormous amplification of middling talents had now replaced Sonny Rollins, Miles, Thelonius Monk, Jimmy Dorsey, Tommy Dorsey—let us not go down memory lane, but let us also not pretend that we have not lost the entrance.

Clamor is the stimulus. It is there to overcome the numb silence of the corporate presence. You can play jazz in a graveyard, but you cannot play it in a corporate park. For that you need electronic blast. Power imprinted upon emptiness is money.

Now, in Woodruff Park, the crowd came alive at the sight of Clinton. It would be hard, at this point, to argue that his appetites had really hurt his career. After all, he had done no more than take an agreeable political premise—press the flesh—and carry it forward to a natural conclusion.

Good old Bill, the dean decided, had raised the perilous sport of tomcatting into a state-of-the-art tool that probably helped him to read the national mood. He had been closer to that mood than the Republicans. After the bombing in Oklahoma City, the people needed reassurance that things could get better. The salesman from Hope had been smart enough to provide a box of toys. In Chicago at the convention he said—and he would repeat it often—"Every library and classroom in America connected to the information superhighway by the year 2000."

What no one seemed ready to contemplate was that the information superhighway was only too well named: It was a real superhighway, efficient yet deadening. Masses of quickly available processed information would soon bear the same relation to culture that a superhighway presents to a country road. One's memory will not retain much of Colorado or South Carolina if you drive through them on an Interstate. Memories, like etchings, are fixed by attention to detail—by working one's way along a two-lane road full of towns, cheap stores, and little courthouse squares.

With the World Wide Web, we will be given the screen of a monitor rather than the page of a book. But the people wanted the technological world. It was simpler. All the values could be compressed into one—power. Clinton gave off the confidence that he could help them get it, and when the dean saw the way black kids looked at Clinton, he was, despite himself, moved. Clinton had the power to offer them the hope of future power.

Yes, Clinton's sunny public nature connected these kids to a vision of their future: They would go to college, they would succeed. Like others, they would gain power. The country was starved for that kind of promise. Dole's range went from elegant to dour. He was not the most optimistic man in America. Of course, he was not. He was all too aware of the basic problem—too much money was going to the top.

Dole might even have had a chance if he had been able to say, "I'm opposed to big government, but I'm also opposed to giving corporations those tax write-offs and subsidies. The largest part of the 15 percent tax cut will come from ending corporate welfare as we know it."

Of course, he could not say it. You could not be a loyal Republican and speak in that manner, not unless you were Pat Buchanan. But Dole was not Buchanan. So there was never the thickness of a width of dental floss between the real economic programs of the Democrats and the Republicans. The only gap was in the candidates: They were far apart in temperament.

Dole's war wound had branded him. If something in his soul would never give up, something else might never be at rest. For Dole's right hand, seen up close, was a small dark object, not unlike a shrunken head, and this resemblance was so striking that one would not have been surprised to see long hair growing out of it. Who could contemplate the pain of carrying such a dark affliction as part of your body when you are a tall and handsome man? How much of his personality was nested in that shrunken right hand? It had made his sensitivity to others acute. If Dole was speaking to an audience, one had to do no more than look at his right hand and ponder its effect upon him. His left hand would come over to protect it.

So, for what it was worth, the dean had come to his conclusion. He would vote for Clinton. It was a dangerous choice, and he disliked two-thirds of what Clinton stood for. He had a certain fondness for Dole, who had at least taken a few wild chances, such as 15 percent and Jack Kemp. There was certainly no question that the press plane following Dole had been a living carnival in the air, while the media traveling with Clinton had been, of necessity, serious. Who but priests can attend a pharaoh?

Yet, it would have to be Clinton. If the dean was going to vote (and his vote for President was all but meaningless for the category of President, since he lived in Massachusetts, and in no way could Clinton ever lose there), still, it would be equal to betting on a game. How could one watch a professional contest if no bet was on the line? The dean was betting that a star, unlike a leading man, is always capable of greatness. In Clinton's case, it would not be the kind of greatness that the dean was likely to admire—it would be too managed. But at least Clinton had the potential to be, in one way at least, a great President. He could bring blacks and whites together. To some degree, at any rate. That might be more important for America's future than anything else right now (with the divine exception of reducing the enormous ratio between wealth and poverty).

So the dean had his epiphany in Georgia and came back to Massachusetts to write about the campaign while he followed the last week and a half in the newspapers. And, of course, the oldest law of journalism and police work came into effect: It always happens when you are not there.

Dole grew angrier at Clinton over the last ten days as the polls refused to lift him rapidly enough to offer any hope of victory, even though Ross Perot had, by now, become a potent scourge to the Clintons. Perot declared: "It's like saying, 'Bonnie and Clyde, we want you to be president of a bank. But for heaven's sake, quit robbing the banks, would you?' "

Perot said more. He spoke of how America could not afford to have the White House under investigation for the next two years. You could feel Clinton losing votes even as Perot spoke, but then, every one of Perot's ideas made some kind of sense, except for his idea of himself. Concerning himself, he was hopeless. With Perot, you did not have to worry about any technological warp the TV set might introduce into your perceptions. Perot had a personality as strong as a turnip sealed for three months in a plastic container. He was far beyond the warp system of TV. If Perot were ever elected, the country would go mad. For he had a voice guaranteed to bring out the worst in all, and his intellectual habits were meaner than his voice. He had a solution he would bring to all our grievous problems, and he would reveal it soon. When? Why, in some soon-to-come hour. Time was not an element. Ross Perot was higher than time. There is no limit to the shamelessness located in the skewed brain cells of the very rich.

Dole took one more gambit. For the last ninety-six hours of the campaign, he went on his marathon. He spoke in something like thirty cities in the last four days. With very little sleep, he was close to incoherent. To save himself from verbal breakdown, he began to repeat each sentence.

"He's no good," he would say, "he's no good." Stop. "Honor and trust, honor and trust." It was as if both halves of his much-divided soul were now obliged to show up for each and every utterance. Of course, by now, both sides of him—the good guy, the bad guy—were beginning to agree with each other. We are always full of energy when the best and worst in us are moving in the same direction. "I will bring integrity back to the White House," said Dole, "and I won't have any drug dealers over for dinner." His voice was gone. His speeches were down to ten minutes, to five minutes.

"Integrity, character, honor, duty, country, decency." Stop. "While I still have my voice, I want you to know. I'll keep my word."

It was not for naught. Perot had become the attack dog that Kemp had refused to become and Dole had not quite known how to be, and Clinton, always vulnerable when caught at the trough, was hurt seriously by the newest gate—Indogate. Clinton must have lost four or five points at the end, a crucial loss, since the Congress would still be Republican.

It was Dole who looked like the winner on election night. As he made his speech of concession, he looked quieter and nicer and more decent and happy than ever before on television, but then, by his own lights, he had saved his honor. His party, in danger of despising him for the ineptitude of his campaign, had seen him make amends with his ninety-six-hour marathon. He had probably moved the Senate and the House of Representatives over to the Republicans in those four last days. Now he would be honored until his death (unless he went back into politics), and so one had the pleasure of looking at the rarest political animal of them all—a completely happy defeated candidate.

As for the dean, his vote took a turn or two. He too was put off by Indogate. While the Republicans certainly took in vast sums from wealthy Americans who were probably as charmless as any Midas of an Indonesian, Clinton had done it again. He might have the makings of a great man, but could he swim fast enough to escape the polluted sea of his past?

Meanwhile, November 2, on C-SPAN, the dean heard a television address given originally by Ralph Nader on October 25 at the All Souls Unitarian Church in Washington, D.C. And after all these months, the dean found at last that he could be moved to moral respect for a candidate.

"We have tens of millions of youngsters," said Nader, "sitting on the couch thirty, forty hours a week, watching TV, watching video. . . . They're more out of shape, our pre-teenagers, more out of shape, more flabby, more overweight than any pre-teenagers since we started recording their physical state in 1990. They're not out in the backyard, kicking the can, playing with kids in the neighborhood. They're

sitting gazing, gazing, learning the lessons of modern corporate huck-
sterism on television and video: Violence is a solution to life's problems. Low-grade sensuality, from junk food to soft porn. And
addiction, above all addiction, because that means more sales and
more profits.

"The children are growing up even more corporate. Ever listen
to their vocabulary? It would shame Esperanto with the sparseness of
their vocabulary. 'You know, kinda . . . cool . . . you know, look, like,
kinda, sorta, cool, you know . . .' [*Laughter*] That's growing up corporate. . . . We all grow up corporate. That's how we're controlled. We
are participants in our own domination if we accept the way corporations look at the world."

So the dean decided to vote for Nader. To hell with Clinton. To
hell with his own epiphany and ithyphallic revivals. He would vote for
Nader. But when an election official passed him the ballot in Province-
town, Massachusetts, he discovered that Nader was not on it. No
Greens in Massachusetts—how odd. What was more odd in retrospect
is that it never occurred to the dean to write in his vote on the ballot.
He did what, at last count, 49.2 percent of all voting Americans did:
He sighed. He voted for Clinton. It was a profound sigh.

Would America never have a major candidate to give again some
promise that politics could become as great and exciting as our
dream? There was something immeasurably insolent in the way politicians patronized the American heart. Marilyn Monroe once commented on the way strangers could be awfully rude to her. "I guess,"
she said, "when they say those things, they think they're only doing it
to your clothing."

From *George* (January 1997)

# 1200 B.C.   THE BATTLE
## OF KADESH

### 1.

"In those days, we still made camp in the same manner as in the age of Thutmose the Great. So, on this morning, the pavilion of the King was erected in the middle of the officers' tents, and the royal chariots were on all four sides. This square was surrounded by our cattle and provenance, and infantrymen were placed to the outside, their tall shields planted vertically on the ridge of an earthwork dug the night before. In that way, we were like a fortress of four walls of shields, and you even entered through gates, except they were not real gates, just the road and a platoon of infantrymen either side of that opening. Inside, you could stroll about, and visit your friends. If not for my message, it might have been good to feel like a soldier again. On ordinary days little made me happier than to be inside a camp, even if many did nothing but snore, or sharpen the blade of a dagger for one hour and then another.

"On this day, in the expectation that we might still be marching into battle—what life had an army without rumors?—many a Nubian put on his helmet, and would not take it off. These blacks, some in leopard skins, some wearing long white skirts with an orange sash slung from the right shoulder, made quite a sight. The blacks liked to be seen, and I watched five of them arguing in one place, and ten sitting so quietly in another that their silence was stronger than clamor, curious soldiers about whom we charioteers disagreed, some saying the Nubians would prove brave in combat, others said no. I knew they were strong, but I thought of them as horses, brave until frightened, and much in love with their plumage. Like horses, the Nubians would put at least one yellow feather at the top of their leather helmets. What a contrast they made to the Syrians who often had bald heads, no helmets, and big black beards.

"About the time I realized it would be afternoon before my King might see me, all discomfort went away, and I relaxed in the sun with other charioteers and told of my adventures, keeping the best to myself, and walked back and forth through the inner and outer square, the goodness of Ra warming my flesh, so that at last I was down to no more than my sandals and a loincloth, lolling about like half the soldiers on that ground, and the day grew lazy. I stopped for a while at the shop of the Royal Carpenter to tell him of the loss of my cart, but he was too busy to care, for he was putting together a chariot from two broken buggies, and promised to do better for me than that, since his workmen could return you six chariots ready for battle out of seven half-dismembered carcasses, and I listened to him while he stood in the middle of his shop with chariot wheels in one stack, the spokes for wheels in another pile, and heaps of broken parts on the ground. I did not know how he would ever be able to move.

"Then I watched other infantrymen carrying paniers of water up from the ford to a large leather bag hung from three sticks in the center of camp, and horses being walked to the blacksmith shop. I watched soldiers drinking wine, and a few were wrestling, and two others led a couple of cows to the field kitchen. I smelled the sweat of the day and the odor of roasting meat. Two of the soldiers drinking wine began to skirmish with daggers. They had been doing it for a long time and knew how to lunge at each other, then stop short. A Sherden, sweating like a fountain in his red and blue woolen cape, was beating a donkey who had gotten his nose into a bag of provisions. The food so excited the beast that he promptly got an erection. The Sherden kept beating on him and the donkey kept scampering away but never lost his excitement, nor took his head out of the bag, not while I watched. Next to him, another donkey, excited by all this, was rolling in the dust.

"Most of the men were sleeping. The afternoon grew lazier still, and I could feel the fatigue of all the days of the march that had brought these troops this far, and then felt my own fatigue, and went back to a tent I was sharing with other charioteers and fell asleep on a ground-cloth, only to be awakened by word the King would see me now. In bewilderment, still dreaming of forests and thieves, I stood up, threw water on my face from a bowl, and went over to the King's pavilion. I had been dreaming of the Hittites and saw a road where they planted sharpened stakes, and Egyptian soldiers were dying on them. Slowly in my dreams, bodies slid down the stakes. My bowels were cold. I took a slug of wine from a skin, and that made me sweat. Looking like a man whose insides must belong to others, I entered the great tent of Ramses the Second.

"It was as much a fine house as a tent. He had not only His sanctuary for prayer, and His bedroom, but a dining room as well, and then a great room for anyone to whom He would give audience. On this day many officers and Generals and the Prince, Amen-khep-shu-ef, were with Him, yet when I entered He was so impatient that He began to speak before I had finished touching my head to the ground. 'Would you,' He asked, 'give up the richest province of your lands without striking a blow?'

" 'My Lord, I would try to fight like the Son-of-Ra.'

" 'Yet, some here tell Me that the King of Kadesh is two days' march on the other side, and dares not come nearer. He is a fool. I will let all know his shame. The stone I put up to celebrate my victory will show that the name of the King of Kadesh is equal to what you see between a whore's thighs!'

"It was hot in the tent from the sun coming down on the other side of the leather, and hot again from forty officers' bodies, but the greatest heat came from Usermare, my Pharaoh. He was like a fire on a hot day in the desert.

" 'Who says he will not defend Kadesh?' I asked.

"My Pharaoh pointed to two shepherds sitting quietly in a corner. By the dust of their long robes, they looked as if they had been traveling with their animals for a hundred days. Now, with smiles that showed their teeth—the teeth that were left—they bowed seven times. Then the older spoke, but in his own language. The Overseer-of-Both-Languages, one of our Generals, exchanged the Bedouin's words for ours, but only after each breath the shepherd took, and he took many breaths.

" 'O Beloved Ramses, Adored-by-Truth,' I heard, 'does not the Good and Great God know happiness when He cuts off the head of His enemy? Does that not give Him more delight than a day of pleasure?'

"I saw my Pharaoh smile.

"The shepherd spoke in a long slow grave voice as deep and full of echo as any prophet, 'O You-who-are-the-Majesty-of-Horus-

and-Amon-Ra, You-Who-are-firm-on-His-horse-and-beautiful-in-His-chariot, know that we have come to Your throne of gold'—and indeed my Usermare-Setpenere was sitting on a small chair of solid gold—'to speak for our families. They are among the greatest of the great families who are sworn to Metella, King of Kadesh and chief of the Hittites. Yet our families say that Metella is our chief no longer, because his blood has become the color of water. His force is to Yours as the eye of the rabbit to the eye of the bull. Metella sits in the land of Aleppo and cannot find the courage to march to Kadesh. So our families have sent us to You, as a pledge of their desire to become Your subjects.'

" 'I am honored,' said Usermare-Setpenere, 'because I know you tell the truth. He who does not tell the truth before Me is a man who will soon lose the limb that makes children. Behold, he must look upon his lost parts with both eyes before his eyes are sent to join the lost parts.'

"Never had I heard my Pharaoh speak that way, but then I had never felt such heat come off His body. 'I believe these men are telling the truth,' He said, 'how dare they lie?' But in the same anger, He turned to me and said, 'Do you believe them?' When I was silent, He laughed. 'You don't? You believe they are so brazen as to deceive your Pharaoh?'

" 'I believe them,' I said. 'I think they tell the truth that is the truth of their family. Yet it is several days since they have left. While they have been making their journey to us, so may the armies of the King of Kadesh have also been traveling. O You-of-the-Two-Great-Houses,' I said, so frightened that I also struck my head seven times to the ground, 'in the dawn, this morning, as I descended from the hills, I saw to the north, near Kadesh, an army.'

" 'You say an army?'

" 'I saw the light of an army. I saw the light that is made by lances, and swords, and the polished metal on shields.'

" 'But you did not see the swords?' asked the Prince Amen-khep-shu-ef. 'Only the light?'

" 'Only the light,' I admitted.

" 'The light is from the river that flows around the walls of Kadesh,' said the Prince. A good many of the Generals laughed. When our Pharaoh did not, however, they were silent. Now I knew why the heat that came from my Pharaoh was so strange. The lion, Hera-Ra, was not by His side. I remembered then how much of the heat used to come from the beast. Yes, the Generals were now silent before Usermare-Setpenere the way once they had been silent before Hera-Ra.

" 'On your travels, what did you hear about the King of Kadesh?' I now was asked.

" 'That Metella hides in the forest near the city,' I said quickly. 'That he has a large army. That he will come on us suddenly.'

" 'It is untrue,' roared the Pharaoh. Under the black and green of His cosmetic, I saw how the whites of His eyes were red. 'It is untrue,' He repeated, 'yet I believe it is true.' He glared at me as if I had taunted Him.

"A discussion began whether to break camp in the dawn and march to Kadesh with the first two divisions, or, whether—and here I could not keep silent and was soon in the debate—it would be wise to wait one more day. Let the last two divisions come through the gorge. 'Then,' I said, 'we can march onto the great plain with a horn to the left and a horn to the right.' I said 'horn' because I remembered that on the day we traveled to His tomb, Usermare had told me how Thutmose the Great never said 'wing' or 'flank.' He spoke of His Armies as if He had a head and two horns, a Mighty Bull.

"My Pharaoh nodded. He looked into Himself and saw His Chariot at the center of a great army on a great field with two horns, and I thought, He will give the order to wait. But Prince Amen-khep-shu-ef also knew His father, and said, 'On that great field we may wait for another week, while the King of Kadesh does not come. Our men will fight with each other. They will desert. We will look foolish, and our horn will crumble.'

"The Pharaoh nodded to that as well. Now, the council was concluded. He gave the order. We would break camp in the dawn. That evening, Usermare-Setpenere stood on the cage that held His lion. One night in the forests of Lebanon, Hera-Ra had eaten one of our soldiers. So a cage had been built for him next morning. Now our Pharaoh spoke to all of us from the top of that cage, while Hera-Ra roared beneath.

" 'The battle of Megiddo was won by the Great Pharaoh, Thutmose the Third. The King, Himself, led the way of His troops. He was mighty at their head like a flame. So will I be mighty at your head.' The soldiers cheered. I knew again that I was part of an army, for the evening was red once with its own light, and red again with our cheers. 'Thutmose went forth to slay barbarians,' said our King, 'and none was like Him. He conquered all the enemy Princes even though their chariots were wrought with gold.' We cheered again. Each time our Pharaoh spoke of gold, we cheered. 'All fled before Thutmose,' said our King. 'In such fear did they run that their clothing was left behind.' A great snickering laugh huge as a river of mud came out of us. 'Yes, they abandoned their chariots of gold and silver'—we gave a sigh like the whisper of moonlight on water—'and the people of Megiddo pulled their soldiers over the wall by what was left of their skin. In this hour, the armies of Thutmose could have captured the city.' Here, our King paused. 'But they did not,' He said. 'Our soldiers gave all their attention to the plunder left on the field. So they lost the treasures that were in the city. The men of Megiddo were stretched on the field like fish, but the army of Thutmose picked at their bones like gulls.' A groan came up from us. 'Do not act,' said Ramses, 'like gulls. The city that was not taken on that day had to be besieged for a year. The army of Thutmose had to work like slaves to cut down forests so that they could build walls to approach the walls of Megiddo. And the work was not done until all of the wall of Megiddo was surrounded by the wall of Thutmose. It was a year's work. The city starved, but in that time, they also hid their gold. It was lost to us. No good slaves were taken. Only the plague-ridden greeted the armies of Thutmose. So I say to you that we will fight a great battle, but none of you will take plunder until I give My word! It is Asiatic hands I want to see on the pile, not Egyptian.'

"We cheered. We cheered with fear in our throats and disappointment in our loins at the thought of less plunder, but we cheered, and the lion roared. Next morning at dawn after a night when few of us could sleep, we broke camp and crossed the ford at Shabtuna. Although the water in the deep places came to our chest, not a man nor a horse was drowned. Disturbed, however, in their nests at the riverbank, beetles gathered like clouds and came between us and the sun. The swarm of their flight was so thick that it left us in shadow. No one saw a good sign in the rising of these beetles.

"Once we were across, we formed our ranks and set out on the great hard plain in the valley of the Orontes that leads to Kadesh. Its soil is as baked as a parade ground. May I say that our horses and our chariot wheels rode over the bodies of all the beetles that had tired of flight. We left the mark of our route as much behind us as if we had trampled through a field of berries. Beetles were in our hair and clothing like a pestilence.

"Again I could feel the impatience of my Ramses. He was in the vanguard of the march. His charioteers, taken together with His Household Guard of the strongest Sherdens and Nubians, giants all, had, counting everyone, not five hundred men. We were certainly in the van. There was a clear distance behind us and the first troops of the Division of Amon. Worse. Looking back from a rise, I could see how far we had marched this morning across the plain. But the troops of Ra were just crossing the ford. It would be half a day before the Division of Ptah could follow. As for Set, those men were still jammed in the gorge. They would be no use to any of us until night.

"All the same, I was happy to be in the van. The dust was less. Clouds rose from the hard-baked clay of this plain to drive away the beetles, and such clouds drifted back on Amon and its five thousand marching men. It would have been like passing through smoke to ride with that division.

"How we must have been visible from Kadesh! Through the dust, we could see the city in the distance there where the sky met the hills. Kadesh was not an hour's ride away on a fast horse, yet would take us until afternoon, because now we were winding through lightly forested rises, and could see ahead no more and so could not go forward without pause, but had to send out scouts, then wait for their return.

"I was carrying a weight in my chest like the heart of a dead man. Yet, I felt neither weak nor spineless, but even in the midst of my oppression, alert, as if throngs were waiting inside me for the battle to begin. I tried to think of what I would do if I were Metella, the King of Kadesh, and where in these woods would I choose to attack the Household Guard of the Pharaoh so that I could capture my great Ramses? Then it seemed to me I would prefer to wait until half the division of Amon was past, or even half the Division of Ra, so that I could strike at a large force when it was stretched out on the trail of the forest as long and vulnerable as a worm you could cut in half. Still, the effort of trying to think as if I were someone other than myself, especially a foreign King, made me know vertigo, and I supposed I was living with a fearful gift from the secret whore of the King of Kadesh. Maybe I was not trying to think like this Metella so much as I was indeed living in the thoughts that came from his heart. If that were so then our vanguard would go forward untouched and the Division of Amon as well. It would be on Ra that the thunder would fall.

"My fear was replaced by woe. At this instant, we were in no danger, yet in a greater danger. I could never tell this to Usermare-Setpenere. He was riding with His son Amen-khep-shu-ef in my place. That left me as a driver for no one better than the Overseer-of-Both-Languages. This fellow was a General called Utit-Khent, but, of course, this name, 'Mistress of Expeditions,' was only an army joke. He was said to have a rectum like the mouth of a bucket. So I knew again my Pharaoh's anger. He would have me share a chariot with such a man. Of course, He was now listening to the advice of His son. So soon as He discovered the power of my thoughts to reach into the thoughts of our enemy, so might I be His driver again. In the meantime, Utit-Khent babbled along about the dust, but in so clever a way I began to laugh for, lo, he pointed out there were Gods for every fish and cat, and the God of beetles was a Great God, but no deity ever bothered to become God of the dust. You could not name such a God. He was harmless, this General, a clown for other Generals, he commanded no men, and had been a flunky for Prince Amen-khep-shu-ef, but I had to wonder if this poor Utit-Khent had once been a strong soldier but had grown weak serving Usermare.

"We were not on a bad trail, indeed it was more like a road wide enough for one chariot to pass another. That was comfortable and it was cool in the forest under the heat of midday, but none of us were comfortable—Kadesh was too near. Besides, you had to wonder where a squadron of chariots could strike at us. While the forest reached to the road in most places, still we also crossed fields, and an army could hide at their edge. Five thousand men could charge down on five hundred, yet now my good King, impatient at delay, did not bother anymore to send out scouts. He must have believed the gates to Kadesh were open.

"Into the early afternoon we traveled, and passed another wood, and many a cultivated field, even saw a farmer or two who ran off at the sight of us, but we kept moving with the river Orontes at our right, and this river was shallow here and slow-moving, and had several fords wide enough for an army, if Metella wished to attack from the other bank. Still, nothing happened, and we came around a turn in our road and saw before us, there in full view to the north, the walls and towers of Kadesh, and no Hittite army was drawn up in front of it. There was nothing before us but the river which wound around its walls to the left. We had been marching so long to reach this town, so many days on the Nile and in the desert and the mountains, that I think my good King could not stop, not yet, but must keep going while He passed the city on our right hand. Soon, the walls would be behind us, and here, as if confused by the absence of any soldiers, or even any face in the windows of the towers of Kadesh, in this silence of the hills where the largest sound was the groaning of our chariot wheels, not a large sound, for we hardly strained on the level ground, Ramses the Second finally gave the order, and in a thin wood with many small fields and scattered trees, we halted beside the river in a place too steep to cross. The three open sides to our square that looked out on the land were quickly faced off with our shields, and an earthworks to support the shields was begun by the Nubians right about the Pharaoh's pavilion. Here we waited in silence, no sound but the digging. The Division of Amon soon followed, and built a larger square around our square, which enabled the King's Guard to move back from the Orontes. Now, the Division of Amon had the river for a fourth side. There was still not a sound from the town.

"Around us you could hear the echo of the five thousand men of Amon digging away, although with no great effort. In another hour we might be moving again. So they carried on with the ease of men unharnessing their horses, feeding their beasts and their own mouths, and in all this unyoking of the provision trains, there was a feeling of safety at the size of our numbers. Only I felt oppressed in my breath. Even though I did not want to fight beside Utit-Khent, still I worked on the chariot I might yet have to ride with him, grinding the bronze rim of the wheels with a rare hard stone I carried in my leather bag until the edge of the wheel was sharp as a knife. That would not last for long, but, oh, what cruelty a wheel, freshly honed, could commit on the body of a fallen man. All the while, I continued to feel heavy in my lungs. When we came to this camping ground, I had seen no sign of another army, no litter whatsoever, and the red pine needles of the forest floor were smooth. Yet they did not look smooth so much as swept back into order. I had the feeling an army had been here before us, even this morning, and wondered how easily pine needles could conceal their traces. Besides, I could smell the God of the pine trees and He was strange.

"Men kept coming to the Pharaoh's pavilion with little pieces of equipment. Here was a wagon-spoke unfamiliar to us, or a broken leather cinch with a strange-smelling oil. More and more did a sentiment become powerful to me that the forest was stale. Then I thought if I were Metella, yes, I would stay on this north side of Kadesh well hidden by the forest, even as Usermare-Setpenere moved forward from the south. Only when He came up to the walls, would I cross the river to the east and hide on the other side to keep the city between us. Then, if He came even further north to this place, so would I move altogether to the south and still be hidden by the walls of Kadesh. That way I could cross the river in the place where there were many fords and strike into the middle of the division of Ra, there in that open field south of the city.

"Even as I was considering such maneuvers, an outcry began in our camp. Two Asiatics had just been brought in by scouts, their faces covered with blood. Soldiers in the middle of cooking a meal stared as the captors led these prisoners to the pavilion of the Pharaoh. Then came many screams and the sound of the flail. By the time I entered the King's tent, the backs of the prisoners were as bloody as their features, and I was glad I could not see their expression.

"Each bite of the flail whipped loose a piece of skin large as your palm. Usermare-Setpenere now pulled off a strip from the prisoner's shoulder like a ribbon of papyrus, and threw it to the ground. Then He said: 'Speak the truth.' That Hittite could not have known a word of our language, but he knew the voice, he knew the eyes that looked at him. The light from those eyes was as full of flame as the sun. So to Usermare-Setpenere, by way of Utit-Khent, he said, 'O Son of Ra, spare my back.'

" 'Where is your miserable King of the Hittites?'

" 'Behold,' cried the Asiatic in his language, and 'behold' said our Overseer-of-Both-Languages in our language, 'Metella the King of Kadesh has gathered many nations in great numbers. His soldiers cover the mountains and valleys.'

"He continued to speak even as Amen-khep-shu-ef was twisting this man's arm behind his neck. I thought his shoulder would dislocate, for even the bleeding stopped, so white did his back become from the pressure. Yet the scout said it all, every word, waiting each few words for Utit-Khent to express what he had said, all the while swallowing his groans. Now, Usermare-Setpenere raised His sword. 'Where is Metella now?'

"He could hold out no longer: 'O my Lord, Metella is waiting on the other bank of the river.'

"I thought the sword would fall. It hovered. Instead, our King let go of the Hittite, and turned to us. 'See what you have told Me,' He cried out, 'see how you have spoken of the King of Kadesh as a coward who flees.' Now I thought He would take the sword to His own son. The Prince struck His head to the ground seven times, and must have had many thoughts, for when He looked up, He said, 'My Lord, let Me ride back to tell the Division of Ptah. We will need them.' When our King gave a slow nod, as if forced to agree despite His wrath, the Prince was out of the tent, and at once, I suppose, on His way, although none of us were able to know what another did, for in the next moment, chaos fell upon us. I heard a far-off din, a nearer uproar, and then the voice of a hundred horses, a most fearful clamor, a pandemonium, the shock and crash of chariots. We did not know that the shattered legions of the Division of Ra, horses without chariots and charioteers without horses, were now running our way, infantrymen chasing wagon trains pulled at a gallop by horses without drivers, and all of this disorder came down on us. Only later would I learn that the Division of Ra had been cut in half even as I had foreseen it, there in the road where they were long indeed like a worm. Now the rear of Ra was running back to the Division of Ptah, and the front half was on us in their rout, some already falling under the first chariots of the first Hittites, while the survivors were staggering up to the shields and earthworks of the outer square of Amon. In this clamor, we saw the sky become as dark as the metal in an infantryman's dagger.

## 2.

"I could tell you," said Menenhetet to our own Pharaoh, and to my mother and father, "of how we spoke of this battle later, when each man would tell it to his own advantage. Then, it was only by comparing the lies that you could begin to look for the truth. But that was later. At this moment, there was nothing but noise, and much confusion. Yet I do not find it hard to remember how I felt through all of that long afternoon to follow when so many of us were nearer to the dead than the living, because I never felt so alive. I can still see the spear that passes to the left of my shoulder, and the sword that misses my head. Once more—it is as near to me as falling from my bed in a dream—I am thrown out from the Pharaoh's Chariot by the shock of a lance against my shield. It was the greatest battle of all wars, and in my four lives I never heard of anything like it. Of course, my mind did not speak to me on that day as on others, and it is true that the most unusual moments and the most unimportant passed equally like separate strangers, but I remember that in the instant when the clamor first beat about our camp, Usermare-Setpenere turned to me, and said, 'Take your shield and ride in My Chariot,' and I who had dreamed of this moment down the Nile, in the dust of Gaza, and through the mysteries of Tyre, could only nod my head and think that the work I had spent in sharpening the wheels of the chariot of Utit-Khent was work worse than lost, for Utit-Khent would probably cut his own leg off falling out of the chariot, and such is the shock of battle where events become as shattered as broken rocks whose pieces fly in all directions, so I was seeing fragments of what was yet to happen, and Utit-Khent certainly did fall out of his chariot, and his leg was mangled by the wheel I had sharpened even as his horses in panic ran over him.

"As I say, all I could feel at the instant was that I must now find my leather bag and my stone and begin to sharpen the wheels of His

Chariot. But even to have such a thought was stupid. A squad of soldiers—the Royal Guard of the Chariot-of-the-Mighty-Bull—were forever polishing the gold and silver filigree, and working many royal
stones on the treads—you could lose your finger running it along His
wheels. So I climbed up instead on the cage of the lion to get a better
view of all that was happening about us. Immediately, Hera-Ra started
roaring beneath like a drunken madman, hooking at his cage so furiously I almost fell off. Standing on those slats, the beast thumped my
feet with his tail and shoulders and head, while I looked in all four directions, my organs in an uproar to match a confusion of sights multi-
tudinous as the foam of the Very Green. I could certainly see the
King's square surrounded on all four sides, for the larger square built
in such haste by the soldiers of Amon was now lost. Beyond our square
was a chaos and a carnage. The Division of Amon were fleeing their
meals, their games, their tents, their wagon trains, and their animals.
While our inside square stood fast for the Pharaoh, outside I could see
no more than a few of ours to face hordes of Hittites overrunning us
so quickly they were caught already in their own rush. These Asiatics
were not riding in one careful rank behind another of charioteers in
perfect order the way we Egyptians like to advance, no, just a mob of
hundreds of chariots, three men in each, wearing odd yellow hats, nor
did they fight with bow and sword, but tried to run everything down
with their axes. In this din, our chariots, at least those still fighting,
kept weaving in and out, our charioteers, some even at this hour with
the reins around their waist, were pulling bows, quick as sparrows
fighting boars. The enemy was so big and clumsy that I even saw two
Hittite chariots crash into each other, three men in one catapulted out
even as the other three were hurled to the ground. Yet over every hill,
through these thin woods, came more ranks of Hittite chariots, some
at a run, some at a walk, and then I saw the nearest thirty or forty,
maybe a squadron, riding at a gallop toward the King's square itself.
They charged our breastworks, up and over, and nearly all spilled.
Those who did not, landed among the strongest of the Pharaoh's
Sherdens who seized these Asiatic horses by the bridle, and held their
footing long enough to turn the horses' necks and halt the chariot, at
which moment, other Sherdens ripped the horses' bellies with their
daggers. Then they pulled off the Hittites. Of the thirty who charged
into our square, not one was left, and I, like a boy quick with excitement on the cage of Hera-Ra, had only an instant to see that the
Pharaoh, His head down, His eyes closed, was still praying. Out of His
mouth I heard these words: 'In the Year Five of My Reign, third

month of the third season, on this Day Nine of Epiphi, under the majesty of Horus, I, Ramses Meri-Amon, the Mighty Bull, Beloved of Maat, King of Upper and Lower Egypt, Son of Ra Who am given life forever'—so I heard Him call on all His names, and even as a shaduf lifts its pail of water up the hill, so was my Pharaoh pumping up His blood as though the very water of the Land of the Dead must be lifted into His heart until He feared no death, and the dead as well as the living would listen: 'I, Who am mighty in valor, strong as a bull, Whose might is in My Limbs like fire'—so He kept speaking while on the battleground of woods and fields outside our square I saw a horse go over backward with an arrow in its neck, down on its own chariot with its own three Hittites, and one of our charioteers with a short spear in his chest fell forward onto the shaft between his two horses. On their backs, everywhere, were dead men staring at the sky. The nearest was farther away than I could throw a stone, yet, brilliant as a bird's eye was his eye. I could see it. Near him lay another dead man clutching his genitals. Then I saw a man whose arm was caught in the hub of a chariot wheel, and a Hittite came along and hacked at his head with an axe. All the while, most of our army was running into the woods. I could not believe in what panic were the men of Amon.

"Now my Pharaoh had finished praying and He unhooked the door to the cage of Hera-Ra, who came out. Then, to my surprise, Usermare-Setpenere leaped into His Chariot on the driver's side. I, thereby, to the other, and He rode in a circle through our square, nearly striking some of our own men as He called, 'We are going to attack. We are going to attack.'

"Six chariots, seven, now eight, followed in our circle. Others saluted but did not move until the next time around. Now others joined, but not enough.

" 'Follow Me,' said Usermare-Setpenere, and with a force of twenty chariots, He rode at full speed to the southern side of our square, choosing the lowest place in the earth wall, and we drove over it and down the other side, banging against one another badly; but then we were on the field, Hittite chariots before us in every direction, and, when I dared to look behind, half of our force was still with us. The other half had not dared to make it over the wall. We were surrounded already, if you could speak in such a way when our Pharaoh, having pumped the courage of the dead into every one of His limbs, not to speak of the force of Strength-of-Thebes and Maat-is-Satisfied, fastest horses of any land, and Hera-Ra bounding at our side, his roars louder than an avalanche of rock down a cliff, were, all of us, galloping through every bewilderment of battle so fast that none, not even our own men, could keep up with us, although some tried. The Hittites parted before our passage, as well as any poor Egyptians from Amon or Ra whom we passed, and for the length of a field, through a wood, and down another field, not one arrow was shot at us, not one did we shoot, and no Hittite came near, not man nor chariot—perhaps they were all afraid of the brilliance of the chariot of Usermare-Setpenere and the face of Hera-Ra, bounding beside us.

"Behind, like a tail that becomes so stretched the end must pull off, were our charioteers. I knew what it cost to keep up with the Pharaoh over rough ground, and only a few stayed with us now. When I dared to look, for I felt as if my good life depended on keeping eyes to the front, I could see how some of our men were surrounded by Hittites, and some had turned back, or were fighting their way back, and still my Ramses the Second galloped south, no one more happy, nobody so brave, nobody so handsome—He looked as if the sun shone out of His eyes. 'We'll break through,' He shouted, 'and find the troops of Ptah. We'll kill these fools when we come back,' and with that, we met a hundred Hittite chariots waiting in the next field.

"Now I saw more battle than a man could fight. Never will I be certain how many of our chariots were still with us, if any. For when our Ramses drove with His golden vehicle full-force into the center of these heavy Hittite carts with their three men, there was nothing for the next few minutes I saw whole. So I saw the spear that came at my shield and the axe that just missed my head. I saw Hera-Ra leap across three men of one chariot onto the horses of another. I saw him hanging upside-down with his muzzle on a horse's neck. Hidden from the arrows of the Hittite charioteers, he clung to the horse, his jaw on the blood of the stallion's throat, the claws of his hind legs opening the belly, until the horse stood up in such extremity of pain that his mate stood up too, both screaming, and they fell backward on their drivers, even as Hera-Ra leaped from the horse to a man and bit off an arm, or most of an arm, I could not believe what I saw, all from the side of my eye, between the movements of my shield, a hundred arrows seeming to come at once, all at the Pharaoh, as if no one could think of the horses nor of me in view of His golden presence. Those arrows were wild, but not the ones I blocked. They came at us hard as birds flying full tilt into a wall, and their points came through the leather of my shield, evil as the nose of your enemy.

"All the while, Ramses the Second would draw His bow and loose an arrow at full gallop, swerve by one Hittite chariot, then another, and was so adept we could stop, wheel, then charge away to stop short again as chariots converged on ours. 'Your sword,' He shouted, and there, not moving, two of us against three on either side, we fought back to back with our swords against their six axes, only it was not so unequal as that, for Hera-Ra charged one chariot, then another, and with such bloody fury that others did not come near, and we were free again, we had broken through, we were on our way to the south once more, we could reach the Division of Ptah, so we thought, so we shouted to each other, only to find another hundred Hittites facing us in still another phalanx.

"Sometimes a few of our own chariots caught up so we were not always alone, but five times we fought like this, five times we drove into a mass of men and horses so thick the only forest you saw was swords, armor, axes, horses, limbs, and chariots turning over. Vehicles raced by empty of riders, and ran into one another. The trees quivered. Ramses' great bow, which nobody but He could draw, had a force to drive its arrow through a man so hard it could knock him from the chariot to the ground, yet these sights I saw in fragments like the eye of a face on the shard of a pot. So, for instance, did I see a Hittite hold up a man who was expiring in the flood of a wound, while two others galloped away in a chariot without reins. The third Hittite had fallen off already. Many a soldier was trampled by horses or run over by wheels—I saw so many of those Hittite wheels with their eight spokes that I dreamed of them for years, foul dreams, the little wheels puckered as a strange anus, and there were sights full of folly: I even saw a Hittite attacking his own horse in harness; such was the fever that the fellow killed the beast with his axe. Maybe it had tried to run him down. I did not know, I never saw more, I was ducking a blow, sticking a lance, or reeling from the impact of the Pharaoh's body against me when He slammed our horses through a sharp turn, once I even fell off, landed on my feet and jumped up again. My lungs knew the fire of the Gods. I saw Hera-Ra leap at three men, who stood motionless in their chariot, transfixed by the loss of their horses. They were still looking at their useless reins as he clawed down on them.

"Loose horses were everywhere. I saw one on broken front legs, trying to rear, and a charioteer lay on the ground, holding the tail of this horse until the animal flopped around to bite him. Another man was all alone in his wagon, his horses walking in stupor with loose reins. Then the man fainted, and I saw him slide to the ground. To the other flank was a riderless horse trying to crawl into a fallen chariot. It was a madness. One pair of horses, stripped of all three men, tried to dash over a collision of other chariots but stumbled, and the empty chariot catapulted overhead while the horses stampeded into the ground. I never heard such a scream come from animals before. The worst was a howl from a steed Usermare-Setpenere struck in the chest with an arrow when it tried to leap between our stallion and mare. Everywhere, beasts in panic were defecating as they ran. On it went. We would think we had broken through the Hittites only to see another phalanx to the south, and we would attack again, even break through, but on the sixth attempt, we saw a thousand Hittites coming toward us in orderly formation.

" 'It can't be done,' I said to Him, 'we can't get out!' He glared at me then as if I were the worst coward ever seen, and said, 'Strengthen your heart. I will lay them in the dust!' I looked at those thousand soldiers and at my King's face, and in it was the expression I have seen in the eyes of mad beggars when they believe they are sons of the Pharaoh, yes, my Ramses the Second could swear to destroy all who called themselves Hittites, and I could feel His certainty so powerfully that I believed in it myself, although in a different way, and I said, 'Let us return, my King, to Your Pavilion, and we will gather Your troops and fight and destroy these Hittites from there,' and on that word, He wheeled our horses and we went charging back to the north, back to the remnants of the King's square that was two hills, three fields, and I do not know how many small woods away.

"There were enemy everywhere, and none of our chariots to be seen, yet no Hittites came to intercept us. They were all too busy plundering the deserted camp of the Division of Amon. So we swept back into the King's square and heard the cheers of all the men who were left. Officers came running forward as we halted, telling in great excitement how they had defended our square by the north side, the south side, the west, and even by the river until the Hittites had retreated—with all their thousands, they had failed to take the square—but Ramses listened with wrath. To hear of their exploits, you would have thought we had none of our own, yet the arrows were still sticking in the quilting of our horses and the face of Hera-Ra was more red with the blood of the Hittites than the chest of a man laid open with a sword. I could not believe how red was the brightness of blood when you saw a great deal of it."

Menenhetet paused. "In what I have told you, there is not the heart of what I truly felt. Those sentiments were magnificent. During all that time we tried to break through to the south, I had been like a God, I felt twice my size—even as They are twice our height—and I was four times my strength, even as Gods know the power of four arms for each of Their shoulders. Never had I been so tireless in so heavy a work, and never was my breath so close to Them. I could have fought through the afternoon and night with the love I knew for Ramses and the horses and all that came forth from how we moved together. Often as not, I had no more than to think of a quick turn to the left for my King to perform the move, and, as if given vision in the back of my head, knew to swing my shield when a flight of arrows came down on us, never did I know as in those moments that we live for Them to see us, see us well, and thereby let us feel like Gods ourselves. I could no more have fled from the field than cut off my feet, at least so long as the Gods were with me, yet I lost them in the instant I saw the chariots of the thousand Hittites, except I do not know if I really did, for I was not full of fear when I saw that frightening sight, merely cool and calm and tired, my arm was suddenly heavy, and the voice that spoke to me was the same God's voice I heard in the flame of the hottest combat, still the same voice now said in my ear, 'Do not let this fool attack, or you are both dead,' and I say to You that the voice was amused—it is the word—It was amused, yet so fine and quiet a voice I could swear I did not hear from Amon with His mighty tongue but the soft tone of Osiris Himself. Who else would dare to speak of my Pharaoh as a fool? Only the Lord Osiris Who gave me the advice to return quickly to the King's Pavilion. And so I said to myself, 'Even if I am the son of Amon, it is Osiris who saved me today.'

"Now we were back in the middle of the Household Guard, and in the joy of our return, so did I feel the strength of the Gods once more. My height doubled again, at least to myself, and I desired combat so much I felt the swelling of my member, and did not know whether to laugh or cry out in exultation. I saw Hera-Ra bounding about, licking our soldiers' faces with his bloody face, and mighty for a cat was his member, also fully extended, he was one in good spirits with me. I do not know if it was the blood on the field or the jubilation of these troops that they had held their square, maybe it was the early fermentation of the dead bodies around us before their seven souls and spirits had begun to depart, but I can only say that the air in our nostrils was like a rose at evening when the light of the sun is also the color of rose, just so fine smelled the air with our desire for new combat. I thought again of my mother's story at how she awoke at my father's side and a God brilliant in the gold of His breastplate was above her, and the hut was filled with a perfume lovelier than any she had ever smelled.

"Now I knew what she had known, and it was equal to the tender odor of this air, and whether we owed it to Amon or Osiris, I could hardly say, but I was moved to climb onto the cage of Hera-Ra, and this so pleased him that he, in turn, walked with humorous thumps of his paws into the space beneath where he began to purr. Only then did I look out to all four sides, and the Hittites with their thousand chariots and a thousand more behind were walking their horses toward us in two great semicircles coming in from the west and the south. To our north was devastation. All of Amon and Ra were long departed, and I saw nothing but corpses, abandoned chariots, shattered tents, and provision wagons being plundered now by the Hittites on the field. The wisdom of Osiris must still have been with me, for I whispered to my King, 'At the east by the river, the line of Asiatics is thin.' It was true—fewer Hittites were there than on any of the other sides of our square, indeed the river was not two hundred paces away, and so He, adding the force of Amon to the mind of Osiris, shouted to the brave Household troops on all our four fronts, 'Come with Me. To the river!' Leaving our flanks and rear unprotected, Ramses mounted His Chariot and we took off at a gallop, followed by our remaining chariots, and foot soldiers from all four sides.

"There were not fifty steps from our line of shields on the east side to their line, and we crossed before you could blink three times. That was just as well since I never saw so many arrows coming our way. They surprised me. A moment before, these Hittites by the river had been somnolent, as desultory in shooting at us, as we at them. So long as arrows went back and forth from one entrenchment to another, you collected what fell, and soon the arrows you returned to the Hittites were sent back again. All the same, I was amazed at the number that now came at us as we galloped across. I heard foot soldiers cry out as they were struck, and then in the full shock of combat, for so it is, full shock, we slammed into the shields before us, and our good horses, Maat and Thebes, took us up over the earthworks of the Hittites, and we came down on their chariots with all our own chariots behind us.

"I do not know what it is like to fall into a river and be dashed over rocks. Since I cannot swim, I will never know, except I do, for the golden chariot of my King, stronger than any beast and beautiful as a God, was met by three Hittite chariots at once. With nine men, six horses, and three heavy carts did we collide, and all four of the vehicles went over, I think, it is certain we did. I remember striking the ground and the King with me, and our chariot coming over on us, its wheel, much blunted now, still scoring my back, then we were bouncing up and the horses were trumpeting, and even as I was coming off the ground, so His Chariot was up again as well, I do not know how unless it kept tumbling with the horses, it was His, after all, and we jumped on once more, and rode in a circle, firing arrows into the Hittites. With it all, these collisions, bumps, falls, and recoveries had been happening as slowly as you would slide down a mountain in a dream. Never had I had as much time to arrange my body for each new shock, nor been this quick with my feet.

"Neither can I tell You how well we fought. It was nothing like the maneuvers we had practiced for years, no orderly sweep of rank on rank, no herding of infantry into a corner, no, we were in a rush to drive them to the river and fast, very fast, before other Hittites overran the King's square we had just left. Maybe it was the desperation of where we were, no front, no rear, no flanks, and probably no King's Pavilion to return to, but we fought like Hera-Ra, and so great was our lust to win a victory on this dreadful day that we were forever jumping in and out of our chariots, Ramses and I often fighting back to back, and many a soldier we wounded, and more than a few we killed, and back to our chariot against new Hittites. Everywhere I could see our vehicles circling their heavy carts with our skillful turns. On the ground, the Nubians were impaling Hittites with their short spears. I saw a man bite the nose off another man, and more than one Nubian had his yellow sash turn red. Three Hittites galloped by, and one of them had an axe in his hand and an arrow in his buttocks. He kept looking backward as if to see who had bitten him.

"We drove them all into the river. Foot soldiers, chariots, charioteers, even their Princes. It was fierce, but our swords were strong, our desperation was the virtue of war itself, and snorting, sobbing, growling at each other, charioteers on foot and infantrymen so crazed they leaped up on loose horses, we fought them to the edge of the embankment of the river, and then one Hittite chariot went over, down the bank and into the stream, a scream, a splash, they were washing away. Speak of rock and a rapid river, the river was narrow here and deep, and downstream a rapids began with many rocks. The first chariot to go shattered on those rocks, and I heard water swallow up the middle of a man's cry.

"Now, river at their back, the desperation of these Hittites matched our own, but we were close to a triumph here and our soldiers were berserk. Since we had overrun their campfires, some of us seized burning branches and hurled them, and I even saw a Sherden swinging a leg of half-cooked beef, and Hittites fought back with torches, and with daggers, and sword against sword, and axe against sword. We pushed them all in, every last man who had not fallen on the field, and the few who clung to the slope of the wet and precipitous bank were struck in the face with arrows, although one of our Nubians was so emblazoned by now with the heat of battle that he slid down the bank to push a Hittite in, and failed. Both men drowned instead, biting at each other, arms around each other's throats.

"What a sight! We stood at the riverbank and cheered, breathless and sobbing we cheered. It sounded like the demented wails you hear in a funeral procession, and over the water we looked, and there were sights no one would ever see again. A horse was swimming downstream with a Hittite trying to climb its back, and falling off, and trying again until he slipped off and drowned, but the horse reached the other bank, and other Hittites pulled the animal out of the water. There was a Prince washed up next, that I knew by his purple raiment, and the Hittites held him upside-down until I could not believe the liquid that poured out of the man's throat, and later I heard he was the Prince of Aleppo, no less. So I saw royalty held by its heels, and then my eye flew to another Hittite, who was sinking. Clearly I saw him wave farewell to the land as he went under the water, and another man swept by right beneath me, his arms around his horse's neck as if he would kiss the creature, and he was speaking to his animal, I heard him weep with love before the rocks struck him and the horse. Behind him went a man who had already drowned, but so fat he floated with an arrow in his belly. I even saw one soldier make it with his animal to the other bank, and crawl ashore and lie there dying from a wound. As he expired, his horse licked his hand.

"Then we saw the Hittites come out on the other bank of the river. Out of the woods they emerged, too far for any of our arrows to reach, and I, practiced at making a quick count of a hundred men in a field, or a thousand, here saw something like eight thousand. I was happy they were on the other side of the river at this place where there was no ford, though I must say so soon as our Ramses saw them, that was equal to destroying His pleasure at what we had gained, whatever it was.

" 'Attack again,' He cried. 'To the west.'

"I never knew if my King was wise in battle, but then wisdom is a word by which one judges a man not a God, and He never looked to see if His command was followed. Instead He charged back over the old camping ground that lay within the entrenchment of our four sides, and everywhere were plundering Hittites, their backs to us and their faces to the ground. Like maggots on meat, they were as blind. The fools were so hungry for spoil they had stopped short of bearing down on us from the rear while we were at the river. Instead, they attacked our riches. Two hundred of them were ransacking the King's Pavilion when we came back. We set fire to them there. In that way I could never understand my Pharaoh. No one loved His treasures more than Himself, yet so great was His heat in battle that He was the first to pick up a burning log and throw it on His tents, and a hundred of us added to the blaze, indeed our chariots ran a relay from the campfire to the fine stuff of His tent itself. Its walls were now collapsing upon the Hittites plundering within, and as they ran out, their beards on fire, their woolen capes on fire, even their groins on fire, our Nubians met them with short clubs, and cracked the heads of these fools on fire, twice fools for they died with the plunder in their arms. The stink of the leather of the King's burning tents was even worse than the odor of burning flesh. Yet the smell was like a marrow to give us blood for the battle. I felt vigor in my sword, as if even the metal could know exhaustion and look for new spirit.

"We destroyed the Hittites in the King's Pavilion and came down like a scourge on the petty plunder of the wagon trains. We took back our four sides and were a square again. Again, we gave a cheer. The two semicircles of Asiatic chariots who had been advancing upon us at a walk now stopped some hundreds of paces from our lines. They, too, were busy at plundering, but it was their own infantrymen they stripped. For those soldiers were still picking up the spoil left behind by the troops of Amon until the Hittite chariots scourged them like big animals eating little animals.

"Now the King's Pavilion was down. Its leather was consumed. White ashes lay on the ground, and some still glowed. My Ramses said, 'Who will bring Me our God?' and the Captain of the Nubians pointed his finger at one of his blacks, a giant of a man with a huge belly, something in build like Amon Himself, and the black stepped into the hot ash and ran to the middle of the fallen tents, picked up the blackened statue—may I say it took all his strength—and staggered out. Given its weight, the Nubian had to hold it against his body, and his breast was burned, and his belly, his hands, his forearms, and his feet, yet once he had set the God down by my King's feet, so did Usermare-Setpenere kiss him, kiss this black—what honor could be so great as for a black to be kissed by the Pharaoh?—and then my Ramses knelt beside Amon, and in the tenderest voice began to speak to Him, talking only of His great love equal to the rapture of the sky at evening, and He took one end of His skirt and wiped all that was black from the God's face, kissing the God on the lips even though His own mouth blossomed at once into two great blisters which He wore in combat. A frightening sight it made, for now He could only speak out of the swollen rope of His upper and lower lips.

"I would have wondered at the power of the black to bear such pain, and even the love for Amon that would lead my Pharaoh to seek such pain, but at that moment a broken feather flew loose from the headdress of Maat-is-Satisfied and drifted to my feet. When I picked it up, the feather was heavy with the blood and grime of battle and moved in my hand like a knife, it had weight. I knew enough to kiss it. So soon as I did, a terrible heat went out of my Pharaoh's lips into mine, and, lo, I, too, was now to fight with white and swollen blisters upon my lips.

"Can I tell You of the rest of the day? Our battle, You remember, had begun under a dull and heavy sky. In that gloom, so strange to our Egyptian eyes, the sweat was cold on our bodies whenever we paused for breath, and our thirst was dry and cold and as desperate in our throats as our situation itself. Now it was easier, and on these scenes, the skies parted, and the Sun was revealed. We were warm in the late afternoon and grew stronger. It was then my Pharaoh lost all sense of how much we were outnumbered. Without a word to any but myself, out of the very warmth He felt from the Sun, and the burn on His mouth, with the reins hardly flogging our good horses, and Maat and Thebes no longer horses to me, but giants, may I say, in the bodies of horses this day, so did He gallop toward the largest circle of Hittites and at such a speed that we came to where they had put up the tent of the Hittite leaders, and in that place, before their phalanxes, alone with me again, my King approached their flags and standards. We were all but surrounded by a circle of the Asiatics' chariots. Hera-Ra roared at them with such fury that I think each enemy was afraid to draw his bow for fear the lion might attack his face alone. I do not know why they did not charge, but there was peace for this moment on the battleground as if no one could move, and even Hera-Ra was silent at last.

" 'I am with Amon in the great battle,' said Ramses the Second, I am the Lord of Light,' and He raised His sword until the sun glittered upon it, and then jumped down from His chariot, and walked ten steps toward the Hittite leaders.

" 'Tie the lion,' He commanded me, and He waited, sword in hand, until I tethered Hera-Ra to our chariot. Then He held up the forefinger of His hand as a way of saying He wanted to fight their best soldier.

"From the Hittite leaders came forth a Prince with a terrible face. His beard was lean, and one eye was as flat as a stone, the other was bright. He, too, was dismounted, and in the moment Usermare saw him, I think my King was not at ease.

"They began to fight. The Hittite was fast and his movements were even quicker than the strokes of my Good and Great God. If this Prince had been as strong with his blade as my King, it would have ended soon, but Usermare attacked with such force that the other went back in a circle away from His great arm. Still, the Hittite's parries blocked the sword of the Sun from above and below, and now, given the chance, he struck back. Behold, there was blood on my King's leg. He limped now, and moved more slowly, and the look in His eye was not good. He breathed like a horse. I could not believe it—the sword of the Hittite grew bolder. Soon he began to attack, and my Lord retreat. The weight of all these hours of fighting was on His mouth, and, then, fending an overhead blow from the Prince, my Ramses' nose was broken by His own shield. I thought He was lost, and it may be that He was, but the end of the fight was interrupted. For the lion had become so agitated that I had to cut him loose from the tether or he would have turned on the horses.

"The Hittite, seeing the beast bound toward him, lost no time running back to his own people, and, Usermare, much fatigued, leaned on His sword. The lion licked His face. A sound like the bellowing of hippopotami came forth from the Hittites, and I was certain they would charge us where we stood. If so, we were done. Usermare might not have the strength to lift His sword, and then the lion and I would be alone. Yet at that moment, a Hittite trumpet blew. I heard a call for their retreat. Now, to my astonishment, they moved out quickly, leaving their royal tent behind.

"I was certain of a trap. I could not believe they would leave such spoils for us. Not when they were so strong. Yet in the next moment, I saw their reason. The Division of Ptah had come on to the field at last. The phalanxes of its chariots were moving up fast from the south. So the Hittites were now in a rush to reach the gates of Kadesh before Ptah crossed the line of their retreat. We had been left alone on the field.

"I think my King had a vision then. It was other sights He saw. I can only tell you that He staggered across to the abandoned tent and emerged with a bull in His arms made of gold. It was the God of these Asiatics, and had great furled wings, and the face, not of a bull, but of a beautiful man with a long Syrian beard. It also had the pointed ears of a monster, and a castle in the shape of a tower was its hat. I had never seen a God like this. He was screaming now, in some harsh language of the Asiatics, a hideous host of lamentations, and must have been naming all the larger catastrophes, locusts, and boils for being deserted by His troops. In truth, it was the most horrible voice I ever heard. It spoke through the blistered lips of my Pharaoh, the oaths resounding in Usermare's throat until He threw the God to the ground. Whereupon fumes came from the mouth, yes, from the golden mouth of this bull-beast came smoke, I swear it. I did not know how my Pharaoh could be called the Mighty Bull of Amon, yet here before us was another bull, also a God, with wings, and a beard. It was then I saw the face of the secret whore of Kadesh. It was her features I saw on the winged bull, a beautiful woman's face with a beard. So I knew that the cries of this voice came from Metella's God. We were hearing His agony that the battle was lost. Maybe it is in war that you come to the place where the rainbow touches the earth, and much that has been hidden is simple.

### 3.

"With the departure of the Hittites, the fields were empty. We were alone, as I say, and Hera-Ra raised his head and gave a lonely cry. It was a sound of much confusion as if the animal did not know whether we were victorious or desolate. In the distance I could see the legions of Ptah give up their attempt to reach the gates of Kadesh before the Hittites. They wheeled instead toward the King's square. Yet my Pharaoh disdained to raise an arm to greet them. We returned over these bloody anguished fields to the sound of many an injured cry and more than a few of the dying to give us a cheer. One fellow even managed to make a sound with his head half off. You saw nothing but the hole in his neck out of which he seemed to speak. My Pharaoh, however, ignored the pandemonium with which our soldiers cheered and as we came through the opening of our square, He drove to the ruins of His Pavilion in silence. He did not dismount.

"Even as His officers came toward us, bowing, then crawling forward on their knees, so did He speak only to the horses. 'You,' He said, 'are My great horses. It is you who rode with Me to repulse the nations, and you were under My hand when I was alone with the enemy.' If there had been sparks when He struck the sword of others in combat, now there was flame in His eye as He looked at His officers. They did not even dare to beat their heads to the ground. 'Here,' He said, pointing to the horses, 'are My champions in the hour of danger. Let them know a place of honor in My stables, and let their food be given to them when I am fed.' Now, He stepped down from His Chariot and caressed each of their noses. They gave an answer in voices full of pleasure. Their feathers were in shreds and their hides were red, their legs shivered in fatigue, but they called forth a thanks to Him. Then my Ramses heard the voice of His officers.

" 'O Great Warrior,' they cried out. It was a babble, however, of one hundred names of praise in six or seven languages, and all in a rush. 'O Twice-a-Great-House,' they cried, 'You have saved Your Army. There is no King that fights like You.'

" 'You,' He said to them in return, 'did not join Me. I do not remember the names of those who are not beside Me when I am in the midst of the enemy. But here is Meni who is My shield,' and He put His arm about me, and patted my buttock as if I were a horse. 'Look,' He said to all those officers. 'With My sword I have struck down thousands, and multitudes have fallen before Me. Millions have been repulsed.'

"They all cheered," said my great-grandfather. "Some had fought, and some had even fought a lot. Many were bloody with their wounds. Yet they listened in shame and lowered their heads and when the Generals of the Division of Ptah came forward to greet our Monarch at this reunion, He did not thank them for saving the day, nor reward His son Amen-khep-shu-ef for the rigors of that ride to join the legions of Ptah, but only remarked, 'What will Amon say when He hears that Ptah left Me alone on this great day? I slaughtered the enemy beneath My wheels but other chariots were not there, and neither was My infantry. I, and I alone, was the tempest against their chiefs.'

"We could only bow. A desolation worse than the swords of the Hittites was being felt. His officers touched the ground, they struck their heads, they lamented. I, in the most peculiar of positions, also bowed, but out of caution, and tried to keep from smiling. I thought that perhaps I was in error and should, unlike the others, remain standing so that my King should never mistake me for them, and I wondered if His mind had not taken a wrench from the screams of that Asiatic God who roared out of His throat. I did not know, but my King was soon silent and sat by Himself, alone by the blackened statue of Amon, and with the linen of His own skirt cleaned the soot from the belly and limbs of Amon, and pressed His forehead to the golden brow in a long embrace.

"We surrounded Him in silence. We waited. As the gold of the late afternoon lowered with the sun, and evening was near, He said,

'Tell the men they may begin the counting of the dead.' By these words the Officers knew they might speak to Him again.

"Yet, I know He lifted His head from the brow of Amon with the greatest regret. So long as He sat with His forehead touching the golden forehead of the Great God, so did He see a sunset behind His closed eyes and feel the peace of our Egyptian wisdom enter His mind and pass into the scourged flesh of His throat and mouth. I could not believe it but when He looked up, the blisters were gone from His lips. (They still remained on mine.) So I could see that in all the splendor of the pure gold out of which Amon was made, there was also balm as cool as dew. What merits in this metal of the Sun!

"Soon, the counting of the hands was begun. We used to lay the hands of thieves in a heap outside the gate of the palace, even as we do now, but, in that time of Ramses the Great, the counting of hands was also done after battle. Usermare-Setpenere stood in His Chariot and soldiers came forward in a line from the Household troops to be followed by the soldiers of Amon. Many hundreds, then thousands of these soldiers passed one by one before the Pharaoh on this night even though we did not know yet if all of the battle had taken place or it was only the first day. Metella still had his infantry and his chariots, and both were inside the gates of Kadesh. They might come out to-morrow. So we could not say whether we had won or must get ready for the dawn. But the field where we fought this afternoon was ours for tonight, and that is like having another man's woman. She may go back to him tomorrow, but no one can tell you tonight that you have lost. So the longer this evening went on, the more it became a night of pleasure. As if in contempt for that enemy who had gone behind his walls, we lit so many campfires that the field was scarlet and gold, and its light prevailed through the darkness like a glow of sunset on one of those miraculous evenings when night itself still hovers, or so it seems, on the last, and then the very last, and then beyond the last light of evening and nobody loses their shadow. So was our field luminous on this night, and the light came from that part of the sun which entered the trees in their youth, and now came forth again while the wood was ablaze.

"All through the night, our fires burned, and through the same night, Usermare-Setpenere stood in His Chariot under a full moon and received the severed hands of the slain Hittites one by one. Since He spoke to no one but the soldier who came before Him on His right hand, and then to the scribe who sat at His left hand entering the name of the fellow bringing in the trophy, so was I able to move away often and come back. Yet on all that long evening, for so long indeed as the line lasted, so did Usermare-Setpenere stand in the same place on His Chariot and never move His feet. I realized once again how to be near Him was to gain all knowledge of how a God might act when He is in the form of a man. He looks so much like a man and yet reveals divinity by even the smallest of His moves. In this case, it was that He did not move His feet. To receive a thousand men, and another thousand, then another, to take into one's right hand the severed hand of a man dead since this afternoon, or dead in the last hour—we were still killing our prisoners—to inquire the name of the soldier who has given over to you this cold hand, or this warm hand, then tell it to the scribe, then throw the hand on the pile without ever moving one's feet, was an exhibition of such poise that one saw the mark of a God. He never moved His feet. Each time He cast another hand onto the pile, and may I say the pile grew until it was the size of a tent, He threw it with the same grace by which He steered Maat and Thebes when the reins were about His waist, that is, He did the task perfectly. One could not think of another way to have done it. He was showing us the nature of respect. The right hand of a dead warrior, the same right hand that might have seized His own in a treaty, having been given to Him, so did He cast it onto the pile with care, and to the place where by His eye it belonged. The pile grew like a pyramid whose corners are rounded, and never did He allow the base to become too broad nor the top too blunted. Yet He was also careful to avoid the vanity of building too fine a peak, for then one misplaced throw could destroy the shape. No, these hands were added to the pile in a harmony between the height and the base that was equal to the harmony with which our Ramses received His soldiers." Here Menenhetet closed his eyes as if to recollect whether it was all so perfect as in his description.

When he began to speak again, he said, "You may be certain that the calm of this ceremony was not matched by the scenes on our campground so recently a battlefield, and now a campground again. It is one matter to kill a man in battle, another to find time at that instant to cut off his hand. Oh, there were sights even in the worst of it when your chariot was overturned, yet through the spokes you'd still see one of ours on his knees sawing away at the wrist of some Hittite he'd just dropped. You'd even see some fellows so blind and red-faced for their trophies that they did not see the Hittite who came up behind, killed them, and started to cut off their lips, the lips! Can you imagine if we had lost the battle to the Asiatics this day?

"You can see then that no good soldier would stop to claim a hand during the tides in and out of such a battle. Figure then the disputes that arose among us that evening when men who had been the bravest on the field were without a prize at night. Those hands were worth much to a soldier. You were able to say your name to the Pharaoh, and have it put on a list. Benefits, even a promotion, could follow. Besides, it was humiliation to go through battle and not have a hand to show. What, after all, were you doing? I can promise that fights broke out. When one squadron of chariots who had fought with the King's Household discovered that a company of infantrymen from Amon, the first to run, were now approaching the Pharaoh's line with a larger collection of hands than the charioteers themselves, a second war nearly began among our own. Soon the officers were in a council to make peace on this matter.

"They knew there would be terrible argument unless they agreed on some allotment. A fracas could spew forth in front of the Pharaoh. So, forcibly, we had to declare how many Hittites were slain by each company. That way we could determine the numbers of hands to be passed out, platoon by platoon. If it came to five for every eight soldiers in one company, you may be certain the five strongest men then seized their hands regardless of how they had fought that afternoon. Let me tell you—more than one ear got bitten off in the little fights that continued. Given the outrage of real warriors who had been passed over, not to speak of the bravado of many a big fellow who had been a coward earlier but was not remembering it that way now, we embarked on a night I will not soon forget. Another fifty of our own must have perished before the darkness was done.

"It was worse with the captured Hittites. Wherever one was not guarded by brave and responsible officers, he soon lost his right hand. More than a few bled to death. More than a few had the stump bound with a leather thong and went on to live and be brought back to Egypt. Naturally, they could expect the prosperous future of a slave with one hand. All the while, those of our men who had not been allotted a trophy went searching the bloody ground with their torches, and some even dared to cut the hands off our own slain, although to be caught in such an act was equal to losing your arm. After all, everyone's trophy would be tainted tomorrow if some of the hands proved to be Egyptian, so, count on it, every dead soldier of ours who was found mutilated at the wrists was stripped of his few clothes and his face soon made unrecognizable—I will spare you more. Even so, the corpse still looked like one of ours in the morning. With or without a face, a dead and naked Egyptian does not look like a naked Asiatic. We have less hair on our bodies.

"Speak of hair, these poor Hittites had beards like thickets and probably hoped to protect their necks from a sword. They also had hair on their head as tough as the hide of a helmet and that may have been to shield their skulls from our clubs. Small use now. Even a helmet cannot protect you from all blows. As the night went on, we used these captives, we gorged on them, we devoured them, of that I will speak. Everywhere was the comic if piteous sight of ten or twenty Hittites all tied with their hands behind their necks, the same cord binding them to the throat of the next fellow, until when told to walk, twenty would hobble along in a lockstep, their eyeballs squeezed out of the heads by terror, their necks at an angle, yes, so hunched up and bound together you could mistake them for a clump of figs on a string, except that these figs groaned frequently from the pain of their bonds. May I say their captors guarded them poorly. Any gang of soldiers who came blundering along could cut off the first or last on the line—it was too much work to untie a captive in the middle. Then you would see some sights in the blaze of the campfires. Many a poor Asiatic's beard was treated like the groin of a woman, and his buttocks as well; why, you would see five men working on one fellow who had already been turned into a woman, and one poor captive was even put into harness like a horse while our soldiers played with him as they would never dare play with a horse. This Hittite could not even get his mouth open to scream—it was filled near to choking. Picture the fury of the man who straddled his head.

"You would have thought with all the blood we had seen this day that some would want no more. But blood is like gold and feeds the appetite. You could not smell it enough and some could not even taste it to their full content. All of us, despite the discomfort of being covered by it, sticky with it, crusted over, came, sooner or later, to want more. It was like fresh cosmetic over old. Blood was now as fascinating as fire and nearer to us. You could never travel to the center of a fire, but the blood was here in everybody's breath. We were like the birds who collected in a million and infinity on this battlefield and would feed through the night on all they could tear from the flesh of the slain. They would fling themselves into the air with a heavy tilting of the earth as we came near and give a clap of sound like thunder, but it was only the uproar of their wings breaking away from us and the blood. Then there were the flies. They enraged us with their bites as if they now carried the fury of those we had killed. In the pestilence of those insects, I brooded much on the nature of wounds, and thought of how a man's power goes out of his flesh when he is injured, and travels into the arm of the man who gave the wound. On the other hand, so soon as you laid a cut into a man, you could treat his pain. If you were sorry for what you had done, you could spit on your hand and that might reduce the suffering of your victim. The Nubians had told me so. But if you wished to irritate his wound, you did well to drink hot and burning juices, or wine heated over a fire. Then would his wound be inflamed. So I was thinking of the Hittites who had given me the cuts and slashes I knew on my chest, my arms, and my legs, and I looked about until I could find a Hittite sword. All through the night, I oiled this blade and took care to bury it in cool leaves so that it would ease the festering of my body tomorrow. I also drank hot wine to irritate the wounds I had left on my enemies.

"I remember some of us even took the heads of Hittites and put them on long pointed sticks. While others held torches, we waved them aloft. We stood on one side of the river, across from the walls and gates of Kadesh, and we mocked them in the night while the banks began to stink from the early corruption of the bodies and would be a monstrosity in hot days to come.

"As we stood at the river, arrows came our way from the walls, not many, so few as to make me wonder at the thousands of Hittite soldiers who had not fought today—why were they silent with their arrows?—it hardly mattered now. We were so drunk that when one of us, a charioteer next to me, was struck with a spent arrow in his chest, the point going just deep enough to stick in his flesh, and thereby oblige him to remove it, he threw the head and shaft away, rubbed the wound with his hand, and with a laugh, licked the blood from his fingers. When his chest still bled, he painted his skin with it. When still it bled, he cut some locks from the beard of the dead Hittite on his pole and stuffed that into the hole in his chest."

"There is," said my mother in a sudden intrusion on this story, "nothing to compare to the monstrousness of men." As she spoke, I was close to her feelings, twice close because of pretending to be asleep, and I lived in her emotions once more. Never had her rage been greater at my great-grandfather, yet I could also feel her courage to scold him sink into itself as she looked at his face, for she was also much excited. Her belly had an ache of expectation that settled in my head like the pain of a tooth. It was enough to make me cry out.

Menenhetet merely shook his head. "On the other side of the river," he said, "at the top of a tower, was a woman who looked out at us and saw the Hittite whose beard had been shorn of a lock. She began to scream. Maybe it was the face of her lover that she recognized, or her husband, or a father or a son, but I tell you her shrieks tore the sky. Her moans were bottomless. I have heard women cry in that way ever since. We know those who make such sounds at any funeral. Hypocrisy is the possession of such women. For their grief speaks of the terrible end of all things in their heart, yet a year later that same woman will be with a new man."

My mother answered in a deep voice. "Women search," she said, "for the bottom of their grief. If they can find it, they are ready for another man. Why, if I were ever to weep for a lover and learn that my sorrow was bottomless, I would know he was the man I must follow into the Land of the Dead. But I cannot be certain of such feelings until I wail." She gave my great-grandfather a triumphant look, as if to say: Have you ever believed you could be that man?

Our Pharaoh, Ptah-nem-hotep, gave a small smile. "Your account, dear Menenhetet, has been so exceptional that I have had ten questions on every turn of the battle, yet I did not wish to divert your thoughts. Now, however, since Hathfertiti, out of the depth of her feelings, has spoken to you, let me ask: What are the sentiments of My ancestor, Usermare-Setpenere, during all of this, this dreadful night? Does He really see none of it? Do His feet, in truth, not move?"

"They never moved. I had been, as I said, standing near Him, and I would also, as I said, go away. When I came back the pile would be higher, but nothing else had changed, unless it was the mood of the Pharaoh. That grew more profound. No matter how well one came to know Him, even if you were to see Usermare-Setpenere every day, be certain you would not approach with ease. If you found Him jovial, then even from some paces away, you would feel the same as you did on entering a room full of sunlight. When He was angry, you were aware of that before coming through the door. On the battlefield, His fury was so great it served as our shield. The Hittites could not see into the dazzling light that came from His sword. The horses of our enemy were afraid to charge. One does not ride up to the sun!

"As this night went on, however, I saw He was not only the Beloved-of-Amon, Blessed-by-the-Sun, but also a King to live with the Lord Osiris in darkness and be familiar with the Land of the Dead. It is certain that the longer He conducted this ceremony of asking each soldier his name, repeating it to the scribe, and making a throw of the hand onto the pile, so did the weight of His presence grow heavier on me until I would have known with my eyes closed that I was somewhere in the presence of Ramses, just as a blind man can tell that he has stepped into a cave, even a large cave. On this night, my King filled the darkness, and the air near Him, unlike the fires of the camp-ground, the red lick of the flames, or the breath of us drunks, was an air cool with the chill of the cave. He was observing the spirits of the dead, or at least that much of them as could be known by their hands. Even as we appreciate something of a stranger by taking his fingers in greeting, so could my Ramses know a little about each of the enemy soldiers as He held their last manifest for an instant. So He under-stood a bit of the character of the fellow and his death. Never had I seen my Monarch brood in such a way, and His mood continued to deepen until it was much like the sound that holds your ears in the roar of the Very Green.

"Indeed, as I stood near Him, which is to say as I entered the cave He inhabited this night, I could not know if each thought I compre-hended was mine or my Pharaoh's. I only knew that the longer I looked at this pile of hands turning to silver in the moonlight, the more I thought of how the power of the Hittites was now in our pos-session, and we owned the field. They could not put the curse of their dead on us so long as our Pharaoh touched each evil thought in the hand of each lost soldier, and drew strength from it for future battles. So did my Pharaoh hold the fortunes of our Two-Lands together.

"I stayed so near to Him for so long that whenever I left to go wandering around the campground, I think I shared a part of His thoughts. Or maybe it was no more than the keenness of His nose for what was next. I know I was hardly surprised to come over a hillock and there between two rocks find Hera-Ra half-asleep under the full moon. I do not know if the lion had never been put back in his cage or whether some of our soldiers had set him loose, but he was quiet and only half-awake. Still, such were the fires of this night on this field just a hill away from the solemnities of our Pharaoh that Hera-Ra now gave a great broad grin at the sight of me, rolled over on his back, spread his legs, showed me the depth of his anus and the embrace of his front paws and invited me to roll on his belly. I never knew the day I would have been that brave. Not in four lives. I patted his mane, kissed him on the cheek. With a grunt and a growl, he rolled over again, got up, and burped in my face to give a sour whiff of all the blood he had drunk; but then, my breath with its wine could have pleased him no better. At any rate, we were now friends enough to go for a walk. I do not know if I ever felt any more life, health, and strength than making the tour of that flame-filled bloody field with ten thousand of our madmen spread over all of these meadows and a thousand fires you could look into for a carouse, yet I was the only one with a lion! It was a wealth of sights—more buttocks than faces!

"Let me say that there were also women among us. A company of camp followers had marched along with the Division of Set, for these were the soldiers last to arrive and they came in on the full moon. They were famous as a lot of fornicators and buggerers, this Division of Set. The tortures that had been tried up to now on the captured Hittites were nothing compared to the practices of the fresh troops who had just joined us.

"They had done little that day but march, and toward the end, as they got word of our victory out of the mouth of some messengers from the Division of Ptah, they had broken into their provisions and were drunk when they arrived. Now lines of men were waiting before each whore brought in by these soldiers from Set (who incidentally were collecting Hittite spoil in recompense). I saw more ways of making love that night than I would see again in three full lives. Since there were more men than women, it behooved you, if you had concern for your own buttocks, to see who was behind. I swear, it was a disgrace. Those Nubians are big, and it is the practice of their males to use one another until they are rich enough to afford a wife. On this night, woe to the poor Egyptian soldier if he waited in front of a Nubian, for he was soon on his knees, Egyptian or not. We are a smaller people. That night, a good deal of our strength was given over to the Nubians and the Libyans, and for what good return? To be able to shoot the few arrows you had left into the loose cave of a mongrel whore? The rush was so great in the fires of this night that many a man could not wait for his place at the front, and so took the girl between her cheeks, while she was busy up forward, and thereby made a three-backed beast, a copulation of serpents. Now, a new man was at her mouth, and another in the third man's bottom. They looked worse than those captives who had been tied like figs. Others, waiting, kept yelling, 'Hurry up, hurry up.' Over it all was the smell of sweat. I could smell the buttocks of half an army. A fit husband was that odor to blood and smoke. I would speak of these acts as abominations but it was less than what was yet to come. Besides, I will offer no judgment. After all, is not our word for a night-camp the same as one of our expressions for fornication? I can only say I was part of it, and much stimulated. I swear, if it were not the Night of the Pig, you would not know so much of this. Enough that Hera-Ra and I moved through campfires and snoring drunks, through lovers and plunderers and scavengers, even past the groans of our wounded—for in the middle of it all, men were still dying, our men mostly (theirs already gone)— our amputees and our belly-gutted fevered, dying first of thirst, then of wine given them to drink. Sometimes you could not tell the oaths of pleasure from the wails of the doomed. Through such cries did Hera-Ra and I walk among the flames. Occasionally the lion would trample over a group of copulators, squeezing their grapes, so to speak, and many a soldier, catching the breath of the lion in his nose, or the wild look in his eye (and Hera-Ra, even when feeling like a kitten, had the wildest pale-green eye anyone had ever seen), would, staring face to face with such a beast, lose his erection for this night and more. Such frights, like a sword, cut you off. The whores, be it said, loved Hera-Ra. I have never seen women so insatiable, so brutal, so superior in pure joy—it is their art, not a man's. Even in this riot, where one came forth so much more than one wanted that the joys were like the throes of one's death, it was still extraordinary with these women. They were only camp whores with putrid breath, but I saw the gates of the Heavenly Fields open in my loins—these women took the sweetest shoots right into the center of themselves. It must have been all the blood and burning flesh. Maybe Maat approaches with love when all are choking with smoke. You have to wonder how many Generals are conceived on campgrounds such as this.

"But I spoke of burning flesh. You cannot know the hunger that comes to your stomach on a battlefield. It mocks the hunger of your private parts. I was ravenous, and Hera-Ra was ravenous. All of our army was hungry, and after we ate all we had plundered from the Hittites, we broke into our own provision trains. I saw salted quarters of beef thrown into the fire, then pulled out, and sawed up for steaks, one side black, the other red. Then the cow was thrown back again. Soon they were cutting into the dead horses as well.

"It was, however, a peculiar hunger. I do not know for how many I can speak, but each taste of meat gave me the desire to taste another kind. I could not satisfy myself on beef, nor even on horse, although there was something already in the flavor of the cooked blood in a stallion's meat that spoke of strange truths and new strengths. I just kept eating to fill a hole in my intestines. Maybe it was the presence of the lion. He kept poking his snout into the wounds of the dead, and before it was over, many of these men had become as ravenous in their taste—how can I confess it to you? Walking next to that lion, he became my best friend on the field. So I could see into his thoughts as clearly as into my Pharaoh's, and the lion, to my surprise, had a mind.

Now he did not think with words, but with smells and tastes, and every sensation put sights into his eyes. As he ate the raw liver of a dead man—I think he was dead, though he twitched—Hera-Ra was seeing our Pharaoh. I knew, by the gusto with which he chewed, that the valor of our Pharaoh had made him happy, just as happy as the liver of the brave warrior he was eating. Then it turned out that the dead fellow was not so brave after all. A taste of bile came into Hera-Ra's throat. Like a dirty vein through the liver was the secret cowardice of this warrior.

"I watched Hera-Ra nibble on dead men's ears until he found those that pleased him most. It was then I could see that as he ate, he had before him a heaven with stars more brilliant than our own smoke-filled sky so obscured by mist and scud. Indeed, my own mind felt blessed as he ate, for I was learning that our ears are the seat of all intelligence and the very door to the Blessed Fields. Now Hera-Ra began to lick the skin of many a forehead. With deliberation and much choice in his taste, he passed from head to head comparing the taste of their salts. Soon enough, I knew why he enjoyed such licking. For the picture he gained from the forehead that pleased him most was of a soldier running uphill, forcing his face up the hill into a stiff wind; truth, the fellow he finally chose had been a monument of perseverance. Then Hera-Ra ate him by the testicles as well and chewed into the groin. The soft growls of Hera-Ra were enough for me. I realized he had selected this fellow as the very seat of manly strength.

"I must tell you more. Before the night was over, I, too, indulged the meat of a limb, burned it in the fire, took a taste, and knew that the pleasures of a cannibal were going to be mine this night. Suffice it that the first step in what is considered the filth of my habits was taken. It has led me through many a wonder and many a wisdom. But then you do not really wish to hear more of the Battle of Kadesh. Let me say only that human fat, gorged in considerable quantity, has an intoxicating effect. I became as drunk as Hera-Ra."

With these words, Menenhetet shut his mouth and did not speak again.

### 4.

We were left with much curiosity. The silence broke, but only into another silence, and our Pharaoh gave a wise look at the fireflies and said, "I hope you will continue. I would like to know of the next day."

Menenhetet sighed. It was the first sound of fatigue he had uttered on many a breath, and the insects quivered behind their fine linen. Did I see what was not to be perceived, or did the glow of these mites fade in salute to the dawn that came outside the walls of Kadesh when the fires were burning down and exhausted soldiers began to sleep? It is certain that their light was less. But then I could remember Eyaseyab telling me that the finest food for these fireflies was themselves, and they ate each other.

"I do not know how much there is yet to tell," said my great-grandfather. "Metella must truly have been cursed by his secret whore; he did not come out in the morning with his eight thousand infantrymen, nor with what were left of his chariots. Even when we took a captured officer, tied his arms to his chariot, and drove him into the river so that he drowned under their noses, Metella did not come out. I thought he was a fool as well as a coward. He should have attacked. We were so festered and unruly that morning, so entangled in a million and infinity of evil spirits that Metella could have overrun us—unless his troops had also had a night like ours.

"We held a council. Some of our officers spoke of siege, and tried to tell how Thutmose the Great had cut the fruit trees in the groves surrounding these hills in order to build the siege-walls that He brought forward against the walls of Kadesh. In the months ahead, if we did the same, the city could be taken. My Ramses listened, and looked affronted, and said at last, 'I am not a slayer of trees.' By that afternoon, camp was broken.

"It proved no easy departure. First, our dead had to be buried, and our wounded gotten ready for the trip. It took a lot of digging before the bodies were covered over, and the pits were never deep enough. These dead men were pressed down so tightly that a hip, an elbow, or even a head would push up and the birds must have had their pick. Of course, the insects devoured the other half. Seeing those myriads swarm over the pits before they were even covered, I knew the answer to one question forever. I learned why the beetle Khepera is the creature closest to Ra. In the middle of any hot night, beneath the silence, give a moment's attention: You will hear the mightiest sound of them all. It is the drone of insects. What multitudes! They possess the silence.

"Needless to say, a few of our dead were saved from the birds and the maggots. Each division had a platoon of embalmers who carried a sacred table with their wagon, and they soon wrapped the Princes and Generals who had fallen. Even if you were no more than an officer (but also happened to be the dead son of a rich merchant) there was a good chance someone would speak up for your remains. No embalmer could be unaware of the award he would receive in Memphi or Thebes if he delivered a well-wrapped son back to the family. Before it was all over, a hundred officers were stacked with care on the different work carts, and though the task was done in the field, only a few of these wrapped bodies began to stink.

"The wounded were worse. Some lived. Some died. They all stank. The Divisions of Amon, Ra, Ptah, and Set traveled behind each other in so long a line that it took a day to move from the van to the rear. Now we were truly like a worm cut in four pieces. Yet the smell connected us. We moved slowly, a thick river, full of rot, and the screams of the wounded were terrible when their wagons shuddered over the rocks of the gorges.

"Of course, we were all in pain. Who did not have foul cuts and scrapes? I soon grew a dozen boils to meet my other afflictions, and you could feel the poison of these wounds growing in new places even as they were being worked out of the old. Some of us were demented by fevers after the third day, and in the heat of our march, what had seemed a victory quivered before us like a defeat. By the fourth day, we were being attacked. A few of Metella's best troops began to follow, not enough to matter, but in sufficient numbers to raid our rear. They would kill a few, wound a few, and ride away. We would lose time in chasing them, more time in burying our dead. Since the carts for the wounded were filled, foot soldiers were now used as litter-bearers and some dropped from the heat and were left behind and had to catch up again. Others were lost altogether.

"One of the Hittite raids even tried to steal a few of the donkeys transporting the hands. We used more than ten for this purpose alone and each carried two large bags, one for either side of their back. The smell was not atrocious unless you came close—there is finally so little flesh on a hand that the skin dries quickly and by itself—although the odor from one of those baskets (if you were fool enough to put your head in) was as clear to the nostrils as rotten teeth. A true curse. Leave it alone and it would hardly stir. Go too near, and the stench lived in the lining of your nose. Hera-Ra could not keep away. Untethered, he would bother these donkeys in the worst way. Trying to bolt, they tangled in their harness, nearly strangling—donkeys in doubt always climb over one another—and in the confusion, a bag broke. Hera-Ra made a meal of what fell to the ground. I came running up to pull him away since I was the only one he obeyed besides our Pharaoh, but I was late. He had gorged on a dozen of those hands, and then more. Pictures of the Pyramids danced in his brain, then sights of great cities. I had never seen buildings like the ones Hera-Ra now envisioned in his head. They showed thousands of windows and great towers and went to vast heights. It was as if a part of great buildings yet to come was in the knowledge of those hands he ate. Yet what a dreadful meal! Hera-Ra had teeth strong enough to break your bones, although not quite—his mouth was happier in soft flesh which he liked to tear to strings. Now he broke one of his own teeth, and whimpered like a baby at the pain, yet kept on eating—all that unspeakable swallow of leathery skin, cursed smell, dried flesh, together with those little bones of the hand that crunched so hard. All the same, something in their odor drove Hera-Ra to more. He growled in real rage at me when I tried to pull him back. He wanted to take this curse. Some curses we dare—we wish to penetrate them. A dull anger went up from these mutilated hands at this second destruction. But then, that was why Hera-Ra took on such a fury. It gave him visions of the future. Again, I saw buildings high as mountains.

"The lion turned ill from his meal. By the next day, he could not walk. His belly swelled, and his hind legs, which had suffered any number of slashes from Hittite swords, began to fester. On his shoulder, an open hole from the point of a spear turned black. He could not keep the flies away. His tail was too weak to brush them off. We built a large litter and six men carried him, but Hera-Ra's eyes took on the dull shine of a dying fish. I knew the hands in his belly were gripping his vitals, the little bones flaying his intestines like knives.

"My Pharaoh was with us ten times a day. The Royal Wagon's golden walls and golden roof were deserted by Him, and He walked along the litter beside Hera-Ra and held the beast's paw, and wept. I cried as well, not just for love of Hera-Ra, but in the terrible fear of knowing that the animal would not have gotten ill if I had kept him away from the donkeys' bags.

"Once, His tears washing thin lines through the black and green cosmetic about His eyes, Usermare-Setpenere said to me, 'Ah, if I had vanquished that Prince of the Hittites who met Me alone, all would be well with Hera-Ra!' and I did not know whether to nod or deny His words. Who could decide whether it was better to encourage His wrath against Himself or take it on my back—I should have known the answer. My good Pharaoh Ramses the Second was not made to bear His own anger.

"Then the lion died. I wept, and more than I would have believed, and for a little while my sorrow was all for Hera-Ra. I even wept because no man had been my friend so much as that beast.

"Few of the embalmed Princes had also been granted the honor of having their organs properly wrapped. The provision wagon of the embalmers could carry a few sets of Canopic jars, but how many can you treat when it is four jars to each fellow? Even Generals were having their organs thrown to the woods. For Hera-Ra, however, the embalmers used the next to last set of jars, and his wrapping was supervised by Usermare-Setpenere Himself. Indeed, I heard the rage in His voice when He examined the intestines and found bits of broken bone protruding from the coils like arrowheads of white stone. By the look my Pharaoh cast at me, it was clear that I was out of favor again.

"My punishment, however, was not so simple this time. He had me travel with Him often in the Royal Wagon. We sat on chairs of gold and looked through open windows at the chasms of the gorge, while we rocked perilously within. Certain bumps so tipped the wagon (which was high enough inside for us to stand) that we all but went over.

"Sometimes, He would not say a word. Just wept silently. The eye-paint streaked. The Overseer of the Cosmetic Box would repair Him, a nimble fellow, nimble as Nef"—this with a nod to my father— "and we would sit in silence. Sometimes when we were alone (for on occasion the King would wipe all cosmetics from His face and dismiss the Overseer) He would speak briefly and in gloom about the campaign. 'I did not win, I did not lose, and so I have lost,' He said to me once. Since His eyes did not leave my own, I nodded. It was the truth. But not even the Gods love the truth when it scores each breath. Before the day was out, He said to me in the gloom of the carriage, 'You should have given your arm to Hera-Ra before you let him eat those hands.' I bowed. I struck the floor seven times with my head even though the floor of the carriage was bumping like a rock in a fall. It hardly mattered. A sigh, long as the sound of the death that had come out of the lion, now came from the throat of Ramses our Second, a terrible sound as though the eyes of the lion were losing their light once more. What can I tell you? I thought often of the meaning of that sigh, and realized that the death of the lion was the end of Usermare's happiness at the sight of me. In the heart of His rebuke was the thought that if I did not know how much my good fortune depended on the health of His beast, then good fortune and I were best separated.

"We were. By the time the troops returned to Gaza, I was transferred from the Household Guards of Usermare-Setpenere to the charioteers of the Division of Amon, and I may say that no division of the four was in worse repute after Kadesh. Still, we were given a good reception by the natives of Gaza, and I was not surprised. In the last days of our return, people cheered us on the road. A runner traveled in front to tell them that the Armies of Ramses the Second had scourged the Hittites from the field.

"I think my Pharaoh must have listened to His messenger. He had healed from His wounds and looked magnificent. On the last day I would see Him for what would yet be fifteen years, He was on the parade ground at Gaza. There He displayed the winged bull of the Hittites and gave it to the city as a gift. This captured God, He told the multitudes, would protect our eastern frontier. By the next day, we began our march to the Delta, and, once there, sailed up the river to Thebes. I sat in the same crowded galley with my back pressing against the knees of the man sitting behind me, and since the winds were not steady, our trip upriver was even longer than the descent. Soon after our arrival, I was sent on duty into the depths of Nubia. That is to say, my King was banishing me to a distant place called Es-huranib. In command of a small detachment, I went up the Nile as far as a boat could go, and then had twenty-four days of march across a desert whose heat I will not soon forget." Even as he spoke these words, I could see such a desert before me. "In that time," he said, "I gave my farewell to every great and exalted moment I had known. The desert was hotter than the steam that rises from the Land of the Dead, and I was an officer without a true command." He ceased, he nodded, and said, "I think I can end my recollections here."

From *Ancient Evenings* (1983)

# NEFERTIRI
# AND MENENHETET

As Nefertiri told me this tale, so did I remember the Battle of Kadesh, and smell again the field where we roasted meats in the night, and the Division of Set arrived with camp followers. I thought of all the men and women I had known by two mouths or three that night. No sword had been so strong as mine but for the sword of Usermare, and He was in the other field counting hands. I could see again the tent of hands, and blood on earth, red once from the wounds and again by the light of the campfires, and I was returned to the joy of seizing lovers I did not know and entering them. So, the smoke of those fires returned to my chest, and my Queen Nefertiri had thereby warmed me further. In the mirror, Her eyes had the light of campfires. Beneath the woven-air, Her breast rose and fell. Even my awe before Her was no longer like the chill of a temple but more like the cold blue fire of the altar when salt is in the flame.

Now, She set aside the mirror, and gave Her attention to my short linen skirt, only She did not look upon it with desire but calculation, in the way I might approach a new horse before considering whether I wished to mount. Then She gave a sigh. Whether it was at the monumental rage of Usermare if He knew Her thought, or my own not so subtle tortures, I cannot say. However, She most certainly drew a circle around Her head before proceeding to tell me another tale.

That was of still another architect. Back in the era when people were crude, and there were no monuments, there had been a sad reign of a Pharaoh Horus Tepnefer-Intef, a weak King Who stored His plunder in a vault built by the architect Sen-Amon.

Horus Tepnefer-Intef feared for these riches and so the walls of the vault were of great thickness, the stones even chosen by Sen-Amon himself, for he was a mason as well as an architect. At night, however, after his laborers had left, he polished one stone, and set it on so perfect an incline that he could draw it forth from the wall. So Sen-Amon slept with the knowledge that the riches of Pharaoh Tepnefer-Intef were, if he desired, his own. But he was old and stole nothing. He merely visited the vault with his oldest son, and counted the King's fortune.

When Sen-Amon died, his son, however, went in with his younger brother, and they took as much gold as they could carry. Since the Pharaoh also liked to count His hoard, He soon discovered the theft. Full of consternation, He set a trap.

When the thieves returned for more, the lid of a sarcophagus fell on the younger brother, and he cried out: "I cannot escape. Cut off my head so no one will recognize me." His older brother obeyed.

When Tepnefer discovered the headless man, He was frantic with terror. He hung the body by the wall of the main gate and told the guards to arrest whoever would weep beneath. "This was," said Nefertiri, "a terrible act for a Pharaoh to decree. We honor the bodies of the dead. Tepnefer-Intef must have been a Syrian.

"The mother of the poor dead thief did not weep in public, but she told her oldest son to rescue the body of his brother, or she would claim it herself. When he went by the wall at evening, therefore, he fed the guards wine. Soon, they were drunk and asleep, and he cut down his brother and escaped."

"Is that all of Your story?" I asked. I was disappointed. The stone that slid in its socket moved in me as well. As the brothers stole the gold, I had felt a first stirring in myself. Yet now, the thought of a headless body lay on me like the weight of a coffin's cover.

"There is more," said Nefertiri. And She told me that this peculiar King, Tepnefer-Intef, infuriated by the cleverness of the thief, was unable to sleep. Tepnefer-Intef even commanded His daughter, Suba-Sebaq, famous for Her wide-open thighs—"they can only be Syrians," said Nefertiri—to open Her house and receive all men, noble or common, who came to visit. Any of these men would be free to take his pleasure by way of any of Her three mouths if he could entertain Her with a true account of the most wicked deed of his life. So She learned of the escapades of the worst men in the reign of Tepnefer-Intef.

Many of these stories exciting Her, the men learned much of the smell of the meat in the three mouths of Suba-Sebaq, "that slut"—now did Nefertiri's clear voice deepen in my ear. Such was Her excitement that Her thighs came apart and I could see in Her parted hair the eye of Horus gleaming. Then Her voice, rapt as the oncoming of the river, went on to tell of the ingenuity of this oldest son of Sen-Amon. To prepare himself, he cut off the arm of a neighbor who had just died, and concealed it beneath his robes. Then, he went to the Princess. In Her Chambers, he told how he had rescued his brother's body. But when the Princess tried to seize him, he gave Her no more to grasp than the arm of the dead man. It came right out of his robe, and Suba-Sebaq fell backward in a swoon. Then, while She lay beneath him, the thief made love to Her by all three mouths.

"After he left, Tepneter-Intef so admired his boldness that He sent out word He would pardon the fellow. Thereby, the son of Sen-Amon disclosed himself and married Suba-Sebaq and became a Prince whose wife was known by half the men of Egypt."

Now, Nefertiri knelt before me, raised my skirt, seized my swollen but still sleeping snake, gave a small tug with Her slim and playful fingers, said, "Ah, this arm does not come off," and proceeded to give Her beautiful face to my limb. As the royal mouth came down upon my honor, my desire, my terror, my shame, my glory, I began to feel the seven gates of my body with all their monsters and snares, and a great heat, like the burning of the sun, blazed in me. Then I was alone again, and the fires were subsiding. She was no longer on me with Her mouth. "You smell like a stallion," She said. "I have never smelled an unperfumed body before."

I knelt and kissed Her foot, ready like a hound to slaver atrociously upon Her sandal. The sensation of Her lips upon the head of my phallus remained, and that was like a halo. My cock felt as if it were made of gold. A glow rose in me. I could die now. I need feel no shame. The woman of my Pharaoh, Usermare, had given me Her mouth, and so my buttocks were my own again, yes, I could have kissed Her feet and chewed upon Her toes.

"Truly, Kazama, you smell dreadful," She said in Her fondest voice, and wiped Her mouth as if She would never have any more of me. But then, She knelt, and despite Herself, gave one queenly teasing lick of Her tongue, light as a feather, along the length of my shaft, down into the tense bag of my balls, and around, a fleeting lick.

"You stink! You smell of the end of the road," She said, which, in the Court of Usermare, where people spoke so well, was the worst reference you could make to the anus, and I wondered if something out of the marrow of Ma-Khrut's fats, some thirst of the lost Pig, or slime of the hippopotamus, must be oozing forth from me, an abomination, or so I would have said until I saw Nefertiri's face, and another Ka was on it. Her delicate features had their own thirst. She was full of folly.

"Oh, I adore how dreadful you are," She said. "Did you visit the Royal Stables? Did you rub the foam of a stallion's mouth all over your little beauty?" She took another lick.

I nodded. I had indeed gone to the Stables before coming here. I had rubbed myself, and with one of Usermare's horses, no less, back from a ride with his groom and not yet rubbed down, I had managed to get my hand full of the slather of the beast, nor had I known why.

"You are a peasant. Common as Lower Egypt," She said, and teased what I had anointed by way of Her fingertips, clever as starlings' wings, but with Her tongue and lips as well, a flutter into the ferment of my seed.

I knew what a mighty revenge She was taking upon Usermare. She never left the crown of my shaft, indeed She called it that, "the crown," and in a crooning voice, almost so pure as one of Her blind singers, said, "Oh, little crown of Upper Egypt," and laid on the butterfly wings of Her light tongue, "Oh," She said, "doesn't the Upper Crown like to be kissed by Lower Egypt," whereupon Her tongue curled like the cobra that comes forward from the Red Crown, and She laughed at the mating of the two, as if She would laugh again when the White Crown and the Red of Usermare were together on His head, and He was solemn with His ceremony. "Oh, don't you spit at Me," She said, "don't you dare, don't let that wickedness of yours begin to shine, don't let it leap, don't let it dance," all with the sweetest little kisses and tickles of Her tongue, trailing the fingertips of one hand like five little sins into my sack and over my shaft, and all the while She played with words in the way I had so often noticed among the most exalted, but all such games were nothing to what She said to me now. It was as if Her heart had tasted no pleasure in so long that She must croon over my coarse peasant cock (and She called it that) and called it by many other names, for after each tickle of Her tongue, I was "groaner," and "moaner," "knife," and "stud," "inscriber," and "anointer," and then, as if that were not enough, She spoke of my "guide" and my "dirty Hittite," my "smelly thickness," and lo, they were all much like the sound you hear in *mtha*, although a little different each, and then using a word so common as *met*, which I heard every day, now came such sweet caressing sounds as "Do you like the way I tickle your *vein,* My *governor,*" and She gave me a nip with Her teeth, "or is it *death*?" Yet, if it were not for the cleverness of my ears after the Gardens of the Secluded, I might have thought She said, "Do you like the way I tickle your governor, My death, or is it the vein?" some such nonsense, but we were laughing so much, and enjoying ourselves so freely that She began to flip my proud (and now shining) crown against Her lips, and She cooed at it and called it "Nefer" but with a different meaning each time so that it was sweet. "Oh My most beautiful young horse," She said, "My *nefer,* My phallus, My slow fire, My lucky name, My *sma,* My little cock, My little cemetery, My *smat,*" and She swallowed as much of my cock as Her royal throat could take, and bit at the root until I screamed, or near to it, but then She kissed the tip. "Did I hurt My little *hen,* My provider, My *hemsi,* My dwelling place? Oh, is he coming forth?" and indeed I would have been all over Her face and spewing on the woven-air across Her breast, and there to watch Her rub it into Her skin slowly and solemnly as if painting the insult to Usermare upon Her flesh—such was all I saw in Her mind—but the coming-forth turned upon itself with all rude force, clear up my fundament, into my cave, seizing my heart, and drew all the joy in the head of my cock right back into my sack, and I knew we had made no small commotion. Yet I had small fear of that. Her Palace was not like the Secluded where every house had its walls yet every sound belonged to all. Here were no walls around Her rooms. Her bedroom opened to a patio that gave on a garden that ended in an arbor beyond which was a pool. So royal was the air, however, and so sweet and heavy the music of birds, and the cawing and barking of Her falcons and greyhounds, that She had no concern for gossip. Who would care to carry such a tale? Her body servants were not only eunuchs, plump as geese from rich food, but silent as fish. For they were also without their tongues—a considerable cruelty, to be certain, but done, I learned later, not to silence their speech, although it did, but by order of Usermare so they could not lick Her. Indeed, if it would not have made them too hideous in appearance, He would have cut off their lips as well. Of course, He did not protect Himself altogether. Once, later, She whispered to me, "They have marvelous fingers, these Nubians."

I speak of such matters, but by now the desire aroused in me was like a fire that could melt a stone. As I stood before Her, trembling, all but flinging myself and my seed in all directions at once, a fire in my stick, and honey in my bowels, my mind was aflame with the stories She had told, and I had to seize myself at the brink before the cream of my loins was shining on Her queenly face. But I had another desire now, large as Usermare Himself. It was to fuck Her, fuck Her good, good and evil. She was murmuring, "Benben, benbenben," but with such little twists and stops of Her mouth, such a beat of Her breath that as I heard it, benben said all too many words, "Oh, *come forth* with Me, you little *God of evil*, you *fucker*, give Me your *obelisk*"—for that was also a *benben*—and then Her gown of woven-air was gone, and Her field was open before me, Her thighs like slim pillars, and Her altar wet with the passions of my tongue. "*Hath, hath, hath*," She panted like a cat in heat, "Let us *fuck*, let us *fly*. Come into My *flame*, My *fire*, My *hath*, My *cunt*, come into My *snare*, enter My *sepulchre*, Oh, come deep into My *cemetery*, My *sma*, My little *cemetery*, *unite* with Me, *copulate* with Me, come to your *concubine*, *O heaven and earth, hath, hath, hath!*"

We kept looking at one another, She on Her back, I on my knees, and I drew into myself all I could remember of the most reverent moments I had known—anything to hold me from shooting every white arrow at once—I saw the solemnity of Bak-ne-khon-su when he sacrificed the ram, and the grandeur of Usermare as He received the hands of the Hittites, and all such thoughts I took in upon my fires like smoke, my lust steaming on the hot stones of my will. I knew all the madness of the lion. "Would You like," I said to Her, my lips as thick as if they had been beaten, nay, scourged, "would You like my obelisk in You, Queen Hat-shep-sut?"

"In my *cunt*, yes, in My *weeping fish*, oh, speak to My *weeping fish*, enter My *mummy*, come into My *spell*, *work your oars*, work your *spell*, *slaughter* Me, *shet, shet, shet*, oh, come into My *plot*, come into my *ground*, come to My *pool*, yes, fuck your *Ka-t*, fuck your *cunt*."

Yet when I entered, Her breasts looking at me like the two eyes of the Two-Lands, all the reverence I had drawn into myself made me ache with a radiance equal to a rainbow in a storm. Having banked the fires of my balls, I entered Her with the solemnity of a priest who reads a service, and lay upon Her lips, but the lips of Her enclosure were so hot that my fires almost flamed over the river. Then all was calm again, and She was lying on Her back. My obelisk was floating on Her river. She made the sounds of a woman in birth, *aq* and *aqaq*, and yet with all the clarity of a greeting to enter, "*Aq*, please *enter*, come to My *sunrise*, come to My *sunset*, Oh, *aqaq*, *raid Me*, spy into My *entrance*, look on My *uba*, rest in My *Court*, *read the prayer*, rest in My *gate*. *Uba*, *uba* live in My *cave*, move in My *den*, *ri, ri, ri, mover of stone*, you are a *mover of stone*, *haa*, you *travel by sea*, be My *embarcation*, *haa*, My *entrance*. Oh," She said, going suddenly still, "do not *burst into flame*, do not *burn up, haa,* paddle away, *khenn* and *khennu,* oh, slip into My *snare, hem, hem, hem,* crush My *majesty, hu, hu, hu,* let it *rain*"—I heard it all. She sang of the beauties of my testicles (which She held with fingers that had learned the tongueless art of the Nubian), She governed me with words of power, with *heq* and *heha* and *hem,* and as She sang to me, I entered the Land of the Dead that was in all the life of Her, and felt like a noble. She kissed me on the side of my mouth with those lips that had brought royalty to the head of my cock, and our mouths were on one another and our tongues met like woven-air and I felt Her voice on my ear, "*Netchem* and *netchemu* and *netchemut,*" She crooned, "Oh, what a merry fuck you are, *ri, ra, rirara,*" and on Nefertiri's face was such tenderness that *rirara* rose in me and I could not enter enough into my *nefer* of my most beautiful Queen, my *nefer-her,* beautiful like rain in the fourth hour after rising, She was a Goddess, She was Her majesty, and She was shameless. *Tcham,* I fucked Her by *Her youth, Tcham, Tcham, Tcham,* by Her *Sceptre* and Her *youth,* and our hips moving together, She cried out, "*Shep, shep, shepit, shepit,* and all such words like *shepu* and *shepa* and *shepat,* Oh, *light,* oh, *radiance,* oh, *brightness,* oh, *blindness,* oh, *wealth* and *shame, vomit* and *shipwreck, shef, shef, shef, ram* into Me, *swell* into Me, give Me your *weapon,* give me your *power, shefesh, shefesh,* I have your *sword,* I have your *gift,* give Me your *evil,* give Me your *wealth. Khut, khut, khut, tehet, tehet, tehet.* Oh, by the *sacred backbone of Osiris,* give me *tcham, tcham, tcham, qef, qef, qef,* show Me to My Ka, *dead white, dead black,* I am *fortress, ai, ai,* what *light,* what *splendor,* go deeper, you obelisk, fuck Me into glory, take Me to flame, I am *rich,* oh, stop, I am *fire* and *light,* I am your *filth,* your *offal,* your *devils,* your *friends,* your *guide,* oh, good, good, good, give Me your *benben,* evil fucker, *nek, nek, nekk, nekk,* fuck me, slash me, murder me, *aar, aar, aar,* I am your *lion,* your *bird,* your *lock of hair,* your *sin,* I come, oh, I come, I come forth, I am the Pharaoh."

And even as I was rising into a celestial city by a field of golden reeds, there to know a change as great as death itself, I heard the deep sounds of the bowels and the high sounds from the wind in my throat, the cries of my heart roaring in the water rising in me, and I flung myself out to fly to the heavens, or crash on the rocks, and saw the legions of the Land of the Dead and a myriad of faces, all the damned and perfected souls that Nefertiri could command, and rammed into the last gate of Her womb with the moan and groan of a peasant cock, the radiance of Amon blazing in me like the Hidden Sun of my mother's belly, and She rebounded beneath like a beast, Her limbs storming over mine with the strength of Usermare as I was borne aloft, but not by Her so much as by the wrath of my Pharaoh, Who lifted me high like a feather over the flame, and slammed me down like a rock, then gave me another blow and another blow of Her queenly cavern, my tomb. I gave out within Her while the storm still blew, and She washed over me. She came out of every great space that Usermare had left in Her. She was much more powerful than myself.

From *Ancient Evenings* (1983)

# IN PREFACE
# TO THE GOSPEL—I

## An Interview
## on Existentialism and Karma

LAURA ADAMS: How literally does God exist?

MAILER: In a great many ways we can comprehend and in a great many we cannot. All I'm saying is that He does not have to be all-powerful. What is there that makes Him all-powerful? He was powerful enough to have created our solar system, perhaps. And if you ask what are His limits, that might be my guess. But this is babbling. It isn't important where God's limits are. What's significant is the idea that God is not all-powerful, nor is the Devil. Rather it is that we exist as some mediating level between them. You see, this notion does restore a certain dignity to moral choice.

ADAMS: In trying to know what is good or evil aren't you in effect trying to take existentialism to its logical end, that is, to end existentialism?

MAILER: Not end it, seat it. Of all the philosophies, existentialism approaches experience with the greatest awe: It says we can't categorize experience before we've experienced it. The only way we're going to be able to discover what the truth about anything might be is to submit ourselves to the reality of the experience. At the same time, given its roots in atheistic philosophers like Sartre, existentialism has always tended toward the absurd. By way of Sartre, we are to act as if there were a purpose to things even though we know there is not. And that has become the general concept of existentialism in America. But it's not mine. I'm an existentialist who believes there is a God and a Devil at war with one another. Like Sartre in his atheism, I offer a statement of absolute certainty equally founded on the inability to verify it. Atheism is as removed from logical positivism as theology. Still, there has to be something out there beyond logical positivism. I want my brain to live. I want to adventure out on a few thoughts. The fact that I can never demonstrate them is not nearly so important to me as the fact that I may come up with an hypothesis so simple, so central, that I may be able to apply it in thousands of situations. If it begins to give me some inner coherence, if I begin to think that I know more as a result of this philosophy, why not?

ADAMS: But isn't what you've identified as existentialism, extended to its logical end, seeking to know what is finally unknowable?

MAILER: That's not my definition of existentialism. I'd say we find ourselves in an existential situation whenever we are in a situation where we cannot foretell the end.

ADAMS: But isn't to a larger extent your aim in all the work that you've been doing to uncover what is essentially good or evil in our natures and God's nature when that kind of thing is actually unknowable? You seem to have become increasingly obsessed since that time with your inability to know what is good and what is evil.

MAILER: You say I'm obsessed, but where would be the literary proof of that? What books would show that?

ADAMS: Start with the case of Richard Nixon in *Miami and the Siege of Chicago* and *St. George and the Godfather*—your inability to know or to intuit whether Nixon is basically good or basically evil; to know, in *Of a Fire on the Moon,* whether our space program will carry God's vision to the stars or the Devil's; to know in *Why Are We in Vietnam?* whether America has made a Faustian compact with the Devil or whether God is using us for evil ends; whether or not our national leaders and events win or lose us ground in this divine battle. It seems to me that you lead us to this question, with increasing desire to know the answer, in every work.

MAILER: Well, it could be said that all I'm doing is leading people back to Kierkegaard. I'd remind you that I've written this several times: Kierkegaard taught us, or tried to teach us, that at the moment we're feeling most saintly, we may in fact be evil. And that moment when we think we're most evil and finally corrupt, we may, in fact, in the eyes of God, be saintly. The first value of this notion is that it strips us of the fundamental arrogance of assuming that at any given moment any of us have enough centrality, have a *seat* from which we can expound our dogma, or measure our moral value. So we don't have the right to say Richard Nixon is: a) good; b) evil. I might have my opinion of Richard Nixon, but I don't have the right to say that man is evil any more than I have a right to say he is good.

ADAMS: Do you have a clear notion of the good?

MAILER: No. But I have, if you will, I have and I submit to the force of this word, I have a fairly well formed *cloud* of intuitions about the nature of the good, and, like a cloud, it has to a certain degree a structure, and yet the structure is capable of altering quickly, depending on the celestial winds blowing and the less celestial winds. A cloud changes shape quickly but it remains a cloud. It's not just simply an unformed chaos.

ADAMS: You've said that an evil person is someone who has a clear notion of the good and operates in opposition to it.

MAILER: Therefore by my own definition I'm definitely not evil.

ADAMS: All right, but are you wicked?

MAILER: Unquestionably.

ADAMS: By your own terms, which is not knowing what is good or evil in any situation, but upping the ante each time.

MAILER: Upping the ante, yes. I'd say I may be one of the most wicked spirits in American life today. But maybe not. America may be changing faster than I am.

ADAMS: Is it fair to say that your existentialism is leading us to know the nature of good and evil?

MAILER: It's leading us to—well, let me take a detour. People who submit to logical positivism, and go on from there into philosophies as difficult as Wittgenstein's, will answer if you ask, "Why go through these incredible disciplines in order to verify the fact that you're able to verify the wing span of a gnat but not of an archangel?" They will answer, "Well, it isn't what we are able to verify that is interesting so much as that we go through a discipline that enables us to think cogently. We're less likely to go in for sloppy thinking thereafter." That's the value of it. I'd say by going in for my variety of associational, metaphorical thinking (which is, of course, the exact opposite) I may be able eventually to think speculatively without feeling philosophical vertigo. You see, it doesn't take any more illogic to posit that there's a god or devil than it takes to say there is none. The latter statement is absolutely as potent an act of faith. There's a marvelous line in *Jumpers,* the play by Tom Stoppard, to that effect. I paraphrase: "Well, maybe atheism is that crutch people need to protect themselves against having to face the enormity of the existence of God." You know, once you contemplate the notion that there is God and this God may be embattled, the terror you feel is enormous.

ADAMS: It's a terror, but isn't it also paranoia?

MAILER: No. The terror is not that some force is working on you to ruin you. It's another kind of terror: It's that nothing is nailed down. That we are out there—that our lives are truly existential. That we're not going to end up well. Not necessarily. You see, there's always been this sort of passive confidence implicit in Christianity, the confidence that things are going to work out all right. One does have to die, that's true, but if one keeps one's nose reasonably clean, one is going to heaven. That gave security to everybody. The ship of state was built on that security. The ship of state, therefore, doesn't have to travel the stormy seas. Rather, it will be carried by the strongest pallbearers of the nation. And what's happened now is we're entering an existential period in our history, where nothing is nailed down. All the American faiths, one by one, are being exploded. We lived for too long in a paranoid dream world that believed communism was the secret of all evil on earth because it was the social embodiment of the Devil.

ADAMS: That's paranoid.

MAILER: That's paranoid. But I don't believe the Devil is the secret of all evil on earth. I believe something more complicated than that. I think God might be the source of a considerable amount of evil. Because if God is embattled, He could fail to take care, much to His great woe, of people who are devoted to Him, in the same way that a general might have to surrender soldiers on a hill. And those soldiers could give up with great bitterness in their hearts. Of course, the Devil loves to pick up those who die with a curse. Malcolm Muggeridge once had Mother Teresa of Calcutta on a television show with him. Muggeridge, who is by any measure a devoutly religious man, had just written a book about Mother Teresa and obviously revered her. He told me what she used to do in Calcutta. Her order of nuns would take people who were dying on the street and move them into her convent, where they'd die anyway a few days later—they didn't begin to have medicine to take care of them or anything like that—but her notion was, and Muggeridge was moved by this, and I agree that it is a moving idea, that she didn't want them to die with absolutely nothing. She wanted them to be able to come in and get a little attention before they died so they wouldn't go out with a complete bitterness in their hearts. Now, that is a religious woman. The recognition that one not die with a curse is fundamental to any inquiry into what could be the possible nature of God and the Devil. If God is embattled, and can't give fair justice to all, then what of those who do not achieve what they saw as their own fulfillment and thereby become spiritual material for the Devil, if not in this life then in another? We haven't said one word about karma, but my first idea these days is that any attempt to speak of these things makes no sense unless you take into account the peculiar calculus of karma. We may have to recognize that we're not only acting for this life but for other lives. Our past lives and our future lives. Paying dues, receiving awards. Reducing the cost of future dues, for example, by certain acts of abnegation that make no sense to us or our friends, yet ready to dare, on the other hand, sometimes desperate activities because we *are* desperate. The condition in which we live is hurting our karma.

ADAMS: Karma is a word you've used increasingly in the last few years. Is this something new in your metaphysics, or is it a term for something that you've already described?

MAILER: I had come across the word in books but never paid any attention. In about 1953, I think it was in Robinson, Illinois, I went out to visit James Jones in his writers' colony and he and Lowney Handy were talking about karma and I said, "What's all that?" So he gave me the standard explanation. Which is that we are not only reincarnated, but the way in which we are is the reflection, the judgment, the truth, of how we lived our previous life. If you exist in a simple form of karma with no interference by Gods or Devils, a natural flux of karma, then to the degree you lived a life that was artful, your reincarnation was artful. To the degree you lived a life that destroyed the time of others and dredged up all the swamp muds, so you are a creature of the swamp in your next life. The beauty of this may be that there is now good purpose to the swamp. (This isn't Jones' talk any longer, just a more general explanation of karma.) At any rate, Jones went on about it, and I said, "You *believe* in that?" Because I was an atheist and a socialist in those days. He said, "Oh, sure. That's the only thing that makes sense." Well, the line rang in my head for years. "The only thing that makes sense." I thought about it over and over, and in the last three or four years I began to think, Yes, that does make sense. Jones was right.

From *Partisan Review* (Summer 1975)

# IN PREFACE
# TO THE GOSPEL—II

## A Jewish Limb of the
## Judeo-Christian Ethic: Miracles

*Once Zusya prayed to God: "Lord, I love you so much, but I do not fear
you enough! Lord, I love you so much, but I do not fear you enough! Let
me stand in awe of you like your angels, who are penetrated by your awe-
inspiring name." And God heard his prayer, and his name penetrated the
hidden heart of Zusya as it does those of the angels. But Zusya crawled
under the bed like a little dog, and animal fear shook him until he
howled: "Lord, let me love you like Zusya again!" And God heard him
this time also.\**

There is an existential logic in this story that leads to a root in the
meaning of miracles. Zusya is ambitious, he is intellectually ambitious.
He wishes to feel a fear of God because he is secretly confident he will
be able to withstand that fear and so acquire more knowledge of the
universe, more revelation of the secrets of God and Nature. The request is Faustian. Yet God in revealing Himself further to Zusya terrifies him profoundly. Why? Does He terrify Zusya because He is
Jehovah, a God of wrath and rectitude, an essentialist's God? Or is the
fear that comes over Zusya a part of the profound fear God feels Himself, a fear that His conception of Being (that noble conception of
every human as potentially a creature of courage and compassion, art,

\*The extracts in italics are from *Tales of the Hasidim* by Martin Buber.

tenderness, skill, stamina, and imagination, exactly the imagination to carry His conception of Being out into the dark emptiness of the universe, there to war against other more malignant conceptions of Being), yes, precisely this noble conception will not prevail, and instead a wasteful, slovenly, slothful, treacherous, cowardly, and monotonous conception of Being will become the future of man—such a fear must for God be insupportable. It is the heart of existential logic that God's ultimate victory over the Devil is no more certain than the Devil's victory over God—either may conquer man and so give Being a characteristic Good or Evil, or indeed each may exhaust the other, until Being ceases to exist or sinks through seas of entropy into a Being less various, less articulated, less organic, more like plastic than the Nature we know. What a fear is this fear in God that He may lose eventually to the Devil! Or, even worse—both will lose! What abysses of anxiety and pits of woe in such a contemplation! Zusya, asking to fear God more, is given instead a vision of God's fear. Like any other man, Zusya draws back in terror.

But is not one of the secrets of the miracle just here? The miracle is revealed to those who can bear to undergo the terror that accompanies it. If intimacy with God is not merely a communion of love but a sharing of the Divine terror, then the beauty of any miracle delivered by God is always accompanied by a fear proportionate to the beauty. Because a miracle is not merely a breach in the laws of nature, but a revelation of the nature of the God behind Nature. If one cannot endure the fear, one does not deserve the revelation. So our taste for miracles has left us. Man in the Middle Ages lived with dread as a natural accompaniment to his day. His senses uninsulated by the daily use of daily drugs (nicotine, caffeine, aspirin, alcohol, so forth), his mind not guarded by a society that was anti-supernatural, medieval man was therefore able to live with gods, devils, angels, and demons, with witches, warlocks, and spirits. Miracles, while terrifying, were nonetheless a mark of merit. One was honored to receive them. Whereas we reach quickly and in terror for the first chemical that will flatten an affect, deaden our senses, damp our madness, or forestall a miracle. Conversely, we also look to a drug to induce a hallucination—because any visitation produced by a drug is exempt from the terror of engaging the supernatural. For we know, even as the experience is upon us, that we are not privy to a vision beyond the lip of death but merely are offered a derangement of the senses produced by chemicals. Our modern pleasure is that one is witnessing not a miracle but miracle-in-a-theater.

"*And the Fire Abated*"

*The tale is told:*

*The rabbi of Kalev once spent the Sabbath in a nearby village as the guest of one of the Hasidim. When the hour to receive the Sabbath had come, someone suddenly screamed, and a servant rushed in and cried that the barn in which the grain was stored was on fire. The owner wanted to run out, but the rabbi took him by the hand. "Stay!" he said. "I am going to tell you a story." The Hasid stayed.*

*"When our master Rabbi Zusya was young," said the zaddik, "he stoked the stoves in the house of the Great Maggid, for this duty was always assigned to the youngest disciples. Once when he was saying the psalms with great fervor just before the coming of the Sabbath, he was startled by screams from within the house. Sparks had fallen from the stove which he had filled with wood, and since no one was in the living room, a fire had started.*

*" 'Zusya!' he was reproached. 'There's a fire!'*

*" 'No matter,' he replied. 'Is it not written: And the fire abated!' At that very same moment the fire abated."*

*The rabbi of Kalev fell silent. The Hasid, whom he still held by the hand, did not dare move. A moment passed and someone called in at the window that the fire in the barn had gone out.*

Mood is the earth of the miracle, its garden, its terrain. The mood created by a fire is always in some part Satanic. One senses an avid implacable relentless impatience, a greed to consume, a determination to destroy the material before it, indeed a lunatic intensity within the fire to appropriate the Time embodied in the object that is burning. That is why a fire in a fireplace offers comfort. The fire in this case is smaller than ourselves; the material it consumes, the Time it accelerates, are subservient to the mood of calm and benevolence with which we study the fire. We have the ability at any moment to put it out. We are not confronting the force of the devil but rather devil-in-a-theater. In effect, we are dealing with a commonplace miracle. We invoke the supernatural power of fire, but we control it. To primitive man fire was of course always a miracle, a dangerous miracle. He did not know, he could not know—for he had not yet codified the resources of fire—that he would necessarily be able to control it in every contingency. So he approached fire with profound respect, and prayed to various spirits as he put out a fire in order that the demons in the flame be not offended. How natural for him to assume that the intensity of the fire came from the rabidity of the evil contained within the material. By this understanding, it is not insignificant that the grain of the Hasid catches on fire. The grain is his hoarded wealth, his greed, his covetousness. If his heart has been impure and his plans for what he will do with the money he obtains from the sale of the grain are unholy, then the grain—by this unspoken logic—becomes filled with everything that is evil in the Hasid's soul and so begins to smolder, then bursts into flame. The Hasid is ready to run to the barn; the rabbi restrains him. When the Hasid pauses to listen to the speech of the rabbi, he is in effect ready to relinquish his wealth. So what has been evil in him expires, and what has been heat for the flame in the grain is now cooled. Thus might go the religious logic. The question is whether this logic is utterly without foundation in the real. For philosophically is it not as plausible to assume we have a spirit which is communicable to other people and to the very properties of our environment as it is to assume that spirit does not exist or is not communicable? And is it not equally or almost equally comfortable to assume that a fire may be extinguished by a dramatic shift in mood? Let the burden fall on the philosopher who would prove that the existence of a fire can never be affected by a mood.

From *Cannibals and Christians* (1966)

Disraeli once made a speech in Commons to the effect that the most damaging mistake a conservative party could make was to persecute the Jews, since they were naturally conservative and turned to radical ideas only when they were deprived of an organic place in society. The statement is certainly not without interest, but may grasp no more than a part of the truth. It is more likely the instinct of the Jews to be attracted to large whole detailed views of society, to seek intellectual specifications of the social machine, and to enter precisely those occupations that subtly can offer institutional, personal, and legislative possibilities to a man of quick wit and sensible cohesive culture. The precise need of the essentialist, the authoritarian, or the progressive is to have a social machine upon which one can apply oneself. Later, having earned sufficient and satisfactory power, one may tinker with the machine. It is small wonder that the four corners of modern Protestantism are pegged on Judaistic notions, upon a set of social ideas given bulk and mass only by a most determinedly circumscribed conception of heaven, hell, divine compassion, and eternal punishment. For modern man, Judaeo-Christian man, the social world before him tends to become all of existence.

Yet if the Jews have a greatness, an irreducible greatness, I wonder if it is not to be found in the devil of their dialectic, which places madness next to practicality, illumination side by side with duty, and arrogance in bed with humility. The Jews first saw God in the desert— that dramatic terrain of the present tense stripped of the past, blind to the future. The desert is a land where man may feel insignificant or feel enormous. On the desert can perish the last of one's sensitivities; one's end can wither in the dwarf's law of a bleak nature. Or, to the contrary, left alone and in fever, a solitary witness, no animal or vegetable close to him, man may come to feel immensely alive, more portentous in his own psychic presence than any manifest of nature.

### From the Look-out of Heaven

*At a time of great anguish for Israel, Rabbi Elimelekh brooded more and more on his griefs. Then his dead master, the maggid of Mezritch, appeared to him. Rabbi Elimelekh cried out: "Why are you silent in such dreadful need?" He answered: "In Heaven we see that all that seems evil to you is a work of mercy."*

To die before one's time in a gas chamber may offer the good fortune that one does not have to live beyond one's time and be kept alive by medicines that do not reach the disease but only deaden the pain.

In a gas chamber one loses one's life and conceivably saves one's death. If there is eternity, and we possess a soul that can either carry us through life into death, or perish in life and never reach eternity, then the real need for a Messiah would appear where souls are becoming dead rather than lives being lost. By this logic, there would be more unconscious demand for the Messiah in a country at peace than a city at war.

The logic is unassailable if God has no need of Time and merely studies the way we save our souls or lose them. But if there is any urgency in God's intent, if we are not actors working out a play for our salvation but rather soldiers in an army that seeks to carry some noble conception of Being out across the stars, or back into the protoplasm of life, then a portion of God's creative power was extinguished in the camps of extermination. If God is not all-powerful but existential, discovering not only the possibilities but the limitations of His creative powers in the form of the history that is made by His creatures, then one must postulate an existential equal to God, an antagonist, the Devil, a principle of Evil whose signature was the concentration camps, whose joy is to waste substance, whose intent is to prevent God's conception of Being from reaching its mysterious goal. If one considers the hypothesis that God is not all-powerful, indeed not the architect of Destiny but rather the creator of Nature, then evil becomes a record of the Devil's victories over God.

### The Teaching of the Soul

*Rabbi Pinhas often cited the words: "'A man's soul will teach him,'" and emphasized them by adding: "There is no man who is not incessantly being taught by his soul."*

*One of his disciples asked: "If this is so, why don't men obey their souls?"*

*"The soul teaches incessantly," Rabbi Pinhas explained, "but it never repeats."*

If God and the Devil are locked in an implacable war, it might not be excessive to assume their powers are separate, God the lord of inspiration, the Devil a monumental bureaucrat of repetition. To learn from an inner voice the first time it speaks to us is a small bold existential act, for it depends upon following one's instinct which must derive, in no matter how distorted a fashion, from God, whereas institutional knowledge is appropriated by the Devil. The soul speaks once and chooses not to repeat itself, because to repeat a message is to give the Devil in one's psyche a chance to prepare a trap.

### For the Sake of Renewal

*Rabbi Pinhas said: "Solomon, the preacher, says: 'Vanity of vanities, all is vanity,' because he wants to destroy the world, so that it may receive new life."*

If the world, seen through the eyes of Marx, is the palpable embodiment of a vast collective theft—the labor that was stolen from men by other men over the centuries—then one need not retire in terror from the idea that the power of the world belongs to the Devil, and God needs soldiers to overthrow him.

The entrance of the Devil into aesthetics is visible in a new airline terminal, a luxury hotel, a housing project, or a civic center. Their flat surfaces speak of power without vision, their plastic materials suggest flesh without the unmanageable details of blood.

### The Story of the Cape

*A woman came to Rabbi Israel, the maggid of Koznitz, and told him, with many tears, that she had been married a dozen years and still had not borne a son. "What are you going to do about it?" he asked her. She did not know what to say.*

*"My mother," so the maggid told her, "was aging and still had no child. Then she heard that the holy Baal Shem was stopping over in Apt in the course of a journey. She hurried to his inn and begged him to pray she might bear a son. 'What are you willing to do about it?' he asked. 'My husband is a poor book-binder,' she replied, 'but I do have one fine thing I shall give to the rabbi.' She went home as fast as she could and fetched her good cape, her 'Katinka,' which was carefully stowed away in a chest. But when she returned to the inn with it, she heard that the Baal Shem had already left for Mezbizh. She immediately set out after him and since she had no money to ride, she walked from town to town with her 'Katinka' until she came to Mezbizh. The Baal Shem took the cape and hung it on the wall. 'It is well,' he said. My mother walked all the way back, from town to town, until she reached Apt. A year later, I was born."*

*"I, too," cried the woman, "will bring you a good cape of mine so that I may get a son."*

*"That won't work," said the maggid. "You heard the story. My mother had no story to go by."*

One could use that anecdote as an introduction to *An Intelligent Woman's Guide to Existentialism*. Death, despair, and dread, intimations of nothingness, the mystery of mood, and the logic of commitment have been the central preoccupations of the existentialists. In this country, there has been a tendency to add our American obsession with courage and sex. These concerns are the no-man's-land of philosophy. Insubstantial, novelistic, too intimate for the coiled cosmological speculations of metaphysics, irrational and alien to the classical niceties of ethics, utter anathema to the post-Logical Positivists of Oxford, existentialism remains nonetheless the one non-sterile continuation open to modern philosophy, for it is the last of the humanisms. It has not given its unconditional surrender to science.

The existential premise in "The Story of the Cape" is that we learn only from situations in which the end is unknown. As an epistemological scheme it suggests that man learns more about the nature of water by jumping into the surf than by riding a boat. Certainly he learns more about the nature of water if he comes close to drowning. Restated in a framework of Zen, one might say that the nature of experience is comprehended to the degree it is seen in the purity of no concept. A career soldier, armed with the professional necessity to be brave, can go through combat without ever entering an existential moment. His duty is simple. It is to fight until he dies or wins. It is only if he goes through enough combat to exhaust the concept of his duty, and is thus reduced to a man who may either have the will to continue or the desire to quit, that he will have then entered the existential terrain where one discovers authenticity in one's desires.

The logic in searching for extreme situations, in searching for one's authenticity, is that one burns out the filament of old dull habit and turns the conscious mind back upon its natural subservience to the instinct. The danger of civilization is that its leisure, its power, its insulation from nature, so alienate us from instinct that our consciousness and our habits take on an autonomy that can censor even the most necessary communication between mind and instinct. Consciousness, alienated from instinct, begins to construct its intellectual formulations over a void. The existential moment, by demanding the most extreme response in the protagonist, tends to destroy psychotic autonomies in the mind—since they are unreal, they give way first— one is returned closer to the reality of one's personal strength or weakness. The woman in search of a child goes on a pilgrimage in which her end is unknown—she may find the Baal Shem or she may not, but her commitment is complete, and the suggestion intrudes itself that on the long miles of her march, her mind, her habits, and her body were affected sufficiently to dissolve the sterilities of her belly and prepare her for a child.

Her commitment created her new condition. In giving herself to a concept outside herself, the experience she encountered was able to change her. The second woman having heard the story was trying to cheat an existential demand. She was looking not for commitment but obedience to a precedent. And precedent is the spine of all consciousness that is constructed upon a void. Precedent, it can be said, is the description of an event that occurred in the past, and has therefore altered the present in such a way that the same event could not take place again.

From *The Presidential Papers* (1963)

# IN PREFACE
# TO THE GOSPEL—III

**October 22**   ## The Communication
of Christ

Five minutes later was a scene of congratulation on the grass outside
the open arcades of Occoquan Prison. He had signed papers, gone
through a few small formalities, and now stood in front of Leiterman's
camera, speaking into the microphone held by the sound man, Heiss,
while reporters from *The Washington Post* stood by with pads in their
hands, taking every word he said, and he spoke slowly at the rate of
dictation he might have used with a new stenographer.

John Boyle, the Presbyterian Chaplain at Yale, was also there. Released yesterday, he had come out to Occoquan today, and he and
Mailer greeted each other with warmth, next to old buddies now on
the impetus of their bust. But he had also greeted Leiterman with
warmth, Leiterman with his faithful camera—how many hours had
Fontaine and Leiterman and Heiss been waiting for his release, and
in the open celebrative sentiment of being free of jail, and out on
that last unexpected high hurdle—funds of great affection now for
de Grazia also listening to his speech before the camera, and for
Hirschkop now back in some other courtroom, working no doubt
with the same dedicated ferocity to gain a verdict for the next prisoner, yes, in this resumption of the open air after twenty-four hours,
no more, there was a sweet clean edge to the core of the substance of
things—a monumentally abstract remark which may be saved by the
concrete observation that the air was good in his lungs—not often
could Mailer count on such sweet air. Standing on the grass, he felt

one suspicion of a whole man closer to that freedom from dread which occupied the inner drama of his years, yes, one image closer than when he had come to Washington four days ago. The sum of what he had done that he considered good outweighed the dull sum of his omissions these same four days. So he was happy, and it occurred to him that this clean sense of himself must come crashing down soon, but still—this nice anticipation of the very next moves of life itself (all for just an incredibly inexpensive twenty-four hours in jail) must mean, indeed could mean nothing else to Christians but what they must signify when they spoke of Christ within them—it was not unlike the rare sweet of a clean loving tear not dropped, still held, oh he must be salient now, and deliver the best of himself to these microphones and reporters, and in respect to Boyle, pick up some of the Chaplain's language, why not? Some message from the Marchers at the Pentagon had to reach America and Americans.

So he made the following speech:

"Today is Sunday, and while I am not a Christian, I happen to be married to one. And there are times when I think the loveliest thing about my dear wife is her unspoken love for Jesus Christ." Unspoken it was, most certainly. She would wonder if he was mad when she read this, for outside of her profound observance of Christmas Eve and her dedication to decorating a Christmas tree, they never talked about such matters. As a child, she had rarely gone to church, but he knew what he meant—some old pagan spirit of her part-Swedish blood must have carried Christ through all the Southern exposures of her mixed part-Indian blood, crazy American lass, one-time mouther of commercials on television, mother of his two—would they be mighty?—boys, angel or witch, she had a presence like silver, she was on all nights of the full moon near to mad, and he loved her for that quality he could never explain—her unexpected quixotic depths of compassion, yes the loveliest thing about his dear wife was her unspoken love for Jesus Christ.

"Some of us," said Mailer to the reporters and the photographer and the microphone, "were at the Pentagon yesterday, and we were arrested in order to make our symbolic protest of the war in Vietnam, and most of us served these very short sentences, but they are a harbinger of what will come next, for if the war doesn't end next year," then said he, feeling as modest as he had felt on the steps of the Department of Justice, "why, then, a few of us will probably have to take longer sentences. Because we must. You see, dear fellow Americans, it is Sunday, and we are burning the body and blood of Christ in Vietnam. Yes, we are burning him there, and as we do, we destroy the foundation of this Republic, which is its love and trust in Christ." He was silent. Wow.

And Boyle gave him a sidelong look, as if to say, "Watch it, old buddy, they put junior reverends in the cuckoo house for carrying on." But Boyle looked pleased. And the reporters looked pleased. And Fontaine and Leiterman, Leiterman particularly, looked ecstatic, for the end of their movie might be there.

They drove back to Washington in de Grazia's car, and Mailer changed at the hotel, called his wife, caught a shuttle, had a merry ride back with Fontaine, for there were hordes of young girls on the flight and the air between New York and Washington was orgiastic with the breath of release; some promise of peace and new war seemed riding the phosphorescent wake of this second and last day's siege of the Pentagon, as if the country were opening into more and more on the resonance of these two days, more that was good, more that was bad, and Mailer met his wife at P. J. Clarke's for dinner, but their luck was poor—an old girl friend of the novelist passed by, tapped him possessively on the hair, and so he spent the evening in a muted quarrel with his wife, the actress Beverly Bentley.

And a few days later saw his immortal speech on Christ as it was printed in *The Washington Post*. There was no mention of the scene outdoors on the grass. The story went like this:

> Novelist Norman Mailer, using a makeshift courtroom to deliver a Sunday sermon on the evils of the Vietnam war, received the only prison sentence yesterday as justice was meted out in wholesale lots for hundreds of anti-war demonstrators.
>
> In his courtroom speech, Mailer said, "They are burning the body and blood of Christ in Vietnam."
>
> "Today is Sunday," he said, "and while I am not a Christian, I happen to be married to one. And there are times when I think the loveliest thing about my dear wife is her unspoken love for Jesus Christ . . ."
>
> Mailer said he believed that the war in Vietnam "will destroy the foundation of this republic, which is its love and trust in Christ." Mailer is a Jew.

It was obvious the good novelist Norman Mailer had much to learn about newspapers, reporters, and salience.

From *The Armies of the Night* (1968)

# THE GOSPEL ACCORDING TO THE SON

## John the Baptist and the Devil

People said, and it was true when I saw him, that the Baptist wore but one small wrapping of camel's hide to conceal his loins. He was so naked to the sun that he looked darker than any of his visitors, a thin man with a thin beard.

I had also heard how he believed that meat and wine inspire demons to live in one's body; therefore he ate nothing but wild honey and locusts, the poorest food of the poor. Yet it was said that these locusts could devour all the disbelief in the hearts of those who came to John. And the wild honey gave warmth to his voice when he spoke in the words of Isaiah: " 'The crooked shall be made straight and the rough ways made smooth.' "

Yet I had also been told that the locusts he ate kept him harsh in spirit and he would greet penitents by saying: "Generation of vipers, who has warned you to flee from the wrath to come?"

The people would ask: "What shall we do?" And John the Baptist would answer: "Let him who has two coats give one to the man who has none." And he would always speak of the man mightier than himself who was yet to come.

Yet when I first saw his face, I wished to hide my own. For I knew that he would not be long among us. And I knew this as if I heard a beating of wings overhead.

I had joined a group of many people and so I could stare at John before he saw me and was able to watch the pilgrims as they were baptized and departed. I remained. Even in the loneliness of this place in the desert, he still could not see me, for I concealed myself in the shadow of a rock. It was only when the others were gone and the stones were hot from the sun that I came forward. To which he said, "I have waited for you."

His eyes had more light than the sky, yet they were paler than the moon. His thin beard was long. The hair that grew from his ears was matted, and so too was the hair that grew from his cheeks. A wing and a leg of a locust were caught in his beard. I wondered how this man who bathed others and washed himself many times a day could still show such leavings. Yet it was not unfitting. His face was like a ravine and small creatures would live within.

Looking at me, he said, "You are my cousin." Then he said, "I knew that you would come today."

"How can you know?"

He sighed. His breath was as lonely as the wind that passes through empty places. He said, "I have been told to wait for you, and I am tired. It is good that you are here."

I felt so near to him that I soon confessed my sins—I had never done as much for another. I would have deemed it belittling to whatever pride I had as a man. (For my sins were too small.) I might be a master carpenter and thirty years of age, but I felt young before him, and modest and much too innocent for such a grave man. I searched to find evil in myself and came back with no more than moments I could recall of disrespect toward my mother and contests in the night with lustful thoughts. Perhaps there had been a few acts of unkindness when judging others.

"Well," he said, "you can still repent. Our sin is always more than we know." And John came behind me as I entered the water, and with the strength of a desert lion, he seized me by the nose and, with his other hand pressing upon my forehead, thrust me back into the river. Passing so quickly from air to water, I gasped first at my loss of breath and then from all the water I swallowed. Still, in this moment I saw many things, and my life was changed forever.

Was the Holiest descending toward us in the shape of a dove? And when I came up from the water, the dove was on my shoulder. I felt as if much had come back to me from all that had been lost. I was one again with myself—a poor man, but good. And then I felt more. I had a vision of glory. The heavens opened for an instant and it was as if I saw a million, nay, a million million of souls.

I heard a voice, and it came from the heavens. It came into my ear and said: "Before I formed thee in the belly, I knew thee." Fear and exaltation were in me then, and in greater measure than I had ever known. I raised my face to the heavens and said, "Lord God, I am like a child."

And the Lord spoke as He had to the prophet Jeremiah. I heard: "Say not 'I am a child,' for you shall go to all the places that I shall send thee." And I felt as if His finger blessed my mouth even as the beak of the dove touched my lips. His Word came into me like the burning fire in my bones when I was twelve and sick with fever.

Now John withdrew his hand from my head and we stood in the river. Away went the dove. And John and I spoke to each other a little. I will tell of that, and soon. But when I left, I knew that I would never see him again. He began to sing as I left, but it was to the River Jordan, not to me. And the taste of that brown river was still in my mouth and the dust of the desert in my nostrils as I set out on my long march home to Nazareth.

It was late in the afternoon. The light upon the rocks turned to gold. And I could still hear John the Baptist as he sang. Since he knew no song, the music of his throat came forth like the voice of a ram.

I walked with strength. For now I was no longer like other men. My legs took larger strides than before. Now I knew the other man who had lived within the shell of myself, and he was better than me. I had become that man.

A great cloud came over the sky. There was a downpour. A rainbow arose from one end of the desert to touch the other, and above me was the radiance of the Lord. Soon I lay down upon the hot damp sand, and soon I heard His voice. He said: "Stand upon your feet."

When I did, He told me: "Once I spoke to the prophet Ezekiel and he saved our people in Babylon. Now these words given to Ezekiel are for you: 'Son of Man, I send thee to the children of Israel, to a nation that hath rebelled against Me, even unto this very day. For they are impudent children and stiff-hearted. But you will speak My words unto them. Since they are not a people of a strange speech whose words you cannot understand but are the house of Israel, behold! I will make your face strong against their face. So fear them not.'"

Then this voice said into my ear: "Those were My words to Ezekiel. But to you I say: You are My son, and therefore you will be mightier than a prophet. Even mightier than the prophet Ezekiel."

I still had many hours to travel across land I hardly knew. Again I was full of exaltation, and again I was full of fear. I was also weary.

The scrolls I had studied since childhood were not as close to me as the words of this high Lord my God, yet now that He was near, I could only fear Him. For the sound of His voice can be heard in the echo of great rocks when they fall. And I did not know how to serve a Lord who could leave boils upon the flesh of every man and beast in the land of Egypt and cast hail to blight every herb of the field, or fire in the grass until every tree was consumed. I raised my hands toward heaven as if to ask whether I was truly the one to exercise His force. And God said to me, "Since you are not yet strong, do not return to your home. Go up rather into the mountain that is there before you. Go now. In that wilderness, fast among the rocks. Drink the water that is beneath the rocks. But eat no food. Before the sun sets on the last of your days of fast, you will know why I have chosen you."

Soon I learned of His power to protect me. As I climbed, darkness fell and I had to share my ground with serpents and scorpions. Yet none came near. In the morning I climbed further and for much of the day upward on this mountain. And it was worthy of the lamentations of the prophet Isaiah, for one could say that the cormorant and the bittern possessed it.

In every direction was emptiness. On the ramparts of the rock, vultures looked down on me, side by side, every vulture with her mate. It was then I thought of how John the Baptist had asked, on saying farewell: "Did the light of the Lord appear when you were immersed?"

Even as John's eyes stared into mine, I had wondered if the million million of souls that I had seen were the face of the Lord. But to John I said only: "Is it not death and destruction to see Him?"

He replied: "For all but the Christ." Then John said: "Once the Holy Spirit came to me. He was so near that I put my hands before my eyes. But the Holy Spirit said: 'I will let you gaze upon My back,' and He allowed me to see that His back was noble, a noble back." Then John grasped my arm. "I have known since I was a child that my cousin must come after me and replace me. For my mother spoke of how your mother told her of all that had been with her." Now he kissed me on both cheeks. "I baptize with water," he said, "and can cleanse any soul who has truly repented, even as water can extinguish fire. But you will baptize with the Spirit. You will root out evil with God's mercy." And he kissed me again.

It was hard not to remember the breath of John the Baptist when he embraced me, for it was full of all that is in the odor of an exhausted man. And indeed, no matter how often one seeks water to soothe the throat, such an odor cannot be separated from the flesh. A vast fatigue speaks of all that has been lost to one's striving. Yet his skin had been honest and full of the loneliness of the desert and its rocks. And so did he also smell of the waters of the River Jordan and the heavy wisdom of its mud and silt.

At the summit, the rocks stood about like tombs, and the steps between were treacherous. It was midday. The heat of the sun was on me.

I sat in the shadow of a great stone and looked out on the lands of Israel, upon Galilee to the north and Judea to the south. The haze had a golden hue, and I wondered whether one could even see the spires of gold that rose above the hills of the holy city. But I did not think long on Jerusalem; living without food for a day, I was hungry.

Yet I also knew why the Lord had sent me to the summit of this mountain. For it was not enough to be His son and cousin to John the Baptist. I had to pass through trials, and the first test must be not to eat. Even as I said to myself, "I will take no food until sundown," the Lord replied.

I did not see Him, nor did I feel His presence other than His voice (which was in my ear), but He said: "You will fast until I tell you to eat."

So I was without food for that day and the next. And by the fifth day, when the pangs of my stomach had given way to a solemn emptiness of spirit, I felt weak and no longer knew if I had the strength to climb down from this mountain. So I said aloud, "How long, O Lord?" and He replied, "Long. It will be long."

Since I was not there to dispute Him but to follow His will, fasting grew easier. I shielded myself from the sun and came to love the taste of water and the wisdom that is found in the shade of large rocks (until they grow too cold at night for any wisdom). And the air of night was cold. No plants grew on the summit of this mountain. Which was just as well. For there were hours when I could have chewed on their thorns.

In the second week, I had visions of King David and knew that he had committed a great sin. I could not recall the offense, but I did remember that he had been punished, and on his death the Lord had appeared to the son of David, King Solomon, and asked: "What shall I give thee?"

And Solomon replied: "O Lord my God, I know not how to go out nor to come in, and Thy servant is in the midst of Thy people, a great people that cannot be numbered nor counted. Give therefore Thy servant an understanding heart that I may discern between good and bad."

And I recalled how this speech had so pleased the Lord that He said to Solomon: "Because thou hast not asked for a long life nor for riches nor begged for the death of thine enemies but asked for discernment in judgment, then, behold, I have given thee a wise and understanding heart."

And God gave Solomon all that he had not asked for, both riches and honors, until there were no kings as great as Solomon in those days.

But now the voice of the Lord was saying to me: "Solomon did not keep My Commandments. Solomon spoke three thousand proverbs, and his songs were a thousand and five. All people came to hear the wisdom of Solomon, in that he exceeded all the kings of the earth. And these kings brought him silver, ivory, apes, and peacocks. But," said the Lord to my ear, "King Solomon loved many strange women: the daughter of Pharaoh and the women of the Moabites, the Ammonites, the Edomites, the Sedonians, and the Hittites, whereas I had said unto the children of Israel, 'Ye shall not go in to them. For surely they will turn your heart toward their gods.' But Solomon had seven hundred wives and three hundred concubines, and when Solomon was old, his heart was not perfect with Me. I had given him too many gifts. So," said the Lord, "I will not give you riches. And you will never tarry with a woman, or you shall lose the Lord."

He had given me Solomon's sins on which to meditate, and that was an advantage not given to Solomon. I, being without food, had no desire for a woman, nor did I feel at odds with the Lord's decision. My fast continued.

The prophets were often with me in these weeks: Elijah and Elisha, Isaiah and Daniel and Ezekiel. I could recall their words as if they were my own. Before long, I had a dream that made me one with the prophet Elijah, and in this dream I had contests with the prophets of Baal. More than forty such pagan prophets had come to my mountain to sacrifice a bullock, but first they destroyed the Lord's altar on the summit. Then they lacerated themselves with knives to show their devotion to Baal. Blood spurted from the wounds of these prophets and they cried aloud, yet the god Baal could not speak.

Seeing that Baal was silent in my presence, I put twelve large stones on end, to stand for the twelve tribes of the sons of Israel, after which I restored the altar of the Lord. Then I dug a trench around the stones and put wood on the altar and cut the bullock into pieces, laying the raw flesh upon the wood. And then I poured four barrels of water on the sacrifice until this water ran into the trench.

And the fire of the Lord blazed through the meat of the bullock and the sopping wood and the wet stones and licked up all the water that was in the trench. And I beheaded these forty prophets of Baal with a sword, and only then did I awake.

Now it came to me that I was not Elijah but only dreaming of the scroll of Elijah, and the dream had been there to tell me that my fast must continue for forty days and forty nights. For if I did not change my ways or the people of Israel did not change theirs, then all of us were in danger of God's final judgment.

So could I also see how my youth had passed with more thought given to the wood under my tools than to my people. Nor had I listened when Joseph would say: "All share in the sinfulness of Israel because we do not work hard enough to overcome it."

I was yet to learn that I would care about sinners more than for the pious, but now I was content to quote the words of Isaiah to myself: "Though Thy people Israel be as the sand of the sea, yet a remnant shall return." And there, near to the sixth week of my fast, full of the spirit of Isaiah, I hoped that with the aid of this remnant of good Jews I might recover all that had been lost in the nation. So I would repeat the sayings of Isaiah aloud, speaking even into the eye of the sun until my eyes burned and I was obliged to return to the shade. I pondered the prayers I would use with sinners and decided that I would tell them, even as had Isaiah: " 'Wash you, make you clean; put away the evil of your doings; relieve the oppressed.' "

And it was the fortieth day. As evening came, the Lord said to me, "Tomorrow you may step down from the mountain and take food." Hunger came back to me on these words, and I was ravenous.

Yet even as I was thinking of what I would eat, the Lord said, "Tonight, remain on the mountain. A visitor will come."

The visitor soon arrived. And he was as handsome as a prince. He had a gold ornament on a gold chain about his neck, and in this ornament was the face of a ram, bestial yet more noble than any ram I had ever seen. And the hair of this prince was as long as my own and lustrous. He was dressed in robes of velvet that were as purple as the late evening, and he wore a crown as golden as the sun. He had climbed the mountain, yet there was no dust on his robes nor sweat upon his skin. He could be no other than who I thought, and indeed he soon introduced himself. I said to myself, "The Devil is the most beautiful creature God ever made."

His first words were: "Do you know how the prophet Isaiah met his death?"

I was overcome with silence. So I was obliged to listen as he said: "Isaiah was killed by a Jewish king, the pagan Manasseh, cohort of Amon. A bad Jew." The Devil nodded as if he were a good Jew (which I was certain he was not!). Then he held up one finger and spoke again: "This Manasseh, wishing to destroy the religion of his fathers, sent out a royal order that Isaiah was to be uprooted from his home in the city and hunted like an animal. Hearing of this, Isaiah fled, and the soldiers of Manasseh set out after him into the wilderness. There, the prophet looked for a tree with a hollow large enough for a man to stand inside. This sanctuary," said the Devil, "he found in a stout oak with a rotten center, and he placed himself inside it. But the officers of Manasseh discovered where he was hiding and brought a great saw to the tree and cut it in half. Isaiah went screaming into his death. Did you know?" asked the Devil.

"Not of such a death did I hear."

Whereupon he laughed. I felt weakened by this story more than by any deprivation of the fast.

He, however, was not about to cease speaking. "The manner in which Isaiah met his death need not give you large concern," he said, "since you are not a prophet but indeed the Son! To my recollection, which is not small, the Lord has never performed an act of this kind before. Indeed, to look upon you is to give me much to contemplate. For you seem innocent of all that I know."

He looked at me fondly. His eyes were black marble, but there were lights within. He said, "Are you hungry? Are you in need of drink?" And he brought forth a jug of wine and a leg of lamb, well cooked, which I had not seen beneath his robes until he produced them. And now he approached me so closely that my nostrils took in the spirit of the wine and the gravies of the lamb, even the smell of the Devil himself, which penetrated a small cloud of perfume rising from the folds of his robe. I could also perceive how greed came forth from his body. For that was kin to the odor that lives between the buttocks. Therefore I refused his food, but still, the other odors of his body entered my appetite like the savory that comes from an oven when food is roasting. And he, seeing such deliberation, smiled once more and said, "But of course you have no need of food. Being the Son of God, you can as easily command these stones to be bread. Which is proper food for an Essene. However, your garment is neither clean nor free of dust. Indeed, that you are the Son of God surprises me. Why did your Father choose you? Say to Him when next you converse that I salute Him. For do you know? Your Father and I have had much traffic and considerable dispute, and so We are always eager to obtain word of the Other and His doings. Indeed, on those occasions when We meet, I tell Him that men and women are the crown of all He has conceived among the animals and the plants of the field but that it is I, not He, who has a better understanding of this Creation. For His work has given issue to many small creatures and spirits that He hardly knows as well as I do. Of course, I was once His servant, His most trusted servant. Contemplate, then, how well I understand Him."

I was amazed. He did not inspire fear but comfort. Now I knew how it might feel to be a sinner in a low tavern drinking wine. The labors of this long fast were gone; I felt balm come to my limbs. I could talk to the Devil; he was comfortable. If his odor could leave me uneasy, it also offered sympathy to desires I had not yet allowed myself to feel.

Yet if I would allow him much, still I could not agree that God, the Lord of the Universe, did not understand His Creation better than my visitor. "It is not possible," I exclaimed. "He is all-powerful. The heavens and the earth, the stars and the sun, bow before Him. They do not bow to you."

For one moment, Satan snorted like a horse. Was he unwilling to accept the bridle?

"Your Father," said the Devil, "is but one god among many. You might take account of the myriad respected by the Romans. Are we to give no homage to the great will of the Romans? Why, your Father does not even have the power to command His own Jews in their own land even though so many see Him as the only One. You would do better to consider the breadth of His rages; they are unseemly for a great god. They are swollen and without proportion. He issues too many threats. He cannot bear anyone who would dispute Him. Whereas I confide to you that a hint of disobedience and a whiff of treachery are among the joys of life, and are to be ranked with its spoils rather than its evils."

"That is not so," I was able to answer. "My Father is God, and of many dimensions, and of all dimensions." But my words tasted like straw.

The Devil replied, "He is not in command of Himself!"

Nor did the Devil show any fear at what he had said. He continued to speak. "Your Father," he said, "does not have the right to demand complete obedience from His people. He does not comprehend that women are creatures different from men and live with separate understanding. Indeed, your Father has no inkling of women; His scorn for them is shared by His prophets, who speak, so they claim, with His voice. And they do! For rarely will He reprimand them! Look at Isaiah! Tell me that Isaiah does not live in your Father's heart when he says: 'Because the daughters of Zion are haughty and walk with stretched-forth necks and wanton eyes, walking and mincing as they go, therefore the Lord will smite with a scabbard the crown of the head of the daughters of Zion, and the Lord will discover their secret parts.' *Their secret parts,*" repeated the Devil. And he continued to speak with the words of Isaiah: " 'The Lord will take away their bracelets and bonnets, the ornaments of the legs, the earrings, the rings and the nose-jewels, the fine linen, the hoods and the veils. And it shall come to pass that instead of sweet smell there shall be stink; and instead of a girdle, a rent; for lovely hair, there shall be baldness, and burning instead of beauty.' "

"My Father was speaking of the nation of Zion," I said. "So were we taught."

"No," replied the Devil. "He pretends to speak of the nation of Zion. But it is women He belittles. His mighty curses He saves for the men. When He wishes to address the nation of Israel, He is speaking only to men: 'The indignation of the Lord is upon all nations, and His fury upon all their armies: He hath utterly destroyed them, He hath delivered them to the slaughter. Their offal shall come up out of their carcasses and the mountains shall be melted with their blood.' What a rage! His failures burn in His heart! Can He suspect that He may not be all-powerful? No! He does not have enough spirit to say: 'Yes, I have lost, but my soldiers were honest and fought well.' No, He is vengeful. 'The palaces will be forsaken,' says Isaiah, 'the forts and towers shall be dens forever, until the Spirit be poured upon us from on High.'

"But when," asked the Devil, "will the Spirit be poured upon us? Your Father would send you forth to improve the hearts of men when His own heart is caked with the blood of those He has slaughtered. His love of all He has created is choked by His curses. His rages may be mighty, but they do not satisfy His desire. His language reveals how much He adores the grandeur He pretends to despise.

"Tell me that your Father is not filled with an adoration of women. Which He hides from Himself! For He hates their power to entice Him. Ezekiel knows what is in your Father's heart. After all, he heard these words from the Lord: 'I swore unto thee and entered into a covenant with thee, and thou becamest mine. I washed thee with water; yea, I thoroughly washed away thy blood, and I anointed thee with oil. I clothed thee also in broidered work, and fine linen, and I covered thee with silk, with ornaments, and I put bracelets upon thy hands and a chain on thy neck, and earrings in thine ears, and a beautiful crown upon thine head. Thou wast decked with gold and silver; thou didst eat fine bread, and honey, and oil: and thou wast exceedingly beautiful, and thou didst prosper into a kingdom. And thy renown went forth among the heathen for thy beauty which I had put upon thee.' Now," said the Devil, "hear how He complains! He is pitiful in His complaints: 'But thou didst trust in thine own beauty, and played the harlot because of thy renown, and poured out thy fornications on everyone that passed by, and multiplied thy whoredoms. Thou hast also committed fornication with the Egyptians, thy neighbors, great of flesh; and hast played the whore also with the Assyrians because thou wast insatiable.

" 'Wherefore, O harlot, because thy filthiness was poured out, and thy nakedness discovered, therefore I will gather all thy lovers with whom thou hast taken pleasure; and will gather them round about against thee, and give thee into their hand, and they shall throw down thine eminent place, and shall strip thee of thy clothes, and shall take thy fair jewels and leave thee naked and bare, and they shall stone thee, and thrust thee through with their swords. And they shall burn thy houses with fire, and execute judgments upon thee in the sight of many women: and I will cause thee to cease from playing the harlot.'

"Does all this take place," asked the Devil, "in order to scorn Jerusalem? Say rather that your Father's language reeks of desire."

"Your words are pollutions." I hoped to excite enough anger in myself to reply, but I could only repeat: "Your words are poisonous."

Satan replied: "Your Father's tongue is as ripe with lust as my own."

I knew confusion. Could I deny that my loins had quickened as I listened to the repetition of my Father's words?

Now the Devil said: "You believe that you are sitting on the summit of this mountain, but we are no longer there. We have risen to a place above the holy places."

His embrace of my vision was complete. Now I saw the city of Jerusalem, and it was beneath us. For we were no longer seated on the mountain. We were on the highest dome of the Great Temple in Jerusalem.

I felt vertigo.

At that moment the Devil said to me, "Because you are the Son of God, you can feel free to leap! Cast yourself out. Your Father's angels will carry you."

I felt a temptation to jump. But, most suddenly, I did not feel as if I were the Son of God. Not yet!

An abyss was below me. And I knew it would be there for all the generations to come. Whenever they stood on a height, they would live in the wind of that unruly spirit who dwells in our breath and has a terror of the leap. Now the Devil looked at me again with his dark eyes, and the points of light within were like a night of stars; those eyes would promise glory. "If you stay with your Father you will labor for Him," he said. "You will be consumed. Jump! You can save yourself. Jump!"

I would be smashed. But would my extinction be brief? And my return to the living as quick? The Devil had taken me into him. By the light in his dark eyes, I knew his speech even though he said nothing. If I jumped, the Devil would possess me. I would have leaped to my death at his bidding.

But at this moment he said aloud, "You will be reborn. In secret. God will not know. I have the power to distract."

He was telling me of a life to come. It would be bountiful. "All is mine!" cried Satan aloud.

Indeed, greed was godly to him. Out of crude greed would come works of great power. "Those who have loyalty to me," said the Devil, "sit now upon the earth with such command that they never give vent to those little turds, fit only for a goat, that pinch themselves forth from the bony cheeks of your friend John. Why, he will not even shit on the Sabbath! And on other days he carries a small hoe to cover his leavings."

And I, in this same moment, wondered whether I could leap but not fall. Could I fly with angels? By power given to me by the Lord, could I fly?

Could I know? Satan stood between my Father and me. Did he have the power to deny the wings of the angel? I did not jump. I wanted to, but I did not dare. To myself I said, "I will not serve God as a brave son but as a modest one." That was just. Had I not spent more than half my life working carefully with many small movements, equal to equal, with the small mysteries of wood?

And now I had an inkling of why God had chosen Mary and Joseph to be my family. I said, "Get thee hence, Satan." If my voice was weak, I repeated it: "Get thee hence, Satan," and now my voice had more force. It was ready to draw upon the strength that comes from emptiness. And I saw the wisdom of the Lord. For even in fasting is strength, and that was the greatest strength one could bring to bear against the Devil inasmuch as he hated emptiness. Who is more lonely than the Devil? I had the power at last to look into Satan's eyes and say: "It is not you I want. It is my Father." Even as I said this, I knew a small but sharp woe. I was losing something I desired, and I was losing it forever.

But Satan gave a cry like a beast just wounded by the spear. "Your Father," he cried, "will destroy His own Creation. For too little!" And he departed. And I was left with a vision of angels. They gathered about me to bathe my eyes. I slept. Never before had I known such exhaustion.

In the morning I awoke to see myself on this same mountain where I had lived for forty days. Now I was ready to come down. The road to Nazareth would be long and empty. Yet for the next day and the next, no brigands attacked. Which was just as well. My hour with the Devil had left me spent. My breath was foul. Nor did I feel that I had escaped altogether.

I was, however, not distraught. For as I marched, so could I recite the words of Isaiah: " 'Unto us,' " I declared, " 'a child is born; unto us a son is given; and the government shall be upon his shoulders; and his name shall be called wonderful, counselor, the mighty God, the everlasting Father, the prince of peace.' " And if I was too insignificant for such words, I had to suppose that God had chosen me for His son because I had been born and had lived in the midst of common people rather than like a king. Thereby I could understand many small virtues and weak habits in others. If I could increase in my powers (and I knew that He would pass on many powers to me), perhaps the world of men might multiply in virtue with me. So I had begun to believe in my Father. I would labor for Him. Soon He would come to save Jerusalem. He was Lord of the Universe. I would labor with joy. Through Him, comfort would come to those who were sorrowful, and the hungry would be fed, yes, and those sinners in greatest despair would find their sins remitted. And I felt such joy at these thoughts that I could not believe they were my own. Indeed, the Devil must have scraped me sore in my judgment, for I was now ready to do all. But then, on this new morning I was not much afraid of Satan. He had captured only a small part of me. I had been tested, had proved loyal, and now my tongue began to feel clean. As I walked, there was the smallest and sweetest of modest miracles. In this desert waste I came upon a small tree and it bore plums that slaked my thirst and gave a sweet warmth to my limbs. I fell to my knees and blessed my Creator, yet before I could even begin to pray, I came to my feet again.

I was obliged to wonder. Why had the Lord left me alone with Satan? Was it to scourge me of an excess of piety? Before long I would learn that there might be truth in this. There was work to do, and it could not be accomplished on one's knees.

## Faith and Lack of Faith

I was coming to comprehend that one must enter the darkness that lives beneath every radiance of spirit. And I wished to open my apostles to such a truth. I told them of a dream that had visited me each night for seven nights; it was a dream that the Son of Man would go to Jerusalem and be denied by the High Priest and be crucified.

On hearing it, my disciples said, "No, you will live forever. And we will live with you."

Then I knew why darkness lies close to exaltation. If they loved me, it was for my power to work miracles, not because I might teach them to love others. They wished to preach like me, but only to increase their own power, not to preach with love. So I rebuked them, saying: "You savor not the things that be of God but the things that be of men." In the silence that followed these words, the dream was upon me again.

"If I am killed, I will rise again after three days," I said. But I did not know if I spoke the truth.

I looked into their eyes to see if their souls were open. For at just this moment, the miracle of faith would be present or would not. In their eyes I saw no more than a heaviness of spirit. It was the heaviness that speaks of concern for oneself. I had wanted to drive them toward faith, but now I realized that I, too, was not acting out of love for others but was looking for power to convince them. So I sighed at the intricacy of the heart. And they sighed after me, as if we all knew how close we had come to truth yet also knew how far away we were.

# Judas

I was uplifted by the force of my voice and spoke with such strength that the Lord whispered: "Enough! In your speech is the seed of discontent. When you are without Me, the Devil is your companion." And I felt as if the Lord held a thorn to my brow; I no longer knew to whose voice I listened. And I understood that to be the Son of God was not equal to being a Prince of Heaven but instead was my apprenticeship in learning how to speak simply and with wisdom, rather than by bewildering others with the brilliance of one's words; it was to know—most difficult of all—when the Lord was speaking through me and when He was not.

While we waited and worked to keep our spirits together, I had my times of doubt. I had labored in so many ways to reach the hearts of my fellow Jews, good men, even pillars of the community, but so many had wanted nothing to do with me.

It was then I had the longest conversation I would know with Judas. For, in an hour of doubt, I asked him: "Why do they not join me? How can they not wish to enter the Kingdom of Heaven?"

He was ready to tell me. "It is," Judas said, "because you do not understand them. You speak of the end of this world and our entrance into another realm. But a moneylender or a merchant does not want this world to end. He is comfortable with his little triumphs, and he wishes to be able to brood on the losses of his day. So he is at home with everything that proves a little cleaner or a little filthier than it was supposed to be. He lives for the play of chance. That is why he is so pious when he does not play. He suspects that the Lord would never approve of chance, yet here is he, enjoying life to the degree that it is a game and not a serious matter. Except for money. Gold is the center of philosophy for such a person, and salvation is there to contemplate in one's thoughts, but not in one's actions. He could even live with what you say about salvation, except that you ask for too much. You tell him to give everything of himself to it. So you offend him profoundly. You want the world to end in order that glory can come for all of us. Your merchant knows better. A little of this, a little of that, and the Highest One to be revered—at a great distance, of course."

"You speak," I said, "as if you agree with them."

"In my thoughts I am often closer to them than I am to you."

"Then why are you with me?"

"Because many of your sayings are closer to me than any enjoyment I receive by witnessing their games. Having grown up among them, I know what is in their hearts, and I detest them. They continue to believe they are good. They see themselves as rich in charity, in piety, and in loyalty to their people. So I scorn them. They not only tolerate the great distance between the rich and the poor, they increase it."

"Then you are with me?"

"Yes."

"Is it because I know that we cannot reach the Kingdom of Heaven until there are no rich and no poor?"

"Yes."

"Still, you almost speak as if you do not care about entering the Kingdom of Heaven."

"God strike me, but I do not believe in it."

"But you say you are with me. Why, then, are you with me?"

"Can you bear the truth?"

"I am nothing without it."

"The truth, dear Yeshua, is that I do not believe you will ever bring us all to salvation. Yet in the course of saying all that you say, the poor will take courage to feel more equal to the rich. That gives me happiness."

"That alone?"

"I hate the rich. They poison all of us. They are vain, undeserving, and wasteful of the hopes of those who are beneath them. They spend their lives lying to the lowly."

I hardly knew what to reply. He had left me not unhappy. Indeed, I was all but merry. For I could see that he would work for me, and work hard. So, he would help to bring us all to salvation. What a smile of joyous disbelief would be on his face when we entered the gates together. Only then would he see how all I said came truly from my Father.

I loved Judas. In this hour I loved him more even than I loved Peter. If all my disciples would dare to be as truthful with me as Judas had been, then I could be stronger and accomplish many things.

"If," I now asked, "I ceased to labor—by even a jot or a tittle—for the needs of the poor, would you see less of value in me?"

"I would turn against you. A man who is ready to walk away from the poor by a little is soon ready to depart from them by a lot."

I had to admire this man. Judas had not seen the glory I knew. Yet his beliefs were as powerful to him as were mine to me. Yes, he was more admirable even than Peter, whose faith was as blind as a stone and so could be split by a larger stone.

So too did I know that trouble might arise between Judas and me. For he had none of the accommodation that my Father had given to my heart to make me ready for those trials that could come upon us unforeseen.

I can also say that this conversation with Judas was wondrous for clearing disarray. At last all seemed to be in order. We were ready. I could hardly believe we were ready to set out at last for Jerusalem, but it was a good morning. If none of us were without fear, we were touched by happiness as well. For we had not been enslaved by our fear. Our legs knew their own joy.

Then, and only then, did we truly step out. And in the vigor of our march, many began to believe that in two days when we were close enough to see Jerusalem, the Kingdom of God would appear. The Lord would be among us.

## An Entrance into Jerusalem

Since I wished my people to feel heartened by our entrance into Jerusalem, I sent forth two of my disciples and told them: "Go into this village before us and ask for a colt on whom no man has ever sat. When you find one, bring him to me. Tell them that the Lord is in need of such an animal."

And they went away and soon found a colt, young and spirited, and led him back. I sat upon this animal, which, until now, had been ignorant of a rider, and I held to its mane. For if I could not subdue such a young beast, how then could I calm the uproar in the hearts of men awaiting me at the Temple?

In time, the colt jumped less and pranced more, and we were able to walk in procession. And I liked the animal. I also felt as hungry as if I might never eat again.

Whereupon, seeing a fig tree that was heavy with leaves, I trotted toward it in order to take my fill. Yet on its branches I found no ripe figs.

Did an ill wind blow toward us? I said to the fig tree, "Let no man eat fruit from you again."

But a weight came upon my heart for cursing the roots of another. "I am the Son of God," I told myself, "yet also a man; by a thread does man live without heedless destruction."

So I also knew that Satan still clung to me. Like a hawk who searches the fields below for one small creature, then swoops for the kill, so had I scourged the tree.

Now the crowd of men and women who walked ahead of me took branches from the palms we passed and strewed them on my path. They sang, "Hosannah! Blessed is he who comes in the name of the Lord. Blessed is the kingdom of our David who comes in the name of the Lord. Hosannah in the highest." And some cried out, "Blessed is the king who comes in the name of the Lord." These people of Jerusalem (and most had not seen me before) were full of favor; in the windows, many waved. Word of our good deeds had come to Jerusalem before us.

Yet I did not forget the fig tree. Its branches would now be bare. Such thoughts made me brood upon the end of the city of Tyre. A thousand years ago it had dwelt in splendor, renowned for its tables of ebony, its emeralds and purple linens, its stalls of honey and balm, its coral and agate and chests of cedar. Yet the sea had washed it all away. Would this yet be said of Jerusalem, as wealthy in this hour as Tyre once had been?

I gazed upon great white buildings with columns so tall that I could not know whether I beheld a temple or a seat of Roman government. I said to myself, "A good name is rather to be chosen than great riches," but the words were too pious (for my heart had leaped at the sight of these riches). So I also said: "The mouth of a strange woman is a deep pit. And a great city is like a strange woman."

Yet I could not scorn Jerusalem. The people of Israel lived with as much magnificence now as in the time of King Solomon, when his palanquin had been made from cedar of Lebanon, its pillars fashioned of silver, its base of gold. The seat of the palanquin was purple and its claws had been wrought by the daughters of Jerusalem. Wondrous was Jerusalem in the time of Solomon, and wondrous was it now.

Yet my followers could hardly share such glory. I saw a Roman noble stop before our procession and stare at our hundreds walking by twos and by threes and fours in the lane. Some were well attired, but most of my people were in plain clothing, or in rags.

I, too, now stared at this throng that belonged to me. The people of Jerusalem were joining us in large numbers; and I was seeing as many faces as there are aspects of man. Among those who followed were many who could be counted as less than believers but were rather among the curious and the tormented and the cynical, and these last were accompanying us to jeer at the Pharisees and thereby repay them for old rebukes.

Some of these new followers were solemn. So in their eyes shone the hope that I might provide a new piety that weighed upon them less than their old piety, which had turned drab in their hearts from too much repetition of the same prayers. And there were children who looked on all the sights and laughed at the wonder of God's bounty when it came to the faces of people; they were the closest to joy. There were also men with the fearful dissatisfaction of boredom on their brow.

And there were the poor. In their eyes I saw great need, and new hope, and much depth of sorrow; they had been disappointed many times. And I spoke to all, good and evil equally, as if they were one, since changes for the better can occur rapidly at times like these. In a bad man, evil and good can shift more quickly than in a good man; bad men are familiar with their sins and often weary of the struggle to deny remorse.

As the throng increased, so was the colt full of many wicked spirits, but they were young and without the foul odors of more practiced devils. Still, my beast would buck, and I knew it was in his mind to throw me over his head onto the stones of the road. Yet I rode him. He was the colt for me. And for this moment I felt like the master of good and evil.

Only at this moment, however. For as I approached the Temple, I grew solemn with awe. I could not believe I was more than a Jew with a modest trade approaching a great and consecrated edifice. We were coming near to the Temple of Temples, and they had built it on a mount.

Even before I came to it, I remembered that its steps would rise from courtyard to courtyard, facing ever more august chapels and sacred sanctuaries, and there would be one chamber into which only the High Priest could enter and then only on one day of the year. That was the Holy of Holies. I was the Son of God, but I was also the child of my mother and so my respect for the Temple was, with each breath, growing larger than my urge to change all that was within. I shivered when the men and women in front of me, on mounting an incline in the road, began to cheer, and soon I too, on mounting the hill, saw the Temple walls.

But as I took in the sight, so did I also know that the future of this magnificence was in peril. In years to come, enemies would be ready to tear down the walls until nothing would remain but one wall. Hardly a stone would be left to rest upon another. All this would pass unless the priests of the Temple came to understand that my message was from the Lord.

Sitting upon the colt, I wept openly at my first sight on this morning of the Great Temple. It was beautiful, but it was not eternal. And I thought of the words of Amos, who had said: "The houses of ivory shall perish." It was then that I dismounted, and continued on foot.

Having climbed the steps of the entrance, I came into the Temple itself. Beyond the first gate was a large court where all could exchange money and goods. How one had to admire the beards of these men of Mammon! They had been curled by a warm iron and were immaculate in their pride. So these moneylenders looked like peacocks. And the priests also looked like peacocks as they moved among them. All was vanity. At home, their tables would be bountiful, while the poor sat in the stinking alleys of the city.

I wrapped silence about me like a holy cloth that others would not dare to touch. I sat alone on a stone bench and looked at how these people cast money into the alms box. Many who were rich cast much. But then came a poor woman, and her shawl was threadbare; she threw in her small coin. My heart leaped.

I called to those disciples who were near and said: "This poor woman has put in more than all the rich. They leave a tithe of their abundance. She gave her living. So she has turned money into a tribute to the Lord. The wealthy give only to impress each other."

I thought of money and how it was an odious beast. It consumed everything offered to it. What slobbering was in such greed! I thought of how the rich are choked with the weight of gold, and their gardens grow no fruit to satisfy them. There is oppression in the perfume of the air, and none of the rich man's blooms bring happiness. For his neighbor is wealthier than himself and his gardens are more beautiful. So are the rich always envious of the next man's gold.

Here, in the outer court of the Temple, surrounded by these moneylenders, I spoke to all, and my voice was my own. I said: "No man can pay allegiance to two masters. For he will cling to the one he needs and, in secret, despise the other. You cannot serve God and Mammon."

Then I heard the Devil speak to me for the first time since I had been with him on the mountain. He said: "Before it is over, the rich will possess you as well. They will put your image on every wall. The alms raised in your name will swell the treasure of mighty churches; men will worship you most when you belong to me as much as to Him. Which is just. For I am His equal." And he laughed. He knew what he would say next:

"Greed is a beast, you say, but note this! Its defecations are weighed in gold. Isn't gold the color of the sun from which all things grow?"

The Lord chose to reply in my other ear: "Everything he says makes sense until it does no longer. He gives this speech to all who catch his eye, and his eye is only for the best, and most beautiful, whom I have fashioned with great hope. He scorns those who are modest but remain with Me."

And this was more than my Father ever said again about Satan, but at this moment it gave little force to my faith. Did my Father speak well of the meek because they were the only ones who remained loyal to Him and to me? How full of chaos was such a thought! I fell prey to a wrath greater than any I had known before.

In the eyes of the moneylenders, greed was as sharp as the point of a spear; the rage of Isaiah came to me. In his words, I cried out: " 'These tables are a pool of vomit. In such filth, nothing is clean!' "

And I overturned each of the tables before me. I threw them over with the money that was on them, and I exulted as the coins gave small cries on striking the stones of the courtyard. Each possessor ran after his lost coins like the swine of Gadarene as they rushed into the sea.

Then I knocked over the seats of those who sold doves and I opened the cages. On this commotion of wings the multitude who were with me came forward and cheered at this defiance of usury.

I said: "My house shall be known before all nations as a house of prayer. Whereas you are men of Mammon and have made it a den of thieves."

Indeed it was the truth. Men who sought Mammon were thieves. They were thieves even if they had never stolen a cup of wheat. Their greed stripped virtue from all who would emulate them.

Soon the priests would be speaking of this act in all the sanctuaries within this Great Temple. For the priests, like the moneylenders, also kept their accounts with God separate from their accounts with

Mammon. And how quick they were to water all the vines of cupidity that grew on one side of their soul.

# A Dialogue with a Scribe

I could see that the scribe who addressed me as Master wanted to continue our discourse. He asked: "What, by your understanding, is the first Commandment of them all?"

I answered: " 'The Lord, our God, is one Lord.' This must be the first Commandment. The second is to love thy neighbor as thyself."

The scribe said: "To love one's neighbor as oneself is more than all burnt offerings and sacrifices."

He was wise in the way he spoke to me. Could he be the Master of the Book in this Great Temple? His manners were as subtle as his well-curled beard. And his speech was as handsome as his appearance. Yet his eyes were pale like the faded blue of the sky when the sky is white. So I did not trust him. Still, I listened as he said: "Here, we are all circumcised. We share a single faith. Many of us in this Temple believe that you have not come here to rend us asunder but to bring us nearer to one another. And this we still believe, even though disruption has followed you like the dust before a storm." He paused to great effect. All among us were now listening to him. "Still," he said, "there are storms that cleanse. So I would ask of you, Master, when will the Kingdom of God be with us?"

As he spoke, I could hear the same two voices that live side by side in many a Pharisee. Their speech is often endowed with good manners, but there is also quiet mockery in their utterance and this is as finely sifted into their courtesies as powder into sand. Nonetheless, I listened. For he was not without some desire to believe that I was the Son of Man. It was possible that the priests who had sent him were also ready to listen. We spoke, therefore, as men who were equal. Only in the second hour did he reveal his knowledge of the scrolls, and thereby began a gentle dispute over the working of cures on the Sabbath.

"Do you recall the verse," he asked, "that says: 'And while the children of Israel were in the wilderness, they found a man that gathered sticks upon the Sabbath day, and they brought him to Moses and

Aaron and to all the congregation. But the Lord said to Moses, "The man shall surely be put to death: all the congregation shall stone him." And the congregation took him outside the camp and did stone him and he died.' " The scribe now said, "That was a thousand years ago, and our congregation today would not stone such a man. Yet the principle may remain. You shall not work on the Sabbath."

I replied that I had answered this question many times. "If you circumcise a babe on the Sabbath," I told him, "then you may also lift the scales from the blind and flex the limbs of the halt."

But here he began to speak with such skill that I did not know how or where to interrupt.

He said, "I have been waiting for all of this year to talk with you. For I have thought of your works, Master, and I would say, even as the prophet Samuel said to King Saul: 'Rebellion is the sin of witchcraft.' Contemplate what I have just said. If you come from Him whom you will not declare but wish us to believe is the Lord, why not say as much? For if you refuse to declare yourself, suffering could result from your good deeds. Your cures could appear to us as witchcraft and full of the bright fire of rebellion. We in the Temple fear that fire. We have labored for ten hundred years to learn what is in the Book. Many have died for the five books of the Torah. Yet with the strength of our beliefs we have built the walls of this Temple. We are able to live by the light it provides us. It is the same light that was given to us by the deeds of our martyrs. They died for our scrolls and our laws. So I would remind you, even as it is written in First Maccabees, that King Antiochus, a heathen king, was set over us, and he declared to his whole kingdom that we should now be one people, Jews and gentiles alike. And all were ordered to obey the laws of this new religion even if it was not ours.

"The gentiles agreed. To our shame, many Israelites also consented to a faith that worshipped idols. Indeed, so many accepted these edicts of Antiochus that the only clear measure of a man who was still a good Jew came to be that you could kill him before he would profane the Sabbath.

"Then, King Antiochus commanded us to abstain from circumcising our children. Whoever did not obey would die. Good Israelites had to flee Jerusalem. The priests of King Antiochus then placed swine upon the altar. Whoever was found with the Book was put to death. When soldiers found infants who were circumcised, they killed them. And they hung the priests who performed the circumcision.

"We learned then," said the scribe, "that our Book could not restrain evil unless all of us gave absolute obedience to the laws of the

Book. When we listen, therefore, to what you say, we do not always hear your understanding of the ten hundred years of the Book. Nor do we feel your recognition of the martyrs who died for the Law. Instead, we see that in your haste to serve God, you encourage publicans, sinners, even the uncircumcised. You rush to destroy all that you have learned in all the years of your schooling. Do you not comprehend that blind rejection of the Law is as evil as idolatry?"

I could hear more and more sounds of assent among those who listened. Some of my own people were muttering that he was right. And many had wept as he spoke of the deaths of these martyrs.

I was slow to reply. "Do not think," I told him, "that I am here to deny the Law or the prophets. I have not come to destroy but to fulfill." Here I stopped, and looked into his pale eyes. "Unless the righteousness of my followers exceeds the righteousness of your scribes and Pharisees, we shall not enter the Kingdom of Heaven."

Before he could reply, I added: "All that you say is just if people observe the Book. But they do not. This land of Israel has committed so many great sins that the Lord now looks upon the people of Israel as living in whoredom. Are we not supposed to find a way to save the whore?"

The scribe answered in a tone so light and so full of the wings of confidence that his words danced upon his tongue; in that moment I heard Satan stir in his throat. For he said: "Save the whore? Yes, you will finish by saying to gentiles, a people who are not your people, 'You are my people,' and they will say, 'You are my God.'" And the scribe laughed softly. All the mockery he had mixed into his courtesy settled over me. It was as if he had seen all things evil and wise where I had not. So he knew to a certainty that gentiles were ignorant and worshipped statues whereas he, like other good Pharisees, was of the Chosen.

I did not speak until I could find the words I sought. And then I spoke in Hebrew, even as I had read it in the Book. "From the words of Ezekiel," I said: " 'My sheep were scattered because there is no shepherd, and they became meek to all the beasts of the field when they were scattered. Neither did My shepherds search for My flock, but fed themselves. Behold, I am against the shepherds.' "

"And these shepherds," the scribe answered, "are kin to me? Can it be that this is what you say?"

I was thinking that even a drunken man would know what it was now politic to say. I was lacking in all knowledge of how to offer what would gain the most and offend the least. But then I had no desire to be politic. I wanted these Pharisees to remember my words forever.

"I look," I told the scribe, "to gather my flock from all places, from wherever they have been scattered. So I do not despise those who are uncircumcised or those who are ignorant of the Book."

"Are you saying that you would give a light to the gentiles?" he asked.

"Yes," I said. "That would be for the salvation of all." The scribe was silent; I think he was weary. He had studied the teachings of the great prophets, and they had dreamed of the hour when God would bring salvation to Israel. But it had not come to pass. Was the scribe wondering whether this Galilean and his peasants could know more about salvation than our heroes and prophets, even the kings of the glorious and holy past?

I continued to speak. "The Lord," I said, "has made my mouth a sharp sword. In the shadow of His hand He has hidden me. He has told me: 'Raise up the tribes of Jacob and the strong reserve of Israel.' But He also said: 'I will give you a light to the gentiles in order that you may be My salvation unto all the ends of the earth.'"

To which the scribe said, "Is that not blasphemy?"

I replied, "It is what my Father has said."

On these words he left. With him went many who agreed with his thoughts. A large number. I was alone again with my followers.

# Mary Magdalene

The dawn was cool, and I, feeling restored, was ready to go again to the Temple and sit beneath a sacred tree. I would teach.

But on the road that went by the Mount of Olives, Pharisees stood in my path, and with them was a woman. They said: "Master, this woman was taken in adultery. She was caught in the very act. The Law commands that she be stoned. What will you say?"

I knew that they would look to accuse me of leniency toward sinners. Therefore I gave my eyes neither to the woman nor to them. "You shalt not commit adultery," I said. "Whoever looks on a woman with lust has committed adultery in his heart." These words were for the young men among them whose eyes reflected their delight that they could stare openly at this woman taken in adultery; I also knew that their thoughts would soon provide idle hands with other forms of delight. To myself, I thought: If thy hand offend thee, cut it off.

This woman before me must have within her every filth and effluence of the Devil's spew, fornication being the most powerful instrument of the Devil. So these Pharisees stood confidently before me, certain that I would find a way to pardon her and thereby admit that I was ready to traffic with whores. But I did no more than stoop down to the earth. And with my finger I wrote in the dust as though I had not heard them.

Their minds were rich with calculation. They knew that to an Essene, unseemly fornication leads directly to the Fire. They would know how much I had learned from the scrolls about the perils of an unclean woman. Indeed, they had read the same scrolls. I remembered what was written of Jezebel in the Second Book of Kings; this Jezebel, a princess, had been thrown down from the high window of a tower, and her blood spattered upon the wall; courtiers rode horses over her and left her underfoot. When the king saw this, he said, "Bury this cursed woman, for she is a king's daughter." But they found no more of her than the skull and the feet and the palms of her hands. So they came and told him and he said, "This is the word of the Lord: 'Dogs shall eat the flesh of Jezebel and the carcass of Jezebel shall be as dung upon the field.' "

Now, I hardly dared to look upon this woman whom the Pharisees had brought to me. Instead, I continued to write with my finger in the sand. If I did not know what I wrote, so I did not let them see it either.

To myself, I whispered from the book of Proverbs: " 'The lips of a strange woman are honey and her mouth is smoother than oil, but the other end is as bitter as wormwood, as sharp as a two-edged sword. Her ways are loose. So do her feet take her down to death, those same feet once so swift in running after mischief.' "

I did not look at her. Peter had come to sit beside me on the ground, and he unrolled the scroll that he carried with him to read when we would rest, and he always carried the scroll, even if he read with great difficulty.

Yet he was close to my thoughts, for he pointed to a passage with his stout finger, twice as thick as one of mine, and in the old Hebrew tongue whispered: "It says: 'On account of a whorish woman is a man brought to a piece of bread.' " When I nodded to go on, he whispered further: " 'An adulterous woman eateth and wipeth her mouth and sayeth, "I have done no wickedness." ' "

I kept nodding in order to keep myself from stealing a look upon this woman. To myself I recited the words of Ezekiel: " 'The Babylonians came to the harlot Aholibah and took her into the bed of love, and they defiled her and she was polluted with them so she discovered her nakedness, yet she did multiply her whoredoms for she doted upon men whose issue is like the issue of horses.' "

Despite myself, I gazed at last upon the woman taken in adultery.

As I feared, she was beautiful. The bones of her face were delicate, and her hair flowed down her back. With art, she had painted her eyes. She was gentle even as her mouth was proud and foolish.

My abhorrence of fornication had filled my years with thoughts of lust. I had suffered the ravages of unspent fury. But now I heard the soft voice of a spirit. Was her angel searching for mercy? I was offered a vision of this woman in the fumes of sin. And with a stranger! Even so, she was a creature of God. She might be near the Lord in ways I could not see, even—could it be?—in the wallow of fornications with strangers. Was she, then, so different from the Son of Man? He too must be close to all strangers. Yes, she could even be close to God all the while that the hands of the Devil embraced her body. Her heart could be one with God even as her body was close to the Devil.

So when these Pharisees, having been as silent and patient as fishermen, now asked me again, saying, "Moses and the Law command us. Such a woman should be stoned. What do you say?" I lifted myself up and spoke not only to my disciples but to the circle of scribes and Pharisees. I said: "If thy hand offend thee, cut it off." When they looked at me, I told them: "It is better to enter the other life maimed than to have two hands to take into hell." Then I saw fear in their eyes. "If your eye offend thee," I told them, "pluck it out. It is better to enter the Kingdom of God and see only with the eye that is left than have both eyes look into the flames. In hell-fire, the worm that eats at your flesh does not die." I was amazed. I felt cleansed of disturbance toward this woman, and by my own words. So I also said: "He that is without sin among you, let him cast the first stone."

A tumult arose. It was so sudden and of such force that I nearly lost my balance and had to stoop once more and write again in the dust as if I cared more for what my finger could say to the earth than for all of them.

Soon, and with each moment, their fury began to abate. Before long it had fled. Now they were pained by their own misdeeds.

I saw them go away. They left one by one, commencing with the oldest man among them. (He had, perhaps, the most sin to support.)

The last to leave was young, and may have been near to innocent. I was alone. Even Peter had departed. Only the woman stood before me.

I could not bring myself to look into her eyes, then I did. In so doing, I still could not see her eyes. Instead, like a dream offered by Satan, I heard a verse from the Song of Songs. "The joints of thy thighs are like jewels, the work of a master's hand" were the words I heard, "and thy navel is like a round goblet." I told myself that I was in the presence of evil angels. For I could find my own evil, and it was rich and dark and begging to be cast forth from me. And these evil angels were so powerful that I knew I must be wary of the beauty of this woman.

So I chose to speak to her in the words of the prophet Ezekiel. I said: " 'Behold your sin. It is written: "I will raise up thy lovers, and they shall come against thee with chariots and wheels, and they shall deal furiously with thee; they shall take away thy nose and ears and thy residue shall be devoured by fire. They shall also strip thee out of thy clothes and take away thy fair jewels. Thus will I make thy lewdness to cease immediately and thy whoredoms be brought out of the land of Egypt, so that thou shall not remember Egypt anymore." ' "

And this harlot, whose eyes were as purple as the last hour of evening, said gently, "I do not wish to lose my nose."

I said, "Woman, where are your accusers? Has no man accused you?"

She said, and her voice was modest, "No man is here to accuse me, Lord."

I said, "Neither do I condemn thee. Go!"

Yet it was not enough. For within this woman remained every echo of her whoredom. So I said: "Where can you go? Are you not bound still to fornication with strangers?"

She replied: "If you do not condemn me, then do not pass judgment. Without the flesh there is no life."

She was vain. She was strong. And I could see that she was wed to the seven powers of the Devil's wrath and to their offspring: the seven demons. So I must attempt to cast out these seven powers and demons. I knew they would come forth slowly. And indeed, when they did come forth, it was one by one, and they clawed at all good spirit between us. Some were sly and some were lewd, and more than one was hideous—seven powers and demons.

The first was Darkness and its demon was treachery. Indeed, I was to realize even as I named each one that I had learned more from

Satan than he wished to tell me. So I knew that Desire was the second power and pride would be its demon. And the third was Ignorance, with a huge appetite for the meat of swine, a gluttonous demon. Love of Death was the fourth power and its demon could be no less than the lust to eat another. For nowhere is our knowledge of death closer to us than when devouring flesh from a fellow human. The fifth power sought Whole Domain and its demon worked to defile all spirit; the good spirit that had come to this woman and myself was much buffeted as this demon came forth. And the sixth power was Excess of Wisdom. Its demon had the urge to steal a soul. Of them all, the last power was the most fearful. It was the Wisdom of Wrath; its demon was the lust to lay waste a city. Such were the seven powers and demons I drew forth from her. Only then could I say: "Go and sin no more." And she left.

Afterward I would learn that her name was Mary and she was from Magdala in Tiberias, a city where many Jews had died in war against the Romans. Their bones now lay under the foundations of the buildings that had been erected by the victors. So this woman Mary Magdalene had committed adultery upon the ground of our martyrs. Yet I did not regret what I had done. For by half she was gentle, and that half belonged to God. Nor did I know that I would see her again. Yet I did.

# A Resurrection

There are some who say that there was an earthquake and the angel of the Lord descended from heaven to roll back the stone from the door. Since the raiment of this angel was as white as snow, the guards fled.

Others say that very early on the morning of the third day, even as death can bring together the harlot and the woman who is virtuous, so did Mary Magdalene come to the sepulchre, where she met Mary my mother. And they agreed to perform proper rites for me. But now that they were there, who would roll away the stone?

Yet when they looked, they saw that the tomb was open. They could enter. Inside, they met a young man who wore a long white garment, and he said: "You seek Jesus of Nazareth, but he is risen. Tell his disciples that he goes before you into Galilee and there you shall see him."

This may be close to the truth. For I know that I rose on the third day. And I also recall that I left the sepulchre to wander through the city and the countryside, and there came an hour when I appeared among my disciples. I said to them: "Why are you sad?" And they did not recognize me. They thought I was a stranger in Jerusalem and did not know what had happened. They even said to me, "Our sorrow is for Jesus of Nazareth, who was a mighty prophet. But our rulers have crucified him."

I said to them: "Behold my hands and my feet!" And Thomas looked and, seeing the holes, he asked to feel them (which is why he is known to this day as Doubting Thomas). But the sight of these wounds allowed them to believe. Soon, all who were there began to say that I had been received in heaven and was seated on the right hand of God. In any case, I had by then wandered away and they could no longer see me. All the same, my disciples went forth and preached that the Lord was with them. And they came at last to believe that they had the power to cast out devils. They spoke with new tongues, and when they laid hands on the sick, a few recovered.

But the Jews were much divided by my death. Many went forth with my disciples and became new followers, calling themselves Christian; others remained close to the Temple and argued among themselves for a hundred years over whether I was or was not the Messiah.

The rich among them, and the pious, prevailed; how could the Messiah be a poor man with a crude accent? God would not allow it!

Still, it must also be said that many of those who now call themselves Christian are rich and pious themselves, and are no better, I fear, than the Pharisees. Indeed, they are often greater in their hypocrisy than those who condemned me then.

There are many churches in my name and in the name of my apostles. The greatest and holiest is named after Peter; it is a place of great splendor in Rome. Nowhere can be found more gold.

God and Mammon still grapple for the hearts of all men and all women. As yet, since the contest remains so equal, neither the Lord nor Satan can triumph. I remain on the right hand of God, and look for greater wisdom than I had before, and I think of many with love. My mother is much honored. Many churches are named for her, perhaps more than for me. And she is pleased with her son.

My Father, however, does not often speak to me. Nonetheless, I honor Him. Surely He sends forth as much love as He can offer, but His love is not without limit. For His wars with the Devil grow worse. Great battles have been lost. In the last century of this second millennium were holocausts, conflagrations, and plagues worse than any that had come before.

Yet it is believed by most that God gained a great victory through me. And it may be that the Devil was not clever enough to comprehend the extent of my Father's wisdom. For my Father knew how to recover from debacle and disaster. Some fifty or more years after my death, the Gospel According to John was composed, and the work of this John (unknown to me) may have been illumined by my Father, because John's words proved unforgettable. They said: "God so loved the world that He gave His only begotten son that whosoever believed in him should not perish but have eternal life." So powerful is the force of this message that no other prophet has ever been followed by as many who were ready to die in his name. Of course, I was not only a prophet but His son.

Nonetheless, the truth is more valuable even than the heavens. Thereby, let it be understood: My Father may not have vanquished the Devil. Less than forty years after I died on the cross, a million Jews were killed in a war against Rome. The Great Temple was left with no more than one wall. Still, the Lord proved as cunning as Satan. Indeed, He understood men and women better than did the Devil. For my Father saw how to gain much from defeat by calling it victory. Now, in these days, many Christians believe that all has been won for them. They believe it was already won before they were born. They believe that this victory belongs to them because of my suffering on the cross. Thereby does my Father still find much purpose for me. It is even by way of my blessing that the Lord sends what love He can muster down to that creature who is man and that other creature who is woman, and I try to remain the source of love that is tender.

Yet I must also remind myself of Pontius Pilate, who said that in peace there was no truth, and in truth, no peace. For that reason I do not bring peace but a sword. I would wage war on all that makes us less than we ought to be, less generous. I would not want the Devil to convince me that the quarries of our greed are a noble pit and he is the spirit of freedom. But then, who but Satan would wish to tell us that our way should be easy? For love is not the sure path that will take us to our good end, but is instead the reward we receive at the end of the hard road that is our life and the days of our life. So I think often of the hope that is hidden in the faces of the poor. Then from the depth of my sorrow wells up an immutable compassion, and I find the will to live again and rejoice.

All selections from *The Gospel According to the Son* (1997)

# AFTER DEATH
# COMES LIMBO

Limbo was a house of many mansions. Mailer's spirits, while hardly free—they whipped around his soul like electrons orbiting a ring—began, nonetheless, to awake. The telling monotonies of Limbo (all those faceless fornications that rang in the ears, those stupors that drifted like bad weather, apathies piling on apathies like old newspapers, the crackle of static, and the playback of cocktail gabble, the gluttony of red wine taken on top of white wine on top of harshly cooked food, or the holes in one's memory now plugged by electronic hum, plus the horror of contemplating falls from heights where one did not want to find oneself, and all the stations of the cross of feeling empty while waiting for subway trains and airline shuttles and waitresses in busy lunchrooms), yes, all such items had so far been experienced in Limbo as direct punishment. Now, however (as his spirits awake), he came to perceive that it was all part of bad spiritual ecology—exactly *such* a category—bad spiritual ecology.

Mailer began to believe that this enforced immersion in every sensation, episode, glut, glop, and repellent handle of experience (his vision filled with nothing but the faces of digital watches, the smell of pharmacies, the touch of polyester shirts, the wet wax paper of Mc-Donald's hamburgers, the air of summer when traffic jams and shrieks of stereo as the volume is jacked-up—not to mention the nausea that plastic highball glasses will give to the resonance of booze) was not necessarily a set of items to scourge him around one eternity before dispatching him to another but might be instead his own natural field of expiation. In place of his soul expiring, or suffering some whole damnation now, he might still be part of his own karmic chain and going through a purification of those misspent hours before being thrown back into the contest again. A joke returned to his ears. "It's a great day for the race," said the elevator operator in the acrylic uniform in the Formica-paneled cage. "What race?" said the passenger. "The human race," said the elevator operator, and laughed his way up the ascension.

All who died were guilty. In part, at least, they were guilty, and conceivably they were innocent in part, and Limbo, thought Mailer, might even be the charity to suppose that innocence, if it wanted to go back to the race, was in need of education. Limbo, on the consequence, took all those moral stances embedded in concrete and wrenched them askew. In the mansion, there was that human, for instance, who held the award for the most faithful church attendance over two decades in the American Midwest; now he was pissing and moaning up a storm at the injustice of being here. Still, he was guilty. The inhabitants were all judged by one fine measure: Had they or had they not wasted more of the soul's substance than was required by the exigencies of their life? Since his first perception offered here was that the most consumable substance of the soul was nothing more than time, that Time, whole and mysterious bed of light, electricity, and force, was invested, like the true fund of the realm, in every soul, it followed as a consequence that Time was not to be wasted but rather, whatever the warp of one's upbringing, was to be spent, all neurotic, psychotic, screwball, timid, stingy, spendthrift, violent, or fear-filled habits taken into account, was still to be spent as wittily, cheerfully, and/or bravely as possible.

That was the standard of Limbo. Time was not to be wasted. It came over one, even on emerging from the first stupefying sleep (and therefore beginning to suffer monotony, apathy, and the boredom that comes from being out of Time), that this dreadful experience, these appalling emptinesses of the spiritual gut that came from existing now in seamless non-dark non-light units punctuated by no breath, was still a course in orientation over spiritual ills. For instance, the Midwestern churchgoer now inhabited a cell (in this penitentiary of the heavens) next to one of the world's worst cons, a man who had killed three prisoners before dying himself over the twenty years of his Lewisburg stretch. Yet the con was here for another kind of crime—he had put in more man-hours watching TV than any other convict in the federal system. All the same, the two were installed side by side—their crimes against the cosmos were apparently not dissimilar. They had both wasted their stuff, and egregiously. The churchgoer had perpetuated this by the brute sterility of his church attendance: The complacency of his performance (that is to say, the spiritual stagnation at the center of his complacency) had been a powerful miasma to lay on the spirit of three young ministers, who in succession grew old at accelerated rates looking into his professionally empty eyes—he had certainly spoiled more of existence than he had sustained. The con, in his turn, had poisoned the livelier possibilities of many a young wolf and punk whose burgeoning shit-oriented libido would somehow drain out after sauntering past that corner of the inmates' lounge where the con was ensconced by the set. Considering how immense was his potential violence, just so flattened had been the prison's rec-room mood by that act of his will that chose to do time quietly, watch TV, and get out—at which, in fact, he failed, for he kept killing other convicts. The con's real mission in life, and he knew it, was to outwit the guards, stifle alarm systems, and climb unclimbable prison walls. The logics of Limbo were not easily available, and yet the message, as one took it through the now non-corporeal equivalent of one's pores, was that something in the cosmos would have prospered more if the con had climbed the wall instead of imbibing TV, even as the churchgoer could have stirred beneficial forces in the universe by catching an X-rated movie or two.

Given the iron law of such logic, Mailer came to recognize that he would have done less damage to his being by going to a church or a temple once in a while rather than increase the total of his appearances on television.

Indeed, it was this particular piece of moral knowledge he was obliged to ingest right after his emergence from the first stupefying sleep-out. It was to recognize that every dull thing one had done to the universe (filling out crossword puzzles one did not wish to fill, taking the Eastern Airlines shuttle when other transportation was available), every hour one had voided thereby of fresh and keen desire to be used, the air around one, in consequence, suffocated by psychic exhaust, had now to be breathed again, the air of the stifled past to be swallowed, digested, suffered, and then stuffed into the ongoing baggage of one's karma. This mansion of Limbo was here to bring you face to face with those sins for which there are no tears, even as a husband and wife cannot weep if they lose a potentially heartfelt piece of ass by watching TV all night; yes, this corner of Limbo (a clean and well-appointed place suggestive of the interior of a picture tube on a black-and-white set—that is, all curved, silver, and gray, an odorless impalpability of fluorescence in an eternity of flickering) was now apparently ready to teach him, that is, teach his soul, something new. That meant, on reflection, that he might still have a soul. Something in himself exactly like the Old Center seemed certainly not to have ceased, that part at least of himself he had always thought wiser than the rest of him (that part which took pains to mash an invisible egg on his head after a rotten remark) was coming to recognize that his tour through Limbo (if indeed a tour and not an ongoing punishment) would ask him to meditate at length and presumably to purpose on those yaws and palls of his life that had passed through TV. He was going to be obliged to regard his own wretched collaboration with the multimillion-celled nausea-machine, that Christ-killer of the ages— television. (Let us say it takes a Jew not wholly convinced of the divinity of Christ to see that is who the tube is killing.) And he shuddered through the now-familiar, if minimal, retchings of Limbo while remembering how on numerous occasions with each of his nine children he had closed the doors of his own resistance to TV and let the little fuckers keep looking at the screen because it *pacified* them, which is to say took the lividity of their five-year-old nerves and slowly (that is, faster than sight) and buzzingly cauterized their nerve ends just the right bloody bit, no blood seen. Again the guilt that cannot be alleviated by tears stirred like sludge in his own small part of the great cosmic gut. Yes, there was a malignancy present in the bowels of existence, and it was video.

From *Pieces and Pontifications* (1982)

# THE HARBORS OF THE MOON

I know
a town
that
sails
the
sun

I know
a town
where
light
is dry
and
boats
come
home
with
silver
in their
hold

where
boats
come
home
with
silver
in their
hold

(Do not
grieve
the
death
of
little
fish
They
are
lights
that
search
the
deep)

I know
a town
with
sighs
of sea

white
with
the
tides
of me

white
as the
spine
of the
sea.

From *Deaths for the Ladies (and Other Disasters)* (1962)

# Acknowledgments and Appreciations

In the course of working on this book, Jason Epstein and I had a small disagreement about the editing. He wanted to include nothing but the best of what might be my best pieces, and I wanted to put in a few that could not be characterized in such fashion. These small debates were, however, useful. They advanced the theme. "I don't want an anthology," I declared. "I would like the book to offer some hint at a social and cultural history over these last fifty years."

"All right," said Epstein, "but put the emphasis on the best pieces." I set out to keep both of us happy, but I did have my rationale. I wanted a social history. It would provide a narrative. While no author can interest readers to the point where they will consume everything in an anthology, one could, with the hint of a narrative, put together a book that would prove sufficiently interesting for a few readers to go all the way straight through—first page to last. If you could do that for one fabulous reader in a hundred, then perhaps half or more of your other readers might remain interested for several hundred consecutive pages.

In any event, the book has been constructed with the idea that no magazine piece and no excerpt from a novel or work of non-fiction had to be considered sacrosanct. I proceeded to cut and trim each piece to my needs. If I was going to offer a very long book that would tell a story taking place over more than fifty years, then by all means such a massive book must still be as short as possible. So I made deletions wherever possible—sometimes to old references that would mean nothing to most readers, sometimes to repetitions of theme. (My criticisms of modern architecture must appear, I expect, in half of the magazine pieces I've written since 1960.) Occasionally, since this had become an out-of-category volume influenced by one of the most monumental works of American literature, nothing less than *U.S.A.*, by John Dos Passos, I even took the liberty of improving old sentences. Nor did I indicate the changes. They are never crucial. They never alter an idea to conform to a new time, they just improve the prose an agreeable bit, no more, and I leave no marks of elision or footnotes—it would have scarred a few pages with unnecessary gaps. Indeed, I did no more than a good copy editor might bring to a new manuscript.

I would add to my earlier dedication to my good, trusted, and dear friends Robert Lucid and J. Michael Lennon the acknowledgment that they helped me with an exceptional commitment of their time and their literary resources. Often, they would remind me of writing I had forgotten and, indeed, were always ready to debate me over the merits of certain selections, thereby developing my sense of what might be the richest choice. Any initial concept, however, of *best* parts is, of course, open to everyone's rejection: "Why was my favorite piece not included?" is bound to be a prevailing criticism. In any case, I started with a pool of five thousand pages that I thought were certainly good enough, but then in a different period of one's life, one might have chosen a different set of pieces. One does not write, after all, to make some pages superior to others—one writes in the attempt to capture a subject. Enrich a particular context for a reader and a swath of ordinary writing can seem to be good, while much fine writing unsupported by a sense of period or place can appear to be no more than an island of good prose. So, my debt to Lennon and to Lucid is for their good friendship—they gave me a sense of personal context that was invaluable for deciding on the dimensions and relations of this book.

A further acknowledgment goes without pause to Jason Epstein, who is probably our nearest successor to Maxwell Perkins. While no two men could be more unalike, it can be comfortably stated that Epstein is probably the last mandarin in American letters. No surprise then if his assistant, Joy de Menil, is resourceful, patient, and full of ideas, most of them good. In addition, I would offer an accolade to Veronica Windholz for her talented and sensitive copyediting, and an appreciation to Elizabeth Adams, Beth Pearson, and Jon Lindgren.

Being unable to conceive of an acknowledgment to Judith McNally that will pay proper respect to the way she keeps my literary house in order, I will content myself with remarking that the list of her fine and, by times, formidable qualities often puts my virtues to shame.

Last, and certainly not least, let me give appreciation to my wife, Norris, whose warm presence and subtle influence have created a domestic climate that not only allows one to thrive at work but even to love the idea that there is work to do and it is worth doing. Since all praise in these personal matters is invariably embarrassing to both the donor and the recipient, leave it that one had to curb a tendency to be hyperbolic in these remarks.

"Truman Capote" is from "A Small and Modest Malignancy, Wicked and Bristling with Dots" from *Pieces and Pontifications* (Boston: Little Brown and Company, 1982).

"The Shits Are Killing Us" and "Hip, Hell, and the Navigator" are from *Advertisements for Myself* (New York: G. P. Putnam's Sons, 1959).

"The Jewish Princess" is from *Marilyn* (New York: Grosset & Dunlap, 1973). Reprinted by permission of Lawrence Schiller.

"The Time of Her Time" is from *Advertisements for Myself* (New York: G. P. Putnam's Sons, 1959).

"Modene—I" is from *Harlot's Ghost* (New York: Random House, Inc., 1991).

"Superman Comes to the Supermarket—I" is from *The Presidential Papers* (New York: G. P. Putnam's Sons, 1963).

"Modene—II" is from *Harlot's Ghost* (New York: Random House, Inc., 1991).

"Superman Comes to the Supermarket—II" is from *The Presidential Papers* (New York: G. P. Putnam's Sons, 1963).

"First Lady in Waiting" is from "An Evening with Jackie Kennedy" from *The Presidential Papers* (New York: G. P. Putnam's Sons, 1963).

"Superman Comes to the Supermarket—III" is from *The Presidential Papers* (New York: G. P. Putnam's Sons, 1963).

"Modene—III" is from *Harlot's Ghost* (New York: Random House, Inc., 1991).

"A Word from the Author" is previously unpublished.

"An Open Letter to Fidel Castro" is from "Open Letter to John Fitzgerald Kennedy and Fidel Castro" from *The Presidential Papers* (New York: G. P. Putnam's Sons, 1963).

"Washington—I: Preparing for the Bay of Pigs," "Washington—II: Until Just Before the Bay of Pigs," "Miami—I: The Day After the Bay of Pigs," "Washington—III: Keeping Up with Modene," "Miami—II: Artime and Castro," and "Miami—III: Poisoning Castro" are all from *Harlot's Ghost* (New York: Random House, Inc., 1991).

"New York—I: Whom?" is from the preface to "Open Letter to John Fitzgerald Kennedy and Fidel Castro" from *The Presidential Papers* (New York: G. P. Putnam's Sons, 1963).

"Marilyn and Arthur Miller" is from *Marilyn* (New York: Grosset & Dunlap, 1973). Reprinted by permission of Lawrence Schiller.

"A Mighty Mother" and "Oswald and Marina in Minsk" are from *Oswald's Tale: An American Mystery* (New York: Random House, Inc., 1995).

"Journalists," "The Mafia," and "The Death of Benny Paret" are from "10,000 Words a Minute" from *The Presidential Papers* (New York: G. P. Putnam's Sons, 1963).

"The Six Time Zones Between Dallas and Paris" is from *Harlot's Ghost* (New York: Random House, Inc., 1991).

"Fort Worth to Dallas," "A High-Powered Rifle," and "A Visit to Lubyanka" are from *Oswald's Tale: An American Mystery* (New York: Random House, Inc., 1995). Reprinted by permission of Lawrence Schiller.

"Terribly Bad Characters" is from *Harlot's Ghost* (New York: Random House, Inc., 1991).

"A Hero to Himself," "The Widow's Elegy," and "The Third Widow" are from *Oswald's Tale: An American Mystery* (New York: Random House, Inc., 1995).

"An American Dream" is from *An American Dream* (New York: Bantam Doubleday Dell Publishing Group, 1965).

"A Debate with William Buckley" is from *The Presidential Papers* (New York: G. P. Putnam's Sons, 1963).

"My Hope for America," "A Speech at Berkeley on Vietnam Day," and "A Happy Solution to Vietnam" are from *Cannibals and Christians* (New York: Bantam Doubleday Dell, 1966).

"Why Are We in Vietnam" is from *Why Are We in Vietnam?* (New York: Henry Holt & Company, 1967). Copyright ©1982 by Norman Mailer. Reprinted by permission of Henry Holt & Company.

"Metaphor Versus Science" is from "Our Argument at Last Presented" from *Cannibals and Christians* (New York: Bantam Doubleday Dell, 1966).

"The Liberal Party," "Toward a Theater of Ideas," "A Transfer of Power," and "The Marshal and the Nazi" are from *The Armies of the Night*. Copyright © 1968 by Norman Mailer. Reprinted by permission of Dutton Signet, a division of Penguin Putnam Inc.

"Bobby Kennedy," "Gene McCarthy in Cambridge," "Miami Beach, August 2–8," "Chicago, August 24–29," "Property," "A Massacre on Michigan Boulevard," and "Convention's End" are from *Miami and the Siege of Chicago* (New York: World Publishing Company, 1968).

"The Psychology of Astronauts," "Wernher Von Braun," "Red and Mollie," "Lift-off," "The Greatest Week," and "The Dream of the Future's Face" are from *Of a Fire on the Moon* (Boston: Little Brown and Company, 1971).

"The Raging Affair: Kate Millett and Henry Miller" and "Millett and D. H. Lawrence" are from *The Prisoner of Sex* (Boston: Little Brown and Company, 1971).

"Brooding over Abortion" is from *St. George and the Godfather* (New York: Arbor House, 1972).

"Togetherness" is from *Deaths for the Ladies (and Other Disasters)* (New York: G. P. Putnam's Sons, 1962).

"The Cavett Show with Gore Vidal and Janet Flanner" is from "A Small and Modest Malignancy, Wicked and Bristling with Dots" from *Pieces and Pontifications* (Boston: Little Brown and Company, 1982). Material from the transcript of *The Dick Cavett Show* is used by permission of Daphne Productions, Inc.

"St. George," "Candidate Emeritus," "A Visit to Dr. Kissinger," "Pat Nixon," "Nixon Comes to Miami," and "Into the Credibility Gap" are from *St. George and the Godfather* (New York: Arbor House, 1972).

"Interview with Ehrlichman" was originally published in *Chic* magazine in 1976 as "A Conversation between Norman Mailer and John Ehrlichman."

"A Harlot High and Low" is from *Pieces and Pontifications* (Boston: Little Brown and Company, 1982).

"Nixon's Fall" was originally published in "Talk of the Town" in the May 20, 1974, issue of *The New Yorker.*

"The Faith of Graffiti" is from *The Faith of Graffiti* (New York: Praeger, 1974).

"Bantu Philosophy," "King of the Flunkies," "The Run," "The Impresario," "The Dressing Room," "Right Hand Leads," "The Man in the Rigging," and "A Long Collapsing Two Seconds" are from *The Fight* (Boston: Little Brown and Company, 1975).

"Christ, Satan, and the Presidential Candidate" appeared in *The New York Times Magazine* on September 26, 1976.

"Brenda, Johnny, and Gary," "Gary and Nicole," "The Guns," "Back in Jail," and "Gilmore and Gibbs" are from *The Executioner's Song* (Boston: Little Brown and Company, 1979). Reprinted by permission of Lawrence Schiller.

"The Embalming" is from *Ancient Evenings* (Boston: Little Brown and Company, 1983).

"Excerpts from *Tough Guys Don't Dance*" is from *Tough Guys Don't Dance* (New York: Random House, Inc., 1984).

"The Best Move Lies Close to the Worst" appeared in *Esquire*, October 1993.

"Huckleberry Finn—Alive at 100" appeared as "Alive at 100" in *The New York Times Book Review*, December 9, 1984.

"A Speech on Salman Rushdie" is from *The Rushdie Letters: Freedom to Speak, Freedom to Write*. (Lincoln: University of Nebraska Press, 1993). Reprinted by permission of University of Nebraska Press and the International Centre Against Censorship.

"The Best of Abbie Hoffman" was originally published as the foreword to *The Best of Abbie Hoffman* (New York: Four Walls, Eight Windows, 1989).

"A Review of *American Psycho*" was originally published in *Vanity Fair*, March 1991.

"Creationism Revisited" is from *Harlot's Ghost* (New York: Random House, Inc., 1991).

"How the Wimp Won the War" was originally published in *Vanity Fair*, May 1991.

"By Heaven Inspired" was originally published in *New Republic*, October 12, 1992.

"Madonna" was originally published as "Like a Lady" in *Esquire*, August 1994.

"The War of the Oxymorons" was originally published in *George*, November 1996.

"How the Pharaoh Beat Bogey" was originally published in *George*, January 1997.

"The Battle of Kadesh" and "Nefertiri and Menenhetet" are from *Ancient Evenings* (Boston: Little Brown and Company, 1983).

"An Interview on Existentialism and Karma" is from "An Interview with Laura Adams" from *Pieces and Pontifications* (Boston: Little Brown and Company, 1982).

"A Jewish Limb on the Judeo-Christian Ethic: Miracles" is from "Responses and Reactions" from *The Presidential Papers* (New York: G. P. Putnam's Sons, 1963).

"The Communication of Christ" is from *The Armies of the Night*. Copyright © 1968 by Norman Mailer. Reprinted by permission of Dutton Signet, a division of Penguin Putnam Inc.

"John the Baptist and the Devil," "Faith and Lack of Faith," "Judas," "An Entrance into Jerusalem," "Dialogue with a Scribe," "Mary Magdalene," and "A Resurrection" are from *The Gosepl According to the Son* (New York: Random House, Inc., 1997).

"After Death Comes Limbo" is from "A Small and Modest Malignancy, Wicked and Bristling with Dots" from *Pieces and Pontifications* (Boston: Little Brown and Company, 1982).

"The Harbors of the Moon" is from *Deaths for the Ladies (and Other Disasters)* (New York: G. P. Putnam's Sons, 1962).

## ABOUT THE AUTHOR

NORMAN MAILER was born in 1923 in Long Branch, New Jersey, and grew up in Brooklyn, New York. After graduating from Harvard, he served as a rifleman in the South Pacific during World War II. He published his first book, *The Naked and the Dead,* in 1948. Mailer won the National Book Award and the Pulitzer Prize in 1968 for *The Armies of the Night* and was awarded the Pulitzer Prize again in 1980 for *The Executioner's Song.* He has directed four feature-length films, was a co-founder of *The Village Voice* in 1955, ran unsuccessfully for mayor of New York in 1969, and was president of the American PEN from 1984 to 1986.